Readings in Artificial Intelligence and Databases

Edited by

John Mylopolous
University of Toronto

and

Michael Brodie
GTE Laboratories, Inc.

MORGAN KAUFMANN PUBLISHERS, INC.
SAN MATEO, CALIFORNIA

President and Editor *Michael B. Morgan*
Production Manager *Shirley Jowell*
Production Assistant *Elizabeth Myhr*
Copy Editor *Lynn Dupre*
Cover Designer *Rick Van Genderen*
Typesetter *Technically Speaking Publications*

Library of Congress Cataloging-in-Publication Data
Readings in artificial intelligence and databases.

Bibliography: p.
Includes index.
1. Artificial intelligence. 2. Expert systems
(Computer science) 3. Data base managemnt.
I. Mylopoulos, John. II. Brodie, Michael L.
Q335.R4118 1988 006.3 88-31989
ISBN 0-934613-53-2

Morgan Kaufmann Publishers, Inc.
Editorial Office: 2929 Campus Drive, San Mateo, California 94403
Order from: P.O. Box 50490, Palo Alto, California 94305

Printed in the United States of America

92 91 90 89 88 5 4 3 2 1

Contents

Acknowledgments vii

Introduction 1

Chapter 1 Introduction to AI and Databases

1.1 Database Management: A Survey 10
M.L. Brodie and F. Manola

1.2 Knowledge Representation and Reasoning 35
H. Levesque

1.3 The Programmer as Navigator 52
C.W. Bachman

1.4 Relational Database: A Practical Foundation for Productivity 60
E.F. Codd

1.5 Making Believers Out of Computers 69
H. Levesque

Chapter 2 Representation and Semantics

2.1 Entity-Based Representations 83

2.1.1 Limitations of Record-Based Information Models 85
W. Kent

2.1.2 The Entity-Relationship Model: Towards a Unified View of Data 98
P.P.-S. Chen

2.1.3 Using Semantic Networks for Database Management 112
N. Roussopoulos and J. Mylopoulos

2.1.4 Database Abstractions: Aggregation and Generalization 138
J.M. Smith and D.C.P. Smith

2.2 Semantic Data Models and Knowledge Representations 154

2.2.1 A Language Facility for Designing Database-Intensive Applications 156
J. Mylopoulos, P.A. Bernstein and H.K.T. Wong

2.2.2 The Functional Data Model and the Data Language DAPLEX 168
D. Shipman

2.2.3 On the Design and Specification of Database Transactions 185
M.L. Brodie and D. Ridjanovic

2.2.4 An Overview of the KL-ONE Knowledge Representation System 207
R. Brachman and J. Schmolze

2.3 Logic and Databases 230

2.3.1 Logic and Databases: A Deductive Approach 231
H. Gallaire, J. Minker and J-M. Nicolas

2.3.2 On Closed World Databases 248
R. Reiter

2.3.3 Logic For Data Description 259
R. Kowalski

2.4 Data/Knowledge Base Semantics 272

2.4.1 Semantics of Databases: The Semantics of Data Models 273
H. Biller and E. Neuhold

2.4.2 An Essential Hybrid Reasoning System: Knowledge and Symbol Level Accounts of KRYPTON 293
R. Brachman, V. Pigman-Gilbert and H. Levesque

2.4.3 Towards a Logical Reconstruction of Relational Database Theory 301
R. Reiter

2.5 Representation Issues: Knowledge Incompleteness 327

2.5.1 The Logic of Incomplete Knowledge Bases 328
H. Levesque

2.5.2 Incomplete Information in a Relational Database 342
T. Imielinsky and W. Lipski

Chapter 3 Performance Issues

3.1 Retrieval, Deduction, and Query Processing 361

3.1.1 A Framework for Choosing a Database Query Language 363
M. Jarke and Y. Vassiliou

3.1.2 An Amateur's Introduction to Recursive Query Processing Strategies 376
F. Bancilhon and R. Ramakrishnan

3.1.3 Deductive Question-Answering on Relational Data Bases 431
R. Reiter

3.1.4 Knowledge Retrieval as Limited Inference 444
A.M. Frisch and J. F. Allen

3.2 Data/Knowledge Base Integrity 456

3.2.1 Fast Maintenance of Integrity Assertions Using Redundant Aggregate Data 457
P.A. Bernstein, B. Blaustein and E. Clarke

3.2.2 A Sophisticate's Introduction to Database Normalization Theory 468
C. Beeri, P.A. Bernstein and N. Goodman

3.2.3 The Programming Language Aspects of ThingLab, a Constraint-Oriented Simulation Laboratory 480
A. Borning

3.2.4 Logic for Improving Integrity Checking in Relational Data Bases 497
J.-M. Nicolas

3.3 Implementation Techniques 510

3.3.1 Access Path Selection in a Relational DBMS 511
P.G. Selinger, M.M. Astrahan, D.D. Chamberlin, R.A. Lorie and T.G. Price

3.3.2 The Notions of Consistency and Predicate Locks in a Database System 523
K.P. Eswaren, J.N. Gray, R. Lorie and I.L. Traiger

3.3.3 Implementation of Integrity Constraints and Views by Query Modification 533
M. Stonebraker

3.3.4 Rete: A Fast Algorithm for the Many Pattern/Many Object Pattern Match Problem . . 547
C.L. Forgy

3.4 Data/Knowledge Management Systems 558

3.4.1 System R: Relational Approach to Database Management 560
M.M. Astrahan, M.W. Blasgen, D.D. Chamberlin, E.P. Eswaren, J.N. Gray, P.P. Griffiths, W.F. King, R.A. Loric, P.R. McJones, J.W. Mehl, G.R. Putzolu, I.L. Traiger, B.W. Wade and V. Watson

3.4.2 Storage and Access Structures to Support a Semantic Data Model 583
A. Chan, S. Danberg, S. Fox, W.K. Lin, A. Nori and D. Ries

3.4.3 A Modular Toolkit For Knowledge Management 592
G. Lafue and R. Smith

3.4.4 Inclusion of New Types in Relational Database Systems 599
M.R. Stonebraker

3.4.5 On the Evaluation Strategy of EDUCE 607
J. Bocca

Epilogue 621

Future Intelligent Information Systems: AI and Database Technologies Working Together 623
M.L. Brodie

Personal Statement: Computer Science and Concern for Our Planet, Michael L. Brodie 643

Bibliography 645

Credits 675

Index 679

Acknowledgments

We offer our special thanks to the following people for their help and encouragement in putting together this volume. Alex Borgida, Ray Reiter, Frank Manola, Umesh Dayal, Sharma Chakaravarthy, Jack Orenstein, Sunil Sarin, and Arnie Rosenthal helped tremendously with advice and encouragement at a time when our own ideas about this volume were still rather unfocused. We thank them for their suggestions and ideas on the structure and contents of this book. The reviewers of the text, Ron Brachman, Herve Gallaire, Richard Fikes, and Carlo Zaniolo, provided useful critiques of the table of contents (not to mention jokes about the amusing histories of AI and database research), which guided us during the final stages of this project. Mike Morgan was generous with his moral support and gentle (not always subtle) prodding. We are very grateful for the patient assistance provided by Marina Haloulos and Jingwen Fang at the University of Toronto; Pamela Talbourdet at GTE Labs; and Shirley Jowell at Morgan Kaufmann. This project would not have been possible without them. We also thank the University of Toronto and GTE Labs for providing infrastructure support for this project and for our research work in general. John Mylopoulos benefited tremendously from a research fellowship awarded by the Canadian Institute for Advanced Research. Michael Brodie is grateful to Bill Griffin, Director of the Computer and Intelligent Systems Lab at GTE, for providing continued support of basic and experimental research in AI and databases.

John Mylopoulos*
Michael Brodie†
September 1988

---

* Fellow, Canadian Institute for Advanced Research, Department of Computer Science, University of Toronto, 10 King's Road, Toronto, Canada M5S 1A4.

† GTE Laboratories, Incorporated, 40 Sylvan Road, Waltham, MA 02254.

Introduction

In the early 1950s computer science was motivated by pioneers with visions for what machines might be able to do. Their visions were on imagined functions, not on specific technologies. As research began to focus on specific problems and problem domains, specialized fields and related technologies evolved. Artificial intelligence (AI) developed techniques to account for reasoning processes of various kinds. Databases developed techniques for efficient retrieval and manipulation of large, shared information bases.

AI and databases are now two mature research fields (at least by computer-science standards; each has won two Turing awards). Since their common origin in the pioneers' visions, the two fields have diverged and have become surprisingly unaware of each other's work. Each field has seen periods of considerable attention and research and has produced important technologies around which industries have developed. AI and databases are currently looking for ways to consolidate and broaden their domains of application. It is now time for the two technologies to come together, to begin to achieve the visions of early and current pioneers in computer science.

The overlap between the two fields has been an active area of interest since the disciplines' very beginnings. It is based on the need for AI as well as database systems to manage, access, and reason about large amounts of possibly shared information. For AI, these *knowledge bases* contain (representations of) "knowledge" about an application domain (for example, the rules of chess, game opening strategies, and the like) and knowledge of how to perform a task relevant to that application domain (for instance, how to choose a chess move using rules of thumb). For databases, the information is represented in *databases* that represent many database applications and that can be thought of as large, shared data structures, stored on secondary storage, accessed concurrently by multiple users, and possibly distributed over several machines and locations.

To deserve their name, knowledge bases have to be endowed with a semantics — i.e., with an account of what their contents **say** about the application domain, as well as with appropriate inference mechanisms compatible with this account.* By and large, the inference mechanisms offered have been deductive, although abductive and inductive ones also have found important uses, particularly in areas where the system under

* This is a somewhat idealized view of knowledge bases; although few people would disagree that a semantic account is crucial for a knowledge base, pragmatic considerations often have led to a different practice, which emphasized ad hoc inference mechanisms and ignored semantics; [ISRA83], [BM86a] and more recently [LEVE87] contain pertinent discussions of this point.

development had to exhibit some form of "judgment" based on the contents of its knowledge base.

On the other hand, efficiency and robustness considerations have played a fundamental role in the development of databases as a research area. The system managing a database, the *database management system* (*DBMS*), **has** to provide efficient access to secondary storage, error recovery to deal with database operations that may abort for any reason, optimization facilities for queries to be evaluated with respect to the database, system security mechanisms to ensure that only authorized database accesses and manipulations occur, and means for allowing multiple users to access a single database with a warranty that they will not interfere with one another in a destructive way. A consequence of the concern for efficiency and robustness is that a database, unlike a knowledge base, has to be provided with one or more languages for data definition (to be used by database designers) and for database query and manipulation (to be used by database users).

The distinction between databases and knowledge bases is not a sharp one and has been the subject of some controversy [BROD86], [WEID84], and [SMIT86]. To some, databases are "simple" knowledge bases, where only propositions of a limited form are allowed, thus simplifying the task of generating inferences [BL86]. To others, databases are mere data structures (relations, records) with no semantics [BM86a]. Fortunately, it is becoming increasingly apparent that the distinction, whatever it is, is gradually disappearing as database research focuses on more powerful semantics including active objects (e.g., rules, object methods) and AI research focuses on knowledge bases that include rules, frames, facts, and data; on knowledge-base system performance and robustness; and on shared or cooperative knowledge-base systems.

A BRIEF HISTORY OF THE FIELD

Prehistory

Even before the advent of electronic computers, people dreamed of a mechanized information-retrieval system. In an article published in 1945, Vannevar Bush described a workstation he called memex, intended aid scholarly research and writing [BUSH45]. In his words, memex was to be "a device in which an individual stores his books, records, and communications, and which is mechanized so that it may be consulted with exceeding speed and flexibility. It is an enlarged intimate supplement to his memory. . ." Memex was supposed to be able to store large amounts of information and to deal with handwritten marginal notes. Many of the requirements for the construction of a memex machine are addressed by present-day and forthcoming technologies for personal workstations [GOTL86]; other requirements will be addressed once large knowledge bases can be managed effectively by computers.

Another pioneering article by Alan Turing [TURI51] proposed the now famous "Turing test" for machine intelligence, in which a machine imitates a (not necessarily truthful) human in a question-answering session. The topic of Turing's paper is whether machines can think, and how we might try to provide an objective answer to that question. It is noteworthy for the purposes of this volume that at the very heart of the test lies a (large!) information repository and a machine that can access and reason with the repository to give humanlike responses to input queries.

John McCarthy's [McCAR58]* offered a fairly concrete proposal for a program, *advice taker*, that accepts new information with which it reasons about its actions, thereby improving its performance. This is a seminal paper for AI in general and for knowledge representation in particular. Some of its premises, such as the representation of knowledge about situations and actions in terms of logical formulas, are now taken for granted. Others, such as the notion that a system can improve its performance through external advice, are still topics of active research. In either case, this paper posed a challenge for AI that this is still being addressed. It prescribed much of what followed in AI on the general topic of knowledge-based systems. In addition, it provided a technical framework, perhaps for the first time, for the construction of systems that build up a knowledge base incrementally and that reason with respect to that knowledge base for the purpose of performing some task.

Successive work broadened the scope of the challenge and offered alternatives for its fulfillment. Fischer Black [BLAC64] proposed a system that realizes aspects of McCarthy's advice

* A version of the original paper with additional technical detail appears in [MINS68] and is reprinted in [BL85].

taker and in so doing encounters the problem of developing efficient theorem-proving techniques. Bertram Raphael [RAPH64] built a "semantic information retrieval" system, SIR, which stored information on a primeval network and could efficiently retrieve information without having to rely on general-purpose theorem proving. Several other systems were developed, in the same period that exhibited "deductive-retrieval" capabilities and, in several cases, a restricted natural-language interface—notably [COOP64], [AS68], [DARL65], [LM67], and many others.

Another wave of research results was triggered by J.A. Robinson's resolution principle [ROBI65] which led to new and relatively more efficient general-purpose theorem provers. [RG68] introduces the resolution principle to the deductive information-retrieval problem. Another important milestone in the same period is W. Woods' work on question answering based on natural language [WOOD68], which led to the LUNAR system [WKN72]. LUNAR could respond to English queries about a database of information concerning lunar rock samples. Woods' work is important not only for its contributions to natural-language processing, but also for its principled adherence to a procedural, rather than truth-theoretic, semantics. It was preceded by several other systems, and proposals for systems, that allowed question answering in English with respect to an information base, such as [GWCL62], [LIND62], and [KBDF71].

The principal idea underlying databases—namely, shared data—first arose in the mid-1950s in FORTRAN programs that provided common areas by means of which such programs could access the same data items. Operating-system–supported device-access methods (e.g., basic direct-access method, indexed sequential-access method) evolved in the late 1950s and became common in second- and third-generation operating systems in the early 1960s. Also in the mid-1950s, the notion of nonshared data records arose in simple file systems, such as IBM's Formatted File System in 1961. The idea of linking data records to represent more complex structures (e.g., CPM networks in engineering) evolved in the late 1950s and early 1960s. Traditional business data processing developed the notion of master and detail records, which evolved into two forms of hierarchical structures. COBOL repeating groups implemented embedded hierarchies (e.g., an address consists of street number, street name, city, etc.), whereas SHARE's 9PAC system supported hierachically structured links between data records (e.g., employee records are linked to the corresponding manager record, which is linked to its corresponding manager record, etc.). These hierarchical structures formed the beginnings of hierarchically structured databases. Network databases evolved as C. Bachman used linked lists based on the work of Newell, Simon, and Shaw [NSS59], the language IPL V [NEWE63], hierarchical data structures from 9PAC, and list-processing concepts from the then-new LISP concepts of J. McCarthy [McCAR58]. At this early stage, there was a clear need in many applications for structuring, sharing, and reasoning about large information bases. There was no distinction between AI and databases. Indeed, pioneering AI work both motivated what are now database concepts and influenced database techniques and structures, such as list processing and linked data structures.

In 1959, the Conference on Data Systems Languages (CODASYL) established two committees to develop a common business language. The "short-term" committee developed COBOL, whereas the "long-term" committee, under the title of the CODASYL List Processing Task Group, began to investigate database concepts. To gain business respectability (i.e., to distance itself from computer science and AI), the committee changed its name to the CODASYL Database Task Group (DBTG). In 1969, the DBTG published its specification of the network data model, language, and DBMS [CODA71].

In the late 1960s T. Codd of IBM developed a complete, general-purpose programming language based on set theory and logic, which he called *relational programming*. At that time, PL/1 was being promoted as IBM's language of the future. Rather than designing his language to compete with PL/1 as a programming language, Codd selected the data-related features of his language (as PL/1 was particularly weak as a database language), which he called a data sublanguage. This work [CODD70] became the basis for the relational data model, and for relational languages and DBMSs. More important, it became the basis of much of today's database theory and systems technology.

DBMSs evolved in several distinct families [CODA69] [SIBL76] [FS76]. Report-generator systems started with General Electric's 1956 Report Generator, which evolved into the RPG and the MARK series of systems. Bachman's Integrated Data Store (IDS) from General Electric in 1962 became the basis for many database innovations, such as rollback, recovery, and checkpoints (1964); on-line transaction processing (1966); concurrency control and deadlock-detection mechanisms (1968); as well as basic ideas that came to be known as data independence, foreign keys, and referential integrity. The 1969 DBTG specification provided the basis for the network family of DBMSs, which included Cullinane's 1970 IDMS (IDS rewritten for an IBM/360 by B.F. Goodrich and first sold by tire sales representatives) and UNIVAC's DMS1100. Hierarchical DBMSs evolved from traditional business data processing. Specifically, IMS started as a joint project between North American (later Rockwell) and IBM in 1965, and became an IBM product in 1969. Prototype relational DBMSs were developed at IBM (System R [ABCE76]) and at many universities (e.g., INGRES [SWKH76]). Although there are now over 300 commercial relational DBMSs, the market is dominated by IBM's DB2 on large computers and Ashton-Tate's dBase products (over 2,700,000 sold) on PCs. It is significant that it took 15 years for Codd's relational concepts to appear in a major IBM DBMS product.

Although database concepts date back to the early 1950s, there was little database research until after 1969. Database concepts and systems evolved initially in industry, as described. The 1969 DBTG specification [CODA71], Codd's article on relational databases [CODD70], and Bachman's Turing award paper (1.3) marked the beginnings of the database research field in industry and universities. For example, in 1972, Bayer and McCreight [BM72] published their work on B-trees, one of the core access methods for modern DBMSs. Industrial requirements continue to motivate database research. For example, the American National Standard's ANSI-SPARC group promoted research in conceptual schemas and multilayered architectures [ANSI75], which ultimately led to systems-interconnection ideas, such as the Open Systems Interconnection (OSI) model currently being investigated in industry and universities. Database concepts and systems issues are discussed in the survey by Brodie and Manola (1.1).

From Dawn to Midday: More Modelling Power for Databases

By the mid-1970s both AI and databases had well-established research frameworks, national and international conferences, and a growing corpus of research results and tradition. Among databases researchers and practitioners, each of the three predominant data models—the hierarchical [TL76], network [TF76], and relational [CHAM76] models—had its supporters and detractors [MMC76]. Although the interest in computer-based information systems with deductive capabilities and natural-language front ends had persisted from the previous decade, a new insight was instrumental in the evolution of a common viewpoint: Data models were expressively inadequate for sophisticated application domains. [SS75] presents one of the earliest and most eloquent statements of the inadequacies of the relational model.* Its criticisms generally apply to the other data models of the day, more to some than to others.† At the first Very Large Databases (VLDB) Conference, in September 1975, some of the early "semantic" data models were proposed as extensions of conventional data models to "capture more semantics" [CODD79] (i.e., to provide better modelling facilities for representing knowledge about some application domains)—notably Peter Chen's Entity-Relationship model (2.1.2) and Roussopoulos (2.1.3). John and Diane Smith were particularly influential during this period ([SS77a], (2.1.4) [SS78]) in focusing database research on other areas of computer science in search of tools to enhance the expressiveness of data models.

The period between 1975 and the early 1980's is characterized by considerable interest in database circles for so-called *semantic data models* (i.e., data structures with a computationally tractable modelling framework [BROD84] [HK87]). They were intended to offer some expressiveness beyond classical data models while remaining within the overall methodological framework of database research. The number of semantic data models proposed during this period, well over 50, is an indication of the degree of interest in the topic. Most of these models share with Chen's work the primitive ontological notions of entity and relationship, adopting at the same time *abstraction mechanisms* as means for structuring the database. So-called *frame-based* knowledge representation languages in AI in the same period bear some similarity to their semantic data model cousins as many of them stress the notion of *frame*

* See [Kent, Section 2.2] for a more in-depth discussion of the modelling woes of conventional data models.

† Several data models, including the binary model of G. Bracchi, P. Paolini and G. Pelagatti [BPP76] and M. Senko's DIAM I and II [SENK75], did claim to offer better modelling facilities than the predominant data models provided.

[MINS75] (*concept, unit, class,...*), and provide various forms of organization, including generalization hierarchies, slots, and the like.

A parallel development of the period is the emergence of the concept of *deductive databases*, based on the observation that a database can (or should) be viewed as a collection of ground atomic formulas rather than a data structure and query processing as (deductive) inference. This simple change of perspective has offered new insights, a foundation for a database semantics and a direction for their extension to knowledge bases. The *Logic and Databases* workshop held in Toulouse in 1977 [GM78] is generally considered as the founding meeting of what is becoming an influential research trend of importance to both databases and AI. The original meeting was followed by others ([GMN81] [GMN84]). The trend has been strengthened by apparent similarities in goals and methodology with theoretical research on the relational model (see, for example, the technical programme of conferences on *Principles of Database Systems* (*PODS*)). A careful account of the relationship and differences in perspective between the two research frameworks can be found in Reiter (2.3.2), while Bancilhon (3.1.2) surveys a research topic (recursive query processing) that is of mutual interest.

Much has been said about the relative merits of entity-based models and deductive databases, mirroring in many respects analogous discussions on "declarative-procedural controversy" [WINO75], the former claiming pragmatic advantages, and the latter claiming the high ground on formality and foundational concerns. In retrospect, the advantages of these schools of thought appear to be complementary rather than mutually exclusive. For entity-based data models, they include a useful ontology and some useful ideas for dealing with organizational issues (a crucial concern for complex application domains), whereas for deductive databases, advantages are based on the availability of a well-established formal semantic framework.

Beyond Midday: Consolidation Period

The 1980s have been characterized by a consolidation of principles and further exploration of the interaction between AI and databases. A series of conferences, workshops, and journals have provided a forum for discussion, exchange of ideas and insights, and presentation of technical papers. These include interdisciplinary workshops at Pingree Park [BZ81], Intervale [BMS84], Kiawah [KERS86], Islamorada [BM86], Chania [ST88], Washington [MINK87] and many others. These meetings have encouraged the development of a common terminology and research methodology. In addition, international conferences such as the international Entity Relationship conference held on a regular basis since the first meeting in 1979 [CHEN79], and the Expert Database Systems conferences [KERS85] [KERS86] initiated by the Kiawah workshop, have provided an audience that is explicitly interested in an AI–databases interaction.

Several prototype implementations of extended DBMSs have also been reported, starting with ADAPLEX [Chan, 3.4.2] and including GEM [ZANI83], POSTGRES [Stonebraker, 3.4.4], Galileo [AGO88], Taxis [NCLB87], EXODUS [CDFG86], and many others. In addition, there have been early results on the development of complete methodologies for the design of databases, including requirements analysis, conceptual design, and implementation [CERI83], [ADD85], [TF80], [TEOR82], [TYF86]. Since 1986, an entire industry, called computer-aided software engineering (CASE), has evolved to provide automated database-design tools. As was the case with DBMSs, research in CASE became respectable in late 1988 after 150 CASE tools appeared on the market.

One of the methodological issues that surfaced during this period concerns the adoption of an **evolutionary** or **revolutionary** approach to the development of prototype DBMSs, offering advanced modelling and inference mechanisms [MYLO86]. Some projects have adopted and extended existing software. Others have attempted to build their systems from scratch, hoping that global optimization will compensate for the additional implementation effort involved. Another methodological issue that attracted attention due to the increased industrial presence of expert systems concerns the cooperation of an expert system with a database. Early approaches to the problem attempted a **loose coupling** of the two systems, based on communication between two independent systems; other approaches opt for a **tight coupling**, where the system managing the expert-system knowledge base is endowed with some DBMS facilities [JV83].

Object-oriented databases constitute another recent trend that bears some relevance to this volume (see [DD86], [BANC88], [BB84], [BUTL87],

[FISH87], [LOCH85], [MSOP86], [MD86], and to another book in this series, *Readings in Object-Oriented Databases* [ZM89]). The premise for this work is that a database consists of *objects*, a concept adopted from programming languages in the tradition of Simula and Smalltalk [GR83] and with many uses in AI programming [SB86]. This trend overlaps to some extent with work on entity-based data models. The ultimate goal here seems to be to extend the data types supported by the DBMS, to support software reusability, as well as to enhance modelling power. As in many other object-oriented approaches, the proposed tools for object-orientation include *encapsulation* as a means for partitioning databases and *message passing* as fundamental control structure.

The reader should not expect to find a deep integration of these AI and database concepts, trends, and systems. Although there has been some progress, significant integration has yet to occur. There are deep, open research issues, such as the development of global ontologies, which must encompass not only multiple knowledge representations but also multiple data models. More progress has been made concerning the construction of systems that incorporate both AI and database technologies, but much remains to be done. The reader is strongly encouraged to contribute to AI–database integration. Researchers are also encouraged to take advantage of the 30 years of technology and research results from the AI, database and AI–database areas. This volume is one starting point for this work.

STRUCTURE OF THE BOOK

This volume is a collection of key papers on the topics of AI and databases, selected for readers with an undergraduate computer-science background in both AI and databases. The text includes survey papers to refresh the reader's background of key concepts and to present a "bird's eye" view of important topics within the two fields that have been the subject of much research. The volume consists of four chapters. The first chapter introduces relevant topics from AI and databases. Two chapters deal with modelling and performance issues, respectively. The final chapter is an epilogue. The volume also contains a bibliography and an index of AI and database terms.

A few words are in order for topics that are **not** covered in the book, the most notable example being *natural-language front ends* to databases. To some extent, this topic is covered in another volume of the *Readings in AI* series [GSW86]. The interested reader may also refer to [WOOD73], [HARR79], and [BMS86] for important references on the subject. A second area of interaction between the two fields that is not covered here involves *expert-system applications* in the design of databases or in the improvement of the performance of a particular database system. [BGM85a] offers a typical example of the former use of expert systems, whereas [KING81] provides a good example of the latter kind, focusing on the problem of query optimization.

The first chapter includes recently written surveys of databases and knowledge representaton in addition to papers written by prominent researchers in the two fields. It is intended as a review of basic concepts as well as a presentation of profound insights into the significance of the results in these fields. For more information on databases, see relevant textbooks (e.g., [ULLM82] [ULLM88] [DATE81] [DATE83]). For knowledge representation, an excellent source of basic material is provided by [BL86], another volume in the *Readings in AI* series.

The second chapter, *Representation and Semantics*, focuses on the modelling tools that have been suggested for advanced data models, and contrasts these with parallel proposals for knowledge representation. The first section, *Entity-Based Representations*, includes early proposals for extending data models; it is followed by a section on *Semantic Data Models and Knowledge Representations*, which looks at a second group of such proposals that are generally more recent, more ambitious, and further developed. The third section presents three papers on *Logic and Databases*, including a survey; the fourth section presents three different ways of looking at *Database/Knowledge-Base Semantics*. A final section presents two different ways of addressing incompleteness in a database or knowledge base, by showing how certain kinds of incomplete information can be represented, then by studying the problem of information retrieval in the presence of such incomplete information. This is only one example of a representation issue where AI and database perspectives lead to quite different results. Others include the representation of temporal and spatial information and of inexact information.

The third chapter, *Performance Issues*, addresses questions of efficiency and robustness. The first section, *Retrieval, Deduction, and Query*

Processing, compares the means that have been offered for accessing a database or knowledge base, including deduction with respect to a knowledge base, retrieval from a data structure, and query processing by a DBMS. The second section, *Database and Knowledge-Base Integrity*, presents alternative views of what does it mean for a database or knowledge base to satisfy an integrity constraint, of how to implement an enforcement mechanism, and of what can be done if a constraint is violated. The third section of this chapter describes important *Implementation Techniques* (mostly, but not exclusively for databases). The last section presents implemented *Database and Knowledge-Base Management Systems*.

The final section, entitled *Epilogue*, presents a current view of the need, importance, status, and challenges of AI–database integration. It is based on an invited talk at the 1988 AAAI and VLDB Conferences, thus marking the importance of the topic or at least the level of concern for it in the AI and database communities. The *Epilogue* discusses database technology applied to AI and vice versa, and the technology that would result from the integration as a basis for the next generation of computing. It presents the results of a survey on AI–database integration conducted in late 1988 with AI and database researchers and practitioners around the world.

The extensive bibliography is a partial list of key papers from the last 30 years of AI–database literature. The introduction to each chapter acts as a guide to articles cited in the bibliography that are relevant to the topic of the chapter. The Subject Index covers principle topics and AI and database terminology.

Chapter 1

Introduction to AI and Databases

This chapter contains papers that present the basic concepts underlying AI and databases. These papers also describe the origins of the two areas and the trends that are setting new directions for AI and database research and technology, such as AI–database integration. The chapter opens with two recent survey papers, "Database Management: A Survey" by Michael L. Brodie and Frank Manola (1.1), and "Knowledge Representation and Reasoning" by Hector Levesque (1.2).

The third paper of the chapter (1.3), "The Programmer as Navigator" by Charlie Bachman, is the 1973 Turing Award Lecture, earned for contributions to the development and industrial acceptance of database technology. Bachman argues in favour of a new view of data processing, which replaces the concepts of machine memory and file with that of a network of records. The lecture is a powerful argument in favour of a database-based rather than a file-based perspective of data processing. It came at a time when debate had already started on the relative advantages and disadvantages of the "established" data models of the day, the hierarchical, network data model largely a result of work by Bachman, and the relational model developed by T. Codd [CODD70]. Bachman's postscript, written in 1986, reviews the dramatic evolution of DBMSs and the roles of the programmer over the 13 years since the Turing Award Lecture. Bachman looks to the future and to the integration of DBMS and other technologies such as AI, communications, and programming languages.

The fourth paper (1.4), "Relational Database: A Practical Foundation for Productivity" by Ted Codd, is the 1981 Turing Award Lecture, by which time the relational model was fully established in the research community as the preeminent data model because of its simplicity and elegance. However, industrial acceptance did not come until the mid-1980s, due partly to inertia and partly to the unexpected difficulty of developing efficient relational DBMSs. Codd's lecture is an overview of the impressive progress made in the development of the relational model as well as in the implementation and use of commercial relational DBMSs.

The occasion for the lecture material presented in the fifth paper (1.5), "Making Believers Out of Computers" by Hector Levesque, was the award of the Computers and Thought prize in 1985. The prize is given every 2 years to the most promising young AI researcher. Levesque examines, from a semantic and a computational viewpoint, the essence of the problem of building computers that are "believers" of the information that they contain, rather than are merely passive information "managers." Another theme of the paper is the development of computationally tractable knowledge-representation schemes. One method suggested by Levesque for avoiding computational intractability is to represent knowledge in a *vivid* form (i.e., in a restricted form that reduces retrieval to simple database-style lookup). [SK88] presents several complexity results on how difficult it is to transform nonvivid knowledge bases to vivid ones using defaults.

Database Management: A Survey

Michael L. Brodie and Frank Manola
GTE Laboratories Incorporated

ABSTRACT *The objective of Database Management technology is to provide general-purpose mechanisms for managing large, shared data repositories. This chapter presents the basic concepts, techniques, and tools of database management. Data modelling, data models, and database languages are described together with their application in database design, and development database management systems and implementation issues are outlined. The chapter concludes by discussing the current challenges that are driving advances in database technology and by identifying the future directions for database management research. Database motivations and concepts are compared and contrasted with those in Artificial Intelligence.*

1. Database Management Technology: Concepts, Techniques, and Tools

During the past 30 years, databases have evolved from simple file systems to collections of data that concurrently serve a wide community of users and numerous distinct applications. For example, an insurance company might store data for policies, claims, investments, personnel, payroll, and planning in one database. Databases can vary in size from very small to very large (e.g., from hundreds to millions of records), and can be designed to support a single user or thousands of on-line users.

Typically, a database is a resource for an organization (e.g., insurance company) for which three human roles are distinguished in relation to its design, development, and use. A database administrator (DBA) is responsible for designing and maintaining the database. Application programmers design and implement database transactions and application interfaces (e.g., screens). Finally, end-users use prepared database applications and, possibly, high-level database query languages.

The design and development of databases and their applications can be described as follows: Given the information and processing requirements of an information system, construct a representation of the information system that captures the static (i.e., information content) and dynamic (i.e., processing operations) properties needed to support the required transactions and queries. To the greatest extent possible, the static and dynamic properties common to all applications should be represented in the database. To be independent of any particular application, a database should represent the properties common to all applications. The process of capturing and representing these properties in the database is called **database design**.

The representation resulting from database design must be able to meet ever-changing requirements of existing or new applications or be modified easily to do so. A major objective of database design is **data independence,** which concerns insulating the database and the associated applications from logical and physical changes. Ideally, the database could be changed logically (e.g., add new entities or objects) or physically (e.g., change access structures) without affecting existing applications, and applications could be added or modified without affecting the existing database.

Static properties include objects, object properties (sometimes called attributes), and relationships among objects. Dynamic properties include query and altering operations on objects and relationships among operations (e.g., to form complex operations called transactions). Properties that cannot be expressed conveniently as objects or object properties are expressed as semantic integrity constraints. A **semantic integrity constraint** is a logical condition expressed over objects (i.e., database states) and operations (i.e., state transitions). The following are examples of integrity constraints:

Written May 1987, revised September 1988. Appeared in *Fundamentals of Knowledge Base Management Systems*, J.W. Schmidt and C. Thanos (eds.), Springer Verlag, 1988, also in [MB88].

Each student must have a unique student number.

For each enrollment, there must be both a student and a course.

Student enrollment in a course must not exceed the enrollment limit for that course.

To enroll in a course, a student must meet the prerequisites for that course.

A manager must earn more than the employees managed.

The results of database design are schema, transaction, and query definitions. A schema defines the static properties of a database, while transactions and queries define the dynamic properties. A **schema** consists of definitions of all application object types, including their attributes, relationships, and static constraints. Corresponding to the schema will be a data repository called a **database** which consists of instances of objects and relationships defined in the schema. A particular class of processes within an application (e.g., paying benefits within an insurance company database) may need to access only some of the static properties of a predetermined subset of the objects. Such a subset, which is called a **subschema** or **view**, is derived from the schema much as a query is defined (e.g., Find/Create subschema using all employees in the investment department).

Associated with the schema concept is a notion of **logical database integrity**. A database exhibits logical integrity if the values in the database are legal instances of the types in the schema and if all semantic integrity constraints are satisfied.

The purpose of a database is to answer queries and to support database transactions. A **query** can be expressed as a logical expression over the objects and relationships defined in the schema and results in identifying a logical subset of the database. A **transaction** consists of several database query and altering operations over objects in a subschema and is used to define application events or operations. Transactions are atomic in that all steps of a transaction must be completed successfully or the entire transaction must be aborted (i.e., no part of a transaction is committed before the whole transaction is completed). The primary criteria for the database is that it exhibit logical and physical integrity and remain secure in the face of potential errors or malicious use by multiple users or transactions.

A **data model** is a collection of mathematically well-defined concepts that help one to reason about data and to express the static and dynamic properties and integrity constraints for an application. (In practice, most data models have been developed intuitively. Formal definitions, if they exist, have been given subsequently) They include concepts for defining schemas, subschemas, integrity constraints, queries, and transactions. A data model includes a constrained-type system (i.e., fewer types than a high-level programming language) for defining objects and operations on objects. Unlike most AI knowledge representation schemes, data models provide a procedural semantics based on elementary database altering operations (i.e., insert, update, and delete) and on the concept of an update transaction. Altering and query operations are an essential part of a data model.

A **data** model defines the **concepts** that underlie the **tools** and **techniques** used to support the design, development, and use of databases. It provides the syntactic and semantic basis for tools such as user interface languages. **Data Definition Languages** (DDL) provide means for defining schemas and subschemas. **Data Manipulation Languages** (DML) are used to write database applications. **Query Languages** (QL) are provided for writing queries and reports. Many database languages combine query, manipulation, and subschema definitions. These languages can be provided on a stand-alone basis, embedded as call statements in a host language such as COBOL (these two cases are typical in commercial systems), or integrated directly into high-level programming languages such as ADAPLEX [SFL83] and TAXIS [MW80] [ALBA86].

The techniques for applying the concepts, supported by the tools, is the domain of database administration. DBAs manage all resources needed to effectively design, develop, and maintain database systems. The DBA role is becoming increasingly automated as database design and development tools are developed (discussed in Section 4).

The main database tool is the **database management system** (DBMS) (see [DATE83, DATE86, ULLM82, ULLM88, SB83]). The hypothetical **DBMS Architecture** [CCA82] (in Figure 1) illustrates the four typical component groups that provide the functions of a centralized (nondistributed) DBMS: (1) user interface processors; (2) schema processors; (3) database administration aids; and (4) core database manager. In Figure 1, the boxes represent sets of components, the circles individual components, and the lines the use of a component by either an end user (labelled "E") or by another component.

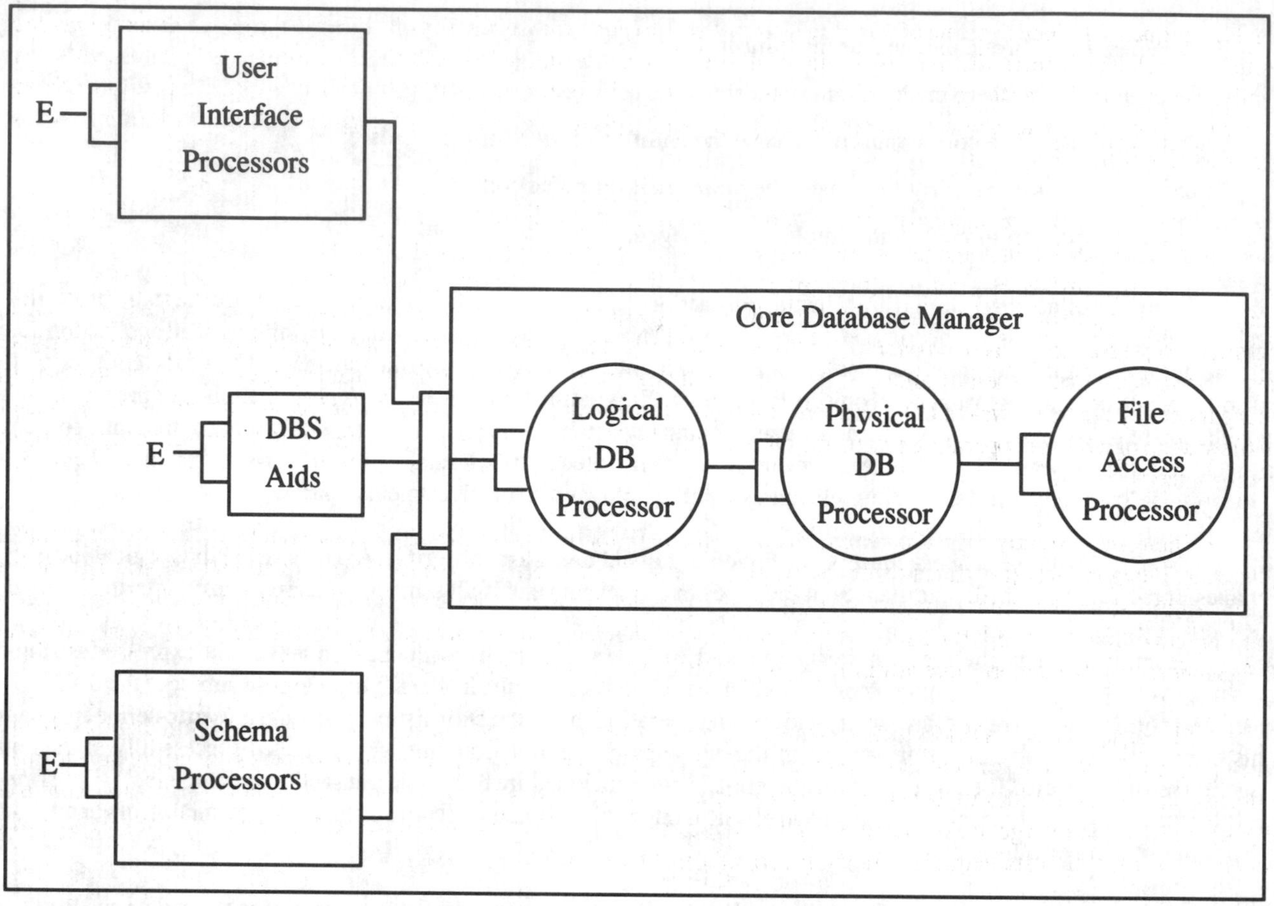

Figure 1. Hypothetical DBMS Architecture

User interface processors support user interactions with the DBMS. These components include QL translators, host programming language or DML translators, and other interfaces such as graphics-based or natural-language interfaces, and tools such as editors to assist users in construction of their requests. These components translate requests into a common interface form defined by the core database manager (e.g., relational algebra).

Schema processors support the definition and maintenance of database definitions expressed using the DDL. This database control data includes definition of logical and physical database structures (e.g., schemas, subschemas, views), semantic integrity constraint definitions, access control definitions, etc., and other information determined during the database design process. Schema processors translate DDL data into internal forms that are used by the DBMS in processing requests. Typically, relational DBMSs do not distinguish between applications and database control data with respect to storage management. Hence, schema processors typically utilize the core database manager for retrieving, updating, and storing database control data.

Database administration aids, such as data dictionary/directories and database design aids, support database administration functions. These functions require data that is processed by the schema processors and stored by the core database manager.

The core database manager components are the central elements of the DBMS. They provide the storage and retrieval facilities for all application and control data stored in the system. The core database manager provides interfaces to the user interface and schema processors and to the database administration aids. The common interface for all user interface processors provides facilities for manipulating the logical data structures defined by the DBMS's data model. The core database manager translates requests defined in terms of this logical interface into data storage commands, using the database descriptions defined through the schema processors. It also provides buffering, query optimization, and other performance enhancement services. Finally, it manages the sharing of the data resources by serializing transactions and other operations against the database, performing recovery management, providing multithreaded scheduling, and supporting audit, cost accounting, and other administrative functions.

The core database manager conceptually consists of three distinct components. The logical database processor component translates database operations expressed in terms of the DBMS's (logical) data model into physical operations on the underlying storage structures. Storage structures that exist for performance reasons, such as indexes, are not visible in the logical data model, but operations on them are visible at the physical level. The physical database processor component translates operations expressed in terms of physical operations on database storage structures into operations on (usually operating system) files. The physical level generally allows specification and manipulation of units of data (e.g., a *page*) that will be accessed from secondary storage in one physical I/O operation. Typically, the functions of the file access processor component are provided by the file system of whatever operating system the DBMS is designed to run on. These functions include various sorts of file system access methods.

There are currently over 400 commercial DBMSs that run on mainframe and microcomputers. They typically support the classical data models (i.e., **hierarchic**, **network**, and **relational**). Since the mid-1970's, relational DBMSs have become widely used and are becoming the main technology for general-purpose database management. The 1980's has seen the development of hundreds of DBMSs for workstations, including personal computers and Lisp machines. These newer, smaller DBMSs increasingly support more advanced data models (discussed in Section 2).

Major advances in DBMS technology have been sparked by the identification of fundamentally difficult problems in developing data-intensive applications. Solutions to these problems have been built into the DBMS system software to provide application developers with simple and innovative *abstractions* for solving the problems. This approach has made it feasible to develop and maintain large-scale database applications. While the abstractions are conceptually simple, they have spawned pioneering research thrusts to implement them correctly and efficiently.

Since the 1960's, three major abstractions have been developed for large, shared database applications. First, the **data independence** abstraction allowed application developers to ignore details of how the information was physically organized on storage devices, or how to efficiently access it for processing queries. Second, the **transaction atomicity** abstraction allowed applications to ignore the effects of other applications that may be concurrently accessing shared information, and also allowed shared databases to be recoverable after system crashes. Third, the **location independence** abstraction permitted applications to access distributed (and possibly heterogeneous) information repositories without worrying about where the data was located.

Three new database abstractions are now being developed in response to new application requirements. First, the **object** abstraction has recently been introduced to support the modelling and processing requirements of many new information types. These requirements differ substantially from those of the conventional record-oriented data handled effectively by conventional DBMSs. Second, to accommodate stringent performance requirements such as those found in real-time and other time-critical applications (e.g., process control), the concept of an active controller is being developed to provide a **self-monitoring** abstraction. Conventional DBMSs can become a serious performance bottleneck for these applications due to their need to constantly poll the DBMS for the latest data. The active controller continually monitors the database and reports relevant events to the requesting application as they occur; it also dynamically schedules its workload to satisfy specified time constraints. Third, the **staging independence** abstraction is being developed for workstation-based applications that need access to large, shared information repositories located on separate machines. Currently such applications are themselves responsible for locating the data, communicating with a database server or file server, and then downloading the data into the workstation, refreshing the downloaded extract as needed, and staging data between the workstation and the back-end server. Typically, these tasks are performed in an *ad hoc* fashion. Research is now being focused on staging independence for workstation object managers to provide the illusion that all required knowledge/data is in the workstation's address space and is private to the application. The benefit of these new abstractions will be a dramatic reduction in application software complexity, and hence in the cost of developing, maintaining, and modifying application software to satisfy evolving application requirements. These new abstractions are discussed in Section 4.

The basic paradigm for advances in database technology is that concepts and techniques provide the basis for the development of the next generation of DBMSs and related tools. Data modelling concepts are developed in response to requirements of new, data-intensive applications. For example, the relational data model and associated languages were developed for record-oriented applications over large, shared databases. Ideally, techniques are developed for database modelling based on the concepts (e.g., normalization, view design, and view integration were developed for relational database design). The concepts and techniques must be understood and proven to support the representation and processing requirements for the intended application classes. Then, the next-generation DBMS and its associated processors are built. Finally, tools are developed to support database design and development techniques for the new DBMS.

The rest of this chapter discusses the concepts, techniques, and tools that underlie the current generation of DBMSs and the requirements of new applications that are already leading to the next generation of DBMSs. Data modelling, data models, and database languages were described in this section together with their application in database design and development. Database management systems and implementation issues are outlined in Section 3. Section 4 concludes the chapter by discussing the current challenges that are driving advances in database technology and by identifying the future directions for database management research.

2. Data Modelling, Data Models, and Database Languages

Database system design and development deals with the application of database technology for building high-quality, low-cost database or information systems. Database design involves the design of both the static and dynamic properties of database applications. It results in definitions of both data (i.e., schemas and subschemas) and processes (i.e., transactions, queries, and reports). Database development involves the implementation of the database design and results in an executable database system.

The size and complexity of the database system design and development process requires powerful concepts, techniques, and tools to support design, development, and management of the design and development process. Recently, database system design and development has matured from loose collections of *ad hoc* techniques to relatively well-understood, proven methods. This coming of age has spurred the development, since 1985, of over 150 commercial products that automate aspects of the design and development process. This emerging technology, called Computer Aided Software Engineering (CASE), is discussed in Section 4. This section describes the concepts (principally data models), techniques, and tools (principally languages) for database design and development.

The database system design and development life cycle provides a framework for the related tasks. It includes eight steps: information resource management, requirements analysis and specification, conceptual design, logical design, distributed design, physical design, implementation, and operation [TEOR82].

Information resource management (IRM) is the management of the data, people, and processes that produce information that serves a business or functional need. IRM focuses on enhancing productivity within a corporation by taking a comprehensive view of systems development. Once the IRM step has identified the organization's need for a database system, the life cycle begins. The requirements step defines the information and processing requirements that the database system must meet.

Database design is levelled to produce successively more detailed database designs (i.e., schemas and transactions) that meet the successively more detailed requirements. The conceptual, logical, and physical design steps provide the levelling in which each step involves a different level of abstraction guided by an appropriately detailed data model. Conceptual design is done in terms of a conceptual data model (e.g., entities, relationships, and transactions in the Entity-Relationship data model) [CHEN76, TYF86]. Logical design involves translating the conceptual design into a logical design in terms of a logical data model such as the relational, network, or hierarchical data models. Physical design involves translating the logical design into a physical design in terms of the physical data model of the target DBMS (i.e., the precise details of the DBMS). This involves selecting the most efficient data encodings, data structures, storage element sizes, indexes, access paths, and algorithms to meet performance and maintenance requirements.

The distributed design step, required for distributed databases, follows the logical design step and is typically expressed in terms of the logical data model. The implementation step involves translating the physical design into executable DDL and DML statements that can produce the executable database system.

The remainder of this section describes logical data models and the associated languages, and the motivations for more advanced semantic data models. The concepts of data model and data languages came about with the relational data model [CODD70, CHAM76] after early DBMSs were developed in industry. Discussions of data model concepts can be found in [DATE86, ULLM82, BROD84, HK87].

The classical data models are based on common concepts (e.g., records, attributes, relationships, unique valued identifying fields) that were inherited from their ancestors, simple file systems. However, the notation and some concepts are unique to each model. Hierarchic [TL76] and network [TF76] data models represent objects in records that are organized, using 1:N binary relationships, as nodes in trees and networks, respectively. These data models provide primitive operations and record-at-a-time navigational facilities.

Unlike the relational languages, hierarchic and network languages are more representational (i.e., users must deal with more storage and implementation features), but they have a richer set of inherent constraints (e.g., built-in relationship types). The navigational and representational aspects of these languages are historical; set-oriented, non-navigational and less representational languages have been proposed for these models.

The following example illustrates concepts common to hierarchical and network data models. Figure 2 illustrates a schema for a database concerning parts. Objects are represented by labelled boxes. Relationships are represented by labelled, directed edges. Single-headed directed edges represent 1:1 relationships. Doubled-headed edges represent 1:N relationships. This schema does not directly support N:M relationships between SUPPLIER and PART (i.e., a part is supplied by several suppliers and a supplier can supply several parts) and between ORDER and PART. Representing an N:M relationship in network schemas requires the introduction of "link" record, as illustrated in Figure 3. Figure 2 is a network schema with a strict hierarchical structure (i.e., each object has one "parent" or "owner"). Hence, Figure 2 can be considered a hierarchical schema. Figure 3 has objects with two "owners" (e.g., PART-ORDER is owned by both PART and ORDER), and hence it is not a hierarchy.

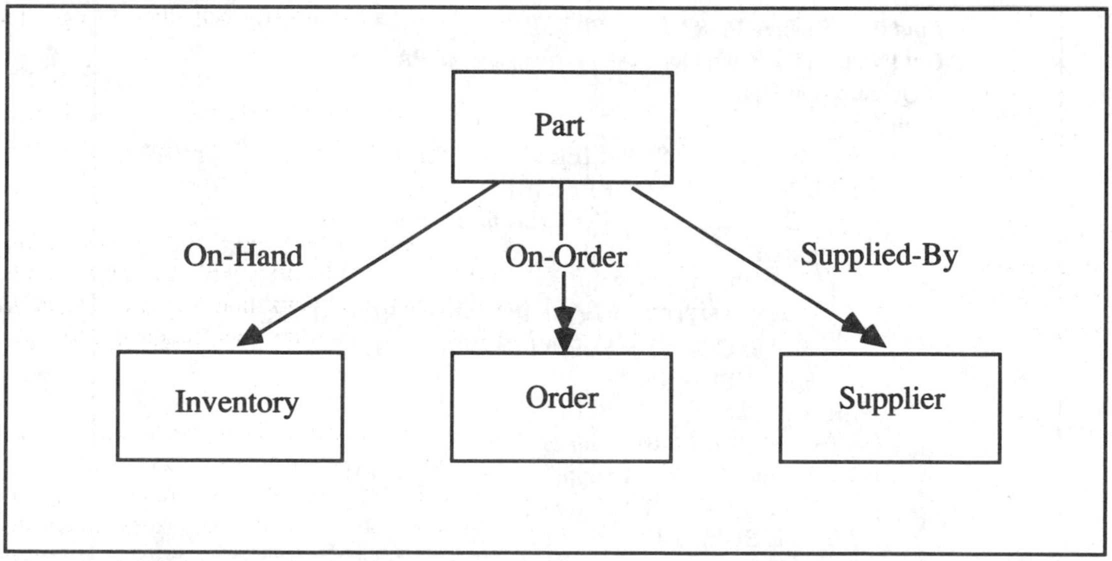

Figure 2. Network PART SCHEMA with 1:M Relationships

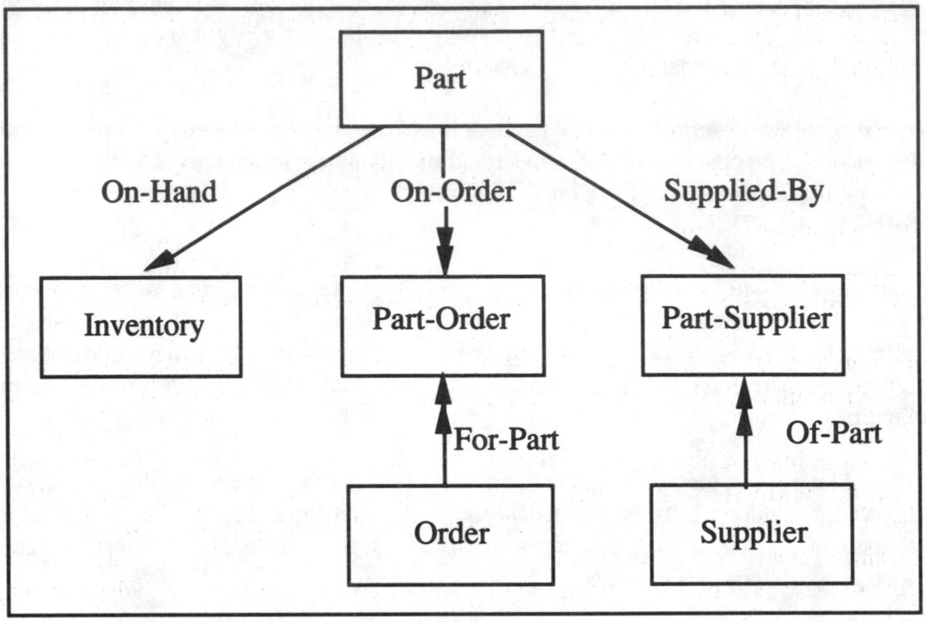

Figure 3. Network PART SCHEMA with N:M Relationships

Hierarchic and network queries and transactions are navigational. They follow logical connections from one record to another reading and writing information as they go. The navigational transaction in Figure 4 orders parts from a preferred supplier for those parts in the given list that have less than 17 in the inventory. The transaction is written against the schema in Figure 2. Note the two nested loops in the transactions.

```
For each P in PART-LIST

Do:
    Find PART where PART.P#=P.P#
    Get INVENTORY via ON-HAND from current PART
    If Quantity-On-Hand < 17
    Then Do
        SUPLOOP: Get next SUPPLIER via SUPPLIED-BY from current PART
            If SUPPLIER.S# = O.PREFERRED-S#
            Then Do: Insert via ON-ORDER for current PART
                ORDER (DATE = today, PART# = P.P#,
                    SUPPLIER = P.S#,
                    QUANTITY-ON-ORDER = PART.RE-ORDER,
                    DISCOUNT = SUPPLIER.DISCOUNT);
                End SUPLOOP
            End do;
        Else If SUPPLIER is last within SUPPLIED-BY
            Then Print ("Preferred Supplier" P.PREFERRED
                "of PART" P.P# "missing")
            Else End SUPLOOP;
    End do;
End do;
```

Figure 4. Recorded-at-a-Time Navigational Transaction

The relational data model is based on the mathematical concept of a relation, on set theory, and on predicate calculus. A relation is a set of n-tuples. A tuple can be used directly to represent both objects and N:M, n-ary relationships. Figure 5 illustrates a relation representing an enrollment object.

```
ENROLLMENT(STUDENT#, COURSE#, TERM, GRADE)
STUDENT(STUDENT#, ...)
COURSE(COURSE#, ...)
```

Figure 5. ENROLLMENT: An N:M Relationship Between STUDENT and COURSE

Enrollment represents both an n-ary relation between the four attributes and an N:M relationship between STUDENT and COURSE objects (i.e., a student can enroll in N courses and a course can have M students enrolled).

The relational algebra and calculus provide a set-oriented query and access facility that can also be used to define schemas and constraints. Figure 6 illustrates a relational schema equivalent to the network PARTS schema given in Figure 2. Objects here are represented by relations. Attributes that take part in the key are underlined. Relationships are value-based, that is, a relationship can be established by matching values of corresponding attributes (via a join operator). For example, a join between ORDER and PART based on equal PART# values establishes the ON-ORDER relationships in Figure 2. As with the network schema, a "link" relation must be added to represent an N:M relationship, as in Figure 7.

```
PART (PART#, COLOR, WEIGHT, RE-ORDER)
SUPPLIER (SUPPLIER#, PART#, ADDRESS, DISCO UNT)
ORDER (DATE, PART#, SUPPLIER#, QUANTITY-ON-ORDER, DISCOUNT)
INVENTORY (PART#, QUANTITY-ON-HAND)
```

Figure 6. Relational PART SCHEMA with 1:N Relationships

```
PART (PART#, COLOR, WEIGHT, RE-ORDER)
SUPPLIER (SUPPLIER#, ADDRESS, DISCOUNT)
PART-SUPPLIER (PART#, SUPPLIER#)
ORDER (ORDER#, DATE)
ORDER-ITEM (ORDER#, PART#, SUPPLIER#, QUANTITY-ON-ORDER, DISCOUNT)
INVENTORY (PART#, QUANTITY-ON-HAND)
```

Figure 7. Relational PART SCHEMA with N:M Relationships

The transaction in Figure 8 is a relational version of the navigational transaction in Figure 4.

```
For each P in PART-LIST, S in SUPPLIER, I in INVENTORY
    where P.PART# = I.PART#
    and I.QUANTITY-ON-HAND < 17
    and S.PART# = P.PART
    and P.PREFERRED-S = S.S#:
Insert ORDER (DATE = today, PART# = P.PART#,
        SUPPLIER# = S.SUPPLIER#, DISCOUNT = S.DISCOUNT,
        QUANTITY-ON-ORDER = PART.RE-ORDER);
```

Figure 8. Set-Oriented Relational Transaction

Whereas the navigational form explicitly uses two nested loops, the set-oriented form uses no explicit loops. The relational query processor determines an execution strategy for processing the set.

Due to the need for higher level data modelling concepts (i.e., at the conceptual level) and to an ever-growing need to capture more meaning of the information stored in a database (if only by improved data representation and organization) (see [SS75] for one of the earliest and most eloquent statements of inadequacies of the relational data model, see also [KENT78] and [KENT79]), a new generation of data models evolved, called **semantic data models** [BROD84] [HK87]. Some of these models were extensions of classical data models, whereas others were developed in response to other influences. Some semantic data models were defined based on mathematical theories, mostly first order logic, in order to make use of well-understood semantics and to rely on associated computational and analytical tools. For example, Reiter [REIT84] proposed a reformulation of the relational data model based on the proof theory of first order logic, thereby providing a direct means to extend the semantics of the model. Most semantic data models were influenced by semantic networks. They are generally object-oriented and provide at least four types of primitive relationships between objects: classification (instance-of), aggregation (part-of), generalization (is-a), and cover (member-of).

Data models differ in their capabilities for expressing static and dynamic properties of applications. Properties that can be expressed directly in one model may require more complex expressions in other data models. For example, a generalization relationship between objects would have to be expressed by complex expressions using the relational model, whereas it could be defined directly using semantic data models that support generalization. Typically, DBMSs enforce properties expressed in the schema by detecting and preventing updates that would result in a database that violates the schema. **Semantic integrity constraints** express properties that cannot be expressed directly in terms of the objects and operations of the data model. They must be enforced, typically at great cost, by applications. Advances in data models arise by enhancing their capabilities for expressing objects, object relationships, and operations. Advances in DBMSs occur when they are extended to directly support the enhanced data models.

The representation of **object relationships** is an essential capability of data models. File systems do not explicitly support relationships. The hierarchic and network data models provide direct means for representing 1:1, 1:N, and restricted N:M relationships between objects. The relational data model provided direct means (the n-ary relation) for representing general N:M relationships (as in the above example). Semantic data models influenced by semantic networks attempt to model more application-oriented relationships (e.g., married-to, works-for, is-part-of, likes). Some data models provide a small, fixed set of relationship types with which all application relationships must be represented (e.g., using the hierarchic data model, all relationships must be hierarchic). Other data models provide general mechanisms for representing any application relationship (e.g., a labelled edge in a semantic network). Some data models support semantic relativism in that there is no distinction between objects and relationships [BR84].

Query and altering operations define the dynamic semantics of a data model. Altering operations define the update semantics of database objects. Query operations define the querying power of the database. Different operations produce different data models, even over the same data structures, just as different inference mechanisms over the same data structures produce different knowledge representation schemes. It can be argued that the network and relational data models differ largely in their operations and not in their data structures.

Database language research is an integral part of data model research. A major thrust of formal database theory and (informal) database semantics research has been to define the semantics of database languages. The results have provided well-defined objects and relationships (for semantic data models). The semantics referred to concern the meaning of queries (i.e., the precise definition of the evaluation of queries over a database and the correctness of query evaluation algorithms).

Data model research has focused on logical aspects of databases and on concepts, tools, and techniques for database design [BROD84] [TF80]. The primary concerns have been for the logical representation of objects. Theoretical work has been done in the areas of defining data model semantics [REIT84], treating of null values, database design techniques based on the relational data model (normalization) [MAIE83, ULLM82, TYF86], specifying and verifying of schemas and transactions, analysis of query languages, query processing, query optimization, view update, (universal relation) interfaces, constraint analysis, applying logic to a variety of traditional database problems, and the development of deductive databases [GMN84].

Database theory establishes the power of relational languages (e.g., transitive closure cannot be expressed). Significant work has been done on the interfacing of programming languages with DBMSs (e.g., loose coupling via workspaces or cursors [AC76], integration with a host language [SFL83]). Other database language research has concentrated on user interfaces and database front ends. Topics in this area include natural language and graphics interfaces to databases, database environments [REIN84], and human factors [SHNE80].

Database theory has produced dependency theory (normalization) [ULLM82, MAIE83], which addresses some aspects of logical design. Algorithms have been developed for aspects of the view integration problem (i.e., designing a global schema from several overlapping views or subschemata). In addition, (intuitive) methodologies have been developed for logical design [OST84, OLLE88]. Other methodologies, based on software engineering principles, have been proposed for the design of both schemata and transactions at the conceptual level [BR84, BMS84]. Database design and development environments to support such methodologies are discussed in Section 4 and [REIN84].

Data models are related to knowledge representation in AI [BMS84]. Issues of common interest include expressive power, modelling capabilities (e.g., abstraction), languages, inference (i.e., search), truth management (i.e., integrity maintenance), and formal definition of the representations. There is some controversy between AI and Database people about what is modelled in databases [BLP84, BM86b]. Database people contend that databases model parts of the real world (i.e., information systems applications). Some AI people contend that databases do not provide interpretations in which individuals (e.g., objects in the real world) are identified with representations in the database that are used in any reasoning. They claim that databases store and manipulate data structures (at the symbol level) as opposed to representing knowledge (as perceived at the knowledge level) and supporting inference. A middle ground between these extremes is that DBMSs provide some interpretation but depend largely on user intuition and that databases do represent knowledge and provide elementary inference capabilities. Most attempts to integrate AI and Database concepts have concerned data models and knowledge representation. As discussed in Section 4, such an integration involves integrating the data models with semantic or knowledge models in AI and enhancing AI systems with the powerful computational models underlying DBMSs.

3. DBMS Systems Issues

Database systems and implementation issues include concurrency control [ESWA76], query optimization [SACL79], data structures and algorithms, performance evaluation, database systems reliability, database machines, DBMS architectures, security, and distributed databases [LR82]. These topics are discussed in DBMS texts such as [DATE86, DATE83, ULLM82, ULLM88].

DBMS architectures consist of the DBMS components (discussed in Section 1), the interfaces between the components, and the languages presented to users. DBMS architectures are studied in order to understand data and control flows within the DBMS, to improve system modularity, and to identify system interfaces that might be candidates for standardization. An early example of an architecture developed for standards-related purposes, called the ANSI/SPARC Framework [ANSI75] [DATE86], identified more than 40 components and interfaces. A major contribution of the framework was the three-schema approach (i.e., external schemata for user views, a conceptual schema that integrated external schemata, and an internal schema that defines physical storage structures). The architecture described in Section 1 is another example of a standards-related architecture. The development of relational DBMSs such as INGRES [STON76] and SYSTEM R [AC76] resulted in a few well-understood DBMS architectures [SB83] to support conventional DBMS functionality. More recent DBMSs have been developed to support the three-schema approach, in order to provide for greater data independence. Current research on advanced DBMS architectures reflects the need to integrate new types of components to support advanced DBMS applications (see Section 4).

A database query is expressed, using a QL, as a high-level description of the data to be accessed (as illustrated in Section 2). Typically, there is more than one possible set of physical database operations that will process the query (i.e., access the required data). **Query optimization** concerns the development of efficient plans for processing queries over a database [JK84, KRB85]. Such plans are developed based on a cost model that reflects the characteristics of the storage structures and access methods available within the DBMS, and information about the data itself maintained by the DBMS. The processing of queries that involve relational operations such as selection, projection, and join operations is well understood. Optimization research has concentrated on the more expensive database operations, which for centralized databases is the join operation, and which for distributed databases is intersite processing (e.g., queries over databases in multiple sites) [YC84]. Database theory has provided query decomposition algorithms, query simplification mechanisms based on tableau, and semi-join theory for optimizing joins [MAIE83].

Integrity maintenance attempts to ensure that a database remains consistent with a set of predefined integrity constraints after each update. Integrity constraints can be thought of as queries that must always return a true value. Hence, integrity maintenance is closely associated with query processing. Although the semantic issues for integrity constraints are relatively well-understood (e.g., declarative expressions of semantic integrity constraints) and some computational results exist, a theory or body of techniques do not support their efficient maintenance.

Since databases are primarily shared resources, a DBMS must process many concurrent requests (transactions). The objective is to provide the maximum amount of concurrent access while preventing requests from interfering with the correct operation of other transactions (e.g., two requests modifying the same data at the same time). Concurrency control mechanisms attempt to provide correct, concurrent access to a DBMS by two or more database transactions [BHG87].

Currently, the primary correctness criterion is "serializability," meaning that the effect of running the transactions concurrently is the same as the effect of some serial (nonconcurrent) execution of the transactions [ESWA76]. This means that a transaction need have no knowledge that any other transactions are running. A well-developed theory exists for serializability, and techniques exist for verifying that individual concurrency control mechanisms are correct according to this criterion. Various mechanisms, based on locking and timestamping, have been devised to synchronize accesses to shared data in order to guarantee this criterion.

Current research is directed at identifying correctness criteria other than serializability that may be appropriate in some applications, and that may require less computational overhead than mechanisms that guarantee serializability (see Section 4).

Data structures and algorithms research was well established before database research began. The results of most research into storage and access structures are directly applicable to databases. Recent database research has addressed dynamic storage structures, including hashing, B-trees [BM72], and index sequential directories. Some well-known heuristics exist for physical database design, and a general theory is beginning to emerge for file structures. Recently there has been a resurgence of interest in the design and analysis of dynamic hashing based, in part, on results from computational complexity of retrievals and updates and motivated by the need to store new types of data (e.g., spatial) and to support new types of processing (e.g., spatial search, recursion [BR86]). General references on some data structures and algorithms are [HS77, HS78].

Performance evaluation of database systems is an emerging research area. Individual algorithms and their data structures have been studied in depth (e.g., B-trees), and some attempts have been made to study entire systems (e.g., queuing models). A framework for performance prediction has been proposed based on an analytical queuing networks. Such a framework would be used to investigate the interdependencies between various systems and application design decisions. To date, however, no comprehensive theory, model, or techniques have been developed.

Database reliability and recovery involve the protection of valuable data against accidental or malicious destruction, or unauthorized access in general [HR83]. Reliability requires facilities to recover data in the applications' transient address space and in the database from crashes. Besides system (i.e., hardware and software) crashes, recovery from media (i.e., secondary storage device) crashes, and application-initiated aborts, is also required.

Conventional DBMSs provide a variety of recovery schemes, based on logging of update operations, periodic checkpointing of the entire database, and shadow page techniques [LORI77]. These techniques guarantee that transactions are executed *atomically*, i.e., if a crash occurs during the execution of a transaction, the system will recover to a state in which either all the updates of the transaction will be reflected (if the transaction had already been *committed*) or none will (if the transaction had not been committed). Although many techniques exist [VERH78], a general theory has yet to evolve.

Database security concerns mechanisms for defining and ensuring only authorized access to databases [DENN83]. Conventional DBMS security mechanisms involve using passwords to identify authorized users, and associating with individual users or user groups specific access rights to collections of data, such as relations or user views. In some cases, users may be allowed to grant their access rights to still other users. Parallel activity, primarily under government sponsorship, has been directed at developing database systems that can be formally verified to enforce security policies defined for managing classified information. This research has addressed problems of preventing users from inferring data they are not authorized to access from data they are authorized to access. Multilevel security (i.e., supporting different security levels on the same system) remains an open research area.

Distributed DBMSs (DDBMSs) provide the appearance of a centralized database when, in fact, there are two or more distinct (e.g., geographically distant) databases [CERI84]. The use of distributed databases is motivated by the need for one or more applications to share and access data that resides in different locations (e.g., accounts at individual bank branches) as they would a single database (e.g., the database of all accounts in all branches). Distributed databases offer several potential advantages: efficiency (e.g., increased parallelism, processing local data locally), reliability (e.g., site failure does not make the system fail), and modularity (e.g., easier to add new nodes than to modify a centralized system). Distributed database systems are either homogeneous (i.e., each site runs the same DBMS) or heterogeneous. In addition to distribution tasks, described below, heterogeneous DBMSs involve the complex task of translating between multiple systems and data models [LR82].

The problems of centralized DBMSs are more complex in DDBMS. Reliability is more complex since there are multiple sites plus communication networks, each of which could fail. To improve reliability, multiple copies of data are frequently maintained on different sites so that the data will be available even if sites go down. This also improves performance by increasing opportunities for parallel access and by placing data near where it will be used. However, it complicates update processing because the system must ensure that updates to data are correctly propagated to all copies of the data, and that concurrency control is maintained during this propagation. Similarly, query optimization is complicated because the optimizer may choose from among multiple copies of data, each involving differing communication delays. Moreover, since there are potentially multiple sites involved in processing a given query, it may be possible to produce an evaluation strategy that allows multiple sites to work in parallel in satisfying a query. The methods used for querying, updating, and concurrency control must accommodate the failure of any system component at any time by retaining sufficient information to recover from the failure without adversely impacting data consistency. Problems also arise due entirely to the distributed environment (e.g., data allocation, heterogeneous databases, data replication, atomicity of distributed transactions).

Generally, the theory of query processing, concurrency control, and recovery in distributed databases is about as well developed as the corresponding theory for centralized databases for traditional database applications (e.g., record-oriented data), even though more complicated techniques are required [DATE83, ULLM82, ULLM88]. Current research is directed at allowing more loosely coupled databases, and guaranteeing the continuous operation of systems in the face of network partitions (communication and site failures that sever all communication paths between two or more subsets of the sites) [SARI86].

Only now are commercial DDBMSs beginning to appear, usually with some restriction on their ability to provide a completely centralized view of the distributed data. Four such commercial DDBMSs are Relational Technology's INGRES/NET [DATE86] (an early release of INGRES/STAR, a fully distributed version of the INGRES DBMS), Oracle's SQL-Star, Tandem Computers' NonStop SQL, and Sybase Inc.'s SYBASE. Many research prototype DDBMSs exist including homogeneous systems such as SDD-1 [RBFG80], R* [WDHL82], and DDM [CDFG83], and heterogeneous systems such as SIRIUS-DELTA [LBEF82] and MULTIBASE [LR82].

Database machine research concerns direct hardware support of database processing for dramatic improvements in processing speed over very large databases. It now appears that the original conception of database machines will not provide the performance improvements originally expected. Current research is directed at new forms of database hardware (e.g., parallel processing, in-core databases, very large cache memories) as well as at architectures in which such hardware can be used. In addition, commercial products incorporating specialized hardware for database processing have been introduced, including the Britton-Lee IDM and the Teradata DBS/1012 [DATE86].

4. Future Directions

The technical challenges driving database technology today arise as attempts are made to apply this technology in new and more challenging applications (see [BBLM88]). Organizations are increasingly attempting to provide environments that allow integrated access to more and more of their data. For decentralized organizations, this requires distributed database capabilities. Since these organizations frequently have existing data that cannot be converted to a common format (either because of specialized requirements or cost-benefit tradeoffs), heterogeneous database capabilities are often required. As integrated access is provided, and organizations increasingly rely on databases for crucial information, the reliability, integrity, and security of the data are becoming serious concerns, in both military and civilian applications. Performance is becoming increasingly important as increasing numbers of users access the database, individual accesses become more demanding (with less reliance on batch reports, and more on *ad hoc* queries or user-friendly displays), databases become larger, and applications requiring real-time response are addressed.

These issues are further complicated as database technology is applied to types of data not previously stored in databases, such as speech, signals of various types, text, geometric data (engineering designs, cartographic data), imagery, and AI knowledge representations; and is used in support of the specialized programs that require and process such data (e.g., engineering design tools, image and signal processing systems, and expert systems). Such data types frequently involve highly specialized data structures with very large storage requirements and with processing programs that often access data in patterns for which conventional database techniques were not designed.

To respond to these challenges, system architectures will have to be increasingly innovative, drawing on many technologies. Specialized hardware can be used to improve performance. Tighter coupling and active cooperation can be used between database and other system components such as operating systems and applications. Knowledge-based techniques can be applied to increase the *intelligence* of DBMS components. Recent advances in areas usually considered a part of database technology (such as data models, query processing, and concurrency control) can be applied.

Advances are also required in techniques (e.g., methodologies) and tools for designing databases and database applications, as well as in tools for designing database system components and architectures themselves. Currently, the number of design choices available to both database and application designers is so large that designers are often overwhelmed, and, lacking sophisticated tools, design is largely *ad hoc* and is based on experience and intuition. There are even more design choices for database system architectures that address the above challenges. Current research is addressing improvements in system design methodologies, supporting tools, and integrated environments in which those tools can be effectively used. The remainder of this section discusses new directions in database research that are responding to the new challenges.

Knowledge base management systems (KBMS) are an example of a new class of system being studied in response to requirements of new knowledge-based applications [BM86a, WIED84, BL86]. A KBMS would provide highly efficient management of large, shared knowledge bases for knowledge-based systems. It will have to deal with information at two levels: the knowledge level and the computational, or symbol, level. The knowledge level can provide mechanisms for the development, refinement, and debugging of a knowledge representation scheme (e.g., data model and the associated knowledge base) for a particular application and for evaluating its adequacy, soundness, completeness, consistency, validity, etc. The computational level, on the other hand, can provide tools for the efficient implementation of a knowledge base, and operations for information retrieval, manipulation, and management.

KBMS technology will require a deep integration of database and AI technologies [BM86b] [BROD88]. DBMS technology will provide the core technology at the computational level. Key features will include traditional database management functions for large, shared databases such as (semantic) data models; languages (i.e., definition, query/browsing, manipulation, transaction); semantic integrity definition and maintenance; storage/search structures; search and update optimization; concurrency; security; error recovery; and distribution of data and processes. AI technology will provide the basis for the knowledge level which will provide the means with which to represent and reason about the knowledge base represented at the computational level. Based on the similarity between the relational data model and logic, such an integration is being attempted in an area now called deductive databases [GMN84].

The development of **advanced data models** (and associated languages) is directed at extending data models to capture new data types required by the new applications of databases mentioned above, as well as providing a more faithful enterprise model within the database. This requires more than just the capability to store the raw bits required to represent new data types in digital form (although in some cases architectural changes will be required to do even this, as described below). For the DBMS to perform efficient query processing, concurrency control, integrity constraint enforcement, and storage management, key aspects of the semantics of these new data types must be captured. For example, query processing over spatial data requires the ability to specify and evaluate operations and predicates involving spatial properties of objects and their spatial relationships.

Two approaches to capturing these semantics are being pursued. The first approach consists of defining the data model with certain specialized semantics built in. For example, considerable work has been done on data models with specialized built-in temporal semantics [SNOD86]. Similarly, specialized models have been defined to handle images [CHAN81], CAD/CAM applications [KATZ84], and so on. This approach can result in a model which, although well adapted to a particular application, is not very flexible in coping with other applications, or evolving in unanticipated directions.

The second approach attempts to provide flexibility by defining **extensible data models**. These data models allow new data types or constructs to be added to the model as required by the particular application involved. They must provide facilities for both syntactically defining the new types (naming them, defining their structure, and the predicates and operations that apply to them), and defining the behaviour of the new types (in terms of the semantics of the operations and predicates).

Extensibility can be provided by adding a simple abstract data type definition facility to a conventional data model, such as the relational model [STON83]. This approach allows the new types to be accessed within the framework of the conventional data model (e.g., as new types of data items). A more recent development is the *object-oriented DBMS* [DD86, ZM89], which encapsulates both the data and operations of the new types, using the object concept from object-oriented programming languages. This is a direct implementation of the object abstraction mentioned in Section 1. Object-oriented approaches encapsulate how elements of the data model are implemented, thus improving data independence, and provide a uniform basis (often based on message-passing) for interfaces. In their full generality, they are also inherently parallel. The development of object-oriented approaches in database technology parallels in many respects the development of object-oriented and actor approaches in AI. This approach appears to be promising in dealing with many of the research issues involving databases, specifically the development of new DBMS architectures, real-time processing, very large databases, interfaces, and multimedia databases. A comparison of some of these models can be found in [HS87].

Extensible DBMSs (i.e., those based on extensible data models) require some way to specify the semantics of operations and predicates defined for new data types. In the simplest cases, procedures must be written in conventional programming languages to implement the operations that apply to the new types or to invoke specialized processors in the case of more complex types. These procedures are then linked to the DBMS in some way. More recent systems, particularly in the object-oriented DBMSs, effectively integrate programming languages with the DBMS for this purpose, Database processing is also increasingly a requirement for programs that must access a database for any purpose. The result is research in the development of languages allowing tighter coupling between conventional programming facilities and databases. New extensible and object-oriented DBMSs include POSTGRES [SR86], Galileo [AGO88], Taxis [NCLB87], and EXODUS [CDFG86].

With most programming languages and expert system shells — even object-oriented ones like Smalltalk, KEE, and CommonLoops — data and knowledge objects in the program's address space exist only as long as the program executes. To make an object persist beyond the lifetime of a single program execution, the programmer must include explicit instructions to save the object on stable storage, usually in a file on disc. Conversely, to reuse an object that was created in an earlier execution, or by some other program, the programmer must include explicit instructions to fetch the object from stable storage.

Modern **database programming languages** address some of these problems by integrating a programming language (or expert system shell) and a DBMS. They allow some distinguished programming language data types to be persistent (e.g., the type *relation* in PASCAL/R [SCHM77]; *entity types* in ADAPLEX [SFL83]). These languages incorporate powerful high-level query facilities that allow the programmer to fetch a set of data objects from the database in one access. Also, by allowing database operations to be bracketed in transactions, they support the controlled sharing of concurrently accessed data objects. However, the programmer is still responsible for translating between two type systems (and two address spaces), that of the transient objects in the program's address space, and that of the persistent objects in the database. Finally, the concurrency control mechanisms provided by conventional DBMSs may be too stringent and restrictive for the new applications described above.

Recent work on **persistent programming languages** is predicated on the principle of *orthogonal persistence* [ATKI83], i.e., *any* instance of any programming language data type should be allowed to persist, not just some distinguished types. This principle has motivated the design of persistent programming languages and object managers for them (e.g., GemStone — a persistent extension of Smalltalk [MAIE86]; Trellis/Owl [OBRI86]; and Galileo [ALBA86]). Ideally, these object managers must support the concept of staging independence described in Section 1, since they must make invisible to the programmer whether an object being referenced is in the database or is a temporary object in the program's workspace.

The development of such languages blurs the distinction between *programming* and *database* languages, the distinction between an application program and a specification of behavioural object semantics, and the distinction between the application code and the database itself. The development of declarative programming techniques also has this effect. An example of this is logic programming, in which both data and *program* are represented by statements in logic. The similarity between logic programming statements and tuples in relational databases has induced considerable work investigating the connection between logic and database systems [GMN84]. This work has contributed to a better understanding of database semantics, and can be expected to make further contributions in the future [BROD88].

Database interface research is addressing issues related to those of database languages in trying to define convenient interfaces to database systems having new capabilities, and incorporating new data types. For example, image and CAD/CAM databases are naturally dealt with using graphics-based interfaces rather than conventional query languages. The object-oriented approach used for designing extensible data models also facilitates the development of more flexible database interfaces. Database interfaces are an important area for the application of AI technology, in such areas as natural-language interfaces and *expert* display composition facilities [FRIE84].

Information or database systems continue to grow in sophistication (as described above), complexity, and size. A relatively new requirement is to integrate database technology with currently disjoint technologies such as graphics, communications, expert systems, and special-purpose processing. This leads to new issues concerning the design of database system architectures that include the previously mentioned technologies on a variety of computers, often in new distributed, workstation environments. The result is a significant increase in the complexity of database systems design and development and of the design and development process itself. As a result, **database design and development** is increasingly challenged to deliver powerful concepts, techniques, and tools for building and maintaining these systems with high quality and at low cost. Database design and development research is now focused on powerful and comprehensive information system design and development environments.

Since 1985, over 150 commercial tools to support database design and development have become available within a new CASE industry. CASE tools are intended to support the entire life cycle. Their use will require significant education as the vast majority of database design is currently done only at the physical level. Currently they are being evaluated and applied by less than 10% of the intended database design community. This very new technology is not at all well developed. Current tools support limited methodology management, graphic input of database designs and requirements, the production of documents and reports, analysis, and the generation of executable DDL statements that correspond to the input design with few implementation considerations and with no physical design or optimization.

Current research is directed at comprehensive design and development support environments with powerful data modelling capabilities, tool sets, process and methodology management, design databases for storing products of design tasks, user-friendly interfaces to present the rich functionality, facilities for explaining and justifying automated design decisions, more powerful documentation of the design process, support of interaction with external systems (e.g., data dictionaries), and architectures that support multiple designers working on separate workstations.

Research on design techniques is required in several areas before more tools can be developed. Such areas include physical optimization and design, distributed database design (e.g., data replication, fragmentation), design verification (e.g., by simulation or analysis), and database redesign (i.e., restructuring and reorganization). Expert system technology is particularly appropriate for physical design (i.e., automating database designers' knowledge and experience about real DBMSs and support systems). Knowledge-based approaches are being investigated for other knowledge-intensive tasks.

Two issues pose even greater challenges than those mentioned above. The first is the very practical need to integrate design and development concepts, techniques, and tools for database systems with those for the more established areas such as systems analysis and software engineering. The second concerns the concept of a comprehensive design environment which is tailorable to fit the particular design and development standards, techniques, and practices of the organizations that they will support.

The design and implementation of **DBMS architectures** to address the new requirements described earlier is also an extremely active area of database research. These architectures require the careful assignment of tasks to components, designing the individual components (and providing required processing support) to perform the tasks, and providing for intercomponent communications. Components potentially involved in these new architectures include DBMSs, operating systems, programming languages, knowledge-based components, and specialized high-performance hardware [MB86].

The importance of careful design in these architectures can be illustrated by the fact that database and knowledge-based system can be integrated today by simply providing the knowledge-based system with an interface to a conventional DBMS. However, such systems have very poor performance due to fundamental mismatches between the two types of systems. As a result, it is anticipated that efficiently integrating database and knowledge-base technology will involve the development of new architectures that, in turn, efficiently integrate the heterogeneous and possibly distributed components that are required to support specialized processing and interfaces, together with general database facilities. For a more detailed discussion of these issues see [BM86a, MB88].

The use of object-oriented approaches in the development of these architectures is extremely attractive. These approaches encapsulate the implementation of individual components (e.g., whether they are implemented as software or using special-purpose hardware: whether output is the result of computation, database search, or knowledge-based reasoning processes), and thus provide for the easy integration of heterogeneous components, many of which may be capable of operating in parallel, and can thus take advantage of new, high-performance parallel computer architectures. Systems developed on this basis are also more easily adapted to the workstation-oriented architectures that are increasingly appearing.

Advances in the implementation techniques that are used within individual components are also required. For example, within DBMSs, advanced storage and access methods must be developed for the physical data structures required to store new data types, for new computer architectures on which they may be implemented, and for new storage technologies, such as optical disks, that may be involved. Related advances are required to support more flexible database restructuring and reorganization, in order to provide the degree of data independence potentially possible with even today's DBMSs, as well as to support rapidly changing application requirements in the future.

Advanced optimization and planning techniques will be required both within these architectures as a whole, and within DBMS components of such architectures. This is true even though object-oriented approaches are used, since in many applications the full generality of the object-oriented message passing paradigm is not required: messages must flow in predefined patterns that can be optimized. Query optimization techniques are commonly used to improve the performance of database systems, but were not designed to produce execution plans that satisfy time constraints as required for **real-time processing**. Addressing this problem requires techniques for the simultaneous optimization of multiple queries to meet a set of constraints, and the development of cost models to accurately predict execution times. New applications necessitate expanding the class of queries that can be optimized [FREY87] (e.g., to include transitive closure, recursion [BR86], aggregation, and quantifiers). Query processors must use additional information about the data (such as semantic integrity constraints) to reduce query evaluation costs, and to extend known query optimization techniques to more advanced data models, e.g., [DAYA83]). In extensible (e.g., object-oriented) data models, this will require that the query optimizer itself be extensible.

Optimization and planning capabilities must also be extended to include active components, such as the active DBMS component required to support the self-monitoring abstraction described in Section 1, and the tighter coupling between programming languages and database languages described earlier in this section. Ideally, in order to *efficiently* support the staging independence required by this type of language coupling, the DBMS must be able to predict when data will be required by an application (which may be operating on a workstation separate from the DBMS), and prestage the data into the workstation (rather than waiting for a data fault to trigger the staging). This requires understanding by the DBMS of application data access characteristics. Ideally, as DBMSs become more *intelligent*, cooperative planning between such DBMSs and knowledge-based applications can take place to improve performance still further [MB86].

Advances in optimization and planning are also required for **concurrency control**. Concurrency control mechanisms based on the serializability criterion are too restrictive for many new applications. First, these applications deal with large complex objects and with long-lived activities (e.g., design, software development and maintenance, problem solving). Under serializability, *long transactions* either lock out a large part of the database for a long period (the pessimistic approach) or defer setting locks at the risk of aborting when it tries to commit (the optimistic approach). Second, the conventional model assumes that concurrent transactions necessarily *conflict* and hence must be precluded from concurrently accessing shared data. For many applications (e.g., knowledge-based applications), a different paradigm is appropriate, viz., that the concurrent programs are *cooperating* to perform some global task (design, planning, scheduling, problem solving, etc.) [GREI87]. It may be desirable for some programs to see the partial results of computations performed by others.

Various mechanisms have been proposed to support long transactions and cooperation. *Multilevel atomicity* permits a set of transactions to be recursively partitioned into equivalence classes providing finer units of concurrency. Synchronizing transactions within the same equivalence class less strictly than transactions from different equivalence classes permits greater throughput. *Check-in/check-out* of objects into/from the shared knowledge/data base (objects are checked out in a few specified modes) provides more flexibility for permitting or precluding concurrent check-out by any other program. *Blackboard* mechanisms support posting messages, partial results, and *notification* by the DBMS to transactions that various concurrent activities are ongoing. More sophisticated mechanisms include preanalysis to determine how best to schedule potentially conflicting activities; generalizations of optimistic concurrency control that permit the concurrent creation of multiple versions of an object, followed by the invocation of an arbitration procedure to resolve inconsistencies among these versions; and packaging of special synchronization methods with each object. Most advanced systems and research prototypes support a fixed subset of these mechanisms.

In a cooperative work environment, the problem of **recovery** is complex. As discussed earlier, *transactions* are typically long, and weaker criteria than serializability may be used. Consequently, dependencies (e.g., exchanging partial results) may be set up between application programs running at different sites. When one program crashes, dependent problems may have to be rolled back or notified to run *compensating* transactions to achieve some desired level of consistency. Compensation is appropriate when it is more important to save performed work than to guarantee strict consistency (e.g., temporary inconsistencies can be tolerated). Recording dependency information and compensation is a relatively unexplored area in cooperative work; however, it has been studied in the context of highly available distributed database systems that must continue to operate after a network partition [SARI86].

Conventional **DBMS recovery techniques** have been generally adopted in object managers for persistent programming languages [MAIE86]. The persistent virtual memory described in [THAT86] goes even further. By logging every operation, it can recover after a crash not just a *clean* point (i.e., results of committed transactions), but to the exact state at which the crash occurred. Such techniques avoid repeating valuable work done by long, uncommitted transactions.

5. 1987 Epilogue

Information systems will continue to grow in sophistication, complexity, and size. Future information systems will be expected to acquire, maintain, retrieve, manipulate, and present many different kinds of information. Requirements such as user-friendly interfaces, powerful reasoning capabilities, shared access to large information bases, and cooperative problem solving all with high performance and low cost have been generally accepted and are increasingly critical. As a result database design and development is increasingly challenged to deliver powerful concepts, techniques, and tools for building and maintaining these systems with high quality and at low cost. While the current new generation of DBMSs is being built and applied, more advanced application requirements lead to new concepts and techniques that the new generation DBMSs cannot efficiently support.

Database technology for building and supporting these new applications is far from meeting these requirements. Despite major achievements in every area of Computer Science, the gap between what is required and what database technology can deliver is widening. This is in marked contrast to dramatic advances in individual areas such as hardware technology, knowledge-based systems, distributed processing, graphics, user interfaces, etc. The critical challenge in meeting the demand for high-quality, low-cost database systems cannot be addressed successfully by individual technologies. Rather, it depends critically on our ability to integrate technologies, such as Artificial Intelligence and Databases, to meet the challenge (see [BROD88]). One reason for the urgency of this task is that dramatic advances in hardware technology have made computers available to an ever-growing community of potential users, all of whom have definite information processing needs.

In the coming five years, the major technology challenge for database technology and Computer Science, as a whole, will be **technology integration**.

6. 1988 Epilogue

Most developments in the year since the above epilogue was completed are continuations of ideas and trends described in the survey. The primary trend has remained the extension of database technology to support all types of shared, persistent objects for all types of systems. This is a movement from the management of simple data types (e.g., relations with simple character or number fields) in largely centralized, homogeneous systems to management of objects regardless of the object type, the client system, and the host machine type or location.

The trends have matured to the point of producing commercial systems with object-oriented and integration capabilities. The last year has seen the introduction of commercial object-oriented DBMSs (OODBMS)), which have become a major research area [MEYR87]. The emphasis now in OODBMS research is on the tight integration of the many related concepts (e.g., support for user-defined, shared persistent data types, advanced concurrency control techniques, database programming facilities, and others mentioned in the survey).

Another development is the appearance of commercial products designed to couple knowledge-based systems with database systems. An example is IntelliCorp's KEEconnection product [INTE87], which allows the KEE knowledge-based system shell to access database data as if it is part of the KEE knowledge base, automatically formulating database queries to move data between the database and knowledge base. While tighter coupling between the two types of systems is possible, this product illustrates commercial realization of what previously were only experimental ideas. By 1988, most commercial knowledge-based system shells and many commercial AI languages provide ways to access one or more commercial DBMSs.

Still another development is the appearance of SQL as both a de facto and de jure standard for database query languages. The language had already been widely adopted by implementors of database systems, and the development of an ANSI standard for the language formalized the process. It will be increasingly difficult to compete in the commercial DBMS marketplace without supporting an SQL interface. Moreover, the fact that most DBMS products either do now or will soon support an SQL interface means that linking different DBMSs together in distributed database configurations will be easier than it otherwise would be.

A final significant development is the increasing potential use of heterogeneous distributed database technology. A number of recent initiatives are based on using this technology to integrate databases (as well as application programs) belonging to different organizations, allowing the exchange of data, and creating a larger integrated system as a result. An example is the Defense Department's Computer-Aided Logistics Support initiative [CALS86], which is intended to allow multiple contractors on the same project to exchange information (both with the government and each other) in digital form, including specifications, drawings, and manuals (including both text and graphics).

Acknowledgment

We are grateful to both Umeshwar Dayal and Jack Orenstein for their comments and suggestions.

7. Bibliography

[ALBA86]
Albano, A., et al. "A Strongly Typed, Interactive Object-Oriented Database Programming Language," in [DD86].

[AGO88]
Albano, A., G. Ghelli, and R. Orsini, "The Implementation of Galileo's Persistent Values," in [ABM88], 253-264.

[ATKI83]
Atkinson, M.P., et al. "An Approach to Persistent Programming," *Computer Journal* 26, No. 4 (1983):360-365.

[ABM88]
Atkinson, M.P., and O. Peter Buneman, "Types and Persistence in Database Programming Languages," *ACM Computing Surveys 19,* No. 2, June 1987.

[ANSI75]
ANSI/X3/SPARC, "Study Group on DBMS Interim Report," *SIGMOD FDT Bulletin 7*, No. 2, 1975.

[AC76]
Astrahan, M. M., D. D. Chamberlin, et al., "System R: Relational Approach to Database Management," *ACM Trans Database Systems*, 1, 1976.

[BR86]
Bancilhon, F., and R. Ramakrishnan, "An Amateur's Introduction to Recursive Query Processing," *Proc. 1986 SIGMOD Int'l Conference on Management of Data,* Washington, D.C., May 1986.

[BM72]
Bayer, R., and E. McCreight, "Organization and Maintenance of Large Ordered Indexes," *Acta Informatica, 1, 3* (1972), 173-189.

[BHG87]
Bernstein, P. A., V. Hadzilacos, and N. Goodman, *Concurrency Control and Recovery in Database Systems*, Addison-Wesley, Reading, MA, 1987.

[BL86]
Brachman, R. J., and H. J. Levesque, "What Makes a Knowledge Base Knowledgeable? A View of Databases from the Knowledge Level," in Larry Kerschberg, ed., *Expert Database Systems* (Menlo Park, CA:Benjamin/Cummings Publishing Co., February 1986).

[BMS84]
Brodie, M. L., J. Mylopoulos, and J. W. Schmidt (eds.), O*n Conceptual Modelling: Perspectives from Artificial Intelligence, Databases, and Programming Languages*, Springer-Verlag, New York, 1984.

[BR84]
Brodie, M. L., and D. Ridjanovic, "On the Design and Specification of Database Transactions," in [BMS84].

[BROD84]
Brodie, M. L., "On the Development of Data Models," in [BMS84].

[BM86a]
Brodie, M. L., and J. Mylopoulos (eds.)., *On Knowledge-Base Systems: Integrating Artificial Intelligence and Database Technologies*, New York: Springer-Verlag, May 1986.

[BM86b]
Brodie, M.L., and J. Mylopoulos, "Knowledge Bases and Databases: Semantic vs. Computational Theories of Information," in *New Directions for Database Systems*, Gad Ariav and Jim Clifford (eds.), New York: Ablex, 1986.

[BROD88]
Brodie, M.L., "Future Intelligent Information Systems: AI and Database Technologies Working Together," in [MB88].

[BBLM88]
Brodie, M.L., D. Bobrow, V. Lesser, S. Madnick, and D.C. Tsichritzis, "Future Artificial Intelligence Requirements for Database Systems," in Kerschberg, L. (ed.), Expert Database Systems: Proceedings of the Second International Conference, Benjamin/Cummings Publishing Co., Menlo Park CA, 1988.

[CALS86]
Office of the Assistant Secretary of Defense (Acquisition and logistics), "Automated Logistic Systems, Part I — Computer Aided Logistic Support (CALS)," Report to the Committees on Appropriations of the U.S. House of Representatives and the U.S. Senate, Washington, DC, March 28, 1986.

[CDFG86]
Carey, M.J., D.J. DeWitt, D. Frank, G. Graefe, M. Muralikrishna, J.E. Richardson, and E.J. Shekita, "The Achitecture of the EXODUS Extensible DBMS," in [DD86], 52-65.

[CCA82]
Computer Corporation of America, "An Architecture for Database Management Standards," *NBS Special Publication* 500-86, National Bureau of Standards, January 1982.

[CERI84]
Ceri, S., and G. Pelagatti, *Distributed Databases: Principles and Systems*, McGraw-Hill, New York, 1984.

[CHAM76]
Chamberlin, D.D., "Relational Database Management Systems," in [SIBL76].

[CDFG83]
Chan, Q., U. Dayal, S. Fox, N. Goodman, D. Ries, and D. Skeen, "Overview of an Ada Compatible Distributed Database Manager," *Proc. ACM SIGMOD Conf. 83*, San Jose, CA, May 1983.

[CDFG83]
Chan, A., U. Dayal, S. Fox, N. Goodman, D. Ries, and D. Skeen, "Overview of an Ada Compatible Distributed Database Manager," Proceedings *ACM SIGMOD International Conference on Management of Data*, San Jose, CA, May 1983.

[CHAN81]
Chang, S.-K. (ed.), "Pictorial Information Systems," *Computer*, 14, 11, November 1981.

[CODD70]
Codd, E. F., "A Relational Model for Large Shared Data Banks," *Comm. ACM*, Vol. 13, No. 6, June 1970, pp. 377-387.

[CHEN76]
Chen, P.P.-S., "The Entity-Relationship Model — Toward a Unified View of Data," *ACM Trans, Database Systems 1*, No. 1 (March 1976).

[DATE83]
Date, C. J., *An Introduction to Database Systems*, Volume II, Addison-Wesley, Reading, MA 1983.

[DATE86]
Date, C. J., *An Introduction to Database Systems*, 4th ed., Addison-Wesley, Reading, MA, 1986.

[DAYA83]
Dayal, U., "Processing Queries over Generalization Hierarchies in a Multidatabase System," *Proc. 9th International Conference on Very Large Databases*, Florence, Italy, October-November 1983.

[DENN83]
Denning, D. E. R., *Cryptography and Data Security*, Addison-Wesley, Reading, MA, 1983.

[DD86]
Dittrich, K., and U. Dayal (eds.), *Proc. International Workshop on Object Oriented Database Systems*, IEEE Computer Society Press, 1986.

[ESWA76]
Eswaran, K.P., J.N. Gray, R.A. Lorie, and I.L. Traiger,"The Notions of Consistency and Predicate Locks in a Database System," *CACM 19*, no.11 (November 1986):624-633.

[FREY87]
Freytag, J.C., "A Rule-Based View of Query Optimization," Proceedings *ACM SIGMOD International Conference on Management of Data*, 1987.

[FRIE84]
Friedell, M., "Automatic Synthesis of Graphical Object Descriptions," *Computer Graphics*, 16, 3, July 1984.

[GMN84]
Gallaire, H., J. Minker, and J-M. Nicolas, "Logic and Databases: A Deductive Approach," *ACM Computing Surveys* Vol. 16, No. 2, June 1984.

[GREI87]
Grief, I., and S. Sarin, "Data Sharing in Group Work," to appear in *ACM TOOIS* (1987).

[HS87]
Hardwick, M., and D. L. Spooner, "Comparison of Some Data Models for Engineering Objects," *IEEE Computer Graphics and Applications*, 7, 3, March 1987.

[HS77]
Horowitz, E., and S. Sahni, *Fundamentals of Data Structures*, Computer Science Press, Inc., Potomac, MD, 1977.

[HR83]
Haerder, T., and A. Reuter, "Principles of Transaction-Oriented Database Recovery," *ACM Computing Surveys*, Vol. 15, No. 4, December 1983.

[HS78]
Horowitz, E., and S. Sahni, *Fundamentals of Computer Algorithms*, Computer Science Press, Inc., Potomac, MD, 1978.

[HK87]
Hull, R., and R. King, "Semantic Database Modelling: Survey, Applications and Research Issues," *ACM Computing Reviews 19*, No. 3, September 1987.

[INTE87]
IntelliCorp Inc., "KEEconnection: A Bridge Between Databases and Knowledge Bases," 1987.

[JK84]
Jarke, M., and J. Kock, "Query Optimization in Database Systems," *ACM Computing Surveys,* Vol. 16, No. 2, June 1984.

[KATZ84]
Katz, R. (ed.), *(IEEE) Database Engineering Bulletin,* 7, 2, June 1984 (Special Issue on Engineering Data Management).

[KENT78]
Kent, W., *Data and Reality,* North Holland, Amsterdam, 1978.

[KENT79]
Kent, W., "Limitations of Record-Based Information Models," *ACM Transactions on Database Systems 6*, No. 4, December 1981.

[KRB85]
Kim, W., D. Reiner, and D. Batory (eds.), *Query Processing in Database Systems*, Springer-Verlag, New York, NY, February 1985.

[LR82]
Landers, T., and R. L. Rosenberg, "An Overview of MULTIBASE," in *Proc. 2nd International Symposium on Distributed Databases*, H. J.Schneider (ed.), Berlin, W. Germany, September 1982.

[LORI77]
Lorie, R.A., "Physical Integrity in a Large Segmented Database," *ACM Transactions on Database Systems*, Vol. 2, No. 1 (March 1977).

[LBEF82]
Litwin, W., J. Baudenant, C. Esculier, A. Ferrier, A. M. Glorieux, J. La Chimia, K. Kabbai, C. Moulinoux, P. Rolin, and C. Stranget, "SIRIUS Systems for Distributed Database Management," in *Distributed Databases*, H. J. Schneider (ed.), North Holland, 1982.

[MB86]
Manola, F., and M.L. Brodie, "On Knowledge-Based System Architectures," in [BRO86a].

[MAIE83]
Maier, D., *The Theory of Relational Databases*, Computer Science Press, Potomac, MD, 1983.

[MAIE86]
Maier, D., J. Stein, A. Otis, and A. Purdy, "Development of an Object-Oriented DBMS," *Proc. 1986 Object-Oriented Programming Systems Languages and Applications* (Portland, OR), (Sept. 29, 1986):472-482.

[MEYR87]
Meyrowitz, N. (ed.), "OOPSLA '87 Conference Proceedings," (ACM) *SIGPLAN Notices*, Vol. 22, No. 12, December 1987.

[MW80]
Mylopoulos, J., and H. Wong, "Some Features of the Taxis Data Model," *Proc. 6th International Conference on Very Large Databases*, Montreal, Quebec, Canada, October 1980.

[MB88]
Mylopoulos, J., and M.L. Brodie, *Readings in Artificial Intelligence and Databases*, Morgan Kaufman, San Mateo, CA, 1988.

[NCLB87]
Nixon, B., L. Chung, D. Lauzon, A. Borgida, J. Mylopoulos, M. Stanley, "Implementation of a Compiler for a Semantic Data Model: Experiences with Taxis," Proceedings *ACM SIGMOD International Conference on Management of Data*, 1987.

[OBRI86]
O'Brien, P., B. Bullis, and C. Schaffert, "Persistent and Shared Objects in Trellis/Owl," in [DD86].

[OST84]
Olle, T. W., H. G. Sol, and C. J. Tully (eds.), *Information Systems Design Methodologies: A Feature Analysis*, North Holland, Amsterdam, September 1984.

[OLLE88]
Olle, T.W., et al., *Information Systems Methodologies: A Framework for Understanding*, Addison-Wesley, Reading, MA, October 1988.

[RBFG80]
Rothnie, J. B., P. A. Bernstein, S. Fox, N. Goodman, M. Hammer, T. A. Landers, C. Reeve, D. W. Shipman, and E. Wong, "Introduction to a System for Distributed Databases (SDD-1)," *ACM Trans. Database Systems*, 5, 1, March 1980.

[REIN84]
IEEE Database Engineering Newsletter, D. Reiner (ed.), Special Issue on Database Design Techniques, Tools, and Environments, December 1984.

[REIT84]
Reiter, R., "Towards a Logical Reconstruction of Relational Database Theory," in [BMS84].

[SARI86]
Sarin, S.K., "Robust Application Design in Highly Available Distributed Databases," *Proc. Fifth Symp. Reliability in Distributed Software and Database Systems* (1986).

[SS75]
Schmid, J., and J.R. Swenson, "On the Semantics of the Relational Model," Proceedings *ACM SIGMOD International Conference on Management of Data*, San Jose, CA, May 1975.

[SCHM77]
Schmidt, J.W., "Some High Level Language Constructs for Data of Type Relation," *ACM Transactions on Database 2*, No. 3, 1977.

[SB83]
Schmidt, J.W., and M.L. Brodie, *Relational Database Systems Analysis and Comparison,* Springer-Verlag, New York, NY, 1983.

[SACL79]
Selinger, P.G., M.M. Astrahan, D.D. Chamberlin, R.A. Lorie, and T.G. Price, "Access Path Selection in a Relational Database Management System," Proceedings *ACM-SIGMOD International Conference on Management of Data*, Boston, May 30-June 1, 1979, 23-34.

[SHNE80]
Shneiderman, B., *Software Psychology*, Winthrop, Cambridge, MA, 1980.

[SIBL76]
Sibley, E.H. (ed.), "Special Issue: Data-Base Management Systems," *ACM Computing Surveys, 8, 1 (March 1976).*

[SFL83]
Smith, J. M., S. A. Fox, and T. Landers, "ADAPLEX Rationale and Reference Manual," Technical Report CCA-83-08, Computer Corporation of America, Cambridge, MA, May 1983.

[SNOD86]
Snodgrass, R., "Research Concerning Time in Databases: Project Summaries," *SIGMOD Record*, 15, 4, December 1986.

[STON76]
Stonebraker, M., et al., "The Design and Implementation of INGRES," *ACM Trans. Database Systems*, 2, 3, September 1976.

[STON83]
Stonebraker, M., "Application of Abstract Data Types and Abstract Indices to CAD Data," *Proc. ACM SIGMOD Conference on Engineering Design Applications*, 1983.

[SR86]
Stonebraker, M., and L.A. Rowe, "The Design of POSTGRES," Proceedings *ACM SIGMOD International Conference on Management of Data*, Washington, DC, May 1986, 340-355.

[TF76]
Taylor, R.W., and R.L. Frank, "CODASYL Data-Base Management Systems," in [SIBL76].

[TF80]
Teorey, T.J. and J.P. Fry, *"The Logical Record Access Approach to Dàtabase Design," ACM Computing Surveys 12*, No. 2, 1980.

[TEOR82]
Teorey, T.J., and J.P. Fry, *Design of Database Structures*, Prentice-Hall, Englewood Cliffs, NJ, 1982.

[TL76]
Tsichritzis, D.C., and F.H. Lochovsky, "Hierarchical Data-Base Management," in [SIBL76].

[TYF86]
Teory, T.J., D Yang, and J.P. Fry, "A Logical Design Methodology for Relational Databases Using the Extended Entity-Relationship Model," *ACM Computing Surveys,* Vol. 18, No. 2, June 1986.

[THAT86]
Thatte, S.M., "Persistent Memory: A Storage Architecture for Object-Oriented Database Systems," in [DD86].

[VERH78]
Verhofstad, J. S. M., "Recovery Techniques for Database Systems," *ACM Computing Surveys*, 10, 2, June 1978.

[ULLM82]
Ullman, J. D., *Principles of Database Systems*, Computer Science Press, Potomac, MD, 1982.

[ULLM88]
Ullman, J.D., *Principles of Database and Knowledge-Base Systems*, Volume 1, Computer Science Press, Potomac, MD, 1988.

[WIED84]
Wiederhold, G., *Database Design*, Second Edition, McGraw-Hill, 1983.

[WDHL82]
Williams, R., D. Daniels, L. Haas, G. Lapis, B. Lindsay, P. Ng, R. Obermarck, P. Selinger, A. Walker, P. Wilms, and R. Yost, "R*: An Overview of the Architecture," *Proc. 2nd International Conference on Databases: Improving Usability and Responsiveness*, Jerusalem, Israel, 1982.

[YC84]
Yu, C.T, and C.C. Chang, "Distributed Query Processing," *ACM Computing Surveys,* Vol. 16, No. 4, December 1984.

[ZM89]
Zdonik, S.B., and D. Maier, *Readings in Object-Oriented Databases*, Morgan Kaufman, Los Altos, 1989.

Ann. Rev. Comput. Sci. 1986. 1:255–87

KNOWLEDGE REPRESENTATION AND REASONING[1]

Hector J. Levesque[2]

Department of Computer Science, University of Toronto, Toronto, Ontario M5S 1A4 Canada

The notion of a *representation of knowledge* is at heart easy to understand. It simply has to do with writing down, in some language or communicative medium, descriptions or pictures that correspond in some salient way to the world or a state of the world. In artificial intelligence (AI) we are concerned with writing down descriptions of the world in which an intelligent machine might be embedded in such a way that the machine can come to new conclusions about its world by manipulating these symbolic representations. David Israel characterizes this "representation problem" as follows:

> All parties to the debate agree that a central goal of research is that computers must somehow come to "know" a good deal of what every human being knows about the world and about the organisms, natural or artificial, that inhabit it. This body of knowledge—indefinite, no doubt, in its boundaries—goes by the name "common sense." The problem we face is how to impart such knowledge to a robot. That is, how do we design a robot with a reasoning capacity sufficiently powerful and fruitful that when provided with some subbody of this knowledge, the robot will be able to generate enough of the rest to intelligently adapt to and exploit its environment? (68, p. 37)

Despite the apparent simplicity of this goal, the research area of knowledge representation (KR) has a long, complex, and as yet nonconvergent history.[3]

[1]This review draws heavily from work done with Ron Brachman. I also thank Jim des Rivières, Bart Selman, and John Tsotsos, for helping with an earlier version of the document. Financial support was received from the Natural Sciences and Engineering Research Council of Canada.

[2]Fellow of the Canadian Institute for Advanced Research.

[3]Research in KR originated with a single paper written by John McCarthy in 1958, and republished as (89).

Even though many current AI programs have a knowledge base (KB) containing symbolic descriptions in some "representation scheme" along the lines described above, there is still significant disagreement among researchers about many of the most fundamental issues. Part of the problem is that KR has evolved (and absorbed material) from a number of research areas with quite different goals and methods, such as psychology (in terms of realistic human memory models), linguistics (representations of word senses), philosophy (the nature of concepts and propositions), logic (varieties of formal reasoning), and computer science (information systems). For a closer look at this amazing diversity, see (131a), a very revealing questionnaire about KR answered by the researchers themselves.

But a more coherent interpretation based primarily on logic and computer science appears to be emerging. So rather than recapitulate the history of KR, this article takes a definite stand on the nature of the research. KR is intimately connected with reasoning, because an AI system will almost always need to generate explicitly at least some of what has been implicitly represented. Moreover, for sufficiently expressive representation languages, calculating these implications may be too demanding computationally, and so compromises are necessary. Knowledge representation, then, can be thought of as the study of what options are available in the use of a representation scheme to ensure the computational tractability of reasoning.

The idea of constructing systems that perform their tasks by reasoning with explicitly represented knowledge is just a working hypothesis about how to achieve generality, flexibility, modularity, and the like in complex systems. In the next section, we examine this hypothesis in more detail, and we show how it leads to a view of KR that is grounded in logic, on the one hand, and computational complexity, on the other. In fact, the main theme of this article is that we can understand much of KR research as attempts to reconcile simultaneously the demands of logical coherence and computational tractability.

Perhaps the most interesting type of KR research that is not well covered by this emphasis on the demands of tractable reasoning has been the attempt to formalize commonsense knowledge of the world. Indeed, Hayes argues (61) that the most pressing task for KR research is to analyze what kinds of knowledge need to be represented in specific subject areas, without too much concern (initially, at least) for how the knowledge will be represented or whether it can be effectively used by any system. This leads to a very different view of KR—a view that concentrates on formal representational theories of domains of general interest such as the properties of time (3, 95, 134), space (75), and liquids (60). Two collections of research papers in this style of "applied" KR research have been published (10, 66). For more comprehensive surveys of KR, see (6) and (105). An excellent general introduction to KR (and much of AI) is found in (107). Finally, an annotated collection of thirty of the most influential papers in the area has been published (22).

1. THE KNOWLEDGE REPRESENTATION HYPOTHESIS

The basic assumption underlying KR (and much of AI) is that thinking can be usefully understood as mechanical operations over symbolic representations. This hypothesis is, in fact, quite old, much older than computers, and seems to have originated with the philosopher Leibniz (1646–1716):

> There is little doubt, however, that Leibniz' ideas, which far outstripped in detail and understanding any earlier hints, were his own spontaneous creation. "While I was yet a boy with a knowledge only of common logic, and without instruction in mathematics, the thought came to me, I know not by what instinct, that an analysis of ideas could be devised, whence in some combinatory way, truths could arise and be estimated as though by numbers" (*Elementa Rationis*). He was thereafter constantly occupied with such notions and attempted to contrive an alphabet of thought, or *characteristica universalis*, which would represent ideas in a logical way, not things in a pictorial way, and would be mechanical in operation, unambiguous, and nonquantitative. (*The Encyclopedia of Philosophy*, Vol. 4, p. 538)

Just as there is a calculus of arithmetic, where numerical expressions are formally manipulated in a value-preserving way, so might there be a calculus of thought, where propositional expressions could be formally manipulated in a truth-preserving way.

This agrees remarkably well with most current views of KR within AI. Many AI systems represent knowledge as explicitly as possible, and (relatively) declaratively, in some formal language. The term *knowledge-based system* (or KBS) is currently popular in AI. An AI system can be described as knowledge-based not because knowledge is required to build it, nor just that it behaves as if it had knowledge, but rather that its architecture includes explicit KBs that are more or less direct symbolic encodings of the knowledge of the system. This is certainly true of Expert Systems [see (135), for example], currently the most visible and plentiful type of AI system.

This is not to say that all AI systems exhibiting knowledge are knowledge based in this sense. A typical game-playing program, for instance, might act as if it believed that it should bring its knight out early in the game. Yet this could be the result of applying a complex evaluation function to the leaves of a generated game tree. Specifically, there need not be any symbolic structure anywhere in the program corresponding to that belief. But according to the *Knowledge Representation hypothesis* (131), intelligence (or at least a certain kind of generality, versatility, etc.) is best served by explicitly representing in the data structures of a program as much as possible of what a system needs to know.

Implicit in this hypothesis[4] are two major properties that the structures forming a KB must satisfy:

- For the structures to represent knowledge, it must be possible to interpret them *propositionally*, that is, as expressions in a language with a *truth theory*. We should be able to point to one of them and say what the world would have to be like for it to be true.
- The system should act the way it does because of the presence of these structures. Clearly, the hypothesis would not be satisfied in a system where the KB was completely ignored (like comments in a program, for example).

The key point is that an account of cognitive activity in terms of computational operations over propositionally interpreted structures imposes constraints on how a KBS can be realized. First of all, it rules out data structure operations that do not respect (in some sense) the propositional interpretation of a KB (e.g. reversing the words of a sentence). Secondly, because of the causal role of a KB, it rules out operations that are not computationally manageable. In other words, the operations on a KB need to be semantically coherent without demanding more than what any computer can be expected to do. To better understand these constraints, we need to examine what it means to operate on structures in a way that respects their semantic interpretation.

2. KNOWLEDGE REPRESENTATION AND LOGIC

Wanting to deal with truth-preserving operations over symbolic structures puts us into the domain of *logic*. Indeed, standard formal logic is a perfect example of a system that deals with symbolic structures (its well-formed formulas) and operations over them that, on the one hand, can be defined purely formally (as specified by a proof theory) and, on the other hand, can be shown to preserve semantic properties (as specified by a truth theory).

For a detailed explanation of formal logic see, for example, (97). Recall, however, that there are two major relationships of interest defined over the sentences of a logical language.

- *logical consequence* A sentence α is a logical consequence of a set of sentences S (written $S \models \alpha$) iff any interpretation of the logic that makes every sentence in S true also makes α true. A sentence is *valid* if it is a logical consequence of the empty set.

[4]It is worth keeping in mind that this is only a working hypothesis. Perhaps its strongest defense is that it seems to be "the only game in town", but even there, alternative trends appear to be emerging (123). For a criticism of this hypothesis on more philosophical grounds, see (39).

- *derivability* A sentence α is derivable from a set of sentences S (written $S \vdash \alpha$) iff there is a sequence of sentences $\alpha_1, \ldots, \alpha_n$ where α_n is α, such that each α_i either is an element of S, or a logical axiom, or follows from earlier α_j's by a rule of inference. A sentence is a *theorem* if it is derivable from the empty set.

Once a language has been fixed, the logic must specify the allowable interpretations, on the one hand, and the axioms and rules of inference, on the other.

The main point is that derivability in formal logic is defined in a way that does not mention what the formulas are intended to mean. Yet soundness and completeness properties can establish links between the two: A sentence will be derivable from a set of sentences precisely when it is a logical consequence of that set. For logics that are sound and complete, this is the sense in which purely formal operations can be shown to preserve semantic properties, as required by the KR hypothesis.

Logic however, does not guarantee the computational tractability of the operations of its proof theory. The derivability of a formula depends on the existence of a certain sequence of formulas, but not on whether or not that sequence can be found purely mechanically, or in a reasonable amount of time. So it is not immediately obvious how logic can be made to play the causal role required by the KR hypothesis.

Indeed, the role of formal logic in KR has been hotly contested from the very beginning.[5] Part of the problem concerns the history and goals of KR and their differences from those of symbolic logic. After Leibniz, the next big advance in formal logic was the work of Frege at the turn of the century who, along with Russell, Peano, and others, gave logic much of the flavor it has today. The goal of this early work was to put mathematics and mathematical reasoning on a sound theoretical footing. Indeed the major application of symbolic logic until recently, and one of the success stories of twentieth century mathematics, was the analysis of formal theories of sets and numbers.

The goals of KR, however, were always quite different, and perhaps much more in line with Leibniz' original dream. On the one hand, KR schemes were being used to represent the semantic content of natural language concepts (e.g. 125, 128), and on the other, to represent psychologically plausible memory models (e.g. 109, 112). In neither case was there a clear relationship to formal languages of any kind [as Woods, among others, has pointed out (141)]. Gradually, however, KR schemes began to be used as a very flexible and modular way to represent the facts that a system needed to know to behave intelligently in a complex environment [an early example is (137)].

This view of KR, involving propositional representations of the beliefs of a system, along the lines of the KR hypothesis, has slowly come to dominate the field. With it has come an emerging consensus about at least some of the issues relating KR and logic. For example, the need for a truth theory for representation languages is generally acknowledged. Without some concrete specification of the meaning of a notational convention, what is implied by an expression in that language is unclear, and comparisons to other notational systems are impossible (57). Also, it is generally accepted that some form of deductive reasoning will be necessary to extract what is implicit in the explicit beliefs to which a system has access. When a KBS needs to know something about its domain, it must use the symbolic structures representing what it knows in order to decide what is true or false about the world. In general, there is no guarantee that what it needs to know will be represented directly in these data structures, but it may very well be logically implicit in these structures.

Suppose, for example, that a medical diagnosis system needs to know whether or not a patient P is allergic to medication M before prescribing a treatment. It may be the case that the KB in question has a structure representing the fact that

Patient P is allergic to medication M.

For instance, there may be a table in a database relating patients to the medicines to which they are allergic. In this case, the system can determine by retrieval alone whether or not it can use M. On the other hand, suppose the KB has explicitly represented only the following facts:

Patient P is allergic to medication M*.

and

Anybody allergic to M* is also allergic to M.

In this case, it will be necessary to determine facts that are only implicitly represented in order to be able to decide what medication can be prescribed. In general, a KBS will be concerned not with what is explicitly represented in a KB but, rather, with what these structures taken together tell about its application domain. In other words, the main concern of a KBS is what information is contained either implicitly or explicitly in a collection of propositionally interpreted data structures.

To a first approximation then, if we restrict our attention to the yes-no questions about the world that a system might be interested in, a KR system has to be able to determine the logical consequences of what is present in the KB. In other words, given a yes-no question α, and a KB understood as a

[5] To get an idea of the range of opinions involved at various points, see (58, 99, 102, 111).

collection of sentences, a KR system must be able to determine whether or not $KB \models \alpha$.[6] So if, as a starting point, we now fix the representation language to be the first-order predicate calculus (or FOL)[7], we can give a very precise definition of $KB \models \alpha$ (and thus, the reasoning service to be provided by the KR system). Moreover, if we assume that the KB can be understood as a finite set of sentences and let KB stand for their conjunction, then because of soundness, completeness, and other properties of FOL, $KB \models \alpha$ iff the sentence $(KB \supset \alpha)$ is derivable from no premises, that is, it is a theorem of FOL. Thus, the question-answering operation becomes one of *theorem proving* in FOL.

2.1 The Problem

The good news in reducing the KR service to theorem proving is that we now have a very clear, very specific notion of what the KR system should do; the bad news is that it is also clear that this service cannot be provided. The fact is that deciding whether or not a sentence of FOL is a theorem is unsolvable [again, see (97)]. Moreover, even if we restrict the language practically to the point of triviality by eliminating the quantifiers, the decision problem, though now solvable, does not appear to be solvable in anywhere near reasonable time.[8] It is important to realize that this is a property not of particular algorithms that have been discovered so far, but of the problem itself: There cannot be an algorithm that does the test for theoremhood correctly in a reasonable amount of time. This bodes poorly, to say the least, for a service that is supposed to be only a part of a larger KBS.

One aspect of these intractability results is that they deal with the worst-case behavior of algorithms. In practice, a given theorem-proving algorithm may work quite well. In other words, a given program might behave properly for a very wide range of questions, even though there will always be questions whose answers will not be returned for a very long time, if at all. How serious is the problem, then? To a large extent this depends on the kind of question asked of a KR subsystem. The worst-case prospect might be perfectly tolerable in a mathematical application where a question is an open problem in mathematics. Provided that progress is being made, a user might be quite willing to stop and redirect a theorem prover after a few months, if it seems to be thrashing. Worst-case behavior is irrelevant; this might be the only case of interest.

But imagine, on the other hand, a robot that needs to know about its external world (such as whether or not it is raining outside, where its umbrella is, and so on) before it can act. If this robot has to repeatedly invoke a KR utility as a subroutine on a wide range of questions, the worst case prospect is much more serious. To be bogged down on a logically difficult but low-level subgoal and be unable to continue without human intervention is clearly an unreasonable form of behavior for something aspiring to intelligence.

But "on the average" the robot might do alright. The trouble is that nobody seems to be able to characterize what an "average" case might be like. As responsible computer scientists, we should not be providing a general inferential service if all that can be said about it is that by and large it will probably work satisfactorily. If the KR service is to be a module in a larger system and if it is not available for introspection or control, then it had better be dependable both in terms of its correctness and the resources it consumes. Unfortunately, this rules out a service based on theorem proving (in full first-order logic).

2.2 Some Pseudo-Solutions

There are at least two fairly obvious ways to minimize the intractability problem. The first is to push the computational barrier as far back as possible. An entire subarea of AI called *Automatic Theorem Proving* (ATP) studies techniques for avoiding redundancies and speeding up certain operations in theorem provers.[9] Significant progress has been achieved here, which allows open questions in mathematics to be answered (136, 143). Along similar lines, VLSI and parallel architectural support no doubt will improve the performance of theorem provers (85).

The second way to make theorem provers more usable is to relax our notion of correctness. A very simple way of doing this is to make a theorem-proving program always return an answer after a certain amount of time. If it has been unable to prove either that a sentence or its negation is implicit in the KB, it could assume that it was independent of the KB and answer "unknown" (or maybe reassess the importance of the question and try again). This form of error (i.e. one introduced by a resource-limited theorem prover), is not nearly as serious as returning a "yes" for a "no", and is obviously preferrable to an answer that never arrives.[10]

[6] In this view of a KR system, the service it provides to a knowledge-based system depends only on the truth theory of the language of representation. No commitment is necessary about how such a service can be realized, if indeed it can. This is in keeping with what we have called elsewhere a *functional* view of KR (see 18, 79), where the service performed by a KR system is defined separately from the techniques a system might use to realize that service.

[7] See (97) for details on this language. In what follows, we will have reason to consider other languages as well, but mainly as departures from FOL.

[8] The problem is now co-NP-hard, meaning that it is strongly believed to be computationally intractable (see 52).

[9] A useful introduction to ATP is (86). An overview of the research in the area can be found in (142).

[10] See (108, 139) for a fuller discussion of resource-limited processing. Many of these ideas were eventually incorporated into the KRL (11) representation language.

However, from the point of view of KR, both of these are only pseudo-solutions. Clearly, the first one alone does not help us guarantee anything about an inferential service. The second one, on the other hand, might allow us to guarantee an answer within certain time bounds but would make it very hard for us to specify what that answer would be. If we think of the KR service as reasoning according to a certain logic, then the logic being followed is immensely complicated (compared to that of FOL) when resource limitations are present. Indeed, the whole notion of the KR system calculating what is implicit in the KB (which was our original goal) would have to be replaced by some other notion that went beyond the truth theory of the representation language to include the inferential power of a particular theorem-proving program. In a nutshell, we can guarantee getting an answer, but not the one we wanted.

2.3 *Knowledge Representation as Compromise*

So there are serious problems with a KR service that attempts to calculate in a reasonable amount of time what is logically implicit in a KB. In this review we demonstrate that much of the research in KR can be construed as trading off a certain generality offered by FOL for a more tractable form of inference. To see where this trade-off between expressiveness and tractability originates, we should first look at the use of the expressive power of FOL in KR and how it differs from its use in mathematics.

In the study of mathematical foundations, the main use of FOL is in the formalization of infinite collections of entities. So, for example, we have first-order theories of numbers and sets that use quantifiers to range over these classes, and conditionals to state the properties that these entities have. This is exactly how Frege intended his formalism to be used.

In KR, on the other hand, the domains being characterized are usually finite. The power of FOL is used not so much to deal with infinities but to deal with *incomplete knowledge* (77, 78, 102).[11] Consider the kind of facts[12] that might be represented using FOL:

1. $\neg$Student(john).

Sentence 1 says that John is not a student, without saying what he is.

2. Parent(sue,bill) $\vee$ Parent(sue,george).

Sentence 2 says that either Bill or George is a parent of Sue, but it does not specify which one is the parent.

3. $\exists x$ Cousin(bill,x) $\wedge$ Male(x).

Sentence 3 says that Bill has at least one male cousin, but it does not say who that cousin is.

4. $\forall x$ Friend(george,x) $\supset$ $\exists y$ Child(x,y).

Sentence 4 says that all of George's friends have children, without saying who those friends or their children are, or even if there are any.
The main feature of these examples is that FOL is used not to capture complex details about the domain but to avoid having to represent details that may not be known. The expressive power of FOL determines not so much what can be said but what can be left unsaid.

For a system that has to be able to acquire arbitrary knowledge in a piecemeal fashion, there may be no alternative to full logical reasoning with a language as expressive as FOL. But we may be able to get by with much less. In what follows, we examine KR research by considering three distinct ways of reducing the computational demands on a general KR reasoning service.

1. *special-purpose languages* By limiting what can be expressed in a KR language, we can rule out certain forms of weak statements allowed by full FOL. Certain types of incomplete knowledge may not be representable, but full logical reasoning may now be within reach. The result, then, is a KB that is forced to be more complete because of the inexpressiveness of its representation language.
2. *models of limited reasoning* Another possibility is to leave the expressiveness unchanged, but to give up trying to ferret out all the implications of an incomplete KB by considering a form of implication that is weaker than full logical consequence. Because only some of the possibilities admitted by an incomplete KB will be considered during reasoning, an incomplete KB ends up being treated as if it were more complete.
3. *defaults and assumptions* Finally, we can leave the language and its logic unchanged but can transform the incomplete KB itself into one that is more complete. By making assumptions based on the absence of contradicting evidence, a KR system may come to conclusions not necessarily implied logically by the original KB. The result of this type of reasoning is that an incomplete KB will be made more complete by filling in the holes in what it knows.

So the view of KR we are considering here is certainly based on logic, but not necessarily classical logic. Rather than dealing with a very expressive language (i.e. FOL), and inferences that are logically complete and sound, we are concerned with inexpressive languages and with logics that are classically incomplete and unsound. First, we will look at some special-purpose KR

[11] A KB is said to be incomplete if it tells us that one of a (possibly infinite) set of sentences is true without telling us which.

[12] The use of FOL to capture *terminology* or laws is somewhat different [see (20) for details].

languages, focussing on their expressive limitations. Next, we will look at logics of knowledge and belief and how these can be made to provide a weaker notion of implication than that of standard logic. Finally, we will examine some of the research in nonmonotonic reasoning in an attempt to characterize the use of defaults and assumptions. In all cases, the main point is that there is much to be gained by looking at the logical form of what is being represented and how the necessary reasoning can be kept (or at least has a hope of being kept) computationally tractable.

As for other sources on this topic outside of AI, there is unfortunately almost nothing in philosophy on managing the dual concerns of logic and computational complexity [a notable exception is (27)]. There have been results in theoretical computer science and mathematical logic in special cases of logics that are computationally manageable (e.g. see 83), but none of these results focus on whether these special cases are representationally significant. Although the issues addressed here provide a very useful perspective on KR research, they are only beginning to be examined in depth.

3. SPECIAL-PURPOSE LANGUAGES

A KR language with restricted expressive power is simply a language whose expressions can be understood propositionally, but without being closed under the normal logical operations of disjunction, existential quantification, and so on. Given that various types of incomplete knowledge will no longer be representable in such a language, the logical consequences of a KB can often be calculated using efficient special-purpose techniques, for example, avoiding, time-consuming (or infinite) case analyses and their equivalents.

Consider, for instance, information that we may have about two positive integral quantities m and n expressed in a first-order logical language that has symbols for the arithmetic operations and relations. So, for example, we might know that $2m - n = 6$ and that either $mn = 80$ or $m^2 < 5n$. If we call these two facts E and add to them Q, the single axiom of Robinson's system of arithmetic (97), then what follows logically is a number of properties of m and n, such as that $2m + n > 20$. This means that this property (call it P) is implicit in a KB that contains E and Q. Moreover, standard theorem proving (among other methods) can be used to discover this, since $((E \wedge Q) \supset P)$ must be a theorem of first-order logic.

But suppose that instead of E, we know E', which says that $2m - n = 6$ and $m + n = 15$. Again, P follows from E' and Q, and again, we could determine this using first-order theorem proving. But since our knowledge about m and n is expressible as a pair of linear equations, there is a much better way to do this: Solve the set of equations (using Gaussian elimination with back substitution) and calculate directly whether or not P is true of these values. In general, k equations can be solved in roughly k^3 operations, and assuming a unique solution, P can be checked in a linear number of operations.[13] Specialized techniques like this are not possible in general, and sets of linear equations are only a small subset of what can be expressed in the full language of first-order arithmetic. But it is nonetheless a very rich and useful subset. So it makes sense to build systems whose input language is restricted to lie in this subset.

Much of the work in KR has involved inventing new KR formalisms and embedding these within KR systems. In retrospect, a good proportion of this research can be seen as the search for useful compromises between expressive power, on the one hand, and tractability of reasoning, on the other (80). In fact, with the possible exception of nonmonotonic facilities (see Section 5 below), these formalisms can almost inevitably be understood as subsets of classical first-order logic.

3.1 Databases

The most obvious restriction to the form of a KB is what might be called *database form*. The idea is to restrict a KB to contain only the kind of information that can be represented in a simple standard database. Consider, for example, a very trivial database that deals with university courses. If we had to characterize in FOL the information contained in the database, we might use a collection of function-free atomic sentences like

Course(csc248)	Dept(csc373,ComputerScience)	Enrollment(psy400,42)
Course(mat100)	Dept(his100,History)	

In other words, a standard tabular database characterizes exactly the positive instances of the various predicates. But more to the point, since we never end up with sentences like

Dept(mat100,Mathematics) $\vee$ Dept(mat100,History),

certain kinds of incomplete knowledge cannot be represented.

There is, moreover, additional hidden information in a standard database that makes it even more complete. Consider the question

How many courses are offered by the Computer Science Department?

The knowledge expressed by the above FOL sentences is insufficient to answer the question: Nothing says that Computer Science has at least two courses (since "csc373" and "csc248" could be names of the same individual), and nothing says that it has at most two courses (since there could be courses

[13] This will be true of any P that can be evaluated directly once the values of its variables are known. So, for example, any P that does not use quantifiers has this property.

other than those mentioned in the list of sentences). But a database system could answer the question successfully by interpreting it as (something like)

> How many tuples in the COURSE relation have ComputerScience in their Dept field?

This is a question not about the world being modelled but about the data itself. To be able to reinterpret it as the intuitive question about courses and departments (rather than as one about tuples and fields), we need to account for additional information taking us beyond the stored data itself. In particular, we need FOL sentences of the form

$c_i \neq c_j$, for distinct constants c_i and c_j,

stating that each constant represents a unique individual. In addition, for each predicate, we need a sentence similar in form to

$\forall x[\text{Course}(x) \supset x = \text{csc248} \vee \ldots \vee x = \text{mat100}]$,

saying that the only instances of the predicate are the ones named explicitly.[14] If we now consider a KB consisting of all of these sentences, a KR system would indeed conclude (just like its database management counterpart) that there were exactly two Computer Science courses.

The main observation here is that answering questions with a KB in database form is much easier than in the general case. Because there is no incompleteness in our knowledge, inference reduces to simple calculation. We do not, for instance, have to reason by cases or by contradiction, as we might in a more general setting, and we can represent symbolically what is known about the world using sets of tuples, exactly like a standard database system. Then, to infer the number of courses of a certain type, all we have to do is count how many appropriate tuples appear in the COURSE relation. From this perspective, a database is a knowledge base whose limited form permits a very special form of inference.

Although database languages are almost always too weak for AI purposes, the limitations they impose on the logical form of a KB are found in many KR languages. There is very close structural correspondence between some part of the KB and the domain of interest: For each entity in the domain, there is a unique representational object that stands for it; for each relationship that it participates in, there is some sort of connection in the KB that corresponds to it. In a very real sense, that part of the KB is an *analogue* of the domain of interest, not so different from other analogues such as maps or physical models. The main advantage of having such an analogue is that it can be used directly to answer questions about the domain. Calculations on the model itself play the role of more general reasoning procedures (much the way arithmetic can replace reasoning with Peano's axioms). The disadvantage of an analogue, however, should also be clear: There are certain kinds of facts about the domain that it cannot leave unsaid.[15] In this sense, an analogue representation can be viewed as a special case of a propositional one, where the information it contains is relatively complete.

3.2 Logic Programs

The second restriction on the form of a KB that we will consider is a generalization of the previous one found in programs written in PROLOG (73), PLANNER (62), and related languages.[16] A KB in logic program form contains a collection of first-order sentences (called Horn sentences) of the form

$\forall x_1 \ldots x_n[P_1 \wedge \ldots \wedge P_m \supset P_{m+1}]$ where $m \geq 0$ and each P_i is atomic.

In the case where $m = 0$ and the arguments to the predicates are all constants, the logic program form coincides with the database form. As in the database case, since we are interested in more than just the universe of terms, we again have to include additional facts in the KB. In general, the resulting KB will be infinite, since it must contain all sentences of the form $(s \neq t)$, for any two distinct terms formed using function and constant symbols appearing in the KB. As before, the KB must also contain a version of the closed world assumption, which is now the negation of every ground atomic sentence not implied by the Horn sentences in the original KB.

The net result is a KB that once again has complete knowledge of the world (within a given language),[17] but this time it requires nontrivial inference to answer questions. The necessary reasoning is the *execution* of the logic program. For example, given a KB in logic program form consisting of

```
parent(bill,mary).
parent(bill,sam).
parent(X,Y), female(Y) ⊃ mother(X,Y).
female(mary).
```

[14]This is one form of what has been called the *closed world assumption* (118).

[15]The same is true for the standard analogues. A map does not allow you to say, for example, that a river passes through one of two widely separated towns, without specifying which town. Similarly, a plastic model of a ship cannot tell us that the ship it represents does not have two smokestacks, without also telling us how many it does have. This is not to say that there is no uncertainty associated with an analogue, but that this uncertainty is limited in various ways. See (82, 129, 130) for more information and see (51) for the use of analogues in problem solving.

[16]See Section 5.2 for another view of the procedural school of KR.

[17]Notice that it is impossible to state in a KB of this form that $(P \vee Q)$ is true without stating which one is true, or that $\exists x P(x)$ is true without saying what x is.

we know exactly who the mother of Bill is, but only after having executed the program.

In some sense, the logic program form does not provide any computational advantage to an FOL reasoning system, since determining if a ground atomic sentence is implied by a collection of Horn sentences (containing function symbols) is undecidable.[18] On the other hand, the form is much more manageable than in the general case, since the necessary inference can be split very nicely into two components: a *retrieval* component that extracts (atomic) facts from a database by pattern-matching, and a *search* component that tries to use the nonatomic Horn sentences to complete the inference. In actual systems like PROLOG and PLANNER, moreover, the search component is (partially) under user control, giving the user the ability to incorporate domain-specific control knowledge. The only purely automatic inference is the retrieval component.

This suggests a different way of looking at the inferential service provided by a KR system (without even taking into account the logical form of the KB). Instead of automatically performing the full deduction necessary to answer questions, a KR system could manage a limited form of inference and leave to the rest of the knowledge-based system (or to the user) the responsibility of intelligently completing it. As suggested in (50), the idea is to take the "muscle" out of the automatic component and leave the difficult part of reasoning as a problem that the overall system can (meta-)reason about and plan to solve (54).[19] It is clear that one of the major attractions of PROLOG is its programmability, and its potential for integrating procedural and declarative concerns, rather than its power as a KR language.[20]

3.3 Semantic Networks

Whereas databases and logic programs have been studied quite independently of KR, semantic networks are much more of a pure KR phenomenon.[21] The first observation about a KB in this form is that it only contains unary and binary predicates. For example, instead of representing the fact that John's grade in cs100 was 85 by

Grade(john, cs100, 85),

we might postulate the existence of objects called "grade-assignments" and represent the fact about John in terms of a particular grade-assignment g_1 as

$$\text{Grade-assignment}(g_1) \wedge \text{Student}(g_1,\text{john}) \wedge \text{Course}(g_1,\text{cs100}) \wedge \text{Mark}(g_1,85).$$

This part of a KB in semantic net form is also in database form: a collection of function-free ground atoms, along with sentences stating the uniqueness of constants and closed world assumptions.

The main feature of a semantic net (and of frames, below), however, is not how individuals are handled, but the treatment of the unary predicates (which we will call *types*) and the binary ones (which we will call *attributes*). First, types are organized into a taxonomy, which, for our purposes, can be treated as a set of sentences of the form[22]

$$\forall x[B(x) \supset A(x)].$$

Finally, there are sentences that place constraints on an attribute as it applies to instances of a type:

$$\forall x[B(x) \supset \exists y(R(x,y) \wedge V(y))] \quad \text{or} \quad \forall x[B(x) \supset R(x,c)].$$

One property of a KB in this form is that it can be represented by a labelled directed graph (and displayed in the usual way). The nodes are either constants or types, and the edges are labelled either with an attribute or with the special label *is-a*. The significance of this graphical representation is that it allows certain kinds of inference to be performed by simple graph-searching techniques. For example, to find out if a particular individual has a certain attribute, it is sufficient to search from the constant representing that individual, up *is-a* links, for a node having an edge labelled with the attribute. By placing the attribute as high as possible in the taxonomy, all individuals below it can *inherit* the property. Computationally, any improvement in the efficiency of graph-searching will improve the performance of inference in a KB of this form (although in general, of course, graph-theoretic operations can be as intractable as any other operations).

In addition, for better or for worse, the graph representation suggests different kinds of inference based more directly on the structure of the KB than on its logical content. For example, we can ask for the connection between two nodes and answer by finding a path in the graph between them.[23] Another example is to use the *is-a* taxonomy for default reasoning.[24] For

[18]In many simple Expert System applications, however, the problem is solvable because no function symbols (except for constants) are used.

[19]This topic is discussed further in Section 4.

[20]For more information on PROLOG as a programming language, see (29, 74).

[21]Originally, semantic networks were proposed as models of associative memory (e.g. 112). Gradually they came to be used for general KR purposes, but not without some confusion regarding how they were to be interpreted (15, 16, 141). For a collection of research papers demonstrating some of the variety in semantic network representations, see (47).

[22]See (16, 59) for a discussion of some of the subtleties involved here.

[23]Quillian (113) proposed a "semantic intersection" approach to answering questions in his original work on semantic nets. See also (30) for later work on the same topic.

[24]Default reasoning is discussed in detail in Section 5.

instance, the *elephant* node can have a *color* link to the value *gray*, but anything below *elephant* (such as *albino-elephant*) can be linked to a different color value. To infer the color of an individual only requires searching up the taxonomy for a value, and stopping when the first one is found, preempting any higher values.[25] The trouble with this type of reasoning is that, with only a procedural account like the one above, it is very easy to lose the import of exactly what is being represented (17).

3.4 Frames

The final form we consider—frame descriptions—is mainly an elaboration of the semantic network form.[26] The emphasis, in this case, is on the structure of the types themselves (usually called *frames*) in terms of their attributes (now called *slots*). Typically, the kind of detail associated with the slots of a frame includes

1. *values*, stating exactly what the attribute of an instance should be. Alternatively, the value may be just a *default*, in which case an individual inherits the value, provided it does not override it.
2. *restrictions*, stating what constraints must be satisfied by attribute values. These can be *value* restrictions, specified by a type that attribute values should be instances of, or *number* restrictions, specified in terms of a minimum and a maximum number of attribute values.
3. *attached procedures*, providing procedural advice on how the attribute should be used. An *if-needed* procedure explains how to calculate attribute values if none have been specified; an *if-added* procedure explains what should be done when a new value is discovered.

Like semantic networks, frame languages tend to take liberties with logical form, and the developers of these languages have been notoriously lax in characterizing their truth theories (17, 59). Restricting ourselves to a noncontroversial subset of a frame language, we might have descriptions like

(Student
  with a dept is computer-science and
  with ≥ 3 enrolled-course is a
    (Graduate-Course with a dept is a Engineering-Department)).

This is intended to be a structured type that describes Computer Science students taking at least three graduate courses in departments within Engineering. If this type had a name (say *A*), we could express the type in FOL by a "meaning postulate" of the form

$$\begin{aligned}\forall x A(x) \equiv [&\text{Student}(x) \wedge \text{dept}(x, \text{computer-science}) \wedge \\ &\exists y_1 y_2 y_3\ (y_1 \neq y_2 \wedge y_1 \neq y_3 \wedge y_2 \neq y_3 \wedge \\ &\quad \text{enrolled-course}(x,y_1) \wedge \text{Graduate-Course}(y_1) \wedge \\ &\qquad \exists z(\text{dept}(y_1,z) \wedge \text{Engineering-Department}(z)) \wedge \\ &\quad \text{enrolled-course}(x,y_2) \wedge \text{Graduate-Course}(y_2) \wedge \\ &\qquad \exists z(\text{dept}(y_2,z) \wedge \text{Engineering-Department}(z)) \wedge \\ &\quad \text{enrolled-course}(x,y_3) \wedge \text{Graduate-Course}(y_3) \wedge \\ &\qquad \exists z(\text{dept}(y_3,z) \wedge \text{Engineering-Department}(z)))].\end{aligned}$$

Similarly, it should be clear how to state equally clumsily[27] in FOL that an individual is an instance of this type.

One interesting property of these structured types is that we do not have to explicitly assert that one of them is below another in the taxonomy. The descriptions themselves implicitly define a taxonomy of *subsumption*, where type *A* is subsumed by type *B* if, by virtue of the form of *A* and *B*, every instance of *A* must be an instance of *B*. For example, without any world knowledge at all, we can determine that the type

(Person with every male friend is a Doctor)

subsumes

(Person with every friend is a (Doctor with a specialty is surgery)).

Analytic relationships like subsumption are useful properties of structured types that are not available in a semantic network where all of the types are essentially atomic (20). In the KRYPTON KR language (18, 19), a full first-order KB is used to represent facts about the world, but subsumption information is also available. The reason for this is that while subsumption can be defined in terms of logical implication,[28] there can be very good special-purpose "description matching" algorithms for calculating these relationships (21). Again, because the logical form is sufficiently constrained, the required inference can be much more tractable.

3.5 Other Possibilities

One final class of special-purpose language worth mentioning are those that are geared to specific subject matters. For example, the representation of

[25] For more complex examples of reasoning based directly on the form of semantic networks, see (121) and (140).

[26] The theory of frames in KR was first presented in (99), although many of the ideas were already "in the air". KRL (11–13) and KL-ONE (14, 23) are perhaps the most representative KR languages based on these ideas.

[27] These sentences are especially awkward in FOL because of the number restrictions. For example, the sentence "There are a hundred billion stars in the Milky Way Galaxy" would be translated into an FOL sentence with on the order of 10^{22} conjuncts.

[28] Specifically, type *A* is subsumed by type *B* iff the meaning postulates for *A* and *B* logically imply $\forall x[A(x) \supset B(x)]$.

knowledge about time proposed by Allen (3) is clearly limited in what kinds of knowledge it can represent. The payoff is that there is a special-purpose algorithm for deciding if knowledge about a collection of temporal intervals is consistent. In a similar vein, Schubert (126, 127) discusses a limited representation for knowledge about parts, where questions about whether or not one object is an ultimate subpart of another can be answered in constant time. Of course, in some sense, the input languages to linear equation solvers, circuit simulators, and program compilers can all be thought of as restricted representation languages that admit very specialized forms of reasoning. Additional domain independent but special-purpose reasoning situations are described in (25).

One final aspect of this approach involves combining more than one special-purpose language in what is called a *hybrid* system. Examples of such systems are the above-mentioned KRYPTON, CAKE (120), and Oppen's co-operating decision procedures (106). The issue in these systems is how to make multiple reasoners co-operate, that is, solve complementary parts of a reasoning problem by exchanging the right sort of information, with a minimum of redundancy.[29] The promise of such systems (which is only starting to be realized) is the possibility of efficiently handling representation languages that are more expressive than those of the subreasoners.

4. MODELS OF LIMITED REASONING

So far, we have considered keeping the reasoning task tractable by limiting the KR language and thus restricting the set of implications to be computed by a KR service. But there are other possibilities. In this section, we consider another approach that leaves the language intact but uses a weaker form of implication.

Technically, there are at least two ways to achieve this. The obvious one is to use (or develop) a nonstandard logic with a different semantics leading to a weaker notion of logical consequence. However, this would force us to give up all of the usual properties of classical logic. Another approach, and one that has received more attention in KR, is to preserve the standard notion of logical consequence, but to augment the language with a knowledge or belief operator, so that the sentence $B\alpha$ is to be read as "the KB believes that α".[30] The idea is to take seriously the concept of belief built into the term "knowledge representation" and to formalize explicitly a weaker sense of belief in terms of the semantics of $B\alpha$. So, instead of basing a KR service on whether or not α is a logical consequence of a set of sentences S, we consider whether or not believing α is a logical consequence of believing the elements of S according to the augmented logic.[31]

4.1 Logical Omniscience

The first formal logic of belief along these lines originated with Hintikka (64) and was based on a *possible-world semantics*.[32] The idea, roughly, is to acknowledge in the semantics that things might have happened differently from the way they did in fact occur, and possible worlds are theoretical entities that index into this space of possibilities. The important point is that within a given interpretation, certain sentences can be true in some possible worlds and false in others. A belief state, then, is characterized by a set of possible worlds, and what is considered to be believed in a belief state is precisely what is true in all of those worlds. So having no opinion on some sentence simply means that it will come out true in some of these possible worlds and false in others.

As is, however, the possible-world model does not formalize a type of belief that is more restricted than the KR service described so far. It suffers from *logical omniscience* (65): At any given point, the set of sentences considered to be believed in this model is closed under logical consequence. It is built into possible-world semantics that if α is believed and α logically implies β, then β is believed as well. A number of attempts have recently been made to formalize a more limited notion of belief. Before looking into them, it should be noted that the main emphasis in this research has been to accurately model the beliefs of an agent, and none of these models have yet been applied in a direct way to the design of new KR architectures.

4.2 The Syntactic Approach

When talking about what an agent actually believes, we want to be able to distinguish between believing only α and $(\alpha \supset \beta)$ on the one hand, and believing α, $(\alpha \supset \beta)$ and β, on the other. While the picture of the world is the same in both cases, only the second involves realizing that β is true. This is somewhat of a problem semantically, since the two sets of beliefs are true in precisely the same possible worlds and so are, in some sense, semantically indistinguishable. Thus, in the possible-worlds approach to belief (as in 77,

[29]Hybrid systems should be distinguished from those with multiple representation languages that do not attempt to avoid redundancy or to pass information among multiple reasoners, such as the systems described in (1, 5, 26).

[30]Strictly speaking, the term "knowledge" is inappropriate, since what is represented in a KB is typically not required to be true; at the very least, we should be talking about belief. Because of this, and to be consistent with most philosophers, we use the term "belief" throughout.

[31]Another reason for preferring this approach is that it quite naturally generalizes to deal with beliefs about other beliefs (by using a B operator within the scope of another). This allows facts about self-knowledge to be expressed, which has applications discussed in Section 5.

[32]See (67) for an introduction to possible worlds and the modal logics based on them.

100, 101), it is impossible to distinguish between the two cases. But if the two belief sets are semantically indistinguishable, they are certainly syntactically distinguishable. This might suggest that any realistic model of belief will have to include (something isomorphic to) an actual set of sentences to distinguish between the two belief states above. In other words, part of what will constitute a belief state in this *syntactic* approach to belief are the actual sentences that are believed.

A number of variants of the syntactic model of belief have been proposed (32, 40, 43, 91, 104). Perhaps the most sophisticated one is by Konolige (70–72). In his case, a belief state is characterized by an initial set of sentences (representing a base set of beliefs) and a set of logically sound deduction rules for obtaining new derived beliefs. Logical omniscience is avoided by allowing the deduction rules to be logically incomplete. Among other things, Konolige is able to demonstrate how many variants of the possible-world model can be seen as special cases of his model, where the deduction rules are required to satisfy certain properties. Moreover, Konolige's model allows introspection to be characterized very naturally and concretely using a submodel (with different base beliefs and deduction rules), which is the system's model of itself.

With or without deduction rules, the syntactic approach suffers from a serious defect that is, in some sense, the opposite of the problem with possible worlds. A possible-world semantics is too *coarse-grained* to model belief in that it cannot distinguish belief sets that logically imply the same set of sentences. The syntactic approach, on the other hand, is too *fine-grained* in that it considers any two sets of sentences as distinct semantic entities and, consequently, different belief sets. In general, $B\alpha$ will logically imply $B\beta$ only if α and β are identical. So, for example, a system that believes that $(\alpha \vee \beta)$ is true is not even required to believe that $(\beta \vee \alpha)$ must also be true.

Of course, the syntactic approach can be embellished by requiring that belief sets satisfy certain additional properties, for example, respecting the commutativity of disjunction. The trouble with this kind of stipulation is that it does not show the source of this property, namely that a disjunction is true exactly when one of the disjuncts is. Clearly, it would be preferable to have a model of belief where restrictions on belief sets followed from the definition of belief, that is, a model based in some way on a concept of truth rather than on a collection of ad hoc restrictions to sets of sentences.

4.3 Impossible and Partial Worlds

Recent research in KR has attempted to deal with the problem of logical omniscience by using a generalized notion of possible world. Logical omniscience (and the attendant computational difficulty) is a direct result of the characterization of belief states as sets of possible worlds. If the agent only believes that α is true, the set of worlds will be all those where α is true: some, for example, where β is true, others, where β is false. However, because valid sentences will also be true in all of these possible worlds, the agent is thought of as believing them just as if they were among his actual beliefs. In terms of the possible worlds, there is no way to distinguish α from a valid sentence.

One solution is to make this notion of what an agent thinks the world is like be more relevant to what he actually believes. This can be done by replacing the possible worlds by a different kind of semantic entity that does not necessarily deal with the truth of all sentences. In particular, sentences not relevant to what an agent actually believes (including some valid ones) need not get a truth value in one of these partial possible worlds [which we call *situations*, following (7)]. In fact, we can think of possible worlds as those limiting cases where every sentence has a truth value. Indeed, the concept of a possible world being *compatible* with a situation is intuitively clear: Every sentence whose truth is supported by the situation should be true in that possible world, and every sentence whose falsity is supported should be false. Also, we can allow for situations that have no compatible possible worlds. These are situations that support both the truth and falsity of some sentence. Although they can never be real, such impossible situations can be imagined and are very useful, since they allow an agent to have an incoherent picture of the world.[33]

The "trick," then, that underlies the models of belief is to identify belief with a *set of situations* rather than with a set of possible worlds. This has the following effect (roughly): Not all valid sentences have to be believed, since situations can fail to support them by being partial. Also, because of impossible situations, beliefs need not be closed under logical consequence. For example, a situation can support both α and $(\neg\alpha \vee \beta)$, without supporting β, by supporting both α and its negation.

Although there were certainly antecedents in the philosophical literature (e.g. 114), the first proposal for using this kind of logic in a computer system was by Belnap (8). He sought to use *relevance logic* (4), which embodies these situations (in terms of four truth values), as a means of dealing with the partiality and potential inconsistency of information presented to a machine. The relation of logical consequence in this type of relevance logic (called *tautological entailment*) is a strict subset of the relation of logical consequence in classical logic. Levesque (81) showed how to use these ideas to establish a formal model of belief parallel to the one based on possible worlds. More importantly, Levesque described a KR service based on this weaker notion of implication and proved that the required inference was indeed more

[33]Although they are used here, impossible situations are not strictly necessary to model inconsistent beliefs, as is discussed later.

computationally tractable (for a language without quantifiers) than the one based on classical logic.

As the foundation for a KR service, relevance logic does have serious drawbacks, however. As mentioned above, it is the impossible situations that allow beliefs to be open under logical consequence: Any agent whose belief state is characterized by a set of possible situations always believes β if α and $(\neg\alpha \vee \beta)$ are believed. Intuitively, one would like to say that failing to believe β results from failing to put the other two beliefs together, rather than allowing for the possibility that both α and its negation might be true. The idea is to have a model where believing a conjunction is not the same thing as believing both of the conjuncts; it should require putting the two conjuncts together. This type of model is presented in (43) and illustrates how logical omniscience can be avoided without requiring impossible situations.

Another problem with the taulogical entailment relation of relevance logic is that the obvious first-order version of it is undecidable (110). This means that a computationally manageable model of belief dealing with full first-order logic cannot be derived simply from propositional versions. Three (related) proposals for dealing with full first-order logic are found in (49, 76, 110). Finally, the relevance logic approach by itself gives no indication of how to deal with beliefs about beliefs, for suggestions in this regard see (43).

5. DEFAULTS AND ASSUMPTIONS

As discussed earlier, avoiding incomplete knowledge is an important way to keep the reasoning of a KR service tractable. In fact, in many cases where knowledge is incomplete, a useful strategy is to make assumptions to complete this knowledge, to reason with the enlarged (tractable) belief set, noting what assumptions are in effect, and perhaps later to retract those conclusions derived from assumptions invalidated by new information. For example, given only that Clyde is an elephant, one may assume (until there are reasons to believe otherwise) that Clyde is gray. Any reasoning that then depends on this color would not need to be duplicated for the gray and nongray cases. The hypothesis is that it will be sufficiently advantageous to deal with relatively complete KBs even if it is occasionally necessary to retract assumptions (and conclusions drawn from them) in the face of conflicting evidence. In other words, provided that assumptions are chosen judiciously, there will be real computational advantage to building systems that do not allow for all of the possibilities admitted by the information they possess.

5.1 The Source of Assumptions

This way of completing a KB presumes that there will be principles for selecting assumptions that are most likely to be correct and least likely to require (costly) retraction. Fortunately, this seems to be the case. The most obvious source of assumptions are *defaults*, which come in a number of forms (117):

the closed world assumption (see Section 3.1) Given a collection of facts about some situation, a common assumption is that any relationship that cannot be inferred to hold among the entities being discussed in fact does not hold (116). Among other things, this assumption allows one to avoid having to specify relationships that do not hold.[34] A similar assumption appears in some *is-a* hierarchies in semantic networks (16), where concepts are assumed to be disjoint unless they share descendants. Other related assumptions are *domain closure* (90), where entities whose existence is not implied are assumed not to exist, and the *unique name assumption* (116), where distinct names are taken to represent distinct entities.

the frame assumption Any system that has to reason about the effects of actions must deal with what exactly is not changed by the occurrence of an action. Since any action will tend to have a very localized effect, a common assumption is that nothing is changed by an action except for what is known to be changed. So, for example, moving an object normally does not change its color and, even less likely, the color of other distant objects. This type of assumption was built into some AI planning systems such as STRIPS (46). However, while the problem of circumscribing the effects of actions is one that was recognized very early in AI [see (94) or (115)], it remains to be solved satisfactorily [see (35) and (48) for suggestions as to why].

prototypes Much of what we know about various categories of objects involves properties that almost always apply. So, for example, polar bears are normally white, birds normally fly, and so on. Also, there seems to be fairly clear evidence that people understand the world based very much on notions of normality and abnormality (122). While there have been proposals in the literature for dealing with these probabilistically (53, 55, 144), another possibility is to understand these probabilities as (meta-theoretic) evidence for why these defaults are reasonable assumptions to make. That is, if there is sufficiently high probability that a polar bear will be white, then there is an equally good chance that the default assumption will not have to be revised.

locality assumptions Another powerful source of default assumptions is based on aspects of a "current" context. In communication, one can often fill in details in an elliptical utterance based on using "here," "now," and "me" when the place, time, or person involved is not mentioned. More generally, the context of conversation will introduce entities that can be used as defaults in later discourse (e.g. see 125). Similarly, when planning to achieve an effect, appropriate instruments might default to those readily at hand.

[34]This assumption is certainly used in standard databases where only positive information is stored. This is also related to the "negation as failure" of PROLOG [28, 119].

Overall, because there are so many sources of default assumptions that do indeed seem to work in a majority of cases, reasoning in this manner seems perfectly justifiable. In fact, Reiter claims (117, p. 218) that "Default reasoning may very well be the rule rather than the exception since normally we act in the presence of incomplete knowledge."

Finally, as pointed out in (82), there seem to be cases where assumptions can be made without the benefit of the statistical justification of defaults. If it turns out that the subject of a potential assumption is not likely to be the subject of later information, it may still be worth making some assumption for computational reasons, as it will be unlikely later to give rise to a conflict. So, for example, given information that a dog chased a cat around a tree, one might assume that the direction of the chase was clockwise, even though statistically, it could go either way.[35] Of course, the real trick here will be to find principles for making assumptions that take into account not only possible computational gains but also the likelihood of errors and their severity.

5.2 Truth Maintenance

One branch of KR research has focussed on appropriate mechanisms for managing families of assumptions and keeping track of justifications to allow a graceful backing out. These have been called *truth maintenance systems* (or sometimes *reason* maintenance systems) (36, 37, 88). Of particular interest in this area are those systems that are explicit about the assumptions being carried or being excluded, such as (33) and (87).[36] Most of this work, however, deals with efficient mechanisms for actually implementing truth maintenance. This in turn derives from earlier work on *procedural representations* of knowledge, where a major focus of attention was the control of reasoning, especially during the kind of backtracking that arises as a result of defeated assumptions. This procedural school began more or less with the PLANNER representation language (62, 63) and received perhaps a last push in the AMORD system (34). A general discussion of the issues involved in this approach to representation can be found in (57, 102, 138). Ultimately, the problem of truth maintenance is that of *belief revision* and theory evolution: what beliefs should be discarded in the face of conflicting evidence [e.g. see (2) and also (38) for a survey of work in this area].

5.3 Nonmonotonic Reasoning

The major conceptual issue faced by KR systems that must reason with assumptions is what kinds of assumptions there are and what is the appropriate logic for reasoning with them. This has led to the development of a branch of AI called *nonmonotonic reasoning*. The idea, roughly, is this. Ordinary reasoning in a KBS is monotonic: The set of conclusions that can be drawn from a body of information grows as the body of information grows (since anything logically implied by a set of sentences is also implied by a superset of that set). But when the body of information in question also contains potential assumptions to be made (barring information to the contrary), the set of conclusions need not grow monotonically, since new information may very well invalidate previous assumptions.

The area of formal nonmonotonic reasoning has recently become a very active and fruitful one. Although no KR systems have been designed to incorporate the general principles, and very little is currently known about the impact of nonmonotonic reasoning on the tractability of the reasoning problem, a number of formalisms capturing different aspects of the problem have been proposed and analyzed.

An early collection of work in this area appears in (9). In this volume, three formalisms for nonmonotonic reasoning are proposed. All of them are based on modifications to classical first-order logics, but unfortunately none of them enjoy the benefit of a semantic account. The first proposal, by Reiter (118), is called *default logic*. Theories in this logic consist of two parts: a base set of standard first-order sentences, and a set of default rules specified by triples of formulas. The proof-theoretic understanding of a default rule is that given (an instance of) the first formula, the third formula can be inferred provided that the second one has not been. An *extension* of a default theory is any consistent minimal set of sentences containing the base set, which is both deductively closed and closed under the default rules. Reiter's interpretation is that any such extension constitutes a reasonable set of beliefs given the base set and defaults, and he shows how certain default theories may have none or more than one such extension. The nonmonotonicity of default logic arises from the fact that an extended base set may prohibit the application of certain default rules.

The second nonmonotonic formalism, called *nonmonotonic logic*, was proposed by McDermott & Doyle (96). In this case, a standard first-order language is augmented with a unary sentential operator M, where $M\alpha$ is to be read as "α is consistent." Their version of an extension of a base set of sentences is any minimal superset that is deductively closed and has the property that $M\alpha$ is an element of the extension whenever $\neg\alpha$ is not an element. Unlike Reiter, the authors identify belief with the set of sentences

[35] Indeed, in "visualizing" a described situation, we are filling in a large number of visually significant details that need not be implied by anything in the original description nor by statistically relevant defaults. So, for example, it is hard to think about Ronald Reagan standing beside Margaret Thatcher without thinking of them from a specific point of view with one of them on the left and the other on the right.

[36] Interestingly enough, Shapiro and Martins argue that relevance logic is the appropriate framework for maintaining a network of assumptions, quite independently of its role in limiting reasoning (as discussed in Section 4.3).

that are members of all such extensions, even though such a belief set need not itself be an extension. The nonmonotonicity arises here from the fact that as the base set grows, fewer $M\alpha$ sentences will be added to an extension.

The third formalism is called *circumscription* and is due to John McCarthy (92). The idea is to take any finite set of first-order sentences as the base and "circumscribe" a predicate in it by adding to the base an infinite collection of sentences (as specified by a circumscription schema). The intent of these sentences is to make the extended theory state that the predicate is as small as possible, given the base set. The way this is done for a predicate P is to include in the collection a sentence for each open first-order formula ϕ with the same number of arguments as P. What this sentence says is that if the base sentences with P replaced by ϕ are true and ϕ is a subset of P, then ϕ and P are equal. The net effect is to prohibit any property (specifiable by an open formula) from simultaneously satisfying the base sentences and being a proper subset of the circumscribed predicate. In other words, the extended theory makes the circumscribed predicate minimal. This is nonmonotonic, because any change to the base set (additive or not) will lead to a different extended theory, since every sentence in that theory uses the base set directly.

Since the publication of these three formalisms, there has been extensive research on their properties. It is generally agreed that the first two have serious drawbacks. In Reiter's model, domain-dependent knowledge has to be encoded in inference rules, more or less ruling out a semantic account for the logic (103); McDermott & Doyle's proposal appears to be based on a notion of consistency that is inappropriate for the job but is best understood in terms of a logic of knowledge or belief (103). Circumscription remains the most successful of the three and certainly the one that has received the most attention (e.g. 41, 84, 119). It does have expressive drawbacks, however, and new versions of it are under active investigation (e.g. 93, 98).

Gaining in popularity is an attempt to understand nonmonotonicity in terms of explicit knowledge and belief. Thus, in (56, 69, 77, 103) a general form of nonmonotonicity is explained in terms of the inherent nonmonotonicity of self-knowledge. The idea is that certain kinds of assumptions are based on a lack of other beliefs (31). For example, one might be willing to believe that there is no city in New Zealand larger than Los Angeles based on a belief that one would know if there were such a city. So belief in the lack of a certain belief is sufficient to make the assumption. But this is a nonmonotonic process, since beliefs about what one does not believe must surely be revised as new beliefs are acquired. On the other hand, it is not clear that all nonmonotonic reasoning behaves this way. For example, the fact that birds generally fly seems to have nothing to do with what is or is not believed at any given point.

At this stage of research, the computational relevance of this work remains somewhat questionable. For the three formalisms described above, it appears (counter-intuitively) that reasoning with assumptions and defaults is even more difficult than reasoning without them.[37] From a computational standpoint, the formalizations seem to be moving in the wrong direction. Not that systems have been unable to take computational advantage of defaults. As discussed in Section 3.3, the use of defaults goes back to Quillian and the very early semantic networks (112), and it remains a major feature of inheritance hierarchies (16, 44, 132, 133). Defaults were also a major part of the frame concept (99) as can be seen in representation languages like KRL (11). But it has often been much easier to construct systems that reason in certain (nonmonotonic) ways than to justify the correctness of that reasoning. Indeed, systems whose behavior seemed appropriate at first glance were later shown to exhibit reasoning anomalies (42, 45). So it remains to be seen how the computational promise of nonmonotonic reasoning can be correctly realized.

6. CONCLUSION

According to the Knowledge Representation hypothesis, intelligent behavior ultimately depends on explicitly represented knowledge. No other design strategy as yet seems plausible to explain behavior, or have it depend in a flexible way on what one is told, or to isolate the assumptions that govern it, or to achieve any number of other desirable traits. But KR by itself does not solve anything unless a system is able to reason effectively with what it has explicitly represented. Specifically, if reasoning needs to be performed automatically as part of a larger task, it must be dependable both in terms of what it calculates and how long it takes. Thus, KR, as it has been presented here, is the study of what information can be extracted, in a computationally dependable way, from what forms of represented knowledge. In other words, it investigates the area within the confines of the KR hypothesis. In some sense, theorem proving with classical first-order logic is the base camp for this investigation, but as this review attempts to show, there is much to be learned from excursions into nearby regions.

[37] In fact, in the first two cases, applying an assumption depends on that assumption being consistent with some theory of the world. But for sufficiently expressive languages like that of FOL, the consistent sentences are not even recursively enumerable.

Literature Cited

1. Aikins, J. 1983. Prototypical knowledge for expert systems. *Artif. Intell.* 20(2): 163–210
2. Alchouron, C., Gardenfors, P., Makinson, D. 1985. On the logic of theory change: partial meet contraction and revision functions. *J. Symbol. Logic* 50(2):510–30
3. Allen, J. 1983. Maintaining knowledge about temporal intervals. *Commun. ACM* 26(11):832–43
4. Anderson, A., Belnap, N. 1975. *Entailment: The Logic of Relevance and Necessity*. Princeton, NJ: Princeton University Press
5. Attardi, G., Simi, M. 1981. Consistency and completeness of OMEGA, a logic for knowledge representation. In *Proc. Int. Jt. Conf. Artif. Intell., Vancouver, BC*, pp. 504–10
6. Barr, A., Davidson, J. 1981. Representation of knowledge. In *The Handbook of Artificial Intelligence*, ed. A. Barr, E. Feigenbaum, pp. 141–222. Los Altos, Calif: W. Kaufmann
7. Barwise, J., Perry, J. 1983. *Situations and Attitudes*. Cambridge, Mass: Bradford Books, MIT Press
8. Belnap, N. 1977. A useful four-valued logic. In *Modern Uses of Multiple-Valued Logic*, ed. J. Dunn, G. Epstein, pp. 8–37. The Netherlands: Reidel
9. Bobrow, D. 1980. *Special Volume on Non-Monotonic Reasoning. Artif. Intell.* 13(1, 2)
10. Bobrow, D. 1984. *Special Volume on Qualitative Reasoning about Physical Systems. Artif. Intell.* 24(1–3)
10a. Bobrow, D., Collins, A., eds. 1975. *Representation and Understanding: Studies in Cognitive Science*. New York: Academic
11. Bobrow, D., Winograd, T. 1977. An overview of KRL, a knowledge representation language. *Cognitive Sci.* 1(1):3–46
12. Bobrow, D., Winograd, T. 1979 KRL: another perspective. *Cognitive Sci.* 3(1):29–42
13. Bobrow, D., Winograd, T., the KRL Research Group. 1977. Experience with KRL-0: one cycle of a knowledge representation language. In *Proc. Int. Jt. Conf. Artif. Intell. Cambridge, Mass.*, pp. 213–22
14. Brachman, R. 1978. A structural paradigm for representing knowledge. *BBN Rep. 3605, Bolt Beranek & Newman, Cambridge, Mass.*
15. Brachman, R. 1979. On the epistemological status of semantic networks. See Ref. 47, pp. 3–50
16. Brachman, R. 1983. What is-a is and isn't: an analysis of taxonomic links in semantic networks. *IEEE Comput.* 16(10):30–36
17. Brachman, R. 1985. I lied about the trees (or, defaults and definitions in knowledge representation). *AI Mag.* 6(3):80–93
18. Brachman, R., Fikes, R., Levesque, H. 1983. KRYPTON: a functional approach to knowledge representation. *IEEE Comput.* 16(10):67–73
19. Brachman, R., Gilbert, V., Levesque, H. 1985. An essential hybrid reasoning system: knowledge and symbol level accounts of KRYPTON. In *Proc. Int. Jt. Conf. Artif. Intell., Los Angeles, Calif.*
20. Brachman, R., Levesque, H. 1982. Competence in knowledge representation. In *Proc. Natl. Conf. Am. Assoc. Artif. Intell., Pittsburgh, Pa.*, pp. 189–92
21. Brachman, R., Levesque, H. 1984. The tractability of subsumption in frame-based description languages. In *Proc. Natl. Conf. Am. Assoc. Artif. Intell., Austin, Texas*, pp. 34–37
22. Brachman, R., Levesque, H., eds. 1985. *Readings in Knowledge Representation*. Los Altos, Calif: Morgan Kaufmann
23. Brachman, R., Schmolze, J. 1985. An overview of the KL-ONE knowledge representation system. *Cognitive Sci.* 9(2):171–216
24. Deleted in proof
25. Bundy, A., Byrd, L., Mellish, C. 1985. Special-purpose, but domain-independent, inference mechanisms. In *Progress in Artificial Intelligence*, ed. L. Steels, J. Campbell, pp. 93–111. London: Ellis Horwood
26. Charniak, E. 1981. A common representation for problem-solving and language-comprehension information. *Artif. Intell.* 16(3):225–55
27. Cherniak, C. 1984. Computational complexity and the universal acceptance of logic. *J. Philos.*, 81(12):739–58
28. Clark, K. 1978. Negation as failure. See Ref. 51a, pp. 293–322
29. Clocksin, W., Mellish, C. 1981. *Programming in* PROLOG. New York: Springer-Verlag
30. Collins, A., Loftus, E. 1975. A spreading-activation theory of semantic processing. *Psychol. Rev.* 82(6):407–28
31. Collins, A., Warnock, E., Nelleke, A., Miller, M. 1975. Reasoning from incomplete knowledge. See Ref. 10a, pp. 383–416
32. Creary, L. 1979. Propositional attitudes: Fregean representation and simulative reasoning. In *Proc. Int. Jt. Conf. Artif. Intell., Tokyo*, pp. 176–81
33. de Kleer, J. 1986. An assumption-based TMS. *Artif. Intell.* 28(2):127–62
34. de Kleer, J., Doyle, J., Steele, G., Sussman, G., 1977. AMORD: explicit control of reasoning. In *Symp. Artif. Intell. Program. Lang., Rochester, NY*, pp. 116–25
35. Dennett, D. 1986. Cognitive wheels: the frame problem of artificial intelligence. In *Minds, Machines, and Evolution*, ed. C. Hookway. Cambridge, England: Cambridge Univ. Press
36. Doyle, J. 1982. A glimpse of truth-maintenance. In *Artificial Intelligence: An MIT Perspective*, ed. P. Winston, R. Brown, pp. 119–35. Cambridge, Mass: MIT Press
37. Doyle, J. 1983. The ins and outs of reason maintenance. In *Proc. Int. Jt. Conf. Artif. Intell. Karlsruhe, FRG*, pp. 349–51
38. Doyle, J., London, P. 1980. A selected descriptor-based bibliography to the literature on belief revision. *SIGART Newsl.* 71:7–23
39. Dreyfus, H. 1981. From micro-worlds to knowledge representation: AI at an impasse. In *Mind Design*, ed. J. Haugeland, pp. 161–204. Cambridge, Mass: MIT Press
40. Eberle, R. 1974. A logic of believing, knowing and inferring. *Synthese* 26: 356–82
41. Etherington, D., Mercer, R., Reiter, R. 1984. On the adequacy of predicate circumscription for closed-world reasoning. In *The Non-Monotonic Reasoning Workshop, New Paltz, NY*, pp. 70–81
42. Etherington, D., Reiter, R. 1983. On inheritance hierarchies with exceptions. In *Proc. Natl. Conf. Am. Assoc. Artif. Intell., Washington DC*, pp. 104–8
43. Fagin, R., Halpern, J. 1985. Belief, awareness and limited reasoning. In *Proc. Int. Jt. Conf. Artif. Intell., Los Angeles, Calif.*, pp. 491–501
44. Fahlman, S. 1979. *NETL: A System for Representing and Using Real-World Knowledge*. Cambridge, Mass: MIT Press
45. Fahlman, S., Touretzky, D., van Roggen, W. 1981. Cancellation in a parallel semantic network. In *Proc. Int. Jt. Conf. Artif. Intell., Vancouver, BC*, pp. 257–63
46. Fikes, R., Nilsson, N. 1971. STRIPS: a new approach to the application of theorem proving to problem solving. *Artif. Intell.* 2(3–4):189–208
47. Findler, N., ed. 1979. *Associative Networks: Representation and Use of Knowledge by Computers*. New York: Academic
48. Fodor, J. 1983. *The Modularity of Mind*. Cambridge, Mass: Bradford Books, MIT Press
49. Frisch, A. 1985. Using model theory to specify AI programs. In *Proc. Int. Jt. Conf. Artif. Intell., Los Angeles*, pp. 148–54
50. Frisch, A., Allen, J. 1982. Knowledge representation and retrieval for natural language processing. *Tech. Rep. TR 104, Dep. Comput. Sci., Univ. Rochester, NY*
51. Funt, B. 1980. Problem-solving with diagrammatic representations. *Artif. Intell.* 13(3):201–30
51a. Gallaire, H., Minker, J., eds. 1978. *Logic and Databases*. New York: Plenum
52. Garey, M., Johnson, D. 1979. *Computers and Intractability: A Guide to the Theory of NP-Completeness*. San Francisco: W. H. Freeman
53. Garvey, T., Lowrance, J., Fischler, M. 1981. An inference technique for integrating knowledge from disparate sources. In *Proc. Int. Jt. Conf. Artif. Intell., Vancouver, BC*, pp. 319–25
54. Genesereth, M. 1983. An overview of meta-level architecture. In *Proc. Natl. Conf. Am. Assoc. Artif. Intell., Washington, DC*, pp. 119–24
55. Ginsberg, M. 1984. Non-monotonic reasoning using Dempster's rule. In *Proc. Natl. Conf. Am. Assoc. Artif. Intell., Austin, Texas*, pp. 126–29
56. Halpern, J., Moses, Y. 1984. Towards a theory of knowledge and ignorance: preliminary report. In *The Non-Monotonic Reasoning Workshop, New Paltz, NY*, pp. 125–43
57. Hayes, P. 1974. Some problems and non-problems in representation theory. In *AISB Summer Conf. Univ. Sussex*, pp. 63–79
58. Hayes, P. 1977. In defence of logic. In *Proc. Int. Jt. Conf. Artif. Intell., Cambridge, Mass.*, pp. 559–65
59. Hayes, P. 1979. The logic of frames. In *Frame Conceptions and Text Understanding*, ed. D. Metzing, pp. 46–61. Berlin: de Gruyter

60. Hayes, P. 1985. Naive physics I: ontology for liquids. See Hobbs & Moore 1985, pp. 71–107
61. Hayes, P. 1985. The second naive physics manifesto. See Hobbs & Moore 1985, pp. 1–36
62. Hewitt, C. 1969. PLANNER: a language for proving theorems in robots. In *Proc. Int. Jt. Conf. Artif. Intell., Washington, DC*, pp. 295–301
63. Hewitt, C. 1972. Description and theoretical analysis (using schemata) of PLANNER, a language for proving theorems and manipulating models in a robot. *Tech. Rep. TR-258, AI Lab., MIT, Cambridge, Mass.*
64. Hintikka, J. 1962. *Knowledge and Belief: An Introduction to the Logic of the Two Notions*. Ithaca, NY: Cornell Univ. Press
65. Hintikka, J. 1975. Impossible possible worlds vindicated. *J. Philos.* 4:475–84
66. Hobbs, J., Moore, R., eds. 1985. *Formal Theories of the Commonsense World*. Norwood, NJ: Ablex
67. Hughes, G., Cresswell, M. 1968. *An Introduction to Modal Logic*. London: Methuen
68. Israel, D. 1983. The role of logic in knowledge representation. *IEEE Comput.* 16(10):37–42
69. Konolige, K. 1982. Circumscriptive ignorance. In *Proc. Natl. Conf. Am. Assoc. Artif. Intell., Pittsburgh, Pa.*, pp. 202–4
70. Konolige, K. 1983. A deductive model of belief. In *Proc. Int. Jt. Conf. Artif. Intell., Karlsruhe, FRG*, pp. 377–81
71. Konolige, K. 1984. *A deduction model of belief and its logics*. PhD thesis. Dep. Comput. Sci., Stanford Univ., Palo Alto, Calif.
72. Konolige, K. 1985. A computational theory of belief introspection. In *Proc. Int. Jt. Conf. Artif. Intell., Los Angeles*, pp. 502–8
73. Kowalski, R. 1974. Predicate logic as a programming language. In *IFIP Congress, Stockholm*, pp. 569–74
74. Kowalski, R. 1979. *Logic for Problem Solving*. Amsterdam: Elsevier North-Holland
75. Kuipers, B. 1979. On representing commonsense knowledge. See Ref. 47, pp. 393–408
76. Lakemeyer, G. 1986. Steps towards a first order logic of implicit and explicit belief. In *Theoretical Aspects of Reasoning about Knowledge: Proc. 1986 Conf.*, ed. J. Halpern, pp. 325–40. Los Altos, Calif: Morgan Kaufmann
77. Levesque, H. 1981. *A formal treatment of incomplete knowledge bases*. PhD thesis, Dep. Comput. Sci., Univ. Toronto, Ontario
78. Levesque, H. 1983. The logic of incomplete knowledge bases. See Ref. 105, pp. 165–86
79. Levesque, H. 1984. Foundations of a functional approach to knowledge representation. *Artif. Intell.* 23(2):155–212
80. Levesque, H. 1984. A fundamental tradeoff in knowledge representation and reasoning. In *Proc. Bienn. Conf. Can. Soc. Comput. Stud. Intell., London, Ontario*, pp. 141–52
81. Levesque, H. 1984. A logic of implicit and explicit belief. In *Proc. Natl. Conf. Am. Assoc. Artif. Intell., Austin, Texas*, pp. 198–202
82. Levesque, H. 1986. Making believers out of computers. *Artif. Intell.* In press
83. Lewis, H. 1978. Complexity of solvable cases of the decision problem for the predicate calculus. In *Proc. 19th IEEE Symp. Found. Comput. Sci.*, pp. 35–47
84. Lipschitz, V. 1985. Closed-world databases and circumscription. *Artif. Intell.*, 27(2):229–236
85. Loganantharaj, R. 1985. *Theoretical and implementational aspects of parallel link resolution in connection graphs*. PhD thesis. Dep. Comput. Sci., Colo. State Univ., Fort Collins
86. Loveland, D. 1978. *Automated Theorem Proving: A Logical Basis*. New York: North-Holland
87. Martins, J., Shapiro, S. 1983. Reasoning in multiple belief spaces. In *Proc. Int. Jt. Conf. Artif. Intell., Karlsruhe, FRG*, pp. 370–73
88. McAllester, D. 1980. *The Use of Equality in Deduction and Knowledge Representation*. MS thesis. AI Lab., Mass. Inst. Technol., Cambridge
89. McCarthy, J. 1968. Programs with common sense. See Ref. 98a, pp. 403–18
90. McCarthy, J. 1977. Epistemological problems in artificial intelligence. In *Proc. Int. Jt. Conf. Artif. Intell., Cambridge, Mass.*, pp. 1038–44
91. McCarthy, J. 1979. First order theories of individual concepts and propositions. In *Machine Intelligence*, ed. J. Hayes, D. Michie, L. Mikulich, 9:129–47. Chichester, England: Ellis Horwood
92. McCarthy, J. 1980. Circumscription—a form of non-monotonic reasoning. *Artif. Intell.* 13(1,2):27–39
93. McCarthy, J. 1984. Applications of circumscription to formalizing commonsense knowledge. In *The Non-Monotonic Reasoning Workshop, New Paltz, NY*, pp. 295–324
94. McCarthy, J., Hayes, P. 1969. Some philosophical problems from the standpoint of artificial intelligence. In *Machine Intelligence*, ed. B. Meltzer, D. Michie, 4:463–502. Edinburgh: Edinburgh Univ. Press
95. McDermott, D. 1982. A temporal logic for reasoning about processes and plans. *Cognitive Sci.* 6(2):101–55
96. McDermott, D., Doyle, J. 1980. Non-monotonic logic I. *Artif. Intell.* 13(1,2): 41–72
97. Mendelson, E. 1964. *Introduction to Mathematical Logic*. New York: Van Nostrand Reinhold
98. Minker, J., Perlis, D. 1984. Protected circumscription. In *Workshop on Non-Monotonic Reasoning, New Paltz, NY*, pp. 337–43
98a. Minsky, M., ed. 1968. *Semantic Information Processing*. Cambridge, Mass: MIT Press
99. Minsky, M. 1981. A framework for representing knowledge. In *Mind Design*, ed. J. Haugeland, pp. 95–128. Cambridge, Mass: MIT Press
100. Moore, R. 1977. Reasoning about knowledge and action. In *Proc. Int. Jt. Conf. Artif. Intell., Cambridge, Mass.*, pp. 223–27
101. Moore, R. 1980. Reasoning about knowledge and action. *Tech. Note 191, Artifi. Intell. Cent., SRI Int., Menlo Park, Calif.*
102. Moore, R. 1982. The role of logic in knowledge representation and commonsense reasoning. In *Proc. Natl. Conf. Am. Assoc. Artif. Intell., Pittsburgh, Pa.*, pp. 428–33
103. Moore, R. 1983. Semantical considerations on nonmonotonic logic. In *Proc. Int. Jt. Conf. Artif. Intell., Karlsruhe, FRG*, pp. 272–79
104. Moore, R., Hendrix, G. 1979. Computational models of belief and the semantics of belief sentences. *Tech. Note 187, Artifi. Intell. Cent., SRI Int., Menlo Park, Calif.*
105. Mylopoulos, J., Levesque, H. 1983. An overview of knowledge representation. In *On Conceptual Modelling: Perspectives from Artificial Intelligence, Databases, and Programming Languages*, ed. M. Brodie, J. Mylopoulos, J. Schmidt, pp. 3–17. New York: Springer-Verlag
106. Nelson, G., Oppen, D. 1979. Simplification by cooperating decision procedures. *ACM Trans. Program. Lang. Sys.* 1(2):245–57
107. Nilsson, N. 1980. *Principles of Artificial Intelligence*. Palo Alto, Calif: Tioga
108. Norman, D., Bobrow, D. 1975. On data limited and resource limited processing. *Cognitive Psychol.* 7:44–64
109. Norman, D., Rumelhart, D., eds. 1975. *Explorations in Cognition*. San Francisco: W. H. Freeman
110. Patel-Schneider, P. 1985. A decidable first-order logic for knowledge representation. In *Proc. Int. Jt. Conf. Artif. Intell., Los Angeles*, pp. 455–58
111. Pentland, A., Fischler, M. 1983. A more rational view of logic. *AI Mag.* 4(4):15–18
112. Quillian, M. 1967. Word concepts: a theory and simulation of some basic semantic capabilities. *Behav. Sci.* 12: 410–30
113. Quillian, M. 1968. Semantic memory. See Ref. 98a, pp. 227–70
114. Rantala, V. 1982. Impossible world semantics and logical omniscience. *Acta Philos. Fenni.* 35:106–15
115. Raphael, B. 1971. The frame problem in problem solving systems. In *Artificial Intelligence and Heuristic Programming*. New York: American Elsevier
116. Reiter, R. 1978. On closed world databases. See Ref. 51a, pp. 55–76
117. Reiter, R. 1978. On reasoning by default. In *Proc. Conf. Theor. Issues Nat. Lang. Process, Univ. Ill. Urbana-Champaign*
118. Reiter, R. 1980. A logic for default reasoning. *Artif. Intell.* 13(1,2):81–132
119. Reiter, R. 1982. Circumscription implies predicate completion (sometimes). In *Proc. Natl. Conf. Am. Assoc. Artif. Intell., Pittsburgh, Pa.*, pp. 418–20
120. Rich, C. 1980. Knowledge representation languages and predicate calculus: how to have your cake and eat it too. In *Proc. Natl. Conf. Am. Assoc. Artif. Intell., Pittsburgh, Pa.*, pp. 193–96
121. Rieger, C. 1976. An organization of knowledge for problem solving and language comprehension. *Artif. Intell.* 7(2):89–127
122. Rosch, E., Mervis, C. 1975. Family resemblances: studies in the internal structure of categories. *Cognitive Psychol.* 7:573–605
123. Rosenschein, S. 1986. Formal theories of knowledge in AI and robotics. *New Generation Comput.* 3(4): In press
124. Schank, R. 1973. Identification of conceptualizations underlying natural language. In *Computer Models of Thought and Language*, ed. R. Schank, K. Colby, pp. 187–247. San Francisco: W. H. Freeman
125. Schank, R. 1975. *Conceptual Informa-*

tion Processing. Amsterdam: North-Holland

126. Schubert, L. 1979. Problems with parts. In *Proc. Int. Jt. Conf. Artif. Intell., Tokyo*, pp. 778–84
127. Schubert, L., Papalaskaris, M., Taugher, J. 1983. Determining type, part, color, and time relationships. *IEEE Comput.* 16(10):53–60
128. Simmons, R. 1973. Semantic networks: their computation and use for understanding English sentences. See Ref. 124, pp. 63–113
129. Sloman, A. 1971. Interactions between philosophy and artificial intelligence: the role of intuition and non-logical reasoning in intelligence. *Artif. Intell.* 2:209–25
130. Sloman, A. 1975. Afterthoughts on analogical representation. In *Proc. Conf. Theoretical Issues in Natural Language Processing, Cambridge, Mass*, pp. 164–68
131. Smith, B. 1982. Reflection and semantics in a procedural language. *Tech. Rep. MIT/LCS/TR-272, Mass. Inst. Technol., Cambridge*

131a. 1980. *Special Issue on Knowledge Representation. SIGART Newsl.*, Vol. 70

132. Touretzky, D. 1984. Implicit ordering of defaults in inheritance systems. In *Proc. Natl. Conf. Am. Assoc. Artif. Intell., Austin, Texas*, pp. 322–25
133. Touretzky, D. 1984. *The mathematics of inheritance systems*. PhD thesis. Dep. Comput. Sci., Carnegie-Mellon Univ., Pittsburgh, Pa.
134. Vilain, M. 1982. A system for reasoning about time. In *Proc. Natl. Conf. Am. Assoc. Artif. Intell., Pittsburgh, Pa.*, pp. 197–201
135. Waterman, D., Hayes-Roth, F., ed. 1978. *Pattern-Directed Inference Systems*. New York: Academic
136. Winker, S. 1982. Generation and verification of finite models and counter-examples using an automated theorem prover answering two open questions. *J. ACM* 29(2):273–84
137. Winograd, T. 1972. *Understanding Natural Language*. New York: Academic
138. Winograd, T. 1975. Frame representations and the declarative/procedural controversy. See Ref. 10a, pp. 185–210
139. Winograd, T. 1980. Extended inference modes in reasoning by computer systems. *Artif. Intell.* 13(1–2):5–26
140. Winston, P. 1975. Learning structural descriptions from examples. In *The Psychology of Computer Vision*, ed. P. Winston, pp. 157–209. New York: McGraw-Hill
141. Woods, W. 1975. What's in a link: foundations for semantic networks. See Ref. 10a, pp. 35–82
142. Wos, L., Pereira, F., Hong, R., Boyer, R., Moore, J., et al. 1985. An overview of automated reasoning and related fields. *J. Autom. Reason.* 1(1):5–48
143. Wos, L., Winker, S., Smith, B., Veroff, R., Henschen, L. 1984. A new use of an automated reasoning assistant: open questions in equivalential calculus and the study of infinite domains. *Artif. Intell.* 22(3):303–56
144. Zadeh, L. 1983. Commonsense knowledge representation based on fuzzy logic. *IEEE Comput.* 16(10):61–66

1973 ACM Turing Award Lecture

The Turing Award citation read by Richard G. Canning, chairman of the 1973 Turing Award Committee, at the presentation of this lecture on August 28 at the ACM Annual Conference in Atlanta:

A significant change in the computer field in the last five to eight years has been made in the way we treat and handle data. In the early days of our field, data was intimately tied to the application programs that used it. Now we see that we want to break that tie. We want data that is independent of the application programs that use it—that is, data that is organized and structured to serve many applications and many users. What we seek is the *data base*.

This movement toward the data base is in its infancy. Even so, it appears that there are now between 1,000 and 2,000 true data base management systems installed worldwide. In ten years very likely, there will be tens of thousands of such systems. Just from the quantities of installed systems, the impact of data bases promises to be huge.

This year's recipient of the A.M. Turing Award is one of the real pioneers of data base technology. No other individual has had the influence that he has had upon this aspect of our field. I single out three prime examples of what he has done. He was the creator and principal architect of the first commercially available data base management system—the Integrated Data Store—originally developed from 1961 to 1964.[1,2,3,4] I-D-S is today one of the three most widely used data base management systems. Also, he was one of the founding members of the CODASYL Data Base Task Group, and served on that task group from 1966 to 1968. The specifications of that task group are being implemented by many suppliers in various parts of the world.[5,6] Indeed, currently these specifications represent the only proposal of stature for a common architecture for data base management systems. It is to his credit that these specifications, after extended debate and discussion, embody much of the original thinking of the Integrated Data Store. Thirdly, he was the creator of a powerful method for displaying data relationships—a tool for data base designers as well as application system designers.[7,8]

His contributions have thus represented the union of imagination and practicality. The richness of his work has already had, and will continue to have, a substantial influence upon our field.

I am very pleased to present the 1973 A.M. Turing Award to Charles W. Bachman.

The Programmer as Navigator

by Charles W. Bachman

This year the whole world celebrates the five-hundredth birthday of Nicolaus Copernicus, the famous Polish astronomer and mathematician. In 1543, Copernicus published his book, *Concerning the Revolutions of Celestial Spheres*, which described a new theory about the relative physical movements of the earth, the planets, and the sun. It was in direct contradiction with the earth-centered theories which had been established by Ptolemy 1400 years earlier.

Copernicus proposed the heliocentric theory, that planets revolve in a circular orbit around the sun. This theory was subjected to tremendous and persistent criticism. Nearly 100 years later, Galileo was ordered to appear before the Inquisition in Rome and forced to state that he had given up his belief in the Copernican theory. Even this did not placate his inquisitors, and he was sentenced to an indefinite prison term, while Copernicus's book was placed upon the Index of Prohibited Books, where it remained for another 200 years.

I raise the example of Copernicus today to illustrate a parallel that I believe exists in the computing or, more properly, the information systems world. We have spent the last 50 years with almost Ptolemaic information systems. These systems, and most of the thinking about systems, were based on a "computer centered" concept. (I choose to speak of 50 years of history rather than 25, for I see today's information systems as dating from the beginning of effective punched card equipment rather than from the beginning of the stored program computer.)

Just as the ancients viewed the earth with the sun revolving around it, so have the ancients of our information systems viewed a tab machine or computer with a sequential file flowing through it. Each was an

Author's address: Honeywell Information Systems, Inc., 200 Smith Street, Waltham, MA 02154.

The abstract, key words, etc., are on page 654.
1–8 Footnotes are on page 658.

adequate model for its time and place. But after a while, each has been found to be incorrect and inadequate and has had to be replaced by another model that more accurately portrayed the real world and its behavior.

Copernicus presented us with a new point of view and laid the foundation for modern celestial mechanics. That view gave us the basis for understanding the formerly mysterious tracks of the sun and the planets through the heavens. A new basis for understanding is available in the area of information systems. It is achieved by a shift from a computer-centered to the database-centered point of view. This new understanding will lead to new solutions to our database problems and speed our conquest of the n-dimensional data structures which best model the complexities of the real world.

The earliest databases, initially implemented on punched cards with sequential file technology, were not significantly altered when they were moved, first from punched card to magnetic tape and then again to magnetic disk. About the only things that changed were the size of the files and the speed of processing them.

In sequential file technology, search techniques are well established. Start with the value of the primary data key, of the record of interest, and pass each record in the file through core memory until the desired record, or one with a higher key, is found. (A primary data key is a field within a record which makes that record unique within the file.) Social security numbers, purchase order numbers, insurance policy numbers, bank account numbers are all primary data keys. Almost without exception, they are synthetic attributes specifically designed and created for the purpose of uniqueness. Natural attributes, e.g. names of people and places, dates, time, and quantities, are not assuredly unique and thus cannot be used.

The availability of direct access storage devices laid the foundation for the Copernican-like change in viewpoint. The directions of "in" and "out" were reversed. Where the input notion of the sequential file world meant "into the computer from tape," the new input notion became "into the database." This revolution in thinking is changing the programmer from a stationary viewer of objects passing before him in core into a mobile navigator who is able to probe and traverse a database at will.

Direct access storage devices also opened up new ways of record retrieval by primary data key. The first was called randomizing, calculated addressing, or hashing. It involved processing the primary data key with a specialized algorithm, the output of which identified a preferred storage location for that record. If the record sought was not found in the preferred location, then an overflow algorithm was used to search places where the record alternately would have been stored, if it existed at all. Overflow is created when the preferred location is full at the time the record was originally stored.

As an alternative to the randomizing technique, the

Copernicus completely reoriented our view of astronomical phenomena when he suggested that the earth revolves about the sun. There is a growing feeling that data processing people would benefit if they were to accept a radically new point of view, one that would liberate the application programmer's thinking from the centralism of core storage and allow him the freedom to act as a navigator within a database. To do this, he must first learn the various navigational skills; then he must learn the "rules of the road" to avoid conflict with other programmers as they jointly navigate the database information space.

This reorientation will cause as much anguish among programmers as the heliocentric theory did among ancient astronomers and theologians.

Key Words and Phrases: access method, attributes, calculated addressing, celestial mechanics, clustering, contamination, database, database key, database set, deadlock, deadly embrace, entity, hash addressing, overflow, owner, member, primary data key, Ptolemy, relationship, retrieval, secondary data key, sequential file, set, shared access, update, Weyerhaeuser

CR Categories: 3.74, 4.33, 4.34, 5.6, 8.1

index sequential access technique was developed. It also used the primary data key to control the storage and retrieval of records, and did so through the use of multilevel indices.

The programmer who has advanced from sequential file processing to either index sequential or randomized access processing has greatly reduced his access time because he can now probe for a record without sequentially passing all the intervening records in the file. However, he is still in a one-dimensional world as he is dealing with only one primary data key, which is his sole means of controlling access.

From this point, I want to begin the programmer's training as a full-fledged navigator in an n-dimensional data space. However, before I can successfully describe this process, I want to review what "database management" is.

It involves all aspects of storing, retrieving, modifying, and deleting data in the files on personnel and production, airline reservations, or laboratory experiments —data which is used repeatedly and updated as new information becomes available. These files are mapped through some storage structure onto magnetic tapes or disk packs and the drives that support them.

Database management has two main functions. First is the inquiry or retrieval activity that reaccesses previously stored data in order to determine the recorded status of some real world entity or relationship. This data has previously been stored by some other job, seconds, minutes, hours, or even days earlier, and has been held in trust by the database management system. A database management system has a continuing responsibility to maintain data between the time when it was stored and the time it is subsequently required for retrieval. This retrieval activity is designed to produce the information necessary for decision making.

Part of the inquiry activity is report preparation. In the early years of sequential access storage devices and the resultant batch processing, there was no viable alternative to the production of massive file dumps as formatted as reports. Spontaneous requirements to examine a particular checking account balance, an inventory balance, or a production plan could not be handled efficiently because the entire file had to be passed to extract any data. This form of inquiry is now diminishing in relative importance and will eventually disappear except for archival purposes or to satisfy the appetite of a parkinsonian bureaucracy.

The second activity of database management is to update, which includes the original storage of data, its repeated modification as things change, and ultimately, its deletion from the system when the data is no longer needed.

The updating activity is a response to the changes in the real world which must be recorded. The hiring of a new employee would cause a new record to be stored. Reducing available stock would cause an inventory record to be modified. Cancelling an airline reservation would cause a record to be deleted. All of these are recorded and updated in anticipation of future inquiries.

The sorting of files has been a big user of computer time. It was used in sorting transactions prior to batch sequential update and in the preparation of reports. The change to transaction-mode updating and on-demand inquiry and report preparation is diminishing the importance of sorting at the file level.

Let us now return to our story concerning the programmer as navigator. We left him using the randomizing or the index sequential technique to expedite either inquiry or update of a file based upon a primary data key.

In addition to a record's primary key, it is frequently desirable to be able to retrieve records on the basis of the value of some other fields. For example, it may be desirable, in planning ten-year awards, to select all the employee records with the "year-of-hire" field value equal to 1964. Such access is retrieval by secondary data key. The actual number of records to be retrieved by a secondary key is unpredictable and may vary from zero to possibly include the entire file. By contrast, a primary data key will retrieve a maximum of one record.

With the advent of retrieval on secondary data keys, the previously one-dimensional data space received additional dimensions equal to the number of fields in the record. With small or medium-sized files, it is feasible for a database system to index each record in the file on every field in the record. Such totally indexed files are classified as inverted files. In large active files, however, it is not economical to index every field. Therefore, it is prudent to select the fields whose content will be frequently used as a retrieval criterion and to create secondary indices for those fields only.

The distinction between a file and a database is not clearly established. However, one difference is pertinent to our discussion at this time. In a database, it is common to have several or many different kinds of records. For an example, in a personnel database there might be employee records, department records, skill records, deduction records, work history records, and education records. Each type of record has its own unique primary data key, and all of its other fields are potential secondary data keys.

In such a database the primary and secondary keys take on an interesting relationship when the primary key of one type of record is the secondary key of another type of record. Returning to our personnel database as an example—the field named "department code" appears in both the employee record and the department record. It is one of several possible secondary data keys of the employee records and the single primary data key of the department records.

This equality of primary and secondary data key fields reflects real world relationships and provides a way to reestablish these relationships for computer processing purposes. The use of the same data value as a primary key for one record and as a secondary key for a set of records is the basic concept upon which data structure sets are declared and maintained. The Integrated Data Store (I-D-S) systems and all other systems based on its concepts consider their basic contribution to the programmer to be the capability to associate records into data structure sets and the capability to use these sets as retrieval paths. All the COBOL Database Task Group systems implementations fall into this class.

There are many benefits gained in the conversion from several files, each with a single type of record, to a database with several types of records and database sets. One such benefit results from the significant improvement in performance that accrues from using the database sets in lieu of both primary and secondary indices to gain access to all the records with a particular data key value. With database sets, all redundant data can be eliminated, reducing the storage space required. If redundant data is deliberately maintained to enhance retrieval performance at the cost of maintenance, then the redundant data can be controlled to ensure that the updating of a value in one record will be properly reflected in all other appropriate records. Performance is enhanced by the so-called "clustering" ability of databases where the owner and some or most of the members records of a set are physically stored and accessed together on the same block or page. These systems have been running in virtual memory since 1962.

Another significant functional and performance advantage is to be able to specify the order of retrieval of the records within a set based upon a declared sort field or the time of insertion.

In order to focus the role of programmer as navigator, let us enumerate his opportunities for record access. These represent the commands that he can give to the database system—singly, multiply or in combination with each other—as he picks his way through the data to resolve an inquiry or to complete an update.

1. He can start at the beginning of the database, or at any known record, and sequentially access the "next" record in the database until he reaches a record of interest or reaches the end.
2. He can enter the database with a database key that provides direct access to the physical location of a record. (A database key is the permanent virtual memory address assigned to a record at the time that it was created.)
3. He can enter the database in accordance with the value of a primary data key. (Either the indexed sequential or randomized access techniques will yield the same result.)
4. He can enter the database with a secondary data key value and sequentially access all records having that particular data value for the field.
5. He can start from the owner of a set and sequentially access all the member records. (This is equivalent to converting a primary data key into a secondary data key.)
6. He can start with any member record of a set and access either the next or prior member of that set.
7. He can start from any member of a set and access the owner of the set, thus converting a secondary data key into a primary data key.

Each of these access methods is interesting in itself, and all are very useful. However, it is the synergistic usage of the entire collection which gives the programmer great and expanded powers to come and go within a large database while accessing only those records of interest in responding to inquiries and updating the database in anticipation of future inquiries.

Imagine the following scenario to illustrate how processing a single transaction could involve a path through the database. The transaction carries with it the primary data key value or database key of the record that is to be used to gain an entry point into the database. That record would be used to gain access to other records (either owner or members) of a set. Each of these records is used in turn as a point of departure to examine another set.

For example, consider a request to list the employees of a particular department when given its departmental code. This request could be supported by a database containing only two different types of records: personnel records and department records. For simplicity purposes, the department record can be envisioned as having only two fields: the department code, which is the primary data key; and the department name, which is descriptive. The personnel record can be envisioned as having only three fields: the employee number, which is the primary data key for the record; the employee name, which is descriptive; and the employee's department code, which is a secondary key which controls set selection and the record's placement in a set. The joint usage of the department code by both records and the declaration of a set based upon this data key provide the basis for the creation and maintenance of the set relationship between a department record and all the records representing the employees of that department. Thus the usage of the set of employee records provides the mechanism to readily list all the employees of a particular department following the primary data key retrieval of the appropriate department record. No other record for index need be accessed.

The addition of the department manager's employee number to the department record greatly extends the navigational opportunities, and provides the basis for a second class of sets. Each occurrence of this new class includes the department records for all the departments managed by a particular employee. A single employee number or department code now provides an entry point into an integrated data structure of an enterprise. Given an employee number, and the set of records of departments managed, all the departments which he manages can be listed. The personnel of each such department can be further listed. The question of departments managed by each of these employees can be asked repeatedly until all the subordinate employees and departments have been displayed. Inversely, the same data structure can easily identify the employee's manager, the manager's manager, and the manager's manager's manager, and so on, until the company president is reached.

There are additional risks and adventures ahead for the programmer who has mastered operation in the n-dimensional data space. As navigator he must brave dimly perceived shoals and reefs in his sea, which are created because he has to navigate in a shared database environment. There is no other obvious way for him to achieve the required performance.

Shared access is a new and complex variation of multiprogramming or time sharing, which were invented to permit shared, but independent, use of the computer resources. In multiprogramming, the programmer of one job doesn't know or care that his job might be sharing the computer, as long as he is sure that his address space is independent of that of any other programs. It is left to the operating system to assure each program's integrity and to make the best use of the memory, processor, and other physical resources. Shared access is a specialized version of multiprogramming where the critical, shared resources are the records of the database. The database records are fundamentally different than either main storage or the processor because their data fields change value through update and do not return to their original condition afterward. Therefore, a job that repeatedly uses a database record may find that record's content or set membership has changed since the last time it was accessed. As a result, an algorithm attempting a complex calculation may get a somewhat unstable picture. Imagine attempting to converge on an iterative solution while the variables are being randomly changed! Imagine attempting to carry out a trial balance while someone is still posting transactions to the accounts! Imagine two concurrent jobs in an airline reservations system trying to sell the last seat on a flight!

One's first reaction is that this shared access is nonsense and should be forgotten. However, the pressures to use shared access are tremendous. The processors available today and in the foreseeable future are expected to be much faster than are the available direct access storage devices. Furthermore, even if the speed of storage devices were to catch up with that of the processors, two more problems would maintain the pressure for successful shared access. The first is the trend toward the integration of many single purpose files into a few integrated databases; the second is the trend toward interactive processing where the processor can only advance a job as fast as the manually created input messages allow. Without shared access, the entire database would be locked up until a batch program or transaction and its human interaction had terminated.

The performance of today's direct access storage devices is greatly affected by patterns of usage. Performance is quite slow if the usage is an alternating pattern of: access, process, access, process, . . . , where each access depends upon the interpretation of the prior one. When many independent accesses are generated through multiprogramming, they can often be executed in parallel because they are directed toward different storage devices. Furthermore, when there is a queue of requests for access to the same device, the transfer capacity for that device can actually be increased through seek and latency reduction techniques. This potential for enhancing throughput is the ultimate pressure for shared access.

Of the two main functions of database management, inquiry and update, only update creates a potential problem in shared access. An unlimited number of jobs can extract data simultaneously from a database without trouble. However, once a single job begins to update the database, a potential for trouble exists. The processing of a transaction may require the updating of only a few records out of the thousands or possibly millions of records within a database. On that basis, hundreds of jobs could be processing transactions concurrently and actually have no collisions. However, the time will come when two jobs will want to process the same record simultaneously.

The two basic causes of trouble in shared access are interference and contamination. *Interference* is defined as the negative effect of the updating activity of one job upon the results of another. The example I have given of one job running an accounting trial balance while another was posting transactions illustrates the interference problem. When a job has been interfered with, it must be aborted and restarted to give it another opportunity to develop the correct output. Any output of the prior execution must also be removed because new output will be created. *Contamination* is defined as the negative effect upon a job which results from a combination of two events: when another job has aborted and when its output (i.e. changes to the database or messages sent) has already been read by the first job. The aborted job and its output will be removed from the system. Moreover, the jobs contaminated by the output of the aborted job must also be aborted and restarted so that they can operate with correct input data.

A critical question in designing solutions to the shared access problem is the extent of visibility that the application programmer should have. The Weyerhaeuser Company's shared access version of I-D-S was designed on the premise that the programmer should not be aware of shared access problems. That system automatically blocks each record updated and every message sent by a job until that job terminates normally, thus eliminating the contamination problem entirely. One side effect of this dynamic blocking of records is that a deadlock situation can be created when two or more jobs each want to wait for the other to unblock a desired record. Upon detecting a deadlock situation, the I-D-S database system responds by aborting the job that created the deadlock situation, by restoring the records updated by that job, and by making those records available to the jobs waiting. The aborted job, itself, is subsequently restarted.

Do these deadlock situations really exist? The last I heard, about 10 percent of all jobs started in Weyerhaeuser's transaction-oriented system had to be aborted for deadlock. Approximately 100 jobs per hour were aborted and restarted! Is this terrible? Is this too inefficient? These questions are hard to answer because our standards of efficiency in this area are not clearly defined. Furthermore, the results are application-dependent. The Weyerhaeuser I-D-S system is 90 percent efficient in terms of jobs successfully completed. However, the real questions are:

—Would the avoidance of shared access have permitted more or fewer jobs to be completed each hour?

—Would some other strategy based upon the detecting rather than avoiding contamination have been more efficient?

—Would making the programmer aware of shared access permit him to program around the problem and thus raise the efficiency?

All these questions are beginning to impinge on the programmer as navigator and on the people who design and implement his navigational aids.

My proposition today is that it is time for the application programmer to abandon the memory-centered view, and to accept the challenge and opportunity of navigation within an *n*-dimensional data space. The software systems needed to support such capabilities exist today and are becoming increasingly available.

Bertrand Russell, the noted English mathematician and philosopher, once stated that the theory of relativity demanded a change in our imaginative picture of the world. Comparable changes are required in our imaginative picture of the information system world.

The major problem is the reorientation of thinking of data processing people. This includes not only the programmer but includes the application system designers who lay out the basic application programming tasks and the product planners and the system programmers who will create tomorrow's operating system, message system, and database system products.

Copernicus laid the foundation for the science of celestial mechanics more than 400 years ago. It is this science which now makes possible the minimum energy solutions we use in navigating our way to the moon and the other planets. A similar science must be developed which will yield corresponding minimum energy solutions to database access. This subject is doubly interesting because it includes the problems of traversing an existing database, the problems of how to build one in the first place and how to restructure it later to best fit the changing access patterns. Can you imagine restructuring our solar system to minimize the travel time between the planets?

It is important that these mechanics of data structures be developed as an engineering discipline based upon sound design principles. It is important that it can be taught and is taught. The equipment costs of the database systems to be installed in the 1980's have been estimated at $100 billion (at 1970 basis of value). It has further been estimated that the absence of effective standardization could add 20 percent or $20 billion to the bill. Therefore, it is prudent to dispense with the conservatism, the emotionalism, and the theological arguments which are currently slowing progress. The universities have largely ignored the mechanics of data structures in favor of problems which more nearly fit a graduate student's thesis requirement. Big database systems are expensive projects which university budgets simply cannot afford. Therefore, it will require joint university/industry and university/government projects to provide the funding and staying power necessary to achieve progress. There is enough material for a half dozen doctoral theses buried in the Weyerhaeuser system waiting for someone to come and dig it out. By this I do not mean research on new randomizing algorithms. I mean research on the mechanics of nearly a billion characters of real live business data organized in the purest data structures now known.

The publication policies of the technical literature are also a problem. The ACM SIGBDP and SIGFIDET publications are the best available, and membership in these groups should grow. The refereeing rules and practices of Communications of the ACM result in delays of one year to 18 months between submittal and publication. Add to that the time for the author to prepare his ideas for publication and you have at least a two-year delay between the detection of significant results and their earliest possible publication.

Possibly the greatest single barrier to progress is the lack of general database information within a very large portion of the computer users resulting from the domination of the market by a single supplier. If this group were to bring to bear its experience, requirements, and problem-solving capabilities in a completely open exchange of information, the rate of change would certainly increase. The recent action of SHARE to open its membership to all vendors and all users is a significant step forward. The SHARE-sponsored Working Conference on Database Systems held in Montreal in July (1973) provided a forum so that users of all kinds of equipment and database systems could describe their experiences and their requirements.

The widening dialog has started. I hope and trust that we can continue. If approached in this spirit, where no one organization attempts to dominate the thinking, then I am sure that we can provide the programmer with effective tools for navigation.

Footnotes to the Turing Award citation on page 653 are:

[1] A general purpose programming system for random access memories (with S.B. Williams). Proc. AFIPS 1964 FJCC, Vol. 26, AFIPS Press, Montvale, N.J., pp. 411–422.

[2] Integrated Data Store. *DPMA Quarterly* (Jan. 1965).

[3] Software for random access processing. *Datamation* (Apr. 1965), 36–41.

[4] Integrated Data Store—Case Study. Proc. Sec. Symp. on Computer-Centered Data Base Systems sponsored by ARPA, SDC, and ESD, 1966.

[5] Implementation techniques for data structure sets. Proc. of SHARE Working Conf. on Data Base Systems, Montreal, Canada, July 1973.

[6] The evolution of data structures. Proc. NordDATA Conf., Aug. 1973, Copenhagen, Denmark, pp. 1075–1093.

[7] Data structure diagrams. Data Base 1, 2 (1969), Quarterly Newsletter of ACM SIGBDP, pp. 4–10.

[8] Set concepts for data structures. In *Encyclopedia of Computer Science*, Amerback Corp. (to be published in 1974).

Related articles are:

The evolution of storage structures. *Comm. ACM 15*, 7 (July 1972), 628–634.

Architectural Definition Technique: its objectives, theory, process, facilities and practice (with J. Bouvard). Proc. 1972 ACM SIGFIDET workshop on Data Description, Access and Control, pp. 257–280.

Data space mapped into three dimensions; a viable model for studying data structures. Data Base Management Rep., InfoTech Information Ltd., Berkshire, U.K., 1973.

A direct access system with procedurally generated data structuring capability (with S. Brewer). *Honeywell Comput. J.* (to appear).

Postscript

The Programmer as Navigator, Architect, Communicator, Modeler, Collaborator, and Supervisor

CHARLES W. BACHMAN
Bachman Information Systems, Inc.

Thirteen years have passed since the writing of the Turing Award paper entitled, "The Programmer as Navigator." Databases have become common, even popular. Some programmers navigate. Others join. I have spent considerable effort in arguing the merits of the network (CODASYL) data model and in extending it for greater modeling power.[1,2,3,4] Arguments and debates concerning data models waxed hot and heavy and have now pretty much simmered down. Today, the only reasonable consensus is that one can do useful work with DBMSs based upon any of the popular data models, even with those DBMSs that have no apparent affinity to any particular data model.

The Programmer as Architect

The study of the architecture of computer-based information systems has progressed well in this period. Two projects, important in their own right, were instrumental in bringing this subject to the forefront. The ANSI/X3/SPARC Study Group on Database Management (1972–1977) reported[5] its architecture of data storage and retrieval. This was one of the first attempts to clearly understand and document the layers of software and human activity involved in the process of data storage and retrieval. It went further and identified and described the interfaces between the various software modules and between them and their human counterparts (administrators, database designers, and programmers). It was significant that this report identified both administrative and run-time interfaces. This project was instrumental in establishing the concept of a *conceptual schema*[6] as a higher level abstraction of information structure definitions, which is independent of data representation.

The Programmer as Communicator

The International Organization for Standardization, through its ISO/TC97/SC16, established (1979–1982) the Reference Model for Open Systems Interconnection. This Reference Model is an architectural master plan for data communications established as an international standard[7] with the intent that it be the controlling and integrating standard for a series of more detailed standards to follow. This architecture identified seven layers of processing involved in and supporting communication between application processes. Each layer was specified in terms of its "administrative entities,"[8] "processing entities," "services," and "protocols." For the processing entities of each layer, there were four important interfaces to be established and standardized:

(1) the *services* that a processing entity offers to the processing entities in the layer immediately above;
(2) the communication *protocol* by which a processing entity communicates with other processing entities in the same layer;
(3) the *use*, by the processing entities of one layer, of the services provided by the processing entities of the layer immediately below;
(4) the administrative *protocol* by which a processing entity is controlled by the administrative entities within the same layer.

The detailed standards, developed subsequently for each layer, spell out the individual protocols, services, and service usage.

The vision and scope of this work can be seen in part by reviewing some of the discussions relating to addressability. How large should the address space be to identify all the processing entities that might wish to communicate with one another? One discussion followed this scenario:

> There will be close to 10 billion people in the world by the end of the year 2000 (10 billion addresses).
>
> Assume that, on the average, 100 robots will be working for each of these people (1 trillion addresses).
>
> Plan for unforeseen contingencies and a useful address space life of 25 years; so multiply by 10 (10 trillion addresses).
>
> Assume that the assignment of address is made through the political processes starting with the United Nations and that 99 percent of the addresses are effectively unavailable for applications level communications (1 quadrillion addresses).

Thus 1 quadrillion addresses is about the right order of magnitude for the address space being considered. This is a 1 followed by 15 zeros in the decimal system, or a 1 followed by approximately 50 zeros in the binary system.

This year the work on ISO standards for Open Systems Interconnection has received a great boost in support in the United States by the creation of COS (Corporation for Open Systems). COS is an industry-wide organization of users, carriers, and manufacturers formed to encourage the implementation of the ISO standards and to provide the testing environment so that a new or revised implementation can be validated for adherence to the ISO standards.

The author, in his capacity as the chairman of ISO/TC97/SC16 reporting to ISO/TC97, recommended to TC97 that it develop a "reference model for computer-based information systems."[9,10] This extended reference model would be used to place all of ISO/TC97's work on computers and information systems into perspective and thus highlight the areas most critical for further standardization.

[1] Bachman, C. W. Why restrict the modeling capability of the CODASYL data structure sets? In *Proceedings of the AFIPS National Computer Conference*, vol. 46. AFIPS Press, Reston, Va., 1977.

[2] Bachman, C. W., and Daya, M. The role concept in data models. In *Proceedings of the 3rd Very Large Database Conference*, 1977.

[3] Bachman, C. W. The structuring capabilities of the molecular data model (partnership data model). In *Entity-Relationship Approach to Software Engineering*. Elsevier Science, New York, 1983.

[4] Bachman, C. W. The partnership data model. Presented at the Fall 1983 IEEE Computer Conference (Washington, D.C.).

[5] ANSI/X3/SPARC/Study Group—Database Management Systems. *Framework Report on Database Management Systems*. AFIPS Press, Reston, Va., 1978.

[6] ISO/TC97/SC5/WG3. Concepts and terminology for the conceptual schema. January 15, 1981.

Author's address: Bachman Information Systems, Inc., 4 Cambridge Center, Cambridge, MA 02142.

[7] ISO. Computers and Information Systems—Open Systems Interconnection Reference Model. Standard 7498. American National Standards Institute, New York, N.Y.

[8] The word "entity" is used in the ISO/TC97 world to mean an active element that plays some part in the communication process. I have used the adjectives "processing" and "administrative" to distinguish the communication-time entities from the set-up-time entities. This usage of the word entity contrasts with its use in the data modeling world where the word entity means something that exists and about which something is known.

In 1984–1985, ISO/TC97 reorganized its committee structure creating a new subcommittee, ISO/TC97/SC21, which has assumed the former responsibilities of SC16 and has been given the additional responsibility of defining the architecture of data storage and retrieval. With time this responsibility should grow to include the aspects of data integrity and data security, since it is not possible to create a complete architecture for data storage and retrieval and data communication without their being integrated with the aspects of integrity and security.

The Programmer as Modeler

I have invested a good deal of my time in these 13 years in extending the conceptual schema work of ANSI/SPARC Study Group on DBMS, joining it with my work on data communications and formal description techniques. The scope of the original conceptual schema work was limited to the information that existed in the business and to its data formats as stored in files and databases (internal schema) and as viewed by programs (external schema). My goal was to extend this abstraction to include descriptions of all the *active agents* (people, computer programs, and physical processes) that were the users of the information, the *communication paths* that they use, and the *messages* that are exchanged.

I wanted to extend this abstraction further to include the rules that governed the behavior of the users of the information. These extended conceptual schemata have been called "enterprise models" or "business models".

Why build a business model? First, as a means of defining the information processing requirements for an organization in a manner that is equally clear to the user community and to the data processing community. Second, to provide the basis for automating the process of generating application software. I define the term *application software* to include database and file descriptions, the application programs, and the environmental control parameters required to install the required files and programs in the computers and to control their operation.

The step of translating a business model into the set of application software required to support that model is the step of translating the *what* of the business world into the *how* of the computer and communications world. This translation requires three additional elements over and above the business model as the formal specification:

1. It requires *information* about the quantities, rates, and response times that must be satisfied.

2. It requires *information* about the available processors, storage, and communication hardware and *information* about the available compilers, DBMSs, communication systems, transaction monitors, and operating systems.

3. It also requires the *expertise* to understand the operating and performance characteristics of the available software and hardware options and how to best use them to meet the functional and quantitative requirements in a cost-effective way.

This performance and optimization expertise has been embodied in the persons of real people, the database designers, application programmers, and system programmers. The best of them are very, very good, but the work of many has been disappointing. All these activities are expensive and more time consuming then any one would wish.

The Programmer as Collaborator

This shortage of good people has started us looking for a means of automating the work of database designers and systems and application programmers. This automation is difficult, as the process of translating the business model into efficient application software is not completely deterministic. There are frequently several alternative approaches with different dynamics and costs. Real expertise and judgment are involved. This difficulty has led to the examination of the tools and techniques coming out of the world of artificial intelligence, where there has been an emphasis on domains of imperfect knowledge.

The AI world, with its knowledge-based software system, has considerable experience developing interactive systems, where a resident human expert can collaborate with a "cloned" expert, which is built into the software to achieve some otherwise difficult task. Together they can carry out all the needed translations between the conceptual level of abstraction and the physical level taking into consideration the performance problems and opportunities.

Programmer as Supervisor

It is reasonable to think that these cloned experts, who are embodied in knowledge-based (expert) systems, will improve with time. As this happens, the role of the resident human expert (database designer, application programmer, or systems programmer) will progressively shift from that of a collaborator with the knowledge-based system to that of the supervisor. This supervisor will be responsible for checking the work of the knowledge-based system, to see that it has covered all modes of operation and all likely operating conditions. After checking and requesting any appropriate modifications, the human expert as supervisor will be required to countersign the final design, just as the engineering supervisor countersigns the work of the engineering staff. In business information systems, nothing goes into production without its being reviewed and someone's taking responsibility for it.

Summary

It is somewhat poetic to see the functional joining of database technology with AI technology. Poetic, because the early (1960) documentation of list processing in the artificial intelligence literature provided the basis for the linked lists used as the first and still most prevalent implementation mode for databases. The confusion between the concept and most prevalent implementation mode of the data structure set has been troublesome. There are a number of well-known techniques[11] for implementing data structure sets, each with its own performance characteristics, while maintaining the functional characteristics of the set.

It will be interesting to see whether the knowledge and implementation expertise of the database world will be able to make a significant contribution to the LISP and AI world as it reaches for commercial applications where the knowledge bases are large and concurrently shared among many distributed, cooperating AI workstations. Here performance and responsiveness are tied to the successful operation of shared virtual memories for knowledge-base purposes.

[9] Bachman, C. W. The context of open systems interconnection within computer-based information systems. In *Proceedings of Gesellschaft für Informatik*, Jan. 1980.

[10] Bachman, C. W., and Ross, R. G. Toward a more complete reference model of computer-based information systems. *J. Comput. Standards 1* (1982); also published in *Comput. Networks 6* (1982).

[11] Bachman, C. W. Implementation of techniques for data structure sets. In *Proceedings of SHARE Workshop on DataBase Systems* (Montreal, Canada, July, 1973).

The 1981 ACM Turing Award Lecture

Delivered at ACM '81, Los Angeles, California, November 9, 1981

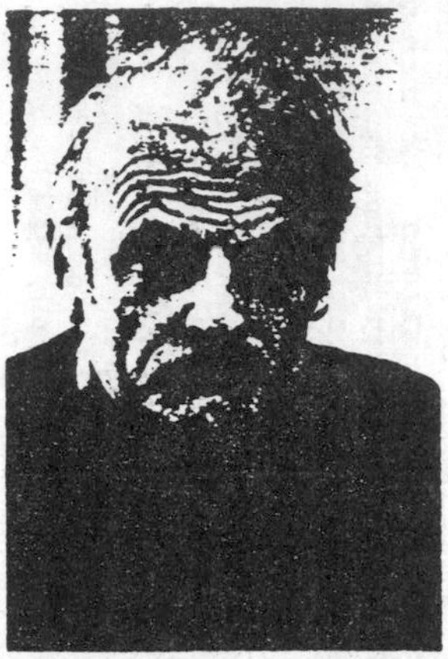

The 1981 ACM Turing Award was presented to Edgar F. Codd, an IBM Fellow of the San Jose Research Laboratory, by President Peter Denning on November 9, 1981 at the ACM Annual Conference in Los Angeles, California. It is the Association's foremost award for technical contributions to the computing community.

Codd was selected by the ACM General Technical Achievement Award Committee for his "fundamental and continuing contributions to the theory and practice of database management systems." The originator of the relational model for databases, Codd has made further important contributions in the development of relational algebra, relational calculus, and normalization of relations.

Edgar F. Codd joined IBM in 1949 to prepare programs for the Selective Sequence Electronic Calculator. Since then, his work in computing has encompassed logical design of computers (IBM 701 and Stretch), managing a computer center in Canada, heading the development of one of the first operating systems with a general multiprogramming capability, contributing to the logic of self-reproducing automata, developing high level techniques for software specification, creating and extending the relational approach to database management, and developing an English analyzing and synthesizing subsystem for casual users of relational databases. He is also the author of *Cellular Automata*, an early volume in the ACM Monograph Series.

Codd received his B.A. and M.A. in Mathematics from Oxford University in England, and his M.Sc. and Ph.D. in Computer and Communication Sciences from the University of Michigan. He is a Member of the National Academy of Engineering (USA) and a Fellow of the British Computer Society.

The ACM Turing Award is presented each year in commemoration of A. M. Turing, the English mathematician who made major contributions to the computing sciences.

Relational Database: A Practical Foundation for Productivity

E. F. Codd
IBM San Jose Research Laboratory

It is well known that the growth in demands from end users for new applications is outstripping the capability of data processing departments to implement the corresponding application programs. There are two complementary approaches to attacking this problem (and both approaches are needed): one is to put end users into direct touch with the information stored in computers; the other is to increase the productivity of data processing professionals in the development of application programs. It is less well known that a single technology, relational database management, provides a practical foundation for both approaches. It is explained why this is so.

While developing this productivity theme, it is noted that the time has come to draw a very sharp line between relational and non-relational database systems, so that the label "relational" will not be used in misleading ways. The key to drawing this line is something called a "relational processing capability."

CR Categories and Subject Descriptors: H.2.0 [Database Management]: General; H.2.1 [Database Management]: Logical Design–*data models*; H.2.4 [Database Management]: Systems

General Terms: Human Factors, Languages

Additional Key Words and Phrases: database, relational database, relational model, data structure, data manipulation, data integrity, productivity

Author's Present Address: E. F. Codd, IBM Research Laboratory, 5600 Cottle Road, San Jose, CA 95193.

1. Introduction

It is generally admitted that there is a productivity crisis in the development of "running code" for commercial and industrial applications. The growth in end user demands for new applications is outstripping the capability of data processing departments to implement the corresponding application programs. In the late sixties and early seventies many people in the computing field hoped that the introduction of database management systems (commonly abbreviated DBMS) would markedly increase the productivity of application programmers by removing many of their problems in handling input and output files. DBMS (along with data dictionaries) appear to have been highly successful as instruments of data control, and they did remove many of the file handling details from the concern of application programmers. Why then have they failed as productivity boosters?

There are three principal reasons:

(1) These systems burdened application programmers with numerous concepts that were irrelevant to their data retrieval and manipulation tasks, forcing them to think and code at a needlessly low level of structural detail (the "owner-member set" of CODASYL DBTG is an outstanding example[1]);

(2) No commands were provided for processing multiple records at a time—in other words, DBMS did not support *set processing* and, as a result, programmers were forced to think and code in terms of iterative loops that were often unnecessary (here we use the word "set" in its traditional mathematical sense, not the linked structure sense of CODASYL DBTG);

(3) The needs of end users for direct interaction with databases, particularly interaction of an unanticipated nature, were inadequately recognized—a query capability was assumed to be something one could add on to a DBMS at some later time.

Looking back at the database management systems of the late sixties, we may readily observe that there was no sharp distinction between the programmer's (logical) view of the data and the (physical) representation of data in storage. Even though what was called the logical level usually provided protection from placement expressed in terms of storage addresses and byte offsets, many storage-oriented concepts were an integral part of this level. The adverse impact on development productivity of requiring programmers to navigate along access paths to reach the target data (in some cases having to deal directly with the layout of data in storage and in others having to follow pointer chains) was enormous. In addition, it was not possible to make slight changes in the layout in storage without simultaneously having to revise all programs that relied on the previous structure. The introduction of an index might have a similar effect. As a result, far too much manpower was being invested in continual (and avoidable) maintenance of application programs.

Another consequence was that installation of these systems was often agonizingly slow, due to the large amount of time spent in learning about the systems and in planning the organization of the data at both logical and physical levels, prior to database activation. The aim of this preplanning was to "get it right once and for all" so as to avoid the need for subsequent changes in the data description that, in turn, would force coding changes in application programs. Such an objective was, of course, a mirage, even if sound principles for database design had been known at the time (and, of course, they were not).

To show how relational database management systems avoid the three pitfalls cited above, we shall first review the motivation of the relational model and discuss some of its features. We shall then classify systems that are based upon that model. As we proceed, we shall stress application programmer productivity, even though the benefits for end users are just as great, because much has already been said and demonstrated regarding the value of relational database to end users (see [23] and the papers cited therein).

2. Motivation

The most important motivation for the research work that resulted in the relational model was the objective of providing a sharp and clear boundary between the logical and physical aspects of database management (including database design, data retrieval, and data manipulation). We call this the *data independence objective.*

A second objective was to make the model structurally simple, so that all kinds of users and programmers could have a common understanding of the data, and could therefore communicate with one another about the database. We call this the *communicability objective.*

A third objective was to introduce high level language concepts (but not specific syntax) to enable users to express operations upon large chunks of information at a time. This entailed providing a foundation for set-oriented processing (i.e., the ability to express in a single statement the processing of multiple sets of records at a time). We call this the *set-processing objective.*

There were other objectives, such as providing a sound theoretical foundation for database organization and management, but these objectives are less relevant to our present productivity theme.

[1] The crux of the problem with the the CODASYL DBTG owner-member set is that it combines into one construct three orthogonal concepts: one-to-many relationship, existence dependency, and a user-visible linked structure to be traversed by application programs. It is the last of these three concepts that places a heavy and unnecessary navigation burden on application programmers. It also presents an insurmountable obstacle for end users.

3. The Relational Model

To satisfy these three objectives, it was necessary to discard all those data structuring concepts (e.g., repeating groups, linked structures) that were not familiar to end users and to take a fresh look at the addressing of data.

Positional concepts have always played a significant role in computer addressing, beginning with plugboard addressing, then absolute numeric addressing, relative numeric addressing, and symbolic addressing with arithmetic properties (e.g., the symbolic address $A + 3$ in assembler language; the address $X(I + 1, J - 2)$ of an element in a Fortran, Algol, or PL/I array named X). In the relational model we replace positional addressing by totally associative addressing. Every datum in a relational database can be uniquely addressed by means of the relation name, primary key value, and attribute name. Associative addressing of this form enables users (yes, and even programmers also!) to leave it to the system to (1) determine the details of placement of a new piece of information that is being inserted into a database and (2) select appropriate access paths when retrieving data.

All information in a relational database is represented by values in tables (even table names appear as character strings in at least one table). Addressing data by value, rather than by position, boosts the productivity of programmers as well as end users (positions of items in sequences are usually subject to change and are not easy for a person to keep track of, especially if the sequences contain many items). Moreover, the fact that programmers and end users all address data in the same way goes a long way to meeting the communicability objective.

The *n*-ary relation was chosen as the single aggregate structure for the relational model, because with appropriate operators and an appropriate conceptual representation (the table) it satisfies all three of the cited objectives. Note that an *n*-ary relation is a mathematical set, in which the ordering of rows is immaterial.

Sometimes the following questions arise: Why call it the relational model? Why not call it the tabular model? There are two reasons: (1) At the time the relational model was introduced, many people in data processing felt that a relation (or relationship) among two or more objects must be represented by a linked data structure (so the name was selected to counter this misconception); (2) Tables are at a lower level of abstraction than relations, since they give the impression that positional (array-type) addressing is applicable (which is not true of *n*-ary relations), and they fail to show that the information content of a table is independent of row order. Nevertheless, even with these minor flaws, tables are the most important conceptual representation of relations, because they are universally understood.

Incidentally, if a data model is to be considered as a serious alternative for the relational model, it too should have a clearly defined conceptual representation for database instances. Such a representation facilitates thinking about the effects of whatever operations are under consideration. It is a requirement for programmer and end-user productivity. Such a representation is rarely, if ever, discussed in data models that use concepts such as entities and relationships, or in functional data models. Such models frequently do not have any operators either! Nevertheless, they may be useful for certain kinds of data type analysis encountered in the process of establishing a new database, especially in the very early stages of determining a preliminary informal organization. This leads to the question: What is a data model?

A data model is, of course, not just a data structure, as many people seem to think. It is natural that the principal data models are named after their principal structures, but that is not the whole story.

A data model [9] is a combination of at least three components:

(1) A collection of data structure types (the database building blocks);

(2) A collection of operators or rules of inference, which can be applied to any valid instances of the data types listed in (1), to retrieve, derive, or modify data from any parts of those structures in any combinations desired;

(3) A collection of general integrity rules, which implicitly or explicitly define the set of consistent database states or changes of state or both—these rules are general in the sense that they apply to any database using this model (incidentally, they may sometimes be expressed as insert–update–delete rules).

The relational model is a data model in this sense, and was the first such to be defined. We do not propose to give a detailed definition of the relational model here—the original definition appeared in [7], and an improved one in Secs. 2 and 3 of [8]. Its *structural part* consists of domains, relations of assorted degrees (with tables as their principal conceptual representation), attributes, tuples, candidate keys, and primary keys. Under the principal representation, attributes become columns of tables and tuples become rows, but there is no notion of one column succeeding another or of one row succeeding another as far as the database tables are concerned. In other words, the left to right order of columns and the top to bottom order of rows in those tables are arbitrary and irrelevant.

The *manipulative part* of the relational model consists of the algebraic operators (select, project, join, etc.) which transform relations into relations (and hence tables into tables).

The *integrity part* consists of two integrity rules: entity integrity and referential integrity (see [8, 11] for recent developments in this latter area). In any particular application of a data model it may be necessary to impose further (database-specific) integrity constraints, and thereby define a smaller set of consistent database states or changes of state.

In the development of the relational model, there has always been a strong coupling between the structural, manipulative, and integrity aspects. If the structures are defined alone and separately, their behavioral properties are not pinned down, infinitely many possibilities present themselves, and endless speculation results. It is therefore no surprise that attempts such as those of CODASYL and ANSI to develop data structure definition language (DDL) and data manipulation language (DML) in separate committees have yielded many misunderstandings and incompatibilities.

4. The Relational Processing Capability

The relational model calls not only for relational structures (which can be thought of as tables), but also for a particular kind of set processing called *relational processing*. Relational processing entails treating whole relations as operands. Its primary purpose is loop-avoidance, an absolute requirement for end users to be productive at all, and a clear productivity booster for application programmers.

The SELECT operator (also called RESTRICT) of the relational algebra takes *one* relation (table) as operand and produces a new relation (table) consisting of selected tuples (rows) of the first. The PROJECT operator also transforms *one* relation (table) into a new one, this time however consisting of selected attributes (columns) of the first. The EQUI-JOIN operator takes *two* relations (tables) as operands and produces a third consisting of rows of the first concatenated with rows of the second, but only where specified columns in the first and specified columns in the second have matching values. If redundancy in columns is removed, the operator is called NATURAL JOIN. In what follows, we use the term "join" to refer to either the equi-join or the natural join.

The relational algebra, which includes these and other operators, is intended as a yardstick of power. It is *not* intended to be a standard language, to which all relational systems should adhere. The set-processing objective of the relational model is intended to be met by means of a data sublanguage[2] having at least the power of the relational algebra *without making use of iteration or recursion statements.*

Much of the derivability power of the relational algebra is obtained from the SELECT, PROJECT, and JOIN operators alone, provided the JOIN is not subject to any implementation restrictions having to do with predefinition of supporting physical access paths. A system has an *unrestricted join capability* if it allows joins to be taken wherein *any* pair of attributes may be matched, providing only that they are defined on the same domain or data type (for our present purpose, it does not matter whether the domain is syntactic or semantic and it does not matter whether the data type is weak or strong, but see [10] for circumstances in which it does matter).

Occasionally, one finds systems in which join is supported only if the attributes to be matched have the same name or are supported by a certain type of predeclared access path. Such restrictions significantly impair the power of the system to derive relations from the base relations. These restrictions consequently reduce the system's capability to handle unanticipated queries by end users and reduce the chances for application programmers to avoid coding iterative loops.

Thus, we say that a data sublanguage L has a *relational processing capability* if the transformations specified by the SELECT, PROJECT, and unrestricted JOIN operators of the relational algebra can be specified in L without resorting to commands for iteration or recursion. For a database management system to be called *relational* it must support:

(1) Tables without user-visible navigation links between them;

(2) A data sublanguage with at least this (minimal) relational processing capability.

One consequence of this is that a DBMS that does *not* support relational processing should be considered *non-relational*. Such a system might be more appropriately called *tabular*, providing that it supports tables without user-visible navigation links between tables. This term should replace the term "semi-relational" used in [8], because there is a large difference in implementation complexity between tabular systems, in which the programmer does his own navigation, and relational systems, in which the system does the navigation for him, i.e., the system provides *automatic navigation*.

The definition of relational DBMS given above intentionally permits a lot of latitude in the services provided. For example, it is not required that the full relational algebra be supported, and there is no requirement in regard to support of the two integrity rules of the relational model (entity integrity and referential integrity). Full support by a relational system of these latter two parts of the model justifies calling that system *fully relational* [8]. Although we know of no systems that qualify as fully relational today, some are quite close to qualifying, and no doubt will soon do so.

In Fig. 1 we illustrate the distinction between the various kinds of relational and tabular systems. For each class the extent of shading in the S box is intended to show the degree of fidelity of members of that class to the structural requirements of the relational model. A similar remark applies to the M box with respect to the manipulative requirements, and to the I box with respect to the integrity requirements.

m denotes the minimal relational processing capability. **c** denotes relational completeness (a capability corresponding to a two-valued first order predicate logic without nulls). When the manipulation box M is fully shaded, this denotes a capability corresponding to the

[2] A data sublanguage is a specialized language for database management, supporting at least data definition, data retrieval, insertion, update, and deletion. It need not be computationally complete, and usually is not. In the context of application programming, it is intended to be used in conjunction with one or more programming languages.

Fig. 1. Classification of DBMS.

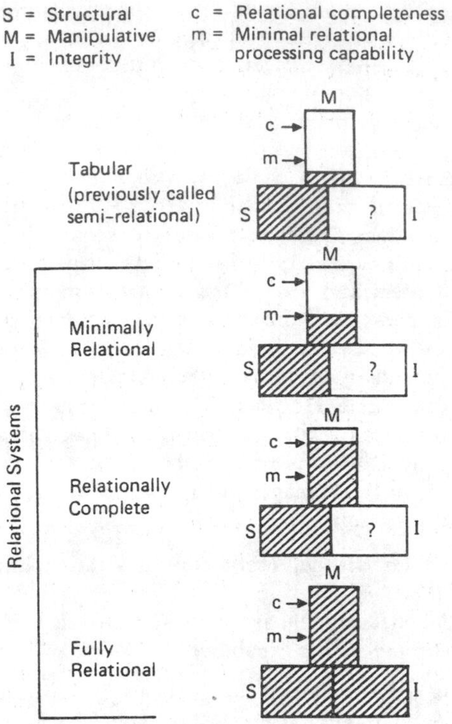

full relational algebra defined in [8] (a three-valued predicate logic with a single kind of null). The question mark in the integrity box for each class except the fully relational is an indication of the present inadequate support for integrity in relational systems. Stronger support for domains and primary keys is needed [10], as well as the kind of facility discussed in [14].

Note that a relational DBMS may package its relational processing capability in any convenient way. For example, in the INGRES system of Relational Technology, Inc., the RETRIEVE statement of QUEL [29] embodies all three operators (select, project, join) in one statement, in such a way that one can obtain the same effect as any one of the operators or any combination of them.

In the definition of the relational model there are several prohibitions. To cite two examples: user-visible navigation links between tables are ruled out, and database information must not be represented (or hidden) in the ordering of tuples within base relations. Our experience is that DBMS designers who have implemented non-relational systems do not readily understand and accept these prohibitions. By contrast, users enthusiastically understand and accept the enhanced ease of learning and ease of use resulting from these prohibitions.

Incidentally, the Relational Task Group of the American National Standards Institute has recently issued a report [4] on the feasibility of developing a standard for relational database systems. This report contains an enlightening analysis of the features of a dozen relational systems, and its authors clearly understand the relational model.

5. The Uniform Relational Property

In order to have wide applicability most relational DBMS have a data sublanguage which can be interfaced with one or more of the commonly used programming languages (e.g., Cobol, Fortran, PL/I, APL). We shall refer to these latter languages as *host languages*. A relational DBMS usually supports at least one end-user oriented data sublanguage—sometimes several, because the needs of these users may vary. Some prefer string languages such as QUEL or SQL [5], while others prefer the screen-oriented two-dimensional data sublanguage of Query-by-Example [33].

Now, some relational systems (e.g., System R [6], INGRES [29]) support a data sublanguage that is usable in two modes: (1) interactively at a terminal and (2) embedded in an application program written in a host language. There are strong arguments for such a *double-mode* data sublanguage:

(1) With such a language application programmers can separately debug at a terminal the database statements they wish to incorporate in their application programs—people who have used SQL to develop application programs claim that the double-mode feature significantly enhances their productivity;

(2) Such a language significantly enhances communication among programmers, analysts, end users, database administration staff, etc.;

(3) Frivolous distinctions between the languages used in these two modes place an unnecessary learning and memory burden on those users who have to work in both modes.

The importance of this feature in productivity suggests that relational DBMS be classified according to whether they possess this feature or not. Accordingly, we call those relational DBMS that support a double-mode sublanguage *uniform relational*. Thus, a uniform relational DBMS supports relational processing at both an end-user interface and at an application programming interface *using a data sublanguage common to both interfaces*.

The natural term for all other relational DBMS is *non-uniform relational*. An example of a non-uniform relational DBMS is the TANDEM ENCOMPASS [19]. With this system, when retrieving data interactively at a terminal, one uses the relational data sublanguage ENFORM (a language with relational processing capability). When writing a program to retrieve or manipulate data, one uses an extended version of Cobol (a language that does not possess the relational processing capability). Common to both levels of use are the structures: tables without user-visible navigation links between them.

A question that immediately arises is this: how can a data sublanguage with relational processing capability be interfaced with a language such as Cobol or PL/I that can handle data one record at a time only (i.e., that is incapable of treating a set of records as a single operand)? To solve this problem we must separate the following two actions from one another: (1) definition of the relation to be derived; (2) presentation of the derived relation to the host language program.

One solution (adopted in the Peterlee Relational Test Vehicle [31]) is to cast a derived relation in the form of a file that can be read record-by-record by means of host language statements. In this case delivery of records is delegated to the file system used by the pertinent host language.

Another solution (adopted by System R) is to keep the delivery of records under the control of data sublanguage statements and, hence, under the control of the relational DBMS optimizer. A query statement Q of SQL (the data sublanguage of System R) may be embedded in a host language program, using the following kind of phrase (for expository reasons, the syntax is not exactly that of SQL)

DECLARE C CURSOR FOR Q

where C stands for any name chosen by the programmer. Such a statement associates a *cursor* named C with the defining expression Q. Tuples from the derived relation defined by Q are presented to the program one at a time by means of the named cursor. Each time a FETCH per this cursor is executed, the system delivers another tuple from the derived relation. The order of delivery is system-determined unless the SQL statement Q defining the derived relation contains an ORDER BY clause.

It is important to note that in advancing a cursor over a derived relation the programmer is *not* engaging in navigation to some target data. The derived relation is itself the target data! It is the DBMS that determines whether the derived relation should be materialized *en bloc* prior to the cursor-controlled scan or materialized piecemeal during the scan. In either case, it is the system (not the programmer) that selects the access paths by which the derived data is to be generated. This takes a significant burden off the programmer's shoulders, thereby increasing his productivity.

6. Skepticism About Relational Systems

There has been no shortage of skepticism concerning the practicality of the relational approach to database management. Much of this skepticism stems from a lack of understanding, some from a fear of the numerous theoretical investigations that are based on the relational model [1, 2, 15, 16, 24]. Instead of welcoming a theoretical foundation as providing soundness, the attitude seems to be: if it's theoretical, it cannot be practical. The absence of a theoretical foundation for almost all non-relational DBMS is the prime cause of their *ungepotchket* quality. (This is a Yiddish word, one of whose meanings is patched up.)

On the other hand, it seems reasonable to pose the following two questions:

(1) Can a relational system provide the range of services that we have grown to expect from other DBMS?

(2) If (1) is answered affirmatively, can such a system perform as well as non-relational DBMS?[3]

We look at each of these in turn.

6.1 Range of Services

A full-scale DBMS provides the following capabilities:

- data storage, retrieval, and update;
- a user-accessible catalog for data description;
- transaction support to ensure that all or none of a sequence of database changes are reflected in the pertinent databases (see [17] for an up-to-date summary of transaction technology);
- recovery services in case of failure (system, media, or program);
- concurrency control services to ensure that concurrent transactions behave the same way as if run in some sequential order;
- authorization services to ensure that all access to and manipulation of data be in accordance with specified constraints on users and programs [18];
- integration with support for data communication;
- integrity services to ensure that database states and changes of state conform to specified rules.

Certain relational prototypes developed in the early seventies fell far short of providing all these services (possibly for good reasons). Now, however, several relational systems are available as software products and provide all these services with the exception of the last. Present versions of these products are admittedly weak in the provision of integrity services, but this is rapidly being remedied [10].

Some relational DBMS actually provide more complete data services than the non-relational systems. Three examples follow.

As a first example, relational DBMS support the extraction of all meaningful relations from a database, whereas non-relational systems support extraction only where there exist statically predefined access paths.

As a second example of the additional services provided by some relational systems, consider views. A *view* is a virtual relation (table) defined by means of an expression or sequence of commands. Although not directly supported by actual data, a view appears to a user as if it were an additional base table kept up-to-date and in a state of integrity with the other base tables. Views are useful for permitting application programs and users at terminals to interact with constant view structures, even when the base tables themselves are undergoing structural changes at the *logical* level (providing that the pertinent views are still definable from the new base tables). They are also useful in restricting the scope of

[3] One should bear in mind that the non-relational ones always employ comparatively low level data sublanguages for application programming.

access of programs and users. Non-relational systems either do not support views at all or else support much more primitive counterparts, such as the CODASYL subschema.

As a third example, some systems (e.g., SQL/DS [28] and its prototype predecessor System R) permit a variety of changes to be made to the logical and physical organization of the data dynamically—while transactions are in progress. These changes rarely require application programs to be recoded. Thus, there is less of a program maintenance burden, leaving programmers to be more productive doing development rather than maintenance. This capability is made possible in SQL/DS by the fact that the system has complete control over access path selection.

In non-relational systems such changes would normally require all other database activities including transactions in progress to be brought to a halt. The database then remains out of action until the organizational changes are completed and any necessary recompiling done.

6.2 Performance

Naturally, people would hesitate to use relational systems if these systems were sluggish in performance. All too often, erroneous conclusions are drawn about the performance of relational systems by comparing the time it might take for one of these systems to execute a complex transaction with the time a non-relational system might take to execute an extremely simple transaction. To arrive at a fair performance comparison, one must compare these systems on the same tasks or applications. We shall present arguments to show why relational systems should be able to compete successfully with non-relational systems.

Good performance is determined by two factors: (1) the system must support performance-oriented physical data structures; (2) high-level language requests for data must be compiled into lower-level code sequences at least as good as the average application programmer can produce by hand.

The first step in the argument is that a program written in a Cobol-level language can be made to perform efficiently on large databases containing production data structured in tabular form with no user-visible navigation links between them. This step in the argument is supported by the following information [19]: as of August 1981, Tandem Computer Corp. had manufactured and installed 760 systems; of these, over 700 were making use of the Tandem ENCOMPASS relational database management system to support databases containing production data. Tandem has committed its own manufacturing database to the care of ENCOMPASS. ENCOMPASS does not support links between the database tables, either user-visible (navigation) links or user-invisible (access method) links.

In the second step of the argument, suppose we take the application programs in the above-cited installations and replace the database retrieval and manipulation statements by statements in a database sublanguage with a relational processing capability (e.g., SQL). Clearly, to obtain good performance with such a high level language, it is essential that it be compiled into object code (instead of being interpreted), and it is essential that that object code be efficient.

Compilation is used in System R and its product version SQL/DS. In 1976 Raymond Lorie developed an ingenious pre- and post-compiling scheme for coping with dynamic changes in access paths [21]. It also copes with early (and hence efficient) authorization and integrity checking (the latter, however, is not yet implemented). This scheme calls for compiling in a rather special way the SQL statements embedded in a host language program. This compilation step transforms the SQL statements into appropriate CALLs within the source program together with access modules containing object code. These modules are then stored in the database for later use at runtime. The code in these access modules is generated by the system so as to optimize the sequencing of the major operations and the selection of access paths to provide runtime efficiency. After this precompilation step, the application program is compiled by a regular compiler for the pertinent host language. If at any subsequent time one or more of the access paths is removed and an attempt is made to run the program, enough source information has been retained in the access module to enable the system to re-compile a new access module that exploits the now existing access paths *without requiring a re-compilation of the application program.*

Incidentally, the same data sublanguage compiler is used on ad hoc queries submitted interactively from a terminal and also on queries that are dynamically generated during the execution of a program (e.g., from parameters submitted interactively). Immediately after compilation, such queries are executed and, with the exception of the simplest of queries, the performance is better than that of an interpreter.

The generation of access modules (whether at the initial compiling or re-compiling stage) entails a quite sophisticated optimization scheme [27], which makes use of system-maintained statistics that would not normally be within the programmer's knowledge. Thus, only on the simplest of all transactions would it be possible for an average application programmer to compete with this optimizer in generation of efficient code. Any attempts to compete are bound to reduce the programmer's productivity. Thus, the price paid for extra compile-time overhead would seem to be well worth paying.

Assuming non-linked tabular structures in both cases, we can expect SQL/DS to generate code comparable with average hand-written code in many simple cases, and superior in many complex cases. Many commercial transactions are extremely simple. For example, one may need to look up a record for a particular railroad wagon to find out where it is or find the balance in someone's savings account. If suitably fast access paths are supported (e.g., hashing), there is no reason why a high-level language such as SQL, QUEL, or QBE should result in less efficient runtime code for these simple transactions than a lower level language, even though such transactions make little use of the optimizing capability of the high-level data sublanguage compiler.

7. Future Directions

If we are to use relational database as a foundation for productivity, we need to know what sort of developments may lie ahead for relational systems.

Let us deal with near-term developments first. In some relational systems stronger support is needed for domains and primary keys per suggestions in [10]. As already noted, all relational systems need upgrading with regard to automatic adherence to integrity constraints. Existing constraints on updating join-type views need to be relaxed (where theoretically possible), and progress is being made on this problem [20]. Support for outer joins is needed.

Marked improvements are being made in optimizing technology, so we may reasonably expect further improvements in performance. In certain products, such as the ICL CAFS [22] and the Britton-Lee IDM500 [13], special hardware support has been implemented. Special hardware may help performance in certain types of applications. However, in the majority of applications dealing with formatted databases, software-implemented relational systems can compete in performance with software-implemented non-relational systems.

At present, most relational systems do not provide any special support for engineering and scientific databases. Such support, including interfacing with Fortran, is clearly needed and can be expected.

Catalogs in relational systems already consist of additional relations that can be interrogated just like the rest of the database using the same query language. A natural development that can and should be swiftly put in place is the expansion of these catalogs into full-fledged active dictionaries to provide additional on-line data control.

Finally, in the near term, we may expect database design aids suited for use with relational systems both at the logical and physical levels.

In the longer term we may expect support for relational databases distributed over a communications network [25, 30, 32] and managed in such a way that application programs and interactive users can manipulate the data (1) as if all of it were stored at the local node—*location transparency*—and (2) as if no data were replicated anywhere—*replication transparency*. All three of the projects cited above are based on the relational model. One important reason for this is that relational databases offer great decomposition flexibility when planning how a database is to be distributed over a network of computer systems, and great recomposition power for dynamic combination of decentralized information. By contrast, CODASYL DBTG databases are very difficult to decompose and recompose due to the entanglement of the owner-member navigation links. This property makes the CODASYL approach extremely difficult to adapt to a distributed database environment and may well prove to be its downfall. A second reason for use of the relational model is that it offers concise high level data sublanguages for transmitting requests for data from node to node.

The ongoing work in extending the relational model to capture in a formal way more meaning of the data can be expected to lead to the incorporation of this meaning in the database catalog in order to factor it out of application programs and make these programs even more concise and simple. Here, we are, of course, talking about meaning that is represented in such a way that the system can understand it and act upon it.

Improved theories are being developed for handling missing data and inapplicable data (see for example [3]). This work should yield improved treatment of null values.

As it stands today, relational database is best suited to data with a rather regular or homogeneous structure. Can we retain the advantages of the relational approach while handling heterogeneous data also? Such data may include images, text, and miscellaneous facts. An affirmative answer is expected, and some research is in progress on this subject, but more is needed.

Considerable research is needed to achieve a rapprochement between database languages and programming languages. Pascal/R [26] is a good example of work in this direction. Ongoing investigations focus on the incorporation of abstract data types into database languages on the one hand [12] and relational processing into programming languages on the other.

8. Conclusions

We have presented a series of arguments to support the claim that relational database technology offers dramatic improvements in productivity both for end users and for application programmers. The arguments center on the data independence, structural simplicity, and relational processing defined in the relational model and implemented in relational database management systems. All three of these features simplify the task of developing application programs and the formulation of queries and updates to be submitted from a terminal. In addition, the first feature tends to keep programs viable in the face of organizational and descriptive changes in the database and therefore reduces the effort that is normally diverted into the maintenance of programs.

Why, then, does the title of this paper suggest that relational database provides only a foundation for improved productivity and not the total solution? The reason is simple: relational database deals only with the shared data component of application programs and end-user interactions. There are numerous complementary technologies that may help with other components or aspects, for example, programming languages that support relational processing and improved checking of data types, improved editors that understand more of the language being used, etc. We use the term "foundation," because interaction with shared data (whether by program or via terminal) represents the core of so much data processing activity.

The practicality of the relational approach has been proven by the test and production installations that are already in operation. Accordingly, with relational systems we can now look forward to the productivity boost that we all hoped DBMS would provide in the first place.

Acknowledgments. I would like to express my indebtedness to the System R development team at IBM Research, San Jose for developing a full-scale, uniform relational prototype that entailed numerous language and system innovations; to the development team at the IBM Laboratory, Endicott, N.Y. for the professional way in which they converted System R into product form; to the various teams at universities, hardware manufacturers, software firms, and user intallations, who designed and implemented working relational systems; to the QBE team at IBM Yorktown Heights, N.Y.; to the PRTV team at the IBM Scientific Centre in England; and to the numerous contributors to database theory who have used the relational model as a cornerstone. A special acknowledgement is due to the very few colleagues who saw something worth supporting in the early stages, particularly, Chris Date and Sharon Weinberg. Finally, it was Sharon Weinberg who suggested the theme of this paper.

Received 10/81; revised and accepted 12/81

References

1. Beeri, C., Bernstein, P., Goodman, N. A sophisticate's introduction to database normalization theory. *Proc. Very Large Data Bases*, West Berlin, Germany, Sept. 1978.
2. Bernstein, P.A., Goodman, N., Lai, M-Y. Laying phantoms to rest. Report TR-03-81, Center for Research in Computing Technology, Harvard University, Cambridge, Mass., 1981.
3. Biskup, J.A. A formal approach to null values in database relations. *Proc. Workshop on Formal Bases for Data Bases*, Toulouse, France, Dec 1979; published in [16] (see below) pp 299–342.
4. Brodie, M. and Schmidt, J. (Eds), Report of the ANSI Relational Task Group., (to be published ACM SIGMOD Record).
5. Chamberlin, D.D., et al. SEQUEL2: A unified approach to data definition, manipulation, and control. *IBM J. Res. & Dev., 20,* 6, (Nov. 1976) 560–565.
6. Chamberlin, D.D., et al. A history and evaluation of system R. *Comm. ACM, 24,* 10, (Oct. 1981) 632–646.
7. Codd, E.F. A relational model of data for large shared data banks. *Comm. ACM, 13,* 6, (June 1970) 377–387.
8. Codd, E.F. Extending the database relational model to capture more meaning. *ACM TODS, 4,* 4, (Dec. 1979) 397–434.
9. Codd, E.F. Data models in database management. *ACM SIGMOD Record, 11,* 2, (Feb. 1981) 112–114.
10. Codd, E.F. The capabilities of relational database management systems. *Proc. Convencio Informatica Llatina*, Barcelona, Spain, June 9-12, 1981, pp 13–26; also available as Report 3132, IBM Research Lab., San Jose, Calif.
11. Date, C.J. Referential integrity. *Proc. Very Large Data Bases*, Cannes, France, September 9–11, 1981, pp 2–12.
12. Ehrig, H., and Weber, H. Algebraic specification schemes for data base systems. *Proc. Very Large Data Bases*, West Berlin, Germany, Sept 13–15, 1978, 427–440.
13. Epstein, R., and Hawthorne, P. Design decisions for the intelligent database machine. *Proc. NCC 1980, AFIPS, Vol. 49., May 1980*, pp 237–241.
14. Eswaran, K.P., and Chamberlin, D.D. Functional specifications of a subsystem for database integrity. *Proc. Very Large Data Bases*, Framingham, Mass., Sept. 1975, pp 48–68.
15. Fagin, R. Horn clauses and database dependencies. *Proc. 1980 ACM SIGACT Symp. on Theory of Computing*, Los Angeles, CA, pp 123–134.
16. Gallaire, H., Minker, J., and Nicolas, J.M. *Advances in Data Base Theory.* Vol 1, Plenum Press, New York, 1981.
17. Gray, J. The transaction concept: virtues and limitations. *Proc. Very Large Data Bases*, Cannes, France, September 9–11, 1981, pp 144–154.
18. Griffiths, P.G., and Wade, B.W. An authorization mechanism for a relational database system. *ACM TODS, 1,* 3, (Sept 1976) 242–255.
19. Held, G. ENCOMPASS: A relational data manager. Data Base/81, Western Institute of Computer Science, Univ. of Santa Clara, Santa Clara, Calif., August 24–28, 1981.
20. Keller, A.M. Updates to relational databases through views involving joins. Report RJ3282, IBM Research Laboratory, San Jose, Calif., October 27, 1981.
21. Lorie, R.A., and Nilsson, J.F. An access specification language for a relational data base system. *IBM J. Res. & Dev., 23,* 3, (May 1979) 286–298.
22. Maller, V.A.J. The content addressable file store—CAFS. *ICL Technical J., 1,* 3, (Nov. 1979) 265–279.
23. Reisner, P. Human factors studies of database query languages: A survey and assessment. *ACM Computing Surveys, 13,* 1, (March 1981) 13–31.
24. Rissanen, J. Theory of relations for databases—A tutorial survey. *Proc. Symp. on Mathematical Foundations of Computer Science*, Zakopane, Poland, September 1978, Lecture Notes in Computer Science, No. 64, Springer Verlag, New York, 1978.
25. Rothnie, J.B., Jr. et al. Introduction to a system for distributed databases (SDD-1). *ACM TODS, 5,* 1, (March 1980) 1–17.
26. Schmidt, J.W. Some high level language constructs for data of type relation. *ACM TODS, 2,* 3, (Sept 1977) 247–261.
27. Selinger, P.G., et al. Access path selection in a relational database system. *Proc. 1979 ACM SIGMOD International Conference on Management of Data*, Boston, MA, May 1979, pp 23–34.
28. ———, SQL/Data system for VSE: A relational data system for application development. IBM Corp. Data Processing Division, White Plains, N.Y., G320-6590, Feb 1981.
29. Stonebraker, M.R., et al. The design and implementation of INGRES, *ACM TODS, 1,* 3, (Sept. 1976) 189–222.
30. Stonebraker, M.R., and Neuhold, E.J. A distributed data base version of INGRES. *Proc. Second Berkeley Workshop on Distributed Data Management and Computer Networks*, Lawrence-Berkeley Lab., Berkeley, Calif., May 1977, pp 19–36.
31. Todd., S.J.P. The Peterlee relational test vehicle—A system overview. *IBM Systems J., 15,* 4, 1976, 285–308.
32. Williams, R. et al. R*: An overview of the architecture. Report RJ3325, IBM Research Laboratory, San Jose, Calif., October 27, 1981.
33. Zloof, M.M. Query by example. *Proc. NCC, AFIPS Vol 44*, May 1975, pp 431–438.

Making Believers out of Computers*

Hector J. Levesque**
Department of Computer Science, University of Toronto, Toronto, Ontario, Canada M5S 1A4

Recommended by Daniel G. Bobrow and Patrick J. Hayes

To someone unfamiliar with Artificial Intelligence, all of the activity that is taking place at this IJCAI conference must be very puzzling. And the current fuss about what is called a "knowledge-based system" (KBS) must be a total mystery. For one thing, there is an amazing amount of talk about *knowledge*. There are even advertisements in *The AI Magazine* reminding us of the value of knowledge. How bizarre! A stranger to AI must wonder who exactly it was that thought that *lack* of knowledge was better.

On closer examination, the idea of a KBS is not totally vacuous. The idea is not just to construct systems that *exhibit* knowledge, but to *represent* that knowledge somehow in the data structures of the program, and to have the system perform whatever it is doing (diagnosing diseases, controlling a power plant, explaining its behaviour, or whatever) by manipulating that knowledge explicitly. Now as anyone who reads the ads can tell you, we can achieve expert-level performance by following these principles and applying vast amounts of domain-dependent knowledge.

While not totally vacuous, this strikes me as a form of buck-passing. What we have done, in effect, is to replace the problem of doing computer medical diagnosis (say) by the problem of getting a computer to apply large amounts of domain-dependent knowledge. Unfortunately this is a type of information processing that we know very little about. How is it possible at all? How does the behaviour of a KBS vary with the amount of knowledge and the kind of knowledge made available to it? What are the limits of KBSs? These are fundamental questions that need to be answered to properly understand KBSs. But to do so, we need *theoretical* foundations. To take an example from nuclear physics, there is only so much that you can learn about nuclear reactors—their properties and limitations—from site visits. Sooner or later, you have to step back and learn a little bit about nuclear physics itself. This poses somewhat of a problem in AI since almost all of the activity that takes place is applied. I am going to assume that there is no shortage of information about the applied end of AI and concentrate here almost exclusively on the theoretical aspects of KBSs.[1]

My work has dealt with a number of (more or less disconnected) topics in the foundations of KBSs, and what I intend to do here is to reconstruct a more general picture of the area, pointing out along the way places where I think I have made a contribution.[2] To start with, I am going to talk about computing and thinking from a very general standpoint. Then I will focus on properties of one kind of thinking, by examining in turn a computationally very difficult case, a somewhat easier case, and finally, what can be done about that most difficult case. Along the way, I am going to have some suggestions for making believers out of computers,[3] and a few speculations to keep things lively. Anyone paying sufficient attention to what I say should have no trouble finding something to disagree with.

1. Computers and Thought

This being a Computers and Thought Lecture, I thought that it might be a good idea to go the the very beginning and ask

What does computing have to do with thinking anyway?

There are obviously forms of computing that seem to have very little to do with thinking, such as shuffling around numbers in an array, and there seem to be forms of thinking that have little to do with computing, such as musing about your Uncle Wiggily in Connecticut. But what is there in the intersection?

The idea that there is *anything* there at all goes way back to the philosopher Leibniz in the 17th century, well before computers. His idea was that just as there was a calculus of *numbers*, where you could combine numeric expressions using the rules of arithmetic and arrive at answers in a purely mechanical way, so could there be a calculus of *ideas*, where you could combine propositional expressions—sentences, if you like—using the rules of logic and, again, arrive at answers in a purely mechanical way. But how can this possibly work?

*This is a slightly revised transcription of a lecture presented upon receipt of the 1985 Computers and Thought Award of the International Joint Conferences on Artificial Intelligence. The lecture was intended to be a retrospective on my own work for a fairly broad audience. I took a stab at clarifying the original where I could, but I would have had to overhaul it completely to make it scholarly or technically precise.

** Fellow of the Canadian Institute for Advanced Research. Some of the work discussed here was done while I was employed by the Schlumberger AI Lab (*née* Fairchild).

Artificial Intelligence **30** (1986) 81–108

[1] But don't confuse "theoretical" with "technical". I was specifically instructed to keep the talk nontechnical.

[2] However, as will become apparent, I will not be able to properly acknowledge my intellectual debt to the many other researchers working in this area.

[3] The tradition in AI has been use the term "knowledge" even though the truth of what is represented is not being claimed. The term "belief" is more appropriate, but I will, by and large, follow tradition and stick to the other one.

1.1. The cocktail party domain

To get a feel for it, what I want you to do is to imagine that you are at a cocktail party of some sort, and having nothing better to do, you decide to try to figure out who is married to whom. Now, by watching Jack very carefully, you might come to the conclusion that

Jack is married to either Jan or Jill.

Later in the party, you might overhear a conversation and discover that

Nobody is married to Jan.

Now being of sound mind (at this stage of the party), you immediately come to believe that

Jack is married to Jill.

The question is how can we get computers to do this kind of thinking,[4] without requiring them to know who Jack and Jill are, or what it means to be married, or any of these very complicated notions?

The answer, as any student of logic knows, is that it does not really matter what these sentences are about. So, for example, if we were thinking instead about who *owed money* to whom in terms of facts like

Jack owes money to either Jan or Jill.
Nobody owes money to Jan.

we would still come out with an analogous conclusion:

Jack owes money to Jill.

Similarly, if we were going to reason about who was *afraid* of whom at the same party, again we come to a similar conclusion:

Jack is terrified of either Jan or Jill.
Nobody is terrified of Jan.

so,

Jack is terrified of Jill.

[4]I will only be dealing with (more or less deductive) *reasoning*, even though there are many other kinds of thinking (such as learning and belief revision) that are certainly within the computational realm.

The reasoning in all three cases is based on the *form* of the sentences not on what their individual terms mean.

To see a further example of this, look at Fig 1. In case you have never seen anything like this before, it is not a division, but how you calculate square roots by hand (i.e., $\sqrt{56169}$ is 237). There seems to be an ever-dwindling number of people that know how to perform this operation. The one thing almost nobody knows is exactly *why* it works. We usually end up just pushing digits around. So, for example, at one point, you take the 2 and the 3 of 237, double it, and write 46 down in the bottom left-hand corner. There is this kind of magic that goes on throughout the calculation. It is important to remember this kind of formal manipulation. To those who would say that computers cannot possibly think since all they do is push symbols around, we might answer that (by the same argument) the people who know how to take square roots do not *really* know how to take square roots at all, since they also just push symbols around. Of course, thinking *feels* like a lot more than just symbol manipulation, and I will have more to say about that later.

1.2. Logic

The point that I want to make now is that you can get correct answers on the basis of strictly syntactic manipulations. In the case of numbers, the idea of an *answer* is fairly clear. What do I mean by an answer when talking about manipulating sentences? Think of it as the ability to imagine and describe what the world would be like if a collection of sentences were true. In more scientific terms, we are concerned with the *logical implications* of a collection of sentences. And what do I mean by "logic"? One thing that I do not mean is a particular language with upside down "A"s and backward "E"s. Nor do I mean that particular characteristic that Mr. Spock has and Bones does not—a cold, unfeeling, inhuman, kind of behaviour as in the sentence:

With impeccable *logic*, he proceeded to destroy the universe.

What I *do* mean by the term is a certain scientific study of *implication*, that is, when the truth of one sentence is *implicit* in the truth of others. This, I claim, is what reasoning is for in the first place: to extract implicit information.

```
      2 3 7
  2 | 56169
    | 4
 43 | 161
    | 129
467 |  3269
    |  3269
```

FIG 1. Long-hand square root calculation.

So, for example, if the world is such that

John is married to Susan.

and

Bill is married to Pat.

it cannot help but also be a world where

Both John and Bill are married.

The truth of this sentence is already present in the truth of the first two. A slightly more complex example (that I stole from Bob Moore) is the following. Imagine a world where

Jack is looking at Ann but Ann is looking at George.

and

Jack is married but George is not.

I claim that in such a world, we have that

A married person is looking at an unmarried one.

To see why, think of Ann's situation: if she is married, then because she is looking at George, *she* is the married person looking at an unmarried one; on the other hand, if she is not married, because Jack is looking at her, *he* is the married person looking at an unmarried one. Either way, the conclusion follows, so the information is already implicit in the first two sentences.

This connection between implication and reasoning is perhaps misleading. One thing I do not mean by logical implication is what might be called "rational inference". So, for example, consider starting with the sentence

Pat is a computer scientist.

and coming to the conclusion that

Pat is male.

This is, of course, an absolutely reprehensible chauvinistic prejudice or, as it is called in AI, a plausible default assumption. Now the assumption may or may not be justified in certain cases, but either way, the information that Pat is male is certainly not *implicit* in the information that Pat is a computer scientist. This type of reasoning, however, is an important one, and I will have more to say about it later.

Let's regroup. We are dealing with KBSs whose abilities derive at least in part by reasoning over an explicit knowledge base. By a *knowledge base*, I mean a collection of data structures that have two properties: we can interpret them as sentences that constitute at least part of the knowledge that the system exhibits; and second, they influence the behaviour of the system in the right way (i.e., they just don't *sit there* like comments in a program). What I want to focus on in particular is a certain component of a KBS called the *knowledge representation system*. Its job is to manage the knowledge base for the overall system. So it will be the one to select the data structures to use to represent the knowledge and to apply reasoning methods that are appropriate for dealing with these data structures. In other words, it is the knowledge representation system that has to worry about applying all of this domain knowledge. What I want to do now is look in a very general way at what is involved in this task, and, in particular, how bad things can get for this component.

2. A Difficult Case

Imagine that it is time to eat at the party and, as you are sitting down, you start reviewing what you know about the party-goers. In particular, you notice the seating arrangement with Jan, Jack, Susan, and so on, around the table. You also recall the facts you know about who is married to whom: John is married to Susan, George is not married, and so on. Now I want to suppose that you are interested in determining whether or not certain general constraints are satisfied by the seating arrangement at the table. So, for example, you might want to see if anyone is sitting beside his or her spouse. This is not too difficult to figure out on the basis of what you know so far. Basically, you can use a data structure that looks like this the one in Fig 2. This is a fairly easy and straightforward calculation. Let's now consider a difficult one.[5]

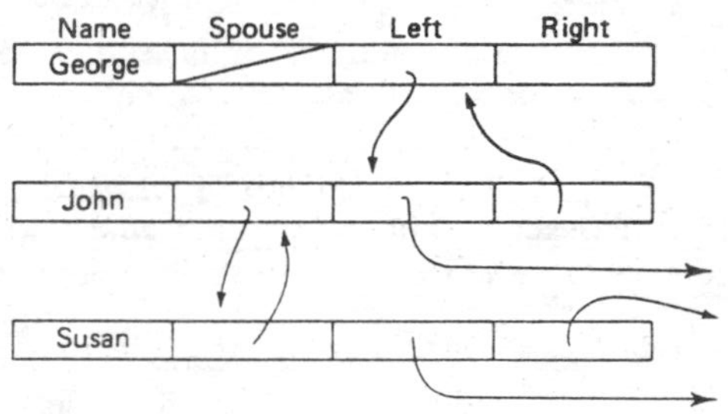

FIG 2. Data structures for table calculation.

[5]*Warning*. AI folks tend to be a fairly optimistic lot. They do not like to spend a whole lot of *time* talking about "worst cases", and get very nervous if you dwell on these for too long. This *should* be kept in mind as I press on.

2.1. Combinatorial explosions

Suppose that all you know about Jack is that he is married to either Jan or to *Jill*. If you are interested in determining a wide range of constraints that might be satisfied by the current seating arrangement (without acquiring any additional information), the best you might be able to do is to consider both possibilities. If, moreover, what you know about Bill is that he is married to either Pat or Ann, you now have four possibilities to consider, depending on whether Jack is married to Jill or to Jan and whether Bill is married to Pat or to Ann. It should be clear what is going to happen here: as the number of facts of this type grows, the number of possibilites that you would have to consider in the worst case becomes enormous. If you imagine a machine going through these possibilities one after another to determine if the constraint is satisfied, it is going to be at it for a *long* time (see Fig 3). As the figure shows, even if we speed up the machine to way beyond current technology, and look at a million million possibilities per second, we are still nowhere near being able to handle one hundred such facts. Even if you imagine a million machines as powerful as these, it still seems that the ability to deal with a hundred such facts is well beyond reach, not to mention reasoning with two hundred or a thousand of them.

This is the combinatorial explosion at its most devastating, and a few observations are in order. First of all, knowledge engineering is not going to help us in a case like this. There is nothing very domain-specific going on; I could just as well be reasoning about who owed money to whom. There is no real knowledge that is going to help with all these possibilities, and consequently no experts for dealing with them either.

Secondly, massive parallelism is not going to help us here either. If a processor is powerful enough to simulate other processors, it will not really matter how many we have; we are only going to get a constant factor speed up. If I have a billion Cray computers, I'm only going to be able to do a billion times as much as if I had just one.[6] With fewer machines, or less powerful ones (as in the connectionist models), I will be able to do even less. It might seem strange to say *only* a billion Cray computers, but for certain combinatorial problems, even this kind of power is just no match. For other types of problems, parallelism will make an enormous difference (and more on this later), but if forced to look at *all* of these possibilities, massive parallelism is not going to help.

Facts	Possibilities	Time (1)	Time (2)	Time (3)
1	2	—	—	—
2	4	—	—	—
5	32	—	—	—
10	1024	—	—	—
25	30 million	30 secs.	—	—
50	10^{15}	30 years	20 mins.	0.001 secs.
100	10^{30}	10^{16} years	30 billion years	30000 years

FIG. 3. Combinatorial explosions. (1) Looking at a million possibilities a second. (2) Looking at a million million possibilities a second. (3) A million machines in parallel, each looking at a million million possibilities a second.

Finally, there is the issue of whether or not we really are forced into looking at all of these possibilities. Unfortunately, it appears that no matter how we go about it, we will have to do roughly this amount of work in the worst case. Clever reasoning is not going to help. It was recently shown, for example, that the worst case of resolution theorem-proving will perform as badly as this [1]. There just does not seem to be much point in searching for good data structures or clever algorithms to handle the general case. The difficulty seems to be inherent in the particular information-processing problem itself.[7]

2.2. The relevance of worst cases

What is all this emphasis on *worst* cases (the ever-optimistic AI person asks)? Why not talk about *average* cases, a much more significant (and reassuring) statistic? The trouble is that nobody seems to be able to decide what an average collection of sentences is, or even what an average *sentence* is. Consequently, we do not know very much about average case behaviour of reasoners one way or another.

But a more serious objection is the following: what if the worst case hardly ever arises in practice? Why should we be spinning our wheels analyzing things that never come up in real life? The argument is simple. If indeed these cases are so rare (and we know this for a fact), we should be able to restrict our attention (with virtually no loss of generality) to a different information-processing problem where these worst cases have been eliminated *by definition*. It is hard to imagine knowing for certain that the troublesome cases will rarely arise without knowing what those cases are. Of course, for this new information-processing problem, we will end up with new worst cases to look at, so the issue has merely been postponed. Thus, there will always be realistic worst cases to consider.

But why should we *care* about them? I think there are two good reasons. First of all, if we think of knowledge representation and reasoning as being a component in a larger system, we want that component to be very well behaved. In systems where life-and-death decisions are being made, it is *not*

[6] Levesque's Parallelism Truism states that for any *n*, *n* sufficiently powerful processors are only *n* times better than just one.

[7] We have to hedge a little bit here since while the NP-complete problems are strongly believed to be intractable, there is as yet no *proof* that they might not have good algorithms.

enough to get the right answer; you have to get the right answer *at the right time*. You often cannot afford to wait. For this reason, I think we want components that are to be used as black boxes in larger systems to be predictable not only with regard to the answers they produce, but also in the effort they may require. So understanding the worst case behaviour of such a component is just part of good software engineering practice.

There is a second reason for being concerned about worst case behaviour, and this has to do with well-founded models of belief. If we want to explain intelligent behaviour as resulting from the application of large amounts of knowledge, it had better *not* be the case that to apply large amounts of knowledge, we have to have intelligence in the first place, or our explanation is going to get into an infinite regress. In other words, sooner or later (at some metalevel), we are going to have to be able to *apply* knowledge without *requiring* more knowledge (at a higher metalevel) to do so. This is not to say that we can't always explain what is taking place at one level in terms of more basic operations one level up. The point is that if we claim that the way to deal with a difficult reasoning task is to reason about how to deal with it, then this second reasoning task had better not be more difficult than the first, and ultimately had better result in a reasoning task that *can* be handled directly. While it makes sense to have knowledge-based vision, knowledge-based diagnosis, knowledge-based this and that, what I am suggesting is that in the end it does not make sense to have a knowledge-based application of knowledge. For knowledge representation and reasoning, the slogan is

> The knowledge-based buck stops here!

We have to be able to get by, at some level, with dumb reasoners that may very well end up making poor choices and hitting the worst cases, yet still produce intelligent behaviour overall.

All this concern about worst cases is really to the effect that we would like to avoid the micro-world problem. We want to be able to *prove* that our simple models will scale up, and will indeed work in the real world on vast amounts of information. To do this, what we have to do is examine how they might behave without being able to rely on lucky guesses, or magic, or homunculi, or little intelligent subsystems, or various other things that could allow them to avoid worst cases.

All this might be starting to sound like one of those games where you can't win, you can't tie, and you can't change the rules. So it's probably not a game we really want to play. But what is? This, I suggest, raises an important scientific problem, namely

> What kinds of information can be extracted from what forms of sentences in a computationally dependable way?

Note that is not an issue of domains or algorithms. If the required processing is sufficiently demanding, it does not really matter what the information is about, or how clever you can be in choosing data structures. The issue is really the information-processing *task* itself: what kind of information do you need to extract, and how hard is it going to be to extract it? The necessary analysis will have to be based on the mathematics of *logic* to tell us what information we should be looking for, and the mathematics of *computational complexity* to tell us how difficult it will be to extract this information.[8]

3. A Much Easier Case

Having said all this, let's move away from the worst case and look at a much more encouraging one. Can we, in general, characterize a form of thinking that is guaranteed to be computationally tractable? There is a common lore associated with this question having to do with the history of AI. It goes something like this:

> In the early days of AI, we had a model of intelligence based on powerful general methods such as resolution, heuristic search, means-end analysis, and so on. The end result of this view of AI was inevitably combinatorial explosions and disaster. Now, in the enlightened era of knowledge-based AI, instead of general methods, we use large amounts of domain-dependent knowledge, and instead of combinatorial explosions, we end up with expert systems that work.

This seems a little too slick to me, and I think that it begs an important and relevant question:

> Why should it be computationally easy to apply large amounts of domain-dependent knowledge?

Even if you assume that some of that knowledge is about how to use other knowledge, why should it be easy to make all of it accessible to a computer? The answer, I think, is that although the *amount* of knowledge needed is large (and it has always been large, even in the early days), what we have discovered is that we can get by with very limited *kinds* of knowledge. The searching and reasoning problems are much the same as they have always been, but because we are using limited types of knowledge, the search space is much smaller, and combinatorial explosions can be contained.

[8]However, the logic we require may turn out to be a very nonstandard one, for reasons to be discussed later, and the complexity theory we will use will end up being at the low end of the computational spectrum.

To convince ourselves of the soundness of these intuitions, Ron Brachman and I investigated a small reasoning problem in isolation [2]. The problem involved matching descriptions and, in particular, determining whether one description was more specific than another. What we found was a good algorithm for dealing with a very simple language of descriptions. But we proved that a slightly more complex one was computationally intractable. The conclusion that we drew from this mathematical experiment was the existence of a cliff separating the doable from the (worst case) un-doable (see Fig. 4). Imagine all reasoning tasks on a straight line with the trivial at one end and the unsolvable at the other. It appears that there is a point where a very small change in the form of the problem is enough to push you over the brink.

3.1. Complete knowledge

As I hinted in earlier examples, the major source of difficulty when it comes to reasoning is *incomplete knowledge*. This is also the area that I have looked at the most in my own research [3–7] and is, in many ways, the main theme of this lecture. A knowledge base (or KB) is called *incomplete* if it tells us that one of a number of sentences is true but doesn't tell us which.[9] So, for example, a KB that tells us that Jack is married to either Jan or Jill without telling us which of the two he is married to would be incomplete. This is a form of incompleteness that arises due to a *disjunction*. But it can also arise with other logical operators: *existentials*, as when all we know is that Jack is married to somebody, but not whom; *negations*, as when all we know is that Jan is not Jack's wife, without knowing who is; *universals*, as when we know that all of the computer scientists at the party like Szechuan food, without knowing who those computer scientists are. From here on, however, I will mostly use disjunctive knowledge as the standard case of incompleteness.

A *complete* KB, on the other hand, could only tell us that Jack was married to either Jan or Jill if it told us which one. So complete knowledge has a certain property that we might call *decomposability*: if we want to find out if a disjunction is true, all we have to do is ask about each disjunct independently; for existentials, we need only find out if a substitution instance is true; similarly for conjunctions, and so on. So in the case of a complete KB, we can find out about any complex proposition we care about by breaking it apart and looking at the pieces individually, and then combining the answers, a technique that does not work when the KB is incomplete. In fact, we can extract the answers to these subquestions in *parallel*, so here is a case where parallelism will make a big difference.

After we have broken up a complex question that we are interested in into its parts, what we are left with is finding out what the KB tells us about the atomic sentences, such as whether or not John is married to Susan. But can this type of atomic question be answered reasonably quickly given a KB that is complete? Sometimes. The answer depends on the form of the complete KB, that is to say, how it is *structured*. Since we are concerned with finding a type of thinking that is guaranteed to be tractable, I would like to pursue this point further.

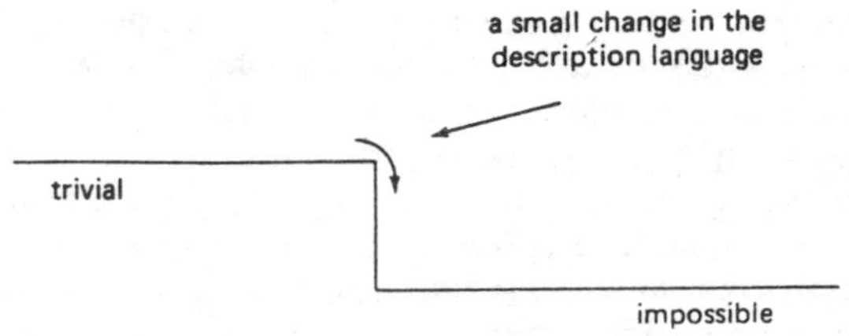

FIG 4. The computational cliff.

3.2. Vivid knowledge

Assume (temporarily) that our KB is just a list of sentences of some sort, where each sentence can be thought of as a list of words. It will be important to distinguish at this stage between the *content* of a KB and its *form*. The content of the KB is what it tells us about the world; the form of the KB is the actual data structures used to represent that content.[10]

Consider two KBs that represent information about the behaviour of Jack and Dan at the party. The first contains the sentences[11]

Dan drank exactly 7 ounces of gin.
Jack drank exactly 6 ounces of gin.

The second KB contains the sentences

Jack and Dan together polished off a 13 ounce bottle of gin.
Dan had precisely one more drink (1 ounce) than Jack.

Note that (modulo arithmetic) the information about how much each drank is the same in each case. You can solve the equations in the second KB and end up with the first, or you can add and subtract the amounts in the first KB and end up with the second. The difference between the two is in the way they

[9] This definition allows a KB that fails to deal with a topic at all (as most do) to still be complete.

[10] These correspond roughly to what Newell has referred to in [8] (and I have pursued in [6, 9, 10]) as the knowledge and symbol levels, respectively.

[11] I will use this font when I am referring to symbols actually present in a KB.

express this information. The first KB tells us what Jack drank in a single atomic sentence, quite independent of any other in the KB. The second KB tells us what Jack drank in a form that has to be assembled from pieces in more than one location. The same applies to Dan. If indeed we are interested in what each individual drank as a simple property of our cocktail party domain (as opposed to *only* caring about why the bottles are empty), then the first KB has information in a form that is ready to be used, while the second KB has information in a form that will almost certainly require more processing. In some sense, the first KB has the "answers" to the second. Even if we were mainly concerned with what groups of people drank (such as whether Jack and Dan together drank more than twice what Bill, Susan, and Henry did), we would still be better off with the equations solved, since it is so easy from there to determine the truth of a very wide range of constraints. By generalizing this example, it should be clear that a KB like the second one might be complete but still require a lot of processing to answer simple questions. But what I really want to focus on are those KBs that are like the first one.

I want to consider a complete KB whose form satisfies a certain constraint that I call *vividness*. The two main properties of a KB whose form is vivid are the following:

(1) There will be a one-to-one correspondence between a certain class of symbols in the KB and the objects of interest in the world.

(2) For every simple relationship of interest in the world, there will be a type of connection among symbols in the KB such that the relationship holds among a group of objects in the world if and only if the appropriate connection exists among the corresponding symbols in the KB.

The first KB about Jack and Dan above was vivid since representations of both individuals were directly connected to representations of the amount they drank. The second KB, by the same criterion, was not. A simpler example is depicted in Fig 5. This is a world with two individuals in it, one being the husband of the other. We also have a simple vivid KB beside it where Jack stands for the first individual, Jill stands for the second, and standing for the

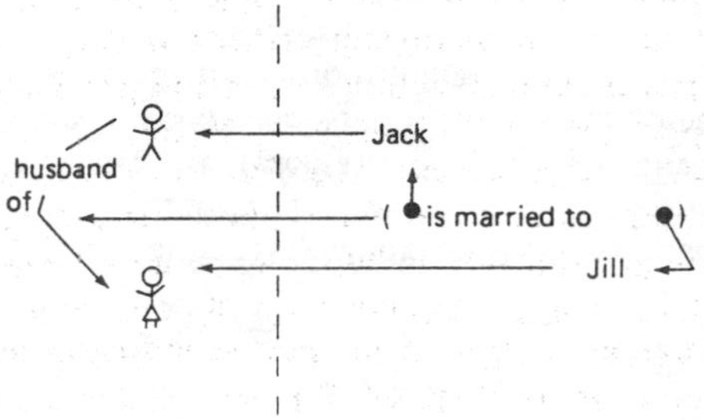

Fig 5. Vivid KB.

husband relationship is a connection involving co-occurrence in a sentence of the form ...is married to... (with the husband in the first position of the sentence).

Now I am being fairly hazy about what I mean by vivid,[12] but two observations about what is *not* intended are in order. First of all, vivid does not mean exact, precise, or unambiguous. So, for example, you can have

Bill is related to Henry.

as part of a vivid KB, if this is the relationship (at the level of detail) that you care about. Similarly, you can have

John knows the meaning of democracy.

if knowing the meaning of democracy is a simple property of individuals that is of concern. Second, vividness is not a characteristic of how a KB is going to be used. It is true (but misleading to say) that a KB could be vivid for certain operations but not for others. The vividness of a KB depends only on its relevant *subject matter*. The only way it could vary from operation to operation is if the domain of discourse varied as well as, for instance, when a KB is made to deal with a new relationship in the world.

My main concern regarding vivid KBs is the following: they are, in some sense, *analogues* of the domain. By that I mean that we can operate on them directly as if they were the domain itself. The easiest way to see this is to consider a counting example. Suppose you are interested in finding out how many computer scientists at the party are husbands. In general, you might have to do all sorts of reasoning to answer this question, perhaps even discovering after all of this that you do not have enough information. Even with a complete KB where there is guaranteed to be enough information to answer the question, it may be necessary to perform time-consuming deductive operations to extract what is only implicitly there. But with a vivid KB, the situation is quite different. We can handle the question simply by asking how many symbols appearing at the start of a sentence of the form

...is a computer scientist.

[12] I am being especially vague about what I mean by a "connection" among symbols. Data structure pointers are the simplest case, but ultimately we may want to allow for symbols jointly satisfying some predicate that is computable in bounded time. What we do *not* want to allow for is a connection that depends on nonlocal criteria such as whether or not the entire KB logically implies something or other. If all we really cared about were KBs represented as standard lists of sentences, we could be much more specific about what those sentences would have to look like, namely collections of ground atomic sentences, coupled with closed-world assumptions of various sorts.

also appear at the start of a sentence

...is married to... .

Just as you can find out how many smokestacks a ship has by counting their representatives on a toy model, or how far apart two cities are by measuring the distance between their representatives on a map, direct calculations on a vivid KB can be used to determine what is true in the domain of discourse. So the KB is an analogue, albeit a propositional one.

This property of vivid KBs suggests an answer to a curious puzzle:

> Thinking may sometimes *feel* like much more than symbol manipulation, but this could be an illusion caused by the very close correspondence between symbols in a vivid KB and what they are about.

In other words, when a KB is vivid, operations that depend purely on its represented form can easily be mistaken for operations that depend on what those forms designate. More cryptically, a vivid KB is a model (in the logical sense) of itself, a property not shared by all logical theories.

Given a KB that is vivid, we can go quite a bit further towards optimizing the form of its information. First and foremost, we can get rid of *sentences* with all their redundancy, and replace them by tables of some sort, making something like a database, as in Fig 6. Similarly, we might consider using a form that is very connected like the kind found in semantic networks. What we are getting from these data structures are variations on how easy it will be to move from one piece of information to another, that is, variations on the patterns of connectivity.[13] It is interesting to speculate that perhaps this is *all* that data structures can provide us with. Note that how to optimize a KB form in this way is very application-dependent, quite unlike what I have been saying about handling incomplete knowledge.

Name	Age	Occupation ...
Jack	32	Computer Scientist
Jill	30	Physician
	⋮	

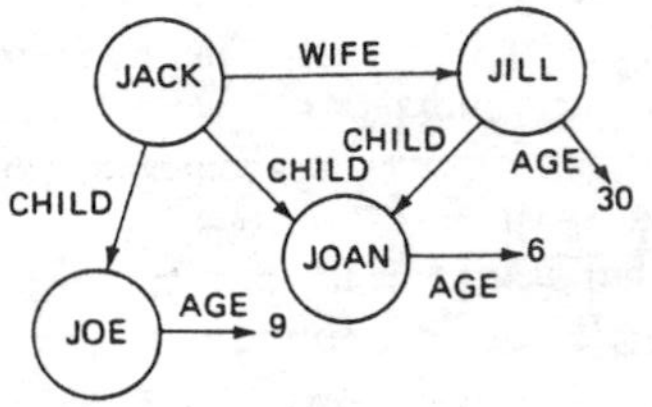

FIG 6. A database and a semantic network.

But the main property of vivid KBs is that we *can* indeed get very efficient worst case reasoning behaviour over them, since the type of reasoning that is necessary is so very limited.[14] In some sense, we get the opposite of a combinatorial explosion in that, given suitable database style indexing schemes, the number of facts that can be handled in a reasonable amount of time is very large.[15] To recap, then, when a KB is complete, reasoning with it reduces to the problem of determining what the KB says about the atomic propositions. And when the KB is also vivid in form, this problem can be efficiently handled by database retrieval techniques. So we are going to be able to deal with vast amounts of knowledge, if it happens to be complete in content and vivid in form.

This leads to an even more curious conjecture:

> If the performance is right, we need never worry about what is *relevant* to a particular situation, but can afford to take *everything* that is known into account.

In other words, for something like a vivid KB, a *holistic* approach to reasoning and belief revision might actually work.

3.3. The ubiquity of completeness and vividness

Let's step back for a moment. Why, then, should we care about knowledge that is represented vividly? The first reason, as I have argued, is that it is eminently tractable. But so what? Sure databases can be very large and still be guaranteed to work, but what does this have to do with the kind of knowledge needed in everyday commonsense situations? The second reason is that, in fact, vivid knowledge shows up all over the place.

Consider, for example, standard information sources. When you look in a telephone book for someone's phone number, you expect to see a string of digits. If, instead, what you saw was a description that correctly stated that the last digit was the 17th digit in the decimal expansion of π, you would be very disappointed. That's not a vivid description, it's a depressing one! And so it goes for other information sources like encyclopedias, atlases, and the like.

[13]There are also interestingly different sorts of optimization. For example, by connecting symbols to numerals, we can stipulate that two symbols are to be considered connected when their associated numbers satisfy some property. This allows us to push the notion of connectivity into the domain of numbers. An example of this is a representation of a transitive relation like *left of* that exploits the fact that the *less than* predicate on numbers is also transitive.

[14]In fact, the reasoning is *so* simple that it is tempting not to think of it as *logical reasoning* at all. Tempting, but wrong. The fact of the matter is that because a vivid KB is so explicit, calculating what is logically implicit in it generally reduces to retrieving what is explicit.

[15]For example, a census information database might easily contain hundreds of millions of records.

They all attempt to present vivid information because this is the kind of information that we think of as ultimate *answers* to questions, as opposed to information requiring further calculation and reasoning.

But perhaps the main source of vividly represented knowledge is *pictorial information*. We can all imagine looking at a picture and realizing that what it shows us is that

John's jacket is all white.

We can also imagine looking at a picture that tells us that

John's jacket is all black.

But try to imagine a picture that only shows you that

John's jacket is either all white or all black.

This uncertainty, easy to convey in a sentence, is impossible to display in a picture. In general, pictorial information is just not closed under disjunction.[16]

The situation here is complex, however. Pictorial information can certainly be *imprecise*, for example, because of grain and limited resolution. Pictorial information can also be *ambiguous*, as in some optical illusions (like the Necker cube) and all the usual properties of a two-dimensional projection. Pictorial information can also have *blind spots* because of occlusions, harsh lighting conditions and the like. So overall, pictorial information can be very uncertain and require careful interpretation. But note that this type of uncertainty is much the same as the kind I have claimed is present in vivid KBs.[17] In other words, there is a kind of incompleteness that analogues such as pictures have, but the possibilities admitted by this incompleteness are relatively limited. Specifically, the possibilities have to be *similar*. It is very easy to imagine looking at a picture and saying

It's Jan or her twin sister Joan.

But it is hard to imagine looking at a picture and saying

It's Jan or a lunar landscape.

without seriously insulting Jan.

Of course, the difference between having a picture of Jan and one of her twin sister may be quite *significant* overall, for example if it depicts one of them in a compromising situation. No matter how similar the cases are *visually*, there may be no alternative to careful inspection and a deliberate and time-consuming case analysis. However, in the vast majority of cases, this won't be necessary. In fact, just the opposite. We are often able to replace incomplete knowledge by knowledge that is complete, and indeed vivid, but *vague*. So, for example, faced with the disjunctive fact that Fred plays a DX-7 or DX-9 synthesizer, we might get by with a vague (but nondisjunctive) version of this which says that Fred plays an FM digital synthesizer, assuming that the difference is insignificant (e.g., anything we know about one applies to the other). Much the same phenomenon seems to occur with interval arithmetic. For many (though not all) operations, we can think of an interval as a number (albeit a fuzzy one) and operate on it *directly*, rather than having to reason by cases about all of the (similar) numbers described by the interval. Thus we can think of *approximations* (and other types of equivalence classes) as almost vivid representations, that permit analogue kinds of operations when the bounds are tight enough, and otherwise revert to case analyses.[18]

There is a lot of research that can and should be done to clear up these issues.[19] But the main point that I want to make is that pictorial information is limited in form, and so can be exploited *relatively* efficiently. Overstating the case somewhat, the reason we should care about vividness is that we are constantly bombarded with vividly represented knowledge that has been extracted perceptually from the world.

One of the areas this observation may help clarify is our obvious success in problem-solving situations where we can rely on *visualization*, such as in the

[16]In other words, it is *not* the case that for every two pictures *A* and *B*, there will be a third picture that shows us a world that is either as *A* shows us or as *B* shows us, no more and no less. There need not always be a picture that is ambiguous in depicting what one of two other pictures depicts. See [11] for a very enlightening discussion of this property of pictures, and [12] for an attempt at refuting this position.

[17]One important exception here is blind spots. I have insisted that vivid KBs incorporate some form of closed-world assumption, so that negative questions could be answered directly. Pictures with occlusions violate this constraint, and so typically cannot tell us what is *not* present in a scene (i.e., there may or may not be a dog behind the barn, as far as the picture shows). Interestingly enough, "semi-vivid" KBs, without any form of closed-world assumption, can be reasoned with as efficiently as their vivid counterparts. The only difference is that semi-vivid KBs tell us nothing about what does not exist or the relationships that do not hold, and so "negative" questions are really outside their area of expertise.

[18]A slightly more complex form of an almost vivid representation involves taking a vivid representation, and making a *parametrized* one by replacing parts of it by *variables*. Equality testing, for instance, now becomes pattern matching, slightly more complex perhaps, but a far cry from general reasoning about equality.

[19]The whole area of vivid *descriptions*, for example, needs analysis. To take one simple example we might be able to understand *procedures* as descriptions of behaviour (or classes of behaviour, better) that are vivid enough that running over them in a certain way actually *produces* the described behaviour, something obviously not true of general behavioural descriptions. It remains to be seen whether or not this view of procedural descriptions as just special (vivid) cases of declarative ones tells us anything about the controversy surrounding these notions.

case of geometry, or reasoning about sets using Venn diagrams. This is to be contrasted with the great difficulty we have with certain kinds of word puzzles, or solving purely logical tautologies. A first explanation might state that we have been primed by evolution to deal effectively with visual information, as opposed to linguistic information, a relative late-comer. But perhaps a better explanation is that visual information is *inherently* more tractable than unrestricted linguistic information, and that all that evolution has done is taught us to exploit this fact.

But if vivid knowledge is so great, why not *only* deal with it? Well, in general, there will always be circumstances where we do not have complete knowledge and hence, will not be able to represent it in vivid form. But it is not hard to show that complete knowledge can always be "compiled" into vivid form. However, there can be very good reasons for not doing so: a vivid KB can be very large, even infinitely so. In such cases, it is much better to derive implicit information only as it is required. Since the KB is complete, the reasoning involved can be handled by specialized techniques.

An application of this principal can be found in expert systems. In its simplest form, we are dealing with atomic data and a collection of if-then rules coupled with closed-world assumptions.[20] The resulting KBs are typically complete but not vivid in form. So some reasoning is required, but a simple form of it (backward-chaining) is often sufficient. On the other hand, it has been suggested that there might be applications where forward-chaining, mass storage technology, and database retrieval methods would be more appropriate. But this depends on complex time/space trade-off issues, and remains an open question.

We can summarize what I have been saying so far as a first heuristic for making believers out of computers (or KBSs that work):

Heuristic 1. Focus on languages where only complete knowledge is representable, and represent as much as possible of it in vivid form.

Although not normally thought of in these terms, a wide range of systems have input languages that are constrained in this way. Examples are database systems, linear equation solvers, standard circuit simulators, and even program interpreters. Imagine trying to solve equations given only input like "$2x + 3y = 3,7$, or 19", or trying to execute a program presented by descriptions like "The statement that follows the assignment to the variable x is not a *go to*."

[20]The easiest way to see if closed-world assumptions are in effect is to ask if the *absence* of anything in the KB counts for something. An example of this in expert systems is when a diagnosis is selected because no better ones can be *found*, as opposed to the system somehow establishing (on the basis of what is present in the KB) that no better ones *exist*. Similar closed-world reasoning occurs in natural language parsers.

We are so used to dealing with complete and vivid descriptions that it seems ridiculous to worry about the other kind.

A fall-back position related to this heuristic is to at least isolate parts of a KBS that can be handled efficiently by building systems that incorporate multiple reasoners optimized to special-purpose languages and reasoning tasks.[21] An example of this is the KRYPTON system that I worked on with Ron Brachman, Richard Fikes, and Victoria Pigman [13–15]. In this system, we had a full first-order logic theorem prover, as well as a very special-purpose description matcher of the kind that I talked about earlier in connection with the computational cliff.

4. The Difficult Case Revisited

So far, I have only suggested how to deal with knowledge that is complete, and especially knowledge that is represented vividly. But clearly any self-respecting KBS will occasionally have to venture outside this safe area. If this very rarely happens, then there is no problem. But what exactly should a well-behaved thinking system do with large amounts of incomplete knowledge? It should certainly *not* get stuck reasoning until it's too late. But what then? What I would like to do now is propose two related methods for dealing with incomplete knowledge. It should be understood at the outset, though, that these are very preliminary suggestions, and that a lot more research is needed.

4.1. Unsound reasoning

Consider the following sentence:

Jill is standing beside her husband Jack and glaring at him in disbelief.

One thing to notice about this is that without even trying to figure out what Jack did at the party, you can't help but fill in a wide range of other details involved in the situation. In particular, it is *very* hard to think about this without seeing Jack either to the left of Jill or to her right, or what Jill is wearing, or even where her hands are, and so on.

What seems to be happening here is that thinking is being reduced to visualizing, that is a *described* situation is being treated as if it were an *observed*

[21]If not multiple reasoners, we should at least have a way of informing a general-purpose reasoner that it is dealing with a specialized problem. I take the attempt to control theorem provers by using special procedural connectives (e.g., forward-only implication) to be along these lines.

one. As discussed earlier, pictorial information is limited in form; if a picture of Jack and Jill is sufficiently clear, unambiguous, and unobstructed to show certain details, it can't help but give us many others (such as their relative positions).[22] So we end up throwing in a whole lot of detail. The net result is information that seems much more *vivid* than the original linguistic description.

This is a form of thinking that I referred to earlier when I talked about concluding that Pat was male given only that Pat was a computer scientist. The vivid knowledge we are talking about here (e.g., that Jack is taller than Jill and standing to her left) is not logically implicit in the original information. So this is an example of what is called *logically unsound* thinking. Not necessarily *incorrect*, mind you, and possibly quite justified. The property is only that the truth of the conclusions is not implicit in the original sentence.

This type of thinking shows up repeatedly. So, for example, when you thought about Jill standing beside Jack at the party, did you imagine everyone pressed against the wall because of a Sherman tank in the room? Probably not. On the other hand, did you imagine Jill as wearing something? Probably yes. We seem to have no trouble inferring either the existence or nonexistence of objects. Similarly, we include details on the basis of normality or typicality conditions. If I tell you, for instance, that Jack spilled coffee on a polar bear rug and ask you what was the colour of that rug, the answer "white" comes to mind immediately. But, interestingly enough, it is hard to think about the sentence

> Jack leaned close to Jan and whispered something in her ear.

without choosing an ear. Here, no normality conditions seem to be involved. This seems to suggest that scripts, frames, prototypes, and the like are inadequate by themselves for filling in this kind of detail. That is, it is hard to believe we should use a default-ear-to-whisper-in slot in some frame to do the job.

How to make sense of this kind of unsound thinking? One aspect that seems to be involved is knowledge about knowledge. If pressed to explain our thinking, we might reason as follows:

> I am aware of all the large objects here at the party.
> I have not noticed that there is a Sherman tank here.
> So there is no tank here, since if there was one, I would have noticed it.

This kind of pattern appears again and again. So if Jill were naked at the party, or if the polar bear rug was not white, I would know about it; but I do not know about it, so it isn't true.

The interesting fact about this pattern of reasoning is that viewed this way, it really is no longer unsound. That is, the conclusion about the Sherman tank does indeed follow from the two premises. Moreover, the second premise is almost certainly true since most of us would be quite aware of what we had not yet observed at the party. So the only dubious belief is the first one that relates what exists to what is believed to exist.[23] Nonetheless, because the reasoning is sound (but perhaps based on false beliefs), we can attempt to characterize it in a new extended logic. There are two requirements. First, we have to be able to express knowledge in a language that talks not only about the *world*, but what is *known* about the world, and allows the two to be related. Second, we have to arrange things so that what is not known is logically implicit in our specification of what is. Otherwise, our KBs would have to stipulate explicitly both what is and what is not known.

My doctoral dissertation [4] made some progress on the first of these issues, and some effort has been directed toward the second [16,17]. But tough conceptual and computational problems remain in the formalization of these notions. In particular, the best theories we have of defaults and reasoning of this nature (so-called "nonmonotonic" reasoning, see [18]) predict that it will be *more difficult* to reason with defaults than without! If this were right, given that this type of reasoning can lead to serious errors, not to mention requiring revision as more is learned, *why would we bother*? Perhaps the computational gains to be had from vividness will give us a more plausible view of default reasoning and the like. An ideal theory of defaults would explain not only what interferences they sanction, but also what is to be gained by them, taking into account the ease of reasoning in the expanded vivid KB, the likelihood of error, and the cost of belief revision.[24]

So a lot more research is required. Nevertheless, we can state our second heuristic for making believers that work:

Heuristic 2. Make incomplete knowledge more vivid by filling in details by using defaults and closed-world assumptions derived from knowledge about knowledge.

A weaker but related suggestion is that sometimes knowledge can be made more vivid by filling in details almost randomly (as in the ear-whispering example), as long as errors are not too serious or revisions too likely or costly.

[22] Again, this is something that unrestricted sentences, on the other hand, can easily avoid. In many ways, the expressive power of general propositional representations is precisely in what they allow us to leave unsaid.

[23] This amounts to belief in a type of closed-world assumption.

[24] In this model, for example, the statistical component of defaults would show up not as part of any explicit belief (as in "The polar bear rug is white, with probality 0.896."), but as part of a metatheoretic justification for why an unequivocal assumption (i.e., "The polar bear rug is white.") is cost-effective overall.

4.2. Incomplete reasoning

The second way of dealing with incomplete knowledge that I wish to discuss is more generally applicable than the previous one. But it's more complex, so I will only sketch the essential ideas. Suppose someone comes up to you at the party and tells you that

> Either John is a lawyer or Henry is eating cheese.

or that

> George is standing beside someone with brown hair.

or that

> If Jack is married, it is not to Jan.

You would probably look at this person, shake your head, and wonder exactly what the *point* was. These sentences sound like *clues* in some kind of logic puzzle, one of those "The man who owns the zebra lives next door to the orange juice drinker," sort of things.

One thing to notice about this kind of information is that we *are* able to deal with it as is, without first demanding to know if John is a lawyer, or who exactly George is standing beside, or who, if anyone, Jack is married to. But we do so by going into a special "puzzle mode": we roll up our sleeves, get out pencil and paper, and start figuring. In particular, we monitor our progress very carefully, since we have no way of knowing at the outset whether or not we are going to be successful in sorting out the implications.

But what should happen with this kind of information in normal, everyday thinking? The goal here is to get *some* understanding quickly, and not to spend unbounded amounts of time thinking about the situation. This means, of course, claiming ignorance occasionally even when the answers are implictly there. But for normal thinking, this is no doubt correct. So whereas before I was talking about logically unsound thinking, now I am suggesting that we consider *logically incomplete* thinking.

How can we account formally for this type of reasoning? Imagine again someone telling you that [25]

> Jack is not married to Jan.

Notice that there is an overwhelming tendency to believe that this tells us something about Jack and Jan together. Otherwise, why was *she* brought into it? Apart from logic games, it's as if the sentence was really of the form

> Jack is ... to Jan.

where the ellipsis stands for some relationship holding between Jack and Jan. This suggests that we may consider treating the negated sentence as if it were

> Jack is not-maried to Jan.

where "not-married" is the name of that relationship. What does this buy us? Obviously, if we understand x being not-married to y exactly when x is not married to y, then the new sentence implies exactly what the previous one did. *But*, and this is the key point, if we take "not-married" to be the name of a new mysterious relationship that we know nothing about (or more precisely, that we are not willing to analyze for now), we get a different set of implications with two very important properties.

First, by replacing the negation by an atomic sentence, we have made the information once again look *vivid*. Vague, of course, because of not-married, but vivid nonetheless. In other words, the sentence is no longer incomplete information about who is married to whom, but vivid information about who is not-married to whom. This artificially simplified logical form (from a negation to an atomic sentence) does not express the uncertainty of the original.

Second, this simplification of logical form leads to sound reasoning. If we take the logical consequences of the not-married sentence, we get sentences like

> Jack is not-married to Jan or Joan.

and

> Either Pat is a computer scientist or somebody is not-married to Jan.

and so on. Each of these (when "not-married" is now expanded) is a logical implication of the original negation. However, the converse does not hold. Suppose, for example, that it is known that

> Jack is married to either Jan or Jill.

Then this coupled with the original negation implies that

> Jack is married to Jill.

But no such conclusion follows from the not-married sentence, since we have lost the connection between not being married and being not-married. Specifically, we have lost the *contradiction* in being married and being not-married at

[25] In what follows, I am going to focus on manipulating a negated sentence only, since I have done some research along these lines [19]. But similar manipulations could be performed on the disjunctive or existential sentences above.

the same time. This, as it turns out, is essential for normal *modus ponens* reasoning. So the reasoning is sound but logically incomplete.

To analyze precisely which implications were preserved by this scheme and which were not, I developed a new logic of belief, where beliefs were closed only with respect to this weaker form of implication [19]. Semantically, what this amounted to was allowing for interpretations where the truth of an atomic sentence was *independent* of that of its negation (as in the "married" and "not-married" relationships), so that both or neither could be true. The requirement that this logic placed on belief was that if a sentence came out true under every interpretation that made all the beliefs true, then that sentence had to also be a belief. It turns out that this closure condition corresponds exactly to a well studied (and independently motivated) branch of logic called relevance logic [20]. But just as importantly, I was also able to prove in [19] that this requirement on belief was computationally manageable.[26]

I should point out, however, that relevance logic as a basis for incomplete thinking does have its problems, and that much needs to be done to iron these out. Nonetheless, the direction looks very promising, and leads to our final heuristic for making believers out of computers:

Heuristic 3. Make incomplete knowledge appear more vivid by rephrasing it in a simplified logical form whose implications are sound.

The corollary to this heuristic is that you should *only* work on the full set of logical implications in a special puzzle mode, where progress can be monitored very carefully.[27] In other words, fully automatic, sound, and complete theorem proving is for proving theorems, not for mundane reasoning.

5. Conclusion

We have come a long way from a simple-minded view of thinking based on logic. The usual picture of logic is that it involves a very expressive language, coupled with a sound and complete inference regime. What I have suggested here, from the desire to deal with large amounts of knowledge within tolerable resource bounds, is looking at very weak languages (e.g., where only vivid knowledge is expressible), unsound inference (e.g., based on defaults) and incomplete inference (e.g., based on simplified logical forms). In all cases, though, I believe the development can be formal, rigourous, and indeed, *logical*.

Let me briefly summarize the main points.

- Knowledge-based systems need to apply large amounts of knowledge.
- It must be possible at some level to apply knowledge without first requiring more knowledge to be applied at a higher level.
- Certain forms of knowledge are inherently intractable, and cannot be fully applied within reasonable resource bounds.
- A special kind of knowledge (namely that which is complete in content and vivid in form) can be fully applied.
- The application of knowledge can also be made computationally tractable by making it logically unsound and incomplete in a principled way.

A few comments about relevant future work are in order. Obviously, the whole area of vivid and complete knowledge needs to be analyzed much more carefully. Two especially promising topics involve graceful degradations of vivid knowledge (e.g., approximations) and the replacement of incomplete knowledge by knowledge that is vague but vivid in form.[28] The whole area is begging for a careful mathematical analysis, sensitive to issues of logic and computational complexity. Another topic that requires investigation is that of logically unsound reasoning, but again dealing with it from a simultaneous logic and complexity standpoint. We need to understand in a precise computational sense why making assumptions is a good idea. A fourth topic that needs further investigation from a logic and complexity perspective is that of logically incomplete reasoning, avoiding the anomalies of relevance logic while preserving computational tractability.[29] Finally, I think it will be very illuminating to look at how knowledge-based systems—systems that derive their abilities from reasoning—relate to non-knowledge-based systems, and I think that the work of Rosenschein and Pereira on this topic (e.g., [25]) is well worth pursuing.

So what does all this mean in *practical* terms? With any talk on theoretical issues, there is invariably the problem of relating it to normal everyday practice. To take an example from nuclear physics again, if what you are mainly interested in is a reactor that does not leak radiation, a talk on neutrinos is not going to help you a lot. What I hope can be extracted from this presentation is a framework for understanding some of the limitations involved in a wide class of systems. In the case of nuclear physics, if someone comes up to you and tells you "I'm going to do fusion", you might ask him a number of questions such as, "How are you going to get the plasma hot enough?", "How are you going to keep it hot?", and so on. In the case of expert systems, the

[26]A serious restriction was necessary for the result: it applies only to a quantifier-free language whose sentences are all in conjunctive normal form, with negations appearing only in front of atomic sentences. Note that even with this restriction, however, *full* logical implication is still (strongly believed to be) intractable.

[27]Ideally, activity here would be *planned* and reasoned about just like any other. In particular, a system might decide to acquire additional information to complete its knowledge, or just give up if the reasoning becomes too demanding. But as I said earlier, this metalevel reasoning had better be no harder than the object-level reasoning. One sufficient condition is that enough metalevel knowledge be vivid in form.

[28]The work that Hobbs has done on granularity [21] may be relevant here.

[29]There are at least three papers in the IJCAI proceedings this year [22–24] that address this issue.

same kinds of questions arise. If someone comes up to you and tells you, "I'm going to handle partial knowledge", you might consider asking "How are you going to limit the reasoning?" or "How are you going to keep the cases down to a manageable number?".

The more general implication of what I have been discussing is that a certain kind of thinking can be very difficult for people to perform, and that perhaps this is not a *biological* peculiarity, but is inherent in the information-processing task itself. We should therefore not expect our computer systems to be any *better* at it. Of course, as we learn more, we may come to believe that there is no reason why they should be any *worse* at it.

Let me conclude by thanking all of the IJCAI people, especially Steve Crocker, Phyllis O'Neil, and Tom Kazsmarek for their help in the presentation, Ron Brachman and John Mylopoulos for all they have done for me over the years, and a group of people too numerous to describe vividly here for their help and inspiration.[30]

Finally, as far as the cocktail party I used as an example is concerned, I would just like to tell you that it ended okay, and that there was no real damage done except to the polar bear rug and to Jack's reputation.

REFERENCES

1. Haken, A., The intractability of resolution, Ph. D. Thesis, Department of Mathematics, Universty of Illinois at Urbana-Champaign, 1984.
2. Brachman, R., and Levesque, H., Tractability of subsumption in frame-based description languages, in: *Proceedings Fourth National Conference on Artificial Intelligence*, Austin, TX (1984) 34–37.
3. Levesque, H., The interaction with incomplete knowledge bases: A formal treatment, in: *Proceedings Seventh International Joint Conference on Artificial Intelligence*, Vancouver, BC (1981) 240–245.
4. Levesque, H., A formal treatment of incomplete knowledge bases, Tech. Rept. No. 3, Fairchild Laboratory for Artificial Intelligence Research, Palo Alto, CA, 1982.
5. Brachman, R.J. and Levesque, H., Competence in knowledge representation, in: *Proceedings Second National Conference on Artificial Intelligence*, Pittsburgh, PA (1982) 189–192.
6. Levesque, H., Foundations of a functional approach to knowledge representation, *Artificial Intelligence* **23** (1984) 155–212.
7. Levesque, H., A fundamental tradeoff in knowledge representation and reasoning in: *Proceedings Fifth CSCSI/SCEIO Conference*, London, Ont. (1984) 141–152.
8. Newell, A., The knowledge level, *The AI Magazine* **2** (2) (1981) 1–20.
9. Brachman, R. and Levesque, H., What makes knowledge bases knowledgeable? A view of databases from the knowledge level, in: *Proceedings First International Workshop on Expert Database Systems*, Kiawah Island, SC (1984) 69–78.

[30] Financial support was received from the National Sciences and Engineering Research Council of Canada. A special thanks to Jim des Rivières, Russ Greiner, Graeme Hirst, Ray Reiter, Bart Selman, and John Tsotsos for helping me with the written version of this lecture. It was my idea to include all the falsehoods, though.

10. Brachman, R. and Levesque, H., Knowledge level interfaces to information systems, in: *Proceedings Workshop on Knowledge Management Systems*, Islamoroda, FL, 1985.
11. Sober, E., Mental representations, *Synthese* **33** (1976) 101–148.
12. Howell, R., Ordinary pictures, mental representations, and logical forms, *Synthese* **33** (1976) 149–174
13. Brachman, R.J., Fikes, R.E. and Levesque, H., KRYPTON: A functional approach to knowledge representation, *IEEE Computer* **16** (10) (1983) 67–73.
14. Brachman, R., Fikes, R.E. and Levesque, H., KRYPTON: Integrating terminology and assertion, in: *Proceedings Third National Conference on Artificial Intelligence*, Washington, DC (1983) 31–35.
15. Brachman, R.J., Gilbert, V.P. and Levesque, H., An essential hybrid reasoning system: Knowledge and symbol level accounts of KRYPTON, in: *Proceedings Ninth International Joint Conference on Artificial Intelligence*, Los Angeles, CA (1985) 532–539.
16. Moore, R.C., Semantical considerations on nonmonotonic logic, in: *Proceedings Eighth International Joint Conference on Artificial Intelligence*, Karlsruhe, F.R.G. (1983) 272–279.
17. Halpern, J. and Moses, Y., Towards a theory of knowledge and ignorance: Preliminary report, in: *Proceedings Non-Monotonic Reasoning Workshop*, New Paltz, NY (1984) 125–143.
18. Reiter, R. A logic for default reasoning, *Artificial Intelligence* **13** (1980) 81–132
19. Levesque, H., A logic of implicit and explicit belief, in: *Proceedings Fourth National Conference on Artificial Intelligence*, Austin, TX (1984) 198–202; Revised as Fairchild Tech. Rept. No. 653, FLAIR Tech. Rept. No. 32, 1984.
20. Anderson, A.R. and Belnap, N.D., *Entailment: The Logic of Relevance and Necessity* 1 (Princeton University Press, Princeton, NJ, 1975).
21. Hobbs, J.R., Granularity, in: *Proceedings Ninth International Joint Conference on Artificial Intelligence*, Los Angeles, CA (1985) 432–435.
22. Fagin, R. and Halpern, J., Belief, awareness, and limited reasoning: Preliminary report, in: *Proceedings Ninth International Joint Conference on Artificial Intelligence*, Los Angeles, CA (1985) 491–501.
23. Patel-Schneider, P.F., A decidable first-order logic for knowledge representation, in: *Proceedings Ninth International Joint Conference on Artificial Intelligence*, Los Angeles, CA (1985) 455–458.
24. Frisch, A.M., Using model theory to specify AI programs, in: *Proceedings Ninth International Joint Conference on Artificial Intelligence*, Los Angeles, CA (1985) 148–154.
25. Rosenchein, S.J., Formal theories of knowledge in AI and robotics, in: *Proceedings Workshop on Intelligent Robots: Achievements and Issues*, SRI International, Menlo Park, CA (1984) 237–252.

Received April 1986

Chapter 2

Representation and Semantics

This chapter focuses on modelling concepts, techniques, and tools for advanced data models, and contrasts these with parallel proposals for knowledge representation in AI. Although enhanced modelling capabilities have always motivated AI research, they have only recently become a major focus in database research, as DBMSs are being extended to support application domains beyond the traditional business context. The chapter contains 17 papers, grouped into five topic sections: Entity-Based Representations, Semantic Data Models and Knowledge Representation, Logic and Databases, Data/Knowledge Base Semantics, and Representation Issues.

2.1 Entity-Based Representations

The first paper in this section (2.1.1), Bill Kent's "Limitations of Record-Based Information Models," presents a careful account of the modelling difficulties that arise when we use records as atomic building blocks. Kent's paper provides a rationale for the extensions to the classical data models proposed in the other papers in this chapter. The reader will find insights into the choice of the modelling features included in these extensions. A longer version of the paper has appeared in book form [KENT78]. Related criticisms and motivations for entity- and object-oriented data modelling can be found in the seminal papers by Abrial [ABRI74] and Schmidt and Swenson [SS75], and in [SS77a], [BROD84], and [HK87]. Related discussions on AI knowledge-representation schemes can be found in [WOOD75], [BRAC79], [ISRA83], [IB84], [ISRA86], and [BL86].

The second paper (2.1.2), Peter Chen's "The Entity-Relationship Model: Towards a Unified View of Data," was presented in the first *Very Large Databases Conference (VLDB)* in September 1975 and was later published in the first issue in 1976 of the *ACM Transactions on Database Systems* (*TODS*). The entity-relationship (E-R) model, noted for its simplicity and the availability of a clean graphical notation, was quickly adopted by practitioners looking for a tool to describe information in their databases at the *conceptual level.* By 1979, there was sufficient interest to warrant a series of international conferences on the "E-R approach" [CHEN79]. Although the vast majority of practical database design is still done at the logical and physical levels, use of E-R design at the conceptual level is growing rapidly. The E-R model has become the de facto standard for conceptual database design in practice, particularly since the onslaught of automated CASE tools, almost all of which support some variant of E-R design. Due to its acceptance and to its limitations, the E-R model has become the basis for improvements and advanced modelling concepts (e.g., it lacks a reasonable query language and the now-accepted modelling concepts discussed in subsequent papers in this section).

The third paper (2.1.3), "Using Semantic Networks for Database Management" by Nick Roussopoulos and John Mylopoulos, was also presented at the first VLDB Conference. Although its motivation is the same as Chen's, it proposes semantic networks for conceptual descriptions of the contents of a database. The proposal (see [ROUS76] for more details) was perhaps premature, as semantic networks were being criticized during that period for their lack of semantics [WOOD75], [SCHU76]. The paper is most interesting because of its advocacy of the wholesale use of AI techniques. The careful reader may note an early version of the classification operation for semantic networks (e.g., [Brachman, 2.2.4]) in the graph-matching operation used in the paper.

The fourth and final paper of the section (2.1.4), "Database Abstractions: Aggregation and Generalization" by John and Diane Smith, focuses on the extension of the relational model to provide *abstraction mechanisms* for the design of logical schemata. The motivation here comes from programming languages, where the notion of abstraction has played an important role. The abstraction mechanisms bear similarities to the AI structuring mechanisms for semantic networks proposed by Roussopoulos and Mylopoulos. Database design principles related to these abstractions are given in [SS78]. A major objective for the design of data models is to identify a small number of modelling primitives for which there are computationally efficient implementations. In contrast, AI knowledge-representation schemes are designed more for their expressive power than for their potential implementation efficiency. For example, aggregation and generalization have become widely accepted as both simple and practically important data-modelling primitives, and efficient implementations have been developed. In contrast, user-defined relationships possible in many AI schemes, such as semantic networks, are not widely accepted in practical modelling, and efficient implementation techniques do not exist. The epilogue, written for this volume in 1988, presents the authors' original motivations, a clarification, and the relationship of their work to current ideas such as object models.

Limitations of Record-Based Information Models

WILLIAM KENT
IBM Corporation

Record structures are generally efficient, familiar, and easy to use for most current data processing applications. But they are not complete in their ability to represent information, nor are they fully self-describing.

Key Words and Phrases: records, information model, data model, semantic model, conceptual model, normalization, first normal form, entities, relationships
CR Categories: 3.70, 4.33, 4.34

INTRODUCTION

Records provide an excellent tool for processing information that fits a certain pattern. Other kinds of information do not fit as well into record structures. In all cases, the use of record structures depends on supplementary information, often reflected only in the special-purpose application programs written to process the data, and which may or may not still be remembered by the users of the data. Record structures do not provide the semantically self-describing base needed for conceptual schemas [2, 3, 21], or for generalized query processors or other end-user facilities.

In their capacity as data processing *tools,* records have a desirable versatility. That is, a given construct (e.g., field names, or compound fields) can be used for different purposes at different times. Unfortunately this virtue becomes a vice for semantic modeling: one has to know the special usage of each construct in each case, and there is no general rule for deducing the underlying semantic structure. While some information cannot be represented in records, other information can be represented in so many ways as to become ambiguous.

Models which provide additional file structure around the records (e.g., sequencing, hierarchies, CODASYL networks) overcome some of the functional limitations. None of them overcome all the limitations. Furthermore, by building on top of record structures, they retain all the underlying ambiguities. In some cases, they simply add more options for representing something which could already be represented in several ways in record structure.

This paper would be pointless if there were not any alternatives, but there are. There are various models which are essentially graph structured, based on such primitive concepts as binary relations, or entities and relationships. Such models tend to be more functionally complete in their information processing capability, and more precise in their semantic modeling. (We are not arguing their economic superiority to record structures for bulk data processing in today's applications.) A number of these are listed in the concluding section of this paper. We do not try to explain or defend these models. Our main purpose is to collect some problems concerning record structures (many of which have already been mentioned in the literature), as a resource to help defend alternative models. Nevertheless, much of the discussion is cast in terms of entities and relationships. The motivation for this paper originated in attempts to reconcile record structures with the characteristics of entities and relationships.

Author's address: General Products Division, IBM Corporation, 555 Bailey Avenue, P.O. Box 50020, San Jose, CA 95150.

"RECORD" DEFINED

By *record* we mean here a fixed sequence of field values, conforming to a static description usually contained in catalogs and/or in programs. The description consists mainly of a name, length, and data type for each field. Each such description defines one *record type* (or, in relational terms, a "relation" or "table"). My remarks apply to any data model based on this kind of construct. This clearly includes the traditional hierarchical, relational, and (CODASYL) network models. (For introductions to these models, see [7, 9–13, 42, 43].) It also includes approaches mentioned in [2] and [18], to the extent that they speak of such things as "conceptual records." (It should be noted that such constructs are not mentioned in [3].) The comments also apply to the entity-relationship model of [8], which is really driven by record structures (relations) rather than by entities and relationships as the primitive concept (his Level 1 constructs appear to be constrained to match his Level 2 information structure).

Some record formats allow a certain variability by permitting a named field or group of fields to occur more than once within a record (i.e., as a list of values or sets of values). We will use the term *normalized system* to refer to systems which do not permit repeating groups or fields. This follows the relational model, which excludes such repetitions via its normalization requirements (specifically, first normal form [9, 20]).

BASIC ASSUMPTIONS BEHIND RECORD STRUCTURES

Record structure presumes a horizontal and vertical homogeneity in data: horizontally, each record of a given type contains the same fields; and vertically, a given field contains the same "kind" of information in each record.

Homogeneity of Relevant Facts

The records of a given type in a file describe a set of things in the real world (e.g., employees). Record structure fits best when the entire population has the same kinds of attributes (e.g., every employee has a name, address, department, salary, etc.). While exceptions are tolerated, the essential configuration is that of a homogeneous population of records, all having the same fields.

Although commercial data processing naturally focuses on areas which fit this pattern, the pattern does not always hold. In many cases, although a certain group of individuals constitutes a single "kind" of thing, there is considerable variation in the facts relevant to each individual in that set.

Consider clothing. While we can agree that pants, socks, underwear, and hats are all items of clothing, it would be very hard to define a conventional "clothing" record type. There are many field names which are relevant; not many of them apply to any one kind of clothing. Consider: size, waist size, neck size, sleeve length, long or short sleeves, cup size, inseam length, button or zipper, sex, fabric type, heel size, width, color, pattern, pieces, season, number, collar style, cuffs, neckline, sleeve style, weight, flared, belt, waterproof, formal or casual, age, pockets, sport, washable, etc. How would you design the record format for clothing records?

Clothing is by no means the only such category. Tools, furniture, vehicles, and people are just a few other categories having inhomogeneous attributes over their populations.

The more that information deviates from the norm of homogeneity, the less appropriate is the record configuration. There are certain techniques for accommodating variability among instances in a record structure, but these need to be used sparingly. If there is considerable variation over a population, then the solutions become cumbersome and inefficient. Such solutions include:

(1) Define the record format to include the union of all relevant fields, where not all the fields are expected to have values in every record. (Often "maiden name" is defined as part of a record format for all employees, though it is only relevant to married females.) Thus many records might have null values in many fields. Furthermore, the limited relevance is not defined to the system; it is only the pattern of usage (and, sometimes, validation logic in programs) which reflects the limitation.

(2) Allow the same field to have different meanings in different records. Unfortunately, such a practice is never defined to the system. With respect to any processing done by the system, that field appears to have the same significance in every record occurrence. It certainly has only one field name, which in these cases usually turns out to be something totally uninformative, like CODE or FIELD 1. It is only the buried logic in application programs which knows the significance of these fields, and the different meanings they have in different records.

Such inhomogeneity is especially vexing if it affects an attribute we would like to use as an identifier. If it does not apply to all individuals in the set, then it cannot be used as a "key" for the record type. This situation is fairly common. The employees of a multinational corporation might not all have social security numbers, or employee numbers. Some books do not have "International Standard Book Numbers" (ISBN), others do not have Library of Congress numbers, and some have neither. Library of Congress numbers are also given to things which are not books (e.g., films and recordings); those would not have ISBN's. Oil companies have their individual conventions for naming their own oil wells, and the American Petroleum Institute has also assigned "standard" names to some wells—but not all.

The function needed here is equivalent to "self-naming" fields, i.e., redefining the concept of record to mean a chain of relevant field names and their values.

Homogeneity Within Fact Type

That was a kind of "horizontal" homogeneity, i.e., each record containing the same fields. There is also a "vertical" homogeneity assumed. Within a record type, a given field is expected to contain the same kind of value in every record, as though a certain kind of fact always involved the same kinds of objects.

Again, this is not always true. Suppose that company cars can be assigned either to employees or to departments. If employees are normally identified by six numeric digits and departments by four alphanumeric characters, how do we design a "vehicle assignment" record? Assignment is a simple fact, to which one might naively expect to be able to address a simple inquiry: "to whom is car 97 assigned?" In such a case, we might like a two-part answer: the type of the assignee (employee or department), plus the identification of the individual assignee (in a format which depended on the assignee type).

We could design a record format with four fields: vehicle number, assignee type, employee, and department. The second field would tell us the assignee type, and hence whether to look for the assignee name in the third or fourth field. We assume, of course, that only one of the last two fields is filled in—but there is not likely to be any system facility to enforce that. Thus the multifield format introduces a data integrity hazard. And, as far as the record definitions convey any meaning to the system, we have here three independent facts about vehicles, with no interdependence among the three. The data structure bears little resemblance to the semantic structure of the underlying relationships. (We have, incidentally, created a horizontal inhomogeneity. The employee field is relevant for some vehicles, and the department field for others. They are never both relevant for the same vehicle.)

If, later on, cars can be assigned to other kinds of things with different identifier formats (e.g., to divisions, or to branch offices) then the record formats have to be redesigned with additional fields for the new assignee types. The validation gets more complicated: only one of the last *n* fields may contain a value. And the file may have to be physically reloaded for each format change.

Another approach is to provide distinct record types, one for each type of assignee. The fields in one record type would be vehicle number and employee, in another they would be vehicle number and department, and so on. Each record type has its own name; instead of "vehicle assignment" being a single kind of fact, we have many kinds: "vehicle-employee assignments," "vehicle-department assignments," etc. (One is required to believe that employees and departments cannot have the same relationships with vehicles. A relationship between an employee and a vehicle is necessarily "different" from a relationship between a department and a vehicle.) Instead of going to one record type (or naming one relationship) to find the assignment of a vehicle, one now has to know how many such record types there are—and their names—and be prepared to interrogate each one of them. It is even worse if you are interested in some other information about the vehicle, not its assignment. That information might be in any one of the record types. Validation is still a problem: there is no system facility to keep the same vehicle from appearing in more than one record type (i.e., having more than one assignee). Extensions are difficult, too: every new assignee type requires the introduction of another record type. And changing a vehicle's assignment is cumbersome, if the assignee type is also changing; a record of one type has to be deleted and a record of another type inserted.

Neither multifield records nor multiple record types offer a good solution to the vertical inhomogeneity problem. These approaches look even worse if there is inhomogeneity on both sides of the relationship. Suppose that instead of vehicle assignments, we were recording more general equipment assignments. Assignable equipment might include vehicles, furniture, tools, etc., each potentially having its own identifier formats. If there are *m* kinds of assignable equipment and *n* kinds of assignees, then the multifield approach requires $m + n + 2$ fields (two type fields), with only four fields containing values in any one record. The multiple record type approach would require $m \times n$ record types.

Still another solution to vertical inhomogeneity is to make it disappear. One way is to relax the field definition to a level that is general enough to handle all necessary identifier formats; a varying character string would do the job. Vehicle assignment records are then reduced to two fields again, where the second field might contain employee numbers, department codes, or the identifiers for any other kinds of assignees. Only users (and the code in their programs) know which is which, and what to do with them. The system is unable to furnish services such as syntax checking of the field values, or following a path to the corresponding employee or department record (by matching key values, as in the relational join), or verifying that a referenced employee or department does, in fact, exist.

This solution also fails if things in different categories might accidentally have the same identifiers (e.g., in the general equipment assignments, if a vehicle registration number might happen to be the same as a tool inventory number). Which points out that the vertical inhomogeneity problem is not simply a record format problem. Even if the record formats are compatible (e.g., employees and departments both having four-character codes), one has to guard against different entity types occurring in the same field if they might have the same identifiers.

But on the other hand, we do not have to have multiple entity types to encounter vertical inhomogeneity. Identifier formats can vary even within a single entity type. Employee numbers might differ in various subsidiaries of a corporation, or within a multinational corporation. Ship registry formats differ according to the country of registry. Oil companies have different formats for identifying their oil wells. The soldiers in a United Nations military group are likely to have different kinds of serial numbers. And so on.

There is still another way to force the disappearance of vertical inhomogeneity. One can provide a uniform reference to all the entities involved by aggregating them into one "supertype" and giving them a new arbitrary identifier, e.g., an "assignee number." (Analogous to such familiar constructs as "taxpayer identification number," or "capital equipment inventory number.") This permits assignees to be referenced uniquely and carefully in the assignment records, with a well-defined and checkable identifier format. Unfortunately, all of the entities involved have now acquired a new and additional identifier for which values have to be assigned, and by which they have to be recognized in various contexts. And, in some cases a readable name (perhaps the department name) is replaced by an unintelligible code number, which has to be looked up somewhere else.

What could such an identifier represent? In a record structure, it should be the key of a record type, i.e., an "assignee" record type. But if we also wanted to have employees and departments represented in distinct record types, we have a conflict. The type of a record is either "department" or "assignee"; it cannot be both.

Still another drawback of this "supertype" approach is that it has to be reapplied for each different kind of multitype fact (i.e., potentially for each case of vertical inhomogeneity). Entities get aggregated one way for equipment assignment records, another way to keep track of who manufactures what, another way for who owns what, another way as "employers" (which might be people, companies, schools, government agencies, foreign organizations, etc.), perhaps still another way as "taxpayers," and so on. Each of these is potential grounds for another supertype, with its own identifier scheme. This touches on the problem of multiple types for an individual, which we will get to later; the immediate concern is that an individual might become attached to a great many serial numbers, potentially one for each aggregation to which it belonged.

Vertical inhomogeneity can introduce still another record formatting problem. The identifiers involved may differ in more than just length and character set (e.g., numeric vs. alphabetic). There may be differences in "structure," e.g., if qualified naming is involved. Consider a company in which the name of a department is unique within its division, but not necessarily within the company as a whole. Then corporate records would have to refer to a department using two fields: a department name plus a division name (serving as a qualifier for the department). At this point, it is not at all clear how many fields there are in a corporate vehicle assignment record. If assigned to an employee, there are two: vehicle number and employee number. When the assignee is a department, there are three fields: vehicle number, department name, and division name. (If we had to describe this relationship in terms of the relational model, we might have to call it a relation of degree two and a half, on the average.)

To net it all out, the record structure is not well suited to information exhibiting "vertical inhomogeneity." The function required here is equivalent to allowing a single fact (field) to include both a type and value, where the syntax and structure of the value depended on the type.

PRESUMPTIONS UNDERLYING TRADITIONAL IMPLEMENTATIONS

Although not intrinsic to the record structure, a number of features characterize most traditional implementations of record processing systems. These include such things as the separation of descriptions and data, minimal requirements for descriptions, and resistance to changing descriptions.

Descriptions Are Not Information

Information is obtained from a record structure by extracting the values of fields, and it is only field values which supply information. One can answer the question "who manages the Accounting department?" by finding a certain field which contains the manager's name. But it is not likely that the file can provide an answer to "how is Henry Jones related to the Accounting department?" There are no fields in the file containing such entries as "is assigned to," "was assigned to," "on loan to," "manages," "audits," "handles personnel matters for," etc. Depending on how the records are organized, the answer generally consists of a field name or a record type name, which are not contained in the records. To a naive seeker of information from the database (e.g., via a high-level query interface), it is not at all obvious why one question may be asked and the other may not.

It is not just that he cannot get an answer; the interfaces do not provide any way to frame the question. The data management systems do not provide a way to ask such questions whose answers are field names or record type names.

Then consider the following questions:

(1) How many employees are there in the Accounting department?
(2) What is the average number of employees per department?
(3) What is the maximum number of employees currently in any department?
(4) What is the maximum number of employees permitted in any department?
(5) How many more employees can be hired into the Accounting department?

If the maximum number of employees permitted is fixed by corporate policy, then a system offering advanced validation capabilities is likely to place that number into a constraint in a database description, outside the database itself. Our naive seeker of facts will then again find himself unable to ask the last two questions. He might well observe that other things having the effect of rules or constraints are accessible from the database, such as sales quotas, departmental budgets, head counts, safety standards, etc. The only difference, which does not matter much to him, is that some such limits are intended to be enforced by the system, while others are not. It is not at all obvious to him why he can ask some questions and not others.

This suggests that we should represent such descriptions and constraints in the same format—and in the same database—as "ordinary" information, but with the added characteristic that they are intended to be executed and enforced by the data processing system.

There is, of course, an inherent difference between descriptions and other data, with respect to update characteristics. Changes to descriptions imply differences in the system's behavior, ranging from changes in validation procedures to physical file reorganizations implied by format changes. Thus the system has to be aware of, and control, changes to descriptions. But such descriptions need not be inherently different for retrieval purposes. And even with respect to update, the method need not be inherently different as perceived by users. It is only necessary that the authorization to do so be carefully controlled, and that the consequences be propagated into the system. There is already a precedent for such update controls: many implementations forbid the modification of key fields of records.

Some Descriptions Are Not Needed

While such things as field names and record types can be factored out of the data [32], they do not always wind up in the catalogs (record descriptions) either. Sometimes they do not appear anywhere in the data management system at all. Catalogs are maintained primarily for the benefit of the system, not for users, and tend to contain only such information as is needed for the performance of system services. Quite often, only key fields are described, for which the system may provide such services as indexing, ordering, and uniqueness checking. Other fields might only be described in the declarations local to the various application programs, with no assurance that such descriptions are consistent with each other.

One of the major contributions of the relational model is to treat all fields in a record as constructs requiring description to the data management system.

Field Names Are Only Place Holders

When provided at all, field names are used by record management systems only to designate some space within a record. This suffices for the system to provide its services, such as matching keys or sequencing. And, certainly, one name is adequate for this purpose. But for information modeling, we may want to attach several labels to a field, indicating perhaps the kind of entity which may occur there (e.g., "date") and its relationship to the subject of the record— its reason for occurring in the record (e.g., "termination").

In practice, there has been no discipline in the usage of field names. Sometimes they name the entity type, sometimes the relationship, sometimes a hybrid of the two ("termination-date"), sometimes an identifier type ("social security number"), and sometimes nothing intelligible ("code 1," "field *x*"). And even when they do name entity types or relationships, field names are just mnemonic aids to human users, rather than anything which can be used by a system service to establish semantic connections. If the field name specifies the entity type, it is not likely to be the same as the corresponding record type name (while a record type might be named "dept-rec," the corresponding field in an employee record might be named "deptno"). The same entity type might be spelled differently in different field names ("dept," "deptnum," "deptno," etc.). And nothing prevents the same field name from meaning entirely different things in different records.

The relational model does improve on this situation by providing for both "selector" (column) names and "domain" names, but there is still relatively little discipline imposed. Domain names often specify identifier types rather than entity types [19]. Thus "social security number" and "employee number" are likely to be specified as the domains of two fields, giving no clue that the same entity might be named in both places. Even if the domain name identified an entity type, it might or might not be the same name as the record type representing those entities. And domain names give no clue when one entity type is a subset of another; unequal domains appear to be disjoint.

Some implementations of the relational model do not incorporate the domain construct at all.

Stability of Relevant Facts

Another implication of record formats, and of the file plus catalog configuration, is that the kinds of facts relevant to an entity are predefined and are expected to remain quite stable. It generally takes a major effort to add fields to records.

While this may be acceptable and desirable in many cases, there are situations where all sorts of unanticipated information needs to be recorded, and a more flexible data structure is needed.

The need to record information of unanticipated meaning or format is crudely reflected in provisions for "comments" fields or records. These consist of unformatted text, in which system facilities can do little more than search for occurrences of words. Thus ironically, we have the two extremes of rigidly structured and totally unstructured information—but very little in between.

CORRELATION WITH INFORMATION CONCEPTS

For information modeling purposes, one has to account for such concepts as entities and entity types, relationships and attributes, and naming. These are discussed in the following sections.

ENTITIES AND TYPES

There is a natural inclination to identify entities with records, since a record has the sense of being an integral object. It is an elementary unit of creation and destruction, as well as of data transmission, and records are classified into types just as entities are. Such a correspondence between entities and records would be enormously simplifying, giving us information modeling as a free by-product of data management technology.

Arguments against such a modeling approach are hampered by the lack of a good operational definition of the term "entity." But we can suggest some difficulties in reconciling record structures with certain "intuitively obvious" characteristics of entities. Thereafter we can either conclude that records have limited value for information modeling, or else adjust our intuitions about entities in order to get a better fit with record concepts.

The questions which might be asked to test the hypothesis that records represent entities are: How well do their characteristics match? Is there a 1:1 correspondence between them?

A Record Does Not Have All the Facts

Many facts have the form of a relationship between two entities (e.g., a department and an employee). Although it concerns both entities, such a fact is not likely to be replicated in the records representing both entities. At most, it will usually be included in the record of only one of the entities involved.

Quite often the fact will not occur in the record corresponding to either one. If the fact is a many-to-many relationship, such as employees and their skills, then normalized record systems do not permit the necessary repeating field to occur in either the employee record or the skill record. Normalized systems constrain a record to be a collection of single-valued facts. If a class has one instructor, then that can be mentioned in the class record, but not if there might be several instructors.

Thus a record cannot be characterized as containing "all the facts" about an entity.

Entities Are Not Always Single-Typed

If we intend to use a record to represent a real world entity, there is some difficulty in equating record types with entity types. It seems reasonable to view a certain person as a single entity (for whom we might wish to have a single record in an integrated database). But such an entity might be an instance of several entity types, such as person, employee, dependent, customer, stockholder, taxpayer, parent, instructor, student, mammal, physical object, property (slaves?), etc. it is difficult, within the current record processing technologies, to define a record type corresponding to each of these, and then permit a single record to simultaneously be an occurrence of several of the record types.

Note that we are not dealing with a simple nesting of types and subtypes: all employees are people, but some customers and stockholders are not. Nor are subtypes mutually exclusive: some people are employees, some are stockholders, and some are both.

In order to fit comfortably into a record-based discipline, we need to perceive entity types as though they did not overlap. We should perhaps think of customers and employees as always distinct entities, sometimes related by an "is the same person" relationship. But we then have to make arbitrary decisions about the placement of common information such as addresses and birthdates. Furthermore, one has to be very careful about the number of entities being modeled. If an employee is a stockholder, there will be two records for him; is he two entities? If a committee has five employees and five stockholders, how big is the committee?

(Bachman and Daya [4] and Smith and Smith [40] propose models in which multiple records can represent the multiple types, or roles, of an entity.)

Type Is Not Always Homogeneous

Even within a single type, there may be facts and naming conventions which are relevant to some occurrences and not others. These points were covered in the earlier discussion of horizontal homogeneity.

Entities Without Records

Most of the things mentioned in a database do not have any distinct records to represent them. These are the things we treat as attributes of other things, such as salaries, colors, birthdates, birthplaces, employers, spouses, addresses, etc. (While such things may be mentioned in multiple records, I do not think we can say they are "represented" by any one record.) Unfortunately, apart from the listing of examples, it is difficult to identify precise criteria for deciding whether something is an entity, and whether it is to be represented by a record.

In a normalized system, an entity might also fail to be represented by a single record if there did not happen to be any single-valued information about the entity. Suppose one had in mind to treat projects as entities, but all the information to be maintained about them turned out to be multivalued (in relational terms, we find no functional dependences on projects). That is, our projects can have multiple managers, multiple objectives, multiple start and stop dates, multiple budgets, and so on. Each such fact needs to be maintained in a distinct intersection record, and there might be no motivation to define a single record type or relation to represent the projects themselves. One would have record types (relations) called "project-manager," "project-objective," "project-dates," and so on, but none called simply "project."

Entities With Many Records

We might have too many records. As mentioned earlier, a common solution to the problem of overlapping types (e.g., employees and stockholders) is to define them as disjoint types, and allowing an entity (person) to be represented by a record in each type.

The "generalization" approach of Smith and Smith [40] yields multiple records per entity; it is not clear that any one of them could be said to "represent" the entity. The approach of Bachman and Daya [4] is similar in this respect, but they do postulate one underlying record (never materialized) per entity.

More generally, there is no discipline preventing the definition of several record types corresponding to one entity type. That is, we could have several record types defined over the same key, with each record type containing different attributes of the subject entity. One might be tempted to do this for economic reasons, e.g., to group together attributes which tend to be accessed together, or to physically segregate rarely used data. Regardless of the motivation, such a configuration is permitted in all record-based systems. Thus none of these systems really has a well-defined semantic establishing a 1:1 correspondence between entities and records.

Records Without Entities

Normalized systems require many-to-many facts to be represented in distinct record types of their own (so-called intersection records). Employee-skill records are a good example. What entity does one of these records represent? Not the employee, nor the skill. If it represents anything at all, the record represents the *relationship* between the employee and the skill. This might suggest the principle that relationships are entities, and ought in general to be represented by records. But some relationships are not represented by records, e.g., the relationship between an employee and his department. (That relationship is recorded in an employee record, but not represented by a distinct record of its own.) Obviously, it is only the many-to-many relationships which must be represented by distinct records (in a normalized system); are they the only ones which are entities?

There are three ways to take a consistent view of this situation:

(1) All relationships are entities, and some records represent multiple entities (as the same record "represents" both an employee and his relationship to a department).
(2) Relationships are not entities, and intersection records do not represent entities.
(3) Some relationships are entities and some are not depending on whether or not they are represented by intersection records.

It is a matter of judgment as to whether any of these views is acceptable.

Depending on what definitions we like, some intersection records might not even represent relationships. You might wish to consider the color of a car to be an attribute, and not a relationship. But if cars are multicolored, then their colors must be split out into separate car/color intersection records. Does the attribute now become a relationship? Is it an entity? What entity does the record represent?

If we do not care to think of such multivalued attributes as being entities in themselves, then we again have records which do not represent entities.

Records With Many Entities

If there is a 1:1 correspondence between certain entities, then a single record might be perceived as "representing" all of them. Employees and spouses provide an example, in a monogamous society. Since each spouse occurs in exactly one employee record, one could view these records as representing spouses just as well as employees. The perception is even more plausible if the spouses are uniquely identified (as they might be, by social security number), and if they occurred in every record (if, perhaps, company policy required all employees to be married).

Summary

"Entity" is not very well defined, for our purposes. To be absolutely fair, we should only conclude that record structures do not correspond to everyone's intuitions about the characteristics of entities. But it is quite difficult to establish a definition of "entity" which puts it in 1:1 correspondence with a normalized record, unless one starts with that as the definition.

RELATIONSHIPS

One Concept, Many Representations

A binary relationship is a fairly simple concept: a named link between two entities. But there are about a half dozen ways to implement binary relationships in record structures. (Schmid and Swenson [31] make a similar analysis.)

Most of these ways to implement binary relationships involve pairing identifiers of the two entities in one record. It might be in the record representing one entity or the other. It might be in a separate record (intersection record) representing the relationship itself. And it might be embedded in a record representing some other entity altogether (an employee record may include a relationship between the employee's spouse and the spouse's employer).

These alternatives correspond to several combinations in which the two entity identifiers might occur as keys in a record. One or the other might be the key, or they might together constitute the key, or neither might be in the key.

(Actually, there are other possibilities as well. One identifier or the other might be a subset of the key, which probably violates third normal form. Or they might together constitute a subset of the key, in which case they might be part of a compound name—to be discussed later. Or they might each constitute a key for the record, if there was a 1:1 relationship between them.)

In addition, a relationship might be represented indirectly, being implied by other relationships. If projects are assigned to single departments, and if each employee works on all of his department's projects, then the way to discover if an employee works on a certain project is to match the department numbers in the employee and project records. That is, an employee's assignment to a department and a project's assignment to the department together imply the employee's working on the project.

In record management systems which provide file structure in addition to record structure, even more options become available. Relationships might be represented by file order, or by the linkage of records into hierarchies or (CODASYL) sets.

For information modeling, the problem is what to do with this plethora of options [12, 26]. Why is it necessary to make such choices? What are the criteria? Do the criteria have anything to do with the semantics of the information, as distinguished from the economics of storing or processing the data? Do all users have to know which options have been chosen, and to adapt their processing accordingly?

Normalized systems reduce the number of options for one-to-many and many-to-many relationships, and generally force them to be treated differently from each other. (But not necessarily; one-to-many relationships can be represented in separate intersection records, though they hardly ever are.) Some differences force the information modeler to prematurely impose processing techniques on end users: one-to-many relationships can often be altered by updating field values, while many-to-many relationships in intersection records can only be altered by deleting and inserting records.

Relationships Are Not Described

The various representations available for relationships are often used for other purposes as well. Thus record descriptions rarely provide clear evidence of the presence of relationships—neither explicitly nor implicitly. A record with multi-field keys might represent a relationship, or the keys might constitute a qualified name for an entity. If neither field is in the key (e.g., spouse and spouse's employer), there is no mention at all of the relationship; the two fields appear to be independent facts about the employee.

There is no regular way to reflect the name of the relationship in the file description. Sometimes it is a record type name (intersection records), sometimes it is a field name (or a part of one), and sometimes it does not occur at all (e.g., implied relationships, or joins). When file structure is available, the relationship name might also be a (CODASYL) set name or, again, it might not occur at all if represented by file order or hierarchical structure.

And, when the relationship names do occur as field names, there is no discipline. There is rarely any clue in the field name (or even in a relational domain name, if provided) as to the record type representing the related entity. Consider a generalized query processor asked to find the name of the manager of a certain department. The department record probably has a field named MANAGER (perhaps with a domain named EMPLOYEE NUMBER). What tells the processor to look into a record type named EMP-RECS to find the name of the employee whose number occurs in that field?

Sometimes the field name combines the relationship and the entity type ("assigned-dept").

The same field name might signify the same or different relationships in different records, and different names might be used for the same relationship in different records. Since field names cannot be duplicated within a record, a relationship occurring more than once in a given record necessarily has different names (in a credit application, "employer" and "spouse's-employer" refer to occurrences of the same relationship).

In a good model for relationships, one might expect some direct way to declare relationships, specifying a name and some characteristics, without having to choose among a variety of (ambiguous) representational alternatives.

Attributes

There does not seem to be an effective way to characterize "attributes," or to distinguish them from relationships. Ironically, the most dominant correlate seems to be with record structures: if a field value is the key of some other record, then it represents a relationship; otherwise it is an attribute. This need to map things into recordlike terms seems to be the main force motivating a distinction between attributes and relationships. If we did not have a record-based implementation in mind, the distinction might go away [35].

NAMING, SYMBOLIC REFERENCE

In a pure record structure, most facts (relationships, attributes) are represented by including in one record symbolic identifiers of two or more things (e.g., employee number and department number, or employee number and salary) [32]. Such symbolic reference admits references to nonexistent entities (entities whose corresponding records are missing). Symbolic reference forces a strong interaction between the concepts of identifier and entity type, and encounters problems with synonyms and with changeable names.

When simple labels are not conveniently available, the record model permits arbitrary combinations of facts to be specified as identifiers capable of distinguishing among entity occurrences. This, in turn, leads to further problems, unless a number of constraints on the selected facts are carefully observed. Furthermore, in using such identifiers to refer to entities, multiple fields serve the function of a single field—generating ambiguities in the structure of the information represented by the record.

Simple Identifiers

To the extent that a record represents an entity (i.e., signifies its existence), symbolic reference permits references to nonexistent entities. A department number can occur in an employee record even if no corresponding department record exists. At best, there might be some check that the field contains a "plausible" department name, in terms of its syntax: the right number of the right kinds of characters. (In the proposals of Schmid and Swenson [31] and Smith and Smith [39] such existence dependences can be expressed and maintained.)

When arbitrary identifiers are assigned, such as employee numbers, then there is little question of uniqueness of identifier. But when some fact about the entity is given double duty as an identifying label for that entity, one has to be quite careful that the fact does, in fact, uniquely determine the entity. Presidential elections can be identified by the year in which they occur—provided we are absolutely certain there is no possible circumstance under which another presidential election might be held in the same year.

Symbolic identifiers rarely provide absolute identification of entities. At best, the identifiers are unique within entity type. One cannot tell which entity is being referenced just by examining a field value; one has to have supplementary knowledge as to which entity type is involved. Nothing in the data tells us whether 123456789 identifies a person or a machine. Such information is almost never included with the data, nor with the record description. That is, a field description rarely specifies the entity type, or record type, whose keys will occur in that field. The domain construct of the relational model provides limited assistance in this area, as mentioned in the earlier discussion of field names.

In a pure record structure (one with no pointers or other file structure interconnecting the records), the only way to detect a reference to the same thing in several records is to find a match in some corresponding field values. (For example, that is the basis of the relational join.) Synonyms and aliases interfere with this process. At best, one could execute a chain of path-following operations, if one knew which record types provided which synonym linkages. That is the only way to detect that, e.g., a social security number in one record referred to the same person as an employee number in another record.

There are often several *kinds* of identifiers by which an entity can be identified uniquely, such as employee numbers and social security numbers. One now has to know not only which entity type is being referenced in the field, but also which kind of identifier is being used. And one has to know which other record type to go to in order to "translate" one name type into the other.

In an obvious way, the extent of an entity type affects the choice of identifier. Facts which are unique over a small set of entities may not be unique over a larger set.

Presidential elections in one country can be identified simply by the year of occurrence. But if the entity type were perceived as a larger set of elections, then the identification would have to include additional facts, such as the office (governor, mayor, etc.) and political unit involved (name of the country, state, city, etc.).

In a converse way, identifiers can affect the perception of entity types. In order to provide record keys, it is often necessary to arbitrarily choose one kind of identifier as a "primary" identifier for an entity. Two constraints then impose boundaries on entity types: a key value is meaningful within exactly one record type, and each record of the type must contain a key value. That is, key values must be in 1:1 correspondence with the set of entities represented, and the tendency is to think of a set as an entity type if it corresponds to the scope of a unique identifier. Unfortunately, different kinds of identifiers may have overlapping but unequal scopes, leading to conflicting choices of entity types. Employee numbers, social security numbers, military service numbers, etc., each identify different sets of people, each leading to a different concept of the "entity type" involved. When identified by ISBN's, books constitute a different entity type from films. When identified by Library of Congress numbers, they are all publications. Thus in general, the varying scopes of identifiers can have an excessive and potentially confusing influence on the establishment of entity types. If names were not tied so intimately to types, it might be possible to deal with types more naturally.

The tight coupling between types and names forces vertical homogeneity, i.e., the inability to represent facts which involve multiple entity types. The name formats are likely to be different between types; when the formats are the same, names might not be unique across types.

Sometimes an entity can have multiple identifiers of the *same* kind. A person can have several social security numbers, and a book might have several ISBN's. Names and addresses can be spelled and abbreviated in a variety of ways. Again, it becomes harder to detect references to the same entity when different identifiers are used. (Consider the difficulty of purging duplicates out of a mailing list.) Furthermore, these identifiers cannot all occur in the record which represents the entity (assuming normalized records), and they certainly cannot all be keys of the record. At most, one of them has to be arbitrarily selected as the primary identifier. For the others, a new intersection record type has to be defined, with each such record "translating" one secondary identifier into a primary identifier. Now, if some record contains a secondary identifier, it is necessary to know that the field is not a key into the entity record type, but must first be translated via the intersection records. If the field might contain either primary or secondary identifiers, then the retrieval algorithm is even more complex. (And, incidentally, one might ask what entities are being represented by the intersection records. They are a distinct record type from the one representing the entities. Their keys are the secondary identifiers, with a separate record for each one, hence several records per entity.)

Sometimes the identifier chosen for an entity is not, strictly speaking, the name of that entity, but of a related entity. This practice can confuse the underlying semantic structure of the information. Many facts are available, for example, about elections. One might reasonably expect to ask, in a symmetric way, who won Election No. 10 and when Election No. 10 was held. But if elections are named by their dates, e.g., the "1948 election," it suddenly becomes absurd to ask when it was held. Strictly speaking, we are dealing with an unnamed entity being identified by means of a related entity, but the record descriptions give no hint of this structure. (If it disturbs you to think of a year as being a related entity, then imagine that presidents could only be elected once, and we therefore named elections by their winners. Then it becomes equally absurd to ask who won the "Truman election," although it is meaningful to ask who lost it, and when it occurred.)

Another way to see the semantic problem is in terms of functional dependences. On an entity level, an election uniquely determines its date and its winner, and hence dates and winners ought to be functionally dependent on elections. But if the relation representing this information contains only a date column and a winner column, then there is no way to express these two functional dependences. In effect, the existence of three distinct entities is not acknowledged in any way. This is one respect in which relations and functional dependences do not mirror relationships among entities.

And, finally, it is not sufficient for a fact to uniquely identify an entity. In order to be useful in a record structure, it had better be an unchangeable fact. It is highly undesirable to have to change that fact in every place where the entity is referenced. Thus while a phone number might uniquely determine an office at any given moment, it is not a good way to identify offices if the phones tend to be moved around.

Compound Identifiers

All of these concerns—and more—apply when compound facts are used to identify entities in records.

We use for an example the identification of dependents of employees, perhaps for a benefits database. Names of dependents are certainly not unique, but we might assume that no employee has two dependents with the same name. Then a dependent could be identified by the combination of his name and the related employee's identifier (as in [8]). (We will refer to that related employee as the "sponsor.")

To begin with, the concerns about uniqueness, existence, synonyms, scope, and changeability must be examined more carefully, because there are more facts involved.

We are depending on the uniqueness of names of one employee's dependents, which might be a questionable assumption if the employee has adopted children, or has remarried, or if the employee's parents, grandchildren, siblings, etc. also qualified as dependents in addition to his children. More simply, his child and spouse might have the same name.

In references to the dependent from other records we have, as before, no assurance that the dependent record itself exists. But a second level of existence dependence is now introduced. In order for the dependent's identification to be meaningful, there must be some assurance that the sponsor's employee record also exists.

Synonyms can easily arise, if a dependent was related to more than one employee. The dependent has as many valid identifiers as he has sponsors. A compound identifier thus need not even be restricted to a many-to-one relationship. If all we are after is the ability to select dependents, then all we need is that no employee have two dependents with the same name. The relationship could be many-to-many.

This gives us a one-way uniqueness. A qualified name identifies exactly one dependent, but we cannot tell whether two qualified names might refer to the same dependent. If two employees had a dependent named "Joe," what indicates whether it is the same dependent? Special pains must be taken to detect that the dependents of several employees might be the same person, in order to properly coordinate benefits. A separate "translation" record type is now needed to establish the equivalences between identifiers. (And the synonym problem is compounded if the sponsors themselves have synonyms.)

It is possible to designate one identifier (involving one sponsor) as the "primary" identifier of the dependent. But it may be necessary in some situations to permit any identifier to be used, requiring a search of both the translation records and the dependent records. Furthermore, this leads to a potential violation of the constancy requirement: a dependent's primary sponsor will change if that sponsor leaves the company but the dependent is still related to other employees. Then all references to that dependent have to be modified. In fact, it is probably not a good idea to use employees to qualify dependent names in an implementation which forbids modification of record keys.

Scope of identifiers is, of course, still a crucial concern. The facts chosen for the compound name must be relevant and known for all occurrences of the entity type being identified. For example, if the company charitably expanded its benefits program to provide aid to all needy people in the community, then some recipients would not have any related employee to use in their identifiers. Some other form of identification would have to be devised.

So far, all these problems of compound names have just been extensions of similar problems which existed for simple names. A whole new set of problems derives from the fact that compound names force an entity to be referenced by multiple fields in a record.

There is a three-way ambiguity. Multiple fields in a record are used to represent three distinct semantic constructs: the compound name of an entity, a relationship among entities, or multiple independent facts about an entity.

Spurious Joins. The resemblance between compound names and independent facts can lead to "phantom entities" and spurious joins. Whenever an employee number and a person's name occur in any two fields of a record, this could be construed as the compound identifier of a dependent. In particular, a relational join can be performed over such fields.

An employee's name and his manager's employee number, in one record, could be matched up with a customer's name and his salesman's employee number in another record, in the mistaken belief that such pairs of fields constituted qualified names for the same person. More simply, a dependent record might include another employee number field besides his sponsor (e.g., a benefits administrator); a join could be done on the wrong employee field, mistaking this person for a dependent of that other employee (who might not even have any dependents).

The domain concept in the relational model is supposed to control joinability. In relational theory, joins may only be performed on columns based on the same domains, presumably assuring that the same entity is occurring on both sides as a "link." The problem is that relations are fundamentally defined as aggregations of single columns, each column based on a domain. There is no concept of a domain encompassing multiple columns, although entities may be identified by multiple columns. The domain concept cannot be applied in such a way that two columns in a relation must always be treated as a unit, and may only be joined with other pairs of columns defined to constitute similar units. In the current example, the two fields might have separate domains specified as "employee number" and "person name"; there is no place to establish "dependents" as a domain. And even if the second domain was specified as "dependent name," it still could be paired with any other employee number in the same record.

Thus domains do not readily correspond to entity types, when the entities are identified by compound names.

Reducibility Dilemma. The resemblance between compound names and independent facts leads to a dilemma in the theory of reducible relations [15, 16, 19, 29].

Consider a person's birthday. On the face of it, this is an elementary (irreducible) fact—a simple binary relationship between a person and a certain day in the past. And, if we happen to represent dates in Julian notation (one field), then birthday actually has the structure of an elementary fact. But if we choose to change the *naming* of the date to the more conventional notation involving three fields, then we have a record containing four fields. This record can now be reduced to three binary records: person and year, person and month; and person and day of month. The original birthday record can always be recovered by joining these three.

The same analysis, and ambiguity, applies whenever a composite naming convention is selected for an entity. City of birth, for example, is an irreducible fact if globally unique city codes are used; it is reducible if the city is identified by the composite of, e.g., city, state, and country names.

Composite names are in general *not* precisely equivalent in function to simple unique identifiers for the same entities. Composite names almost always convey additional information; when used in lieu of simple names they necessarily change the underlying structure of the information. A simple name simply designates an entity; a composite name does that, but it simultaneously informs us about other related entities. A city code simply designates a city; the conventional notation may additionally tell us the state and country in which it is located. A Julian date simply designates a certain day (if we do not bother to do certain computations); the conventional notation additionally tells us the year and month in which it occurred, as well as the day of the month. In the role of designating a single entity, a compound name could be part of an irreducible fact; in the role of providing auxiliary information about related entities, it leads to reducibility.

Confusion of Subject. The resemblance between compound names and relationships confuses the subject matter of a record, namely the question of what entity is being represented by a record. A record having employee number and dependent name as a compound key might be a dependent record (representing a dependent), or it might be an intersection record representing the relationship between an employee and a dependent. In the first case, it would be appropriate to include the dependent's age in the record, since that is a fact about the dependent:

EMPLOYEE-NUM	DEPENDENT-NAME	AGE

.... key ....

In the second case, the record might specify the kinship between the dependent and the employee:

EMPLOYEE-NUM	DEPENDENT-NAME	KINSHIP

.... key ....

The first fact is really about the dependent alone, while the second is about the relationship between the dependent and an employee. But the structure of the two in "irreducible" form is indistinguishable. Thus if naming conventions are not separated from entity representation, "irreducible" records still do not model the structure of information unambiguously. (To see the significance, compare what happens to the preceding two structures if dependents were named simply, e.g., by social security numbers.)

In unreduced records, a composite key is likely to be serving both roles simultaneously. It would not be unusual to see the two records shown above combined into one (since they have the same key), containing both age (a fact about the dependent) and kinship (a fact about the relationship). It is thus ambiguous as to which entity is really represented by this record.

Ironically, although "intersection records" are commonly accepted as the construct which represents many-to-many relationships, it is, in fact, hard to know which records are serving as intersection records.

Surrogates

A precise model of information should distinguish carefully between the structure of entities being modeled and the various structures of names which might be associated with them. This implies a distinction in the model between entities and traditional data items.

Some alternative models suggest that some sort of an internal construct be used to represent an entity, acting as a "surrogate" for it [1, 19]. This surrogate would occur in data structures wherever the entity is referenced, and naming problems would at least be isolated by keeping structured or ambiguous identifiers off to one side, outside the structures representing attributes and relationships.

Since these surrogates must eventually be implemented inside the computer in some form of symbol string, it is sometimes held that such surrogates are themselves nothing but symbolic identifiers.

It is useful to be aware of some fundamental differences between surrogates and ordinary identifiers:

(1) A surrogate might not be exposed to users. Only ordinary identifiers need pass between user and system. In concept, models involving surrogates can behave as though a fact (e.g., the assignment of an employee to a department) was treated in two stages. First, the surrogates corresponding to the employee and department identifiers are located (i.e., name resolution). Then the two surrogates are placed in association with each other, to represent the fact.

(2) Users do not specify the format, syntax, structure, uniqueness rules, etc. for surrogates.

(3) Surrogates are globally unique, and have the same format for all entities. The system does not have to know the entity type (or the identifier type) before knowing which entity is being referenced, or before knowing what the surrogate format will be.

(4) Surrogates are purely information-free. They do not imply anything about any related entities, nor any kind of meaningful ordering.

SEMANTIC STRUCTURE AND THIRD NORMAL FORM

In the absence of any additional discipline, it is difficult to guess the semantic structure implied by a record format. A given field might include multiple facts by encoding, or with internal punctuation. A given fact might occur in any of several fields: in one of our example vehicle assignment records, the assignee would occur in the third field of some records and the fourth field of other records. A given field might give information about different things in different records: a clever programmer might design a single "maiden name" field to refer either to an employee or to the employee's spouse, depending on which was female. In general, the possibility of tricks such as these obscures the underlying semantic structure.

The semantic structure suggested by a relation under the discipline of third normal form [11, 20] is one in which each record represents a single "subject" entity (identified by the key), with the other fields being "direct" facts about the subject entity. That is, the nonkey fields are functionally dependent on the key, and there are no other functional dependences.

There are some difficulties here also. In the first place, the role of functional dependences in relational theory is unclear, at least as reflected in implementations. The assumption tends to be that functional dependences (if specified at all) have been used during the design phase of the database to insure that relations are in third normal form, and then discarded. They do not seem to be present at run time to explain the semantic structure of the data.

Secondly, functional dependences deal only with 1:*n* relationships and not *m*:*n* relationships. However, some recent work [14] offers extensions into this area.

Thirdly, functional dependences merely specify dependences without naming the relationships involved. Thus, e.g., it cannot be determined whether several functional dependences (between different pairs of columns) are based on the same relationship. Consider, for example, a credit application record containing the applicant, employer, spouse, and spouse's employer. Functional dependences give no clue that the same relationship exists between the first and second columns as between the third and fourth.

Furthermore, third normal form allows several keys to remain in the same relation, even if they identify different entities. This can occur when entities are in a 1:1 relationship, as with employees and spouses. One of the keys is typically selected as "primary," which can suggest that only one entity (e.g., the employee) is the subject of the record. If functional dependences are discarded after the database design phase, there is nothing left to dispel this illusion. The remaining structure implies, for example, that "spouse's birthdate" is not an attribute of the spouse, but only of the employee. The structure is vulnerable to update anomalies, with the implication that the "spouse" and "spouse's birthdate" attributes of an employee may be updated independently of each other.

Still another concern is that it may not be possible to model the *attributes* of 1:*n* and 1:1 relationships, because only "full" functional dependences are considered in the determination of third normal form. A full functional dependence is based on the "smallest" possible subject which determines the related fact. Thus while the relationship between an employee and his department may have an assignment-date attribute, that date is not "fully" dependent on both employee and department. There is only one (current) assignment date for each employee, and hence that date has a full functional dependence on the employee alone. (That is, knowing the employee is sufficient to determine the date.) To the extent that only full dependences are considered, functional dependences distort the semantic structure of information. Attributes of 1:*n* and 1:1 relationships are always transformed into attributes of one of the related entities. Only the attributes of *m*:*n* relationships are preserved in functional dependences.

Finally, the most serious concern is that functional dependences are expressed on the name level rather than the entity level. One consequence is the failure to model the existence of entities whose names are given to other entities (as in the earlier example of elections named via years or winners).

Another consequence is that dependences are only expressed when the subjects are uniquely named. In the example of employees and spouses, functional dependences on the spouses would only be expressed if the spouses were uniquely named (as by social security number). In the more common case, no functional dependences could be written, since the same spouse *name* might occur in different records with different birthdates, employers, etc. Spouses would not in any way be designated as the subjects of any information, or as candidate keys. (We could uniquely identify spouses by the combination of spouse name and employee number, as a qualified name. But functional dependences based on this pair of fields would not be full dependences, since the attributes—such as "spouse's birthdate"—are uniquely determined by employee number alone. As mentioned earlier, such nonfull dependences are discarded in the determination of third normal form.)

Because of the dependence on naming, a large number of relationships in a typical database fail to be reflected in functional dependences, and hence fail to be subject to the discipline of third normal form. In a personnel file, attributes of such things as previous employers, banks, schools, relatives, etc. tend to be duplicated by embedding in multiple employee records. The functional dependence between a school and its address could not be specified, because several schools might have the same name. Hence, if several employees attended the same school, the address of that school might be included in each employee's record, without violating third normal form. All such cases are exposed to the update anomalies which third normal form is supposed to prevent.

A special case of this problem is not only tolerated but in fact encouraged by the relational model. Compound keys, in which the name of an entity includes the name of a related entity, plainly constitute a replication of information, thereby violating the spirit if not the letter of third normal form.

Consider an earlier example, where departments were uniquely named only within divisions, so that company records had to use a compound of department name qualified by division name. On the entity level, a department uniquely determines its division (a given department is, after all, in only one division). But on the name level, a department name does *not* uniquely determine the corresponding division—that is precisely why qualification is needed in the first place. Hence no functional dependence can be written here, even though there is a many-to-one relationship between the entities involved.

A department's division is mentioned in every record which references that department. If the division of a department changes, that single fact must be changed wherever that department is mentioned—precisely what third normal form should avoid.

There is a pragmatic solution. The update problem is best dealt with by legislating it away: forbid the update of keys. This is common in most implementations, though not a formal part of relational theory.

Third normal form is very sensitive to naming conventions. Giving departments globally unique identifiers would represent no real change in the semantic structure of the information. But a functional dependence could now be written between departments and divisions, and the records in question would no longer be in third normal form.

To conclude: records in third normal form can include a great many relationships which are not suggested at all in the record descriptions, even in the form of functional dependences.

CONCLUSIONS

We have outlined a number of ways in which record structures fail to model the semantics of information accurately and unambiguously. Other models deal with these problems, with varying degrees of success. A discussion of such alternatives is generally beyond the scope of this paper.

Just briefly, we can observe that file structures (hierarchies, CODASYL sets) overcome some functional limitations, but by increasing rather than decreasing the variety of representational alternatives. Bachman and Daya [4] and Smith and Smith [40] address some of the problems of types, but still in a record-based framework. Binary relation (or "elementary fact") models are generally more successful in coping with the modeling problems, though none have done so completely. Such models are more directly based on semantic concepts, e.g., entities and the network of relationships among them, rather than on recordlike structures. The model described by Biller and Neuhold [5] is excellent in this respect. Other models along these lines include the works (referenced below) of Abrial, Bracchi, Falkenberg, Griffith, Hall, Roussopoulos, Schmid, Senko, and Sowa.

ACKNOWLEDGMENTS

Many people made valuable comments on earlier versions of this paper, including Chris Date, Bob Engles, Bob Griffith, Roger Holliday, Lucy Lee, and especially Paula Newman, who suggested some of the ideas. I am also deeply indebted to the referees, especially Mike Senko, who instigated major improvements in the paper.

REFERENCES

1. Abrial, J.R. Data semantics. In *Data Base Management,* J. W. Klimbie and K. L. Koffeman, Eds., North-Holland Pub. Co., Amsterdam, 1974.
2. ANSI/X3/SPARC. Study Group on Data Base Management Systems. Interim Rep., Feb. 1975; also FDT (Bulletin of ACM SIGMOD) *7,* 2 (1975).
3. The ANSI/X3/SPARC DBMS Framework. Report of the Study Group on Data Base Management Systems, D. Tsichritzis and A. Klug, Eds., AFIPS Press, Montvale, N.J., 1977.
4. Bachman, C.W., and Daya, M. The role concept in data models. Proc. Third Int. Conf. Very Large Data Bases, Database (ACM) *9,* 2 (Fall 1977), SIGMOD Record (ACM) *9,* 4 (Oct. 1977), 464–476.
5. Biller, H., and Neuhold, E.J. Semantics of data bases: The semantics of data models. *Inform. Syst. 3,* 1 (1978).
6. Bracchi, G., Paolini, P., and Pelagatti, G. Binary logical associations in data modeling. In *Modelling in Data Base Management Systems,* G. M. Nijssen, Ed., North-Holland Pub. Co., Amsterdam, 1976.
7. Chamberlin, D.D. Relational data base management systems. *ACM Comptng. Surveys 8,* 1 (March 1976), 43–66.
8. Chen. P.P.S. The entity-relationship model: Toward a unified view of data. *ACM Trans. Database Syst. 1,* 1 (March 1976), 9–36.
9. Codd, E.F. A relational model of data for large shared data banks. *Comm. ACM 13,* 6 (June 1970), 377–387.
10. Codd, E.F. Normalized data base structure: A brief tutorial. ACM SIGFIDET Workshop on Data Description, Access, and Control, San Diego, Nov. 1971, pp. 1–18.
11. Codd, E.F. Further normalization of the data base relational model. In *Data Base Systems* Courant Computer Science Symposia 6, R. Rustin, Ed., Prentice-Hall, Englewood Cliffs, N.J., 1972; also IBM Res. Rep. RJ909.
12. Codd, E.F., and Date, C.J. Interactive support for non-programmers: The relational and network approaches. ACM SIGMOD Workshop on Data Description, Access, and Control (Vol. 2), May 1974, pp. 11–41; also IBM Res. Rep. RJ1400.
13. Date, C.J. *An Introduction to Database Systems,* Addison-Wesley, Reading, Mass., Second ed., 1977.
14. Fagin, R. Multivalued dependencies and a new normal form for relational databases. *ACM Trans. Database Syst. 2,* 3 (Sept. 1977), 262–278; also IMB Res. Rep. RJ1812.
15. Falkenberg, E. Concepts for modelling information. In *Modelling in Data Base Management Systems,* G. M. Nijssen, Ed., North-Holland Pub. Co., Amsterdam, 1976.
16. Falkenberg, E. Significations: The key to unify data base management. *Inform. Syst. 2,* 1 (1976), 19–28.
17. Griffith, R.L. Information structures. IBM Tech. Rep. TR03.013, IBM, San Jose, Calif., May 1976.
18. Data Base Management System Requirements. Joint Guide-Share Data Base Requirements Group, Nov. 1970.
19. Hall, P.A.V., Owlett, J., and Todd, S.J.P. Relations and entities. In *Modelling in Data Base Management Systems,* G.M. Nijssen, Ed., North-Holland Pub. Co., Amsterdam, 1976.
20. Kent, W. A primer of normal forms. Tech. Rep. TR02.600, IBM, San Jose, Calif., Dec. 1973.
21. Kent, W. New criteria for the conceptual model. In *Systems for Large Data Bases,* P. C. Lockemann and E. J. Neuhold, Eds., North-Holland Pub. Co., Amsterdam, 1977.
22. Kent, W. Entities and relationships in information. In *Architecture and Models in Data Base Management Systems,* G.M. Nijssen, Ed., North-Holland Pub. Co., Amsterdam, 1977.
23. Kerschberg, L., Ozkarahan, E.A., and Pacheco, J.E.S. A synthetic English query language for a relational associative processor. Proc. Second Int. Conf. Software Eng., San Francisco, 1976, pp. 505–519.
24. Klimbie, J.W., and Koffeman, K.L., Eds. *Data Base Management,* North-Holland Pub. Co., Amsterdam, 1974. (Proc. IFIP Working Conf. Data Base Management, Cargese, Corsica, France, April 1974.)
25. Lockemann, P.C., and Neuhold, E.J., Eds. *Systems for Large Data Bases,* North-Holland Pub. Co., Amsterdam, 1977. (Proc. Second Int. Conf. Very Large Data Bases, Sept. 1976, Brussels.)
26. Nijssen, G.M. Two major flaws in the CODASYL DDL 1973 and proposed corrections. *Inform. Syst. 1* (1975), 115–132.
27. Nijssen, G.M. *Modelling in Data Base Management Systems,* North-Holland Pub. Co., Amsterdam, 1976. (Proc. IFIP TC-2 Working Conf., Freudenstadt, W. Germany, Jan. 1976.)
28. Nijssen, G.M. *Architecture and Models in Data Base Management Systems,* North-Holland Pub. Co., Amsterdam, 1977. (Proc. IFIP TC-2 Working Conf., Nice, France, Jan. 1977.)
29. Rissanen, J., and Delobel, C. Decomposition of files, a basis for data storage and retrieval. IBM Res. Rep. RJ1220, IBM Res. Lab., San Jose, Calif., May 1973.
30. Roussopoulos, N., and Mylopoulus, J. Using semantic networks for data base management. Proc. Int. Conf. Very Large Data Bases, 1975, pp. 144–172. (available from ACM, New York)
31. Schmid, H.A., and Swenson, J.R. On the semantics of the relational model. Proc. ACM SIGMOD Int. Conf. Manage. of Data, 1975, pp. 211–223.
32. Senko, M.E., Altman, E.B., Astrahan, M.M., and Fehder, P.L. Data structures and accessing in data base systems. *IBM Syst. J. 12* (1973), 30–93.
33. Senko, M.E. The DDL in the context of a multilevel structured description: DIAM II with FORAL. In *Data Base Description,* B.C.M. Douque and G. M. Nijssen, Eds., North-Holland Pub. Co., Amsterdam, 1975, pp. 239–257; also IBM Res. Rep. RC5073.
34. Senko, M.E. Information systems: Records, relations, sets, entities, and things. *Inform. Syst. 1,*

1 (1975), 1–13.

35. SENKO, M.E. DIAM as a detailed example of the ANSI SPARC architecture. In *Modelling in Data Base Management Systems,* G. M. Nijssen, Ed., North-Holland Pub. Co., Amsterdam, 1976.
36. SHARMAN, G.C.H. A new model of relational data base and high level languages. Tech. Rep. TR. 12.136, IBM United Kingdom, Feb. 1975.
37. ACM SIGFIDET Workshop on Data Description, Access, and Control, Nov. 1971, San Diego, Calif., E. F. Codd and A. L. Dean, Eds.
38. ACM SIGMOD International Conference on Management of Data, May 1975, San Jose, Calif., W. F. King, Ed.
39. SMITH, J.M., AND SMITH, D.C.P. Database abstractions: Aggregation. *Comm. ACM 20,* 6 (June 1977), 405–413.
40. SMITH, J.M., AND SMITH, D.C.P. Database abstractions: Aggregation and generalization. *ACM Trans. Database Syst. 2,* 2 (June 1977), 105–133.
41. SOWA, J.F. Conceptual graphs for a data base interface. *IBM J. Res. and Develop. 20,* 4 (July 1976), 336–357.
42. TAYLOR, R.W., AND FRANK, R.L. CODASYL data base management systems. *ACM Comptng Surveys 8,* 1 (March 1976), 67–104.
43. TSICHRITZIS, D., AND LOCHOVSKY, F.H. Hierarchical data base management systems. *ACM Comptng. Surveys 8,* 1 (March 1976), 105–124.
44. Proceedings of the International Conference on Very Large Data Bases, Framingham, Mass. 1975. (available from ACM, New York)
45. Proc. of the Second Int. Conf. Very Large Data Bases, Brussels, 1976.
46. Proceedings of the Third International Conference on Very Large Data Bases, Oct. 1977, Tokyo, Japan, Joint Issue Data Base *9* (ACM) 2 (Fall 1977), SIGMOD Record (ACM) *9,* 4 (Oct. 1977).

Received June 1977; revised February 1978 and June 1978

The Entity-Relationship Model—Toward a Unified View of Data

PETER PIN-SHAN CHEN
Massachusetts Institute of Technology

A data model, called the entity-relationship model, is proposed. This model incorporates some of the important semantic information about the real world. A special diagrammatic technique is introduced as a tool for database design. An example of database design and description using the model and the diagrammatic technique is given. Some implications for data integrity, information retrieval, and data manipulation are discussed.

The entity-relationship model can be used as a basis for unification of different views of data: the network model, the relational model, and the entity set model. Semantic ambiguities in these models are analyzed. Possible ways to derive their views of data from the entity-relationship model are presented.

Key Words and Phrases: database design, logical view of data, semantics of data, data models, entity-relationship model, relational model, Data Base Task Group, network model, entity set model, data definition and manipulation, data integrity and consistency
CR Categories: 3.50, 3.70, 4.33, 4.34

1. INTRODUCTION

The logical view of data has been an important issue in recent years. Three major data models have been proposed: the network model [2, 3, 7], the relational model [8], and the entity set model [25]. These models have their own strengths and weaknesses. The network model provides a more natural view of data by separating entities and relationships (to a certain extent), but its capability to achieve data independence has been challenged [8]. The relational model is based on relational theory and can achieve a high degree of data independence, but it may lose some important semantic information about the real world [12, 15, 23]. The entity set model, which is based on set theory, also achieves a high degree of data independence, but its viewing of values such as "3" or "red" may not be natural to some people [25].

This paper presents the entity-relationship model, which has most of the advantages of the above three models. The entity-relationship model adopts the more natural view that the real world consists of entities and relationships. It incorporates some of the important semantic information about the real world (other work in database semantics can be found in [1, 12, 15, 21, 23, and 29]). The model can achieve a high degree of data independence and is based on set theory and relation theory.

The entity-relationship model can be used as a basis for a unified view of data. Most work in the past has emphasized the difference between the network model and the relational model [22]. Recently, several attempts have been made to reduce the differences of the three data models [4, 19, 26, 30, 31]. This paper uses the entity-relationship model as a framework from which the three existing data models may be derived. The reader may view the entity-relationship model as a generalization or extension of existing models.

This paper is organized into three parts (Sections 2–4). Section 2 introduces the entity-relationship model using a framework of multilevel views of data. Section 3 describes the semantic information in the model and its implications for data description and data manipulation. A special diagrammatric technique, the entity-relationship diagram, is introduced as a tool for database design. Section 4 analyzes the network model, the relational model, and the entity set model, and describes how they may be derived from the entity-relationship model.

2. THE ENTITY-RELATIONSHIP MODEL

2.1 Multilevel Views of Data

In the study of a data model, we should identify the levels of logical views of data with which the model is concerned. Extending the framework developed in [18, 25], we can identify four levels of views of data (Figure 1):

(1) Information concerning entities and relationships which exist in our minds.

(2) Information structure—organization of information in which entities and relationships are represented by data.

(3) Access-path-independent data structure—the data structures which are not involved with search schemes, indexing schemes, etc.

(4) Access-path-dependent data structure.

In the following sections, we shall develop the entity-relationship model step by step for the first two levels. As we shall see later in the paper, the network model, as currently implemented, is mainly concerned with level 4; the relational model is mainly concerned with levels 3 and 2; the entity set model is mainly concerned with levels 1 and 2.

2.2 Information Concerning Entities and Relationships (Level 1)

At this level we consider entities and relationships. An *entity* is a "thing" which can be distinctly identified. A specific person, company, or event is an example of an entity. A *relationship* is an association among entities. For instance, "father-son" is a relationship between two "person" entities.[1]

A version of this paper was presented at the International Conference on Very Large Data Bases, Framingham, Mass., Sept. 22–24, 1975.
Author's address: Center for Information System Research, Alfred P. Sloan School of Management, Massachusetts Institute of Technology, Cambridge, MA 02139.

[1] It is possible that some people may view something (e.g. marriage) as an entity while other people may view it as a relationship. We think that this is a decision which has to be made by the enterprise administrator [27]. He should define what are entities and what are relationships so that the distinction is suitable for his environment.

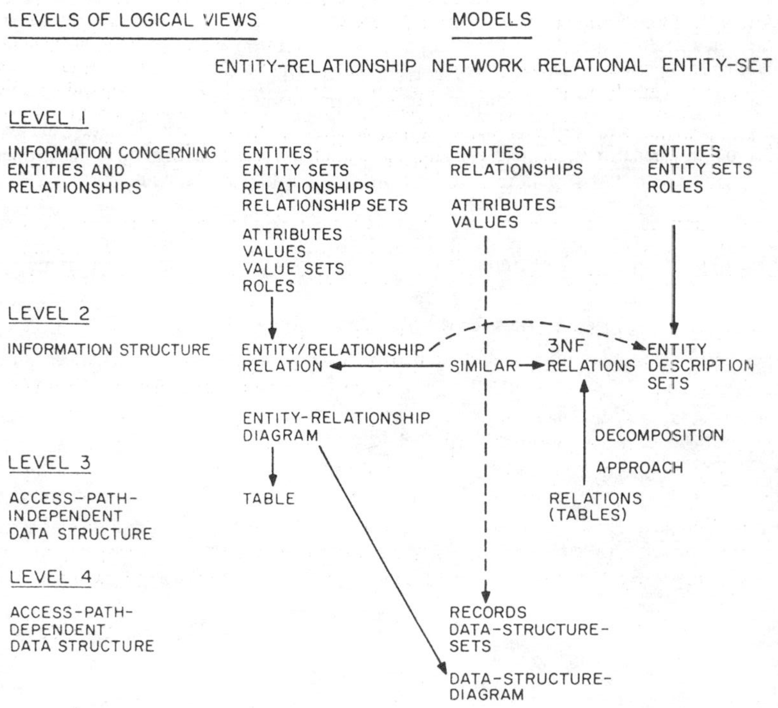

Fig. 1. Analysis of data models using multiple levels of logical views

The database of an enterprise contains relevant information concerning entities and relationships in which the enterprise is interested. A complete description of an entity or relationship may not be recorded in the database of an enterprise. It is impossible (and, perhaps, unnecessary) to record every potentially available piece of information about entities and relationships. From now on, we shall consider only the entities and relationships (and the information concerning them) which are to enter into the design of a database.

2.2.1 Entity and Entity Set. Let e denote an entity which exists in our minds. Entities are classified into different *entity sets* such as EMPLOYEE, PROJECT, and DEPARTMENT. There is a predicate associated with each entity set to test whether an entity belongs to it. For example, if we know an entity is in the entity set EMPLOYEE, then we know that it has the properties common to the other entities in the entity set EMPLOYEE. Among these properties is the aforementioned test predicate. Let E_i denote entity sets. Note that entity sets may not be mutually disjoint. For example, an entity which belongs to the entity set MALE-PERSON also belongs to the entity set PERSON. In this case, MALE-PERSON is a subset of PERSON.

2.2.2 Relationship, Role, and Relationship Set. Consider associations among entities. A *relationship set*, R_i, is a mathematical relation [5] among n entities, each taken from an entity set:

$$\{[e_1, e_2, \ldots, e_n] \mid e_1 \in E_1, e_2 \in E_2, \ldots, e_n \in E_n\},$$

and each tuple of entities, $[e_1, e_2, \ldots, e_n]$, is a *relationship*. Note that the E_i in the above definition may not be distinct. For example, a "marriage" is a relationship between two entities in the entity set PERSON.

The *role* of an entity in a relationship is the function that it performs in the relationship. "Husband" and "wife" are roles. The ordering of entities in the definition of relationship (note that square brackets were used) can be dropped if roles of entities in the relationship are explicitly stated as follows: $(r_1/e_1, r_2/e_2, \ldots, r_n/e_n)$, where r_i is the role of e_i in the relationship.

2.2.3 Attribute, Value, and Value Set. The information about an entity or a relationship is obtained by observation or measurement, and is expressed by a set of attribute-value pairs. "3", "red", "Peter", and "Johnson" are values. Values are classified into different *value sets*, such as FEET, COLOR, FIRST-NAME, and LAST-NAME. There is a predicate associated with each value set to test whether a value belongs to it. A value in a value set may be equivalent to another value in a different value set. For example, "12" in value set INCH is equivalent to "1" in value set FEET.

An *attribute* can be formally defined as a function which maps from an entity set or a relationship set into a value set or a Cartesian product of value sets:

$$f: E_i \text{ or } R_i \to V_i \text{ or } V_{i_1} \times V_{i_2} \times \cdots \times V_{i_n}.$$

Figure 2 illustrates some attributes defined on entity set PERSON. The attribute AGE maps into value set NO-OF-YEARS. An attribute can map into a Cartesian product of value sets. For example, the attribute NAME maps into value sets FIRST-NAME, and LAST-NAME. Note that more than one attribute may map from the same entity set into the same value set (or same group of value sets). For example, NAME and ALTERNATIVE-NAME map from the entity set EMPLOYEE into value sets FIRST-NAME and LAST-NAME. Therefore, attribute and value set are different concepts although they may have the same name in some cases (for example, EMPLOYEE-NO maps from EMPLOYEE to value set EMPLOYEE-NO). This distinction is not clear in the network model and in many existing data management systems. Also note that an attribute is defined as a function. Therefore, it maps a given entity to a single value (or a single tuple of values in the case of a Cartesian product of value sets).

Note that relationships also have attributes. Consider the relationship set PROJECT-WORKER (Figure 3). The attribute PERCENTAGE-OF-TIME, which is the portion of time a particular employee is committed to a particular project, is an attribute defined on the relationship set PROJECT-WORKER. It is neither an attribute of EMPLOYEE nor an attribute of PROJECT, since its meaning depends on both the employee and project involved. The concept of attribute of relationship is important in understanding the semantics of data and in determining the functional dependencies among data.

2.2.4 Conceptual Information Structure. We are now concerned with how to organize the information associated with entities and relationships. The method proposed in this paper is to separate the information about entities from the infor-

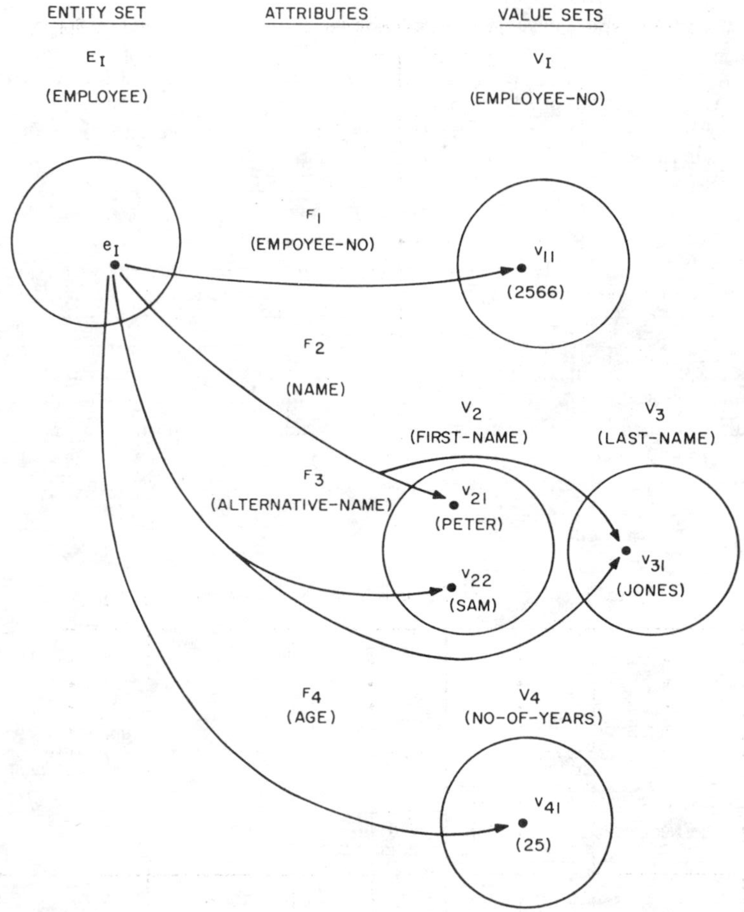

Fig. 2. Attributes defined on the entity set PERSON

mation about relationships. We shall see that this separation is useful in identifying functional dependencies among data.

Figure 4 illustrates in table form the information about entities in an entity set. Each row of values is related to the same entity, and each column is related to a value set which, in turn, is related to an attribute. The ordering of rows and columns is insignificant.

Figure 5 illustrates information about relationships in a relationship set. Note that each row of values is related to a relationship which is indicated by a group of entities, each having a specific role and belonging to a specific entity set.

Note that Figures 4 and 2 (and also Figures 5 and 3) are different forms of the same information. The table form is used for easily relating to the relational model.

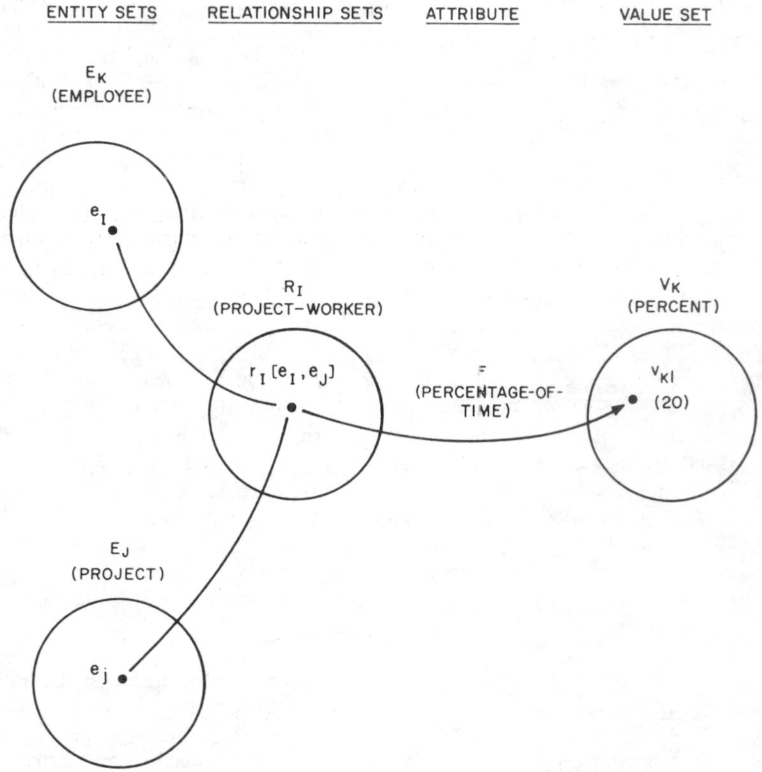

Fig. 3. Attributes defined on the relationship set PROJECT-WORKER

2.3 Information Structure (Level 2)

The entities, relationships, and values at level 1 (see Figures 2–5) are conceptual objects in our minds (i.e. we were in the conceptual realm [18, 27]). At level 2, we consider representations of conceptual objects. We assume that there exist direct representations of values. In the following, we shall describe how to represent entities and relationships.

2.3.1 Primary Key. In Figure 2 the values of attribute EMPLOYEE–NO can be used to identify entities in entity set EMPLOYEE if each employee has a different employee number. It is possible that more than one attribute is needed to identify the entities in an entity set. It is also possible that several groups of attributes may be used to identify entities. Basically, an *entity key* is a group of attributes such that the mapping from the entity set to the corresponding group of value sets is one-to-one. If we cannot find such one-to-one mapping on available data, or if simplicity in identifying entities is desired, we may define an artificial attribute and a value set so that such mapping is possible. In the case where

ATTRIBUTE / ENTITY SET AND VALUE SET	F_1 (EMPLOYEE-NO)	F_2 (NAME)		F_3 (ALTERNATIVE-NAME)		F_4 (AGE)
E_I (EMPLOYEE)	V_1 (EMPLOYEE-NO)	V_2 (FIRST-NAME)	V_3 (LAST-NAME)	V_2 (FIRST-NAME)	V_3 (LAST-NAME)	V_4 (NO-OF-YEARS)
e_1	v_{11} (2566)	v_{21} (PETER)	v_{31} (JONES)	v_{22} (SAM)	v_{31} (JONES)	v_{41} (25)
e_2	v_{12} (3378)	v_{23} (MARY)	v_{32} (CHEN)	v_{24} (BARB)	v_{33} (CHEN)	v_{42} (23)
⋮	⋮	⋮		⋮		⋮

Fig. 4. Information about entities in an entity set (table form)

ROLE	WORKER	PROJECT	RELATIONSHIP ATTRIBUTE: F (PERCENTAGE-OF-TIME)
ENTITY SET / VALUE SET	E_I (EMPLOYEE)	E_J (PROJECT)	V_K (PERCENTAGE)
	e_{I1}	e_{J1}	v_{K1} (20)
	⋮	⋮	⋮

Fig. 5. Information about relationships in a relationship set (table form)

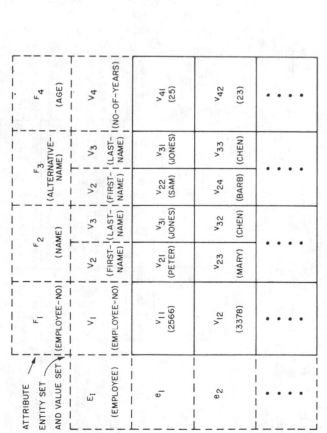

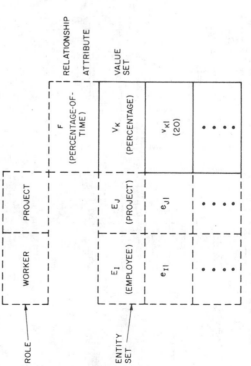

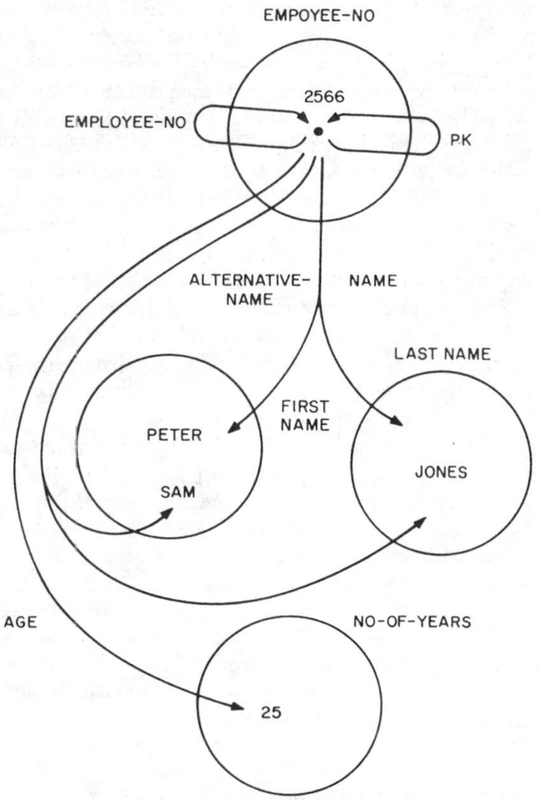

Fig. 6. Representing entities by values (employee numbers)

several keys exist, we usually choose a semantically meaningful key as the *entity primary key* (PK).

Figure 6 is obtained by merging the entity set EMPLOYEE with value set EMPLOYEE–NO in Figure 2. We should notice some semantic implications of Figure 6. Each value in the value set EMPLOYEE–NO represents an entity (employee). Attributes map from the value set EMPLOYEE–NO to other value sets. Also note that the attribute EMPLOYEE–NO maps from the value set EMPLOYEE–NO to itself.

2.3.2 Entity/Relationship Relations. Information about entities in an entity set can now be organized in a form shown in Figure 7. Note that Figure 7 is similar to Figure 4 except that entities are represented by the values of their primary keys. The whole table in Figure 7 is an *entity relation*, and each row is an *entity tuple*.

Since a relationship is identified by the involved entities, the *primary key of a relationship* can be represented by the primary keys of the involved entities. In

	EMPLOYEE-NO (PRIMARY KEY)	NAME		ALTERNATIVE-NAME		AGE
ATTRIBUTE	EMPLOYEE-NO	NAME		ALTERNATIVE-NAME		AGE
VALUE SET (DOMAIN)	EMPLOYEE-NO	FIRST-NAME	LAST-NAME	FIRST-NAME	LAST-NAME	NO-OF-YEARS
ENTITY (TUPLE)	2566	PETER	JONES	SAM	JONES	25
	3378	MARY	CHEN	BARB	CHEN	23
	⋮	⋮	⋮	⋮	⋮	⋮

Fig. 7. Regular entity relation EMPLOYEE

Figure 8, the involved entities are represented by their primary keys EMPLOYEE-NO and PROJECT-NO. The role names provide the semantic meaning for the values in the corresponding columns. Note that EMPLOYEE-NO is the primary key for the involved entities in the relationship and is not an attribute of the relationship. PERCENTAGE-OF-TIME is an attribute of the relationship. The table in Figure 8 is a *relationship relation*, and each row of values is a *relationship tuple*.

In certain cases, the entities in an entity set cannot be uniquely identified by the values of their own attributes; thus we must use a relationship(s) to identify them. For example, consider dependents of employees: dependents are identified by their names and by the values of the primary key of the employees supporting them (i.e. by their relationships with the employees). Note that in Figure 9, EMPLOYEE-NO is not an attribute of an entity in the set DEPENDENT but is the primary key of the employees who support dependents. Each row of values in Figure 9 is an entity tuple with EMPLOYEE-NO and NAME as its primary key. The whole table is an entity relation.

Theoretically, any kind of relationship may be used to identify entities. For simplicity, we shall restrict ourselves to the use of only one kind of relationship: the binary relationships with $1:n$ mapping in which the existence of the n entities on one side of the relationship depends on the existence of one entity on the other side of the relationship. For example, one employee may have n ($= 0, 1, 2, \ldots$) dependents, and the existence of the dependents depends on the existence of the corresponding employee.

This method of identification of entities by relationships with other entities can be applied recursively until the entities which can be identified by their own attribute values are reached. For example, the primary key of a department in a company may consist of the department number and the primary key of the division, which in turn consists of the division number and the name of the company.

Therefore, we have two forms of entity relations. If relationships are used for identifying the entities, we shall call it a *weak entity relation* (Figure 9). If relationships are not used for identifying the entities, we shall call it a *regular entity relation* (Figure 7). Similarly, we also have two forms of relationship relations. If all entities in the relationship are identified by their own attribute values, we shall call it a *regular relationship relation* (Figure 8). If some entities in the relationship are identified by other relationships, we shall call it a *weak relationship relation*. For example, any relationships between DEPENDENT entities and other entities will result in weak relationship relations, since a DEPENDENT entity is identified by its name and its relationship with an EMPLOYEE entity. The distinction between regular (entity/relationship) relations and weak (entity/relationship) relations will be useful in maintaining data integrity.

	PRIMARY KEY		
ENTITY RELATION NAME	EMPLOYEE	PROJECT	
ROLE	WORKER	PROJECT	
ENTITY ATTRIBUTE	EMPLOYEE-NO	PROJECT-NO	PERCENTAGE-OF-TIME (RELATIONSHIP ATTRIBUTE)
VALUE SET (DOMAIN)	EMPLOYEE-NO	PROJECT-NO	PERCENTAGE
RELATIONSHIP TUPLE	2566	31	20
	2173	25	100
	⋮	⋮	⋮

Fig. 8. Regular relationship relation PROJECT-WORKER

	PRIMARY KEY		
ENTITY RELATION NAME	EMPLOYEE		
ROLE	SUPPORTER		
ENTITY ATTRIBUTE	EMPLOYEE-NO	NAME	AGE (RELATIONSHIP ATTRIBUTE)
VALUE SET (DOMAIN)	EMPLOYEE-NO	FIRST-NAME	NO-OF-YEARS (RELATIONSHIP ATTRIBUTE)
ENTITY TUPLE	2566	VICTOR	3
	2173	GEORGE	6
	⋮	⋮	⋮

Fig. 9. A weak entity relation DEPENDENT

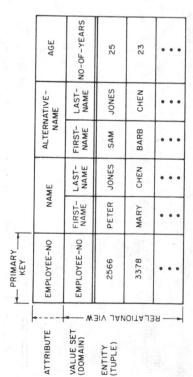

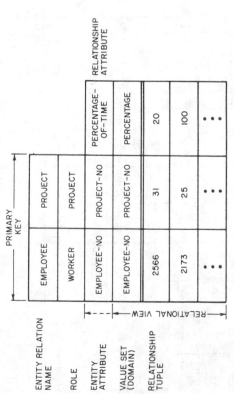

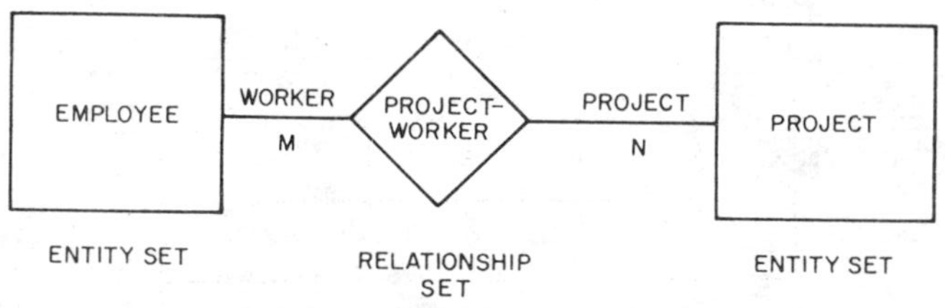

Fig. 10. A simple entity-relationship diagram

3. ENTITY-RELATIONSHIP DIAGRAM AND INCLUSION OF SEMANTICS IN DATA DESCRIPTION AND MANIPULATION

3.1 System Analysis Using the Entity-Relationship Diagram

In this section we introduce a diagrammatic technique for exhibiting entities and relationships: the entity-relationship diagram.

Figure 10 illustrates the relationship set PROJECT–WORKER and the entity sets EMPLOYEE and PROJECT using this diagrammatic technique. Each entity set is represented by a rectangular box, and each relationship set is represented by a diamond-shaped box. The fact that the relationship set PROJECT–WORKER is defined on the entity sets EMPLOYEE and PROJECT is represented by the lines connecting the rectangular boxes. The roles of the entities in the relationship are stated.

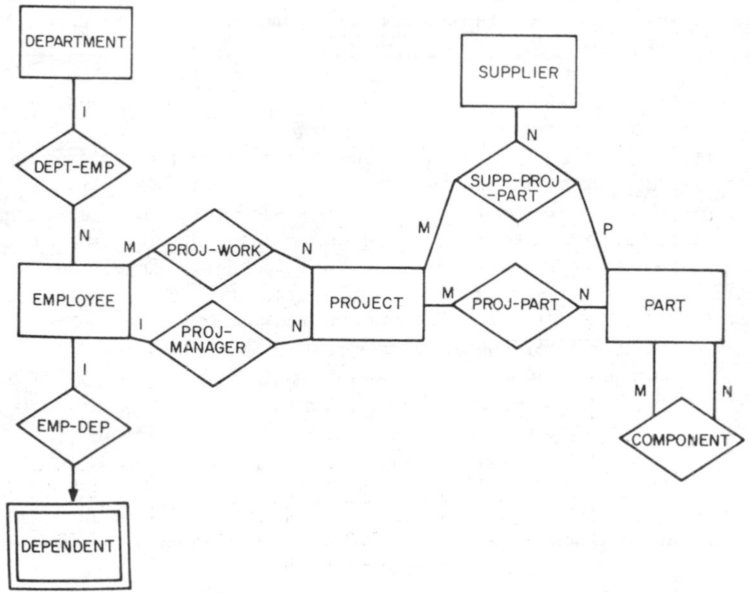

Fig. 11. An entity-relationship diagram for analysis of information in a manufacturing firm

Figure 11 illustrates a more complete diagram of some entity sets and relationship sets which might be of interest to a manufacturing company. DEPARTMENT, EMPLOYEE, DEPENDENT, PROJECT, SUPPLIER, and PART are entity sets. DEPARTMENT–EMPLOYEE, EMPLOYEE–DEPENDENT, PROJECT–WORKER, PROJECT–MANAGER, SUPPLIER–PROJECT–PART, PROJECT–PART, and COMPONENT are relationship sets. The COMPONENT relationship describes what subparts (and quantities) are needed in making superparts. The meaning of the other relationship sets need not be explained.

Several important characteristics about relationships in general can be found in Figure 11:

(1) A relationship set may be defined on more than two entity sets. For example, the SUPPLIER–PROJECT–PART relationship set is defined on three entity sets: SUPPLIER, PROJECT, and PART.

(2) A relationship set may be defined on only one entity set. For example, the relationship set COMPONENT is defined on one entity set, PART.

(3) There may be more than one relationship set defined on given entity sets. For example, the relationship sets PROJECT–WORKER and PROJECT–MANAGER are defined on the entity sets PROJECT and EMPLOYEE.

(4) The diagram can distinguish between $1:n$, $m:n$, and 1:1 mappings. The relationship set DEPARTMENT–EMPLOYEE is a $1:n$ mapping, that is, one department may have n ($n = 0, 1, 2, \ldots$) employees and each employee works for only one department. The relationship set PROJECT–WORKER is an $m:n$ mapping, that is, each project may have zero, one, or more employees assigned to it and each employee may be assigned to zero, one, or more projects. It is also possible to express 1:1 mappings such as the relationship set MARRIAGE. Information about the number of entities in each entity set which is allowed in a relationship set is indicated by specifying "1", "m", "n" in the diagram. The relational model and the entity set model[2] do not include this type of information; the network model cannot express a 1:1 mapping easily.

(5) The diagram can express the *existence dependency* of one entity type on another. For example, the arrow in the relationship set EMPLOYEE–DEPENDENT indicates that existence of an entity in the entity set DEPENDENT depends on the corresponding entity in the entity set EMPLOYEE. That is, if an employee leaves the company, his dependents may no longer be of interest.

Note that the entity set DEPENDENT is shown as a special rectangular box. This indicates that at level 2 the information about entities in this set is organized as a weak entity relation (using the primary key of EMPLOYEE as a part of its primary key).

3.2 An Example of a Database Design and Description

There are four steps in designing a database using the entity-relationship model: (1) identify the entity sets and the relationship sets of interest; (2) identify semantic information in the relationship sets such as whether a certain relationship

[2] This mapping information is included in DIAM II [24].

set is an 1:n mapping; (3) define the value sets and attributes; (4) organize data into entity/relationship relations and decide primary keys.

Let us use the manufacturing company discussed in Section 3.1 as an example. The results of the first two steps of database design are expressed in an entity-relationship diagram as shown in Figure 11. The third step is to define value sets and attributes (see Figures 2 and 3). The fourth step is to decide the primary keys for the entities and the relationships and to organize data as entity/relationship relations. Note that each entity/relationship set in Figure 11 has a corresponding entity/relationship relation. We shall use the names of the entity sets (at level 1) as the names of the corresponding entity/relationship relations (at level 2) as long as no confusion will result.

At the end of the section, we illustrate a schema (data definition) for a small part of the database in the above manufacturing company example (the syntax of the data definition is not important). Note that value sets are defined with specifications of representations and allowable values. For example, values in EMPLOYEE-NO are represented as 4-digit integers and range from 0 to 2000. We then declare three entity relations: EMPLOYEE, PROJECT, and DEPENDENT. The attributes and value sets defined on the entity sets as well as the primary keys are stated. DEPENDENT is a weak entity relation since it uses EMPLOYEE.PK as part of its primary key. We also declare two relationship relations: PROJECT-WORKER and EMPLOYEE-DEPENDENT. The roles and involved entities in the relationships are specified. We use EMPLOYEE.PK to indicate the name of the entity relation (EMPLOYEE) and whatever attribute-value-set pairs are used as the primary keys in that entity relation. The maximum number of entities from an entity set in a relation is stated. For example, PROJECT-WORKER is an m:n mapping. We may specify the values of m and n. We may also specify the minimum number of entities in addition to the maximum number. EMPLOYEE-DEPENDENT is a weak relationship relation since one of the related entity relations, DEPENDENT, is a weak entity relation. Note that the existence dependence of the dependents on the supporter is also stated.

```
DECLARE   VALUE-SETS      REPRESENTATION    ALLOWABLE-VALUES
          EMPLOYEE-NO     INTEGER (4)       (0,2000)
          FIRST-NAME      CHARACTER (8)     ALL
          LAST-NAME       CHARACTER (10)    ALL
          NO-OF-YEARS     INTEGER (3)       (0,100)
          PROJECT-NO      INTEGER (3)       (1,500)
          PERCENTAGE      FIXED (5.2)       (0,100.00)

DECLARE   REGULAR ENTITY RELATION EMPLOYEE
          ATTRIBUTE/VALUE-SET:
               EMPLOYEE-NO/EMPLOYEE-NO
               NAME/(FIRST-NAME, LAST-NAME)
               ALTERNATIVE-NAME/(FIRST-NAME,LAST-NAME)
               AGE/NO-OF-YEARS
          PRIMARY KEY:
               EMPLOYEE-NO

DECLARE   REGULAR ENTITY RELATION PROJECT
          ATTRIBUTE/VALUE-SET:
               PROJECT-NO/PROJECT-NO
          PRIMARY KEY:
               PROJECT-NO

DECLARE   REGULAR RELATIONSHIP RELATION PROJECT-WORKER
          ROLE/ENTITY-RELATION.PK/MAX-NO-OF-ENTITIES
               WORKER/EMPLOYEE.PK/m
               PROJECT/PROJECT.PK/n      (m:n mapping)
          ATTRIBUTE/VALUE-SET:
               PERCENTAGE-OF-TIME/PERCENTAGE

DECLARE   WEAK RELATIONSHIP RELATION EMPLOYEE-DEPENDENT
          ROLE/ENTITY-RELATION.PK/MAX-NO-OF-ENTITIES
               SUPPORTER/EMPLOYEE.PK/1
               DEPENDENT/DEPENDENT.PK/n
          EXISTENCE OF DEPENDENT DEPENDS ON
          EXISTENCE OF SUPPORTER

DECLARE   WEAK ENTITY RELATION DEPENDENT
          ATTRIBUTE/VALUE-SET:
               NAME/FIRST-NAME
               AGE/NO-OF-YEARS
          PRIMARY KEY:
               NAME
               EMPLOYEE.PK THROUGH EMPLOYEE-DEPENDENT
```

3.3 Implications on Data Integrity

Some work has been done on data integrity for other models [8, 14, 16, 28]. With explicit concepts of entity and relationship, the entity-relationship model will be useful in understanding and specifying constraints for maintaining data integrity. For example, there are three major kinds of constraints on values:

(1) Constraints on *allowable values* for a value set. This point was discussed in defining the schema in Section 3.2.

(2) Constraints on *permitted* values for a certain attribute. In some cases, not all allowable values in a value set are permitted for some attributes. For example, we may have a restriction of ages of employees to between 20 and 65. That is,

$$\text{AGE}(e) \in (20,65), \text{ where } e \in \text{EMPLOYEE}.$$

Note that we use the level 1 notations to clarify the semantics. Since each entity/relationship set has a corresponding entity/relationship relation, the above expression can be easily translated into level 2 notations.

(3) Constraints on *existing values* in the database. There are two types of constraints:

(i) Constraints between sets of existing values. For example,

$$\{\text{NAME}(e) \mid e \in \text{MALE-PERSON}\} \subseteq \{\text{NAME}(e) \mid e \in \text{PERSON}\}.$$

(ii) Constraints between particular values. For example,

$$TAX(e) \leq SALARY(e),\ e \in EMPLOYEE$$

or

$$BUDGET(e_i) = \sum BUDGET(e_j),\ \text{where } e_i \in COMPANY,\ e_j \in DEPARTMENT \text{ and } [e_i,e_j] \in COMPANY\text{-}DEPARTMENT.$$

3.4 Semantics and Set Operations of Information Retrieval Requests

The semantics of information retrieval requests become very clear if the requests are based on the entity-relationship model of data. For clarity, we first discuss the situation at level 1. Conceptually, the information elements are organized as in Figures 4 and 5 (on Figures 2 and 3). Many information retrieval requests can be considered as a combination of the following basic types of operations:

(1) Selection of a subset of values from a value set.

(2) Selection of a subset of entities from an entity set (i.e. selection of certain rows in Figure 4). Entities are selected by stating the values of certain attributes (i.e. subsets of value sets) and/or their relationships with other entities.

(3) Selection of a subset of relationships from a relationship set (i.e. selection of certain rows in Figure 5). Relationships are selected by stating the values of certain attribute(s) and/or by identifying certain entities in the relationship.

(4) Selection of a subset of attributes (i.e. selection of columns in Figures 4 and 5).

An information retrieval request like "What are the ages of the employees whose weights are greater than 170 and who are assigned to the project with PROJECT-NO 254?" can be expressed as:

$\{AGE(e) \mid e \in EMPLOYEE,\ WEIGHT(e) > 170,$
$[e, e_j] \in PROJECT\text{-}WORKER,\ e_j \in PROJECT,$
$PROJECT\text{-}NO(e_j) = 254\};$

or

{AGE(EMPLOYEE) | WEIGHT(EMPLOYEE) > 170,
[EMPLOYEE,PROJECT] ∈ PROJECT-WORKER,
PROJECT-NO(EMPLOYEE) = 254}.

To retrieve information as organized in Figure 6 at level 2, "entities" and "relationships" in (2) and (3) should be replaced by "entity PK" and "relationship PK." The above information retrieval request can be expressed as:

{AGE(EMPLOYEE.PK) | WEIGHT(EMPLOYEE.PK) > 170
(WORKER/EMPLOYEE.PK,PROJECT/PROJECT.PK) ∈ {PROJECT-WORKER.PK},
PROJECT-NO (PROJECT.PK) = 254}.

To retrieve information as organized in entity/relationship relations (Figures 7, 8, and 9), we can express it in a SEQUEL-like language [6]:

```
SELECT    AGE
FROM      EMPLOYEE
WHERE     WEIGHT > 170
AND       EMPLOYEE.PK =
          SELECT    WORKER/EMPLOYEE.PK
          FROM      PROJECT-WORKER
          WHERE     PROJECT-NO = 254.
```

It is possible to retrieve information about entities in two different entity sets without specifying a relationship between them. For example, an information retrieval request like "List the names of employees and ships which have the same

Table I. Insertion

level 1	level 2
operation: insert an entity to an entity set	*operation:* create an entity tuple with a certain entity-PK *check:* whether PK already exists or is acceptable
operation: insert a relationship in a relationship set *check:* whether the entities exist	*operation:* create a relationship tuple with given entity PKs *check:* whether the entity PKs exist
operation: insert properties of an entity or a relationship *check:* whether the value is acceptable	*operation:* insert values in an entity tuple or a relationship tuple *check:* whether the values are acceptable

Table II. Updating

level 1	level 2
operation: • change the value of an entity attribute	*operation:* • update a value *consequence:* • if it is not part of an entity PK, no consequence • if it is part of an entity PK, •• change the entity PKs in all related relationship relations •• change PKs of other entities which use this value as part of their PKs (for example, DEPENDENTS' PKs use EMPLOYEE'S PK)
operation: • change the value of a relationship attribute	*operation:* • update a value (note that a relationship attribute will not be a relationship PK)

Table III. Deletion

level 1	level 2
operation: • delete an entity *consequences:* • delete any entity whose existence depends on this entity • delete relationships involving this entity • delete all related properties	*operation:* • delete an entity tuple *consequences* (applied recursively): • delete any entity tuple whose existence depends on this entity tuple • delete relationship tuples associated with this entity
operation: • delete a relationship *consequences:* • delete all related properties	*operation:* • delete a relationship tuple

age" can be expressed in the level 1 notation as:

$$\{(\text{NAME}(e_i),\text{NAME}(e_j)) \mid e_i \in \text{EMPLOYEE}, e_j \in \text{SHIP}, \text{AGE}(e_i) = \text{AGE}(e_j)\}.$$

We do not further discuss the language syntax here. What we wish to stress is that information requests may be expressed using set notions and set operations [17], and the request semantics are very clear in adopting this point of view.

3.5 Semantics and Rules for Insertion, Deletion, and Updating

It is always a difficult problem to maintain data consistency following insertion, deletion, and updating of data in the database. One of the major reasons is that the semantics and consequences of insertion, deletion, and updating operations usually are not clearly defined; thus it is difficult to find a set of rules which can enforce data consistency. We shall see that this data consistency problem becomes simpler using the entity-relationship model.

In Tables I–III, we discuss the semantics and rules[3] for insertion, deletion, and updating at both level 1 and level 2. Level 1 is used to clarify the semantics.

4. ANALYSIS OF OTHER DATA MODELS AND THEIR DERIVATION FROM THE ENTITY-RELATIONSHIP MODEL

4.1 The Relational Model

4.1.1 The Relational View of Data and Ambiguity in Semantics. In the relational model, *relation*, R, is a mathematical relation defined on sets $X_1, X_2, \ldots, X_n$:

$$R = \{(x_1, x_2, \ldots, x_n) \mid x_1 \in X_1, x_2 \in X_2, \ldots, x_n \in X_n\}.$$

The sets $X_1, X_2, \ldots, X_n$ are called *domains*, and $(x_1, x_2, \ldots, x_n)$ is called a *tuple*. Figure 12 illustrates a relation called EMPLOYEE. The domains in the relation

ROLE		LEGAL	LEGAL	ALTERNATIVE	ALTERNATIVE	
DOMAIN	EMPLOYEE-NO	FIRST-NAME	LAST-NAME	FIRST-NAME	LAST-NAME	NO-OF-YEARS
TUPLE	2566	PETER	JONES	SAM	JONES	25
	3378	MARY	CHEN	BARB	CHEN	23

Fig. 12. Relation EMPLOYEE

are EMPLOYEE-NO, FIRST-NAME, LAST-NAME, FIRST-NAME, LAST-NAME, NO-OF-YEAR. The ordering of rows and columns in the relation has no significance. To avoid ambiguity of columns with the same domain in a relation, domain names are qualified by *roles* (to distinguish the role of the domain in the relation). For example, in relation EMPLOYEE, domains FIRST-NAME and LAST-NAME may be qualified by roles LEGAL or ALTERNATIVE. An *attribute name* in the relational model is a domain name concatenated with a role name [10]. Comparing Figure 12 with Figure 7, we can see that "domains" are basically equivalent to value sets. Although "role" or "attribute" in the relational model seems to serve the same purpose as "attribute" in the entity-relationship model, the semantics of these terms are different. The "role" or "attribute" in the relational model is mainly used to distinguish domains with the same name in the same relation, while "attribute" in the entity-relationship model is a function which maps from an entity (or relationship) set into value set(s).

Using relational operators in the relational model may cause semantic ambiguities. For example, the join of the relation EMPLOYEE with the relation EMPLOYEE-PROJECT (Figure 13) on domain EMPLOYEE-NO produces the

PROJECT-NO	EMPLOYEE-NO
7	2566
3	2566
7	3378

Fig. 13. Relation EMPLOYEE-PROJECT

[3] Our main purpose is to illustrate the semantics of data manipulation operations. Therefore, these rules may not be complete. Note that the consequence of operations stated in the tables can be performed by the system instead of by the users.

		LEGAL	LEGAL	ALTERNATIVE	ALTERNATIVE	
PROJECT-NO	EMPLOYEE-NO	FIRST-NAME	LAST-NAME	FIRST-NAME	LAST-NAME	NO-OF-YEARS
7	2566	PETER	JONES	SAM	JONES	25
3	2566	PETER	JONES	SAM	JONES	25
7	3378	MARY	CHEN	BARB	CHEN	23

Fig. 14. Relation EMPLOYEE–PROJECT' as a "join" of relations EMPLOYEE and EMPLOYEE–PROJECT

relation EMPLOYEE–PROJECT' (Figure 14). But what is the meaning of a join between the relation EMPLOYEE with the relation SHIP on the domain NO–OF–YEARS (Figure 15)? The problem is that the same domain name may have different semantics in different relations (note that a role is intended to distinguish domains in a given relation, not in all relations). If the domain NO–OF–YEAR of the relation EMPLOYEE is not allowed to be compared with the domain NO–OF–YEAR of the relation SHIP, different domain names have to be declared. But if such a comparison is acceptable, can the database system warn the user?

In the entity-relationship model, the semantics of data are much more apparent. For example, one column in the example stated above contains the values of AGE of EMPLOYEE and the other column contains the values of AGE of SHIP. If this semantic information is exposed to the user, he may operate more cautiously (refer to the sample information retrieval requests stated in Section 3.4). Since the database system contains the semantic information, it should be able to warn the user of the potential problems for a proposed "join-like" operation.

4.1.2 Semantics of Functional Dependencies Among Data. In the relational model, "attribute" B of a relation is *functionally dependent* on "attribute" A of the same relation if each value of A has no more than one value of B associated with it in the relation. Semantics of functional dependencies among data become clear

SHIP-NO	NAME	NO-OF-YEARS
037	MISSOURI	25
056	VIRGINIA	10

Fig. 15. Relation SHIP

in the entity-relationship model. Basically, there are two major types of functional dependencies:

(1) Functional dependencies related to description of entities or relationships. Since an attribute is defined as a function, it maps an entity in an entity set to a single value in a value set (see Figure 2). At level 2, the values of the primary key are used to represent entities. Therefore, nonkey value sets (domains) are functionally dependent on primary-key value sets (for example, in Figures 6 and 7, NO–OF–YEARS is functionally dependent on EMPLOYEE–NO). Since a relation may have several keys, the nonkey value sets will functionally depend on any key value set. The key value sets will be mutually functionally dependent on each other. Similarly, in a relationship relation the nonkey value sets will be functionally dependent on the prime-key value sets (for example, in Figure 8, PERCENTAGE is functionally dependent on EMPLOYEE–NO and PROJECT–NO).

(2) Functional dependencies related to entities in a relationship. Note that in Figure 11 we identify the types of mappings ($1{:}n$, $m{:}n$, etc.) for relationship sets. For example, PROJECT–MANAGER is a $1{:}n$ mapping. Let us assume that PROJECT–NO is the primary key in the entity relation PROJECT. In the relationship relation PROJECT–MANAGER, the value set EMPLOYEE–NO will be functionally dependent on the value set PROJECT–NO (i.e. each project has only one manager).

The distinction between level 1 (Figure 2) and level 2 (Figures 6 and 7) and the separation of entity relation (Figure 7) from relationship relation (Figure 8) clarifies the semantics of functional dependencies among data.

4.1.3 3NF Relations Versus Entity-Relationship Relations. From the definition of "relation," any grouping of domains can be considered to be a relation. To avoid undesirable properties in maintaining relations, a normalization process is proposed to transform arbitrary relations into the first normal form, then into the second normal form, and finally into the third normal form (3NF) [9, 11]. We shall show that the entity and relationship relations in the entity-relationship model are similar to 3NF relations but with clearer semantics and without using the transformation operation.

Let us use a simplified version of an example of normalization described in [9]. The following three relations are in first normal form (that is, there is no domain whose elements are themselves relations):

EMPLOYEE (EMPLOYEE–NO)
PART (PART–NO, PART–DESCRIPTION, QUANTITY–ON–HAND)
PART–PROJECT (PART–NO, PROJECT–NO, PROJECT–DESCRIPTION,
PROJECT–MANAGER–NO, QUANTITY–COMMITTED).

Note that the domain PROJECT–MANAGER–NO actually contains the EMPLOYEE–NO of the project manager. In the relations above, primary keys are underlined.

Certain rules are applied to transform the relations above into third normal form:

EMPLOYEE' (EMPLOYEE–NO)
PART' (PART–NO, PART–DESCRIPTION, QUANTITY–ON–HAND)

PROJECT' (PROJECT-NO, PROJECT-DESCRIPTION, PROJECT-MANAGER-NO)
PART-PROJECT' (PART-NO, PROJECT-NO, QUANTITY-COMMITTED).

Using the entity-relationship diagram in Figure 11, the following entity and relationship relations can be easily derived:

entity relations	PART'' (PART-NO, PART-DESCRIPTION, QUANTITY-ON-HAND)
	PROJECT'' (PROJECT-NO, PROJECT-DESCRIPTION)
	EMPLOYEE'' (EMPLOYEE-NO)
relationship relations	PART-PROJECT'' (PART/PART-NO, PROJECT/PROJECT-NO, QUANTITY-COMMITTED)
	PROJECT-MANAGER'' (PROJECT/PROJECT-NO, MANAGER/EMPLOYEE-NO).

The role names of the entities in relationships (such as MANAGER) are indicated. The entity relation names associated with the PKs of entities in relationships and the value set names have been omitted.

Note that in the example above, entity/relationship relations are similar to the 3NF relations. In the 3NF approach, PROJECT-MANAGER-NO is included in the relation PROJECT' since PROJECT-MANAGER-NO is assumed to be functionally dependent on PROJECT-NO. In the entity-relationship model, PROJECT-MANAGER-NO (i.e. EMPLOYEE-NO of a project manager) is included in a relationship relation PROJECT-MANAGER since EMPLOYEE-NO is considered as an entity PK in this case.

Also note that in the 3NF approach, changes in functional dependencies of data may cause some relations not to be in 3NF. For example, if we make a new assumption that one project may have more than one manager, the relation PROJECT' is no longer a 3NF relation and has to be split into two relations as PROJECT'' and PROJECT-MANAGER''. Using the entity-relationship model, no such change is necessary. Therefore, we may say that by using the entity-relationship model we can arrange data in a form similar to 3NF relations but with clear semantic meaning.

It is interesting to note that the decomposition (or transformation) approach described above for normalization of relations may be viewed as a bottom-up approach in database design.[4] It starts with arbitrary relations (level 3 in Figure 1) and then uses some semantic information (functional dependencies of data) to transform them into 3NF relations (level 2 in Figure 1). The entity-relationship model adopts a top-down approach, utilizing the semantic information to organize data in entity/relationship relations.

4.2 The Network Model

4.2.1 Semantics of the Data-Structure Diagram. One of the best ways to explain the network model is by use of the *data-structure diagram* [3]. Figure 16(a) illustrates a data-structure diagram. Each rectangular box represents a record type.

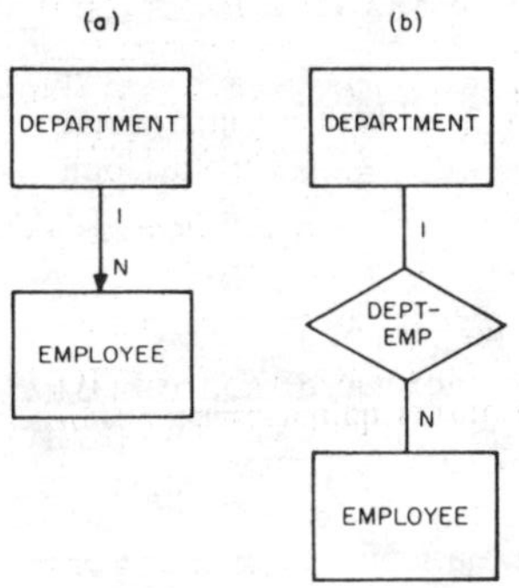

Fig. 16. Relationship DEPARTMENT-EMPLOYEE
(a) data structure diagram
(b) entity-relationship diagram

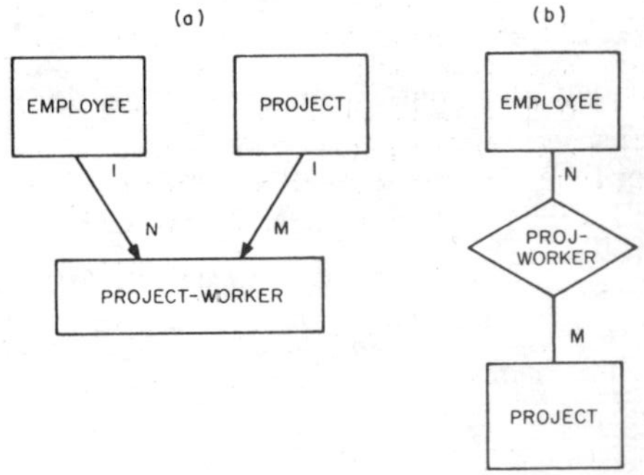

Fig. 17. Relationship PROJECT-WORKER
(a) data structure diagram
(b) entity-relationship diagram

The arrow represents a data-structure-set in which the DEPARTMENT record is the *owner-record*, and one owner-record may own n ($n = 0, 1, 2, \ldots$) *member-records*. Figure 16(b) illustrates the corresponding entity-relationship diagram. One might conclude that the arrow in the data-structure diagram represents a relationship between entities in two entity sets. This is not always true. Figures 17(a) and 17(b) are the data-structure diagram and the entity-relationship diagram expressing the relationship PROJECT-WORKER between two entity types EMPLOYEE and PROJECT. We can see in Figure 17(a) that the relationship PROJECT-WORKER becomes another record type and that the arrows no longer represent relationships between entities. What are the real meanings of the arrows in data-structure diagrams? The answer is that an arrow represents an $1{:}n$ relationship between two *record* (not entity) types and also implies the existence of an access path from the owner record to the member records. The data-structure diagram is a representation of the organization of records (level 4 in Figure 1) and is not an exact representation of entities and relationships.

4.2.2 Deriving the Data-Structure Diagram. Under what conditions does an arrow in a data-structure diagram correspond to a relationship of entities? A close comparison of the data-structure diagrams with the corresponding entity-relationship diagrams reveals the following rules:

1. For $1{:}n$ binary relationships an arrow is used to represent the relationship (see Figure 16(a)).

2. For $m{:}n$ binary relationships a "relationship record" type is created to represent the relationship and arrows are drawn from the "entity record" type to the "relationship record" type (see Figure 17(a)).

3. For k-ary ($k \geq 3$) relationships, the same rule as (2) applies (i.e. creating a "relationship record" type).

Since DBTG [7] does not allow a data-structure-set to be defined on a single record type (i.e. Figure 18 is not allowed although it has been implemented in [13]), a "relationship record" is needed to implement such relationships (see

[4] Although the decomposition approach was emphasized in the relational model literature, it is a procedure to obtain 3NF and may not be an intrinsic property of 3NF.

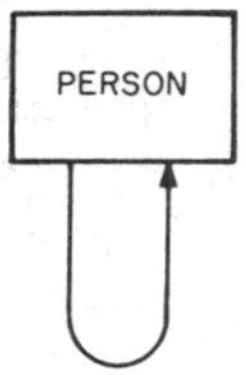

Fig. 18. Data-structure-set defined on the same record type

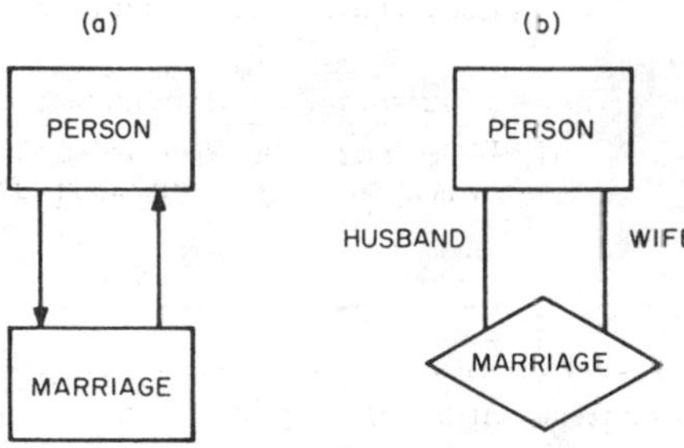

Fig. 19. Relationship MARRIAGE (a) data structure diagram (b) entity-relationship diagram

Figure 19(a)) [20]. The corresponding entity-relationship diagram is shown in Figure 19(b).

It is clear now that arrows in a data-structure diagram do not always represent relationships of entities. Even in the case that an arrow represents a $1:n$ relationship, the arrow only represents a unidirectional relationship [20] (although it is possible to find the owner-record from a member-record). In the entity-relationship model, both directions of the relationship are represented (the roles of both entities are specified). Besides the semantic ambiguity in its arrows, the network model is awkward in handling changes in semantics. For example, if the relationship between DEPARTMENT and EMPLOYEE changes from a $1:n$ mapping to an $m:n$ mapping (i.e. one employee may belong to several departments), we must create a relationship record DEPARTMENT-EMPLOYEE in the network model.

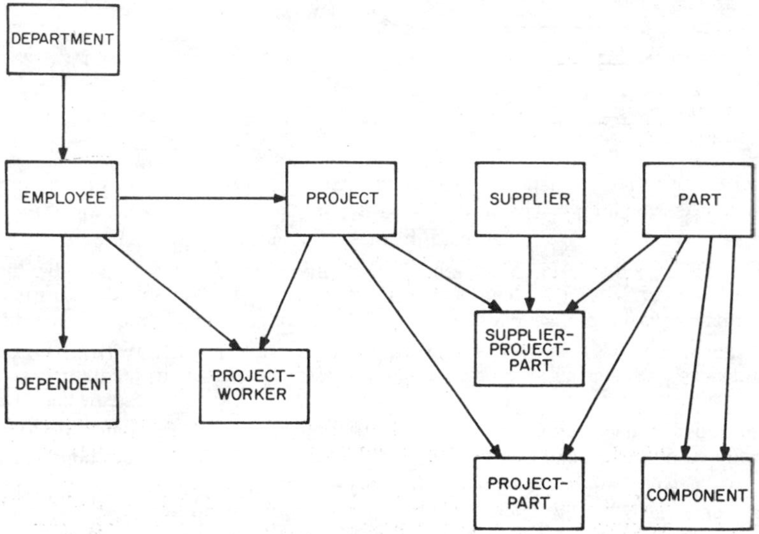

Fig. 20. The data structure diagram derived from the entity-relationship diagram in Fig. 11

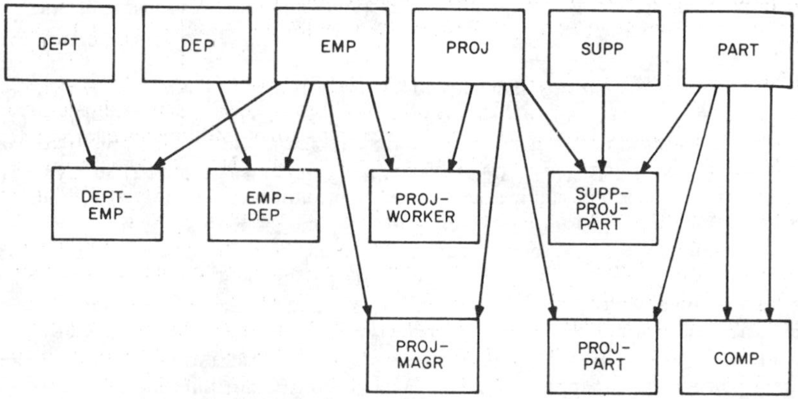

Fig. 21. The "disciplined" data structure diagram derived from the entity-relationship diagram in Fig. 11

In the entity-relationship model, all kinds of mappings in relationships are handled uniformly.

The entity-relationship model can be used as a tool in the structured design of databases using the network model. The user first draws an entity-relationship diagram (Figure 11). He may simply translate it into a data-structure diagram (Figure 20). using the rules specified above. He may also follow a discipline that every entity or relationship must be mapped onto a record (that is, "relationship records" are created for all types of relationships no matter that they are $1:n$ or $m:n$ mappings). Thus, in Figure 11, all one needs to do is to change the diamonds to boxes and to add arrowheads on the appropriate lines. Using this approach three more boxes—DEPARTMENT-EMPLOYEE, EMPLOYEE-DEPENDENT, and PROJECT-MANAGER—will be added to Figure 20 (see Figure 21). The validity constraints discussed in Sections 3.3–3.5 will also be useful.

4.3 The Entity Set Model

4.3.1 The Entity Set View. The basic element of the entity set model is the entity. Entities have names (*entity names*) such as "Peter Jones", "blue", or "22". Entity names having some properties in common are collected into an *entity-name-set*, which is referenced by the *entity-name-set-name* such as "NAME", "COLOR", and "QUANTITY".

An entity is represented by the entity-name-set-name/entity-name pair such as NAME/Peter Jones, EMPLOYEE-NO/2566, and NO-OF-YEARS/20. An entity is described by its association with other entities. Figure 22 illustrates the entity set view of data. The "DEPARTMENT" of entity EMPLOYEE-NO/2566 is the entity DEPARTMENT-NO/405. In other words, "DEPARTMENT" is the role that the entity DEPARTMENT-NO/405 plays to describe the entity EMPLOYEE-NO/2566. Similarly, the "NAME", "ALTERNATIVE-NAME", or "AGE" of EMPLOYEE-NO/2566 is "NAME/Peter Jones", "NAME/Sam Jones", or "NO-OF-YEARS/20", respectively. The description of the entity EMPLOYEE-

NO/2566 is a collection of the related entities and their roles (the entities and roles circled by the dotted line). An example of the *entity description* of "EMPLOYEE-NO/2566" (in its full-blown, unfactored form) is illustrated by the set of role-name/entity-name-set-name/entity-name triplets shown in Figure 23. Conceptually, the entity set model differs from the entity-relationship model in the following ways:

(1) In the entity set model, everything is treated as an entity. For example, "COLOR/BLACK" and "NO-OF-YEARS/45" are entities. In the entity-relationship model, "blue" and "36" are usually treated as values. Note treating values as entities may cause semantic problems. For example, in Figure 22, what is the difference between "EMPLOYEE-NO/2566", "NAME/Peter Jones", and "NAME/Sam Jones"? Do they represent different entities?

(2) Only binary relationships are used in the entity set model,[5] while n-ary relationships may be used in the entity-relationship model.

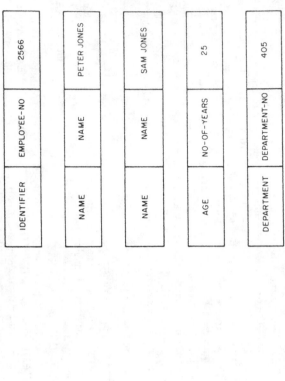

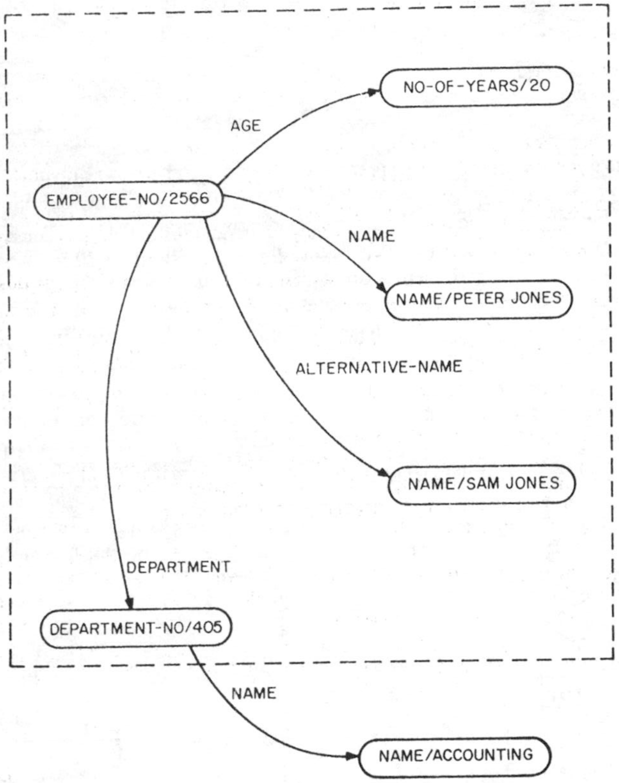

Fig. 22. The entity-set view

THE ENTITY-RELATIONSHIP MODEL TERMINOLOGY	ATTRIBUTE OR ROLE	VALUE SET	VALUE
THE ENTITY SET MODEL TERMINOLOGY	"ROLE-NAME"	"ENTITY-NAME-SET-NAME"	"ENTITY-NAME"
	IDENTIFIER	EMPLOYEE-NO	2566
	NAME	NAME	PETER JONES
	NAME	NAME	SAM JONES
	AGE	NO-OF-YEARS	25
	DEPARTMENT	DEPARTMENT-NO	405

Fig. 23. An "entity description" in the entity-set model

4.3.2 Deriving the Entity Set View. One of the main difficulties in understanding the entity set model is due to its world view (i.e. identifying values with entities). The entity-relationship model proposed in this paper is useful in understanding and deriving the entity set view of data. Consider Figures 2 and 6. In Figure 2, entities are represented by e_i's (which exist in our minds or are pointed at with fingers). In Figure 6, entities are represented by values. The entity set model works both at level 1 and level 2, but we shall explain its view at level 2 (Figure 6). The entity set model treats all value sets such as NO-OF-YEARS as "entity-name-sets" and all values as "entity-names." The attributes become role names in the entity set model. For binary relationships, the translation is simple: the role of an entity in a relationship (for example, the role of "DEPARTMENT" in the relationship DEPARTMENT-EMPLOYEE) becomes the role name of the entity in describing the other entity in the relationship (see Figure 22). For n-ary ($n > 2$) relationships, we must create artificial entities for relationships in order to handle them in a binary relationship world.

ACKNOWLEDGMENTS

The author wishes to express his thanks to George Mealy, Stuart Madnick, Murray Edelberg, Susan Brewer, Stephen Todd, and the referees for their valuable sug-

[5] In DIAM II [24], n-ary relationships may be treated as special cases of identifiers.

gestions (Figure 21 was suggested by one of the referees). This paper was motivated by a series of discussions with Charles Bachman. The author is also indebted to E.F. Codd and M.E. Senko for their valuable comments and discussions in revising this paper.

REFERENCES

1. Abrial, J.R. Data semantics. In *Data Base Management*, J.W. Klimbie and K.L. Koffeman, Eds., North-Holland Pub. Co., Amsterdam, 1974, pp. 1–60.
2. Bachman, C.W. Software for random access processing. *Datamation 11* (April 1965), 36–41
3. Bachman, C.W. Data structure diagrams. *Data Base 1*, 2 (Summer 1969), 4–10.
4. Bachman, C.W. Trends in database management—1975. Proc., AFIPS 1975 NCC, Vol. 44 AFIPS Press, Montvale, N.J., pp. 569–576.
5. Birkhoff, G., and Bartee, T.C. *Modern Applied Algebra*. McGraw-Hill, New York, 1970
6. Chamberlin, D.D., and Raymond, F.B. SEQUEL: A structured English query language Proc. ACM-SIGMOD 1974, Workshop, Ann Arbor, Michigan, May, 1974.
7. CODASYL. Data base task group report. ACM, New York, 1971.
8. Codd, E.F. A relational model of data for large shared data banks. *Comm. ACM 13*, 6 (June 1970), 377–387.
9. Codd, E.F. Normalized data base structure: A brief tutorial. Proc. ACM-SIGFIDET 1971 Workshop, San Diego, Calif., Nov. 1971, pp. 1–18.
10. Codd, E.F. A data base sublanguage founded on the relational calculus. Proc. ACM-SIGFIDET 1971, Workshop, San Diego, Calif., Nov. 1971, pp. 35–68.
11. Codd, E.F. Recent investigations in relational data base systems. Proc. IFIP Congress 1974, North-Holland Pub. Co., Amsterdam, pp. 1017–1021.
12. Deheneffe, C., Hennebert, H., and Paulus, W. Relational model for data base. Proc IFIP Congress 1974, North-Holland Pub. Co., Amsterdam, pp. 1022–1025.
13. Dodd, G.G. APL—a language for associate data handling in PL/I. Proc. AFIPS 1966 FJCC, Vol. 29, Spartan Books, New York, pp. 677–684.
14. Eswaran, K.P., and Chamberlin, D.D. Functional specifications of a subsystem for data base integrity. Proc. Very Large Data Base Conf., Framingham, Mass., Sept. 1975, pp 48–68.
15. Hainaut, J.L., and Lecharlier, B. An extensible semantic model of data base and its data language. Proc. IFIP Congress 1974, North-Holland Pub. Co., Amsterdam, pp. 1026–1030.
16. Hammer, M.M., and McLeod, D.J. Semantic integrity in a relation data base system. Proc Very Large Data Base Conf., Framingham, Mass., Sept. 1975, pp. 25–47.
17. Lindgreen, P. Basic operations on information as a basis for data base design. Proc. IFIP Congress 1974, North-Holland Pub. Co., Amsterdam, pp. 993–997.
18. Mealy, G.H. Another look at data base. Proc. AFIPS 1967 FJCC, Vol. 31, AFIPS Press, Montvale, N.J., pp. 525–534.
19. Nijssen, G.M. Data structuring in the DDL and the relational model. In *Data Base Management*, J.W. Klimbie and K.L. Koffeman, Eds., North-Holland Pub. Co., Amsterdam, 1974, pp. 363–379.
20. Olle, T.W. Current and future trends in data base management systems. Proc. IFIP Congress 1974, North-Holland Pub. Co., Amsterdam, pp. 998–1006.
21. Roussopoulos, N., and Mylopoulos, J. Using semantic networks for data base management. Proc. Very Large Data Base Conf., Framingham, Mass., Sept. 1975, pp. 144–172.
22. Rustin, R. (Ed.). Proc. ACM-SOGMOD 1974—debate on data models. Ann Arbor, Mich., May 1974.
23. Schmid, H.A., and Swenson, J.R. On the semantics of the relational model. Proc. ACM-SIGMOD 1975. Conference, San Jose, Calif., May 1975, pp. 211–233.
24. Senko, M.E. Data description language in the concept of multilevel structured description: DIAM II with FORAL. In *Data Base Description*, B.C.M. Dougue, and G.M. Nijssen, Eds., North-Holland Pub. Co., Amsterdam, pp. 239–258.
25. Senko, M.E., Altman, E.B., Astrahan, M.M., and Fehder, P.L. Data structures and accessing in data-base systems. *IBM Syst. J. 12*, 1 (1973), 30–93.
26. Sibley, E.H. On the equivalence of data base systems. Proc. ACM-SIGMOD 1974 debate on data models, Ann Arbor, Mich., May 1974, pp. 43–76.
27. Steel, T.B. Data base standardization—a status report. Proc. ACM-SIGMOD 1975, Conference, San Jose, Calif., May 1975, pp. 65–78.
28. Stonebraker, M. Implementation of integrity constraints and views by query modification. Proc. ACM-SIGMOD 1975, Conference, San Jose, Calif., May 1975, pp. 65–78.
29. Sundgren, B. Conceptual foundation of the infological approach to data bases. In *Data Base Management*, J.W. Klimbie and K.L. Koffeman, Eds., North-Holland Pub. Co., Amsterdam, 1974, pp. 61–95.
30. Taylor, R.W. Observations on the attributes of database sets. In *Data Base Description*, B.C.M. Dougue and G.M. Nijssen, Eds., North-Holland Pub. Co., Amsterdam, pp. 73–84.
31. Tsichritzis, D. A network framework for relation implementation. In *Data Base Description*, B.C.M. Douge and G.M. Nijssen, Eds., North-Holland Pub. Co., Amsterdam, pp. 269–282.

Using Semantic Networks for Data Base Management

Nicholas Roussopoulos

John Mylopoulos

Department of Computer Science
University of Toronto

ABSTRACT

This paper presents a semantic model of data bases. The model assumes the availability of a semantic network storing knowledge about a data base and a set of attributes for the data base. The use of the semantic net in generating a relational schema for the data base, in defining a set of semantic operators and in maintaining the data base consistent is then demonstrated.

1. INTRODUCTION

The usefulness of Data Base Management Systems (DBMSs) is severely restricted by their failure to take into account the semantics of data bases. Although all three models (Hierarchical, Network and Relational) provide a logical view of the data base in terms of data structures and a set of operators on them, they fail to incorporate the semantics of the data base into these data structures and operators.

Some of the problems that are not handled adequately by existing models are listed below. For reasons of economy, we will discuss the relational model only, although similar criticisms apply to the other models as well.

(a) **What do attributes and relations mean?** Each user must know what the attributes and relations of a relational schema mean, otherwise he cannot use them. The methods that are available for solving this problem (data dictionaries) are in their infancy and are restricted to primary relations only.

(b) **How do we choose a relational schema for a particular data base?** Some work has been done on this problem using the concept of functional dependency [1,3,7,14]. It has been argued elsewhere [9], and we concur, that this concept is not adequate for expressing the semantic relationships that may exist between items constituting a data base, and that a new, more semantic, approach may be needed.

(c) **When do data base operations make sense?** Apart from obvious syntactic considerations, the only constraints on the execution of a particular data base operation the current systems can account for are related to cost and security. On the other hand, there are many semantic pointers that could be used to determine whether an operation makes sense or not.

This work was partially supported by the Department of Communications of Canada and by the National Research Council of Canada. Authors' address: Dept. of Computer Science, Artificial Intelligence Group, University of Toronto, Ontario, M5S 1A7, Canada.

(d) **How do we maintain the data base consistent?** With the semantics of the data base excluded from the relational model the effect insertions, deletions and updates have on the data base is only understood by the user in terms his/her subjective view of what the information in the data base means. Thus consistency becomes a subjective notion and this can easily lead to its violation.

Our approach to data base management is based on the availability and use of a semantic network which stores knowledge about the data base being considered. Given this semantic network, we proceed to tackle the problems mentioned above, and others, always refering back to the net whenever a question arises regarding the meaning of the data base.

It should be clear to the reader that any system which uses the semantic approach we are proposing here will be expensive, since it has to account for information about, as well as in the data base. It is our position, however, that many problems data base management faces today will not be solved until the semantics of the data base are included in the designer's as well in the user's viewpoint of the data base.

The semantic model we will develop is in several respects an extension of Codd's relational model [2]. Two first attempts to use the semantics of a data base in order to derive the relational schema in such a way that some consistency constraints can be posed on it are due to Deheneffe et al [6] and Schmid and Swenson [13]. Both papers use a simple-minded representation for the semantics of a data base and provide consistency rules for addition-deletion operations on the data base. Another work that must be mentioned because it is our starting point in this research is the TORUS project whose aim was to provide a natural language front end for a data base management system [9]. In the process of designing and implementing a prototype version of TORUS we have reached many of the conclusions that are presented in this paper.

The paper assumes that a data base is presented in terms of the set of attributes to be used and a semantic network representation of the knowledge defining the meaning of the data base. It then considers some of the problems mentioned earlier, namely the generation of the relational schema, the definition of semantic operators with data base counterparts, and the maintenance of consistency for the data base, demonstrating in each case how the availability of the semantic net can be of use.

Section 2 gives an introduction of the representation we will use for knowledge about a data base. Section 3 considers the generation of the relational schema from the semantic net. Section 4 provides semantic operators and their data base counterparts. Finally, section 5 discusses consistency of data bases and gives four examples to demonstrate the uses of the semantic net regarding this problem.

2. REPRESENTING KNOWLEDGE ABOUT A DATA BASE

In this section we discuss the representation of knowledge that will be used in the rest of the paper. This representation is based on semantic networks as developed by the TORUS project and more complete descriptions of its features and uses can be found elsewhere [9,10,11]. A major extension to the TORUS representation had to be introduced in order to allow it to handle quantification, which is rather important for expressing queries about the data base.

The section consists of two parts. In the first, we introduce the representation and discuss various aspects of its use, notably the generation of context and the integration of new information to the semantics net (graph-fitting). In the second, we describe the representation of quantification that we will use.

2.1. The Semantic Net and its Uses.

The semantic net is a labelled directed graph where both nodes and edges may be labelled. The labels of nodes will only be used for reference purposes and will usually be mnemonic names. The labels of edges, on the other hand, will have a number of associated semantic properties and inferences.

There are four types of nodes: ***concepts***, ***events***, ***characteristics*** and ***value-nodes*** which are used to represent ideas making up the knowledge related to a particular data base.

Concepts are the essential constants or parameters of the world we are modelling and specify physical or abstract objects.

Events are used to represent the actions which occur in the world. Their representation is based on a case-grammar model, (Fillmore [8]), and consists of an event node and several nodes that specify who plays the *roles* (or fills the *cases*) associated with this event. For example,

```
western.united ←— agent,source —— supply ———— destination —→ eastern.co.
                                    |
                                  object
                                    ↓
                                part.#.7305
```

represents an instantiation of the event 'supply' with 'western.united' playing the role of "agent" and "source", 'eastern.co.' playing the role of "destination' and 'part.#.7305' being the supplied part.

The list of cases we will use and their abbreviations has as follows: agent (a), affected (aff), topic (t), instrument (i), result (r), source (s), destination (d) and object (o). The names of these cases are intended to be self-explanatory.

Characteristics are used to represent states (situations) or to modify concepts, events or other characteristics. A characteristic may be considered to be a binary relation mapping elements from its domain, those nodes to which the characteristic may apply, to its range, those values which the characteristic may take. For example, ADDRESS maps LEGAL.PERSON (the set of persons and institutions) into the set of possible address.values. Graphically, a characteristic is represented as a node labelled by the name of the characteristic, with a "ch" ("characterize") edge pointing to an element of the domain and a "v" ("value") edge pointing to the corresponding value:

```
john.smith ←— ch —— address —— v —→ 65 st. george st.,toronto,canada
```

"True" characteristics are usually natural attributes of concepts but characteristics can also be used as abbreviations of more complicated situations where we wish to omit unnecessary detail. In some circumstances such abbreviations are mappings from a cross-product domain to a range and we use a "wrt" ("with-respect-to") edge to indicate the second argument. For example, PRICE characterizes PARTS with respect to SUPPLY, producing a DOLLAR.VALUE:

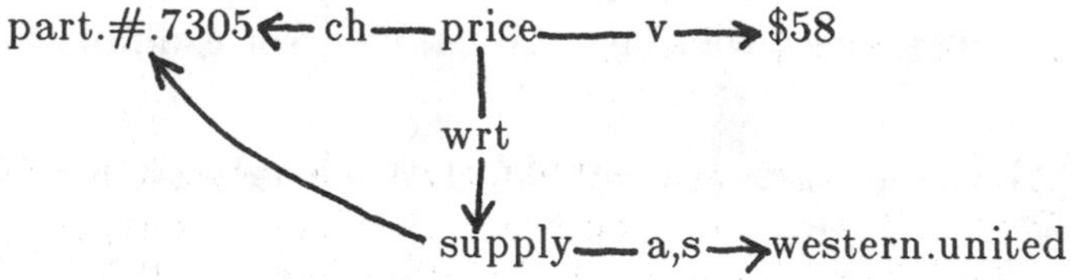

We will distinguish four types of characteristics, depending on the relation defined between the domain and the range of the characteristic: many-to-many, many-to-one, one-to-many and one-to-one. Below we give examples of the four different types, demonstrating the graphical notation we will use for each kind:

PERSON⇐ch═ADDRESS═v⇒ADDRESS.VALUE
(many-to-many)
PHYSICAL.OBJECT⇐ch═WEIGHT—v→WEIGHT.VALUE
(many-to-one)
PERSON← ch—POSSESSION═v⇒PHYSICAL.OBJECT
(one-to-many)
PART←ch—PART.#–v→PART.#.VALUE
(one-to-one)

Thus a person can have several addresses and at the same time several persons may have the same address, each physical object has a unique weight but a weight cannot be associated to a unique physical object; a physical object is possessed by a unique person but a person does not possess a unique object. Finally, a part has a unique part number and each part number is associated to a unique part.

Value-nodes represent values of characteristics such as an address ('65 st. george st., ontario, canada'), a weight ('65lbs'), a dollar value ('$53.70'), a name ('john smith') etc.

In addition to these types of entities, we will sometimes use mathematical predicates and functions such as SET.MEMBER, SET.DIFFERENCE, NUMERIC.DIFFERENCE etc. Two examples of such nodes, and the types of edges we associate to them, are given below:

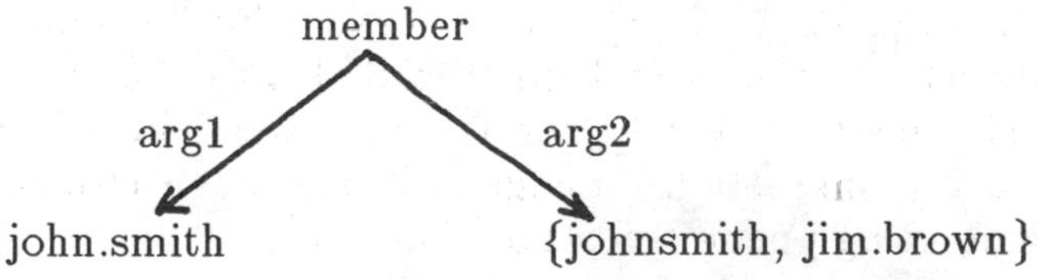

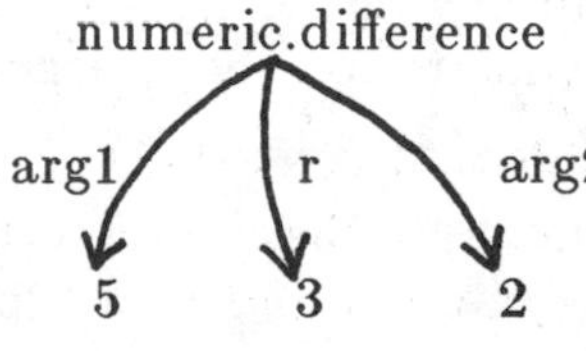

The "r"-labelled edge is the result edge that is also used for events.

The nodes that constitute the semantic net will be divided into two classes: one, relating to generic concepts, events, characteristics and value-nodes describes the possible or allowable states of affairs in our domain of discourse. This class we will informally call the "upstairs" of the semantic net, in contrast to the second class, its "downstairs", where we keep instantiations or particular occurances of ideas. Note that each generic node can be thought of as the possibly empty or possibly infinite set of its instantiations. Similarly, "upstairs" nodes will have identifies given in capital letters whereas "downstairs" ones willhave their names given in small letters. For example, in

PHYSICAL.OBJECT⇐ch═WEIGHT—v→WEIGHT.VALUE

the nodes are generic and the fact described by this graph is "physical objects can have a weight whose value is an instantiation of the generic node WEIGHT.VALUE; moreover the relation between PHYSICAL.OBJECT and WEIGHT.VALUE is many-to-one. On the other hand,

peter.wells←ch—weight—v→140lbs

specifies that the instantiation 'peter.wells' has weight '140lbs'. This graph could be meaningless if the item 'peter.wells' is not recognized as an instantiationof PHYSICAL.OBJECT, and '140lbs' as an instantiation of WEIGHT.VALUE. Thus structures which include generic nodes serve in a certain sense as templates that must be matched by structures that consist of instantiations only, if the latter are to be meaningful to the semantic network.

In the representation of 'peter.wells weighs 140lbs' we have introduced a simplification that we intend to use throughout this paper: we have named the node that represents the person named 'peter.wells' with the name 'peter.wells'. A more complete representation of this would have been

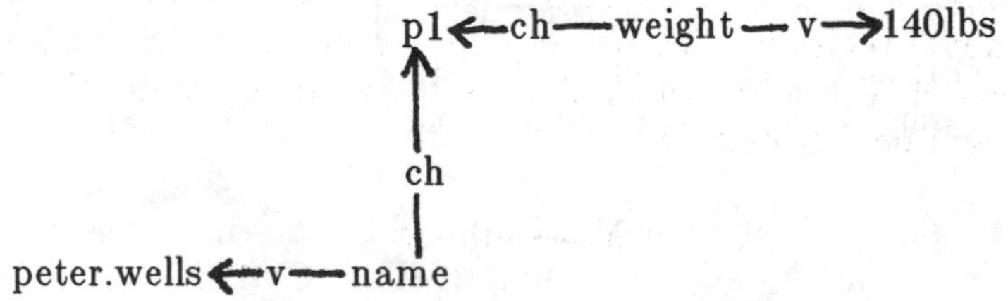

where p1 is an arbitrary identifier. In general, when we have one-to-one characteristic for a certain class of concepts we will often omit this characteristic from the representation altogether and we will use the value-nodes associated to that characteristic as replacements for the characterized concepts. This way, assuming that NAME is an one-to-one characteristic, we replace the structure

p1←ch—name—v→peter.wells

by a single node labelled 'peter.wells'.

The apparatus we have described so far is sufficient for the representation of most isolated phenomena, but we need the ability to represent larger chunks of knowledge. We achieve this by introducing *scenarios*.

A "scenario" is a collection of events, characteristics and mathematical predicates related through causal connectives such as "prerequisite" ("prereq") and "effect".

One may regard a scenario as a pattern or template which when matched by a structure, causes various kinds of inferences and predictions to be made. Moreover, only structures which are matched by some of the scenarios on the semantic net are meaningful to the system. Consider, for example, the notion of 'suppliers supply projects with parts', which we can represent as shown in fig. 2.1(a). This is a general scenario that will be matched by any instantiation of supply if the latter is to make any sense at all. Another scenario that involves 'supply' is shown in fig. 2.1(b) and represents the meaning of 'honest.ed supplies auto.parts' which means that 'honest.ed' is willing/equipped /in contract to supply AUTO.PARTS. Note that some project has to be assumed as the destination of such 'supply' actions as well. Another 'supply'-related scenario is given in fig. 2.1(c) and means 'honest.ed supplies bad.boy with auto.parts.made.by.ford'. Again the 'supplying' is supposed to be taking place on a regular basis, possibly after a mutual agreement. Yet another scenario related to 'supply' involves particular cases where 'honest.ed supplies bad.boy with a certain quantity of parts on a certain date'. Fig. 2.1(d) shows the scenario for this situation and notes the effects of any such 'supply' action has: the parts must have been ordered by 'bad.boy', and 'bad.boy' must pay 'honest.ed' because the latter supplied the parts. This is a partial instantiation of a more general scenario shown in fig. 2.1(e). Finally, fig. 2.1(f) shows a particular instantiation of the 'supply' event of fig. 2.1(d), which may correspond to a statement such as 'honest.ed supplied bad.boy on may 12, 1973 with (a quantity of) 500 mufflers at the price of $63.20 each and that he received a total of $31,600.00'.

In fig. 2.1 we presented six different scenarios or instantiations of scenarios that are obviously related semantically. We will now describe the overall organization of the semantic network, in other words, how are all these scenarios put together to form the semantic network. This organization will be defined in terms of "axes" or "dimensions".

The first axis we will discuss is called "SUB" because it is based on the subset (set-theoretic containment) relation. We will say that node X is a SUBnode of node Y if the set of instantiations of X is a subset of the set of instantiations of Y. The SUB relation between X and Y will be denoted by

$$Y \text{—sub} \rightarrow X$$

or simply

$$Y \longrightarrow X$$

If X is downstairs, the relation between Y and X is one of "instantiation" or "example-of". We will continue to use an unlabelled edge to denote such relations, since the fact that X is downstairs is already specified by its name (small letters). Fig. 2.2 shows a portion of the SUB axis for concepts that may be related to a Suppliers-Projects-Parts data base.

In general, we can organize (partially order) the concept occuring in our domain of discourse into a hierarchy representable by its Hasse diagram. It is important to note that (semantic) properties of concepts are inhereited along the SUB axis. For example,

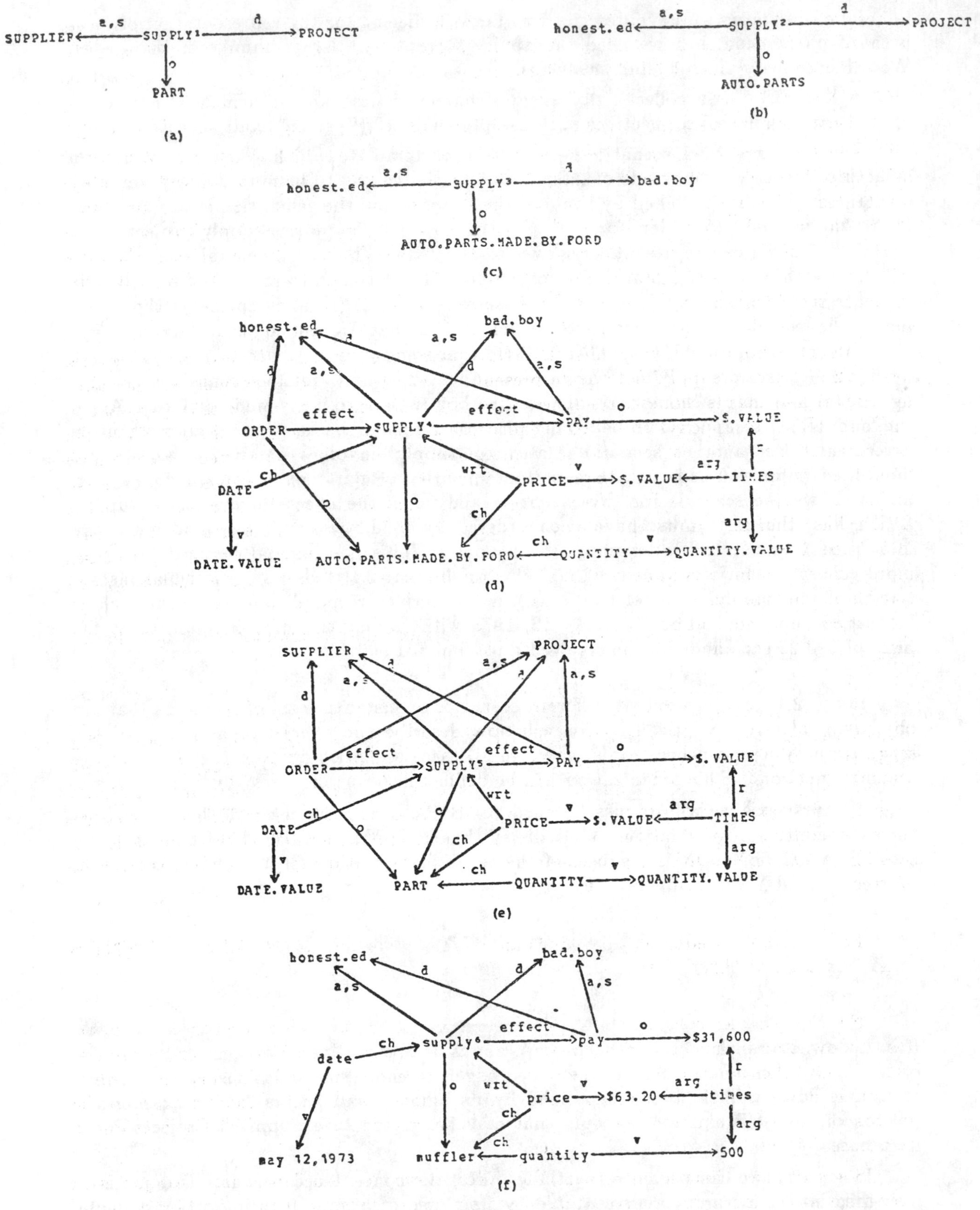
SUPPLIER
a,s
SUPPLY¹
d
PROJECT
o
PART
(a)
honest.ed
a,s
SUPPLY²
d
PROJECT
o
AUTO.PARTS
(b)
honest.ed
a,s
SUPPLY³
d
bad.boy
o
AUTO.PARTS.MADE.BY.FORD
(c)
honest.ed
bad.boy
ORDER
effect
SUPPLY⁴
PAY
$.VALUE
DATE
ch
wrt
PRICE
$.VALUE
TIMES
arg
r
DATE.VALUE
AUTO.PARTS.MADE.BY.FORD
QUANTITY
QUANTITY.VALUE
(d)
SUPPLIER
PROJECT
ORDER
SUPPLY⁵
PAY
$.VALUE
DATE
PRICE
$.VALUE
TIMES
DATE.VALUE
PART
QUANTITY
QUANTITY.VALUE
(e)
honest.ed
bad.boy
date
supply⁶
pay
$31,600
price
$63.20
times
may 12,1973
muffler
quantity
500
(f)

fig. 2.1

since SUPPLIERs are COMPANYs which are INSTITUTIONs, which are LEGAL.PERSONs, and since any LEGAL.PERSON can have an ADDRESS, a SUPPLIER can have an ADDRESS. This property of the SUB axis is a very important memory-saving device.

Scenarios are also organized on the SUB axis. Thus the six structures of SUPPLY given in fig. 2.1 can be organized as shown in fig. 2.3. It should be noted that cases or other characteristics of events which are not explicitly represented on the net are inherited from its lowest super-event that fills those cases or characteristics. The reader should note that indeed the SUB relations do hold between the various SUPPLY nodes, as claimed on fig. 2.3. It must also be noted that for an event E with cases C1, C2,...,Cn to be placed below another event E' with cases C1', C2',...,Cn' on the SUB axis, it must be that E is a subset of E', but also Ci is a subset of Ci' for $1 \leq i \leq n$.

Another important axis is the "DEF(initional)" one. Let us go back to the scenario of fig. 2.1(e) and the $SUPPLY^5$ node present there. Here we are obviously talking abut a sequence of events that starts when a SUPPLIER begins to make arrangements to SHIP PARTs to a PROJECT and ends when the latter receives them. Thus the scenario of fig. 2.1(e) is semantically ambiguous since it does not specify what does DATE refer to, the date the shipment is made or the date it is received. In order to define how does one $SUPPLY^5$ (something) and what does DATE refer to, we use the DEF axis. Fig. 2.4 shows the scenario that defines $SUPPLY^5$ in terms of the events SHIP and RECEIVE. The figure shows how are the cases of $SUPPLY^5$ related to cases in the scenario, but also how is DATE defined (here we define it as the date on which the shipment was made)

In general, the DEF axis enables us to give more details about events and characteristics.

Concepts can also be defined in terms of scenarios which specify the roles of those concepts. For example, PARTS.MADE.BY.FORD is defined as the concept filling the object case of the event MANUFACTURE whose agent case is filled by 'ford'. This definition of AUTO.PARTS.MADE.BY.FORD is indicated on the net by a "cdef" labelled edge, see fig. 2.5. The role of concept definitions is very important for the so called "membership problem". In order words "cdefs" denote the sufficient and necessary conditions for membership in a particular class. In the example of PARTS.MADE.BY.FORD, a part belongs into this class iff it has been manufactured by 'ford'.

Finally, another edge which defines an axis is the "part" edge (a DEPARTMENT is "part" of a COMPANY, a WHEEL is "part" of a CAR, etc.)

Representing knowledge on the semantic network has the advantage that this information can be examined and reasoned about provided that there is an appropriate interpreter. On the other hand, this represenation is expensive and for any universe of discourse there will be "peripheral" knowledge for which general reasoning may not be necessary. We will represent such knowledge in terms of functions which we associate to corresponding nodes on the semantic net.

Some of these functions we will call "recognition functions" because their job is to recognize instances of a class by using syntactic or semantic information. For example, dates can be recognized by syntactic string matching rules while the "cdef" axis has to

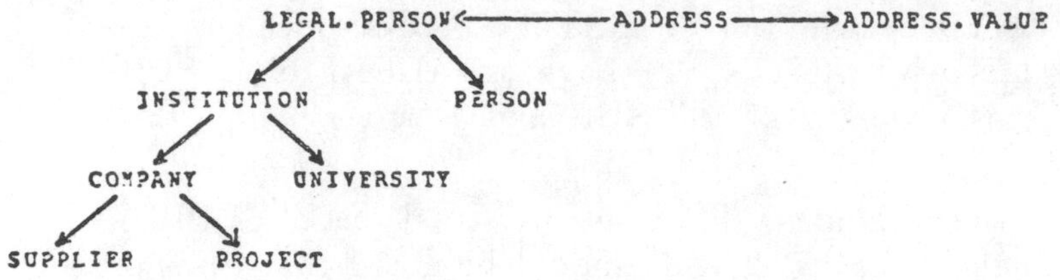

fig. 2.2

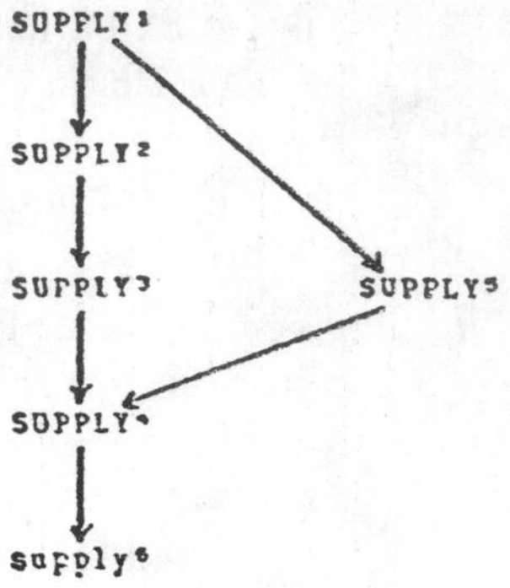

fig. 2.3

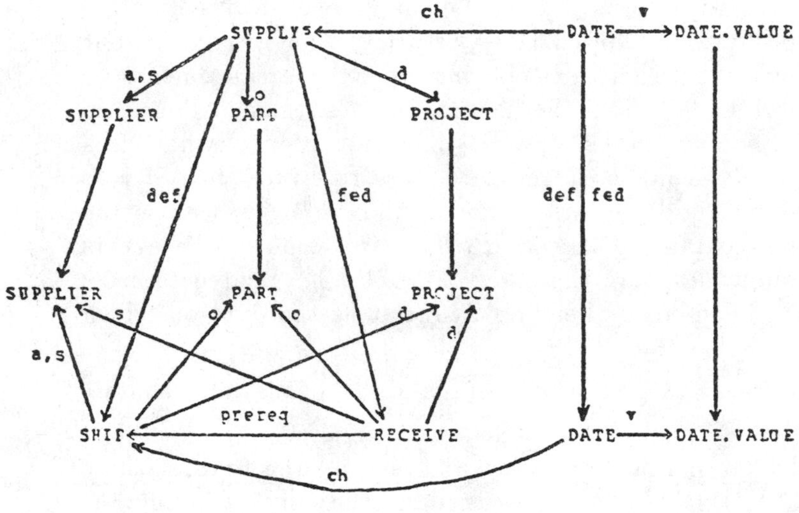

fig. 2.4

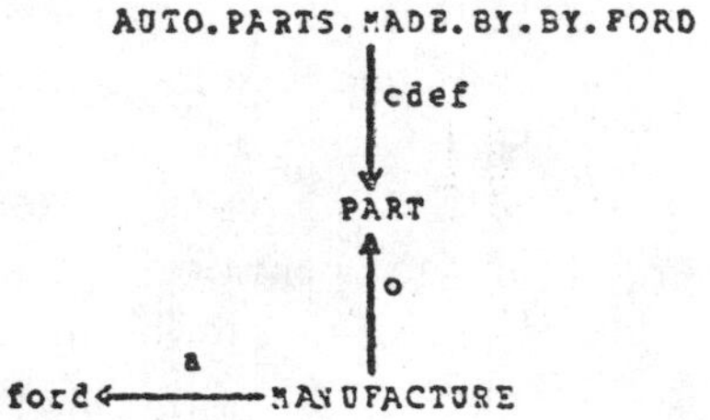

fig. 2.5

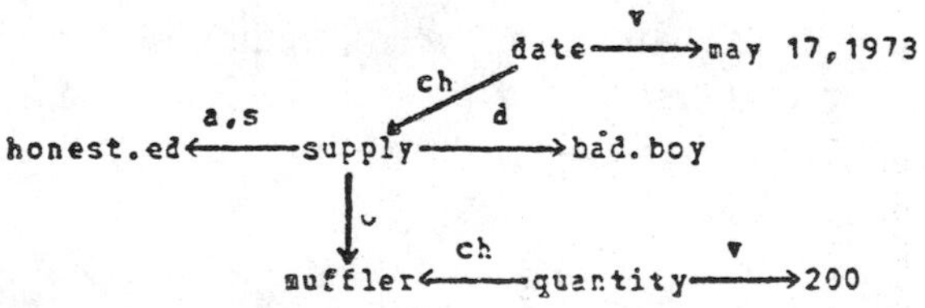

(a)

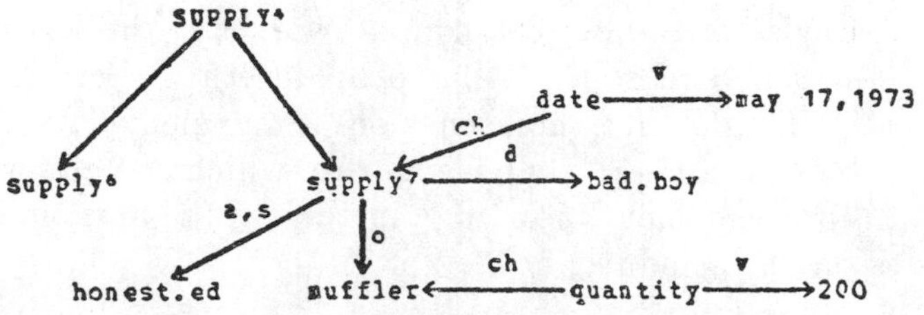

(b)

fig. 2.6

be used in order to determine whether or not a particular part belongs to the class of AUTO.PARTS.MADE.BY.FORD. Value-nodes in general do have associated recognition functions. "Mapping functions" are useful for mapping structures from one level of the represenation to another. For example, mapping functions may be used to replace every instantiation of SUPPLY by the explicit DEFinition of SUPPLY on the semantic net. "Definitional functions" are used to define procedures for performing particular actions (RETRIEVE all tuples that satisfy a given description, UPDATE something in the data base, MOVE a block, etc.). The nodes of the net that have associated definitional functions will have their names preceded and followed by *'s. For example,

system←a—*retrieve*—o→?←v—part.#—ch→muffler

the function "retrieve" will perform the retrieval of the part number of the part 'muffler' and it will replace the question mark by this value.

It is important to stress that knowledge can be represented in either procedural or declarative form and which form is used is strictly an issue of trading cost for "understanding power".

We turn our attention now to some uses of the semantic network in accomplishing "understanding". There are two uses we will discuss: the generation of "context" during a dialog and the "integration" of new information to the already existing semantic network (graph-fitting). We discuss these uses partly to give some justification for the representation we have described so far, and partly because some aspects of these uses are closely related to semantic problems of data bases (see sections 4.3 and 5).

The presence of a network entity in the context represents the system's expectation that this item is or will be relevant to the current dialogue. When new information, which has been predicted, enters the dialogue, its relevance can be explained by the "generation path" taken to create the expectation. Consider, for example, the statements:

'honest.ed send out a shipment yesterday.'

and

'there were 300 snow-tires and 50 mufflers.'

Here, we can generate part of the context of SHIP when the first sentence is "understood". Part of this context is the event of $SUPPLY^5$ according to the scenario of fig. 2.4. Once $SUPPLY^5$ with 'honest.ed' as agent-source is in, the object case of this $SUPPLY^5$ (i.e. AUTO.PARTs) also enters the context. When the second statement is presented, it can be "understood" in terms of the existing context, since both 'snow-tires' and 'mufflers' are AUTO.PARTs. By "understood" we mean here that an interpreter can infer what is the relationships of the sentence to what was said before.

In generating the context one has to take into account the semantics of the various edge labels. To give an example, whenever we have the configuration

A—effect→B

every instantiation of A implies strongly an instantiation of B, while every instantiation of B implies weakly an instantiation of A. This means that when a node enters the context, it has a "strength" value attached, which specifies how reliably it can be inferred from the already existing context. More informationon the context mechanism can be found in [10].

A part of the procedure for integrating new input to the semantic network will have to be done by an algorithm which we call "graph-fitting". Assume that the semantic network includes the scenarios of fig. 2.1 and that the new sentence

'honest.ed supplied bad.boy with 200 mufflers on may 17, 1973'

is presented to the system. The system's job is to construct the graph of fig. 2.6(a) representing the meaning of this sentence, and then to integrate this graph with the semantic network (fig. 2.6(b)). To accomplish that, the graph-fitting algorithm may start from the most generic $SUPPLY^1$ node, making sure that all the cases of the input 'supply' may be placed below the cases of the generic $SUPPLY^1$. Once this has been accomplished, it may try to see whether there are any SUPPLY events below the generic one which are matched by the input 'supply'. The scenario of fig. 2.3(b) is chosen and a test is again performed to make sure that the input 'supply' in fact matches the $SUPPLY^4$ already on the net. This process is repeated until it is not longer possible to move the input graph any further down along the SUB axis. A portion of the net resulting from the integration is shown in fig. 2.6(b).

Note that if there is a context at the time the above sentence is presented for integration, with a SUPPLY node on it, the graph-fitting algorithm will begin with that SUPPLY rather than the most generic one since the lower is the most relevant and an instantiation of it is expected.

2.2. A representation for quantification.

In this section we present an extension of the TORUS representation which allows the representation of simple quantified statements. TOPUS avoided this issue because of its complexity and because primitive types of quantification can be handled by other means, as we will see below. However, many queries to a data base management system such as

> 'Give me all suppliers who supply all auto-parts to all projects located in Houston'

obviously involve many nested (universal) quantifiers. The need to be able to represent the meaning of such queries has forced us to consider the problem of quantification.

The semantic network, as we described it so far, can handle some aspects of quantification. For example, statements such as

'Every supplier is a company'

and

'Every supplier supplies some parts to some projects'

can be handled through "sub" and case edges respectively.

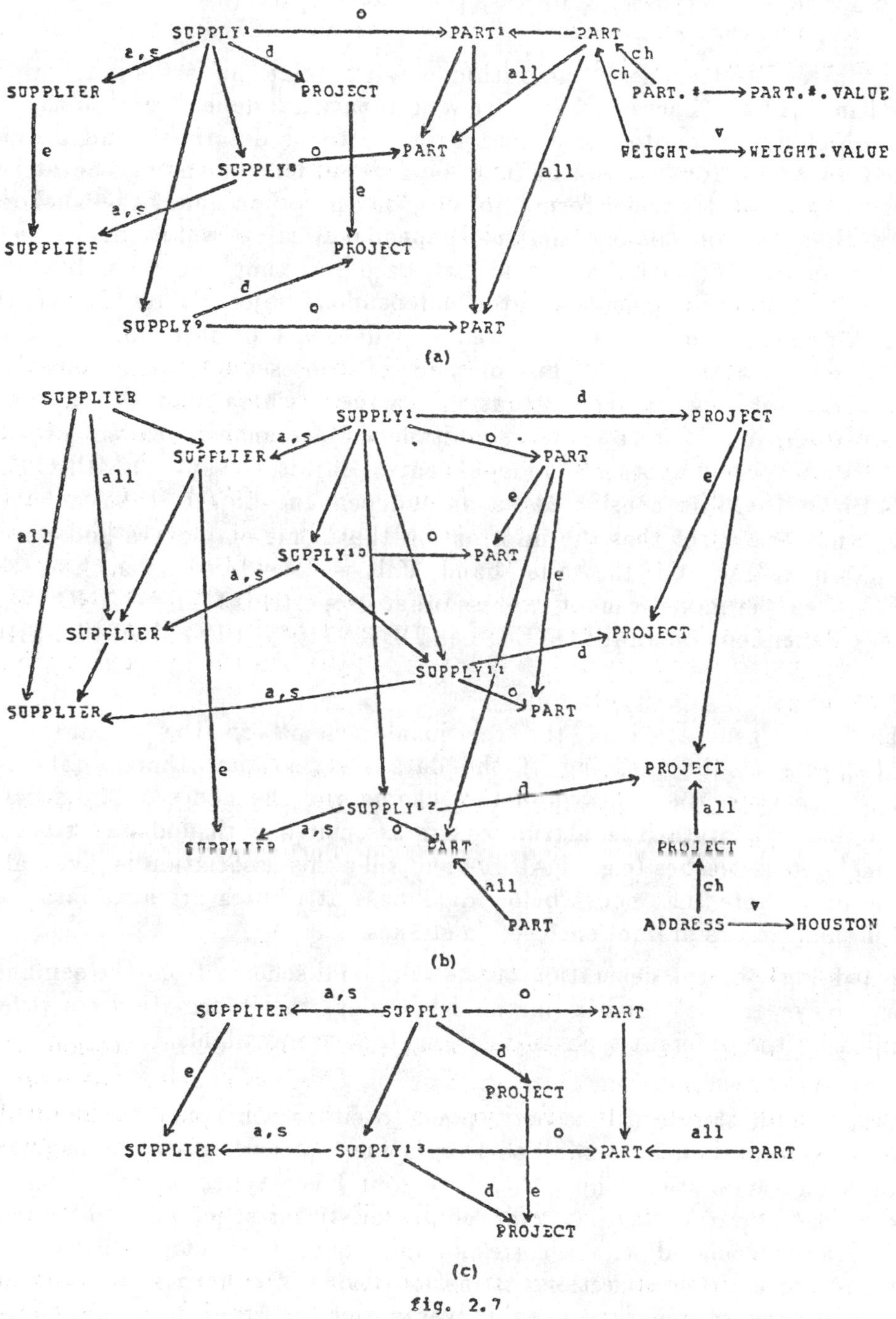
SUPPLY¹
o
PART¹
PART
ch
all
ch
a,s
d
SUPPLIER
PROJECT
PART.#
PART.#.VALUE
e
o
PART
v
WEIGHT
WEIGHT.VALUE
SUPPLY⁸
all
e
a,s
SUPPLIER
PROJECT
d
o
SUPPLY⁹
PART
(a)
SUPPLIER
d
SUPPLY¹
PROJECT
a,s
o
SUPPLIER
PART
all
e
e
all
o
SUPPLY¹⁰
PART
a,s
e
SUPPLIER
PROJECT
d
SUPPLY¹¹
a,s
o
SUPPLIER
PART
e
PROJECT
d
all
SUPPLY¹²
a,s
o
SUPPLIER
PART
PROJECT
all
ch
v
PART
ADDRESS
HOUSTON
(b)
a,s
o
SUPPLIER
SUPPLY¹
PART
e
d
PROJECT
a,s
o
all
SUPPLIER
SUPPLY¹³
PART
PART
d
e
PROJECT
(c)

fig. 2.7

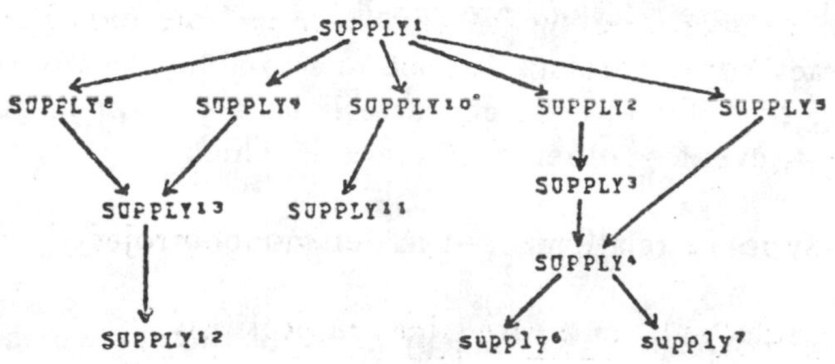
SUPPLY¹
SUPPLY⁸
SUPPLY⁹
SUPPLY¹⁰
SUPPLY²
SUPPLY⁵
SUPPLY³
SUPPLY¹³
SUPPLY¹¹
SUPPLY⁴
SUPPLY¹²
supply⁶
supply⁷

fig. 2.8

3. GENERATING THE RELATIONAL SCHEMA

The first attempts to generate algorithmically the relational schema for a data base are described in [7,14,1]. These papers start with functional dependency as the primitive in terms of which the semantics of a data base are to be described, and provide algorithms which generate from the set of functional dependencies among the attributes, a functional schema in 3rd normal form. In [13], on the other hand, the authors argue, convincingly, that the concept of functional dependency is not sufficient for the expression of all semantic information about a data base and they choose a different set of semantic primitives. These primitives are "independent objects", "characteristics" and "associations" and they have been inspired by the effect of insertions, deletions and modifications on a data base. This method of representing semantics runs into difficulties, however, when a situation arises where an item, such as TRAINING.PROGRAM, can be viewed simultaneously as an independent object and as a characteristic of another independent object, say EMPLOYEE. If TRAINING.PROGRAM is considered as an independent object, then deletion of an instance of it has the effect that the information that some employees had been trained by this program is lost. On the other hand, if it is considered as a characteristic of EMPLOYEE, then the model cannot express other properties of TRAINING.PROGRAM which are not dependent on EMPLOYEE, i.e. DURATION, PROGRAM.DESRIPTION, etc.

We base the generation of the relational schema on the semantic net that represents (aspects of the meaning of the data base so that there exists a natural correspondence between the relations of the schema and the nodes of the semantic net. We are assuming that data base attributes are associated with nodes of the net whose names are enclosed in slashes (e.g. /PART/) and that this association is given along with the semantic net. Note that nodes below data base attributes are also data base attributes even if their names are not enclosed in slashes.

A methodology for the generation of the relational schema from the semantic net is given below. Keys are not used in our model because the information conveyed in the keys is implied by the different types of relations that are available.

The relations in the data base correspond to either concepts or semantic relationships between concepts, such as the "part" relationship, and relationships that involve an event or a characteristic. Thus, there are four basic types of data base relations, named "concepts", "part", "event" and "characteristic" respectively. The relations in the data base are associated with a corresponding concept, event or characteristic node on the net and store either collections of instantiations of concepts, events and characteristics or collections of generic concepts, events and characteristics. The nodes which are associated with data base relations are called "realized".

Note that characteristic relations can be one-to-many, many-to-one and many-to-many, but not one-to-one. One-to-one characteristics are mapped onto attributes in the relation of the concept, event or other characteristic which they characterize.

The four types of relations used in our model are:

A. *Concept-relations* correspond to concept nodes of the net which are data base attributes. Their names are identical to the names of the concepts to which they are associated with and have as attributes the concept itself and the names of the value-nodes of their one-to-one characteristics which are data base attributes. For example, the concept /PART/ on the network, fig. 3.1, is mapped onto the relation

PART (PART, PART.#.VALUE, WEIGHT.VALUE)

in the data base. The PART concept on the net is underlined as an indication that this concept is realized. Note that the attribute PART in the above relation stands for PART.NAME.VALUE, while the relation named */PART/* stands for the concept PART. As mentioned in section 2.1, the two nodes have been identified on the net.

B. *Part-relations* correspond to "part" relationships between data base attributes of the net. Their names are identical to the containing concept name and have as attributes the names of both containing and contained concepts. For example, consider the concept */COMPANY/* in fig. 3.2. The "part" relationship is mapped onto the data base relation:

COMPANY(COMPANY, DEPARTMENT)

Again the attribute COMPANY stands for COMPANY.NAME.VALUE, while the relation named *COMPANY* stands for the concept node COMPANY. The concept *COMPANY*, (underlined), indicates that there is a data base relation where the instances of the relationship "part" are stored. Note that the containing concept also has a concept data base relation associated with it to store its one-to-one characteristics and that there is one part-relation for each "part" relationship of it.

C. *Event-relations* correspond to event relationships among data base attributes of the net. Their names are identical to the names of the events to which they are associated and have as attributes the names of their case-nodes, the names of the value-nodes of their one-to-one characteristics and the value-nodes of one-to-one characteristics of their cases which are not inherited from supernodes. For example, the event *SUPPLY* on the net, (fig. 3.3), is mapped onto the relation:

SUPPLY(SUPPLIER, PROJECT, PART, DATE.VALUE,
QUANTITY.VALUE, $.VALUE)

in the data base. The *SUPPLY* event node on the net is underlined as an indication that this object is realized and that if a supplying action is requested, it can be retrieved from the *SUPPLY* relation in the data base.

D. *Characteristic-relations*. There are three different kinds of characteristic relations to account for the three different types of mappings, many-to-one, one-to-many and many-to-many. Their names are identical to the characteristic nodes and have as attributes the concepts they characterize, the names of value-nodes of one-to-one characteristics of their cases which are not inherited from supernodes, the names of their value-nodes, and the names of the value-nodes of other one-to-one characteristics characterizing the characteristics themselves. Consider the semantic net of figure 3.4. This is mapped onto the data base relation:

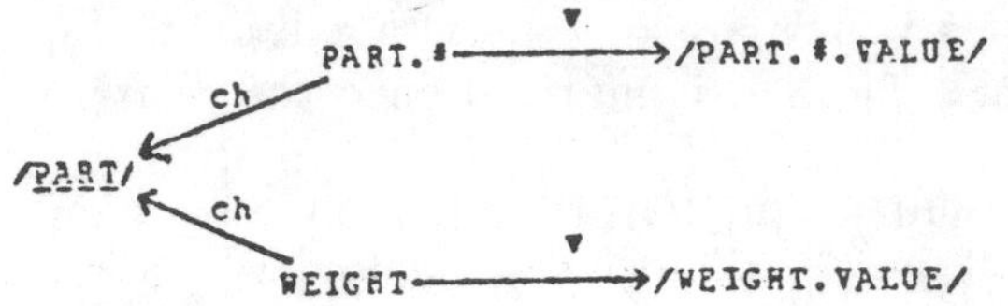

fig. 3.1

fig. 3.2

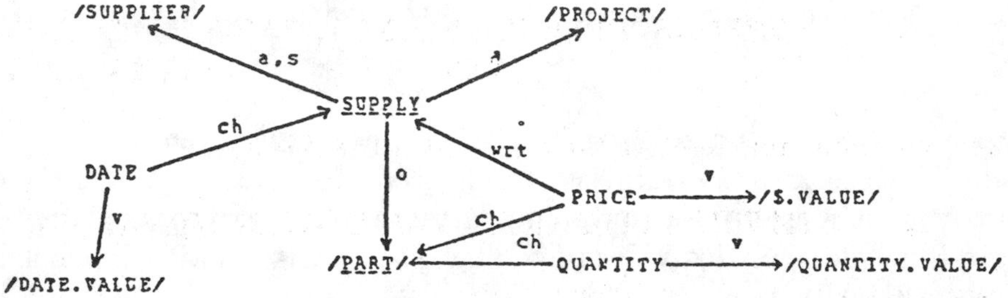

fig. 3.3

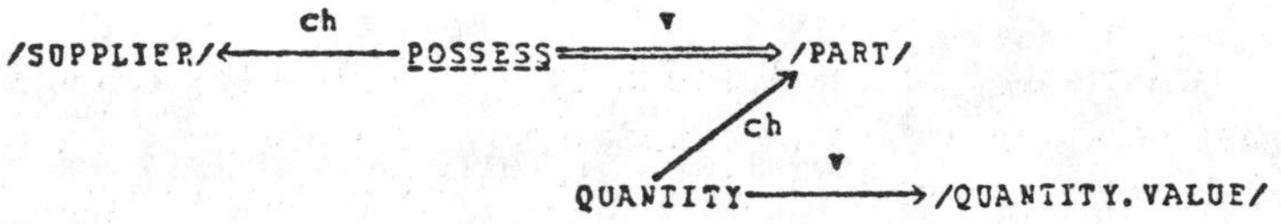

fig. 3.4

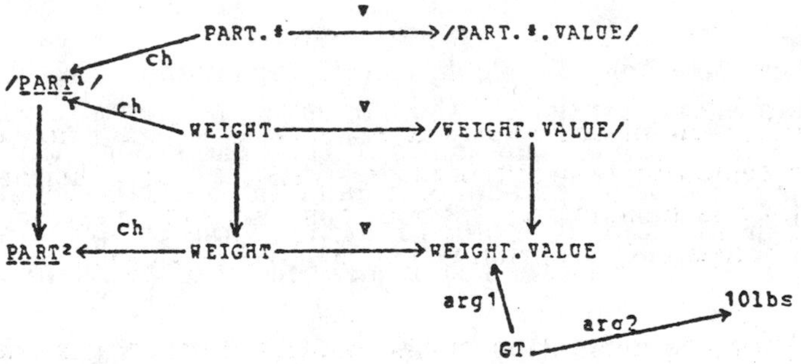

fig. 4.1

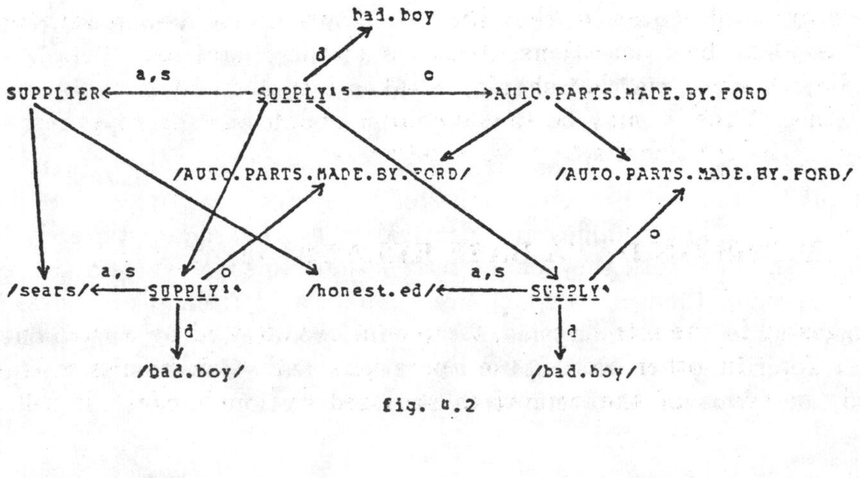

fig. 4.2

POSSESS(SUPPLIER, PART, QUANTITY.VALUE)

which is associated to the node *POSSESS*.

As one can see, concepts can be relations and/or attributes. Below we give an example where a concept is a relation and an attribute at the same time. Consider the network of fig. 3.3, where the concept */PART/*, (at the bottom of the diagram), is one of the attributes in

SUPPLY(SUPPLIER, PROJECT, PART, DATE.VALUE,
QUANTITY.VALUE, $.VALUE)

and has a certain value domain. At the same time, the relation

PART(PART, PART.#.VALUE, WEIGHT.VALUE)

which corresponds to the same /PART/ node is a concept relation that stores the values of the domain of the attribute PART in *SUPPLY* along with its one-to-one characteristics inherited from node /PART/ in fig. 3.1.

The partial ordering of realized nodes by the SUB edge reflects a partial ordering onto the data base relations which correspond to those nodes. Given a relation r associated with a node n of the net, we will use the terms "superrelation", "subrelation" to specify relations r1 and r2 which are associated to nodes n1 and n2 respectively such that

n1— n→n2

Contrary to Codd's view of the relational schema as a "flat" collection of independent relations, [5], the semantic network organizes relations in a heirarchy which explicitly states the semantic relationships among relations. This enables the model, as we will see later, to maintain consistency of primary and derived relations.

Our method for the generation of the relational schema is based on the primitive blocks for building the semantic net (concepts, events and characteristics). The justification for using it is that since those primitives are the smallest semantic entities accessable in our representation, they are also natural units for semantic operations that correspond to data base insertions, deletions and modifications. On the other hand, there may be other criteria that should be taken into account in the process of generating the schema. Thus, it may be that scenarios should also serve as semantic blocks in terms of which the relational schema is constructed.

4. OPERATIONS ON DATA BASE RELATIONS

As suggested in the introduction, the operations allowed by a model must be ones it can account for. In other words, the operations and their results must be explained (interpreted) in terms of the primitives provided by the model. It follows from this premise that for our semantic model we must provide "semantic operators", in contrast to the data base operators defined by the relational model [2]. By a "semantic operator" we mean here an operator which takes as arguments (operands) one or more nodes of the net and constructs a new node or nodes related semantically to those it was obtained from.

Since some nodes on the net have associated relations or attributes of the data base, a semantic operator may have a corresponding data base operation. It is important to stress, however, that in our model the starting point for the definition of operators is the semantic net not the data base. The data base operators are defined by studying the effect semantic operators must have on the data base.

All semantic operators we will define are set-theoretic in nature and can be directly related to manipulations of the SUB axis.

This definition of the semantic operators are given informally in section 4.1. As part of each definition, we give an English expression of the semantic operator. It must be noted that we do so for the reader's convenience in understanding the meaning of the operators. We do not assume the existence of a natural language analyzer for our model. The data base operators we will use can be defined algebraically, as in [4], but this will not be done in this paper.

Section 4.2 describes when and how is a data base operation executed as a result of the execution of a corresponding semantic operation. Section 4.3 considers when is a semantic operation "legal" and whether there is always a corresponding data base operation.

4.1. The semantic and their corresponding data base operators

a. Selection

The semantic operator of selection on a node n consists of creating a subnode below n which has more restricted semantic properties that node n. For example, the expression

'parts which have weight greater than 10lbs'

operates on node $PART^1$ and results in node $PART^2$ of fig. 4.1. The data base operator of selection is defined as the selection of tuples of a relation according to certain condition(s) on one or more attribute value(s) and results in a subrelation of the operand relation. Returning to our example, if selection is applied to relation $PART^1$ associated to node $PART^1$ it results in a relation $PART^2$ in the data base and it is associated to node $PART^2$ of fig. 4.1.

b. Union

Union operates on two nodes n1 and n2 and results in a new node nr which

i. is below every node n that is above n1 and n2

ii. is above n1 and n2

iii. inherits all common characteristics and/or cases of n1 and n2.

For example

'cases of supplying auto.parts.made.by.ford carried out by honest.ed or sears with bad.boy as destination'

operates on the two $SUPPLY^4$ and $SUPPLY^{14}$ nodes on fig. 4.2 and results in node $SUPPLY^{15}$, also shown on the figure.

The corresponding data base operator of union takes as arguments two relations associated with nodes n1 and n2 respectively and creates a new relation which is associated with nr. Its attributes are those of the operand relations that correspond to the common characteristics and/or cases of n1 and n2. Thus the new $SUPPLY^{15}$ relation obtained from the union of

$SUPPLY^4$ (honest.ed, bad.boy, AUTO.PARTS.MADE.BY.FORD)

and

$SUPPLY^{14}$(sears, bad.boy, AUTO.PARTS.MADE.BY.FORD)

is

$SUPPLY^{15}$(SUPPLIER, bad.boy, AUTO.PARTS.MADE.BY.FORD)

c. Intersection

Intersection operates on two nodes n1 and n2 and results in a new node nr which

i. is above every node that is below n1 and n2

ii. is below n1 and n2

iii. inherits all characteristics and/or cases of n1 and n2.

For example,

'parts that have been ordered by some project and possessed by some supplier'

operates on nodes $PART^3$ and $PART^4$ of fig. 4.3 and results in node $PART^5$ also shown on the figure.

The corresponding data base operator of intersection takes as arguments two relations associated with nodes n1 and n2 respectively and creates a new relation which is associated with nr. Its attributes are those of the operand relations that correspond to the characteristics and/or cases of nr. In the above example, the new relation $PART^5$, created from the intersection of $PART^3$ and $PART^4$, has the same form as $PART^3$ and $PART^4$ and is associated with node $PART^5$.

d. Difference

Difference operates on two nodes n1 and n2, (n1-n2), and results in a new node nr which

i. is below n1

ii. is connected with n2 by an edge pointing to it and labelled "none"

iii. inherits all characteristics and/or cases of n1.

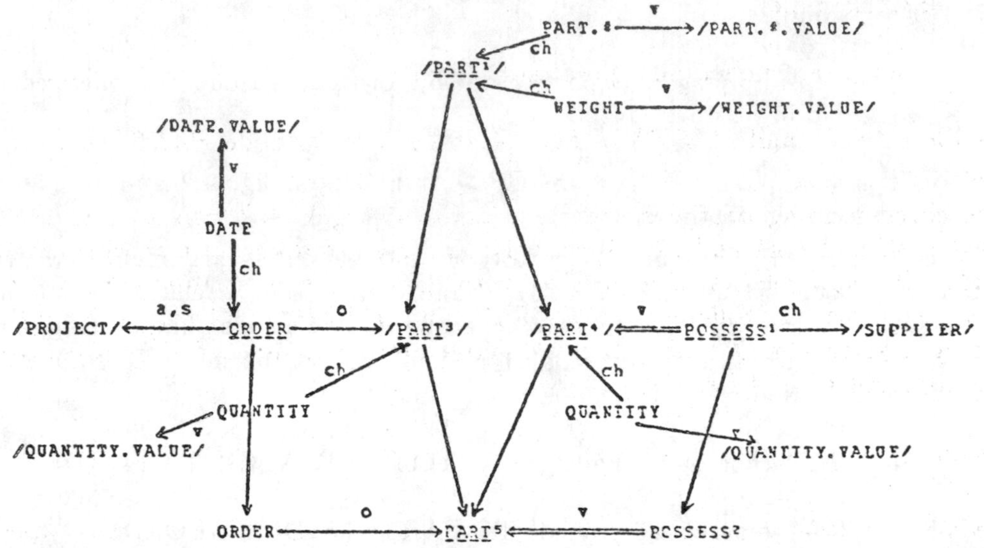
PART.#
/PART.#.VALUE/
/PART¹/
WEIGHT
/WEIGHT.VALUE/
/DATE.VALUE/
DATE
/PROJECT/
ORDER
/PART³/
/PART⁴/
POSSESS¹
/SUPPLIER/
QUANTITY
/QUANTITY.VALUE/
QUANTITY
/QUANTITY.VALUE/
ORDER
PART⁵
POSSESS²

fig. 4.3

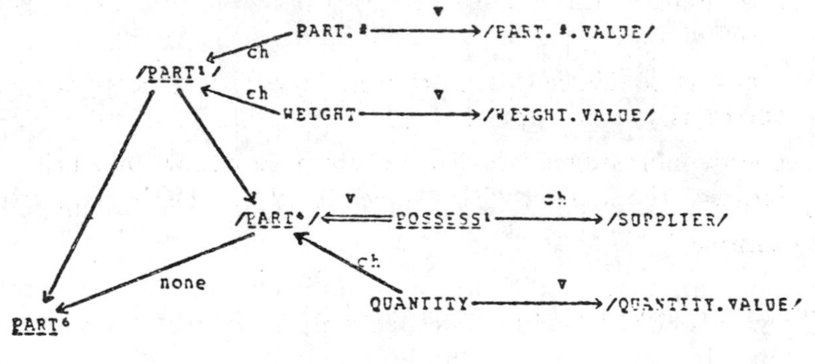
PART.#
/PART.#.VALUE/
/PART¹/
WEIGHT
/WEIGHT.VALUE/
/PART⁴/
POSSESS¹
/SUPPLIER/
none
QUANTITY
/QUANTITY.VALUE/
PART⁶

fig. 4.4

For example,

'parts that no supplier possesses'

operates on $PART^1$ and $PART^4$ of fig. 4.4 and results in node $PART^6$ also shown in the figure.

The corresponding data base operator takes as arguments two relations r1 and r2 associated with nodes n1 and n2 respectively, and creates a new one rr which is subrelation of r1. The new relation is associated with nr and has as attributes those of r1. In the above example the difference of $PART^1$ and $PART^4$, ($PART^1$ - $PART^4$), will result in a relation $PART^6$ which has the same attributes as $PART^1$ and is associated with the node $PART^6$ of fig. 4.4.

e. Division

Division is the semantic operator that is related to our representation of quantification. It takes as arguments

i. an event or characteristic node n (the dividend)

ii. a node nd (the divisor), and a case-node n1 of n, over which division is to be applied

iii. one or more case-nodes n2, n3,.. of n with respect to which the division is to be applied

It results in

i. a new node nr below n

ii. new nodes nr1,nr2,.., case-nodes of nr corresponding one-to-one with the cases of n

iii. a new edge labelled "all" from nd to nr1 to indicate the node over which the division was applied

iv. one or more edges labelled "e" from n2,n3,.. to nr2,nr3,.. respectively to indicate the node(s) with respect to which the division was applied.

For example,

'suppliers possessing all parts ordered by project pj1'

operates on node $POSSESS^1$ and $PART^7$ over node $PART^4$ with respect to node $SUPPLIER^1$ on fig. 4.5 and results in nodes $POSSESS^3$, $PART^8$ and $SUPPLIER^2$, as shown on fig. 4.5, along with the appropriate links created by the division.

The corresponding data base operator of division takes as arguments

i. an event or a characteristic relation (dividend) associated with node n

ii. a concept relation (divisor) associated with node nd

iii. an attribute of the dividend relation over which the division is to be applied (corresponding to node n1)

iv. one or more other attributes of the dividend relation with respect to which the division is to be applied (corresponding to nodes n2,n3,..)

It results in a subrelation of the dividend relation and is associated with node nr. Thus in our example,

POSSESS[1](PART, SUPPLIER, QUANTITY.VALUE)
(dividend)

PART[7](PART, PART.#.VALUE, WEIGHT.VALUE)
(divisor)

are divided and result in

POSSESS[3](PART, SUPPLIER, QUANTITY.VALUE)

which is associated with *POSSESS*[3] in fig. 4.5.

Note that our data base division is slightly different from the one given in [4]. In our definition an extra argument is provided which specifies the attribute(s) with-respect-to which division is applied. Thus the dividend relation does not have to be binary.

4.2. Execution of data base operators

Consider the statements

'find all parts which have weight greater than 10lbs'

and

'honest.ed increased the prices of parts which have weight greater than 10lbs'

Both statements involve the execution of the (semantic) selection operator, as shown in fig. 4.1. The question is whether the data base selection operator must be executed at the same time or whether its execution can be deferred. In the case of the first statement execution of the data base selection operator appears necessary, so that the FIND command can be carried out. For the second statement, however, creation of a new relation through the data base selection operator may be altogether unnecessary.

Our general position on this issue is that data base operations are not carried out when corresponding semantic ones are, but rather, when definitional functions (see section 2.1) corresponding to system commands -such as "find", "update", "insert", "delete", etc.- are executed.

4.3. "Legality" of semantic operations

The data base operations we have defined, like the original ones introduced by Codd, place certain restrictions on the relations that may serve as their operands. For example, it is not possible to take the union of the relations

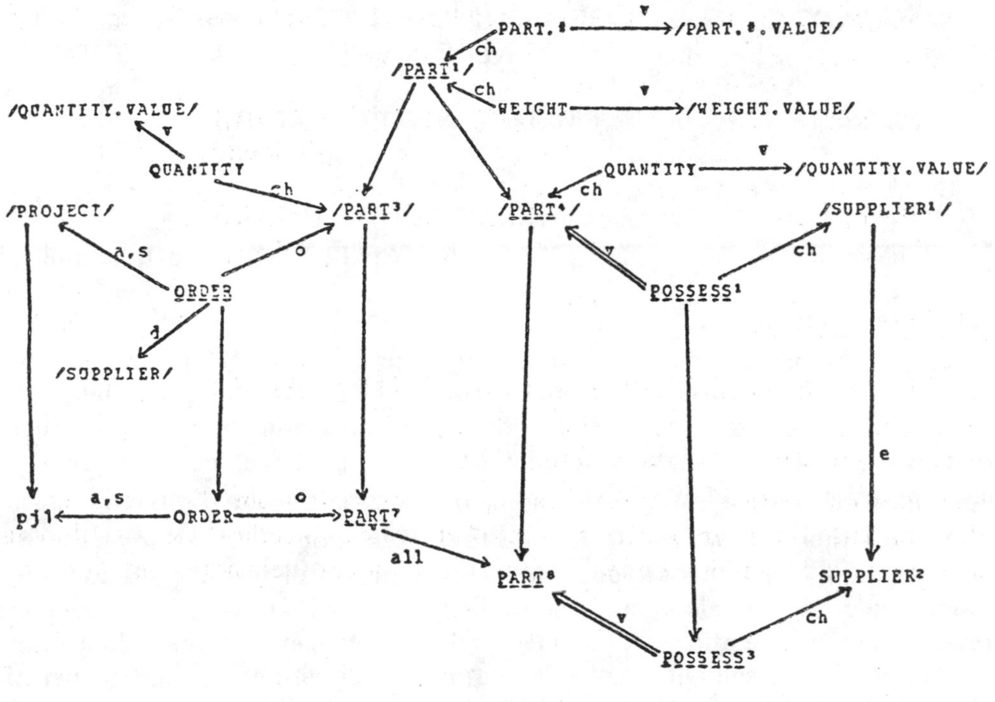
PART.#
/PART.#.VALUE/
v
ch
/PART¹/
ch
WEIGHT
/WEIGHT.VALUE/
/QUANTITY.VALUE/
QUANTITY
/QUANTITY.VALUE/
/PROJECT/
/PART³/
/PART⁴/
/SUPPLIER¹/
a,s
o
ORDER
POSSESS¹
d
/SUPPLIER/
e
pj1
ORDER
PART⁷
all
PART⁸
SUPPLIER²
POSSESS³

fig. 4.5

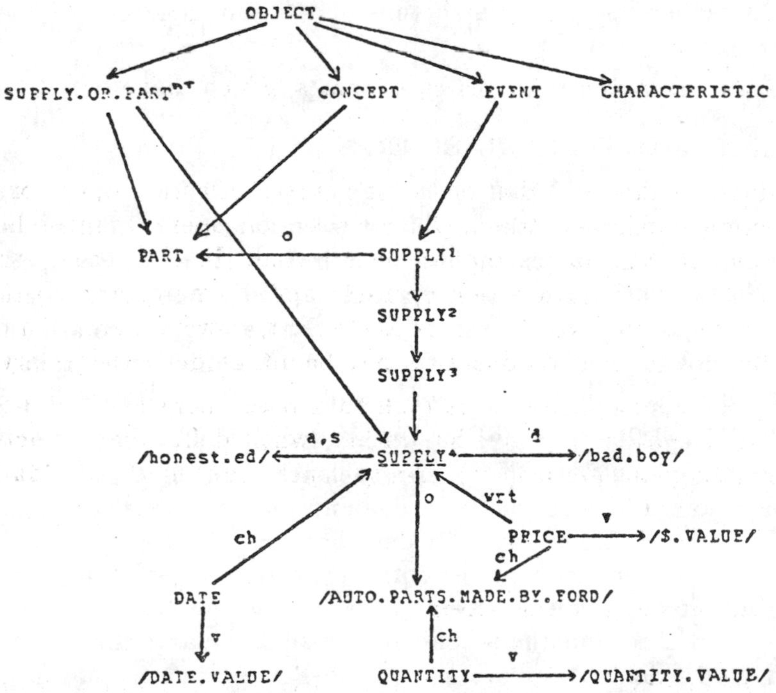
OBJECT
SUPPLY.OR.PART
CONCEPT
EVENT
CHARACTERISTIC
PART
o
SUPPLY¹
SUPPLY²
SUPPLY³
a,s
d
/honest.ed/
SUPPLY⁴
/bad.boy/
o
vrt
ch
PRICE
/$.VALUE/
ch
DATE
/AUTO.PARTS.MADE.BY.FORD/
v
ch
/DATE.VALUE/
QUANTITY
/QUANTITY.VALUE/

fig. 4.6

SUPPLY^4(honest.ed, bad.boy, AUTO.PARTS.MADE.BY.FORD, DATE.VALUE, \$.VALUE, QUANTITY.VALUE)

and

PART^1(PART, PART.#.VALUE, WEIGHT.VALUE).

On the other hand, the expression

> 'cases where honest.ed supplied auto.parts.by.ford, or parts supplied to projects'

can cause the creation of the node marked nr on the net, and it can therefore be said to "make sense". The node OBJECT in fig. 4.6 is the highest node on the net with respect to the SUB axis. The conclusion to be drawn from this example is that semantic operators are more general than data base ones and that there will be situations where the data base operation associated to a semantic one cannot be carried out.

Given that there are no restrictions on the application of semantic operators similar to those that exist for data base ones, the reader may still wonder whether there is at least a measure of "strangeness" that could be introduced to make the model suspicious of expression such as the above. Such measures of "strangeness" are in fact possible and depend directly on the semantic net representation. Thus, any semantic operation that causes the creation of a node so high on the SUB axis, and therefore so far removed from what would normally be expected to be of interest (e.g. through context), may raise questions on a system's part regarding the user's credibility, infallibility, sanity, or whatever. What action the system takes depends on the designer of the system. Our point is that as long as the semantic model is used, there are no clear cut "illegal" semantic operations, although some semantic operations are rendered more expected and less "strange" than others because of the structure of the semantic net and its associated mechanisms (e.g. context).

5. MAINTAINING THE DATA BASE CONSISTENT

Consistency is an important issue in data base management and some efforts have been made to account for it. For example, normalization [3] and insertion, deletion and modification rules [6,13] were introduced to avoid certain kinds of anomalies caused by the execution of such operations on the data base. These techniques are only applicable to primary relations, not to derived ones. They are not meant to maintain the data base consistent throughout insertion, deletion or modification operations but instead they describe what the user can or cannot do in order to avoid some inconsistencies.

As was done in previous sections, we approach this issue by first defining what are the semantic implications of insertions, deletions and modifications on the net, and from those we derive the appropriate sequence of data base operations to be performed. Two basic features of our semantic model are essential in the process of maintaining data base consistency. The first one is the relative position on the net of the information to be inserted, deleted or modified and the second is the different axes and other edges available in the model which define the various relationships among attributes and relations of the data describing here will keep the data base consistent with respect to the semantic net. Thus, if the net is inadequate, so will be the notion of consistency that will be derived from it.

This section includes four examples which will demonstrate how the semantic model maintains a data base consistent. Space considerations force us to use the tiny semantic net described so far which has very limited knowledge, as we will demonstrate in the fourth example.

Example 1. Consider the statement

'honest.ed supplied bad.boy with 100 tables on July 15, 1974'.

Although this statement is meaningful it has no place in the world of our data base. The semantic net (as it has been described so far) only knows 'honest.ed' as a source of parts and since 'tables' are not parts, the statement is immediately rejected and no change is made to the data base.

Example 2. Consider now the statement

'honest.ed supplies bad.boy with cadillac fenders'.

Since 'cadillac fenders' are parts there exists a position on the net where this information can be placed. This position is below $SUPPLY^2$ on fig. 2.1(b). Note that this information cannot be moved any further down the SUB axis because although $SUPPLY^3$ on fig. 2.1(c) has 'honest.ed' and 'bad.boy' as agent-source and destination respectively, its object case is PARTS.MADE.BY.FORD which does not match 'cadillac fenders' (made by GM). Accordingly, this instantiation of $SUPPLY^2$ is inserted as a data base tuple is $SUPPLY^2$ is realized. Similarly, the samê tuple is inserted to all superrelations of $SUPPLY^2$

In both examples given so far the recognition functions (see section 2.1) for PARTs and AUTO.PARTS.MADE.BY.FORD play an important role in maintaining the integrity of the data base while the SUB axis is used for maintaining consistency. Also note that the process of graph-fitting a query to the data base is instrumental in determining what should be done about the query.

Example 3. Our third example demonstrates how consistency is maintained for primary as well as derived relations. Consider the statement

'supplier dominion electric now possesses 83 generators'

The position of this statement on the net is below $POSSESS^1$ shown in figures 4.3-4.5. Node $POSSESS^1$ is realized (underlined) and thus the appropriate tuple conveying the new information is inserted to the data base. Similar insertions must be made for all superrelations of $POSSESS^1$, if any.

When this new information is inserted in $POSSESS^1$, it may cause inconsistencies to other relations namely $PART^5$, $PART^6$ and $POSSESS^3$ which store

'parts that have been ordered by some project and possessed by some suppliers'

'parts that no supplier possesses'
and

'suppliers possessing all parts ordered by pj1'

respectively (see section 4.1). The semantic model can detect what is affected by the new information by searching below $POSSESS^1$ along the SUB axis and by matching the new information against other scenarios. Partially matched scenarios, created by semantic operations, may be affected, in which case the data base operations which created their associated data base relations are executed again.

Example 4. Our last example concerns deletions. Consider the statement

'sears no long supplies bad.boy with
auto.parts.made.by.ford'

Its position is exactly the same as the position of $SUPPLY^{14}$ on fig. 4.2. Note that $SUPPLY^{14}$ is a generic event which might have instantiations and/or generic subevents. Deletion of the relation $SUPPLY^{14}$ must be followed by deletion of all its subrelations, if any, in order to maintain consistency. The reason for this is that $SUPPLY^{14}$ is the connecting event between $SUPPLY^{15}$ and its associated relation and the other subevents of $SUPPLY^{14}$ which are not applicable any more. It should be pointed out that any information about 'auto.parts.made.by.ford supplied by sears to bad.boy in the past will be lost once these changes to the net and the data base have been made. This is not a deficiency of our model but rather of the network we use. If one wants to extend the data base's world to include information about the past, then a "time" axis [11] has to be included in the net, which will specify the period of applicability for each scenario.

Returning to our example, the tuple that corresponds to the deletion of $SUPPLY^{14}$ will be removed from the relation $SUPPLY^{15}$. In general, deletion of a tuple from a relation r must be followed by deletions of the same tuple from all the subrelations of r while deletions of the same tuple from superrelations of r corresponding to higher level scenarios may follow if those scenarios match partially the information to be deleted.

Modifications of the data base are handled using the same techniques as for insertions and deletions.

6. CONCLUSIONS.

We have presented a semantic model of data bases which assumes the availability of a semantic network storing knowledge about a data base and a set of attributes for the data base. The use of the semantic net in generating a relational schema for the data base, in defining a set of semantic operators and in maintaining the data base consistent is then demonstrated and it is shown that the model does not distinguish between primary and derived relations of a data base.

The description of the semantic model is by no means complete. More work has to be done to establish that the association of relations to basic building blocks of the semantic net (concepts, events and characteristics) is adequate, that the set of semantic operators we have proposed is in fact sufficient and that other aspects of consistency, integrity, cost and security can be handled by the semantic net representation we have proposed so far. We believe, however, that the results of this paper set the foundations of a semantic model for data bases, with respect to goals as well as methodology.

ACKNOWLEDGEMENT

The authors would like to thank Phil Cohen and Hans Schmid for their helpful comments.

REFERENCES

1. Bernstein, P.A., Swenson, J.R., Tsichritzis, D., "A unified approach to functional dependencies and relations", Proc. of ACM SIGMOD Workshop, San Francisco, May 1975.
2. Codd, E.F., "A Relational Model of Data for Large Shared Data Banks", Comm. ACM, vol. 13, no. 6, June 1970, 377-387.
3. Codd, E.F., "Further Normalization of the Data Base Relational Modle", Courant Computer Science Symposia 6, Data Base Systems, New York City, May 24-25, 1971, Prentice-Hall.
4. Codd, E.F., "Relational Completeness of Data Base Sublanguages", Courant Computer Science Symbosia 6, Data Base Systems, New York City, May 24-25, 1971, Prentice-Hall.
5. Codd, E.F., "Recent investigations in Relational Data Base Systems", Proc. of IFIP 1974, North Holland Pub. Co., Amsterdam 1974, 1017-1021.
6. Deheneffe, C., Hennebert, H., Paulus, W., "Relational Model for Data Base", Proc. of IFIP 1974, North Holland Pub. Co., Amsterdam 1974, 1022-1025.
7. Delobel, C., Casey, R.G., "Decomposition of a Data Base and the Theory of Boolean Switching Functions", IBM Jouranl of Research and Developments, Vol. 17, No. 5, SEpt. 1973, pp. 374-386.
8. Fillmore, C., "The case for case", In Universals in Linguistic Theory, Bach, E. and Harms, R., (eds.), Holt, Rinehart and Winston Inc., Chicago, Illinois, 1968.
9. Mylopoulos, J., Borgida, A., Cohen, P., Roussopoulos, N., Tsotsos, J., Wong, H., "TORUS: A Natural Language Understanding System for Data Management", Proceedings of the 4-th International Joint Conference on AI, Tbilisi, USSR, Sept. 1975.
10. Mylopoulos, J., Cohen, P., Borgida, A., Sugar, L., "Semantic Networks and the Generation of Context", Proceedings of the 4-th International Joint Conference on AI, Tbilisi, USSR, Sept. 1975.
11. Mylopoulos, J., Borgida, A., Cohen, P., Roussopoulos, N., Tsotsos, J., Wong, H., "The TORUS Project: Progress Report", In preparation, Dept. of Computer Science, University of Toronto.
12. Reason, C., Sugar, L., "Reference Determination and Context, as applied to TORUS", Unpublished report, Dept. of Computer Science, University of Toronto, Toronto 1975.
13. Schmid, H.A., Swenson, J.R., "On the Semantics of the Relational Data Model", Proceedings of SIGMOD Conference, San Jose, May 1975.
14. Wang, C.P., Wedekind, H.H., "Sequent synthesis in logical data base design", IBM Journal Research and Development, vol. 19, no. 1, January 1975, pp. 71-77.

Database Abstractions: Aggregation and Generalization

JOHN MILES SMITH and DIANE C.P. SMITH
University of Utah

Two kinds of abstraction that are fundamentally important in database design and usage are defined. Aggregation is an abstraction which turns a relationship between objects into an aggregate object. Generalization is an abstraction which turns a class of objects into a generic object. It is suggested that all objects (individual, aggregate, generic) should be given uniform treatment in models of the real world. A new data type, called generic, is developed as a primitive for defining such models. Models defined with this primitive are structured as a set of aggregation hierarchies intersecting with a set of generalization hierarchies. Abstract objects occur at the points of intersection. This high level structure provides a discipline for the organization of relational databases. In particular this discipline allows: (i) an important class of views to be integrated and maintained; (ii) stability of data and programs under certain evolutionary changes; (iii) easier understanding of complex models and more natural query formulation; (iv) a more systematic approach to database design; (v) more optimization to be performed at lower implementation levels. The generic type is formalized by a set of invariant properties. These properties should be satisfied by all relations in a database if abstractions are to be preserved. A triggering mechanism for automatically maintaining these invariants during update operations is proposed. A simple mapping of aggregation/generalization hierarchies onto owner-coupled set structures is given.

Key Words and Phrases: data model, relational database, database design, aggregation, generalization, data abstraction, data type, integrity constraints, knowledge representation
CR Categories: 3.65, 3.69, 3.79, 4.29, 4.33, 4.34

1. INTRODUCTION

An *abstraction* of some system is a model of that system in which certain details are deliberately omitted. The choice of the details to omit is made by considering both the intended *application* of the abstraction and also its *users*. The objective is to allow users to heed details of the system which are *relevant* to the application and to ignore other details.

In some applications a system may have too many relevant details for a single abstraction to be *intellectually manageable*. Such manageability can be provided by decomposing the model into a *hierarchy* of abstractions. A hierarchy allows relevant details to be introduced in a controlled manner. The abstractions on any given level of the hierarchy allow many relevant details to be (temporarily) ignored in understanding the abstractions on the next higher level.

One advantage of such an "abstraction hierarchy" is the capability for different users to access the model at different levels of abstraction. For example, if the underlying system is a commercial enterprise, executive users may access global information while clerical users may access detailed information. In this way a single model can be shared among several diverse users without compromising their access requirements. Another advantage of an abstraction hierarchy is an enhanced *stability* of the model as the application, or the system itself, evolves. A change in a detail which is ignored at higher levels of the model will leave these higher levels unaffected. Some changes of course will permeate from a low level to a high level.

A *relation* in Codd's relational schema supports two distinct forms of abstraction. We call these forms of abstraction "aggregation" and "generalization." *Aggregation* refers to an abstraction in which a relationship between objects is regarded as a higher level object. In making such an abstraction, many details of the relationship may be ignored. For example, a certain relationship between a person, a hotel, and a date can be abstracted as the object "reservation." It is possible to think about a "reservation" without bringing to mind all details of the underlying relationship—for example, the number of the room reserved, the name of the reserving agent, or the length of the reservation.

Generalization refers to an abstraction in which a set of similar objects is regarded as a generic object. In making such an abstraction, many individual differences between objects may be ignored. For example, a set of employed persons can be abstracted as the generic object "employee." This abstraction disregards individual differences between employees—for example, the facts that employees have different names, ages, and job functions.

When an appropriate *structuring discipline* is imposed, Codd's relational schema can simultaneously support both hierarchies of aggregation abstractions and hierarchies of generalization abstractions. In a previous paper [4] we proposed a structuring discipline suitable for aggregation abstractions. The present paper develops a structuring discipline for generalization abstractions and integrates it with the one previously proposed for aggregation abstractions.

The benefits of such a structuring discipline are:

(i) abstractions (sometimes called views) pertinent to different database users can be effectively integrated and consistently maintained;
(ii) stability (sometimes called data independence) of models can be provided under several kinds of evolutionary change;
(iii) highly structured models can be supported without a significant loss in intellectual manageability;
(iv) a more systematic approach to database design, particularly of database procedures, can be developed;
(v) more efficient implementations are possible since more assumptions can be made about high level structure.

In [4] we contrasted the primitives for expressing aggregation abstractions that are found in programming languages with those that are needed in databases. We

This work was partially supported by the National Science Foundation under Grant MCS75-09903.
Authors' address: Computer Science Department, University of Utah, Salt Lake City, UT 84112.

showed how to adapt Hoare's *Cartesian product* structure[1] [2] so that it may be used to define relational models. This adaptation leads to several insights about the role of *aggregation* abstractions in databases. The present work can be regarded as an adaptation of Hoare's *discriminated union* structure[2] [2] to relational models. This adaptation leads to insights about the role of *generalization* abstractions in databases.

Database research has been almost exclusively concerned with aggregation (for example, Codd's normal forms [1]) while generalization has been largely ignored. The reason for this is probably that in simple models generalization can usually be handled, fairly satisfactorily, on an ad hoc basis. Interestingly, artificial intelligence (AI) research on knowledge bases has been principally concerned with generalization (for example, Quillian's semantic networks [3]) while aggregation has not been fully exploited. By combining aggregation and generalization into one structuring discipline, we are cross-fertilizing both the database and AI areas.

Section 2 develops a philosophy for representing generalization abstractions in Codd's relational schema. This philosophy leads to a powerful **generic** structure for defining relational models. This structure is described in Section 3. Section 4 examines how the **generic** structure may be used to handle various modeling situations. Section 5 considers five properties of a relational model which must remain invariant during update operations. These invariant properties form a (partial) axiomatic definition of the **generic** structure. A set of rules for maintaining these invariants is developed by using semantic considerations. Section 6 offers concluding remarks on several aspects of the **generic** structure, including database design methods, implementation techniques, and access languages.

2. GENERALIZATION ABSTRACTIONS

The object of this section is to develop a philosophical position on the nature and representation of generalizations. First we motivate why it is important to represent generalizations in models of (aspects of) the real world. Then we consider hierarchies of generalizations and discuss some of their properties. Finally, we investigate the representation of generalizations as Codd relations.

We will use the term "generalization" in the following way: *A generalization is an abstraction which enables a class of individual objects to be thought of generically as a single named object.* Generalization is perhaps the most important mechanism we have for conceptualizing the real world. It is apparently the basis for natural language acquisition—the child moves from the observation of specific dogs to a model of dogs in general. It allows us to make predictions about the future on the basis of specific events in the past—if this fire and that fire have burned my hand, then perhaps fires in general will burn my hand.

In designing a database to model the real world, it is essential that the database schema have the capability for explicitly representing generalizations. This will allow naming conventions in the model to correspond with natural language and enable users to employ established thought patterns in their interactions with the database. In particular the explicit naming of generic objects allows the following capabilities: (i) the application of operators to generic objects; (ii) the specification of attributes of generic objects; and (iii) the specification of relationships in which generic objects participate. Essentially we want to allow generic objects to be treated uniformly with, and to have the same capabilities as, all other kinds of objects. The first capability above is clear enough; however, it may be worth giving some examples of the second and third capabilities.

[1] Similar to PASCAL's record structure.

[2] Similar to PASCAL's record variant structure.

Table I. Generic objects participating in a relationship

affiliation:

profession	society
computer scientist	ACM
computer scientist	IEEE
doctor	AMA
trucker	Teamsters
electrical engineer	IEEE

Suppose we have generalized a class of individual objects into a named generic object. Information which "summarizes" attributes of the individuals can be attached as attributes of the generic object. For example, since all dogs have "sharp teeth" and "four legs," this information can be attached as an attribute of the generic object "dog." This information could be attached redundantly as attributes of individual dogs. However, this disguises the fact that dogs in general have these attributes rather than just the individuals mentioned.

As another example, we might generalize a class of truck drivers into the generic object "trucker." We may not be interested in the pay rate of each individual truck driver, but only in the average (maximum, minimum) pay rate of truck drivers in general. This pay rate information belongs as an attribute of the generic object "trucker."

A generic object, like an individual object, can participate in a relationship with other objects. For example, we can take the relationship between "professions" and their affiliated "societies." Particular professions include "trucker," "computer scientist," and "doctor"—all of which are generic objects. This relationship, called "affiliation," is represented in Table I. Notice that "profession" is a generalization of the class which includes "trucker," "computer scientist," and "doctor."

We now examine the properties of a *hierarchy* of generic objects. To fix the discussion, we make this examination via a specific example. We assume that a model must be constructed for the set of vehicles owned by some large organization such as a government agency or an industry. These vehicles include many diverse types such as trucks, submarines, bicycles, and helicoptors.

Figure 1 illustrates one particular decomposition of "vehicle" into lower level generic objects. Note that individual vehicles are not explicitly represented. Each generic object should be thought of as defining a class of individual vehicles. The

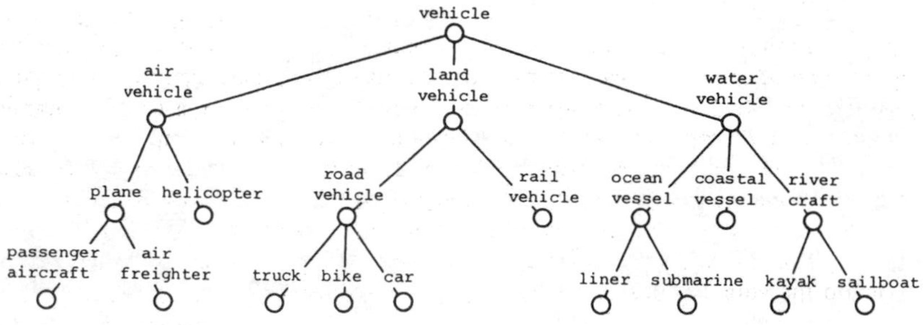

Fig. 1. A generic hierarchy over vehicles

figure indicates, for example, that "truck," "bike," and "car" can be generalized to the notion "road vehicle"; that "road vehicle" and "rail vehicle" can be generalized to the notion "land vehicle"; and that "land vehicle," "air vehicle," and "water vehicle" can be generalized to the notion "vehicle."

Let G be an object in a generic hierarchy. To represent G as a Codd relation, we must select a set of attributes which are common to *all* individuals in the class of G. For example, in representing "vehicle" we may include the attributes "identification number," "manufacturer," "price," and "weight." These attributes are common to all vehicles. In representing "road vehicle" we may include the previous attributes and others such as "number of wheels" and "tire pressure." These attributes are common to all road vehicles; however, the latter two attributes are *not* common to all vehicles. In representing "truck" we may include all the previous attributes and others such as "engine horsepower" and "cab size." These attributes are common to all trucks; however, the latter two attributes are *not* common to all road vehicles.

Now an individual truck will be a member of each of the classes "vehicle," "road vehicle," and "truck." However, the relevant attributes of this truck will vary from class to class. When this truck is considered as an individual *vehicle*, any attributes which distinguish trucks from other *vehicles* will be irrelevant. When this truck is considered as an individual *road vehicle*, any attributes which distinguish trucks from other *road vehicles* will be irrelevant. In general an individual object will have more relevant attributes the lower the generic level of the class in which it appears. We call the attributes of an individual object that are relevant to a class G the *G-attributes* of that object.

The generic hierarchy shown in Figure 1 has two characteristics that do not belong to all generic hierarchies. The first characteristic is that it is a tree (i.e. no generic object is the immediate descendant of two or more generic objects). The second characteristic is that the immediate descendants of any node have classes which are mutually exclusive. Generic hierarchies which do not have these characteristics are shown in Figures 2 and 3, respectively. Our method for representing generic hierarchies as Codd relations can accommodate these general forms of generic hierarchy.

Figure 2 indicates that "helicopter" can be generalized in two ways—either to "motorized vehicle" or to "air vehicle." Figure 3 illustrates a decomposition of

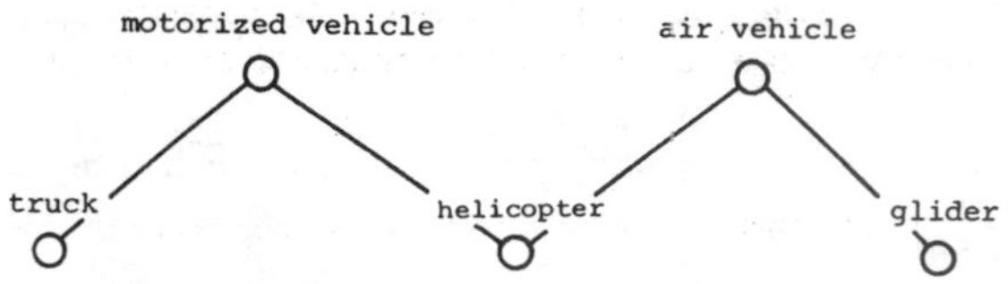

Fig. 2. A generic hierarchy which is not a tree

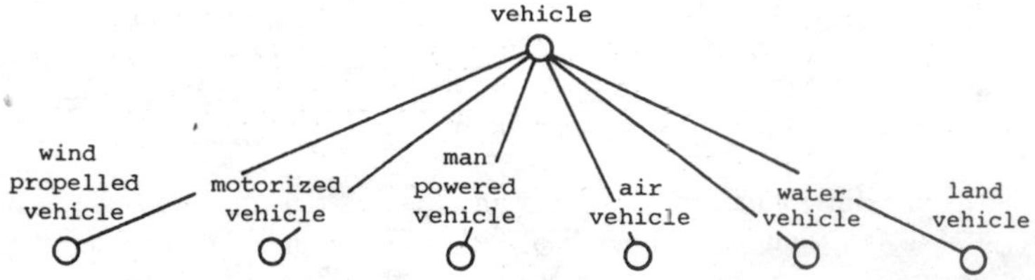

Fig. 3. A generic hierarchy in which the immediate descendants of a node do not form mutually exclusive classes

"vehicle" into two distinct kinds of generic object. One kind of generic object is concerned with the method of vehicle propulsion (wind, human, motor). The other kind of generic object is concerned with the principal medium through/on which the vehicle moves (air, water, land). Some of these descendant objects do not have disjoint classes. For example, some vehicles are both motorized and move through the air. The classes for "motorized vehicle" and "air vehicle" therefore have some common members.

Our method for representing a generic heirarchy requires that the immediate descendants of any node be partitioned into groups. Each group must contain generic objects whose classes are mutually exclusive. In practice this grouping can usually be made quite easily from semantic considerations. For example, the descendants in Figure 3 would be grouped as: {wind propelled vehicle, motorized vehicle, man powered vehicle} and {air vehicle, water vehicle, land vehicle}. The first group contains mutually exclusive classes which correspond to alternative types of "propulsion system." The second group contains mutually exclusive classes which correspond to different types of "transit medium."[3]

We call a mutually exclusive group of generic objects sharing a common parent a *cluster*. We say that a cluster *belongs to* its parent generic object. For example, we may talk about the two clusters belonging to "vehicle" in Figure 3. A leaf node in a generic hierarchy has no cluster belonging to it. In Figure 1 every non-leaf generic object has exactly one cluster belonging to it. In Figure 2 the cluster belonging to "motorized vehicle" and the cluster belonging to "air vehicle" have a common element—helicopter..

We shall find it necessary to give each cluster a (meaningful) name. This name

[3] If amphibious vehicles were of interest, the generic object "amphibious vehicle" would be included as an alternative to "air vehicle," "water vehicle," and "land vehicle."

should be chosen so that it is descriptive of the generic objects in the cluster. For example, the name of the cluster {wind propelled vehicle, motorized vehicle, man powered vehicle} may be "propulsion category." The name of the cluster {air vehicle, water vehicle, land vehicle} may be "medium category."

We will now describe a method for representing a generic hierarchy as a hierarchy of Codd relations. We create one relation for each generic object in the hierarchy. Assume G is a generic object such that (i) I is the class of individual objects associated with G, (ii) $A_1, \ldots, A_n$ are the G-attributes, and (iii) $C_1, \ldots, C_m$ are the names of clusters belonging to G. G is represented by the Codd relation:

G:

A_1	...	A_n	C_1	...	C_m
...	...	...	...	...	...
v_1	...	v_n	v_{n+1}	...	v_{n+m}
...	...	...	...	...	...

where (i) there is one and only one tuple for each individual in I; (ii) if an individual has a value v_i for attribute A_i, then its tuple contains v_i in domain A_i; (iii) if an individual is also included in generic object v_{n+j} in cluster C_j, then its tuple contains v_{n+j} in domain C_j; and (iv) if an individual is *not* also included in any generic object in cluster C_j, then its tuple contains a blank (—) in domain C_j.

Table II illustrates how Codd relations may appear (at some point in time) for the generic objects "vehicle," "motorized vehicle," and "air vehicle" in Figure 4. Notice that one consequence of the representation method is the appearance of relation names as values in domains. For example, the domains "medium category" and "propulsion category" in the relation "vehicle" have relation names as values. This allows us to employ Codd's relational operators in the manipulation of generic objects. As we shall see in Section 4, it also allows us to use a uniform method for representing relationships in which objects, either generic or individual, participate.

We call the domain in a relation which contains the name of a descendant relation the *image domain* for that descendant. For example, the domain "medium category" in the relation "vehicle" is the image domain for the descendant relations "land vehicle," "air vehicle," and "water vehicle." There is a one-to-one correspondence between clusters in a generic hierarchy and image domains in its relational representation.

Notice that in Table II, with the exception of the image domains, all domains in "vehicle" are inherited by its descendant relations "motorized vehicle" and "air vehicle." Although this domain inheritance may often be appropriate in relational models, we do not insist that it must occur. This allows generalization abstractions to be represented in the manner most appropriate to their users.

It is clear that a great deal of information occurs redundantly in a relation hierarchy. This is perfectly acceptable provided there is some way to *implement* a relation hierarchy such that (i) storage space is not wasted owing to data duplication, and (ii) consistency of redundant information can be maintained. This issue is further discussed in Section 6.

Table II. Examples of Codd relations for three generic objects from the hierarchy of Figure 4

vehicle:

iden. num.	manufacturer	price	weight	medium category	propulsion category
V1	Mazda	65.4	10.5	land veh.	motorized veh.
V2	Schwin	3.5	0.1	land veh.	man powered veh.
V3	Boeing	7,900	840	air veh.	motorized veh.
V4	Aqua Co	12.2	1.9	water veh.	wind propelled veh.
V5	Gyro Inc	650	150	air veh.	motorized veh.

motorized vehicle:

iden. num.	manufacturer	price	weight	horse-power	fuel capacity	motor category
V1	Mazda	65.4	10.5	150	300	rotary veh.
V3	Boeing	7,900	840	9600	2600	jet veh.
V5	Gyro Inc	650	150	1500	2000	rotary veh.

air vehicle:

iden. num.	manufacturer	price	weight	maximum altitude	takeoff distance	lift category
V3	Boeing	7,900	840	30	1000	plane
V5	Gyro Inc	650	150	5.6	0	helicopter

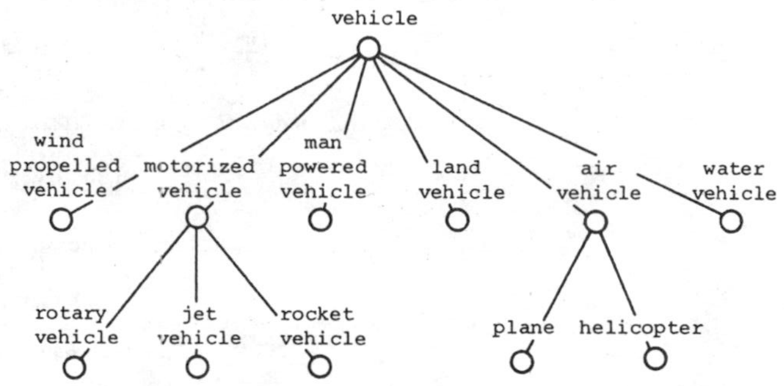

Fig. 4. A generic hierarchy over vehicles

3. THE GENERIC STRUCTURE

We now describe a structuring primitive for specifying generalizations in relational models. In [4] we introduced the types **collection** and **aggregate** and declared a relation R by writing:

```
var R: collection of aggregate [keylist]
                s1: {key} R1;
                ...
                sn: {key} Rn
              end
```

In this declaration "keylist" contains the selectors for the key domains of R. The curly brackets around "**key**" indicate that it does not always have to occur. Now R can actually be thought of as the name of a generic object. To define the position of the generic object R in a generic hierarchy, we only need to specify its descendants in this hierarchy. This suggests that the structure shown in Figure 5 is appropriate for defining Codd relations.

We use the term **generic** rather than the looser term **collection** to indicate that a generic object is being defined. The **generic** structure simultaneously specifies two abstractions: (i) It specifies R as an aggregation of a relationship between objects R_1 through R_n, and (ii) it specifies R as a generalization of a class containing objects R_{11} through R_{mp_m}. The domains with selectors s_{k1} through s_{km} are image domains. If no image domains are specified, then the **generic** structure is the same as the **collection** structure of [4].

Before discussing the five syntactic requirements of the **generic** structure, we define the three relations of Table II. These definitions are shown in Figure 6. Note in the definition of "vehicle" that its generic descendants are listed following "**generic**" and its aggregate descendants are listed following "**aggregate**." The generic descendants are grouped into clusters, and each cluster is associated with the selector of its corresponding image domain. In this case the image domains have selectors MC and PC.

We shall not discuss the first two syntactic requirements in Figure 5—these are explained in [4]. Requirement (iii) demands that each generic descendant of R be declared elsewhere as a generic object in its own right. In Figure 6 this is illustrated by the declarations of "motorized vehicle" and "air vehicle." Furthermore, these

```
var R: generic
          sk1 = (R11, ... , R1p1);
            ...
          skm = (Rm1, ... , Rmpm)
        of
        aggregate [keylist]
          s1: {key} R1;
            ...
          sn: {key} Rn
        end
```

where:

(i) R_i $(1 \le i \le n)$ is either a generic identifier (in which case "**key**" must appear) or a type identifier (in which case "**key**" must not appear);
(ii) "keylist" is a sequence of s_i's $(1 \le i \le n)$ separated by commas;
(iii) each R_{ij} $(i = 1, 1 \le j \le p_1; \dots ; i = m, 1 \le j \le p_m)$ is a generic identifier whose key domains are the same as those of R;
(iv) each s_{ki} $(1 \le i \le m)$ is the same as some s_j $(1 \le j \le n)$;
(v) if s_{ki} is the same as s_j, then the type "{**key**} R_j" is the range $(R_{i1}, \dots , R_{ip_i})$.

Fig. 5. The **generic** structure

```
var vehicle:
  generic
    MC = (land vehicle, air vehicle, water vehicle);
    PC = (motorized vehicle, man powered vehicle, wind propelled vehicle)
  of
  aggregate [ID#]
      ID#: identification number;
        M: manufacturer;
        P: price;
        W: weight;
       MC: medium category;
       PC: propulsion category
  end

var motorized vehicle:
  generic
    MTC = (rotary vehicle, jet vehicle, rocket vehicle)
  of
  aggregate [ID#]
      ID#: identification number;
        M: manufacturer;
        P: price;
        W: weight;
       HP: horsepower;
       FC: fuel capacity;
      MTC: motor category
  end

var air vehicle:
  generic
    LC = (plane, helicopter)
  of
  aggregate [ID#]
      ID#: identification number;
        M: manufacturer;
        P: price;
        W: weight;
       MA: maximum altitude;
       TD: takeoff distance;
       LC: lift category
  end
```

Fig. 6. Definitions for the relations in Table II

descendant objects must all have the same key domains as R. This requirement allows us to reference individual objects in a uniform way regardless of the generic class in which they appear. An occasionally useful exception to this rule is that if s_{ki} is in the key of R, then it does not have to appear in the key of any R_{ij} $(1 \le j \le p_i)$. If it did appear, the domain would have the same value for each individual in R_{ij}. For example, suppose PC was declared as belonging to the key of "vehicle" in Figure 6. If we then added "propulsion category" as a new domain in the relation "motorized vehicle" in order to satisfy requirement (iii), this domain would have the same value ("motorized vehicle") in every individual.

Requirement (iv) ensures that each specified cluster is associated with a particular (image) domain. Requirement (v) ensures that each image domain can actually assume as values the generic identifiers listed in its associated cluster. For example, in the definition of "vehicle" in Figure 6, the type "medium category" must be defined (elsewhere) as ranging over the identifiers "land vehicle," "air vehicle," and "water vehicle."

If the definition of a relation satisfies the five syntactic requirements, this is no guarantee that the definition specifies a meaningful aggregation abstraction and a meaningful generalization abstraction. We now consider what additional requirements are necessary for meaningful abstractions to be specified. These requirements must be semantic and somehow related to our intuitive understanding of the real world.

Since databases are usually designed to model the real world as we understand it, we can safely require that all object names in a relation definition be natural language nouns. These nouns then provide the bridge between our intuitive understanding of the real world and its intended reflection in the relation definition. If natural language nouns are not used, any discussion of the meaningfulness of a relation definition seems moot.

Assuming that R, each R_i, and each R_{ij} (in Figure 5) are all natural language nouns, five semantic conditions are necessary for a relation definition to specify an aggregation and a generalization:

(i) Each R-individual must determine a unique R_i-individual.
(ii) No two R-individuals determine the same set of R_i-individuals for all R_i whose selectors are in "keylist."
(iii) Each R_{ij}-individual must also be an R-individual.
(iv) Each R-individual classified as R_{ij} must also an R_{ij}-individual.
(v) No R_{ij}-individual is also an R_{ik}-individual for $j \neq k$.

By an R (R_i or R_{ij})-individual, we mean an instance of the generic object R (R_i or R_{ij}) as it occurs in the real world.

The first two conditions are necessary for an aggregation abstraction and are discussed in [1]. The remaining three conditions are necessary for a generalization abstraction. Condition (iii) ensures that R_{ij} is a subclass of R and thus that R_{ij} can be generalized to R. For example, in Table II, the motorized vehicles V1, V3, and V5 are also vehicles. Condition (iv) ensures that R_{ij} contains all R-individuals classified as belonging to R_{ij}. For example, in Table II, "motorized vehicle" contains all vehicles so classified in "vehicle." Condition (v) ensures that clusters contain mutually exclusive classes.

We say that a relation is *well-defined* if its definition satisfies the five semantic requirements above.

4. MODELING WITH THE GENERIC STRUCTURE

The objective of this section is to show how aggregation and generalization abstractions are used in designing real world models. When aggregation and generalization are employed separately, they can only model relatively simple situations. However, by employing them together, we will see that a rich variety of models can be defined. We first describe a graphical representation for relation definitions. This notation makes models much easier to visualize.

The notation is based on the observation that aggregation and generalization are independent activities. Given a particular object, generalizations of this object can be considered independently of relationships in which the object participates. This suggests a graphical notation in which generalization and aggregation are represented *orthogonally*. We have chosen to represent aggregation in the plane of the page, and generalization in the plane perpendicular to the page. The **generic** structure of Figure 5 is denoted graphically in Figure 7.

High level aggregate objects will appear toward the top of the page and low level aggregate objects toward the bottom. Aggregation therefore occurs *up* the page. High level generic objects will appear (in a simulated three-dimensional space) in the surface of the page and low level generic objects will appear below the surface. Generalization therefore occurs *out of* the page.

Suppose that we must model the "employees" of a certain company. Let's assume that this company has three different types of employees at some point in time—truckers, secretaries, and engineers. Information must be maintained about each individual employee—though different kinds of information are required depending on the type of employee. In addition information must be maintained about each generic type of employee.

Specifically, assume that the attributes "employee ID#," "name," "age," and "employee type" are important for *all* individual employees. The necessary additional attributes for each employee type are given in the following table.

employee type	additional attributes
trucker	vehicle ID#, number of license endorsements
secretary	typing speed
engineer	highest degree, type (mech, elec, etc.)

For each generic type of employee the following attributes must be recorded: number of employees (size), number of vacant positions (vacancies), hiring agency (agency).

We will now construct a relational model which meets the preceding require-

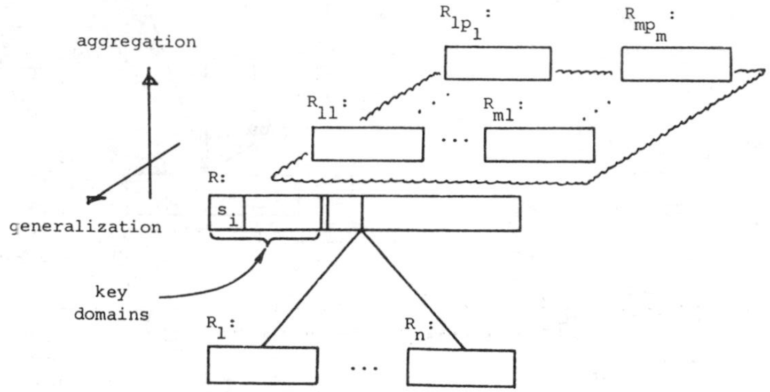

Fig. 7. A graphical notation for the **generic** structure

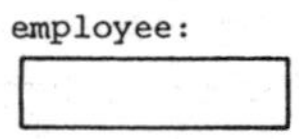

Fig. 8. Initial model for "employee"

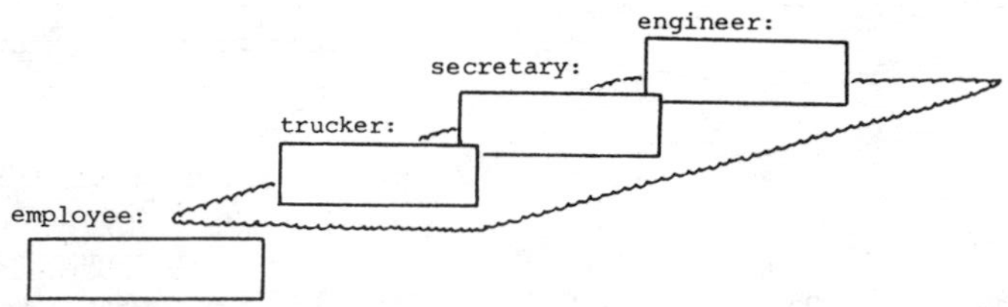

Fig. 9. Decomposition of "employee" in the generalization plane

ments. Since the most abstract object that must be represented is "employee," the initial model contains precisely this object. This is shown in Figure 8. The next step is to decompose this object in both the aggregation and generalization planes. We have decided to decompose first along the generalization plane. In this plane the components of "employee" are the generic objects "trucker," "secretary," and "engineer." These three objects form a single cluster. The model then appears as in Figure 9.

We now decompose "employee" in the aggregation plane. There are four attributes of an employee that must be recorded: employee ID#, name, age, and employee type. We therefore include four objects as the components of "employee." These objects are included in Figure 10. With the exception of "employee-type," the components of "employee" are *primitive* objects—that is, they are only thought of as a whole. The object "employee-type," however, has several components which are important. These correspond to the attributes: typename, size, vacancies, and agency. All these components are primitive. The model now appears as in Figure 10.

We can now continue to develop the model by decomposing any object (which is not already decomposed) along either plane. Since we are not interested in any subtypes of "employee-type," this object is not decomposed along the generalization plane. For similar reasons, we do not decompose "trucker," "secretary," or "engineer" along the generalization plane. However, these three objects must each be decomposed into (primitive) objects in the aggregation plane. These decompositions are included in Figure 11. To avoid cluttering the figure, we have left incomplete the lines which should connect each of the objects "emp. ID#," "name," and "age" with each of the objects "trucker," "secretary," and "engineer." Finally, we can choose selectors and keys for each object. The relational model then appears as in Figure 11.

Definitions for the relations "employee" and "employee-type" are given in Figure 12. Notice that the relation "employee-type" describes details about "trucker," "secretary," and "engineer" when they are thought of as generic objects. The relation "employee" refers to these details through the image domain (i.e. the domain with selector "TN"). This allows each individual employee to

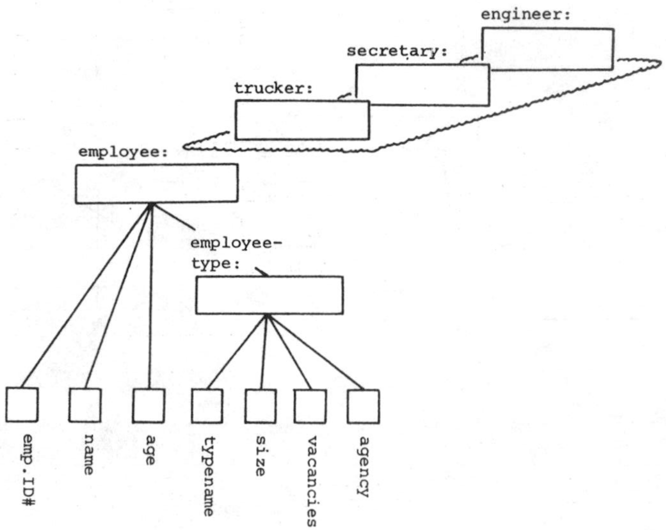

Fig. 10. Decomposition of "employee" in the aggregation plane

refer to all the generic properties of the employee subclass to which it belongs.

In general a relation R may have several clusters in the generalization plane which belong to it. For each cluster C there will be a corresponding relation referenced from R in the aggregation plane. This relation will describe the attributes (if any) of the generic objects in C. We can summarize this general property of relational models as: *The generic components of an abstract object R have their attributes defined in relations which are aggregate components of R.*

We now consider the modeling of various additional aspects of the real world related to employees. As our first aspect, assume that the "trade unions" affiliated with different employee types must be modeled. The attributes of a trade union that are relevant include its name, address, and senior officer. Figure 13 shows the object "trade union" in the aggregation plane of "employee"—the generalization plane is omitted (see Figure 10).

We are also interested in the "affiliation" of employee types with trade unions. We therefore form an abstract object "affiliation" as an aggregation of "employee-type" and "trade union." Let's assume that an important attribute of an affiliation is the person empowered to speak for union members of a particular employee type. An appropriate object, say "spokesman," must therefore be included as an additional component of "affiliation." When this is done, the model appears as in Figure 14. With selectors and keys appropriately chosen, a definition of "affiliation" is given below:

```
var affiliation:
  generic of
  aggregate [TN, UN]
```

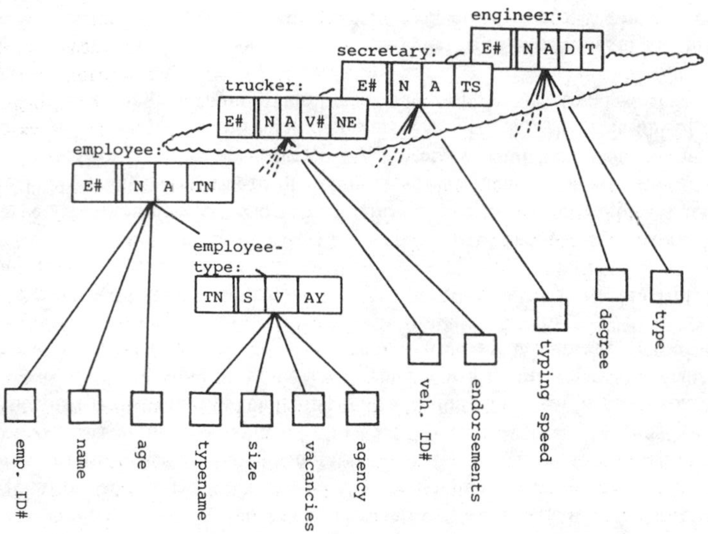

Fig. 11. A relational model for "employee"

var employee:
  generic
    TN = (trucker, secretary, engineer)
  of
  aggregate [E#]
      E#: emp. ID#;
      N: name;
      A: age;
    TN: **key** employee-type
  end
var employee-type:
  generic of
  aggregate [TN]
    TN: typename;
      S: size;
      V: vacancies;
    AY: agency
  end

Fig. 12. Definitions for "employee" and "employee-type" in Figure 11

    TN: **key** employee-type;
    UN: **key** trade union;
      S: spokesman
  end

This definition specifies a relationship over generic objects.

We next consider some relationships over the generalization plane of "employee" (Figure 10). Let's assume that the company where the employees work owns a fleet of vehicles (including cars and trucks). We will model the relationship between employees and vehicles determined by employee usage of vehicles. In particular trucks are used by truckers for hauling materials and cars are used by engineers to visit distant sites. No other (official) vehicle use is permitted. The representation of "employee" and "vehicle" in the generalization plane is shown in Figure 15.

There are two ways that this relationship between employees and vehicles could be modeled. One way is to abstract a *single* relationship between "employee" and "vehicle" as an aggregate object (say, "trip"). Unfortunately this approach is too general to fully capture the intended relationship. It would seem that *any* employee could take *any* vehicle on a trip—including a secretary driving a truck. Furthermore, there is no distinction between trips where materials are hauled and trips where engineers visit a site. It is very likely that different attributes of a trip are important depending on which kind of trip it is.

The second way of modeling the required relationship between employees and vehicles is to decompose it, in the generalization plane, into two relationships—

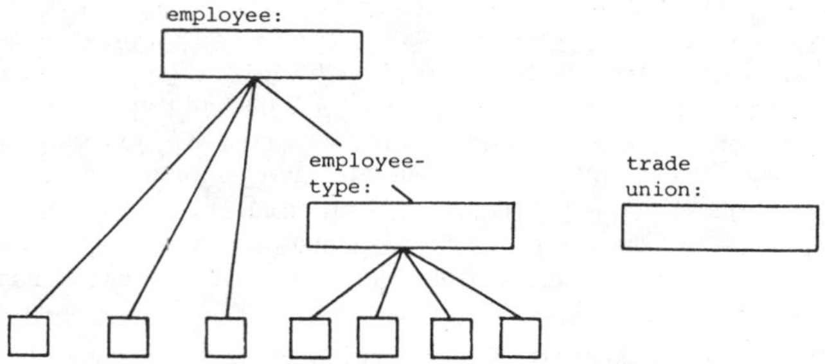

Fig. 13. "Trade union" incorporated in the aggregation plane of "employee"

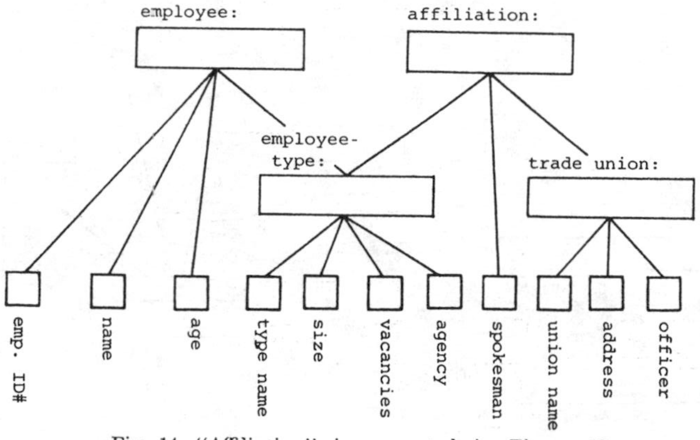

Fig. 14. "Affiliation" incorporated in Figure 13

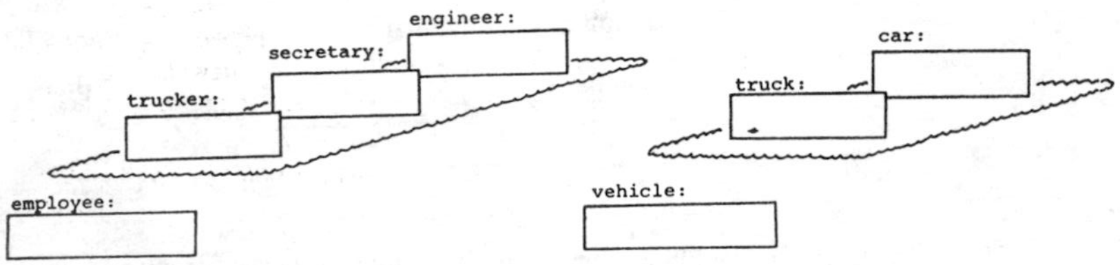

Fig. 15. Decomposition of "employee" and "vehicle" in the generalization plane

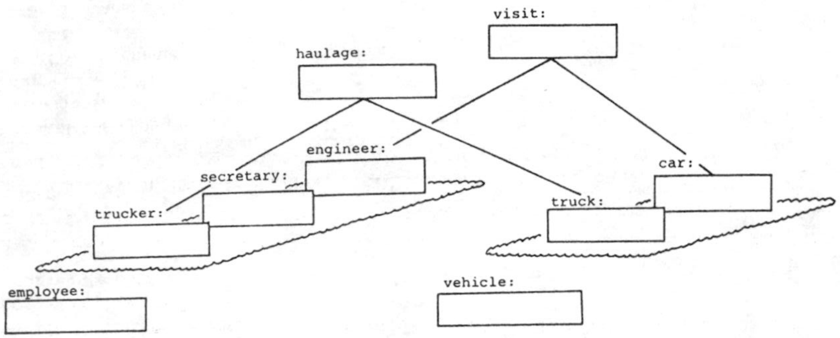

Fig. 16. "Haulage" and "visit" incorporated in Figure 15

one between "trucker" and "truck" and the other between "engineer" and "car." The first relationship can be abstracted as the aggregate object "haulage" and the second as "visit." These objects are shown in Figure 16.

The main advantage of this second approach is that the model is a more precise representation of reality. This makes the model more understandable and thus less prone to erroneous access and manipulation. Furthermore, the model expresses real world constraints on "haulage" and "visit"—namely that "haulage" must relate truckers to trucks and "visit" must relate engineers to cars. If these constraints are enforced during update operations, then certain integrity problems (e.g. secretaries who drive trucks) can be avoided. Another advantage is that by restricting "haulage" and "visit" to explicit subsets of "employee" and "vehicle" there is more scope for optimizing retrieval operations at a lower level of implementation.

Let's consider another example of a relationship over the generalization plane of employee. We assume that the assignment of secretaries to engineers must be modeled. The most direct way of modeling this relationship is to abstract an object (say, "assignment") as an aggregation of "secretary" and "engineer." The object "assignment" is shown on the right in Figure 17. Although this relationship could be modeled as an aggregation of "employee" and "employee," to do so would create unnecessary ambiguity.

The previous three relationships (haulage, visit, and assignment) all have the property that employees of some, but not all, types participate. We now examine a relationship in which employees of all types participate. Consider the relationship

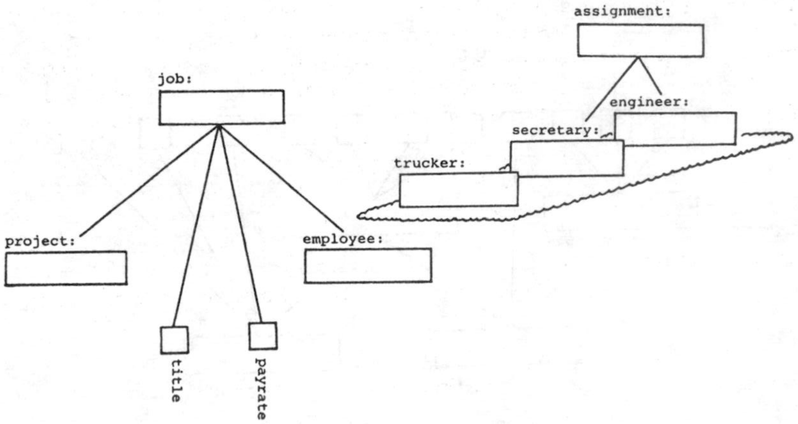

Fig. 17. "Assignment" and "job" incorporated in Figure 16

between employees and projects which identifies the jobs employees hold on projects. We assume that a given employee may hold jobs on several projects simultaneously but not several jobs on the same project. This relationship is best modeled by aggregating "employee" and "project" into an abstract object (say, "job"). Other attributes of "job" such as "title" and "payrate" may be introduced. The object "job" is shown in Figure 17.

A definition of "job," with appropriate choices for selectors and key, is given below:

```
var job:
  generic of
  aggregate [E#, P#]
       E#: key employee;
       P#: key project;
        T: title;
      PR: payrate
  end
```

The key "E#, P#" is chosen since, by the constraints given above, jobs are in one-to-one correspondence with employee-project pairs. The definition assumes that no decomposition of "job" in the generalization plane is of interest. Alternatively, suppose some model users are interested in specific types of jobs. Let's assume that among the projects is one to develop modems and another to upgrade printers. Some users may want to think of "modem project job" and "printer project job" as generic objects. Figure 18 shows how the model appears when these objects are incorporated as descendants of "job" in the generalization plane.

Let's examine why Figure 18 expresses the appropriate structure. First, since we are decomposing job into generic objects (in the generalization plane), a new object must be introduced (in the aggregation plane) which is a generalization of these objects (thought of as individuals). This follows from the requirement of the

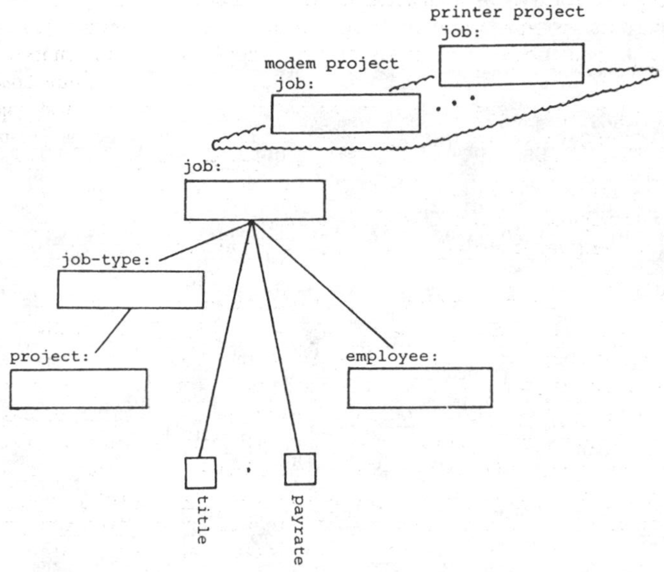

Fig. 18. Effect of decomposing "job" in the generalization plane

generic structure that each cluster have its own image domain. This new object is called "job-type" and is a component of "job." "Job-type" may itself be decomposed into its attribute objects.

Second, note that each job type is the abstraction of all jobs belonging to a certain project. Thus one attribute of a job type is the project to which all its jobs belong. Accordingly, in Figure 18 "project" is shown as an attribute of "job-type." "Project" is no longer a *direct* component of "job" as in Figure 17—it is now an *indirect* component via "job-type." Definitions of "job" and "job-type" are given below:

```
var job:
  generic
    TN = (modem project job, ... , printer project job)
  of
  aggregate [E#, TN]
     E#: key employee;
      T: title;
     PR: payrate;
     TN: key job-type
  end

var job-type:
  generic of
  aggregate [TN]
     TN: typename;
      P#: key project;
     AP: average payrate
  end
```

Note that "job" is an example of a relation in which the key contains an image domain.

The introduction of "job-type" illustrates a form of *restructuring* that may often become necessary as the application of a model evolves. In the initial application users may be interested in a general class C of objects. As the application evolves, certain users may become interested only in the subcategory of C-objects whose A attribute is some value v_1, while others may become interested in the subcategory whose A attribute is v_2. These *subcategories of C with respect to attribute A* must then be represented as a cluster in the generalization plane of C. In Figure 18 the cluster {modem project job, ... , printer project job} represents a subcategorization of "job" with respect to "project."

In general, if it becomes necessary in an existing model to subcategorize an object O with respect to attribute A, the following restructuring is required: (i) Define a new object S which abstracts the class of subcategories; (ii) replace in O the domain which references A by a domain which references S; (iii) if the key of O contains the selector for A, replace it with the selector for S; and (iv) insert in S a domain which references A.

5. RELATIONAL INVARIANTS

We first consider the properties of relations that must remain invariant during update operations. We then examine each update operation in turn and consider methods for ensuring the invariance of these properties. The update operations we consider are:

insert—this operation is performed when a new individual object becomes of interest;

delete—this operation is performed when an existing individual object ceases to be of interest; and

modify—this operation is performed when the details of an existing individual object are subject to change.

In Section 3 we stated the conditions that must be satisfied by the real world objects named in a relation definition in order for the definition to express abstractions. If an object R is being defined in terms of the aggregate components R_i and the generic components R_{ij}, these conditions are:

(i) Each R-individual must determine a unique R_i-individual.
(ii) No two R-individuals determine the same set of R_i-individuals for all R_i whose selectors are in "keylist."
(iii) Each R_{ij}-individual must also be an R-individual.
(iv) Each R-individual classified as R_{ij} must also be an R_{ij}-individual.
(v) No R_{ij}-individual is also an R_{ik}-individual for $j \neq k$.

It is important that the relations and tuples which represent these real world objects at some point in time satisfy a corresponding set of conditions. This ensures that the relations faithfully represent the abstract structure of the real world. In stating these conditions the following definitions are useful.

Let t be a tuple in R_{ij}. A *parent image* of t is a tuple t′ in R for which: (i) t and t′ have the same values in all common domains and (ii) t′.s_{ki} has the value "R_{ij}." Semantically speaking, a tuple and its parent image both describe the same real world individual; however, the parent image is at a higher level of generalization.[4] If t′ is a parent image of t, we say that t is a *child image* of t′.

We can now state the conditions for a relation, together with its aggregate and generic components, to represent abstractions:

(i) For each R-tuple t, if t.s_i is nonblank, then when R_i is a generic identifier t.s_i is the key of an R_i-tuple, and when R_i is a type identifier t.s_i is of type R_i.
(ii) No two distinct R-tuples have the same key.
(iii) Each R_{ij}-tuple has a parent image in R.
(iv) For each R-tuple t, if t.s_{ki} is nonblank and has the value R_{ij}, then R has a child image in R_{ij}.
(v) No R-tuple has a child image in both R_{ij} and R_{ik} for $j \neq k$.

We call these five conditions *relational invariants*.[5] They are a transformation of the prior five conditions in accordance with the method of representing generic objects as relations. There is one minor exception embodied in the first and fourth invariants. In practice it is necessary to permit the occurrences of blanks (which mean "unknown" or "don't care") in some domains. The first and fourth invariants make allowance for this possibility.

The relational invariants can be thought of as constraining a relation to represent an "abstract object." These invariants must be satisfied by *every* relation in a relational model irrespective of the kind of abstract object the relation represents. In addition each relation must usually satisfy a set of invariants (often called "integrity constraints") which are peculiar to that relation alone. These invariants constrain a relation to the representation of a *particular kind* of abstract object. Since the relational invariants apply to every relation, they are the most fundamental form of integrity constraint.

Users do not normally interact with a database at the level of primitive update operations such as insert, delete, and modify. In most cases these primitives are used to construct higher level update operations called *transactions*. The notion of a transaction allows the difference between the relational invariants and special integrity constraints to be characterized in another way. The relational invariants must be satisfied before and after each user initiated update operation. However, special integrity constraints need only be satisfied before and after each transaction.

We now discuss the maintenance of the relational invariants during update operations. Throughout this discussion we assume an idealized situation in which (i) the model correctly abstracts the real world structure at the time of update, (ii) all update information accurately reflects the attributes of real world individuals, and (iii) all users have full access rights to all relations. This idealized situation allows us to ignore the separate issues of special integrity constraints and

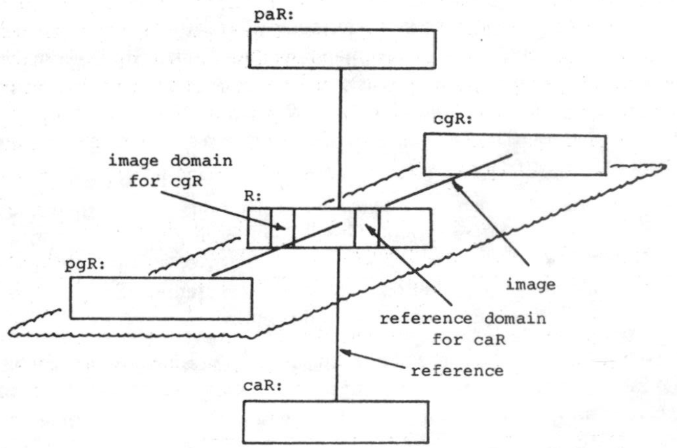

Fig. 19. A relation R and its paR, caR, pgR, and cgR relations

access control. We contend that these issues are best attacked *after* methods have been developed to maintain the relational invariants.

The following abbreviations will be useful in the subsequent discussion. Consider a relational model M which contains, among others, a relation R. Relative to R, we say that a relation is:

paR if it is a *p*arent in the *a*ggregation plane of *R*;
caR if it is a *c*hild in the *a*ggregation plane of *R*;
pgR if it is a *p*arent in the *g*eneralization plane of *R*;
cgR if it is a *c*hild in the *g*eneralization plane of *R*.

Figure 19 illustrates how a relation R is "connected" to its paR, caR, pgR, and cgR relations.

In Table III we summarize methods for maintaining the relational invariants during update operations. Each type of update operation (insert, delete, modify) is considered in a separate table. Each table records the effect on the five invariants of performing an update operation on a tuple t with key k in a relation R.

It is assumed that the relational invariants are satisfied prior to the update operation. Each table shows how the invariants could be violated as a result of the update operation and also what action can be taken to correct each violation. The action is always to perform an update operation on one or more paR, caR, pgR, or cgR relations. These actions may in turn cause further violations and thus update operations on other relations. In this way a single user initiated update operation can trigger additional update operations which propagate along both aggregation and generalization planes.

We first explain some entries in the tables of Table III and then examine some important properties of triggered operations. As is usual in relational models, we assume that no tuple is ever allowed to have a blank in a key domain. This should be the *only* reason for disallowing a "correct" update operation.

The only time that invariant (ii) can be violated by a correct update is when a

[4] A tuple may have several parent images, though each must be in a different relation (for example, consider the hierarchy of Figure 2).
[5] These invariants may be used as axioms to specify (in the manner of Hoare [2]) the semantics of the generic structure. Other axioms are required in addition to the five invariants.

duplicate tuple is inserted. In this case the corrective action is simply to delete one duplicate. Invariant (v) can never be violated given our correctness assumptions. Invariants (i), (iii), and (iv) can be violated by any correct update. In each case the corrective action is in accordance with the abstract structure of relational models. Let's consider a few examples.

Table III. Maintenance of the relational invariants during update operations. Part 1
(Part 2 appears on next page.)

INSERT

Invariant	Possible violation after insertion	Method for correcting violation
i)	t references a non-existent tuple in some caR relation R'	*insert* a tuple in R' with the appropriate key values and blanks elsewhere
ii)	t occurs twice in R	*delete* either occurrence of t
iii)	t does not have a parent image in some pgR relation R'	if a tuple with key k already occurs in R' then *modify* this tuple so that it becomes the parent image of t otherwise *insert* a parent image in R' (use blanks where values are unknown)
iv)	t does not have a required child image in some cgR relation R'	*insert* a child image in R' (use blanks where values are unknown)
v)	none	

DELETE

Invariant	Possible violation after deletion	Method(s) for correcting violation
i)	a tuple in some paR relation references a non-existent R-tuple	a) *modify* the tuple so that the reference is replaced by a blank (only possible if reference is not part of tuple's key) b) *delete* the tuple
ii)	none	
iii)	a tuple in some cgR relation has no parent image in R	*delete* the tuple
iv)	a tuple in some pgR relation does not have a required child image in R	a) *modify* the tuple by replacing its image domain value by a blank (only possible if image domain is not part of tuple's key) b) *delete* the tuple
v)	none	

Table III. Part 2
(Part 1 appears on previous page.)

MODIFY

Invariant	Possible violation after insertion	Method for correcting violation
i)	t references a non-existent tuple in some caR relation R'	*insert* a tuple in R' with the appropriate key values and blanks elsewhere
	(key domain modification) a tuple in some paR relation references a non-existent R-tuple	*modify* the tuple so that it references t
ii)	none	
iii)	t does not have a parent image in some pgR relation R'	*modify* t's old parent image so that it becomes t's (new) parent image
	a tuple in some cgR relation R' has no parent image in R	if image domain for R' is modified then *delete* the tuple otherwise *modify* the tuple so that t becomes its parent image
iv)	t does not have a required child image in some cgR relation R'	if image domain for R' is modified then *insert* a child image in R' (use blanks where values are unknown) otherwise *modify* t's old child image in R' so that it becomes t's (new) child image.
	a tuple in some pgR relation does not have a required child image in R	*modify* the tuple so that t becomes its child image
v)	none	

Suppose we violate invariant (i) by inserting a tuple t. This means that t must reference a nonexistent tuple in some relation R′. To correct this violation we must insert an appropriate tuple (say t′) in R′. Lacking other input information, the only detail we know about t′ is its key (which appears in t). Blanks must therefore be inserted in the nonkey domains of t′. Semantically, the effect of this corrective action is to introduce the abstract object t′ which is known to participate in the relationship t.

Suppose we violate invariant (iii) by deleting a tuple t. This means that the tuple (say t′), which was the child image of t, no longer has a parent image in R. To correct this violation we must delete the tuple t′. This corrective action reflects the semantic requirement that an object which does not appear in a class at a high level of generalization cannot appear in a class at a lower level of generalization.

Suppose we violate invariant (iv) by modifying a tuple t. There are two ways in which such a violation can occur. The first way is when t, after modification, has a value (say R′) in some image domain (say d) and yet t has no child image in R′. In this case the corrective action depends on whether or not d was changed by the modify operation. If d was not changed then t's old child image in R′ must be modified to make it t's new child image—all the information required already occurs in t. If d was changed then a child image must be inserted into R′. The key of this child image is contained in t—however, blanks will have to be inserted in any domain whose value is not contained in t.

The second way in which a violation can occur is when t's old parent image (say t′) no longer has a child image in R. In this case the corrective action is to modify t′ so that it becomes once again the parent image of t. In all cases the corrective action reflects the semantic requirement that the details of an abstract object must be consistent no matter what the level of generalization of the class in which it appears.

Examination of Table III will reveal that there are two methods for correcting violations of invariants (i) and (iv) following a delete operation. Each of these methods is semantically appropriate for certain situations. Let's consider invariant (i) first. Suppose we have an abstract object x which has an object y as an aggregate component. The question is whether x should be deleted if y is deleted. The answer seems to depend on the context.

For example, suppose a certain car has a "radio" and a "unibody" as two of its aggregate components. If the radio is destroyed, the car is normally considered to remain in existence. However, if the "unibody" is destroyed, then the car is normally considered to have also been destroyed. Since such questions about deletion can only be answered within a higher semantic framework, it is necessary to leave open the decision of how invariant (i) is maintained. When transactions are designed, the programmer can select which option is most appropriate relative to the integrity constraints he wants to maintain.

Similar considerations apply to invariant (iv). Suppose we have a general class x of objects which includes all objects from a more special class y. The question is whether an object should be deleted from x if it is deleted from y. For example, suppose that an object ceases to be a "Ford car." Since it is not very meaningful to change the manufacturer of a car, the presumption is that the object has ceased to be a "car" of any sort. On the other hand, suppose that an object ceases to be a "red car." Since it is very easy to repaint a red car in the color blue, the presumption might be that the object still remains a "car." The decision as to how invariant (iv) should be maintained under deletion operations must therefore be left to a higher level of modeling.

From the previous discussion, it should be clear that the maintenance procedures in Table III are designed to reflect the abstract structure of the real world. In principle, therefore, no matter what relational model is involved, triggered sequences of update operations should reflect "natural" side effects of an original user defined update. However, if we disregard our real world interpretation and consider the question formally, it is not at all easy to verify that sequences of triggered updates will necessarily be well behaved.

Conceptually, triggered updates are propagated simultaneously along many paths. What happens when two paths cross? Can one triggered update undo the work of another? Is the net result of a user defined update independent of the order in which triggered updates are scheduled? Can a sequence of triggered updates become cyclic? If a triggered update cannot be accepted (because invariant (ii) or (v) would be violated), then the sequence of triggered updates must be backed up and the original update disallowed. How do we know that no "correct" user defined update will be disallowed for this reason?

We would require that any invariant maintenance procedure satisfy at least the following three properties:

(i) The propagation of triggered updates must eventually terminate.

(ii) The overall effect, after propagation terminates, is independent of the order in which triggered updates are scheduled.

(iii) A "correct" user defined update is only disallowed when it requires a blank to be inserted in a key domain.

We call these properties *termination*, *determinancy*, and *compliancy*. We conjecture that the invariant maintenance procedure of Table III satisfies all three properties.

6. CONCLUDING REMARKS

In this section we discuss several aspects of the **generic** structure, including database design methods, implementation techniques, and query languages. We will begin with database design methods—the discussion will first concentrate on "normal forms" and then move on to consider design methodology.

In Section 3 we said that a relation is well defined if it satisfies the five relational invariants. Codd [1] and others have proposed several *normal forms* which are also supposed to capture some notion of a "good" relation. What is the relationship between a well-defined relation and a normal-form relation?

Essentially, normal forms are an attempt to formalize the notion of "basic aggregate object" in terms of the concept of functional dependency. These normal forms are not intended to, and do not, address properties of generalization. Given an aggregate object, these normal forms are useful in deciding whether the object is basic (i.e. that the object has no other object embedded within it). However, normal forms are not, at present, able to distinguish what is, or is not, an aggregate object.

Intuitively an aggregate object is something that we can *name* with a noun (or noun phrase) and presumably think of as a whole. By requiring relations to be named, the **aggregate** structure captures this aspect of an aggregate object. Normal forms do not explicitly consider naming and as a result normal-form relations may be effectively unnameable (except by a sentential description). For example, the relation R in Figure 20 satisfies (we believe) all published normal forms. However, the relation does not represent an aggregate object because it has, apparently, no name which satisfies the semantic requirements for being well defined.

R(man, property value, woman, property value)

Tuple $\langle x, y, z, w\rangle$ *is in R iff x owns a piece of property worth y, z owns a piece of property worth w, and* $y > w$.

(Assume that both men and women can own several pieces of property.)

Fig. 20. A normal-form relation which is effectively unnameable

On the other hand, while the **aggregate** structure is a stronger attempt at capturing the notion of "aggregate object," it does not capture the notion of "basic." We suggest, therefore, that "well-defined relation" and "normal-form relation" are complementary criteria for use in database design. Once well-defined relations have been discovered, their internal dependency structure may be checked against normal-form criteria. If a well-defined relation is not in normal form, it may (or may not) be appropriate to further decompose the relation.

In [4] we suggested a methodology for database design which leads to aggregate objects and then to well-defined relations. However, this methodology did not consider decomposition in the generalization plane (i.e. single-level generic hierarchies were implicitly assumed). The methodology can be extended in the obvious way to consider decomposition in both planes. There may be a marginal advantage to decomposing in the generalization plane before decomposing in the aggregation plane. This is because each cluster introduced in the generalization plane requires a new object to be inserted in the aggregation plane.

We now comment on techniques for implementing relational models at lower levels. In such an implementation there are two factors to consider: (i) how the relational *structure* is represented, and (ii) how the relational *invariants* are maintained. One consideration in choosing the structure representation is to save storage space by eliminating redundant information. Such information occurs in both the aggregation and generalization planes. In the aggregation plane it occurs as a result of key values being repeated up the hierarchy. In the generalization plane it occurs when attribute values (key or nonkey) are repeated up the hierarchy. One effect of the relational invariants is to ensure that all redundant information is consistent. Therefore, by removing as much redundancy as possible, the relational invariants should be maintainable in the most efficient manner.

Preliminary investigation indicates that relational models can be represented in terms of DBTG (Database Task Group) "owner-coupled set" structures so that no redundancy occurs. For the aggregation plane, each hierarchic branch becomes a different set type with the upper relation as member type and the lower relation as owner type. Each set instance contains as members all tuples which reference the owner tuple. For the generalization plane, each collection of all hierarchic branches from a given relation becomes a different set type with the upper relation as owner type and all descendant relations as member types. Each set instance contains as members all child images of the owner tuple. It seems likely that most of the relational invariants can be maintained using DBTG Data Definition Language options—however, this issue is not yet fully resolved.

Finally, we discuss some issues associated with access languages for relational models. When we began our study of generalization and its representation in relational models, we had assumed that a higher order query language would be essential to exploit the rich hierarchic structure. It seemed that higher order variables would be needed to range over higher order relations (i.e. relations of relations, etc.) in addition to first order variables which range over first order relations (i.e. relations of individuals).

However, we had underestimated the power of abstraction. Our motivation for the **generic** structure was to provide uniform treatment for all kinds of objects—individual, aggregate, and generic. This means that higher order relations are structurally identical to first order relations. As a result a first order query language appears to be adequate for all relational models no matter how many levels of generalization they contain. In essence, by imposing an appropriate structuring discipline, we have been able to exploit a richness that was already implicit in Codd's original work.

Despite the fact that a first order language may be adequate for querying, there are strong reasons for developing higher order primitives for applications programming. Consider the following query over the relational model of Figure 11:

> *"Find out what type of employee E5 is, and then retrieve his record for that employee type."*

This query can be conveniently expressed in two parts as shown below.

Part 1:
```
R ← RESTRICT (employee to E# = E5);
S ← PROJECT (R on TN);
RETRIEVE S;
```

Part 2 (assuming response to Part 1 is "trucker"):
```
T ← RESTRICT (trucker to E# = E5);
RETRIEVE T;
```

The first part returns E5's employee type (say "trucker"), and the second part retrieves E5's record from "trucker." In this case the user has to formulate the second part from information obtained in the first part.

If this query were to be implemented as an application program, the user would be "replaced" by a case statement as shown below.

```
READ X;
R ← RESTRICT (employee to E# = X);
S ← PROJECT (R on TN);
T ← case S of
        trucker: RESTRICT (trucker to E# = X);
        secretary: RESTRICT (secretary to E# = X);
        engineer: RESTRICT (engineer to E# = X)
    end
RETRIEVE T;
```

The problem with using the case statement is that the program becomes *dependent* on the generic components of "employee" *at one point in time.* If a new type of employee is hired (say "guard") then the program will not work when the input happens to be the employee number of a guard.

This "time dependency" can be removed with the aid of a higher order operator which we will call SPECIFY. Given the name of a relation, SPECIFY will return the relation so named. We can now rewrite the preceding program as shown below.

```
READ X;
R ← RESTRICT (employee to E# = X);
S ← PROJECT (R on TN);
T ← SPECIFY S;
U ← RESTRICT (T to E# = X);
RETRIEVE U;
```

The new program is independent of the generic components of "employee" at all points in time.

The introduction of higher order primitives can thus increase the stability of programs as the database evolves in accordance with the real world. It is not clear what other higher order operators are useful besides SPECIFY. As far as we know, these aspects of applications programming have yet to be investigated.

ACKNOWLEDGMENTS

We are grateful for the comments of R.W. Taylor and the anonymous referees on an earlier version of this paper.

REFERENCES

1. Codd, E.F. Further normalization of the data base relational model. In *Courant Computer Science Symposium 6: Data Base Systems*, Prentice-Hall, Englewood Cliffs, N.J., May 1971, pp. 33–64.
2. Hoare, C.A.R. Notes on data structuring. In *APIC Studies in Data Processing No. 8: Structured Programming*, Academic Press, New York, 1972, pp. 83–174.
3. Quillian, M.R. Semantic memory. In *Semantic Information Processing*, M.I.T. Press, Cambridge, Mass., 1968, pp. 227–268.
4. Smith, J.M., and Smith, D.C.P. Database abstractions: Aggregation. To appear in *Comm. ACM* in June 1977.

Received November 1976; revised February 1977

1988 Epilogue*

Our original goal in this work was to find a theoretically sound, and practically useful, method for designing a database schema. Methods proposed at the time did not seem satisfactory to us. Third form normalization [BERN76] was perplexing; it seemed to work in many cases but made impractical assumptions. E-R models [CHEN76] were easier to understand but made some unintuitive distinctions that were difficult to apply. Semantic networks [RM75] avoided the distinctions but seemed too general and unconstrained for database design. In searching for a solution, we became inspired by Hoare's article [HOAR72] on abstraction and data structures.

From Hoare, it appeared that a satisfactory object type system could be built on just a few fundamental abstraction mechanisms. Ultimately, we recognized three distinct abstractions which we came to call "aggregation", "generalization" and "classification". These abstractions correspond to the set-theoretic operations of cartesian product, union, and set creation respectively. It seemed to us that these were the ideal primitives for structuring a database schema. The primitives should give strong guidance to the designer, the resulting designs should be easier to understand in whole and in part, and update semantics should be free of anomalies. We felt that clear principles of practical database schema design could be articulated once the basic ideas were worked out.

This paper, and its companion [SS77] explore the basic ideas of abstraction in database models. In reviewing the paper over a decade later, it appears that most of the ideas have survived the test of time, and our deeper understanding of data models. The examples in the paper illustrate well the practical role that abstraction can play in database design. However, the syntax for object type definitions, and its reliance on "keys", looks dated. One regret is that the paper does not cleanly separate classification from generalization. In fact, the term "generalization" is used ambiguously for both concepts. This ambiguity is cleared up in later papers. The application of aggregation and generalization to database design is covered more fully in [SS78].

While working on database abstractions, we became familiar with the ideas of "abstract data types" [LZ74]. This latter work also deals with abstraction but is focussed (to our way of thinking) on hiding physical details about how an object is implemented on a computer system. In contrast, our work is focussed on hiding logical details about complex objects. Our abstractions are important even if the objects are never physically implemented. Physical and logical abstractions are complementary and both must be captured in programming environments. We formulated these observations in a position paper [SMIT78].

We have mixed feelings now about our decision in the paper to portray object type hierarchies as closely coupled with the relational model. At the time we thought that this would aid comprehension and show how the ideas applied to relational database design. Unfortunately, some readers have assumed that the abstraction concepts apply only to the relational model. In retrospect, the paper would have been better had we used abstract data types, instead of relations, to define each object type in a hierarchy. This would have made it clear that aggregation, generalization, and classification are really concepts for constructing object-oriented systems in general, and not just relational databases.

It was not until [SS79b], that we reformulated our ideas to incorporate abstract data types. We defined a simple object-oriented data model and included a predicate language for defining operations on object types. The result was a high-level, albeit rudimentary, persistent object-oriented programming language. From a present day perspective, the language appears as a strange combination of features from Smalltalk and Prolog. To demonstrate the generality of the language, we showed how it could be used to define system programming objects, such as "stack" or "symboltable", as well as database objects. In [SS79a], we described specifically how the language can be applied to database design. Due to the pressure of other responsibilities, it was at this point that the thread of our work on aggregation and generalization came to an end.

Under the influence of languages like Smalltalk, generalization hierarchies are now fundamentally associated with object type systems. Classification is also being increasingly exploited, although for reasons of implementability, its full power is not always available. We feel that aggregation is still undervalued and underutilized in object type systems. This is unfortunate as the full generality of these type systems will not be available until all three forms of abstraction can be uniformly and recursively applied.

---

* Citations in this epilogue refer to entries in the bibliography for this volume.

2.2 Semantic Data Models and Knowledge Representations

This section presents four papers covering the period from 1975 to 1980. It describes work based on some form of E-R representations. The semantic data models presented in the first three papers can be seen as advances on earlier proposals (some of which appear in the previous section). There have been many other proposals for semantic data models. [BROD84] summarizes their main features, and [HK87] present a comprehensive and up-to-date survey of such proposals. [BORG85], [AB87a], and [ALBA85] compare such proposals. Other literature on the semantic data-model includes [WM77], [BPP76], [MW80], [BB84], [KM84], [KM85], and [MO86]. [BL85] is an excellent source for the key literature on knowledge representation.

The first paper of the section (2.2.1), "A Language Facility for Designing Interactive Database-Intensive Systems" by John Mylopoulos, Phil Bernstein, and Harry Wong, was first presented at the 1978 SIGMOD conference. It proposes a comprehensive and uniform framework for modelling data objects that constitute the database, transactions that operate on these objects, exceptions that can arise in the execution of these transactions, and exception handlers used to deal with such exceptions. Taxis has been provided with a formal semantics [BW81], has been extended to offer a version of Petri nets intended for modelling long-term processes [BARR81], and has been implemented [NCLB87]. Taxis has been one of the most influential languages that combine advanced AI and database concepts. [MBGM86] presents a recent overview of the research results of the entire project.

The second paper (2.2.2), "The Functional Data Model and the Data Language DAPLEX" by Dave Shipman, was first presented at the 1979 SIGMOD conference. It adopts the notions of entity and function to develop DAPLEX, a data definition, manipulation, and query language. DAPLEX is the best-known functional data model (others are described in [KP75], [HR85], [HUDS86]), and was influential in semantic data-model and data-language research. Functional data models have not been strongly related to the long tradition of functional languages and schemes in AI. A recent example of a functional scheme in AI is [BFL83]. Two other influential semantic data models, RM/T [CODD80] and RIGEL [RS79], also were presented at the same conference. Early in 1980, the Computer Corporation of America (CCA) adopted DAPLEX for many of its advanced database projects, including one that led to ADAPLEX, an extension of ADA that supports database-management facilities (see [Chan, 3.4.2]).

One premise of database technology is that it is useful to factor out, from all applications, data that could be shared by other applications (see both [Bachman] and [Brodie and Manola, 1.1]). Unfortunately, this separation makes it difficult for database designers to "impart meaning" to their databases, and for end users to grasp that meaning. This observation has led to proposals for semantic data modelling that provide facilities for modelling the *behavioural* as well as the *structural* features of a database. The third paper of the section (2.2.3), "On the Design and Specification of Database Transactions" by Michael L. Brodie and Dzenan Ridjanovic, offers one of the most thorough treatments available in the literature for describing the behavioural properties of a database. This approach is also addressed by [ABRI74], [DZ81], [KM84], and [Mylopoulos, this section]. The approach adopted in the paper, and in many subsequent proposals, is to specify operations that are meaningful for each entity type, explicitly in the conceptual schema (in the spirit of abstract data types [LZ84]). Such encapsulation of structure and behaviour is one of the main ideas underlying the now-popular object-oriented databases. An epilogue for this third paper, written recently by Brodie and Ridjanovic, outlines trends in data modelling since 1980.

The fourth and last paper of the section (2.2.4), "An Overview of the KL-ONE Knowledge Representation System" by Ron Brachman and Jim Schmolze, presents an overview of KL-ONE, a knowledge-representation language based on semantic nets. The language was developed by Ron Brachman and colleagues at Bolt, Beranek, and Neuman. It was clearly influenced by [WOOD75] in its careful stand on semantic issues, and also by [MINS75] in the facilities it provides for the organization of concepts. In turn, KL-ONE has been one of the most influencial knowledge-representation languages, mostly because of its treatment of semantic issues and the availability of an implementation. KRYPTON [BFL83], NIKL [MOSE83], and KL-TWO [VILA85] are KL-ONE descendants. [SB81] is the proceedings of one of a series of workshops whose participants have included KL-ONE designers, implementors, and *users*. KL-ONE shares its ancestry with frame-based representation schemes (e.g., [FK85],

[MINS75], [WINO75], FRL, KRL [BW77], and [HAYE79]), which in turn share ancestry with the data models based on abstract data types and object-orientation discussed earlier in this chapter. Unlike their object-oriented cousins, frame-based schemes emphasize flexibility at the expense of the benefits of encapsulation or information hiding.

A Language Facility for Designing Database-Intensive Applications

JOHN MYLOPOULOS
University of Toronto
PHILIP A. BERNSTEIN
Harvard University
and
HARRY K. T. WONG
IBM Research Laboratory

TAXIS, a language for the design of interactive information systems (e.g., credit card verification, student-course registration, and airline reservations) is described. TAXIS offers (relational) database management facilities, a means of specifying semantic integrity constraints, and an exception-handling mechanism, integrated into a single language through the concepts of *class*, *property*, and the *IS-A* (generalization) *relationship*. A description of the main constructs of TAXIS is included and their usefulness illustrated with examples.

Key Words and Phrases: applications programming, information system, relational data model, abstract data type, semantic network, exception handling
CR Categories: 3.70, 3.73, 4.22, 4.29, 4.33, 4.34, 4.39

1. INTRODUCTION

1.1 Motivation

A primary goal of database management is the reduction of software costs by promoting data independence. In the database literature, practical aspects of the development of applications software that use a database system are often treated as peripheral to the main thrust of database research. Until recently, applications programming has usually been considered in the context of a data sublanguage embedded in a conventional applications programming language. Some of the better examples of this approach include papers by Date [5] and Schmidt [17].

This work was supported in part by the National Science Foundation under Grant ENG77-05720, in part by the National Research Council of Canada, and in part by the Division of Applied Sciences at Harvard University.
Authors' addresses: J. Mylopoulos, Department of Computer Science, University of Toronto, Toronto, Ont., M5S 1A7, Canada; P.A. Bernstein, Aiken Computation Laboratory, Harvard University, Cambridge, MA 02138; H.K.T. Wong, IBM Research Laboratory, San Jose, CA.

A more recent trend is to design the programming language with database facilities as a single unit [16, 22]. This paper takes a step along this path by presenting an applications programming language that tightly integrates data with the procedures that use it (in the style, say, of SIMULA [4]).

Our language, called TAXIS,[1] is designed primarily for applications systems that are highly interactive and make substantial use of a database. These applications, which we call interactive information systems (IIS), are characterized by their handling of large volumes of transactions that are short, of predictable structure, and update intensive. Examples include credit card verification, student-course registration, and airline reservations. By applying our tools to a more limited domain, we can customize them to the domain. Also, by defining our problem more narrowly than that of "applications systems," it will be easier to evaluate the efficacy of our approach.

In the future, we see TAXIS at the center of a programming system that would permit a designer to interactively build an IIS with the help of specialized text-editing and graphics facilities. The system would include a relational database management system (DBMS). The DBMS provides an interface into which the database operations of the IIS can be compiled.

1.2 Design Principles

TAXIS is eclectic, combining concepts from three areas of computer science research: artificial intelligence (AI), programming languages, and database management. From AI we have used the concept of semantic network for data and procedure modeling [2, 11]. From programming languages we have borrowed the concept of abstract data type [12, 18] and exception handling [21]. Finally, from database management we have built on the concept of a relational database [8].

These ideas are married to form a concise language framework, yielding a novel and powerful collection of facilities. First, the semantic network modeling constructs represent a qualitative improvement in abstraction mechanisms over conventional programming languages. Database operations can work on hierarchies of objects, instead of independent tuples and relations (similar to [20]). Data can thereby be manipulated at varying levels of abstraction. We extend our semantic structures beyond relations and apply them equally to procedures, integrity constraints, and exception handling.

Second, by associating operations with the data they use, the semantics of the *database* can be represented in the applications program. This is in contrast to the sharp distinction between DDL and DML in most database languages. The semantic information can be used by the compiler to solve many integrity, security, and concurrency problems at compile time.

Finally, since the application is described in a formal semantic model, "meta-level" commands allow the application description itself to be manipulated by programming language commands. This permits database administrator functions to peruse the logical design on-line.

Four principles guided much of the TAXIS design:

(1) The language must offer relations and associated operations for database

[1] Taxis (τάξις): Greek noun meaning order as in "law and order" or class as in "social class," "university class," etc.

management, transactions for the specification of application programs, and exception-handling facilities to enhance the development of interactive systems.

(2) Each conceptual object represented in the language must have associated semantics that involve both a behavioral and a structural component. These semantics are expessed in terms of the notions of class, property, and the *IS-A* hierarchy (cf. "generalization" in [20]).

(3) As much of the language as possible should be placed into the framework of classes, properties, and the *IS-A* hierarchy.

(4) The schema (i.e., the collection of classes, along with their properties and the associated *IS-A* hierarchy) should be compilable into a language such as Pascal, enriched with a relation data type and associated operations (as proposed, for instance, in [17]).

The first principle is a consequence of the intended scope of the language. The second reflects our belief that much of the difficulty of designing and implementing IISs (usually translated into high costs of initial implementation and maintenance) is due to the lack of appropriate programming constructs in "conventional" languages (e.g., Cobol and PL/I) for handling the semantics of any one application. The third and fourth principles are the results of our concern for linguistic uniformity and efficiency. We consider both of them quite important given the multiplicity of sources of ideas and the complexity of the problem at hand.

Section 2 of the paper discusses the basic entities that constitute a TAXIS program. Section 3 describes the *IS-A* hierarchy as an organizational principle (abstraction mechanism) for the classes constituting a program. In Section 4 we present more details about the different categories of classes. Concluding remarks and directions for further research appear in Section 5.

The presentation of the language is rather informal and necessarily sketchy due to space limitations. The interested reader is referred to [14, 25] for more details.

2. OBJECTS AND PROPERTIES

There are three types of objects in TAXIS: *tokens*, which represent constants; *classes*, which describe collections of tokens; and *metaclasses*, which describe collections of classes.

2.1 Tokens and Classes

Tokens are the constants of a TAXIS program. For example, *john-smith* (representing the particular person called John Smith), '*SMITH,JOHN,B*' (representing the string SMITH,JOHN,B), and 7 (representing the number 7) are all tokens. Tokens are denoted throughout the paper by identifiers in lowercase letters and numerals; strings are delimited by single quotes.

A class is a collection of tokens sharing common properties. If a token *t* is an element of the collection associated with a class *C* we say that *t is an instance of C*. It may be helpful for the reader to compare TAXIS classes with SIMULA classes or programming language types as points of reference.

Some sample classes are *PERSON*, whose instances are tokens such as *john-smith*, representing particular persons, *PERSON-NAME*, whose instances are (string) tokens, such as '*SMITH,JOHN,B*' that can serve as proper names, and *INTEGER*, whose instances are integers such as 7. We use identifiers in uppercase letters to denote classes.

We call the collection of all tokens which are instances of a class *C the extension of C*.

2.2 Properties

Classes and tokens have properties through which they can be related to other classes and tokens. Some of the properties that may be associated with the class *PERSON* represent the following information:

"each person has a name, an address, an age, and a phone number"
"each person's name consists of a first and last name and possibly a middle initial"

For tokens, properties represent specific facts rather than abstract rules such as those presented above. Thus, *john-smith* will have properties expressing facts such as

"*john-smith*'s name is '*SMITH,JOHN,B*', his address is 38 Boston Dr., Toronto, his age is 32, and his telephone number is 762-4377"

Properties are triples consisting of one or more *subjects*, an *attribute*, and a *property value* (or *p-value*). For example, *PERSON* may have the following properties:

⟨*PERSON, name, PERSON-NAME*⟩

⟨*PERSON, address, ADDRESS-VALUE*⟩

⟨*PERSON, age, AGE-VALUE*⟩

⟨*PERSON, phone#, PHONE-VALUE*⟩

The same applies for properties of tokens, i.e.,

(*john-smith, name,* '*SMITH,JOHN,B*')

(*john-smith, address, john-smith's-address*)

(*john-smith, age,* 32)

(*john-smith, phone#,* 7624377)

Note that the properties of *PERSON* provide information about the structure of instances of that class, while the properties of *john-smith* specify the structure of the token itself. This distinction was already made in the notation just introduced for properties, with the properties of a class delimited by angular brackets and those of a token by parentheses. We call the former type of property *definitional* and the latter *factual*.

Some properties may have more than one subject. For example,

⟨(*FLIGHT#, DATE*), *flt, FLIGHT*⟩

defines a (definitional) *complex property* with subjects the classes *FLIGHT#* and *DATE* and *p*-value the class *FLIGHT*. This property may represent the information:

"each combination of a flight number and a date has an associated flight"

As the reader may have suspected, there is a strong relationship between the definitional properties of a class and the factual properties of its instances. The relationship may be expressed in terms of the following property induction principle.

Property Induction Principle. The definitional properties of a class induce factual properties for its instances.

If classes $C_1, \ldots, C_n$ are the subjects of a definitional complex property with attribute p, the TAXIS expression $(C_1, \ldots, C_n) \,..\, p$ (or $C_1 \,..\, p$ if $n = 1$) returns the p-value of that property. For example, *PERSON* .. *age* returns the class *AGE-VALUE*, while (*FLIGHT#*, *DATE*) .. *flt* returns *FLIGHT*. In other words, " .. " is a "schema selector" and allows the traversal of the schema defined with a TAXIS program by its classes and their definitional properties. For the " .. " operator to be unambiguous, no two definitional properties can have the same subject(s) and attribute.

Turning to factual properties, if $\langle (C_1, \ldots, C_n), p, C \rangle$ is a definitional property and t_i is an instance of C_i, $1 \le i \le n$, then $(t_1, \ldots, t_n).p$ (or $t_1.p$ if $n = 1$) evaluates to an instance of C, say t, such that $\langle (t_1, \ldots, t_n), p, t \rangle$ is a factual property. Thus *john-smith.age* returns 32 while (802, *may*-1-1979).*flt* returns the particular flight associated with those two tokens through the *flt* property (i.e., the property with attribute "*flt*").

2.3 Metaclasses

If one wishes to represent the information

"the average age of (known) persons is 28"

or

"the number of (known) flights is 473"

he may be tempted to express these facts by

⟨*PERSON*, *average-age*, 28⟩

⟨*FLIGHT*, *cardinality*, 473⟩

However, this representation is incorrect since definitional properties represent information about the structure of instances of a class, not the class itself. Instead, factual properties must be used to represent these facts:

(*PERSON*, *average-age*, 28)

(*FLIGHT*, *cardinality*, 473)

But to be consistent with the property induction principle, these factual properties must be induced by definitional properties which have the classes *PERSON* and *FLIGHT* as instances. This observation leads to the introduction of a third type of TAXIS object called *metaclass*. A metaclass is similar to a class in every respect, except that its instances are classes rather than tokens. For instance, the metaclass *PERSON-CLASS* may be defined with instances of all classes whose instances denote persons (e.g., *PERSON*, *STUDENT*, *EMPLOYEE*, *MANAGER*). Then the definitional property

⟨*PERSON-CLASS*, *average-age*, *AGE-VALUE*⟩

allows the association of an *average-age* factual property with every instance of *PERSON-CLASS*.

(*PERSON*, *average-age*, 28)

(*STUDENT*, *average-age*, 19), etc.

We refer to the relationships between a token (class) and the class (metaclass) it is an instance of as the *INSTANCE-OF* relationship.

Generally, a TAXIS program includes tokens which can only have factual properties associated with them, classes which can have factual and definitional properties, and metaclasses which can only have definitional properties. For a more sophisticated treatment of the *INSTANCE-OF* relationship which allows an arbitrary number of levels of metaclasses, see [11] and [19]. We expect that the three levels allowed in TAXIS will suffice for most practical situations.

For metaclasses, we use identifiers in uppercase letters which end in *-CLASS*. As with classes, the collection of all instances of a metaclass is called its extension.

2.4 Examples

Classes and metaclasses are defined by specifying their name and their simple properties. For example, the metaclass *PERSON-CLASS* can be defined by

```
metaclass PERSON-CLASS with
  attribute-properties
    average-age: AGE-VALUE;
end
```

Here *PERSON-CLASS* is defined to have one simple (i.e., noncomplex) property

⟨*PERSON-CLASS*, *average-age*, *AGE-VALUE*⟩

The metaclass definition also specifies that the property defined is of the **attribute-property** category which means that the *average-age* factual property of an instance of *PERSON-CLASS* may change with time. Generally, every definitional property defined in a TAXIS program is classified into a unique *property category* at the time of its definition, which determines the functional and operational characteristics of the property.

Property categories allow the specification of information such as that the function defined by a property is time varying or 1-1 or should be used in a particular manner when instances of its subject(s) are created. The following examples illustrate the different uses of property categories.

The class *PERSON* can now be defined as an instance of the metaclass *PERSON-CLASS* by

```
PERSON-CLASS PERSON with
  keys
    person-id: (name, address);
  characteristics
    name: PERSON-NAME;
    address: ADDRESS-VALUE;
    phone#: PHONE-VALUE;
  attribute-properties
    age: AGE-VALUE;
    status: STATUS-IN-CANADA;
end
```

According to this definition, *PERSON* has two attribute (i.e., time-varying) properties and three characteristic properties which are time invariant. The key property described in the definition of *PERSON* specifies the complex property

((*PERSON-NAME, ADDRESS-VALUE*), *person-id, PERSON*)

Thus ('*SMITH, JOHN, B*', *john-smith's-address*).*person-id* returns the person with '*SMITH, JOHN, B*' as name and *john-smith's-address* as address, if any. If there is none, the expression returns the special TAXIS token **nothing**.

The class *FLIGHT* can be defined in a similar fashion:

```
VARIABLE-CLASS FLIGHT with
  keys
    flt: (flight#, date);
  characteristics
    flight#: {|1::999|}
    departure: [|city: CITY, country: COUNTRY|];
    destination: [|city: CITY, country: COUNTRY|];
    aircraft: AIRCRAFT-TYPE;
    date: DATE-VALUE;
  attribute-properties
    seats-left: NONNEGATIVE-INTEGER;
end
```

Here *VARIABLE-CLASS* stands for a special metaclass whose instances can have their collections of tokens changed in terms of explicit insertions or removals. Thus, since *FLIGHT* is an instance of *VARIABLE-CLASS*, it can have tokens added to or removed from its collection of instances. Clearly, variable classes behave very much like relations [3]. *PERSON* can also be made an instance of the metaclass *VARIABLE-CLASS*, in addition to its being an instance of *PERSON-CLASS*, by relating the metaclasses *PERSON*- and *VARIABLE-CLASS* through the *IS-A* relationship. This is discussed in more detail in Section 3.

The class defined by {|1::999|} is *finitely defined* in the sense that it has a finite, time-invariant collection of instances which includes all integers from 1 to 999. Since this class does not have an associated name, it can only be referenced through expressions such as *PERSON* .. *flight#*.

The class defined by [|*city*: *CITY*, *country*: *COUNTRY*|] has as instances all tuples with the first component an instance of *CITY* and the second an instance of *COUNTRY*. Classes such as this are instances of the special metaclass *AGGREGATE-CLASS*. Generally, an instance of *AGGREGATE-CLASS*, say *A*, has a collection of instances which is the cross product of the collections of instances of classes that serve as *p*-values of *A*'s characteristic properties. In this respect, aggregate classes are quite different from variable classes.

In other words, if aggregate class C has characteristic properties $p_1, \ldots, p_n$ with *p*-values $C_1, \ldots, C_n$, respectively, and if the extensions of these classes are $\text{ext}(C_1, \sigma), \ldots, \text{ext}(C_n, \sigma)$ in some database state σ, then

$$\text{ext}(C, \sigma) = \text{ext}(C_1, \sigma) \times \text{ext}(C_2, \sigma) \times \cdots \times \text{ext}(C_n, \sigma).$$

The class [|*city*: *CITY*, *country*: *COUNTRY*|] could have been defined separately.

```
AGGREGATE-CLASS LOCATION with
  characteristics
    city: CITY;
    country: COUNTRY;
end
```

with *LOCATION* replacing [|*city*: *CITY*, *country*: *COUNTRY*|]. If that second method were used,

FLIGHT .. *departure* = *FLIGHT* .. *destination*

With the original definition of *FLIGHT*, however, the above equality does not hold. In other words, each class definition that appears in a TAXIS program causes the introduction of yet another class in the schema described by the program.

Turning to some of the classes mentioned in the definitions presented so far, let us first define *PHONE-VALUE* as

```
FORMATTED-CLASS PHONE-VALUE with
  {|'('|} @ REPEAT(DIGIT, 3) @ {|')'|} @ REPEAT(DIGIT, 7)
end
```

Formatted classes (i.e., instances of *FORMATTED-CLASS*) have as instances all strings which are consistent with a given string pattern. In particular, *PHONE-VALUE* instances have the format '(*ddd*)*ddddddd*' where *d* is any digit. Here {|')'|} defines a class with only instance the string ')', and *A* @ *B* defines a class with instances strings obtained by concatenating an instance of *B* to an instance of *A*. Moreover,

REPEAT(*A*, *n*) ≡ *A* @ *A* @ ⋯ @ *A* (*n* times)

Finally, *DIGIT* is assumed to be the class {|'0', '1', . . . , '9'|}.

It was mentioned in the introduction that all TAXIS constructs are treated within the framework described so far. Thus transactions are classes too. For example, the transaction *RESERVE-SEAT* may be defined as follows:

```
TRANSACTION-CLASS RESERVE-SEAT with
  parameter-list
    reserve-seat: (p, f);
  locals
    p: PERSON;
    f: FLIGHT;
    x: INTEGER;
  prereqs
    seats-left?: f. seats-left > 0;
  actions
    make-reservation:
      insert-object in RESERVATION with
          person ← p, flight ← f;
    decrement-seats: f. seats-left ← f. seats-left − 1;
    assign-aux variable: x ← f. seats-left;
  returns
    rtrn: x;
end
```

The above definition specifies the parameter list of *RESERVE-SEAT* through the **parameter-list** property which defines a complex property

⟨(*PERSON*, *FLIGHT*), *reserve-seat*, *RESERVE-SEAT*⟩

Local properties (**locals**) define either parameters or local variables of the transaction. The body of the transaction is given in terms of zero or more prerequisite, action, and result properties (**prereqs, actions, result,** respectively) whose *p*-values are invariably expressions. Finally, the returns property (**returns**) associates with a transaction an expression to be evaluated when execution of the body of the transaction has been completed. The value of the expression is also the value returned by the transaction.

It is assumed in the definition of *RESERVE-SEAT* that *RESERVATION* has already been defined as a variable class and that it has two characteristics with attributes *person* and *flight*, respectively. Thus the **insert-object** expression inserts another instance into the extension of this class and sets its two characteristic properties to *p* and *f*, respectively. The other two action properties decrement the *seats-left* property of *flight f* by 1 and set the local variable *x* to the value to be returned by the transaction.

A transaction class is similar to a variable class in that it has a time-varying extension. When an expression involving a call to *RESERVE-SEAT* is evaluated, a new token is first created and added to the extension of *RESERVE-SEAT*. This token is essentially an execution instance of *RESERVE-SEAT*, and the factual properties associated with it indicate the values of local variables at any one time. In fact, for the expressions which appear inside the transaction, mention of a local variable or parameter, i.e., *p*, *f*, or *x* for *RESERVE-SEAT*, is interpreted as equivalent to *self.p*, *self.f*, *self.x*, where *self* denotes the execution instance with respect to which these expressions are evaluated. Something analogous applies to **prereqs, actions, result,** and **returns** properties which initially have *p*-value **unknown** (another special TAXIS token), until the corresponding expression has been evaluated. From that point on, the *p*-value of such a property is the value returned by the expression. Thus if the identifier *make-reservation* appears in an expression, before the *make-reservation* **action** property is evaluated its value is **unknown**, while after it is evaluated, it is the value returned by the **insert-object** expression.

As mentioned earlier, execution of a transaction begins by adding a token to the extension of the transaction (class). Execution then proceeds by evaluating each prerequisite *p*-value expression to make sure that it returns the value **true**. If any of the prerequisite expressions are found to have a value other than **true**, an *exception* is said to arise and execution is suspended. Otherwise, action expressions and then result expressions, which must also return **true** values, are evaluated. Thus prerequisite and result properties can be thought of as preconditions and postconditions which must be satisfied if execution of the transaction is to be meaningful. If they are not, an exception is raised and an exception-handling transaction is called to correct the situations. The exception-handling mechanism of TAXIS is discussed in Section 4.4.

When the *p*-value of a definitional property $\langle (C_1, \ldots, C_n), p, T \rangle$ is a transaction, the meaning of the property changes in that T specifies not the type of *p*-values of factual properties induced by $\langle (C_1, \ldots, C_n), p, T \rangle$, but rather an algorithm for getting them. For example, suppose the property

⟨*PERSON*, *birthdate*, *COMPUTER-BIRTHDATE*⟩

is added to the definition of *PERSON* where

```
TRANSACTION-CLASS COMPUTE-BIRTHDATE with
  parameter-list
    birthdate: (p);
  returns
    rt: this-year - p.age;
end
```

and *this-year* is an identifier that denotes the current year. Clearly, to every particular person this property associates not an instance of *COMPUTE-BIRTHDATE*, but rather a token returned by the *p*-value of the *rt* property.

This convention of treating transactions as a means for obtaining *p*-values rather than as types of *p*-values is consistent with the SIMULA class concept. Thus in TAXIS

p. birthdate ≡ *COMPUTE-BIRTHDATE*(*p*)

where *p* is an instance of *PERSON*. Similarly, for the parameter-list complex property associated with *RESERVE-SEAT*,

(*prsn*, *flt*).*reserve-seat* ≡ *RESERVE-SEAT*(*prsn*, *flt*)

3. THE *IS-A* HIERARCHY

We envision a TAXIS program as a large collection of tokens, classes, and metaclasses interconnected through their properties. Perhaps the most important feature of TAXIS is the facility it provides for organizing the collection of classes and metaclasses into a hierarchy (taxonomy).

3.1 Preliminaries

The *IS-A* (generalization) relationship is defined over classes and metaclasses. Informally, we say that (*A IS-A B*) where *A*, *B* are both classes (metaclasses) if every instance of *A* is an instance of *B*. For example, (*ADULT IS-A PERSON*) specifies that every adult is a person and (*CHILD IS-A PERSON*) that every child is a person.

If (*A IS-A B*) then every definitional property of *B* is also a definitional property of *A*. Moreover, *A* can have additional properties that *B* does not have at all, or it can redefine some of the properties of *B*. For example, the class *ADULT* inherits the *name*, *address*, and *phone#* properties of *PERSON* but must redefine the *age* property by restricting *age* *p*-values to instances of the class *OVER*-18. Similar remarks apply for *CHILD* which, in addition, has the *guardian* property that *PERSON* does not have at all. In defining the classes *ADULT* and *CHILD*, one need not mention the properties these classes share with *PERSON*:

```
VARIABLE-CLASS ADULT is-a PERSON with
  attribute-properties
    age: OVER-18;
end
VARIABLE-CLASS CHILD is-a PERSON with
  attribute-properties
    age: UNDER-18;
    guardian: ADULT;
end
```

Properties cannot be redefined arbitrarily. For example, redefinition of *age* only makes sense if (*UNDER*-18 *IS-A AGE-VALUE*). As the reader may have suspected, the *IS-A* relationship referred to above is the reflexive transitive closure of the relationship **is-a** used in class definitions.

3.2 *IS-A* Relationship Postulates

The formal properties of the *IS-A* relationship can be summarized in terms of the following postulates:

I. All classes (metaclasses) constituting a TAXIS program are organized into an *IS-A* hierarchy in terms of the binary relation *IS-A* which is a partial order.

II. There is a most general (maximum) and a most specialized (minimum) class with respect to *IS-A* called, respectively, *ANY* and *NONE*. Similarly, there is a most general and a most specialized metaclass called, respectively, *ANY-CLASS* and *NO-CLASS*.

III. (Extensional *IS-A* Constraint) If (*C IS-A D*) for classes (metaclasses) *C* and *D*, then every instance of *C* is also an instance of *D*.

IV. (Structural *IS-A* Constraint) If (*A IS-A B*) and *B* is the subject of a definitional property $\langle (C_1, \ldots, B, \ldots, C_n), p, D \rangle$, then *A* is also the subject of a definitional property $\langle (C_1, \ldots, A, \ldots, C_n), p, E \rangle$ and moreover (*E IS-A D*).

Note that these postulates define *necessary* not sufficient conditions for the *IS-A* relationship to hold.

It is assumed that there exist classes *ANY-FORMATTED*, *ANY-VARIABLE*, *ANY-TRANSACTION*, etc., which are specializations of *ANY* and below which one finds all formatted classes, variable classes, etc. For example, the definition given earlier

```
VARIABLE-CLASS FLIGHT with
    ...
end
```

places *FLIGHT* below *ANY-VARIABLE* and is therefore equivalent to

```
VARIABLE-CLASS FLIGHT is-a ANY-VARIABLE with
    ...
end
```

For metaclasses the *IS-A* hierarchy must be defined explicitly by the TAXIS user. For example, the metaclass *PERSON-CLASS* should be a specialization of *VARIABLE-CLASS*, as suggested in Section 2.4, and for this purpose its definition should be changed to

```
metaclass PERSON-CLASS is-a VARIABLE-CLASS with
    ... (as before)
end
```

After this change, all instances of *PERSON-CLASS* are also instances of *VARIABLE-CLASS* according to Postulate III, and therefore *PERSON* is a variable class.

The Hasse diagram of the *IS-A* relationship need not be a tree. For example, the definition

```
PERSON-CLASS MALE-STUDENT is-a MALE, STUDENT with
    ...
end
```

makes *MALE-STUDENT* a specialization of *MALE* and *STUDENT* which may not be *IS-A*-comparable.

The class *ANY* has as instances all tokens available to a TAXIS program, while *NONE* has no instances at all. Similarly, *ANY-CLASS* has all classes as instances, while *NO-CLASS* has no instances at all.

3.3 More on Seat Reservations

We return to the world of persons, flights, and seat reservations to illustrate the use of the *IS-A* hierarchy.

First, let us define a few specializations of previously defined classes.

```
INTERNATIONAL-FLIGHT# := {|500::999|} is-a FLIGHT..flight#
FLIGHT#-WITHIN-CANADA := {|1::499|} is-a FLIGHT..flight#
```

places the finitely defined classes with extensions the ranges 500 :: 999 and 1 :: 499, respectively, below *FLIGHT* . . *flight#* (= {|1 :: 999|}) on the *IS-A* hierarchy. Similarly,

```
CANADA := {|'CANADA'|} is-a COUNTRY
```

makes *CANADA* a class with a single instance. Presumably, *COUNTRY* has as instances many other strings such as '*USA*', '*CHINA*', and '*GREECE*', in addition to '*CANADA*'.

It is now possible to define two specializations of *FLIGHT*

```
VARIABLE-CLASS INTERNATIONAL-FLIGHT is-a FLIGHT with
  characteristics
    flight#: INTERNATIONAL-FLIGHT#;
end

VARIABLE-CLASS FLIGHT-WITHIN-CANADA is-a FLIGHT with
  characteristics
    flight#: FLIGHT#-WITHIN-CANADA;
    departure: [|country: CANADA|] is-a FLIGHT..departure;
    destination: [|country: CANADA|] is-a FLIGHT..destination;
end
```

When a class is defined "on-line" in terms of the match-fix operators {|, |} or [|, |], one can place it at the same time on the *IS-A* hierarchy, as illustrated in the *departure* and *destination* properties of *FLIGHT-WITHIN-CANADA*. Of course, since the aggregate class defined by [|*country*: *CANADA*|] is a specialization of *FLIGHT* . . *departure* (= [|*city*: *CITY*, *country*: *COUNTRY*|]), it has two (not one) characteristic properties, as *city* is inherited.

According to the definition of *RESERVE-SEAT*, the definitional complex property

$$\langle (PERSON, FLIGHT), \textit{reserve-seat}, RESERVE\text{-}SEAT \rangle$$

is part of the TAXIS program being constructed. It follows then from Postulate IV (the structural *IS-A* constraint) that any combination of specializations of the classes *PERSON* and *FLIGHT* must have a *reserve-seat* complex property whose *p*-value, a transaction, is a specialization of the transaction *RESERVE-SEAT*. Intuitively, this means that the *reserve-seat* for, say, *CHILD*, and *INTERNATIONAL-FLIGHT* must have at least the prerequisites, actions, and results of *RESERVE-SEAT* and possibly more of each. For example, suppose that we wish to enforce a (rather conservative) constraint whereby each child must be accompanied by his/her guardian on an international flight. This is clearly a constraint concerning the transaction (*CHILD, INTERNATIONAL-FLIGHT*) . . *reserve-seat*. It can be added to that transaction as a prerequisite as follows:

```
prereq accompanied-by-guardian? on
  (CHILD, INTERNATIONAL-FLIGHT) . . reserve-seat is
  not ((p.guardian, f). reservation = nothing)
```

This definition adds *accompanied-by-guardian?* as a prerequisite property of the transaction (*CHILD, INTERNATIONAL-FLIGHT*) . . *reserve-seat*, which, of course, also inherits all properties of *RESERVE-SEAT*. The expression (*p.guardian, f*).*reservation* has value **nothing** when there is no instance identified by the key value (*p.guardian, f*) in the (variable) class *RESERVATION*; otherwise, it returns the instance of *RESERVATION* identified by that key value.

As another example, suppose that any person (adult or child) entering Canada must be a citizen, landed-immigrant, or visitor:

```
prereq can-enter-canada? on
    (PERSON, INTERNATIONAL-FLIGHT) . . reserve-seat is
    p.status instance-of {|'CITIZEN', 'LANDED-IMMIGRANT', 'VISITOR'|}
      or not f.destination.country = 'CANADA'
```

As a final example of how specializations of *RESERVE-SEAT* might be modified to suit particular combinations of specializations of *PERSON* and *FLIGHT*, suppose that the income tax office must be notified for any citizens or landed immigrants leaving Canada:

```
action notify-income-tax-people on
  (ADULT, INTERNATIONAL-FLIGHT) . . reserve-seat is
  if (p.status = 'CITIZEN' or p.status = 'LANDED-IMMIGRANT'
    and f.departure.country = 'CANADA'
    and not (f.destination.country = 'CANADA')
  then NOTIFY-INCOME-TAX-PEOPLE(p, f)
```

This action has no effects if its Boolean condition is not true.

Once these properties have been added to their corresponding transactions, the expression (*p, f*).*reserve-seat* has quite different meaning depending on whether *p* is an adult, a child, or just a person and *f* is an international or local flight. Generally,

$$(p, f).reserve\text{-}seat \equiv (Type(p), Type(f)) \,..\, reserve\text{-}seat(p, f)$$

where *Type*(*x*) returns (one of) the least general class that has *x* as an instance. If there is more than one such class, then it is assumed that choosing between them does not affect the value or the side effects caused by the call.

The examples presented illustrate the following points about the *IS-A* relationship.

(1) It is not only data objects that can be organized into an *IS-A* hierarchy but also semantic integrity constraints, expressed as prerequisites, results, and database actions.

(2) Parts of the *IS-A* hierarchy determine the structure of other parts through the definition of properties. For example, the part of the *IS-A* hierarchy which appears below the transaction *RESERVE-SEAT* is structurally homomorphic to the cross product of the *IS-A* hierarchies which appear below *PERSON* and *FLIGHT*. This is a direct consequence of Postulate IV (the structural *IS-A* constraint) and it can serve as a powerful guiding principle for the construction of a TAXIS program.

4. MORE ON CLASSES AND METACLASSES

We return to the topic of classes and metaclasses in order to provide additional details about them.

4.1 Variable Classes

The built-in metaclass *VARIABLE-CLASS* has the special feature that only its instances can have their extensions altered through the expressions **insert-object, remove-object**. For example,

```
VARIABLE-CLASS PASSENGERS with
  p: PERSON
end
```

defines an instance of *VARIABLE-CLASS* which initially has no instances of its own. However,

```
insert-object in PASSENGERS with p ← john-smith
```

adds a new token to the extension of *PASSENGERS* with "*p*" *p*-value the person *john-smith*, and returns that new token as value. A token *x* can be removed from the extension of a class *C* through the expression

```
remove-object x from C
```

Note that when a token is added to the extension of a class, it is also added to the extensions of all its generalizations, and when it is removed from a class, it is removed from the extensions of all its specializations. Thus Postulate III for the *IS-A* relationship is never violated as a result of an insertion or removal of a token.

In addition to **insert-object** and **remove-object**, TAXIS provides three other QUEL-like ([7]) expressions which allow general searches of the extension of one or more variable classes. Thus the expression

```
for x in EMPLOYEE
  for y in MANAGER
    retrieve into FATCATS with name ← x.name, sal ← x.sal
      where x.dept = y.dept and x.sal > y.sal
```

retrieves into the variable class *FATCATS* employees making more than one of their managers. Note that the assumption (*MANAGER IS-A EMPLOYEE*) implies that *MANAGER* has the properties of *EMPLOYEE*, in particular, *sal* and *dept*.

In addition to **retrieve, append** and **delete** expressions are also provided and are similar in form and semantics to **retrieve** (or corresponding QUEL commands).

Variable classes are the only classes which are allowed to have key properties. Going from a key to the corresponding token is handled in terms of the mechanisms already introduced. Thus if *address*-1 is a particular address,

('SMITH, JOHN, B', address-1).person-id

returns either the person identified by this key or **nothing**.

The attribute factual properties of a variable class instance can be changed through the *update operator* "←". For instance,

john-smith.age ← 35

changes *john-smith*'s *age* from whatever it was to 35.

4.2 Aggregate Classes

A second important category of classes consists of instances of the built-in metaclass *AGGREGATE-CLASS*. The extension of an aggregate class is determined at all times by the cross product of the extensions of its *p*-values. For example, the extension of the aggregate class [| *city*: *CITY*, *country*: *COUNTRY* |] is the cross product of the extensions of *CITY* and *COUNTRY*. The only way to change the extension of an aggregate class is to change the extension of one of its *p*-values.

Instances of aggregate classes can be referenced but never created or destroyed. Thus

[*city*: *'TORONTO'*, *country*: *'CANADA'*]

references a tuple which is an instance of any aggregate class whose extension includes the tuple (*'TORONTO'*, *'CANADA'*). We call the tokens referenced through the matchfix operators [,] ***aggregates***.

All the simple properties of an aggregate class are characteristic properties and cannot be changed for any one aggregate. However, there is an expression in TAXIS which allows the identification of an aggregate related to a given one with respect to some of its components. For example, if *x* is the aggregate [(*'TORONTO'*, *'CANADA'*] then the expression

x **but** *city* ← *'MONTREAL'*

identifies the tuple obtained from *x* by replacing its *city* *p*-value with *'MONTREAL'*.

4.3 Finitely Defined Classes

Instances of the built-in metaclass *FINITELY-DEFINED-CLASS* have their extensions specified once and for all at the time they are defined, e.g.,

CANADIAN-METROPOLES := {| *'MONTREAL'*, *'TORONTO'*, *'VANCOUVER'* |}

or

INTERNATIONAL-FLIGHT# := {|500 :: 999|} **is-a** *FLIGHT#*

Finitely defined classes are very similar to Pascal scalar types. For instance, the functions *succ* and *pred* return the successor or predecessor of an instance in the ordering of instances specified by the class definition. Similarly, there are special relations *lt*, *gt*, *le*, *ge* which compare two instances of a finitely defined class with respect to this ordering.

4.4 Test-Defined Classes

Aggregate, finitely defined, and formatted classes are all special cases of the general collection of *test-defined classes*. Such classes are characterized by the fact that membership in their extension is determined by a transaction defined for this purpose:

((*ANY*, *TEST-DEFINED-CLASS*), *test*, *TEST-TRANSACTION*)

This complex property specializes for aggregate classes to

((*ANY-AGGREGATE*, *AGGREGATE-CLASS*), *test*, *TEST-AGGREGATE*)

where *AGGREGATE* is a specialization of *ANY* with all possible aggregates as instances. Similarly, we have

((*ANY-FINITELY-DEFINED*, *FINITELY-DEFINED-CLASS*), *test*, *FINITE-TEST*))

and

((*STRING*, *FORMATTED-CLASS*), *test*, *FORMAT-TEST*)

where *STRING*'s extension contains all strings and *TEST-AGGREGATE*, *FINITE-TEST*, and *FORMAT-TEST* are all specializations of *TEST-TRANSACTION*. The essence of these three transactions was already given in the discussion of aggregate, finitely defined, and formatted classes. For instance, *TEST-AGGREGATE*(*x*, *C*) checks that the components of aggregate *x* are instances of the *p*-values of *C*'s attribute properties. *FINITE-TEST*(*x*,*C*), on the other hand, checks whether *x* is one of the tokens defined to be in the extension of *C*. Generally, if *C* is a test-defined class, then

x **instance-of** *C* ≡ (*Type*(*x*), *Type* (*C*)) . . *test* (*x*,*C*)

Not all test transactions are predetermined as they are for aggregate, finitely defined, and formatted classes. For example, we can define the metaclass

metaclass *TRAVELER-TO-CANADA-CLASS* **is-a** *TEST-DEFINED-CLASS*

and then the transaction

```
TRANSACTION-CLASS TEST-TRAVELER-TO-CANADA is-a TEST-
  TRANSACTION with parameter-list
    test:(p, class);
  locals
    p: PERSON;
    class: TRAVELER-TO-CANADA-CLASS;
  returns
    rtrn: not (nothing =
        get-object x from RESERVATION
          where (x.person = p and
                x.flight.destination.country = 'CANADA'))
end
```

thereby setting up the definitional property

((*PERSON*, *TRAVELER-TO-CANADA-CLASS*), *test*, *TEST-TRAVELER-TO-CANADA*)

Now, the class defined by

TRAVELER-TO-CANADA-CLASS TRAVELER-TO-CANADA **is-a** *PERSON*

has as instances all persons who have booked a reservation for a flight with a destination in Canada.

4.5 Expressions

Expressions can only appear in TAXIS programs as p-values of prerequisite, action, result, or return properties.[2]

Conditional, block, and looping constructs are provided in the language for the construction of compound expressions from simpler ones.

Expressions are classes and can have definitional properties of their own (which associate exceptions with them). However, expressions are special types of classes in two respects:

(1) their extension is invariably empty;
(2) their *IS-A* hierarchy is determined by the following rule: If $\langle T,p,E \rangle$ and $\langle T',p,E' \rangle$ and (T *IS-A* T'), then (E *IS-A* E'), where T, T' are transactions, and E, E' are expressions.

Thus there is no need to specify explicitly the *IS-A* hierarchy of expression classes since that is determined by the transactions to which they are attached.

The fact that expression classes have empty extensions means that Postulate III (the extensional *IS-A* constraint) is trivially satisfied for expressions. As a replacement we propose the following postulate.

III′ (Behavioral *IS-A* Constraint) (a) If E, E' are Boolean expressions and (E *IS-A* E'), then it must be that $E \rightarrow E'$ (E implies E') and E causes at least the side effects of E'.

(b) If E, E' are non-Boolean expressions and (E *IS-A* E'), then it must be that when *value* $(E) \neq$ **nothing**, *value* (E) = *value* (E') and moreover E causes at least the side effects of E'.

Consider, for example, a specialization of the *RESERVE-SEAT* transaction, say T, for which the prerequisite *seats-left?* must be redefined. It makes sense, according to the Postulate III′ (the behavioral *IS-A* constraint), to redefine it as

prereq *seats-left?* **on** T **is** *f.seats-left* > 10,

since (*f.seats-left* > 10) → (*f.seats-left* > 0). The redefinition, however,

prereq *seats-left?* **on** T **is** *f.seats-left* > 0 **or** *p.age* < 2

is inappropriate because

(*f.seats-left* > 0 **or** *p.age* < 2) ↛ *f.seats-left* > 0)

Similarly, the block expression E defined by

```
begin
  insert-object in RESERVATIONS with
    person ← p, flight ← f;
  insert-object in PASSENGERS with p ← p;
end
```

can be made a specialization of *RESERVE-SEAT*.. *make-reservation* because its side effects, which involve two insertions, include those of *RESERVE-SEAT*.. *make-reservation*. The same statement is not true if the first **insert-object** expression is deleted from E.

Postulate III′ (the behavioral *IS-A* constraint) is formalized in [25] and its consequences are discussed.

4.6 Transactions

We have already presented the basic categories of properties one can associate with a transaction. Through prerequisites, actions, and results, the TAXIS user can "factor out" a transaction body into semi-independent constraint checks and actions that may be associated with a transaction directly, during its definition, or indirectly, through inheritance.

4.7 Exceptions

We have adapted Wasserman's [21] procedure-oriented exception-handling mechanism with modifications that allow exceptions and exception-handling to be treated within the framework of classes, properties, and the *IS-A* relationship.

Exception classes are defined and organized into an *IS-A* hierarchy, like all other classes. The built-in metaclass *EXCEPTION-CLASS* has as instances all exception classes which are also specializations of the built-in class *ANY-EXCEPTION*. For a particular TAXIS program, or a collection thereof, we may have below *ANY-EXCEPTION* the classes *SECURITY-EXCEPTION*, *CONSTRAINT-EXCEPTION*, etc. Below these, one may wish to attach exception classes such as

```
EXCEPTION-CLASS NO-SEATS-LEFT is-a CONSTRAINT-EXCEPTION with
  attribute-properties
    pers: PERSON;
    flt: FLIGHT;
end
```

When an instance of this exception class is created (i.e., is *raised*), its factual properties are assigned p-values through which one can obtain information about the circumstances under which the exception was raised.

Exceptions are raised when a prerequisite or result expression evaluates to a value other than **true**. To specify which exception is raised, one must associate with a prerequisite or result p-value, which is always an expression class, an exception class. For *RESERVE-SEAT*, for example, this can be done either by replacing the *seats-left?* property of the transaction with

```
TRANSACTION-CLASS RESERVE-SEAT with
   ...
  seats-left?: f.seats-left > 0 exc
    NO-SEATS-LEFT (pers: p, flt: f);
   ...
end
```

or by adding a definitional property to the p-value of the *seats-left?* property with

exception-property *exc* **on** *RESERVE-SEAT*.. *seats-left?* **is** *NO-SEATS-LEFT* (*pers*: *p*, *flt*: *f*)

[2] This discussion does not apply to expressions involving @, [|,|], and (|,|) which define new classes and are evaluated at compilation time.

In both cases, the associations *pers*: *p*, *flt*: *f* indicate the *p*-values to be assigned to the factual properties of the *NO-SEAT-LEFT* instance raised when the prerequisite *seats-left*? fails.

When an exception is raised within a transaction *T*, it is up to the caller of *T* to specify what should be done to handle it. Such specifications come in the form of complex properties called *exception-handlers* that take as subjects an expression *E* and an exception *EXC* and *p*-value an exception-handling transaction T_h. When an instance of *EXC* is raised during the evaluation of *E*, then T_h is called with the exception raised as its only argument. Suppose, for example, that the transaction *CALLER* calls *RESERVE-SEAT* or one of its specializations during the execution of one of its actions, say *act*. To indicate that the transaction *FIND-ALTERNATIVE* should be called if the exception *NO-SEATS-LEFT* is raised, we write

```
TRANSACTION-CLASS CALLER with
    ...
  actions
    ...
    act: RESERVE-SEAT(p1, f1)
          exc-handler eh for NO-SEATS-LEFT is
             FIND-ALTERNATIVE
    ...
end
```

which defines the complex property

((*RESERVE-SEAT*(p1, f1), *NO-SEAT-LEFT*), *eh*, *FIND-ALTERNATIVE*)

Now, if an instance of *NO-SEATS-LEFT* is raised during the evaluation of *RESERVE-SEAT* (*p*1, *f*1), *FIND-ALTERNATIVE* will be called with the newly created exception instance as argument. From the properties of this instance, *FIND-ALTERNATIVE* will determine the circumstances of the exception and, we hope, what should be done.

Treating exceptions and exception-handling in terms of classes, properties, and the *IS-A* relationship means that the already existing *IS-A* hierarchy of data classes and transactions can be used to structure exception-handling within any one TAXIS program. We illustrate this point by extending the example we have used so far so that if a *NO-SEATS-LEFT* instance is raised for a child, it is not only for the child that an alternative is found but also for his or her guardian. First, we create a specialization of *NO-SEATS-LEFT*:

```
EXCEPTION-CLASS NO-SEAT-FOR-CHILD is-a NO-SEATS-LEFT with
  attribute-properties
    guardian: ADULT;
end
```

Then we redefine the exception property *exc* of the *seats-left*? prerequisite for the transaction (*CHILD*, *INTERNATIONAL-FLIGHT*) . . *reserve-seat*

```
exception-property exc on (CHILD, INTERNATIONAL-FLIGHT) . .
    reserve-seat . . seats-left? is
  NO-SEAT-FOR-CHILD (pers: p, flt: f, guardian: p.guardian)
```

Finally, we augment the exception handler *FIND-ALTERNATIVE* for the exception-handling property *eh* of *CALLER* . . *act* and *NO-SEAT-FOR-CHILD*:

```
action find-alternative-for-guardian-too on
  (CALLER . . act, NO-SEAT-FOR-CHILD) . . eh is
  /*remove the child's guardian from the flight flt and reserve a seat for him or her as
  well on the alternative flight selected*/
```

According to this, another action property is added to the (transaction) class specified by the expression (*CALLER* . . *act*, *NO-SEAT-FOR-CHILD*) . . *eh*. *CALLER* . . *act* evaluates to the expression class *RESERVE-SEAT*(*p*1, *f*1) (see definition of *CALLER*), and *RESERVE-SEAT*(*p*1, *f*1), *NO-SEATS-LEFT* have a complex property *eh* whose *p*-value is the (exception-handling) transaction *FIND-ALTERNATIVE*. It follows then that the expression (*CALLER* . . *act*, *NO-SEAT-FOR-CHILD*) . . *eh* evaluates to a specialization of *FIND-ALTERNATIVE* which inherits all the actions of that transaction in addition to the new action defined by the *find-alternative-for guardian-too* action.

We will not present code for the new action defined for the exception-handler of *NO-SEATS-LEFT* exceptions. It is worth noting, however, that the *IS-A* hierarchy of exception-handlers is patterned after that of *PERSON*, *FLIGHT*, and their specializations, along with the transactions that operate on them.

When an exception-handling transaction completes it execution, control returns to the point where the exception was raised and the expression following the prerequisite or result where the exception was raised is evaluated. Thus each prerequisite or result expression *E* can be interpreted as a conditional expression

if *E* **then nil else**. . .

where the blank is filled by the caller of the transaction where *E* appears.

5. CONCLUSIONS

Several other research efforts are related and/or have influenced our work. PLAIN [22] is one of the few examples of a language designed with goals similar to those of TAXIS. The main difference between the two languages is that PLAIN does not use the *IS-A* relationship as a structuring construct for data or procedures. We have adapted PLAIN's exception-handling mechanism, but modified it to make it consistent with the TAXIS framework. Moreover, due to the structure of transactions, we have managed to restrict the kind of situation under which an exception is raised to failure of a prerequisite or a result.

A recent proposal in [13] for the use of type hierarchy is basically identical to the *IS-A* hierarchy described in this paper. Our work seems to differ from Mealy's only in that his is applied to EL1 data structuring mechanisms [23] rather than the design of an application language.

Our *IS-A* hierarchy is also similar to the generalization hierarchy proposed in [20], although we do not use the "unique key" assumption they impose on their hierarchy, nor do we use their notion of image domains which defines a particular implementation of the *IS-A* relationship within a relational database framework. Another difference between *IS-A* and the generalization hierarchy proposed by the Smiths is that it is possible to redefine a property for a specialization of a class in TAXIS (subject to Postulate IV structural *IS-A* constraint), but that is not the case for the generalization hierarchy. We consider this ability to redefine properties (by specializing their *p*-values) an important component of the structuring mechanism offered by the *IS-A* relationship. Hammer and McLeod [6] and Lee and Gerritzen [9] have also proposed data models which offer an *IS-A* relationship.

The treatment of the *INSTANCE-OF* relationship in TAXIS is based on the treatment this relationship receives in PSN (procedural semantic network formalism) described in [10, 11]. However, PSN allows an arbitrary number of metaclass levels, as well as the possibility for a class to be an *INSTANCE-OF* itself. We have avoided such a scheme because experience has taught us that two levels of classes are sufficient for most situations. Lee [8] and Smith and Smith [19] also offer proposals concerning the *INSTANCE-OF* relationship.

The high-level relational database operations of QUEL (e.g., **retrieve** [7]) are very similar to the compound expressions used to manipulate variable classes. Obviously, variable classes share many features with relations of the relational model. In embedding variable classes in a programming language we have taken a very different approach from that described in [17] which treats relations as data objects that can be created dynamically as results of relational operations. Instead, in TAXIS *no classes* (variable or otherwise) can be created as results of run-time operations. We rejected Schmidt's proposal very early in our work because it raises a design dilemma for which we do not have a good solution: either we allow the inclusion of classes in TAXIS programs that do not have the usual TAXIS semantics (i.e., properties and a position on the *IS-A* hierarchy), contrary to design principle (2) of Section 1, or we include run-time facilities for obtaining the TAXIS semantics for derived classes, as done in [15], contrary to design principle (4).

Finally, Abrial's work [1] has been very influencial in directing us toward "data models" or "representation schemes" [26] which offer procedural as well as data-oriented facilities for the definition of a model.

From an AI point of view, our work is a direct descendant of PSN, with much of the power of the formalism left out to accommodate the design principles of TAXIS.

As far as contributions are concerned, we believe that this paper has provided evidence on how a framework involving classes, properties (of classes), the *IS-A* relationship, and to a lesser extent the *INSTANCE-OF* relationship, can be used to account not only for data-oriented (declarative, to use the terminology in [26]) aspects of a model of some enterprise, but also procedural ones, e.g., expressions, exceptions, and transactions.

Acceptance of the TAXIS framework for the design of IISs can have far-reaching consequences:

(1) It provides a methodology for dealing with semantic integrity constraints, which in TAXIS are treated as prerequisite and result properties of transactions and are organized into an *IS-A* hierarchy consistent with those defined for data classes and operations on them.

(2) It provides a general design methodology based on "stepwise refinement by specialization" as opposed to "stepwise refinement by decomposition" [24], which has been the main design tool used so far in program development. For data structures, an account of what stepwise refinement by specialization means and how it relates to stepwise refinement by decomposition has already been given in [20]. TAXIS proposes a similar framework for *all* aspects concerning a program design, not just its data structures. Further evidence for the importance of this notion is provided in [25].

There are four directions along which research on TAXIS is proceeding:

(1) Formalization. TAXIS offers some unusual constructs and a formal definition of what they mean appears highly desirable. Wong [25] provides an axiomatization of the language as well as a denotational semantics to account for these constructs. A by-product of this work is the ability to prove TAXIS programs correct with respect to some logical specification.

(2) Definition of Input/Output Facilities. TAXIS does not offer input/output facilities at this time. To extend it in order to have it provide such facilities, we are considering the possibility of using the same framework (classes et al.) for the definition of all syntactic and pragmatic aspects of a user interface.

(3) Implementation. A TAXIS parser and code generator, and possibly an interactive system through which a designer can use TAXIS, is an important step toward testing the language. Also, there are important theoretical problems such as the mapping of variable and transaction classes into relations and procedures, respectively.

(4) Applications. Apart from the design of individual IISs in TAXIS, we wish to explore the possibility of extending TAXIS to make it suitable for the design of IISs from one particular applications area, say, accounting or inventory control.

ACKNOWLEDGMENTS

We would like to thank Teresa Miao for typing this paper.

REFERENCES

1. Abrial, J.R. Data semantics. In *Data Management Systems*, J.W. Klimbie and K. L. Koffeman (Eds.), North Holland Pub. Co., Amsterdam, 1974.
2. Brachman, R. On the epistemological status of semantic networks. In *Associative Networks*, N. Findler (Ed.), Academic Press, New York, 1979.
3. Codd, E.F. A relational model for large shared data banks. *Commun. ACM 13*, 6 (June 1970), 377–387.
4. Dahl, O.J., and Hoare, C.A.R. Hierarchical program structures. In *Structured Programming*, O.J. Dahl, E. Dijkstra, and C.A.R. Hoare (Eds.), Academic Press, New York, 1972.
5. Date, C.J. An architecture for high level language database extension. *Proc. 1975 ACM SIGMOD Conf.*, pp. 101–122.
6. Hammer, M., and McLeod, D. The semantic data model: A modeling mechanism for database applications. *Proc. 1978 ACM SIGMOD Conf.*, pp. 26–36.
7. Held, G., Stonebraker, M., and Wong, E. INGRES: A relational data base system. *Proc. Nat. Computer Conf.*, Anaheim, Calif., 1975, pp. 19–22.
8. Lee, R., On the semantics of instance in database modeling. Working Paper, Dep. Decision Sci., Wharton School, Univ. Pennsylvania, Philadelphia, 1978.
9. Lee, R., and Gerritzen, R. A hybrid representation for database semantics. Tech. Rep. 78-01-01, Dep. Decision Sci., Wharton School, Univ. Pennsylvania, Philadelphia, 1978.
10. Levesque, H. A procedural approach to semantic networks. M.Sc. thesis (Tech. Rep. 105), Dep. Computer Sci., Univ. Toronto, Toronto, Canada, 1977.
11. Levesque, H., and Mylopoulos, J. A procedural semantics for semantic networks. In *Associative Networks*, N. Findler (Ed.), Academic Press, New York, 1979.

12. Liskov, B., Snyder, A., Atkinson, R., and Schaffert, C. Abstraction mechanisms in CLU. *Commun. ACM 20*, 8 (Aug. 1977), 564–576.
13. Mealy, G. Notions. In *Current Trends in Programming Methodology*, vol. 2, R. Yeh (Ed.). Prentice-Hall, Englewood Cliffs, N.J., 1977.
14. Mylopoulos, J., Bernstein, P., Wong, H.K.T. A preliminary specification of TAXIS: A language for interactive systems design. Tech. Rep. CCA-78-02, Computer Corp. of America, 1978.
15. Roussopoulos, N. A semantic network model of databases. Ph.D. dissertation (Tech. Rep. 104), Dep. Computer Sci., Univ. Toronto, Toronto, Canada, 1976.
16. Rowe, L.A., and Shoens, K.A. Data abstraction, views and updates in RIGEL. *Proc. 1979 ACM SIGMOD Conf.*
17. Schmidt, J.W. Some high level language constructs for data of type relation. *ACM Trans. Database Syst. 2*, 3 (Sept. 1977), 247–261.
18. Shaw, M., Wulf, W.A., and London, R.L. Abstraction and verification in ALPHARD: Defining and specifying iteration and generators. *Commun. ACM 20*, 8 (Aug. 1977), 553–563.
19. Smith, J., and Smith, D.C.P. A database approach to software specification. Tech. Rep. CCA-79-17, Computer Corp. of America, 1979.
20. Smith, J., and Smith, D.C.P. Database abstractions: Aggregation and generalization. *ACM Trans. Database Syst. 2*, 2 (June 1977), 105–133.
21. Wasserman, A.I. Procedure-oriented exception-handling. Tech. Rep. 27, Lab. Medical Inf. Sci., Univ. California, San Francisco, 1977.
22. Wasserman, A.I., Sherniz, D.D., and Handa, E.F. Report on the programming language PLAIN. Lab. Medical Inf. Sci., Univ. California, San Francisco, 1978.
23. Wegbreit, B. The treatment of data-types in EL1. *Commun. ACM 17*, 5 (May 1974), 251–264.
24. Wirth, N. Program development by step-wise refinement. *Commun. ACM 14*, 4 (April 1971), 221–227.
25. Wong, H.K.T. Design and verification of interactive information systems. Ph.D. dissertation, Dep. Computer. Sci., Univ. Toronto, Toronto, Canada. To appear.
26. Wong, H.K.T., and Mylopoulos, J. Two views of data semantics: Data models in artificial intelligence and database management. *INFOR 15*, 3 (Oct. 1977), 344–382.

The Functional Data Model and the Data Language DAPLEX

DAVID W. SHIPMAN
Computer Corporation of America

DAPLEX is a database language which incorporates:

(1) a formulation of data in terms of entities;
(2) a functional representation for both actual and virtual data relationships;
(3) a rich collection of language constructs for expressing entity selection criteria;
(4) a notion of subtype/supertype relationships among entity types.

This paper presents and motivates the DAPLEX language and the underlying data model on which it is based.

Key Words and Phrases: database, language, functional data model
CR Categories: 4.22, 4.33

1. INTRODUCTION

1.1 The Goals of the Language

DAPLEX is a data definition and manipulation language for database systems, grounded in a concept of data representation called the functional data model. DAPLEX may be considered to be a syntactic embodiment of the functional data model and throughout this paper the two terms will be used interchangeably.

A fundamental goal of DAPLEX is to provide a "conceptually natural" database interface language. That is, the DAPLEX constructs used to model real-world situations are intended to closely match the conceptual constructs a human being might employ when thinking about those situations. Such conceptual naturalness, to the extent it has been achieved, presumably simplifies the process of writing and understanding DAPLEX requests, since the translation between the user's mental representation and its formal expression in DAPLEX is more direct.[1]

[1] To some extent this "naturalness" has been a goal of other data models. For example, the "simplicity" which is often cited as an objective of the relational data model [7] is similar to naturalness in some respects, but it also includes the notions of minimality (i.e., a small number of data constructs) and nonredundancy (i.e., representation of a single "fact" only once in the database). These latter attributes of the relational model are almost certainly not characteristic of the way humans model the world. DAPLEX is prepared to sacrifice these goals in favor of a more natural representation.

Author's present address: Massachusetts Institute of Technology, Research Laboratory of Electronics, Room 36-597, Cambridge, MA 02139.

The basic constructs of DAPLEX are the *entity* and the *function*. These are intended to model conceptual objects and their properties. We may, for example, model a particular student and the courses he is taking as entities, with the function "course of" defined to map one to the other. (A DAPLEX function, in general, maps a given entity into a *set* of target entities.)

Often some properties of an object are derived from properties of other objects to which it is related. For example, assume that courses have an "instructor of" property. We may then consider an "instructors of" property which relates students to their instructors. Such a property would be based on the "instructor of" property of those courses in which the student is enrolled. The principle of conceptual naturalness dictates that it be possible for users to treat such derived properties as if they were primitive. This follows, for example, from the observation that properties which are "derived" in one database formulation may be "primitive" in another, even though the same real-world situation is being modeled. Such alternative representations of the same facts are modeled in DAPLEX by the notion of *derived function*.

The problem of database representation is complicated by the fact that no single model of reality may be appropriate for all users and problem domains. The properties which are considered relevant and the mechanisms by which they are most naturally referenced vary across differing world views. Even the decision as to what constitutes an object depends on the world view assumed. Some users might prefer, for example, to view the enrollment of a student in a course as an entity having its own properties, while for others, dealing with enrollments as objects would be unnatural and awkward. To cope with these issues, DAPLEX provides for the construction of separate *user views* of the database. Because user views are specified in terms of derived functions, complex interrelationships among views may be accommodated.

In short, the DAPLEX language is an attempt to provide a databae system interface which allows the user to more directly model the way he thinks about the problems he is trying to solve.

1.2 A Quick Look at DAPLEX

Consider the query,

> "What are the names of all students taking EE courses from assistant professors?"

In DAPLEX this is expressed as

```
FOR EACH Student
  SUCH THAT FOR SOME Course(Student)
    Name(Dept(Course)) = "EE" AND
    Rank(Instructor(Course)) = "ASSISTANT PROFESSOR"
  PRINT Name(Student)
```

(DAPLEX requests can be read in an English-like manner: "For each student such that, for some course of the student, the name of the department of the course is EE and the rank of the instructor of the course is assistant professor, print the name of the student.")

Figure 1 is a graphic representation of the data description for the database against which this query is issued. The rounded enclosures indicate entity types

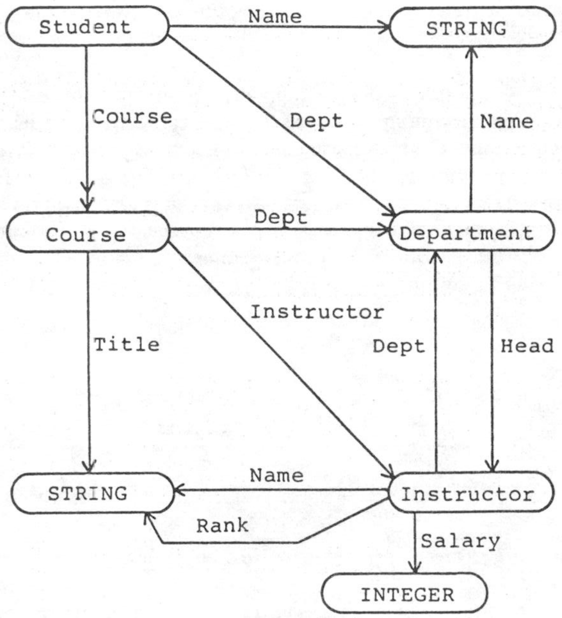

Fig. 1. The university database.

and the arrows depict functions mapping their argument types into their result types.[2]

In this example the FOR EACH statement iterates over a set of entities of type "Student", executing its for-body, the PRINT statement, for each member of the set. Here, the set of entities under consideration has been qualified by a SUCH THAT clause. SUCH THAT will consider all "Student" entities, testing them against a qualifying predicate. The qualification here further involves quantification as indicated by the phrase "FOR SOME Course(Student)". Within this phrase, the variable "Student" refers to the particular student under consideration by SUCH THAT. "Course" is a function defined over students that returns a set of course entities. If the following Boolean predicate is true for at least one of the courses, then the student entity will pass the SUCH THAT qualification. This Boolean predicate consists of two comparisons joined by the Boolean operator AND. Notice the nested functional notation here. In the expression "Name(Dept(Course))", "Course" refers to the particular "Course" entity under consideration by the FOR SOME phrase. When the "Dept" function is applied to this entity, the result is a "Department" entity indicating the department under which the course is offered. "Name" is a function which may be applied to "Department" entities to return the STRING entity which indicates the name of the department. This STRING entity is compared to the string "EE".

[2] The formal DAPLEX description of this database is given in the following section. Readers familiar with the AI literature will recognize that we are essentially dealing with a form of *semantic net* [13]. It should also be pointed out that the simple graphical notation indicated here is not adequate to represent the full power of the data description capability.

1.3 Relation to Previous Work

Data modeling has been one of the major themes of database research over the past ten years. DAPLEX is an outgrowth of this work. As extensive summaries of the field appear elsewhere [1, 10, 12], only particularly relevant research will be discussed here.

The notion of a functional data model was first introduced by Sibley and Kershberg [15]. This work explored the use of the functional approach as a tool for modeling the data structures representable under the three dominant data models (hierarchical, relational, and network). However, the payoff resulting from the concept of derived functions was not recognized.

The semantic data model of McLeod and Hammer [9, 12] does recognize the potential inherent in the notion of derived data. In addition, this work includes a great deal of pioneering research into the descriptive capabilities needed to represent, in the database, useful semantic properties of the real world being modeled. This work, however, has not concentrated on extracting the underlying primitives of the proposed model or on expressing its ideas within a concise notational framework. To a large extent, DAPLEX is an attempt to provide such a framework for many of the ideas in this model.

In a concurrent effort, Buneman [5] has developed a functional notation for data which incorporates many of the concepts underlying the functional data model proposed here. His notation is based on the functional programming (FP) notation advocated by Backus [4]. While Buneman's notation is not entirely suitable as a user interface language, it may well be useful as an internal representation for portions of the DAPLEX syntax.

In addition, some reference should be made to the work of Smith and Smith [16], whose explorations of the issues of generalization and aggregation lead directly or indirectly to many of the concepts embodied in DAPLEX; to the work of Bachman [3], whose role model bears many similarities to the use of types in DAPLEX; and to the work of Kent [11], who argues persuasively of the disadvantages of record-based data modeling. Rowe and Shoens [14] introduced the notion of procedural encapsulation of view updates. System R [2] and INGRES [17] both employ data dictionaries defined in terms of the native data model.

Many, if not most, of the ideas incorporated in DAPLEX have been adapted from previous work in database management. What is significant about DAPLEX is the fact that these ideas have been integrated into a single framework, the functional data model, and expressed in a syntax which tends to avoid unnecessary awkwardness.

The remainder of this paper includes sections describing data definition, data manipulation, derived data, metadata, and applications examples. It should be pointed out that the study of the DAPLEX language and its implications is a continuing effort and that details of the design should be considered preliminary. No implementation currently exists. The appendix presents the complete specification of the language as it stands.

```
DECLARE Student ( ) ⇒» ENTITY
DECLARE Name (Student) ⇒ STRING
DECLARE Dept (Student) ⇒ Department
DECLARE Course (Student) ⇒» Course

DECLARE Course ( ) ⇒» ENTITY
DECLARE Title (Course) ⇒ STRING
DECLARE Dept (Course) ⇒ Department
DECLARE Instructor (Course) ⇒ Instructor

DECLARE Instructor ( ) ⇒» ENTITY
DECLARE Name (Instructor) ⇒ STRING
DECLARE Rank (Instructor) ⇒ STRING
DECLARE Dept (Instructor) ⇒ Department
DECLARE Salary (Instructor) ⇒ INTEGER

DECLARE Department ( ) ⇒» ENTITY
DECLARE Name (Department) ⇒ STRING
DECLARE Head (Department) ⇒ Instructor
```

Fig. 2. Data description.

2. DATA DEFINITION

2.1 The DECLARE Statement

Figure 2 illustrates the data definition statements needed to express the data structure which is graphically presented in Figure 1. All of the statements shown here are DECLARE statements. They establish functions in the system. Functions are used to express both entity types and what we have been calling the "properties" of an entity.

Let us consider a number of the statements in this description. First, we look at

DECLARE Name(Student) ⇒ STRING

This states that "Name" is a function which maps entities of type "Student" to entities of type STRING. STRING is one of a number of entity types provided by the system along with such other types as INTEGER and BOOLEAN. The statement

DECLARE Dept(Student) ⇒ Department

states that "Dept" is a function which applied to a "Student" entity returns an entity of type "Department". It is important to remember that when the "Dept" function is applied, a department entity itself is returned, not a department number or other identifier. These two functions are called *single-valued* as they always return a single entity. (Strictly speaking, single-valued functions return a set of entities consisting of a single element.) Single-valued functions are indicated by use of a single-headed arrow (⇒) in their definition. An example of a *multivalued* function, indicated by the double-headed arrow (⇒»), is

DECLARE Course(Student) ⇒» Course

Here the "Course" function, applied to a "Student" entity, returns a set of entities of type "Course". A multivalued function may return the empty set.

All function applications evaluate to sets of entities in the mathematical sense; that is, the sets are considered unordered and do not contain duplicates.[3]

The functions we have examined so far take a single argument. It is also possible for functions to take no arguments. For example,

DECLARE Student ( ) ⇒» ENTITY

Here the function "Student" evaluates to a set of entities. ENTITY is the system-provided type of all entities. By convention, zero-argument functions define entity types. Thus the statement above has a dual purpose; it declares the function "Student" and it defines the entity type "Student". All and only those entities returned by the "Student" function are of type "Student".

Multivalued functions are initialized to return the empty set. Single-valued functions must be explicitly initialized by the user.[4] Further instantiation of functions takes place through update statements, discussed in Section 3.4.

2.2 Multiple Argument Functions

We have just considered functions of zero and one argument. However, functions taking any number of arguments may be declared. For example, we could augment the data description of Figure 2 with the statement

DECLARE Grade(Student, Course) ⇒ INTEGER

The "Grade" function might return the grade which "Student" obtained in "Course".

Other data modeling mechanisms often force the creation of new entity types in such a situation, for example, [6]. In these systems it is necesssary to view, for example, the enrollment of a student in a course as a conceptual object, and then to assign a "grade of" property to that "object." With DAPLEX, the mandatory creation of such potentially unnatural entity types is avoided.

A difficulty with the function declaration above is that it specifies the function "Grade" as well defined for every "Student"–"Course" pair, while in fact the function should only exist for those courses in which the student is enrolled. The more sophisticated declaration that follows circumvents this problem:

DECLARE Grade(Student, Course(Student)) ⇒ INTEGER

2.3 Function Inversion

The reader may be concerned that DAPLEX functions map in only one direction. Thus, given a "Course" entity, we may apply the function "Instructor" to obtain the instructor of the course. But, given an "Instructor" entity, how do we determine the courses he teaches? This problem is solved through the use of function inversion, as illustrated by

```
DEFINE Course(Instructor) ⇒»
  INVERSE OF Instructor(Course)
```

---

[3] As we see later, however, the language does include facilities which allow the user to associate orders with certain sets of entities.

[4] Formally, single-valued functions are initialized to a particular entity which is only of type ENTITY. Because the value of the function is of the wrong type, any reference to the function will cause a run-time error. Further, the transaction (i.e., top-level DAPLEX statement) will abort if the function has not been properly initialized by the end of the transaction (see Appendix, Section A2.2.2).

```
DECLARE Person ( ) =>> ENTITY
DECLARE Name (Person) => STRING

DECLARE Student ( ) =>> Person
DECLARE Dept (Student) => Department
DECLARE Course (Student) =>> Course

DECLARE Employee ( ) =>> Person
DECLARE Salary (Employee) => INTEGER
DECLARE Manager (Employee) => Employee

DECLARE Instructor ( ) =>> Employee
DECLARE Rank (Instructor) => STRING
DECLARE Dept (Instructor) => Department
```

Fig. 3. Subtypes.

We now have a function "Course" which can be applied to "Instructor" entities. In so doing, we have entered the domain of derived functions (notice the keyword DEFINE has replaced DECLARE). Section 4 is devoted to the definition and use of derived data, and in that section the subject of function inversions is taken up again.

2.4 Subtypes and Supertypes

Rather than declare "Student" and "Instructor" entities, as is done in Figure 2, the more general specification given in Figure 3 might be used. Here, by defining students as persons and instructors as employees, who in turn are persons, we have implied a number of *subtype* and *supertype* relationships.

In Figure 3 the "Student" function is defined to return a set of "Person" entities. That is, the set of "Student" entities is a subset of the set of "Person" entities. This implies that any "Student" entity also has the "Name" function defined over it since it is necessarily a "Person" entity as well.

Similar comments apply to the specification of the "Employee" type, as well as to the "Instructor" type, a subtype of the type "Employee". An "Instructor" entity has "Name", "Salary" and "Manager" functions specified over it as well as "Rank" and "Dept".

The mechanisms discussed above organize types into a hierarchy. However, use of the INTERSECTION OF or UNION OF operators, described in Section 4, results in a lattice of entity types.

2.5 Function Names

A single entity may be a member of several types. A particular "Student" entity, for example, may be an "Instructor" entity as well. This can give rise to potential ambiguities in function invocation. Earlier, the "Course" function was defined over "Instructor" entities to return the courses the instructor teaches. But the "Course" function was also declared above to map a "Student" entity into the courses the student is taking. When we apply the function "Course" to an entity which is both a "Student" and an "Instructor", which courses do we get?

The resolution of this dilemma lies in the fact that the two "Course" functions *are different functions*. Consequently they are given different *internal names* even though their *external names* are the same. Such a situation is generally referred to as "function name overloading." The internal name of a function is generated by enclosing in square brackets the external function name and the argument types over which it was originally specified. Thus the internal names of our two functions are [Course(Instructor)] and [Course(Student)].

Which function is chosen depends on the role the argument entity plays in the user's request. If the entity is currently being viewed as a student, then [Course(Student)] is applied. If it is being viewed as an instructor, then [Course(Instructor)] is applied instead.

The formal notion of *role*, discussed in Section 3.6, is used to achieve these results. Briefly, role associates an entity type with every expression in the language. External function names are disambiguated by determining the role of their argument expressions.

2.6 Ordered Data

Order forms a natural part of a user's conception of reality and consequently has been incorporated into the design of DAPLEX. An explicit ordering facility eliminates the need for the artificial "ordering attributes" sometimes required with other data models.

Any multivalued function may have an order associated with the members of the set it returns. In particular, types may be ordered by associating an order with the zero-argument function which defines the type.

Orders may be system maintained or user maintained. A system-maintained ordering is based on the evaluation of expressions defined over the elements of the set to be ordered. An example would be the ordering of instructors by rank and salary, or the ordering of students by the number of courses which they are taking. User-maintained orders are defined explicitly via update statements in the language. Examples might include the ordering of the musical notes in a melody, the ordering of the stops on a subway line, or the ordering of statements in a computer program.

The syntax relevant to orders is rather conventional. The reader is directed to the appendix for further details.

3. DATA MANIPULATION

3.1 Expressions and Statements

The basic elements of the DAPLEX syntax are statements and expressions. Statements direct the system to perform some action and include the data definition statements and FOR loops. Expressions, which always appear within statements, evaluate to a set of entities. As seen in the example query of Section 1, expressions may involve qualification, quantification, Boolean operators, and comparisons. Figure 4 presents a decomposition and labeling of the syntactic units of this query according to the syntax specification of the appendix.

3.2 Some Syntactic Tricks

This section discusses two syntactic devices, namely, nested function calls and implicit looping variables, which are designed to increase the "conceptual conciseness" of DAPLEX. A conceptually concise language is one which reduces the need for introducing artificial elements when formally specifying a query.

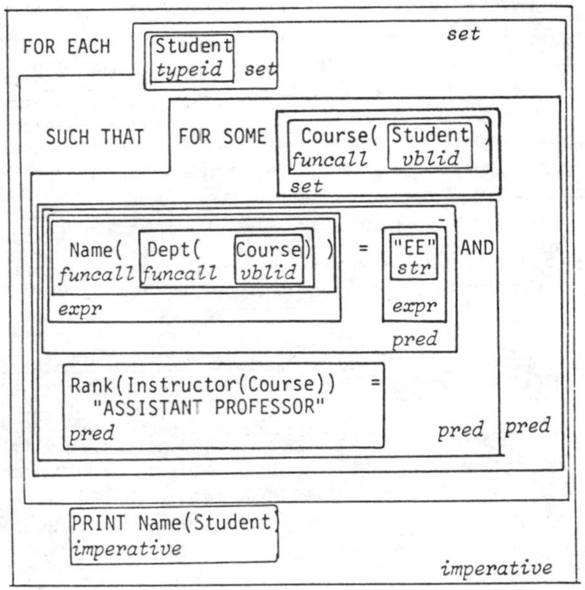

Fig. 4. Anatomy of a request.

The functional notation readily lends itself to functional nesting. Consider the following predicate from Figure 4:

Rank(Instructor(Course)) = "ASSISTANT PROFESSOR"

The advantage of such a construct is that it is not necessary to introduce the additional instructor variable which would be required if function nesting were not permitted. In languages without function nesting, the above predicate would have to be expressed as something analogous to the following:

```
FOR SOME Instructor
  Instructor(Course) = Instructor AND
  Rank(Instructor) = "ASSISTANT PROFESSOR"
```

Another way the language is made conceptually concise is through the use of implicitly declared looping variables. Consider the query, "Which employees earn more than their managers?" This could be expressed in DAPLEX as

```
FOR EACH X IN Employee ( )
  SUCH THAT Salary (X) >
    Salary(Manager (X))
  PRINT Name(X)
```

However, the following semantically equivalent rendition is preferred, since it avoids the introduction of the explicit looping variable "X":

```
FOR EACH Employee
  SUCH THAT Salary(Employee) >
    Salary(Manager(Employee))
  PRINT Name(Employee)
```

In the later query, the symbol "Employee" is used in two distinct senses. In the first line, it refers to the entity type "Employee" and references the entire set of "Employee" entities.[5] In succeeding lines the symbol "Employee" is a looping variable. It is bound successively to the members of the iteration set, as is the symbol "X" in the former query.

Each set expression in DAPLEX has associated with it a reference variable. Operators which iterate over the set, such as FOR EACH and SUCH THAT in the preceding example, successively bind this variable to the entities in the iteration set. The reference variable typically appears in the body of the iterating operator and references the particular entity being considered in the current iteration. By using the IN operator, the user is able to explicitly specify the reference variable associated with a set. Otherwise the reference variable is implicitly declared, usually to be the same symbol as the first identifier in the set expression.[6]

Although the implicit variable declaration results in more readable requests, the explicit form is provided in DAPLEX for two reasons. The first is that this syntax is expected to be easier for a database front end (such as a natural language front end) to generate. The second is that there are circumstances in which two or more variables must range over the same set of entities and in which implicit variable declarations would assign both variables the same name. Such usage is illustrated in the following (exceedingly) awkward rendition of the preceding query.

```
FOR EACH X IN Employee
  SUCH THAT FOR SOME Y IN Employee
    Y = Manager (X) AND
    Salary (X) > Salary (Y)
  PRINT Name (X)
```

It is important to note, however, that it is almost never necessary to use explicit reference variables. Through such techniques as nested functional notation, DAPLEX eliminates the need for multiple variables ranging over the same set in nearly all cases. In fact, a good rule of thumb is that whenever explicit ranging variables must be specified, the query is probably poorly formulated.

3.3 Aggregation

Aggregation functions include AVERAGE, TOTAL, COUNT, MAXIMUM, and MINIMUM. Consider the request, "How many instructors are in the EE department?"

```
PRINT COUNT (Instructor
  SUCH THAT Name (Dept(Instructor)) = "EE")
```

The argument to the COUNT function is a set of "Instructor" entities, and COUNT simply returns the cardinality of that set.

[5] "Employee" here is equivalent to "Employee( )." In general, a symbol which is a type name evaluates to the set of entities of that type, *unless* the symbol has been already bound in the local context to a particular entity. Such binding of symbols occurs, for example, with formal parameters (see Section 4.1) and with the explicit and implicit looping variables discussed in this section.

[6] The precise rules for implicit declaration of reference variables are given in the appendix. Note that although this symbol is often a type name, it need not be.

The set orientation of DAPLEX presents a problem for aggregation in general. Assume we wish to know the average salary of instructors in the EE department. We cannot take the average of the *set* of such salaries because the set notion does not allow duplicates. (The average of $15,000, $25,000, and $15,000 would be $20,000 if we simply took the average of the set of salaries.) The following notation resolves this problem. "What is the average salary of instructors in the EE department?"

```
PRINT AVERAGE (Salary(Instructor) OVER Instructor
  SUCH THAT Name (Dept(Instructor)) = "EE")
```

The semantics of this query are as follows. The OVER operator takes a set specification and an expression defined over members of that set. Here the set involved is a particular set of "Instructor" entities. This set does not contain duplicates. For each member of this set, the given expression is evaluated. (Note that "Instructor" in this expression is an implicit looping variable.) Each resulting value is included in the average independent of whether or not duplicate values are present. Strictly speaking, the OVER expression evaluates not to a set but to a bag.[7] The cardinality of the bag is the same as the cardinality of OVER's set operand.

3.4 Updating

Update statements are used to specify the value returned by a function when applied to particular entities. Some examples illustrate the syntax involved. "Add a new student named Bill to the EE department and enroll him in 'Systems Analysis' and 'Semiconductor Physics',"

```
FOR A NEW Student
  BEGIN
  LET Name (Student) = "Bill"
  LET Dept (Student) = THE Department SUCH THAT
      Name (Department) = "EE"
  LET Course (Student) =
      {THE Course SUCH THAT Name (Course) =
            "Systems Analysis",
       THE Course SUCH THAT Name (Course) =
            "Semiconductor Physics"}
  END
```

The following illustrates the incremental updating of multivalued functions. "Drop 'Introductory Physics' from John's courses and add 'Organic Chemistry',"[8]

```
FOR THE Student SUCH THAT Name (Student) = "John"
  BEGIN
  EXCLUDE Course (Student) =
    THE Course SUCH THAT Name (Course) =
      "Introductory Physics"
  INCLUDE Course (Student) =
    THE Course SUCH THAT Name (Course) =
      "Organic Chemistry"
  END
```

[7] A *bag*, sometimes called a *multiset*, is a set which may contain duplicate elements.
[8] A less awkward version of this request is presented in Section 4.1.

3.5 Function Evaluation

Update statements set the value a function is to return when it is applied to particular arguments. In the context of a DAPLEX expression, however, a function's arguments are not always individual entities but rather sets of entities. This is simply a result of the fact that the argument to a function is an expression, and expressions, in general, evaluate to a set. When a function is evaluated, the result is the union of all entities returned by the function applied to all members of its argument set. Thus, "List all courses taken by EE students,"

```
FOR EACH
    Course (Student SUCH THAT Dept (Student) = "EE")
  PRINT Title (Course)
```

The argument to the "Course" function here is a set of "Student" entities. The evaluation of the function returns the set of all courses taken by any of these students. Note that each course is listed only once.[9]

A corollary to the function evaluation convention is that functions with null set arguments evaluate to the null set.

3.6 Value, Role, and Order

We are now ready to consider some of the more subtle aspects of expression evaluation in DAPLEX. Three components are associated with every expression evaluation. These are the expression *value*, the expression *role*, and the expression *order*. The expression value is the set of entities returned by evaluating the expression. The expression role is the entity type under which these entities are to be interpreted when resolving external function name ambiguities. The expression order is the ordering associated with these entities.

So far in our discussions we have been almost exclusively concerned with expression value. Clearly, it is the most important aspect of expression evaluation.

An expression's role is used only in determining internal function names (see Section 2.5). The role of an expression can always be determined by a static analysis of the request and the data description; accessing of the actual database is not required.

An expression's order is only relevant when the expression is used with the operator FOR EACH . . . IN ORDER, with expressions involving the keywords PRECEDING and FOLLOWING and with predicates which compare two entities based on their order. Otherwise the order is ignored.

The value, role, and order of an expression are calculated from the value, role, and order, respectively, of its subexpressions. The appendix gives complete rules for obtaining value, role, and order for each of the expression types in DAPLEX.

The following example illustrates the use of expression role. "Among the students who are also instructors, list those who are taking a course which

[9] Had we, for some reason, desired duplicate courses to be listed, the query would have been expressed as

```
FOR EACH Student SUCH THAT Dept (Student) = "EE"
  FOR EACH Course (Student)
    PRINT Title (Course)
```

they teach,"

```
FOR EACH Student SUCH THAT
  SOME Course (Student) =
    SOME Course (Student AS Instructor)
  PRINT Name (Student)
```

The operator AS converts the role of an expression without affecting its value or order. In the first use of the function name "Course", the argument to the function has the role "Student". Therefore, the internal function name for this invocation is [Course (Student)]. In the second use of the function name "Course", the argument to the function has been converted to have the role "Instructor". Consequently, the internal function name for this invocation is [Course (Instructor)]. It should also be noted that the AS expression evaluates to the null set (and consequently the qualifying predicate evaluates to FALSE) when the current "Student" is not of type "Instructor".

3.7 General-Purpose Operators and Control Structures

It is intended that DAPLEX be embedded in a general-purpose high-level language. Consequently, syntax for general-purpose operators and control structures are not specified here, as this would be supplied by the high-level language. Nonetheless, the examples here have made use of such constructs (e.g., PRINT, AND, BEGIN . . . END are all assumed to be supplied by the high-level language). The semantics in these cases should be cl.

4. DERIVED DATA

4.1 The DEFINE Statement

The use of derived data dramatically extends the naturalness and usability of a database system. In the context of the functional data model, "derived data" is interpreted to mean "derived function definitions." Essentially we are defining new properties of objects based on the values of other properties. Derived functions are specified by means of DEFINE statements.[10]

To define a function "Instructor" over "Student" entities which returns the instructors of courses the student is taking, use

```
DEFINE Instructor(Student) ⇒
  Instructor(Course(Student))
```

The function "Instructor" may now be used in queries exactly as if it had been a primitive function. The user need not be aware that it is derived data.

As another example, assume we wish to define a "grade point average" property of students:

```
DEFINE GradePointAverage(Student) ⇒
  AVERAGE(Grade(Student, Course)
    OVER Course(Student))
```

[10] Derived functions behave as if their values were recomputed on each access. This does not imply, however, that they actually need be. An implementation strategy which stored the derived function values would be perfectly acceptable so long as it produced the same values as a recompute-on-each-access strategy. This would involve updating a stored value when the values on which it is based have changed.

"Student" is being used as a formal parameter within the body of the DEFINE statements above. When the derived function is evaluated, this variable is bound to the actual argument supplied. In cases where a function takes more than one argument of the same type, the IN operator can be used.[11] Thus, to define a Boolean function which compares two students on the basis of their respective grade point averages, use

```
DEFINE Brighter(S1 IN Student, S2 IN Student) ⇒
  GradePointAverage(S1) > GradePointAverage(S2)
```

Derived functions mayalso be defined over the system-supplied entity types. For example,

```
DEFINE Student(STRING) ⇒ INVERSE OF Name(Student)
DEFINE Course(STRING) ⇒ INVERSE OF Title(Course)
```

These functions map a STRING into a set of "Students" or "Courses", respectively. The update request presented earlier in Section 3.4 can now be written more straightforwardly as follows: "Drop 'Introductory Physics' from John's courses and add 'Organic Chemistry',"[12]

```
FOR THE Student("John")
  BEGIN
  EXCLUDE Course(Student) =
    THE Course("Introductory Physics")
  INCLUDE Course(Student) =
    THE Course("Organic Chemistry")
  END
```

4.2 Conceptual Abstractions

Consider the query, "Which instructors earn over twice the average salary for instructors in their departments?" In the DAPLEX rendition that follows, the query is broken into three parts. First, a function mapping departments to their instructors is defined. Next, a property of "instructors' average salary" is defined for departments. Finally, this property is used to find the desired instructors.

```
DEFINE Instructor(Department) ⇒
  INVERSE of Department(Instructor)
DEFINE InstAvgSal(Department) ⇒
  AVERAGE (Salary(Instructor)
    OVER Instructor(Department))
FOR EACH Instructor
  SUCH THAT
    Salary(Instructor) >
      2•InstAvgSal(Dept(Instructor))
  PRINT Name(Instructor)
```

This request illustrates a profound capability of derived functions: the ability to specify and name conceptual abstractions. This ability is the essence of structured programming, abstract data types, and subroutines. It lies at the core

[11] This is not a special case but follows from the fact that the function arguments specified in DECLARE and DEFINE statements may be arbitrary DAPLEX expressions (see the appendix).

[12] Yet another version of this request appears in Section 4.4.

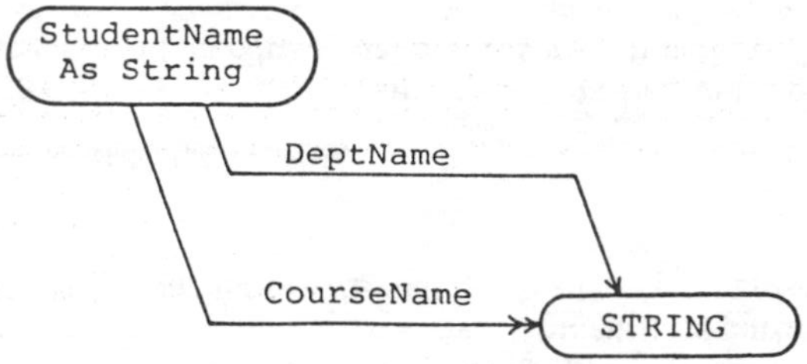

Fig. 5. A user view.

of good software engineering practice. Derived data provides this capability in DAPLEX.

4.3 User Views

For reasons of convenience a user may not wish to see the database as depicted in Figures 1 and 2, but rather as it is depicted in Figure 5. Here, the only user-defined entity type is "StudentName", a subtype of STRING, and all of the functions over "StudentName" return STRING entities. The derived function definitions that follow convert the original database to this new view:

```
DEFINE StudentName( ) =>> Name(Student( ))

DEFINE DeptName(StudentName AS STRING) =>
  Name(Dept(THE Student (StudentName)))

DEFINE CourseName(StudentName AS STRING) =>>
  Title(Course(THE Student(StudentName)))
```

These definitions provide the user with access to the functions he desires. For example, "What department is Mary in?" can be expressed as[13]

```
PRINT DeptName("Mary")
```

User views are often for purposes of security as well as convenience. That is, not only may it be desirable for the user to have access to the new definitions but also for him to be prevented from directly invoking the underlying functions. To accomplish this, the new user view is defined in a different name space (i.e., different "module" or "package") from the old view.[14] A secure system, then, would only allow the user to access the name space in which the new view is defined. In addition to this security consideration, the name space distinction is needed when certain function renamings take place. For example, if the new view were to reference the course titles of a student with a function called "Course" rather than one called "CourseName," separate name spaces would be needed to distinguish this new "Course" function from the original one.

4.4 Updating Derived Data

Suppose we have the following update request expressed over the view constructed in the preceding section, "Change Jack's department to Biology",

```
LET DeptName("Jack") = "Biology"
```

There are several cnceivable interpretations of this request in terms of the underlying primitive functions. The first, and most plausible, is that Jack is to be registered in the Biology department; that is,[15]

```
LET Dept(THE Student("Jack")) = THE Department("Biology")
```

The second, somewhat less plausible, is that the name of Jack's current department, say the Mathematics department, is to be changed to "Biology"; that is,

```
LET Name(Dept(THE Student("Jack"))) = "Biology"
```

Yet a third alternative, similar to the proposal of Dayal [8] for updating views in the relational data model, would be to create a new department which is given the name "Biology" and to which Jack is assigned; that is,

```
FOR A NEW Department
  BEGIN
  LET Name(Department) = "Biology"
  LET Dept(THE Student("Jack")) = Department
  END
```

It is not possible for the system to intuit which of these three meanings is desired.

In DAPLEX, the semantics for updating derived data are explicitly provided by the user. This is accomplished with the PERFORM . . . USING construct. For example, updates to the derived function "CourseName" might reasonably be defined as follows:

```
PERFORM
  INCLUDE CourseName(StudentName AS STRING) = Title
USING
  INCLUDE Course(THE Student(StudentName)) =
    THE Course(Title)

PERFORM
  EXCLUDE CourseName(StudentName AS STRING) = Title
USING
  EXCLUDE Course(THE Student(StudentName)) =
    THE Course(Title)
```

With these update specifications, the request presented earlier in Sections 3.4

[13] Some discussion of the use of the AS STRING phrase in the preceding definitions is in order. As the example illustrates, these functions are not defined over entities of type "StudentName" but rather over entities of type STRING (but only those STRING entities which also happen to be names of students). That is, the internal names of these functions are [DeptName(STRING)] and [CourseName(STRING)]. Had we instead used

```
DEFINE DeptName(StudentName) =>
  Name(Dept(THE Student(StudentName)))
```

a function with internal name [DeptName(StudentName)] would have been defined and then we would have had to express "What department is Mary in?" as

```
PRINT DeptName("Mary" AS StudentName)
```

Since an AS phrase must be used somewhere, it is preferable to include it once in the definition of the function rather than require it every time the function appears in a request.

[14] The "package" or "module" facility is assumed to be provided by the high-level language (see Section 3.7).

[15] We are assuming for these examples a previous definition,

```
DEFINE Department(STRING) =>> INVERSE of Name(Department)
```

and 4.1 may be expressed even more succinctly, "Drop 'Introductory Physics' from John's courses and add 'Organic Chemistry',"

```
EXCLUDE CourseName("John") = "Introductory Physics"
INCLUDE CourseName("John") = "Organic Chemistry"
```

The PERFORM . . . USING statement directs the system to execute the body of the statement whenever the indicated update operation is performed. It is important to point out that this facility merely allows users to provide the *illusion* of derived data updating. The system does not, for example, validate the PERFORM . . . USING statement to ensure that it results in the intended derived data update. Finally, it should be noted that a derived data update is illegal unless an appropriate PERFORM . . . USING directive has been declared.

4.5 Some Special Operators for Defining Functions

In this section we examine the operators INVERSE OF, TRANSITIVE OF, INTERSECTION OF, UNION OF, DIFFERENCE OF, and COMPOUND OF. These operators are used only in function definitions.

To invert the function [Instructor(Course)], we could use

```
DEFINE Course(Instructor) ⇒ Course SUCH THAT
  Instructor = Instructor(Course)
```

It is more convenient, however, to define this function as

```
DEFINE Course(Instructor) ⇒
  INVERSE OF Instructor(Course)
```

A simple modification of this syntax allows us to define transitive closures. For example,

```
DEFINE Superior(Employee) ⇒
  TRANSITIVE OF Manager(Employee)
```

The function [Superior(Employee)] returns the set containing the manager of the employee, the manager's manager, the manager's manager's manager, etc.

The INTERSECTION OF, UNION OF, and DIFFERENCE OF operators may be used to form set intersections, unions, and differences. They are most useful in creating new types. For example,

```
DEFINE StudentTeacher( ) ⇒
  INTERSECTION OF Student, Instructor
```

The COMPOUND OF operator is used to create derived entities corresponding to the elements of the Cartesian product of its operands. As an example, assume that we wish to view the enrollment of a given student in a particular course as a "thing" designated by an entity. We could define the set of enrollment entities by

```
DEFINE Enrollment( ) ⇒
  COMPOUND OF Student, Course(Student)
```

In addition to defining the set of "Enrollment" entities and the "Enrollment" entity type, the system implicitly defines the two functions "Student" and "Course" to operate over entities of type "Enrollment". These return the "Student" and "Course" entities upon which the compound entity was based. The entity is fully specified by the values of these system-defined functions. That is, no two "Enrollment" entities correspond to the same "Student"–"Course" entity pair. If the set of students or their courses are altered, the set of enrollments automatically reflects this change.

4.6 Constraints

Assume we wish to enforce the constraint that a department's head must come from within the department. We could define the following function over "Department" entities:

```
DEFINE NativeHead(Department) ⇒
  Dept(Head(Department)) = Department
```

This function will evaluate to TRUE for those departments which satisfy the desired constraint and to FALSE for those which do not. By inserting the keyword CONSTRAINT, we define a *constraint* which instructs the system to abort any update transactions which leave the function value FALSE for any department. Thus

```
DEFINE CONSTRAINT NativeHead(Department) ⇒
  Dept(Head(Department)) = Department
```

Constraints may also be specified over the database as a whole. For example, to ensure that the number of managers is always less than the number of nonmanagement employees, use

```
DEFINE Manager( ) ⇒ Manager(Employee( ))
DEFINE NonManager( ) ⇒ DIFFERENCE OF Employee, Manager
DEFINE CONSTRAINT TooManyChiefs( ) ⇒
  COUNT(Manager( )) < COUNT(NonManager( ))
```

The *trigger* capability is related to that for constraints. When a trigger has been installed over a function definition, a specified imperative is executed whenever the function changes from FALSE to TRUE. To inform the department head whenever more than 45 students are enrolled in a class, we might use[16]

```
DEFINE Student(Class) ⇒ INVERSE OF Class(Student)
DEFINE TRIGGER Overbooked(Class) ⇒
    COUNT(Student(Class)) > 45
  SendMessage(Head(Dept(Class)), "Overbooked:",
      Title(Class))
```

5. DATABASE SYSTEM CONSIDERATIONS

5.1 Data Description as Data

The data description is itself data. In a DAPLEX system implementation, the data description can be queried as ordinary data. The design of the data description for the data description, that is, the metadescription, is not specified here and depends, to some extent, on the details of system implementation. In any

[16] In this request "SendMessage" is a procedure defined in the high-level language.

case, of course, it is possible for individual users to define their own view of the data description.

The metadescription includes entities of type FUNCTION. A special system function APPLY is also provided. APPLY takes one or more arguments, the first of which is a function entity, and returns the value of that function applied to the remaining arguments.

Access to metadata is especially useful in building sophisticated interfaces (e.g., natural language front ends) for the naive user, who is often unfamiliar with the structure of the database he is using.

5.2 Updating Metadata

Metadata is normally updated using DECLARE and DEFINE statements. It is also possible for users to update the data description using update statements operating over entities of type FUNCTION. Such updates do not directly update the metadata but instead manipulate a system-provided metadata user view. PERFORM . . . USING statements trap updates to the metadata user view and perform whatever system-internal measures are necessary (such as allocating storage or establishing indices) to effect the desired metadata update.

5.3 Storage Attributes

Storage attributes are associated with each function as metadata. The storage attributes direct the system as to how the data are to be physically organized on the storage medium. Like other metadata, storage attributes may be updated via the metadata user view. These storage attributes indicate how functions are to be internally represented, which data items are to be located near each other, and whether indexed access via function values is to be provided. For derived functions, the storage statements can indicate whether the function values are to be physically stored or recomputed each time they are referenced. A general discussion of storage considerations is beyond the scope of this paper.

6. EXAMPLE APPLICATIONS

6.1 DAPLEX Front Ends

The data modeling capabilities of DAPLEX incorporate those of the hierarchical, relational, and network models, the principal database models in use today. This suggests the possibility of DAPLEX front ends for existing databases and database systems.

As an example, consider a relational version of the database of Figures 1 and 2. This is illustrated in Figure 6. Figure 7 shows the isomorphic DAPLEX description. It is clear that the relational model is a subset of the functional model since the isomorphic DAPLEX description of any relational database will be subject to the following limitations:

(1) No multivalued functions are allowed.
(2) Functions cannot return user-defined entities.
(3) Multiple-argument functions are not allowed.
(4) There are no subtypes.

Having specified the isomorphic description, and assuming the existence of a

STUDENT

STUD#	NAME	DEPT#

COURSE

COURSE#	TITLE	DEPT#	INSTRUCTOR#

ENROLLMENT

STUD#	COURSE#

INSTRUCTOR

INSTRUCTOR#	NAME	RANK	DEPT#	SALARY

DEPARTMENT

DEPT#	NAME	HEAD#

Fig. 6. Relational data description.

suitable data manipulation translator, DAPLEX requests can be written against the relational database. However, the full benefits of the DAPLEX approach will not be available because of the limitations in the underlying data model. What is needed is to define derived functions which provide a more convenient view of the database. The additional definitions in Figure 8 transform the description of Figure 7 to conform to that of the original DAPLEX example of Figure 2. Having specified these functions, we may now write DAPLEX queries as if we were working with the DAPLEX database.

The derived functions of Figure 8 can be thought of as adding semantic information which is not expressible in the relational data model. Figure 9 shows the steps for transforming a DAPLEX request into a relational request in the data language QUEL [8]. Figure 9a shows the original request. After the substitutions indicated by derived function definitions are performed, the query will

```
DECLARE Student( ) ⇒ ENTITY
DECLARE Stud#(Student) → INTEGER
DECLARE Name(Student) → STRING
DECLARE Dept#(Student) → INTEGER

DECLARE Course( ) ⇒ ENTITY
DECLARE Course#(Course) → INTEGER
DECLARE Title(Course) → STRING
DECLARE Dept#(Course) → INTEGER
DECLARE Instructor#(Course) → INTEGER

DECLARE Enrollment( ) ⇒ ENTITY
DECLARE Stud#(Enrollment) → INTEGER
DECLARE Course#(Enrollment) → INTEGER

DECLARE Instructor( ) ⇒ ENTITY
DECLARE Instructor#(Instructor) → INTEGER
DECLARE Name(Instructor) → STRING
DECLARE Rank(Instructor) → STRING
DECLARE Dept#(Instructor) → INTEGER
DECLARE Salary(Instructor) → INTEGER

DECLARE Department( ) ⇒ ENTITY
DECLARE Dept#(Department) → INTEGER
DECLARE Name(Department) → STRING
DECLARE Head#(Department) → INTEGER
```

Fig. 7. The relational description in DAPLEX.

```
DEFINE Dept(Student) → Department SUCH THAT
  Dept#(Department) = Dept#(Student)
DEFINE Course(Student) →  Course SUCH THAT
  FOR SOME Enrollment
    Stud#(Student) = Stud#(Enrollment) AND
    Course#(Enrollment) = Course#(Course)
DEFINE Dept(Course) → Department SUCH THAT
  Dept#(Course) = Dept#(Department)
DEFINE Instructor(Course) → Instructor SUCH THAT
  Instructor#(Instructor) = Instructor#(Course)
DEFINE Dept(Instructor) → Department SUCH THAT
  Dept#(Instructor) = Dept#(Department)
DEFINE Head(Department) → Instructor SUCH THAT
  Instructor#(Instructor) = Head#(Department)
```

Fig. 8. Definitions for the functional view.

```
     FOR EACH Student SUCH THAT
       FOR SOME Course(Student)
(a)      Name(Dept(Course)) = "EE" AND
         Rank(Instructor(Course)) = "ASSISTANT PROFESSOR"
       PRINT Name (Student)

     FOR EACH Student SUCH THAT
       FOR SOME (Course SUCH THAT
         FOR SOME Enrollment
           Stud#(Student) = Stud#(Enrollment) AND
           Course#(Enrollment) = Course#(Course))
         (FOR SOME (Department SUCH THAT
(b)            Dept#(Department) = Dept#(Course))
           Name(Department) = "EE")
         AND
         (FOR SOME (Instructor SUCH THAT
               Instructor#(Instructor) = Instructor#(Course))
           Rank(Instructor) = "ASSISTANT PROFESSOR")
       PRINT Name(Student)

     FOR EACH Student SUCH THAT
       FOR SOME Course
       FOR SOME Enrollment
       FOR SOME Department
       FOR SOME Instructor
         Stud#(Student) = Stud#(Enrollment) AND
(c)      Course#(Enrollment) = Course#(Course) AND
         Dept#(Department) = Dept#(Course) AND
         Name(Department) = "EE" AND
         Instructor#(Instructor) = Instructor#(Course) AND
         Rank(Instructor) = "ASSISTANT PROFESSOR"
       PRINT Name(Student)

     RANGE OF S IS Student
     RANGE OF C IS Course
     RANGE OF E IS Enrollment
     RANGE OF D IS Department
     RANGE OF I IS Instructor
(d)  RETRIEVE S. Name WHERE
       S.Stud# = E.Stud# AND
       E.Course# = C.Course# AND
       D.Dept# = C. Dept# AND
       D.Name = "EE" AND
       I.Instructor# = C.Instructor# AND
       I.Rank = "ASSISTANT PROFESSOR"
```

Fig. 9. Steps in request translation.

appear as shown in Figure 9b. This query can be reorganized using simple syntactic transformations to arrive at the representation in Figure 9c. The corresponding QUEL query is shown in Figure 9d.

6.2 Database Networks

The notion of DAPLEX front ends can be adapted to provide an interface to a network of dissimilar database management systems, as illustrated in Figure 10. An isomorphic DAPLEX description is written for each of the local databases in

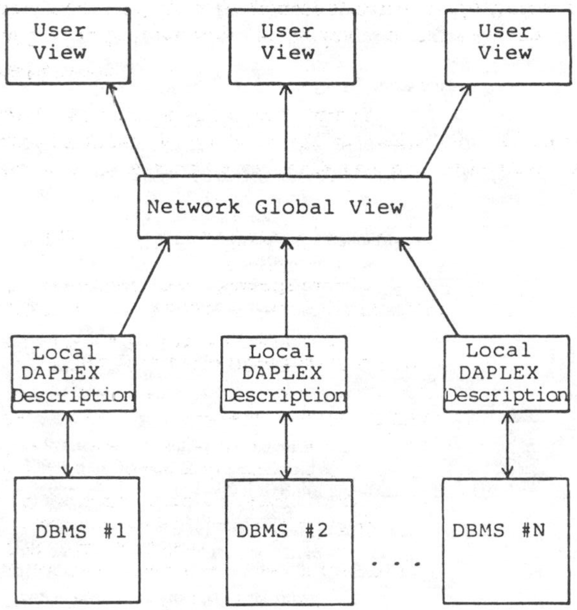

Fig. 10. Networked databases.

the network. These are then converted, via view mechanisms, into a common unified view of the entire network database. DAPLEX provides the global language by which this database is accessed. Individual user views may be defined over the global database as necessary.

7. CONCLUSION

The principal characteristics of DAPLEX can be summarized as follows:

(1) Data is modeled in terms of entities. Database entities are meant to bear a one-to-one correspondence to the "real-world" entities in the user's mental conception of reality.

(2) Relationships between data are expressed as functions, exploiting an established programming metaphor. Identical functional notation is used to reference both "primitive" and "derived" relationships. Conceptual conciseness is enhanced through the use of nested function reference. Functions may be multivalued, returning sets of entities.

(3) The request language is based on the notion of looping through entity sets. Expressions in the language are, in general, set valued. Sets are specified using the functional notation with special operators for qualification and quantification. A simple aggregation semantics, also based on looping, is incorporated. Looping variables are typically declared implicity.

(4) Computational power is provided through the general-purpose operators of a high-level language. While not emphasized in this paper, this capability is crucial to the development of realistic applications systems.

(5) Derived functions allow users to represent arbitrary entity relationships directly by defining them in terms of existing relationships. We have seen one example request (in Sections 3.4, 4.1, and 4.4) become progressively simpler through the introduction of appropriate derived functions. In effect, the derived function capability allows application semantics to be encoded into the data description, thereby allowing requests to be expressed directly in terms of those semantics. Updating of derived relationships is supported through procedures explicitly supplied by the user.

(6) Entity types are defined as functions taking no arguments. Notions of subtype and supertype follow naturally from this formulation.

(7) User views are implemented in terms of derived functions. It was shown how DAPLEX views may be constructed over existing databases represented in terms of traditional models, thus lending support to the use of DAPLEX as a "universal" database language for heterogeneous networked databases.

APPENDIX. SPECIFICATION OF DAPLEX

A1. Syntax

The DAPLEX syntax is described in terms of the syntax specification language proposed by Wirth [18]. To quote the original proposal describing the specification language:

> This meta language can therefore conveniently be used to define its own syntax, which may serve here as an example of its use. The word *identifier* is used to denote *nonterminal symbol*, and *literal* stands for *terminal symbol*. For brevity, *identifier* and *character cflare not defined in further detail.*
>
> *syntax* = {*production*}.
> *production* = *identifier* "=" *expression* ".".
> *expression* = *term* {"|" *term*}.
> *term* = *factor* {*factor*}.
> *factor* = *identifier* | *literal* | "(" *expression* ")" | "[" *expression* "]" | "{" *expression* "}".
> *literal* = """" *character* {*character*} """".
>
> Repetition is denoted by curly brackets, i.e. {*a*} stands for $\epsilon | a | aa | aaa | \ldots$. Optionality is expressed by square brackets, i.e. [*a*] stands for $a|\epsilon$. Parentheses merely serve for grouping, e.g. $(a|b)c$ stands for $ac|bc$. Terminal symbols, i.e. literals, are enclosed in quote marks (and, if a quote mark appears as a literal itself, it is written twice), which is consistent with common practice in programming languages.

In Figure 11 we define the DAPLEX syntax itself.

A2. Semantics

A2.1 *Expressions*

expr = *set* | *singleton*.

Expressions evaluate to either singletons or sets.

A2.1.1 *Sets*. The properties of a *set* are its value, role, order, and reference variable. Value, role, and order are discussed in Section 3.6. The reference variable is used as the formal parameter or looping variable corresponding to the *set*. In the syntactic specifications that follow, digit suffixes may be appended to symbols for purposes of reference.

set = mvfuncall.

Value: the *set* returned by the multivalued function application
Role: that of *mvfuncall*
Order: that of *mvfuncall*
Reference Variable: the *funcid* in the *mvfuncall*

set = typeid.

Value: the set of entities of this type (this usage is vald only when the *typeid* identifier is not currently bound as a reference variable)
Role: *typeid*
Order: that of the type
Reference Variable: *typeid*

set = "{" *singleton* { "," *singleton* } "}".

Value: a *set* consisting of the listed *singletons* (All *singletons* must have the same type)
Role: the type of the *singletons*
Order: the listed order
Reference Variable: none (if a reference variable is desired it must be explicitly declared using the IN operator)

set = set1 "SUCH" "THAT" *pred.*

Value: those members of *set1* for which *pred* is true (in evaluating *pred*, the reference variable is bound to the member of *set1* being tested)
Role, order, reference variable: that of *set1*

set = set1 comp singleton.

Value: those members of *set1* bearing the *comp* relationship to the *singleton*
Role, order, reference variable: that of *set1*

set = set1 comp quant set2.

Value: those members of *set1* bearing the *comp* relationship to the specified quantity of members of *set2* (in evaluating *set2*, the reference variable of *set1* is bound to the member under consideration)
Role, order, reference variable: that of *set1*

set = identifier "IN" *set1.*

Value, role, order: that of *set1*
Reference Variable: identifier

set = expr "AS" *typeid.*

Value: those members of *expr* which are of the specified type
Role: *typeid*
Order, reference variable: that of *expr*

```
program = {statement}.
statement = declarative | imperative.
declarative = "DECLARE" funcspec ("→"|"⇒") expr [order]|
  "DEFINE" funcspec ("→"|"⇒")
    (expr|
     "INVERSE" "OF" funcspec)|
     "TRANSITIVE" "OF" expr|
     "COMPOUND" "OF" tuple|
     ("INTERSECTION"|"UNION") "OF" expr {"," expr}|
     "DIFFERENCE" "OF" expr "," expr |
    )[order].
   "DEFINE" "CONSTRAINT" funcspec "→" boolean|
   "DEFINE" "TRIGGER" funcspec "→" boolean imperative|
   "PERFORM" update "USING" imperative.
funcspec = funcid "(" [tuple] ")".
tuple = expr {"," expr}.
expr = set | singleton.
set = mvfuncall | typeid |
   "{" [singleton {"," singleton}] "}"|
   set "SUCH" "THAT" pred|
   set comp (singleton | quant set)|
   identifier IN set | expr AS typeid|
   "(" set ")" | gpset.
singleton = constant | vblid | svfuncall | aggcall | pred |
   "THE" set | "A" "NEW" typeid|
   "THE" set ("PRECEDING"|"FOLLOWING") singleton |
   "(" singleton ")" | gpsingleton.
svfuncall = funcall.
mvfuncall = funcall.
funcall = funcid "(" [tuple] ")".
aggcall = aggid "(" bag ")".
bag = expr | singleton "OVER" tuple.
pred = boolean |
   "FOR" (singleton | quant set) pred|
   (singleton | quant set) comp (singleton | quant set)|
   quant set ("EXIST"|"EXISTS").
comp = ">"|"<"|"="|"EQ"|"NE"|"LT"|"GT"|"LE"|"GE".
quant = "SOME"|"EVERY"|"NO"|
   ("AT" ("LEAST"|"MOST")|"EXACTLY") integer.
integer = singleton.
string = singleton.
boolean = singleton.
constant = int | str | bool.
int = digit {digit}.
str = """" character {character} """".
bool = "TRUE"|"FALSE".
imperative = forloop | update | gpimperative
forloop = "FOR" "EACH" set [order] imperative |
   "FOR" singleton imperative.
order = "IN" "ORDER"
       {"BY" [("ASCENDING"|"DESCENDING")] singleton}.
update = "LET" svfuncall "=" singleton |
   ("LET"|"INCLUDE"|"EXCLUDE") mvfuncall "=" expr|
   "INSERT" mvfuncall "=" (singleton | set [order])
       ("PRECEDING"|"FOLLOWING") singleton |
vblid = identifier.
typeid = identifier.
funcid = identifier.
aggid = identifier.
```

Fig. 11. DAPLEX syntactic specification.

set = "(" *set1* ")".

Value, role, order, reference variable: that of *set1* (this construct is used only for syntactic grouping)

set = *gpset*.

gpset is a *set*-valued expression in the general-purpose syntax. Value, role, order, and reference variable are not specified here.

A2.1.2 *Singletons*. Only value, role, and reference variable need be specified for *singletons*, as the order is trivial.

singleton = *constant*.

Value: that of the *constant*
Role: the type of the *constant*
Reference Variable: none

singleton = *vblid*.

Value: *vblid* must be bound to a particular entity
Role: that of the *expr* for which this is the reference variable
Reference Variable: *vblid*

singleton = *svfuncall* | *aggcall*.

Value: the entity returned by the single-valued function or aggregation application
Role: that of *svfuncall* or *aggcall*
Reference Variable: the *funcid* in the *svfuncall* or *aggid* in *aggcall*

singleton = *pred*.

Value, role, reference variable: that of *pred*

singleton = "THE" *set*.

Value: The single member of *set* (if *set* evaluates to more than one member an error is flagged)
Role, reference variable: that of *set*

singleton = "A" "NEW" *typeid*.

Value: a new entity of the specified type
Role: *typeid*
Reference Variable: *typeid*

singleton = "THE" *set* ("PRECEDING" | "FOLLOWING") *singleton*.

Value: the member of *set* preceding or following *singleton* according to the order of *set* (*singleton* must be a member of *set*)
Role, reference variable: that of *set*

singleton = "(" *singleton* ")".

Value, role, reference variable: that of *singleton*

singleton = *gpsingleton*.

gpsingleton is an entity valued expression in the general-purpose syntax. Value, role, order, and reference variable are not specified here.

A2.1.3 *Predicates*. The role of all predicates is BOOLEAN, and there is no reference variable, thus only value needs to be specified.

pred = *boolean*.

Value: that of the *boolean* constant or expression

pred = "FOR" *singleton pred1*.

Value: that of *pred1* evaluated with *singleton*'s reference variable bound to the value of *singleton*

pred = "FOR" *quant set pred1*.

Value: TRUE if *pred1* evaluates to true for the specified quantity of members of *set*, FALSE otherwise

pred = *singleton1 comp singleton2*.

Value: TRUE if *singleton1* bears the *comp* relation to *singleton2*, FALSE otherwise (the reference variable of *singleton1* is bound to the value of *singleton1* during evaluation of *singleton2*)

pred = *singleton comp quant set*.

Value: TRUE if *singleton* bears the *comp* relation to the specified quantity of members of *set*, FALSE otherwise (the reference variable of *singleton* is bound to the value of *singleton* during evaluation of *set*)

pred = *quant set comp singleton*.

Value: TRUE if the specified quantity of members of *set* bear the relation *comp* to *singleton*, FALSE otherwise (the reference variable of *set* is bound to the member under consideration during the evaluation of *singleton*)

pred = *quant set1 comp quant set2*.

Value: TRUE if the specified quantity of members of *set1* bears relation *comp* to the specified quantity of members of *set2*, FALSE otherwise (the reference variable of *set1* is bound to the member under consideration during the evaluation of *set2*, the scope of the first quantifier extends over that of the second)

pred = *quant set* ("EXIST" | "EXISTS").

Value: TRUE if the specified quantity of members of *set* exist, FALSE otherwise (note that this predicate is vacuously TRUE for the quantifier EVERY)

comp = ">"|"<"|"="|"EQ"|"NE"|"LT"|"GT"|"LE"|"GE".

The comparators >, <, LT, GT, LE, and GE require that their operands have the same role. In such cases the comparisons are with respect to that role's order. The operators =, EQ, and NE do not require their operands to have the same role. In such cases, the comparison is based solely on the values of the operands.

quant = "SOME"|"EVERY"|"NO"|
("AT" ("LEAST"|"MOST")|"EXACTLY") *integer*.

The quantifier semantics should be self-evident.

A2.1.4 *Miscellaneous Expressions*

svfuncall = *funcall.*
mvfuncall = *funcall.*
funcall = *funcid* "(" [*tuple*] ")".
tuple = *expr* {"," *expr*}.

svfuncalls are those invoking single-valued functions, *mvfuncalls* those invoking multivalued functions. The value returned by the *funcall* is the union of the results obtained by applying the function to each element of *tuple*. The elements of *tuple* are constructed in the following way. This method allows *exprs* in *tuple* to contain the reference variables of preceding *exprs*. First, the first *expr* is evaluated to return a set of entities. Then, for each member of the set, the reference variable for the first *expr* is bound to the member of the set and the second *expr* is evaluated. This continues until all of the constituent *exprs* have been processed. Note that when reference variables of preceding *exprs* are not present, *tuple* simply evaluates to the cross product of the *expr* sets. Example: The tuple "Student ( ),Course(Student)" refers to those student-course pairs for which the course is a course of the student.

The *funcid* and the roles of the argument *exprs* specify a particular internal function name. It is this function which is applied to the argument values. The internal function name is determined in the following manner in order to avoid ambiguous reference. First, the set is constructed consisting of all internal names which have the specified *funcid* and proper number of arguments and which are defined over the types or the supertypes of the types which are the roles of the argument *expr*. If this set is empty, the *funcall* is illegal (undefined). The designated internal name is that member, *M*, of this set such that, for every argument position, there exists no other member defined over some subtype of the type over which *M* is defined at that argument position. If there is no such *M*, then the function reference is illegal (ambiguous). Example: If "expr1" has role "type1," "expr2" has role "type2," "super1" is a supertype of "type1" but not of "type2," "super2" is a supertype of "type2" but not of "type1," and the only internal names are "[*F*(type1,super2)]" and "[*F*(super1,type2)]", then the reference "*F*(expr2,expr1)" is illegal (undefined) and the reference "*F*(expr1,expr2)" is illegal (ambiguous).

aggcall = *aggid* "(" *bag* ")".
bag = *expr* | *singleton* "OVER" *tuple.*

In the case of *expr*, each element of the *set* is passed to the aggregator specified by *aggid*. In the case of an OVER phrase, *singleton* is evaluated for each element of *tuple* and the result is passed to the aggregator. During evaluation of *singleton*, the reference variables for each constituent expression of *tuple* are bound to the corresponding element of the expression value.

A2.1.5 *Typed Expressions and Constants*

integer = *singleton1.*
string = *singleton2.*
boolean = *singleton3.*
constant = *int* | *str* | *bool.*
int = *digit* {*digit*}.
str = """"" *character* {*character*} """"".
bool = "TRUE"|"FALSE".

singleton1 must be of type INTEGER. *singleton2* must be of type STRING. *singleton3* must be of type BOOLEAN. *ints* have type INTEGER, *strs* STRING and *bools* BOOLEAN.

A2.2 *Statements*

program = {*statement*}.
statement = *declarative* | *imperative.*

programs consist of *statements* which are either *declaratives* or *imperatives.*

A2.2.1 *Declaratives*

declarative =
"DECLARE" *funcspec* ("⇒"|"⇛") *expr* [*order*].
funcspec = *funcid* "(" [*tuple*] ")".

This declares primitive functions, which are directly updatable. If "⇒" is used, the function is single-valued; if "⇛", it is multivalued. If the function takes arguments, the type of the function is the role of *expr*. If there are no arguments, the *funcid* is implicitly declared to be a *typeid* and the function has type *funcid*, which is considered a subtype of the role of *expr*. The order of the function is determined by *order*. The internal name of the function is constructed from the *funcid* and the roles of the *exprs* in *tuple.*

declarative =
"DEFINE" *funcspec* ("⇒"|"⇛") *expr* [*order*].

This declares a derived function. The value of a derived function is computed on each invocation by evaluating *expr*. This evaluation is done with the reference variables of the *exprs* in *funcspec* bound to the corresponding actual arguments. Type, order and internal function name are determined as for actual primitive functions. It is not possible to directly update a derived function, however the PERFORM . . . USING construct allows such updates to be simulated.

declarative = "DEFINE" *funcspec1* ("⇒"|"⇛")
"INVERSE" "OF" *funcspec2* [*order*].

funcspec1 and *funcspec2* must specify one-argument functions. The role of the argument *expr* in *funcspec1* must be the same as the type of *funcspec2*. The value of a *funcall* on the new function will be those entities which, when supplied as arguments to the function specified by *funcspec2*, return the actual argument in the *funcall*. The type of *funcspec1* is the role of the *expr* argument in *funcspec2*, and the default order is the order of that type.

declarative = "DEFINE" *funcspec* ("⇒"|"⇛")
"TRANSITIVE" "OF" *expr* [*order*].

funcspec must involve exactly one argument which must have the same role as *expr*. *expr* must contain the reference variable for the formal argument in *funcspec*. The value of the defined function is the union of the values of *expr* evaluated with the reference variable bound to the actual function argument and to all other values which the function returns.

declarative = "DEFINE" *funcspec* ("⇒"|"=»")
"COMPOUND" "OF" *tuple* [*order*].

funcspec must specify a zero-argument function. The new type being defined will be a subtype of ENTITY and will include one entity for each element of *tuple*. For each *expr* component of *tuple*, the system will implicitly define an access function. The access function will map entities of the new type into the corresponding component of the tuple associated with the entity. The *funcid* of the access function is the reference variable of the corresponding *expr* in *tuple*.

declarative = "DEFINE" *funcspec* ("⇒"|"=»")
("INTERSECTION"|"UNION") "OF" *expr* {"," *expr*} [*order*].
declarative = "DEFINE" *funcspec* ("⇒"|"=»")
"DIFFERENCE" "OF" *expr* "," *expr* [*order*].

A derived function is declared. If the function takes arguments, then each of the *exprs* must be of the same type which becomes the type of the function. If the function takes no arguments, a new type is being defined. The function is of that type, which is considered to be a subtype of each of the roles of the *exprs*. The value of the function is the intersection, union or difference of the sets obtained by evaluating the *exprs*. In the case of functions which take arguments, this evaluation takes place with the reference variables of the *funcspec* arguments bound to the corresponding actual values.

declarative =
"DEFINE" "CONSTRAINT" *funcspec* "⇒" *boolean*.

The function is defined as if the keyword CONSTRAINT were not present. In addition, if any top-level statement (i.e., a program statement) completes with the function having the value FALSE for any arguments, the statement is aborted; that is, any updates it had performed are undone.

declarative =
"DEFINE" "TRIGGER" *funcspec* "⇒" *boolean imperative*.

The function is defined as if the keyword TRIGGER and the *imperative* were not present. In addition, whenever the function becomes TRUE for any arguments, *imperative* is executed. This execution is performed with the reference variables of the *funcspec* arguments bound to the entities for which the function has become true. When multiple triggers are activated, the order of execution of the corresponding *imperatives* is arbitrary.

declarative = "PERFORM" *update* "USING" *imperative*.

update specifies a statement which updates a derived function. *update* will contain a *funcspec* and a *vblid* which formally represents the value to which the derived function is to be set. *imperative* typically contains this *vblid* as well as the reference variable for the formal arguments of the *funcspec*. When an update statement is executed which corresponds to the format of update, then these variables are bound to the actual parameters appearing in the update statement and *imperative* is executed. The *imperative* would presumably effect the desired update to the derived function but this is not guaranteed nor is it checked for. Use of the A NEW operator against a derived type will have the effect of INCLUDEing the new entity in that type and all its supertypes. These implicit INCLUDEs also trigger a matching PERFORM . . . USING imperative.

A2.2.2 *Imperatives*

imperative = *forloop* | *update* | *gpimperative*.

The *gpimperatives* are imperative statements in the general-purpose language and are not further specified here.

forloop = "FOR" "EACH" *set* [*order*] *imperative*.

The *imperative* is executed for each member of *set* with the reference variable for *set* bound to that member. If *order* is supplied without any BY-phrases then the members of *set* are processed according to the order associated with *set*. If *order* is supplied with BY-phrases then the members of *set* are processed in the order specified by the BY-phrases. Otherwise, the order of processing is arbitrary.

forloop = "FOR" *singleton imperative*.

imperative is executed with the reference variable of *singleton* bound to the value of *singleton*.

update = "LET" *svfuncall* "=" *singleton*.

The value returned by the function referenced by *svfuncall* when applied to the actual arguments in *svfuncall* is changed to the value of *singleton*. The role of *singleton* and that of *svfuncall* must be the same.

update = ("LET"|"INCLUDE"|"EXCLUDE") *mvfuncall* "=" *expr*.

The value returned by the function referenced by *mvfuncall* when applied to the actual arguments in *mvfuncall* is changed. For LET, it becomes the value of *expr*. For INCLUDE, it becomes the union of the current value of *mvfuncall* and that of *expr*. For EXCLUDE, it becomes the difference of the current value of *mvfuncall* and that of *expr*. The role of *expr* and that of *mvfuncall* must be the same. If an update statement has the effect that some *funcall* returns an incorrect type, that *funcall* is illegal, and the situation must be corrected before the *program statement* is exited. No update statement for explicitly deleting entities from the database is provided, since entities are effectively deleted when they can no longer be referenced. This is typically done by excluding the entity from all of the types in which it participates.

update = "INSERT" *mvfuncall* "=" (*singleton1* | *set* [*order*])
("PRECEDING"|"FOLLOWING") *singleton2*.

mvfuncall must refer to an explicitly ordered function. The value of the *mvfuncall* becomes the union of its previous value and the value of *singleton1* or *set*. If a *set* is specified, the elements are partially ordered with respect to *singleton2* (which must be a current value of *mvfuncall*) as indicated by the

PRECEDING/FOLLOWING keyword. If *order* is supplied, then it specifies their new relative order within *mvfuncall*, otherwise they are mutually unordered. If any inserted elements are already being returned by *mvfuncall*, then they are reordered. The roles of *expr*, *singleton* and *mvfuncall* must be the same.

A2.2.3 *Orders*

order = "IN" "ORDER" {"BY" [("ASCENDING"|"DESCENDING")] *singleton*}.

The order syntax is used to specify a partial order for a *set*. When used in a function declaration or definition, the absence of a BY-phrase indicates that an explicitly ordered function is being defined. When used in a FOR EACH or INSERT statement, the absence of a BY-phrase indicates that the existing order associated with the *set* is to be used. When multiple BY-phrases are included, the first is the primary ordering, the second the secondary ordering, the third the tertiary ordering, etc. The partial order for each BY-phrase is determined by evaluating *singleton* for each member of the *set* with the reference variable for the *set* bound to that member. The relative order of the members of *set* is that of the relative order of the corresponding values of *singleton* relative to the order associated with *singleton*'s role. While *order* may specify a total order, it in general specifies a partial order. In the case of the FOR EACH statement and expressions involving PRECEDING/FOLLOWING or the *comp* operators, however, a total order is required. In these cases, the system supplies an arbitrary total order which conforms to the partial order. However, this total order is guaranteed not to change during the execution of any single statement.

ACKNOWLEDGMENTS

The author wishes to thank the many members of the Cambridge area database community for their helpful discussions and criticisms of the DAPLEX design. Special thanks are due Jim Rothnie for helping the author develop an understanding of the significance of the proposed approach and for his long-standing personal encouragement.

REFERENCES

1. Special Issue on Data-Base Management Systems. *ACM Comput. Surv. 8*, 1 (March 1976), 1–151.
2. Astrahan, M.M., et al. System R: Relational approach to database management. *ACM Trans. Database Syst. 1*, 2 (June 1976), 97–137.
3. Bachman, C.W., and Daya, M. The role concept in database models. *Proc. Int. Conf. Very Large Databases*, Tokyo, Japan, Oct. 1977, pp. 464–476.
4. Backus, J. Can programming be liberated from the von Neumann style? A functional style and its algebra of programs. *Commun. ACM 21*, 8 (Aug. 1978), 613–641.
5. Buneman, P., and Frankel, R.E. FQL—A functional query langauge. *Proc. ACM SIGMOD Conf.*, Boston, Mass., May–June 1979, pp. 52–58.
6. Chen, P.P.S. The entity-relationship model: Toward a unified view of data. *ACM Trans. Database Syst. 1*, 1 (March 1976), 9–36.
7. Codd, E.F. A relational model of data for large shared data banks. *Commun. ACM 13*, 6 (June 1970), 377–387.
8. Dayal, U., and Bernstein, P.A. On the updatability of relational views. *Proc. 4th Int. Conf. Very Large Databases*, Berlin, West Germany, Sept. 1978. pp. 368–377.
9. Hammer, M., and McLeod, D. The semantic data model: A modelling mechanism for database applications. *Proc. 1978 SIGMOD Conf.*, Austin, Tex., May 1978, pp. 26–35.
10. Kent, W. *Data and Reality*. North-Holland, Amsterdam, 1978.
11. Kent, W. Limitations of record-based information models. *ACM Trans. Database Syst. 4*, 1 (March 1979), 107–131.
12. McLeod, D. A semantic data base model and its associated structured user interface. Ph.D. Dissertation, Dep. Electrical Engineering and Computer Science, M.I.T., Cambridge, Mass., 1978.
13. Quillian, H.R. Semantic memory. In *Semantic Information Processing*, M. Minsky, Ed. M.I.T. Press, Cambridge, Mass., 1968.
14. Rowe, L., and Shoens, K. Data abstraction views and updates in RIGEL. *Proc. ACM SIGMOD Conf.*, Boston, Mass., May–June 1979, pp. 71–81.
15. Sibley, E.H., and Kershberg, L. Data architecture and data model considerations. *Proc. AFIPS Nat. Computer Conf.*, Dallas, Tex., June 1977, pp 85–96.
16. Smith, J.M., and Smith, D.C.P. Database abstractions: Aggregation and generalization. *ACM Trans. Database Syst. 2*, 2 (June 1977), 105–133.
17. Stonebraker, M., Wong, E., Kreps, B., and Held, G. The design and implementation of INGRES. *ACM Trans. Database Syst. 1*, 3 (Sept. 1976), 189–222.
18. Wirth, N. What can we do about the unnecessary diversity of notation for syntactic definitions? *Commun. ACM 20*, 11 (Nov. 1977), 822–823.

Received March 1979; revised November 1979; accepted August 1980

On the Design and Specification of Database Transactions

Michael L. Brodie
Computer Corporation of America

Dzenan Ridjanovic
University of Minnesota

ABSTRACT *A complete design and specification of database transactions must include both structural and behavioural properties. Structure deals with states and static properties while behaviour concerns state transitions and dynamic properties. Database design techniques emphasize the importance of behaviour but seldom provide for modelling and integrating behaviour* and *structure.*

This chapter presents concepts, tools, and techniques for the design and specification of behavioural and structural properties of database transactions. The concepts, tools, and techniques result from the integration of programming language (PL) and database (DB) technologies. Design principles from PLs (e.g., *abstraction and refinement), are applied to DB design and a new DB design principle, called localization, is proposed. PL concepts such as procedural abstractions, abstract data types, control structures, and specification techniques are integrated with DB concepts such as data abstractions, integrity constraints, data structures, and data models to produce a semantic data model for the conceptual design of databases and their associated transactions. The integration is based on the correspondence between the structure of complex databases and the structure of the associated transactions. In the proposed methodology, hierarchies of transactions and their constituent actions are designed in correspondence with the hierarchies designed to relate objects. As proposed in both artificial intelligence and PLs, design and specification are leveled. Gross design is done using graphic notation while detailed design is done using a conventional predicate based specification language. Appropriate concepts, tools, and techniques are presented for each level. The methodology is adequate for most database applications. However, complex and critical database applications* (e.g., *critical patient care, nuclear power plants) require precise, structured specifications. An appropriate formal specification technique, based on functional programming, is introduced. Formal specifications support increased precision and permit automated analysis and verification. The motivation for this work is similar to that for precise specifications in PLs. However, the existence of a database changes the nature of the problem and the required solution.*

The relationship between this chapter and other chapters is presented in a concluding Epilogue.

1. Motivation

Database applications have both structural and behavioural properties. *Structure* refers to states and static properties (*i.e.*, entities and their relationships). *Behaviour* refers to state transitions and dynamic properties (*i.e.*, operations and their relationships). A complete design and specification of a database application must include both structure and behaviour. For example, only part of the semantics of *hotel-reservation* is given in the structural properties represented by the relation *hotel-reservation (reservation#, hotel, room, person, arrival-date, departure-date)* represented in Figure 1.1. The semantics of actions that alter *hotel-reservation*, such as *insert-hotel-reservation, delete-hotel-reservation*, and *update-hotel-reservation*, is needed to complete the definition. The actions can then be used to design more complex operations such as *cancel-reservation, make-group-reservation*, and *convert-reservation-to-registration.* Database design requires concepts, tools, and techniques for modelling both structure and behaviour.

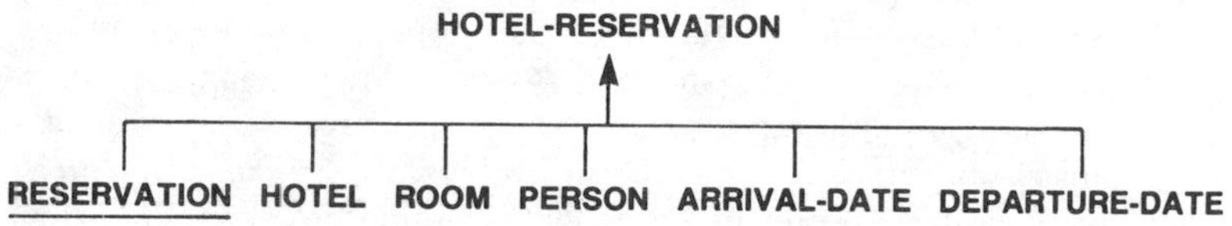

Figure 1.1 *Hotel-Reservation Object Scheme*

A principal objective of database design has been to extract as many structural properties as possible from programs that will access the database in order to define conceptual and external schemas. Consequently, many excellent concepts, such as semantic data models, were developed to deal with structure explicitly and abstractly (see the database overview by Ridjanovic, Brodie, and McLeod). Some behavioural properties are defined implicitly by structural properties. The remaining behavioural properties are defined using insert, update, and delete primitives and procedural abstractions not included in data models. The separate treatment of structure and behaviour complicates design, specification, modification, and semantic integrity analysis. Increasingly, the database emphasis on structure is shifting to include behaviour [SUNA78] (and the chapters by Borgida, Mylopoulos and Wong and by King and McLeod).

In the programming language area, behavioural properties are considered to be more abstract (*i.e.*, representation-free) than structural properties. As a result many excellent concepts, such as procedural and control abstractions, have been developed to deal explicitly and abstractly with behaviour. Some structural properties are specified implicitly by behavioural properties (*e.g.*, abstract data types). The emphasis on behaviour is currently shifting in light of recent interest in data abstractions (see the chapter by Shaw) and object-oriented programming.

2. Active and Passive Component Modelling

This chapter presents concepts, tools, and techniques for the design and specification of database applications and an associated design methodology called Active and Passive Component Modelling (ACM/PCM) [BROD81a] [BS82c] [RB82a] [RB82b] [RB82d].

Two principles are used in ACM/PCM to manage the complexity of database design: the principle of abstraction and the principle of localization. The *principle of abstraction* is the suppression of some detail in order to emphasize more appropriate detail (see the chapter by Shaw). ACM/PCM integrates behaviour and structure by means of data abstractions and abstract data types. Data abstraction here refers to composition rules used to compose higher level data objects from its constituents. Both structural and behavioural properties of each application object are defined completely in an integration of data abstraction and abstract data type. The *principle of localization* leads a designer to model each property of an application object independently (localized) and then to integrate the properties to produce a complete design. Concepts and tools are presented for the design and specification of data and procedural abstractions using the principle of localization.

Behaviour modelling concepts are presented as extensions of the semantic hierarchy model [SS77b]. The additions are a structural abstraction and forms of control and procedural abstraction with which to compose abstract operations. These behavioural abstractions are similar to the structural abstractions used to compose abstract objects from primitive objects.

In ACM/PCM, three levels are distinguished: the transaction level, the conceptual level, and the database level. The levels are similar to those in the ANSI/SPARC architecture. The transaction level, like the external schema level, is designed for specific application and end user needs. *Transaction modelling* involves the design and specification of structural and behavioural properties of transactions, queries, and reports. The conceptual level, like the conceptual schema level, is designed to meet the common needs of all known transactions. *Conceptual modelling* involves the design and specification using data abstraction of an abstract data type (*i.e.*, structure and actions) for each application object. The database level, like the internal schema level, involves the implementation and maintenance of the properties specified at the other levels using existing software (*e.g.*, DBMSs and programming languages). Modelling at all three levels involves behaviour and structure. This chapter focuses on behaviour modelling at the conceptual and transaction levels. The design and specification of database structure is described in more detail elsewhere [BROD80a] [BROD81a] [BROD82] [RB82a] [RB82b] [RB82c].

The result of applying ACM/PCM to an application is not only a deep structure (hierarchy) of objects but also a corresponding deep structure (hierarchy) of procedures. A procedure hierarchy, called a transaction-action hierarchy, goes across the three levels and defines the invocation hierarchy of the transaction. The concept of procedure hierarchies is used extensively in the chapter by Borgida, Mylopoulos, and Wong.

ACM/PCM integrates operation (action and transaction) modelling with event modelling. An action is a behavioural property of one object and can be invoked to produce a state transition for the object. A transaction is composed of actions and produces a collection of logically related state transitions called an event. Hence, a class of events is designed by modelling a transaction. This approach to event modelling has several advantages. First, behavioural relationships among actions are used explicitly to define legal event classes. As the chapter will show, behavioural relationships (composition rules) among actions can be deduced directly from the structural relationships among the corresponding objects. Second, time can be modelled to the extent that actions and transactions can be invoked to run in sequence or in parallel.

Modelling in ACM/PCM proceeds in two steps. First, properties are designed at a gross level of detail. Then, the properties are specified precisely in an incremental way. The design levels are intended to support abstraction through incremental design as is intended for the design and conceptual schema approach presented in the chapter by King and McLeod. This chapter presents object schemes and behaviour schemes as design aids for gross design and semi-formal and formal behaviour specifications for precise design.

3. Structure Modelling

3.1 Extended Semantic Hierarchy Model (SHM+)

For the design and specification of structural properties of database applications, SHM+ provides one structural concept, the object, and four forms of data abstraction for relating objects: classification, aggregation, generalization, and association. The data abstractions are fundamental for most semantic data models. Classification, aggregation, and generalization are being used in various forms [SS77b] (and the chapters by Borgida, Mylopoulos and Wong and by McLeod and King) whereas association has only recently been formalized [BROD81a] [RB82a] [RB82c].

Classification is a form of abstraction in which a collection of objects is considered as a higher level object class. An *object class* is a precise characterization of all properties shared by each object in the collection. An *object* is an instance of an object class if it has the properties defined in the class. Classification represents an ***instance-of*** relationship between an object class in a schema and an object in a database. For example, an object class *employee* that has properties *employee-name, employee-number,* and *salary* may have as an instance the object with property values "John Smith," 402, and $50,000. Classification is used in conceptual modelling to identify, classify, and describe objects in terms of object classes. In the remainder of the chapter, "object" is used to refer to object classes and the associated objects except when the two concepts must be distinguished.

Aggregation, generalization, and association are used to relate objects. Some properties of an object are determined through inheritance by the role it plays in one or more of these relationships. *Aggregation* is a form of abstraction in which a relationship between *component objects* is considered as a higher level *aggregate object.* This is the ***part-of*** relationship. For example, an *employee* may be an aggregate of components *employee-number, employee-name,* and *salary. Generalization* is a form of abstraction in which a relationship between *category objects* is considered as a higher level *generic object.* This is the ***is-a*** relationship. For example, the generic *employee* may be a generalization of categories *secretary* and *manager* (*i.e., secretary* ***is-a*** *employee* and *manager* ***is-a*** *employee*). *Association* is a form of abstraction in which a relationship between *member objects* is considered as a higher level *set object.* This is the ***member-of*** relationship. For example, the set *trade-union* is an association of *employee* members and the set *management* is an association of *employee* members.

The important features of aggregation, generalization, and association are expressed in the following predicate calculus and set theoretic expressions: (when P is a predicate, let the set of P_s denote $\{x|P(x)\}$).
Aggregation: Let A be the aggregate with components P_i.

$$A(x) <=> \exists y_1, \ldots, y_n P_1(x,y_1) \ \& \ \ldots \ \& \ P_n(x,y_n)$$

$$x \in A_s <=> x \in \{z | \exists y_1 P_1(z,y_1)\} \ \& \ \ldots \ \& \ x \in \{z | \exists y_n P_n(z,y_n)\}$$

Generalization: Let G be the generic with categories C_i.

$$C_i(x) => G(x)$$

$$x \in C_{i_s} => x \in G_s \ or \ C_{i_s} \subset G_s$$

Association: Let S be the set type and M be the member type.

$$S(x) <=> \forall y (y \in x => M(y))$$

$$x \in S_s <=> x \in P(M) \text{ where } P(x) \text{ is the power set over } x.$$

The predicate calculus and set theoretic expressions are intended to give intuition into the concepts. The expressions, however, do lose some of the richness of the concepts such as abstraction (suppression of details) and property inheritance. It is essential to completely define the semantics of these concepts (see the chapter by Reiter). The concepts presented in this chapter are defined precisely in [BROD82] by means of predicate axioms and in [RB82a] [RB82c] by means of sets and functions.

Aggregation bears some similarity to the artificial intelligence (AI) concept of frames (see the Knowledge Representation Overview by Mylopoulos and Levesque). A component of an aggregate corresponds to a slot in a frame. Like slots, components, as defined in this chapter, have both static (data structure) and dynamic (operation) properties. Defaults, such as exist in frames, have not been addressed in aggregation with the exception of identifying essential components. Defaults would be an excellent concept to integrate into aggregation hierarchies. Frames and aggregation, as defined here, differ, just as prototypes differ from types. An "instance" of a prototype need not have all properties given in the frame, whereas a type instance must have all the properties defined in the aggregate. (For a further discussion of this distinction see Hewitt's conclusion at the end of the book.) Hence, SHM+ provides not only a frame-like knowledge representation mechanism, it also provides generalization and association for structuring frame-like representations.

The three forms of abstraction provide techniques for structure modelling: composition/decomposition, association/membership (which emphasizes set oriented design as a special case of composition/

decomposition), and generalization/specialization which all take advantage of property inheritance. The use of generalization is discussed in detail in the chapter by Borgida, Mylopoulos, and Wong. Aggregation and association support upward inheritance in which properties of the components or members are inherited by the aggregate or set. For example, the properties of the components *employee-name, employee-number,* and *salary* are inherited as properties of the aggregate *employee.* Aggregates and sets are designed by *decomposition* into, or *composition* from, components or members without concern for their properties. Generalization supports downward inheritance in which all properties of a generic object are inherited by each of its category objects. For example, the categories *secretary* and *manager* inherit all properties of the generic *employee.* Categories are designed by *specialization* in which only those properties that distinguish the category object from the generic object are defined. For example, a *secretary* is defined as an *employee* who has the distinguishing property of *typing-speed.* Alternatively, a generic object can be generalized from the common properties of distinct objects. Property inheritance supports abstraction, modularity, and consistency, since essential properties of an object are defined once and are inherited in all relationships in which it takes part.

Structure modelling at the conceptual level involves the identification and relationship of all objects required for an application. Aggregation, generalization, and association can be applied to compose objects to form aggregates, generics, and sets, and to decompose objects into components, categories, and members. Repeated application of composition/decomposition results in aggregation and association hierarchies. The repeated applications of generalization/specialization results in generalization hierarchies. An object can simultaneously take part in all three kinds of hierarchies provided by the orthogonal nature of the abstractions.

The design of the abstraction hierarchies for complex database applications is a complex process. The principle of localization is used to design these hierarchies step by step. Only one application object and objects immediately related by aggregation, generalization, and association are considered at one time. The combined result of structure modelling is a conceptual model of the application that reflects the complexity of the application being modelled. The complexity can be reduced by reapplying localization to ignore particular details and to consider each object independently as an aggregate, component, generic, category, set, or member.

Structure modelling at the transaction level involves identifying objects and relationships in the conceptual model that need to be accessed by a transaction. Objects and relationships not in the conceptual model but needed by the transaction may be introduced as local to the transaction. These local objects, relationships, and associated actions are called virtual and explained in detail in [RB82a] [RB82d].

3.2 Object Schemes

In structure modelling, a semantic data model aids in identifying and relating structural properties and in specifying those properties precisely. These two roles are at different levels of precision and form the basis of a two step modelling process. First, the gross structural properties (*e.g.,* objects and their relationships) are designed. Second, the fine details of those properties are specified. SHM+ provides design tools for both steps. Object schemes are used for gross structure design. A structure specification language, Beta [BROD80a] [BROD81a] [BROD82] [BS82c], is used for structure specification. Similarly, the chapter by King and McLeod proposes two kinds of schema.

An object scheme, like a data structure diagram and an E-R diagram, graphically represents the objects and structural relationships of a database application. An *object scheme* is a directed graph in which nodes are strings denoting objects, and edges identify aggregation, generalization, and association relationships between objects. The graphic notation for the three forms of abstraction is given in Figure 3.1.

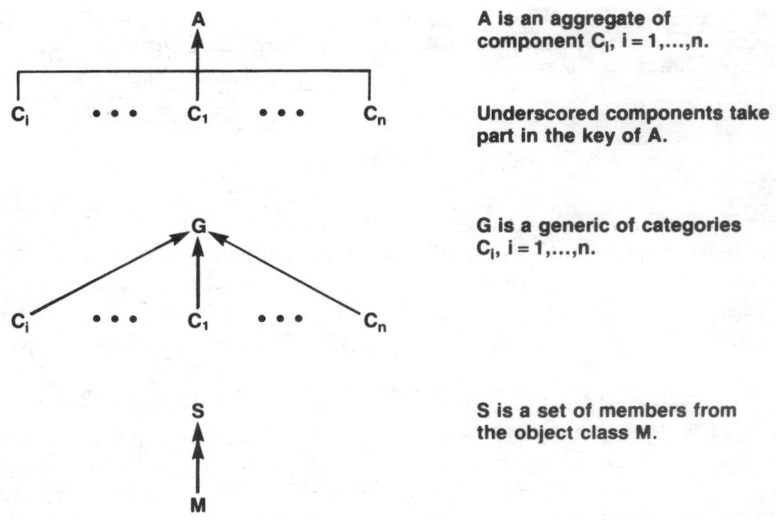
A
C_i ••• C_1 ••• C_n
A is an aggregate of component C_i, i = 1,...,n.
Underscored components take part in the key of A.
G
C_i ••• C_1 ••• C_n
G is a generic of categories C_i, i = 1,...,n.
S
M
S is a set of members from the object class M.

Figure 3.1 *Object Scheme Notational Conventions*

The result of applying composition/decomposition and generalization/specialization to a single object can be represented, according to the principle of localization, in one or more object schemes. Figure 3.2 contains two object schemes for *employee.*

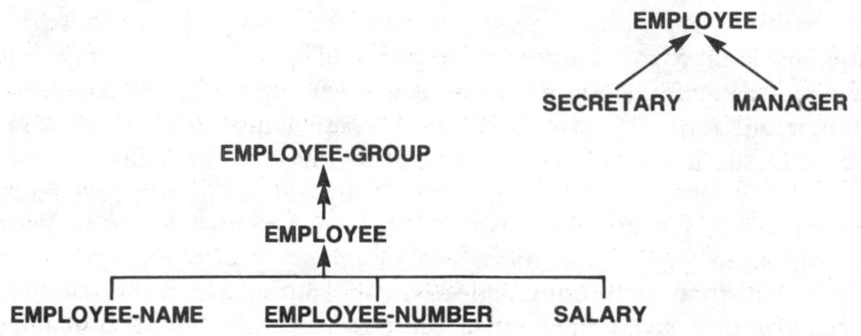

Figure 3.2 *Employee Object Schemes*

Using the principle of localization, additional properties of objects in an object scheme can be modelled by extending the object scheme or by designing independent object schemes. Object schemes can be composed/decomposed and generalized/specialized. In transaction modelling, object schemes for each object involved in a transaction can be combined to form a transaction object scheme. In conceptual modelling, an object scheme containing all objects and relationships can be created by combining the object schemes of either all transactions or of each independent object (*e.g.,* these alternatives correspond to view integration and conceptual schema design). Subsequently, object schemes for new transactions can be abstracted from the object scheme of the conceptual model and by introducing, if necessary, virtual objects.

Using object schemes, the gross design of structure takes advantage of abstraction and modularity. Detailed information about constituent objects can be ignored when designing an object. Many structural properties can be assumed through property inheritance.

Object schemes have been presented as a design aid for SHM+ databases. However, they also can be used with most other data models. Effective techniques exist [RB82a] for mapping SHM+ object schemes to each of the "classical" data models. Due to the fundamental nature of SHM+, object schemes also can be used as a graphic design aid for most semantic data models. Specifically, object schemes can be used with the semantic data models that support semantic relativism [MS81] such as SHM [SS77b], TAXIS [MBW80], SDM [HM81], and RM/T [CODD79]. According to semantic relativism, an object can be considered both independently and in terms of any relationship in which it takes part. In turn, a relationship can be considered as an object. Depending on one's point of view, properties of objects can be considered as attributes, entities, or relationships; a distinction is not forced by the model but can be made by the observer.

Object schemes offer advantages over data structure diagrams, E-R diagrams, and relation schemes. The major advantage is that object schemes, in supporting semantic relativism, support the principles of abstraction and localization. A second advantage is that object schemes distinguish aggregation and association. These two fundamental concepts are only implicitly represented in relations and in 1:N relationships of data structure and E-R diagrams. Hence, object schemes can be more precise. A distinct advantage over relation schemes is that object schemes can be used to represent higher order relations (*i.e.,* relationships between relations).

4. Behaviour Modelling

For the design and specification of behavioural properties of database applications, SHM+ provides primitive database operations on objects, three forms of control abstraction with which to compose application-oriented operations, and two forms of procedural abstraction: *actions* for conceptual modelling and *transactions* for transaction modelling. The three forms of control abstraction are direct analogs to the three forms of data abstraction (aggregation, generalization, and association). They are fundamental to function theory, hence, to all programming languages.

Each database operation is either an altering or a retrieval operation over a single instance of an object class. The altering operations are ***INSERT, DELETE, UPDATE*** (*e.g.,* ***INSERT*** *employee,* ***UPDATE*** *employee-salary,* and ***DELETE*** *employee-group*). Altering operations ensure SHM+ semantics for each role an object plays (*e.g.,* aggregates can be inserted only if their essential components exist; deleting a generic causes its dependent categories to be deleted). Retrieval operations for object values are: ***FIND*** an object in the database, ***CREATE*** an object using a defined procedure, and ***REQUEST*** an object (interactively) from the user.

Control abstractions are used to relate operations to form higher-level, composite operations. The three forms of control abstraction sequence, choice, and repetition are *behavioural analogs* of the three forms of data abstraction. Aggregation corresponds to either *sequence* or *parallel* relationship of operations. An operation on an aggregate is composed of either a sequence or parallel of operations, one for each component. The essence here is that there is a fixed number of possibly different operations. For example, an action *insert-hotel-reservation* on *hotel-reservation* (Figure 1.1) for a given hotel over given dates might be composed of a sequence of operations to create a *reservation#*, request a *person,* reserve a *room,* plus ***INSERT*** the *hotel-reservation.* Generalization corresponds to *choice* (*e.g.,* if-then or case control structures). An operation on a generic is composed of a choice of operations, one for each category (case is used for nonoverlapping categories; sequence or parallel of if-then control structures is used for overlapping categories). For example, a *hire-employee* action on *employee* (Figure 3.2) consists of a choice of two insert operations, one for *secretary* and one for *manager*, plus ***INSERT*** the *employee.* Association corresponds to *repetition* (*e.g.,* do-while or for-each control structures used in the framework of either sequence or parallel control structures). An operation on a set is composed of an operation that is applied in sequence or parallel to each member of the set. The essence here is that there is an undetermined (at compile time) number of identical operations. For example, an action *dissolve-employee-group* on the object *employee-group* (Figure 3.2) is composed of a delete operation for each *employee*, plus ***DELETE*** the *employee-group.* The three forms of control abstraction can be used to define all partial recursive (*i.e.,* computable) functions [DAVI58]. Hence, they are sufficient for all application-oriented operations. Although the above data structure-control structure correspondence is only an analogy, it gives considerable insight into the relationship between data and its related operations, hence between structure modelling and behaviour modelling.

Behaviour modelling at the conceptual level involves the identification, design, and specification of actions for each object. Many of the modelling concepts here are based on abstract data types. An *action* is a conceptual level, application-oriented operation designed, using the principle of localization, for *one* object to ensure that all properties of the object are satisfied. An action is designed from a single database altering operation by providing the necessary invocation context. Before invoking the database operation, certain preconditions must be met, and actions on other objects may be necessary. After the actions are invoked, a postcondition must be checked and the database operation is executed. For both pre- and postconditions, exception handling must be designed. The *insert-hotel-reservation* operation described earlier has as a precondition that the *hotel* exists and that an appropriate *room* be available on the desired dates. If the precondition is true then the room must be reserved by invoking other operations. The postcondition ensures that the room is reserved and that the *hotel-reservation* can be ***INSERT***ed.

Actions provide the only means of altering an object. This ensures the semantic integrity of an object since all constraints on the object must be satisfied by all attempts to alter it. An *action local scope* includes the object of interest and all objects immediately related by aggregation, generalization, and association. An *action complete scope* is inferred from the hierarchy of invoked actions. The database operation can alter only the object of interest. All other objects are accessed by means of actions. Actions provide a degree of modularity that aids design and redesign. For example, redefining *insert-hotel-reservation* effectively and consistently redefines all operations that invoke it.

The behaviour of an object is completely defined by its actions. Typically, an object has one insert, one delete, and zero or more update actions. The *hotel-reservation* object has one insert, one delete, and two update actions (one update to alter *hotel* and *room,* and another to alter the *dates*). The purpose of designing actions for an object is that they may be used to construct any legal, application-oriented operation at the transaction level that would access it.

The behavioural and structural properties of an object constitute an abstraction that completely defines the semantics of the object. The result of conceptual modelling, the conceptual model of the application, is a network of abstractions related by the three forms of abstraction. In terms of structure there is a hierarchy of objects. In terms of behaviour there is a hierarchy of actions. The purpose of conceptual modelling is to provide an adequate basis for the design of all application-oriented objects and operations at the transaction level.

Behaviour modelling at the transaction level involves the identification, design, and specification of transactions. A *transaction* is an application-oriented operation at the transaction level that alters *one* or *more* objects. A *transaction scope* includes all objects accessed in the transaction. A transaction is designed from actions on objects in the scope by providing an appropriate invocation context. The invocation context of a transaction provides a particular *behavioural view* of the underlying conceptual model just as derivation rules and constraints provide particular *structural views.* Preconditions, action invocations, postconditions, and exception-handling are required, as is the case with actions. However, unlike actions there is no database operation.

Transactions are designed to fulfill specific user requirements. Consider two transactions for use by clerks at a hotel's front desk. The first, *cancel-reservation,* checks that the *reservation* exists, invokes the *delete-hotel-reservation* action, and ensures that the *reservation* was deleted. The second transaction, *convert-reservation-to-registration* is used to create a *hotel-registration* from an arriving guest's *hotel-reservation.* The precondition checks that the *hotel-reservation* exists, verifies the reservation information, and ensures that the room is available. The transaction then creates, finds, or requests registration information and invokes the actions *insert-hotel-registration* and *delete-hotel-reservation*. The postcondition checks the success of the actions. Both transactions provide different invocation contexts for the *delete-hotel-reservation* action, thereby ensuring the same constraints on *hotel-reservation*. Both transactions were designed abstractly (*i.e.*, without concern for the details of the actions involved, exception handling, *etc.*).

To ensure the semantic integrity of database applications there is a strict invocation hierarchy. Transactions are the only means for end users to alter the database. Transactions invoke actions that are the only means of altering objects. Each action invokes a single database operation to alter a single object. Both actions and transactions are well-defined logical units that have well-defined scopes, pre- and postconditions, and effects on the database. Typically, transactions have been used as a unit of physical integrity (*e.g.*, concurrency [BHR80]). Design using the SHM+ and ACM/PCM treats actions and transactions as units of semantic integrity.

Behaviour modelling is done, together with structure modelling, in a two step process that reduces the amount of detail to be considered at one time (incremental or refinement design). First the gross behavioural properties are designed. Actions and transactions are identified and related to objects. Then, aided by the gross designs, the fine details of actions and transactions are specified. As a result of this process the structure of the resulting invocation hierarchy, called the transaction-action hierarchy, corresponds directly to the structure of the object hierarchy.

SHM+ provides design and documentation aids for both behaviour design and behaviour specification. Behaviour schemes are used for the design of gross behavioural properties. Behavioural specifications are used to specify those properties precisely. Behaviour schemes and specifications provide designer, user, and implementor guidance and form a basis for semantic integrity analysis.

5. Behaviour Schemes

A behaviour scheme is an explicit graphical representation of the gross properties of a single action or transaction. Schemes provide graphical means for designing behavioural properties of database applications, as do paths in the chapter by King and McLeod and scripts in the chapter by Borgida, Mylopoulos, and Wong. Three forms of control abstraction, (*i.e.*, sequence or parallel, choice, and repetition) are used to represent the behavioural relationships between an action (or transaction) and its constituent operations. There is a constituent operation for each object in the action local scope or transaction scope. Constituent operations and their relationships are represented by adding behavioural information to an object scheme. This facilitates the explicit modelling of behaviour at a gross level of detail. Behaviour schemes integrate structural and behavioural properties in one representation.

A *behaviour scheme* for an action (transaction) is an object scheme that includes each object in the local scope (transaction scope), plus an operation label on each edge, one label for each constituent operation. An operation label indicates the nature of a constituent operation by naming the database operation(s) on which it is based and by giving an invocation context by means of an arrow (→). The arrow points to the object on which the operation is invoked and points from the object that invoked it. A double arrow (=>) is used to distinguish the action or transaction from the constituent operations. The relationship between operations is given by the forms of abstractions.

Figure 5.1 gives the notation for behavioural relationships and invocation contexts for behaviour schemes by adding operation edge notation to the object scheme notation given in Figure 3.1. In Figure 5.1, T_1, T_2, and T_3 name actions or transactions; $O_1, O_2, \cdots, O_n$ and O name constituent operations.

Although most constituent operations are based on one action, they can be composed by sequence or parallel, choice, and repetition of one or more actions. Operation edges name the database operations on which the action is based. The syntax for operation names is given by the grammar,

```
OP ::= insert|update|delete|find|request|create|noop

       |OP  V  OP|OP  &  OP|OP*
```

where "&" indicates *and* (for sequence or parallel); "V" indicates *or* (for choice); and "*" indicates zero or more repetitions.

To construct behaviour schemes (Figures 5.2 and 5.3) for the insert and delete from *hotel-reservation* object scheme (Figure 1.1), some details must be known about the component objects. *Reservation#* is generated automatically by the system. *Hotel* and *room* objects exist independently of the *reservation*. *Person*, *departure-date*, and *arrival-date* exist only in the context of a *reservation*.

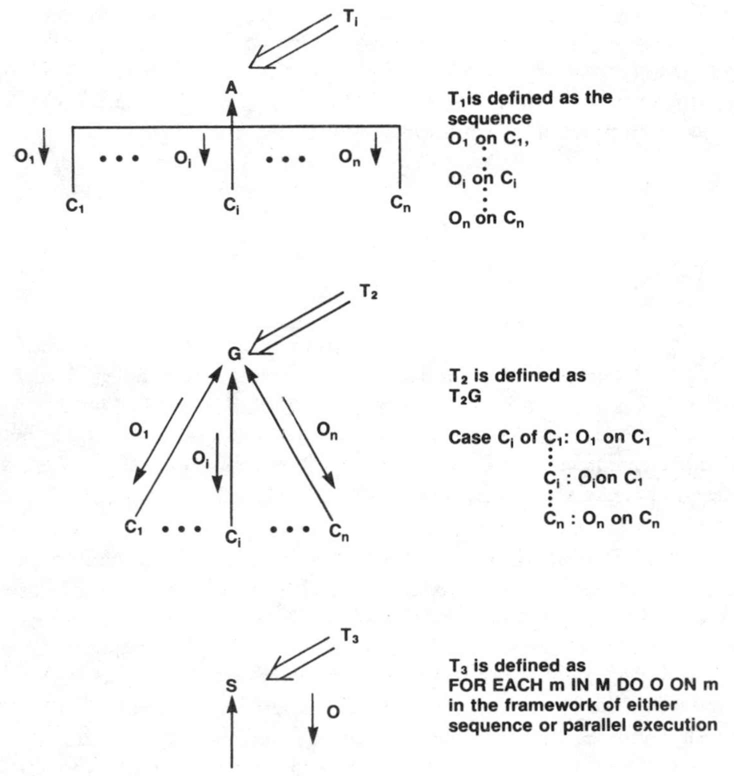

Figure 5.1 *Behavioural Relationships in Behaviour Schemes*

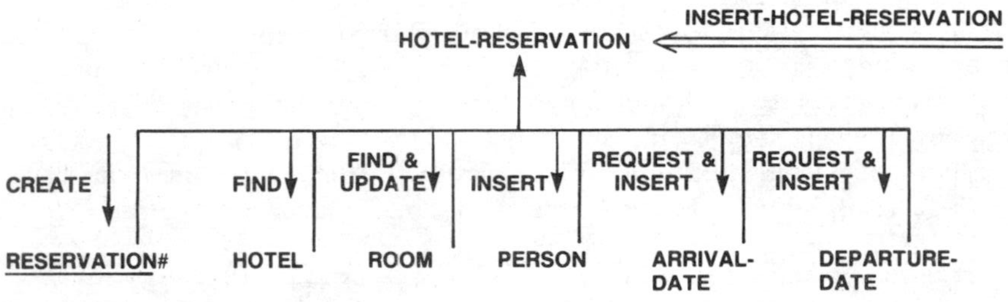

Figure 5.2 *Insert-Hotel-Reservation Action Scheme*

Now, consider designing a transaction scheme for the transaction *convert-reservation-to-registration*. First, an object scheme is designed for the transaction scope. To represent the behavioural relationship between a transaction and its constituent actions, a transaction object (virtual object) is introduced and related to each object in the scope. The *transaction* object in Figure 5.4 is an aggregate of objects in the scope.

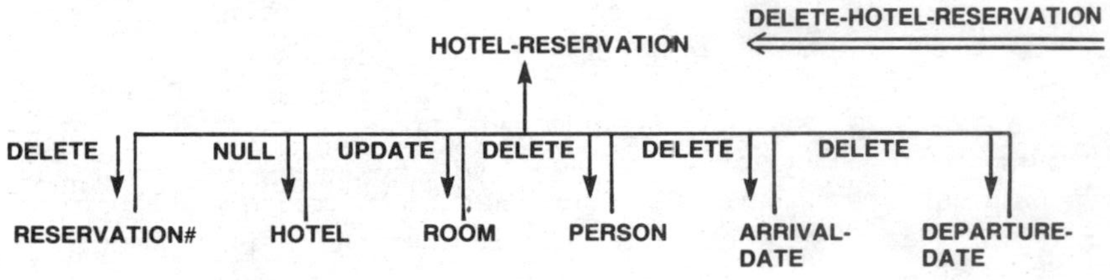

Figure 5.3 *Delete-Hotel-Reservation Action Scheme*

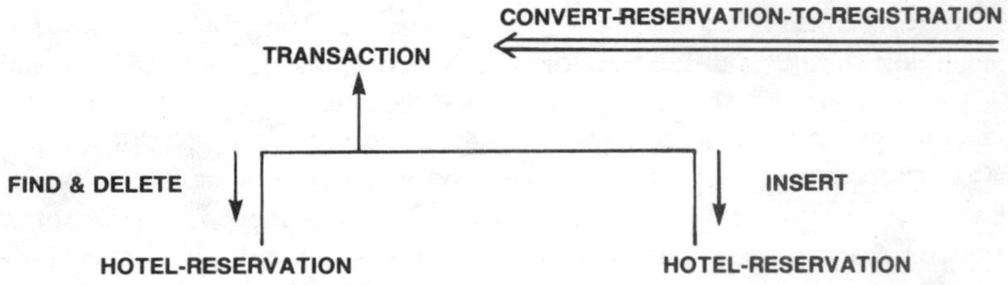

Figure 5.4 *Convert-Reservation-to-Registration Transaction Scheme*

Using behaviour schemes, the design of gross behavioural properties of actions and transactions can be done explicitly and abstractly taking advantage of modularity. The effect of an operation is considered explicitly in terms of constituent operations, their relationship, and invocation context. Detailed information about constituent objects, hence parameters, can be ignored, as can the details of actions on those objects. Those actions can be designed using separate behaviour schemes and can be invoked by any object to which the action object is related. The insert and delete actions represented in Figures 5.2 and 5.3 can be used to design other transactions that alter *hotel-reservation*. This modularity simplifies the design process and ensures the semantic integrity of the object. The semantics of the transaction represented in Figure 5.4 is relatively complex but its design has been simplified by using action and transaction schemes.

Behaviour schemes have been presented in terms of SHM+; however, they are more generally applicable. As discussed earlier, object schemes can be used in conjunction with many data models.

Correspondingly, behaviour schemes can be used for the gross design of actions and transactions over those models as long as the data model rules are satisfied (*e.g.*, triggered delete for hierarchies, storage and removal constraints for networks, referential integrity for relations [RB83], and structure invariants for models based on the semantic hierarchy model) [BROD81a].

Behaviour schemes and SHM+ provide control and procedural abstractions for behaviour modelling not provided for in data structure and E-R diagrams, relation schemes, and the semantic data models mentioned earlier. Behaviour schemes provide explicit means for the design and representation of behavioural properties at a gross level of detail. More important, behaviour schemes can be used to design and represent both structural *and* behavioural properties of database applications.

Due to abstraction and modularity inherent in object and behaviour schemes, gross conceptual modelling can precede or follow gross transaction modelling. If transaction modelling is done first, the resulting object schemes can be integrated by identifying common objects in transaction scopes and applying composition/decomposition and generalization/specialization. Then, action schemes can be designed for objects in the conceptual model and compared with the transaction schemes for completeness. When conceptual modelling is done first, and when new transactions are being designed, a transaction scope can be derived from the conceptual model and virtual objects, and transaction schemes can be designed using existing actions and virtual actions [RB82a] [RB82d]. Experience with SHM+ has shown that neither transaction nor conceptual modelling should be completed independently, but that design is an iterative process. Generally, a preliminary design of transaction schemes aids substantially in conceptual modelling, which is then followed by complete transaction modelling.

6. Behaviour Specifications

To complete behaviour modelling, the fine details of actions and transactions designed using behaviour schemes must be specified. This is done in a behaviour specification that is a complete definition of the behavioural properties of an action or transaction. Such specifications should be precise, abstract, formal, and easy to use and modify. To be complete, all properties must be defined precisely and explicitly. Typically this means many constraints on each operation. A specification is abstract if it gives a minimum amount of detail to define the operation (*e.g.*, implementation detail should be excluded). Formal (possibly automated) techniques can be applied for semantic integrity analysis of formal specifications and for database transaction verification. Finally, due to the size, complexity, and evolutionary nature of database applications, specifications should be easily constructed, understood, and modified. This requires that specifications be structured. Structured specifications enable (among other things) abstraction to be applied during the specification of complex applications, specifying partial functions (constraints), and the manipulation (*e.g.*, modification and composition) of specifications.

Many techniques have been proposed for the specification of behaviour. In the programming language area the principal techniques include axiomatics [HW73], predicate transformers [DIJK76], algebra [GH78], functions [LMW79], and the Vienna Development Method (VDM) [BJ78]. With the exception of VDM, these techniques treat structural properties implicitly, hence they are inappropriate for structural properties of databases. All techniques require mathematical sophistication, making them somewhat difficult to use. With the exception of the functional approach, constraints are difficult to specify and modify. None of these techniques permit the specification structuring and modification essential for complex database applications. Consequently, these techniques have not proved practical for large scale systems.

Object and behaviour schemes are abstract and easy to use and modify, but they are neither precise nor do they have associated analysis techniques. Formal techniques that support analysis and verification are precise but are often difficult to use. The gap between graphical and mathematically formal techniques is large. This chapter proposes an intermediate step between graphical object and behaviour schemes and a formal technique for analysis and verification. The intermediate step involves specifying behaviour using the axiomatic and predicate transformer techniques. These predicate behaviour specifications can be used for semantic integrity analysis of database transactions. They are adequate for most database applications. However, particularly complex applications, with many objects, relationships, and constraints, require the precision and analysis that only advanced formal approaches have so far been able to provide [BG80b] [WIRS82] [WB81] [WPPD83]. Specifically, structuring and modification of specifications, not supported by axiomatic and predicate transformer techniques, are essential for complex database applications. For critical database applications (*e.g.*, critical patient care, nuclear power plant operation) verification techniques are essential. The extension of the functional technique [LMW79] is proposed here as a promising candidate for structuring and modifying transaction specifications and for verifying transaction specifications and their corresponding programs [RB82a] [RB82e].

6.1 Predicate Specifications

The form of the behaviour specifications proposed here is based on the axiomatic and predicate transformer techniques. Databases are treated explicitly since behaviour specifications refer to objects for which a structure specification is given. Axioms and inference rules for the structure specification language are given elsewhere [BROD82]. A behaviour specification is given in terms of constraints expressed as predicates; hence, they can be both abstract and precise. For most database applications, constraints are readily constructed and modified by adding and deleting predicates.

Actions and transactions have similar components based on the form:

$$N\,(V)\;I, O, L : P\,\{A\}\,Q, D$$

N is the operation name and V is a parameter list. I, O, L defines the operation's scope (local scope for an action, transaction scope for a transaction) by naming: I, the objects accessed through actions and retrieval operations; O, the object altered through the database operation, D; and L, the objects local to the operation. The effect of the operation is specified in terms of a precondition, P; an active role, A; a postcondition, Q; and possibly a database operation D. P and Q are lists of predicates and A is composed of zero or more action invocations.

An action alters one object, O, directly by means of an SHM+ primitive ***INSERT***, ***UPDATE***, or ***DELETE*** operation, D, and can access objects, I, that are immediately related to O by means of actions in A. $P\{A\}Q$ constitutes the precondition to be satisfied to ensure the successful execution of D. $P\{A\}Q$ must check or establish every relationship between O and objects in I. The potential complexity of $P\{A\}Q$ warrants its being considered in three parts. P ensures that A can be invoked. The actions in A appropriately alter the objects in I to ensure the desired relationships. Q checks the success of A.

A transaction can access any collection of objects only by means of their actions, hence, O and D are empty. I and L define the transaction scope. P is the precondition that determines whether A can proceed. A is composed of actions that achieve the desired effects of the transaction which are checked by the postcondition Q.

A predicate behaviour specification has the form:

$$N\,(V)\;I, O, L : P\{\,\}Q, D$$

The effect of an action or transaction (*i.e.*, exactly *what* it does), is completely defined by $P\{\,\}Q,D$. The active role A defines *how* the effect is achieved and is therefore excluded as inappropriate detail for a specification. The effect of an operation is specified in terms of simple predicates (these predicates are simple for most databases) in P and Q that can be precise, abstract, semi-formal, and easy to specify and modify.

As an example, consider the specification of the *insert-hotel-reservation* action (Figure 6.1) guided by the action scheme in Figure 5.2.

```
ACTION insert-hotel-reservation (h,p)
IN (n: reservation#, h: hotel, r: room, p: person
   a: arrival-date, d: departure-date)
OUT (hotel-reservation)
PRECONDITION: hotel-exists (h)?
              legal-person (p)?
POSTCONDITION: room-reserved (n,h,r,a,d)?
DB-OPERATION: INSERT hotel-reservation (n,h,r,p,a,d)
```

Figure 6.1 *Insert-Hotel-Reservation Action Specification*

First, the scope I and O is determined directly from the object scheme. O is *hotel-reservation* and I includes all of its components. Second, the parameter list V is determined by considering how objects are to be retrieved. The action scheme indicates that *reservation#* is to be created and that *arrival-date* and *departure-date* are to be requested interactively from the user within the active role. *Person* is to be inserted, hence, is input via a parameter. *Hotel* and *room* are to be found in the database. As a design decision, it is stated that reservations be made by giving a hotel name and that rooms can be reserved automatically by giving the *hotel, arrival-date,* and *departure-date*. Hence, *hotel* and *person* are the parameters. The precondition checks the validity of the input parameters. The only requirement for the success of the database operation, ***INSERT*** *hotel-reservation,* is that the active role ensures that an appropriate room is found and reserved. The postcondition is expressed as a predicate that checks this requirement.

The action specification for *delete-hotel-reservation* (Figure 6.2) and the transaction specification for *convert-reservation-to-registration* (Figure 6.3) can be similarly designed from their respective behaviour schemes (Figures 5.3 and 5.4).

6.2 Specifying Predicates and Exception Handling

Predicates in the pre- and postconditions, P and Q, are used to detect and handle errors and exceptional conditions. The failure of any predicate in P and Q causes the operation to be terminated. The failure of Q additionally requires that the effects of the active role be undone. Exception handling in this approach, unlike that using triggers

```
ACTION delete-hotel-reservation (n)
IN (n: reservation#, r: room)
OUT (hotel-reservation)
PRECONDITION: hotel-reservation-exists (n)?
POSTCONDITION: room-freed (h,r,a,d)?
DB-OPERATION: DELETE hotel-reservation (n)
```

Figure 6.2 *Delete-Hotel-Reservation Action Specification*

```
TRANSACTION convert-reservation-to-registration (n1)
SCOPE (n1: hotel-reservation, n2: hotel-registration)
PRECONDITION: reservation-verifies (n1)?
              room-available (n1)?
POSTCONDITION: hotel-reservation-cancelled (n1)?
               hotel-registration-exists (n2)?
```

Figure 6.3 *Convert-Reservation-to-Registration Transaction Specification*

and database procedures, is used only to undo the effects of an incomplete or unsuccessful active role. This approach is based on the small, limited scope (local scope) of actions that are units of logical integrity.

Due to the principle of localization, exception handling for the pre- and postconditions is ignored in action and transaction specifications. It is specified separately using predicates and procedures, combined with action and transaction specifications, to complete them.

Predicates are specified using predicate calculus (based on PASCAL/R syntax [SCHM77]) over objects in the scope. In addition, each predicate also can have exception handling specified for the failure of the predicate. For example, the predicate *hotel-reservation-exists (r)* used in the precondition of the *delete-hotel-reservation* specification (Figure 6.2) is specified as:

```
hotel-reservation-exists (R) :=
   some h in hotel-reservation (h.reservation# = R)
```

Additionally, exception handling could be specified for the predicate's failure. For example, there could be an interaction with the hotel clerk to retrieve other identifying information for the desired *hotel* or an alternative *hotel*.

6.3 Object Class Specifications

Generally, structure and behaviour modelling are quite separate. Structural properties of an object are designed and defined in schemas and subschemas. Behavioural properties are defined by all programs that alter the object. New programs are defined using primitive altering operations that extend, and possibly alter or conflict with, existing properties. While each program should not be concerned with all properties of the objects they alter, these properties must be maintained consistently.

Typically, to relate structural and behavioural properties, new constraints are defined independently of programs and schemas. The constraints are implemented using assertions, triggers, database procedures, on conditions, check clauses, *etc.* These techniques implement constraints as side effects of operations. Hence, the properties of objects are defined implicitly and explicitly, in three different forms, and in different places throughout an application definition. This complicates design, definition, modification, and semantic integrity analysis.

Using SHM+, structure and behaviour specifications of an object are integrated to form an object class (integration using data abstractions to form abstract data types). An object class is a complete definition of the properties of an object. It consists of a structure specification and an action specification for each action available on objects of the class. An action specification refers to structure specifications by naming the object in its local scope. All properties to be altered by an action are stated explicitly in $P\{\}Q,D$. Abstraction (*i.e.*, the suppression of irrelevant detail) is applied in designing and specifying object classes. The modular nature of abstractions aids in semantic integrity and modification. The integration using data abstraction to form abstract data types borrows the good features of abstract data types but still allows database retrieval by a query language.

7. Action and Transaction Programs

An action or transaction program is constructed by adding an active role to the associated behaviour specification. The design of an active role is guided by both the behaviour specification and the behaviour scheme.

The following syntax is used to illustrate action program design:

```
ACTION  <action name>(<parameter list>)
IN  (<object list>)
OUT  (<object list>)

if  <precondition>
then  <active role>
{else  terminate action}

if  <postcondition>
then  <database operation>
{else  undo active role and terminate action}
```

The backout actions given in the ***else*** clauses are handled in the pre- and postcondition predicates. The database operations are denoted ":+" for ***INSERT***, ":&" for ***UPDATE*** and ":-" for ***DELETE*** following the syntax of PASCAL/R.

The active role is a number of action invocations related by some control constructs. The actions can be deduced from operation labels on behaviour schemes. Control structures can be determined from the forms of abstraction relating to the objects (Figure 5.1) and from details given by the operation label.

```
ACTION insert-hotel-reservation (h,p)
IN (n: reservation#, h: hotel, r: room, p: person,
    a: arrival-date, d: departure-date)
OUT (hotel-reservation)
 if hotel-exists (h) and
    legal-person (p)
 then request-arrival-date (a)
      request-departure-date (d)
      create-reservation# (n)
      reserve-room (n,h,r,a,d)
 if room-reserved (n,h,r,a,d)
 then hotel-reservation :+ (n,h,r,p,a,d)
```

Figure 7.1 *Insert-Hotel-Reservation Action*

For example, the *insert-hotel-reservation* program (Figure 7.1) can be designed by adding to its specification (Figure 6.1) active role details expressed in its action scheme (Figure 5.2). Aggregation results, in this example, in a sequence of action invocations. Inserts of *arrival-date, departure-date,* and *person* occur directly in the database operation. *Hotel* is found in the precondition. The remaining operations are achieved through four action invocations. Abstraction aids in the design of active roles. Designers need know only *what* actions do, not *how* they do it. In the design of *insert-hotel-reservation* it is necessary to know that given n, h, a, and d, *reserve-room* reserves a room and returns a reference to it in the result parameter r. It is not necessary to know the algorithm or human interaction needed to reserve the room. *Delete-hotel-reservation* (Figure 7.2) and *convert-reservation-to-registration* (Figure 7.3) were designed similarly.

```
ACTION delete-hotel-reservation (n)
IN (n: reservation#, r: room)
OUT (hotel-reservation)
 if hotel-reservation-exists (n)
 then delete-room-reservation (n,h,r,a,d)
 if room-freed (h,r,a,d)
 then hotel-reservation :- n
```

Figure 7.2 *Delete-Hotel-Reservation Action*

```
TRANSACTION convert-reservation-to-registration (n1)
SCOPE (n1: hotel-reservation,
       n2: hotel-registration)
 if reservation-verifies (n1) and
    room-available (n1)
 then delete-hotel-reservation (n1)
      insert-hotel-registration (n2)
 check hotel-reservation-cancelled (n1)
       hotel-registration-exists (n2)
```

Figure 7.3 *Convert-Reservation-to-Registration Transaction*

8. Functional Specifications

This section is intended to give intuition into the formal specification and verification technique underlying SHM+ and ACM/PCM. For very complex database applications, side-effects of actions, expressed through their active roles, can refer to a large portion of a database. The associated chain of action invocations can be represented as a hierarchy of actions that is invoked by the transaction. For these transaction-action hierarchies, predicate behaviour specifications can become complex and very detailed, hence difficult to manage and modify. Predicate specifications are not structured. Functional specifications, however, can be easily structured in a hierarchy of functions that specifies a corresponding transaction-action hierarchy. Regardless of the hierarchy's size, every function is of manageable size and its place in the hierarchy is precisely defined. The structuring and modifying of behaviour specifications is based on the principle of localization and the algebraic nature of the functional technique.

A specification of a database program (transaction or action) is a given function, called the *intended database program function*. A function domain is represented by a sequence of application objects called the *input state vector*. A function range is represented by an identically ordered sequence of the same objects (possibly altered), called the *output state vector*. Using the principle of localization and defining, in every state vector, only the object of interest and its related input data, the size of intended database program functions becomes manageable. In general, an intended database program function f, with state vector sv, is given in the form illustrated in Figure 8.1. The output state vector (sv') indicates that some objects in the input state vector (sv) are altered.

$$f(sv) = \begin{cases} (sv') & \textit{if} \text{ objects in (sv) satisfy certain properties } \textit{and} \text{ active role is successful} \\ (sv) & \textit{else.} \end{cases}$$

Figure 8.1 *Database Program Function Specification*

The meaning of a database program is a computed database program function that completely determines a mapping from the input state vector to the output state vector. More precisely, given a database program *DP* (·*DP* denotes a program syntax) its semantics is the function [*DP*] computed by the program *DP*. [*DP*] is the functional composition of the computed functions of the database programs, SHM+ primitives, and the control abstractions used in *DP*. Computed functions of the primitives and control abstractions are given by definition [RB82a] [RB82e].

A database program *DP* is correct with respect to its specification (the intended program function) f if and only if

$$f = [DP]$$

where

1. The number of arguments in state vectors must agree
2. Domains must agree (*i.e.*, f and [*DP*] are defined on exactly the same objects)

Due to the principle of localization, each function (or database program) in a hierarchy of transactions and actions is of manageable size. However, the hierarchy can be very deep when it is used for very complex database applications. The associated verification method [LMW79], which is convenient for a small number of relatively small programs, can be time- and space-consuming for large transaction-action hierarchies. Hence, there is a need for the new verification method that takes advantage of the hierarchical structure and the principle of localization. Such a technique is being developed [RB82a] [RB82e].

9. Conclusions

Due to the complex, evolutionary nature of database applications and to the growing need for precision and semantic integrity, database designers are faced with increasingly more complex requirements. They face such problems as "where to start," "how to proceed," "what representations to use," and "model correctness and completeness." Database research has provided semantic data models and design methodologies for modelling structure but little guidance for modelling behaviour. Since database design and specification is incomplete without a definition of its behaviour, note that concepts, tools, and techniques are required for behaviour modelling and should be integrated with their structural counterparts for structure modelling.

This chapter presents and illustrates concepts, tools, and techniques for behaviour modelling of database applications. The primary goals are the integration of control and procedural abstractions with data abstractions, and the development of tools to aid designers in applying the forms of abstraction. Sequence or parallel, choice, and repetition are control abstractions that are the behavioural analogs of the forms of data abstraction: aggregation, generalization, and association. Control abstractions are used to compose abstract operations from primitive operations, just as forms of data abstraction are used to compose abstract objects from primitive objects. Actions and transactions are procedural abstractions used to represent abstract operations. Procedural abstractions permit modularity in behaviour modelling just as data abstractions provide modularity in structure modelling. Also, data abstraction object properties (aggregation, generalization and association) and abstract data type object properties (actions and transactions) are integrated to form an object class that is an abstract, complete, and precise characterization both of the structural and behavioural properties of the object. SHM+ is a storage model that attempts to integrate the fundamental concepts of (semantic) data models and programming languages.

This chapter also introduces three specification techniques: a graphical technique for gross design, a semiformal predicate based technique for a detailed specification of most database applications, and a formal, functional technique for applications where precision and analysis with verification are critical. All three techniques are based on SHM+. The more informal techniques were derived from the functional technique, with the goal of providing techniques that are easy to use and understand while maintaining precision and soundness. It is shown that behaviour schemes and predicate behaviour specifications can be used to design and specify behavioural properties explicitly, abstractly, and in a modular fashion. Although the concepts, tools, and techniques are presented in the context of ACM/PCM and SHM+, they are more generally applicable due to the fundamental concepts on which SHM+ is based [RB82c] [RB82f].

Finally, the chapter presents ACM/PCM, a design methodology that incorporates the above results for the design and specification of database applications. A distinctive contribution of ACM/PCM is that it provides a database transaction design and specification techniques that are fully integrated with structure design. There is a cost associated with the precise specification of database applications and the adopting of the principle of localization. ACM/PCM leads to a large number of small procedures. Since more properties are being modelled there is a possibility of over-specification and undesirable rigidity. These problems have ramifications for design and redesign. However, a disciplined database application development process significantly increases project success in terms of time, cost, and customer satisfaction. ACM/PCM does not resolve a number of important problems. For example, the decomposition of an application into the appropriate data abstractions is not resolved, but design aids are provided to support it. Also, the design and specification of queries and reports are not addressed.

ACM/PCM has been used by novices and by experts to design and specify a number of database applications: a university registration system, a hotel reservation system, soccer team management, a real estate sales management system, and a criminal court scheduling system. The criminal court system has been implemented many times following ACM/PCM. Although the main implementation tool was PASCAL/R (each version entailing approximately 10,000 lines of code), COBOL and the CODASYL system DMS1100 were also used. This experience has been used to refine and test the concepts, tools, and techniques. The greatest benefit of the approach is the guidance provided to manage the complexity of the application semantics on one hand and of the design and development process on the other hand.

10. Epilogue

This chapter discusses several concepts that are fundamental to other chapters in the book.

Abstraction. Both data abstraction (aggregation, generalization and association) from DBs and abstract data types (object class specifications) from PLs are used to design and specify structure and behaviour of database applications. Aggregation and generalization are used in the chapters by Borgida, Mylopoulos and Wong; King and McLeod; and Reiter. Generalization/specialization hierarchies and property inheritance are used for both objects and operations. This chapter provides a user with hierarchies that are based on all three data abstractions. Association hierarchies are used to emphasize a set oriented design of database transactions. King and McLeod use the simple form of generalization hierarchies where the properties are inherited only by attribute restrictions. Abstract data types are used in the chapters by Krieg-Brueckner; Reimer, Schmidt and Mall; Shaw; Stonebraker; and Zilles. Stonebraker uses abstract data types in a simplified way to represent properties of relation attributes. This chapter uses abstract data types to represent more complex objects and integrates the notions of data abstraction and abstract data types that provide an important communication path between DBs and PLs. The property inheritance concept from AI is not fully used in the behavioural design.

Localization. Localization is a concept addressed for the first time in this chapter. It is used to design properties separately and then to combine them to obtain the complete design. One of the consequences of applying the principle of localization is that the action local scopes are precisely defined by the underlying object and its relationship with immediately related objects. In part, the principle resembles the notion related to partitioning and focusing from AI used in the chapter by Rich.

Incremental design. Incremental design from AI and stepwise refinement from PLs are used in several chapters. The chapters by King and McLeod; Rich; and this chapter go from the level of gross design (informal text, diagrams, schemes, syntactical cliches) toward the more detailed and formal designs. King and McLeod present two levels (design and conceptual schemas) that are not essentially different by the level of details. This chapter provides more levels (object and behaviour schemes, semi-formal predicates, formal functions, programs), thus providing a smooth transition between levels. Beside the different levels of precision, the chapter presents three different levels of modelling (transaction, conceptual, and database), thus partitioning the levels of precision.

Kinds of modelling. It is obvious from the book that there are shifts in research directions in the three areas. Behavioural aspects (events, transactions, actions) are becoming more important in DBs, and structural aspects (persistent and more complex objects) are becoming more important in PLs. This chapter uses control structures from PLs to design database behaviour. Integration is done using the concepts of data abstraction and abstract data types. The same control structures are used to design both behaviour and structure. In the chapter by Borgida, Mylopoulos and Wong, separate mechanisms are used to design composition of more complex structures and operations. Constraints, exceptions, incomplete knowledge, and side-effects are the other kinds of modelling that are considered more often. Procedural abstractions from PLs are used to design events, transactions, and actions. In the chapter by King and McLeod, events from DBs and procedures from PLs appear to be similar. In this chapter, an event is described as an instance of a transaction concept. Transactions and actions are shown to be special kinds of procedures that have precisely defined constituents. An action is an application-oriented operation at the conceptual level designed for one object (only one database operation is invoked) in order to ensure that all properties of the object are satisfied (preconditions are checked, the other actions are invoked, and postconditions are checked). A transaction is an application-oriented operation at the transaction level (view-oriented procedure) that alters one or more objects by using actions and not database operations.

Integration of different concepts, tools, and techniques. There are many useful existing concepts, tools, and techniques from AI, DBs, and PLs. It seems that we do not need the new concepts, but we need to combine them into an integrated whole (see Zilles' conclusion at the end of the book) in order to develop new tools, techniques, and systems that are capable of solving current problems in conceptual modelling. This chapter attempts to integrate abstract data types from PLs, data abstractions from DBs, aspects of property inheritance from AI, and view oriented objects and operations (useful abstractions that are not so rigid as abstract data types) from DBs. Our impression is that the successful integration of these concepts will provide useful systems for conceptual modelling of real-world applications.

This chapter is based on Brodie, M.L., "On Modelling Behavioural Semantics of Databases," *Proc. 7th International Conference on Very Large Databases*, Cannes, France, September 1981.

11. References

[BG80b] [BHR80] [BJ78] [BROD80a] [BROD81a] [BROD82] [BS82c] [CODD79] [DAVI58] [DIJK76] [GH78] [HM81] [HW73] [LMW79] [MBW80] [MS81] [RB82a] [RB82b] [RB82c] [RB82d] [RB82e] [RB82f] [RB83] [SCHM77] [SS77b] [SUNA78] [WB81] [WIRS82] [WPPD83]

Discussion

What is impressive about this work is the completeness of the whole process of design, specification, and implementation, and the fact that both structural and behavioural properties of applications are not only designed but also integrated.

The chapter describes a strict application of divide and conquer to logical database design. The authors isolate concepts for abstraction and design, and provide a methodology with which to apply these concepts in order to come up with a uniform design. They provide concepts, tools, and techniques in an integrated approach for the database transaction design, specification, modification, integrity analysis, and documentation.

Database applications have both structural and behavioural properties. In the past, structural properties were emphasized. However, structural properties capture only a part of the semantics of database applications. Behavioural properties must also be specified. The approach places equal emphasis on database (structure) design and transaction (behaviour) design in order to achieve an integrated result.

Traditional DB models provide structural abstractions and primitive operations, but no means for designing complex operations. One contribution of the chapter is that it provides procedural abstractions appropriate for modelling database transactions from primitive operations. Operations are divided into three types: transactions, actions, and primitive operations. The different types are used to design strict operation invocation hierarchies that mirror the corresponding object hierarchies. Transactions invoke actions, and actions invoke primitive operations. Each type of operation is used at a different modelling level. Transactions are used at the transaction (application) level, actions are used at the conceptual level, and DB primitive operations are used at the database (implementation) level. An action is the behavioural property of *one* object. An object can have more than one action. A transaction is a controlled collection of actions on *several* objects.

The Approach

The approach is based on three principles: abstraction (for structural and behavioural properties), localization (design properties separately, then combine them to get the desired result), and refinement (gross design followed by detailed design, specification, and implementation).

Since the design of database applications is not yet well understood (*i.e.*, cannot be expressed algorithmically), the authors took an empirical approach. Several large, complex database applications were designed. Using existing semantic modelling concepts, they developed and refined a methodology. The target specification and implementation vehicle was the relational data model plus PASCAL (*i.e.*, PASCAL/R) although the methodology applies to any DBMS (a CODASYL DBMS was also used). The goal was to develop a high level semantic model for data and procedures. The model was to be object oriented and was to include transaction concepts, hence it had to be at a higher level than the relational model. Methodological concepts that were proven to be effective in practice were embedded into the model. Hence, the research paradigm was to go from methodology to model to implementation. This covers the complete spectrum in the development of database applications.

The major concern is the integration of structural and behavioural modelling. The authors provide a technique to control action and transaction design using rules analogous to those for object composition. The design of behavioural properties is guided by structural properties.

SHM+: A Semantic Data Model

The approach is based on an object oriented semantic data model, called SHM+, rather than on a record oriented data model such as that of the relational data model. SHM+ uses the traditional structuring concepts of classification, aggregation, and generalization and introduces a new concept called association. These concepts are referred to as forms of abstraction since they are used to combine objects into higher level (*i.e.*, more abstract) objects.

Classification is used to define an object class from the instances of the class. Aggregation is used to define compound objects from its parts. Generalization is used to define generic objects from their categories. Association is used to determine a set of objects from its members.

Classification is a relationship between a type and its instances, whereas aggregation, generalization, and association are relationships between types. The type relationships are the important ones for modelling. Any one type can simultaneously have aggregation, generalization, and association relationships with other types. An object can be viewed simultaneously as an aggregate of parts, as a generic of categories, and as a set of members. Alternatively, an object can be a part, a category, and a member in other types.

Defining Data Model Concepts

The notions of aggregation, generalization, and association may be clear to those in the DB community who developed them; however, they may not be clear to others, such as those in the AI and PL communities. The concepts must be defined precisely for those who will use them for modelling. Precision aids not only our understanding of the concepts but also our investigations of the properties of the concepts. For example, the authors claim that their concepts support disjoint types, multiple hierarchies, multiple inheritance, and nonhierarchical structures.

A framework is required to define and use new, complex semantic data models concepts. English does not appear to be adequate. A formal framework such as axiomatics or FOL appears to be more appropriate. In a previous paper, Brodie defined the concepts axiomatically. Developing the axiomization was a valuable process in formulating the concepts, but the result was formidable. Over 150 axioms were required to define the static properties alone. Intuition can be lost due to the large amount of detail.

Mary Shaw: "Some day we will come to understand that specifications, just like code, must be organized carefully if they are to be readable or maintainable."

The chapter presents single sentence definitions of each of the concepts in FOL and in set theory. The definitions do not capture all of the properties. They are intended to avoid the problems of jargon and to provide intuition and a basis for understanding and communicating. A major disadvantage of FOL, set theory, and axiomatics is their inability to handle dynamic properties. Not only must procedurality be defined for database applications, it must be integrated with the definition of the static properties. In any case, any semantic data model must be precisely defined for the community that will use it. The ideal framework or formalism has yet to be determined.

Structure Design

Structure design proceeds in three steps: gross design, detailed design (specification), and type definition. A graphical notation, called object schemes, is used to characterize gross structural properties. An object scheme is a directed graph in which nodes represent objects and edges represent the relationship between objects. There are three kinds of edge, one for each form of abstraction. Object schemes are used to document database designs and to guide the detailed design, which is expressed using the specification language for SHM+ databases. If the type specification is not implemented directly on the target DBMS, then an appropriate type or schema definition must be generated. There is an algorithm for generating relational schemes from SHM+ specifications. Roughly speaking, one object corresponds to one relation. Primary and foreign keys are used to represent the relationships that must be maintained by all operations accessing the relations. For this reason, relation types (relations and their operations) are implemented as abstract data types. The chapter describes structure design briefly and refers to the authors' detailed methodology called Active and Passive Component Modelling (ACM/PCM).

Behaviour Modelling Concepts

For behavioural modelling, three kinds of concepts are provided: primitive DB operations, two forms of procedural abstraction (actions and transactions), and three forms of control abstraction. The DB primitive operations are those of the target DBMS, typically insert, delete, and update. An action consists of a single DB operation and an appropriate invocation context. Transactions are application or user oriented operations and can be defined over any collection of objects. Transactions are designed or composed from actions (the modules or building blocks for transactions) together with an appropriate invocation context. An invocation context is specified by means of preconditions, postconditions, and exceptions. Integrity of objects is always maintained since only actions (which are predefined, meaningful operations) can be used to access objects.

Events and Generalized Schemas

An event is something that happens in time. A procedure represents a class of events just as a data type represents a class of data values. Hence, a class of events in a database application is represented by an action or transaction. In that sense, the concept of schema is generalized in this work to include action and transaction definitions as well as data definitions.

Behaviour Modelling

Following the authors' goal of integrating structure and behaviour, behaviour design follows structural design closely. Gross behaviour design involves designing behaviour schemes from the already designed object schemes. A behaviour scheme is used to represent the properties of an action on an object or a transaction over a collection of objects related by aggregation, generalization, and association. A behaviour scheme is an object scheme with edges added to indicate the constituent operations of an action or transaction and the objects they act on.

Detailed behaviour design, which is guided by behaviour schemes, results in high level action and transaction specifications. There are two levels of behaviour specification, a semiformal, predicate specification and a formal, functional specification. In each case, the same format is used for both actions and transactions. Transactions differ from action specifications because transactions have larger scopes and they cannot invoke DB primitives. The final step in behaviour design is the generation of programs for actions and transactions. Specifications are used systematically for program generation. As with specifications, action and transaction programs follow the same pattern. For uniformity, the authors attempt to use the same syntax and design concepts for actions and transactions wherever possible.

Analogies Between Structure and Behaviour

The authors develop an appealing analogy between structural and behavioural concepts in order to integrate structure and behaviour. The analogy is based on the assumption that the structure of objects mirrors that of the associated operations, and vice versa. The claim is that control structures (used for organizing programs) are the behavioural counterparts of data structures (used for organizing data). More specifically, the claim is that aggregation, generalization, and association are adequate and necessary for relating or structuring objects as well as operations, at least in database applications. The authors point out that it is an analogy and cannot be pushed too far.

The analogy can be explained as follows. Aggregation applied to objects (components) produces an aggregate or record type data structure. An operation over an aggregate consists of a fixed number of possibly different operations in sequence or in parallel, one for each component. Hence, aggregation relates the aggregate data structure and the sequence or parallel control structure. Generalization applied to objects (categories) produces a generic data structure or type hierarchy. An operation over a type hierarchy consists of an operation on the generic followed by a choice of operations, one for each category in the hierarchy. Hence, generalization relates type hierarchies and choice (case or if..then) control structure. Finally, association applied to objects (members) produces a set data structure. An operation over a set consists of one operation repeated for each member of the set. Hence, association relates the set data structure and iteration or the "do while" control structure.

There are several appealing features of the analogy. The first is elegance. Only three concepts are necessary for modelling both structure and behaviour. The second is integration. The analogy establishes a strong relationship between structure and behaviour. Data structure can be used to determine transaction structure, and vice versa. On this basis, structure and behaviour modelling can be integrated. The third is a possible completeness argument. Since sequence, choice, and iteration are necessary and sufficient to express all computable functions, database transaction can be expressed by using them. The hope is that any data structure also can be expressed using them.

Intuition gained by means of the proposed correspondence between structure and behaviour has been useful in understanding database transactions. The fact that complex objects naturally decompose into rather deep aggregation, generalization, and association hierarchies led to the discovery that the associated transactions naturally decompose into a similar deep structure. The authors therefore developed the concept of transaction-action hierarchies and the associated strict invocation hierarchies in which transactions invoke actions that invoke DB operations.

Epilogue

1988

This work, which began in 1978 and was first published in 1981, was an early investigation of what is now called object-oriented data models and languages. Although the concept of object-oriented databases has advanced considerably, the message of the paper is now more important than it was ten years ago. It offers concepts for currently open problems in the little studied area of object-oriented information system design methodologies.

The premise of the paper was that data models and languages, especially those intended for applications semantically richer than traditional business processing, should be designed to meet the modelling requirements of the application domain and to support effective design. That is, powerful design methodologies should be developed in cooperation with the supporting data models and languages.

The research goal was to develop more powerful concepts (i.e., data models), techniques (i.e., design methodologies), and tools (e.g., database languages and transforms) to support information system design and development. The added power was to be able to capture more properties of the application than was possible with existing classical and semantic data models.

The relational data model provided the elegant, simple idea of a table with which to represent all business processing entities. Database constraints were used to represent properties that could not readily be captured as static properties of tables. These constraints typically prevented illegal updates to entities. Like demons in AI, such constraints are *ad hoc* mechanisms that are difficult to design effectively and to execute efficiently.

Missing from data models were means for modelling dynamic properties of database applications. For dynamic properties, most data models had elementary concepts (e.g., basic read and write operations with implicit or non-existent control structures), tools (e.g., the entity-relationship model had no query or update languages), and techniques (i.e., few with design methodologies, none addressing dynamic properties).

The research approach was to apply abstract data type and object-oriented concepts to persistant objects for information system design and development. The basic idea was to encapsulate static and dynamic properties of entities in objects which are defined by object classes. The concepts included: user defined object classes, inheritance of static and dynamic properties, polymorphism (i.e., each object had the same basic operation names used to invoke object-specific operations), information hiding, and complex objects (i.e., objects composed of objects).

The starting point was to develop a means to model dynamic properties explicitly in terms of meaningful queries and transactions against objects. The paper proposes concepts (i.e., actions) and tools (i.e., linear and graphical languages, and translation between them) designed to support a proposed transaction design technique. These constituted the means for modelling the behavioural properties of objects to complement existing means for modelling the structural properties of objects.

Traditional abstract data type concepts had to be extended to accommodate structural properties of persistant objects as they are seen in the database world (e.g., object attributes, relationships, and boundaries). This was done by integrating (i.e., placing equal emphasis on) static and dynamic properties via a strong analogy between data and control structures.

The lack of design methodologies for the classical data models posed major problems in the effective use of traditional databases. The problems are being addressed by a tidal wave of design methodologies and over 120 associated commercial products, called Computer Aided Software Engineering (CASE) tools. Over 30,000 copies of CASE tools for database design have sold in under three years. Although most CASE tools are weak and non-integrated, the commercial CASE trend has done more for database design and development in three years than the research community did in the previous ten years. Open problems in this area include: support of transaction/ behavioural design; tools that do expert level design, especially physical design; tool suites to cover the entire life cycle; integration of database design, analysis, and program generation tools; integrated design databases/dictionaries; version and configuration control; intelligent design guidance/explanation; re-design/re-engineering; database migration; and the ability to tailor tool suites to support specific software engineering requirements. There will likely be a significant reduction in the number of CASE tools on the market; however, over 200,000 copies could sell by 1992.

Now that object-oriented databases are providing important concepts for expanding the scope of information management, the premise of the paper is more important than ever. Currently, there are few ideas for object-oriented design methodologies. Most such work is being done by CASE product companies rather than by universities. The lack of an object-oriented design methodology is more severe due to the additional complexity of designing both behavioural and structural properties of objects. The power of object-oriented data models is that they provide primitive concepts (i.e., object class) that can be used to support the modelling requirements of any application domain. The requirements are best understood by designing the intended application object classes. Hence, object-oriented design methodologies are critical to the entire design and development process. As mentioned above, the methodology, data model, and language should all be developed to support each other.

The paper offers a few concepts towards that end, including: the integration of structure and behaviour, the principles of abstraction and localization, and the concepts underlying the object-oriented information system design methodology. The principle of localization may be the most valuable concept in the paper.

Ten years has also uncovered mistakes. The distinction between actions and transactions should be dropped. Actions (operations, messages) are composed of actions just as objects are composed of objects. Two design levels are completely adequate. Conceptual level design involves application-oriented actions. Database level design involves mapping actions onto the data model/language of the target DBMS. The concept of *action* presented in the paper corresponds more closely to the basic operations of a persistant object. All objects have the same names for basic operations; however, the semantics of each operation is specific to the object on which it is invoked. Considered in this light, persistant objects exhibit polymorphism and the common protocol provides a basis for an object algebra for persistent objects. The analogous relational algebra was one of the most powerful features for objects of type relation in the relational data model. An object algebra was developed for the Probe Data Model (PDM). Perfecting such an algebra is one of the major challenges in object-oriented data models.

Reference

[PDM] Manola, F., and U. Dayal, "PDM: An Object-Oriented Data Model," in Dittrich, K., and U. Dayal (eds.), *Proc. Intl. Workshop on Object-Oriented Database Systems,* Washington, IEEE Computer Society Press, 1986.

Michael L. Brodie*
Dzenan Ridjanovic†
February 1988

* GTE Laboratories Incorporated
40 Sylvan Road
Waltham, MA 02254
(Brodie@gte-labs.csnet)

† Laval University
Faculty of Administrative Science
Quebec City, Quebec
CANADA G1K 7P4
(Ridjanod@lavalvm2.bitnet)

References

[BG80a] Bobrow, D. and Goldstein, I., "Representing Design Alternatives," *Proc. Society for Study of Artificial Intelligence and Simulation of Behavior Conference*, Amsterdam, The Netherlands, July 1980.

[BHR80] Bayer, R., H. Heller, and A. Reiser, "Parallelism and Recovery in Database Systems," *ACM Transactions on Database Systems,* Vol. 5, No. 2, June 1980.

[BJ78] Bjorner, D. and C.B. Jones, *The Vienna Development Method,* Springer-Verlag, New York, 1978.

[BROD80a] Brodie, M.L., "The Application of Data Types to Database Semantic Integrity," *Information Systems,* Vol. 5, No. 4, 1980.

[BROD81a] Brodie, M.L., "Association: A Database Abstraction for Semantic Modelling," *Proc. 2nd International Entity-Relationship Conference,* Washington, D.C., October 1981.

[BROD82] Brodie, M.L., "Axiomatic Definitions for Data Model Semantics," *Information Systems,* Vol. 7, No. 2, 1982.

[BS82c] Brodie, M.L. and E.O. Silva, "Active and Passive Component Modelling: ACM/PCM," in [OSV82], pp. 41-91.

[BZ81] Brodie, M.L. and S.N. Zilles (eds.), *Proc. Workshop on Data Abstraction, Databases, and Conceptual Modelling, SIGART Newsletter,* No. 74, January 1981; *SIGMOD Record,* Vol. 11, No. 2, February 1981; *SIGPLAN Notices,* Vol. 16, No. 1, January 1981.

[CODD79] Codd, E.F., "Extending the Database Relational Model to Capture More Meaning," *ACM Transactions on Database Systems,* Vol. 4, No. 4, December 1979, pp. 397-434; IBM Research Report RJ2599, San Jose, CA, August 1979.

[DAVI58] Davis, M., *Computability and Unsolvability,* McGraw-Hill, New York, 1958.

[DIJK76] Dijkstra, E.W., *A Discipline of Programming,* Prentice-Hall, Englewood Cliffs, NJ, 1976.

[GH78] Guttag, J.V. and J.J. Horning, "The Algebraic Specification of Abstract Data Types," *Acta Informatica,* Vol. 10, 1978, pp. 27-52.

[HM81] Hammer, M. and D. McLeod, "Database Description with SDM: A Semantic Database Model," *ACM Transactions on Database Systems,* Vol. 6. No. 3, September 1981.

[LMW79] Linger, R.C., H.D. Mills and B.I. Witt, *Structured Programming Theory and Practice,* Addision-Wesley, Reading, MA, 1979.

[MBW78] Mylopoulos, J., P.A. Bernstein and H.K.T. Wong "A Preliminary Specification for TAXIS," Technical Report CCA-78-02, Computer Corporation of America, Cambridge, MA, January 1978.

[MS81] McLeod, D. and J.M. Smith, "Abstraction in Databases," in [BZ81].

[OSV82] Olle, T.W., H.G. Sol and A.A. Verjn-Stuart, "Information Systems Design Methodologies: A Comparative Review," *Proc. IFIP TC 8 Working Conference on Comparative Review of Information Systems Design Methodologies,* Noordwijkerhout, Netherlands, May 1982, Elsevier North-Holland, Amsterdam, The Netherlands, 1982.

[RB82a] Ridjanovic, D. and M.L. Brodie, "Semantic Data Model-Driven Design, Specification and Verification of Interactive Database Transactions," Computer Corporation of America, Cambridge, MA, April 1982.

[RB82b] Ridjanovic, D. and M.L. Brodie, "Defining Database Dynamics with Attribute Grammars," *Information Processing Letters,* Vol. 14, No. 3, May 1982.

[RB82c] Ridjanovic, D. and M.L. Brodie, "Definition of Fundamental Concepts and Tools for Semantic Modelling of Data and Associated Operations," submitted for publication.

[RB82d] Ridjanovic, D. and M.L. Brodie, "Disciplined Methodology for Database Transaction Design," submitted for publication.

[RB82e] Ridjanovic, D. and M.L. Brodie, "Functional Specification and Implementation Verification of Database Transactions," submitted for publication.

[RB82f] Ridjanovic, D. and M.L. Brodie, "Conceptual Modelling of Office Procedures," submitted for publication.

[RB83] Ridjanovic, D. and M.L. Brodie, "Action and Transaction Skeletons: High Level Language Constructs for Database Transactions," *Proc. 1983 SIGPLAN Conference,* San Francisco, CA, June 1983.

[SCHM77] Schmidt, J.W., "Some High Level Language Constructs for Data of Type Relation," *ACM Transactions on Database Systems,* Vol. 2, No. 3, September 1977.

[SUNA78] Sunagren, B., "Database Design in Theory and Practice," *Proc. 4th International Conference on Very Large Database,* West Berlin, September 1978.

[WB81] Wirsing, M. and M. Broy, "An Analysis of Semantic Models for Algebraic Specifications," *International Summer School on the Theoretical Foundations of Programming Methodology,* Marktoberdorf, 1981.

[WIRS82] Wirsing, M., "Structured Algebraic Specifications," *Proc. AFCET Symposium for Computer Science,* Paris, France, March 1982.

[WPPD83] Wirsing, M., P. Pepper, H. Partsch, W. Dosch and M. Broy, "On Hierarchies of Abstract Data Types," *Acta Informatica,* 1983.

An Overview of the KL-ONE Knowledge Representation System*

RONALD J. BRACHMAN
Schlumberger Palo Alto Research

JAMES G. SCHMOLZE
BBN Laboratories Inc.

KL-ONE is a system for representing knowledge in Artificial Intelligence programs. It has been developed and refined over a long period and has been used in both basic research and implemented knowledge-based systems in a number of places in the AI community. Here we present the kernel ideas of KL-ONE, emphasizing its ability to form complex structured descriptions. In addition to detailing all of KL-ONE's description-forming structures, we discuss a bit of the philosophy underlying the system, highlight notions of taxonomy and classification that are central to it, and include an extended example of the use of KL-ONE and its classifier in a recognition task.

1. INTRODUCTION

KL-ONE is a system for representing knowledge in Artificial Intelligence programs, more or less in the tradition of semantic networks and frames. Literally speaking, KL-ONE (a k a KLONE) is an implementation of some ideas about the structure of descriptions and their use in reasoning, a computational incarnation of what have been called *structured inheritance networks* (or *SI-Nets,* see Brachman, 1978, in press, b).[1] But its utility has gone well beyond that of an implementation.

KL-ONE first appeared in 1977 as the initial implementation of a representational paradigm described in the first author's Ph.D. dissertation (Brachman, 1978, in press, b). The original work developed a level of representation that was independent of any particular domain, but whose primitives were more explicitly geared to the task of AI knowledge representation than those of predicate logic.[2] This level of representation—for better or worse called the ''epistemological level''—tried to deal carefully with ideas of ''description,'' ''attribute,'' ''concept,'' ''role,'' ''inheritance,'' and ''instantiation,'' which were treated in a somewhat informal manner in previous representation systems. In that regard, the work owes much to Woods (1975) and Brachman (1977), which criticized various inconsistencies and ambiguities in semantic network systems.[3]

KL-ONE was originally used in two systems at Bolt Beranek and Newman Inc.: a system for intelligent information presentation (Zdybel, Greenfeld, Yonke, & Gibbons, 1981) and a large prototype natural language understanding system (Brachman et al., 1979; Sidner, Bates, Bobrow, Brachman, Cohen, Webber, & Woods, 1981). In these two contexts, KL-ONE provided a useful set of primitives for forming descriptions of the objects of the domain, as well as an inference mechanism for deriving the consequences of the use of descriptions in particular situations (see the Appendix for an example of KL-ONE's utility in the natural language system). Since then, the representation system has grown, its representational facilities have matured, and its user community has expanded. It has inspired several new research efforts.[4] Its research community has had three workshops (see, for instance, Schmolze & Brachman, 1982), and KL-ONE has

* The history of the ideas in KL-ONE is too complex to recount here, and the number of contributors to this whole area of work makes it inevitable that we will forget to mention many who deserve to be acknowledged. At the very least, we would like to extend our thanks to these people, who have been intimately involved with KL-ONE, KL-TWO, and Krypton: Danny Bobrow, Rusty Bobrow, Phil Cohen, Richard Fikes, Mike Freeman, Jeff Gibbons, Victoria Gilbert, Brad Goodman, Norton Greenfeld, Austin Henderson, David Israel, Henry Leitner, Hector Levesque, Bob Lingard, Tom Lipkis, Bill Mark, Peter Patel-Schneider, Candy Sidner, Mark Stefik, Marc Vilain, David Wilczynski, Bill Woods, Martin Yonke, and Frank Zdybel.

This research was supported in part by the Defense Advanced Research Projects Agency under Contract N00014-77-C-0378. Views and conclusions contained in this paper are the authors' and should not be interpreted as representing the official opinion or policy of DARPA, the U.S. Government, or any person or agency connected with them.

Correspondence and requests for reprints should be sent to Ronald J. Brachman, AT&T, Bell Laboratories, 600 Mountain Avenue, Murray Hill, NJ 07974.

[1] KL-ONE has as an integral part a language for specifying descriptions and occasionally the name has been used to refer to just that language. However, the implementation comprises much more than the language; it includes facilities for building and saving KL-ONE networks, querying a network, etc. That is why ''system'' is probably the most appropriate descriptor for KL-ONE.

[2] The languages of mathematical logic were developed for the precise expression of mathematical propositions and the generation of their consequences using combinatorial rules of proof. See Israel (1984), especially section 4.2, for a detailed discussion on the appropriateness of logic as an AI knowledge representation language. Also, see Brachman, Fikes, and Levesque (1983) for a discussion of the role of logic vis-a-vis AI description languages.

[3] For an introduction to semantic networks, and a more detailed justification of the kind of representation exemplified by KL-ONE, see Brachman (1979). A brief recap is presented in section 2.1 of this paper.

[4] The first author is now working exclusively on one of these (Brachman et al., 1983), and the second author is working on a new implementation of KL-ONE (Moser, 1983).

been used in systems for understanding and generating natural language, interactive information retrieval, question-answering about system utilities and natural language command execution, computer system configuration, and office procedures modeling. KL-ONE has also influenced work in philosophy and psychology (Cohen, 1982; Rifkin, 1985).

With all of this, KL-ONE has achieved a status afforded to few efforts in the brief history of Artificial Intelligence: Over a significant period of time (at least eight years) and over a large number of projects, it has served as the foundation for some very basic research in knowledge representation (Brachman, 1983; Brachman, in press, a; Israel, 1983; Israel & Brachman, 1984), and at the same time has provided representational support in a number of implemented AI systems. Over its history, the language of KL-ONE has of course changed. However, throughout its many implementations (at least three in Interlisp as well as versions in SmallTalk (Fikes, 1982), PROLOG (Freeman, Hirschman, McKay, Miller, & Sidhu, 1983), SNePs (Tranchell, 1982), and GRASPER (Woolf, 1982), KL-ONE has maintained an unchanging central core of ideas and representational philosophy. It is probably this representational kernel that is responsible for the interest in, and longevity and utility of, KL-ONE, and it is this kernel of ideas to which we address ourselves in this paper.

In the KL-ONE kernel discussed here, we concentrate heavily on the static structure of and interrelations between descriptions. A great deal of the recent work on knowledge representation in AI has concentrated on the forms of representations, and the work on KL-ONE is no exception. Unfortunately, the representation forms developed do not wear their applicability on their sleeves (this is just as true of logic and English as representation languages as it is of KL-ONE or KRL). Throughout the text, we do mention inferences that follow from structuring a domain in a KL-ONE knowledge base and such automatic deductions are a central benefit of representing knowledge with KL-ONE. The only place, however, that we try to address a seriously complicated use of KL-ONE is in the Appendix.

2. LANGUAGE STRUCTURE AND PHILSOPHY

KL-ONE principally provides a language for the explicit representation of conceptual information based on the idea of *structured inheritance networks* (Brachman, 1978, 1979, in press, b). Before going into the details of KL-ONE structures, we will first sketch the philosophy underlying the development of the language.

KL-ONE is intended to represent general conceptual information and is typically used in the construction of the knowledge base of a single reasoning entity. A KL-ONE knowledge base can be thought of as representing the beliefs of the system using it. Thus KL-ONE fits squarely into the currently prevailing philosophy for building reasoning systems. This approach to knowledge-based systems is characterized by what Brian Smith (1982) calls the "knowledge representation hypothesis":

> Any mechanically embodied intelligent process will be comprised of structural ingredients that (a) we as external observers naturally take to represent a propositional account of the knowledge that the overall process exhibits, and (b) independent of such external semantical attribution, play a formal but causal and essential role in engendering the behavior that manifests that knowledge. (p. 2)

In other words, KL-ONE provides a language for expressing an *explicit set of beliefs* for a rational agent.[5]

KL-ONE aspires to a bipartite view of the knowledge-representation task. Over the course of its development, we began to tease out the distinction between KL-ONE constructs whose intent was primarily for elaborating descriptions and those whose intent was for making statements. In a sense, KL-ONE was beginning to divide into two different formalisms—one for *assertion* and one for *description*. These two parts would serve to represent the beliefs of the system and the terms out of which the belief sentences would be constructed, respectively.[6]

While KL-ONE never really split into formally distinct sublanguages, we often speak as if it had. The intent behind the different kinds of constructs is quite different. In particular, the descriptional part of KL-ONE allows one to form a variety of descriptive terms out of other descriptive terms using a small set of description-forming operators. This yields an extensible repertoire of terms—a conceptual vocabulary—that can be used to make assertions. For example, we can form a compound KL-ONE description corresponding to "a man from Betelgeuse" using the KL-ONE descriptions for "a man" and "Betelgeuse." However, simply forming this description asserts nothing about any particular man or star, as structures in the description language have no assertional import by themselves (but see section 4). The assertional part, on the other hand, makes use of terms from the description language to make statements about the world. The assertional capabilities in KL-ONE are somewhat impoverished as compared, say, to a first order language with equality; they include only statements of existence, of coreference of description, and of identity of individual constants (all in a particular context). For example, we might form a description like "the person giving the talk" and use it to assert that such a person exists (in say, context C1). We could then establish another description—say, "a man from Betelgeuse"—as coreferential with the first and thereby make the

[5] Such a set of beliefs expressed in some representation language is what is typically meant by the term *knowledge base*.

[6] This line of thought is more developed in Brachman et al. (1983); the separation between definition and assertion is one of the *raisons d'être* of the Krypton system.

statement (in C1), "the person giving the talk is a man from Betelgeuse." This latter type of construct—a predication—is a legitimate object of belief, whereas descriptions by themselves are not.

This paper describes the KL-ONE language and system as of the summer of 1982, which marks the end of a chapter of our work in knowledge representation. Until then, most of our work on KL-ONE had focused on description formation, with very little attention paid to making assertions (we felt that existing formalisms, such as predicate logic, were adequate for this task). Since that time, our thoughts about description formation have extended the work described herein, and we have begun to focus more intensively on the assertion language. This work has been taken up in the context of two new experimental representation systems, Krypton (Brachman et al., 1983) and KL-TWO (Moser, 1983).

2.1 Epistemological Primitives

KL-ONE is, in a sense, an "object-centered" language. Its development has proceeded from traditional semantic networks, but its principal structures do not directly represent either propositions or sets as did those of several earlier semantic net systems (e.g., see Hendrix, 1979, and Schubert, Goebel, & Cercone, 1979).[7] Instead, the principal element of KL-ONE is the *structured conceptual object,* or *Concept.*[8]

Our view of these objects comes from a careful analysis of early trends in semantic networks and more recent trends in knowledge representation in general. As discussed in Brachman (1979) and Woods (1975), the history of network representations is fraught with imprecision on the meanings of nodes and links. One can find links in networks being used to represent implementational pointers, logical relations, semantic relations (e.g., "cases"), and arbitrary conceptual and linguistic relations. Network schemes consistent with structures at any one of these "levels" (implementational, logical, conceptual, linguistic—see Brachman, 1979) can be compared and tested for adequacy, but unfortunately, most of the existing formalisms mix structures from two or more of these levels. This yields confusing notations and makes for great difficulty in explaining the interpreter for a semantic network system.

Bearing in mind the value of consistency at a single level of network primitive, we have set out to capture an adequate set of primitive elements for representing a broad spectrum of concepts. We have attempted to determine a reasonable set of underlying object and relation types for knowledge structuring. To the extent that we can formalize this in a grammar for well-formed conceptual structures, we have defined what might be called an "epistemology." This is not a theory of any particular domain—one builds that on top of this level—but part of a generative theory of the structure and limits of thought for a rational agent.[9] KL-ONE thus comprises a fixed set of "epistemologically primitive" structure types (e.g., "Concept," "Role") and structure-forming operations (e.g., "specialization," "restriction," "differentiation"). We have attempted to understand the important features of the internal structure of concepts, and to embody them in a language that is expressively powerful and fairly natural to use.

2.2 Primitive and Defined Concepts

KL-ONE separates its descriptions into two basic groups: *primitive*[10] and *defined.* When specifying domain knowledge in KL-ONE, one usually first specifies some primitive types, which are then typically followed by other types (either primitive or defined) that are specified in terms of them.

For example, if our domain were planar geometry, we might begin with POINT and LINE SEGMENT as atomic, primitive types; these would be represented in KL-ONE by *primitive Concepts.* We might also decide that the concept of a polygon was useful to represent, but while we had several necessary properties of polygons in hand, we did not want to attempt to characterize fully its necessary and sufficient conditions. In this case, POLYGON would also have to be a primitive Concept. However, KL-ONE allows primitive Concepts to have defined properties; that is, it treats primitive Concepts as incomplete definitions. This means that we could include in its specification the fact that a polygon—by definition—has three or more sides that are line segments. (Nonatomic but still primitive concepts are also discussed in Israel, 1983.)

Once given the POLYGON Concept, we could specify TRIANGLE as a *defined Concept* derived from it. Namely, a triangle is exactly a polygon

[7] "Object-centeredness" is a characteristic of many of the current representation systems. Its prominence seems to arise from the convenience of indexing knowledge through the entities that the knowledge is about, and the whole area of "object-oriented programming" has grown up in parallel. See Brachman (in press, section 4.2) and Nilsson (1980, section 9.1), for discussions of this feature.

[8] KL-ONE object types will be capitalized throughout this article.

[9] KL-ONE does not commit one to any particular domain primitives but rather provides a representational foundation out of which domain primitives can be specified. Generally speaking, a representer ("knowledge engineer" in some circles) selects his domain primitives with a particular set of useful inferences in mind. See Amarel (1968) for an example of how a change in domain-level primitives can help solve a problem.

KL-ONE also takes a strong stand on names. As has been pointed out (for instance, see Brachman, in press, a; Israel & Brachman, 1984; McDermott, 1982; and Woods, 1975), suggestive names can do more harm than good in semantic networks and other representation schemes. Atomic labels attached to nodes in KL-ONE are purely for user convenience and hold no significance for any KL-ONE functions.

[10] "Primitive" here refers to domain concepts for which we are incapable of giving full necessary and sufficient definitions. In the previous subsection, we discussed primitive objects and operations for the KL-ONE language.

with three sides. TRIANGLE becomes a new term in the description language, defined to be nothing more than "a polygon with exactly 3 sides," a definition that gives both necessary and sufficient conditions for being a triangle. Given a plane figure that is at least a polygon and has three sides (it may have other properties), the figure is a triangle simply on the basis of the meaning of the term. On the other hand, given the primitive specification for polygons, even an object satisfying the description would not be guaranteed to be a polygon. For example, a particular geometric figure with three sides that were line segments might not be a polygon—it might not be closed.

Although a primitive Concept does not provide sufficient conditions, it can specify a rich variety of necessary conditions. The notion of *natural kind terms* such as *dog* or *lemon,* may be related to this last point, because it is usually assumed that it is not possible to completely define such terms. Even so, it is probably important to allow elaboration of natural kind terms in KL-ONE, and some of this might be specified with necessary conditions. For example, *mammal* and *cat* are both natural kinds, and there is an important relationship between them that we might want to represent, namely, that cats are necessarily mammals (see Kripke, 1980, esp. pp. 122–128). KL-ONE allows a Concept for cats to be specified that includes that relationship.

Another important type of knowledge about natural kinds and other real-world categories is default or typicality information. KL-ONE as yet does not address this directly, although we do comment on it in section 7.

3. NETWORKS AND THE NOTION OF A CLASSIFIER

As mentioned earlier, KL-ONE is based on the idea of *structured inheritance networks.* What this amounts to is that it is convenient to think of a KL-ONE knowledge base as a type of semantic network with a roughly hierarchical organization of general types (called *Generic Concepts*). The "structured inheritance" aspect refers to the fact that an implementation must preserve a complex set of relations between description parts as one moves down the specialization hierarchy; the details of this will become evident later.

In KL-ONE the network implementation follows from the structure of the description language. That there is a type hierarchy as the backbone of a KL-ONE knowledge base is derived from the fact that KL-ONE descriptions are always formed from other, more general KL-ONE descriptions. The specialization relations implicit in these compound descriptions (e.g., to move rather abruptly to the domain of electronic mail, "message from AAAI-OFFICE@SUMEX" is a compound description that implicitly specializes "message") are naturally envisioned in a directed graph structure. While it is easy to think of KL-ONE structures in terms of nodes and links, this is only an incidental byproduct of the relations implicit in the language of Concepts and Roles.

Given two KL-ONE descriptions, an important question to consider is whether one *subsumes* the other—that is, whether an instance of one is always an instance of the other. In semantic nets, this question usually comes down to looking from one node up the hierarchy to see if another happens to lie on a superset path. In KL-ONE, the subsumption question can also be answered by looking up a hierarchy, with one crucial difference. Because the network is simply a byproduct of the structure of terms in the language (the network is not itself the language), not all network-derived subsumption inferences are valid unless the hierarchy completely reflects all of the relations implicit in the descriptions in question. In other words, the descriptions must be in their proper places in the network before any conclusions can be drawn.

This gives rise to the notion of a *classifier* (Schmolze & Lipkis, 1983), which is a mechanism for taking a new KL-ONE description and putting it where it belongs in the hierarchy. It is in the right place if it is below all descriptions that subsume it, and if it is above all descriptions that it subsumes.[11] Classification provides an important inference capability to a system using KL-ONE, and a detailed example of its use appears in the Appendix.

All in all, then, KL-ONE knowledge bases have a network flavor, with the links standing for what we have called the "epistemologically primitive" relations among concepts. The network is a reflection of the implicit subsumption (and other) relations among the descriptions that its nodes stand for.

4. GENERIC CONCEPTS AND BASIC TAXONOMY

As mentioned, the principal elements of KL-ONE descriptions are Concepts, of which there are several types. The most important type is the *Generic Concept,* the KL-ONE equivalent of a "general term" (Quine, 1960)—potentially many individuals in any possible world can be described by it. For example, a KL-ONE knowledge base might have Generic Concepts for

[11] There are differences in philosophy on computing subsumption in different KL-ONE-based systems. In Krypton (Brachman et al., 1983), the subsumption relation is computed directly from the descriptions, and is only stored in a network for later computational convenience. In KL-ONE, the network is computed first from the forms of descriptions, and subsumption questions are always read off from the hierarchy. In either case, it is important to have a means of computing subsumption independent from a simple network lookup. This independent means of determining subsumption makes soundness an important property of KL-ONE, as opposed to many other semantic network systems, whose only semantics is "what the interpreter does."

animal, mammal, human, female human, woman, etc., each of which are descriptions that could be used to describe many individuals in the world.

In fact, as already hinted, some of these Generic Concepts may be formed out of the others (the Generic Concept *HUMAN* would have *MAMMAL* as a component, for example[12]). There are several structure-forming operations available for building Concepts,[13] which bring together one or more general Concepts and a set of restrictions on those Concepts. More specifically, the components of a Concept are

- its subsuming Concepts (its *superConcepts*).
- and its local internal structure expressed in
  - *Roles,* which describe potential relationships between instances of the Concept and those of other closely associated Concepts (i.e., its properties, parts, etc.), and
  - *Structural Descriptions,* which express the interrelations among the Roles.

To be well-formed, a KL-ONE Concept must have more than one superConcept (if there are no local restrictions), differ from its superConcept in at least one restriction, or be primitive. A Concept with no local restrictions is defined as the conjunction of its superConcepts.

The Roles and Structural Descriptions of a Concept are taken as a set of restrictions applied to its superConcepts. Thus, a superConcept serves as a proximate genus, whereas the local internal structure expresses essential differences, as in classical classificatory definition (Sellars, 1917). It should be noted that its superConcepts and set of restrictions are the only KL-ONE structures that contribute to the meaning of a Concept.

As mentioned in section 3, when one specifies a Concept like *HUMAN* in terms of one like *MAMMAL,* one is implicitly specifying that the more general subsumes the more specific. Subsumption of descriptions has the following consequence: If Concept *A* subsumes Concept *B,* then every individual that can be described by *B* can also be described by *A*.[14] So, by specifying the Concept *HUMAN* such that the Concept *MAMMAL* subsumes it—in other words, so that the property of being a human includes the property of being a mammal—one is specifying that any human must be a mammal.

[12] We will use upper-case, italic letters when writing the names of Generic Concepts, which KL-ONE allows one to specify for convenience. The names carry no meaning for the system.

[13] From this point on, we will use "Concept" to mean "Generic Concept," except when "Concept" alone would be ambiguous.

[14] More precisely, *A* subsumes *B* if, and only if, in all possible interpretations, the extension of *A* is a superset of the extension *B*. We have specified a formal extensional semantics for at least part of KL-ONE (see Schmolze & Israel, 1983).

We often refer to the network structure formed by the subsumption relationships between Concepts as a "taxonomy." Whereas a Concept like *WOMAN* might be subsumed by all of *THING, ANIMAL, HUMAN,* and *FEMALE-ANIMAL,* the taxonomy usually indicates only the direct subsumption relations. Because this relation is transitive, the relation between *WOMAN* and, say, *ANIMAL* can still be read off of the network. This is typical of semantic network taxonomies, and makes the notation more readable.

For example, the simple taxonomy of Figure 1 shows for each Concept only the proximate genus. Each ellipse represents a Generic Concept; the subsumption relation is denoted by a *superC* link, which is depicted by a wide arrow. The superC link is sometimes called a superC *cable* because, as we will see, other links may be associated with it.

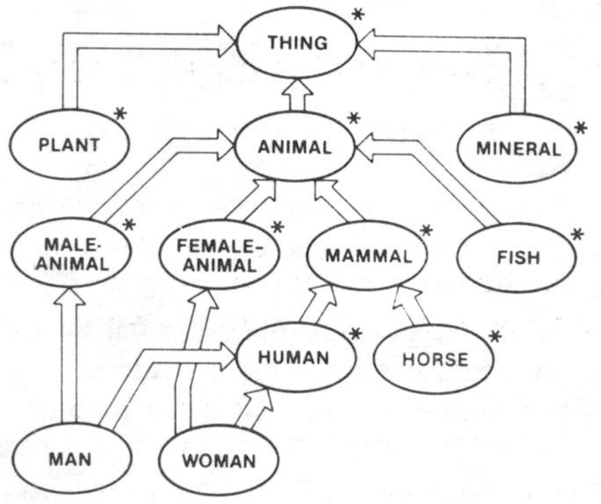

Figure 1. A simple KL-ONE network of Generic Concepts.

In using a compact notation for Concepts, wherein only "local" information is indicated, we must be careful not to neglect certain inferences that are dictated by the meaning of the subsumption relation. First, as mentioned, a Generic Concept actually subsumes all Generic Concepts below it, either immediately, or otherwise.[15] Also, because a Concept is defined in terms of its superConcepts, all of the restrictions (the essential differences) of the parents must apply to the children. In order to achieve this effect, the KL-ONE system provides *inheritance* facilities. Regarding our example, all component restrictions of the Concept *MAMMAL* would be inherited by *HUMAN* (see the sections on Roles and Structural Descriptions for the exact specification of these restrictions). So, if the Concept *MAMMAL* included components that meant that mammals were warm-blooded animals, the Concept *HUMAN* would inherit those same components.

[15] From this point on, the notions of "above" and "below" will be used interchangeably with "subsumer" and "subsumee," respectively.

Figure 1 illustrates some other points about KL-ONE networks. For one thing, KL-ONE taxonomies always have a single root Concept, usually named *THING*. *THING* subsumes all other Concepts and is the only one that has no superConcepts. For another, as we discussed in section 2.2, some Concepts are fully defined by their components and some are not. In Figure 1, the Concepts with an asterisk are primitive, the others are defined.

You may also note in Figure 1 that a Generic Concept can have many superConcepts as well as subConcepts. The Concept *WOMAN* has both *FEMALE-ANIMAL* and *HUMAN* as its superConcepts. Hence, both *FEMALE-ANIMAL* and *HUMAN* subsume *WOMAN*. The Concept *WOMAN* in this case is defined to be just the conjunction of the two.

Finally, it is important to reiterate that a Concept like *MAMMAL* does not derive any of its meaning from the Concept *HUMAN*. A Concept's meaning is strictly determined by its subsuming Concepts plus the information associated specifically with the Concept.[16]

5. ROLES, RESTRICTION, AND DIFFERENTIATION

The Role is the primary component of a Concept. A Role acts like a generalized attribute description, representing potential relationships between individuals of the type denoted by the Concept and other individuals. In other words, Roles are the KL-ONE equivalent of two-place predicates.

KL-ONE distinguishes Roles from their fillers. The difference is motivated essentially by the "attributive/referential" distinction in the philosophy of language (Donnellan, 1966). Imagine a situation in which an alligator's tail has fallen off. We might remark, "The alligator's tail lay wriggling on the ground." Or, we might say something like, "Don't worry, the alligator's tail will grow back again." The "tails" talked about must be different in the two cases—in the first, we are referring to the previous filler, the actual piece of protoplasm that used to be the alligator's tail. In the second, because the previous tail will not reattach itself to the alligator, we must mean something else by "alligator's tail." We are in fact talking in a general way about anything that will eventually play the role of "tail" for the alligator. KL-ONE lets us distinguish statements about an actual known role filler and a potential one by providing an explicit structure for the description of potential fillers, the Role.

[16] There has been considerable discussion among KL-ONE users as to whether or not KL-ONE should be able to represent exhaustion or mutual exclusion among a Concept's subsumees. If it did, then a Concept could possibly gather part of its definition from those it subsumes, in the case of exhaustion, or "sibling" Concepts (Concepts that share the same subsuming Concept), in the case of mutual exclusion. However, KL-ONE does not support either, although KL-TWO (Moser, 1983) does. Krypton (Brachman et al., 1983) allows mutually exclusive terms to be defined.

There are several different types of Roles of which the Generic RoleSet is the most important. RoleSets (in general, used to mean Generic RoleSet) capture the notion that a given functional role of a Concept (e.g., sender of a message, upright of an arch, officer of a company, input to a program) can be played by several different entities for just one individual. A RoleSet captures the commonality among a set of individual role players (e.g., what all officers of a given company will have in common by definition).

A pictorial representation of a Concept of a message is shown in Figure 2, where *MESSAGE* represents a simple type of electronic message. Here, we see that *MESSAGE* has *THING* as a subsumer (because this is true of all Concepts, *THING* will not appear in any other figures). Each of the encircled squares depicts a Generic RoleSet, of which *MESSAGE* has five. (For convenience, KL-ONE allows Roles to be named, and in this paper we have named all Roles after the relations they represent. Role names appear in the text as italicized, capitalized words.) The RoleSets in the figure are connected to *MESSAGE* by unnamed links that merely denote that the RoleSets are components of *MESSAGE* (we sometimes call the link "has-role").

The quoted sentence at the bottom of Figure 2 is a JARGON statement specifying the Concept. JARGON is a stylized, restricted, Englishlike language for describing KL-ONE objects and relationships. It has two important properties: It is usually easier for a novice to understand a JARGON statement than its equivalent in the graphical notation, and an interpreter exists that can translate most JARGON statements into appropriate KL-ONE structures.[17]

RoleSets themselves have structure. Descriptions of potential fillers are specified with a *Value Restriction (V/R)*. In Figure 2 we see that the RoleSet *Sender* has a Value Restriction of *PERSON*. The system interprets Value Restrictions as *necessary* type restrictions on RoleSet fillers, and so the senders of messages must be persons. No cancellation of Value Restrictions is allowed (for example, in this ontology, senders of *any* subtype of message must be persons—see section 7). Cases arise where several Value Restrictions are applicable to a RoleSet filler (these cases will be apparent as the inheritance mechanism is explained). If more than one V/R is applicable at a given RoleSet, the restrictions are taken conjunctively.

Because the functional roles defined by RoleSets can be played by more than one individual at a time, RoleSets also have *Number Restrictions* to express cardinality information. A Number Restriction is a pair of numbers, a lower and upper bound, defining the range of cardinalities for sets of role-player descriptions. We use "NIL" for infinity in cases where there is

[17] We have taken some liberties with JARGON in our figure captions to improve readability. For the complete story on what JARGON actually can do, see Woods (1979).

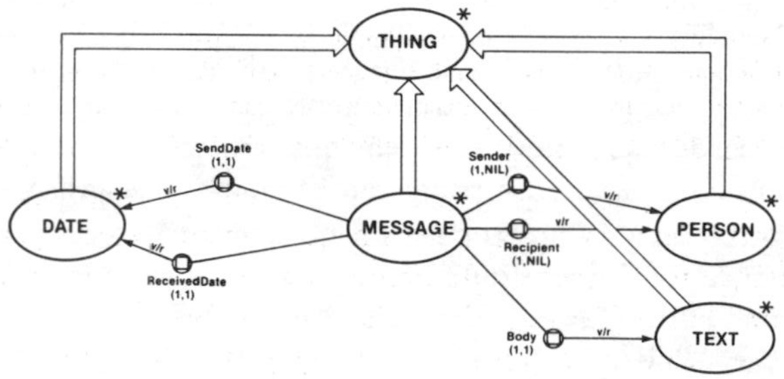

"A MESSAGE is, among other things, a THING with at least one Sender, all of which are PERSONs, at lease one Recipient, all of which are PERSONs, a Body, which is a TEXT, a SendDate, which is a DATE, and a ReceivedDate, which is a DATE."

Figure 2. The Primitive Concept *MESSAGE*.

no finite upper bound. Thus the Number Restrictions in Figure 2 (written in parentheses near the RoleSets) indicate that any *MESSAGE* has at least one *Sender,* at least one *Recipient,* exactly one *Body,* exactly one *SendDate,* and exactly one *ReceivedDate.*

5.1. RoleSet Restriction

In section 4 we defined the subsumption relation between Concepts, which reflects how one Concept can be specified in terms of another. The *restriction* relation[18] between Role Sets allows a similar specification, but with respect to the components of a RoleSet. In Figure 3, we have shown the Concept *STARFLEET-MESSAGE,* which represents messages sent by Starfleet commanders. There is a link labeled "restricts" from the RoleSet on the lower Concept to *Sender,* which means that this lower RoleSet denotes a subset of the relation denoted by *Sender,* and in this case, that subset is restricted to senders who are Starfleet commanders.

We define restriction with the following: If Concept *A* with RoleSet *Ra* subsumes Concept *B,* and if RoleSet *Rb* of *B* restricts *Ra,* then every set of fillers of *Rb* satisfies all restrictions on *both Ra* and *Rb.* Moreover, *Ra* and *Rb* designate the same two-place relation.

Restriction does not specify a new Role, rather it adds constraints on the fillers of a Role with respect to some Concept. These constraints include those specified by both Value Restrictions and Number Restrictions, such as in Figure 4. For a *MESSAGE* to be a *PRIVATE-MESSAGE,* it must have

[18] For most of KL-ONE's history, this has been called "modification," but "restriction" is more appropriate.

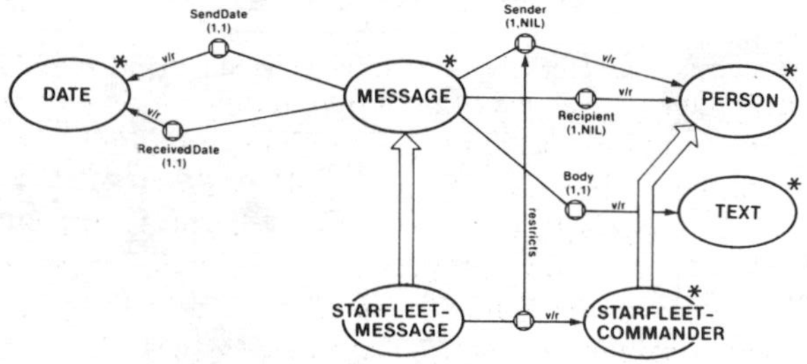

"A STARFLEET-MESSAGE is a MESSAGE, all of whose Senders are STARFLEET-COMMANDERS."

Figure 3. A Defined Concept that uses Role restriction.

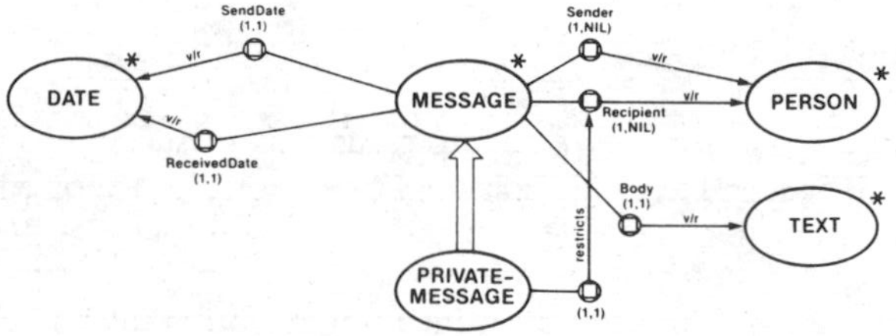

"A PRIVATE-MESSAGE is a MESSAGE with exactly one Recipient."

Figure 4. Another Defined Concept that uses restriction.

exactly one *Recipient.* Our graphical notation unfortunately does not distinguish newly introduced RoleSets (such as *Recipient* for *MESSAGE*) from already inherited RoleSets whose components are just being further restricted (such as *Recipient* for *PRIVATE-MESSAGE*). The only way to tell them apart is that the latter have "restricts" links pointing away from them. By convention, restricted RoleSets inherit the names of the RoleSets they restrict, so in Figure 4 the restricting RoleSet inherits the name "Recipient."

The figures in this paper emphasize the local Concept-forming operations and thus do not usually include the inherited components of a Concept. However, it should be kept in mind that the meaning of a Concept includes not only its local restrictions, but its inherited components as well. Just for reference, Figure 5 illustrates the "true" picture of the Concept *PRIVATE-MESSAGE.* It shows the Concept with all of its components. Note that when queried, the KL-ONE implementation provides inherited information about a Concept or Role, thus performing an important kind of inference at retrieval time. If one tried to draw a picture of *PRIVATE-MESSAGE* solely from the results of querying the system about the components of a *PRIVATE-MESSAGE,* the result would be as in Figure 5.

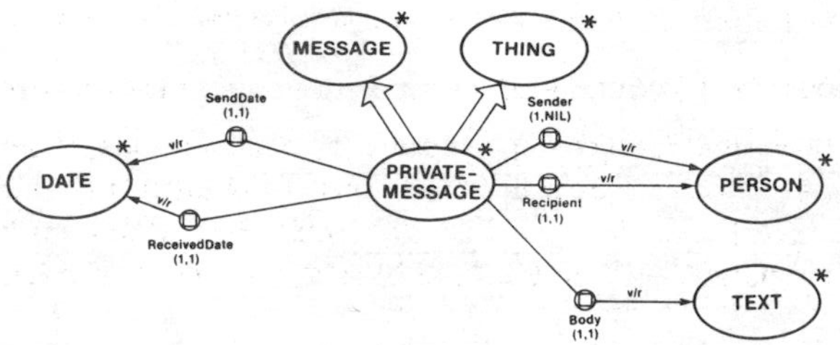

Figure 5. A depiction of all inherited components of a Concept.

5.2. RoleSet Differentiation

RoleSet *differentiation* is one of KL-ONE's unique features. A RoleSet differentiates another when the former denotes a subrelation of the relation denoted by the latter. The motivation for differentiation comes from the fact that KL-ONE Roles are intrinsically set descriptions, with potentially many fillers for a given Role; differentiation allows the specification of subRoles that are to be filled with subsets of the fillers of the Roles they differentiate. For example, one might want to differentiate the *Officer* Role of *COMPANY* into *President, Vice President,* etc. KL-ONE allows definitional knowledge common to all types of officers to be associated with the *Officer* Role, and that specific to president, etc., to be associated with the subRoles of *officer*. Further, a differentiation relation between *President* and *Officer* specifies that any president of a company is, by definition, an officer of that company.

Figure 6 demonstrates differentiation with the Concept *CC-MESSAGE,* which splits the *Recipient* RoleSet of *MESSAGE* into two parts, *To-Recipient* and *CC-Recipient*. Many electronic mail facilities allow the separation of recipients of messages into two categories: those to whom the message is primarily addressed (the fillers of the *To-Recipient* RoleSet), and those who should receive the electronic equivalent of a carbon copy (the fillers of the *CC-Recipient* RoleSet). Differentiation lets one specify that the *To-Recipient* is indeed a *Recipient,* and that this is a necessary condition.

The behavior of differentiating RoleSets (e.g., *To-Recipient* in the figure) with respect to Value Restrictions is the same as in the case of Role restriction. A subRoleSet inherits the Value Restriction of the RoleSet it differentiates. When specifying a subRoleSet, one may also specify additional constraints for the Value Restriction. In such cases, both the inherited Value Restriction and the locally specified one must apply (i.e., their conjunction must apply). On the other hand, Number Restriction inheritance works a little differently than in the case of restriction. Because the essence of differentiation is the specification of a subset, only the maximum can be inherited.

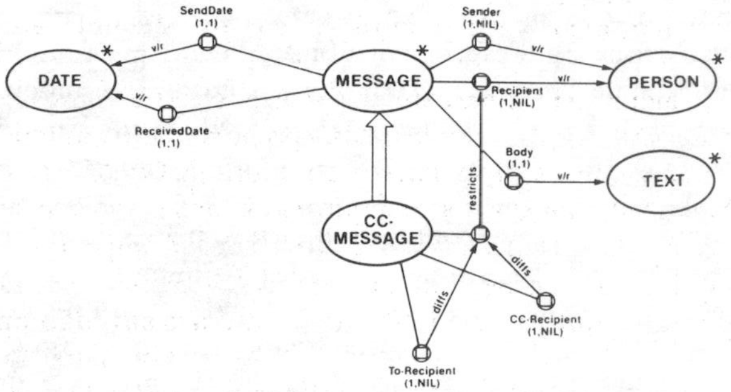

"A CC-MESSAGE is a MESSAGE, at least one of whose Recipients is a To-Recipient, and at least one of whose Recipients is a CC-Recipient."

Figure 6. A Concept that uses RoleSet differentiation.

If no minimum is specified at the subRole, the minimum is taken to be 1 (not the minimum of the parent). Note that a differentiating RoleSet also inherits the name(s) of the RoleSet it differentiates. This is approriate since by definition all fillers of the subRoleSet are also fillers of the parent (a to-recipient is also a recipient).

It is important to note that the information associated with a differentiating RoleSet specifies necessary conditions, but not sufficient ones. In this regard, the relation denoted by such RoleSets can be thought of as primitive. For our *CC-MESSAGE* Concept, we have not specified precisely under what conditions a Recipient is either a *To-Recipient* of a *CC-Recipient* or neither.[19]

We can define RoleSet differentiation a little more formally with the following:

> If RoleSet *Rb* differentiates RoleSet *Ra,* then any pair of individuals that satisfy the relation denoted by *Rb* also satisfy the relation denoted by *Ra*. Furthermore, all individuals in the range of the relation denoted by *Rb* satisfy the Value Restrictions of both *Ra* and *Rb*. The maximum (cardinality of the image of the relation for any individual in the domain) specified in the Number Restriction of *Ra* is also the maximum for *Rb,* unless a smaller maximum is specified directly at *Rb*. The minimum for *Rb* is 1, unless a larger minimum is specified directly at *Rb*.

Both restricting RoleSets and differentiating RoleSets can themselves be restricted and/or differentiated (for differentiation, as long as the maxi-

[19] The Structural Description mechanism, which will be covered briefly later, was designed to provide the missing part of the definitions of Roles. While interesting work is proceeding using special cases of SDs (see, for example, Freeman & Tomlinson, 1982; Freeman, Hirschman, McKay, & Palmer, 1983), the details of the Role-defining mechanism have not yet been worked out satisfactorily.

mum is greater than 1) in the specification of other Concepts. Thus, except for the subtlety about Number Restrictions, differentiation between RoleSets is similar to subsumption between Concepts. KL-ONE actually supports a *Role taxonomy* akin to its basic Concept taxonomy.

At this point, we have described enough of KL-ONE to explain the classifier. We will continue with the remainder of the KL-ONE syntax immediately thereafter.

6. CLASSIFICATION OF KL-ONE CONCEPTS

The classifier takes a newly specified Concept and determines the subsumption relations between it and all other Concepts in a given network. In some cases subsumption is specified directly, as in Figure 3, where *MESSAGE* was specified as *STARFLEET-MESSAGE's* subsumer. Indirectly, this also implies other cases of subsumption due to transitivity—e.g., in the same figure all subsumers of *MESSAGE* also subsume *STARFLEET-MESSAGE* (in this case only *THING*). However, classification also discovers cases of subsumption not readable from the Concept specification by simple means, and in such cases, the classifier adds the appropriate superC links.

An example of the classifier discovering a subsumption relation is shown in Figures 7 and 8. In Figure 7, we specify Concept *X* as "a *MESSAGE* with exactly one *Recipient* and whose *Sender* is a *STARFLEET-COMMANDER*." This specification does not make transparent the fact that *STARFLEET-MESSAGE* subsumes *X*, but the classifier will discover that relation and add a superC link (as shown in Figure 8).[20]

The classifier takes all components of a Concept's specification into account (only some of which have been described so far). We have shown informally (though not here) that the classifier's algorithm is sound, i.e., any subsumption relations discovered by the classifier are legitimate, but not complete, i.e., it does not discover all subsumption relations.[21] While no formal specification of its incompleteness has been made, the cases missed by the classifier have not proven problematic in applications of KL-ONE to date.

The effect of the classifier is to automate the placement of new Concepts into a KL-ONE taxonomy. The proper place for a Concept is above those Concepts it subsumes (its subsumees) and below those that subsume it (its subsumers). Not only does this simplify the task of creating static knowledge bases (because the system takes some of the work out of the user's hands), it supports dynamic creation of descriptions (Concepts) during the execution of some task.

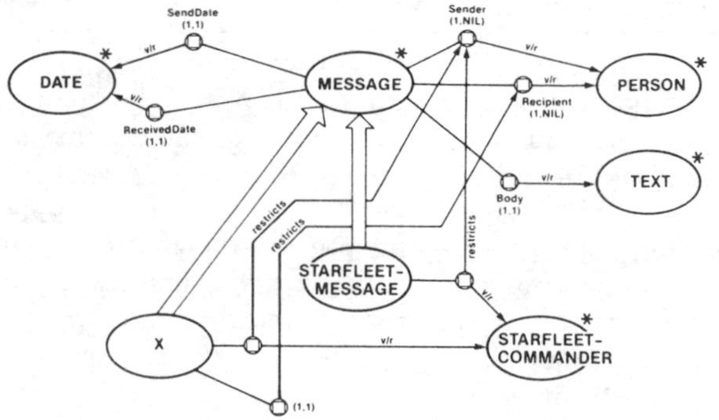

"A MESSAGE with exactly one Recipient, and all of whose Senders are STARFLEET-COMMANDERs."

Figure 7. Before classifying the Concept X.

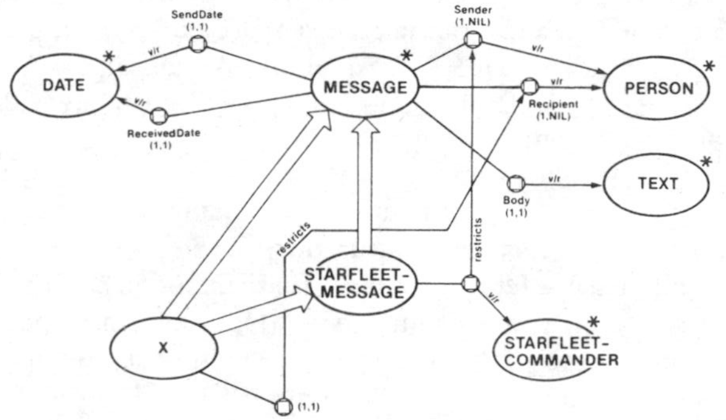

Figure 8. After classifying Concept X.

In addition, the classifier performs a class of inferences that has been found to be very useful for several AI applications. A typical use of KL-ONE is the following. First, a static knowledge base is created that contains general information. Then, a reasoning task is begun that creates many new descriptions as representations of partial results. These descriptions are classified, and the discovered subsumers and/or subsumees are used to continue the reasoning process. The Appendix treats an example of this in some depth.

An important use of the classifier is for generalized search. If one forms a search pattern into a Concept (call it *PATTERN*), classification will

[20] The classifier will also discover that *X* is a *PRIVATE-MESSAGE*, although this is not shown in Figure 8.

[21] The issues of soundness and completeness for the KL-ONE classifier are addressed in Schmolze and Lipkis (1983). Krypton (Brachman et al., 1983) opts for a simpler language in order to guarantee completeness for the subsumption algorithm.

discover other Concepts that *PATTERN* subsumes. If the target of the search is also described by some Concept (call it *TARGET*), and if the pattern matches the target, then *PATTERN* will subsume *TARGET*. Hence, the first phase of a search process can be accomplished by using classification to restrict the search-space of possible target descriptions.

The classifier is an important contribution of KL-ONE, and we will demonstrate its utility with an extended example in the Appendix. The classifier's algorithm will not be described in this paper (but see Lipkis & Mark, 1981; Schmolze & Israel, 1983; Schmolze & Lipkis, 1983).

7. A NOTE ON DEFAULT VALUES AND CANCELLATION

As has been stated throughout this paper, all components of a Concept specify (at least) necessary conditions for individuals that the Concept can describe. This also applies to components that a Concept inherits from its subsumers. Thus, it would be inappropriate to "cancel" an inherited component and KL-ONE does not allow any such cancellation.

The lack of cancellation of Value Restrictions might appear problematic from the point of view of representing "exceptions" (e.g., three-legged elephants—see Fahlman, 1979). However, if we were to allow cancellation of components within Concepts, then these components would be reduced in status from necessary conditions to default assertions. We feel that such nonnecessary conditions are more appropriately expressed outside of the taxonomy. Furthermore, cancellation would derail the classifier. For example, the classifier would have its hands tied if Roles expressed defaults: A given Concept could be forced to fit almost anywhere, because all we would need to do is cancel the Roles that don't match up. In this way, *THREE-LEGGED-ELEPHANT* could just as well subsume *FOUR-LEGGED-ELEPHANT* as be subsumed by it. See Brachman (in press, a) for more about this problem.

We intend, instead, to allow statements of default rules *between Concepts* only. Thus (when implemented), one would *not* represent elephants' typically having four legs as in Figure 9. Instead, one would assert something like

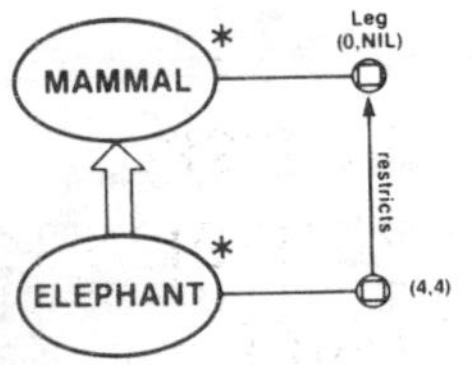

Figure 9. Not the way to describe elephants.

$$\frac{\text{Elephant}(x) : \text{M}[\text{Four-legged-mammal}(x)]}{\text{Four-legged-mammal}(x)}$$

in the manner of Reiter (1980). That is, "unless you have information to the contrary, assume of an elephant that it is also a four-legged-mammal." This leaves the Concepts of *ELEPHANT* and *FOUR-LEGGED-MAMMAL* distinct (as they should be) and inviolate. KL-ONE seems to be different from many of today's representation languages precisely because of its reliance upon necessary conditions rather than default assertions.

8. INDIVIDUAL CONCEPTS

KL-ONE provides structures that are suitable for uniquely describing individuals. The primary unit for individual description is the *Individual Concept*, which is similar to the Generic Concept but can be used to describe at most one individual in a particular context. As with Generic Concepts, nothing is asserted about any particular individual when an Individual Concept is formed. Actual use of Concepts to make statements is the responsibility of the assertion language (section 10).

Each Individual Concept must individuate some Generic Concept, as does *MESSAGE.1* in Figure 10 (shaded ellipses in the Figure denote Individual Concepts, shaded arrows denote the *Individuates* link). The Individual Concept carries the same meaning as the Generic Concept it individuates, together with the fact that there can be at most one individual described by it per context (i.e., if there are two individuals, x and y, such that an Individual Concept describes both x and y; then $x=y$).

An Individual Concept also has associated Role descriptions that serve to describe the actual individual fillers of the Roles inherited from its parent Concept. There are two kinds of Roles that can be components of Individual Concepts: *IRoles* and *Particular RoleSets*. An IRole represents the binding of two individuals together in a relation. The relation is the one denoted by the parent RoleSet of the IRole (IRoles are always descended from Generic RoleSets). The two individuals are the one represented by the Individual Concept and the one that is described as filling the IRole. IRoles are the way to instantiate with arguments the two-place relations represented by RoleSets. For example, in Figure 10, there is an IRole (depicted as a filled-in square) that corresponds to the *Sender* RoleSet of *MESSAGE*. The link connecting the two is called the "satisfies" link. The other labeled link emanating from the IRole is called "val," and it leads to a description of the sender of *MESSAGE.1*. (The unlabeled link connecting the Individual Concept to the IRole is the "has Role" link.) Thus, if some individual is

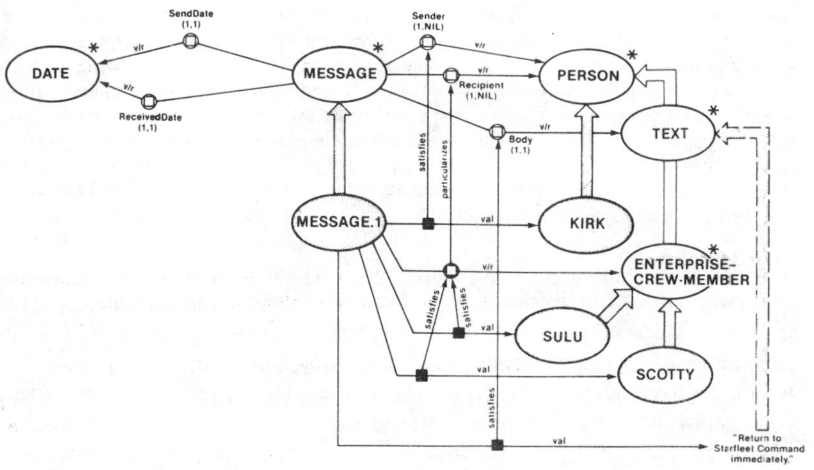

"The MESSAGE with a Sender that is KIRK, a Body that is "Return to Starfleet Command immediately.", whose Recipients are all ENTERPRISE-CREW-MEMBERs, one of which is SULU, and one of which is SCOTTY."

Figure 10. An Individual Concept.

described by *MESSAGE.1,* its *Sender* will be described by the Individual Concept *KIRK*. *KIRK* is simply an individual *PERSON* about which (for simplicity) we offer no further information.

A Particular RoleSet is to an Individual Concept just as a Generic RoleSet that restricts a parent RoleSet is to a Generic Concept. It represents the set of fillers of the Role for the particular individual rather than some generic set of fillers. It has associated further restrictions upon fillers of the relation it represents, just as the Generic RoleSet does. These restrictions constrain all fillers of the Role and are taken conjunctively with restrictions inherited from the parent Role. For example, in Figure 10, a Particular RoleSet of *MESSAGE.1* further restricts the *Recipient* RoleSet of *MESSAGE* by adding a new Value Restriction—*ENTERPRISE-CREW-MEMBER*. For this *MESSAGE.1,* there are at least two recipients, one of which is described by *SCOTTY*, and one by *SULU.* Note that the IRoles, specifying these particular bindings, are descended from the Particular RoleSet and that there is exactly one for each filler (IRoles intrinsically have cardinality 1, whereas Particular RoleSets are like other RoleSets and have Number Restrictions). There is no restriction against more recipients for *MESSAGE.1* because the Number Restriction is (1,NIL). If the Particular RoleSet had constrained the Number Restriction to be (2,2), then all recipients would be accounted for.

It should be noted that Individual Concepts, as described here, are primitive. Their Role filler descriptions specify necessary conditions, but there are no sufficient conditions for uniquely determining the referent of an Individual Concept.

As a final note, we should mention that in the KL-ONE implementation a Role filler can also be a Lisp object. The IRole for *Body* shows a Lisp string as the description of the *Body* of *MESSAGE.1.* In our KL-ONE implementation, each Lisp object is treated as an Individual Concept of a *Lisp-Type* Concept. In this case, there is an implicit "individuates" link from the string to the Concept TEXT.

9. STRUCTURAL DESCRIPTIONS

In earlier sections we covered some of the ways that Generic Concepts can be formed from their superConcepts by adding restrictions. Each of the types of "essential difference" presented so far (Value Restriction, Number Restriction, etc.) has involved restricting only a single Role at a time. A moment's thought about descriptions that occur in realistic knowledge bases reveals that we need a facility to form Concepts by constraining the relation between more than one Role of the same Concept.

The compositional apparatus introduced so far yields Concepts that, for all intents and purposes, have all of their Roles independent of one another. But, generally speaking, the functional roles that we want to represent are *inter*dependent. For example, the vertical clearance of an arch is a function of the location of its lintel and the surface the arch is standing on; or, we might characterize an "important-message" as one whose sender is the supervisor of the recipient. In KL-ONE, these kinds of relations among Roles are specified with *Structural Descriptions.*

The need to handle the various possible relations among Roles makes the technical details of Structural Descriptions (SDs) a bit messy. However, the intent is straightforward—an SD allows the formation of a description whose essential difference with its proximate genus is a relationshp among more than one of its Roles.

Before we present some of the details of the two types of SDs currently in KL-ONE, we should mention another motivation for their existence. While KL-ONE Roles can be given "names," these are meaningless strings as far as the system is concerned. In the structure presented before this section, we have seen how Roles describe actual or potential fillers, but nothing (except our wishful thinking) gives a Role its intended meaning as the description of a functional role to be played. In addition to providing a way to specify a new Concept whose difference from its parent is a constraint between Roles, SDs can add substance to the names attached to Roles. For example, the buyer in a transaction is the person to whom goods go in exchange for legal tender provided by that buyer. The Structural Description mechanism allows us to describe such a transaction in terms of two connected giving events (the giving of money and the giving of goods in exchange); the relation of the *Buyer* Role to the *Giver* and *Receiver* Roles of those giving events defines the role being played by the buyer in the transaction.[22]

9.1 Role Value Maps

As mentioned, there are actually two types of SDs in KL-ONE. The simpler of these is called the *Role Value Map (RVM).* This special kind of Structural Description was introduced into the system for convenience. In the course of the use of KL-ONE in a natural language understanding system, it was often necessary to express the equality of two sets of Role fillers. Such relations could presumably be expressed with the more general SD facility, but would tend to involve more complex notation. So KL-ONE introduced a special notation to allow one to say things like "the grandparents of a person are exactly the same as the parents of the parents of that person."[23]

The crucial representational ingredient needed here is something that allows access to the Roles of a Concept from within an RVM. That is, to express equality between two Roles' fillers, we need some notation that allows us to access those Roles. Thus, the heart of an RVM resides in two pointers to Roles, or *Role Chains,* that are taken to stand for the sets of fillers of the Roles in an instance.

Figure 11 illustrates the simple structure of a Role Value Map. It shows the *PRIVATE-MESSAGE* and *IMPORTANT-MESSAGE* Concepts; the latter is intended to represent messages from the immediate supervisors of their recipients. The RVM is drawn as a diamond, and its two pointers, x and y, access the Roles whose fillers are to be equated (the Role Chains are drawn as dashed lines). In this case, the x pointer stands for the set of the senders of an instance of *IMPORTANT-MESSAGE* (in this case there will always be only one filler of the *Sender* Role), and the y pointer indicates the immediate supervisors of the recipients of the message (again, we expect only one). This latter Role Chain indicates how Roles can be composed to form constraints on embedded Role descriptions. One can think of Role Chains as a varia-

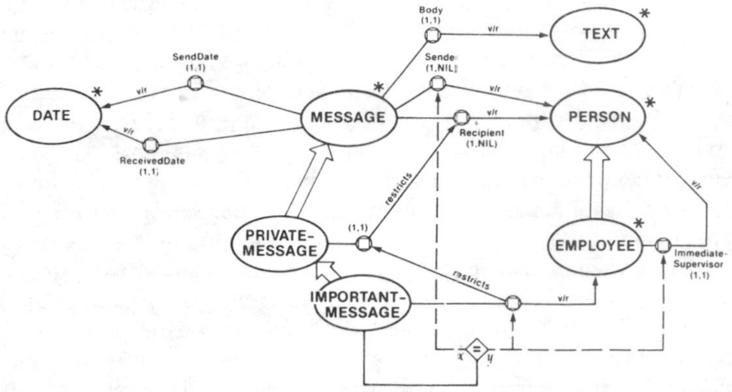

"An IMPORTANT-MESSAGE is a PRIVATE-MESSAGE whose Recipient is an EMPLOYEE, and whose Sender is the same as the ImmediateSupervisor of its Recipient."

Figure 11. A Role Value Map.

tion of functional composition where the functions are set-valued, e.g., "ImmediateSupervisor(Recipient (IMPORTANT-MESSAGE))".

Note that the Role Value Map is strictly a part of *IMPORTANT-MESSAGE,* even though one of the Roles it accesses comes from *MESSAGE.* The Role Value Map is the essential difference between *IMPORTANT-MESSAGE* and *PRIVATE-MESSAGE.* Because subConcepts always inherit the Roles of their superConcepts, the constraint can use the *Sender* and *Recipient* Roles at *IMPORTANT-MESSAGE,* but it does not affect them, except in the context of *IMPORTANT-MESSAGE.*[24]

A Role Value Map specifies a necessary and sufficient condition. Thus, the RVM in *IMPORTANT-MESSAGE's* specification requires that each instance of IMPORTANT-MESSAGE satisfy the following: The set of persons that are the senders of the particular *MESSAGE* is the same set as the immediate supervisors of the recipients of that very same *MESSAGE.* Any *PRIVATE-MESSAGE* that satisfies this constraint is, by definition, an *IMPORTANT-MESSAGE.* The converse is also true—any *IMPORTANT-MESSAGE* satisfies the constraint.

KL-ONE allows a variation on the kind of RVM illustrated in Figure 11 that specifies a *subset* relation between sets of Role Chain fillers. It is depicted by a diamond surrounding a set inclusion symbol, and in such a case the set indicated by the x pointer is taken to be a subset of the one indicated by the y pointer.

[22] In light of this, it is easy to see that the Role Differentiation mechanism of KL-ONE discussed in section 5.2 allows only the *primitive* derivation of new Roles from old ones. That is, if I specify the role of *BUYER* of a *TRANSACTION* as a subRole of *Participant* of an *ACTIVITY* by differentiation, I know nothing about what makes the filler the buyer (rather than, say, the seller). We have always envisioned a definitional mechanism whereby we could specify completely what it means to be a buyer (in terms of the other participants and goods in the transaction). SDs are the beginning of a mechanism sufficient to do this, but there is still a long way to go before Roles can be fully defined in KL-ONE.

[23] We have also implemented special-purpose routines for processing this set of relations.

[24] This is a place where the particular graphical notation may be more of a hindrance than a help.

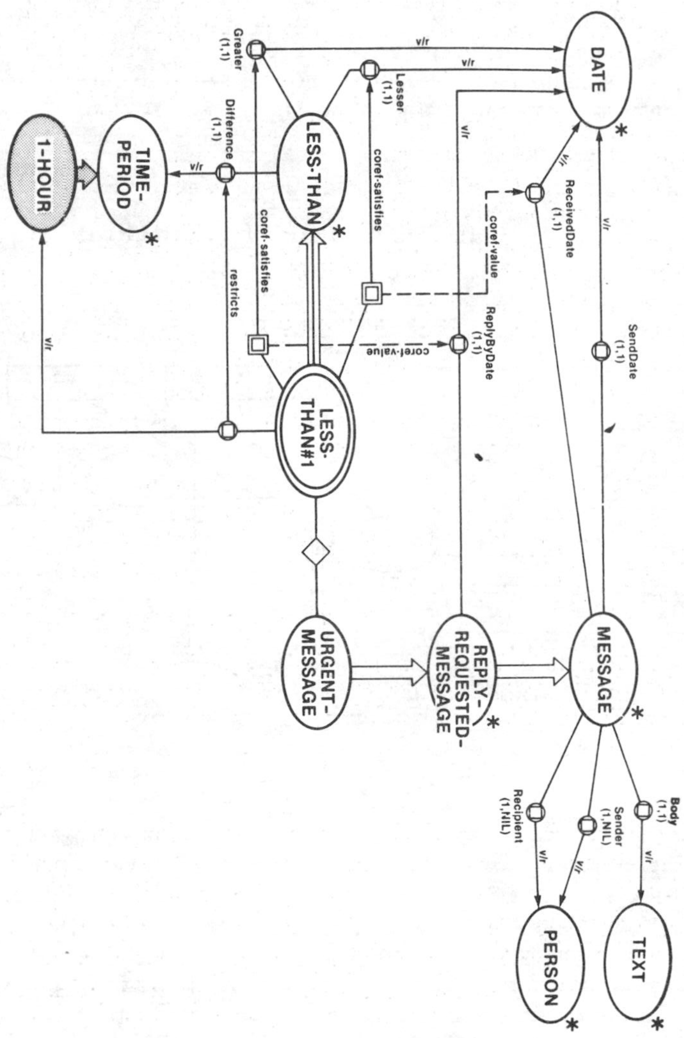

"A REPLY-REQUESTED-MESSAGE is, among other things, a MESSAGE with a ReplyByDate, which is a DATE."

"An URGENT-MESSAGE is a REPLY-REQUESTED-MESSAGE whose ReceivedDate and ReplyByDate satisfy a LESS-THAN whose Lesser is the ReceivedDate, whose Greater is the ReplyByDate, and whose Difference is 1-HOUR."

Figure 12. A Structural Description that uses another Concept.

9.2. Structural Descriptions

The second, more general type of Structural Description allows us to express how the Roles of a Concept interrelate (and how they relate to the Concept as a whole) in terms of other Concepts in the network. Rather than just express a subset or equality relation between sets of Role fillers, these SDs can relate Roles in arbitrary ways by using Concepts defined elsewhere.

There are two fundamental aspects to the relation of two Roles using KL-ONE Concepts. First, there is simply getting access to those Concepts in such a way that their use in defining a new Concept does not inadvertently change their meaning or assert the existence of any individuals. One can make an analogy here to a similar phenomenon in programming languages: Functions can be defined in one place and used in definitions of other functions. This analogy points up the second aspect of KL-ONE's SD mechanism: Once we have an embedded "call" to a Concept, we need to bind the formal arguments of the called Concept to the actual arguments to be used in the context of the call. While programming languages typically use argument order to achieve the correspondence between actuals and formals, KL-ONE's philosophy advocates using explicit links; thus the KL-ONE structure that implements SDs is unhappily complicated.

For an illustration of some of the details of SDs, consider Figure 12, wherein we define the concept of an "urgent message" as one that requires response within one hour. We do this in terms of our familiar *MESSAGE* Concept and a Concept called *"LESS-THAN,"* which we presume is accounted for elsewhere in the network. The idea is to use the *LESS-THAN* to express a relation between the *ReceivedDate* of an *URGENT-MESSAGE,* and a new Role that we will call *"ReplyByDate."* The received-date will have to be less than 1 hour before the reply-by-date. For modularity, we introduce the new *ReplyByDate* Role at a Concept called *"REPLY-REQUESTED-MESSAGE"* ("among other things" appears in the specification of this Concept, because we are presuming that there is more to requesting a reply than adding a single field to a message).

The way that the KL-ONE structure in the figure expresses the relation we need is the following: the SD (the diamond in the figure) has associated with it a version of the *LESS-THAN* Concept. The structure of this internal version of *LESS-THAN* is isomorphic to that of the regular, Generic version. Because, however, its use is to be restricted to this particular definition of *URGENT-MESSAGE,* it itself is not a Generic but rather a version of the Concept "parameterized" by the surrounding context (the rest of the *URGENT-MESSAGE* structure). It is this *Parametric Individual Concept* (*LESS-THAN#1*) that represents the "call" to *LESS-THAN* within *URGENT-MESSAGE.*

Once we have the internal version of *LESS-THAN* to work with, all we need is to bind the "actual" Roles to the "formal" ones. This is achieved by means of Role Chains, exactly as we saw with Role Value Maps in the previous section. In this case, we bind the *ReceivedDate* to the *LesserRole* of *LESS-THAN#1,* and the *ReplyByDate* to its *Greater* Role. *LESS-THAN#1,* its Roles, and some of the links in the SD are drawn slightly differently than they are in the case of *LESS-THAN,* because their function is somewhat different than in the Generic Case. *LESS-THAN#1* is drawn as a double ellipse, and its relation to *LESS-THAN* is shown by a wide, 3-line arrow that depicts the *parametric individuates* relation. The Roles of *LESS-THAN#1* are defined by *Coref-Satisfies* links to the corresponding RoleSets of *LESS-THAN,* and their bindings are defined by *Coref-Value* Role Chains.

We should add one more technical note. In Figure 12, the Coref-Value links point directly from Roles of *LESS-THAN#1* to RoleSets of *URGENT-MESSAGE* (actually, they point to RoleSets that *URGENT-MESSAGE* inherits). In general, Coref-Value links can be Role Chains and have the same properties as Role Chains for RVMs. When used with Parametric Individual Concepts, the Role Chain can also point directly to the enclosing Concept in order to express the participation of the instance's "self"—that is, the thing as a whole—in a relationship.

10. ASSERTIONAL LANGUAGE

As mentioned earlier, the description formation part of KL-ONE has a complementary assertion-making part. We have tried carefully to distinguish between purely descriptional structure and assertions about coreference, existence, etc. All of the structure mentioned above (Concept, Roles, etc.) is purely descriptional. All assertions are made relative to a *Context* and thus do not affect the (descriptive) taxomony of generic knowledge. We anticipate that Contexts will be of use in reasoning about hypotheticals, beliefs, and desires.

One asserts the existence of some thing satisfying a description (i.e., Concept) by connecting it to a *Nexus* within a particular *Context.* This connecting link is called a *Description Wire.* A Nexus is a structureless entity which serves as a locus of coreference statements; it holds together various descriptions, all of which are taken to specify the same object in the Context. Nexuses have been conveniently thought of as corresponding to things in the world; KL-ONE, however, makes no such commitment. The Description Wires are also taken to be in the Context. Contexts are at the moment simply collections of Nexuses and Description Wires. Thus, a Context can act as a "world," which comprises a set of statements about existence and description coreference.[25]

In Figure 13 (the Nexuses are small circles, the Contexts rectangles, and the Description Wires squiggly lines), we have Nexus N1 in Context C1 asserting that a Vulcan named Spock is the First Officer of the Enterprise, whereas in Context C2 these same descriptions are used in a different way by Nexuses N2 and N3 to assert that the First Officer of the Enterprise is a person named Uhura and a Vulcan named Spock is the Captain of the Enterprise. We should note that KL-ONE at the moment does not support any meaningful relations between Contexts, although a hierarchy of Contexts can be created by putting the meta-anchor (i.e., a Nexus—see section 11.1) of one Context into another Context.

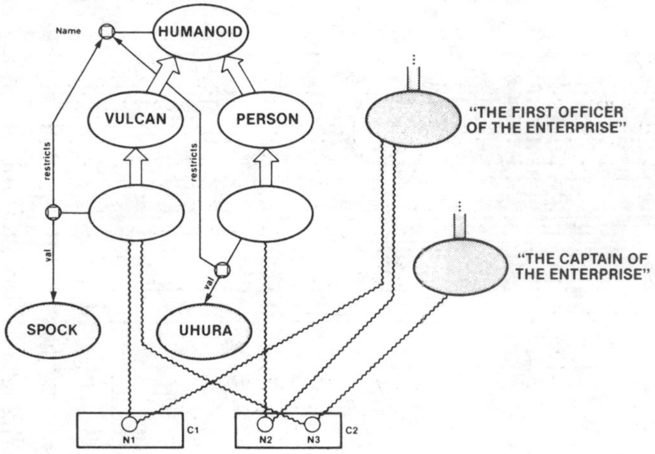

Figure 13. Some KL-ONE assertions.

11. ADDITIONAL KL-ONE FACILITIES

11.1 Metadescription

Nexuses allow us to come as close to reference to objects outside the system as is possible in this kind of representation environment. In addition to the use of Nexuses as surrogates for outside entities, KL-ONE allows reference to internal entities (e.g., Concepts) as well. Thus one can *metadescribe* a KL-ONE object *in KL-ONE.* Of course, to do this, the system needs to have the Concepts of a KL-ONE Concept, a KL-ONE Role, a KL-ONE Role Value Map, etc. These are not yet part of the implemented system.

[25] Co-"reference" is not quite the right term, because the objects "referred to" need not exist. *Co-specification of description* is probably a better term (see Sidner, 1979).

In order to construct a metadescription, one uses the same type of structure used in constructing a regular description. Each KL-ONE structure is considered implicitly to have a corresponding Nexus that is known to exist in a "KL-ONE base level" Context.[26] Metadescriptions are simply descriptions (usually expressed in terms of the Concepts *KL-ONE-CONCEPT, KL-ONE-ROLE,* etc.) attached to those Nexuses by means of the Description Wire mechanism mentioned earlier. In the future, we expect to study how further to exploit metadescription in KL-ONE. The KL-ONE system might provide automatic access to a complete metadescription of any other description and also allow one to affect the KL-ONE interpreter by restricting these metadescriptions in a manner similar to that of Brian Smith's (1982) 3-LISP. The primary questions in this effort deal with the details of such a system, and more importantly, the determination of exactly what leverage one gains by using it.

11.2 Attached Procedures and Data

The final feature of KL-ONE to be touched on here is the ability to attach procedures and data to structures in the network. This is purely a programming convenience—attached procedures and data are outside of KL-ONE and have no semantically justifiable place in the epistemology. Hence, this section deals strictly with our implementation.

The attached procedure mechanism is implemented in a very general way. Procedures are attached to KL-ONE entities by *interpretive hooks (ihooks)* (see Smith, 1978), which specify the set of situations in which they are to be triggered. An interpreter function operating on a KL-ONE entity causes the invocation of all procedures inherited by or directly attached to that entity by ihooks whose situations match the intent of that function. Situations include things like "Individuate," "Restrict," "Create," "Remove," etc. In addition to a general situation, an ihook specifies when in the execution of the interpreter function it is to be invoked ("PRE-" and "POST-" for conditional execution, or "WHEN-" for side effects).

Procedures attached to the conceptual taxonomy can make KL-ONE work like a special kind of object-oriented programming system. We make no claims about this use of the system (but see Goodwin, 1979)—the procedures are not themselves written in KL-ONE, and there can be no guarantee that an attached procedure will honor the integrity of the network. The facility itself is supported only in a very simple way.

Finally, a facility has been incorporated to attach arbitrary data to KL-ONE Concepts. The data is stored in property list format and is inherited along superC cables. A second attached data facility exists which simply provides a property list format without inheritance.

[26] We have on occasion called these Nexuses *meta-anchors* in the manner of Smith (1978).

12. CONCLUSION

Work on KL-ONE continues, but much has been accomplished in the several years since its birth. Most importantly, the language has provided the basis for much further research and development in Artificial Intelligence and has helped focus a large number of people on some important facets of knowledge representation. It has also provided a practical foundation for a number of application systems.

On the technical side, KL-ONE has pioneered the idea of constructing a representation out of "epistemological" primitives and has provided a first set of such primitives for examination and experimentation. It has also instigated first-class status for Roles (a k a slots) in frame-based knowledge representation systems, including the potential for multiple fillers and explicit differentiation into subRoles. Further, KL-ONE has helped begin serious investigation of the separation of the representation task into descriptional and assertional components. It has also initiated serious research into the interaction of Roles through its Structural Description and Role Value Map mechanisms.

There is much more research to be done on representations derived from KL-ONE (i.e., Krypton and KL-TWO), but through it all, the kernel of KL-ONE survives.

REFERENCES

Amarel, S. (1968). On representation of problems of reasoning about actions. In D. Michie (Ed.), *Machine Intelligence 3.* Edinburgh: Edinburgh University Press.

Bobrow, R. J. (1979a). The RUS natural language parsing framework. In *Research in natural language understanding, annual report* (Report No. 4274). Cambridge, MA: Bolt Beranek and Newman.

Bobrow, R. J. (1979b). Semantic interpretation in PSI-KLONE. In *Research in natural language understanding, annual report* (Report No. 4274). Cambridge, MA: Bolt Beranek and Newman.

Brachman, R. J. (1977). What's in a Concept: Structural foundations for semantic networks. *International Journal of Man-Machine Studies, 9,* 127–152.

Brachman, R. J. (1978). *A structural paradigm for representing knowledge.* (Tech. Rep. No. 3605). Cambridge, MA: Bolt Beranek and Newman.

Brachman, R. J. (1979). On the epistemological status of semantic networks. In N. V. Findler (Ed.), *Associative networks: Representation and use of knowledge by computers.* New York: Academic.

Brachman, R. J. (1983). What is-a is and isn't: An analysis of taxonomic links in semantic networks. *IEEE Computer, 16*(10), 30–36.

Brachman, R. J. (in press, a). I lied about the trees. *AI Magazine 6*(3).

Brachman, R. J. (in press, b). *A structural paradigm for representing knowledge.* Norwood, NJ: Ablex.

Brachman, R. J., Bobrow, R. J., Cohen, P. R., Klovstad, J. W., Webber, B. L., & Woods, W. A. (1979). *Research in natural language understanding, annual report* (Tech. Rep. No. 4274). Cambridge, MA: Bolt Beranek and Newman.

Brachman, R. J., Fikes, R. E., & Levesque, H. J. (1983). Krypton: A functional approach to knowledge representation. *IEEE Computer, 16*(10), 67–73.

Cohen, B. C. (1982). *Understanding natural kinds.* Unpublished doctoral dissertation, Stanford University, CA.

Donnellan, K. (1966). Reference and definite descriptions. *Philosophical Review, 75,* 281–304.

Fahlman, S. E. (1979). *NETL: A system for representing and using real-world knowledge.* Cambridge, MA: M.I.T. Press.

Fikes, R. E. (1982). Highlights from Klone Talk. In J. G. Schmolze & R. J. Brachman (Eds.), *Proceedings of the 1982 KL-ONE Workshop, BBN Report No. 4842.* Cambridge, MA: Bolt Beranek and Newman. (Also published as FLAIR Tech. Rep. No. 4, Fairchild Laboratory for Artificial Intelligence Research, Palo Alto, CA).

Freeman, M. W., & Tomlinson, C. J. (1982). Towards a calculus of structural descriptions. In J. G. Schmolze & R. J. Brachman (Eds.), *Proceedings of the 1981 KL-ONE Workshop, BBN Report No. 4842.* Cambridge, MA: Bolt Beranek and Newman. (Also published as FLAIR Tech. Rep. No. 4, Fairchild Laboratory for Artificial Intelligence Research, Palo Alto, CA).

Freeman, M., Hirschman, L., McKay, D., Miller, F., & Sidhu, D. (1983). Logic programming applied to knowledge-based systems, modeling and simulation. In *Proceedings of Conference on Artificial Intelligence.* Oakland University, Rochester, MI.

Freeman, M., Hirschman, L., McKay, D., & Palmer, M. (1983). KNET: A logic-based associative network framework for expert systems. (Tech. Rep.). Paoli, PA: Research and Development Division, SDC—A Burroughs Company.

Goodwin, J. W. (1979). *Taxonomic programming with Klone.* (Tech. Rep. LiTH-MAT-R-79-5). Linköping, Sweden: Informatics Laboratory, Linköping University.

Hendrix, G. G. (1979). Encoding knowledge in partitioned networks. In N. V. Findler (Ed.), *Associative networks: Representation and use of knowledge by computers.* New York: Academic.

Israel, D. J. (1983). On interpreting network formalisms. *Computers and mathematics with applications—special issue on computational linguistics, 9*(1), 1–14.

Israel, D. J. (1984). A short companion to the naive physics manifesto. In J. Hobbs & R. Moore (Ed.), *Formal theories of the common sense world.* Norwood, NJ: Ablex.

Israel, D. J., & Brachman, R. J. (1984). Some remarks on the semantics of representation languages. In M. L. Brodie, J. Mylopoulos, J. W. Schmidt (Eds.), *On conceptual modelling: Perspectives from artificial intelligence, databases, and programming languages.* New York: Springer Verlag.

Kripke, S. A. (1980). *Naming and necessity.* Cambridge, MA: Harvard University Press.

Lipkis, T., & Mark, W. (1981). *Consul note 5, The consul classifier.* Marina del Rey, CA: USC/Information Sciences Institute.

McDermott, D. (1982). Artificial intelligence meets natural stupidity. In J. Haugeland (Ed.), *Mind design.* Cambridge, MA: MIT Press.

Moser, M. G. (1983). An Overview of NIKL, The new implementation of KL-ONE. In C. Sidner, M. Bates, R. Bobrow, B. Goodman, A. Haas, R. Ingria, D. Israel, D. McAllester, M. Moser, J. Schmolze, M. Vilain, *Research in knowledge representation for natural language understanding, annual report* (BBN Report No. 5421). Cambridge, MA: Bolt Beranek and Newman.

Nilsson, N. J. (1980). *Principles of artificial intelligence.* Palo Alto, CA: Tioga.

Quine, W. V. O. (1960). *Word and Object.* Cambridge, MA: M.I.T. Press.

Reiter, R. A. (1980). A logic for default reasoning. *Artificial Intelligence, 13,* 81–132.

Rifkin, A. (1985). *A deontic model of natural categories: featural definitions, cross-classification, and context sensitivity.* Unpublished doctoral dissertation, City University of New York, NY.

Schmolze, J. G., & Brachman, R. J. (1982, June). *Proceedings of the 1981 KL-ONE workshop.* (Tech. Rep. No. 4842). Cambridge, MA: Bolt Beranek and Newman. (Also published as FLAIR Tech. Rep. No. 4, Fairchild Laboratory for Artificial Intelligence Research, Palo Alto, CA.)

Schmolze, J., & Israel, D. (1983). KL-ONE: Semantics and classification. In C. Sidner, M. Bates, R. Bobrow, B. Goodman, A. Haas, R. Ingria, D. Israel, D. McAllester, M. Mosler, J. Schmolze, & M. Vilain, *Research in knowledge representation for natural language understanding, annual report, (BBN Report No. 5421).* Cambridge, MA: Bolt Beranek and Newman.

Schmolze, J. G., & Lipkis, T. A. (1983). Classification in the KL-ONE knowledge representation system. In *Proceedings of the Eighth International Joint Conference on Artificial Intelligence.* Karlsruhe, W. Germany.

Schubert, L. K., Goebel, R. G., & Cercone, N. J. (1979). The structure and organization of a semantic net for comprehension and inference. In N. V. Findler (Ed.), *Associative networks: Representation and use of knowledge by computers.* New York: Academic.

Sellars, R. W. (1917). *The essentials of logic.* Cambridge, MA: The Riverside Press.

Sidner, C. L. (1979). *Towards a computational theory of definite anaphora comprehension in English discourse.* (Tech. Rep. AI-TR-537). Cambridge, MA: Artificial Intelligence Laboratory, M.I.T.

Sidner, C. L., Bates, M., Bobrow, R. J., Brachman, R. J., Cohen, P. R., Webber, B. L., & Woods, W. A. (1981). *Research in knowledge representation for natural language understanding, annual report.* (Tech. Rep. No. 4785). Cambridge, MA: Bolt Beranek and Newman.

Smith, B. C. (1978). *Levels, layers, and planes: The framework of a theory of knowledge representation semantics.* Unpublished master's thesis, Artificial Intelligence Laboratory, Massachusetts Institute of Technology, Cambridge, MA.

Smith, B. C. (1982). *Reflection and semantics in a procedural language.* Unpublished doctoral dissertation, Artificial Intelligence Laboratory, Massachusetts Institute of Technology, Cambridge, MA.

Tranchell, L. M. (1982). *A SNePs implementation of KL-ONE.* (Tech. Rep. 198). Buffalo, NY: Dept. of Computer Science, State Univ. of New York at Buffalo.

Woods, W. A. (1975). What's in a link: Foundations for semantic networks. In D. G. Bobrow & A. Collins (Eds.), *Representation and understanding: Studies in cognitive science.* New York: Academic.

Woods, W. A. (1979). *Theoretical studies in natural language understanding, annual report* (Tech. Rep. No. 4332). Cambridge, MA: Bolt Beranek and Newman.

Woods, W. A. (1983). What's important about knowledge representation? *IEEE Computer,* 1983, *16*(10), 22–27.

Woolf, B. (1982). An intelligent tutor for beginning programmers. In J. G. Schmolze & R. J. Brachman (Eds.), *Proceedings of the 1981 KL-ONE Workshop, BBN Report No. 4842.* Cambridge, MA: Bolt Beranek and Newman. (Also published as FLAIR Tech. Rep. No. 4, Fairchild Laboratory for Artificial Intelligence Research, Palo Alto, CA).

Zdybel, F., Greenfeld, N. R., Yonke, M. D., & Gibbons, J. (1981). An information presentation system. In *Proceedings of the Seventh International Joint Conference on Artificial Intelligence.* Vancouver: International Joint Conferences on Artificial Intelligence.

APPENDIX
AN EXAMPLE USING KL-ONE AND THE CLASSIFIER

In this appendix we present an example of a system using KL-ONE. From a natural language understanding (NLU) context (Brachman et al., 1979), we have chosen to describe a part of the process that translates English sentences into representations of their meanings.

The example has been chosen because it shows a system

- creating KL-ONE structures during a complex process,
- making use of classification, and
- using structures and procedures that go "outside" of KL-ONE in order to capture that which KL-ONE cannot.

We include the latter because the use of KL-ONE typically entails more than what can be "said" in KL-ONE per se. Woods (1983) calls this type of use the "conceptual coat rack" approach, and we will see this as the example is developed.

The NLU system in question uses the RUS parser (Bobrow, 1979a) to translate English sentences into the equivalent of parse trees, and it uses PSI-KLONE (Bobrow, 1979b) to translate these parses into KL-ONE representations of the meanings of the corresponding sentences. PSI-KLONE proceeds in two phases. First, it translates parsed sentences into a more structured syntactic representation. From this, interpretation rules are used to create the actual meaning representations. The two representations used by PSI-KLONE are in KL-ONE.

Before proceeding, we note that we have simplified the description of PSI-KLONE for presentation purposes. Also, the output of PSI-KLONE is not a representation of the final meaning of the sentence but a *literal semantic interpretation* that becomes the input to the portion of the system that deals with pragmatics.

The KL-ONE representation of a sentence's syntactic structure is built by PSI-KLONE by making use of a *syntaxonomy*. This is a group of Concepts in a network, each denoting a class of sentence fragments. They are distinguished from each other by both grammatical considerations and the particular words used in the fragments. For example, *NP* is a Concept denoting noun phrases (based on grammar only) and *PERSON-NP* is a Concept denoting noun phrases that, in turn, denote people (based on both grammar and particular nouns that refer to people). With each Concept in the syntaxonomy, we associate one or more interpretation rules that map descriptions of sentence fragments into semantic representations. The semantic interpretation process for a sentence S is as follows:

1. Sentence S is parsed.
2. A representation of the parse vis-à-vis the syntaxonomy is created (call it S′).
3. The KL-ONE classifier is invoked to find all legitimate superConcepts of S′ that are not already known. In particular, we are interested in those superConcepts that are in the syntaxonomy because they have interpretation rules associated with them.
4. Some set of interpretation rules are now applicable to S′, namely, those rules that are applicable to the superConcepts of S′. By using inheritable attached data (see section 11.2) to store the interpretation rules, the KL-ONE system automatically calculates this set.
5. A special interpreter executes the interpretation rules to produce the semantic interpretation.

Thus, the Concepts in the syntaxonomy are used both as a discrimination net for determining which interpretation rules apply and as a mechanism for inheriting the appropriate interpretation rules. Furthermore, the classifier performs the bulk of the discriminating.

An interesting feature of RUS and PSI-KLONE is that all of these steps can proceed in parallel. When the parser has found a sentence fragment, it immediately passes it along to the process concerned with finding its analog in the syntaxonomy, while the parser returns to the remainder of the sentence. As soon as the fragment's analog in the syntaxonomy is found, its inherited interpretation rules are executed and the corresponding literal semantic representation is constructed. Thus, RUS and PSI-KLONE proceed simultaneously. The purpose of this parallelism is two-fold. First, it can be an effective use of low-level parallel hardware. Second, because the parse of a sentence is often semantically ambiguous and some parses may be semantically incoherent (such as "round square") we reduce the search space for semantically coherent interpretations with the following. Because the interpretation rules can detect incoherent sentence fragments, PSI-KLONE provides immediate feedback to the parser as soon as an incoherent fragment is detected. The parser, in turn, immediately dispenses with all possible parses that involve the incoherent fragment. If this were not done, the parser might generate many parses that all included the same incoherent fragment. So, by intermingling parsing and interpretation, the search space is reduced.

In the remainder of this section, we will demonstrate in some detail how KL-ONE helps significantly in the discrimination process, i.e., in finding a sentence's analog in the syntaxonomy. Space limitations will not allow us to show the use of interpretation rules. Our example sentence is:

> "That professor teaches undergraduates about Lisp on Thursday."

Figure 14 shows a parse tree for it. The sentence is a clause with a logical subject that is a noun phrase (NP) consisting of a determiner "That" and noun "professor." The clause's head verb is the verb "teaches" and its logical object is the noun phrase "undergraduates." It also has two prepositional phrase (PP) modifiers, "about Lisp" and "on Thursday."

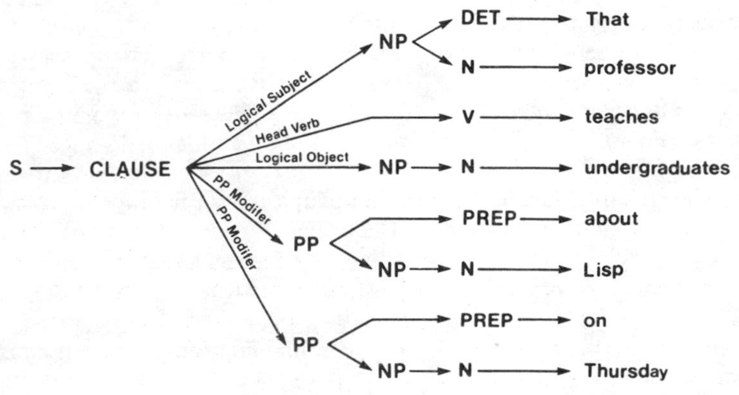

Figure 14. A parse tree for the example sentence.

In Figure 15, we depict a portion of the syntaxonomy that includes its most general Concepts. The Concept *PHRASE* is a primitive Concept that denotes all phrases. It has no further KL-ONE structure, so no more can be said about it. *PHRASE* has three immediate subConcepts, which are all primitive as well: *NP, CLAUSE,* and *PP.* These Concepts denote noun phrases, clauses, and prepositional phrases, respectively, all of which are types of phrases. We have drawn *NP* and *PP* with dashed lines to indicate that their entire KL-ONE structure is not shown here; we will show that later. Another primitive Concept is *VERB,* which denotes all verbs, and it

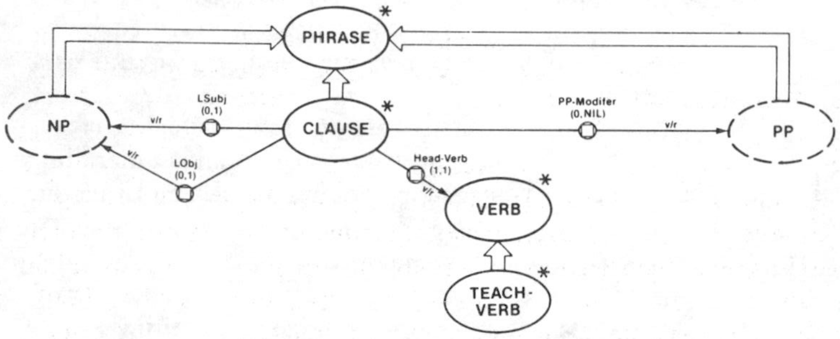

Figure 15. The top of the syntaxonomy: Phrases and Clauses.

has a primitive subConcept *TEACH-VERB,* which denotes all verbs that refer to teaching. Throughout this section, we will only include Concepts that pertain to our example sentence.

The Concept *CLAUSE* is shown in its entirety, and although it is primitive, it has several RoleSets. Thus, while these RoleSets specify necessary conditions for clauses, KL-ONE cannot express sufficient conditions for them. The RoleSet *LSubj* denotes the logical subject of a clause. It has a Value Restriction of *NP* and a Number Restriction of "(0,1)." This means that each *CLAUSE* need not have a logical subject, but if it does, it can have at most one. Also, each logical subject must be a noun phrase. The RoleSet *LObj* denotes the logical object of a clause. From its Value and Number Restrictions, we can see that each clause can have at most one logical object and each must be a noun phrase. *Head-Verb* denotes the head verb of a clause, and its Value Restriction is *VERB.* Thus, each clause must have exactly one head verb and each head verb must be a verb. The final RoleSet, *PP-Modifier,* denotes prepositional phrase modifiers. A clause can have any number of them, each of which must be a prepositional phrase.

The RUS parser begins by examining our example sentence from left to right while looking for certain sentence fragments and passing them along to PSI-KLONE. PSI-KLONE places a fragment's analog in the syntaxonomy and then builds the literal semantic interpretations of each fragment. The ability to build such interpretations is a test of semantic coherence (if the semantic interpreter fails, the fragment is incoherent); the result of the process is passed back to the RUS parser. RUS does not need to parse an entire sentence before calling upon PSI-KLONE, however, it does impose a certain order upon the fragments it sends:

1. It first parses enough of a sentence, which is a clause, to find a plausible head verb. PSI-KLONE is informed that a clause has been found with the given head verb and with the remaining constituents unspecified.
2. Next, RUS passes the logical subject of the clause to PSI-KLONE. If it must parse further in order to obtain the logical subject, it does so. Otherwise, it does so without further parsing. This strategy of parsing as needed is followed throughout.
3. The logical object is passed next.
4. Pre-modifiers of the clause are passed, from right-most to left-most.
5. Post-modifiers are passed, from left-most to right-most.
6. Finally, PSI-KLONE is informed that the clause is complete.

Getting back to our example, RUS first passes this message along to PSI-KLONE:

A clause was found that will be named "cl#teaches." Its head verb is "teaches," which is a verb; cl#teaches is incomplete.[27]

PSI-KLONE will use 3 dictionaries. One dictionary maps terms in the communication language into terms in the syntaxonomy, such as mapping "clause" to the Concept *CLAUSE*. Another dictionary maps words to their morphological roots, such as mapping "teaches" to "teach." A third maps a particular word (that is a morphological root) along with its grammatical category into the syntaxonomy Concept that best describes it. For example, "professor" as a noun is best described by the Concept *TEACHER-NOUN*.[28]

Using these dictionaries, PSI-KLONE finds that clauses are represented by *CLAUSE* and it begins to construct an Individual Concept of *CLAUSE*, which it calls *CL#TEACHES*. PSI-KLONE also sees that "teaches" is a verb, and it looks up the morphological root of "teaches," which is "teach," and finds that it is best described by the Concept *TEACH-VERB*. So, it creates an Individual Concept of *TEACH-VERB* for "teaches," which it calls *VB#TEACHES*. This verb happens to be a complete fragment, so PSI-KLONE calls upon the classifier to find all legitimate superConcepts of *VB#TEACHES*.[29] However, because it has no structure other than its parent Concept, no new superConcepts are found. And as it happens, there are no interpretation rules associated with just verbs, so the verb is accepted as being semantically coherent, as there are no contraindications. Returning to the clause, PSI-KLONE finds the RoleSet *Head-Verb*, which indicates that the Value Restriction for head verbs of clauses is *VERB*. "Teaches" satisfies this restriction, so no problems are reported. It also checks the Number Restriction, which is satisfied. Now PSI-KLONE adds an IRole whose *val* is *VB#TEACHES*, and that *satisfies Head-Verb* from *CL#TEACHES*. However, because our clause is incomplete, PSI-KLONE does nothing more with *CL#TEACHES* and it returns to RUS with

Clause cl#teaches is represented by the Individual Concept *CL#TEACHES*. It is OK so far. Its head verb is represented by the Individual Concept *VB#TEACHES*, which is complete and coherent.

[27] We use an English version of the actual communication language.

[28] This third dictionary contains information that may not seem suitable for a mechanism as simple as a dictionary. But keep in mind that the output of PSI-KLONE becomes the input to the part of the system that deals with pragmatics, and it is there that much of the complexity of language is dealt with. For example, if "professor" had actually been used to refer to a robot, then *TEACHER-NOUN* (which is constrained to apply to *people* who are teachers) would, in the end, be inappropriate. However, we allow this "mistake" for now and rely upon the pragmatics component to deal with it.

[29] Unfortunately, the actual implementation of the classifier does not work with Individual Concepts, so PSI-KLONE is forced to use only Generic Concepts for this task. However, extending the classifier to perform as explained in this section would be simple and straightforward.

RUS now knows the syntaxonomy analogs of the fragments it has passed, and RUS is responsible for keeping track of this. Figure 16 shows the current representation of *CL#TEACHES*.

Concepts for nouns and noun phrases are shown in Figure 17. On the top left side is the Concept *NOUN*, which denotes all nouns, and its descendant Concepts. *NOUN* is a primitive Concept without any further structure, and it has 3 immediate descendants, *TIME-NOUN*, *PERSON-NOUN*, and *SUBJECT-NOUN*, denoting nouns that describe time, people, or subjects, respectively (where subjects include history, computer science, Lisp, etc.). Each of these is primitive and without further structure. *PERSON-NOUN* is further distinguished by *STUDENT-NOUN*, denoting nouns that describe students, and *TEACHER-NOUN*, denoting nouns that describe teachers.

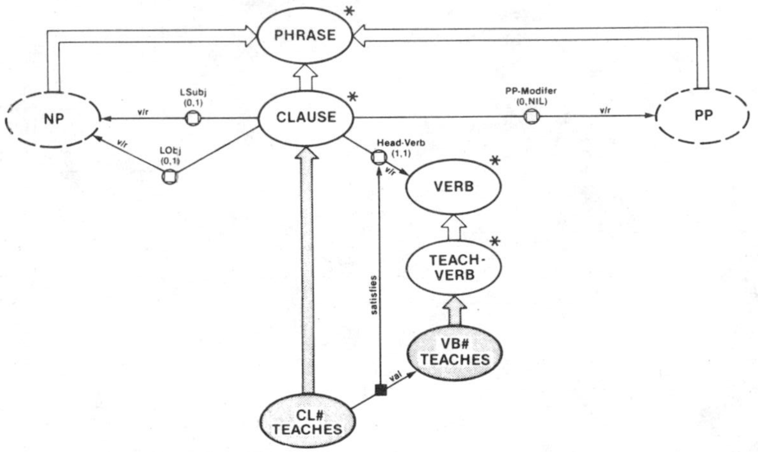

Figure 16. Partial representation of sentence: with head verb only.

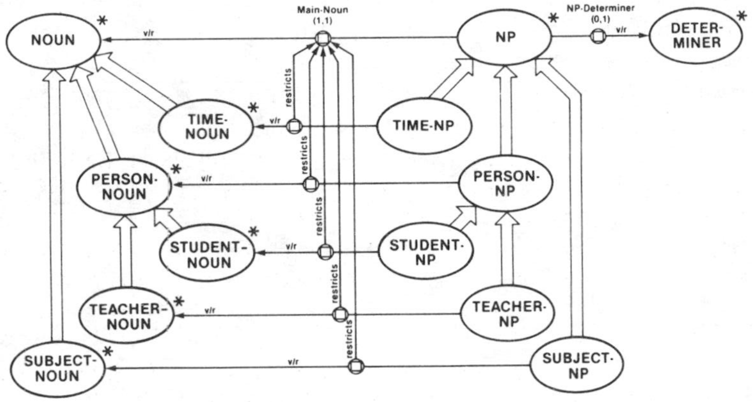

Figure 17. Part of the syntaxonomy: Nouns and Noun Phrases.

On the top right side of Figure 17 is the Concept *NP,* which denotes noun phrases. Although it is primitive, it has a RoleSet called *Main-Noun* whose Value Restriction is *NOUN* and Number Restriction is "(1,1)." *Main-Noun* denotes the main noun of a noun phrase, so each noun phrase must have exactly one main noun and it must be a noun. *NP* has another RoleSet *NP-Determiner,* which denotes the determiner of a noun phrase. The Number Restriction here states that there can be at most one determiner per noun phrase and it must be an instance of *DETERMINER,* a primitive Concept that denotes determiners.

A descendant of *NP* is *TIME-NP,* and this is our first defined Concept. Because it is defined, its complete meaning can be determined from the network. *TIME-NP* specializes *NP,* so each instance of *TIME-NP* must be a noun phrase. Furthermore, the RoleSet at *TIME-NP* restricts *Main-Noun* and has a Value Restriction of *TIME-NOUN.* Its Number Restriction of "(1,1)" is the same as that of its parent Concept, *NP.* Thus, each instance of *TIME-NP* is just a noun phrase whose main noun is a noun describing time. *PERSON-NP, STUDENT-NP, TEACHER-NP,* and *SUBJECT-NP* are specified similarly, and they are defined Concepts that denote noun phrases describing, respectively, people, students, teachers, and subjects.

Returning to our process, RUS passes along the logical subject of our sentence:

> Clause cl#teaches has a logical subject, to be named "np#prof," that is a noun phrase; np#prof has "professor" as its main noun and "That" as its determiner; np#prof is complete, but cl#teaches is not.

PSI-KLONE now constructs the Concept *DET#THAT* for "That," an Individual Concept of *DETERMINER.* For "professor," it constructs a Concept *N#PROF* that individuates *TEACHER-NOUN,* which it determines from its dictionaries. Finally, it constructs *NP#PROF,* an Individual Concept of *NP* with a *Main-Noun* of *N#PROF* and a *NP-Determiner* of *DET#THAT.* Since *DET#THAT, N#PROF,* and *NP#PROF* are complete, they are classified. For *DET#THAT* and *N#PROF,* no new information is discovered. However, the classifier finds that *NP#PROF* is also an Individual Concept of *TEACHER-NP.* Thus, it inherits interpretation rules that are applicable to such noun phrases, and we will assume that these rules generate a coherent interpretation. Finally, the Concept *CL#TEACHES* is expanded to include the logical subject, as shown in Figure 18. PSI-KLONE returns to RUS with:

> Clause cl#teaches is still OK. Its logical subject is represented by the Individual Concept *NP#PROF,* with a coherent interpretation of. . . .

Here, the interpretation for the noun phrase "That professor" is passed back to RUS; we have not shown that interpretation.

In a similar fashion, RUS passes along the logical object "undergraduates" and PSI-KLONE creates its analog, *NP#UNDERGRADS,* and ex-

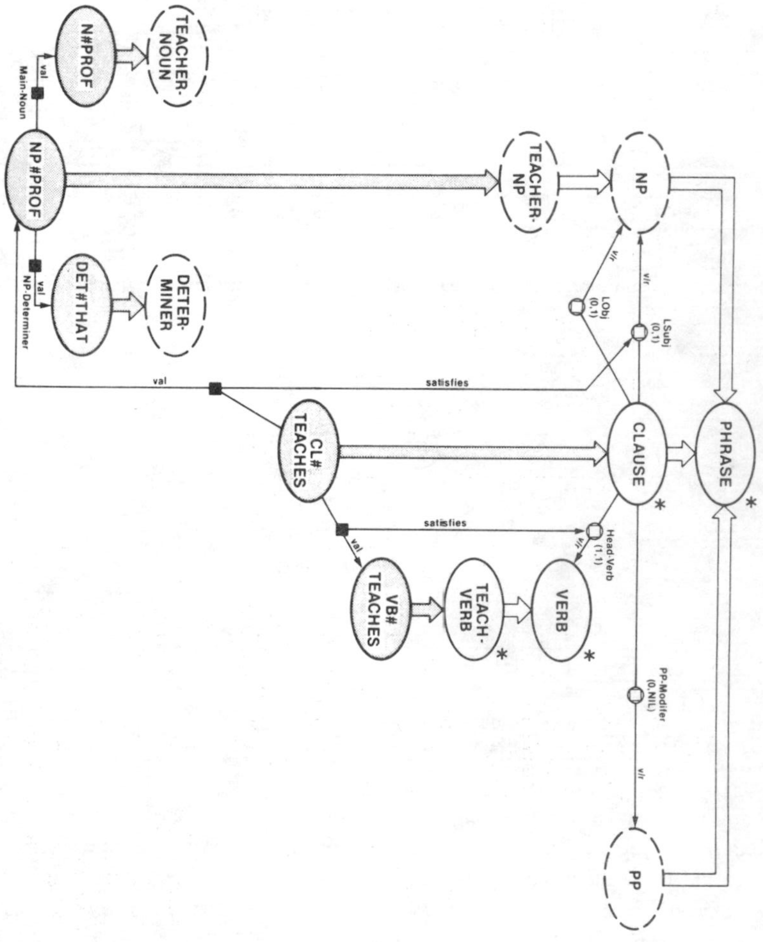

Figure 18. Partial representation of sentence: logical subject added.

pands the representation of *CL#TEACHES* as shown in Figure 19. Actually, the word "undergraduates" has an analog as a noun, *N#UNDERGRADS*, and as a noun phrase, *NP#UNDERGRADS*.

The syntaxonomy also includes Concepts for prepositional phrases, as shown in Figure 20. *PP* denotes all prepositional phrases (PPs), *PP-Prep* denotes the preposition of a PP, and *PP-Object* denotes its object. We can see that a PP must have exactly one preposition that must be a preposition, where *PREPOSITION* denotes all prepositions. Also, each PP must have exactly one object which must be a noun phrase. *ABOUT-PREPOSITION* denotes a singleton set, the preposition "about," and the various Concepts for types of noun phrases were described earlier.

Here there are several defined Concepts. *ABOUT-PP* denotes just those PPs whose preposition is the word "about." *TIME-PP* denotes just those PPs whose objects refer to time. *ABOUT-SUBJECT-PP* denotes just those PPs whose object refers to a subject and whose preposition is the word "about."

Now we can continue with the handling of the two PPs in our example. Using its dictionaries and the classifier, PSI-KLONE finds that "about Lisp" is an instance of *ABOUT-SUBJECT-PP*, which we will call *PP#LISP*. Similarly, "on Thursday" is found to be an instance of *TIME-PP*, which we will call *PP#THURS*. For the sake of brevity, in our discussion we have dispensed with the Individual Concepts for each of "about," "Lisp," "on," and "Thursday," and how they relate to *PP#LISP* and *PP#THURS*. In the actual system, of course, these are accounted for. This completes the clause, and simultaneously, the sentence, so RUS signals that the end of the clause has been reached. The representation of *CL#TEACHES* as it stands now is shown in Figure 21. However, before we show PSI-KLONE's final steps, we must first explain the final portion of the syntaxonomy, as shown in Figure 22.

Here we have specified several defined subConcepts of *CLAUSE* and we have used RoleSet differentiation for the first time in this section. *TIME-PP-CLAUSE* has a RoleSet called *Time-PP-Modifier* that differentiates the *PP-Modifier* RoleSet of *CLAUSE*, which means that *some* of a clause's PP modifiers can be also be instances of *Time-PP-Modifier*. The Value Restriction for *Time-PP-Modifier* is *TIME-PP*, which was shown earlier to denote PPs whose objects refer to time. Its Number Restriction is "(1,NIL)." Therefore, an instance of *TIME-PP-CLAUSE* is a clause that has at least one PP modifier that satisfies the constraints of *Time-PP-Modifier*. However, we must remember that RoleSet differentiation describes *necessary, but not sufficient* conditions. Thus, *KL-ONE* cannot independently recognize that two objects stand in the relation denoted by *Time-PP-Modifier*, just as it can't do the same for, say, *Head-Verb*. Only some outside sources can do

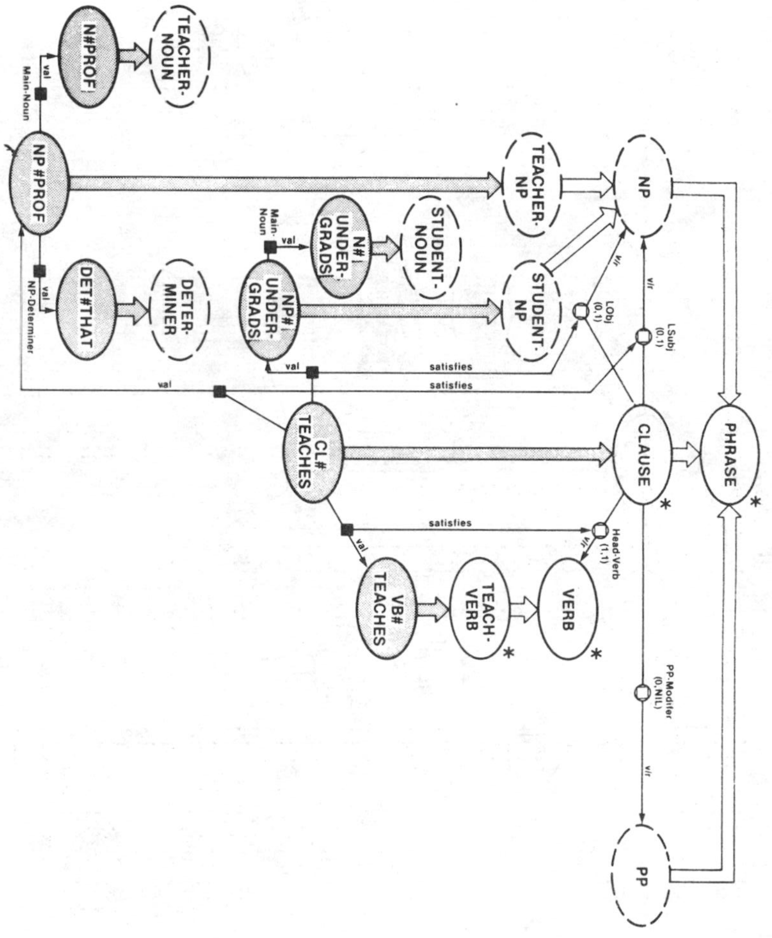

Figure 19. Partial representation of sentence: logical object added.

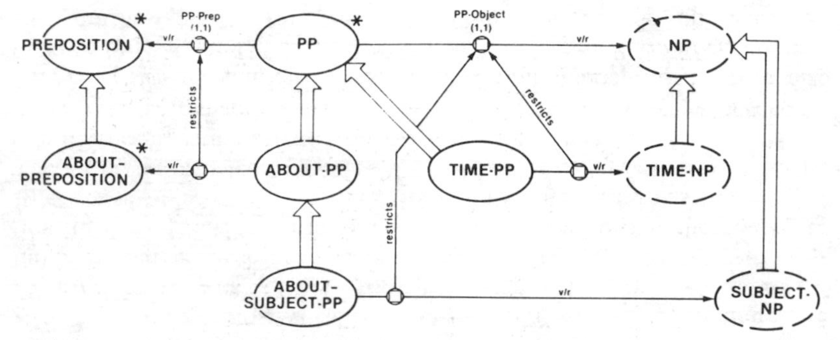

Figure 20. Part of the syntaxonomy: Prepositional Phrases.

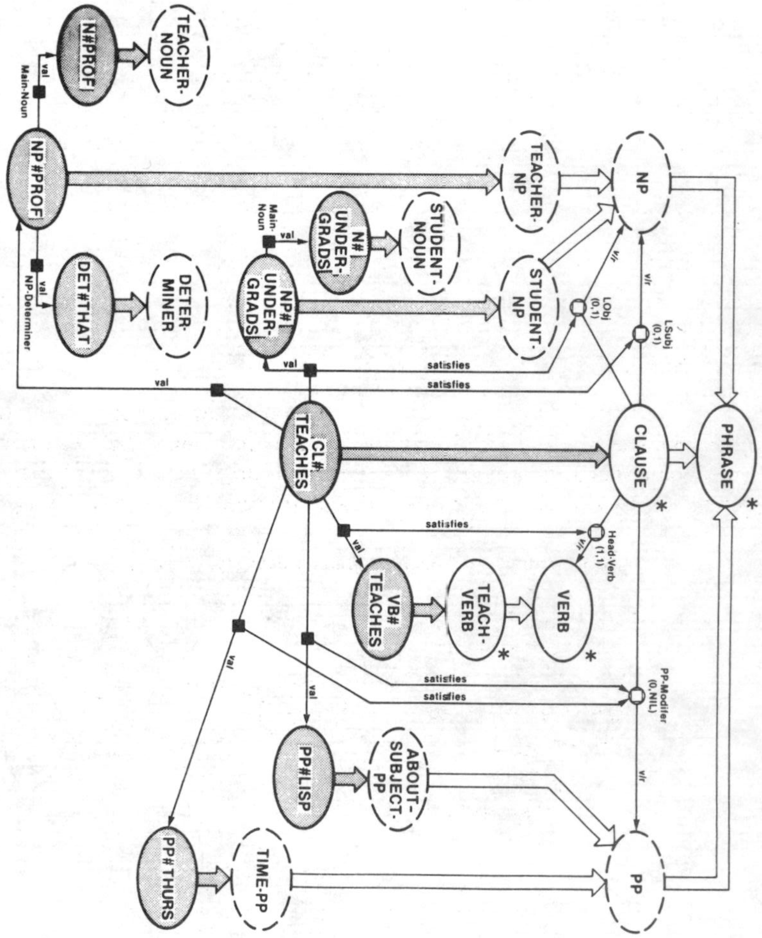

Figure 21. Representation of sentence with all constituents.

that. However, our intended meaning of *Time-PP-Modifier* is exactly as if these conditions were sufficient, i.e., it denotes those clauses that have at least one PP modifier whose object refers to time. Unfortunately, we cannot say this presicely in KL-ONE.

ABOUT-SUBJECT-CLAUSE is specified similarly to *TIME-PP-CLAUSE*. The only difference here is that we differentiate *PP-Modifier* to form *About-Subject-PP-Modifier*. As with *Time-PP-Modifier*, our intended meaning is as if the necessary conditions represented in KL-ONE were sufficient as well, i.e., *ABOUT-SUBJECT-CLAUSE* denotes those clauses with at least one PP modifier whose preposition is "about" and whose object refers to subjects.

The meaning of *TEACH-STU-CLAUSE* follows easily. It denotes just those clauses with a head verb that refers to teaching and a logical object that refers to students.

So, before PSI-KLONE can classify the analog for the entire clause, *CL#TEACHES*, it must enforce our intended meanings for the RoleSets *Time-PP-Modifier* and *About-Subject-PP-Modifier*. In other words, whenever it determines that some PP is a modifier of a clause, it must also test whether it satisfies the relations denoted by those two RoleSets. This requires an additional mechanism in PSI-KLONE that we will not describe due to space limitations. However, given our intended meanings for these RoleSets, we can see that "about Lisp" satisfies the meaning of *About-Subject-PP-Modifier* and that "on Thursday" satisfies the meaning of *Time-PP-Modifier*.

We now classify *CL#TEACHES* and find it has several new parent Concepts, *TIME-PP-CLAUSE, ABOUT-SUBJECT-CLAUSE,* and *TEACH-STU-CLAUSE*. This is represented by forming a Concept that is just the conjunction of these parent Concepts, and having *CL#TEACHES* individuate it. Figure 23 shows this; the unnamed Concept is defined to be just the conjunction of its parent Concepts.

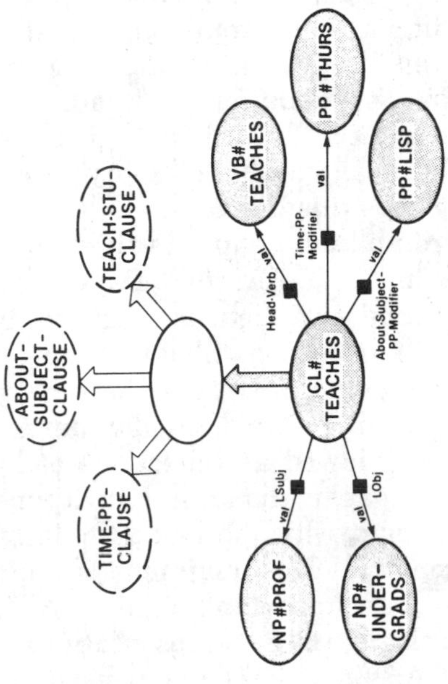

Figure 23. Final representation of sentence: after classification.

We assume that appropriate interpretation rules are inherited from the newly discovered parent Concepts and that PSI-KLONE makes a coherent interpretation. RUS and PSI-KLONE are now done with the sentence, and we are done with our discussion.

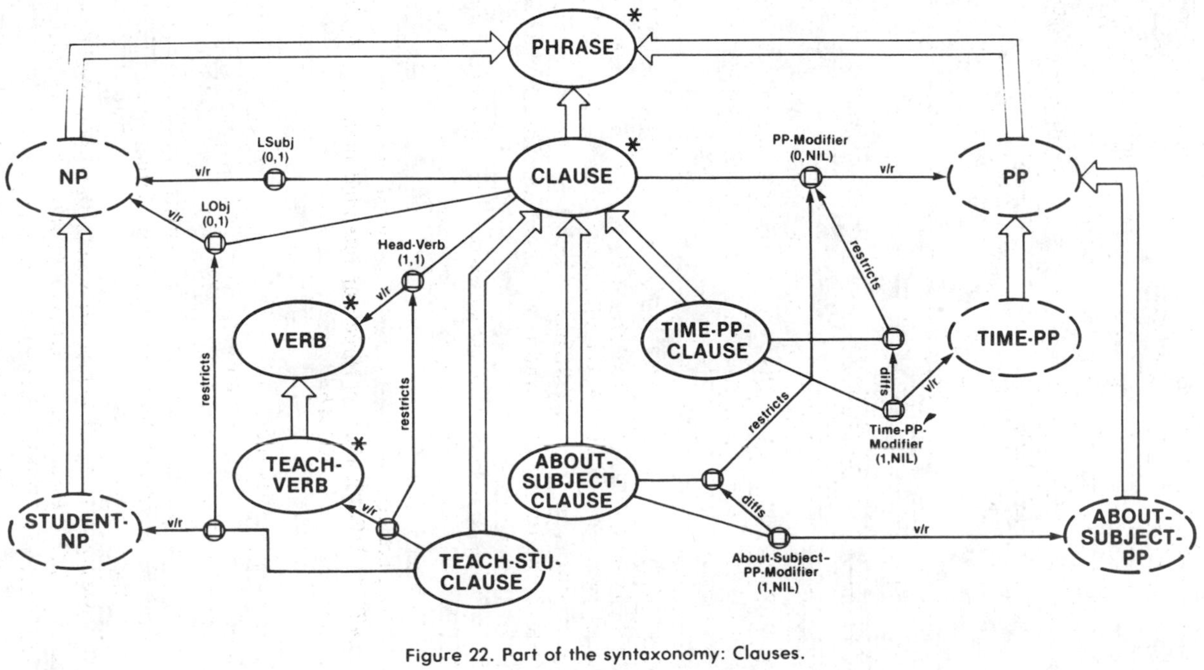

Figure 22. Part of the syntaxonomy: Clauses.

2.3 Logic and Databases

The application of logic to database theory and practice has become an influential research framework for AI and databases, as well as for other areas of computer science. The first paper of this section (2.3.1) is "Logic and Databases: A Deductive Approach" by Herve Gallaire, Jack Minker, and Jean-Marie Nicolas. It is a thorough survey of research in the related research written by three of the primary contributors and most influential protagonists of the work. Deductive databases have their roots in logic programming, which has been the focus of much research (see [KOWA74], [VK76], [CP81], [BK82], [LOGI82], and [LOGI83]), as has deductive databases ([GM78], [HARE80], [GALL81], [GALL83], [GRAY84], [LT85], and [BJ86]).

"On Closed World Databases" by Ray Reiter, the second paper (2.3.2), is a seminal paper not only of logic and databases but also of database research itself. It points out that query evaluation with respect to a database is based on a hidden assumption that *everything you do not know to be true may be assumed to be false*, which Reiter calls the *closed-world assumption*. The paper has had tremendous impact because it presents one of the first thorough discussions of the nonmonotonic nature of databases (and knowledge bases). It is equally important from a methodological viewpoint, as it gives a vivid illustration of the value of the reformulation of databases in logical terms. The paper "Towards a Logical Reconstruction of Relational Database Theory" [Reiter, 2.4.3] further develops this theme.

The third and final paper in this section (2.3.3), Bob Kowalski's "Logic for Data Description," presents a lucid argument against the traditional distinction between databases and programs. Instead, the paper adopts a logic-programming viewpoint, arguing that both databases and programs can be viewed as collections of logical formulas. The paper dismisses criticisms against (first-order) logic, which focus on the latter's monotonicity property. The treatment of nonmonotonicity has been an important research topic for proponents of logic-based representations in recent years [McCAR80] [REIT87], suggesting that the dismissal was perhaps premature.

Logic and Databases: A Deductive Approach

HERVÉ GALLAIRE

Compagnie Générale d'Électricité Laboratoire de Marcoussis, Marcoussis, France

JACK MINKER

University of Maryland, Computer Science Department, College Park, Maryland

JEAN-MARIE NICOLAS

ONERA-CERT, Département d'Informatique, Toulouse, France

The purpose of this paper is to show that logic provides a convenient formalism for studying classical database problems. There are two main parts to the paper, devoted respectively to conventional databases and deductive databases. In the first part, we focus on query languages, integrity modeling and maintenance, query optimization, and data dependencies. The second part deals mainly with the representation and manipulation of deduced facts and incomplete information.

Categories and Subject Descriptors: H.2.1 [**Database Management**]: Logical Design—*data models*; H.2.3 [**Database Management**]: Languages—*query languages*; H.2.4 [**Database Management**]: Systems—*query processing*

General Terms: Deductive Databases, Indefinite Data, Logic and Databases, Null Values, Relational Databases

CONTENTS

INTRODUCTION
- I.1 Relational Model
- I.2 Mathematical Logic
- I.3 Databases Viewed through Logic

1. CONVENTIONAL DATABASES
   - 1.1 Query Languages
   - 1.2 Integrity Constraints
   - 1.3 Query Optimization
   - 1.4 Database Design
2. DEDUCTIVE DATABASES
   - 2.1 Definition of Deductive or Logic Databases
   - 2.2 Definite Deductive Databases (DDDBs)
   - 2.3 Indefinite Deductive Databases (IDDDBs)
   - 2.4 Logic Databases
3. CONCLUSION

ACKNOWLEDGMENTS

REFERENCES

INTRODUCTION

As emphasized by Codd [1982], theoretical database studies form a fundamental basis for the development of homogeneous and sound database management systems (DBMS), which offer sophisticated capabilities for data handling. A comprehensive study of the many problems that exist in databases requires a precise formalization so that detailed analyses can be carried out and satisfactory solutions can be obtained. Most of the formal database studies that are under way at present are concerned with the relational data model introduced by Codd [1970], and use either a specially developed database theory [Maier 1983; Ullman 1982] or other formal theories such as mathematical logic as their framework. The purpose of this paper is to provide an overview and a survey of a subfield of logic as it is applied to databases. We are mostly concerned with the application of logic to databases, where logic may be used both as an inference system and as a representation language; we primarily consider relational type databases. Some important efforts in the application of other aspects of logic theory to databases (e.g., see Maier [1983], Ullman [1982], and the references provided there) or those that deal with nonrelational (i.e., hierarchical and network) databases (e.g., see Jacobs [1982] and Jacobs et al. [1982]) are not covered here.

The use of logic for knowledge representation and manipulation is primarily due to the work of Green [1969]. His work was the basis of various studies that led to so-called question-answering systems, which are concerned mainly with a highly deductive manipulation of a small set of facts, and thus require an inferential mechanism provided by logic. Similar techniques have been adapted to databases to handle large sets of facts, negative information, open queries, and other specific database topics. These techniques have given rise to what is called deductive databases. However, the use of logic to study databases is not restricted to providing deductive capabilities in a DBMS; the pioneering work of Kuhns [1967, 1970] also uses logic for conventional databases to characterize answers to queries.

Aside from the introduction and conclusion to this paper, there are two main sections, which are devoted respectively to conventional databases and deductive databases. In this introduction we provide background material to familiarize the reader with the terminology used throughout the paper, introducing the reader to concepts in relational databases, to the area of mathematical logic, and to the basic relationships between logic and databases. Section 1 is an extended and revised version of material that appeared in Gallaire [1981]. This material shows how logic provides a formalism for databases, and how this formalism has been applied to conventional databases. Its use in query languages, integrity modeling and maintenance, query evaluation, and database schema analysis is described. In Section 2 we show how logic extends relational databases to permit deduction and describe how logic provides a sound basis for a proper treatment and understanding of null values and incomplete information.

In the remainder of this introduction, we first describe the main concepts of the relational data model. Following this, we specify what is meant by mathematical logic, focusing on logic relevant to databases rather than logic in general. Finally, we briefly introduce two ways in which databases can be considered from the viewpoint of logic.

I.1 Relational Model

To define a relational model we need some concepts. A *domain* is a usually finite set of values. The *Cartesian product* of domains $D_1, \ldots, D_n$ is denoted by $D_1 \times \cdots \times D_n$ and is the set of all tuples $(x_1, \ldots, x_n)$ such that for any i, $i = 1, \ldots, n$ $(x_i \in D_i)$. A *relation* is any subset of the Cartesian product of one or more domains. A database (instance) is a finite set of finite relations. By a finite relation we mean that the extension of the relation (i.e., the totality of all tuples that can appear in a relation) is finite. The arity of a relation $R \subseteq D_1 \times \cdots \times D_n$ is n. One may envision a relation to be a table of values. Names are generally associated with the columns of these tables; these names are called *attributes*. Values of an attribute associated with column i of a relation are taken from domain D_i. A relation R with attributes $A_1, \ldots, A_n$ defines a relation scheme denoted as $R(A_1, \ldots, A_n)$, whereas the specific relation R (i.e., the relation with specified tuples) is said to be an *instance* or *extension* of the relation scheme.

Not all instances of a relation scheme have meaningful interpretations; that is, they do not correspond to valid sets of data according to the intended semantics of the database. One therefore introduces a set of constraints, referred to as *integrity constraints*, associated with a relation scheme

Current address of Hervé Gallaire and Jean-Marie Nicolas: European Computer-Industry Research Centre (ECRC), Arabellastrasse 17, D-8000 München 81, FRG.

to ensure that the database meets the intended semantics. Integrity constraints may involve interrelationships between relations.

To summarize, a database scheme consists of a collection of relation schemes together with a set of integrity constraints. A database instance, also called a database state, is a collection of relation instances, one for each relation in the database scheme. A database state is said to be valid if all relation instances that it contains obey the integrity constraints. In this paper, values in database/relation instances are referred to as elements, constants, or individuals, depending on the context.

To manipulate data in a relational database, a language is introduced. One may introduce an algebraic language based on algebraic operators, or a calculus language, which we discuss in the following section. In an algebraic language we need only two operators for our purposes: the project and join operators. Given a relation R, and X a set of attributes of R, then the *projection* of R on X is $\{s[X] | s \in R\}$, where $s[X]$ is a tuple constructed from s by keeping all and only those components that belong to attributes in X. Given two relations R and S, the *natural join* $R * S$ is formed by computing the Cartesian product, $R \times S$, selecting out all tuples whose values on each attribute common to R and S coincide, and projecting one occurrence of each of the common attributes. For a more thorough presentation of the relational model, the reader is referred to Date [1977, 1981] and Ullman [1982]. See also Delobel [1980] and Maier [1983] for an overview and a survey of relational database theory.

I.2 Mathematical Logic

As is true for any formal system, mathematical logic relies upon an object language, a semantics or interpretation of formulas in that language, and a proof theory.

As the *object language* we shall use a first-order language such as that of the first-order predicate calculus. Primitive symbols of such a language are (1) parentheses, (2) variables, constants, functions, and predicate symbols, (3) the usual logical connectors, $\neg$ (not), & (and), $\vee$ (or), $\rightarrow$ (implication), $\leftrightarrow$ (equivalence), and (4) quantifiers, $\forall$ (for all), $\exists$ (there exists). Throughout the paper we use lowercase letters from the start of the alphabet to represent constants ($a, b, c, \ldots$), those from the end of the alphabet to represent variables (u, v, w, x, y, z), and letters such as ($f, g, h, \ldots$) to denote functions.

A *term* is defined recursively to be a constant or a variable, or if f is an n-ary function and $t_1, \ldots, t_n$ are terms, then $f(t_1, \ldots, t_n)$ is a term. There are no other terms. We usually assume that a term in the context of databases is function free; that is, it is either a constant or a variable.

If P is an n-ary predicate symbol and $t_1, \ldots, t_n$ are terms, then $P(t_1, \ldots, t_n)$ is an *atomic formula*. An atomic formula or its negation is a *literal*. *Well-formed formulas* (wffs) are defined recursively as follows. An atomic formula is a wff. If w_1 and w_2 are wffs, then $\neg(w_1)$, $(w_1) \vee (w_2)$, (w_1) & (w_2), $(w_1) \rightarrow (w_2)$, and $(w_1) \leftrightarrow (w_2)$ are wffs. A *closed* wff is one that does not contain any *free* variable (i.e., it contains only quantified variables and constants).

In dealing with wffs it is sometimes convenient to place them in a normal form. A wff is in *prenex normal form* if all quantifiers appear in front of the formula. The wff corresponding to the statement "Every teacher has a diploma" is

$$(1)\quad (\forall x\ \forall y)(\text{TEACH}(x, y) \rightarrow (\exists z)\text{DIPLOMA}(x, z)).$$

It is indeed possible to place all quantifiers in front of the formula to achieve the prenex normal form (see Chang and Lee [1973] for details). When this is done, formula (1) becomes formula (2):

$$(2)\quad (\forall x)(\forall y)(\exists z)(\neg\text{TEACH}(x, y) \vee \text{DIPLOMA}(x, z)).$$

Similarly, the prenex normal form of the wff

$$(3)\quad (\forall x)(\forall y)(((\exists z)(P(x, z)\ \&\ P(y, z))) \rightarrow (\exists u)Q(x, y, u))$$

is

$$(4)\quad (\forall x)(\forall y)(\forall z)(\exists u)(\neg P(x, z) \vee \neg P(y, z) \vee Q(x, y, u)).$$

A prenex formula is in *Skolem normal form* when all existential quantifiers are eliminated by replacing variables they quantify with arbitrary functions of all universally quantified variables that precede them in the formula. These functions are called Skolem functions; a Skolem function of 0 arguments is called a Skolem constant. A *clause* is a disjunction of literals, all of whose variables are implicitly universally quantified. The Skolem normal form of (2) is

$$(5)\quad \forall x\ \forall y(\neg\text{TEACH}(x, y) \vee \text{DIPLOMA}(x, f(x, y))),$$

where the existentially quantified variables are eliminated and replaced by Skolem functions. Similarly, the Skolem normal form of (4) is

$$(6)\quad (\forall x)(\forall y)(\forall z)(\neg P(x, z) \vee \neg P(y, z) \vee Q(x, y, g(x, y, z))),$$

where the existentially quantified variable u has been eliminated and replaced by the Skolem function $g(x, y, z)$. When a wff is in Skolem normal form, all the quantifiers remaining in the front of the formula may be eliminated since all variables that remain are, by convention, universally quantified. Formula (5), above, may be replaced by

$$(7)\quad \neg\text{TEACH}(x, y) \vee \text{DIPLOMA}(x, f(x, y)).$$

Thus

$$\neg A_1 \vee \cdots \vee \neg A_m \vee B_1 \vee \cdots \vee B_n,$$

where the A_1 and the B_j are positive literals, is a clause. We shall write a clause in an equivalent form as

$$A_1\ \&\ \cdots\ \&\ A_m \rightarrow B_1 \vee \cdots \vee B_n.$$

In a clause, whenever n is equal to 0 or 1, the clause is said to be a *Horn clause*. If both m and n are equal to 0, there are no atoms on the left- or right-hand side of the implication sign, and the clause is called the *empty clause*. A clause (a literal) in which no variables appear is called a *ground clause* (*ground literal*). Every closed, well-formed formula may be placed in clause form. We note that the transformation of a wff into prenex normal form preserves equivalence, but this is not the case for transformations into Skolem or clause form. The latter transformations only preserve satisfiability, which is sufficient for provability purposes.

Two complementary aspects of wffs are of interest. One deals with *semantics* (or *model theory*), the specification of truth values to wffs, whereas the other deals with *proof theory*, the derivation of a wff from a given set of wffs.

I.2.1 Semantics: Model and Interpretation

In semantics we are concerned with interpretations, where an *interpretation* of a set of wffs consists of the specification of a nonempty set (or domain) E, from which constants and variables are given values. Each n-ary function symbol is assigned a function from E^n to E. Each n-ary predicate is assigned a relation on E^n.

In an interpretation with domain E, a closed wff is either true or false, whereas a (open) wff with n ($n \geq 1$) free variables determines a set of n-tuples (i.e., a relation) on E^n. Each of these n-tuples is such that when its components are substituted for the corresponding free variables in the open wff, then in this interpretation, the closed wff that is obtained is true. If the set of n-tuples is empty, then the open wff is said to be false, and if the set of n-tuples coincides with E^n, then the open wff is said to be true. Broadly, the truth value of a closed wff is obtained as follows. If R is the relation assigned to a n-place predicate symbol P, then $P(e_1, \ldots, e_n)$ evaluates to true if $\langle e_1, \ldots, e_n\rangle \in R$; otherwise it evaluates to false. Now, if w_1 and w_2 are closed wffs, $\neg w_1$ evaluates to true if w_1 is false; otherwise it evaluates to false. w_1 & w_2 evaluates to true if both w_1 and w_2 are true; otherwise it evaluates to false. $w_1 \rightarrow w_2$ evaluates to true if either w_1 is false or w_2 is true; otherwise it evaluates to false. Well-formed formulas constructed using the other logical symbols may be evaluated similarly. Finally, if x is a variable in w, $\forall x w(x)$ (respectively, $\exists x w(x)$) evaluates to true if for all elements e_1 in E (respectively, there is an element $e_1 \in E$ such that) $w(e_1)$ is true; otherwise it evaluates to false.

A *model* of a set of wffs is an interpretation in which all wffs in the set are true. A wff w is said to be a *logical consequence* of a set of wffs W iff w is true in all models of W. This is denoted by $W \models w$.

I.2.2 Syntax: First-Order Theory

The first-order predicate calculus is a formal system that has as object language a first-order language, a set of axiom schemas (the logical axioms), and two inference rules: *modus ponens* and *generalization.*

When other wffs are added as axioms, the formal system that is obtained is called a *first*-order theory. The new axioms are called *nonlogical* or (*proper*) axioms. A first-order theory is essentially characterized by its nonlogical axioms. A set of nonlogical axioms could be, for example,

Man(Turing),

$(\forall x)(\text{Man}(x) \rightarrow \text{Mortal}(x))$.

A *model* of a theory is an interpretation in which all axioms are true; logical axioms are, in fact, chosen to be true in all interpretations. For the above theory, setting

$$\text{Man(Turing)} = \text{True},$$

$$\text{Mortal(Turing)} = \text{True}$$

yields a model since it makes all statements in the above theory true. A wff w is *derivable* from a set of wffs W in a theory $T(W \vdash w)$ iff w is deducible from W and from the axioms of T by a finite application of the inference rules.

Using the inference rule of modus ponens, which states that from p and $p \rightarrow q$ one can conclude q, we obtain from the above theory the derived result: Mortal(Turing). If W is empty, then w is a *theorem* of T ($\vdash_T w$, or equivalently $T \vdash w$). Whenever T is clear, we shall write $W \vdash w$ for $W \vdash_T w$.

Inference rules other than modus ponens and generalization can be used to derive theorems; in fact most theorem-proving techniques are based on the inference rule termed the Robinson Resolution Principle [Robinson 1965], which applies to wffs in clausal form.

The Robinson Resolution Principle is a rule of inference that permits a new clause to be derived from two given clauses; further, the derived clause is satisfiable (i.e., has a model) if the two given clauses are satisfiable. In the context of databases assumed to be function free, the principle can be described in terms of the following example. From

C1: $\neg P(a, b, c) \vee Q(d, e)$, and

C2: $P(x, y, z) \vee R(x, y)$,

one obtains the derived clause

C3: $Q(d, e) \vee R(a, b)$.

The clause C3 is found by considering the literals in the two clauses that have the same predicate name, but one is negated and the other is not. The only predicate of this type is P. One then determines if the two atoms $\{P(a, b, c), P(x, y, z)\}$ can be made identical by some substitution to the variables, where a, b, and c are assumed to be constants and x, y, and z are assumed to be variables. The substitution $\{a/x, b/y, c/z\}$ is such a substitution, and is to be read: Substitute a for x, b for y, and c for z. One then eliminates the two literals made identical by the substitution (said to be unified) from each clause, forms the disjunction of the remaining literals in the two clauses, and applies the unifying substitution to the remaining literals to obtain the derived clause. Thus in this example the clause C3 is derived.

The resolution principle is used mostly to carry out refutation proofs: In order to prove $W \vdash w$, one tries to show that W and $\neg w$ are not simultaneously satisfiable. As resolution preserves satisfiability, if one can, by resolution from the clausal forms of W and $\neg w$, derive the empty clause, then W and $\neg w$ cannot simultaneously be satisfiable. For example, $\neg P(a, b, c)$ and $P(x, y, z)$, where x, y, and z are variables, would resolve to yield the empty clause.

A resolution proof consists of applying resolution to all clauses in the original set, adding those newly derived clauses to the set, and iterating the process.

The most important relationships between the semantic and the syntactic approaches are soundness and completeness. An inference system is *sound* iff for all W and w, whenever $W \vdash w$, it implies that $W \models w$; it is *complete* iff for all W and w, whenever $W \models w$, it implies that $W \vdash w$. The inference rules of modus ponens and generalization are complete and sound for the propositional calculus. Similarly, resolution refutation is complete and sound for first-order theories: The empty clause is derived if and only if the initial clause (which is negated to apply resolution) is a theorem in the theory. However, there is an element of undecidability; if the clause proposed to be proved is not a theorem, the inference process may never terminate. Resolution refutation is also complete and sound. The meaning of completeness and soundness is that the same results are obtained by using semantics, which deals with truth assignments, and provability, which deals with inference rules.

The reader should refer to Enderton [1972] and Mendelson [1978] for general background on logic and to Chang and Lee [1973] and Loveland [1978] for more material on the resolution principle.

I.3 Databases Viewed through Logic

Before considering the formalization of databases in terms of logic, we shall mention some assumptions that govern query (and integrity constraint) evaluation of databases. On the one hand, these assumptions express a certain implicit representation of negative facts (e.g., "Paul is not the father of Peter:" ¬Father(Paul, Peter)) and, on the other hand, they make precise the universe of reference to which queries refer. There are three such assumptions:

(1) The *closed world assumption* (CWA), also called convention for negative information, which states that facts not known to be true are assumed to be false (i.e., $\neg R(e_1, \ldots, e_n)$ is assumed to be true iff the tuple $\langle e_1, \ldots, e_n \rangle$ fails to be found in relation R).

(2) The *unique name assumption*, which states that individuals with different names are different.

(3) The *domain closure assumption*, which states that there are no other individuals than those in the database.

Answers to "For all" queries or queries involving negation are obtained by using the above hypotheses. For example, the query, "Who is not a Full Professor?", addressed to a database whose current state consists of

Full-Prof.(Jean),
Full-Prof.(Paul),
Associate-Prof.(Andre),
Assistant-Prof.(Pierre),

will get as an answer {Pierre, Andre}. Indeed, the domain closure assumption restricts the individuals to be considered to the set {Jean, Paul, Pierre, Andre}. Furthermore, according to the unique name assumption, one gets the following: Pierre ≠ Jean, Pierre ≠ Paul. Consequently, Pierre ∉ Full-Prof., which, according to the closed world assumption, leads to ¬Full-Prof.(Pierre). The second element of the answer, ¬Full-Prof.(Andre), is obtained in a similar way.

We note that one way to avoid calling for the domain closure assumption is to consider as acceptable queries (and integrity constraints) only expressions that restrict their own reference domain. This is the case for any expression of the relational algebra and for the so-called class of definite (or safe, or range-restricted) logical formulas (see Section 1.1.1).

Although the query evaluation process in any DBMS (implicitly) works under the above hypotheses, these assumptions were made explicit and clearly understood only through a logical formalization of databases.

As first characterized by Nicolas and Gallaire [1978], a database can be considered from the viewpoint of logic in two different ways: either as an *interpretation* (of a first-order theory) or as a (first-order) *theory.* When considered from the viewpoint of interpretations, queries (and integrity constraints) are formulas that are to be evaluated on the interpretation using the semantic definition of truth. From the viewpoint of a theory, queries and integrity constraints are considered to be theorems that are to be proved. The interpretation viewpoint and the theory viewpoint respectively formalize the concepts of conventional and deductive databases.

Reiter [1984] and Kowalski [1981a] have investigated these two approaches more thoroughly. Reiter refers to the two approaches as the *model-theoretic view* and the *proof-theoretic view*, respectively, whereas Kowalski refers to them as the *relational structure view* and the *logic database view.*

The three terms "interpretation," "model," and "relational structure" are closely related. A model is an interpretation that makes all axioms true. The "relational structure" view means that queries are evaluated by assuming the database entries to be true. All these terms relate to the semantic definition of truth. We shall use the term "model-theoretic view" for these three terms throughout this paper. The three terms "theory," "proof theoretic," and "logic database" connote that, in order to determine answers to queries, one derives data from axioms. We use the term "proof theoretic" for these terms throughout the paper.

Both Kowalski and Reiter have shown that, although conventional databases are generally considered from a model-theoretic view, they can also be considered from the proof-theoretic view and can thus be considered as a particular logic database.

This section provides an intuitive characterization of these two views of a database through the perspective of logic. Further details are provided in Section 2 of this paper for the proof-theoretic view.

Let DB be an instance of a relational database. Then DB consists of a set of relations (i.e., a relation R for each relation schema $R(A_1, \ldots, A_n)$) and a set of integrity constraints, IC. Let D be the union of the underlying domains of all attributes that occur in the relation schema. Now define a first-order language L to consist of an n-place predicate symbol $\mathbf{R}$ for each n-ary relation in DB and a set of constants, one for each element in D; the language is assumed to have no function symbols. DB can be seen as an interpretation of formulas of the language as defined in Section I.2, and the formulas of L can be evaluated in this interpretation as follows: Variables range over the domain D, and $\mathbf{R}(e_1, \ldots, e_n)$ is true iff $\langle e_1, \ldots, e_n\rangle \in R$. The language can be extended to include arithmetic comparison operators ($<, =, >, \leq, \geq$) as particular predicate symbols, which are assigned their usual interpretation.

If the integrity constraints in IC are expressed as formulas of L, then the database DB will be a valid database state iff every constraint in IC evaluates to true in DB, that is, iff DB is a model of IC. We note that, according to the very definition of an interpretation, the evaluation of logical formulas (on an interpretation) is done in accord with the closed world, unique name, and domain closure assumptions stated at the beginning of this section.

The above constitutes a description of the model-theoretic view of a database. The proof-theoretic view of DB is obtained by constructing a theory T that admits DB as a unique model. Then for any wff w in L, $T \vdash w$ iff w is true in DB.

The process of defining T consists of making its (proper) axioms precise. The axioms (see Reiter [1984]) are of three kinds:

(1) *Assertions.* For any relation R in DB and any tuple $\langle e_1, \ldots, e_n\rangle \in R$, an axiom $\mathbf{R}(e_1, \ldots, e_n) \in T$.

(2) *Particularization Axioms.* Particularization axioms explicitly state the evaluation hypotheses that, in the model-theoretic view, are conveyed by the notion of interpretation:

(i) *The completion axioms.* There is one such axiom for any relation R in DB. If $\langle e_1^1, \ldots, e_1^n\rangle, \ldots, \langle e_p^1, \ldots, e_p^n\rangle$ are all the tuples in R, it is written as

$$\forall x_1 \cdots \forall x_n(R(x_1, \ldots, x_n) \rightarrow (x_1 = e_1^1 \;\&\; \cdots \;\&\; x_n = e_1^n) \vee \cdots \vee (x_1 = e_p^1 \;\&\; \cdots \;\&\; x = e_p^n)).$$

The completion axiom effectively states that the only values tuples that the relation R can have are

$$\langle e_1^1, \ldots, e_1^n\rangle, \ldots, \langle e_p^1, \ldots, e_p^n\rangle.$$

(ii) *The unique name axioms.* If $e_1, \ldots, e_q$ are all the individuals in DB, the unique name axioms are

$$(e_1 \neq e_2), \ldots, (e_1 \neq e_q),$$
$$(e_2 \neq e_3), \ldots, (e_{q-1} \neq e_q).$$

(iii) *The domain closure axiom.* This is

$$\forall x((x = e_1) \vee (x = e_2) \vee \cdots \vee (x = e_q)).$$

(3) *Equality Axioms.* Equality axioms are needed since the axioms in (2) involve the equality predicate. These axioms specify the usual properties of equality:

- *reflexivity:*

$$\forall x(x = x).$$

- *symmetry:*

$$\forall x \forall y((x = y) \rightarrow (y = x)).$$

- *transitivity:*

$$\forall x \forall y \forall z((x = y) \;\&\; (y = z) \rightarrow (x = z)).$$

- *principle of substitution of equal terms:*

$$\forall x_1 \cdots \forall y_n(P(x_1, \ldots, x_n) \;\&\; (x_1 = y_1) \;\&\; \cdots \;\&\; (x_n = y_n) \rightarrow P(y_1, \ldots, y_n)).$$

Let us briefly give the underlying reason why T admits DB as a unique model (up to an isomorphism). The only interpretation of T in which the domain closure axioms and the unique name axioms are all satisfied is such that their individuals are in one-to-one correspondence with elements in D. Thus all the possible models of T have the same domain as DB (up to an isomorphism). For any such model M, since its domain is fixed, in order to be different from DB, it must assign to at least one $\mathbf{R}$ a relation R' different from R. But this is not possible. Indeed, if a tuple $\langle e_1, \ldots, e_n\rangle$ belongs to R but not to R', then M does not satisfy one of the axioms in (1). Conversely, if $\langle e_1, \ldots, e_n\rangle$ belongs to R' but not to R, then M does not obey the completion axiom associated with $\mathbf{R}$.

As defined above T provides the proof-theoretic view of DB. According to this view, DB satisfies a constraint w in IC iff $T \vdash w$. Furthermore, the answer to a query formulated as $W(x_1, \ldots, x_p)$—where $x_1, \ldots, x_p$ are the free variables in the formula W—consists of those p-tuples $\langle e_1, \ldots, e_p\rangle$ such that $T \vdash W(e_1, \ldots, e_p)$.

It is worth noting that, although according to this view query (and integrity constraint) evaluation calls for proof techniques, DB is and remains a conventional (i.e., nondeductive) database. No other (positive) facts than those explicitly stated in (1) can be derived from T.

At this stage one may notice that the above proof-theoretic view is not intended to be used directly as a basis for a DBMS implementation. The combinatorial complexity of the particularization axioms would lead to inefficient systems, but, as emphasized by Reiter [1984], the value of this view is found in the generalizations that it suggests for databases: (1) Add some disjunctive facts or existentially quantified literals among the assertions and one obtains a database with null values and incomplete information; (2) suppress from the set of ICs some of its formulas and add those formulas as axioms to the theory and one obtains a new theory that is a deductive database. However, the formulation of the completion axioms then has to be reconsidered, as is seen in Section 2. Except for work in deductive databases, the applications of logic to databases has mainly referred, either explicitly or implicitly, to the model-theoretic view. This work is reported upon in Section 1.

1. CONVENTIONAL DATABASES

The goal of Section 1 is to show how logic can provide formal support to study classical database problems, and in some cases, how logic can go further, helping to comprehend and then to solve them. We describe contributions published in the literature that relate to logic and databases with respect to query languages, integrity modeling and maintenance, query evaluation, and database schema analysis.

1.1 Query Languages

1.1.1 Toward Relational Calculus

One of the first impacts of logic on databases was the use of its language as a basis for defining assertional query languages. This can be done in any one of four ways [Pirotte 1976, 1978], depending on whether one-sorted or many-sorted languages [Enderton 1972] are used and whether tuples of relations or elements of domains are considered as primitive objects [Ullman 1980]. In fact, only two out of these four possibilities have been truly exploited: the so-called *domain relational calculus* (DRC, one sorted/elements of domains) and the *tuple relational calculus* (TRC, one sorted/tuples of relations). Both of these languages have the same expressive power [Ullman 1980]. The respective pioneering and fundamental efforts of Kuhns [1967] and Codd [1972] are shown in each of these two cases. We shall focus on the DRC.

As described in Section I.3, the reason for considering the language of logic as a basis for defining query languages is that a relational database (instance) can be viewed as an interpretation of a first-order language. Thus the answer to a formula $W(x_1, \ldots, x_p)$, where $x_1, \ldots, x_p$ are the free variables in W, considered as a query, is the set of p-tuples $\langle e_1, \ldots, e_p \rangle \in D^P$ such that $W(e_1, \ldots, e_p)$ is true. However, when considered as queries, some formulas may be "unreasonable" [Kuhns 1967], since their answer may be different in two database states, where the relations they refer to are the same. A typical example is the formula $\neg\mathbf{R}(x_1, \ldots, x_n)$, which characterizes all tuples in D^n except those that are in R as opposed to $P(x_1, \ldots, x_n)$ & $\neg\mathbf{R}(x_1, \ldots, x_n)$.

A semantic characterization of formulas that can be considered to be reasonable queries led to the notions of *definite* formulas [Kuhns 1967] and *safe* formulas [Ullman 1980]. Roughly, such formulas are domain independent since they self-restrict the range of the variables that they contain.[1] However, once these classes were defined, a new problem appeared, that of finding machine-recognizable criteria for determining whether a given formula is definite (or safe). Unfortunately, as proved by Di Paola [1969] and Vardi [1981], the decision problem for definite formulas is recursively unsolvable. Thus what remained to be done was to look for the largest of its subclasses that was recursive. This was one of the motivations for various authors who introduced purely syntactically defined subclasses of definite formulas such as "proper" [Kuhns 1970], range separable [Codd 1972], acceptable [Artaud and Nocolas 1974], range restricted [Nicolas 1979a, 1979b], and evaluable [Demolombe 1982] formulas.

Using many-sorted logic as a basis for defining query languages while considering elements of domains as primitive objects was exploited by Pirotte [1978] (see also Minker [1978b] and Reiter [1978b]). In such a case each sort is assigned to a database domain, and the well formedness of formulas is checked with regard to sort requirements. Languages obtained in this manner have the same expressive power as the preceding ones.

Many-sorted languages offer a more "precise" definition of the model, but they freeze to some extent any evolution of the application. In that respect one should note how important the issue of *knowledge representation* is to many applications, not only in the database field, but also in artificial intelligence and programming languages. An important workshop sponsored by SIGART, SIGMOD, and SIGPLAN brought to light many points common to these fields [Brodie and Zilles 1980] (see, e.g., papers by Codd [1980], Lacroix and Pirotte [1980], and Mylopoulos [1980]).

Two additional points indicating the importance of a relational calculus language are that Codd [1972] proposed it as a reference for measuring the "completeness" of query languages (discussed below), and query languages known to be "user friendly" (e.g., Query-by-example, Zloof [1977] and Quel, Stonebraker et al. [1976]) are based on it. However, improvements to user interfaces are still required, regardless of the query language.

1.1.2 Extensions to Query Languages

In this section we argue that logic supports powerful extensions to basic query languages in two directions: natural languages and programming languages. Logic languages are close to natural languages. In addition to Codd [1972], who used this argument to support the relational calculus as a yardstick to measure other languages, many linguists have also made this observation; thus querying databases using natural language has been and is a subject of active research [Colmerauer 1973; Colmerauer and Pique 1981; Dahl 1982; Moore 1981; Warren 1981; Woods 1967].

Several authors have questioned Codd's proposal to "define" completeness (i.e., expressiveness) of query languages with reference to a language (relational calculus) whose expressiveness had not been assessed from a semantic viewpoint. This proposal has also been questioned because some well-known operations on data such as the transitive closure of a relation [Aho and Ullman 1979] and aggregation operations used to compute sums, averages, and other operations are not expressible either in the relational calculus or in the relational algebra. This completeness notion has thus attracted much discussion.

Bancilhon [1978] and Paredaens [1978] have shown that, when restricted to finite relations, the relational calculus and the relational algebra are both complete in the sense that for a given database they can express all (and only those) relations whose extension is definable over the set of all domains of that database. This completeness definition is still restrictive as one cannot, for instance, express the transitive closure of a relation with a single expression independently of the extension of that relation. To attain such a capability, various authors proposed that the relational calculus or relational algebra be embedded in a host language [Aho and Ullman 1979; Chandra and Harel 1979, 1980]. Such an embedding will allow a simple expression (i.e., a program in the host language) to define an operator, for example, transitive closure, from the primitive constructs of the host language (such as iteration, recursion, or least fixed points). In some cases, all computable functions can be expressed; this is the ultimate notion of completeness.

Of course, the host language can be a logic programming language. Its expressive power attains completeness, according to Cooper [1980], or can be limited to subsets of computable functions. But logic offers an alternative way to provide extensions such as those that motivate the embedding of the query language (logic) in a host programming logic language. Indeed, the same effect is obtained by extending the representation and manipulation capabilities of the database system itself (rather than of the query language); this is precisely the idea of the deductive database system, where the database system is a theory, usually first order, with nonunit axioms (e.g., see Gallaire and Minker [1978]).

Accepting the view that a database system consisting of a theory that contains nonunit axioms is similar to extending the host language of a database system may not be entirely apparent. Harel [1980], in a review of the book edited by Gallaire and Minker [1978], attempts to refute the above view, but provides no convincing arguments. The database theory view has many theoretical advantages, if not practical ones, which are developed in Section 2 of the paper. Harel [1980] provided another critique of the work presented by Gallaire and Minker [1978], namely that some queries are not characterizable in first-order logic and hence the language must be extended to a higher order language. Although it is true that such extensions may yield answers to queries, that is, relation extensions that may not be first-order definable (e.g., the transitive closure of a relation), the query language remains precisely first order in the database-theoretic view, and may possibly remain first order in a model-theoretic view, depending on the choice of

[1] It turns out, and it is not fortuitous, that "reasonable" queries precisely correspond to formulas that avoid calling for the domain closure assumption (see Section I.3).

the host logic programming language. Thus the second critique need not apply. The possible failure to note the distinction between regarding a database an an interpretation or as a theory may have been the cause for the comments by Harel as conjectured by Kowalski [1981b].

1.1.3 *Null Values*

Null values are a special case of the incomplete information problem that is addressed further in Section 2. Null values have been investigated in the ANSI/X3/SPARC [1975] report. Although many different meanings can be ascribed to missing or null values in the instance of a relation, most researchers have dealt primarily with "attributes applicable but values are unknown," whereas only a few deal with "value does not exist" [Zaniolo 1981]. An unknown value can be represented readily in a database, but problems arise with respect to its manipulation and interpretation in a query language.

A model-theoretic approach is to define a three-valued logic [Codd 1979], based on the truth values {true, false, undefined}. The logical connectors truth definition is extended appropriately: Should any component in a tuple be unknown, the corresponding literal has the truth value true, false, or undefined, depending on whether one obtains a literal that is systematically true, systematically false, or either true or false when substituting any value for unknown. This approach has been criticized by several authors [Grant 1977; Vassiliou 1979] because the theory does not provide for several unknown values. Some of the unknown values may be known to be equal even though their precise values are unknown. Furthermore, an expression should be evaluated globally, and not recursively in terms of its subexpressions, in order to infer some of the external knowledge from the incomplete internal knowledge. As a typical example, if the age of John is unknown, the expression

$$\exists x(\text{Age}(\text{John}, x) \ \& \ x < 60)$$
$$\lor \ (\text{Age}(\text{John}, x) \ \& \ x \geq 60)$$

should receive the value true although both operands of the disjunction have value undefined.

Lipski [1979] defines information which *surely*, alternatively *possibly*, can be extracted from a database in the presence of unknown values. He then defines a query language that encompasses such modal operators. Although such an approach has been criticized on grounds of efficiency [Vassiliou 1980], where a denotational semantics approach is specified, Imielinski and Lipski [1981] improve upon Lipski's earlier approach and define systems capable of handling null values when subsets of the relational operators are used.

Where does logic stand in tackling this problem? As already noted, Codd's approach can be considered to be a model-theoretic approach. Other approaches that use logic as a basis and are more general encompass more forms of incomplete information such as indefinite data. Data are said to be indefinite if they are of the form $P(a) \lor Q(b)$, and it is unknown whether $P(a)$ is true, $Q(b)$ is true, or both are true. Reiter [1983, 1984] gives precise solutions to some of these issues on the basis of the proof-theoretic view of databases with null value and indefinite data. The theory that models such a database is obtained from the theory given for a standard database in Section I.3 by the addition of a new class of axioms that stand for facts with null values (Skolem constants in logical terms) and for indefinite data and by a reformulation of the particularization axioms that account for the presence of these new axioms. For details on these axioms see Reiter [1984]. Grant and Minker [1983] provide a precise algorithm to answer queries on such databases for a subclass of such data when null values are contained within the given domain of elements and only positive ground clauses are permitted.

Three additional approaches to the problem of null values use a tool from metalanguage techniques. In Levesque [1981] a language is defined that extends predicate calculus in that one can refer to the state of the database and thus to what is currently known. Both the semantics and proof theory are covered, cases where one can fall back on predicate calculus are studied, and connections with nonmonotonic logic (described in Section 2) are stressed and shown to yield a simpler semantics of the concept of nonmonotonicity. It becomes possible to specify that not all tuples of a relation are known and to query a database as to what is known and what is not known. A slightly different framework is provided by Konolige [1981], who uses a metalanguage based on first-order logic to describe information known about the domain of discourse (i.e., the actual world) and the database language. Queries are specified in the metalanguage. Some queries can be translated into a database language and hence can be evaluated. Others cannot be answered from the database; that is, they have no equivalent answer because of the incompleteness of the data. Both of these approaches can be dealt with within a general framework investigated by Bowen and Kowalski [1982]. They consider predicate logic as an object language and as a metalanguage where the provability relation of the object language can be formulated in the metalanguage. One can reason at the metalanguage level and at the same time provide answers at the object language level.

At this time the results discussed above tend to be more theoretical than practical. In the case of null values, a more practical solution combining logic and relational algebra has been studied by Biskup [1981], who also further investigates Codd's proposals, providing them with a sound foundation and arguing for their practical applicability [Biskup 1982]. In the case of more general incomplete information, we mention here the work by Bossu and Siegel [1981], where a promising approach based on model theory is taken, and the work by Minker [1982]. Finally, an interesting complement to logic for handling null values can be found in Siklossy and Lauriere [1982]. As mentioned above, work in artificial intelligence that deals with nonmonotonic logics is relevant to this topic. The interested reader is referred to papers in the 1980 special issue of the *Artificial Intelligence Journal* on nonmonotonic logic [AIJ 1980].

1.2 Integrity Constraints

1.2.1 *Formulation and Enforcement*

Database consistency is enforced by integrity constraints, which are assertions that database instances (states) are compelled to obey. Integrity constraints have been classified according to various criteria. The first criterion distinguishes between state constraints, which characterize valid database states, and transition constraints, which impose restrictions on the possible state transitions of a database. Among state constraints different subclasses can be isolated: for example, *type constraints*, which require the arguments of relations to belong to specified domains, or *dependency constraints*, which are discussed in Section 1.4.

As stated by Ullman [1980], a fundamental idea concerning integrity constraints is that query languages can be used to express them, although transition constraints require special attention [Casanova and Bernstein 1979; Florentin 1974; Nicolas and Yazdanian 1978]. It is therefore not surprising that various authors have used a first-order language to study integrity constraints and have appealed to both the model-theoretic and the proof-theoretic logical views.

The model-theoretic view is exploited by Nicolas and Yazdanian [1978] for characterizing those integrity constraints in a database that might be falsified by a given update, and must consequently be evaluated to determine whether the resulting database state is valid. Once such a constraint, say C, has been selected, one can take advantage of the fact that C is known to be satisfied in the state before the update, in order to derive (according to the update) a simplified form of C, say $S(C)$, such that $S(C)$ is satisfied in the new database state iff C is satisfied, and the evaluation cost of $S(C)$ is less than or equal to the evaluation cost of C. Then the evaluation of $S(C)$ can be substituted for the evaluation of C, thus reducing the cost of integrity constraint checking. Such a simplification method, which relies upon truth, preserving instantiations of formulas, is defined by Nicolas [1979a, 1979b] for constraints expressed in the domain relational calculus.

An implementation of this simplification method is reported upon by Homeier [1981]. A similar method was also introduced later by Blaustein [1981] for constraints expressed in the tuple relational calculus. Finally, in Casanova and Bernstein [1979] the same database logical view is used to define a data manipulation language with a logic system that permits one to prove whether or not a transaction preserves consistency (see Section 1.2.2).

In addition, Henschen et al. [1984] describe a technique for extracting integrity tests from database constraints expressed as first-order formulas. The tests can be generated at database design time and are applied when updates to the database appear. Of particular interest in this approach is that tests are applied before the update is made.

An alternative formulation of integrity constraints as first-order formulas has been exploited by McSkimin [1976], McSkimin and Minker [1977], Minker [1978b], and Reiter [1981]. Although their work was done in the context of deductive databases, it can be applied equally well to integrity checking in conventional databases. Both approaches consider a (principal) database augmented with a type database. Types are distinguished by unary relations (or Boolean combinations of them); a type database is a set of formulas (represented as a semantic graph in Minker [1978b]), expressing relations among types (e.g., inclusion, and disjointness) and also the inclusion of certain data values to a particular type. The connection between both databases is made via type integrity constraints that force arguments of relations to be of the same type.

Minker uses these integrity constraints to reject queries that are not well formed, such as a query that requires two relations to be joined on attributes that belong to disjoint types. A refutation-like procedure checks the well formedness of a query by using type constraints and the type database.

Reiter [1981] addresses the problem of detecting the violation of these constraints when the database is updated. Both insertions of data and of general laws are considered (integrity constraints on standard databases, axioms in a deductive database). The method relies upon a transformation of these general laws, which are universally quantified formulas, into a form for which simple criteria for the detection of type constraint violations are proposed.

1.2.2 Proving Consistency of Transactions

It is clearly easier to prove the consistency of transactions when data is defined in a formal framework, and integrity constraints and database transactions (which retrieve, insert, delete, and update information) are stated formally and in the same language. Starting from a database state that complies with given constraints, consistency of transactions is proved when the state arrived at after the transaction has been executed also complies with these constraints. In order to prove consistency, a formal system can be provided whose objects are the transactions: A syntax, semantics, and proof theory for reasoning about objects are needed. A transaction is expressible in a programming language, including expressions used to define sets of data upon which the transaction acts; thus transaction languages include data definition languages. If the data definition language itself is endowed with a proof theory, the transaction formal system can use it. This is the case with the logic interpretation of databases.

Casanova and Bernstein [1979, 1980] offer an elegant, albeit theoretical, answer to these problems. The data definition language, viewed through its logic perspective, includes the integrity constraints as axioms of a first-order theory. The transaction language then is embedded in regular programs [Pratt 1976], supported by a formal system, first-order dynamic logic (DL). This embedding is accomplished by expressing the operations of retrieve, insert, delete, and update in terms of assignment, tests, random tuple selection, union, composition, and iteration operators, the semantics of which encompass that of all computable queries (Section 1.1.2). Regular first-order DL [Harel 1979] then is extended to a system called modal dynamic logic (MDL) to reason about such programs. MDL is shown to have the necessary power to prove most essential database questions: consistency, transaction, and serializability of transactions. One should note that this work was also extended to deal with aggregate operators (Section 1.1.2). This approach obviously needs a more practical counterpart. Gardarin and Melkanoff [1979] offer a partial answer, using Hoare's logic rather than dynamic logic.

1.3 Query Optimization

Optimization of query evaluation, or improvement of query evaluation as it might better be termed, has been attacked in many different ways. A traditional approach is to use low-level information such as statistical information about various costs to access individual relations. Systems that have been implemented, for example, System R [Chamberlin et al. 1981; Selinger et al. 1979] and more experimental systems [Demolombe 1980; Grant and Minker 1981], have demonstrated that significant gains in efficiency can be achieved by using such information. However, it is clear that additional gains can be obtained by using higher level information, whether syntactic or semantic.

Syntactic transformations, yielding a logical equivalent of the initial query have been studied by Aho et al. [1979] and Chandra and Merlin [1976]. For example, the query

$$(\exists u, v, w, y, z)R(x, v, w) \\ \& R(x, z, w) \& S(u, w) \\ \& S(u, v) \& S(y, w) \\ \& S(y, v) \& S(y, z),$$

where x is a free variable, can be shown to be equivalent to

$$\exists u, v, w\ R(x, v, w) \& S(u, v).$$

But perhaps the most promising technique is found in the so-called semantic transformations. A first step in that direction was taken by McSkimin [1976] and McSkimin and Minker [1977], who used a form of integrity constraint that describes domains of relations and relates them to each other. Additional information, which takes into account the cardinality of intersections or unions of domains, is used to simplify queries and also to interrupt the process of extracting an answer whenever the additional information justifies it.

A more general approach, related to global problem-solving strategies [Kowalski 1979], is described by King [1981] and Hammer and Zdonik [1980], where the idea of query modification based on general rules is addressed. A set of general rules (integrity constraints and/or deductive laws—see Section 2) such as "a ship carries no more cargo than its rated capacity" or "the only ships whose deadweight exceeds 150 thousand tons are supertankers" [King 1981] can also be used to transform a query submitted by a user into a query less costly to evaluate, eliminating unnecessary relations or propagating constraints. This process then interacts with, and uses information from, a more classical optimizer, which can take into account such factors as indexing of attributes. Obviously a major problem is to control the derivation of queries from the original query. This is a classical problem in artificial intelligence systems, and has been studied by King, who derived a set of heuristics and specified and implemented a plan–generate–test process that gives interesting and practical results. Logic is seen at its best in such applications. Much remains to be done in this important area.

A different use of logic is reported by Warren [1981] in relation to the application of natural language database querying. The underlying database is relational, and logic is used to (1) write a translator from natural language input to an internal representation, (2) represent the internal form of queries as logic formulas, (3) write an optimizer of the querying process, which analyzes the query and uses the traditional type of statistical information already referred to above, to modify the query, and (4) evaluate the query (which could be interfaced to the access level of a standard database management system). The performance of the overall process is very acceptable; the interested reader is referred to Warren [1981] for further details. Warren's approach to optimization is similar to the approach taken by Selinger et al. [1979]. See Chakravarthy et al. [1982] for a discussion of how a logic database may be interfaced with a relational database and related work by Kunifuji and Yokota [1982] and Yokota et al. [1983].

Before leaving this extremely promising field, we note another use of constraints or general laws describing the domain of discourse in the query interpretation process. As discussed by Janas [1979, 1981], whenever a query has an empty answer, a reasonable set of subqueries can be constructed whose failure explains the empty answer of the original query; this reasonable set is obtained by taking particular integrity constraints into account. A reason for not having an answer is that no tuples that currently exist in the database satisfy the query, in which case the subquery that fails can be identified or the constraints of the database are such that no answers that satisfy the query will ever be possible from the database. Such information could be of considerable value to a user. See also Demolombe [1981] for related work.

1.4 Database Design

There is an area where logic plays an increasing role in the specification of data models. In general, there are several methods of formal specification and several formalisms for each method; databases are but one kind of object to formalize, and techniques developed for programming languages in general can be applied. We have seen in Section 1.2.2 how such a specification can be used for a precise purpose: proving the consistency of a transaction. Veloso et al. [1981] provide a comprehensive review of these techniques, for a large part on the basis of logic (see also Borgida and Wong [1981], where logic is used to define the formal semantics of the Taxis data model). Logic is a very important tool in this area, if only because it blends nicely with all the other tools described in this paper for different purposes.

We now turn to data dependencies, a concept central to database design. Data dependencies are special cases of integrity constraints that express structural properties of relations and permit relations to be decomposed, and retain certain properties described below. A number of dependencies of various kinds have been characterized and studied in the literature (see Delobel [1980] and Maier [1983] for comprehensive surveys on dependencies). In this section we see how logic has been used to study the properties of some of these dependencies and, in some cases, define them. We also note that special formal systems have been developed for that purpose (e.g., see Armstrong [1974]). This section is divided into two parts; the first is concerned with studies involving propositional logic, and the second with studies involving first-order logic.

1.4.1 Propositional Logic and Dependencies

Delobel, Fagin, Parker, and Sagiv [Delobel and Parker 1978; Sagiv and Fagin 1979; Sagiv et al. 1981] have shown that an equivalence exists between some dependencies and a fragment of the propositional logic. They have shown that functional dependencies (FDs) [Codd 1970] and multivalued dependencies (MVDs) [Fagin 1977b; Zaniolo 1976] can be associated with propositional logic statements. The equivalence developed between these dependencies and propositional logic extends earlier results of Fagin [1977a] and also Delobel and Casey [1973] that relate FDs to the theory of Boolean switching functions.

The above-mentioned equivalence provides new techniques for proving properties of FDs and MVDs, and for solving the membership problem for those dependencies. Additionally, shorter and simpler proofs have been obtained for important theorems about FDs and MVDs, and strategies developed for special-purpose theorem provers provide efficient algorithms for the membership problem. Furthermore, on the basis of a proof of this equivalence, a characterization of the dependency basis in terms of truth assignments has been given by Fagin [1977b]. This has led to the development of an efficient membership algorithm for FDs and MVDs by Sagiv [1980], which has been supplanted by a faster algorithm by Galil [1982]. As another application of this equivalence, Parker and Delobel [1979] have developed an algorithm to determine whether a set of attributes is a *key* for a relation, that is, whether a set of attributes uniquely determines a tuple in the relation and is itself not contained in any other set of attributes that uniquely determines a tuple.

The equivalence, first established for FDs, was extended later to include MVDs [Sagiv et al. 1981]. It has also been extended to other kinds of dependencies, for example, Boolean dependencies, which are expressions of attributes built using the Boolean operators &, ∨, ¬. For example, $A \vee (B \,\&\, \neg C)$ is a Boolean dependency whose meaning is "for every pair of tuples, either the two tuples agree on attribute A, or the two tuples agree on attribute B and disagree on attribute C." However, although this shows that the equivalence can be extended to some generalization of FDs, it cannot be extended to embedded MVDs (MVDs that hold for a projection of a relation) or to mutual dependencies for which the inferential structure of propositional logic seems to be too weak [Delobel 1978]. Nicolas [1978] was the first to suggest that first-order logic be used. However, before considering first-order logic, we note a similar equivalence result between FDs obtained by Vassiliou [1980], who redefined a FDs interpretation in order to account for null values, and implicational statements of a model propositional logic system. Vassiliou exploited this equivalence, notably, for proving the completeness of a set of inference rules for those "newly interpreted" FDs.

1.4.2 First-Order Logic and Dependencies

By considering dependencies as first-order formulas, one provides advantages similar to those sketched for propositional logic; results from proof theory and model theory can be used to study their properties.

Dependency statements can be expressed as first-order formulas. For example, given a relation scheme $R(ABCD)$, the FD $C \to D$ and the MVD $A \to\to B$ are, respectively, equivalent to the following two first-order formulas:

$$\forall x \cdots \forall v'(R(x, y, z, v) \;\&\; R(x', y', z, v') \to (v = v')),$$

$$\forall x \cdots \forall v'(R(x, y, z', v') \;\&\; R(x, y', z, v) \to R(x, y, z, v)).$$

New kinds of dependencies have been characterized and defined directly as particular first-order formulas. Typical of this are generalized dependency statements (GDs) and their embedded version (EGDs) [Grant and Jacobs 1982], implicational dependencies (IDs) and their embedded version (EIDS), and extended embedded IDs (XEIDs) [Fagin 1980, 1982], and tuple- and equality-generating dependencies [Beeri and Vardi 1980, 1981]. We briefly specify the main results related to these dependencies below.

Essentially, generalized dependencies are Horn clauses that contain no function symbols; they capture FDs, MVDs, JDs (join dependencies), IDs, and some other constraints. Horn clauses are defined in Section I.2 and in Section 2. After studying the implication problem for GDs, Grant and Jacobs [1982] proposed a decision procedure for determining whether a GD is a logical consequence of a set of GDs. This procedure is related to both techniques from automatic theorem proving and the "chase method," a decision procedure for dependencies described by Maier et al. [1979] on the basis of the tableau formalism of Aho and Ullman [1979].

Horn clauses were also used to define EIDs, which were studied to "help bring order to the chaos by presenting certain mathematical properties shared by all (the previously defined) dependencies" [Fagin 1980, 1982]. Among these properties are *domain independence*, which means that whether or not a dependency holds for a relation can be determined independently of the underlying domains of the attributes in the relation, *satisfiability on empty relations* (i.e., relations with no tuples), and *faithfulness* with regard to a version of the Cartesian product called direct product.

As principle results for EIDs, Chandra et al. [1981] have shown that any set D of EIDs admits an Armstrong relation (i.e., a relation that obeys all dependencies in D—and their consequences—but no others) and that the decision problem for this class of dependencies is undecidable. However, a complete set of inference rules has been given for the equivalent class of algebraic dependencies [Yannakakis and Papadimitriou 1982].

On the basis of the formulation of dependencies as first-order formulas, Beeri and Vardi [1980, 1981] have studied the implication problem for a general class of dependencies, the tuple- and equality-generating dependencies (tgds and eqds), and for some of its subclasses. These dependencies, which, in fact, correspond to EIDs, intuitively require that, "if some tuples fulfilling certain conditions exist in the database, then either some other tuples (possibly with unknown values), fulfilling certain conditions, must also exist in the database (tgds), or some values in the given tuples must be equal (eqds)" [Beeri and Vardi 1980, 1981].

In the same work Beeri and Vardi proposed an extension to the chase method (see also Sadri and Ullman [1980, 1982]), which provides a proof procedure for these dependencies and a decision procedure for total dependencies (i.e., nonembedded). A decision procedure is guaranteed to terminate in any case, whereas a proof procedure is not guaranteed to terminate when D does not imply d. It is worth noting that, when described in the formalism of logic, the chase method corresponds to a well-known theorem-proving procedure by refutation (using resolution and paramodulation) [Beeri and Vardi 1981].

We have described results by using logic that relates to conventional relational databases; in the following section, we describe how logic extends conventional databases to permit deduction and sheds new insight into problems concerning negative and incomplete information.

2. DEDUCTIVE DATABASES

A deductive database is a database in which new facts may be derived from facts that were explicitly introduced. We consider such databases here from a proof-theoretic viewpoint as a special first-order theory. In this framework, we focus upon several subjects: the manner in which *negative data* are to be treated in a database, the *null value* problem in which the value of a data item is missing, and *indefinite data* in which one knows, say $P(a) \vee P(b)$ is true, but one does not know if $P(a)$ is true, $P(b)$ is true, or both are true.

We first provide the background for defining deductive databases, and then treat two different kinds of deductive databases: definite and indefinite. It will be seen that assumptions generally made with respect to definite databases do not apply directly to indefinite databases. Finally, we briefly discuss other extensions to deductive databases and logic databases.

For additional material on the subjects of deductive databases or logic and databases not covered in this survey article, see Gallaire et al. [1984], the *Proceedings of the First Conference on Logic Programming* [1982], *the Logic Programming Workshop Proceedings* [1983], *the International Joint Conference on Artificial Intelligence* [1983], *the International Symposium on Logic Programming* [1984], and other conferences devoted to artificial intelligence and logic programming.

2.1 Definition of Deductive or Logic Databases

In general, we shall consider a database to consist of a finite set of constants, say $\{c_1 \cdots c_n\}$, and a set of first-order clauses without function symbols (see Section I.2). Functions are excluded in order to have finite and explicit answers to queries. Initially our theory precludes null values that arise in a database when one has statements such as $(\exists x)P(a, x)$, that is, linked to "a" in the predicate P there is a value, but its precise value is unknown. When one skolemizes the formula $(\exists x)P(a, x)$ and places it in clause form, the clause $P(a, \omega)$ results, where ω is a Skolem constant (i.e., a constant whose value is otherwise unconstrained).

The general form of clauses that will represent facts and deductive laws is

$$P_1 \mathbin{\&} P_2 \mathbin{\&} \cdots \mathbin{\&} P_k \rightarrow R_1 \vee \cdots \vee R_q.$$

It is equivalent to the clause

$$\neg P_1 \vee \cdots \vee \neg P_k \vee R_1 \vee \cdots \vee R_q.$$

The conjunction of the P_i is referred to as the left-hand side of the clause and the disjunction of the R_j as the right-hand side. Since the clauses that we will consider are function free, terms that are arguments of the P_i and R_j are either constants or variables. Whenever any variable that occurs in the right-hand side of a clause also occurs in the left-hand side, the clause is said to be *range restricted*. We shall briefly discuss various types of clauses depending on the respective values of k and q, as in Minker [1983]:

Type 1: $k = 0$, $q = 1$. Clauses have the form

$$\rightarrow P(t_1, \ldots, t_m).$$

(a) If the t_i are constants, $c_{i1}, \ldots, c_{im}$, then one has

$$\rightarrow P(c_{i1}, \ldots, c_{im}),$$

which represents an assertion or a fact in the database. The set of all such assertions for the predicate letter P corresponds to a "table" in a relational database. The arrow preceding an assertion will generally be omitted.

(b) When some, or all, of the t_i are variables, the clause corresponds to a general statement in the database. For example,

$$\rightarrow \text{Ancestor}(\text{Adam}, x),$$

states that Adam is an ancestor of all individuals in the database (the database consists only of human beings). Clearly, such data, which are not range-restricted clauses and therefore assume that all the individuals in the database are of the same "type," appear very seldom.

Type 2: $k = 1$, $q = 0$. Clauses have the form

$$P(t_1, \ldots, t_m) \rightarrow.$$

(a) When all of the t_i are constants, then we have

$$P(c_{i1}, \ldots, c_{im}) \rightarrow,$$

which stands for a negative fact. Negative statements may seem peculiar since relational databases do not contain negative data. We shall return to this topic in a later section.

(b) Some of the t_i are variables. This may either be thought of as an integrity constraint (as a particular Type 3 clause; see below), or as the "value does not exist" meaning for null values (see Section 1.1.3).

Type 3: $k > 1$, $q = 0$. Clauses have the form

$$P_1 \mathbin{\&} \cdots \mathbin{\&} P_k \rightarrow.$$

Such axioms may be thought of as integrity constraints. That is, data to be added to a database must satisfy the laws specified by the integrity condition to be allowed in the database. For example, one may specify an integrity law that states that "no individual can be both a father and a mother of another individual." This may be specified as

$$\text{FATHER}(x, y) \mathbin{\&} \text{MOTHER}(x, y) \rightarrow.$$

If FATHER(JACK, SALLY) is already in the database, an attempt to enter MOTHER(JACK, SALLY) into the database should lead to an integrity violation. This does not rule out other kinds of integrity constraints.

Type 4: $k \geq 1$, $q = 1$. Clauses have the form

$$P_1 \mathbin{\&} P_2 \mathbin{\&} \cdots \mathbin{\&} P_k \rightarrow R_1.$$

The clause may be considered to be either an integrity constraint or a definition of the predicate R_1 in terms of the predicates $P_1, \ldots, P_k$ (such a definition is a deductive law).

Type 5: $k = 0$, $q > 1$. Clauses have the form

$$\rightarrow R_1 \vee R_2 \vee \cdots \vee R_1.$$

If the x_i, $i = 1, \ldots, n$ are constants, then we have an *indefinite assertion*. That is, any combination of one or more R_i is true, but we do not know which ones are true.

Type 6: $k \geq 1$, $q > 1$. Clauses have the form

$$P_1 \,\&\, P_2 \,\&\, \cdots \,\&\, P_k \rightarrow R_1 \vee R_2 \vee \cdots \vee R_q.$$

The clause may be interpreted as either an integrity constraint or the definition of indefinite data. An integrity constraint that states that each individual has at most two parents may be written as

$$P(x_1, y_1) \,\&\, P(x_1, y_2) \,\&\, P(x_1, y_3) \rightarrow (y_1 = y_2) \vee (y_1 = y_3) \vee (y_2 = y_3).$$

As a general rule of deduction we might have

$$\text{Parent}(x, y) \rightarrow \text{Mother}(x, y) \vee \text{Father}(x, y).$$

This general law could also be interpreted as an integrity constraint.

Finally, a clause where $k = 0$, $q = 0$ (the empty clause) denotes falsity and should not be part of a database. Furthermore, we shall call a clause *definite* if its right-hand side consists of exactly one atom (i.e., Type 1b or Type 4).

All the types of clauses defined above, except ground facts (Type 1a), are treated as integrity constraints in conventional databases. In a deductive database some of them may be treated as deductive laws. We shall distinguish two classes of databases: definite databases in which no clauses of either Type 5 or Type 6 appear and indefinite databases in which such clauses do appear.

2.2 Definite Deductive Databases (DDDBs)

2.2.1 *A Formal Definition of DDDBs*

A definite deductive database is defined as a particular first-order theory (together with a set of integrity constraints). This theory is obtained from the theory given for conventional databases in Section I.3 by the addition of a new class of axioms, which stand for the deductive laws, and by a reformulation of the completion axioms, which account for the presence of these new axioms. More precisely, a definite deductive database consists of the following:

(1) *A theory T* whose proper axioms are

- Axioms 1 (the particularization axioms): the domain closure axiom, the unique name axioms, the equality axioms (as given in Section I.3), and the completion axioms (one for each predicate in T) whose formulation is given below.
- Axioms 2 (the elementary facts): a set of ground atomic formulas defined by clauses of Type 1a in Section 2.1.
- Axioms 3 (the deductive laws): a set of function-free definite clauses of Type 4 (or Type 1b) in Section 2.1.

(2) *A set of integrity constraints IC,* which consists of any closed formulas.

The completion axiom for a predicate P is now not only built from the facts related to P (which occur in Axioms 2), but also from the "only if" missing part of the definite clauses defining P (which occur in Axioms 3). For example, let P have the following assertions in T:

$$P(c_i, c_j),$$
$$P(c_p, c_q),$$

and let

$$Q(x, y) \,\&\, R(y, z) \rightarrow P(x, z),$$

and

$$S(x, y) \rightarrow P(x, y),$$

be all the clauses in Axioms 3 that imply P; then, the completion axiom for P is

$$P(x, y) \rightarrow ((x = c_i) \,\&\, (y = c_j)) \vee ((x = c_p) \,\&\, (y = c_q)) \vee (Q(x, y) \,\&\, R(y, z)) \vee (S(x, y)).$$

Such a completion axiom permits one to derive a negative fact $\neg P(d, e)$ whenever $P(d, e)$ is neither in Axioms 2 nor derivable through Axioms 3. Thus from the database just specified we can derive $\neg P(c_i, c_p)$.

In such a deductive database the definition of answers to queries and of the satisfiability of integrity constraints is equivalent to their definition in a conventional database viewed from the proof-theoretic perspective. An answer to a query $W(x_1, \ldots, x_p)$, where $x_1, \ldots, x_p$ are free variables in W, is the set of tuples $\langle c_{i1}, \ldots, c_{ip} \rangle$ such that $T \vdash W(c_{i1}, \ldots, c_{ip})$. Now, a deductive database obeys the integrity constraints in IC iff for any formula ϕ in IC $T \vdash \phi$.

An alternative definition can be given for the satisfiability of integrity constraints: A deductive database obeys the integrity constraints in IC iff $T \cup$ IC (the axioms in T together with the formulas in IC) is consistent [Kowalski 1979]. Since the theory T, as defined above for a definite deductive database, is complete (i.e., for any closed formula W, either $T \vdash W$ or $T \vdash \neg W$), both definitions are equivalent in that case. However, for more general deductive databases whose corresponding theory is not complete, the second definition is less stringent than the first and its impact is worth investigating.

Deductive laws (in Axioms 3) that imply a relation R provide an extended definition for R. The tuples $\langle c_{i1}, \ldots, c_{im} \rangle$ that "satisfy" R are not only those tuples such that $R(c_{i1}, \ldots, c_{im})$ is a fact in Axioms 2, but also those tuples such that $R(c_{i1}, \ldots, c_{im})$ is derivable through the deductive laws. Relations that are jointly defined by deductive laws and elementary facts in a deductive database, called derived relations, constitute a generalization of relations defined as "views" in a conventional database. A "view" is a relation, not stored in the database, that is defined in terms of database relations or other views by a relational algebra (or calculus) expression. A derived relation reduces to a view when

(i) there are no elementary facts in Axioms 2 related to this relation, and
(ii) no recursive deductive law or cycle appears among the deductive laws that imply this relation in Axioms 3.

In such a case, if $E_1 \rightarrow R, \ldots, E_q \rightarrow R$ are all the deductive laws that imply R, this derived relation corresponds to the view $V = E_1 \vee \cdots \vee E_q$. We note that Point (i) is not significant since two different names may be given to the "explicit part" and the "derived part" of a relation. However, Point (ii) has more impact. Some relations may be defined as derived relations, whereas strictly, they cannot be defined as views. A typical example is the Ancestor relation, which is the transitive closure of the Parent relation. Incidentally, we note that the relational calculus (or algebra) may be extended (or embedded into another language) in order to be able to define such a relation as a view. However, since from a model-theoretic viewpoint the transitive closure of a relation is not first-order definable, one has to call for languages that are more powerful than first-order language. But, in a (definite) deductive database defined from a proof-theoretic point of view as above, the Ancestor relation can easily be defined as a derived relation in terms of two deductive laws:

$$(\text{Parent}(x, y) \rightarrow \text{Ancestor}(x, y),$$
$$\text{Ancestor}(x, y) \,\&\, \text{Parent}(y, z) \rightarrow \text{Ancestor}(x, z)),$$

and strictly remain in the context of first-order logic (see Section 1.1.2).

Clearly, on considering the combinatorial complexity of the particularization axioms (Axioms 1), it would be quite inefficient to implement a (definite) deductive DBMS, while clinging to the formal definition of a DDDB given here, namely, to implement such a DBMS as a standard theorem prover that treats axioms in Axioms 1 in the same way as axioms in Axioms 2 or Axioms 3. The solution is similar to what is done for conventional DBMSs. It consists of substituting adequate metarules (or metaconventions) for the particularization axioms, thus obtaining a so-called operational definition of a DDDB. The following section is devoted to this issue.

2.2.2 *An Operational Definition of DDDBs*

Particularization axioms may be eliminated for DDDBs in a way that is similar to conventional databases, thus providing a convenient way to implement corresponding systems. First, calling for the domain closure axiom may be avoided by dealing with range-restricted formulas for query, integrity constraint, and deductive law formulation (see Section 1.1.1). Then, as discussed by Kowalski [1978, 1979] and proved by Clark [1978], the unique name and completion axioms may be removed, provided that negation is interpreted as (finite) failure (see also Jaffar et al. [1983] for a stronger result). The metarule of *negation as failure* states that for any positive literal P, $\vdash \neg P$ iff $\nvdash P$; that is, failure to prove P permits one to infer $\neg P$. Finite failure further requires that all proof attempts terminate. Finally, since the equality axioms were needed only for the presence of the equality predicate in the above axioms, they are no longer required.

To summarize, keeping in mind that any formula now has to be range restricted, from an operational point of view a DDDBs consists of the following:

(1) A set of axioms: Axioms 2 (elementary facts) ∪ Axioms 3 (deductive laws).
(2) A set of integrity constraints: IC.
(3) A metarule: negation as finite failure (nff).

Query answering and integrity constraint satisfiability remain defined as in Section 1.3.1 except that, now "$\vdash$" has to be interpreted as "provable under nff."

Negation as finite failure generalizes in the deductive databases case to the usual assumption underlying conventional databases for negative facts (see Section I.3). The use of this concept was discussed as the "convention for negative information representation" by Nicolas and Syre [1974] and Nicolas and Gallaire [1978], and also described as the "closed world assumption" (CWA)[2] by Reiter [1978a, 1980]. This concept is also used in the artificial intelligence languages PLANNER [Hewitt 1972] and PROLOG [Roussel 1975].

The syntactic definition (i.e., according to proof theory) of negation as failure given above has a semantic (i.e., according to model theory) counterpart. Let G be the set of all possible ground (positive) atomic formulas constructible from the symbols in a given set of definite clauses. A Herbrand model for this set of clauses is a subset of G that makes all the clauses true. It has been shown [Van Emden and Kowalski 1976] that the intersection of all such models is itself a model, and indeed is the minimal model (i.e., it contains the minimal number of atomic formulas). If one substracts the set of atomic formulas in the minimal model from G, the remaining set of atomic formulas is the set of all formulas whose negations may be assumed to be true. These are the same atomic formulas obtained by the CWA. This shows that the CWA and negation as failure assume complete knowledge, and there are no unknown facts. A discussion of the semantic definition of negation as failure can be found in Minker [1982] and Van Emden [1978].

Although the formal and operational definitions of a DDDB are equivalent in the sense that they will give the same answers to queries, they are in fact not strictly equivalent. The formal definition is stated in standard first-order logic, which is monotonic, whereas the use of negation as failure in the operational definition leads to a nonmonotonic logic. A logic is said to be *monotonic* if one is given a theory T (i.e., a set of axioms) in which a formula w can be proved (i.e., $T \vdash w$), then the addition to T of an axiom A still permits one to prove w; that is, $T \cup \{A\} \vdash w$. According to negation as failure, $\neg P(b)$ can be inferred from $\{P(a), Q(b)\}$ but not from $\{P(a), Q(b)\} \cup \{P(b)\}$; thus we have a nonmonotonic logic. For an analysis of the relation between predicate completion and work in artificial intelligence on nonmonotonic logic, the reader is referred to Reiter [1982].

Finally, we note that, as shown by Nicolas and Gallaire [1978] and formally proved by Reiter [1978a], a definite deductive database is always consistent under the CWA. The intuitive reason is that definite clauses preclude the derivation of positive facts from negative facts. We see in Section 2.3 that this is not the case when indefinite clauses are accepted as deductive laws.

2.2.3 *Deductive Laws and Integrity Constraints*

Both deductive laws in Axioms 3 and integrity constraints in IC correspond to general knowledge of the world modeled by the database. Given such general knowledge, we might inquire as to the basis on which one can decide to consider a general rule as a deductive law, and thus incorporate it in Axioms 3, or as an integrity constraint, and thus incorporate it as part of the IC. There is no final answer to this (database design) question, but some suggestions are provided by Nicolas and Gallaire [1978] and Reiter [1978a, 1984]. They are briefly stated below.

(i) If one wants to obtain finite and explicit answers to queries (i.e., sets of tuples of elements in the database), deductive laws have to be function free. Thus general knowledge that corresponds to formulas that do not fulfill this constraint should be treated as integrity constraints. For example, the general knowledge "every teacher has a diploma,"

$$(\forall x\ \forall y(\text{TEACH}(x, y) \rightarrow (\exists z)\text{DIPLOMA}(x, z))),$$

should be treated as an integrity constraint since the clause form of the axiom contains a Skolem function.

(ii) In order to avoid inconsistency with the CWA, one retains as deductive laws only general knowledge that corresponds to definite clauses (and thus use the other clauses as integrity constraints). However, as we shall see in Section 2.3, there is another possibility, which consists of modifying the CWA.

(iii) Since purely negative clauses (i.e., clauses of Type 3 in Section 2.1) will never produce new facts (under the CWA), they need only be used as integrity constraints [Reiter 1978a].

(iv) General knowledge that implies instances of a relation that is completely defined independently of it will not, if used as a deductive law, produce any new valid facts and should be used as an integrity constraint.

For example, the general knowledge, "the age of any person is less than 150,"

$$(\forall x\ \forall y)(\text{Age}(x, y) \rightarrow (y < 150)),$$

used as a deductive law, would always produce facts which are either inconsistent (e.g., $180 < 150$) or redundant (e.g., $35 < 150$). A functional dependency statement such as

$$(\forall x\ \forall x'\ \forall y)(\text{Father}(x, y)\ \&\ \text{Father}(x', y) \rightarrow (x = x')),$$

is another example of this kind. Hence these rules are best used as integrity constraints.

In the two examples above, the implied relations are of a particular kind, and it is generally agreed that they are defined independently of any reference to a specific database. For more standard relations, it is a matter of choice (dependent upon database design) to decide what general knowledge and which assertions will participate in the complete definition of a relation. As an extreme case, in a conventional database it is (implicitly) assumed that every relation (other than views) is completely defined in terms of elementary facts (the tuples in the corresponding table), and thus all general knowledge is used as integrity constraints.

As noted by Kowalski [1979] and as we shall emphasize here, a deductive database can be viewed as a logic program that produces facts (the facts in the minimal model characterized in Section 2.2.2) and whose integrity constraints are the program properties. Modifications to the program (viz. database updates involving either deduction laws or elementary facts) must preserve those properties.

When general knowledge has been partitioned between deductive laws and integrity constraints, they have to be exploited conjointly. Integrity checking in a deductive context is discussed by Nicolas and Yazdanian [1978] and Reiter [1981], and a methodology for updating databases with integrity constraints and deductive laws was suggested by Fagin et al. [1983]. Further, query evaluation and update handling are uniformly treated by dos Santos et al.

---

[2] There is the open world assumption (OWA) corresponding to the CWA that provides a standard interpretation of negation as given with a full first-order theory.

[1981], where deduction provides either an analysis of a state of the database, that is, an answer to a query, or a plan, that is, a sequence of database modifications to reach a desired state. We now focus on deductive laws.

As mentioned in the preceding section, the theory that constitutes a definite deductive database admits a (unique) minimal model. This (minimal) model consists of a set of facts that connotes that these are the facts that are true. These facts constitute the conventional database (CDB) underlying the deductive database. Now, one can choose to exploit the deductive database in either of two ways. The underlying CDB can be kept implicit, in which case the deductive laws, or their compiled form (see Section 2.2.4.2), have to be run at query evaluation time to find the (implicit) deducible facts. The alternative consists of making the underlying CDB explicit. To do so, deductive laws have to be run when new facts are inserted into the database to make explicit the deducible facts. Then query evaluation can be done as in a conventional database. In the first case deductive laws are said to be used as derivation rules, whereas in the second case, they are said to be used as generation rules [Nicolas and Gallaire 1978]. The respective advantages of derivation and generation rules are discussed by Nicolas and Gallaire [1978] and Nicolas and Yazdanian [1982]. We only mention here that, as opposed to derivation paths, "generation paths" stop naturally even when recursive rules or cycles among the rules appear. The interested reader will find a description of a prototype deductive DBMS by using generation rules in Nicolas and Yazdanian [1982].

Finally, we note that exploiting deductive laws as generation rules can be viewed as an automatic revalidation of integrity constraints in a conventional database. This can also be viewed as providing a generalization of "concrete views" [Blaustein 1981], that is, views whose corresponding set of tuples is explicitly stored.

In the following section we focus on proof-theoretic techniques used for exploiting derivation rules.

2.2.4 Inference Methods and Database Access

We shall describe two ways to perform the inference process: the interpretive and the compiled methods.

The *interpretive method* works with a problem solver, using the deductive laws and interleaves search of the extensional DB (which contains the elementary facts, i.e., Axioms 2). In the *compiled approach*, the problem solver uses all of the deductive laws until a point is reached at which either the problem is solved or all that remains is to search for facts in the extensional DB. Both methods work well when deductive laws are assumed to be free of cycles, that is, when there are no recursive axioms. Otherwise, both have difficulties handling the termination problem, that is, detecting at which point no new solutions will be found. However, it should be possible to find such termination conditions, as only a finite number of tuples can be generated as answers to any query to a definite deductive database (function free, with a finite set of constants and consisting of only definite clauses). This problem has been studied by a number of authors [Chang 1981; Kunifuji and Yokota 1982; Minker and Nicolas 1982; Naqvi and Henschen 1984; Reiter 1978c; Shapiro and McKay 1980; Yokota et al. 1983].

2.2.4.1 Interpretive Method of Deduction. We shall describe the interpretive method for the following simple database. Let the facts in the database (the extensional DB) be

$F(e, b_1)$	$M(c, e)$	$H(a, c)$
$F(e, b_2)$	$M(c, f)$	
$F(e, b_3)$	$M(c, g)$	
	$M(g, d)$	

where F, M, and H stand, respectively, for Father, Mother, and Husband. Let the deductive laws be

(A_1) $M(x, y)$ & $M(y, z) \rightarrow GM(x, z)$,

(A_2) $M(x, y)$ & $F(y, z) \rightarrow GM(x, z)$,

(A_3) $GM(z, y)$ & $H(x, z) \rightarrow GF(x, y)$.

Relation GM (Grandmother) is said to be intensionally defined in terms of the extensional relations F and M. Relation GF (Grandfather) is intensionally defined in terms of the extensional relation H and intensional relation GM, and hence in terms of the extensional relations F and M as well. There is no loss of generality in assuming that no relation is hybrid; that is, all relations are either (purely) intensional or (purely) extensional (e.g., see Minker [1982]). We illustrate the interpretive approach, starting from a query $GF(a, y)$:

(1) $GF(a, y)$,

and applying A3, using the Robinson Resolution Principle (Section I.2) yields

(2) $GM(z, y)$ & $H(a, z)$

as the subproblems to be solved. At this point a selection function could be used to provide advice to solve $H(a, z)$ first. The reason for selecting $H(a, z)$ first is that it contains a constant and is presumably easier to satisfy than the case where one arbitrarily looks for a tuple that satisfies $GM(z, y)$ and hopes that the value of z, when substituted into $H(a, z)$, will be in the database. By accessing the database, we find that $H(a, c)$ is in the database and z is bound to c. Now, the subproblem

(3) $GM(c, y)$

remains to be solved. Since there are two ways to solve this last goal on the DB (Axioms A_1 and A_2), a choice is made to select Rule A2, yielding

(4) $M(c, y_1)$ & $F(y_1, y)$,

which now must be solved. These subproblems may be solved in two steps, to obtain one answer, $\{b_1\}$. However, the process is not finished, and backtracking at previous choice points will yield $\{b_2, b_3, d\}$ as further answers. So, for the sake of efficiency, at each step one has to involve a selection function and a choice function. Some of the variants of this basic method have explored the idea of obtaining the whole set of answers at each access to the DB, rather than one at a time [Chakravarthy et al. 1982; Minker 1975a, 1975b, 1978a, 1978b]. Although no termination conditions are known in the general case, one should note that this problem also exists in logic programming, where it is left up to the skill of the programmer to specify a termination condition.

2.2.4.2 Compilation Method of Deduction. Access to the database is delayed in the deductive process until all the work remaining to be done for query evaluation is to access the database. This should allow the possibility for global optimizations of DB accesses. The method was basically described by Chang [1978], Furukawa [1977], Kellogg et al. [1978], Kellogg and Travis [1981], and Reiter [1978b]. Two possible techniques can be used. In the first technique, which could be called a pseudo-compilation technique, only one path at a time is pursued. That is, a single expression involving only extensional relations is produced at a given time; backtracking then produces further expressions. This is clearly a source of redundant work. With the above deductive laws, first one would get the expression

$$M(z, y_1) \ \&\ M(y_1, y) \ \&\ H(a, z),$$

which would be passed over to the DB evaluator, and along a second path one might generate the expression

$$M(z, y_1) \ \&\ F(y_1, y) \ \&\ H(a, z),$$

which has obvious redundancies with the previous expression [Chakravarthy et al. 1982; Kunifuji and Yokota 1982]. The second technique aims at producing an iterative program that synthesizes the set of all retrieval expressions. Let us illustrate it by extending the deductive laws of our previous example to the following intensional recursive relation (Ancestor):

$$F(x, y) \ \&\ A(y, z) \rightarrow A(x, z),$$

$$M(x, y) \rightarrow A(x, y).$$

In this case, a method described by Naqvi and Henschen [1980, 1984] would produce the following program from an initial query $A(?, a)$.

```
z2 := a
eval(F(y2, y1) & M(y1, z2))
                     /likely to access M first/
print(y1)      /there may be several values of y1/
enque(S, y1)
  /put in set S those values not already put into
                                               it/
while(S ≠ empty) do
  y2 := deque(S)        /take the first element/
  eval(F(y3, y2))
  print(y3)
  enque(S, y3)
  end
```

This method is general but suffers from some drawbacks in that some redundancy may still remain. The enque process may be time consuming and the program generated depends on the initial query.

2.3 Indefinite Deductive Databases (IDDDBs)

An indefinite deductive database differs from a definite deductive database (referring to its operational definition) in Axioms 3 and the metarule to handle negation. The difference in Axioms 3, although seemingly minor, will be seen to be substantial. We define Axioms 3′ as follows:

- Axioms 3′: a set of function-free definite or indefinite clauses. An indefinite clause is to the form given by Type 5 or Type 6 in Section 2.1, for example,

$$P(a, b) \vee Q(c, d, e),$$

or

$$R(x, y) \ \&\ T(y, z) \rightarrow P(x, z) \vee Q(x, y, z).$$

More precisely, an *indefinite deductive database* consists of

(1) A set of axioms T, where T = Axioms 2 ∪ Axioms 3′.
(2) A set of integrity constraints IC.
(3) A metarule: generalized negation as failure, described below.

The addition of indefinite clauses changes matters radically. Methods and results that apply to definite deductive databases do not apply to indefinite deductive databases. For example, an indefinite database may be inconsistent under the CWA. Consider a database that consists of a single fact,

$$\text{cat(felix)},$$

and of a single deductive law,

$$\text{cat}(x) \rightarrow \text{black}(x) \vee \text{white}(x).$$

Since black(felix) cannot be proved, application of the CWA leads to

$$\vdash \neg\text{black(felix)}.$$

Similarly, one can also conclude

$$\vdash \neg\text{white(felix)}.$$

But the set

$$\{\text{cat}(x) \rightarrow \text{black}(x) \vee \text{white}(x), \text{cat(felix)}, \neg\text{black(felix)}, \neg\text{white(felix)}\}$$

is obviously inconsistent. Hence the closed world assumption (negation as failure) as defined for definite databases is not applicable to indefinite databases.

The concept of a CWA can be extended to achieve a *generalized closed world assumption* (GCWA) as follows. Let E be the set of all purely positive (possibly empty) clauses not provable. Then assert $\neg P(x)$ iff $P(x) \vee C$ is not provable for any C in E. We also refer to this as *generalized negation as failure.* As in the case of definite databases, one can obtain a semantic interpretation of generalized negation as failure. But, whereas in a definite database there is a unique minimal model, in an indefinite database a set of minimal models arises. The GCWA as defined above was introduced by Minker [1982]. In the case where no general axioms appear other than definite ground clauses, Grant and Minker [1983] have developed an algorithm on the basis of the GCWA to compute answers to queries. Although the GCWA provides a sound formal basis, this notion has not yet been shown to be sufficiently efficient when general axioms are permitted to be directly usable in practice. A variant that may be more promising from a practical point of view was introduced independently, and widely studied by Bossu and Siegel [1981].

The GCWA treats null values correctly, where it is meant here that the null value is among the constants already known in the database. Let the database consist of $\{P(\omega), Q(a), Q(b)\}$, where '$\omega$' is a null value, or Skolem constant that arises from the statement $\exists x P(x)$. If the domain D consists only of $\{a, b\}$, then the existentially quantified statement corresponds to

$$(\exists x P(x)) \leftrightarrow P(a) \vee P(b).$$

Hence $P(\omega)$ is a shorthand notation for $P(a) \vee P(b)$. If one were to replace the entry $P(\omega)$ with $P(a) \vee P(b)$, and the database were treated under the GCWA, one could not conclude $\neg P(a)$ from this database. The null value is then treated correctly. A disadvantage to this approach is that of having to list a potentially long disjunction for a database with many constants in its domain.

Another major difference is that the deduction mechanism needs to be more complex for indefinite databases than for definite deductive databases. Indeed, proof strategies such as input resolution [Chang 1970] and LUSH resolution [Hill 1974], although complete for Horn clauses, are not complete for non-Horn clauses. When dealing with indefinite clauses, a complete proof strategy such as linear resolution [Loveland 1969, 1970; Reiter 1971], linear resolution with selection function (SL) [Kowalski and Kuehner 1971], or linear resolution with unrestricted selection function based on trees (LUST) [Minker and Zanon 1982] is required.

Answers in an indefinite deductive database are no longer definite. That is, if the entire database consists of the single entry $P(a) \vee P(b)$, then the answer to the query $P(x)$? is $x = a + b$, which denotes that either $x = a$ or $x = b$ or both satisfy the query. The problem of indefinite answers is addressed by Reiter [1978b] and Grant and Minker [1983].

Minker and Perlis [1983, 1984] treat a different kind of indefiniteness. Users may know that some of their facts are correct. They may also know that they are not willing to make statements about other facts. That is, the facts may or may not be true. In either a conventional or a deductive database there is no facility available to store facts and specify to the user that these facts may or may not be true. To account for this possibility Minker and Perlis have generalized the concept of circumscription developed by McCarthy [1980] to what they call protected circumscription. They have shown that the user can then obtain answers of the form yes, no, and unknown. Efficient computational techniques are required to make the approach practical. They have also developed a completeness and soundness result for protected circumscription in the case of finitary data, and hence for cases of interest to databases.

2.4 Logic Databases

The presentation of deductive databases given in the preceding sections essentially reflects a view from the perspective of conventional databases, that is, a "DB field" view. Starting with a conventional DB, one introduces some ad hoc deductive capabilities while keeping (as far as possible) the usual DB conventions. For example, only function-free formulas are retained, but clearly, authorizing functions allows more general forms of data to be manipulated (i.e., general terms instead of only constants and variables), which eventually give a different conceptual model to the user (e.g., semantic networks; see Deliyanni and Kowalski [1979] for a discussion as to how semantic networks can be represented in logic). We do not consider an (extended) deductive database as an unconstrained first-order theory because its implementation would be extremely inefficient.

Introducing functions into DB Horn clauses takes the deductive database field closer to the field of logic programming. It is thus not surprising to see the same enhancements carried out for both fields. Horn clauses augmented with negation as failure led to the PROLOG language, which has been demonstrated to be efficient [Roussel 1975]. A PROLOG program is quite similar to a definite deductive database (up to functions). However, this does not mean that a standard interpreter for such a language constitutes a DDBMS that must not only provide us with query facilities, but also with functions for integrity and maintenance of deduced facts. A logic database system would be obtained by combining the above-mentioned facilities with an efficient access method to a large number of facts. Such an integration can be realized in various ways (see Chakravarthy et al. [1982] and Gallaire [1983]). It should be clear that a logic database language could be continuously extended, by providing extensions to negation as failure, incorporating metalanguage capabilities and other capabilities. This could prove useful for databases, as argued by Kowalski [1981a].

3. CONCLUSION

We have attempted to cover results obtained within the framework of mathematical logic applied to databases mainly through the perspective of deductive databases. We have shown how logic applies to query languages, integrity modeling and maintenance, query evaluation, database design through dependencies, representation and manipulation of deduced facts, and incomplete information. However, the field of logic and databases, as it is called, is far from closed; logic provides an appropriate framework for many database problems that still need to be investigated thoroughly. We note some of these problems below. Many of the problems listed below as needing continued research have been drawn from a report to which the first and third authors of this paper contributed [Adiba et al. 1982] (see also Reiter [1984]):

- *Designing natural language query systems*, whatever "natural" means.
- *Optimizing query evaluation based on semantic knowledge*, which is needed, in general, for interactive access to databases and especially in a natural language context.
- *Finding criteria and methods for choosing, between equivalent sets of integrity constraints, a good set*, where "good" means constraint sets that are easy to check and to maintain.
- *Finding criteria to decide which relations should be base relations and which should be derived or hybrid relations*, in other words, what general knowledge should be used as integrity constraints and what should be used as deduction rules.
- *Finding more efficient means for detecting the violation of integrity constraints.*
- *Synthesizing a program preserving integrity from transaction specifications and integrity constraints*, both expressed in logic. Since such a program could also be written in logic (programming), the field of logic and databases appears to be particularly well suited here.
- *Relaxing some of the conditions for a formula to be an integrity constraint* and investigating the interest of such less stringent definitions.
- *Embedding data manipulation languages in programming languages.* In deductive databases one usually considers the deductive component to be part of the DBMS. However, it is possible to interface a (conventional or deductive) DBMS with a logic programming language, for example, PROLOG. Such an integration is accomplished most easily when the DBMS language is predicate calculus oriented; a full integration could result in which the DBMS appears as the part of the programming system specialized to the manipulation of facts.
- *Looking for practical solutions to handle general forms of incomplete information.* Although satisfactory solutions have been found for some incomplete information problems, major developments are needed to be able to handle practical problems. It will be necessary to investigate the concepts of circumscription and protected circumscription to expand their applicability to databases. The investigation of incomplete information is intimately connected with null value problems.
- *Investigating how logic can help in defining the so-called semantic models*, which appear as competitors to the relational model both for classical database applications and for more ambitious applications, where various types of data must be handled (e.g., text, computer-assisted design data, graphics). Such research will pursue problems identical to those in knowledge representation.

As we have attempted to demonstrate in this survey article, the field of logic and databases is important both to conventional and deductive databases. In this connection we note that "logic and databases" as have been described in this paper constitute the core of the work in Japan in the field of knowledge bases in their "Fifth-Generation Project."

Logic, we believe, provides a firm theoretical basis upon which one can pursue database theory in general. There are many research areas that remain to be investigated in addition to those listed above before a full understanding of databases is achieved. We believe that the field of logic and databases will contribute significantly to such an understanding. At the same time, we believe that logic databases may be made practical and efficient, as has been described by the many developments reported on in this survey.

ACKNOWLEDGMENTS

We thank Bob Kowalski and Ray Reiter, whose work in the field of logic and databases has been very influential, and for the many discussions that we have had with them over the past several years. The comments of the referees, the ACM technical editor, and Joachim Biskup on an earlier version of this paper were greatly appreciated.

Support for the work on this paper was received by Hervé Gallaire from Compagnie Générale d'Électricité (CGE), by Jack Minker from the Air Force Office of Scientific Research (AFOSR) under Grant 82-0303, the National Aeronautics and Space Administration (NASA) under Grant NAG-1-51, and the National Science Foundation (NSF) under Grants MCS-7919418 and MCS-8305992, by Jean-Marie Nicolas from the Direction des Recherches, Études et Techniques d'Armements (DRET), the Centre National de la Recherche Scientifique (CNRS-APT Intelligence Artificielle), and the Institut National de la Recherche en Informatique et Automatique (INRIA). We gratefully acknowledge the support that made this work possible.

REFERENCES

ADIBA, M., et al. 1982. Bases de donnes: Nouvelles perspectives. Rapport du groupe BD3 ADI-INRIA, Paris.

AHO, A. V., AND ULLMAN, J. D. 1979. Universality of data retrieval languages. In *Proceedings of the 6th ACM Symposium on Principles of Programming Languages* (San Antonio, Tex., Jan. 29–31). ACM, New York, pp. 110–120.

AHO, A. V., SAGIV, Y., AND ULLMAN, J. D. 1979. Equivalences among relational expressions. *SIAM J. Comput. 8*, 2 (May), 218–246.

ANSI/X3/SPARC 1975. Study Group on DBMS Interim Report. *SIGMOD FDT Bull. 7*, 2, 1975.

ARMSTRONG, W. W. 1974. Dependency structures of database relationships. In *Proceedings of IFIP 74.* Elsevier North-Holland, New York, pp. 580–583.

ARTIFICIAL INTELLIGENCE JOURNAL 1980. *13*, 1, 2; Special issue on nonmonotonic logic.

ARTRAUD, A., AND NICOLAS, J.-M. 1974. An experimental query system: SYNTEX. In *Proceedings of the International Computing Symposium 73.* Elsevier North-Holland, New York, pp. 557–563.

BANCILHON, F. 1978. On the completeness of query languages for relational databases. In *Proceedings of the 7th Symposium on Mathematical Foundations of Computer Science.* Springer-Verlag, Berlin and New York, pp. 112–123.

BEERI, C., AND VARDI, M. Y. 1980. A proof procedure for data dependencies. Tech. Rep., Computer Science Dept., Hebrew Univ., Jerusalem (Aug.).

BEERI, C., AND VARDI, M. Y. 1981. The implication problem for data dependencies. In *Proceedings of the 8th Colloquium on Automata, Languages, and Programming ACTC* (AKKO). Springer-Verlag, Berlin and New York, pp. 73–85.

BISKUP, J. A. 1981. A formal approach to null values in database relations. In *Advances in Database Theory*, vol. 1, H. Gallaire, J. Minker, and J.-M. Nicolas, Eds. Plenum, New York, pp. 299–341.

BISKUP J. A. 1982. A foundation of Codd's relational maybe-operations. Tech. Rep., Computer Science Dept., Univ. of Dortmund, West Germany.

BLAUSTEIN, B. T. 1981. Enforcing database assertions: Techniques and applications, Ph.D. dissertation, Computer Science Dept., Harvard Univ., Cambridge, Mass. (Aug.).

BORGIDA, A., AND WONG, H. K. T. 1981. Data models and data manipulation languages: Complementary semantics and proof theory. In *Proceedings of the 7th Conference on Very Large Data Bases* (Cannes, France, Sept. 9–11). IEEE, New York, pp. 260–271.

BOSSU, G., AND SIEGEL, P. 1981. La saturation au secours de la non-monotonicite. These de 3eme Cycle, Départment d'Informatiques, Université d'Aix-Marseille-Luminy, Marseille, France (June).

BOWEN, K. A., AND KOWALSKI, R. A. 1982. Amalgamating language and metalanguage in logic programming. In *Logic Programming*, K. L. Clark and S. A. Tarnlund, Eds. Academic Press, New York, pp. 153–172.

BRODIE, M. L., AND ZILLES, S. N., Eds. 1980. *Proceedings of the Workshop on Data Abstraction, Databases and Conceptual Modeling* (Pingree Park, Colo., June). *ACM SIGMOD Rec. 11*, 2 (Feb.).

CASANOVA, M. A., AND BERNSTEIN, P. A. 1979. The logic of a relational data manipulation language. In *Proceedings of the 6th ACM Symposium on*

Principles of Programming Languages (San Antonio, Tex., Jan. 29–31). ACM, New York, pp. 101–109.

CASANOVA, M. A., AND BERNSTEIN, P. A. 1980. A formal system for reasoning about programs accessing a relational database. *ACM Trans. Program. Lang. Syst. 2*, 3 (July), 386–414.

CHAKRAVARTHY, U. S., MINKER, J., AND TRAN, D. 1982. Interfacing predicate logic languages and relational databases. In *Proceedings of the 1st Conference on Logic Programming* (Marseille, France, Sept.). Université d'Aix-Marseille-Luminy, Marseille, France, pp. 91–98.

CHAMBERLIN, D. D., ASTRAHAN, M. M., BLASGEN, M. W., GRAY, J. N., KING, W. F., LINDSAY, B. G., LORIE, R., MEHL, J. W., PRICE, T. G., PUTZOLU, F., SELINGER, P. G., SCHKOLNICK, M., SLUTZ, D. R., TRAIGER, I. L., WADE, B. W., AND YOST, R. A. 1981. A history and evaluation of System R. *Commun. ACM 24*, 10 (Oct.) 632–646.

CHANDRA, A. K., AND HAREL, D. 1979. Computable queries for relational data bases. In *Proceedings of the 11th ACM Symposium on Theory of Computing* (Atlanta, Ga., Apr. 30–May 2). ACM, New York, pp. 309–318.

CHANDRA, A. K., AND HAREL, D. 1980. Structure and complexity of relational queries. In *Proceedings of the 21st IEEE Symposium on Foundations of Computer Science* (Syracuse, N.Y., Oct.). IEEE, New York, pp. 333–347. Also in *J. Comput. Syst. Sci. 25*, 1 (Aug. 1982), 99–128.

CHANDRA, A. K., AND MERLIN, P. M. 1976. Optimal implementation of conjunctive queries in relational data bases. In *Proceedings of the 9th ACM Symposium on Theory of Computing* (Boulder, Colo., May 2–4). ACM, New York, pp. 77–90.

CHANDRA, A. K., LEWIS, H. R., AND MAKOWSKY, J. A. 1981. Embedded implicational dependencies and their inference problem. In *Proceedings of the 13th ACM Symposium on Theory of Computing* (Milwaukee, Wis., May 11–13). ACM, New York, pp. 342–354.

CHANG, C. L. 1970. The unit proof and the input proof in theorem proving. *J. ACM 17*, 4 (Oct.) 698–707.

CHANG, C. L. 1978. DEDUCE 2: Further investigations of deduction in relational databases. In *Logic and Databases*, H. Gallaire and J. Minker, Eds. Plenum, New York, pp. 201–236.

CHANG, C. L. 1981. On evaluation of queries containing derived relations in a relational database. In *Advances in Database Theory*, vol. 1, H. Gallaire, J. Minker, and J.-M. Nicolas, Eds. Plenum, New York, pp. 235–260.

CHANG, C. L., AND LEE, R. C. T. 1973. *Symbolic Logic and Mechanical Theorem Proving.* Academic Press, New York.

CLARK, K. L. 1978. Negation as failure. In *Logic and Databases*, H. Gallaire and J. Minker, Eds. Plenum, New York, pp. 293–322.

CODD, E. F. 1970. A relational model of data for large shared data banks. *Commun. ACM 13*, 6 (June), 377–387.

CODD, E. F. 1972. Relational completeness of data-base sublanguages. In *Data Base Systems*, R. Rustin, Ed. Prentice-Hall, New York, pp. 65–98.

CODD, E. F. 1979. Extending the relational database model to capture more meaning. *ACM Trans. Database Syst. 4*, 4 (Dec.), 397–434.

CODD, E. F. 1980. Data models in database management. In *Proceedings of the Workshop on Data Abstraction, Databases and Conceptual Modeling* (Pingree Park, Colo., June), pp. 112–114; *ACM SIGMOD Rec. 11*, 2 (Feb.).

CODD, E. F. 1982. Relational database: A practical foundation for productivity. *Commun. ACM 25*, 2 (Feb.), 109–117.

COLMERAUER, A. 1973. Un systeme de communication homme-machine en francais. Rapport, Groupe Intelligence Artificielle, Université d'Aix-Marseille-Luminy, Marseilles, France.

COLMERAUER, A., AND PIQUE, J. F. 1981. About natural logic. In *Advances in Database Theory* vol. 1, H. Gallaire, J. Minker, and J.-M. Nicolas, Eds. Plenum, New York, pp. 343–365.

COOPER, E. C. 1980. On the expressive power of query languages for relational databases. Tech. Rep. 14-80, Computer Science Dept., Harvard Univ., Cambridge, Mass.

DAHL, V. 1982. On database systems development through logic. *ACM Trans. Database Syst. 7*, 1 (Mar.), 102–123.

DATE, C. J. 1977. *An Introduction to Database Systems.* Addison-Wesley, Reading, Mass.

DATE, C. J. 1981. *An Introduction to Database Systems*, 3rd ed. Addison-Wesley, Reading, Mass.

DELIYANNI, A., AND KOWALSKI, R. A. 1979. Logic and semantic networks. *Commun. ACM 22*, 3 (Mar.), 184–192.

DELOBEL, C. 1978. Normalization and hierarchical dependencies in the relational data model. *ACM Trans. Database Syst. 3*, 3 (Sept.), 201–222.

DELOBEL, C. 1980. An overview of the relational data theory. In *Proceedings of IFIP 80.* Elsevier North-Holland, New York, pp. 413–426.

DELOBEL, C., AND CASEY, R. G. 1973. Decomposition of a database and the theory of Boolean switching functions. *IBM J. Res. Dev. 17*, 5 (Sept.), 484–485.

DELOBEL, C., AND PARKER, D. S. 1978. Functional and multivalued dependencies in a relational database and the theory of boolean switching functions. Tech. Rep. 142, Université de Grenoble, Grenoble, France (Nov.).

DEMOLOMBE, R. 1980. Estimation of the number of tuples satisfying a query expressed in predicate calculus language. In *Proceedings of the 6th International Conference on Very Large Data Bases* (Montreal, Oct. 1–3). IEEE, New York, pp. 55–63.

DEMOLOMBE, R. 1981. Assigning meaning to ill-defined queries expressed in predicate calculus language. In *Advances in Database Theory*, vol. 1, H. Gallaire, J. Minker, and J.-M. Nicolas, Eds. Plenum, New York, pp. 367–395.

DEMOLOMBE, R. 1982. Utilization du calcul des predicats comme langage d'interrogation des bases de données. These de doctorat d'état, ONERA-CERT, Toulouse, France (Feb.).

DI PAOLA, R. A. 1969. The recursive unsolvability of the decision problem for the class of definite formulas. *J. ACM 16*, 2 (Apr.), 324–327.

DOS SANTOS, C. S., MAIBAUM, T. S. E., AND FURTADO, A. L. 1981. Conceptual modeling of database operations. *Int. J. Comput. Inf. Sci. 10*, 5, 299–314.

ENDERTON, H. B. 1972. *A Mathematical Introduction to Logic.* Academic Press, New York.

FAGIN, R. 1977a. Multivalued dependencies and a new normal form for relational databases. *ACM Trans. Database Syst. 2*, 3 (Sept.), 262–278.

FAGIN, R. 1977b. Functional dependencies in a relational database and propositional logic. *IBM J. Res. Dev. 21*, 6 (Nov.), 534–544.

FAGIN, R. 1980. Horn clauses and data base dependencies. In *Proceedings of the 12th Annual ACM-SIGACT Symposium on Theory of Computing.* ACM, New York, pp. 123–134.

FAGIN, R. 1982. Horn clause and database dependencies. *J. ACM 29*, 4 (Oct.), 952–985.

FAGIN, R., ULLMAN. J. D., AND VARDI, M. Y. 1983. On the semantics of updates in databases. In *Proceedings of the 2nd ACM Symposium on Principles of Database Systems* (Atlanta, Ga., Mar. 21–23). ACM, New York, pp. 352–365.

FLORENTIN, J. J. 1974. Consistency auditing of data bases. *Comput. J. 17*, 1, 52–58.

FURUKAWA, K. 1977. A deductive question-answering system on relational databases. In *Proceedings of the 5th International Joint Conference on Artificial Intelligence* (Cambridge, Mass., Aug.), pp. 59–66.

GALIL, Z. 1982. An almost linear-time algorithm for computing a dependency basis in a relational database. *J. ACM 29*, 1 (Jan.), 96–102.

GALLAIRE, H. 1981. Impacts of logic on data bases. In *Proceedings of the 7th International Conference on Very Large Data Bases* (Cannes, France, Sept. 9–11). IEEE, New York, pp. 248–259.

GALLAIRE, H. 1983. Logic databases vs. deductive databases. *Logic Programming Workshop* (Albufeira, Portugal). University of Lisboa, Lisbon, Portugal, pp. 608–622.

GALLAIRE, H., AND MINKER, J., Eds. 1978. *Logic and Data Bases.* Plenum, New York.

GALLAIRE, H., MINKER, J., AND NICOLAS, J.-M., Eds., 1981a. *Advances in Data Base Theory*, vol. 1. Plenum, New York.

GALLAIRE, H., MINKER, J., AND NICOLAS, J.-M. 1981b. Background for advances in data base theory. In *Advances in Data Base Theory*, vol. 1, H. Gallaire, J. Minker, and J.-M. Nicolas, Eds. Plenum, New York, pp. 3–21.

GALLAIRE, H., MINKER, J., AND NICOLAS, J.-M., Eds. 1984. *Advances in Data Base Theory*, vol. 2. Plenum, New York.

GARDARIN, G., AND MELKANOFF, M. 1979. Proving consistency of database transactions. In *Proceedings of the 5th International Conference on Very Large Data Bases* (Rio de Janeiro, Oct. 3–5). IEEE, New York, pp. 291–298.

GRANT, J. 1977. Null values in a relational data base. *Inf. Process. Lett. 6*, 5, 156–157.

GRANT, J., AND JACOBS, B. E. 1982. On the family of generalized dependency constraints. *J. ACM 29*, 4 (Oct.), 986–997.

GRANT, J., AND MINKER, J. 1981. Optimization in deductive and conventional relational database systems. In *Advances in Data Base Theory*, vol. 1, H. Gallaire, J. Minker, and J.-M. Nicolas, Eds. Plenum, New York, pp. 195–234.

GRANT, J., AND MINKER, J. 1983. Answering queries in indefinite databases and the null value problem. Tech. Rep. 1374, Computer Science Dept., University of Maryland, College Park.

GREEN, C. 1969. Theorem proving by resolution as a basis for question-answering systems. In *Machine Intelligence 4*, B. Meltzer and D. Michie, Eds. Elsevier North-Holland, New York, pp. 183–205.

HAMMER, M. T., AND ZDONIK, S. B., JR. 1980. Knowledge-based query processing. In *Proceedings of the 6th International Conference on Very Large Data Bases* (Montreal, Oct. 1–3). IEEE, New York, pp. 137–147.

HAREL, D. 1979. First order dynamic logic. In *Lecture Notes in Computer Science*, vol. 68. Springer-Verlag, Berlin and New York.

HAREL, D. 1980. Review of *Logic and Databases*, H. Gallaire and J. Minker. *Comput. Rev. 21*, 8 (Aug.), 367–369.

HENSCHEN, L. J., MCCUNE, W. W., AND NAQVI, S. A. 1984. Compiling constraint checking programs from first order formulas. In *Advances in Database Theory*, vol. 2, H. Gallaire, J. Minker, and J.-M. Nicolas, Eds. Plenum, New York, pp. 145–169.

HEWITT, C. 1972. Description and theoretical analysis (using schemata) of PLANNER: A language for proving theorems and manipulating models in a robot. AI Memo No. 251, MIT Project MAC, Cambridge, Mass.

HILL, R. 1974. LUSH resolution and its completeness. DCS Memo, No. 78. University of Edinburgh, School of Artificial Intelligence.

HOMEIER, P. V. 1981. Simplifying integrity constraints in a relational database: An implementation. M.Sc. thesis, Computer Science Dept., University of California, Los Angeles.

IMIELINSKI, T., AND LIPSKI, W. 1981. On representing incomplete information in a relational database. In *Proceedings of the 7th International Conference on Very Large Data Bases* (Cannes,

France, Sept. 9–11). IEEE, New York, pp. 389–397.

INTERNATIONAL JOINT CONFERENCE ON ARTIFICIAL INTELLIGENCE 1983. August, 8–12, 1983, Karlsruhe, West Germany.

INTERNATIONAL SYMPOSIUM ON LOGIC PROGRAMMING 1984. Feb. 6–9, 1984, Atlantic City, N.J.

JACOBS, B. E. 1982. On database logic. *J. ACM 29*, 2 (Apr.), 310–332.

JACOBS, B. E., ARONSON, A. R., AND KLUG, A. C. 1982. On interpretations of relational languages and solutions to the implied constraint problem. *ACM Trans. Database Syst. 7*, 2 (June), 291–315.

JAFFAR, J., LASSEZ, J. L., AND LLOYD, J. 1983. Completeness of the negation by failure rule. In *Proceedings of the 8th International Joint Conference on Artificial Intelligence* (Karlsruhe, W. Germany, Aug.), pp. 500–506.

JANAS, J. M. 1979. Towards more informative user interfaces. In *Proceedings of the 5th International Conference on Very Large Data Bases* (Rio de Janeiro, Oct. 3–5). IEEE, New York, pp. 17–23.

JANAS, J. M. 1981. On the feasibility of informative answers. In *Advances in Data Base Theory*, vol. 1, H. Gallaire, J. Minker, and J.-M. Nicolas, Eds. Plenum, New York, pp. 397–414.

KELLOGG, C., AND TRAVIS, L. 1981. Reasoning with data in a deductively augmented data management system. In *Advances in Data Base Theory*, vol. 1, H. Gallaire, J. Minker, and J.-M. Nicolas, Eds. Plenum, New York, pp. 261–295.

KELLOGG, C., KLHAR, P., AND TRAVIS, L. 1978. Deductive planning and path finding for relational data bases. In *Logic and Databases*, H. Gallaire and J. Minker, Eds. Plenum, New York, pp. 179–200.

KING, J. J. 1981. QUIST: A system for semantic query optimization in relational databases. In *Proceedings of the 7th International Conference on Very Large Data Bases* (Cannes, France, Sept. 9–11). IEEE, New York, pp. 510–517.

KONOLIGE, K. 1981. A metalanguage representation of databases for deductive question-answering systems. In *Proceedings of the 7th International Joint Conference on Artificial Intelligence* (Vancouver, B.C., Aug.), pp. 469–503.

KOWALSKI, R. A. 1978. Logic for data description. In *Logic and Data Bases*, H. Gallaire and J. Minker, Eds. Plenum, New York, pp. 77–103.

KOWALSKI, R. A. 1979. *Logic for Problem Solving*. Elsevier North-Holland, New York.

KOWALSKI, R. A. 1981a. Logic as a data base language. In *Proceedings of the Advanced Seminar on Theoretical Issues in Data Bases* (Cetraro, Italy, Sept.).

KOWALSKI, R. A. 1981b. Personal communication.

KOWALSKI, R. A., AND KUEHNER, D. 1971. Linear resolution with selection function. *Artif. Intell. 2*, 3/4, 227–260.

KUHNS, J. L. 1967. Answering questions by computers—A logical study. Rand Memo RM 5428 PR, Rand Corp., Santa Monica, Calif.

KUHNS, J. L. 1970. Interrogating a relational data file: Remarks on the admissibility of input queries. Tech. Rep. TR-511-PR, Rand Corp., Santa Monica, Calif. (Nov.).

KUNIFUJI, S., AND YOKOTA, H. 1982. Prolog and relational databases for the fifth generation computer system. ICOT Rep. D02, Institute for New Generation Computer Technology, Tokyo.

LACROIX, M., AND PIROTTE, A. 1980. Associating types with domains of relational databases. In *Workshop on Data Abstraction, Databases and Conceptual Modeling* (Pingree Park, Colo., June). *ACM SIGMOD Rec. 11*, 2 (Feb.), 144–146.

LEVESQUE, H. J. 1981. The interaction with incomplete knowledge bases: a formal treatment. *Proceedings of the 7th International Joint Conference on Artificial Intelligence* (Vancouver, B.C., Aug.), pp. 240–245.

LIPSKI, W. 1979. On semantic issues connected with incomplete information systems. *ACM Trans. Database Syst. 4*, 3 (Sept.), 262–296.

LOGIC PROGRAMMING WORKSHOP PROCEEDINGS 1983. June 26–July, 1, 1983, Praia da Falesia, Algarve, Portugal. Dept. of Computer Science, University of Lisboa, Lisbon, Portugal.

LOVELAND, D. 1969. Theorem provers combining model elimination and resolution. In *Machine Intelligence*, vol. 4. B. Meltzer and D. Michie, Eds. Elsevier North-Holland, New York, pp. 73–86.

LOVELAND, D. 1970. A linear format for resolution. *Proceedings of the IRIA Symposium on Automatic Demonstration*. Springer-Verlag, Berlin and New York, pp. 147–162.

LOVELAND, D. 1978. *Automated Theorem Proving: A Logical Basis*. Elsevier North-Holland, New York.

MAIER, D. 1983. *The Theory of Relational Databases*. Computer Science Press, Rockville, Md.

MAIER, D., MENDELZON, A. O., AND SAGIV, Y. 1979. Testing implications of data dependencies. *ACM Trans. Database Syst. 4*, 4 (Dec.), 455–469.

MCCARTHY, J. 1980. Circumscription—A form of non-monotonic reasoning. *Artif. Intell. 13*, 27–39.

MCSKIMIN, J. 1976. Techniques for employing semantic information in question-answering systems. Ph.D. dissertation, Dept. of Computer Science, University of Maryland, College Park.

MCSKIMIN, J., AND MINKER, J. 1977. The use of a semantic network in a deductive question-answering system. In *Proceedings of the 5th International Joint Conference on Artificial Intelligence* (Cambridge, Mass., Aug.), pp. 50–58.

MENDELSON, E. 1978. *Introduction to Mathematical Logic*, 2nd ed. Van Nostrand-Reinhold, New York.

MINKER, J. 1975a. Performing inferences over relational data bases. In *ACM SIGMOD International Conference on Management of Data* (San Jose, Calif., May 14–16). ACM, New York, pp. 79–91.

MINKER, J. 1975b. Set operations and inferences over relational databases. In *Proceedings of the 4th Texas Conference on Computing Systems* (Nov.). Univ. of Texas, Austin, pp. 5A1.1–5A1.10.

MINKER, J. 1978a. Search strategy and selection function for an inferential relational system. *ACM Trans. Database Syst. 3*, 1 (Mar.), 1–31.

MINKER, J. 1978b. An experimental relational data base system based on logic. In *Logic and Databases*, H. Gallaire and J. Minker, Eds. Plenum, New York, pp. 107–147.

MINKER, J. 1982. On indefinite databases and the closed world assumption. In *Proceedings of the 6th Conference on Automated Deduction* (New York). Springer-Verlag Lecture Notes in Computer Science, No. 138. Springer-Verlag, Berlin and New York, pp. 292–308.

MINKER, J. 1983. On deductive relational databases. In *Proceedings of the 5th International Conference on Collective Phenomena* (July), J. L. Lebowitz, Ed., *Annals of the New York Academy of Sciences*, vol. 10. New York Academy of Science, New York, pp. 181–200.

MINKER, J., AND NICOLAS, J. M. 1982. On recursive axioms in deductive databases. *Inf. Syst. 8*, 1 (Jan.), 1–13.

MINKER, J., AND PERLIS, D. 1983. On the semantics of circumscription. Tech. Rep., Computer Science Dept., Univ. of Maryland, College Park.

MINKER, J., AND PERLIS, D. 1984. Applications of protected circumscription. In *Proceedings of the Conference on Automated Deduction 7* (Napa, Calif., May). Springer-Verlag, Berlin and New York, pp. 414–425.

MINKER, J., AND ZANON, G. 1982. An extension to linear resolution with selection function. *Inf. Process. Lett. 14*, 4 (June), 191–194.

MOORE, R. C. 1981. Problems in logical form. In *Proceedings of the 19th Annual Meeting of the Association for Computational Linguistics* (June). Association for Computational Linguistics, pp. 117–124.

MYLOPOULOS, J. 1980. An overview of knowledge representation. In *Proceedings of the Workshop of Data Abstraction, Databases, and Conceptual Modeling*, M. Brodie and S. N. Zilles, Eds. (Pingree Park, Colo., June). *ACM SIGMOD Rec. 11*, 2 (Feb.), 5–12.

NAQVI, S. A., AND HENSCHEN, L. J. 1980. Performing inferences over recursive data bases. In *Proceedings of the 1st Annual National Conference on Artificial Intelligence* (Stanford, Conn., Aug.). AAAI, Palo Alto, Calif., pp. 263–265.

NAQVI, S. A., AND HENSCHEN, L. J. 1984. On compiling queries in recursive first-order databases. *J. ACM 31*, 1 (Jan.), 47–85.

NICOLAS, J.-M. 1978. First order logic formalization for functional, multivalued and mutual dependencies. In *Proceedings of ACM-SIGMOD International Conference on Management of Data* (Austin, Tex., June 1, 2). ACM, New York, pp. 40–46.

NICOLAS, J.-M. 1979a. A property of logical formulas corresponding to integrity constraints on database relations. In *Proceedings of the Workshop on Formal Bases for Data Bases* (Toulouse, France). ONERA-CERT, Toulouse, France.

NICOLAS, J.-M. 1979b. Logic for improving integrity checking in relational databases. Tech. Rep. ONERA-CERT, Toulouse, France (Feb.). Also in *Acta Inf. 18*, 3 (Dec.), 227–253.

NICOLAS, J.-M., AND GALLAIRE, H. 1978. Database: Theory vs. interpretation. In *Logic and Databases*, H. Gallaire and J. Minker, Eds. Plenum, New York, pp. 33–54.

NICOLAS, J.-M., AND SYRE, J. C. 1974. Natural question answering and automatic deduction in the system SYNTEX. In *Proceedings of IFIP 1974*. North-Holland, Amsterdam, pp. 595–599.

NICOLAS, J.-M., AND YAZDANIAN, K. 1978. Integrity checking in deductive databases. In *Logic and Databases*, H. Gallaire and J. Minker, Eds. Plenum, New York, pp. 325–346.

NICOLAS, J.-M., AND YAZDANIAN, K. 1982. An outline of BDGEN: A deductive DBMS. Tech. Rep. TR-ONERA-CERT, Toulouse, France (Oct.). Also in *Proceedings of IFIP 83 Congress*. North-Holland, Amsterdam, 1983, pp. 711–717.

PAREDAENS, J. 1978. On the expressive power of relational algebra. *Inf. Process. Lett. 7*, 2 (Feb.), 107–111.

PARKER, D. S., AND DELOBEL, C. 1979. Algorithmic applications for a new result on multivalued dependencies. In *Proceedings of the 5th Conference on Very Large Data Bases* (Rio de Janeiro, Oct. 3–5). IEEE, New York, pp. 67–74.

PIROTTE, A. 1976. Explicit description of entities and their manipulation in languages for the relational database model. Thèse de doctorat, Université libre de Bruxelles, Brussells, Belgium (Dec.).

PIROTTE, A. 1978. High level data base query languages. In *Logic and Data Bases*, H. Gallaire and J. Minker, Eds. Plenum, New York, pp. 409–436.

PRATT, V. R. 1976. Semantical considerations on Floyd–Hoare logic. In *Proceedings of the 17th IEEE Symposium Foundations of Computer Science* (Oct.). IEEE, New York, pp. 409–120.

PROCEEDINGS OF THE 1ST CONFERENCE ON LOGIC PROGRAMMING 1982. Marseille, France (Sept.), Université d'Aix-Marseille-Luminy, Marseille.

REITER, R. 1971. Two results on ordering for resolution with merging and linear format. *J. ACM 18*, 4 (Oct.), 630–646.

REITER, R. 1978a. On closed world databases. In *Logic and Databases*, H. Gallaire and J. Minker, Eds. Plenum, New York, pp. 56–76.

REITER, R. 1978b. Deductive question-answering on relational databases. In *Logic and Data Bases*, H. Gallaire and J. Minker, Eds. Plenum, New York, pp. 149–178.

REITER, R. 1978c. On structuring a first-order database. In *Proceedings of the 2nd Canadian Society for Computer Science National Conference*, Canada (July).

REITER, R. 1980. Equality and domain closure in first-order databases. *J. ACM 27*, 2 (Apr.), 235–249.

REITER, R. 1981. On the integrity of first-order databases. In *Advances in Data Base Theory*, vol. 1, H. Gallaire, J. Minker, and J.-M. Nicolas, Eds. Plenum, New York, pp. 137–158.

REITER, R. 1982. Circumscription implies predicate completion (sometimes). In *Proceedings of the American Association for Artificial Intelligence 82 Conference* (Pittsburgh, Pa., Aug.). AAAI, Menlo Park, Calif., pp. 418–420.

REITER, R. 1983. A sound and sometimes complete query evaluation algorithm for relational databases with null values. Tech. Rep. 83-11, Computer Science Dept., University of British Columbia, Canada (June).

REITER, R. 1984. Towards a logical reconstruction of relational database theory. In *On Conceptual Modeling*, M. Brodie, J. Mylopoulos, and J. W. Schmidt, Eds. Springer-Verlag, Berlin and New York.

ROBINSON, J. A. 1965. A machine oriented logic based on the resolution principle. *J. ACM 12*, 1 (Jan.), 23–41.

ROUSSEL, P. 1975. PROLOG: Manuel de reference et d'utilisation. Tech. Rep., Département d'Informatiques, Université d'Aix-Marseille-Luminy, Marseille, France (Sept.).

SADRI, F., AND ULLMAN, J. D. 1980. A complete axiomatization for a large class of dependencies in relational databases. In *Proceedings of the 17th Annual ACM-SIGACT Symposium on Theory of Computing*. ACM, New York, pp. 117–122.

SADRI, F., AND ULLMAN, J. D. 1982. Template dependencies: A large class of dependencies in relational databases and its complete axiomatization. *J. ACM 29*, 2 (Apr.), 363–372.

SAGIV, Y. 1980. An algorithm for inferring multivalued dependencies with an application to propositional logic. *J. ACM 27*, 2 (Apr.), 250–262.

SAGIV, Y., AND FAGIN, R. 1979. An equivalence between relational database dependencies and a subset of propositional logic. Res. Rep. RJ2500, IBM Research Laboratories, San Jose, Calif. (Mar.).

SAGIV, Y., DELOBEL, C., PARKER, D. S., JR., AND FAGIN, R. 1981. An equivalence between relational database dependencies and a subclass of propositional logic. *J. ACM 28*, 3 (July), 435–453.

SELINGER, P. G., ASTRAHAN, M. M., CHAMBERLIN, D. D., LORIE, R. A., AND PRICE, T. G. 1979. Access path selection in a relational database management system. In *Proceedings ACM-SIGMOD International Conference on Management of Data* (Boston, May 30–June 1). ACM, New York, pp. 23–34.

SHAPIRO, S. E., AND MCKAY, D. P. 1980. Inference with recursive rules. In *Proceedings of the 1st Annual National Conference on Artificial Intelligence*. AAAI, Palo Alto, Calif.

SIKLOSSY, L., AND LAURIERE, J.-L. 1982. Removing restrictions in the relational database model: an application of problem solving techniques. In *Proceedings of the American Association for Artificial Intelligence 82 Conference* (Pittsburgh, Pa., Aug.). AAAI, Menlo Park, Calif., pp. 310–313.

STONEBRAKER, M. R., WONG, E., AND KEEPS, F. 1976. The design and implementation of INGRES. *ACM Trans. Database Syst. 1*, 3 (Sept.), 189–222.

ULLMAN, J. D. 1980. *Principles of Database Systems*. Computer Science Press, Potomac, Md.

ULLMAN, J. D. 1982. *Principles of Database Systems*, 2nd ed. Computer Science Press, Potomac, Md.

VAN EMDEN, M. H. 1978. Computation and deductive information retrieval. In *Formal Description of Programming Concepts*, E. J. Neuhold, Ed. Elsevier North-Holland, New York, pp. 421–440.

VAN EMDEN, M. H., AND KOWALSKI, R. A. 1976. The semantics of predicate logic as a programming language. *J. ACM 23*, 4 (Oct.), 733–742.

VARDI, M. Y. 1981. The decision problem for database dependencies. *Inf. Process. Lett. 12*, 5 (Oct.), 251–254.

VASSILIOU, Y. 1979. Null values in data base management—A denotational semantics approach. In *Proceedings of the ACM-SIGMOD International Conference on the Management of Data* (Boston, May 30–June 1). ACM, New York, pp. 162–169.

VASSILIOU, Y. 1980. Functional dependencies and incomplete information. In *Proceedings of the 6th International Conference on Very Large Data Bases* (Montreal, Oct. 1–3). IEEE, New York, pp. 260–269.

VELOSO, P. A. S., DE CASTILHO, J. M. V., AND FURTADO, A. L. 1981. Systematic derivation of complementary specifications. In *Proceedings of the 7th International Conference on Very Large Data Bases* (Cannes, France, Sept. 9–11). IEEE, New York, pp. 409–421.

WARREN, D. H. D. 1981. Efficient processing of interactive relational database queries expressed in logic. In *Proceedings of the 7th International Conference on Very Large Data Bases* (Cannes, France, Sept. 9–11). IEEE, New York, pp. 272–281.

WOODS, W. A. 1967. Semantics for question-answering systems. Ph.D. dissertation, Rep. NSF-19, Aiken Computation Laboratory, Harvard University, Cambridge, Mass.

YANNAKAKIS, M., AND PAPADIMITRIOU, C. 1982. Algebraic dependencies. *J. Comput. Syst. Sci. 25*, 1 (Aug.), 2–41.

YOKOTA, H., KUNIFUJI, S., KAKUTA, T., MIYAZAKI, N., SHIBAYAMA, S., AND MURAKAMI, K. 1983. An enhanced inference mechanism for generating relational algebra queries. Tech. Rep. 026, ICOT Research Center, Institute for New Generation Computer Technology, Tokyo, Japan.

ZANIOLO, C. 1976. Analysis and design of relational schemata for data base system. Tech. Rep. UCLA Eng. 7769, Dept. of Computer Science, University of California, Los Angeles.

ZANIOLO, C. 1981. Incomplete database information and null values: An overview. In *Proceedings of the Advanced Seminar on Theoretical Issues in Data Bases* (Cetraro, Italy, Sept.).

ZLOOF, M. M. 1977. Query-by-example: A data base language. *IBM Syst. J. 16*, 4, 324–343.

Received February 1983; final revision accepted July 1984.

ON CLOSED WORLD DATA BASES

Raymond Reiter

The University of British Columbia

Vancouver, British Columbia

ABSTRACT

Deductive question-answering systems generally evaluate queries under one of two possible assumptions which we in this paper refer to as the open and closed world assumptions. The open world assumption corresponds to the usual first order approach to query evaluation: Given a data base DB and a query Q, the only answers to Q are those which obtain from proofs of Q given DB as hypotheses. Under the closed world assumption, certain answers are admitted as a result of failure to find a proof. More specifically, if no proof of a positive ground literal exists, then the negation of that literal is assumed true.

In this paper, we show that closed world evaluation of an arbitrary query may be reduced to open world evaluation of so-called atomic queries. We then show that the closed world assumption can lead to inconsistencies, but for Horn data bases no such inconsistencies can arise. Finally, we show how for Horn data bases under the closed world assumption purely negative clauses are irrelevant for deductive retrieval and function instead as integrity constraints.

INTRODUCTION

Deductive question-answering systems generally evaluate queries under one of two possible assumptions which we in this paper refer to as the open and closed world assumptions. The open world assumption corresponds to the usual first order approach to query evaluation: Given a data base DB and a query Q, the only answers to Q are those which obtain from proofs of Q given DB as hypotheses. Under the closed world assumption, certain answers are admitted as a result of <u>failure</u> to find a proof. More specifically, if no proof of a positive ground literal exists, then the negation of that literal is assumed true. This can be viewed as equivalent to implicitly augmenting the given data base with all such negated literals.

For many domains of application, closed world query evaluation is appropriate since, in such domains, it is natural to explicitly represent only positive knowledge and to assume the truth of negative facts by default. For example, in an airline data base, all flights and the cities which they connect will be explicitly represented. Failure to find an entry indicating that Air Canada flight 103 connects Vancouver with Toulouse permits one to conclude that it does not.

This paper is concerned with closed world query evaluation and its relationship to open world evaluation. In the section, Data Bases and Queries, we define a query language and the notion of an open world answer to a query. The section called The Closed World Assumption formally defines the notion of a closed world answer. The section, Query Evaluation Under the CWA, shows how closed world query evaluation may be decomposed into open world evaluation of so-called "atomic queries" in conjunction with the set operations of intersection, union and difference, and the relational algebra operation of projection. In the section, On Data Bases Consistent with the CWA, we show that the closed world assumption can lead to inconsistencies. We prove, moreover, that for Horn data bases no such inconsistencies can arise. Also, for Horn data bases, the occurrence of purely negative clauses is irrelevant to closed world query evaluation. By removing such negative clauses one is left with so-called definite data bases which are then consistent under both the open and closed world assumptions. Finally, in the section, The CWA and Data Base Integrity, we show that these purely negative clauses, although irrelevant to deductive retrieval, have a function in maintaining data base integrity.

In order to preserve continuity we have relegated all proofs of the results in the main body of this paper to an appendix.

DATA BASES AND QUERIES

The query language of this paper is set oriented, i.e. we seek all objects (or tuples of objects) having a given property. For example, in an airline data base the request "Give all flights and their carriers which fly from Boston to England" might be represented in our query language by:

$$< x/Flight,\ y/Airline \mid (Ez/City)Connect\ x,Boston,z \wedge Owns\ y,x \wedge City\text{-}of\ z,England >$$

which denotes the set of all ordered pairs (x,y) such that x is a flight, y is an airline and

$$(Ez/City)Connect\ x,Boston,z \wedge Owns\ y,x \wedge City\text{-}of\ z,England$$

is true. The syntactic objects Flight, Airline and City are called types and serve to restrict the variables associated with them to range over objects of that type. Thus, (Ez/City) may be read as "There is a z which is a city".

Formally, all queries have the form

$$< x_1/\tau_1,\ldots,x_n/\tau_n \mid (Ey_1/\theta_1)\ldots(Ey_m/\theta_m)W(x_1,\ldots,x_n,y_1,\ldots,y_m) >$$

where $W(x_1,\ldots,x_n,y_1,\ldots,y_m)$ is a quantifier-free formula with free variables $x_1,\ldots,x_n,y_1,\ldots,y_m$ and moreover W contains no function signs. For brevity we shall often denote a typical such query by $< \vec{x}/\vec{\tau} \mid (E\vec{y}/\vec{\theta})W >$. The τ's and θ's are called <u>types</u>. We assume that with each type τ is associated a set of constant signs which we denote by $|\tau|$. For example, in an airline data base, $|City|$ might be {Toronto, Boston, Paris,...,}. If $\vec{\tau} = \tau_1,\ldots,\tau_n$ is a sequence of types we denote by $|\vec{\tau}|$ the set $|\tau_1| \times\ldots\times |\tau_n|$.

A <u>data base</u> (DB) is a set of clauses containing no function signs. For an airline data base, DB might contain such information as:

"Air Canada flight 203 connects Toronto and Vancouver."

Connect AC203, Toronto, Vancouver

"All flights from Boston to Los Angeles serve meals."

$(x/Flight)Connect\ x,Boston,LA \supset Meal\text{-}serve\ x$

Let $Q = < \vec{x}/\vec{\tau} \mid (E\vec{y}/\vec{\theta})W(\vec{x},\vec{y}) >$ and let DB be a data base. A set of n-tuples of constant signs $\{\vec{c}^{(1)},\ldots,\vec{c}^{(r)}\}$ is an <u>answer</u> to Q (with respect to DB) iff

1. $\vec{c}^{(i)} \in |\vec{\tau}| \quad i = 1,\ldots,r$ and
2. $DB \vdash \bigvee_{i\le r} (E\vec{y}/\vec{\theta})W(\vec{c}^{(i)},\vec{y})$

Notice that if $\{\vec{c}^{(1)},\ldots,\vec{c}^{(r)}\}$ is an answer to Q, and $\vec{c}$ is any n-tuple of constant signs satisfying 1. then so also is $\{\vec{c}^{(1)},\ldots,\vec{c}^{(r)},\vec{c}\}$ an answer to Q. This suggests the need for the following definitions:

An answer A to Q is <u>minimal</u> iff no proper subset of A is an answer to Q. If A is a minimal answer to Q, then if A consists of a single n-tuple, A is a <u>definite</u> answer to Q. Otherwise, A is an <u>indefinite</u> answer to Q. Finally define $\|Q\|_{OWA}$ to be the set of minimal answers to Q. (For reasons which will become apparent later, the subscript OWA stands for "Open World Assumption".) Notice the interpretation assigned to an indefinite answer $\{\vec{c}^{(1)},\ldots,\vec{c}^{(r)}\}$ to Q: $\vec{x}$ is either $\vec{c}^{(1)}$ or $\vec{c}^{(2)}$ or...or $\vec{c}^{(r)}$ but there is no way, given the information in DB, of determining which. Instead of denoting an answer as a set of tuples $\{\vec{c}^{(1)},\ldots,\vec{c}^{(r)}\}$ we prefer the more suggestive notation $\vec{c}^{(1)} + \ldots + \vec{c}^{(r)}$, a notation we shall use in the remainder of this paper.

<u>Example 1.</u>

Suppose DB knows of 4 humans and 2 cities:

$$|Human| = \{a,b,c,d\} \qquad |City| = \{B,V\}$$

Suppose further that everyone is either in B or in V:

$$(x/Human)Loc\ x,B \vee Loc\ x,V$$

and moreover, a is in B and b is in V:

$$Loc\ a,B \qquad Loc\ b,V$$

Then for the query "Where is everybody?"

$$Q = < x/Human,y/City \mid Loc\ x,y >$$

we have

$$\|Q\|_{OWA} = \{(a,B),(b,V),(c,B) + (c,V),(d,B) + (d,V)\}$$

i.e. a is in B, b is in V, c is either in B or V and d is either in B or V.

Since it is beyond the scope of this paper, the reader is referred to Reiter [1977] or Reiter [1978] for an approach to query evaluation which returns $\|Q\|_{OWA}$ given any query Q.

THE CLOSED WORLD ASSUMPTION

In order to illustrate the central concept of this paper, we consider the following purely <u>extensional</u> data base (i.e., a data base consisting of ground literals only):

$|Teacher| = \{a,b,c,d\}$

$|Student| = \{A,B,C\}$

Teach	
a	A
b	B
c	C
a	B

Now consider the query: Who does not teach B?

$Q = < x/Teacher \mid \overline{Teach}\ x,B >$

By the definition of the previous section, we conclude, counter-intuitively, that

$\|Q\|_{OWA} = \phi$.

Intuitively, we want $\{c,d\}$ i.e. $|Teacher| - \| < x/Teacher|\overline{Teach}\ x,B > \|_{OWA}$. The reason for the counterintuitive result is that first order logic interprets the DB literally; all the logic knows for certain is what is explicitly represented in the DB. Just because $\overline{Teach}\ c,B$ is not present in the DB is no reason to conclude that $\overline{Teach}\ c,B$ is true. Rather, as far as the logic is concerned, the truth of Teach c,B is unknown! Thus, we would also have to include the following facts about Teach:

$\overline{Teach}$	
a	C
b	A
b	C
c	A
c	B
d	A
d	B
d	C

Unfortunately, the number of negative facts about a given domain will, in general, far exceed the number of positive ones so that the requirement that all facts, both positive and negative, be explicitly represented may well be unfeasible. In the case of purely extensional data bases there is a ready solution to this problem. Merely <u>explicitly</u> represent <u>positive</u> facts. A negative fact is <u>implicitly</u> present provided its positive counterpart is <u>not explicitly</u> present. Notice, however, that by adopting this convention, we are making an assumption about our knowledge about the domain, namely, that we know everything about each predicate of the domain. There are no gaps in our knowledge. For example, if we were ignorant as to whether or not a teaches C, we could not permit the above implicit representation of negative facts. This is an important point. <u>The implicit representation of negative facts presumes total knolwedge about the domain being represented.</u> Fortunately, in most applications, such an assumption is warranted. We shall refer to this as the <u>closed world assumption</u> (CWA). Its opposite, the <u>open world assumption</u> (OWA), assumes only the information given in the data base and hence requires all facts, both positive and negative, to be explicitly represented. Under the OWA, "gaps" in one's knowledge about the domain are permitted.

Formally, we can define the notion of an answer to a query under the CWA as follows:

Let DB be an extensional data base and let $\overline{EDB} = \{\overline{P\vec{c}} \mid P$ is a predicate sign, $\vec{c}$ a tuple of constant signs and $P\vec{c} \notin DB\}$
Then $\vec{c}$ is a <u>CWA answer</u> to $< \vec{x}/\vec{\tau} \mid (E\vec{y}/\vec{\theta})W(\vec{x},\vec{y}) >$ (with respect to DB) iff

1. $\vec{c} \in |\vec{\tau}|$ and

2, $DB \cup \overline{EDB} \vdash (E\vec{y}/\vec{\theta})W(\vec{c},\vec{y})$

For purely extensional data bases, the CWA poses no difficulties. One merely imagines the DB to contain all negative facts each of which has no positive version in the DB. This conceptual view of the DB fails in the presence of non ground clauses. For if $P\vec{c} \notin DB$, it may nevertheless be possible to infer $P\vec{c}$ from the DB, so that we cannot, with impunity, imagine $\overline{P\vec{c}} \in DB$. The obvious generalization is to assume that the DB implicitly contains $\overline{P\vec{c}}$ whenever it is not the case that $DB \vdash P\vec{c}$.

Formally, we can define the notion of an answer to a query under the CWA for an arbitrary data base DB as follows:

Let

$\overline{EDB} = \{\overline{P\vec{c}} \mid P$ is a predicate sign, $\vec{c}$ a tuple of constant signs and $DB \nvdash P\vec{c}\}$

Then $\vec{c}^{(1)} + \ldots + \vec{c}^{(r)}$ is a <u>CWA answer</u> to

$< \vec{x}/\vec{\tau} \mid (E\vec{y}/\vec{\theta})W(\vec{x},\vec{y}) >$ (with respect to DB) iff

1. $\vec{c}^{(i)} \in |\vec{\tau}|$ $i=1,\ldots,r$ and

2. $DB \cup \overline{EDB} \vdash \bigvee_{i\leq r} (E\vec{y}/\vec{\theta})W(\vec{c}^{(i)},\vec{y})$

This definition should be compared with the definition of an answer in the previous section. We shall refer to this latter notion as an OWA answer. As under the OWA, we shall require the notions of minimal, indefinite and definite CWA answers. If Q is a query, we shall denote the set of minimal CWA answers to Q by $||Q||_{CWA}$.

Example 2.

We consider a fragment of an inventory data base.

1. Every supplier of a part supplies all its subparts.

   (x/Supplier)(yz/Part)Supplies x,y $\wedge$ Subpart z,y $\supset$ Supplies x,z

2. Foobar Inc. supplies all widgets.

   (x/Widget)Supplies Foobar,x

3. The subpart relation is transitive.

   (xyz/Part)Subpart z,y $\wedge$ Subpart y,x $\supset$ Subpart z,x

Assume the following type extensions:

$|Supplier| = \{Acme, Foobar, AAA\}$

$|Widget| = \{w_1,w_2,w_3,w_4\}$

$|Part| = \{p_1,p_2,p_3,w_1,w_2,w_3,w_4\}$

Finally, assume the following extensional data base:

Supplies	x	y
	Acme	p_1
	AAA	w_3
	AAA	w_4

Subpart	x	y
	p_2	p_1
	p_3	p_2
	w_1	p_1
	w_2	w_1

Then $\overline{EDB}$ is:

Supplies	x	y
	Acme	w_3
	Acme	w_4
	AAA	p_1
	AAA	p_2
	AAA	p_3
	AAA	w_1
	AAA	w_2
	Foobar	p_1
	Foobar	p_2
	Foobar	p_3
	p_1	Acme
	p_1	AAA
	p_1	Foobar
	p_1	p_1
	p_1	p_2
	p_1	p_3
	p_1	w_1
	etc.	

Subpart	x	y
	p_1	p_1
	p_1	p_2
	p_1	p_3
	p_1	w_1
	p_1	w_2
	p_1	w_3
	p_1	w_4
	p_2	p_2
	p_2	p_3
	p_2	w_1
	p_2	w_2
	p_2	w_3
	p_2	w_4
	p_3	p_3
	p_3	w_1
	p_3	w_2
	p_3	w_3
	p_3	w_4
	etc.	

The notion of a CWA answer is obviously intimately related to the negation operators of PLANNER (Hewitt [1972]) and PROLOG (Roussel [1975]) since in these languages, negation means "not provable" and the definition of $\overline{EDB}$ critically depends upon this notion. Clark [1978] investigates the relation between this notion of negation as failure and its truth functional semantics. The need for the CWA in deductive question-answering systems has been articulated in Nicolas and Syre [1974].

Notice that under the CWA, there can be no "gaps" in our knowledge about the domain. More formally, for each predicate sign P and each tuple of constant signs $\vec{c}$, either $DB \vdash P\vec{c}$ or $\overline{EDB} \vdash \overline{P\vec{c}}$ and since, under the CWA the data base is taken to be $DB \cup \overline{EDB}$, we can always infer either $P\vec{c}$ or $\overline{P\vec{c}}$ from $DB \cup \overline{EDB}$. Since there are no "knowledge gaps" under the CWA, it should be intuitively clear that indefinite CWA answers cannot arise, i.e. each minimal CWA answer to a query is of the form $\vec{c}$. The following result confirms this intuition.

Theorem 1.

Let $Q = < \vec{x}/\vec{\tau} | (E\vec{y}/\vec{\theta})W(\vec{x},\vec{y}) >$. Then every minimal CWA answer to Q is definite.

There is one obvious difficulty in directly applying the definition of a CWA answer to the evaluation of queries. The definition requires that we explicitly know $\overline{EDB}$ and, as Example 2 demonstrates, the determination of $\overline{EDB}$ is generally non trivial.

In any event, for non toy domains, $\overline{EDB}$ would be so large that its explicit representation would be totally unfeasible. Fortunately, as we shall see in the next section, there is no need to know the elements of $\overline{EDB}$ i.e. it is possible to determine the set of closed world answers to an arbitrary query Q by appealing only to the given data base DB.

QUERY EVALUATION UNDER THE CWA

It turns out that the CWA admits a number of significant simplifications in the query evaluation process. The simplest of these permits the elimination of the logical connectives $\wedge$ and $\vee$ in favour of set intersection and union respectively, as follows:

Theorem 2.

1. $\| < \vec{x}/\vec{\tau} \,|\, (E\vec{y}/\vec{\theta})(W_1 \vee W_2) > \|_{CWA} = \| < \vec{x}/\vec{\tau} \,|\, (E\vec{y}/\vec{\theta})W_1 > \|_{CWA} \cup \| < \vec{x}/\vec{\tau} \,|\, (E\vec{y}/\vec{\theta})W_2 > \|_{CWA}$

2. $\| < \vec{x}/\vec{\tau} \,|\, W_1 \wedge W_2 > \|_{CWA} = \| < \vec{x}/\vec{\tau} \,|\, W_1 > \|_{CWA} \cap \| < \vec{x}/\vec{\tau} \,|\, W_2 > \|_{CWA}$

Notice that in the identity 2, the query must be quantifier free. Notice also that the identities of Theorem 2 fail under the OWA. To see why, consider the following:

Example 3

$|\tau| = \{a\}$

DB: Pa $\vee$ Ra

$Q = < x/\tau \,|\, Px \vee Rx >$

$\|Q\|_{OWA} = \{a\}$

but

$\| < x/\tau \,|\, Px > \|_{OWA} = \| < x/\tau \,|\, Rx > \|_{OWA} = \phi$

Example 4

$|\tau| = \{a,b\}$

DB: Pa $\vee$ Pb, Ra, Rb

$Q = < x/\tau \,|\, Px \wedge Rx >$

$\|Q\|_{OWA} = \{a+b\}$

but

$\| < x/\tau \,|\, Px > \|_{OWA} = \{a+b\}$

$\| < x/\tau \,|\, Rx > \|_{OWA} = \{a,b\}$

One might also expect that all occurrences of negation can be eliminated in favour of set difference for CWA query evaluation. This is indeed the case, but only for quantifier free queries and then only when DB $\cup$ $\overline{EDB}$ is consistent.

Theorem 3.

If W, W_1 and W_2 are quantifier free, and DB $\cup$ $\overline{EDB}$ is consistent, then

1. $\| < \vec{x}/\vec{\tau} \,|\, \overline{W} > \|_{CWA} = |\vec{\tau}| - \| < \vec{x}/\vec{\tau} \,|\, W > \|_{CWA}$

2. $\| < \vec{x}/\vec{\tau} \,|\, W_1 \wedge \overline{W}_2 > \|_{CWA} = \| < \vec{x}/\vec{\tau} \,|\, W_1 > \|_{CWA} - \| < \vec{x}/\vec{\tau} \,|\, W_2 > \|_{CWA}$

To see why Theorem 3 fails for quantified queries, consider the following:

Example 5

$|\tau| = \{a,b\}$

DB: Pa,a

Then $\overline{EDB} = \{\overline{P}a,b,\ \overline{P}b,a,\ \overline{P}b,b\}$

Let $Q(P) = < x/\tau \,|\, (Ey/\tau)Px,y >$

$Q(\overline{P}) = < x/\tau \,|\, (Ey/\tau)\overline{P}x,y >$

Then $\| Q(P) \|_{CWA} = \{a\}$

$\| Q(\overline{P}) \|_{CWA} = \{a,b\} \neq |\tau| - \| Q(P) \|_{CWA}$

Notice also that Theorem 3 fails under the OWA.

By an atomic query we mean any query of the form $< \vec{x}/\vec{\tau} \,|\, (E\vec{y}/\vec{\theta})Pt_1,\ldots,t_n >$ where P is a predicate sign and each t is a constant sign, an x, or a y.

Theorems 2 and 3 assure us that for quantifier free queries, CWA query evaluation can be reduced to the Boolean operations of set intersection union and difference applied to atomic queries. However, we can deal with quantified queries by introducing the following <u>projection operator</u> (Codd [1972]):

Let $Q = \langle \vec{x}/\vec{\tau}, z/\psi \mid W \rangle$ where W is a possibly existentially quantified formula, and $\vec{x}$ is the n-tuple $x_1, \ldots, x_n$. Then $\|Q\|_{CWA}$ is a set of (n+1)-tuples, and the <u>projection of $\|Q\|_{CWA}$ with respect to z</u>, $\pi_z \|Q\|_{CWA}$, is the set of n-tuples obtained from $\|Q\|_{CWA}$ by deleting the (n+1)st component from each (n+1)-tuple of $\|Q\|_{CWA}$. For example, if $Q = \langle x_1/\tau_1, x_2/\tau_2, z/\psi \mid W \rangle$ and if

$$\|Q\|_{CWA} = \{(a,b,c),(a,b,d),(c,a,b)\}$$

then

$$\pi_z \|Q\|_{CWA} = \{(a,b),(c,a)\}$$

<u>Theorem 4.</u>

$$\|\langle \vec{x}/\vec{\tau} \mid (E\vec{y}/\vec{\theta})W \rangle\|_{CWA} = \pi_{\vec{y}} \|\langle \vec{x}/\vec{\tau}, \vec{y}/\vec{\theta} \mid W \rangle\|_{CWA}$$

where $\pi_{\vec{y}}$ denotes $\pi_{y_1}\pi_{y_2}\cdots\pi_{y_m}$

<u>Corollary 4.1</u>

1. $\|\langle \vec{x}/\vec{\tau} \mid (E\vec{y}/\vec{\theta})\overline{W} \rangle\|_{CWA} = \pi_{\vec{y}} \|\langle \vec{x}/\vec{\tau}, \vec{y}/\vec{\theta} \mid \overline{W} \rangle\|_{CWA}$
$= \pi_{\vec{y}}(|\vec{\tau}| \times |\vec{\theta}| - \|\langle \vec{x}/\vec{\tau}, \vec{y}/\vec{\theta} \mid W \rangle\|_{CWA})$

2. $\|\langle \vec{x}/\vec{\tau} \mid (E\vec{y}/\vec{\theta})W_1 \wedge W_2 \rangle\|_{CWA} = \pi_{\vec{y}}(\|\langle \vec{x}/\vec{\tau}, \vec{y}/\vec{\theta} \mid W_1 \rangle\|_{CWA}$
$\cap \|\langle \vec{x}/\vec{\tau}, \vec{y}/\vec{\theta} \mid W_2 \rangle\|_{CWA})$

Thus, in all cases, an existentially quantified query may be decomposed into atomic queries each of which is evaluated under the CWA. The resulting sets of answers are combined under set union, intersection and difference, but only after the projection operator is applied, if necessary.

<u>Example 6.</u>

$$\|\langle x/\tau \mid (Ey/\theta)Px,y \vee Qx,y\ Rx,y \rangle\|_{CWA}$$
$$= \|\langle x/\tau \mid (Ey/\theta)Px,y\|_{CWA} \cup \pi_y(\|\langle x/\tau, y/\theta \mid Qx,y \rangle\|_{CWA}$$
$$\cap \|\langle x/\tau, y/\theta \mid Rx,y \rangle\|_{CWA})$$

$$\|\langle x/\tau \mid PxQx \vee \overline{Rx} \rangle\|_{CWA} = \|\langle x/\tau \mid Px \rangle\|_{CWA}$$
$$\cap \|\langle x/\tau \mid Qx \rangle\|_{CWA} \cup [|\tau| - \|\langle x/\tau \mid Rx \rangle\|_{CWA}]$$

$$\|\langle x/\tau \mid (Ey/\theta)Px,y \vee Qx,y\ \overline{Rx},y \rangle\|_{CWA}$$
$$= \|\langle x/\tau \mid (Ey/\theta)Px,y \rangle\|_{CWA} \cup \pi_y(\langle x/\tau, y/\theta \mid Qx,y \rangle\|_{CWA}$$
$$- \|\langle x/\tau, y/\theta \mid Rx,y \rangle\|_{CWA})$$

In view of the above results, we need consider CWA query evaluation only for atomic queries.

We shall say that DB is <u>consistent with the CWA</u> iff DB $\cup$ $\overline{EDB}$ is consistent.

<u>Theorem 5.</u>

Let Q be an atomic query. Then if DB is consistent with the CWA, $\|Q\|_{CWA} = \|Q\|_{OWA}$.

Theorem 5 is the principal result of this section. When coupled with Theorems 2 and 3 and the remarks following Corollary 4.1 it provides us with a complete characterization of the CWA answers to an arbitrary existential query Q in terms of the application of the operations of projection, set union, intersection and difference as applied to the OWA answers to atomic queries. In other words, CWA query evaluation has been reduced to OWA atomic query evaluation. A consequence of this result is that we need never know the elements of $\overline{EDB}$. CWA query evaluation appeals only to the given data base DB.

<u>Example 7.</u>

We consider the inventory data base of Example 2. Suppose the following query:

$$Q = \langle x/Supplier \mid (Ey/Widget) Supplies\ x,y \wedge Subpart\ y,p_1 \wedge \overline{Supplies}\ x,p_3 \rangle$$

Then

$$\|Q\|_{CWA} = \pi_y(\|Q_1\|_{OWA} \cap \|Q_2\|_{OWA}) \cap (|Supplier| - \|Q_3\|_{OWA})$$

where

$$Q_1 = \langle x/Supplier, y/Widget \mid Supplies\ x,y \rangle$$

$Q_2 = < x/Supplier,\ y/Widget \mid Subpart\ y, p_1 >$

$Q_3 = < x/Supplier \mid Supplies\ x, p_3 >$

It is easy to see that

$$\|Q_1\|_{OWA} = \{(Foobar,w_1),\ (Foobar,w_2),\ (Foobar,w_3),\ (Foobar,w_4),\ (AAA,w_3),\ (AAA,w_4),\ (Acme,w_1),\ (Acme,w_2)\}$$

$$\|Q_2\|_{OWA} = \{(Acme,w_1),\ (Acme,w_2),\ (AAA,w_1),\ (AAA,w_2),\ (Foobar,w_1),\ (Foobar,\ w_2)\}$$

$$\|Q_3\|_{OWA} = \{Acme\}$$

whence

$$\pi_y(\|Q_1\|_{OWA} \cap \|Q_2\|_{OWA}) = \{Foobar,Acme\}$$

and

$$|Supplier| - \|Q_3\|_{OWA} = \{Foobar,AAA\}$$

Hence

$$\|Q\|_{CWA} = \{Foobar\}.$$

ON DATA BASES CONSISTENT WITH THE CWA

Not every consistent data base remains consistent under the CWA.

Example 8.

DB: Pa V Pb

Then, since DB $\not\vdash$ Pa and Db $\not\vdash$ Pb , $\overline{EDB} = \{\overline{Pa}, \overline{Pb}\}$ so that DB $\cup$ $\overline{EDB}$ is inconsistent.

Given this observation, it is natural to seek a characterization of those data bases which remain consistent under the CWA. Although we know of no such characterization, it is possible to give a sufficient condition for CWA consistency which encompasses a large natural class of data bases, namely the Horn data bases. (A data base is Horn iff every clause is Horn i.e. contains at most one positive literal. The data base of Example 2 is Horn.)

Theorem 6

Suppose DB is Horn, and consistent. Then DB $\cup$ $\overline{EDB}$ is consistent i.e., DB is consistent with the CWA.

Following van Emden [1977] we shall refer to a Horn clause with exactly one positive literal as a definite clause. If DB is Horn, let Δ(DB) be obtained from DB by removing all non definite clauses i.e., all negative clauses. The following Theorem demonstrates the central importance of these concepts:

Theorem 7

If $Q = < \vec{x}/\vec{\tau} \mid (E\vec{y}/\vec{\theta})W >$ and DB is Horn and consistent, then $\|Q\|_{CWA}$ when evaluated with respect to DB yields the same set of answers as when evaluated with respect to Δ(DB). In other words, negative clauses in DB have no influence on CWA query evaluation.

Theorem 7 allows us, when given a consistent Horn DB, to discard all its negative clauses without affecting CWA query evaluation. Theorem 7 fails for non Horn DBs, as the following example demonstrates:

Example 9

DB: $\overline{Pa} \vee \overline{Ra}$, Ra V Sa, Pa

Then DB $\vdash$ Sa

But Δ(DB) = {Ra V Sa, Pa} and Δ(DB) $\not\vdash$ Sa.

Let us call a data base for which all clauses are definite a definite data base.

Theorem 8

If DB is definite then DB is consistent.

Corollary 8.1

If DB is definite then

(i) DB is consistent

(ii) DB is consistent with the CWA.

Corollary 8.1 is a central result. It guarantees data base and CWA consistency for a large and natural class of data bases. Since the data base of Example 2 is definite we are assured that it is consistent with the CWA.

In van Emden [1977], he addresses, from a semantic point of view, the issues of data base consistency under the CWA. He defines the notion of a "minimal model" for a data base as the intersection of all its models. If this minimal model is itself a model of the data base, then the data base is consistent with the CWA. Van Emden goes on to point out some intriguing connections between minimal models and Scott's minimal fixpoint approach to the theory of computation, results which are elaborated in van Emden and Kowalski [1976].

THE CWA AND DATA BASE INTEGRITY

Theorem 7 has an interesting consequence with respect to data base integrity. In a first order data base, both intensional and extensional facts may serve a dual purpose. They can be used for deductive retrieval, or they can function as integrity constraints. In this latter capacity they are used to detect inconsistencies whenever the data base is modified. For example, if the data base is updated with a new fact then logical consequences of this fact can be derived using the entire data base. If these consequences lead to an inconsistency, the update will be rejected.

In general, it is not clear whether a given fact in a data base functions exclusively as an integrity constraint, or for deductive retrieval, or both (Nicolas and Gallaire [1978]). However, if the data base is both Horn and closed world, Theorem 7 tells us that purely negative clauses can function only as integrity constraints. Thus the CWA induces a partition of a Horn data base into negative and non-negative clauses. The latter are used only for deductive retrieval. Both are used for enforcing integrity.

SUMMARY

We have introduced the notion of the closed world assumption for deductive question-answering. This says, in effect, "Every positive statement that you don't know to be true may be assumed false". We have then shown how query evaluation under the closed world assumption reduces to the usual first order proof theoretic approach to query evaluation as applied to atomic queries. Finally, we have shown that consistent Horn data bases remain consistent under the closed world assumption and that definite data bases are consistent with the closed world assumption.

ACKNOWLEDGMENT

This paper was written with the financial support of the National Research Council of Canada under grant A7642. Much of this research was done while the author was visiting at Bolt, Beranek and Newman, Inc., Cambridge, Mass. I wish to thank Craig Bishop for his careful criticism of an earlier draft of this paper.

APPENDIX

Proofs of Theorems

Theorem 1.

Let $Q = < \vec{x}/\vec{\tau} \mid (E\vec{y}/\vec{\theta})W(\vec{x},\vec{y}) >$. Then every minimal CWA to Q is definite.

The proof requires the following two lemmas:

Lemma 1

Let $W_1, \ldots, W_r$ be propositional formulae. Then

$DB \cup \overline{EDB} \vdash W_1 \vee \ldots \vee W_r$

iff $DB \cup \overline{EDB} \vdash W_i$ for some i.

Proof: The "only if" half is immediate.

With no loss in generality, assume that the set of W's is minimal, i.e., for no i do we have

$DB \cup \overline{EDB} \vdash W_1 \vee \ldots \vee W_{i-1} \vee W_{i+1} \vee \ldots \vee W_r$.

Suppose W_1 is represented in conjunctive normal form, i.e. as a conjunct of clauses. Let $C = L_1 \vee \ldots \vee L_m$ be a typical such clause. Then $DB \cup \overline{EDB} \vdash L_i$ or $DB \cup \overline{EDB} \vdash \overline{L_i}$, $i=1,\ldots,m$. Suppose the latter is the case for each i, $1 \le i \le m$. Then $DB \cup \overline{EDB} \vdash \overline{C}$ so that $DB \cup \overline{EDB} \vdash \overline{W_1}$. Since also $DB \cup \overline{EDB} \vdash W_1 \vee \ldots \vee W_r$, then $DB \cup \overline{EDB} \vdash W_2 \vee \ldots \vee W_r$ contradicting the assumption that the set of W's is minimal. Hence, for some i, $1 \le i \le m$, $DB \cup \overline{EDB} \vdash L_i$ so that $DB \cup \overline{EDB} \vdash C$. Since C was an arbitrary clause of W_1, $DB \cup \overline{EDB} \vdash W_1$ which establishes the lemma.

Lemma 2

$DB \cup \overline{EDB} \vdash (E\vec{y}/\vec{\theta})W(\vec{y})$ iff there is a tuple $\vec{d} \in |\vec{\theta}|$ such that $DB \cup \overline{EDB} \vdash W(\vec{d})$.

Proof: The "only if" half is immediate.

Since $DB \cup \overline{EDB} \vdash (E\vec{y}/\vec{\theta})W(\vec{y})$ then for tuples $\vec{d}^{(1)},\ldots,\vec{d}^{(r)} \in |\vec{\theta}|$

$DB \cup \overline{EDB} \vdash \bigvee_{i \le r} W(\vec{d}^{(i)})$

The result now follows by Lemma 1.

Proof of Theorem 1:

Suppose, to the contrary, that for $m \geq 2$, $\vec{c}^{(1)} + \ldots + \vec{c}^{(m)}$ is a minimal CWA answer to Q. Then

$$DB \cup \overline{EDB} \vdash \bigvee_{i \leq m} (E\vec{y}/\vec{\theta})W(\vec{c}^{(i)},\vec{y})$$

i.e.,

$$DB \cup \overline{EDB} \vdash (E\vec{y}/\vec{\theta}) \bigvee_{i \leq m} W(\vec{c}^{(i)},\vec{y})$$

so by Lemma 2 there is a tuple $\vec{d} \in |\vec{\theta}|$ such that

$$DB \cup \overline{EDB} \vdash \bigvee_{i \leq m} W(\vec{c}^{(i)},\vec{d})$$

By Lemma 1, $DB \cup \overline{EDB} \vdash W(\vec{c}^{(i)},\vec{d})$ for some i whence $\vec{c}^{(i)}$ is an answer to Q, contradicting the assumed indefiniteness of $\vec{c}^{(1)} + \ldots + \vec{c}^{(m)}$.

Theorem 2.

1. $$\|<\vec{x}/\vec{\tau}|(E\vec{y}/\vec{\theta})(W_1 \vee W_2)>\|_{CWA} = \|<\vec{x}/\vec{\tau}|(E\vec{y}/\vec{\theta})W_1>\|_{CWA} \cup \|<\vec{x}/\vec{\tau}|(E\vec{y}/\vec{\theta})W_2>\|_{CWA}$$

2. $$\|<\vec{x}/\vec{\tau}|W_1 \wedge W_2>\|_{CWA} = \|<\vec{x}/\vec{\tau}|W_1>\|_{CWA} \cap \|<x/\tau|W_2>\|_{CWA}$$

Proof: 1. follows from Lemmas 1 and 2 and Theorem 1. The proof of 2. is immediate from Theorem 1.

Theorem 3.

If W, W_1 and W_2 are quantifier free, and $DB \cup \overline{EDB}$ is consistent, then

1. $$\|<\vec{x}/\vec{\tau}|\overline{W}>\|_{CWA} = |\vec{\tau}| - \|<\vec{x}/\vec{\tau}|W>\|_{CWA}$$

2. $$\|<\vec{x}/\vec{\tau}|W_1 \wedge \overline{W}_2>\|_{CWA} = \|<\vec{x}/\vec{\tau}|W_1>\|_{CWA} - \|<\vec{x}/\vec{\tau}|W_2>\|_{CWA}$$

Proof: 1. The proof is by structural induction on W. Denote $\|<\vec{x}/\vec{\tau}|W>\|_{CWA}$ by Q(W).

We must prove

$$Q(\overline{W}) = |\vec{\tau}| - Q(W).$$

Case 1: W is $Pt_1,\ldots,t_m$ where P is a predicate sign and $t_1,\ldots,t_m$ are terms.

Suppose $\vec{c} \in Q(\overline{W})$. Let $\Pi(\vec{c})$ be $Pt_1,\ldots,t_m$ with all occurrences of x_i replaced by c_i. Then $DB \cup \overline{EDB} \vdash \overline{\Pi}(\vec{c})$. Since $DB \cup \overline{EDB}$ is consistent, $DB \cup \overline{EDB} \nvdash \Pi(\vec{c})$, i.e. $\vec{c} \notin Q(W)$. Since $\vec{c} \in |\vec{\tau}|$, then $\vec{c} \in |\vec{\tau}| - Q(W)$, so that $Q(\overline{W}) \subseteq |\vec{\tau}| - Q(W)$. Now suppose $\vec{c} \in |\vec{\tau}| - Q(W)$. Then $\vec{c} \notin Q(W)$ so $DB \cup \overline{EDB} \nvdash \Pi(\vec{c})$. But then $DB \cup \overline{EDB} \vdash \overline{\Pi}(\vec{c})$, and since $\vec{c} \in |\vec{\tau}|$, then $\vec{c} \in Q(\overline{W})$, so that $|\vec{\tau}| - Q(W) \subseteq Q(\overline{W})$.

Case 2: W is $U_1 \wedge U_2$.

Assume, for i=1,2 that $Q(\overline{U}_i) = |\vec{\tau}| - Q(U_i)$.

Then
$$\begin{aligned} Q(\overline{W}) &= Q(\overline{U_1 \wedge U_2}) \\ &= Q(\overline{U}_1 \vee \overline{U}_2) \\ &= Q(\overline{U}_1) \cup Q(\overline{U}_2) \quad \text{by Theorem 2} \\ &= [|\vec{\tau}| - Q(U_1)] \cup [|\vec{\tau}| - Q(U_2)] \\ &= |\vec{\tau}| - [Q(U_1) \cap Q(U_2)] \\ &= |\vec{\tau}| - Q(U_1 \wedge U_2) \quad \text{by Theorem 2} \\ &= |\vec{\tau}| - Q(W) \end{aligned}$$

Case 3: W is $U_1 \vee U_2$.
The proof is the dual of Case 2.

Case 4: W is $\overline{U}$.

Assume that $Q(\overline{U}) = |\vec{\tau}| - Q(U)$. Since $Q(U) \subseteq |\vec{\tau}|$, it follows that $Q(U) = |\vec{\tau}| - Q(\overline{U})$. i.e. $Q(\overline{W}) = |\vec{\tau}| - Q(W)$.

$$\begin{aligned} Q(W_1 \wedge \overline{W}_2) &= Q(W_1) \cap Q(\overline{W}_2) \quad \text{by Theorem 2} \\ &= Q(W_1) \cap [|\vec{\tau}| - Q(W_2)] \text{ by 1.} \\ &= Q(W_1) - Q(W_2) \quad \text{since } Q(W_1) \subseteq |\vec{\tau}|. \end{aligned}$$

Theorem 4.

$$\|<\vec{x}/\vec{\tau}|(E\vec{y}/\vec{\theta})W(\vec{x},\vec{y})>\|_{CWA} = \pi_{\vec{y}}\|<\vec{x}/\vec{\tau},\vec{y}/\vec{\theta}|W(\vec{x},\vec{y})>\|_{CWA}$$

where $\pi_{\vec{y}}$ denotes $\pi_{y_1} \pi_{y_2} \ldots \pi_{y_m}$

Proof:

Suppose $\vec{c} \in \| < \vec{x}/\vec{\tau} | (E\vec{y}/\vec{\theta}) W(\vec{x},\vec{y}) > \|_{CWA}$

Then by definition

$$DB \cup \overline{EDB} \vdash (E\vec{y}/\vec{\theta}) W(\vec{c},\vec{y})$$

whence by Lemma 2 there is a tuple $\vec{d} \in |\vec{\theta}|$ such that

$$DB \cup \overline{EDB} \vdash W(\vec{c},\vec{d})$$

i.e., $\vec{c},\vec{d} \in \| < \vec{x}/\vec{\tau}, \vec{y}/\vec{\theta} | W(\vec{x},\vec{y}) > \|_{CWA}$

i.e., $\vec{c} \in \Pi_{\vec{y}} \| < \vec{x}/\vec{\tau}, \vec{y}/\vec{\theta} | W(\vec{x},\vec{y}) > \|_{CWA}$

Now Suppose $\vec{c} \in \Pi_{\vec{y}} \| < \vec{x}/\vec{\tau}, \vec{y}/\vec{\theta} | W(\vec{x},\vec{y}) > \|_{CWA}$

Then for some tuple $\vec{d} \in |\vec{\theta}|$

$$\vec{c},\vec{d} \in \| < \vec{x}/\vec{\tau}, \vec{y}/\vec{\theta} | W(\vec{x},\vec{y}) > \|_{CWA}$$

so that $DB \cup \overline{EDB} \vdash W(\vec{c},\vec{d})$

i.e., $DB \cup \overline{EDB} \vdash (E\vec{y}/\vec{\theta}) W(\vec{c},\vec{y})$

i.e. $\vec{c} \in \| < \vec{x}/\vec{\tau} | (E\vec{y}/\vec{\theta}) W(\vec{x},\vec{y}) > \|_{CWA}$

Theorem 5.

Let Q be an atomic query. Then if DB is consistent with the CWA, $\|Q\|_{CWA} = \|Q\|_{OWA}$.

Proof: The proof requires the following:

Lemma 3

If DB is consistent with the CWA then every atomic query has only definite OWA answers.

Proof:

Let $Q = < \vec{x}/\vec{\tau} | (E\vec{y}/\vec{\theta}) P(\vec{x},\vec{y}) >$ be an atomic query where $P(\vec{x},\vec{y})$ is a positive literal. Suppose, on the contrary, that Q has an indefinite OWA answer $\vec{c}^{(1)} + \ldots + \vec{c}^{(m)}$ for $m \geq 2$. Then

$$DB \vdash \bigvee_{i \leq m} (E\vec{y}/\vec{\theta}) P(\vec{c}^{(i)},\vec{y}) \qquad (1)$$

and for no i, $1 \leq i \leq m$, is it the case that $DB \vdash (E\vec{y}/\vec{\theta}) P(\vec{c}^{(i)},\vec{y})$.

Hence, for all $\vec{d} \in |\vec{\theta}|$, $DB \nvdash P(\vec{c}^{(i)},\vec{d})$ i=1,...,m.

Thus $\overline{P}(\vec{c}^{(i)},\vec{d}) \in \overline{EDB}$ for all $\vec{d} \in |\vec{\theta}|$, i=1,...,m.

Hence, $DB \cup \overline{EDB} \vdash \overline{P}(\vec{c}^{(i)},\vec{d})$ for all $\vec{d} \in |\vec{\theta}|$, i=1,...,m and from (1), $DB \cup \overline{EDB} \vdash \bigvee_{i \leq m} (E\vec{y}/\vec{\theta}) P(\vec{c}^{(i)},\vec{y})$

i.e. $DB \cup \overline{EDB}$ is inconsistent, contradiction.

Proof of Theorem 5:

Let $Q = < \vec{x}/\vec{\tau} | (E\vec{y}/\vec{\theta}) P(\vec{x},\vec{y}) >$ where $P(\vec{x},\vec{y})$ is a positive literal. By Lemma 3 $\|Q\|_{OWA}$ consists only of definite answers. Now

$\vec{c} \in \|Q\|_{OWA}$ iff $\vec{c} \in |\vec{\tau}|$ and $DB \vdash (E\vec{y}/\vec{\theta}) P(\vec{c},\vec{y})$

$\vec{c} \in \|Q\|_{CWA}$ iff $\vec{c} \in |\vec{\tau}|$ and $DB \cup \overline{EDB} \vdash (E\vec{y}/\vec{\theta}) P(\vec{c},\vec{y})$

Hence $\|Q\|_{OWA} \subseteq \|Q\|_{CWA}$.

We prove $\|Q\|_{CWA} \subseteq \|Q\|_{OWA}$. To that end, let $\vec{c} \in \|Q\|_{CWA}$. Then $DB \cup \overline{EDB} \vdash P(\vec{c},\vec{d})$ for some $\vec{d} \in |\vec{\theta}|$.

If $DB \vdash P(\vec{c},\vec{d})$, then $\vec{c} \in \|Q\|_{CWA}$ and we are done.

Otherwise, $DB \nvdash P(\vec{c},\vec{d})$ so that $\overline{P}(\vec{c},\vec{d}) \in \overline{EDB}$

i.e. $DB \cup \overline{EDB} \vdash P(\vec{c},\vec{d})$ and $DB \cup \overline{EDB} \vdash \overline{P}(\vec{c},\vec{d})$

i.e. DB is inconsistent with the CWA, contradiction.

Theorem 6.

Suppose DB is Horn, and consistent. Then $DB \cup \overline{EDB}$ is consistent, i.e. DB is consistent with the CWA.

Proof: Suppose, on the contrary, that $DB \cup \overline{EDB}$ is inconsistent. Now a theorem of Henschen and Wos [1974] assures us that any inconsistent set of Horn clauses has a positive unit refutation by binary resolution in which one parent of each resolution operation is a positive unit. We shall assume this result, without proof, for typed resolution*. Then since $DB \cup \overline{EDB}$ is an inconsistent

*Because all variables are typed, the usual unification algorithm (Robinson [1965]) must be modified to enforce consistency of types. Resolvents are then formed using typed unification. For details, see (Reiter [1977]).

Horn set, it has such a (typed) positive unit refutation. Since all clauses of $\overline{EDB}$ are negative units, the only occurrence of a negative unit of $\overline{EDB}$ in this refutation can be as one of the parents in the final resolution operation yielding the empty clause. There must be such an occurrence of some $\overline{U} \in \overline{EDB}$, for otherwise $\overline{EDB}$ does not enter into the refutation in which case DB must be inconsistent. Hence, $DB \cup \{\overline{U}\}$ is unsatisfiable, i.e. $DB \vdash U$. But then $\overline{U}$ cannot be a member of $\overline{EDB}$, contradiction.

Theorem 7.

If $Q = < \vec{x}/\vec{\tau} | (E\vec{y}/\vec{\theta})W >$ and DB is Horn and consistent, then $\|Q\|_{CWA}$ when evaluated with respect to DB yields the same set of answers as when evaluated with respect to $\Delta(DB)$. In other words, negative clauses in PB have no influence on CWA query evaluation.

Proof: By Theorems 2, 3, and 4 CWA query evaluation is reducible to OWA evaluation of atomic queries whenever DB is consistent. Hence, with no loss in generality, we can take Q to be an atomic query. Suppose then that $Q = < \vec{x}/\vec{\tau} | (E\vec{y}/\vec{\theta})P(\vec{x},\vec{y}) >$, where $P(\vec{x},\vec{y})$ is a positive literal. Denote the value of $\|Q\|_{CWA}$ with respect to DB by $\|Q\|^{DB}_{CWA}$. Similarly, $\|Q\|^{\Delta(DB)}_{CWA}$, $\|Q\|^{DB}_{OWA}$, $\|Q\|^{\Delta(DB)}_{OWA}$. We must prove $\|Q\|^{DB}_{CWA} = \|Q\|^{\Delta(DB)}_{CWA}$. Since DB is consistent and Horn, so also is $\Delta(DB)$ so by Theorem 6, both DB and $\Delta(DB)$ are consistent with the CWA. Hence, by Theorem 5, it is sufficient to prove $\|Q\|^{DB}_{OWA} = \|Q\|^{\Delta(DB)}_{OWA}$. Clearly $\|Q\|^{\Delta(DB)}_{OWA} \subseteq \|Q\|^{DB}_{OWA}$ since $\Delta(DB) \subseteq DB$. We prove $\|Q\|^{DB}_{OWA} \subseteq \|Q\|^{\Delta(DB)}_{OWA}$. To that end, let $\vec{c} \in \|Q\|^{DB}_{OWA}$. Then $DB \vdash (E\vec{y}/\vec{\theta})P(\vec{c},\vec{y})$. Hence, as in the proof of Theorem 6, there is a (typed) positive unit refutation of $DB \cup \{\overline{P}(\vec{c},\vec{y})\}$. Since DB is Horn and consistent, $\overline{P}(\vec{c},\vec{y})$ enters into this refutation, and then only in the final resolution operation which yields the empty clause. Clearly, no negative clause other than $\overline{P}(\vec{c},\vec{y})$ can take part in this refutation, i.e. only definite clauses of DB enter into the refutation. Hence we can construct the same refutation from $\Delta(DB) \cup \{\overline{P}(\vec{x},\vec{y})\}$ so that $\Delta(DB) \vdash P(\vec{c},\vec{y})$ i.e. $\vec{c} \in \|Q\|^{\Delta(DB)}_{OWA}$.

Theorem 8.

If DB is definite, then DB is consistent.

Proof: Every inconsistent set of clauses contains at least one negative clause.

REFERENCES

1. Clark, K.L. [1978] Negation as Failure, In *Logic and Data Bases* (H. Gallaire and J. Minker, Eds.), Plenum Press, New York, N.Y., 1978, 293-322.

2. Codd, E.F. [1972] Relational Completeness of Data Base Sublanguages, In *Data Base Systems* (R. Rustin, Ed.), Prentice-Hall, Englewood Cliffs, N.J., 1972, 65-98.

3. Henschen, L. and Wos, L. [1974] Unit Refutations and Horn Sets, *JACM 21*, 4 (October 1974), 590-605.

4. Hewitt, C. [1972] Description and Theoretical Analysis (Using Schemata) of PLANNER: A Language for Proving Theorems and Manipulating Models in a Robot, *AI Memo No. 251*, MIT Project MAC, Cambridge, Mass., April 1972.

5. Nicolas, J.M. and Gallaire, H. [1978] Data Bases: Theory vs. Interpretation, In *Logic and Data Bases* (H. Gallaire and J. Minker, Eds.), Plenum Press, New York, 1978, 33-54.

6. Nicolas, J. M. and Syre, J.C. [1974] Natural Question Answering and Automatic Deduction in the System Syntex, *Proceedings IFIP Congress 1974*, Stockholm, Sweden, August, 1974.

7. Reiter, R. [1977] An Approach to Deductive Question-Answering, *BBN Report No. 3649*, Bolt, Beranek and Newman, Inc., Cambridge, Mass., Sept. 1977.

8. Reiter, R. [1978] Deductive Question-Answering on Relational Data Bases, In *Logic and Data Bases* (H. Gallaire and J. Minker, Eds.), Plenum Press, New York, N.Y., 1978, 149-177.

9. Robinson, J. A. [1965] A Machine Oriented Logic Based on the Resolution Principle, *JACM 12*, (January 1965), 25-41.

10. Roussel, P. [1975] PROLOG: Manuel de Reference et d'Utilisation, Groupe d'Intelligence Artificielle, U.E.R. de Luminy, Universite d'Aix-Marseille, Sept. 1975.

11. van Emden, M. H. [1977] Computation and Deductive Information Retrieval, Dept. of Computer Science, University of Waterloo, Ont., Research Report CS-77-16, May 1977.

12. van Emden, M.H. and Kowalski, R.A. [1976] The Semantics of Predicate Logic as a Programming Language, *JACM 23*, (Oct. 1976), 733-742.

LOGIC FOR DATA DESCRIPTION

Robert Kowalski

Imperial College

London, England

ABSTRACT

Logic is useful both for describing static data bases as well as for processing data bases which change. Both the static and dynamic management of data bases depends upon the form of definitions: whether data is defined by means of complete if-and-only-if definitions or only by means of the if-halves, whether the only-if half of an if-and-only-if definition is stated explicitly or is assumed implicitly, and whether the only-if assumption is understood as a statement of the object language (in the data base) or as a statement of the meta-language (about the data base). Similar considerations apply to the processing of computer programs. When logic is used to describe information, the conventional distinction between data bases and programs no longer applies.

INTRODUCTION

Taking the relational view of data (Codd [1970]) as our point of departure, we shall compare the n-ary relation representation of n-column tables with the representation by means of binary relations. We shall argue for the utility, even in conventional data bases, of using logic to describe data by means of general laws.

We shall investigate the role of deduction in the processing of new information. In general, new information

(1) may be ignored, if it is already implied by the existing data;

(2) may replace existing data, if they are implied by it;

(3) may be added to the data base if it is independent from the existing data; or

(4) may contradict the data base, in which case consistency can be restored either by abandoning or suitably restricting some sentence which participates in the derivation of contradiction.

The last case is the most interesting. It is the case which applies both when data violate consistency constraints and when exceptions contradict general rules.

We shall argue that both the static and the dynamic management of a data base depends on whether the data is defined by full if-and-only-if definitions or only by the if-halves of the definitions. It depends also on whether the only-if half

A only-if B

of an if-and-only-if definition

A if-and-only-if B

is expressed in the object language

$A \rightarrow B$

or in the meta language

"The <u>only</u> way the conclusion B can be established is by using the sentence $A \leftarrow B$."

When logic is used to represent information, the distinction between data bases and programs disappears. General laws which describe the data function as programs which compute the data when it is required. The relational representation of data in data bases applies with similar benefits to the representation of data structures in programs. The same problem-solving techniques can be used both for data retrieval and program execution, for verifying data base integrity constraints and proving program properties, for updating and modifying data bases and developing programs by successive refinement.

Throughout this paper, except for if-and-only-if definitions, we restrict our attention to the use of Horn clauses. A compact introduction to clausal form and logic programming can be found in other papers (Gallaire et al. [1978]) in this volume.

DATA DESCRIPTION

In relational data bases (Codd [1970]), tables are regarded as relations. For each column of the table, there is a component in the corresponding relation. Thus to an n-column table there corresponds an n-ary relation. Rows of the table are n-tuples of the relation.

As a first approximation, tables and their corresponding relations can be represented in logic by means of assertions. The table

Course	Number	Name	Teacher	Level
	103	Programming	SJG	B.Sc.1
	1.4	Logic	RAK	M.Sc.

for example, can be represented by the assertions

Course(103,Programming,SJG,B.Sc.1)←

Course(1.4,Logic,RAK,M.Sc.)←

In this representation the n-ary relation is named by an n-ary predicate symbol.

An alternative representation, which is suggested by a comparison of logic and semantic networks (Deliyanni and Kowalski [1978]), uses binary predicate symbols.

Isa(103, Course)←

Name(103, Programming)←

Teacher(103, SJG)←

Level(103,B.Sc.1)←

Isa(1.4, Course)←

Name(1.4, Logic)←

Teacher(1.4, RAK)←

Level(1.4, M.Sc.)←

In this representation, each row of the table is named by a constant symbol (e.g. 103 or 1.4) which uniquely identifies the row. The entry i in column C, row r is represented by the assertion

C(r,i)←

Membership of a row r in the table T is also expressed by an assertion

Isa(r,T)←

We shall call the representation of tables by binary relations the <u>binary representation</u>, for short. The representation of n-column tables by n-ary relations will be called the <u>n-ary representation</u>. Notice that, in this terminology, the binary and n-ary representations are always different - even when n equals two.

It has been argued (Deliyanni and Kowalski [1978]) that the binary representation offers several advantages over the n-ary representation. Particularly important for data base applications are that unknown information can be more easily ignored and additional information can be more easily added. It can be argued, moreover, that binary relations offer a better model of data tables. Both binary and n-ary relations formalize the property of tables that the order of rows does not matter. In both cases, different ways of ordering the rows of a table correspond to different ways of ordering assertions. However, binary, but not n-ary, relations capture the additional property of tables that the order of columns does not matter. In the case of binary relations, interchanging the columns of a table corresponds to reordering assertions - which does not affect their meaning. In the case of n-ary relations, interchanging columns corresponds to interchanging components of the relation. The new n-ary relation is generally different from the original one.

Interchanging the last two columns of the Course-table, for example, gives rise to the same set of assertions in the binary representation but to different assertions

Course(103,Programming,B.Sc.1,SJG)←

Course(1.4,Logic,M.Sc.,RAK)←

in the n-ary representation.

More important, from a practical point of view, is that the binary representation is more useful than the n-ary representation for describing data by means of general laws. The direct translation into logic of the general rule

"RAK teaches all logic courses"

for example, is the statement

Teacher(x,RAK ← Name(x,Logic)

"If a course is a logic course than RAK teaches it"

in the binary representation. It can be shown that the same rule cannot be expressed by means of Horn clauses using the n-ary Course-predicate.

The argument in favour of binary relations is an oversimplification. The Marks-table

Marks	Student#	Course#	Grade

and the Plus relation

Plus(x,y,z)   x plus y is z

for example, are more naturally expressed by ternary relations than they are by binary ones. Reconciling these examples with the argument in favour of the binary representation is a problem for which we do not yet have a satisfactory solution. It is related to the problem of defining suitable normal forms for relational data bases (Codd [1970]).

The relational data base model views data as explicitly presented in tables. It provides no facilities for expressing general rules or for representing data computationally. The emphasis on explicit representation of data may be attributable in part to the unsuitability of the n-ary representation for expressing general laws. It may also be due to a belief that conventional data bases do not often conform to general rules. Our own empirical observations lead us to the opposite conclusion.

Conventional tables of data give direct access to information and are easy to read. Like abstract data structures in programming, they provide an abstract view of the data which does not go into the details of its derivation. It does not follow, however, that there are no general rules underlying the data or that making such rules explicit would not be useful. Tables of logrithms, interest tables, the periodic table of the elements, tyre pressure tables, tables of parts and their costs, tables of predicted astronomical phenomena are obvious examples of data tables which are governed by general rules. Depending upon the size of the tables and the complexity of the derivations, such data might be represented more efficiently by means of general rules which compute them when they are necessary rather than by means of tables which store them explicitly.

That general laws are not more apparent in conventionally presented data bases is a consequence, in part, of the computational difficulty of recognising patterns of data and of proposing general laws to account for them. Discovering general laws underlying explicitly presented data is the problem of induction. It is easier to avoid problem-solving altogether and to define the data by menas of general rules in the first place. It is easier, for example, to rule that

"All compulsory, third year, undergraduate courses are held in room 145."

"Radiators, with surface area ≤ 20 square feet, cost £ 2.50 per square foot."

"Front tyre pressure, for the Renault 4, under normal driving conditions, is 18 psi for all brands of tyre, except Sempervite, for which it is 19 psi."

"The university bookstore has a standing order of 10 copies per month of 'Sky and Telescope' magazine for every month of the academic year."

than it is to discover such laws in the unorganized, explicit form of the data. Moreover, if the data base system is able to understand both general laws and specific facts, then there is a positive incentive to organize the data by means of general rules. Using a general rule, instead of many specific facts, has the advantage that the data

is easier to input,
occupies less space, and
is easier to change.

What happens when the data is defined by means of both general laws and their exceptions will be treated later when we discuss the dynamic aspects of data bases.

Perhaps it is less surprising that conventional data base systems are unable to process general laws when we reflect that they are troublesome for administrators as well. The general rule

RAK requires an overhead projector for all his lectures

is an administrator's headache. It is easier to deal with tables of specific room-time-equipment requirements than it is to apply general rules. It is more convenient for the administrator if RAK constructs hiw own entries in the table and keeps the general rules to himself.

A number of proposals (Chang [1976], Kellogg et al. [1978] and Reiter [1978b]) have been made to extend the expressive power of conventional data bases by using logic to define part of the data implicitly while using the conventional data base system to store the rest explicitly. In some cases (Chang [1976]), the restriction is imposed that the implicitly defined relations be distinct from those which are explicitly stored. This restriction simplifies interfacing with the existing data base system, but it imposes unnatural constraints on the data. A typical relation needs to be defined both by means of specific facts and general laws. For example

"Course 203 is held in room 139."

"All compulsory third year undergraduate courses are held in room 145."

DATA QUERY LANGUAGES

The relational view of data provided by the relational data base model is intended more for data query languages than it is for data description. Although logic has been used to describe data and data base queries (Darlington [1969], Minker [1975], and Nicolas and Syre [1974]) independently of the relational data base model, until recently, the relational calculus was the only relational query language to be explicitly formulated in logic. Since then, van Emden [1979] has shown how query-by-example as developed by Zloof [1975] can be expressed in logic in a manner compatible with the n-ary representation of tables. Moreover, Pirotte [1978], using logic as a uniform formalism, has shown how to classify and construct a variety of relational query languages.

Although the relational model views tables as n-ary relations, it can be argued that the relational calculus treats them as binary relations. Given, for example, the tables

Course	Number	Name	Teacher	Level

Lecturer	Number	Name	Group	Office

the query

"What courses do theory group lecturers teach."

can be formulated in both the n-ary and the binary representations

←Ans(x)

Ans(x) ← Course(x,y,u,v),Lecturer(z,u,theory,w)

Ans(x) ← Isa(x,course),Teacher(x,u),Isa(z,lecturer),
Name(z,u),Group(z,theory)

As van Emden [1979] argues, the n-ary representation is like the query-by-example formulation. The binary representation, on the other hand, is like the relational calculus formulation. The relational calculus would use unary type predicates instead of Isa-predicates and unary function symbols instead of binary predicates, i.e.,

Ans(x) ← Course(x), teacher(x) = u,
Lecturer(z), name(z) = u,
group(z) = theory

or more compactly

Ans(x) ← Course(x), teacher(x) = name(z),
Lecturer(z), group(z) = theory .

The difference between the binary relations and the unary functions, however, is more syntactic than semantic.

INTEGRITY CONSTRAINTS

The use of logic to express integrity constraints on data is analogous to the use of logic to express properties of programs. There is no difference in principle between the integrity constraint

"All computer laboratories are held in the afternoons"

and the program property

"All permutations of a list have the same length as the list."

It is uneconomical to develop separate strategies for solving what is essentially the same problem: verifying integrity constraints in data bases and proving properties of programs.

Nicolas and Gallaire [1978] observe that the same general law can be used either as part of the definition of the data or as an integrity constraint. A similar remark holds for programs. When the program property is a specification of the program which can be executed efficiently then it can be used as a program itself.

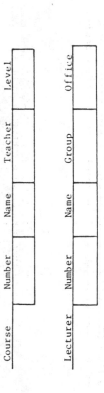

Otherwise it serves as a property with respect to which a more efficient program needs to be consistent.

A DEPARTMENTAL DATA BASE

At Imperial College we are developing a general purpose logic programming system which we intend to use for data base purposes as well as for other programming tasks. The system accepts Horn clause programs including negative procedure calls. The procedure call

not - P

succeeds if all attempts (using Horn clauses) to execute P fail. Clark [1978] has shown that such an interpretation of negation is consistent with interpreting the Horn clauses which define the predicate symbol of P as the if-half of an if-and-only-if definition. The implementation uses PROLOG (Roussel [1975]), data structures but avoids its extralogical language features. Like PROLOG, it executes procedure calls top-down. However, it coroutines procedure calls, automatically tests for loops and, when failure occurs, analyzes bindings of variables in order to control backtracking more intelligently.

Below is a fragment of the data base we are designing to describe our department. A part of the data base concerned with the timetable of courses has been run as a pilot project by David Smith, an undergraduate in our department.

We use function symbols to construct names of individuals. For example, given the two-argument function symbol lect, the constant symbol RAK and the constant symbol 323, the expression lect(RAK,323) names that part of course 323 which consists of RAK's lectures. Similarly stgp(RAK,323) names the part which consists of RAK's study groups. In relational data bases, only integers and character strings are allowed as data objects. There are no data structures corresponding to those constructed using function symbols.

In order to increase readability, we use infix notation for relation symbols. For example, we write (x ≤ y) instead of ≤(x,y). Similarly, we write

(x is occupied in y) instead of Occupied(x,y), etc.

(1) (x is occupied in y) ← (x teaches y)

(2) (x is occupied in y) ← (x attends y)

(3) (x is occupied in y) ← (x is member of committee y)

(4) (x teaches lect(x,y))←

(5) (x teaches stgp(x,y))←

(6) (the hour of lect(RAK,323) is 9:30)←

(7) (the hour of lect(RH,323) is 11:30)←

(8) (the hour of stgp(x,323) is 15:30)←

(9) (the day of lect(RAK,323) is MON)←

(10) (the day of lect(RH,323) is WED)←

(11) (the day of stgp(x,323) is MON)←

(12) (the term of x is II) ← (x is part of 323)

(13) (lect(x,y) is part of y)←

(14) (stgp(x,y) is part of y)←

(15) (the room of lect(x,323) is 139)←

(16) (the room of stgp(x,y) is 222) ← (Year of y is 3)

(17) (the building of x is Huxley) ← (x is part of y),(Dept of y is CCD)

(18) (Year of 323 is 3)←

(19) (Dept of 323 is CCD)←

(20) (AM attends lect(RAK,323))←

(21) (JCA attends lect(RH,323))←

(22) (x attends 323) ← (x is 3rd year student)

(23) (x attends lect(RH,323)) ← (x is M.Sc. student)

(24) (x attends y) ← (x attends z), (y is part of z)

(25) (Capacity of 139 is 50)←

(26) (Capacity of 222 is 25)←

(27) (total of 17 attend lect(RAK,323))←

(28) (total of 39 attend lect(RH,323))←

(29) (total of 16 attend stgp(x,323))←

We intend to use the system to test integrity constraints by defining conditions under which the data base would be inconsistent; for example, if an activity x is held in a room whose capacity is less than the number of people who attend it.

```
Inconsistent(x) ← (the room of x is y), (total of u attend x),
                  (capacity of y is v), (v < u)
```

The system can check for inconsistencies by periodically asking itself to find inconsistent activities via the query

```
←Inconsistent(x)
```

To make an appointment with RAK at 16.30 on Thursday in term II, a user of the data base might pose the query

```
← (RAK is occupied in x), (the hour of x is 16.30),
  (the day of x is Thurs), (the term of x is II)
```

DATA BASES AND PROGRAMS

Conventional data base systems compensate for their inability to express general laws by interfacing with a conventional programming language. The programming language is host to the data base system and provides the possibility of defining data procedurally.

Logic, in contrast, serves as a single uniform language which can be used both for expressing data definitions, queries and integrity constraints, as well as for defining programs. Indeed, when both data bases and programs are formulated in logic, the distinction between them disappears. When logic is used to describe data bases, the general laws behave as procedures. If the procedures are executed bottom-up, then they generate explicit assertions corresponding to conventional tables of data. If the procedures are executed top-down, they compute the data when it is needed. Bottom-up and top-down execution are different but equivalent ways of using the same information (Kowalski [1976]).

When logic is used to define programs, procedures are represented by means of relations which hold between the input and the output. A given input-output relation might be defined both by assertions and by general laws. The general laws are often recursive and the assertions serve as the bases of the recursions. A logic program for symbolic integration, for example, like the one written in PROLOG by Bergman and Kanoui [1973], defines the relationship between a function and its integral both by means of assertions, such as

```
sin(x) is the integral of cos(x)
with respect to x
```

and by general laws, such as,

```
u+v is the integral of u'+v'
with respect to x
if u is the integral of u' with respect to x
and v is the integral of v' with respect to x.
```

The symbolic integration program is a clear example of a program which can also be regarded as a data base.

The distinction between data bases and programs becomes less distinct when we use assertions and procedures instead of terms as data structures. Instead of representing the sequence

```
a,c,b,a
```

by a term

```
cons(a,cons(c,cons(b,cons(a,nil))))
```

as in LISP, we can give it a name, say A, and represent it by the assertions

```
Item(A,o,a)←

Item(A,1,c)←

Item(A,2,b)←

Item(A,3,a)←

Length(A,4)←
```

where Item(x,y,z) means that

```
z is the yth item of x
```

and Length(x,y) means that

```
y is the length of x.
```

Instead of writing a conventional recursive program to reverse a sequence, for example,

$Rev(x,y) \leftarrow Rev^*(x,nil,y)$

$Rev^*(nil,y,y) \leftarrow$

$Rev^*(cons(u,x),z,y) \leftarrow Rev^*(x,cons(u,z),y)$

we can write a non-recursive one. Here rev(x) names the sequence which is the reverse of x.

$Item(rev(x),u,y) \leftarrow Item(x,v,y),\ Length(x,w),(u+v=w)$

$Length(rev(x),y) \leftarrow Length(x,y)$

Programming with data represented by relations is programming at a higher level than with data represented by terms. It is especially suitable for representing data structures such as graphs. A program of this sort was written and run on our logic system at Imperial College by a high school student, Jacob Foguel, during the summer of 1977. The program systhesises organic compounds by searching for appropriate sequences of reactions. Chemical compounds are described by defining the atoms which belong to them and by defining the bonds between atoms. The information that

The bond b of strength s holds between the atoms a_1 and a_2

in the compound c

might be expressed by a single n-ary relationship

$Bond(b,s,a_1,a_2,c) \leftarrow$

or by several binary relationships

(b belongs to c)←

(b bonds a_1)←

(b bonds a_2)←

(b has strength s)←

The initial compound is defined by means of assertions; the goal compound, by a goal statement; and compounds which result from chemical reactions, by general laws. The resulting data-base-program has the same structure as our formulation of the plan-formation problem in Kowalski [1974]. The initial and goal compounds correspond to initial and goal states. Chemical reactions correspond to actions which transform one state into another. Like actions, they are described by specifying (1) the preconditions which must hold true of a compound in order for the reaction to take place, (2) the new bonds which the reaction introduces and (3) the old bonds which the reaction destroys. A frame axiom is necessary to express that bonds which are not destroyed are retained in the new compound. As in plan-formation, the frame axiom states that most of the facts which hold true of a given situation remain true of the new situation which results from performing an action.

Similar to the chemistry program, but more important commercially, are the drug analysis programs written in PROLOG at the ministry of Heavy Industry in Budapest (Futo et al. [1978]). Those programs typically employ binary rather than more general n-ary relations because much of the information about a given drug might be unavailable.

The relational data base community is beginning to feel the need for programming languages which interface with data bases more smoothly than existing programming languages. The design of a programming language by Zloof [1977] based on query-by-example is a significant development in this direction. It is worth observing, however, that logic programming shows how to extend any query language to a programming language:

Simply add a procedure head P to a query $\leftarrow Q$

in order to turn it into a procedure $P \leftarrow Q$.

P consists of the name of a relation together with components which normally occur already in Q . In such a manner, for example, we can turn the query

"What is the number y of hours per year that teacher x teaches?"

into the definition

"The teaching load of x is y if y is the number of hours per year that teacher x teaches."

which behaves as a program for computing teaching loads, when it is interpreted top-down.

The extension of query languages to programming languages permits the definition of recursive procedures, since the same relation can be named in both the procedure head and the procedure body. The ability to pose queries of recursively defined relations is absent in the relational data base query languages, but is present in the programming languages which extend them. The inclusion of recursively defined relations remedies an incompleteness in the original query language (Codd [1972]).

THE DYNAMICS OF EVOLVING DATA BASES

Complex programs and data bases change with time. New information becomes available. Old information is refined. Inconsistencies appear and are resolved.

It is a common misconception to assume that a data base formulated in logic changes only monotonically by expanding its information content. The monotonicity assumption is the basis of Minsky's (Minsky [1975]) criticism of logic for representing human knowledge.

In general the attempt to assimilate new information into an existing data base can give rise to one of four situations.

(1) The existing data base already implies the new information. The implied information need not be added explicitly to the data base.

(2) The new information, together with part of the information in the data base, implies information in the other part of the data base. The implied information can be replaced by the new information.

(3) The new information is independent from the existing data. It is simply added to the data base.

(4) The new information is inconsistent with the existing data base. Consistency can be restored either by abandoning, or by suitably restricting some sentence which participates in, and is indispensible for, the proof of inconsistency.

In the first three cases the data base changes monotonically. In the first case the new data base has the same information content as the original one. In the second case it includes the information in the original data base. In the third case it necessarily contains more information.

It is the fourth case which is most interesting. It includes both the case in which the new data violates existing integrity constraints as well as the case in which it is an exception which contradicts existing general rules. When the data violates an integrity constraint, consistency is maintained by rejecting the data. When the data is an exception which contradicts a general rule, the data is added to the data base and consistency is preserved by adding the exception as an extra condition which restricts the application of the general rule.

The accommodation of exceptions to general rules in an evolving data base provides further support for the thesis that it is easier to construct general rules than it is to discover them. It is easy to add an exception to a general rule, transforming, for example,

```
(the room of lect(x,y) is 145) ← (Year of y is 3),
                                  (y is compulsory)
```

into

```
(the room of lect(x,302) is 139)←

(the room of lect(x,y) is 145) ← (Year of y is 3),
                                  (y is compulsory),
                                  (y is different from 302).
```

It is more difficult to discover the restricted rule and its exceptions by analyzing the explicit form of the data.

Interactive timetabling is a potentially useful application of the dynamic evolution of a data base which describes the activities of a university department. Early versions of the timetable might be defined by ambitiously general laws.

"All 1st year lectures are held in room 314."

"All lectures with more than 50 students are held in room 145."

Conflicts which arise as inconsistencies among the general rules and the integrity constraints would be reconciled by abandoning or restricting the general rules. The search space of possible timetables defined by general rules and their exceptions would be more manageable than the conventional search space of all possible activity-time-place relations defined explicitly, without general rules.

THE MONTONICITY CRITICISM RECONSIDERED

Minsky's monotonicity criticism can be countered by drawing attention to the importance of reconciling inconsistency as a method of nonmonotonically changing a logic data base. The situation is somewhat complicated, however, by the fact that the statement which needs to be abandoned or restricted may be one which is neither explicitly stated nor logically implied by the original data base.

To illustrate the complications, suppose that we have a data base containing <u>only</u> the information

"A and B teach programming and are both professors."

Suppose that we change the data base by adding the new information

"C, who is different from A and B, also teaches programming."

It can be argued, at the informal, natural language level, that the statement

"Everyone who teaches programming is a professor."

holds in the original data base but not in the new one. Addition of the new information nonmonotonically alters the information content of the data base.

Let us see what happens when we try to formalize the argument in logic. If we assume, as we have until now, that the initial data base is represented by means of Horn clauses

Teaches(A,programming)←

Teaches(B,programming)←

Professor (A)←

Professor (B)←

then the statement

Professor(x) ← Teaches(x,programming)

<u>is not a logical consequence</u> of the data base and consequently is not invalidated by the new information

Teaches(C,programming)←

← C = A

← C = B

In order to justify the informal argument, it is necessary to assume that the <u>only information</u> there is to know about the Teaches-relation is the information given in the original data base. We need, at least, to add to the original data base the assumption

"Only A and B teach programming"

x = A, x = B ← Teaches(x,programming)

The statement that everyone who teaches programming is a professor <u>is now a logical consequence</u> of the augmented data base. The new information that C teaches programming is inconsistent with the data base and behaves as an exception to a general rule. Consistency is restored by adding the new information to the data base and by modifying the general rule, replacing it by the more restricted rule.

x = A, x = B, x = C ← Teaches(x,programming)

The revised formulation in logic justifies the informal natural language argument. It makes explicit two considerations which are not stated in the informal argument: (1) the assumption that the only people who teach programming are those we know about in the data base, and (2) the automatic, consistency restoring, modification of the assumption, when we learn that another individual teaches programming.

In general, Minsky's monotonicity criticism of logic can be answered (1) by making explicit the assumption that all the information there is to know is already present in the data base and (2) by recognising that the acquisition of knowledge involves more than simply adding new statements to a data base.

THE IF-AND-ONLY-IF FORMULATION OF DEFINITIONS

The preceding discussion of the monotonicity criticism has brought out a potential difficiency in the use of Horn clauses to express definitions. Horn clauses typically express only the if-halves of definitions, which are completely expressed by using if-and-only-if. The clauses

Teaches(A,programming)←

Teaches(B,programming)←

for example, are only the if-half of the if-and-only-if definition

Teaches(x,programming) ↔ [x = A ∨ x = B]

of the "who teaches programming" relation.

It is not always clear whether it is the full if-and-only-if definition or only the Horn clause if-half which is required for a given relation. This is largely because the if-half alone is sufficient for most useful purposes. It is sufficient, in particular, for computing, in the sense of logic programming, all instances of the relation. The only-if half of the definition may be needed, however, for proving properties of the relation or for answering queries containing universal quantifiers. For example, simply to determine

"Who teaches programming?"

the if-half of the if-and-only-if definition is sufficient. But to answer in the affirmative

"Are all the people who teach programming professors?"

the only-if half is necessary. The fact that the if-half of a definition is sufficient for computing instances of a relation, whereas the only-if half is necessary for proving properties, has been used by Clark and Tarnlund [1977] in their techniques for proving properties of Horn clause logic programs in first-order logic.

There are occasions when only the if-half of a definition is justified. Reiter [1978a] calls the assumption that the data base contains all the information there is to know the closed world assumption. The assumption that there may be more to know is called the open world assumption. Our proposal is to identify the closed world assumption with if-and-only-if definitions and the open world assumption with the if-halves. This has the advantage that the closed world and open world assumptions can be mixed in the same data base, applied to different relations or to different instances of the same relation. Reiter makes an interesting alternative proposal to formalize the closed world assumption by expressing that the individuals named in the data base are the only individuals there are.

Distinguishing whether it is the full if-and-only-if definition or only the if-half which is required is complicated by the fact that in natural language it is common to assert only the if-halves of definitions whether or not the only-if-halves are also intended Even logicians have sanctioned the unstated only-if assumption in the case of inductive definitions. When a logician gives the inductive definition of natural number, for example

(N1) o is a natural number

(N2) if x is a natural number then the successor of x is a natural number

if it is not explicitly stated that

(N3) the only natural numbers are those given by conditions (1) and (2)

it is none-the-less implicitly assumed.

Natural language carries the unstated only-if assumption to the extreme. The classical fallacy of logic is probably an example of this. Assume, for example,

B ← A .

Now suppose

B ←

We may safely conclude

A ←

if we assume that

A is the only condition under which B holds

that is, it was the if-and-only-if definition of B which was intended

B if-and-only-if A

when only the if-half was stated.

It is curious that natural language should be so careless about specifying whether or not the unstated only-if assumption is to be applied. This may be a consequence, in part, of the awkwardness of the if-and-only-if syntax. In data bases, the definition of a relation may be scattered in several places, intermingled with the definition of other relations. In such cases, an if-and-only-if expression at the head of the definition is not appropriate. A more convenient syntax might be one which follows the last clause of the definition and which states that no other clause of the definition follows - an explicit

"and that is all there are"

statement, for example.

AMBIGUITY OF ONLY-IF

The considerations we have just outlined are further complicated by the fact that the only-if assumption is ambiguous.

A if-and-only-if B

can be expressed wholely in the object-language

A ← B

A → B

or the if-half can be expressed (using Horn clauses) in the object language

A ← B

and the only-if-half can be expressed in the meta-language

"The sentence 'A ← B' states the only conditions under which A holds."

The inductive definition of natural number is a simple example. The only-if-half can be expressed in the object language

Numb(x) → {x = o ∨ ∃x' [x=succ(x') ∧ Numb(x')]}

or it can be expressed in the meta-language

"Sentences (N1) and (N2) state the only conditions under which x is a number."

An important practical consequence of the ambiguity is that arguments which need to appeal to the only-if-halves of definitions can be formalized either in the object language or in the meta-language. Proving properties of logic programs is one example. Constructing answers to queries containing negation or universal quantifiers is another.

Consider, for example, the Horn clause logic program which defines the Append relation on lists.

(A1) Append(nil,x,x)←

(A2) Append(cons(x,y),z, cons(x,y')) ← Append(y,z,y') .

Here the expression Append(u,v,w) is to be read as expressing that the list w results from appending the list v to the list u.

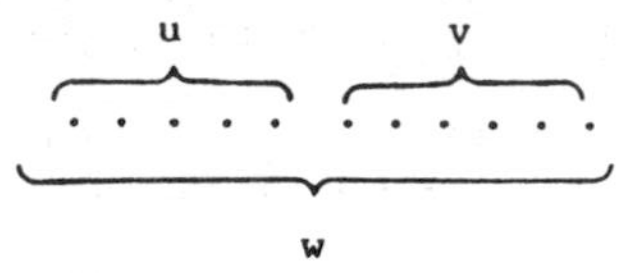

the property that

Append(x,nil,x) holds for all lists x

can be proved either in the object-language or in the meta-language.

The object-level proof is the one constructed by the method of Clark and Tarnlund [1977]. It expresses, in the object language, both the only-if-half of the definition

Append(u,v,w) → {[u = nil ∧ v = w] ∨ ∃x,y,y'[u = cons(x,y) ∧ w = cons(x,y') ∧ Append(y,v,y')]}

as well as the appropriate axiom schema for lists.

The alternative method is to prove the property in the meta-language. Assume that (A1) and (A2) are the only methods for establishing that the Append relation holds among lists. Suppose that A is any list. We need to demonstrate that

(A3) Append(A,nil,A)←

can be proved using only (A1) and (A2). The demonstration is by induction on the structure of A. If A is nil, then there is a one-step proof of (A3) using (A1) alone. If A is cons(B,A'), then by the induction hypothesis there is some n-step proof of

Append(A',nil,A')←.

By adding an extra step to the proof, using (A2), we obtain an n+1 step proof of

Append(cons(x,A'),nil,cons(x,A'))←

for any x and therefore a proof of (A3) in particular.

The object-level and meta-level proofs are similar. They contain similar steps and employ a similar induction on the structure of lists. Their logical status, however, is quite different.

Similar observations apply when the only-if assumption is necessary for answering data base queries. For example, given the Horn clause data base

Teaches(A,programming)←

Teaches(B,programming)←

Professor(A)←

Professor(B)←

the only-if assumption is necessary to justify a positive answer to the question

"Is everyone who teaches programming a professor?"

When the only-if assumption is expressed in the object-language, a typical goal-directed theorem prover reasons backward, trying to establish the goal both by asserting that some individual, say I, teaches programming and by trying to show that I is a professor. Reasoning forward from the assumption that I teaches programming, it uses the only-if assumption to conclude that I is A or I is B. Considering each case in turn, it uses the definition of the Professor relation to show that I is a professor in any case.

When the only-if assumption is expressed in the meta-language, the meta-level theorem prover uses the Horn clause if-half of the definition of the Teaches-relation in order to find all answers to the question

"Who teaches programming?"

← Teaches(x,programming)

for each x=i in the set of all solutions, it uses the Horn clauses defining the Professor-relation to show that

i is a professor

← Professor(i) .

If it succeeds in doing so, it concludes that everyone who teaches programming is a professor.

The two proofs have in common that they both show that everyone who teaches programming is a professor by finding all individuals who teach programming and showing that each of them is a professor. The object-level proof uses the only-if half of the definition to derive a nonHorn clause disjunction which identifies all the individuals who teach programming

$$I = i_1 \vee I = i_2 \vee \ldots \vee I = i_n .$$

The meta-level proof uses the Horn clause if-half of the definition to find the set of all solutions to the problem of finding an individual who teaches programming

$$\{i_1, i_2, \ldots, i_n\} .$$

Both proofs use the Horn clause if-half of the definition of the Professor-relation to show that each i_j (who teaches programming) is a professor.

Given the Horn clause if-half of a relation, the only-if assumption is necessary to show that some instance P of the relation does not hold

← not-P .

The proof can be carried out at the object-level by using the only-if half of the relation to show that none of the conditions which might imply P hold. Or it can be carried out at the meta-level by showing that the search space, determined by all the ways of using the Horn clause definition of the relation to establish P, contains no solutions. Clark [1978] has shown that for any meta-level proof of not-P, of a sufficiently simple kind (using no induction, for example), there exists a structurally similar object-level proof using the object-level only-if half of the definition. Presumably, Clark's proof can be generalized to cover situations requiring induction. If the meta-level proof uses an induction argument to show that an infinite search space contains no solutions, the corresponding object-level proof would use an induction axiom stated in the object language.

CONCLUSIONS

The use of logic for data description abolishes the distinction between data bases and programs. The same techniques apply to problems in both fields. Strategies which apply to the execution of programs apply also to the retrieval of answers to data base queries. Methods for proving properties of programs apply both to verification of integrity constraints and to retrieval of answers to queries involving negation and universal quantifiers. Procedures for maintaining dynamically evolving data bases apply to the evolutionary development and modification of programs.

The need for a single uniform formalism for describing both data bases and programs becomes unarguable once we recognize the existence of a continuum with deterministic programs and explicitly described data bases on opposite extremes. Programs for symbolic integration, synthesis of organic compounds, drug analysis and natural language understanding lie at intermediate positions along the continuum. Conventional formalisms may be suitable for conventional data bases; but logic is useful both for conventional data bases and programs as well as for the computational data bases which lie between the extremes.

ACKNOWLEDGMENTS

I am grateful for the useful discussions I have had with Keith Clark, Bernard Marsh and Marek Sergot. This research was supported by the Science Research Council and aided, in its later stages, by a visiting appointment at the University of Syracuse.

REFERENCES

1. Bergman, M. and Kanoui, H. [1973] Application of Mechanical Theorem Proving to Symbolic Calculus, *Third International Symposium on Advanced Computing Methods in Theoretical Physics*, C.N.R.S., Marseille, June 1973.

2. Chang, C. L., [1976] DEDUCE: A Deductive Query Language for Relational Data Bases, In *Pattern Recognition and Artificial Intelligence* (C. H. Chen, Ed.), Academic Press, Inc., New York, 1976, 108-134.

3. Clark, K. L., Tarnlund, S. A. [1977] A First Order Theory of Data and Programs, *Proceedings IFIP 77*, North-Holland, 1977, 939-944.

4. Clark, K. L. [1978] Negation as Failure, In *Logic and Data Bases* (H. Gallaire and J. Minker, Eds.), Plenum Press, New York, 1978, 293-322.

5. Codd, E. F. [1970] A Relational Model for Large Shared Data Bases, *CACM 13*, 6 (June 1970), 377-387.

6. Codd, E. F. [1972] Relational Completeness of Data Base Sublanguages, In *Data Base Systems* (R. Rustin, Ed.), Prentice-Hall, Englewood Cliffs, N.J., 1972, 65-98.

7. Darlington, J. L. [1969] Theorem Proving and Information Retrieval, In *Machine Intelligence 4* (B. Meltzer and D. Michie, Eds.), American Elsevier Publishing Co., Inc. New York, 1969.

8. Deliyanni, A. and Kowalski, R. A. [1977] Logic and Semantic Networks, Department of Computing and Control Research Report, Imperial College, London, June 1977. Also *Proceedings of the Workshop on Logic and Data Bases*, Toulouse, November 1977.

9. Futó, I., Szeredi, P., and Darvas, F. [1977] Some Implemented and Planned PROLOG Applications, *Workshop of Logic and Data Bases*, Toulouse, November 1977.

10. Gallaire, H., Minker, J. and Nicolas, J.M. [1978] An Overview and Introduction to Logic and Data Bases, In *Logic and Data Bases* (H. Gallaire and J. Minker, Eds.). Plenum Press, New York, 1978, 3-30.

11. Gallaire, H. and Minker, J., Editors [1978] *Logic and Data Bases*, Plenum Press, New York, 1978.

12. Green, C. [1969] Theorem-Proving by Resolution as a Basis for Question Answering Systems, In *Machine Intelligence 4* (B. Meltzer and D. Michie, Eds.), American Elsevier Publishing Co., Inc., New York, 1969, 183-205.

13. Kellogg, C., Klahr, P., Travis, L. [1978] Deductive Planning and Pathfinding for Relational Data Bases, In *Logic and Data Bases* (H. Gallaire and J. Minker, Eds.), Plenum, N.Y., 179-200.

14. Kowalski, R. A. [1974] Logic for Problem-Solving, *Memo No. 75*, Department of Computational Logic, University of Edinburgh, 1974.

15. Kowalski, R. A. [1976] Algorithm = Logic + Control, Research Report, Department of Computing and Control, Imperial College, London, 1976.

16. Minker, J. [1975] Performing Inferences over Relational Data Bases, *Proceedings of 1975 ACM SIGMOD International Conference on Management of Data*, 1975, 79-91.

17. Minsky, M. [1975] A Framework for the Representation of Knowledge, In *The Psychology of Computer Vision* (P. Winsont, Ed.), McGraw Hill, New York, 1975, 211-280.

18. Nicolas, J. M. and Syre, J. C. [1974] Natural Question Answering and Automatic Deduction in the System SYNTEX, *Proceedings IFIP Congress 1974*, North Holland Publishing Co., Stockholm, Sweden, August 1974.

19. Nicolas, J. M. and Gallaire, H. [1978] Data Base: Theory vs. Interpretation, In *Logic and Data Bases* (H. Gallaire and J. Minker, Eds.), Plenum Press, New York, 1978, 33-54.

20. Pirotte, A. [1978] High Level Data Base Query Languages, In *Logic and Data Bases* (H. Gallaire and J. Minker, Eds.), Plenum Press, New York, 1978, 409-436.

21. Reiter, R. [1978] On Closed World Data Bases, In *Logic and Data Bases*(H. Gallaire and J. Minker, Eds.), Plenum Press, New York, 1978, 55-76.

22. Reiter, R. [1978] Deductive Question-Answering on Relational Data Bases, In *Logic and Data Bases* (H. Gallaire and J. Minker, Eds.), Plenum Press, New York, 1978, 149-177.

23. Roussel, P. [1975] PROLOG: Manuel de Reference et d'Utilisation, Groupe d'Intelligence Artificielle, U.E.R. de Luminy, Universite d'Aix-Marseille, Sept. 1975.

24. van Emden, M. H. [1979] Computation and Deductive Information Retrieval, In *Formal Description of Programming Concepts* (E. Neuhold, Ed.), North-Holland, to be published.

25. Zloof, M. M. [1975] Query-by-Example, *Proceedings AFIPS 1975 NCC, Vol 44*, AFIPS Press, Montvale, N. J., 1975, 431-348.

26. Zloof, M. M. and deLong, S. P. [1977] The System for Business Automation (SBA): Programming Language, *CACM 20*, 6 (June 1977), 385-396.

2.4 Data/Knowledge Base Semantics

This section presents three very different methods for addressing semantic issues for a database or knowledge base. The first paper (2.4.1), "Semantics of Databases: The Semantics of Data Models" by Horst Biller and Erich Neuhold, is one of the finest and most comprehensive efforts to address semantic issues for a database. The work is motivated by the *data-equivalence problem* (i.e., deciding when two databases contain the "same" information about the "world"). The reader should not confuse this kind of semantics, where one is interested in interpreting the contents of the database or knowledge base vis-à-vis the "world," with programming- and query-language semantics, where one is interested in interpreting a statement in a formal (computer) language with respect to a data structure. This distinction is made clearly in the paper within a formal framework, but has also been noted elsewhere (e.g., [WOOD75]). Many other database and knowledge-base semantic issues have been addressed elsewhere (data representation [ABRI74], null values [VASS79], data-manipulation languages [CB79] and [BW81], time [CW83], updates [FUV83], and universal relations [MU83]).

The second paper (2.4.2), "An Essential Hybrid Reasoning System: Knowledge and Symbol Level Accounts of KRYPTON" by Ron Brachman, Victoria Pigman-Gilbert, and Hector Levesque, adopts a drastically different approach to data semantics. Here, the semantics of an information base is given denotationally in terms of a collection of "possible worlds," which are consistent with the contents of the information base. The paper also finds a very different use for abstract data types in the context of information bases. Instead of viewing the schema of an information base as a collection of abstract data types (as described in the introduction to Section 2.2 and in the following), this paper views the whole information base as an abstract data type, with associated operations for adding information to or retrieving information from the information base. The information base itself consists of defined *terms* and assertions about the application domain, presumably expressed through the use of the given terms. AI research related to this work concerns hybrid systems [KKW84] and [VILA85], and further knowledge-level issues [BL86].

The third and last paper of the section (2.4.3) is "Towards a Logical Reconstruction of Relational Database Theory" by Ray Reiter. Reiter argues in favour of viewing a relational database as a collection of logical formulas, rather than as a data structure with respect to which queries can be interpreted. The paper examines the axioms required to make the resulting logical theory behave like a relational database. Extensions of such a theory (always within the framework of first-order logic) are also proposed to account for null values and other useful modelling features of semantic data models. This is in many ways a sequel paper to those of Reiter (2.3.2) and Kowalski (2.3.3). The treatment here of null values is relevant to Levesque (1.5) and Imielinski (2.5.2).

Yet another approach to database and knowledge-base semantics, not represented in this section, adopts an abstract-data-type perspective, where different elements of the schema (e.g., *classes, frames, and units*) are given a semantics through associated operations for creating, destroying, and accessing their instances. An interesting feature of this approach is that it is largely self-descriptive and extensible, much in the spirit of LISP.* This approach to semantics has been adopted by object-oriented data models, referenced in the introductions to this volume and in that to Section 2.2. It is consistent with the "proceduralist" view of semantics, which argues that knowing a concept or fact amounts to knowing how to use it in different contexts (see, for example, [WINO75] for an eloquent argument in favour of this perspective). Several papers in this volume, including [Brodie, 2.2.3], [Mylopoulos, 2.2.1], [Shipman, 2.2.2], and [Lafue, 3.4.3], adopt this viewpoint to some extent.

* See [ABRI74] for a particularly striking example of self-description and extensibility.

SEMANTICS OF DATA BASES: THE SEMANTICS OF DATA MODELS

HORST BILLER and ERICH J. NEUHOLD
Institut für Informatik, Universität Stuttgart, D-7000 Stuttgart, Azenbergstr. 12, F.R. of Germany

(*Received* 3 *September* 1976; *in revised form* 10 *March* 1977)

Abstract—The definition of data equivalence depends on a notion of the semantics (i.e. the meaning) of the data stored in a data base. To define the semantics of these data it is very important to distinguish between the things to be modelled in a data base and the language in which they are represented. We introduce an abstract data model which is suited to express the semantics of schemas respectively data instances. To represent this model we propose a logical data definition language (LDDL) and a logical data language (LDL) which as a consequence allow to specify the kind of information which may be stored in the data base and which ensures the correctness and consistency of this information.

1. INTRODUCTION

In several areas of data base management systems the subject of data equivalence is of great importance. For example in the field of data translation methods and languages have been developed to map files from one data base management system into files of another one (i.e. [1-3]) or the architecture of future data base management systems will have to provide flexible mappings between a "conceptual schema" and "external schemas" (see [4] or [5]). In [6] an intuitive definition of data equivalence is given and the translation between files based on this definition is discussed. In the same way the translation languages proposed in recent years rely upon the users intuitive knowledge of the meaning of the files. But to avoid misunderstandings and incorrect data in a data base which is constructed according to the coexistence architecture it is important to develop tools which can be used to assure semantically correct mappings between the different views.

In this paper we introduce two languages called logical data definition language (LDDL) and logical data language (LDL) which are suited to express the meaning of data structures. But first we discuss, how the semantics of data bases can be defined. For this it is important to differentiate between the things which are to be modelled in a data base (the semantic universe of discourse) and the representation languages (see also [7-10]). The (intuitive and implicit) semantics of different data base languages or data models are then expressed by mapping them to our model, the semantics of which are explicitely defined. For this purpose we introduce an abstract model which is suited to express those features of the reality which are to be represented in a data base.

The abstract model consists of a set of abstract states, which in turn contain a set of entities, a set of types which are subsets of the set of entities and a set of relations.

To be able to translate data bases and to assure the semantic correctness it is very important to express explicitly the consistency conditions. In most data models some of them are implicitly contained in the underlying structures. We therefore discuss the consistency constraints with respect to our abstract model. For the specification of these constraints consistency clauses are included in LDDL, which allow to specify those conditions which are of importance for the mappings between the different models and which are needed to assure the correctness of the data base.

Since a data base represents a collection of real world facts[4], i.e. a slice of reality[8], one could try to compare two different data bases on the level of the real world. But then the equivalence of two data bases can never be formally proven, since then we would have to formalize our perception of the reality. With help of the abstract model however formal investigations can be made, as at this level the semantics of data definition and manipulation languages can be treated formally ([11, 12]), and a formal definition of equivalence can be given. However we will discuss later that it is very important to rely on the users understanding of natural languages, since only in this fashion the connection between a data base and the reality about which statements are to be represented can be established.

2. AN INTRODUCTORY EXAMPLE

In this chapter we give a motivation for our approach to the definition of data equivalence. We start with an informal definition of data equivalence:

"Two data bases are equivalent if they represent equivalent facts about a certain slice of reality".

This definition is a consequence of the statement:

"A data base is the collection of data that represents those facts defined to be of interest to an enterprise"[4].

But this definition does not help too much as long as it is not known, how to derive the facts represented by a database and if these facts are known, how to compare them, so that one can state, that they are equivalent.

These problems are illustrated by means of the following example.

Consider the schema A (see [2]) in Fig. 1.

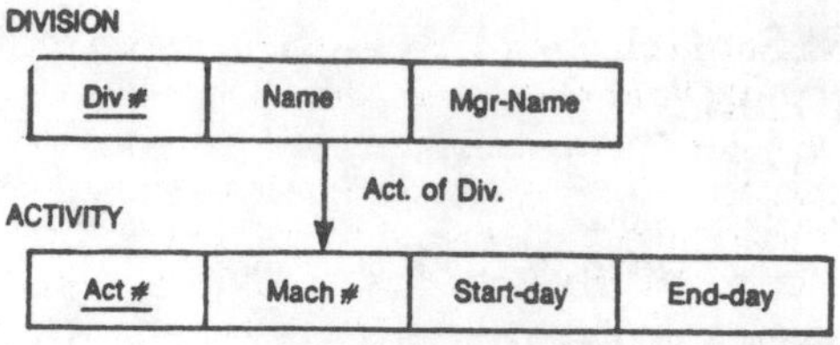

Fig. 1. Schema A.

In this figure the schema of the group relation Act. of Div. is given. DIVISION is a group schema containing the item schemas Div #, Name, Mgr-Name and ACTIVITY is a group schema containing the item schemas Act #, Mach #, Start-day and End-day. In any instance of this schema one instance of the group DIVISION may be connected to zero or more instances of the group ACTIVITY (called an assembly of the group ACTIVITY) and any instance of the group ACTIVITY must be connected to exactly one instance of the group DIVISION. Div # is an identifier of the group DIVISION, i.e. at any moment there must not exist within the data base two instances of the group DIVISION containing the same instance of Div #. Act # is an identifier of the group ACTIVITY relative to the group DIVISION, i.e. at any moment there must not exist two instances of the group ACTIVITY containing the same instance of Act # within one assembly. An instance I_1 of this schema is shown in Fig. 2.

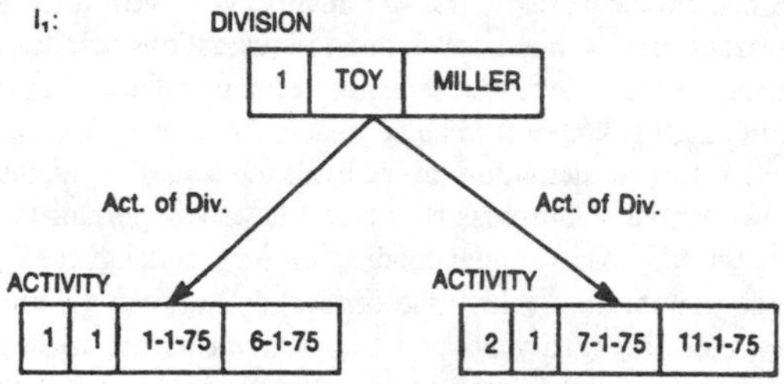

Fig. 2. Instance I_1 of Schema A.

A set of facts possibly represented by this instance is:

F_1 = {Division no. 1 has the name TOY and the manager MILLER,
Activity no. 1 of division no. 1 needs the machine no. 1 from 1–1–75 to 6-1-75,
Activity no. 2 of division no. 1 needs the machine no. 1 from 7-1-75 to 11-1-75}.

To associate F_1 with the instance I_1 we regard group instances to represent objects about which information is stored, i.e. any group instance represents one object.

By applying the function "compression"[2] to the above schema, we generate the schema B of Fig. 3.

The instance I_1 is translated into the instances I_2 and I_3 of schema B (Fig. 4).

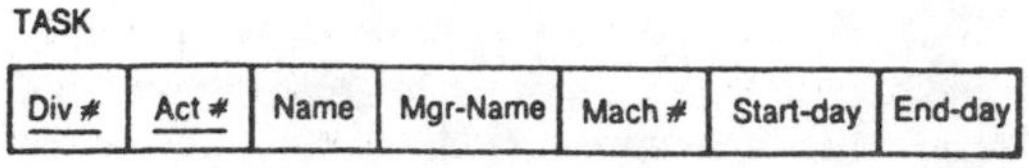

Fig. 3. Schema B.

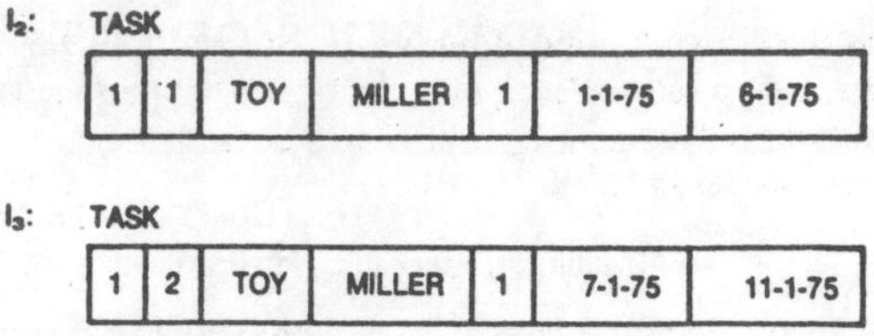

Fig. 4. Instances I_2, I_3 of Schema B.

If we regard group instances again to represent objects in this data base information about the objects "task no. 1 with div no. 1 and act no. 1" and "task no. 2 with div no. 1 and act. no. 2" is represented by these instances. The set of facts then would be

F_2 = {The task with div. no. 1 and act. no. 1 has the name TOY and the manager Miller and needs machine no. 1 from 1-1-75 to 6-1-75; the task with div. no. 1 and act. no. 2 has the name TOY and the manager Miller and needs machine no. 1 from 7-1-75 to 11-1-75}.

To prove that the sets F_1 and F_2 are equivalent is certainly not easily done, at least it is not obvious.

But there exists another possible way of associating facts to the instances F_2 and F_3.

If within one group instance information about several objects might be represented, the instances of the group TASK could represent the set of facts:

F_3 = {The division with div. no. 1 has manager MILLER and name TOY and activity no. 1 of the division no. 1 needs the machine no. 1 from 1-1-75 to 6-1-75; the division with div. no. 1 has manager MILLER and name TOY and activity no. 2 of the division no. 1 needs the machine no. 1 from 7-1-75 to 11-1-75}.

That F_3 is equal to F_1 is quite obvious, since the first sentence of F_3 is the conjunction of the first two sentences of F_1 and the second sentence of F_3 is the conjunction of the first and the third sentence of F_1, and therefore we have shown that the instance I_1 is equivalent to the instances I_2 and I_3 according to the above definition, if the facts represented by I_2 and I_3 are expressed by the set F_3.

The following three issues are the underlying principles in showing the equivalence of the sets of instances $\{I_1\}$ and $\{I_2, I_3\}$:

Firstly one must introduce a representation of facts. In this example we have chosen natural language sentences. A presupposition for this is that we understand these sentences, i.e. that we know the meaning of these sentences with respect to the slice of reality about which data are stored.

Secondly we have to define a mapping from data instances onto facts. By this mapping meaning is attached to the data, i.e. the semantics of the data are defined. This mapping has to be defined for the schema of the data base so that all instances of the same schema are mapped to facts in an analogous way.

Thirdly we have assumed that it is known, whether two sets of natural language sentences are equivalent. Again we presuppose that the natural language is commonly understood. To circumvent the problem to decide, when two sets of sentences are equivalent, we have tried to show that the sets of instances $\{I_1\}$ and $\{I_2, I_3\}$ can be mapped to sets of facts, the equivalence of which can be shown by the application of simple obvious (i.e. logical) rules only.

3. THE SEMANTIC FRAMEWORK

In this Section we introduce precise definitions of what the semantics of data bases are, as needed for investigating the problem of data equivalence. Figure 5 illustrates the connection between the different notions to be defined in this Section. The picture reflects the situation, as it exists at a specific instance of time, let us say *t*.

3.1 *Reality and the real world states*

For each data base system only a part of all possible facts which can be stated about the reality is of interest. So at any instance of time the users would agree that a certain fact is relevant or not. That means a perception and selection process is applied to the reality which extracts a slice of reality [8], the real world state, which is intended to be represented in the data base. At each specific instance of time this slice of reality is called a *real world state.* Therefore the real world is represented by a set of states, which is constructed from all the states which the users agree that they may exist at some point of time. We shall denote this set also as the set of *imaginable real world states.*

The fundamental concepts of the real world which are of relevance in the data base area are *objects,* which possess *properties,* and between which *relationships* may exist. All these concepts cannot be defined formally, but may only be explained in an informal way.

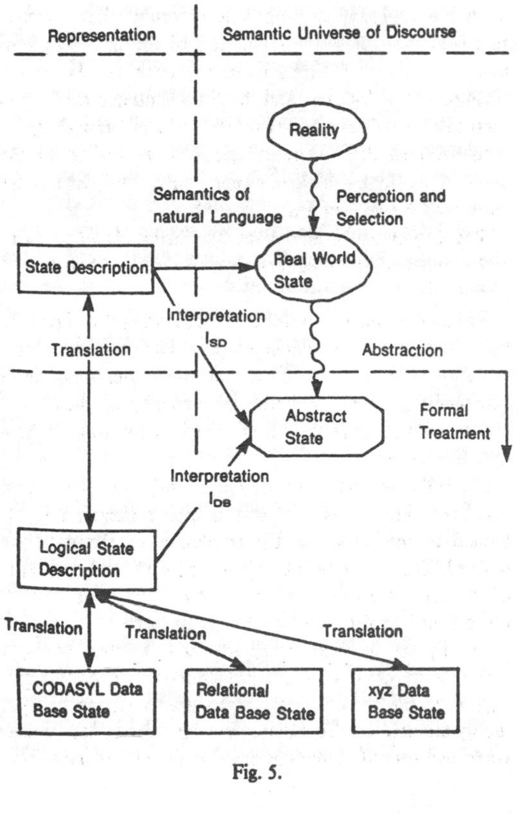

Fig. 5.

An object is anything about which assertions can be made, i.e. something that can appear in the subject or object position of an English sentence. Objects can be *concrete* ("the typewriter *I* use to write this paper") or *abstract* ("the numeric value 2345"), they may be *simple* ("the age 23") or *complex* ("the set of all parts stored in a specific warehouse").

A *property* is denoted by a predicative expression in natural language ("to be an employee", "to be red").

A property can be the conjunction or disjunction of other properties [8, 13]. For example is the property "to be husband" the conjunction of the properties "to be male" and "to be married". We use the term property as it has been introduced in [8], whereas in several papers, for example [14–18] this term is used with a different meaning. A detailed discussion of the differences in the terminology used can be found in [19].

A *relationship* is denoted by natural language verbs, for example "is married to".

Since formal criteria do not exist, which allow to state what an object, property or relationship is, it is possible that the perception process applied by different persons to the same part of reality results in different real world states. We call these different real world states *conceptually different views* in contrast to *syntactically different views* which will be explained later. An example for conceptually different views would be, to regard colours to be objects ("red", "green",...) and to introduce a relationship between colours and objects ("has colour"), or to regard the colour of objects to be properties ("to be red", "to be green").

To view colours as objects as in the first case allows facts about colours to be represented, e.g. "the wave length of the colour red is between 0.65 μ and 0.75 μ", whereas in the second case further facts about colours cannot be represented.

That two real world states are the result of perception processes applied to the same reality cannot be formally proven since the perception process cannot be formalized. However to avoid misunderstandings it is necessary to assure that users which share a data base do not have conceptually different views. Before discussing this problem in detail we first describe how real world states are represented.

3.2 *The state description*

A real world state is completely determined if it is known which objects exist, which properties they possess, and which relationships between objects exist and which do not exist. In other words, a real world state is completely determined if one knows, which facts are correct and which facts are not correct.

A fact can be represented by a predicative English sentence. A set of elementary predicative sentences which completely describes a real world state is called a *state description* [20]. Since we have presupposed that the users agree upon facts to be relevant or not, a real world state can be represented at a certain time *t* by those sentences only, which are true at time *t*, if one defines that all sentences representing facts, which are relevant but not included in the state description, are false. That moreover means that we include in a state description only positive sentences, e.g. sentences which are not formally negated.

An elementary sentence contains three components, a subject, a predicate and an object-part consisting of none, one or several denotations of objects. We assume that an elementary sentence s cannot be split up into a conjunction of other elementary sentences $s_1, s_2, \ldots$, so that for all times t holds:

$$s \Leftrightarrow s_1 \wedge s_2 \wedge s_3 \wedge \ldots$$

The subject as well as the objects denotations need not be simple, they rather can be structured.

Examples of elementary sentences are given in Fig. 6.

"Bill Jones is an employee"
"Division No. 1 has the manager Miller"
"Activity No. 1 of Division No. 1 needs machine No. 1"

Fig. 6. Examples of elementary sentences.

In a formal notation an elementary sentence corresponds to a predicate followed by n object terms, where $n \geqslant 1$. Whether a sentence is elementary or not can only be decided with respect to a certain view of the reality. Consider for example the sentence

"Bill Jones makes 100 dollars per week for working on project alpha".

If we assume that a person might work on several projects at the same time and get different salaries in different jobs, this sentence is an elementary one, since we cannot conclude at all instances of time from "Bill Jones makes 100 dollars per week" and "Bill Jones works on project alpha", that the above sentence is true.

But if we assume that a person might only work on one project at a time, and cannot get several salaries, this sentence could be split into the conjunction

"Bill Jones works on project alpha *and* Bill Jones makes 100 dollars per week".

In this case the above sentence is not an elementary one.

A state description is *true* with respect to a real world state, if all sentences represent facts, which are true with respect to this real world state.

Since we assumed, that all the users of a data base agree on the real world to be represented in the data base, we can now assume that all the users would agree at any point of time, that a given state description is true or that it is false. This means that all users understand a common language (i.e. English) and that we use (a subset of) this language as our representation language for the real world. For example we used English phrases for the representation of our sample objects above and we had to assume a common understanding of "the typewriter *I* use to write this paper".

3.3 *The abstract model and the standard interpretation* I_{SD}

The real world is a conceptualization of the reality as it actually exists, but still it does not lend itself to a formal treatment. But to be able to formalize the semantics of data bases, we need a formally defined universe of discourse. To achieve this goal we introduce an *abstract (world) model* which is a set of *abstract states.* This abstract model is an abstraction of the real world. Several authors have introduced data models to express the semantics of data bases (i.e. [4, 5, 8, 9, 16–18, 21–28]) but we introduce a new name, since some important differences exist which will be discussed later. A detailed comparison of these models with our abstract model can also be found in [19].

An abstract state is a mathematical structure, consisting of a set E, the set of *entities*, a family T, the *types* and a family R, the *relations*, where every type T_i, which is an element of T, is a subset of the set of entities, the set E is the union of all elements of the set T, and with any relation R_i, which is an element of R, a rank n_i is associated, and R_i is a subset of E^{n_i}. All abstract states of an abstract model must contain the same number of types respectively relations.

We do not exclude that in an abstract state a type T_i or a relation R_j does not contain an element, i.e. that $T_i = \phi$ or $T_j = \phi$ holds for some abstract states. We also do not exclude that an entity is an element of two different types in an abstract state.

To discuss the interrelationship between a real world state and an abstract state we must first introduce the *standard interpretation* I_{SD} of a state description.

A standard interpretation is a mapping which assigns entities to noun phrases (mapping noun phrases which denote different real world objects to different entities), types or relations to verb phrases and the value true or false to sentences. A verb phrase is mapped to a type, if it denotes a property, and mapped to a relation, if it denotes a relationship. Since objects may possess several properties, it is possible that an entity is element of several types, and therefore we do not require types to be disjoint. By a standard interpretation in all abstract states the same entities must be assigned to the same noun phrase, and to a verb phrase the types respectively relations with the same index must be assigned. The type respectively relation which is assigned to a verb phrase in an abstract state is called the *extension* [20] of the verb phrase (in the respective abstract state). The set of all extensions of a verb phrase is called the *intension* [20] of the verb phrase.

A sentence of the state description either states that an object possesses a property, or that a relationship between some objects holds. In the first case the sentence is mapped to the value *true*, if the entity, to which the noun phrase of the sentence is mapped, is an element of the type, to which the verb phrase is mapped, otherwise it is mapped to the value *false*. In the second case the entities to which the subject and object parts of the sentence are mapped, let us say $e_1, \ldots, e_n$, form a tuple $(e_1, \ldots, e_n)$. The sentence is mapped to the value *true*, if this tuple is an element of the relation, to which the verb phrase is mapped.

An abstract state is called a *model* of a state description SD, if a standard interpretation exists, so that all sentences of SD are mapped to the value *true*, and all sentences which are not element of SD are mapped to the value *false*. This definition corresponds to the use of the term model in the logic (see, e.g. [29]).

Let SD be a state description which is true with respect to a real world state RW, and let AS be an abstract state which is a model of SD. Then AS is called an abstraction of the real world state RW. An entity e is called the abstraction of an object o, if a noun phrase denoting o in SD is mapped to the entity e, the type T_p is called the abstraction of the property p, if the verb phrase denoting p is mapped to the type T_p, and a relation $R\rho$ is called the abstraction of the relationship ρ, if the verb phrase denoting ρ is mapped to the relation $R\rho$. The fact that the object o possesses the property p, is expressed in the abstract model by the abstraction e of o being an element of T_p, and the fact that the relationship ρ holds between objects $o_1, \ldots, o_n$ with the abstractions $e_1, \ldots, e_n$, is modelled by the tuple $(e_1, \ldots, e_n)$ being an element of the relation $R\rho$.

The interrelation between a state description and an abstract state can be used for a representation of abstract states, by means of which the intended standard interpretation is reflected. Entities are represented by noun phrases, and types and relations are denoted by verb phrases and represented by sets of representations of entities respectively tuples of entities. An example of a representation of an abstract state, which corresponds to the example in Section 1, is given in Fig. 7.

At the end of this chapter we now can define, that the complete abstract model is the set of all abstract states which are models of state descriptions which are true with respect to one of the imaginable real world states.

3.4 *The logical state description and the interpretation* I_{SD}

An abstract state is a representation of facts, which can be used as range of an interpretation of a state of a (physical) data base like a Codasyl data base or a relational data base. A state of such a data base is a set of data instances, each of which can be regarded to be a linguistic representation of one or several facts. The set of all possible, i.e. syntactically correct, states of a data base is determined by specifying a *schema*, i.e. a set of sentences of a data definition language, together with rules, how data instances can be derived from schema entries. Therefore the set of all syntactically correct states of a data base base corresponds to the set of all abstract states of that abstract model, which is the abstraction from the real world to be represented in the data base. The semantics of a data base schema therefore are given by a mapping from the schema to an abstract model, whereas the semantics of a data base state are given by a mapping to an abstract state.

For several reasons representations of abstract states like the one given in Fig. 7 are not very useful for the semantic mappings. First there is a lot of redundancy in such a representation. For example from the name of e_1 "division with div no. 1", one knows that (e_1, e_2) is an element of the relation "division has no". Secondly, since facts are not stated explicitly, one must derive them from the abstract state, so that the interpretation of

$E = \{e_1, \ldots, e_{15}\}$

with

e_1 = "division with div no 1"
e_2 = "div no. 1"
e_3 = "TOY"
e_4 = "manager Miller"
e_5 = "Miller"
e_6 = "activity with act. no. 1 of division with div no. 1"
e_7 = "act. no. 1"
e_8 = "machine with mach. no. 1"
e_9 = "mach. no. 1"
e_{10} = "1-1-75"
e_{11} = "6-1-75"
e_{12} = "activity with act. no. 2 of division with div. no. 1"
e_{13} = "act no. 2"
e_{14} = "7-1-75"
e_{15} = "11-1-75"

$T = \{T_1, \ldots, T_{10}\}$

with

T_1 = "is division"
T_2 = "is number of division"
T_3 = "is division name"
T_4 = "is manager"
T_5 = "is manager name"
T_6 = "is activity"
T_7 = "is number of activity"
T_8 = "is machine"
T_9 = "is number of machine"
T_{10} = "is date"

and

$T_1 = \{e_1\}$ $T_6 = \{e_6, e_{12}\}$
$T_2 = \{e_2\}$ $T_7 = \{e_7, e_{13}\}$
$T_3 = \{e_3\}$ $T_8 = \{e_8\}$
$T_4 = \{e_4\}$ $T_9 = \{e_9\}$
$T_5 = \{e_5\}$ $T_{10} = \{e_{10}, e_{11}, e_{14}, e_{15}\}$

$R = \{R_1, \ldots, R_9\}$

with

R_1 = "division has div. no."
R_2 = "division has name"
R_3 = "division has manager"
R_4 = "manager has name"
R_5 = "division needs activity"
R_6 = "activity has act. no."
R_7 = "activity needs machine from start date"
R_8 = "activity needs machine to end date"
R_9 = "machine has mach no."

where

$R_1 = \{(e_1, e_2)\}$
$R_2 = \{(e_1, e_3)\}$
$R_3 = \{(e_1, e_4)\}$
$R_4 = \{(e_4, e_5)\}$
$R_5 = \{(e_1, e_6), (e_1, e_{12})\}$
$R_6 = \{(e_6, e_7), (e_{12}, e_{13})\}$
$R_7 = \{(e_6, e_8, e_{10}), (e_{12}, e_8, e_{14})\}$
$R_8 = \{(e_6, e_8, e_{11}), (e_{12}, e_8, e_{15})\}$
$R_9 = \{(e_8, e_9)\}$

Fig. 7. Example of an abstract state.

data instances becomes more complex. Thirdly, in defining the standard interpretation of a state description we have presupposed that this mapping can be formally defined. In fact some difficulties could arise which we should better avoid. The meaning of natural language sentences may be ambiguous, the syntax even of elementary predicative natural language sentences is very complex, and the naming of objects is not unique. For example it may be impossible to decide, if two noun phrases denote the same object or not. Fourthly we need a representation of the abstract model, and since the number of imaginable real world states in all reasonable applications will be very high, we cannot represent the abstract model by the set of all abstract states.

We therefore introduce two languages called *l*ogical *d*ata *d*efinition *l*anguage (LDDL) and *l*ogical *d*ata *l*anguage (LDL), which can be used for the unique representation of an abstract model respectively abstract states. A set of LDDL sentences is called a *logical schema* and a set of LDL sentences is called a *logical state description*. These languages then can be used to express the meaning of a schema respectively state of a (physical) data base.

By a logical schema on the one hand a representation of an abstract model is given and on the other hand a set of logical state descriptions which are representations of the abstract states which are elements of this abstract model.

The structure of LDL sentences is similar to the structure of elementary predicative sentences of the state description. They are constructed using entity names, type names and relation names. Both LDDL and LDL are described in Section 4.

The semantics of a logical state description are given by the *interpretation* I_{DB}, a mapping assigning entities to entity names, types to type names, relations to relation names and the value true or false to LDL sentences. The interpretation I_{DB} is discussed in Section 4.4. A formal specification can be found in [30]. Since LDL is a formal language this interpretation can be formally defined. Moreover the names used in LDL are unique so that no ambiguities can arise.

With respect to its semantics LDL possesses the following characteristics:

1. The concepts of the abstract states (i.e. entities, types, relations) are directly expressed in LDL.
2. Different concepts are expressed by different grammatical constructs.
3. All LDL concepts can be interpreted in the abstract states.
4. Concepts of LDL are clearly distinguished from concepts of the abstract states.
5. The representation of abstract states is as "natural" as possible. This means that for example LDL entity names correspond to common language names of the objects from which the entities are abstracted.

None of the data languages proposed in recent years possesses all these characteristics so that we introduce a new language. For example Condition 1 is violated in the entity set model ([10]), since relations are only represented in an indirect fashion, and in [31] where the types must be disjoint. Condition 2 is violated in the relational model ([32]), where a relation may represent an entity as well as a relation of the abstract world state, and in the ANSI/SPARC model, where conceptual records may represent an entity as well as a relation. Condition 3 is violated in the DBTG model [33], since data base keys do not correspond to a concept of the abstract model. Condition 4 is violated in the entity-relationship model [26], since values, which are a concept of the abstract model, are not distinguished from their representation. The rationale for condition 5 follows from the fact that the connection to the real world is given by the state description. If the names of entities do not correspond to object names in the state description, translation rules have to be given for these names, to clarify the intended real world meaning of LDL sentences.

We can now formally define the correctness of a logical state description.

A logical state description LSD is correct with respect to an abstract state, if an interpretation I_{DB} exists, so that all sentences of LSD are mapped to the value *true*, and all LDL sentences which are not contained in LSD are mapped to the value *false*.

A logical schema LS represents an abstract model AM, if for any abstract state AS, which is an element of AM, a logical state description LSD exists, which can be derived from LS and which is correct with respect to AS, and if for any logical state description LSD derivable from LS, an element AS of AM exists so that LSD is correct with respect to AS.

The interrelationship between a logical state description and a state description is given by a translation from LDL sentences into natural language sentences. Since a close correspondence between entity names and noun phrases, and type- and relation names and verb phrases exists, this translation is straightforward. This similarity is used, to tie "real world meaning" to LDL sentences.

3.5 *Syntactical views*

A logical state description is a formal representation of facts. This now will be used to define the semantics of a data base state. As already explained above, a state of a data base is a set of data instances, derived from the data type definitions declared in the schema. From a syntactical point of view data instances are sentences of a formal language, the grammar of which is given by the schema, and by the derivation rules for creating instances from data type definitions. The meaning of these sentences is given by translating them into sets of LDL sentences, the meaning of which is defined as shown in the foregoing sections. In general one data instance is translated into a set of LDL sentences since more than one fact is expressed by a single data instance (see our example of Section 1). An LDL sentence, however, represents a single fact since it is just a formalization of the elementary sentences of a state description.

The translation depends on the grammatical structure of the data instances, which reflects the structure of the corresponding abstract states, i.e. the underlying data model, as well as on the intended meaning of the data base. Therefore it cannot be defined for the different data models and the respective data languages in general it rather must be defined for specific schemas and the corresponding data base states.

The meaning of a data base schema DBS is given by translating it into a logical schema LS, and thereby associating the abstract model represented by LS with DBS. This translation also is the basis for the translation of states derived from DBS to logical state descriptions.

Now we can precisely define, when we consider two data base states derived from different schemas to be equivalent. Two data base states are equivalent if it is possible to translate both into the same logical state description. This means that both represent the same set of facts.

By this definition also a technique for the translation of two data base states, let us say DB_1 and DB_2 with schemas S_1 and S_2, which takes the semantics into account, is given. First one must translate DB_1 into a logical state description, which is always possible if the meaning of the data is known, and afterwards one must construct a state of schema S_2, which can also be translated into this logical state description. The relationship between source and target structures is given by their respective relationship to the same LDL sentences.

Since two data base states, which are equivalent according to our definition, represent the same abstract state and also the same real world state we call them *syntactically different views.* Finally we define, that two data base schemas are equivalent, if they can be translated into the same logical schema. This means they are equivalent, if they represent the same abstract model.

4. THE LOGICAL DATA BASE

In this Section we will give a description of both, LDDL and LDL. Before introducing a syntax for LDDL in Section 4.2, we discuss in Section 4.1 in more detail the characteristics of the abstract model to be expressed by LDDL. In Section 4.3 an example of a schema is given, and finally in Section 4.4 LDL is described.

4.1 *Consistency conditions*

Since we cannot represent the abstract model by the set of representations of all imaginable abstract states, an axiomatic approach is used. In this approach (see also [34]) the abstract model is represented by introducing type names and relation names, and by the specification of axioms, which must hold for any abstract state which is an element of the abstract model to be represented. These axioms are called *consistency conditions,* since they restrict the set of abstract world states to states, which are abstractions of imaginable real world states, i.e. consistent with respect to the users view of the reality. By the consistency conditions the users knowledge of interdependencies between different components of the imaginable real world states is expressed. For example if an object has the property to be female, it cannot be male at the same time. This is expressed by the consistency condition: The types "is male" and "is female" must be disjoint.

Consistency conditions of this kind are called *static consistency conditions* in contrast to *dynamic consistency conditions* (see for example [34, 35]). By dynamic conditions dependencies between abstract states and other (successor) states are expressed. If for example the marital status of a person is represented by the types "is single", "is married", "is widowed" and "is divorced", then an example for a dynamic condition is: An entity which once is an element of the type "is married" can never be an element of the type "is single" again. In the abstract model, as introduced in Section 3.3, only the static aspects of the semantics of data models, i.e. the structure of data base states, are reflected. To deal with the dynamic aspects, i.e. transition between data base states, the model must be changed to contain imaginable sequences of abstract states. The dynamic aspects are needed for the definition of the semantics of data manipulation languages, which will be dealt with in a later paper.

Interdependencies of various state components can only be determined through an investigation of the reality. Therefore formal criteria for their existence and about the ways to produce them cannot be given, and it also will be impossible to prove, that a given set of axioms is complete, that is that only those abstract states are correct which are abstractions of imaginable real world states. Nevertheless if one investigates the examples for consistency conditions given in the literature (see for example [8, 24, 34–39]), it can be seen that only a relatively small number of rules seems to be important.

Most of the above authors formulate the consistency conditions in terms of one special data model. For example in [35] the conditions are classified into domain restrictions and relation restrictions, according to the domains and relations of the relational model. But it will be difficult to translate the conditions formulated in terms of let us say the relational model into conditions formulated in terms of the DBTG model. We therefore formulate the conditions in terms of the abstract model, i.e. entities, types and relations. The transformation of the conditions into different syntactical views of the same abstract model is easily performed, as soon as one knows how entities, types and relations are represented in the respective model. It is important to notice that the conditions formulated in terms of the abstract model are independent of the representation. Some of the conditions given in the following sections therefore are implicitly contained in certain data models. For example in the group schema DIVISION in Fig. 1 of Section 2 the condition is included that a division must have at least zero and at most one name.

4.1.1 *Conditions for types.* A type is a set of entities which is assigned to a property name by the standard interpretation. Since an abstract state must be an abstraction of an imaginable real world state the entities which are elements of a certain type must have some common features according to the intension [20] of the corresponding property name. These features are explained in detail in this section.

4.1.1.1 *Relevant and characteristic types and relations.* A type T_i is called *relevant* to a type T_j (in an abstract model) if in some abstract state, which is element of the abstract model, an entity exists which is element of both types T_i and T_j. Out of this definition follows that, if a type T_i is relevant to a type T_j, T_j is also relevant to T_i. For example, the type "is old" is relevant to the type "is person" and vice versa.

An *n*-ary relation R_i is called *relevant* to a type T_j (in an abstract model), if in some abstract state, which is element of the abstract model, a tuple $(e_1, \ldots, e_n)$ exists, which is an element of the relation R_i, and one of the entities $e_1, \ldots, e_n$ is an element of the type T_j. For example the relation "is spouse of" is relevant to the type "is person". And relation R_i is called relevant to a type T_j in role k (in an abstract model), if in some abstract state, which is element of the abstract model, an entity exists which is an element of the type T_j as well as of the projection of the relation R_i on the kth domain. For example the relation "person owns car" is relevant to the type "is person" in role 1, and to the type "is car" in role 2.

A type T_i is called *characteristic* of a type T_j (in an abstract model), if in all abstract states, which are elements of the abstract model, all entities which are elements of the type T_j are also elements of the type T_i. This definition is reflexive, i.e. a type is characteristic of itself. If the type T_i is characteristic of the type T_j then T_j is a subset of T_i in all abstract states. For example the type "is person" is characteristic of the type "is employee".

A relation R_i is called *characteristic* of a type T_j in role k (in an abstract model), if in all abstract states which are elements of the abstract model the type T_j is a subset of the projection of the relation R_i on the kth domain.

For example the relation "person has birthday" is characteristic of the type "is person" in role 1.

Types and relations, which are relevant to a type T or which are characteristic of a type T, are also called relevant respectively characteristic types or relations of the type T.

The existence of a characteristic relation of a type means, that a dependency between elements of this type and other entities exists which is called *existence dependency*. If for example a binary relation R is characteristic of a type T in role 1, then the existence of an entity e which is element of the type T implies, that an entity e' exists so that the pair (e, e') is an element of the relation R.

In [27] entities are divided into dependent and independent entities, according to this existence dependency. However, this feature of an entity is not stable, since in one abstract state the same entity can be dependent on the existence of another one and in other states it can be independent. Imagine for example an entity of the type "is person", which in some abstract state is also an element of the type "is employee". In this case it is dependent on the existence of an entity of the type "is employer", whereas, if the same person becomes unemployed in another abstract state, the corresponding entity would become independent.

4.1.1.2 *Complete types.* For some types it is known for all abstract states of an abstract model, which entities are elements of that types and which are not. These types are called *complete types.*

Let T_p be the type which is the abstraction of the property p in an abstract state AS. T_p is called complete if in any other state AS' T_p is also the abstraction of the property p. As a consequence of this definition entities may neither be inserted into complete types nor deleted from such types.

Complete types are either defined by axioms or by enumeration. Examples of the first are the types "is integer", "is real", "is string", "is salary" and an example of the latter is the type "is month" = {"january", ..., "december"}. A special subset of the complete types are the *basic types* (for example "is number", "is integer", "is real", "is string"). These types are called basic type since it is assumed that all users agree upon their meaning so that no consistency rules need to be defined for those types. The representation of these types is used as the starting point for the representation of the entities in a data language as will be shown later. In any data language which is used to represent the abstract model, these types are represented by constants. To each of the basic types belongs a set of operations and relations (i.e. the arithmetic operations $+, -, *, /, \ldots$ and the relations $<, >$ to the type "is number"), the meaning of which also is assumed to be known to all users. A basic type together with its relevant operations and relations forms a mathematical structure, which is a triple containing a set of objects (the domain of the structure), a set of operations and a set of relations both defined on the domain.

Some complete types now may be characterized by stating that an isomorphic mapping between a type together with some of its characteristic relations and one of the basic types exists (see also [8]). An example is the type "is salary" together with the relations "sum of salaries" and "difference of salaries" which is defined to be isomorphic to the basic type "is integer" together with addition and subtraction. By stating this isomorphism it is declared, that it is meaningful to add two salaries (the result will also be a salary) but in general that it is not meaningful to add an integer number to a salary, unless a special addition operation between integers and salaries is defined. Since all relations in the abstract model must be defined in the LDDL schema no special axioms for the definition of compatibility of types [35] are needed. Instead the compatibility of types is a consequence of the relation definitions.

4.1.1.3 *The identifying set of a type.* In this section we discuss a semantic feature of types to be expressed by axioms, which later will be seen to be very important for the representation of entities. By the *identifying set* of a type all the types and relations are declared which can be used to uniquely describe entities of a type in contrast to all other entities of the same type. Formally the identifying set is (T) of a type T is defined as follows.

A set of type names and pairs of relation names and numbers

$$(T) = \{T_1, \ldots, T_n, (R_1, i_1), \ldots, (R_m, i_m)\}$$

is called an identifying set of the type T denoted by $is(T)$ if the following conditions are satisfied:

(1) In all abstract states of an abstract model holds: Let e_1 and e_2 be different elements of the type T. Then at least one of the conditions (i) and (ii) must be satisfied.

(i) A type $T_j \in is(T)$ exists so that e_1 is an element of T_j and e_2 is not an element of T_j or vice versa.

(ii) A pair $(R_j, i_j) \in is(T)$ and tuple $r \in R_j$ exists so that $r \cdot i_j = e_1$ and no tuple $r' \in R_j$ exists so that the only difference between r and r' is that $r' \cdot i_j = e_2$ or vice versa.

(2) The set $is(T)$ is *minimal*, i.e. if one of the types $T_1, \ldots, T_n$ or one of the relations $R_1, \ldots, R_m$ is taken off, then condition one is no more satisfied.

Since the first condition must be satisfied in all abstract states, the decision whether a type or a relation is an element of the identifying set cannot be based on formal rules. Rather the declaration of an identifying set is based on the knowledge of the characteristics of the reality which is to be represented.

Examples of identifying sets are given in Fig. 8

Example No.	Type	Identifying Set
1	"is division"	{("division has no", 1)}
2	"is division"	{("division has name", 1)}
3	"activity"	{("activity has act. no", 1), ("division runs activity", 2)}
4	"is person"	{("has name", 1), ("has birthday", 1)}
5	"is company"	{("has reg. no", 1)}
6	"is legal person"	{"is person", "is company", ("has name", 1), ("has birthday", 1), ("has reg. no", 1)}

Fig. 8. Types and identifying sets.

As can be seen from examples 1 and 2 in Fig. 8, for one type several identifying sets may exist. Example 3 shows that several relations may form an identifying set. A legal person is either a company or a natural person. If a legal person is a natural person, it may be identified by its name and birthday, if it is a company it may be identified by its register number.

This concept loosely corresponds to the concept of candidate keys of the relational model. But in contrast to the candidate keys the definition of the identifying sets is not dependent on terms of the representation, it rather is defined in terms of the abstract model. The reader should also notice that every relation which is relevant to a type may be an element of an identifying set of this type. The relations of the abstract model are not divided into those modelling "attributes" which can be used in an identifying set and those modelling "relationships". We also have not required the relations of an identifying set to be functions. For example if we assume, that a person may have several first names and one family name, and that it is impossible, that two persons exist, having the same first names and the same family name, then an identifying set of the type "is person" is given by the set {("has first name", 1) ("has family name", 1)}.

The identifying set of a type can be used to represent the entities in the data language. The representation of elements of a type is reduced to the representation of the entities which are connected to it by relations contained in the identifying set. For this procedure to end, it is necessary, that the elements of some types are represented by constants of the data language.

Two cases exist where a type need not possess an identifying set. The first is, that a type is a basic type or isomorphic to a (subset of a) basic type. In the second case elements of a type are equal with respect to all types and relations, which are contained in the abstract model, i.e. although they are different they are both elements of the same types, and for all relations of which a tuple exists, where one of the two entities is an element, there also exists a tuple, where the other entity is an element. Those entities are called *similar* with respect to the abstract model. Similar entities can occur in an abstract state since in the abstract model only a part of the reality is represented. Therefore it is possible, that two entities are similar although they are abstractions of objects which the user knows to be different. Here difficulties arise with respect to the representation of such entities if only the types and relations of the abstract model are used. This is illustrated by the following example.

Imagine a data base in which information about persons and cars is to be represented. The only relevant relations for the type "is car" are the colour of the car, abstracted by the types "is red", "is blue", ..., the year in which the car was constructed, modelled by a relation "constructed in", defined on the type "is car" and a type "is year", the type of the car, modelled by the types "is Opel", "is Mercedes", ..., and the owner of the car, modelled by a relation "is owner of", defined on the types "is person" and "is car". The relation "is owner of" is many to many, i.e. one person can be owner of several cars and one car can be owned by several persons. Imagine now a real world state, in which a person owns two cars of the type Opel, which were both constructed in 1975 and have the colour blue. The part of the corresponding abstract state which is of importance to our example is shown in Fig. 9.

"is person" = $\{p_1\}$
"has name" = $\{(p_1,$ John Smith")$\}$
"is car" = $\{c_1, c_2\}$
"is blue" = $\{c_1, c_2\}$
"is Opel" = $\{c_1, c_2\}$
"constructed in" = $\{(c_1,$ "1975"), $(c_2,$ "1975")$\}$
"is owner of" = $\{(p_1, c_1), (p_1, c_2)\}$

Fig. 9. An abstract state with two similar entities.

In the abstract state the fact that the cars are different is expressed by the type "is car" containing two entities c_1 and c_2. If we now would represent the entities c_1 and c_2 using all relevant relations and types, we would get for both c_1 and c_2 the representation: "Opel" which is blue, constructed in "1975", owned by "John Smith", i.e. we could not distinguish the two cars. We therefore introduce in this case a special relation "IDENT of car", defined on such types and natural numbers, into the representation, so that the entity c_1 is represented by: "the car 1" and c_2 by "the car 2".

This difficulty seems not to occur in a conceptual representation of the abstract model using a graph (see for example semantic nets[21] or the WEB model[40]), since different entities will be represented by different nodes of the graph and the location (address) in the graph is the differentiating criterion, but we still need a linguistic representation of the abstract model to be able to communicate with the computer. In [14] for all types such an artificial relation is introduced so that any entity is represented by a unique identifier, called surrogate. But thereby the representation of elements of types which possess an identifying set is not as natural as possible, so that the understanding of the real world meaning of the data instances is rendered more difficult than necessary. In our approach artificial identifiers are only used if we are forced to do so by the abstraction process.

4.1.1.4 *Derived types.* The axioms, by which types or relations are defined to be characteristic of a type, are a special case of more complex dependencies between types. For example a type can be a subset of the intersection of other types (the type "is male employee" is the intersection of the types "is male" and "is employee") or an element of a type must either be an element of a type T_1 or an element of a type T_2 (the elements of "is legal person" are either elements of "is person" or of "is company").

We therefore define a *derived* type to be a set of entities which can be defined by means of the set operations union (∪) intersection (∩), and difference (/) out of a set of types and projections of relations on a single domain, and call a derived type T_i to be characteristic of a type T_j, if in all abstract states all elements of T_i are also elements of T_j.

An example for a derived type which is constructed using a type and a relation domain is: The nodes of an acyclic directed graph either possess a predecessor or are a root node, i.e. "is predecessor of". 2∪"is root" is characteristic of "is node".

Between the characteristic types of derived types and those of the types from which it is derived, the following interrelations exist which will be utilized to avoid redundancy in a LDDL schema:

(ch1) If the type T_1 is a subset of the type T_2 then all characteristic types of T_2 are also characteristic of T_1.

(ch2) If the type T_1 is a subset of the intersection of the types t_2 and t_3 then all characteristic types of t_2 *and* t_3 are also characteristic of T_1.

(ch3) If the type T_1 is a subset of the union of the types T_2 and T_3, then holds for all types T_2' and T_3', which are characteristic of T_2 respectively T_3, that $T_2' \cup T_3'$ is characteristic of T_1.

(ch4) If the type T_1 is a subset of the difference of the types T_2 and T_3, then all characteristic types of T_2 are also characteristic of T_1.

Between the identifying sets of a derived type and those types, from which it is derived, the following interrelations exist, which also will be utilized in a LDDL schema:

(id1) If the type T_1 is a subset of the type T_2 and $is(T_2)$ is an identifying set of the type T_2, then either $is(T_2)$ or a subset thereof is an identifying set of T_1.

(id2) If the type T_1 is a subset of the intersection of the types T_2 and T_3, then T_1 is a subset of both T_2 and T_3, and therefore id1 is applicable as well for T_1 and T_2 as for T_1 and T_3.

(id3) If the type T_1 is a subset of the difference of the types T_2 and T_3, then T_1 is a subset of T_2, and therefore (id1) is applicable for T_1 and T_2.

(id4) If a type T_1 is a subset of the union of the types T_2 and T_3 and $is(T_2)$ and $is(T_3)$ are identifying sets of T_2 respectively T_3, then either $\{T_2\} \cup is(T_2) \cup \{T_3\} \cup is(T_3)$ or a subset thereof is an identifying set of T_1.

4.1.2 *Conditions for relations.* An *n*-ary relation is a set of *n*-tuples of entities. By the axioms concerning relations mainly structural characteristics of the relation are expressed, which are known since the relation must be the abstraction of a real world relationship. The most important conditions for relations are the *domain definitions* and the *cardinality restrictions.*

4.1.2.1 *Domain definitions.* By the domain definitions a relation is restricted to subsets of the cartesian product of certain subsets of the set of entities. Several possibilities to define a domain of a relation R exist. The simplest is to state, that the ith domain of R must be a subset of a Type. An example is the relation "division has manager" of the example of chapter one, where the first domain is restricted to the type "is division", and the second domain is restricted to the type "is manager".

It is also possible that a domain of a relation is restricted to a *subset of a type* which is defined by a predicate. An example is the relation "is husband of" defined on subsets of the types "is male person" and "is female person", where the age of the persons must be greater than 18 years.

In general a domain of a relation can be defined to be a *derived type* (see Section 4.1.1) or a specified subset thereof. For example the first domain of the relation "is tax adviser of" is the type "is tax adviser" and the second domain is the union of the types "is person" and "is company". Another example is the relation "income of husband", the first domain of which is the type "is salary", and the second domain is a subset of the first domain of the relation "is husband of", which has been defined above. In case that a domain d_1 of a relation R_1 is defined to be a subset of a domain d_2 of a relation R_2, it is necessary (to avoid cyclic definitions) that d_2 is not itself defined (also not indirectly) to be a subset of d_1. Rather every derived type used in a domain definition must be a subset of a set of entities, which can be defined by means of the set operations union, intersection and difference out of some types.

4.1.2.2 *Cardinality restrictions.* A second kind of axioms to be defined on relations are the *cardinality restrictions* which are a generalization to *n*-ary relations of the notion of cardinality of access functions introduced in [24] for binary relations. Cardinality restrictions are either *minimum restrictions* or *maximum restrictions.* Both are specified for pairs of domain lists of the relation. A domain list of a relation is a list of natural numbers which are less or equal to the degree of the relation.

Let R_i be a relation, l_1 and l_2 domain lists of R_i, (l_1, l_2) the concatenation of l_1 and l_2. and n_{min} and n_{max} natural numbers with $0 \leq n_{min} \leq n_{max}$. Then the cardinality restriction with lower bound n_{min} and upper bound n_{max} holds for the domain lists l_1 and l_2, if the condition

$$(\forall r' \in R_i \cdot l_1)(n_{min} \leq |\{r;\, r \in R_i \cdot (l_1, l_2) \wedge r \cdot l_1 = r'\}| \leq n_{max})$$

holds in all abstract states.

Cardinality restrictions are defined for the entities which actually are elements of a domain of a relation, and not for the type of which the domain is a subset. One should also notice, that they must hold for every abstract state of the abstract model, that means that knowledge of the reality is expressed, so that they cannot be derived by analyzing a special abstract state.

A special case of cardinality restrictions are the *functional dependencies.* A functional dependency between two domain lists of a relation is a cardinality restriction where $n_{min} = n_{max} = 1$.

Some authors state, that functional dependencies exist between types *per se* (see, e.g. [41]). But they only exist within certain relations, since it is possible, that with respect to different relations between the same type in one case a functional dependency exists, whereas in a second case nó functional dependency exists, as can be seen in the following example. In the relation "has birthday" exists a functional dependency between the types "person" and "date", whereas in the relation "is wedding day of" a functional dependency between those types does not exist.

4.1.2.3 *Other conditions for relations.* In this section we only summarize some more relevant conditions. A more detailed description and examples may be found in [30].

Analogous to the complete types and derived types in Sections 4.1.1.2 and 4.1.1.4 *complete relations* and *derived relations* can be defined via consistency conditions. A relation may be the *projection, permutation* or *inverse* of another relation. Relations may be *symmetric, transitive* or a relation may be the *product* of two other relations.

4.1.3 *Other consistency conditions.* Since the consistency conditions reflect the users view of the reality, and since they are only representations of empirical laws, the set of axioms described in Sections 4.1.1 and 4.1.2 certainly is not complete. We have only mentioned those conditions, which reflect essential characteristics of the types and relations, i.e. common features of all entities, which are elements of a type, respectively all tuples, which are elements of a relation, and therefore should be made part of the declarations of types and relations in the LDL schema.

Another reason for restricting ourselves to the above conditions is that by them all conditions which are implicitly contained in the data models proposed in the literature are explicitly expressed. There are many examples of other kinds of consistency conditions, but they are not integrated into the different data definition languages.

Some authors propose to develop special user oriented languages ([36, 42]), or to use data manipulate languages ([35, 38]), to express consistency conditions. In general a static consistency condition is a predicate which must be satisfied by the abstract states. It therefore can be formulated by an expression of a general predicate calculus, in which constants and variables denoting entities, types and relations are used. A general language for expressing consistency conditions therefore will always be only a reformulation of the predicate calculus. Even if in some special cases a special language will be easier to understand for a user there will always be conditions, where one is forced to use a predicate calculus, or which cannot be expressed by a special consistency language.

4.2 *The logical data definition language*

A data definition language is a formal language, the sentences of which are called *schema entries,* and a set of schema entries is called a *schema.* The schema of a data base has a twofold purpose. Firstly it is a representation of the abstract model. We therefore distinguish in LDDL between three kinds of schema entries, i.e. type declarations, relation declarations and consistency conditions. The second purpose of a schema is to define the set of (syntactically) correct data base states, i.e. it must be specified in a schema, how the data instances can be derived. Therefore within a type declaration it must be defined, how the entities of this type are to be represented in the logical data language.

In developing LDDL we tried to meet three main goals.

(1) The meaning of schema entries with respect to the abstract model should be easy to understand.

(2) The consistency conditions for types and relations mentioned in Sections 4.1.1 and 4.1.2 are to be integrated within the type and relation declarations.

(3) Redundancy is avoided.

A complete specification of the syntax and semantics is given in [30].

4.2.1 *Type declarations.* In the following we assume that the basic types are "NUMBER", "INTEGER", "REAL", "STRING", "CHARACTER", "DIGIT", "LETTER" and "SIGN", which are defined together with the usual ordering relations and functions, and need not be defined explicitly in the schema. In general a type declaration has the form

⟨type definition⟩[⟨characteristics⟩]
[⟨identification⟩]
[⟨comment⟩]

Throughout the following section we enclose nonterminals in brackets ⟨ ⟩. The square brackets [ ] indicate that the enclosed clauses are optimal. Before we explain the different clauses we first introduce a concept which is useful to avoid redundancies in the schema.

4.2.1.1 *The nucleus of types.* Let BT be the set of basic types and T' the set of all types which are not basic types. A special subset of T' is called a *nucleus of types* of an abstract model (NOT) and the elements *nucleus types* if the following conditions hold:

(1) In all abstract states of the abstract model holds

$$\bigcup_{b \in BT} bt \cap \bigcup_{n \in NOT} nt = \phi$$

(2) In all abstract states of the abstract model holds

$$\bigcup_{t \in BT \cup NOT} t = \bigcup_{t \in T} t$$

(3) There do not exist two different nucleus types T_1 and T_2, so that for all abstract states T_1 is a subset of T_2.

The condition assures that all types which are neither nucleus types nor basic types may be derived from nucleus types or basic types. Therefore a representation for all entities exists, if a representation for the nucleus types and basic types is given.

Since all three conditions must hold in all abstract states, the nucleus of types of an abstract model cannot be formally derived. We did not include the definition of the nucleus of types into the consistency conditions since it is defined for the purpose of representation and not to assure the consistency of the abstract model.

4.2.1.2 *The type definition clause.* In the type definition clause a type name is introduced together with a description of the elements of the type. We distinguish several cases which are explained in the following. A type may be a basic type, a nucleus type or a derived type. If the type to be defined is a nucleus type, it may either be extensionally or intensionally defined. In the first case it may be defined by enumeration or by an isomorphism to a (subset of) a basic complete type. If the type to be defined is a derived type, it may also be either intensionally defined or extensionally defined. In the second case it may be defined by a predicate or by enumeration. In Fig. 10 the different cases are illustrated.

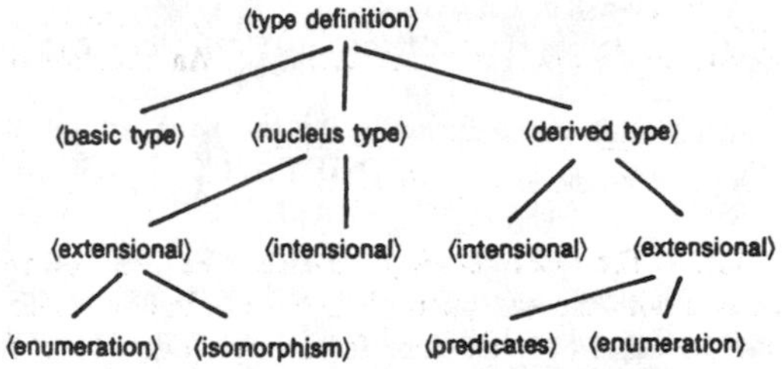

Fig. 10. The different type definition clauses.

The format of the type declaration clause for a basic type is

basic ⟨type name⟩ [*relations* ⟨basic rel op list⟩]
[*functions* ⟨basic func op list⟩].

By this declaration a name of a basic type is introduced together with the relations and functions defined for this type. It is assumed, that the meaning of this type and the relations and functions belonging to it are known, so that a further description is not necessary.

An example is the declaration

basic INTEGER *relations* <, ≤, ≥, >
functions +, −, *, /, **.

The format of a type declaration clause for a nucleus type, defined by enumeration is

type ⟨type name⟩ *elements* ⟨entity repr list⟩

⟨entity repr list⟩ is a sequence of entity instances, as they are explained in Section 4.4.

An example is

type MONTH *elements* january,
february, . . ., december.

Nucleus types, which are isomorphic to a basic type, are declared by

type ⟨type name⟩ *isomorphic to* ⟨set definition⟩
[⟨rel clause⟩] [⟨func clause⟩]
⟨set definition⟩:: = ⟨type name⟩ [*where* ⟨predicate⟩]|
{⟨entity repr list⟩}
⟨rel clause⟩:: = *relations* ⟨rel op pair list⟩|
relations nil
⟨rel op pair list⟩:: = ⟨rel op pair⟩, ⟨rel op pair list⟩|
⟨rel op pair⟩
⟨rel op pair⟩:: = (⟨basic rel op⟩, ⟨defined rel op⟩)
⟨functions⟩:: = *functions* ⟨function def list⟩|
functions nil
⟨function def list⟩:: = ⟨function def⟩, ⟨function def list⟩|
⟨function def⟩
⟨function def⟩:: = ⟨func op pair⟩|⟨function definition⟩
⟨func op pair⟩:: = (⟨basic func op⟩, ⟨defined func op⟩)
⟨function definition⟩:: = ⟨defined func op⟩:
⟨type product⟩ → ⟨type name⟩
⟨type product⟩:: = ⟨type name⟩ × ⟨type product⟩|
⟨type name⟩.

The type is defined to be either isomorphic to a basic type or a subset thereof, which is defined by the predicate expression of the *where* clause, or by the set defined by ⟨entity repr list⟩. Through the relations resp. functions clause is declared, which relations and functions defined for the basic type are also defined for the new type. If the relations respectively functions clause is not specified, all relations respectively functions declared for the basic type are also declared to be defined for the new type. If the second alternative is used, none of the relations or functions declared for the basic type is also defined for the new type.

With the list of relation operators it is possible, to introduce new denotations for the relations of the basic type. The newly introduced relation operator denotes a relation, which is defined for the new type so that the isomorphism holds.

With a function definition it is possible, to introduce function operators. For relation operators and function operators declared through these clauses infix notation is used to preserve inside of the predicate expressions a more natural notation. As we will see a prefix notation is used for the relations introduced with a relation declaration in the schema.

Examples are

type FIRST NAME *isomorphic to* STRING
functions nil
type COUNTRY NAME *isomorphic to* STRING
where length $(x) \leq 20$
functions nil
type SALARY *isomorphic to* REAL
where $100 * x \in$ INTEGER
relations ($<$, less than),
($>$, greater than)
functions (+, +), (−, −), $*$:
SALARY × REAL → SALARY.

In the first type declaration a type FIRST NAME is defined, which is isomorphic to the basic type STRING. The type COUNTRY NAME is isomorphic to a subset of the type STRING. Whereas the concatenation of two strings is a meaningful operation, by which another string is produced, it is not meaningful to concatenate first names and country names. Free variables inside a predicate in the where-clause are assumed to denote elements of the corresponding basic types, and to be bound by an universal quantifier. For the type SALARY the ordering relations are renamed and the function clause declares that addition and subtraction are defined the same as for the real numbers. Multiplication and division are not meaningful operations for salaries and therefore not declared. Instead a special multiplication operation between salaries and real numbers is defined, the result of which is a salary.

The form of an intensional definition of a nucleus type is

type ⟨type name⟩,

i.e. by the declaration only a type name is introduced. Examples are

type PERSON
type DIVISION
type MACHINE.

Intensionally defined derived types are declared by

type ⟨type name⟩ *subset of* ⟨complex set⟩
[⟨qualification⟩]
⟨complex set⟩:: = ⟨type name⟩|
(⟨complex set⟩ ∪ ⟨complex set⟩)|
(⟨complex set⟩/⟨complex set⟩)
⟨qualification⟩:: = *where* ⟨predicate⟩.

The declaration of types, which are used in the complex set clause, must be reducible to nucleus types so that cyclic definitions cannot occur.

Examples are

type LEGAL UNIT *subset of*
(PERSON ∪ COMPANY)

where it is assumed that persons exist which have not the status of legal units (for example children),

type PRESIDENT *subset of* PERSON
type MEMBER OF PARLIAMENT
subset of PERSON
where $(\jmath y)$ (IS AGE OF $(y, x)) \geq$ AGE (25)

i.e. members of parliament must be persons which are older than 25 years. By j we denote the designation operator of predicate logic.

Extensionally defined derived types, which are to be defined using a predicate, are declared by

type ⟨type name⟩ *equal to* ⟨complex set⟩ ⟨qualification⟩.

In contrast to the subset declaration, here all entities, which are described by the complex set and qualification clauses, are also elements of the declared type. Examples are

type OF AGE *equal to* PERSON *where*
$(\jmath y)$ (IS AGE OF $(y, x)) \geq$ AGE (18)
type EVEN NUMBER *equal to* INTEGER *where*
$(\exists y)\ (x = 2 * y)$
type MALE EMPLOYEE *equal to*
EMPLOYEE ∩ MALE.

The last form of the type definition clause for derived types is

type ⟨type name⟩ *elements* ⟨entity repr list⟩ *of*
⟨type name⟩.

Different from the declaration of a nucleus type all elements of the entity list must be elements of a nucleus type. Therefore a derived type defined by enumeration always is a subset of some other type. An example is

type SUMMER MONTH *elements*
June, July, August *of* MONTH.

4.2.1.3 *The characteristic clause.* Like all other clauses with the exception of the type definition clause this clause is optional since for example characteristic types or relations need not exist for nucleus types which are defined by enumeration. Also for a derived type which is a subset of a nucleus type no other characteristics need exist than those of the type which it is derived from.

The characteristic clause has the form

characteristics ⟨char expr list⟩

where a characteristic expression is a predicate which is constructed according to the rules

⟨char expr⟩:: = ⟨elem char expr⟩|
(⟨char expr⟩ ∨ ⟨char expr⟩)|
(⟨char expr⟩ + ⟨char expr⟩)|
¬(⟨char expr⟩)
⟨elem char expr⟩:: = ⟨type name⟩|
⟨relation name⟩|
⟨relation name⟩.⟨integer⟩.

The logical connector + is used to denote the exclusive or, i.e. if $T_1 + T_2$ is characteristic of a type T, then the elements of T must be either elements of T_1 or elements of T_2 but not both. All elements to the list of characteristic expressions are assumed to be connected by the logical "and", so that we do not need this connector for the construction of characteristic expressions. Furthermore it is assumed that types are disjoint, unless the contrary is explicitly stated in the schema—this may be a consequence of the type definition clause or the characteristic clause. Therefore it must not be stated explicitly, that the elements of a type are not also elements of some other type. If a characteristic relation of a type is relevant for this type in one role only, then the relation name alone can be used in a characteristic expression, otherwise the qualified form must be used. Examples are

Characteristics MALE + FEMALE, HAS SOCIAL SEC #,
HAS NAME, HAS BIRTHDAY, HAS ADDRESS

which is the characteristics clause of the type PERSON

characteristics HAS MACH #.

which is the characteristic clause of the type MACHINE

characteristics MARRIED WITH. 1

which is the characteristics clause of the type HUSBAND which is defined to be a subset of the type PERSON, so that all characteristics of the type PERSON also are characteristics of the type HUSBAND and need not be explicitly stated.

characteristics HAS VALUE IN CURRENCY

which is the characteristic clause of the type SALARY, where HAS VALUE IN CURRENCY is a ternary relation between salaries, real numbers and currency designations (i.e. $, DM, ...).

The first example states that persons must be either male or female and that every person must possess a social security #, a name, an age and an address.

4.2.1.4 *The identification clause.* The identification clause has the form

identified by ⟨id set list⟩

where

⟨id set⟩:: = {⟨set specification list⟩}
⟨set specification⟩:: = ⟨type name⟩|
⟨rel specification⟩|
one of ⟨rel specification⟩
⟨rel specification⟩:: = ⟨relation name⟩|
⟨relation name⟩.⟨integer⟩.

The form *one of* ⟨rel specification⟩ is used, if in the identifying set of a type T_i a pair (R_j, i_j) is contained, so that in the relation R_j the i_jth domain is functional dependent of all other domains but not vice versa.

An example is given below. The identification clause also is used to specify, how the elements of a type are represented in LDL. For that purpose we introduce the convention, that the first element of the list of identifying sets is used for the representation of the elements of the type, if the type declared is a nucleus type *and* intensionally defined. As will be shown in Section 4.4 this is sufficient for a nonredundant representation of the abstract states in LDL. To avoid cycles in the representation of entities, the identifying set used for the representation may not contain a relation which is to hold between elements of the type to be represented, or involve entities which themselves are identified by elements of the type to be represented.

Examples are

identified by {HAS DIVISION}, {HAS NAME}

which is the identification clause of the type DIVISION,

identified by {HAS SOCIAL SEC #},
{HAS NAME, HAS BIRTHDAY}

which is the identification clause of the type PERSON and

identified by one of HAS VALUE IN CURRENCY

which is the identification clause of the type SALARY, i.e. a salary is uniquely identified by a pair (value, currency). For example the pair (1000 DM) denotes the same salary as the pair (400 $) if we assume that one mark is equivalent to 0.4 dollars. Divisions are represented by division numbers, persons by social sec. numbers and salaries by pairs of values and currencies.

4.2.1.5 *The comment clause.* The last clause of the type declaration provides the users with a better understanding of the meaning of the type. But the comments are not considered to be consistency conditions to be taken into account by the interpretation of the schema.

The form of the comment clause is

comment/ * ⟨*string*⟩ * /.

An example is the following comment which may be part of the declaration of a type PRESIDENT:

comment/ * The elements of this type are the presidents of the United States * /.

Another example is

comment/ * Persons making more than 1,000,000 $ per year */

which may be part of the declaration of a type RICH PERSON.

4.2.2 *Relation declarations.* By a relation declaration a relation name together with the definition of its domains and of special consistency conditions is introduced. The general form is given by

relation ⟨relation name⟩ [⟨domain declaration⟩]
[⟨consistency constraints⟩]
[⟨comment⟩]

In the following sections we describe the domain declarations and consistency conditions. The comment clause is equal to that of the type declaration in Section 4.2.1.5.

4.2.2.1 *The domain declaration.* The domains of a relation can be defined to be any derived type whereby domains of other relations may also be used. The form of the cause is given by

domains ⟨domain def list⟩

where

⟨domain def⟩:: = *equal to* ⟨set expr⟩ [*where* ⟨predicate⟩]|
⟨subset expr⟩ [*where* ⟨predicate⟩]
⟨set expr⟩:: = ⟨elem set expr⟩|
(⟨set expr⟩ ∩ ⟨set expr⟩)|
(⟨set expr⟩ ∪ ⟨set expr⟩)|
(⟨set expr⟩/⟨set expr⟩)
⟨elem set expr⟩:: = ⟨type name⟩|
⟨relation name⟩ . ⟨integer⟩
⟨subset expr⟩:: = ⟨set expr⟩.

We assume that by the ordering of the domain definitions the ordering of the elements of the tuples of the relation is defined. For this reason it is not necessary to introduce role names [32]. The unqualified form of the domain definition specifies, that the projection of the relation on the corresponding domain is equal to the type described by the set expression whereas in the qualified form it must be equal to the subset of the type defined by the predicate expression. Examples are

relation DIV HAS NAME *domains equal to*
DIVISION, DIVISION-NAME
relation PERSON HAS NAME *domains equal to*
PERSON, NAME
relation HAS TAX ADVISER *domains*
(PERSON ∪ COMPANY), PERSON
relation IS MARRIED TO *domains* MALE
where (jy) (IS AGE OF (y, x)) ≥ AGE (18)
FEMALE
where (jy) (IS AGE OF (y, x)) ≥ AGE (16).

The last example expresses that male persons are only allowed to marry, if they are older than 18 years, whereas female persons are allowed to marry, if they are older than 16 years.

4.2.2.2 The consistency clause. The form of the consistency clause is

⟨condition list⟩

where

⟨condition list⟩:: = ⟨condition⟩ ⟨condition list⟩|
⟨condition⟩

⟨condition⟩:: = *func dep on* ⟨integer list list⟩|
⟨occurrence restrictions⟩|
product of ⟨relation name⟩,
⟨relation name⟩|
union of ⟨relation name list⟩|
inverse of ⟨relation name⟩|
subset of ⟨relation name⟩ . ⟨integer list⟩|
symmetric|
transitive
⟨occurrence restrictions⟩:: = *restricted by* ⟨integer list⟩
⟨integer list⟩ *min* ⟨integer⟩
max ⟨integer⟩
⟨integer list list⟩:: = (⟨integer list⟩), ⟨integer list list⟩|
(⟨integer list⟩).

Since we demand, that all sentences of the state description are elementary ones, the relations of the abstract model are irreducible [14]. If a functional dependency exists at all within a relation, then one domain of the relation must be functional dependent on all other domains, otherwise the relation could be split up into several irreducible relations. Therefore it is sufficient to define in the first clause only the list of attributes, on which the relation is functional dependent. In the occurrence restriction clause the restriction is defined between the first and the second attribute list specified in the clause. In case of specifying the *inverse of* clause in a relation declaration, no other clauses may be specified, since these clauses are specified in the declaration of the inverse relation.

By means of the *subset of* clause it is possible to define, that one relation is a subset of the projection of another relation on the specified domain list, whereby also permutations of the domains can be described. Examples are

relation DIV HAS NAME *func dep on* (1), (2)
relation IS GRANDFATHER OF *product of*
IS FATHER OF, HAS CHILD
relation HAS NAME *union of* DIV HAS NAME,
PERSON HAS NAME
relation IS NAME OF *inverse of* HAS NAME.

4.2.3 *Declaration of consistency conditions.* Besides of the general consistency conditions only one category of the consistency conditions introduced in Section 4.1 has not been discussed so far with the other parts of LDDL. This is the definition of the relevant types of a type. We did not incorporate this definition into the type declaration because it is a symmetric condition, that is if a type T_1 is relevant to a type T_2 then T_2 is also relevant to the type T_1, and no reasons exist, to include the definition into the declaration of one of the types and not into the declaration of the other. To avoid redundancy in the schema, we therefore introduce a separate consistency condition.

As explained in Section 4.1.3 general consistency conditions must be expressed by predicate calculus expressions and we do not suggest a special syntax for the formulation of general conditions.

So we have for the form of consistency conditions

⟨consistency condition⟩:: = ⟨relevance def⟩|
⟨general expression⟩
⟨relevance def⟩:: = *relevant* (⟨type name list⟩)

Through this clause the intersection of the types, which are specified in the type name list, is declared not to be empty in all abstract states.

An example is

relevant (IS GERMAN, MALE, PERSON).

This clause expresses that in some abstract states persons exist, which are Germans as well as male.

4.3 *An example schema*

In this Section we give an example of a LDDL-schema. The example is part of a presidential data base which can be found in [6]. In Fig. 11 an informal definition in terms of flat files and attributes is given.

The data base contains information about presidents and candidates for the presidency of the United States.

The type section of the LDDL schema is given in Fig. 12 and the relation section in Fig. 13.

At the first sight the LDDL schema seems to be much more complex than the flat file schema. This is only the consequence of expressing explicitly semantic knowledge in the LDDL schema, which is implicitly contained in the flat file schema. In the LDDL schema is clearly stated, what kinds of objects and relationships are modelled. For example the PRESIDENT-MARRIAGE file represents three relations (MARRIED WITH, MARRIED ON, HAS CHILDREN WITH), whereas the PRESIDENT file represents the entities of the type president together with a part of its characteristic relations, since the relation HAS OCCUPANCY is represented in a special file. In the flat file schema it is not described that the attribute "FATHER OF PRESIDENT" only contains the father's name, and not a unique identifier for the president's father. Further constraints which are not expressed in the flat file schema are for example, that the value set of the attribute WINNER NAME of the file ELECTION must be equal to the value set of the attribute PRESIDENT NAME in the president file, and that a president need not be married, so that the value set of the attribute

```
PRESIDENT                 PRESIDENT-OCCUPATION
   PRESIDENT-NAME            PRESIDENT-NAME
   DATE-OF-BIRTH             OCCUPATION
   PARTY
   FATHER-OF-PRES
   MOTHER-OF-PRES
                          PRESIDENT-MARRIAGE
                             PRESIDENT-NAME
                             WIFE-NAME
                             DATE-OF-MARRIAGE
                             NO-OF-CHILDREN

ELECTION                  CANDIDATES
   ELECTION-YEAR             ELECTION-YEAR
   WINNER-NAME               CANDIDATE-NAME
                             CANDIDATE-PARTY
                             VOTES-FOR-CANDIDATE
```

Fig. 11. Schema of a Presidential Data Base (underlined fields are collective identifiers).

```
basic STRING relations <, >
             functions length
basic INTEGER relations <, ≤, ≥, >
              functions +, −, *, /
type CANDIDATE
     characteristics HAS NAME, CANDIDATE IN, GOT VOTES IN,
        CANDIDATE OF
     identified by {HAS NAME, CANDIDATE IN}
     comment/*Persons who ran for president of the United States*/
type NAME
     isomorphic to STRING where length (x) ≤ 20
     functions nil
     comment/*Names are person names*/
type ELECTION
     characteristics IN YEAR, CANDIDATE IN, GOT VOTES IN, WINNER OF
     identified by {IN YEAR}, {WINNER OF}
type VOTES subset of INTEGER
           where (0 ≤ x ∧ x < 700)
     comment/*number of votes in electoral college*/
type PARTY elements PEOPLE, DEMOCRATIC, REPUBLICAN
type YEAR isomorphic to INTEGER
          where 1700 ≤ x
type PRESIDENT subset of CANDIDATE
     characteristics IS BORN ON, HAS FATHER, HAS MOTHER,
                     HAS OCCUPANCY, WINNER OF
     identified by {HAS NAME}
type DATE isomorphic to INTEGER functions nil
     characteristics MONTH OF, DAY OF, YEAR OF
     identified by {MONTH OF, DAY OF, YEAR OF}
type DAY isomorphic to INTEGER where (1 ≤ x ∧ x ≤ 31)
type MONTH isomorphic to INTEGER where (1 ≤ x ∧ x ≤ 12)
type OCCUPATION isomorphic to STRING where length (x) ≤ 60
type NO OF CHILDREN subset of INTEGER where (0 ≤ x ∧ x ≤ 20)
```

Fig. 12. The type section of the LDDL schema.

```
relation HAS NAME
        domains CANDIDATE, NAME
        func dep on (1)
relation CANDIDATE IN
        domains CANDIDATE, ELECTION
relation GOT VOTES IN
        domains CANDIDATE, VOTES, ELECTION
        func dep on (1, 3)
relation CANDIDATE OF
        domains CANDIDATE, PARTY
        func dep on (1)
relation IN YEAR
        domains ELECTION, YEAR
        func dep on (1)
relation WINNER OF
        domains PRESIDENT, ELECTION
        func dep on (2)
relation IS BORN ON
        domains PRESIDENT, DATE
        func dep on (1)
relation HAS FATHER
        domains PRESIDENT, NAME
        func dep on (1)
        comments/*relation between presidents and names
        of father*/
relation HAS MOTHER
        domains PRESIDENT, NAME
        func dep on (1)
relation HAS OCCUPANCY
        domains PRESIDENT, OCCUPANCY
        comments/*The relation is many to many*/
relation MONTH OF
        domains MONTH, DATE
        func dep on (2)
relation DAY OF
        domains DAY, DATE
        func dep on (2)
relation YEAR OF
        domains YEAR, DATE
        func dep on (2)
relation MARRIED WITH
        domains equal to MARRIED ON. 1, equal to MARRIED ON. 2
        HAS CHILDREN WITH. 1, 3
relation MARRIED ON
        domains PRESIDENT, NAME, DATE
        func dep on (1, 2), (1, 3)
relation HAS CHILDREN WITH
        domains MARRIED ON. 1, NO OF CHILDREN, MARRIED ON. 2
        func dep on (1, 3)
        restricted by (1) (2, 3) min 1 max 3
```

Fig. 13. The relation section of the LDDL schema.

PRESIDENT-NAME of the file PRESIDENT-MARRIAGE must be a subset of the value set of the attribute PRESIDENT-NAME in the PRESIDENT file. From the example schema it can also be seen, that the LDDL schema may be less redundant than the flat file schema. Since the type PRESIDENT is declared to be a subset of the type CANDIDATE, all characteristics of the type CANDIDATE are also characteristic of the type PRESIDENT, and therefore we need not define the relation between presidents and their party twice, as is done in the flat file schema by the attributes PARTY of the PRESIDENT file and the attribute CANDIDATE-PARTY of the file CANDIDATE.

4.4 *The logical data language* LDL

In this chapter we give a description of the logical data language LDL which is used to represent states of the abstract model. LDL is a formal language the grammar of which is derived from the schema and the derivation rules discussed below. To avoid too much details, we will not give a complete syntax description in this paper but rather will discuss the main principles of the language and give enough examples to allow the reader to get some understanding of the language. The complete description may be found in [30].

Sentences of LDL are either *property instances* or *relation instances*, i.e. and LDL sentence either expresses than an entity is an element of a type, i.e. the corresponding object possesses the property of which the type is an abstraction, or that a tuple of entities is an element of a relation, i.e. the relationship of which the relation is an abstraction holds between the corresponding objects. A LDL data base state is a set of property instances and relation instances which is derived from a LDDL schema, using the type and relation definitions and the consistency rules. The third fundamental notion of LDL are the *entity instances*, which are the representations of entities. To avoid redundancies and difficulties for the correct interpretation of LDL states onto abstract states, every entity should be represented only by exactly one entity instance. In this case for each fact of the real world model exactly one representation by a property instance or relation instance will exist, and it also will be known that two different property- or relation instances will represent different facts. If we introduce different representations for the elements of different types, whereby for example the type name is used within the representation, we obviously cannot avoid to get different representations for the same entity, since the types need not be disjoint. We therefore introduce representations using the type name only for the elements of the nucleus types, whereas the representation of entities belonging to derived types is reduced to the former. Still for every entity at least one representation exists, since every derived type must be by definition a subset of the union of some nucleus types and basic types, and different representations of the same entity can only exist, if it belongs to several nucleus types. We accept this possibility of double representations, to avoid too complex rules for the representation of entities.

Before we introduce the form of property instances and relation instances, we must first discuss the form of entity instances. We start with the elements of the basic types, which are represented by constants.

Examples are the integers

$$-10{,}000, -99, 0, 10, 100{,}000$$

and the strings

xxxxx, +*, HOUSE, MARY-POPPINS.

Nucleus types, which are isomorphic to a basic type and for which an identification clause is not declared, are represented by entity instances of the form

⟨type name⟩ (⟨const⟩)

where ⟨const⟩ must be a representation of an element of the corresponding basic type.

An example is

NAME (WILSON)

which is an entity instance of the type NAME in Fig. 12. For nucleus types defined by axioms or enumeration the representation is already defined in the type declaration clause. For all other nucleus types the identification clause is declared, except for those for which entities similar with respect to the abstract model exist. Elements of these types are represented by entity instances of the form

⟨type name⟩ (⟨integer⟩).

Examples are

car (1), car (2)

which are element of the type CAR as explained in Section 4.1.1.

If the identification clause is declared within the declaration of a type, the first specified identifying set is used for the representation of the elements of this type. A general form of an entity instance is

⟨entity instance⟩:: = ⟨type name⟩ (⟨descriptor list⟩)

where

⟨descriptor list⟩:: = ⟨descriptor⟩, ⟨descriptor list⟩|
⟨descriptor⟩
⟨descriptor⟩:: = ⟨type name⟩|
⟨relation name⟩ (⟨instance list⟩)|
⟨relation name⟩ {⟨instance list list⟩}
⟨instance list⟩:: = ⟨instance⟩, ⟨instance list⟩|⟨instance⟩
⟨instance list list⟩:: = (instance list), ⟨instance list list⟩|
(⟨instance list⟩)
⟨instance⟩:: = ⟨entity instance⟩| *

In the descriptor list the names of the types relevant for the entity to be represented and relation instances of the relevant relations are listed in the same sequence in which they are declared in the identifying clause. The entity to be represented is replaced in these relation instances by the symbol *. The form ⟨relation name⟩ {⟨instance list list⟩} is used if the entity to be represented can be element of several tuples of the relation and the *one of* form is not used for this relation in the declaration of the identifying set.

Examples of this general form of entity instances are

ELECTION (IN YEAR (*, YEAR (1916)))
CANDIDATE (HAS NAME (*, NAME (WILSON)),
CANDIDATE IN (*, ELECTION (IN YEAR
(*, YEAR (1916)))))
DATE (MONTH OF (8, *), DAY OF (8, *), YEAR
OF (1780, *)

which are entity instances of the types ELECTION and CANDIDATE of the schema of Fig. 12

Another example is

PERSON (HAS FIRST NAME
{(*, HANS), (*, JOCHEN)},
HAS FAMILY NAME (*, SCHNEIDER))

which is an entity instance of the type PERSON explained in Section 4.1.1.

By the following rules a simplification for the representation of entities is brought about

(i) the * is omitted.

(ii) If the identifying set contains only characteristic relations, then the names of the relations in the entity instance are omitted.

(iii) If a domain of a relation is defined to be a subset of a single (nucleus) type, then the type name is omitted in the relation instances.

Using these simplifications the above entity instances then are changed to

ELECTION ((1916))
CANDIDATE ((WILSON), (1916))
PERSON ({(HANS), (JOCHEN)}, (SCHNEIDER)).

The general form of property instances now is

⟨type name⟩ (⟨entity instance⟩)

where ⟨entity instance⟩ must be the representation of an entity of a type for which the type name is relevant.

Examples are

PRESIDENT (CANDIDATE (CLEVELAND), (1892)))

or in the simplified form

PRESIDENT ((CLEVELAND), (1892)).

This is the LDL representation of the fact, that the person CLEVELAND which ran for president in 1892 was one of the presidents of the United States.

Finally the general form of relation instances is given by

⟨relation name⟩ (⟨instance list⟩).

Examples are

CANDIDATE OF (((CLEVELAND), (1892)),
(DEMOCRATIC))

or

IS BORN ON ((WASHINGTON), ((2), (22), (1732))).

If a domain of a relation is defined to be a subset of a derived type, then for this domain of the relation instance an entity instance of one of the types, from which the type is derived, is-introduced. The only exception arises, if the derived type possesses an identifying set, which is a subset of the identifying set of the type, from which it is derived. In this case only the subset is used, as can be seen from the above example of an instance of the relation IS BORN ON, where the president is represented by his name only.

Finally we explain the interpretation I_{DB} of a logical state description, i.e. a state of the logical data base with respect to an abstract state.

Type names are mapped to types, relation names are mapped to relations and an entity representation is mapped to an entity, whereby the interpretation of the type names and relation names in the identifying set of the type of which an entity is an element is taken into account.

A property instance, let us say "type" ("entity") is mapped to the value *true*, if I ("entity") $\in I$("type") holds and a relation instance, let us say "relation" ("entity-1", ..., "entity-*n*") is mapped to the value *true*, if (I ("entity-1"), ..., I ("entity-*n*")) $\in I$ ("relation") holds.

5. CONCLUSION

In this paper we have explained a logical frame, within which the semantics of the data in a database can be treated. We have shown, that it is not possible to give a completely formal description of the semantics of a specific data base system in contrast to programming languages, since the reality must be taken into account and one rather must rely on a common understanding of natural languages. This is in contrast to the area of programming languages where completely formal semantics can be given. But with respect to an abstract model the semantics of a data base can be formally defined as shown in [11] and [12].

With respect to the investigations on the equivalence of databases two major areas of work can be seen.

(1) To investigate changing abstract models, one has to derive rules to determine whether two abstract models describe the same slice of reality. These rules can only be based on empirical knowledge but the concepts introduced in this paper should give important guidance to this work.

(2) To define the equivalence of different representations, it is necessary to define precise translation rules between different representations of the same abstract world model. In this paper we have introduced the semantic primitives on which these translations can be based, since LDDL and LDL can be used as a normal form for data representations in the translation process.

REFERENCES

[1] J. P. Fry, R. L. Frank and F. A. Hershey, III: A developmental model for data translation. *Proc. ACM SIGMOD Conference*, Denver, Colorado (Nov. 1972).

[2] S. B. Navathe and J. P. Fry: Restructuring for large data bases: three levels of abstraction. *ACM Trans. on Data Base Systems* 1, 1 (Mar. 1976).

[3] N. C. Shu, B. C. Housel and V. Y. Lum: CONVERT: A high level translation definition language for data conversion. *IBM Res. Rep. RJ* 151 (Feb. 1975).

[4] ANSI/X3/SPARC, Study group on data base management systems: *Interim Report, ANSI* 75-02-08.

[5] G. M. Nijssen: A gross architecture for next generation DBMS. In *Modelling in Data Base Management Systems*. North Holland, Amsterdam (1976).

[6] W. C. McGee: A contribution to the study of data equivalence. In *Data Base Management*. North Holland, Amsterdam (1974).

[7] R. Durchholz and G. Richter: Information management concepts (IMC) for use with DBMS interface. In *Modelling in Data Base Management Systems*. North Holland, Amsterdam (1976).

[8] B. Sundgren: An infological approach to data bases, *Urval Nr. 7, Statistika Centralbyran*, Stockholm (1973).

[9] E. Falkenberg: A uniform approach to data base management. In *Modelling in Data Base Management Systems*. North Holland, Amsterdam (1976).

[10] M. Senko, E. B. Altman, M. M. Astralian and P. L. Felider: Data structures and accessing in database systems. *IBM Systems J.* 12(1), 30–93.

[11] H. Biller and W. Glatthaar: On the semantics of data bases: the semantics of data definition languages. In *Lecture Notes in Computer Science*, Vol. 34, Springer, Heidelberg (1975).

[12] H. Biller, W. Glatthaar and E. J. Neuhold: On the semantics of data bases: the semantics of data definition languages. In *Modelling in Data Base Management Systems*. North Holland, Amsterdam (1976).

[13] W. Glatthaar: A problem oriented input processor supporting problem solving. *Tech. Rep.* Institut für Informatik, Stuttgart (1975).

[14] P. Hall, T. Owleff and S. Todd: Relations and entities. In *Modelling in Data Base Management Systems*. North Holland, Amsterdam (1976).

[15] M. Senko: DIAM as a detailed example of the ANSI/SPARC architecture. In *Modelling in Data Base Management Systems*. North Holland, Amsterdam (1976).

[16] F. Grotenhuis and J. van den Broek: A conceptual model for information processing. In *Modelling in Data Base Management Systems*. North Holland, Amsterdam (1976).

[17] E. Benci, F. Bodart, H. Bogaert and A. Cabanes: Concepts for the design of a conceptual schema. In *Modelling in Data Base Management Systems*. North Holland, Amsterdam (1976).

[18] P. Moulin, J. Randon, M. Teboul, S. Savoysky, S. Spaccapietra and H. Tardieu: Conceptual model as a data base design tool. In *Modelling in Data Base Management Systems*. North Holland, Amsterdam (1976).

[19] H. Biller and E. J. Neuhold: Concepts for the conceptual schema. In *Modelling in Data Base Management Systems*. Proc. of the TC-2 Working Conference in Nice 1977, North Holland, Amsterdam (1977).

[20] R. Carnap: *Meaning and Necessity*. 2nd Edn. University of Chicago Press, Chicago (1956).

[21] N. Roussopoulos and J. Mylopoulos: Using semantic networks for data base management. *Proc. Int. Conf. on Very Large Data Bases*. Framingham, Massachussetts (22–24 Sept. 1975).

[22] G. Bracchi, P. Paolini and G. Pelagaffi: Binary logical association in data modelling. In *Modelling in Data Base Management Systems*. North Holland, Amsterdam (1976).

[23] M. Adiba, C. Delobel and M. Léonard: A unified approach for modelling data in logical data base design. In *Modelling in Data Base Management Systems*. North Holland, Amsterdam (1976).

[24] R. Abrial: Data semantics. In *Data Base Management*. North Holland, Amsterdam (1974).

[25] L. Kershberg, A. Klug and D. Tsichritzis: A taxonomy of data models. *Proc. 2nd Int. Conf. on Very Large Data Bases*. North Holland, Amsterdam (1977).

[26] P. P. Chen: The entity-relationship model: towards a unified view of data. *ACM Trans. Data Base Systems* 1, 1 (Mar. 1976).

[27] H. A. Schmid and J. R. Swenson: On the semantics of the relational model. *Proc. ACM SIGMOD Conference*. San Jose, Calif. (May 1975).

[28] J. Hainant and B. Lechalier: An extensible semantic model of data base and its data language. In *Proc. IFIP Conference* 1974. North Holland, Amsterdam (1974).

[29] R. C. Lyndon: *Notes on Logic.* Van Nostrand, Princeton (1966).

[30] H. Biller: Die Semantik von Datenbanken (in German). *Dissertation*, Institut für Informatik, Stuttgart (1976).

[31] E. Falkenberg: Significations, the key to unify data base management. *Information Systems* 2(1) (Apr. 1976).

[32] E. F. Codd: A relational model for large shared data banks. *Comm. ACM* 13, 6 (June 1970).

[33] *CODASYL Data Base Task Group Report*, ACM, New York (1971).

[34] J. J. Florentin: Consistency auditing of data bases. *Comput. J.* 17, 1 (1974).

[35] K. P. Eswaran and D. D. Chamberlin: Functional specification of a subsystem for data base integrity. *Proc. Int. Conf. on Very Large Data Bases.* Framingham, Massachussetts (22–24 Sept. 1975).

[36] M. M. Hammer and D. J. McLeod: Semantic integrity in a relational data base system. *Proc. Int. Conf. on Very Large Data Bases.* Framingham, Massachussetts (22–24 Sept. 1975).

[37] H. Weber: A semantic model to specify constraints on a relational data base. In *Modelling in Data Base Management Systems.* North Holland, Amsterdam (1976).

[38] M. Stonebraker: Implementation of integrity constraints and views by query modification. *Proc. ACM SIGMOD Conference.* San Jose, Calif. (May 1975).

[39] C. Machgeels: A procedural language for expressing integrity constraints in the coexistence model. In *Modelling in Data Base Management Systems.* North Holland, Amsterdam (1976).

[40] R. Munz: Das WEB-Modell, (in German). *Dissertation*, Stuttgart (1976).

[41] C. P. Wang and H. H. Wedekind: Segment synthesis in logical data base design. *IBM J. Res. Develop.* 19, 71 (1975).

[42] D. J. McLeod: High level domain definition in a relational data base system. *Proc. ACM SIGPLAN/SIGMOD Conf. on Data.* Salt Lake City (Mar. 1976).

AN ESSENTIAL HYBRID REASONING SYSTEM: KNOWLEDGE AND SYMBOL LEVEL ACCOUNTS OF KRYPTON

Ronald J. Brachman
AT&T Bell Laboratories
600 Mountain Ave.
Murray Hill, NJ 07974

Victoria Pigman Gilbert
Schlumberger Palo Alto Research
3340 Hillview Ave.
Palo Alto, CA 94304

Hector J. Levesque[1]
Dept. of Computer Science
University of Toronto
Toronto, Ontario
Canada M5S 1A7

ABSTRACT

Hybrid inference systems are an important way to address the fact that intelligent systems have muiltifaceted representational and reasoning competence. KRYPTON is an experimental prototype that competently handles both terminological and assertional knowledge; these two kinds of information are tightly linked by having sentences in an assertional component be formed using structured complex predicates defined in a complementary terminological component. KRYPTON is unique in that it combines in a completely integrated fashion a frame-based description language and a first-order resolution theorem-prover. We give here both a formal Knowledge Level view of the user interface to KRYPTON and the technical Symbol Level details of the integration of the two disparate components, thus providing an essential picture of the abstract function that KRYPTON computes and the implementation technology needed to make it work. We also illustrate the kind of complex question the system can answer.

I Introduction

Many of today's knowledge representation (KR) systems offer their users a choice of more than one language for expression of domain knowledge. While the idea has been important to the field for many years (*e.g.*, see [Brown and Burton, 1975] [Moses, 1971] [Sloman, 1971]), "multiple representations" seems to have recently become a popular catch phrase. Many of the modern expert system development environments wave the polyglot banner, and except perhaps for some stalwart first-order logicians, most everyone would probably agree that one uniform language will not serve all representational needs.

It is sometimes difficult to discern the true value of multiple languages; some of the commercial development tools seem simply to appeal to "the more the merrier," without any clear idea of how merrier is better. However, on the research front, there have fortunately been some coherent views expressed on the merits of bringing disparate dialects together. The arguments have mainly to do with the naturalness of expressing certain kinds of facts in certain forms (see, *e.g.*, [Rich, 1982]), or with the efficiency of computing some inferences once some datum is massaged into a certain representational form [Genesereth, 1981].[2]

The arguments in favor of naturalness and computational superiority are important ones. However, as we have argued elsewhere [Brachman and Levesque, 1982], there may be a simpler, more basic reason to diversify: an intelligent system has more than one kind of representational need. For example, it is interesting to observe that so far, most KR systems only allow the expression of what we would call *assertional* knowledge—statements of facts or beliefs. If the system uses logic or production rules, the sentential nature of its content is self-evident (*e.g.*, "if the infection is primary bacteremia and ..., then there is suggestive evidence that the organism is bacteroides"). Even if the system uses frames or semantic nets, it is most likely encoding sentences of the form, "elephants are gray", or "Clyde is an armadillo" (see [Brachman, 1985] for more on this).

But what accounts for the meanings of the terms used in these sentences? In addition to representing the beliefs (or, popularly, "knowledge") of a cognitive system, we need to account at least for the complex terms (like *bacteremia* and *armadillo*, above) used in forming those beliefs. In other words, unless we intend to give up the lexical ghost and take all terms as inscrutable atomic primitives, some substantive representational explanation must be given for the *noun phrases* out of which the sentences expressing beliefs are constructed.

We have designed and implemented a complete hybrid reasoning system, called KRYPTON, that is significantly different from other "multiple representation" systems[3] in that it tries to provide exactly such an explanation. Instead of concentrating on multiple ways to perform the same inference, KRYPTON tries to span two fundamentally different types of representation and reasoning. Not only does it provide a language for composing sentences expressing beliefs (using sentential operators of the usual sort, for conjunction, quantification, negation, etc.), it supports the definition of complex predicates to be used in those sentences (with a set of special term-forming operators, for conceptual conjunction, role composition, role value restriction, etc.). Further, KRYPTON supports an appropriate set of inferences over sentences and over complex terms. Thus, KRYPTON is at least minimally competent in both the *assertional* and *terminological* domains.

In this paper, we will describe KRYPTON in some detail mainly by addressing two questions (both of which are crucial for designers of *any* representation system to answer):

1. *Exactly what service is being provided to the user?* The user should know, at some level not dependent on implementation details, what questions the system is capable of answering, and what operations are permitted that allow new information to be provided to it. He needs to know how questions put to a knowledge base will be answered strictly as a function of the information it contains, and not dependent on how the information is represented. In other words, the user requires what Newell [Newell, 1981] calls a *Knowledge Level* account (see also [Brachman and Levesque, 1984b] [Brachman, *et al.*, 1983b] [Levesque, 1984c]).

2. *How does the implementation realize the service promised?* In other words, how, at the *Symbol Level*, is the Knowledge Level account realized? In the case of a hybrid system, the interface between the disparate parts of the hybrid is particularly important.

[1] Fellow of the Canadian Institute for Advanced Research

[2] For an interesting recent paper on this general subject, see [Sloman, 1984].

[3] Except for KL-TWO [Vilain, 1985], whose history is significantly intertwined with that of KRYPTON.

This paper provides detailed Knowledge and Symbol Level accounts of KRYPTON (previous accounts [Brachman, *et al.*, 1983a] [Brachman, *et al.*, 1983b] gave only sketchy and informal details of what a real KRYPTON might be like). We first provide a formal semantics that brings together meanings of terms and the *subsumption* relation with meanings of sentences and *truth valuations*. This leads to a Knowledge Level account of KRYPTON in terms of a set of *operations on knowledge bases*. Subsequently, we explain how, at the Symbol Level, our implementation achieves this functionality in terms of an alteration to the meaning of unification in a resolution theorem-prover. In this section, we concentrate on the assertional component and how term definitions affect it, since details of our terminological component have been provided elsewhere [Brachman, *et al.*, 1983a]. We conclude the paper with some sample inferences drawn by KRYPTON, to illustrate how the two components are indeed tightly integrated, and that the system provides the kind of hybrid reasoning service promised by our Knowledge Level description.

Before we begin, it should be noted that KRYPTON's answers to the two questions posed above are more complicated and also more interesting than they would be for less ambitious systems. In the case of a "non-essential" hybrid that uses multiple representations of the same facts, Question 1 can be finessed with a simple explication of the semantics of the language into which all of the multiple representations can be translated (hopefully a standard one, as with first-order logic in MRS [Genesereth, 1981]), and an account of the translation rules used among the languages. In such systems, the multiple representations are usually not integrated in any important way, so Question 2 has an easy answer.

However, for an essential hybrid like KRYPTON, which attempts to integrate two fundamentally different kinds of representation and reasoning facilities, the picture is more complex. At the Knowledge Level, KRYPTON provides extra functionality over systems based on standard first-order logic; thus, we cannot ask the user to rely on intuitive knowledge of standard formal semantics, but rather must provide a detailed explanation of how the meanings of sentences in the assertional component can be affected by the structure of descriptions in the terminological component. At the Symbol Level, the user needs to know that, in the implementation he is using, complex term definitions really will have the impact on the meaning of the believed sentences advertised in the Knowledge Level account. It is not enough to say that KRYPTON has a frame-style description language for forming terms and a first-order predicate language for forming sentences—we must explain how the interpretations of the sentences by the theorem-prover depend on the definitions of the terms. As the reader will soon see, both the Knowledge Level and Symbol Level accounts must take seriously KRYPTON's hybrid structure.

II Representational Roots

As hinted above, KRYPTON is a hybrid system with two main components, one that specializes in assertional reasoning (the *ABox*), the other in terminological reasoning (the *TBox*). Each component has its own language, and its own inference mechanism.

KRYPTON developed mainly out of work on KL-ONE, a fairly complex representation system based on both semantic networks and frames [Brachman and Schmolze, 1985]. As KL-ONE evolved, it became evident that its strength lay in its ability to form complex *descriptions*. To the extent that you could *say* anything at all with KL-ONE, it was with clearly impoverished assertional facilities. In fact, if frame-based systems in general have any advantage, it comes from their ability to form descriptions, rather than sentences. As pointed out in [Brachman and Levesque, 1982] and [Brachman, *et al.*, 1983b], logical languages like that of first-order predicate calculus are far superior at meeting the needs for belief representations, since they can provide for a kind of noncommittal expression not possible with frame languages.

Given the strength of KL-ONE's terminological facilities and the weakness of its assertional ones, it seemed best to abandon the latter completely, and adopt a language better suited to sentence representation. While we would no doubt have used a more computationally tractable inference framework than full first-order logic if an appropriate one were available,[4] we chose to build our initial KRYPTON ABox on Stickel's connection graph theorem-prover [Stickel, 1982]. While the full first-order resolution mechanism is, in a sense, too powerful for our needs [Levesque, 1984a] [Levesque, 1984b], as a first ABox it turned out to be a remarkably good fit (as will be detailed in Section IV).

The heart of KRYPTON is the connection between the two components: predicates used in the ABox are actually defined in the TBox.[5] Thus, all of the analytic inferences computed by the frame-based TBox must be available for consumption in the logic-based ABox. This paper illustrates at both the Knowledge and Symbol Levels how the ABox benefits from the special-purpose definitional facilities available in the TBox.

Finally, as the reader of earlier papers on KRYPTON will note, there are potentially several versions of the TBox language that could be discussed here. While our implemented TBox includes virtually all of the operators mentioned in [Brachman, *et al.*, 1983b],[6] not all of those operators are tightly integrated with the ABox. Therefore, we have limited our discussion in this paper to those parts of the TBox that currently can affect the meaning of sentences in the ABox. For example, while subsumption for concepts with number restrictions works in the TBox, it is not treated here, since it awaits full integration with the theorem-prover.[7]

III Knowledge Level Operations

Although our basic ABox is a standard first-order predicate logic, its proper integration in KRYPTON demands that complex terms defined in the TBox be available for use as predicates in assertions. Thus, if the resulting assertional capability is considered as a predicate logic, then it is a non-standard one, in that it has both the normal sentential operators and special operators used for constructing complex predicates. In this section we will demonstrate the hybrid semantics necessary to explain the integration. First we present the syntax of KRYPTON's languages and their semantics; we then rigorously specify the interface that a Krypton system presents to an outside user. In particular, we

[4] We are currently working on a relevance-style [Anderson and Belnap, 1975] limited inference mechanism [Patel-Schneider, 1985]; see also [Levesque, 1984b] for properties appropriate to a belief representation.

[5] The mapping between symbols and their definitions is maintained by a *symbol table*, shared by the TBox and ABox. Please consult [Brachman, *et al.*, 1983b] and [Brachman, *et al.*, 1983a] for more on the structure of the system.

[6] More precisely, we have implemented the language exactly as described in [Brachman, *et al.*, 1983b], except for the *VRDiff* operator, which was ommitted for computational reasons as discussed in [Brachman and Levesque, 1984a], and the *DecompRole* operator.

[7] Also, a note about KL-TWO seems in order here. The terminological language in that system is much more extensive than the one discussed here (it is almost a superset of our TBox). Given that, its computational properties are less understood, and the completeness of its subsumption mechanism is somewhat in doubt (it is not clear exactly what is currently implemented and working). On the other hand, KL-TWO uses a much more tractable (propositional) ABox. Also, as reported in [Vilain, 1985], the method of integrating terminology and assertion is quite different in KL-TWO.

will precisely define operations which allow questions to be answered about the world or about the conceptual vocabulary being used, as well as operations which allow new information about the world to be accepted and new terms to be defined.

A. Syntax and Semantics

The language currently implemented in the TBox has two main categories: *concepts* and *roles*, roughly comparable to frames and slots. These are inter-defined by the following simple BNF grammar:

$\langle \textit{concept} \rangle ::= \langle \textit{1-predicate-symbol} \rangle$
$\quad | \; (\textbf{ConGeneric}\ \langle \textit{concept} \rangle_1 \ldots \langle \textit{concept} \rangle_n), \; n \geq 0$
$\quad | \; (\textbf{VRGeneric}\ \langle \textit{concept} \rangle\ \langle \textit{role} \rangle\ \langle \textit{concept} \rangle)$
$\langle \textit{role} \rangle ::= \langle \textit{2-predicate-symbol} \rangle$
$\quad | \; (\textbf{RoleChain}\ \langle \textit{role} \rangle_1 \ldots \langle \textit{role} \rangle_n), \; n \geq 1.$

This language has much in common with many typical frame languages. $\langle \textit{1-predicate-symbol} \rangle$ and $\langle \textit{2-predicate-symbol} \rangle$ are primitive (undefined) concepts and roles. **ConGeneric** allows the conjunction of concepts. **VRGeneric** allows the specification of a type restriction on the filler of a role (*e.g.*, (**VRGeneric** *Paper Author Scientist*) would represent the concept of a paper all of whose authors were scientists). **RoleChain** supports the composition of two-place relations.

For the ABox, the language we will use is that of a pure (that is, function-free) predicate calculus.[8] The grammar, then, is the following:

$\langle \textit{wff} \rangle ::= (\langle \textit{k-predicate-symbol} \rangle\ \langle \textit{var} \rangle_1 \ldots \langle \textit{var} \rangle_k), \; k \geq 0$
$\quad | \; (\textbf{NOT}\ \langle \textit{wff} \rangle)$
$\quad | \; (\textbf{OR}\ \langle \textit{wff} \rangle\ \langle \textit{wff} \rangle)$
$\quad | \; (\textbf{EXISTS}\ \langle \textit{var} \rangle\ \langle \textit{wff} \rangle).$

It is assumed that the other usual logical connectives (conjunction, universal quantification, etc.) can be defined syntactically in terms of the ones provided here (we will use standard logical typography for these when convenient). Note that one- and two-place predicate symbols are both terms of the TBox language and components of the ABox language. To make this intersection explicit, we also define the following categories:

$\langle \textit{TBox-symbol} \rangle ::= \langle \textit{1-predicate-symbol} \rangle$
$\quad | \; \langle \textit{2-predicate-symbol} \rangle$
$\langle \textit{gsymbol} \rangle ::= \langle \textit{k-predicate-symbol} \rangle, \; k \geq 0$
$\langle \textit{gterm} \rangle ::= \langle \textit{gsymbol} \rangle \; | \; \langle \textit{concept} \rangle \; | \; \langle \textit{role} \rangle$

So gterms, as they will be understood here, are either predicate symbols or composite TBox expressions and each gterm has an associated arity (1 for concepts, 2 for roles, and k for each k-place predicate symbol).

The semantics of the TBox and ABox languages is defined in terms of mappings from gsymbols to relations of the same arity over some domain. Given a domain of individuals and such a mapping, it will be possible to specify the extension of every gterm and the truth value of every sentence.[9] For the TBox language, this is defined as follows:

Definition 1 *Let $\mathcal{D}$ be any set. Let $\mathcal{E}$ be any function from gsymbols to relations over $\mathcal{D}$ such that $\mathcal{E}(s)$ has the same arity as s. Then for any gterm e, we define the EXTENSION of e wrt $\mathcal{E}$ by*

1. *The extension of any gsymbol s is $\mathcal{E}(s)$.*
2. *The extension of (***ConGeneric*** $e_1 \ldots e_k$) is the intersection of the extensions of the e_i, and $\mathcal{D}$ if k is 0.*
3. *The extension of (***VRGeneric*** $e_1\ r\ e_2$) is those elements x of the extension of e_1 such that $\langle x, y \rangle$ is in the extension of r only when y is in the extension of e_2.*
4. *The extension of (***RoleChain*** $r_1 \ldots r_k$) is the relational composition of the extensions of $r_1 \ldots r_k$.*

For example, the extension of (**VRGeneric** *Person Child Doctor*) would be the elements x of the extension of *Person* such that any y such that $\langle x, y \rangle$ is in the extension of *Child* is also in the extension of *Doctor*; that is, the complex term stands for those persons whose children are all doctors.[10] Similarly, the extension of (**RoleChain** *Child Child*) is the set of all pairs $\langle x, z \rangle$ such that for some y, $\langle x, y \rangle$ is in the extension of *Child* and $\langle y, z \rangle$ is also in the extension of *Child*; that is, the expression stands for the *Grandchild* relation.

To define the semantics of the ABox language, we need the notion of an *environment*, which is a function from variables to elements of some domain. Given an environment $\mathcal{V}$, a variable x, and an object o, we also define $\mathcal{V}[x/o]$ to be the environment that is exactly like $\mathcal{V}$ except that x is mapped to o. The truth of a wff is defined in terms of a mapping $\mathcal{E}$ and an environment $\mathcal{V}$ as follows:

Definition 2 *Let $\mathcal{D}$ be any set. Let $\mathcal{E}$ be any function from gsymbols to relations over $\mathcal{D}$ such that $\mathcal{E}(s)$ has the same arity as s. Let $\mathcal{V}$ be any environment over $\mathcal{D}$. Then for any wff α, we define the TRUTH of α wrt to $\mathcal{E}$ and $\mathcal{V}$ by*

1. *($p\ x_1 \ldots x_k$) is true iff $\langle \mathcal{V}(x_1), \ldots, \mathcal{V}(x_k) \rangle$ is in the relation $\mathcal{E}(p)$.*
2. *(***NOT*** α) is true iff α is not true.*
3. *(***OR*** $\alpha\ \beta$) is true iff either α or β is true.*
4. *(***EXISTS*** $x\ \alpha$) is true iff for some d in $\mathcal{D}$, α is true wrt to $\mathcal{E}$ and $\mathcal{V}[x/d]$.*

One thing to notice about this definition is that the truth of sentences does not depend on an environment at all and so, as with gterms, the meaning of sentences is strictly a function of the set $\mathcal{D}$ and the mapping $\mathcal{E}$.

So far, the only relation between the semantics of the TBox and the ABox languages is that both depend on the assignment $\mathcal{E}$ of relations to gsymbols. However, the coupling is closer than this since TBox symbols can be *defined*, that is, associated with other gterms which become their definitions. The net effect is to constrain the mapping $\mathcal{E}$ so that the extension of the defined symbol is the same as the extension of the gterm. To make this precise, we introduce the notion of a *symbol table* as follows: a symbol table $\mathcal{S}$ is a function from 1-place predicates to concepts and 2-place predicates to roles; for any TBox symbol g, $\mathcal{S}(g)$ is the gterm which is the definition of g under $\mathcal{S}$. Strictly speaking, we should be careful to avoid circular definitions[11] in a symbol table, but will not do so here. In fact, we will use the convention that a gsymbol is undefined whenever $\mathcal{S}(p)$ equals p itself. In other words, for any gsymbol g, we say that g is *primitive* wrt $\mathcal{S}$ when g equals $\mathcal{S}(g)$.[12]

A key notion given a symbol table $\mathcal{S}$ is that of a mapping $\mathcal{E}$ being an *extension function*:

[8] The actual implementation described below uses function symbols of every arity including constants (0-ary ones). We are omitting these here for simplicity.

[9] By a *sentence*, we mean a closed wff of the ABox language.

[10] As a matter of terminology, we will say that the fillers of the *Child* role are constrained to be in the extension of *Doctor*.

[11] An example of a circular definition might be one where $\mathcal{S}(p)$ is (**ConGeneric** $q\ r$) and $\mathcal{S}(q)$ is (**ConGeneric** $p\ s$).

[12] In particular, we assume that all k-place predicates for k greater than 2 are primitive.

Definition 3 *Let S be a symbol table. $\mathcal{E}$ is an EXTENSION FUNCTION wrt S iff for every gsymbol g, $\mathcal{E}(g)$ is the same as the extension of $S(g)$ wrt $\mathcal{E}$.*

In other words, an extension function is a mapping that obeys the definitions specified by S. For example, if p is defined by S to be the gterm (**ConGeneric** q r), then $\mathcal{E}(p)$, to be an extension function, would have to be the intersection of $\mathcal{E}(q)$ and $\mathcal{E}(r)$.

B. Outcomes and Knowledge Bases

Using the notion of an extension function defined above, we can define what it means to be a *truth valuation* and a *subsumption relationship*, which together will tell us what the world is like and how the gterms relate to each other. We define the first as follows:

Definition 4 *Let S be a symbol table. Let w be a mapping from sentences to {true,false}. w is a TRUTH VALUATION wrt to S iff there is a set $\mathcal{D}$ and an extension function $\mathcal{E}$ wrt S over $\mathcal{D}$ such that $w(\alpha)$ = true iff α is true wrt $\mathcal{E}$.*

So a truth valuation is a mapping from sentences to truth values that follows the definition of truth given earlier and respects the definitions given by S. For example, if p is defined by S to be q, then any truth valuation that says that (**EXISTS** x $(p\ x)$) is true, must also say that (**EXISTS** x $(q\ x)$) is also true.

For terms, we define the subsumption relationship as follows:

Definition 5 *Let S be a symbol table. Let e_1 and e_2 be gterms. e_1 SUBSUMES e_2 wrt S iff for any set $\mathcal{D}$ and any $\mathcal{E}$ that is an extension function wrt S, the extension of e_1 is a superset of that of e_2.*

So, for example, the gterm p always subsumes (**ConGeneric** p r), and if q is defined by S to be (**ConGeneric** p r), then p subsumes q with respect to S (for any p, q, and r).

The notion of an *outcome* is that of a complete specification of what the world is like and how the gterms are interrelated. It is defined by the following:

Definition 6 *An OUTCOME is a pair $(\Rightarrow, w)$ where, for some symbol table S,*

1. *$\Rightarrow$ is the subsumption relationship wrt S (so $\Rightarrow \subseteq$ gterm $\times$ gterm)*
2. *w is a truth valuation wrt S (so w is a function from sentences to truth values).*

Note that an outcome does not determine a unique symbol table. As a very simple example, if the relation $\Rightarrow$ says that the gterms p and (**ConGeneric** q r) subsume each other, it could have been the case that p was defined as (**ConGeneric** q r) or as (**ConGeneric** r q) or even as some other expression that subsumes and is subsumed by (**ConGeneric** r q). The actual syntactic form of the definition of p is not considered to be relevant; what counts is the relationship between p and all other gterms.

While an outcome is a complete specification of what the world and vocabulary are like, a *knowledge base* is considered a partial specification of the same. Formally, we define a knowledge base to be any set of outcomes. (This is the usual convention of treating a partial x as the set of all complete x's that are 'consistent' with it.) So the outcomes that are members of a KB are those that are consistent with the information available to the KB; the outcomes that are not members of the KB are those that can be ruled out based on the information available to the KB. So for example, if a KB knows only that α is true and that p is defined to be (**ConGeneric** q r), the outcomes it will contain are all those where p subsumes (**ConGeneric** q r) and vice-versa, and where α is true. This is not to say that the KB does not know about other truths or subsumption relationships. For example, in all the outcomes in the KB, p also subsumes (**ConGeneric** r s q), and (**OR** α β) is also true. Moreover, for any KB at all, all of its outcomes have the property that p subsumes (**ConGeneric** p q), and every valid sentence of logic comes out true.

C. The Operations on Knowledge Bases

We are now in a position to define what operations are available on these abstract knowledge bases. These are the operations that actually define KRYPTON and the only ones that an implementation has to provide to a user.

First, we have a simple operation to get started. NEWKB creates a new knowledge base that includes no definitions or contingent facts. NEWKB is defined this way:

NEWKB[ ] = $\{(\Rightarrow, w) \mid (\Rightarrow, w)$ is an outcome$\}$.

In other words, the result of NEWKB is the set of all outcomes. Note that this KB does have some nontrivial properties, such as those mentioned at the end of the last section.

There are two ABox operations provided by KRYPTON. The first, called ASK, is used to determine what the world is like according to what is known. Informally, ASK takes a sentence and a KB and returns 'yes' or 'no'. The second, called TELL, is used to inform the KB of what the world is like. It takes a sentence and a KB and returns a new KB that knows that the sentence is true. More formally,

ASK[α,KB] =
  yes, if for each $(\Rightarrow, w)$ in KB, $w(\alpha)$ = true,
  no, otherwise.
TELL[α,KB] = $\{(\Rightarrow, w)$ in KB $\mid w(\alpha)$ = true$\}$.

So TELL rules out the possibility that its argument is false by retaining only those outcomes where it comes out true. Similarly, ASK answers 'yes' precisely when the possibility that α is false has been ruled out.

The TBox equivalent to TELL is called DEFINE. It takes a TBox symbol, a TBox expression and a KB and tells the KB that the symbol is defined by the expression. The equivalent to ASK is called SUBSUMES. It takes two TBox terms and returns 'yes' or 'no' according to whether the first subsumes the second based on what is known about the terms. These are defined as follows:

DEFINE[g, e,KB] = $\{(\Rightarrow, w)$ in KB $\mid g \Rightarrow e$ and $e \Rightarrow g\}$.
SUBSUMES[e_1,e_2,KB] =
  yes, if for each $(\Rightarrow, w)$ in KB $e_2 \Rightarrow e_1$,
  no, otherwise.

The TBox also has operations that have no (current) analogue in the ABox. These operations are questions that return sets of gsymbols, instead of 'yes' or 'no'.[13] The intent is that we should be able to find out what symbols have been defined and to reconstruct, for each such symbol, a definition for it. It may not be the actual definition that was used, but its effect overall would be the same. The three operations are VOCAB, which returns the gsymbols that have been defined; PRIMS, which given a TBox term returns the ultimate primitives[14] that make up the expression; and, ROLEPAIRS, which given a concept, returns a

[13] Stickel's theorem-prover provides answers to some assertional "wh-questions" but the question of an appropriate set for KR purposes is still an open one.

[14] Recall that a primitive is a symbol that has no definition. Thus what constitutes a primitive may vary as definitions are acquired.

list of pairs $\langle c, p \rangle$ where p is a primitive concept and c is a list of primitive roles, and where the gterm constrains the fillers of the chain of c to be in the extension of p. These operations are defined in the following way:

VOCAB[KB] = {p, a gsymbol | there is a
  different gsymbol q such that SUBSUMES[q, p,KB] = yes}.
PRIMS[e,KB] =
  if e is a concept then
    {p, a 1-predicate-symbol | p is not in VOCAB[KB] and
    SUBSUMES[p, e,KB] = yes}
  if e is a role then ($q_1 \ldots q_k$) where
    no q_i is in VOCAB[KB] and
    SUBSUMES[(**RoleChain** $q_1 \ldots q_k$),e,KB] = yes.
ROLEPAIRS[e,KB] = {$\langle(q_1, \ldots, q_k), p\rangle$ |
  neither p nor any q_i is in VOCAB[KB] and
  SUBSUMES[(**VRGeneric** e (**RoleChain** $q_1 \ldots q_k$) p),
      e,KB] = yes}.

Note that a gsymbol is a primitive exactly when it is not defined, that is, when it is not in VOCAB.

Given the details of this Knowledge Level account, there are a number of important properties of KRYPTON that we can prove. For example, it is easy to show that ASK and TELL have the right relationship, *i.e.*, that ASK[α, TELL(α, KB)] = true, for any KB, as well as any subsequent KB (TELL works *monotonically*—anything that is believed continues to be believed as new facts or new definitions are added). Similarly, it can be shown that DEFINE and SUBSUMES have a proper relationship, *i.e.*,

SUBSUMES[s, e, DEFINE(s, e, KB)] = yes
  and
SUBSUMES[e, s, DEFINE(s, e, KB)] = yes   (for any KB).

We can show that all of the logical truths hold in an empty KB, *e.g.*, ASK[$p \vee \neg p$, KB_0] = yes, where KB_0 is the value of NEWKB[ ]. We can show that all of the appropriate subsumption relationships [Brachman and Levesque, 1984a] hold in the TBox, as in, *e.g.*,

SUBSUMES[p_1, (**ConGeneric** p_1 p_2), KB] (for any KB).

It can also be shown that the expanded form of a definition into only primitives (using the results of PRIMS and ROLEPAIRS) is equivalent to the original definition. Finally, and most cogent to the focus of this paper, it can be shown that the ABox and the TBox have the desired relationship. For example, universal assertions that should follow directly from definitions can be shown to do so:

ASK[$\forall x\, Man(x) \supset Person(x)$,
  DEFINE[*Man*, (**VRGeneric** *Person Sex Male*), KB]]
  = yes (for any KB).

In general, because we can prove such things about KRYPTON, this kind of Knowledge Level account plays a vital part in providing a predictable, reliable interface for consumers of the KR service.

IV The KRYPTON Implementation

Having defined the existing KRYPTON interface, we now turn our attention to the way the service is implemented. In general, it is possible to build a hybrid KR system wherein term definitions are expressed in a special language, and then simply translated into sentences in another. This loose kind of integration at least allows a system to take some of the implications of definitions into account. However, integration of this type has two potentially serious problems: first, contingent assertional sentences (even universally quantified biconditionals) simply do not have the same import as definitions and loose integration forces their conflation (contrast "every animal is either not in my field or is a cow" with "every triangle is a three-sided polygon"); second, adding more sentences to a belief-reasoner (*i.e.*, a theorem-prover) will invariably slow it down (see [Stickel, 1985]).

In KRYPTON, we have embodied a tightly integrated hybrid architecture. We have extended the basic inference rule of the assertional reasoning mechanism to take directly into account the structure of definitions by altering the meaning of unification. Thus, definitions of terms have a direct, complete, and correct effect on the reasoning process without slowing it down. Further, the term definition language is kept completely distinct from the assertion-making language, and is a more natural one for forming structured definitions and for drawing definitional (analytic) inferences (*e.g.*, subsumption). As implied above, definitions are first-class citizens in KRYPTON, and are distinct from simple contingent sentences even of similar logical form.

In this section, we describe our alteration to unification in the context of our ABox—Stickel's nonclausal connection graph resolution theorem-prover [Stickel, 1982] [Stickel, 1983] [Stickel, 1985]. This should give the reader a solid idea of how KRYPTON has been made to work, but owing to the brevity of the presentation, it is not intended to be a complete account of the ABox–TBox interface.

A. Connection Graph Theorem-Proving

A connection graph [Kowalski, 1975] is a set of wffs and a set of links between the literals[15] of the wffs. For every literal that occurs in a clause input by the user or as the resolvent in a resolution step, there is a corresponding node in the graph. At the time a clause is entered each of its literals is examined and a link is created between each literal and any other literal for which there exists a unifier that causes them to be complementary. Note that there is a crucial distinction between *forming* a link and *resolving upon* a link. A link should be thought of as a marker for identifying two wffs that can be used in a resolution step. The link makes it easier to find the wffs at resolution time, but does not actually perform the resolution. It appears that in general the pre-computation of possible resolution steps allows connection-graph theorem-proving to proceed faster than ordinary resolution [Kowalski, 1975] [Stickel, 1982].

B. Residues

An important piece of information that is stored on a link is the *residue* between the two literals. A residue can be viewed as a statement that the literals connected by a link are contradictory, provided that some additional information, specifically the negation of the residue, is known. When a resolution step is performed, the residue is added as a disjunct to the resolvent in the place of the resolved-away literals. In a conventional unification step, the residue is "*false*", indicating that the literals are directly contradictory; thus a conventional step adds no additional information to the resolvent. However, in KRYPTON we make extensive use of complex non-empty residues for the TBox links.

For example, if we define in the TBox the concept of a *Person* as something that is both a *Mammal* and a *Thinker*, and we know that *Rover* is not a *Person* and that he is a *Mammal*, then by definition *Rover* must not be a *Thinker*. Therefore, the literals $\neg Person(Rover)$ and *Mammal(Rover)* will be linked together with a residue of $\neg Thinker(Rover)$. This link can be pictured as below, where the literals being linked occur on either side of the horizontal line, and the residue is attached below them:

[15] A literal is an atomic sentence or the negation of one.

$$\neg Person(Rover) \text{———} Mammal(Rover)$$
$$\downarrow$$
$$\neg Thinker(Rover)$$

The residue wff is attached only as information associated with the link, but is not actually added to the graph until the link has been resolved upon in a resolution step. So, in this case, none of the links that would connect $\neg Thinker(Rover)$ to other literals are computed until the parent link is resolved upon. The most important consequence of this is that the residue will not be visible for use by the set of support strategy that the ABox employs to direct the progress of a proof (see below).

C. Proof Procedure and Resolution Strategy

The proof procedure used with a connection graph is quite simple. The kernel of the procedure is as follows:

1. Stop if the graph contains the empty clause.
2. Select any link from the graph.
3. Generate the resolvent.
4. Construct the new graph:
   (a) Delete the link resolved upon.
   (b) Add links for the resolvent.
5. Return to 1.

Once a given pair of literals in a pair of wffs has been resolved upon, literals that are derived in later resolution steps from the resolved-on literals cannot themselves be resolved upon. This follows from the fact that the original link is deleted *before* links are added between literals in the resolvent and other literals in the graph. As a result of this, connection graph resolution does not allow all the resolution steps that other methods might.

An important point to notice about the proof procedure is that it is nondeterministic. That is, the procedure places no restrictions on how the next link to be resolved upon is chosen. A given implementation must be very careful to embody a strategy that guarantees to preserve completeness of the procedure. One obvious constraint on a suitable strategy should be that the choice of link tend to simplify the resultant graph. Another is that only links that are relevant to the query should be resolved upon.

In Stickel's theorem prover, these goals are achieved by the use of a complex evaluation function for determining the next link to schedule and by having the evaluation function use set of support as the basic resolution strategy.[16] The evaluation function also takes into account such things as how deep the search in a given direction has been and how complicated the residue on the link will be. The hope is that it will choose to ignore links that will result in a more complicated graph and that it will abandon paths that seem to be fruitless. While the evaluation function depends on heuristics and is not guaranteed to find the fastest proof in all cases, our experience shows it to work very well.

D. Terminological Link Types

The ABox is made to understand the TBox by the addition of links to the connection graph that are derived from the terminological definitions in the TBox. Just as in the case of normal connection graph theorem-proving, deduction time is saved by pre-computation of possible unification steps. Further, since our definitions are structured and include a subsumption hierarchy, links constructed from them allow multiple deduction steps (*e.g.*, multiple applications of *modus ponens*) to be accomplished at once. Although we cannot provide evidence of it in the small space we have here (but see [Stickel, 1985]), directly changing the connection graph turns out to be potentially far superior to the mere addition of "meaning postulates" in a loosely integrated system.

Our modification involves the addition of four new connection graph link types. The first three are for concept definitions, and the fourth for role definitions. To a first approximation, the links for a concept correspond to (1) links to concepts that subsume the concept, (2) links to concepts that occur (either explicitly or implicitly) as value restrictions in **VRGenerics** for the concept, and (3) links to roles that occur in **VRGenerics** for the concept. Links for the definition of a role are for subchains of that definition that are themselves defined roles. At the very least, this will involve the primitive roles included in the definition.

There are two cases for each of the four basic link types, arising from the necessity and sufficiency of our TBox definitions.[17] These are the cases corresponding to positive and negative occurrences of a term. For example, if we know that *Fred* is a *Person*, then we know that his not being a *Thinker* is immediately contradictory, so given the appropriate facts, this link would be necessary:

$$Person(Fred) \text{———} \neg Thinker(Fred)$$
$$\downarrow$$
$$false$$

The *Rover* link of section IV.B shows a link required by the addition of a negative occurrence of a term.

In the next two sections, we will cover in some detail two of the necessary link types arising from concept definitions. The first of these is between a concept and all concepts that subsume it. The second is between a concept and roles that occur in a **VRGeneric** in the concept's definition.

In what follows, we shall use these definitions:

- *Grandchild*: (**RoleChain** *Child Child*), that is, the *Child* of a *Child*.
- *Woman-Student*: (**ConGeneric** *Woman Student*), that is, somebody that is both a *Woman* and a *Student*.
- *Successful-Grandma*: (**VRGeneric** *Woman Grandchild Doctor*), that is, a *Woman* all of whose *Grandchildren* are *Doctors*.

1. Concept-SuperConcept Linking

A concept P must be linked to concepts that subsume it. For this concept linking, the TBox must supply the names of all concepts that subsume P and also all concepts that it subsumes (information that can be gotten from the TBox using the Knowledge Level operations defined above). The reason for the latter is that we have no way of controlling the order of entry of terms. Finding a concept Q that P subsumes will allow Q to be appropriately linked up when P is encountered.

Positive links: Each positive instance of a concept must be linked to all negative instances of concepts that subsume it when the arguments unify in the conventional fashion. No residue is associated with these links. The *Fred* link of the last section is an example of this link type.

[16] *Set of support* is a general strategy designed to ensure that only links that point into a "support set" are eligible for selection for the next resolution step. At the beginning of a proof the support set contains only the links between the negation of the query and other wffs. When a link is resolved upon, the old link is removed from the set, and all of the links of the resolvent are added.

[17] It should be emphasized that while these link connections may appear complicated, they are not calculated repeatedly. The appropriate links are computed exactly once for each definition, at the time the definition is entered. Therefore the apparent complexity here does not adversely affect the process of deduction.

Negative links: Each negative instance of a concept, P, must be linked to all positive instances of concepts, Q, that are subsumed by primitive concepts occurring as conjuncts in the definition of P when the arguments unify in the conventional fashion. The residue is formed by taking the definition of P, removing those pieces of it that are shared with the definition of Q, and then negating the result. For example, consider

$$\neg Woman\text{-}Student(Sue) \text{ — } Successful\text{-}Grandma(Sue)$$
$$\downarrow$$
$$\neg Student(Sue)$$

If *Sue* is not a *Woman-Student*, but she is a *Successful-Grandma*, then some part of the definition of *Woman-Student* that does not apply to *Successful-Grandma* must not be true for *Sue*. The only piece of *Woman-Student* not included in the other definition is *Student*, so *Sue* must not be a *Student*.

2. Concept–RoleChain Linking

A concept P must be linked to each **RoleChain** that occurs in a **VRGeneric** for it. In order to do this linkage correctly, the TBox must provide the ABox, for each concept, the names of all defined **RoleChains** that occur in that concept, and for each defined **RoleChain**, the names of all concepts in which it occurs.

Positive links: For every role, R, whose definition occurs as a **RoleChain** or a subchain of a **RoleChain** in some **VRGeneric** in the definition of P, link P with the rest of the **VRGeneric** in which R occurs. So, for example, since *Grandchild* is defined as *(***RoleChain** *Child Child)*, *Child* is a defined subchain of *Grandchild*. Therefore, if *Marge* is a *Successful-Grandma* and has a *Child*, then if that *Child* in turn has any *Children*, they must all be *Doctors*.

$$Successful\text{-}Grandma(Marge) \text{ — } Child(Marge, Hope)$$
$$\downarrow$$
$$\forall(x) Child(Hope, x) \supset Doctor(x)$$

Negative links: For every role, R, whose definition occurs as a subchain of a **RoleChain** in some **VRGeneric** in the definition of P, link $\neg P(a)$ and $\neg R(SkF_n(a), SkF_m(a))$ (where SkF_n and SkF_m are both Skolem functions associated with the definition of P). This link has as its residue the negation of the rest of the definition of P, after removing the **VRGeneric** in which R appears.

$$\neg Successful\text{-}Grandma(Charlie) \text{ — } \neg Child(Charlie, x)$$
$$\downarrow$$
$$\neg Woman(Charlie)$$

If *Charlie* has no children, then the **VRGeneric** for *Successful-Grandma* holds vacuously, so for *Charlie* to not be a *Successful-Grandma*, he must fail in the only other requirement, and not be a *Woman*.

3. Other links

In the preceding sections we have outlined two of the major link types in our extension of unification. There are several choices for other links to use to complete the extension. Currently we have implemented one set that, while complete,[18] is probably not the best choice, as it yields some unintuitive links to assure that completeness. We have been exploring other link choices that do not of themselves ensure completeness but can be shown to be sufficient when coupled with the set of support strategy. Another approach that is being considered is to not restrict ourselves to binary links, that is links between two literals, but to instead make use of Stickel's more general *theory resolution* capabilities and use n-ary links [Stickel, 1983] [Stickel, 1985]. For example, instead of the link mentioned in the last section concerning *Charlie* which necessitated the addition of a residue, we might have waited until we had all three literals $\neg Successful\text{-}Grandma(Charlie)$, $\neg Child(Charlie, x)$, and $Woman(Charlie)$, and made a single ternary link containing no residue.

[18]Because of space limitations, we are not saying here what it means to be complete and consistent with respect to our Knowledge Level specification.

V Example Proof

In this final section, we will present a sample use of KRYPTON. We will supply some TBox definitions and a set of ABox facts and then show how KRYPTON goes about answering a query based on that information.

- TBox definitions:
  - Primitive Roles: *Child*
  - Primitive Concepts: *Mammal, Thinker, Woman*
  - Defined Concepts:
    - *Person* (**ConGeneric** *Mammal Thinker*)
    - *NoSon* (**VRGeneric** *Person Child Woman*)
- ABox facts:
  - $Child(Fred, Pat)$
  - $Child(Mary, Sandy)$
  - $NoSon(Fred) \lor NoSon(Mary)$

With the facts above, we should be able to show that there is somebody in the world who is a *Person* and has a *Child* that is a *Woman*, even though we do not know who that somebody is. This query is formulated as $\exists x \exists y[Person(x) \land Child(x, y) \land Woman(y)]$. The intuition behind the proof is that if *Fred* and *Pat* both have children and at least one of them is a *NoSon*, then whichever of them it is is himself a *Person* and has a *Child* that is a *Woman* (given the definition of *NoSon*). That either *Fred* or *Mary* is a *NoSon* is insufficient information for this proof, since the definition of *NoSon* does not require that such a person have a *Child*, merely that if she has a *Child*, then that *Child* is a *Woman*. Note that any proof of this is going to have to use terminological information to know, for example, that the *Child* of whichever of them is a *NoSon* is also a *Woman*.

The proof proceeds by trying to derive a contradiction from the known facts and the negation of the query. Lines 1–3 are the known ABox facts that will be used in the proof. Line 4 is the negation of the query. x and y are used as universal variables.

1. $Child(Fred, Pat)$
2. $Child(Mary, Sandy)$
3. $NoSon(Fred) \lor NoSon(Mary)$
4. $\neg Person(x) \lor \neg Child(x, y) \lor \neg Woman(y)$
5. $\neg Person(Fred) \lor \neg Woman(Pat)$

Normal resolution on 1 and $\neg Child(x, y)$ in 4.

6. $\neg Person(Fred) \lor NoSon(Mary) \lor \neg Child(Fred, Pat)$

By 3, *Fred* is possibly a *NoSon*, which means that all his *Children* are *Women* (from the terminology). Stating that *Pat* is not a *Woman* in 5 has the consequence that *Pat* cannot be *Fred's Child*. In other words, $NoSon(Fred)$ in 3 and $\neg Woman(Pat)$ in 5 resolve away and leave a residue of $\neg Child(Fred, Pat)$.

7. $\neg Person(Fred) \lor NoSon(Mary)$

Normal resolution on 1 and $\neg Child(Fred, Pat)$ in 6.

8. $NoSon(Mary)$

By the definition of *NoSon*, if *Fred* is one then he must also be a *Person*, so $\neg Person(Fred)$ in 7 and $NoSon(Fred)$ in 3 are directly contradictory.

9. $\neg Child(Mary, y) \lor \neg Woman(y)$

This time, if *Mary* is a *NoSon*, she must be a *Person*, so 8 and

$\neg Person(x)$ in 4 are directly contradictory, with *Mary* being substituted for x in the resolvent.

10. $\neg Child(Mary, y)$

If *Mary* is a *NoSon* (as stated in 8), any *Children* she might have must be *Women*. Therefore, if there are no *Women* at all (as stated in 9), then *Mary* must have no *Children*. In this case, the residue, $\neg Child(Mary, y)$, was already part of the resolvent of 8 and 9, so it does not need to be added again.

11. *false*

Normal resolution on 10 and 2.

VI Conclusions

As we have shown, KRYPTON is a tightly integrated hybrid reasoning system that provides both terminological and assertional facilities. At the Knowledge Level, it can be seen that assertional reasoning takes into account the definitions of terms expressed in a special-purpose frame-based description language. At the Symbol Level, it can be seen that this interface is implemented by augmenting a theorem-prover's notion of unification to accommodate definitional relationships between predicates. Our KRYPTON implementation currently runs on a Symbolics 3600.

In some respects, this resembles what Stickel has called "theory resolution" [Stickel, 1983] [Stickel, 1985], wherein non-equational theories can be built directly into the theorem-prover. One could—at the Symbol Level—accurately call KRYPTON an implementation of partial theory resolution, in that we have used the TBox to implement specialized reasoning procedures for certain tasks. However, as discussed in Section III, we have a full formal semantics at the Knowledge Level that supports the first-class citizenship of descriptive terms in KRYPTON. Theory resolution allows us a convenient implementation of this idea, but does not itself provide us with the suitable semantics.

KRYPTON is different, in fact, from most other hybrid approaches in that it directly, and soundly, integrates two fundamentally different kinds of representation and reasoning.

References

[Anderson and Belnap, 1975] Anderson, A. R., and Belnap, N. D., Jr., *Entailment: The Logic of Relevance and Necessity.* Vol. 1. Princeton, NJ: Princeton University Press, 1975.

[Brachman, 1985] Brachman, R. J., "'I Lied About the Trees.'" *AI Magazine*, Vol. 6, No. 3, Fall, 1985.

[Brachman and Levesque, 1982] Brachman, R. J., and Levesque, H. J., "Competence in Knowledge Representation," in *Proc. AAAI-82*, Pittsburgh, August, 1982, 189–192.

[Brachman and Levesque, 1984a] Brachman, R. J., and Levesque, H. J., "The Tractability of Subsumption in Frame-Based Description Languages," in *Proc. AAAI-84*, Austin, TX, August, 1984, 34–37.

[Brachman and Levesque, 1984b] Brachman, R. J., and Levesque, H. J., "What Makes a Knowledge Base Knowledgeable? A View of Databases from the Knowledge Level," in *Proc. First International Workshop on Expert Database Systems*, Kiawah Isl., S. C., October, 1984, 30–39.

[Brachman and Schmolze, 1985] Brachman, R. J., and Schmolze, J. G., "An Overview of the KL-ONE Knowledge Representation System." *Cognitive Science*, **9**(2), April–June, 1985, 171–216.

[Brachman, *et al.*, 1983a] Brachman, R. J., Fikes, R. E., and Levesque, H. J., "Krypton: Integrating Terminology and Assertion," in *Proc. AAAI-83*, Washington, DC, August, 1983, 31–35.

[Brachman, *et al.*, 1983b] Brachman, R. J., Fikes, R. E., and Levesque, H. J. "Krypton: A Functional Approach to Knowledge Representation." *IEEE Computer, Special Issue on Knowledge Representation*, October, 1983, 67–73.

[Brown and Burton, 1975] Brown, J. S., and Burton, R. R., "Multiple Representations of Knowledge for Tutorial Reasoning," in *Representation and Understanding: Studies in Cognitive Science.* D. G. Bobrow and A. Collins, *eds.* New York: Academic Press, 1975, 311–349.

[Genesereth, 1981] Genesereth, M., "The Architecture of a Multiple Representation System," Memo HPP-81-6, Comp. Sci. Dept., Stanford Univ., May, 1981.

[Kowalski, 1975] Kowalski, R., "A Proof Procedure Using Connection Graphs", *JACM*, **22**(4), October, 1975, 572–595.

[Levesque, 1984a] Levesque, H. J., "A Fundamental Tradeoff in Knowledge Representation and Reasoning," in *Proc. CSCSI-84*, London, Ontario, May, 1984, 141–152.

[Levesque, 1984b] Levesque, H. J., "A Logic of Implicit and Explicit Belief," in *Proc. AAAI-84*, Austin, TX, August, 1984, 198–202.

[Levesque, 1984c] Levesque, H. J., "Foundations of a Functional Approach to Knowledge Representation." *Artificial Intelligence*, **23**(2), July, 1984, 155–212.

[Moses, 1971] Moses, J., "Algebraic Simplification: A Guide for the Perplexed." *CACM*, **14**(8), August, 1971, 527–537.

[Newell, 1981] Newell, A., "The Knowledge Level," *AI Magazine*, **2**(2), Summer, 1981, 1–20.

[Patel-Schneider, 1985] Patel-Schneider, P. F., "A Decidable First-Order Logic for Knowledge Representation," *Proc. IJCAI-85.*

[Rich, 1982] Rich, C., "Knowledge Representation Languages and Predicate Calculus: How to Have Your Cake and Eat it Too," in Proc. AAAI-82, Pittsburgh, August, 1982, 193–196.

[Sloman, 1971] Sloman, A., "Interactions Between Philosophy and Artificial Intelligence: The Role of Intuition and Non-Logical Reasoning in Intelligence." *Artificial Intelligence*, **2** (1971), 209–225.

[Sloman, 1984] Sloman, A., "Why We Need Many Knowledge Representation Formalisms," British Computer Society Expert Systems Conference, December, 1984.

[Stickel, 1982] Stickel, M. E., "A Nonclausal Connection-Graph Resolution Theorem-Proving Program," in *Proc. AAAI-82*, Pittsburgh, August, 1982, 229–233.

[Stickel, 1983] Stickel, M. E., "Theory Resolution: Building in Nonequational Theories," in *Proc. AAAI-83*, Washington, DC, August, 1983, 391–397.

[Stickel, 1985] Stickel, M. E., "Automated Deduction by Theory Resolution," to appear in *J. Automated Reasoning*, 1985.

[Vilain, 1985] Vilain, M., "The Restricted Language Architecture of a Hybrid Representation System," *Proc. IJCAI-85.*

Towards a Logical Reconstruction of Relational Database Theory

Raymond Reiter
University of British Columbia

ABSTRACT *Insofar as database theory can be said to owe a debt to logic, the currency on loan is* model theoretic *in the sense that a database can be viewed as a particular kind of first order interpretation, and query evaluation is a process of truth functional evaluation of first order formulae with respect to this interpretation. It is this model theoretic paradigm which leads, for example, to many valued propositional logics for databases with null values.*

In this chapter I argue that a proof theoretic *view of databases is possible, and indeed much more fruitful. Specifically, I show how relational databases can be seen as special theories of first order logic, namely theories incorporating the following assumptions:*

1. *The domain closure assumption. The individuals occurring in the database are all and only the existing individuals.*
2. *The unique name assumption. Individuals with distinct names are distinct.*
3. *The closed world assumption. The only possible instances of a relation are those implied by the database.*

It will follow that a proof theoretic paradigm for relational databases provides a correct treatment of:

1. *Query evaluation for databases that have incomplete information, including null values.*
2. *Integrity constraints and their enforcement.*
3. *Conceptual modelling and the extension of the relational model to incorporate more real world semantics.*

1. Introduction

There is in our midst a small group of researchers whose devotion to logic and databases[1] is viewed with some perplexity by the majority of database theoreticians and practitioners. Their literature is peppered with obscure logical notation and theorems. As befits logicians, they claim privileged sovereignty over the Truth about databases. Can this cabal possibly be saying anything of interest to the database community?

Of course, everyone is at least dimly conscious of some logical debt owed by database theory, if only because the relational calculus relies on a first order language. What other outstanding logical loans are generally acknowledged? Well, a relational calculus query is a first order formula that is *evaluated* with respect to a database of facts. Since logic dictates that formulae have values (truth values) only with respect to *interpretations*, a database is commonly viewed as just that — a first order interpretation in the standard Tarskian sense. The value of a relational calculus query is determined by those instances of its free variables that make the query true with respect to the interpretation specified by the underlying database. This view of a database as a first order interpretation also neatly accommodates the concept of an integrity constraint. Insofar as one can view an integrity constraint as a first order formula, a database can be said to satisfy this constraint iff the constraint is true with respect to the database as interpretation. That is, given a set of integrity constraints, one cannot admit just any interpretation as a correct representation of one's domain of application; the interpretation must be a *model* (again, in the standard Tarskian sense) of the integrity constraints.

I think it is fair to say that, as far as database theoreticians conceive the field in logical terms, it is this *model theoretic* point of view that prevails. A database is a model of some set of integrity constraints, and a query is some formula to be evaluated with respect to this model. Now I invite you to survey the literature of the database logicians. You will, for the most part, find little mention of models and interpretations. Poor Tarski gets short shift here. And the relational algebra at best is granted footnote status. Instead, you will find most theoretical constructs couched in proof theoretic terms. A database is viewed as a set of first order formulae, not as a model. Queries are formulae to be proven, given the database as premises. Satisfaction of integrity constraints is defined in terms of consistency.[2] Considerable

[1] See, for example, [GM78].

[2] I shall provide a different definition in this chapter, but one which nevertheless is proof theoretic.

energy is invested in obtaining algorithms for efficiently finding proofs. In short, the logicians adopt a *proof theoretic* view of database theory.

What, then, is the preferred formal perspective on database theory — the model theoretic or the proof theoretic? Without a careful analysis, of course, one cannot say. This chapter presumes to provide such an analysis. My conclusion will be that both paradigms are reconcilable, but that the proof theoretic view is richer and more fruitful. More precisely, I shall show how, when given a model theoretic database *DB without null values*, one can transform *DB* into a suitable set of first order axioms, such that the resulting first order theory provides a proof theoretic characterization of query evaluation and integrity constraints. By itself this would not be a very exciting result. Curious perhaps, but not exciting. The idea bears fruit only in its capacity for generalization. For now that databases can be perceived as special kinds of first order theories, one can generalize these theories in order to provide answers to a variety of outstanding questions about databases:

1. How can the relational model be extended in order to incorporate more real world knowledge?
2. A number of null values have been proposed. What is their semantics?
3. What really are databases that have incomplete information?
4. What is the correct notion of an answer to a query in the presence of semantically rich databases such as those incorporating the features mentioned in 1-3 above?
5. For such semantically rich databases, what is an appropriate notion of an integrity constraint and what does it mean to satisfy a constraint?

My purpose in this chapter is to show how answers to these questions emerge in a very natural way from a proof theoretic characterization of database theory.

2. Databases and Logic: The Model Theoretic Perspective

This section outlines in some detail what I take to be the model theoretic paradigm in relational database theory.[3] To that end we require some formal preliminaries.

[3] Many of the ideas of this section, in particular the concept of a database as a first order model of a set of integrity constraints, derive from [NG78]. In effect, Sections 2.1-2.3 below formalize this concept.

2.1 First Order Languages

A first order language F is specified by a pair $(\mathcal{A}, \mathcal{W})$ where $\mathcal{A}$ is an alphabet of symbols and $\mathcal{W}$ is a set of syntactically well formed expressions called well formed formulae constructed using the symbols of $\mathcal{A}$. The rules for constructing the formulae of $\mathcal{W}$ are the same for all first order languages F; only the alphabet $\mathcal{A}$ may vary. $\mathcal{A}$ must contain symbols of the following kind, and only such symbols:

Variables: x, y, z, x_1, y_1, z_1, . . . ,
There must be infinitely many of these.

Constants: a, b, c, part17, acme, . . . ,
There may be 0 or more of these, possibly infinitely many.

Predicates: P, Q, R, *SUPPLIES*, *EMPLOYEE*, . . . ,
There must be at least one of these, possibly infinitely many. With each is associated an integer $n \geqslant 0$, its *arity*, denoting the number of arguments it takes.

Punctuation Signs: (,) .,

Logical Constants: $\supset$ (implies), $\wedge$ (and), $\vee$ (or), $\sim$ (not), $\equiv$ (iff).

Notice that function symbols are not included in this alphabet. I omit them because their introduction leads to severe difficulties for database theory [REIT78a] (pp. 173-175). Fortunately, they are not required for a formal treatment of current ideas in databases.

With such an alphabet $\mathcal{A}$ in hand, we can construct a set of syntactically well formed expressions, culminating in a definition of the set $\mathcal{W}$ of well formed formulae, as follows:

Terms
A variable or a constant of $\mathcal{A}$ is a *term*.

Atomic Formulae
If P is an n-ary predicate of $\mathcal{A}$ and $t_1, \ldots, t_n$ are terms, then $P(t_1, \ldots, t_n)$ is an *atomic formula*. $P(t_1, \ldots, t_n)$ is a *ground* atomic formula iff $t_1, \ldots, t_n$ are all constants.

Well Formed Formulae
$\mathcal{W}$ is the smallest set such that:

1. An atomic formula is a well formed formula (wff).
2. If W_1 and W_2 are wffs, so also are $(W_1 \wedge W_2)$, $(W_1 \vee W_2)$, $(W_1 \supset W_2)$, $(W_1 \equiv W_2)$, $\sim W_1$.
3. If x is a variable and W is a wff, then $(x)(W)$ and $(Ex)(W)$ are wffs. Here (x) is a *universal quantifier* and (Ex) an *existential quantifier.*

For the purposes of formally defining a relational database, we won't require arbitrary first order languages; a suitable proper subset of these will do. Accordingly, define a first order language $F = (\mathcal{A}, \mathcal{W})$ to be a *relational language* iff $\mathcal{A}$ has the following properties:

1. There are only finitely many constants in $\mathcal{A}$, but at least one.
2. There are only finitely many predicates in $\mathcal{A}$.
3. Among the predicates of $\mathcal{A}$ there is a distinguished binary predicate = which will function for us as equality.
4. Among the predicates of $\mathcal{A}$ there is a distinguished subset, possibly empty, of unary predicates. Such unary predicates are called *simple types.* Not all unary predicates of $\mathcal{A}$ need be simple types. Such simple types, together with boolean combinations of simple types, will, in part, model the concept of the domain of a relation as it arises in standard database theory.

Given a relational language $R = (\mathcal{A}, \mathcal{W})$ we can define the set of *types* of R as the smallest set such that:

1. A simple type of $\mathcal{A}$ is a type.
2. If τ_1 and τ_2 are types, so also are $(\tau_1 \wedge \tau_2)$, $(\tau_1 \vee \tau_2)$, $\sim\tau_1$.

For a relational language $R = (\mathcal{A}, \mathcal{W})$ it is convenient to define appropriate syntactically sugared *abbreviations* for certain of the wffs of $\mathcal{W}$, as follows:

If τ is a type, then

$$(x/\tau)(W) \text{ abbreviates } (x)(\tau(x) \supset W)$$

$$(Ex/\tau)(W) \text{ abbreviates } (Ex)(\tau(x) \wedge W)$$

where

1. If τ is $(\tau_1 \wedge \tau_2)$ then $\tau(x)$ is $(\tau_1(x) \wedge \tau_2(x))$.
2. If τ is $(\tau_1 \vee \tau_2)$ then $\tau(x)$ is $(\tau_1(x) \vee \tau_2(x))$.
3. If τ is $\sim\tau_1$ then $\tau(x)$ is $\sim\tau_1(x)$.

Here $(x/\tau)(W)$ should be read as: "For all x which are τ, W is the case," and $(Ex/\tau)(W)$ as: "there is an x, which is a τ, such that W is the case." Thus these *type restricted quantifiers* are meant to restrict the possible x's to just those which belong to the class τ. Notice that quantifiers may be restricted only by types, not by arbitrary predicates.

Example 2.1

If *MALE, EMPLOYEE, MANAGER, SUPPLIER,* and *PART* are simple types, the following are type restricted quantified wffs;

$$(x/SUPPLIER)\ (Ey/PART) SUPPLIES(x,y)$$

which abbreviates the ordinary wff

$$(x)[SUPPLIER(x) \supset (Ey)(PART(y) \wedge SUPPLIES(x,y))]$$

i.e., "Every supplier supplies at least one part."

$$(x/MALE \wedge EMPLOYEE \wedge \sim MANAGER)[DEPT(x,13)$$
$$\supset PENSION\text{-}PLAN(x)]$$

which abbreviates the ordinary wff

$$(x)[MALE(x) \wedge EMPLOYEE(x) \wedge \sim MANAGER(x)$$
$$\supset [DEPT(x,13) \supset PENSION\text{-}PLAN(x)]]$$

i.e., "All male employees of department 13 who are not managers belong to the pension plan."

In this example I have omitted a lot of parentheses on the assumption (correct, I hope) that you all know what these formulae *mean.* I shall continue this practice whenever no ambiguity will result.

2.2 The Semantics of First Order Languages

The objective here is to assign a precise meaning to each of the symbols of the alphabet $\mathcal{A}$ of a first order language $F = (\mathcal{A}, \mathcal{W})$ and, using this assignment as a basis, to define the truth values of arbitrary wffs in $\mathcal{W}$ constructed from these symbols. The required definitions are by now standard (see, for example, [MEND64]).

An *interpretation* I *for the first order language* $F = (\mathcal{A}, \mathcal{W})$ is a triple (D,K,E) where

1. D is a non empty set, called the *domain* of I, over which the variables of $\mathcal{A}$ are meant to range.
2. K is mapping from the constants of $\mathcal{A}$ into D (*i.e.*, for each constant c, $K(c) \in D$).
3. E is a mapping from the predicates of $\mathcal{A}$ into sets of tuples of elements of D (*i.e.*, for each n-ary predicate symbol P, $E(P) \subseteq D^n$). $E(P)$ is called the *extension* of P in the interpretation I.

Example 2.2

Consider a relational language $R = (\mathcal{A}, \mathcal{W})$ where the only predicates and constants of $\mathcal{A}$ are the following:

Predicates: $TEACHER(\cdot)$, $COURSE(\cdot)$, $STUDENT(\cdot)$, $TEACH(\cdot,\cdot)$, $ENROLLED(\cdot,\cdot)$, $=(\cdot,\cdot)$.

Simple Types: $TEACHER(\cdot)$, $COURSE(\cdot)$, $STUDENT(\cdot)$.

Constants: A, B, C, a, b, c, d, $CS100$, $CS200$, $P100$, $P200$.

Then the following defines an interpretation for R, with domain $\{A, B, C, a, b, c, d, CS100, CS200, P100, P200\}$:

TEACHER	COURSE	STUDENT	TEACH	ENROLLED	=	
A	CS100	a	A CS100	a CS100	A	A
B	CS200	b	A CS200	a P100	B	B
C	P100	c	B P100	b CS100	C	C
	P200	d	C P200	c P100	a	a
				d CS200	b	b
				d P200	c	c
					d	d
					CS100	CS100
					CS200	CS200
					P100	P100
					P200	P200

Here the tables define the extensions of the predicate symbols *TEACHER*, *COURSE*, *etc.* Notice that, strictly speaking, the domain elements A, B, C, *etc.*, are *not* the same as the constant symbols A, B, C, *etc.*, which are part of our alphabet of symbols. In effect, I have chosen to name the domain elements by the constant symbols. So think of the domain elements in the tables as coloured red, and the constant symbols as coloured black. In subsequent examples I shall freely name domain elements by constant symbols.

Now given an interpretation $I = (D,K,E)$ for a first order language $F = (\mathcal{A}, \mathcal{W})$, let ρ be a mapping from the variables of $\mathcal{A}$ into D (*i.e.*, for each variable $x \in \mathcal{A}$, $\rho(x) \in D$). ρ is called an *environment* for the variables of $\mathcal{A}$. For a given environment ρ, define a mapping:

$\|\cdot\|^{\rho}_{I}$: terms $\rightarrow D$ as follows:

$\|c\|^{\rho}_{I} = K(c)$ for each constant symbol $c \in \mathcal{A}$.

$\|x\|^{\rho}_{I} = \rho(x)$ for each variable $x \in \mathcal{A}$.

Next define a relation $\models_{I,\rho}$ by:

1. $\models_{I,\rho} P(t_1, \ldots, t_n)$ iff $(\|t_1\|^{\rho}_{I}, \ldots, \|t_n\|^{\rho}_{I}) \in E(P)$ for each atomic formula $P(t_1, \ldots, t_n) \in \mathcal{W}$.
2. $\models_{I,\rho} W_1 \wedge W_2$ iff $\models_{I,\rho} W_1$ and $\models_{I,\rho} W_2$.
3. $\models_{I,\rho} W_1 \vee W_2$ iff $\models_{I,\rho} W_1$ or $\models_{I,\rho} W_2$.
4. $\models_{I,\rho} \sim W$ iff not $\models_{I,\rho} W$.
5. $\models_{I,\rho} W_1 \supset W_2$ iff $\models_{I,\rho} \sim W_1 \vee W_2$.
6. $\models_{I,\rho} W_1 \equiv W_2$ iff $\models_{I,\rho} (W_1 \supset W_2) \wedge (W_2 \supset W_1)$.
7. $\models_{I,\rho} (x)W$ iff for all $d \in D$, $\models_{I,\rho[x \rightarrow d]} W$ where $\rho[x \rightarrow d]$ denotes an environment identical to ρ except that this new environment maps the variable x to the domain element d.
8. $\models_{I,\rho} (Ex)W$ iff $\models_{I,\rho} \sim(x)\sim W$.

Finally, define $\models_I W$ iff $\models_{I,\rho} W$ for all environments ρ, in which case W is said to be *true in the interpretation I*. W is *false in the interpretation I* iff for no environment ρ is it the case that $\models_{I,\rho} W$. An interpretation I is a *model* of the wff W iff W is true in I. I is a *model* of a set S of wffs iff W is true in I for each $W \in S$.

Example 2.2 (continued)

The previous interpretation is a model for each of the following formulae:

$$(x)(y)[TEACH(x,y) \supset TEACHER(x) \wedge COURSE(y)] \quad (2.1)$$

$$(x)(y)[ENROLLED(x,y) \supset STUDENT(x) \wedge COURSE(y)] \quad (2.2)$$

$$(x/COURSE)(Ey/TEACHER)TEACH(y,x) \quad (2.3)$$

$$(x/TEACHER)(Ey/COURSE)TEACH(x,y) \quad (2.4)$$

Notice that, on the view that types formalize the concept of "domain of a relation," then (2.1) and (2.2) specify the domains of the relations *TEACH* and *ENROLLED*.[4] Formulae (2.1)-(2.4) can be viewed as integrity constraints that happen to be true in the given interpretation.

Notice also that the logician's fancy definition of truth in an interpretation, involving as it does the notion of an environment ρ for variables, is motivated by the requirement of maintaining the distinction between the objects of the interpretation and the purely syntactic symbols of the first order language. Of course, no one really thinks of

[4] Notice that I have not yet defined the concept of a relation. It should be clear from Example 2.2, however, that *TEACH* and *ENROLLED* will be examples of relations by whatever definition I eventually come up with.

interpretations in this way, at least not in the database setting. Rather, one thinks of the tables of an interpretation as defining a set of propositions. In Example 2.2, the true propositions are *TEACHER*(*A*), *TEACHER*(*B*) , . . . , *ENROLLED*(*d,P*200), =(*a,a*) , . . . , =(*P*200, *P*200). Those propositions not included in this set are treated as false. For example, *TEACHER*(*d*), *TEACH*(*B,CS*100) and =(*A,B*) are false. Then a wff $(x)\ W(x)$ is true in an interpretation iff for every d in the domain of the interpretation, $W(d)$ is true. $(Ex)\ W(x)$ is true iff for some d, $W(d)$ is true. Of course the logical constants $\wedge$, $\vee$, $\sim$, $\supset$ and $\equiv$ are given their usual truth table definitions. Thus, in the case of finite interpretations, determining the truth of an arbitrary wff reduces to purely propositional truth table evaluations.

2.3 Relational Databases Defined

Recall that a relational language $R = (\mathcal{A}, \mathcal{W})$ is a first order language for which $\mathcal{A}$ contains finitely many constants and finitely many predicates, among which is a distinguished equality predicate and possibly some distinguished unary predicates called simple types. Among all of the possible interpretations for a relational language R, we can single out the class of relational interpretations as follows:

Let $R = (\mathcal{A}, \mathcal{W})$ be a relational language. An interpretation $I = (D,K,E)$ for R is a *relational interpretation* for R iff

1. K: constants of $\mathcal{A} \xrightarrow[onto]{1-1} D$ (so that D must be finite).

2. $E(=) = \{ (d,d) \mid d \in D \}$.

The interpretation of Example 2.2 is a relational interpretation.

A *relational database* is a triple (R,I,IC) where:

1. R is a relational language.

2. I is a relational interpretation for R.

3. IC is a set of wffs of R, called *integrity constraints.* In particular, it is required that for each n-ary predicate P distinct from = and the simple types, IC must contain a wff of the form

$$(x_1) \ldots (x_n)[P(x_1, \ldots, x_n) \supset \tau_1(x_1) \wedge \ldots \wedge \tau_n(x_n)]$$

where the τ_i are types. $\tau_1, \ldots, \tau_n$ are called the *domains* of P.

For each predicate P distinct from the simple types, the extension $E(P)$ is called a *relation.* When the context is clear, I shall often refer to a relation by the name of the corresponding predicate P. Thus I will speak of "the relation P" in referring to P's extension.

The integrity constraints IC of a relational database (R,I,IC) are said to be *satisfied* iff I is a model for IC. Wffs (2.1)-(2.4) of Example 2.2 (continued) might well be taken to define a set of integrity constraints in which case Example 2.2, together with its continuation, defines a relational database. The wffs (2.1) and (2.2) then define the domains of the predicates *TEACH* and *ENROLLED*. For this example, the relational database satisfies its integrity constraints.

A few remarks are in order.

1. Since the extension of the equality predicate is the set of all pairs (d,d) of domain elements, $=(d,d')$ is false for all distinct domain elements d,d'. This is in keeping with the universally adopted assumption in database theory that distinctly named individuals are in fact distinct. From our model theoretic perspective, this means that different domain elements denote different individuals, so that in Example 2.2, the proposition =(*P*100,*P*200) is false, whereas =(*P*100,*P*100) is true.

2. Relational database theory generally incorporates a set of arithmetic comparison operators like $<, =, >$ *etc.*, as needed. I have chosen only to represent the equality "operator," primarily because it will play a prominent role in the subsequent theory. It would be a simple matter to modify my definition of a relational database to include the binary predicates $<$, $>$, and indeed any set of desired binary "operators." The basic difference between my approach and the conventional one is that I treat these operators as predicates that are extensionally defined within the theory, whereas conventionally these operators are viewed as procedures whose formal properties are understood by everyone and therefore are not defined within the theory. They are, so to speak, "external operators."

3. The concept of an integrity constraint as defined above corresponds to the so-called *static* integrity constraints or *state laws* of [NY78]. Such constraints are meant to be satisfied by any state of the database. In contrast there is also the concept of a *dynamic* integrity constraint or *transition law* [NY78]. Satisfaction of a dynamic constraint is a function of not just the current state of the database but also of its successor state. I do not, in this chapter, address this latter class of integrity constraints, except to point out their intimate connection with the well known "frame problem" in Artificial Intelligence [RAPH71].

2.4 A First Order Query Language

The query language I will appeal to is one first defined in [REIT77] and used subsequently in [REIT78a] and [REIT80a]. It is obviously a close relative of that used in the domain calculus of [ULLM80] (pp. 116-117).

Queries are defined relative to a given relational language $R = (\mathcal{A}, \mathcal{W})$. Specifically, a *query for* R is any expression of the form $<\vec{x}/\vec{\tau} \mid W(\vec{x})>$ where:

1. $\vec{x}/\vec{\tau}$ denotes the sequence $x_1/\tau_1, \ldots, x_n/\tau_n$, and the x_i are variables of $\mathcal{A}$.
2. Each τ_i is a type composed of simple types of $\mathcal{A}$.
3. $W(\vec{x}) \in \mathcal{W}$ and the only free variables of $W(\vec{x})$ are among $\vec{x} = x_1, \ldots, x_n$. Moreover, all of the quantifiers occurring in $W(\vec{x})$ are type restricted quantifiers.

If $DB = (R,I,IC)$ is a relational database then a query for R is said to be *applicable* to DB. The intention here is that information may be retrieved from a relational database only by posing queries that are applicable to that database.

Intuitively, the query $<\vec{x}/\vec{\tau} \mid W(\vec{x})>$ is meant to denote the set of all tuples of constants $\vec{c} = c_1, \ldots, c_n$ such that each c_i satisfies the type τ_i, and such that the database satisfies $W(\vec{c})$. A formal definition will follow the next example.

Example 2.3

The following are sample queries applicable to the education database of Example 2.2:

Who teaches $P100$?

$$<x/TEACHER \mid TEACH(x,P100)>$$

Who are all of A's students?

$$<x/STUDENT \mid (Ey/COURSE)TEACH(A,y) \wedge ENROLLED(x,y)>$$

What courses does a take, and who teaches them?

$$<x/COURSE,\ y/TEACHER \mid ENROLLED(a,x) \wedge TEACH(y,x)>$$

Who teaches all of the students?

$$<x/TEACHER \mid (y/STUDENT)(Ez/COURSE)TEACH(x,z) \wedge ENROLLED(y,z)>$$

The following queries are not applicable to this database because they involve constants or predicates that are not part of the alphabet of the relational language for the database:

$$<x/TEACHER \mid TEACH(x,MATH100)>$$

$$<x/SUPPLIER \mid (y/PART)SUPPLIES(x,y)>$$

Formally, let $DB = (R,I,IC)$ and let $Q = <\vec{x}/\vec{\tau} \mid W(\vec{x})>$ be a query applicable to DB. A tuple $\vec{c}$ of constants of R's alphabet is an *answer* to Q *with respect to* DB iff

1. $\tau_i(c_i)$ is true in I, $i = 1, \ldots, n$.
2. $W(\vec{c})$ is true in I.

Notice that the concept of an answer is defined only for queries applicable to DB. A query not applicable to DB must involve predicates not contained in R's alphabet and which therefore have no extensions in I, or constants not contained in R's alphabet and which thus have no corresponding domain elements in I. In other words, DB *does not know* about these predicates or constants, in which case the query must be viewed as meaningless.

Finally, notice that there is no correlate in my definition of a query to the notion of a safe [ULLM80] or definite [KUHN67] or range separable [CODD72] query. Essentially these latter restrictions on queries are deemed necessary in order to avoid ever computing the unrestricted complement of a relation; this because such complements are seen as either infinite or undefined. But notice that when a relational database is a triple (R,I,IC), the complement of a type or a relation is finite and perfectly well defined since there are but finitely many individuals in the domain of I. These are the only individuals the database *knows* about; as far as it is concerned *these are all and only the existing individuals.* There is no need for the concept of a safe query.

The source of the safe query constraint in conventional database theory can be traced to the concept of a domain for a relation as the totality of all individuals of a certain kind. Thus, the totality of all parts might be a domain for an inventory database, or the totality of all suppliers. Domains might be infinite, as is the set of all integers. Whether these domains are conceived as being finite or infinite, it is the *completed totality* of such individuals that is somehow seen to be part of the database, despite the fact that in any state of the database only a finite subset of this totality will be explicitly represented. Unrestricted complements of relations are understood to be defined with respect to the completed totality of database individuals, not with respect to the finitely many explicitly present representatives of this totality. Hence the requirement of safe queries.

Now I must confess to a certain discomfort over this notion of complementation with respect to completed totalities. For this totality is never explicitly represented in the database; rather, it is a conceptualization that we, as humans, entertain. There is no way that the database can be said to know about, say, the set of all integers, at least not without some representation of Peano arithmetic. It knows only about some finitely many integers, and precious little about them. It seems to me that queries are about things the database *knows about* (suppliers, integers, *etc.*, that it has explicit representations for). A query $<\bar{x}/\bar{\tau} \mid W(\bar{x})>$ asks for all tuples $\bar{x}$ *known to the database*, satisfying $\bar{\tau}$ and W. In this view, complementation is perfectly respectable. $<x/INTEGER \mid \sim P(x)>$ denotes the set of all integers known to the database for which $\sim P(x)$ is known to be true.

2.5 Some Problems with the Model Theoretic Perspective

The model theoretic paradigm has an elegance and simplicity that accounts, in large measure, for the overwhelming success of Codd's original proposal for a relational model of data [CODD70]. Yet it is not without its difficulties, some of which (*e.g.*, null values) Codd had foreseen, others of which have subsequently emerged. I shall here focus on two such problems with the model theoretic world view.

2.5.1 Databases with Incomplete Information

A variety of phenomena fall under this rubric. I shall consider two of these: disjunctive information and the need for null values.

2.5.1.1 Disjunctive Information

One encounters this problem whenever there is the need to represent a fact of the kind "P is the case, or Q is the case, or . . . " but it is not known which of P, Q, . . . , actually is the case. [LIPS79] proposes a treatment of this situation under certain simplifying assumptions. For the education database of Example 2.2, we face this problem in an attempt to represent the fact "a is enrolled in $P200$ or in $CS200$, but I don't know which." The obvious (and indeed only) approach within the model theoretic framework is to split the given interpretation into three interpretations I_1, I_2 and I_3, each identical to the given one, except that, in I_1, the relation *ENROLLED* contains the additional tuple $(a,P200)$. In I_2 it contains $(a,CS200)$, while in I_3 it contains both $(a,P200)$ and $(a,CS200)$. Then $\bar{c}$ will be defined to be an answer to the query $<\bar{x}/\bar{\tau} \mid W(\bar{x})>$ iff $\tau_i(c_i)$ and $W(\bar{c})$ are all true in all three interpretations I_1, I_2 and I_3. This idea generalizes in the obvious way to the concept of a database involving many interpretations, and the concept of query evaluation requiring truth in all these interpretations. Anyone familiar with the completeness theorem for first order logic will immediately detect proof theory in this observation.

Notice that we cannot avoid the problem of multiple interpretations by treating the formula $ENROLLED(a,P200) \vee ENROLLED(a,CS200)$ as an integrity constraint. For to do so would require that at least one of $(a,P200)$ and $(a,CS200)$ be included in the relation *ENROLLED* in order for this constraint to be satisfied, and we don't know which of these tuples is the case.

2.5.1.2 Null Values

This terminology embraces a multitude of necessary evils in database theory. I shall focus here on just one such null, namely "value at present unknown." In fact this null value has two distinct manifestations: "value at present unknown, but one of some finite set of known possible values," and "value at present unknown, yet *not necessarily* one of some finite set of known possible values." As an example of the former, suppose that in our education database we wish to represent the fact that e is a student who is enrolled in some course, but we don't know which course that is. Suppose further that we know that the only existing courses are the ones mentioned in the database, so that a priori, whichever course that e is taking, it is one of $CS100$, $CS200$, . . . , $P200$. Then our task is to represent the disjunctive fact:

$$ENROLLED(e,CS100) \vee ENROLLED(e,CS200)$$
$$\vee \ldots \vee ENROLLED(e,P200)$$

which is just the problem of disjunctive information discussed above.

As an example of the latter "value unknown" null, consider the ubiquitous "supplier and parts" database which contains a relation *SUPPLIES* (.,.) whose domains are specified by:

$$(x)(y)\,[SUPPLIES(x,y) \supset SUPPLIER(x) \wedge PART(y)]$$

Now suppose that p is a part with no known supplier, but we do know that someone, perhaps one of the known suppliers, perhaps not, does supply it. How shall we represent this fact? The standard approach (see, for example, [CODD79]) is to postulate a new unknown but existing entity ω, a *null value*, then add the tuple (ω,p) to the *SUPPLIES* table, add ω to the *SUPPLIER* table and p to the *PART* table. But ω is an individual with quite a different character from the other known individuals of the database, so it is deemed necessary to augment the conventional truth values {true, false} with a third truth value "unknown" in order to correctly evaluate queries over databases containing such null values. The effect of this third truth value is then an extension of the relational algebra so that, for example, equality and the join operator suitably reflect the intended meaning of this null value.

Notice that *the multiple truth valued approach to null values is a direct and natural consequence of the model theoretic paradigm of relational database theory.* Models are concerned with truth. Since two truth values suffice for the evaluation of wffs in an interpretation without nulls, it is only natural to try inventing new truth values in order to evaluate queries in an interpretation with nulls. Notice also that a correct treatment of nulls is predicated on a prior notion of what these null values *mean.* Without a correct *semantics,* no correct extended relational algebra is possible. On this view, multi-valued logics provide one possible framework within which a semantics for values may be defined. Alas, within this framework it is by no means clear how to extend the relational model to correctly represent null values. Although several approaches exist in the literature (*e.g.,* [BISK81] [CODD79] [WALK80] [VASS79] [ZANI77]), there is no general agreement about which of these, if any, provides a correct semantics for nulls. This difficulty is compounded in the presence of additional kinds of null values (*e.g.,* "no value permitted").

2.5.2 Extending the Relational Model to Incorporate More World Knowledge

It is becoming increasingly evident that the relational model provides limited expressive power, and that extensions to the formalism are required in order to incorporate more real world meaning [CODD79] [BZ81]. The following are typical examples of the kinds of real world knowledge that an extended relational model might accommodate:

1. General facts about the world such as "The subpart relation is transitive" and "All men are mortal."
2. Events: Their sequencing and times of occurrence.
3. Generalization hierarchies (IS-A hierarchies) with property inheritance.

It is true that certain kinds of knowledge can be represented within the model theoretic paradigm by treating this knowledge as an integrity constraint. For example, the fact that the subpart relation is transitive

$$(x/PART)\,(y/PART)\,(z/PART)[SUBPART(x,y) \wedge SUBPART(y,z) \supset SUBPART(x,z)]$$

could be an integrity constraint, thereby forcing the extension of *SUBPART* to be closed under transitivity. But other kinds of information, for example disjunctive information, cannot be treated as integrity constraints, as observed in Section 2.5.1.1. Because of this, and because there are settings in which various forms of inference seem necessary (for example, property inheritance in hierarchies), other approaches to the strict model theoretic have been proposed. I shall return to these issues in Section 4.2 in the context of a proof theoretic view of databases.

3. Databases and Logic: the Proof Theoretic Perspective

My objective in this section is to show how the model theoretic perspective on databases can be reinterpreted in purely proof theoretic terms. Specifically, I shall define a class of first order theories, called relational theories, and prove an equivalence result relating relational theories to relational interpretations. From this it will follow that a definition of a relational database, equivalent to the one presented in Section 2.3, is as a triple (R,T,IC) where T is a relational theory. Then, all prior definitions, involving as they do truth in a relational interpretation, can be reformulated in terms of provability in the theory T. The point of this result, namely its capacity for generalization, will be taken up in Section 4.

3.1 Relational Theories

Imagine given a database (R,I,IC). I shall assume, as I have assumed all along, that the domain elements of I are named using constant symbols of R's alphabet.[5] In addition, instead of viewing the relational interpretation I as a set of tables, think of it as a set of ground atomic formulae. Thus, in Example 2.2, think of the interpretation as being specified by the ground atomic formulae

$$\{TEACHER(A),\ TEACHER(B),\ TEACHER(C),\ \ldots,$$
$$ENROLLED(d,P100), ENROLLED(d,P200),$$
$$=(A,A),\ =(B,B),\ \ldots,\ =(P200,P200)\}.$$

I now propose viewing this set as a first order theory (*i.e.,* as a set of wffs of the underlying relational language).[6] Currently, these wffs are simply ground atomic formulae, but I shall shortly have occasion to modify this set using other kinds of formulae.

---

[5] See the comments of Example 2.2.

[6] In general if $(\mathcal{A}, \mathcal{W})$ is a first order language, then any subset of $\mathcal{W}$ is called a *first order theory* of the language.

Given such a relational interpretation, reinterpreted as a first order theory T, there are various formulae that can be proven, given T as premises. Thus, with reference to Example 2.2 we have the following:

$$T \vdash ENROLLED(c,P100)$$ [7]

$$T \vdash ENROLLED(a,P100) \wedge TEACH(B,P100)$$

$$T \vdash (Ey/COURSE)\, TEACH(A,y) \wedge ENROLLED(a,y)$$

Notice that all of these provable formulae also happen to be true in the original interpretation. However, there are formulae that are true in the interpretation but that are not provable from the corresponding first order theory. For example:

$$(x)[TEACHER(x) \vee COURSE(x) \vee STUDENT(x)]$$

is such a formula. This is not provable because the first order theory T does not know that $A, B, \ldots, P100, P200$ are all and only the existing individuals. As far as T is concerned, there might be other existing individuals in the world. So augment T with the following domain closure axiom:

$$(x)[=(x,A) \vee =(x,B) \vee \ldots \vee =(x,P100) \vee =(x,P200)]$$

In general, if I is a relational interpretation with domain $c_1, \ldots, c_n$, then the *domain closure axiom* for I [REIT80a] is

$$(x)[=(x,c_1) \vee =(x,c_2) \vee \ldots \vee =(x,c_n)]$$

We can also simplify the representation of the equality relation by replacing all of its instances $=(A,A), =(B,B), \ldots, =(P200,P200)$ by the single formula $(x)=(x,x)$. Our transformed first order theory T now consists of the following wffs:

$$(x)=(x,x)$$

$$(x)[\doteq(x,A) \vee =(x,B) \vee \ldots \vee =(x,P100) \vee =(x,P200)]$$

$$TEACHER(A),\ TEACHER(B),\ \ldots,\ ENROLLED(d,CS200),$$

$$ENROLLED(d,P200).$$

Unfortunately, there still remain wffs true in the original interpretation I but unprovable from T, for example all of the inequalities $\sim=(A,B)$, $\sim=(A,C)$, *etc.* So for each pair of distinct constants c,c' of the domain, augment T with the *unique name axioms* $\sim=(c,c')$ [REIT80a]. Since I am proposing to treat equality proof theoretically, we shall also require the standard axioms specifying the intuitive properties that equality should have, namely commutativity, transitivity, and substitution of one term for another term that is equal to it. These axioms will be given below.

Our theory T now contains unique name axioms, together with axioms for equality. The only remaining problem with T is that it fails to treat negation properly. For example, the wff $\sim TEACHER(a)$, while true in I, is not provable from T. The reason is clear enough; T has models in which $TEACHER(a)$ is true. To avoid this, we need a first order wff which says that the only individuals $TEACHER$ can be predicated of are A, B, and C. This can be done using the *completion* of the predicate $TEACHER$:

$$(x)[TEACHER(x) \supset =(x,A) \vee =(x,B) \vee =(x,C)]$$

Similarly, the completion of the predicate $TEACH$ for our education database is

$$(x)\,(y)[TEACH(x,y) \supset =(x,A) \wedge =(y,CS100)$$
$$\vee =(x,A) \wedge =(y,CS200) \vee =(x,B) \wedge =(y,P100)$$
$$\vee =(x,C) \wedge =(y,P200)]$$

We can now augment the theory T for the education example with the completions of each of the predicates of that database. The first order theory that we finally end up with consists of the following formulae:

1. Domain closure axiom:

$$(x)[=(x,A) \vee =(x,B) \vee \ldots \vee =(x,P100) \vee =(x,P200)]$$

2. Unique name axioms:

$$\sim=(A,B),\ \sim=(B,C),\ \sim=(A,a),\ \ldots,$$

3. Equality axioms specifying the reflexivity, commutativity and transitivity of equality, and the principle of substitution of equal terms.
4. The ground atomic facts:

$$TEACHER(A),\ TEACHER(B),\ \ldots,\ ENROLLED(d,P200).$$

5. Completion axioms for each predicate:

$$(x)[TEACHER(x) \supset =(x,A) \vee =(x,B) \vee =(x,C)]$$

$$(x)\,(y)[ENROLLED(x,y) \supset =(x,a) \wedge =(y,CS100) \vee \ldots \vee$$
$$=(x,d) \wedge =(y,P200)]$$

etc.

[7] If W is a set of first order formulae and if w is a first order formula, then $W \vdash w$ means that there is a first order proof of w from premises W.

Notice that *the only model of this theory is the original interpretation* of Example 2.2. Thus, whenever we had occasion to speak of *truth in this interpretation*, we can instead speak of *provability in the theory*. All of which motivates the following definition:

Let $R = (\mathcal{A}, \mathcal{W})$ be a relational language. A first order theory $T \subseteq \mathcal{W}$ is a *relational theory* of R iff it satisfies the following properties:

1. If $c_1, \ldots, c_n$ are all of the constants of $\mathcal{A}$, T contains the domain closure axiom

$$(x)[=(x,c_1) \vee \ldots \vee =(x,c_n)]$$

   T contains the unique name axioms

$$\sim =(c_i,c_j) \quad i, j = 1, \ldots, n \quad i < j$$

2. T contains each of the following equality axioms:

   (i) Reflexivity
   $(x) = (x,x)$

   (ii) Commutativity
   $(x)[=(x,y) \supset =(y,x)]$

   (iii) Transitivity
   $(x)\ (y)\ (z)[=(x,y) \wedge =(y,z) \supset =(x,z)]$

   (iv) Leibnitz' principle of substitution of equal terms:

   For each m-ary predicate symbol P of $\mathcal{A}$,

$$(x_1) \ldots (x_m)\ (y_1) \ldots (y_m)[P(x_1, \ldots, x_m) \wedge$$
$$=(x_1,y_1) \wedge \ldots \wedge =(x_m,y_m) \supset P(y_1, \ldots, y_m)]$$

3. For some set $\Delta \subseteq \mathcal{W}$ of ground atomic formulae, none of whose predicates is the equality predicate, $\Delta \subseteq T$.
   For each m-ary predicate P of $\mathcal{A}$ distinct from the equality predicate define a set C_P of m-tuples of constants by

$$C_P = \{\overline{c} \mid P(\overline{c}) \in \Delta\}.$$

   The set $\{P(\overline{c}) \mid \overline{c} \in C_P\}$ is called the *extension of P in T*.[8]

   Suppose $C_P = \{(c_1^{(1)}, \ldots, c_m^{(1)}), \ldots, (c_1^{(r)}, \ldots, c_m^{(r)})\}$. Then in addition to the wffs of Δ, T contains the following *completion axiom* for P:

$$(x_1) \ldots (x_m)[P(x_1, \ldots, x_m) \supset =(x_1,c_1^{(1)}) \wedge \ldots \wedge =(x_m,c_m^{(1)})$$
$$\vee \ldots \vee =(x_1,c_1^{(r)}) \wedge \ldots \wedge =(x_m,c_m^{(r)})]$$

   If $C_P = \{\ \}$, then P's extension in T is empty, and T's completion axiom is

$$(x_1) \ldots (x_m) \sim P(x_1, \ldots, x_m).$$

4. The only wffs of T are those sanctioned by conditions 1-3 above.

Notice that in a relational theory T the extension of P in T together with P's completion axiom is logically equivalent to the wff

$$(x_1) \ldots (x_m)[P(x_1, \ldots, x_m) \equiv =(x_1,c_1^{(1)}) \wedge \ldots \wedge =(x_m,c_m^{(1)})$$
$$\vee \ldots \vee =(x_1,c_1^{(r)}) \wedge \ldots \wedge =(x_m,c_m^{(r)})]$$

This is the "if and only if form" of the predicate P as defined in [CLAR78]. The idea of using a completion axiom in the above definition derives from Clark's paper.

The following theorem establishes an equivalence between relational theories and relational interpretations.

Theorem 3.1. *Suppose $R = (\mathcal{A}, \mathcal{W})$ is a relational language. Then:*

1. *If T is a relational theory of R, then T has a unique model I which is a relational interpretation for R.*

2. *If I is a relational interpretation for R then there is a relational theory T of R such that I is the only model of T.*

Proof.

1. Let $I = (D,K,E)$ be the following relational interpretation for R:

   (i) $D = \{c_1, \ldots, c_n\}$ where $c_1, \ldots, c_n$ are all of the constants of $\mathcal{A}$.

   (ii) $K(c_i) = c_i,\ i = 1, \ldots, n.$

   (iii) $E(=) = \{(c,c) \mid c \in D\}$

   If P is a m-ary predicate of $\mathcal{A}$ whose completion axiom in T has the form

$$(x_1), \ldots (x_m) \sim P(x_1, \ldots, x_m) \qquad (3.1)$$

   (so that P's extension in T is empty), $E(P) = \{\ \}$. Otherwise P's completion axiom in T has the form

[8] Not to be confused with the concept of the extension of a predicate P in an interpretation.

$$(x_1)\ldots(x_m)[P(x_1,\ldots,x_m) \supset =(x_1,c_1^{(1)}) \wedge \ldots \wedge =(x_m,c_m^{(1)}) \vee \ldots \vee =(x_1,c_1^{(r)}) \wedge \ldots \wedge =(x_m,c_m^{(r)})] \quad (3.2)$$

where the $c_i^{(j)}$ are all constants of $\mathcal{A}$. In this case P's extension in T is $\{P(c_1^{(1)},\ldots,c_m^{(1)}),\ldots,P(c_1^{(r)},\ldots,c_m^{(r)})\}$ and $E(P) = \{(c_1^{(1)},\ldots,c_m^{(1)}),\ldots,(c_1^{(r)},\ldots,c_m^{(r)})\}$.

I is clearly a model of T. To see that I is T's only model notice first that T's domain closure and unique name axioms force any model M of T to have the same domain as I (up to renaming of I's domain elements). Secondly, T's reflexivity axiom forces the extension in M of the equality predicate to be the same as in I. Finally, the extension and completion axiom, in T, of a predicate P together with T's unique name axioms force P's extension in M to be the same as its extension in I.

2. The proof here involves constructing, from I, a relational theory T in the same fashion as in the educational database of Example 2.2. So, given a relational interpretation $I = (D,K,E)$ for R, define a first order theory $T \subseteq \mathcal{W}$ as follows:

(i) If $D = \{c_1,\ldots,c_n\}$ then T contains the wffs

$$(x)[=(x,c_1) \vee \ldots \vee =(x,c_n)]$$

$$\sim=(c_i,c_j) \quad i,j = 1,\ldots,n, \; i<j.$$

(ii) T contains axioms for the reflexivity, commutativity and transitivity of the equality predicate, together with axioms for the principle of substitution of equal terms for each predicate P of $\mathcal{A}$.

(iii) For each m-ary predicate P of $\mathcal{A}$ distinct from the equality predicate:

If $E(P) = \{\,\}$ then T contains the wff (3.1).

If $E(P) = \{(c_1^{(1)},\ldots,c_m^{(1)}),\ldots,(c_1^{(r)},\ldots,c_m^{(r)})\}$ then T contains the wff (3.2), together with each of the wffs $P(c_1^{(i)},\ldots,c_m^{(i)})$ $i = 1,\ldots,r$.

(iv) The only wffs in T are those sanctioned by (i)-(iii) above.

Then T is a relational theory of R and it is not hard to see, as in the proof of 1 above, that I is a unique model of T.

QED

Corollary 3.2. *Suppose T is a relational theory of a relational language R, and that I is a model of T. Then for any wff w of R, w is true in I iff $T \vdash w$.*

Proof. The proof follows from the fact that I must be a unique model of T and the completeness theorem for first order logic.

3.2 A Proof Theoretic Reconstruction of Relational Database Theory

Theorem 3.1 and Corollary 3.2 form the basis for a proof theoretic reconstruction of all the model theoretic concepts and definitions of Section 2. For if (R,I,IC) is a relational database, then we can construct, as in the proof of 2. of Theorem 3.1, a relational theory T of R for which I is T's only model. By Corollary 3.2, the concepts of truth in I and provability from T are equivalent. Conversely, by 1. of Theorem 3.1, any relational theory T defines a unique relational interpretation I, and again, by Corollary 3.2, truth in I is equivalent to provability from T.

Accordingly, we can equivalently define a *relational database* to be a triple (R, T, IC) where R and IC are as before, and T is a relational theory of R. The integrity constraints IC are said to be *satisfied* iff for each $w \in IC$, $T \vdash w$. If $Q = \langle \overline{x}/\overline{\tau} \mid W(\overline{x}) \rangle$ is a query applicable to this database, then an n-tuple $\overline{c}$ of constants of R's alphabet is an *answer* to Q *with respect to this database* iff

1. $T \vdash \tau_i(c_i)$ $i = 1,\ldots,n$ and
2. $T \vdash W(\overline{c})$

4. Generalizing the Proof Theoretic Perspective

In this section I shall show how the proof theoretic view of a relational database as a triple (R,T,IC) admits a variety of generalizations, through modification of the first order theory T.

4.1 Databases That Contain Incomplete Information

Recall that in Section 2.5.1 I discussed two manifestations of the problem of representing incomplete information within the model theoretic paradigm of database theory, namely disjunctive information and null values. Let us return to these problems and determine the

4.1.1 Disjunctive Information

This was the problem of representing disjunctive facts of the form: "P is the case, or Q is, or ... , but I don't know which," and of using such incomplete information in deriving answers to database queries.

Example 4.1

Consider the following relational theory for a supplier and parts world:

PART	*SUPPLIER*	*SUPPLIES*	*SUBPART*
p_1	Acme	Acme p_1	p_1 p_2
p_2	Foo	Foo p_2	
p_3			

where for brevity I use tables to specify the predicate extensions in the theory instead of the ground atomic formulae $PART(p_1)$, $PART(p_2)$, . . . ,$SUBPART(p_1,p_2)$.

Domain Closure Axiom:

$$(x)[=(x,p_1) \vee =(x,p_2) \vee =(x,p_3) \vee =(x,Acme) \vee =(x,Foo)]$$

Unique Name Axioms:

$$\sim=(p_1,p_2),\ \sim=(p_2,p_3),\ etc.$$

Equality Axioms: as usual

Completion Axioms:

1. $(x)[PART(x) \supset =(x,p_1) \vee =(x,p_2) \vee =(x,p_3)]$
2. $(x)[SUPPLIER(x) \supset =(x,Acme) \vee =(x,Foo)]$
3. $(x)(y)[SUPPLIES(x,y) \supset =(x,Acme) \wedge =(y,p_1)$
   $\vee =(x,Foo) \wedge =(y,p_2)]$
4. $(x)(y)[SUBPART(x,y) \supset =(x,p_1) \wedge =(y,p_2)]$

Now suppose that we also wish to represent the disjunctive fact: "Foo supplies p_1 or Foo supplies p_3 but I don't know which." This item of information can be represented by the wff:

$$SUPPLIES(Foo,p_1) \vee SUPPLIES(Foo,p_3) \qquad (4.1)$$

Now one must resist the natural temptation to simply add this wff to the above theory, thinking that one has thereby provided a correct representation of this world. To see why, consider the contrapositive of 3, the completion axiom for *SUPPLIES*:

$$\vee \sim=(y,p_2)]$$

From this and from the unique name axioms we can prove, taking $x = Foo$ and $y = p_1$, the wff $\sim SUPPLIES(Foo,p_1)$. Similarly we can prove $\sim SUPPLIES(Foo,p_3)$. But these two facts are inconsistent with the disjunctive wff (4.1).

The reason for this "anomaly" is clear enough; the completion axiom 3 was designed to say that, of the original theory, the *only possible instances* of *SUPPLIES* are $(Acme,p_1)$ and (Foo,p_2). But the disjunctive wff (4.1) says that *there are other possible instances* of *SUPPLIES*, namely (Foo,p_1) and (Foo,p_3). To accommodate these new possible instances replace the completion axiom 3 by:

3′. $(x)(y)[SUPPLIES(x,y) \supset =(x,Acme) \wedge =(y,p_1)$
$\vee =(x,Foo) \wedge =(y,p_2) \vee =(x,Foo) \wedge =(y,p_1)$
$\vee =(x,Foo) \wedge =(y,p_3)]$

Notice that we can, with 3′, still prove $\sim SUPPLIES(Acme,p_2)$ as before, but we can no longer, as we could before, prove $\sim SUPPLIES(Foo,p_1)$ or $\sim SUPPLIES(Foo,p_3)$. This is precisely what one's intuition about disjunctive facts such as (4.1) would demand.

Now consider representing, in addition to (4.1), the fact

> "If Acme does not supply p_2 then p_2 must be a subpart of p_3."

This can also be represented as a disjunctive wff

$$SUPPLIES(Acme,\ p_2) \vee SUBPART(p_2,p_3) \qquad (4.2)$$

Again we want to include this wff in the theory, but the completion axioms 3′ and 4 must both be modified to accommodate the new possible instances $(Acme,\ p_2)$ and (p_2,p_3) of *SUPPLIES* and *SUBPART*. So replace 3′ and 4 by

3″. $(x)(y)[SUPPLIES(x,y) \supset =(x,Acme) \wedge =(y,p_1)$
$\vee =(x,Foo) \wedge =(y,p_2) \vee =(x,Foo) \wedge =(y,p_1)$
$\vee =(x,Foo) \wedge =(y,p_2) \vee =(x,Acme) \wedge =(y,p_2)]$

4′. $(x)(y)[SUBPART(x,y) \supset =(x,p_1) \wedge =(y,p_2) \vee =(x,p_2) \wedge =(y,p_3)]$

All of which leads to a new theory consisting of:

1. The extensions defined by the tables.
2. The domain closure, unique name, and equality axioms.

3. The completion axioms 1, 2, 3″ and 4′.

4. The disjunctive wffs (4.1) and (4.2).

This theory provides an intuitively correct representation for this incompletely specified world.

These considerations lead to a natural generalization of the concept of a relational database to incorporate disjunctive information, as follows.

Let $R = (\mathcal{A}, \mathcal{W})$ be a relational theory. A wff of $\mathcal{W}$ is called a *positive ground clause* of R iff it has the form $A_1 \vee \ldots \vee A_r$ where each A_i is a ground atomic formula whose predicate is distinct from the equality predicate. The case $r = 1$ is permitted, in which case the clause is simply a ground nonequality atomic formula. A first order theory $T \subseteq \mathcal{W}$ is a *generalized relational theory* of T iff it satisfies the following properties:

1. If $c_1, \ldots, c_n$ are all of the constants of $\mathcal{A}$, T contains the domain closure axiom

$$(x)[=(x,c_1) \vee \ldots \vee =(x,c_n)].$$

T contains the unique name axioms

$$\sim=(c_i,c_j) \quad i,j = 1, \ldots, n \quad i < j$$

2. T contains axioms for the reflexivity, commutativity and transitivity of equality, together with an axiom for the substitution of equal terms for each predicate P of $\mathcal{A}$.

3. For some set $\Delta \subseteq \mathcal{W}$ of positive ground clauses of R, $\Delta \subseteq T$. For each m-ary predicate P of $\mathcal{A}$ distinct from the equality predicate, define a set C_P of m-tuples of constants by

$C_P = \{\vec{c} \mid$ for some positive ground clause $A_1 \vee \ldots \vee A_r$ of Δ and some i, $1 \leqslant i \leqslant r$, A_i *is* $P(\vec{c})\}$

Suppose $C_P = \{(c_1^{(1)}, \ldots, c_m^{(1)}), \ldots, (c_1^{(r)}, \ldots, c_m^{(r)})\}$. Then in addition to the wffs of Δ, T contains the following *completion axiom* for P:

$$(x_1) \ldots (x_m)[P(x_1, \ldots, x_m) \supset =(x_1,c_1^{(1)}) \wedge \ldots \wedge =(x_m,c_m^{(1)})$$
$$\vee \ldots \vee =(x_1,c_1^{(r)}) \wedge \ldots \wedge =(x_m,c_m^{(r)})]$$

If $C_P = \{\ \}$, then T's completion axiom is

$$(x_1) \ldots (x_m) \sim P(x_1, \ldots, x_m).$$

4. The only wffs of T are those sanctioned by conditions 1-3 above.

Notice that the definition of a relational theory of Section 3.1 is a special case of the above definition, in which Δ is a set of ground nonequality atomic formulae. It is natural to define a *generalized relational database* to be a triple (R,T,IC) where T is a generalized relational theory, and R and IC are as before. Similarly, the definition of IC being *satisfied* and the definition of an *answer* to a query are as in Section 3.2.

Generalized relational theories are sufficiently complicated to cause concern about their consistency. Not to worry.

Theorem 4.1. *Every generalized relational theory T is consistent.*

Proof: This is proven by constructing a model of T. Suppose $R = (\mathcal{A}, \mathcal{W})$ and $T \subseteq \mathcal{W}$ is a generalized relational theory. Define an interpretation $I = (D,K,E)$ for R with domain $D = \{c_1, \ldots, c_n\}$ where these are all of the constants of $\mathcal{A}$. Define $E(=) = \{(c,c) \mid c \in D\}$. Then I satisfies the domain closure, unique name, and equality axioms of T. Finally, for each nonequality predicate P of $\mathcal{A}$ define $E(P) = \{\vec{c} \mid \vec{c} \in C_P\}$. Then I satisfies each wff of Δ as well as the completion axioms for each nonequality predicate of $\mathcal{A}$. Hence I is a model of T.

QED

4.1.2 The Semantics of Null Values

The concept of a relational database as developed in Sections 2 and 3 or as generalized in Section 4.1.1 did not accommodate null values. Indeed, as I remarked in Section 2.5.1.2, it is by no means clear what some of these null values even *mean*. My purpose now is to show in some detail how one particular null (namely "value at present unknown, but not necessarily one of some finite set of known possible values")[9] may be defined within the proof theoretic paradigm for database theory.[10]

To focus the discussion, consider the relational theory defined at the beginning of Example 4.1. Suppose we wish to represent the fact:

---

[9] See the discussion of Section 2.5.1.2.

[10] The other most common null value, namely "no value permitted," also has a simple first order representation. For example, suppose *EMP(p,m,s)* denoted that person *p* whose marital status is *m* (*M*arried or *S*ingle) has spouse *s*. Then if John-Doe is single, no value for *s* is permitted. This can be represented by *(s/PERSON)* $\sim$*EMP (John-Doe,S,s)*. I shall not consider such nulls in this chapter.

> "Some supplier supplies part p_3 but I don't know who it is. Moreover, this supplier may or may not be one of the known suppliers Acme and Foo."

This fact may be represented by the first order wff

$$(Ex)SUPPLIER(x) \wedge SUPPLIES(x,p_3) \tag{4.3}$$

which asserts the existence of an individual x with the desired properties. Now we can choose to name this existing individual (call it ω) and instead of (4.3), ascribe these properties to ω directly:

$$SUPPLIER(\omega) \wedge SUPPLIES(\omega,p_3) \tag{4.4}$$

In database terminology, ω is a *null value*. It is called a *Skolem constant* by logicians. Skolem constants, or more generally Skolem functions, provide a technical device for the elimination of existential quantifiers in proof theory (see, for example, [CL73]).

The problem at hand is how to correctly integrate the facts (4.4) into our supplier and parts relational theory. Notice first that ω is a new constant, perhaps denoting the same individual as some known constant, perhaps not. So the unique name axioms remain untouched. The domain closure axiom, however, must be expanded to accommodate this new constant:

$$(x)[=(x,p_1) \vee =(x,p_2) \vee =(x,p_3) \vee =(x,Acme) \vee =(x,Foo) \vee =(x,\omega)] \tag{4.5}$$

Moreover, the completion axioms for *SUPPLIER* and *SUPPLIES* must likewise be expanded:

$$(x)[SUPPLIER(x) \supset =(x,Acme) \vee =(x,Foo) \vee =(x,\omega)] \tag{4.6}$$

$$(x)(y)[SUPPLIES(x,y) \supset =(x,Acme) \wedge =(y,p_1) \vee =(x,Foo) \wedge =(y,p_2) \vee =(x,\omega) \wedge =(y,p_3)] \tag{4.7}$$

If now we add the facts $SUPPLIER(\omega)$ and $SUPPLIES(\omega,p_3)$ to this modified theory we end up with an intuitively correct representation. Notice that in this resulting theory, *the only thing that distinguishes the Skolem constant ω from the "ordinary" constants Acme, Foo, etc., is the absence of unique name axioms for ω.*

Notice also that in this theory we can prove things like $\sim SUPPLIES(Acme,p_2)$, and $\sim SUPPLIES(Foo,p_1)$, but *not* $\sim SUPPLIES(Acme,p_3)$ or $\sim SUPPLIES(Foo,p_3)$. Intuitively, this is precisely what we want. For we know $SUPPLIES(\omega,p_3)$. Moreover, we *don't know* whether ω is the same as, or different than, Acme or Foo.[11] So if we could prove, say $\sim SUPPLIES(Acme,p_3)$, we could also prove $\sim=(\omega,Acme)$, contradicting our presumed ignorance about the identity of ω. What we really have here is a correct formalization of the closed world assumption [REIT78b] in the presence of null values. I shall return to this issue in Section 4.2.4.

One last observation is in order. If we wanted, in addition, to represent the fact:

> "Some supplier (possibly the same as Acme or Foo, possibly not) supplies p_2"

$$(Ex)SUPPLIER(x) \wedge SUPPLIES(x,p_2)$$

we must choose a name for this supplier, say ω', which must be distinct from the name of the previous unknown supplier ω. This is for obvious reasons. Moreover, the domain closure axiom (4.5) and the completion axioms (4.6) and (4.7) must be expanded to take ω' into account. In general, each time a new null value is introduced into the theory, the null must be denoted by a fresh name, distinct from all other names of the theory, and the domain closure and completion axioms must be expanded.

These ideas now can be formalized as follows: Let $R = (\mathcal{A}, \mathcal{W})$ be a relational theory, where the constants of $\mathcal{A}$ are partitioned into two disjoint sets of constants $C = \{c_1, \ldots, c_n\}$ and $\Omega = \{\omega_1, \ldots, \omega_r\}$. Here Ω may be empty, but C may not be. Each ω_i is called a *null value*. As before, a wff of $\mathcal{W}$ is called a *positive ground clause* of R iff it has the form $A_1 \vee \ldots \vee A_m$ where each A_i is a nonequality ground atomic formula. The case $m = 1$ is permitted. A first order theory $T \subseteq \mathcal{W}$ is a *generalized relational theory of R with null values* iff it satisfies the following properties:

1. T contains the domain closure axiom:

$$(x)[=(x,c_1) \vee \ldots \vee =(x,c_n) \vee =(x,\omega_1) \vee \ldots \vee =(x,\omega_r)].$$

Moreover, T contains the unique name axioms:

$$\sim=(c_i,c_j) \quad i < j, \; i, j = 1, \ldots, n.$$

In addition, T *may* contain one or more inequalitites of the following forms:

$$\sim=(\omega_i,c_j) \text{ for some } 1 \leqslant i \leqslant r, \; 1 \leqslant j \leqslant n.$$

$$\sim=(\omega_i,\omega_j) \text{ for some } 1 \leqslant i, \; j \leqslant r, \; i < j.$$

[11] Remember that there are no unique name axioms for ω.

2. T contains the usual equality axioms.

3. For some set $\Delta \subseteq \mathcal{W}$ of positive ground clauses of R, $\Delta \subseteq T$. For each m-ary predicate P of $\mathcal{A}$ distinct from the equality predicate define a set K_P of m-tuples of constants from $C \cup \Omega$ by

$$K_P = \{\vec{k} \mid \text{for some positive ground clause } A_1 \vee \ldots \vee A_m \text{ of } \Delta \text{ and some } i,\ 1 \leqslant i \leqslant m,\ A_i \text{ is } P(\vec{k})\}.$$

Suppose $K_P = \{(k_1^{(1)}, \ldots, k_m^{(1)}), \ldots, (k_1^{(s)}, \ldots, k_m^{(s)})\}$. Then in addition to the wffs of Δ, T contains the following *completion axiom* for P:

$$(x_1) \ldots (x_m)[P(x_1, \ldots, x_m) \supset =(x_1,k_1^{(1)}) \wedge \ldots \wedge =(x_m,k_m^{(1)}) \vee \ldots \vee =(x_1,k_1^{(s)}) \wedge \ldots \wedge =(x_m,k_m^{(s)})]$$

If $K_P = \{\ \}$, then T's completion axiom is

$$(x_1) \ldots (x_m) \sim P(x_1, \ldots, x_m)$$

4. The only wffs of T are those sanctioned by conditions 1-3 above.

The definition of a generalized relational theory of Section 4.1.1 is a special case of the above definition, in which $\Omega = \{\ \}$.

A *generalized relational database with null values* is a triple (R,T,IC) where R and T are as above, and $IC \subseteq \mathcal{W}$ is a set of integrity constraints. The definitions of an *answer* to a query, and of *satisfaction* of the integrity constraints remain the same as before.

Having formalized a class of first order theories that accommodate null values, we can now observe that *the only formal distinction between a null value* $\omega \in \Omega$ *and an "ordinary" constant* $c \in C$ *is that some of the possible unique name axioms for* ω *are absent from the theory.* If in fact all of the unique name axioms for ω were present (the definition does allow this), then ω would be indistinguishable from an "ordinary" constant.

Notice also that generalized relational theories with null values provide for disjunctive information as well, and permit some quite subtle distinctions to be represented. For example:

"Someone supplies p_3 but I don't know who. Whoever it is, it is neither A nor B."

$$(Ex/SUPPLIER)SUPPLIES(x,p_3) \wedge \sim=(x,A) \wedge \sim=(x,B)$$

which, after elimination of the existential quantifier becomes

$$SUPPLIER(\omega) \wedge SUPPLIES(\omega,p_3) \wedge \sim=(\omega,A) \wedge \sim=(\omega,B)$$

"Someone supplies p_2 and someone supplies p_3. I don't know who they are but I do know they are not the same suppliers."

$$(Ex/SUPPLIER)(Ey/SUPPLIER)SUPPLIES(x,p_2) \wedge SUPPLIES(y,p_3) \wedge \sim=(x,y)$$

which becomes

$$SUPPLIER(\omega_1) \wedge SUPPLIER(\omega_2) \wedge SUPPLIES(\omega_1,p_2) \wedge SUPPLIES(\omega_2,p_3) \wedge \sim=(\omega_1,\omega_2)$$

"Someone supplies p_2 or p_3 but I don't know who. I do know it is not A."

$$(Ex/SUPPLIER)[SUPPLIES(x,p_2) \vee SUPPLIES(x,p_3)] \wedge \sim=(x,A)$$

which becomes

$$SUPPLIER(\omega) \wedge [SUPPLIES(\omega,p_2) \vee SUPPLIES(\omega,p_3)] \wedge \sim=(\omega,A)$$

The following result is comforting.

Theorem 4.2. *Every generalized relational theory T with null values is consistent.*

Proof: The proof is constructed by adding enough inequalities to T to yield a generalized relational theory. By Theorem 4.1, this enlarged theory will be consistent in which case so will any subset of it, in particular T itself.

To suitably enlarge T add to it every inequality $\sim=(c_i,\omega_j)$ such that neither this inequality nor the inequality $\sim=(\omega_j,c_i)$ is already present in T. Similarly, add to T every inequality $\sim=(\omega_i,\omega_j)$ for $i \neq j$ such that neither this nor the inequality $\sim=(\omega_j,\omega_i)$ is already present in T. The resulting theory is a generalized relational theory.

QED

One final observation: any generalized relational theory with null values is decidable, basically because the domain closure axiom restricts the class of its models to those whose domains are no larger than the finite set of constants of the theory. Of course testing a wff for theoremhood by testing it for truth in all these models is hardly an exemplary procedure. A theorem proving approach would certainly be preferable. Better still would be a suitable generalization of the relational algebra, but whether this is even possible remains to be seen.

4.2 Conceptual Modelling: Incorporating More World Knowledge

As I remarked in Section 2.5.2, there is a perceived need within the database community to extend the relational model to accommodate more real world knowledge, and many of the required extensions cannot be accommodated by the model theoretic paradigm for relational databases. A bewildering variety of proposals have been advanced in response to this need. Representative examples include the "Tasmanian" relational model [CODD79], TAXIS, an object oriented programming language [MBW80], class oriented data models [HM78], and semantic networks [SOWA76]. Now there are two problems with this embarrassing number of proposals:

1. How can one begin to compare them? In what formal sense could one claim that two such proposals have the same representational "powers," or that one is a generalization of another? Most such proposals involve different representation languages and different (and in some cases underspecified) semantics, making mappings between them virtually impossible.

2. Insofar as the concept of an answer to a query is defined at all, it is defined operationally, for example by a generalization of the relational algebra, or by some set of retrieval routines which may or may not perform inferences. Now these data models are complicated. Therefore these operational definitions for answers to queries are also complicated. Why should one believe that these definitions are *correct* (*i.e.*, that any answer returned will be intuitively appropriate)? Why should one believe that these definitions are *complete* (*i.e.*, that anything that intuitively should be an answer will be returned)?

My purpose in this section is to indicate how a logical framework can alleviate these problems. Specifically, I shall argue that the kinds of real world knowledge that these extended data models attempt to capture have natural representations as first order formulae. If you grant me this claim for the moment, it follows that such non logical data models can be equivalently formalized by suitably restricted classes of first order theories, much as Section 4.1.2 formalized the relational model with disjunctive information and null values as the class of generalized relational theories with null values. Provided this mapping from a non logical data model to a logical one can be done, we would enjoy a number of immediate benefits [REIT80b]:

1. The semantics of the non logical data model would be precisely defined by its logical translation.

2. Two different non logical data models could be compared (say, with respect to their representational "power"), by comparing their translations.

3. The definition of an answer to a query remains the same as in Section 3.2. This is a central point: no matter how one extends one's data models to incorporate more real world meaning, *the definition of an answer to a query remains the same, as long as this extension is first order definable.* This is not to say that one's query evaluation algorithms must resemble the logician's proof procedures. The relational algebra is such an algorithm, and it looks nothing like proof theory. Nevertheless, logic is the final arbiter of the correctness of proposed query evaluation mechanism for any first order definable data model. Thus *we can prove the correctness of proposed query evaluation algorithms.*

4. Similar remarks hold for integrity constraints. The definition of satisfaction of an integrity constraint remains as it was expressed in Section 3.2 for any first order data model. Thus *we can prove the correctness of proposed integrity maintenance algorithms.*

It remains for me to argue that the kinds of real world knowledge that various semantic data models attempt to capture are representable within first order logic. Space limitations prevent an exhaustive or detailed survey of the kinds of knowledge modelled in the database literature, so I shall focus instead on some of the more prominent semantic requirements.

4.2.1 The Representation of Events

First order event based representations have been used extensively in Artificial Intelligence for modelling verbs and their associated case frames for natural language understanding systems [BRUC75]. These ideas translate very naturally into the database setting. The idea is to extend one's ontology to include a new class of individuals of type *EVENT*, and then to postulate various properties that these individuals may possess. For example, in an inventory database, one may want to represent the fact that an order has been received on June 12, 1981, to be filled by Sept. 1, 1981, and which is to be shipped to Acme. The order is for 12 pipewrenches, catalogue number 1376, and for 24 doors, catalogue number 2001, colour brown. This has as its event-based first order representation:

$$(Ex/ORDER{-}EVENT)[DATE{-}RECEIVED(x,\ June\ 12\ 1981)$$

$$\wedge\ DATE{-}TO{-}BE{-}FILLED(x,\ Sept\ 1\ 1981) \wedge SHIP{-}TO(x, Acme)$$

$$\wedge\ GOODS{-}ORDERED(x, pipewrench)$$

$$\wedge\ CATALOGUE{-}NO(x, pipewrench,\ 1376)$$

$\wedge$ *QUANTITY* (*x,pipewrench*, 12) $\wedge$ *GOODS−ORDERED* (*x,door*)

$\wedge$ *CATALOGUE−NO* (*x,door*, 2001) $\wedge$ *QUANTITY* (*x,door*, 24)

$\wedge$ *COLOUR* (*x,door,brown*)]

Associated with any individual of type *ORDER−EVENT* might be an integrity constraint specifying that there must be someone to whom the goods are to be shipped, that there are some goods on order, and that the date the order is received must precede the date it is to be filled.

(*x*/*ORDER−EVENT*) (*Ey*/*DATE*) (*Ez*/*DATE*) (*Eu*/*BUYER*)

(*Ew*/*INVENTORY−ITEM*) [*DATE−RECEIVED* (*x,y*)

$\wedge$ *DATE−TO−BE−FILLED* (*x,z*) $\wedge$ $y<z$

$\wedge$ *SHIP−TO* (*x,u*) $\wedge$ *GOODS−ORDERED* (*x,w*)]

4.2.2 Hierarchies and the Inheritance of Properties

The modelling task here is to provide a first order representation of generalization (IS-A) hierarchies, the properties associated with "classes" in the hierarchy, and how these properties are inherited by classes "lower down" in the hierarchy. These features are common to virtually every attempt in the literature to define data models with more "meaning" (*e.g.*, [CODD79] [HM78] [MBW80] [SS77b]).

For example, consider an educational domain with the hierarchy of simple types (classes) of Figure 4.1. The semantics of this hierarchy can be specified by the following first order wffs:

(*x*)[*UNDERGRADUATE* (*x*) ⊃ *STUDENT* (*x*)]

(*x*)[*GRADUATE* (*x*) ⊃ *STUDENT* (*x*)]

(*x*)[*FRESHMAN* (*x*) ⊃ *UNDERGRADUATE* (*x*)]

(*x*)[*JUNIOR* (*x*)⊃ *UNDERGRADUATE* (*x*)]

etc.,

together with wffs specifying the disjointness of these types, namely:

(*x*)~[*UNDERGRADUATE* (*x*) $\wedge$ *GRADUATE* (*x*)]

(*x*)~[*FRESHMAN* (*x*) $\wedge$ *JUNIOR* (*x*)]

(*x*)~[*FRESHMAN* (*x*) $\wedge$ *SOPHOMORE* (*x*)]

etc.

In addition to this hierarchy, there might be properties that generally hold for simple types "high up" in the hierarchy and that are inherited by any instances of simple types "lower down." For example, it will likely be the case that every student should have a student number:

(*x*/*STUDENT*) (*Ey*/*INTEGER*) *STUDENT−NO* (*x,y*)

This is an example of a *property* associated with the type *STUDENT*. In general a property of the simple type τ is a wff of the form $(x/\tau)\ (Ey/\theta) P(x,y)$ where θ is some type and P is a binary predicate.

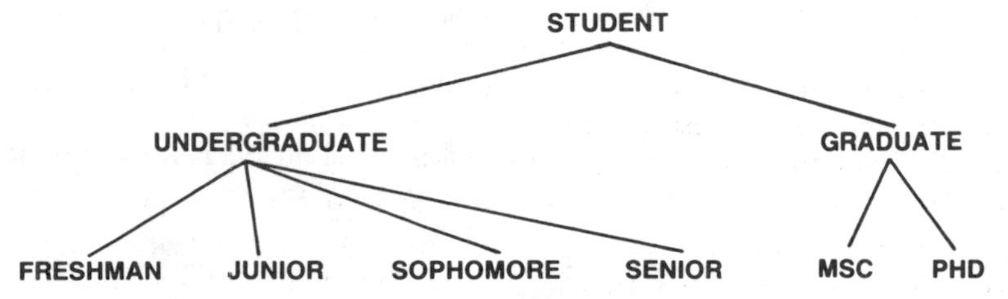

Figure 4.1 *A Hierarchy of Simple Types*

For the example at hand it is easy to see that the following wffs are all *deducible* from the wffs defining the hierarchy, and the student number property:

(*x*/*GRADUATE*) (*Ey*/*INTEGER*) *STUDENT−NO* (*x,y*)

(*x*/*FRESHMAN*) (*Ey*/*INTEGER*) *STUDENT−NO* (*x,y*)

etc.

This is an example of the *inheritance of properties* applying to superclasses down the hierarchy to subclasses. Properties only inherit "downwards." If every freshman must be enrolled in English 100

(*x*/*FRESHMAN*) *ENROLLED* (*x,E* 100)

it does not follow, either intuitively or logically from our representation, that every undergraduate must be enrolled in English 100.

The transitivity of "IS-A" is a simple consequence of the transitivity of "implies." Thus the following is provable:

(*x*)[*MSC* (*x*) ⊃ *STUDENT* (*x*)]

Finally, the concept of a token *t* of a class *C* translates into the logical ground atomic formula *C*(*t*). Thus John Doe as a token of the class *GRADUATE* is represented by *GRADUATE* (*John−Doe*).

4.2.3 Aggregations

This modelling notion was introduced in [HM78] and is also treated in [CODD79] [MBW80]. An aggregation is a set of some kind to which one wishes to ascribe various properties. I shall indicate how to represent aggregations in first order logic by modelling certain aspects of professional societies. The simple type *SET* takes sets as its argument. To improve readability, I use upper case symbols for set variables and constants.

Subset defined:

$$(X/SET)\ (Y/SET)[SUBSET(X,Y) \equiv (z)[MEMBER(z,X) \supset MEMBER(z,Y)]]$$

A professional society is a set of people representing a field. Any member of the society is interested in at least one subfield of this field.

$$(X)[PROF{-}SOC(X) \supset SET(X)]$$

$$(X)[PROF{-}SOC(X) \supset (y)[MEMBER(y,X) \supset PERSON(y)]]$$

$$(X)[PROF{-}SOC(X) \supset (Ex/FIELD{-}TYPE)[FIELD(X,x) \wedge (y)[MEMBER(y,X) \supset (Ez/FIELD{-}TYPE)SUBFIELD(z,x) \wedge INTERESTS(y,z)]]]$$

Notice that this is not a definition of a professional society. The wffs merely define various properties that anything called a professional society must possess.

ACM is a professional society of computer scientists.

$$PROF{-}SOC(ACM)$$

$$FIELD{-}TYPE(cs)$$

$$FIELD(ACM,cs)$$

The executive board of a professional society is a subset of the members of the society and always has a president, a secretary, a treasurer, and members-at-large. Neither the president, treasurer nor secretary may be members-at-large.

$$(X)\ (Y/PROF{-}SOC)[EX{-}BOARD(X,Y) \supset SET(X) \wedge SUBSET(X,Y)]$$

$$(X/SET)\ (Y/PROF{-}SOC)[EX{-}BOARD(X,Y) \supset [(Eu/PERSON)MEMBER(u,X) \wedge PRESIDENT(u,Y)] \wedge [(Ev/PERSON)MEMBER(v,X) \wedge SECRETARY(v,Y)] \wedge [(Ew/PERSON)MEMBER(w,X) \wedge TREASURER(w,Y)]]$$

$$(X/SET)\ (Y/PROF{-}SOC)[EX{-}BOARD(X,Y) \supset (EZ/SET)[SUBSET(Z,X) \wedge MEMBERS{-}AT{-}LARGE(Z,Y) \wedge (x/PERSON)[MEMBER(x,Z) \supset \sim PRESIDENT(x) \wedge \sim SECRETARY(x) \wedge \sim TREASURER(x)]]]$$

Lady Lovelace is a member of ACM's executive board.

$$(EX)EXECUTIVE{-}BOARD(X,ACM) \wedge MEMBER(Lady{-}Lovelace,X)$$

If one replaces the existentially quantified variable X by a Skolem constant Ω (*i.e.*, a null value) this latter wff becomes

$$EXECUTIVE{-}BOARD(\Omega,ACM) \wedge MEMBER(Lady{-}Lovelace,\Omega)$$

Using these wffs together with some of the earlier ones we can deduce, among other things

$$PERSON(Lady{-}Lovelace)$$

$$MEMBER(Lady{-}Lovelace,ACM)$$

A special interest group of a professional society is a set of individuals interested in some subfield of the society.

$$(X)\ (Y/PROF{-}SOC)[SIG(X,Y) \supset SET(X)]$$

$$(X/SET)\ (Y/PROF{-}SOC)\ [SIG(X,Y) \supset (z)\ [MEMBER(z,X) \supset PERSON(z)]]$$

$$(X/SET)\ (Y/PROF{-}SOC)\ (u/FIELD{-}TYPE)\ (v/FIELD{-}TYPE)\ [SIG(X,Y) \wedge FIELD(X,u) \wedge FIELD(Y,v) \supset SUBFIELD(u,v) \wedge (z/PERSON)[MEMBER(z,X) \supset INTERESTS(z,u)]]$$

Notice that one may be a member of a special interest group without being a member of the professional society.

SIGART is a special interest group of ACM for Artificial Intelligence.

$$SIG(SIGART,ACM)$$

$$FIELD(SIGART,ai)$$

Using the wffs on hand we can deduce:

$$SUBFIELD(ai,cs)$$

Suppose *rr* is a member of SIGART.

$$MEMBER(rr,SIGART)$$

We can deduce:

$PERSON(rr)$

$INTERESTS(rr,ai)$

4.2.4 Discussion

I have indicated how a variety of data modelling concepts can be naturally represented as first order formulae. Now my earlier conclusions (Section 4.1) were that various species of relational databases are all formalizable by suitable triples (R,T,IC). It is natural, then, to persevere with this notion and to further generalize relational databases to accommodate these new data modelling concepts. More precisely, insofar as a semantic data model admits first order formulae of a certain kind (*e.g.*, formulae for aggregations), then some of these formulae normally will be viewed as integrity constraints. Put them in IC. The remaining formulae then serve as general world knowledge for the inferential retrieval of answers. Put them in T.

Now this leaves us with the mildly uncomfortable view that, in order to do arbitrary conceptual modelling, we must accept databases (R,T,IC) where T and IC are arbitrary first order theories of the relational language R. While this is essentially true, there are certain constraints that one is likely to impose upon T:

1. It should contain a domain closure axiom.
2. It should contain unique name axioms for the known constants of R (but not necessarily for its null values).
3. T should represent the closed world assumption.

This latter point requires amplification. In [REIT78b] I studied the problem of representing negative information in first order databases without null values. My point of departure was the observation that in conventional relational databases, a negative fact like $\sim SUPPLIES(s,p)$, is held to be true provided its positive part (*i.e.*, $SUPPLIES(s,p)$), is not in the database. In other words, a tuple satisfies the negation of a relation iff the tuple is absent from the relation's table. In keeping with my proof theoretic bias, I generalized this notion to first order theories T as follows:

$$\text{Infer } \sim R(\vec{c}) \text{ iff } T \nvdash R(\vec{c}).$$

This characterization of negation in database theory I termed the *closed world assumption.* For a number of reasons, this particular version of the closed world assumption is unsuitable:

1. It treats null values incorrectly.
2. In the presence of disjunctive information it leads to inconsistencies.
3. Since it is a rule of inference, and not a wff or set of wffs, it is not, strictly speaking, first order representable. It is a meta-notion.

Now there is a different way of viewing the closed world assumption, one which provides a strong clue for its first order representability. For it assumes that the given information about the world being modelled is complete in the sense that *all and only* the relationships that can possibly hold among the known individuals are those implied by the given information. It is this point of view that led to the completion axioms for generalized relational theories with null values (Section 4.1.2). These axioms permit the derivation of negative facts from the theory, but only such facts as do not conflict with the unknown individual property of null values, and which do not lead to inconsistencies with the disjunctive information. In this limited setting, the completion axioms provide a correct first order representation of the closed world assumption.

I do not know whether suitable completion axioms can be formulated for more general first order settings, for example settings representing hierarchies and/or aggregations. Whether this is possible or not, some representation of the closed world assumption is necessary. Moreover, this is not a problem peculiar to a logical view of database theory. Any formalism for extended conceptual modelling must provide for the representation of negative information and its use in query evaluation, although this problem is rarely addressed in the literature.

It is of some interest to observe that variants of the closed world assumption arise in contexts other than database theory, for example in providing a semantics for negation in PROLOG and PLANNER-like programming languages [CLAR78] [AV80], and for Artificial Intelligence applications [MCCA80] [REIT80c]. In particular, Clark and McCarthy provide different but extremely interesting first order approaches to the closed world assumption, approaches well worth investigating for their potential impact on database theory. In this connection [REIT82] shows how, for certain classes of databases viewed as first order theories, McCarthy's formalization of the closed world assumption is a generalization of Clark's.

5. Conclusions

I have, in some detail, carried out a logical reconstruction of various aspects of conventional relational database theory. The value of this logical embedding is, in my view, primarily *semantic;* a number of central concepts in database theory have been given precise definitions. Among these are: databases that have incomplete information, including null values; integrity constraints and what it means for them to be satisfied; queries and their answers; and conceptual modelling and what it might mean to represent more real world knowledge.

As I see it, the major *conceptual* advantage of this logical reconstruction is its uniformity:

1. Representational uniformity. Queries, integrity constraints and facts in the database are all represented in the same first order language.

2. Operational uniformity. First order proof theory is the sole mechanism for query evaluation and the satisfaction of integrity constraints.

This uniformity provides a number of practical advantages:

1. Nonlogical data models can be given precise semantics by translating them into logical terms.

2. Different data models may be compared.

3. Non proof theoretic query evaluation algorithms may be proven correct with respect to the logical semantics of queries.

4. Integrity maintenance algorithms may be proven correct with respect to the proof theoretic definition of constraint satisfaction.

A wide variety of questions have not been explored in the chapter, and they require further research.

1. Can the relational algebra be generalized to deal correctly with null values? With disjunctive information?

2. What is an appropriate formalization of the closed world assumption for arbitrary first order theories?

3. Which first order theories admit efficient query evaluation procedures? In this connection, notice that so-called Horn theories accommodate efficient theorem proving techniques [KOWA79] that can be directly applied to query evaluation.

4. What are some criteria for deciding whether a given wff should be treated as an integrity constraint or as knowledge to be used in deriving answers?

5. Suppose we restrict attention to relational databases as defined in Section 3.2. Determine natural classes of integrity constraints for which efficient and provably correct integrity maintenance algorithms can be found. Contrast this approach to correctness proofs with that of [BBC80].

6. Discussion: Why Logic?

In this chapter I have made some arguments favouring a logical (specifically proof theoretic) perspective for relational database theory. While this logical perspective was couched in the first order predicate calculus, other logics are certainly possible, perhaps even desirable in certain settings. (See, for example, Levesque's chapter on incomplete knowledge bases, or [JACO82].) Exactly which logic as appropriate for conceptual modelling can be a contentious issue, as the chapter by Israel and Brachman indicates, and I do not wish here to take sides in this dispute. But there is a prior issue which I do wish to address, and that is whether logic, whatever its species. is even a suitable formalism for conceptual modelling.

The standard opposing view to the logical paradigm has it that data models are definable by a choice of data representation together with suitable *operations* on the data representation (*i.e.,* by the database operations performed for retrieval, updates, deletions, *etc.,* [TL82]). It is the total constellation of these operations that defines the "meaning" of one's representation. But surely this confuses *implementation* with *specification,* for whatever else it might be, a database is a representation of various things which are *known* (or better, *believed*) *about some aspect of the real world.* Logic provides an abstract *specification* language for expressing this knowledge. The logical formulae which presume to specify this knowledge are things which are either true or false in the real world. Of course, they are intended to be true. Nevertheless, they are open for inspection by the sceptical as well as the curious. For example, in Section 4.2.3, I proposed a collection of formulae specifying what I mean by a professional society. You, in turn, are free to decide whether these formulae are true of the world, and whether there are important features (for your application) of a professional society which I failed to specify. If you agree with my formulae, well and good. If not, then at least we have a solid basis for dispute. Either way, the logical formulae are completely up front; they unambiguously specify exactly what I mean by a professional society, no more, no less. In this sense, logic provides a rigorous specification of meaning. Moreover, it does so at a very high level of abstraction, in the sense that the specification is entirely nonprocedural. It tells us *what* knowledge is being represented. It tells us *what* is meant, for example, by an answer to a query, namely, any tuple of constants which make the query true in all models of the formulae. Similarly, a logic suitable for representing state changes would tell us *what* should be the result of a database update. In no sense does a logical specification include procedures detailing *how* to perform database operations; hence its nonprocedural character.

Of course this emphasis on logic as a specification language ignores a crucial aspect of conceptual modelling, the *implementation* problem. How do we computationally *realize* the abstract logical specification? It is at this implementation level that database operations assume their proper role. A wide variety of options are possible. One extreme is literally to encode the formulae as themselves, and define the database operation for retrieval, say, to be a theorem prover. This approach is advocated by the PROLOG community whenever the formulae are Horn clauses [VANE78]. Another possibility is to represent formulae by a semantic network of some kind, and define the database operation of retrieval by some sort of network interpreter. Usually, such network representations are strongly oriented towards hierarchies and property inheritance, and the associated network interpreter is designed to search up hierarchies for inherited properties [MBW80]. (See Section 4.2.2 for a sketch of a logical specification of such hierarchies. See also [SCHU76a].) Conventional relational database theory encodes ground atomic formulae as themselves (*i.e.*, as a set of relational instances), and the relational algebra supplies the operations for retrieval. Whatever one's choice of data model for realizing a logical specification, this choice will provide a lower level of abstraction, reflecting a concern for implementing the specification, hence a preoccupation with database operations. While necessary, this emphasis on database operations has unpleasant semantic consequences. The semantic effects of certain formulae in the logical specifications are buried in the operations. For example, the effects of the domain closure axiom in the logical specification of a relational database (Section 3.1) are realized in the relational data model by the division operator. The completion axioms are realized by the operation of set difference. *Such axioms are not encoded as part of the data representation, but as data model operations.* The more complex data models become, the more we can expect such operational encodings of specification axioms (not to mention the operational encoding of logical deduction). Provided there is a logical specification to begin with, this makes for good computer science; one can prove that one's data model is a correct realization of the specification.

But what if, as is current practice, a data model is served up without benefit of an abstract specification of the assumptions made by that data model about the world being modelled? Whatever these assumptions might be, they are likely to be buried deeply within the data model's operations. When these are complex operations, how is one to know what the assumptions are? Are they correctly and completely realized by the operations? For that matter, what can "correct" and "complete" even mean in this setting? Without a specification of the "knowledge content" of the database, one which provides a direct connection to the real world being modelled, there can be no concept of the correctness and completeness of a data model's operations. A mature theory of databases will provide for this distinction between a logical specification and its realization by a procedurally oriented data model, and it will require that the operations and data representations of this data model be proven correct and complete with respect to a given specification.

In summary, I have argued the following advantages of logically defined data models for conceptual modelling:

1. Logic is precise and unambiguous. It has a well defined semantics that provides the crucial connection between its formulae and the real world being modelled.

2. Logical data models provide a very high level of abstraction because there are no database operations. They are entirely nonprocedural. They act as specifications of those aspects of the real world being modelled, and of the assumptions one is making about that world.

3. A logical data model is transparent. All and only the knowledge being represented is open for inspection, including assumptions that might otherwise be buried in procedurally oriented data models.

4. Because they are specifications, logical data models can be realized in a variety of ways by procedurally oriented data models. Such data models can be proven correct and complete with respect to the logical specifications that they realize. Since a logical specification provides a connection with the world being modelled (See 1. above), this notion of correctness and completeness is probably the best that one can hope for.

7. Acknowledgments

The bulk of this research was supported by the National Science and Engineering Research Council of Canada under grant A7642. Additional support was provided by NSF Grant MCS-8203954.

I am grateful to David Etherington, Hervé Gallaire, Randy Goebel, Jean Marie Nicolas, Moshe Vardi and K. Yazdanian, all of whom read an earlier draft of this chapter and provided valuable comments and corrections.

8. References

[AV80] [BBC80] [BISK81] [BRUC75] [BZ81] [CL73] [CLAR78] [CODD70] [CODD72] [CODD79] [HM78] [JACO82] [KOWA79] [KUHN67] [LIPS79] [MBW80] [MCCA80] [MEND64] [RAPH71] [REIT77] [REIT78a] [REIT78b] [REIT80a] [REIT80b] [REIT80c] [REIT82] [SCHU76a] [SOWA76] [SS77b] [TL82] [ULLM80] [VANE78] [VASS79] [WALK80] [ZANI77]

Discussion

This chapter uses first order logic (FOL) to express popular DB concepts such as events, hierarchies, and integrity constraints to illustrate the utility of FOL in dealing with issues surrounding the relational data model (RDM).

Current relational database theory is based on model theoretic (MT) notions. The chapter attempts to show that the proof theoretic (PT) approach is better. MT definitions are generalized to PT definitions to provide a good basis for extending RDM theory and to talk precisely about the semantics of extensions, such as those needed for incomplete knowledge (disjunctive information and null values), integrity constraints, and conceptual modelling extensions (events, hierarchies, inheritance, aggregation, and association). The resulting theories are all decidable since the domain of a database (DB) is finite.

Domains

There are at least two different domain notions, one from MT and the other from the RDM. The MT view is that a domain is a set of constants. The DB approach presumes to enumerate all possible values of a domain (like a type in programming language (PL) without the related operations). For example, an *address* domain is the set of *all* possible addresses. Some people attempt to embed as much semantics as possible in the data type of an object (*e.g.,* address and its operations, salary and its operations). In that case, a type such as a string is only a representation of the address object.

Reiter's notion of domain does not make a distinction between type and variable, although such a distinction is generally useful for semantic integrity checking. Reiter claims that such benefits can be gained through axioms (*e.g.,* manager is a subtype of employee). However, the issue here may not be expressibility, but convenience.

Ray Reiter: "This comment implies a misunderstanding of the chapter that addresses *semantic* issues, *not* convenience, efficiency, or implementation. It should be clear that knowledge representation (viewed as an abstract formalism) and database representation (viewed as an implementation) are two different issues."

Extending the RDM Using PT

There are many problems for which the RDM must be extended (*e.g.*, incomplete information, events, and hierarchies). Many of the approaches proposed for these extensions are ad hoc and pose new problems. The RDM can be considered, at a logical level, as a special kind of theory of FOL. The MT approach, the most direct representation for the RDM, cannot deal adequately with the desired extensions. When defining the RDM in the PT approach and one gets not only the RDM but also all the other machinery of FOL with which to resolve other RDM problems. The PT approach provides a proof theory for databases. Using PT, integrity constraints are satisfied if they can be derived from the theory given by the axioms, and queries are answered via proof theory. FOL also can be used to provide a clear semantics for the RDM and its problems and a convenient framework within which to attack the problems.

Reiter proposes that the RDM be extended by using new axioms to handle problems such as disjunctive information and nulls. An example of disjunctive information is "Foo supplies P1 or Foo supplies P3 but I don't know which." The RDM does not permit the information in this statement to be stored or returned. Although there are other such proposed extensions in the literature, their semantics often are not clear. What is meant by the answer to a query in the presence of incomplete information? To understand disjunctive information, you should build a suitable first order theory (in your mind at least) and then use proofs to determine the answer to the query on incomplete information. Having so defined a correct semantics, implement efficient mechanisms to support the semantics, and prove that the implementation corresponds to the given semantics. If one is unhappy with the semantics, then define another. *It is not wise to add a new concept without knowing its semantics.*

It is extremely important that precise specifications be given for any new data model or model extension. If the semantics are not clear, the models or languages are hard to use. In the future, we should not accept a new model or feature without a precise specification that is complete, formal, and unambiguously communicable to its users.

When using a logical formalism to express new models, some things come for free (*e.g.*, means of answering or resolving queries). Papers proposing new models usually give complex ways of retrieving information without demonstrating their correctness. If a data model is specified using FOL, the correct notion of an answer is free. The logic definition correctly characterizes an intuition of how the answer is to be derived, and every answer for which there is an intuition can be retrieved by the same mechanism.

Null Values

In the chapter, null values are special constants about which questions can be asked. There is a recognition problem involving different null values in the RDM literature. For example, if null-x supplies P1 and null-y supplies P3, are null-x and null-y the same? In the PT approach, special constant symbols (W1, W2, . . .) are introduced that may or may not be equal to any existing DB constant. If two null values are the same, one must explicitly state this fact. Contrary to some DB proposals, null values are not an issue for three value logic. The issue is what is provable and what is not. If we can neither prove nor disapprove something it means that we have incompletely specified knowledge. The literature is full of conditions of the form: T *or not*(T) evaluates to unknown if T happens to be unknown, but T *or not*(T) is a tautology and so is always true.

State Versus State Transitions

The chapter considers database theory that has not addressed dynamic aspects of databases. Data structures have received considerable emphasis in DB. Now that many structural problems are solved, there is a growing emphasis on behaviour, the semantics and representation of operations over databases. Being able to express the semantics of events is very important — what actually happens when an event takes place. The chapter avoids state changes because of the frame problem, an open problem in AI. The frame problem is that of stating all the invariants for each state change. For example, if you change the state of a room by opening a window, there are unbelievably many invariants (*e.g.*, people in the room remain seated). A complementary problem is to state all changes for an event. What is to be ignored and what is to be emphasized? For a finite domain (*e.g.*, a DB) one can list all the changes and invariants. But, even if one could state all the invariants and changes there is an inference problem; a change can have many side effects. Some of these issues can be addressed using type hierarchies.

Hierarchies and Property Inheritance

In data models, there are higher-level (higher than 1st order) axioms (or model inherent constraints) stating that all hierarchies of the same type have the same properties. This saves writing the same axioms for every application. The same effect can be achieved in FOL through notational convention rather than resorting to a higher order logic.

To deal adequately with hierarchies in PT, completion axioms are needed which allow you to ask questions about elements that are not part of the hierarchy. These axioms are not well understood. Although they may turn out to be simple, they currently appear to be very difficult.

Logical Modelling and Efficiency

Some first order theories permit more efficient query evaluation than others. This fact is used in the PROLOG community (*e.g.*, Horn clauses provide efficient computation and a PROLOG program can be annotated to improve efficiency). There are two issues here. First, there are many ways to ask the same question. Second, is the efficiency of the system measured by how well it performs on the most efficient representation of a query? In this regard, input for efficient implementation should not be sought at the logical description level but in meta-knowledge (*e.g.*, query optimizers should look for hints in the dictionary, not in the database). Efficiency in the RDM is a different problem. It is hard to define predicates that will help in evaluating optimal search paths.

What is the relationship between FOL and implementation efficiency? How does one theory relate to another on the basis of efficiency, assuming that the theories have equivalent interpretations? There is no known answer to these questions. If one happens to know how PROLOG works, then annotations can be used to take advantage of it. Annotation was used long ago for FORTRAN II but annotated programs were found to be less efficient than the standard compiled programs. The RDM is a subset of FOL that is reasonably efficient to process; maybe other "theories" are even more efficient.

Efficiency concerns representation and not logic. There are several ways of improving representations. One approach is to have the compiler collect data from programs (to be kept as a meta-knowledge) and from users (in exceptional cases). Another approach would be to automatically and incrementally map from one representation, say pure PROLOG, to equivalent and more efficient representations.

Concluding Remarks

There are four main benefits of mapping nonlogical models to logical models.

1. Precise definitions of nonlogical data models.
2. Possibility to compare the representational powers of nonlogical models.
3. Defines precisely the concept of an answer to a query. Hence to prove the correctness of proposed evaluation algorithms for a query.
4. Defines satisfiability of an integrity constraint. Hence, to prove the correctness of proposed integrity maintenance algorithms.

The emphasis in using FOL should be on mental hygiene, rather than on theorem proving. FOL should be used if there are doubts about the clear semantics of new database concepts (*e.g.*, incomplete information). When the semantics of a construct is clear, go back to a level that is convenient for data modelling.

Reiter's chapter, which draws examples from DB literature, makes several questionable assumptions about databases. Examples used in the DB literature do not reflect the size or complexity of real databases. A database is a large collection of data, and database applications form large systems. Toy examples do not illustrate the real problems of designing large database applications. For example, census databases are very complex and have several hundred record types, each with several thousand attributes. Database design and definition become extremely complex. The large number of axioms needed to handle the complexity of database applications, coupled with the size of databases, raises serious questions about the practicality of using FOL for real database applications.

Ray Reiter: "The above comment misses the point of the chapter, which provides a framework for defining the semantics of data models. Implementation issues are not addressed nor is the complexity of actual applications except insofar as this complexity has to do with *representational* issues. If you are trying to capture complex *semantic* properties of the real world in a *data model* then use FOL to define that data model. That is all the chapter says."

The following characterization was proposed from the PL point of view: The essence of database is captured by sets and set oriented operations, and the whole database problem is really just an efficiency problem. The response: The characterization ignores many important aspects. Capturing structural properties by sets is a reasonable thing to do, but much of the semantics cannot be captured by using sets. The concept of transactions is ignored. DB has been in the set oriented framework for a long time. Now more difficult problems are being addressed (*i.e.*, many basic problems faced in PL embedded in data intensive applications).

In conclusion, it is fair to say that some formal system is better than no formal system. Model theory and proof theory have been discussed, but other formal systems are also candidates.

References

[AV80] Apt, K.R. and M.H. Van Emden, "Contributions to the Theory of Logic Programming," Research Report CS-80-12, Department of Computer Science, University of Waterloo, Ontario, Canada, 1980.

[BBC80] Bernstein, P.A., B.T. Blaustein and E.M. Clarke, "Fast Maintenance of Integrity Assertions Using Redundant Aggregate Data," *Proc. 6th International Conference on Very Large Databases,* Montreal, Quebec, Canada, October 1980.

[BISK81] Biskup, J., "Null Values in Data Base Relations," in [GM78].

[BRUC75] Bruce, B., "Case Systems for Natural Language," *Artificial Intelligence,* Vol. 6, pp. 327-360, 1975.

[BZ81] Brodie, M.L. and S.N. Zilles (eds.), *Proc. Workshop on Data Abstraction, Databases, and Conceptual Modelling, SIGART Newsletter,* No. 74, January 1981; *SIGMOD Record,* Vol. 11, No. 2, February 1981; *SIGPLAN Notices,* Vol. 16, No. 1, January 1981.

[CL73] Chang, C.L. and R.C.T. Lee, *Symbolic Logic and Mechanical Theorem Proving,* Academic Press, New York, 1973.

[CLAR78] Clark, K.L., "Negation as Failure," in [GM78].

[CODD70] Codd, E.F., "A Relational Model of Data for Large Shared Data Banks," *Communications of the ACM,* Vol. 13, No. 6, pp. 377-387, June 1970.

[CODD72] Codd, E.F., "Relational Completeness of Database Sublanguages," in R. Rustin (ed.), *Data Base Systems,* Prentice-Hall, Englewood Cliffs, NJ, 1972.

[CODD79] Codd, E.F., "Extending the Database Relational Model to Capture More Meaning," *ACM Transactions on Database Systems,* Vol. 4, No. 4, December 1979, pp. 397-434; IBM Research Report RJ2599, San Jose, CA, August 1979.

[GM78] Gallaire, H. and J. Minker (eds.), *Logic and Data Bases,* Plenum Press, New York, 1978.

[HM78] Hammer, M. and D. McLeod, "The Semantic Data Model: A Modelling Mechanism for Database Applications," *Proc. 1978 ACM SIGMOD International Conference on the Management of Data,* Austin, TX, May–June 1978.

[JACO82] Jacobs, B.E., "On Database Logic," *Journal of the ACM,* Vol. 29, No. 2, April 1982, pp. 310-332.

[KOWA79] Kowalski, R., *Logic for Problem Solving,* Elsevier North-Holland, New York, 1979.

[KUHN67] Kuhns, J.L., "Answering Questions by Computer—A Logical Study," Memorandum RM 2428 PR, Rand Corporation, Santa Monica, CA, December 1967.

[LIPS79] Lipski, W., Jr., "On Semantic Issues Connected with Incomplete Information Databases," *ACM Transactions on Database Systems,* Vol. 4, No. 3, September 1979, pp. 262-296.

[MBW80] Mylopoulos, J., P.A. Bernstein and H.K.T. Wong, "A Language Facility for Designing Interactive Database-Intensive Applications," *ACM Transactions on Database Systems,* Vol. 5, No. 2, June 1980, pp. 27-39.

[MCCA80] McCarthy, J., "Circumscripton—A Form of Non-Monotonic Reasoning," *Artificial Intelligence,* Vol. 13, Nos. 1 and 2, April 1980, pp. 27-39.

[MEND64] Mendelson, E., *Introduction to Mathematical Logic,* Van Nostrand, Princeton, NJ, 1964.

[RAPH71] Raphael, B., "The Frame Problem in Problem-Solving Systems," in N.V. Findler and B. Meltzer (eds.), *Artificial Intelligence and Heuristic Programming,* Edinburgh University Press, Edinburgh, Scotland, 1971.

[REIT77] Reiter, R., *An Approach to Deductive Question-Answering,* BBN Technical Report 3649, Bolt, Beranek and Newman, Inc., Cambridge, MA, September 1977.

[REIT78a] Reiter, R., "Deductive Question-Answering on Relational Databases," in [GM78], pp. 149-177.

[REIT78b] Reiter, R., "On Closed World Data Bases," in [GM78], pp. 55-76.

[REIT80a] Reiter, R., "Equality and Domain Closure in First Order Databases," *Journal of the ACM,* Vol. 27, No. 2, 1989, pp. 235-249.

[REIT80b] Reiter, R., "Databases: A Logical Perspective," in [BZ80], pp. 174-176.

[REIT80c] Reiter, R., "A Logic for Default Reasoning," *Artificial Intelligence,* Vol. 13, 1980, pp. 81-132.

[SCHU76a] Schubert, L.K., "Extending the Expressive Power of Semantic Networks," *Artificial Intelligence,* Vol 7, No. 2, Summer 1976, pp. 163-198.

[SOWA76] Sowa, J.F., "Conceptual Structures for a Database Interface," *IBM Jornal of Research and Development,* Vol. 20, No. 4, July 1976, pp. 336-357.

[SS77b] Smith, J.M. and D.C.P. Smith, "Database Abstractions: Aggregation and Generalization," *ACM Transactions on Database Systems,* Vol. 2, No. 2, June 1977, pp. 105-133.

[TL82] Tsichritzis, D. and F. Lochovsky, *Data Models,* Prentice-Hall, Englewood Cliffs, NJ, 1982.

[ULLM80] Ullman, J.D., *Principles of Database Systems,* Computer Science Press, Potomac, MD, 1980.

[VASS79] Vassiliou, Y., "Null Values in Database Management: A Denotational Semantics Approach," *Proc. 1979 ACM SIGMOD International Conference on Management of Data,* Boston, MA, May 1979, pp. 162-169.

[WALK80] Walker, A., "Time and Space in a Lattice of Universal Relations with Blank Entries," *XPI Workshop on Relational Database Theory,* Stony Brook, NY, June–July 1980.

[ZANI77] Zaniolo, C., "Relational Views in a Database System; Support for Queries," *Proc. IEEE Computer Applications and Software Conference,* Chicago, IL, November 1977, pp. 267-275.

2.5 Representation Issues: Knowledge Incompleteness

This section examines two substantially different treatments of the problem of knowledge incompleteness. In its simplest form, the problem is one of recording, in the information base, the lack of information concerning an attribute (e.g., Mary's telephone number) in a way that does not result in a computationally intractable retrieval operation with respect to the information base. More complex situations can arise in cases of partial knowledge or in ones involving various forms of the closed-world assumption. [ETHE87] presents a recent treatment of the issues that arise when we are reasoning with respect to incomplete information, and relates these issues to recent advances in nonmonotonic reasoning. Related work on null values and incompleteness includes [VASS79], [LIPS79], [VASS80], [REIT83], and [LEVE81].

The first paper (2.5.1), Hector Levesque's "The Logic of Incomplete Knowledge Bases," looks at the expressiveness required of a language intended for the definition of and access to a knowledge base that contains incomplete information. The paper argues that, to talk about the completeness of the knowledge base, one needs to be able to refer to the state of the knowledge base and to how that state relates to the application domain. A language that includes a modal operator (which stands for *it is believed that*) is proposed. The authors show how that language can be used to query a knowledge base. Somewhat surprisingly, they conclude that the knowledge-base–definition language need not use the modal operator because every fact added to the knowledge can be translated to one that uses only first-order logical assertions. The short discussion at the end of the paper evaluating the expressiveness of various proposals for the representation of incomplete knowledge is both thorough and revealing.

The second and final paper in this section (2.5.2), "On Representing Incomplete Information in a Relational Database" by Tomasz Imielinski and Withold Lipski, examines ways of extending the relational model to deal with various types of null values, and the effect such extensions have on relational operations. In particular, the paper proposes conditions that must be satisfied by any semantically meaningful extension of the relational operators intended to deal with operands (tables or relations) that include null values. This work continues earlier research by Lipski [LIPS79]. It is one of the better examples of how limited incompleteness can be represented and dealt with algorithmically in the context of a database (with all the requirements on efficiency that this entails).

The Logic of Incomplete Knowledge Bases

Hector J. Levesque
University of Toronto

ABSTRACT *Some formal representation issues underlying the use of incomplete knowledge bases are discussed. An incomplete knowledge base is one that has only partial knowledge of the application domain. It is argued that a language that can refer to both the application domain and to the state of the knowledge base is required to specify and to question an incomplete knowledge base. A formal logical language with this expressive ability is presented and its semantics and proof theory are defined. It is also shown how different the use of the language must be, depending on whether the interaction involves querying or defining the knowledge base.*

1. Introduction

An important characteristic of any knowledge based system is its interaction with a *knowledge base* (KB) that provides and maintains information about the application domain. In general, there are two distinct modes of interaction between an expert system and its KB: the system will want to *ask* and to *tell* the KB about the application area. The assumption here is that a KB is interesting only as a repository for information about the domain and that the questions and assertions of interest are about the domain and not about the structure of the KB itself. In this chapter, I will examine what special expressive requirements are placed on the language(s) of interaction when a system must deal with a KB that is *incomplete.*

Generally speaking, a KB is incomplete when it does not have all the information necessary to answer a question of interest to the system. In this case, the user of the KB (man or machine) must distinguish between what is *known* by the KB and what is *true* in the intended application area. For example, a KB may know that someone is married without knowing to whom; it may know that one person is younger than another without knowing either person's age. In situations such as these, any interaction with the KB must be based on the understanding that the KB may have only partial knowledge of certain relevant aspects of the application. Specifically, the KB cannot be treated simply as a direct model or analogue of the domain. For instance, with an incomplete KB, one cannot establish how many people there are in the domain by simply counting representational objects of a certain type. Only when a KB is sufficiently complete will there be a structural similarity between the domain and the KB.

The reason incomplete KBs are so important is that, in many applications, the KB undergoes a continual evolution. At each stage, information can be acquired that is potentially very vague or indefinite in nature. More important, a problem solving system cannot simply wait for the KB to stabilize in some final and complete form since this may *never* happen.

When a knowledge based system is forced to depend on an incomplete KB, its ability to make decisions or solve problems is seriously compromised. In some cases, the lack of knowledge can be circumvented by using general defaults [REIT78c], while in other situations, special heuristics are required [CWAM75]. However, no matter how a system plans to deal with incompleteness, it must first be able to determine where this incompleteness lies. In other words, *a system has to find out exactly where knowledge is lacking before it can decide what to do about it.* This suggests that a KB must be capable of providing information not only about the application area, but about itself as well. Thus, the language used to interact with a KB must allow a user to define and inquire about what the KB does and does not know. The major issue of this chapter, then, is what impact this capability will have on the language of interaction.

The approach taken in my work focuses primarily on the formal aspects of this issue. As described in Section 2, I will be dealing with KBs consisting of formulas of the first order predicate calculus. In Section 3, I examine what questions one would like to be able to ask such a KB and conclude that these questions are best phrased in a superset of the predicate calculus I call KL. In Section 4, I examine the language KL in detail and provide a semantics and proof theory. Given this analysis of KL, I then consider it as a language used to interact with a KB. In Section 5, the formulas of KL are used to *query* a KB, and I show that this involves a nonmonotonic version of the language. In Section 6, the formulas of KL are used to *define* a KB, and I indicate why this requires converting the formulas into the language of the KB. In Section 7, I briefly survey how incompleteness has been handled in Database Management and, in Section 8, I discuss how my work could relate to traditional Knowledge Representation.

Three areas of related research should be noted. First of all, my formalization of KL owes much to the work on the logic of knowledge and belief pioneered in [HINT62] and continued in [MOOR80] and [MSHI78] (though my application is somewhat different). Secondly, there has been research on incompleteness from the database area (*e.g.*, [VASS80] [LIPS78]) concentrating primarily on efficient query evaluation. Finally, although the research here does not deal with defaults or assumptions, the work on nonmonotonic reasoning [MD78] [MCDE80] [MCCA80] [REIT80] has provided technical inspiration. Despite the inherent formality of the subject matter, the tone of this chapter is somewhat informal. In particular, three nontrivial results are announced without proof. In each case, the length of the proof would have severely restricted the space available for motivation and discussion of the framework. The interested reader is invited to consult [LEVE81a] for the technical details of these results. This chapter itself is an extension and refinement of [LEVE81b].

2. First Order Knowledge Bases

As described in [GM78], a first order KB is a finite set of closed formulas of first order logic (FOL). I will restrict my attention to formulas that do not contain function symbols other than a (possibly infinite) set of 0-ary symbols called constants. Moreover, it is assumed that there are as many constants as there are entities in the domain of discourse.

A query in this framework is any formula of FOL and is answered by consulting the provability relation $\vdash$ to determine what does and does not follow from the KB. In this chapter, I will consider only closed queries which correspond to yes/no questions. For each query α there are three possible replies:

- *yes*, when $KB \vdash \alpha$
- *no*, when $KB \vdash \neg\alpha$
- *unknown*, when neither $KB \vdash \alpha$ nor $KB \vdash \neg\alpha$

If we allow for inconsistent KBs, there is a fourth possibility which is:

- *both*, when $KB \vdash \alpha$ and $KB \vdash \neg\alpha$

Typically, a first order KB can be factored into two parts, one containing particular facts of the application domain such as

$$\text{Student(bill)},\ \text{Student(joe)},\ \text{Teaches(john,bill)}$$

and the other containing general rules regarding the usage of predicate symbols such as

$$(\forall x)\ \neg\ \text{Teaches}\ (x,x)$$

or

$$(\forall x)[\text{Teacher}\ (x) \equiv (\exists y)\ \text{Teaches}\ (x,y)].$$

The first rule above might be used as an integrity constraint, and the second can be used to deduce who the teachers are.

To avoid having to include within a KB all the "negative" facts about the application such as

$$\neg\ \text{Student(john)},\ \neg\ \text{Teaches(bill,john)},$$

$$\neg\ \text{Teaches(joe,john)},\ \neg\ \text{Teaches(john,joe)},$$

$$\neg\ \text{Teaches(joe, bill)},\ \neg\ \text{Teaches(bill,joe)},$$

an assumption is usually made (once and for all) that the negation of any atomic formula can be inferred from the inability to infer the atomic formula. This is the *closed world assumption* (CWA) [REIT78b] and results in a new view of query evaluation. In this case, a query is answered in terms of

$$KB \vdash_{cwa} \alpha$$

where $\vdash_{cwa}$ is a provability relation that takes the assumption into account. Letting

$$\overline{KB} = \{\neg\ p \mid p \text{ is atomic and } \neg\ KB \vdash p\}$$

then we have

$$KB \vdash_{cwa} \alpha \text{ iff } KB \cup \overline{KB} \vdash \alpha.$$

If the CWA is used along with the assumption that the constants correspond to the entities in the domain,[1] we have the property that for any closed formula α either

$$KB \vdash_{cwa} \alpha \text{ or } KB \vdash_{cwa} \neg\ \alpha.$$

---

[1] What this assumption amounts to is that $\vdash$ is such that any set of sentences containing $\exists x\alpha$ and $\neg\alpha_c^x$ for every constant c is inconsistent. The set of constants need not be finite and there could be other function symbols including additional 0-ary ones.

I will call a KB where no closed query has an unknown answer *complete* since it provides a complete picture of the domain it is intended to model relative to the query language.

In an *incomplete* KB, on the other hand, there are relevant queries having *unknown* as an answer. Consider, for example, a KB that contains

$$[\text{Student(mary)} \vee \text{Student(susan)}]$$

but neither

$$\text{Student(mary)}$$

nor

$$\text{Student(susan)}.$$

In this case, $KB \cup \overline{KB}$ is inconsistent so the CWA cannot be used. This KB only partially describes a world since it specifies that Mary or Susan is a student but does not particularize. Thus, there is a query that is true in the intended application but whose truth cannot be determined on the basis of what is available in the KB.

To say that a KB is incomplete is quite different from the somewhat trivial observation that a KB can never completely capture all aspects of some domain and that therefore unknowns exist. To allow the CWA to be used, queries are normally constrained to deal only with the KB's area of expertise (for example, by restricting the predicate symbols that can be used). Within this narrow area, the KB may indeed be complete. The key point regarding the above KB is that even within its domain of expertise it is incomplete because it does specify that Mary or Susan is a student. So there is, in fact, a *relevant* query (*i.e.*, whether or not Mary is a student), that cannot be answered with certainty.

For the rest of this chapter, I will say that a KB *knows* a formula if it answers *yes* to the query and, for any predicate p and constant c, that c is a *known* p when the formula $p(c)$ is known.

3. The Knowledge Base Query Language

Even though a KB is incomplete and the CWA cannot be used, there may be completeness in certain areas. For example, suppose that

$$KB \vdash (\forall x)[\text{Teacher}(x) \equiv (x = \text{john} \vee x = \text{george})].$$

In this case, not only are John and George teachers, but the KB knows that they are the only teachers. It therefore has a complete picture of the teachers. On the other hand, it may be the case that

$$KB \vdash (\exists x)\text{Teacher}(x)$$

without there being any known teachers. In this situation, the KB knows that there is a teacher but does not know who, indicating, therefore, that is does not have a complete list of teachers. There is, moreover, a third possibility, where it cannot be determined whether or not the KB has complete knowledge of the teachers. For example, suppose that the only thing the KB knows about the teachers is that John is one of them. In this case, it is neither true that

$$KB \vdash (\exists x)[\text{Teacher}(x) \wedge (x \neq \text{john})]$$

nor

$$KB \vdash \neg(\exists x)[\text{Teacher}(x) \wedge (x \neq \text{john})].$$

In other words, the KB may or may not already know all of the teachers. So just as the question

Is John a teacher?

may be answered *yes*, *no*, or *unknown*, the question

Are all the teachers known?

may also be *yes*, *no*, or *unknown*, depending only on what is in the KB.

If the purpose of a query language is to provide an accurate picture of what is and is not available in the KB, we should be able to formulate queries that ask the KB about its incompleteness. The query

$$(\exists x)[\text{Teacher}(x) \wedge (x \neq \text{john})]$$

does not suffice since it asks only if there is a teacher other than John. It may turn out, for example, that

$$KB \vdash \text{Teacher(george)}$$

in which case the query is answered *yes* without telling us whether all the teachers are known. What is really required is the query

$$(\exists x)[\text{Teacher}(x) \wedge x \neq c_1 \wedge x \neq c_2 \wedge \ldots \wedge x \neq c_k)]$$

where the c's are constants ranging over all the teachers known to the KB.

There are a couple of problems with this method of asking whether all the teachers are known. First of all, there could be a very large number of known teachers. In some applications and for some predicates, there may even be an *infinite* number. Secondly, to be able to formulate the query we have to know what these constants are. For a large and complex KB, it could happen that only the KB has this information. One can also imagine situations in which the KB will not divulge this information for security reasons while still being able to answer questions about its incompleteness.

This suggests that the KB itself should keep track of its incompleteness in the same way it maintains knowledge of the application area. One possibility, for example, is to have a predicate

$$\textit{Known-teacher}\ (x)$$

and to allow a KB containing the following:

$$\text{Teacher(john)},\ \textit{Known-teacher}\ (\text{john}),$$
$$[\text{Teacher(george)} \vee \text{Teacher(dan)}],$$
$$\neg\ \textit{Known-teacher}\ (\text{george}),\ \neg\ \textit{Known-teacher}\ (\text{dan}).$$

Granted this arrangement, we can ask whether the KB has a complete list of teachers by the query

$$(\exists x)[\text{Teacher}(x) \wedge \neg\ \textit{Known-teacher}\ (x)]$$

for which the answer here is *yes*, confirming the fact that the KB is incomplete.

The problem with this approach (and any other that involves a direct encoding into FOL) is the management of this extended language. There is a very definite relationship between "Teacher" and "*Known-teacher*" that must be captured somehow. Among other things, we intend that whenever

$$\text{Teacher}(c)$$

is in the KB, then

$$\textit{Known-teacher}(c)$$

is in the KB as well. The closest we can come to expressing this is by an axiom stating that

$$(\forall x)[\text{Teacher}(x) \supset \textit{Known-teacher}(x)].$$

However, this does not work since, for the above KB, it implies that

$$[\textit{Known-teacher}(\text{george}) \vee \textit{Known-teacher}\ (\text{dan})]$$

which is inconsistent with what is already known. Moreover, once we admit that "*Known-teacher*" is a predicate, there is a new source of potential incompleteness for the KB, and thus we will want to be able to ask if the KB has all instances of this predicate:

$$(\exists x)[\textit{Known-teacher}\ (x) \wedge \neg\ \textit{Known-Known-teacher}\ (x)].$$

This, of course, leads to an infinite regression of predicates, none of which are very relevant to the application area. In a nutshell, "*Known-teacher*" should not be a predicate for the simple reason that its truth or falsity does not depend on the domain being modelled but on the model, the KB itself.

The solution, then, is to leave the KB as is but to extend the query language in order to allow questions that refer to the current state of knowledge of the KB. The query language I propose, called KL, contains all of FOL, and in addition has formulas of the form Kα read as

The KB knows that α.

This leaves us with a first order KB while still allowing us to query the KB regarding its incompleteness. In particular, we have a new form of query evaluation

$$\text{KB} \Vdash \alpha$$

where $\Vdash$ is some (as yet to be specified) provability relation and α is any formula of KL possibly containing K's.

For example, to find out whether the KB had a incomplete list of teachers, we must find out whether

$$\text{KB} \Vdash (\exists x)[\text{Teacher}(x) \wedge \neg\ \text{K}[\text{Teacher}(x)]].$$

Similarly, while the query

$$(\exists x)\text{Teacher}(x)$$

can be used to find out whether there are any teachers, the query

$$(\exists x)\text{K}[\text{Teacher}(x)]$$

asks whether the KB knows who any of them are. To be able to define the $\Vdash$ relation, we must first look at the semantics of the language KL itself.

4. The Language KL

The query language KL has the same formation rules as FOL but also includes the rule

$$\text{If } \alpha \in \text{KL then } \text{K}\,\alpha \in \text{KL}.$$

Consequently there are two kinds of formulas in KL. The first, like

$$p(c) \wedge (\exists x) q(x)$$

will be true or false depending only on the interpretation of the constant and predicate symbols. The second, like

$$K[p(c) \wedge (\exists x) q(x)]$$

will be true or false depending only on the KB and on what is known or not known. I will call the latter formulas *pure*. There are also formulas in KL that are mixtures of the two types and whose truth value depends both on the interpretation and the KB. KL also allows for *meta-knowledge* in formulas such as

$$K[(\exists x) K p(x)]$$

which talk about the KB's knowledge of its own knowledge.

The semantic interpretation of a closed formula of KL will depend on both a world description (or interpretation, in the Tarskian sense) and a description of a KB. In general, a KB can be viewed as a partial description of a world and can thus be characterized by a set of world descriptions. If we characterize a KB by a set of world descriptions *m*, we have

> K α is true in the KB described by *m* iff α is true in every world described by an element of *m*.

To make all this more precise, first note that because of the correspondence between constants and entities in the domain, a world description need only assign a truth value to the atomic sentences in order to determine the truth value of all sentences of FOL. Thus, we can define

> the set of world descriptions, $\mathcal{W} = [\text{ATOMS} \rightarrow \text{T,F}]$.

A KB description is, then, just a nonempty set of world descriptions

> the set of KB descriptions, $\mathcal{M} = \{ m \subseteq \mathcal{W} \mid m \neq \emptyset \}$.

The interpretation of any closed formula α is provided by the function Φ.

$$\Phi \in [\text{KL} \times \mathcal{W} \times \mathcal{M} \rightarrow \{\text{T,F}\}] \text{ is defined by}$$

$$\begin{aligned}
\Phi(\alpha, w, m) &= w(\alpha) \text{ when } \alpha \text{ is atomic.} \\
\Phi(\neg\alpha, w, m) &= \text{T iff } \Phi(\alpha, w, m) = \text{F.} \\
\Phi([\alpha \vee \beta], w, m) &= \text{T iff } \Phi(\alpha, w, m) = \text{T or } \Phi(\beta, w, m) = \text{T.} \\
\Phi((\exists x)\, \alpha, w, m) &= \text{T iff for some } c,\ \Phi(\alpha^x_c, w, m) = \text{T.} \\
\Phi(K\alpha, w, m) &= \text{T iff for every } w' \in m,\ \Phi(\alpha, w', m) = \text{T.}
\end{aligned}$$

A formula is *valid* when it is true on every world and KB description. In the case where α is pure, I will use $\Phi(\alpha, m)$ to refer to the truth value of α on the KB described by m.

Turning now to the proof theory for KL, since the language includes FOL as a subset, we will need the two inference rules of FOL: *modus ponens* and *universal generalization*. In fact, these are the only two rules required. As for axioms, we need the axioms of FOL in order to guarantee that negation, implication, and quantification behave properly.

To account for the K operator, we have to realize that it behaves like a provability relation because something is known when it "follows" from what is available in the KB. We will, therefore, insist that the axioms of FOL are known and that the KB is able to perform modus ponens and universal generalization[2] based on what is known. This might be called the assumption of *competence*. As for meta-knowledge, it is convenient to assume that the KB knows the correct truth value of any pure formula. In other words, there is never any reason to tell the KB about itself nor is there any reason to doubt what the KB knows about itself. No matter how incomplete or inaccurate a KB can be about the world, it is assumed to be the final authority on itself. This might be called the assumption of *closure*. Note that this assumption applies only to pure sentences. Fortunately, these can be given a syntactic characterization:

> A formula is *pure* iff every occurrence of a predicate symbol appears within the scope of a K operator.

We therefore have the following axiomatization of the language KL:

[2] The actual form of universal generalization needed here is somewhat special since, among other things, we have to be able to infer a universal sentence from a (possibly infinite) set of positive instances. A finitary version of this inference rule that has this property is presented in [LEVE81a].

Axiom Schemata

- The axioms of FOL
- $K\alpha$ where α is an axiom of FOL
- $K(\alpha \supset \beta) \supset (K\,\alpha \supset K\,\beta)$
- $(\forall x)K\alpha \supset K(\forall x)\,\alpha$
- $\alpha \equiv K\,\alpha$ where α is pure

Rules of Inference

- Modus ponens and Universal Generalization

If we let $\vdash$ denote the provability relation for this axiomatization, then the key result here is that the proof theory is both sound and complete with respect to the semantics given earlier:

Proposition 1. *$\vdash \alpha$ iff α is valid.*

Given this equivalence between the proof theory and the semantics, certain properties of KL are easily verified. For example, we have

$$\vdash K\,\alpha \supset \neg K\,\neg\alpha$$

which says that a KB is always *consistent* since it contains no contradictory information. This is easily verified by noting that no element of $\mathcal{M}$ is empty. One thing to notice is that by the closure property, we have that for any pure α

$$\vdash K\,\alpha \supset \alpha.$$

This is, however, not the case for arbitrary α since, for example, the set

$$\{\neg p(c), Kp(c)\}$$

is satisfiable and, hence, logically consistent. This is a situation in which the KB is behaving properly but just happens to be mistaken about the world. So, in some sense, the K operator should be read as "believe" rather than "know." On the other hand, the kind of belief involved here is very special since a KB will always think it is dealing with knowledge because

$$\vdash K(K\alpha \supset \alpha)$$

for any formula α. In other words, a KB will always believe that what it believes is true. So there is an aspect of *commitment* to what is believed because a KB will never believe it has mistaken beliefs.

5. Queries Revisited

Having examined the semantics and proof theory of KL, we are still faced with the problem of specifying what is meant by

$$KB \Vdash \alpha \text{ where } KB \subseteq FOL \text{ and } \alpha \in KL.$$

The idea here is that this should mean

If all I know is what is in KB, then I know that α.

The tricky part is characterizing the "all" in the above sentence, what Konolige calls "circumscriptive ignorance" [KONO82]. Semantically, this means that $K\alpha$ is true with respect to the knowledge base that has the *least amount* of world knowledge consistent with knowing everything in KB. Thinking of a knowledge base as described by a set of world descriptions, we want the least amount of world knowledge and, thus, the largest possible set.

$$\text{Let } \mathcal{M}(KB) = \{w \mid w \text{ satisfies the KB}\}.$$

Any knowledge base that knows what is in the KB is described by a subset of $\mathcal{M}$ (KB) and therefore has a more refined view of the world. For example, if the KB is empty then $\mathcal{M}$ (KB) is the set of all possible world descriptions. This suggests how query evaluation can be defined semantically:

$$\text{Let } KB \Vdash \alpha \text{ iff } \Phi(K\alpha, \mathcal{M}(KB)) = T.$$

Thus, the answer to a question is *yes* exactly when the question is known to be true in $\mathcal{M}$ (KB). For example, if

$$KB1 = \{Teacher(john)\}$$

then

$$KB1 \Vdash Teacher(john),$$
$$KB1 \Vdash \neg K[Student(bill)],$$
$$KB1 \Vdash (\exists x)K[Teacher(x)],$$
$$KB1 \Vdash K \neg K[Student(bill)],$$
$$KB1 \Vdash \neg K[(\exists x)[Teacher(x) \wedge \neg K\,Teacher(x)]].$$

The last statement above confirms that KB1 knows that it does not know whether or not it has a complete list of teachers.

Note that for any pure α we have that either

$$KB \Vdash \alpha \text{ or } KB \Vdash \neg\alpha$$

since the KB has complete knowledge about itself. Also worth noting is that $\Vdash$ is a nonmonotonic operator because it is not the case that

$$\text{KB1} + \text{Student(bill)} \Vdash \neg\, \text{K[Student(bill)]}.$$

However, unlike a fully general nonmonotonic operator like the one presented in [MD78] or [MCDE80], the $\Vdash$ operator here has been given a simple and natural semantic characterization. Below I will present a theoretic proof analogue of this operator and claim a soundness and completeness type result, but before doing so it is necessary to examine how KL can be used to specify a KB.

6. The Knowledge Base Definition Language

Since, for incomplete KBs, the CWA is not used uniformly, it would be extremely convenient to be able to tell the KB when (if ever) the assumption could be used for special cases. Conversely, we should also be able to tell the KB when the CWA cannot be used. If we let

$$\pi = (\exists x)[\text{Teacher}(x) \wedge \neg \text{KTeacher}(x)]$$

then $\neg\pi$ states that if someone is not currently known to be a teacher then he is not a teacher. So $\neg\pi$ is the CWA relativized to teachers, while π itself is a statement that this assumption cannot be used (because there are teachers other than the currently known ones). The question immediately arises as to whether or not we can add formulas such as π or $\neg\pi$ to a KB, thus generalizing a KB to be any consistent set of formulas from KL instead of FOL.

There are a number of problems with this generalization, but I will address only one that relates to the formula π. The idea here is that we would start off with a KB such as KB1 defined earlier. Since KB1 does not know whether or not John is the only teacher, it is not the case that either

$$\text{KB1} \Vdash \pi \text{ or } \text{KB1} \Vdash \neg\pi.$$

Suppose we consider telling it that it does not have all the teachers and get

$$\text{KB2} = \text{KB1} + \pi$$

If we now want to tell the KB that George is a teacher, we get

$$\text{KB3} = \text{KB2} + \text{Teacher(george)}$$

The problem here is that KB3 still contains π and, consequently, still thinks it is missing a teacher. In fact, no matter how many teachers we tell the KB about, it will still think it is missing at least one. Moreover, if we try to tell it that it finally has all of them by adding $\neg\pi$, then we arrive at an inconsistent KB since it also contains π.

What *should* have happened here is somewhat different. Once we arrived at KB2, the KB should know that it is missing a teacher and hence believe π. However, once a new teacher is added to the KB producing KB3, the KB has no way to decide if this is the last teacher it was missing. So it should be the case (as with KB1) that neither

$$\text{KB3} \Vdash \pi \text{ nor } \text{KB3} \Vdash \neg\pi.$$

In other words, after the introduction of George, the KB should no longer know whether or not it has all the teachers. In fact, the knowledge it had as KB2 is lost when it becomes KB3.

This is a strange kind of nonmonotonicity. The usual symptom of a nonmonotonic logic is that the addition of a new axiom invalidates a previous *theorem*. In our case, the addition of the new axiom invalidated a previous *axiom*. The curious puzzle here is that there is no "belief revision" going on in the sense of a realization that an axiom was incorrectly added to the KB. Similarly, there is no admission of the world having changed in the sense of someone becoming or ceasing to be a teacher. In fact, the only change that has taken place is a change in what is known about the world. But this is enough since π does make reference to the *current* state of the KB. So without admitting that the world has changed or that some previous statement about the world needs revision, we can still maintain that the truth value of π can change by noting that the state of the KB has changed. Thus, π cannot be part of the KB since the state of knowledge it refers to disappears as information is acquired.

The solution to the problem of the addition of π to a KB is, therefore, to treat the formula as ordinary world knowledge where the K operator is used to refer to the current state of the KB. This is only natural since a KB is assumed to have complete knowledge of itself. Consequently, any mention of what is known in a new piece of information must be "referential" and not "attributive." Thus, the addition to the KB must be understood by first resolving these references. In other words, the solution to the problem is not to prohibit additions like π, but rather to allow π in the KB definition language but not the KB itself. For example, KB2 now becomes

$$\text{KB2} = \text{KB1} + \pi = \{\text{Teacher(john)}, (\exists x)[\text{Teacher}(x) \wedge (x \neq \text{john})]\}$$

where we have replaced the open formula

$$\text{K[Teacher(x)]}$$

by a first order formula that resolves this reference with respect to KB1:

$$(x{=}\text{john}).$$

This produces the property that

$$KB2 \Vdash \pi$$

and neither

$$KB3 \Vdash \pi \text{ nor } KB3 \Vdash \neg\pi$$

as desired. Similarly, if we start with KB1 and wish to tell it that it has all the teachers, then we add

$$(\forall x)[\neg K[\text{Teacher}(x)] \supset \neg\text{Teacher}(x)]$$

which for KB1 resolves to

$$(\forall x)[\text{Teacher}(x) \supset (x = \text{john})]$$

again a formula of FOL. Note that if we start with a KB that is missing a teacher such as

$$\{\text{Teacher(john)}, [\text{Teacher(george)} \vee \text{Teacher(dan)}]\}$$

then the attempt to add the CWA for teachers will correctly result in an inconsistency.

The solution I have proposed above presupposes that there always will be a formula of FOL that can be used to resolve any reference to what is known. It is worth noting that this cannot be done independently of a KB since there is no formula α of FOL such that

$$\vdash K\,\pi \equiv K\,\alpha.$$

In this sense, the language KL is more expressive than FOL. Of course, all we really need is a formula for each KB and not a formula that works for every KB. Fortunately, if we assume the availability of an equality predicate and restrict ourselves to *finite* KBs, this can always be done.

Proposition 2. *Assume $KB \subseteq FOL$ finite and $\alpha(x_1,\ldots x_k) \in KL$. There exists a formula $/\alpha/ \in FOL$ (with equality) such that $KB \Vdash (\forall x_1) \ldots (\forall x_k)\,[K\,\alpha \equiv K\,/\alpha/]$.*

The method of allowing all of KL to specify a KB is thus to let

$$KB + \alpha = KB \cup \{/\alpha/\} \text{ for any } \alpha \in KL.$$

Viewed more semantically in terms of world descriptions, we have that

$$\mathcal{M}(KB) \cap \{w \mid \Phi(\alpha, w, \mathcal{M}(KB)) = T\} = \mathcal{M}(KB \cup \{/\alpha/\}).$$

For any formula $\alpha \in KL$, a formula $/\alpha/ \in FOL$ that satisfies the above proposition can be defined by

$$/\alpha/ = \alpha \text{ when } \alpha \in \text{FOL},\quad /\neg\alpha/ = \neg/\alpha/,\quad /(\alpha \supset \beta)/ = (/\alpha/ \supset /\beta/)$$

$$/(\forall x)\alpha/ = (\forall x)/\alpha/ \text{ and } /K\alpha/ = \text{RESOLVE}[/\alpha/].$$

RESOLVE[α] = **If** α *has no free variables*
  then if KB $\vdash \alpha$ **then** $(\forall x)(x = x)$ **else** $\neg(\forall x)(x = x)$
  else /* *Assume x is a free variable of α* and
    $c_1,\ldots,c_k$ *are all the constants in α* or KB */
 $[(x = c_1 \wedge \text{RESOLVE}[\alpha^x_{c_1}]) \vee \ldots \vee (x = c_k \wedge \text{RESOLVE}[\alpha^x_{c_k}]) \vee$
    /* *Assume c is any constant not in α* or KB */
   $(x \neq c_1 \wedge \ldots \wedge x \neq c_k \wedge \text{RESOLVE}[\alpha^x_c]^c_x)]$

The point of this definition is to show a formula that works but obviously not the *shortest* one. Note that although the function RESOLVE is not recursive, it is strictly proof-theoretic. Moreover, it can be shown that

Proposition 3. *$KB \Vdash \alpha$ iff $KB \vdash /\alpha/$ for any $\alpha \in KL$.*

In other words, for any query α in KL, the answer is *yes* exactly when $/\alpha/$ is a (first order) consequence of the sentences in the KB. This defines a purely first order syntactic version of query evaluation that is exactly equivalent to the semantic one defined earlier. Of course, the proof theory is not axiomatic but this is to be expected given that

$$\{\alpha \in KL \mid \Vdash \alpha\}$$

is not recursively enumerable. So, to summarize, although the interaction with a first order KB should allow the language KL to be used, this interaction can be understood in first order terms when the KB is finite.

7. Incompleteness in Database Management

It is perhaps worthwhile at this stage to compare my approach to three other proposals in Database Management that have made special provisions for dealing with incompleteness: the relational model as presented in [CODD79] and [VASS80], the TAXIS model [MW80], and the model advocated by Lipski [LIPS78]. While the three models attempt to deal with a wide variety of issues, my only concern here is the extent to which incompleteness is allowed in the information system (KB, database).

A common feature of the three models is the ability to represent information such as

Mary's supervisor is *unknown*.

over and above specific information like

Bill's supervisor is George.

The supervisor of Mary, in this case, is represented by a *null value* [CODD70] indicating that its exact value is not (yet) known. The intent appears to be the same as knowing that

$$(\exists x)\ \text{Supervisor}\ (x,\text{mary})$$

where, perhaps, it is also known that every student has at most one supervisor:

$$(\forall x)\ (\exists y)\ (\forall z)\ [\text{Student}(x) \land \text{Supervisor}(z,x) \supset y{=}z].$$

A serious limitation of the relational and TAXIS models is that they do not allow information about a null value to be accumulated. If Mary's supervisor is not known, all that can be known about it is that it falls within the domain of supervisors. For example, an assertion such as

$$[\text{Supervisor}(\text{joe}, \text{mary}) \lor \text{Supervisor}(\text{jim}, \text{mary})]$$

which would severely constrain Mary's (unknown) supervisor, cannot be represented even though each disjunct can be. Similarly, a very weak constraint on the null value, such as

$$\neg\ \text{Supervisor}(\text{george}, \text{mary})$$

cannot be handled by either data model.

This particular limitation is not shared by Lipski's model since it allows one to specify a set for each attribute (*e.g.*, supervisor) of each object (*e.g.*, Mary). If the set contains one element, then the value is known; otherwise, the value is only known to be a member of the set. However, the Lipski model is limited in other ways. Like the TAXIS model, it is "object-centered" because everything that is known about the world is expressed in terms of properties of specific objects. There is, consequently, no provision for uncertainty regarding which object is being characterized. For example, statements such as

$$[\text{Supervisor}(\text{joe}, \text{mary}) \lor \text{Supervisor}(\text{joe}, \text{john})]$$

or

$$(\exists x)\,[\text{Student}(x) \land \text{Supervisor}(\text{jim}, x)]$$

cannot be accommodated since, in each case, the student claiming to have a certain supervisor is not known.

Apart from their limited ability to relate null values to known values, none of the three models allow null values to be related to each other. Suppose, for example, that the supervisor of Mary is not known. There is no way of representing the fact that John's (unknown) supervisor is distinct from Mary's,

$$(\exists x)\,[\text{Supervisor}(x, \text{john}) \land \neg\ \text{Supervisor}(x, \text{mary})]$$

or that Bill's is identical to hers,

$$(\exists x)\,[\text{Supervisor}(x, \text{bill}) \land \text{Supervisor}(x, \text{mary})].$$

The implicit assumption is that null values *independently* represent known values. This assumption, when applied to unknown truth values, leads to rules such as

If α and β are *unknown*, then so is $(\alpha \lor \beta)$.

which is quite inappropriate when β is the negation of α .

The limitations of the relational, TAXIS and Lipski models are nicely summarized in a passage from [MOOR80] (p. 137):

> Any system adequate for representing the knowledge of an intelligent being must surely be able to:
>
> - Say that something has a certain property without saying what thing has that property.
> - Say that everything in a certain class has a certain property without saying what everything in that class is.
> - Say that at least one of two statements is true without saying which statement is true.
> - Explicitly say that something is false.
> - Either settle or leave open to doubt whether two nonidentical expressions name the same object.

Note that I made reference to all but the second requirement in my examination of the three models.[3] The crucial point here, however, is that *all* these requirements are based on provisions for various kinds of incompleteness. As the chapter by Reiter points out, the incompleteness admitted by the three models can be accommodated within a FOL framework. In other words, the reason for wanting the expressive

---

3 That requirement will be dealt with in the next section.

power of FOL is not to be able to represent detailed knowledge of a complex domain, but rather to be able to represent very shallow and incomplete knowledge of the domain. It is important to realize that the choice is not so much between a "logical" or a "nonlogical" representation language, but more a decision about what kinds of incompleteness will be tolerated.

My approach differs from these three data models primarily because it allows a much wider variety of incompleteness. The main argument of this chapter is that, given this incompleteness, a more expressive language is required to interact with the KB. It should be noted that Lipski does allow his query language to distinguish between, in my terminology,

$$\text{Supervisor}(\text{joe}, x) \quad \text{and} \quad K[\text{Supervisor}(\text{joe}, x)].$$

The fact that the usefulness of this is questioned in [VASS80] is perhaps explained by the limited forms of incompleteness under consideration. It must be remembered, of course, that the concerns that gave rise to these limitations may be perfectly valid from a database viewpoint (even if they do not coincide with those of knowledge based systems).

8. Incompleteness in Knowledge Representation

Arguments presented in the last section should not be taken to imply that representation languages in Artificial Intelligence do not share the limitations of those in Database Management. Indeed, the "nonlogical" representation schemes (such as KL-ONE [BRAC76], PSN [LM79], NETL [FAHL79], or KRL [BW77]) appear to suffer from the same assertional poverty induced by object centeredness. For these languages and others, reasoning depends upon having a close correspondence between the objects and relationships in the domain and their representational counterparts in a system. In this section, I will briefly suggest a possible unification of the "logical" and "nonlogical" approaches to Knowledge Representation that preserves the advantages of each by completely separating their concerns. The suggestion should be taken as preliminary and in need of much research.[4]

Suppose we are interested in using a predicate "FlyingBird." We would certainly want any KB using this predicate to know that

A. $(\forall x)[\text{FlyingBird}(x) \equiv \text{Bird}(x) \wedge \text{Fly}(x)]$.

If we are interested in modelling a world where penguins are the only birds that do not fly, we should be able to tell the KB that

B. $(\forall x)[\text{FlyingBird}(x) \equiv \text{Bird}(x) \wedge \neg \text{Penguin}(x)]$.

Note that because of possible incomplete knowledge about the world, we should be able to assert (B) and intend it to apply to *all* birds (in that world) and not just the currently known ones. This is again the kind of partial knowledge usually not representable in an object-centered scheme. The main point here, however, is that the import of (B) is quite distinct from that of (A) even though the KB should know that both are true. Specifically, (B) need not be true in a different world, and thus its truth conveys information about the world. The intent of (A), on the other hand, is that it cannot fail to be true and thus conveys no information about the world. If these two statements are to coexist in a KB, they must be distinguished somehow. An important characteristic of both (A) and (B) is that the predicate "FlyingBird" can, in some sense, be eliminated.

A′. $(\forall x)[\text{Bird}(x) \wedge \text{Fly}(x) \equiv \text{Bird}(x) \wedge \text{Fly}(x)]$

B′. $(\forall x)[\text{Bird}(x) \wedge \text{Fly}(x) \equiv \text{Bird}(x) \wedge \neg \text{Penguin}(x)]$.

Once again, (B′) but not (A′) could be false and says something about the world. Moreover, (B′) appears to say the same thing about the world that (B) does. But if (A′) says the same thing as (A), then (A) is not really asserting anything at all.

My claim here is that (A) is best understood not as an assertion (about some world) but as an addition to terminology used when talking about a world. In other words, (A) is best paraphrased by something like

D. $\text{FlyingBird} \leftarrow \lambda x.\ [\text{Bird}(x) \wedge \text{Fly}(x)]$

which defines a predicate in terms of two other predicates. The question of whether (D) is true or false simply does not arise since it is not the kind of linguistic expression that can take a truth value. If we insist on talking about the truth value of (A), we can take the position that it is true in the same way (A′) is true — vacuously and by virtue of the way the language is intended to be used. In its present form, (A) is quite misleading, however, because it looks like (B). Following a distinction made in [WOOD75], I will call statements like (A) that introduce terminology *definitional*, and those like (B) that convey information about a world *assertional*.

Why should a representation scheme that is interested only in expressing knowledge about a world have to deal with statements that carry no information? The answer, I believe, is that definitional mechanisms facilitate the interaction between a user (man or machine) and

[4] See also [BL82] for a further refinement of these ideas.

the KB. The addition of terminology is not a matter of truth or falsity but a matter of convenience to the user. In particular, the definitional mechanisms of a language should help structure and should organize what eventually will be said or asked about the world.

In the previous section, I argued that a "logical" language like KL was essential to allow sufficiently weak assertions to be made about a world. Indeed, the traditional concern of logical languages is precisely to provide adequate assertional facilities of various kinds. The "non-logical" representation languages (and most semantic data models), on the other hand, while weak at the assertional level, do attempt to provide adequate facilities for organizing and structuring the set of terms (predicates, types, classes, concepts, units) being used. For example, the ubiquitous IS-A hierarchy is perhaps best viewed as a mechanism for introducing new terms by specializing or generalizing existing ones rather than as a facility for asserting restricted universal generalizations. The goal need not (and should not) be to supplant or extend the assertional features of the language, any more than the abstraction mechanisms of high level programming languages extend the computational power of lower level languages. Conversely, as Israel and Brachman argue in their chapter, the fact that definitions can be explained away, to a certain extent, at the assertional level cannot be taken as an argument that they are not needed. The assertional and definitional levels each has its own purpose, methodology, and standards of adequacy. It is this separation of concerns that might permit the "logical" and "nonlogical" approaches to be profitably unified within a single representation scheme.

The research reported here deals only with the expressive adequacy of the assertional level but could also have repercussions at the definitional level. For example, new terms are often required for which no necessary and sufficient conditions seem appropriate (*e.g.,* natural kinds). These are sometimes best characterized at the definitional level in terms of prototypes and defaults. In this case, the definitional level has to be able to refer not only to the the world being modelled, but to the state of the KB as well. This, of course, is the original motivation behind my language KL. At any rate, the best way to proceed in this regard remains to be seen.

9. Conclusion

In this chapter, I have considered from a formal standpoint the problem of interacting with an incomplete KB. The motivation behind the research is that, to effectively deal with partial knowledge, a system first must be able to determine the exact limits of what is known. This, in turn, places certain requirements on the language used to interact with a KB. In particular, the language has to be able to refer to the state of the KB as well as to the state of the application domain.

To this effect, I proposed a language KL for interacting with a first order KB and presented a proof theory and semantics which were direct extensions of their FOL counterparts. KL was then applied to query evaluation and I showed that this required a nonmonotonic operator. Semantic and syntactic interpretations of this operator were provided. Finally, KL was applied to KB definition and I demonstrated why this required reducing KL into the language of the KB, FOL. In fact, the net result was that the KB remained first order, but that interaction with it took place in a more expressive language.

Apart from the more practical implications of this work, there remain open questions even within the formal framework. I have not mentioned, for example, what impact the presence of an equality relation or nonconstant terms would have on KL. Also, a method of handling defaults (and exceptions) is a reasonable goal granted that the framework allows one to determine where its application is needed. In summary, the framework provides not only a formal standard against which to measure representation languages, but also a basis for further exploration.

10. References

[BW77] [BRAC76] [BL82] [CODD70] [CODD79] [CWAM75] [FAHL79] [GM78] [HINT62] [KONO82] [LEVE81a] [LEVE81b] [LM79] [LIPS78] [MCCA80] [MSHI78] [MCDE80] [MD78] [MOOR81] [MW80] [REIT78b] [REIT78c] [REIT80] [VASS80] [WOOD75]

Discussion

This chapter presents a very general account of incomplete knowledge, and it should be of interest to knowledge base and database system designers. The account applies to systems whose knowledge base can be expressed in terms of a set of first order formulas. The range of things that can be expressed in this way goes well beyond current Database practice (see also the chapter by Reiter). One way to distinguish between a database and a knowledge base is in terms of the things it is perceived to contain. A (relational) database contains tuples and a query such as: "Is there a tuple e in the EMPLOYEE relation such that e.name = bill will always return true or false." With a knowledge base, on the other hand, one is interpreting the data and reasoning about them so that the answer to a query may be neither true nor false.

The Closed World Assumption (CWA)

All forms of the CWA can be expressed in English as "Anything not known to be true is false." The divergence between different accounts arises in the formulation of "not known." An early proposal that links knowledge (on the part of the database) to provability has problems in dealing with disjunction and null values (see Section 6 of the chapter by Reiter). A different formulation is proposed in this chapter. Another very general formulation called circumscription is due to McCarthy.

The K Operator

In cases where the CWA is not (or cannot be) used, a new kind of query suggests itself. Suppose that we are dealing with a knowledge base about teachers which knows only that John and Bill are teachers. A possible query to this knowledge base is:

1. "Is there a teacher who is not known to the knowledge base"

or, alternatively for this particular knowledge base,

2. "Is there a teacher who isn't John or Bill"

Note that this query is about the knowledge base, not the world. The second formulation of the query is clearly unsatisfactory when there are many known teachers. To represent "known" in the first formulation we might consider introducing a predicate Known-teacher so (1) is reformulated as:

3. "Is there someone who is a teacher and not a known-teacher"

The problem now is that the representation treats the predicates Teacher and Known-teacher as distinct even though they are intimately related. Also, this solution creates a need for other predicates such as Known-known-teacher, *etc.*, for queries that involve nested knowledge statements. Instead of these unsatisfactory solutions, the chapter proposes a *modal operator* K such that K&& is read as:

"The knowledge base knows that &&"

In providing a formal semantics for K we view the knowledge base as an (incomplete) description that fits a set of possible worlds. To evaluate a query such as "K&&" amounts to checking that && is satisfied by all possible worlds described by the knowledge base.

The framework presented in the chapter allows only first order formulas in the knowledge base, although updates and queries are expressed in a modal language, called KL, which includes the operator K. A provability theory has been developed for this language and has been shown to be sound and complete. Without the K operator the theory reduces to first order provability theory.

It is important to note that the designer of the knowledge base does not specify explicitly possible worlds. Instead he tells the knowledge base that, for example, a sentence, FOO, is true, and as a result the set of possible worlds described by the knowledge base is reduced by leaving out worlds that do not satisfy FOO.

Deductive Capabilities

The proposed framework is mainly intended as a way of correctly *understanding incomplete knowledge bases in general and not as a method of implementing specific application problems.* There are, for example, a family of puzzles that deal with constraint satisfaction (given an apparently incomplete description of the solution). We might be given separate lists of first and last names, and also information about where people with these names reside, as well as other information such as: "Smith and Jones drink together," "Bill and Paul live in different cities," *etc.* The problem is to find correspondences between first and last names. However, the use of KL to solve such problems would be somewhat of an overkill. These problems are finite and it is possible to solve them by simply making a table and trying out possibilities until one is found that satisfies all constraints. It should also be noted that use of the framework demands a full-fledged first order theorem prover, which means that the process of finding a solution may be slow and inefficient when compared with other possibilities for solving the problem.

In trying to generate a solution to such puzzles or answers to arbitrary queries expressed in KL, the theorem prover will not necessarily have to replace existential quantifiers with null values.

Concluding Remarks

Once you raise the question of incompleteness for a wide variety of knowledge bases, it is natural to ask such questions as: What is the logic of the situations that may arise? What can be proven about these situations? What would you want to be able to tell and not to tell about the knowledge base? What should updates look like and what should queries return. These are the issues dealt with in this chapter.

In his chapter, Reiter builds (from the bottom up) a closed world and the conditions it must satisfy. This chapter, on the other hand, lays down criteria once and for all in a broad brush stroke for dealing with incomplete knowledge. The broad brush approach exposes technical problems for a very general class of incomplete knowledge bases.

References

[BC75] Bobrow, D. and A. Collins (eds.), *Representation and Understanding,* Academic Press, New York, 1975.

[BW77] Bobrow, D. and T. Winograd, "An Overview of KRL, a Knowledge Representation Language," *Cognitive Science,* Vol. 1, No. 1, January 1977.

[BRAC76] Brachman, R.J., "A Structural Paradigm for Representing Knowledge," BBN Report No. 3605, Bolt, Beranek and Newman Inc., Cambridge, MA, 1976.

[BL82] Brachman, R.J. and H. Levesque, "Competence in Knowledge Representation," *Proc. AAAI National Conference,* Pittsburgh, PA, August 1982, pp. 189-192.

[CODD70] Codd, E.F., "A Relational Model of Data for Large Shared Data Banks," *Communications of the ACM,* Vol. 13, No. 6, June 1970, pp. 377-387.

[CODD79] Codd, E.F., "Extending the Database Relational Model to Capture More Meaning," *ACM Transactions on Database Systems,* Vol. 4, No. 4, pp. 397-434, December 1979; IBM Research Report RJ2599, San Jose, CA, August 1979.

[CWAM75] Collins, A., E. Warnock, N. Aiello and M. Miller, "Reasoning from Incomplete Knowledge," in [BC75].

[FAHL79] Fahlman, S.E., *NETL: A System for Representing and Using Real-World Knowledge,* MIT Press, 1979.

[FIND79] Findler, N.V., *Associative Networks Representation and Use of Knowledge by Computer,* Academic Press, New York, 1979.

[GM78] Gallaire, H. and J. Minker (eds.), *Logic and Data Bases,* Plenum Press, New York, 1978.

[HINT62] Hintikka, J., *Knowledge and Belief: An Introduction to the Logic of the Two Notions,* Cornell Univ. Press, 1962.

[KONO82] Konolige, K., "Circumscriptive Ignorance," *Proc. AAAI National Conference,* Pittsburgh, PA, August 1982.

[LEVE81a] Levesque, H., "A Formal Treatment of Incomplete Knowledge Bases," Ph.D. Thesis, Department of Computer Science, University of Toronto, 1981; also available as Technical Report No. 3, Fairchild Laboratory for Artificial Intelligence Research, Palo Alto, CA.

[LEVE81b] Levesque, H., "The Interaction with Incomplete Knowledge Bases: A Formal Treatment," *Proc. International Joint Conference on Artificial Intelligence,* University of British Columbia, Vancouver, B.C., Canada, 1981.

[LM79] Levesque, H. and J. Mylopoulos, "A Procedural Semantic for Semantic Networks," in [FIND79].

[LIPS78] Lipski, W., Jr., "On Semantic Issues Connected with Incomplete Information Data Bases," PAS Report 325, Institute of Computer Science, Warsaw, Poland, 1978.

[MCCA80] McCarthy, J., "Circumscription—A Form of Non-Monotonic Reasoning," *Artificial Intelligence,* Vol. 13, Nos. 1 and 2, April 1980, pp. 27-39.

[MSHI78] McCarthy, J., M. Sato, T. Hayashi and S. Igarashi, "On the Model Theory of Knowledge," Memo AIM-312, Department of Computer Science, Stanford University, 1978.

[MCDE80] McDermott, D., "Non-Monotonic Logic II: Non-Monotonic Modal Theories," Research Report No. 174, Department of Computer Science, Yale University, February 1980.

[MD78] McDermott, D. and J. Doyle, "Non-Monotonic Logic I," Memo MIT/AIM-486, MIT Laboratory for Artificial Intelligence, 1978.

[MOOR81] Moore, R., "Reasoning about Knowledge and Action," Technical Note 191, Artificial Intelligence Center, SRI International, Menlo Park, CA, 1980.

[MW80] Mylopoulos, J. and H. Wong, "Some Features of the TAXIS Data Model," *Proc. 6th International Conference on Very Large Databases,* Montreal, Quebec, Canada, October 1980.

[REIT78c] Reiter, R., "On Reasoning by Default," *Proc. Second TINLAP Conference,* Urbana, IL, July 1978, pp. 210-218.

[REIT80a] Reiter, R., "Equality and Domain Closure in First Order Databases," *Journal of the ACM,* Vol. 27, No. 2, pp. 235-249, 1980.

[REIT80b] Reiter, R., "Databases: A Logical Perspective," in [BZ80], pp. 174-176.

[REIT80c] Reiter, R., "A Logic for Default Reasoning," *Artificial Intelligence,* Vol. 13, pp. 81-132, 1980.

[VASS80] Vassiliou, Y., "A Formal Treatment of Imperfect Information in Database Management," Ph.D. Thesis, Department of Computer Science, University of Toronto, Canada, 1980.

Incomplete Information in Relational Databases

TOMASZ IMIELIŃSKI AND WITOLD LIPSKI, JR.

Polish Academy of Sciences, Warsaw, Poland

Abstract. This paper concerns the semantics of Codd's relational model of data. Formulated are precise conditions that should be satisfied in a semantically meaningful extension of the usual relational operators, such as projection, selection, union, and join, from operators on relations to operators on tables with "null values" of various kinds allowed. These conditions require that the system be safe in the sense that no incorrect conclusion is derivable by using a specified subset Ω of the relational operators; and that it be complete in the sense that all valid conclusions expressible by relational expressions using operators in Ω are in fact derivable in this system. Two such systems of practical interest are shown. The first, based on the usual Codd's null values, supports projection and selection. The second, based on many different ("marked") null values or variables allowed to appear in a table, is shown to correctly support projection, positive selection (with no negation occurring in the selection condition), union, and renaming of attributes, which allows for processing arbitrary conjunctive queries. A very desirable property enjoyed by this system is that all relational operators on tables are performed in exactly the same way as in the case of the usual relations. A third system, mainly of theoretical interest, supporting projection, selection, union, join, and renaming, is also discussed. Under a so-called closed world assumption, it can also handle the operator of difference. It is based on a device called a conditional table and is crucial to the proof of the correctness of the second system. All systems considered allow for relational expressions containing arbitrarily many different relation symbols, and no form of the universal relation assumption is required.

Categories and Subject Descriptors: H.2.3 [**Database Management**]: Languages—*query languages*; H.2.4 [**Database Management**]: Systems—*query processing*

General Terms: Theory

Additional Key Words and Phrases: Relational database, incomplete information, null values, marked nulls, relational algebra, query language semantics, query processing

1. *Introduction*

Attempts to represent incomplete information in the relational model of data have been made since the very beginning of the relational database theory [3, 7, 8, 10, 12, 13, 18–21, 27, 28, 30, 31, 33, 34]. (See also the extensive bibliography in [22].) The main device in this context has been the *null value*, a special symbol @ allowed as an entry in a table, with its intended meaning being *value at present unknown* (*but the attribute applicable*).

Representing incomplete information in a database immediately raises the much more difficult and important problem of processing this information so that the user can obtain—perhaps partial, but correct—responses to his or her queries on the basis of the incomplete information. In the context of the relational model, this comes down to defining the relational operators on tables with null values in a semantically correct way. The intuitive condition that should be satisfied is the following. If a null value has a specified semantic interpretation, that is, if we assume that a specified relation exists between a table with nulls and the real world, then this relation should be similar for the tables that are arguments of a relational operator and for the table obtained as the result.

Solutions to this problem proposed so far have been in many respects partial and unsatisfactory. Codd's approach [7, 8] is based on a three-valued logic and a so-called null substitution principle, which has been criticized on semantic grounds by Grant [10] and Lipski [20]. Lipski [19–21] and Vassiliou [30] consider, essentially, only the relational operator of selection, where the selection condition can be an arbitrary Boolean combination of atomic conditions. Proposals involving a richer subset of the relational operators—and it is the join that seems to be the main source of difficulty—usually do not give a clear and precise explanation of the sense in which the definitions of relational operators on tables with nulls are semantically correct [7, 8, 18]. An exception is the work of Biskup [3]. However, his definition of, say, a join $T \bowtie U$ of two tables with nulls works correctly when T and U are "independent" but does not necessarily provide a method for correctly evaluating an expression $f(T) \bowtie g(T)$ where f and g are some relational expressions. This is because in the latter case there may be "additional information" implied by the fact that both arguments of the join come from the same table T, and his definition of join is not able to take this into account (this is discussed in more detail at the end of Section 4.) In fact, queries in a relational database are arbitrary relational expressions, so that we should be able to handle correctly relational expressions rather than just single relational operators.

In this paper we formulate the precise conditions that we believe should be satisfied in any semantically meaningful extension of the usual relational operators, such as projection, selection, union, and join, from operators on relations to operators on "incompletely specified relations"—typically, tables with "null values" of different kinds allowed as entries. These conditions are embodied into the definition of a representation system (see Section 3).

Roughly speaking, these conditions require that our system be safe in the sense that no incorrect conclusion is derivable by using a specified subset Ω of the relational operators, and that it be complete in the sense that all valid conclusions expressible by relational operators using operators in Ω are in fact derivable. The intuition behind the notion of a representation system can also be explained in the following way. By performing relational operators over tables with nulls, we may introduce some corruption of information. However, if the query language that the user has at his or her disposal is weak enough, that is, if only a specified subset Ω of the relational operators is available, then this corruption is not visible by the user.

Two representation systems of practical interest are shown. The first, described in Section 4, is based on tables with the usual Codd null values @ (we call them Codd tables). The following is an example of a Codd table.

This work was supported in part by the Polish Academy of Sciences under Contract MR.I.3. The second author was also aided through a visiting appointment by Istituto di Analisi dei Sistemi ed Informatica, Consiglio Nazionale delle Richerche, Roma, Italy.

Some of the results of this paper were presented at the Seventh International Conference on Very Large Data Bases, Cannes, France, September 1981.

Authors' present addresses: T. Imieliński, Rutgers University, Department of Computer Science, Hill Center for the Mathematical Sciences, Busch Campus, New Brunswick, NJ, 08903; W. Lipski, Jr., Laboratoire de Recherche en Informatique, Université de Paris-Sud, Centre d'Orsay, Bât. 490, 91405 Orsay Cedex, France.

SUPPLIER	LOCATION	PRODUCT	QUANTITY
Smith	London	Nails	@
Brown	@	Bolts	@
Jones	@	Nuts	40,000

This table represents the information that Smith, located in London, supplies (an unknown quantity of) nails; Brown supplies bolts; and Jones supplies 40,000 nuts. The system based on Codd tables supports projection and selection, and it is shown that no representation system based on Codd tables can support projection and join at a time.

Section 5 describes some algorithms for correctly evaluating a selection over a Codd table, including the case in which attribute domains are linearly ordered, and the selection condition is an arbitrary Boolean combination of elementary inequalities between attributes or between attributes and values.

The second representation system, presented in Section 6, supports projection, positive selection (with no negation occurring in the selection condition), union, join, and renaming of attributes—this allows for processing arbitrary conjunctive queries [4], as shown in Section 8. It is based on tables allowing many different ("marked") null values, or variables (such tables are called *V*-tables). The following is an example of a *V*-table:

COURSE	TEACHER	WEEKDAY
Databases	x	Monday
Programming	y	Tuesday
Databases	x	Thursday
FORTRAN	Smith	z

This table contains three different variables, x, y, z. Notice that it represents the information that the teacher of the course on databases, though unknown, is the same on Monday and Thursday, a fact not representable by means of a Codd table.

A very desirable property enjoyed by our representation system based on *V*-tables is that all relational operators on *V*-tables are performed in exactly the same way as in the case of the usual relations, treating variables as if they were regular values in appropriate attribute domains (this may be referred to as the *naive evaluation*). It may also be noted that *V*-tables appear in a natural way in the context of updating relational views. Assume, for instance, that a database is given by

SL :

SUPPLIER	LOCATION
Smith	London

SP :

SUPPLIER	PRODUCT
Smith	Nails

and suppose that the relational view

$$\pi_{\text{LOCATION, PRODUCT}}(\text{SL} \bowtie \text{SP})$$

is updated by adding two tuples, ⟨New York, Bolts⟩ and ⟨Los Angeles, Nuts⟩. It is then natural to define the effect of this update to be

SL :

SUPPLIER	LOCATION
Smith	London
x	New York
y	Los Angeles

SP :

SUPPLIER	PRODUCT
Smith	Nails
x	Bolts
y	Nuts

A negative result shown in Section 6 is that, rather surprisingly, no representation system based on *V*-tables can support projection and arbitrary selection (recall that these operators can be supported by Codd tables).

A third representation system, described in Section 7, supports projection, selection, union, join, and renaming and is mainly of a theoretical interest. It is based on an idea of a so-called conditional table and is crucial in the proof of the correctness of the second system. A conditional table is a *V*-table with an additional column, *con*, containing a condition; for example, the conditional table

SUPPLIER	LOCATION	PRODUCT	con
x	London	Nails	$x = \text{Smith}$
Brown	New York	Nails	$x \neq \text{Smith}$

represents the information that nails are supplied either by Smith in London or by Brown in New York, but not by both at a time.

All representation systems considered in this paper allow for relational expressions containing arbitrarily many different relation symbols, and no form of the universal relation assumption [24] is required.

Most of the results of the paper are developed under a so-called open world assumption (see [26]) that, roughly speaking, means that we are not able to represent negative information. In Section 9 we briefly show how the results can be extended in a straightforward manner to a modified interpretation of tables where negative information is representable. It turns out that under such a modified interpretation the system based on conditional tables can also handle the operator of difference, thus supporting the full strength of the relational algebra.

The last section contains conclusions and briefly describes related work, in particular, the work concerning the problem of handling dependencies in the context of *V*-tables, and the relation between *V*-tables and tableaux of Aho, Sagiv, and Ullman [1].

2. *Basic Definitions*

In this section, we give some basic definitions and notation concerning the relational data model ([5]; see also [29]).

Throughout the paper we consider a fixed, finite (unless otherwise stated) set $\mathscr{U}$ of *attributes*. Attributes are usually denoted by A, B, C, and sets of attributes by X, Y, Z, with possible subscripts. A set of attributes, say $\{A, C\}$, is usually written as AC. Associated with every $A \in \mathscr{U}$ is an *attribute domain* $D(A)$. We always assume that $|D(A)| \geq 2$ and we denote $D = \bigcup_{A \in \mathscr{U}} D(A)$. Elements of D are sometimes called *constants*. Elements of $D(A)$, $D(B)$, $D(C)$ are usually denoted by a, b, c, respectively, with possible primes, etc. By a *tuple* on X we mean any mapping t that associates a value $t(A) \in D(A)$ with every $A \in X$. A tuple is usually denoted as a string of values associated with the attributes; for example, ac is a tuple on AC. For a tuple t on X and for any $Y \subseteq X$, we denote by $t[Y]$ the *restriction* of t to Y; for example, if $t = abc$ then $t[AC] = ac$. By a *relation* on X we mean any finite set of tuples on X. If t, r are a tuple and a relation on X, we then write

$$\alpha(t) = \alpha(r) = X,$$

and we call $\alpha(t)$ and $\alpha(r)$ the *type* of t and r, respectively. A *multirelation* of type $\langle X_1, \ldots, X_n \rangle$ is any sequence $\langle r_1, \ldots, r_n \rangle$ in which r_i is a relation on X_i, $1 \leq i \leq n$. Relations are usually denoted by r, s, with possible subscripts, and multirelations by $\mathbf{r}$, $\mathbf{s}$ (conforming to the general convention that boldface indicates multiobjects). The type of multirelation $\mathbf{r}$ is denoted by $\alpha(\mathbf{r})$. By an empty multirelation we mean any multirelation of the form $\mathbf{0} = \langle \varnothing, \ldots, \varnothing \rangle$; formally, we shall assume that there is a different empty multirelation for each type.

For two multirelations $\mathbf{r} = \langle r_1, \ldots, r_n \rangle$, $\mathbf{s} = \langle s_1, \ldots, s_n \rangle$ of the same type, we write $\mathbf{r} \subseteq \mathbf{s}$ if $r_i \subseteq s_i$, $1 \leq i \leq n$. If $\mathbf{r} = \langle r_1, \ldots, r_n \rangle$ and $1 \leq i \leq n$, then we define

$$\mathrm{pr}_i(\mathbf{r}) = r_i.$$

The set of all multirelations of type $\langle X_1, \ldots, X_n \rangle$ is denoted by $\mathscr{R}(X_1, \ldots, X_n)$; in particular, $\mathscr{R}(X)$ is the set of all relations of type X. The set of all multirelations is denoted by $\mathscr{R}$.

The class of all nonempty homogeneous sets of multirelations is denoted by $\mathscr{I}$ (a set $\mathscr{X}$ of multirelations is *homogeneous* if $\alpha(\mathbf{r}) = \alpha(\mathbf{s})$ for all $\mathbf{r}, \mathbf{s} \in \mathscr{X}$). Elements of $\mathscr{I}$ are denoted by $\mathscr{X}$, $\mathscr{Y}$, $\mathscr{Z}$, and the definition of $\alpha(\mathscr{X})$, the type of $\mathscr{X}$, is the natural one.

We consider the usual relational operators:

Projection

$$\pi_Y(r) = \{t[Y] : t \in r\} \qquad (Y \subseteq \alpha(r)).$$

Selection

$$\sigma_E(r) = \{t \in r : E(t) = \mathbf{true}\}.$$

Here E is a *selection condition*; that is, any expression built up from atomic conditions of the form $(A = a)$, $(A = B)$, $A, B \in \mathscr{U}$, $D(A) = D(B)$, $a \in D(A)$ (and truth constants **true**, **false**) by means of the logical connectives $\vee$ (or), $\wedge$ (and), $\neg$ (not). $E(t)$ denotes the truth value obtained by substituting the value $t(A)$ for any occurrence of A in E and evaluating the expression in the natural way. We always assume that $\alpha(r)$ contains all the attributes occurring in E. A selection condition E and the selection operator σ_E is called *positive* if it does not contain the $\neg$ symbol.

We sometimes consider a more general form of selection, where E is *any* mapping from tuples to $\{\mathbf{true}, \mathbf{false}\}$. (Note: The operation $\sigma_{A=B}$ is also called *restriction*.)

Union

$r \cup s$, that is, the usual set-theoretical union.

We always assume that both arguments of union are of the same type.

Join

$$r \bowtie s = \{t : \alpha(t) = X \cup Y \wedge t[X] \in r \wedge t[Y] \in s\},$$

where

$$X = \alpha(r), \qquad Y = \alpha(s).$$

Difference

$r - s = r \backslash s$, that is, the usual set-theoretical difference.

We always assume that both arguments of difference are of the same type.

In Section 8 we also consider the following additional operation.

Renaming (of an attribute)

$$s_B^A(r) = \{s_B^A(t) : t \in r\}$$

where $A \in \alpha(r)$, $B \in \mathscr{U} \backslash \alpha(r)$, $D(A) = D(B)$, and $s_B^A(t)$ is the tuple of type $(\alpha(r)\backslash\{A\}) \cup \{B\}$ with

$$(s_B^A(t))(C) = \begin{cases} t(C) & \text{if } C \in \alpha(r)\backslash\{A\}, \\ t(A) & \text{if } C = B. \end{cases}$$

Intuitively, $s_B^A(r)$ is the result of renaming column A or r to B.

We show in Section 8 how the results of this paper can be extended to another version of relational algebra, based on Cartesian product (see, e.g., [29]) instead of join.

By a *relation name* we mean a symbol R (the letter S is also used) with possible subscripts, with an associated *type* $\alpha(R) \subseteq \mathscr{U}$.

An *instance* of R is any relation r such that $\alpha(r) = \alpha(R)$. An instance is usually denoted by a lowercase version of the letter denoting the relation name.

For any subset Ω of the relational operators of projection (P), selection (S), positive selection (S^+), join (J), difference (D), and renaming (R), a *relational Ω-expression* means any well-formed expression built up from relation names and relational operators in Ω; for example, $\sigma_{A=a}(R_1) \bowtie \pi_{AB}(R_2)$ is a relational PS^+J-expression. A *multirelational Ω-expression* is any sequence $\mathbf{f} = \langle f_1, \ldots, f_k \rangle$ of relational Ω-expressions. Relational and multirelational Ω-expressions are often called simply Ω-expressions; they are usually denoted by f, g, with possible subscripts, and by $\mathbf{f}$, $\mathbf{g}$, respectively. They are assumed to be *typed* in the following sense. We assume that associated with every $\mathbf{f}$ is a sequence $\langle R_1, \ldots, R_n \rangle$ (either clear from the context or given explicity by writing $\mathbf{f}(R_1, \ldots, R_n)$) containing all relation names occurring in $\mathbf{f}$ (and possibly some other relation names). The *argument type* of $\mathbf{f}$ is then defined as

$$\alpha(\mathbf{f}) = \langle \alpha(R_1), \ldots, \alpha(R_n) \rangle.$$

For any $\mathbf{f} = \langle f_1, \ldots, f_k \rangle$ and any multirelation $\mathbf{r} = \langle r_1, \ldots, r_n \rangle$ of type $\alpha(\mathbf{r}) = \alpha(\mathbf{f})$, we define $\mathbf{f}(\mathbf{r}) = \langle f_1(\mathbf{r}), \ldots, f_k(\mathbf{r}) \rangle$ where $f_i(\mathbf{r})$ denotes the relation obtained by substituting r_j for all occurrences of R_j in f_i, $j = 1, \ldots, n$. We also define $\beta(\mathbf{f}) = \alpha(\mathbf{f}(\mathbf{r}))$ and call it the *result type* of $\mathbf{f}$.

It may be mentioned in this context that the relational algebra can be embedded in a natural way into a simple algebraic system called a *cylindric set algebra*, such that all relations considered are of type $\mathscr{U}$ and all relational operators are total (i.e., there are no restrictions on the arguments). This approach has several advantages (i.e., the "complicated" join operator becomes the usual set-theoretical intersection) but leads to infinite relations and creates some problems concerning the finite representability of these relations. This approach is treated in more detail in another paper by the authors [14].

3. *Representation Systems*

In this section we formulate some general conditions that we require to be satisfied in any semantically meaningful extension of the relational algebra to "tables with nulls."

To this end we introduce the notion of a representation system. By a *representation system* we mean a triple $\langle \mathcal{T}, \text{Rep}, \Omega \rangle$ where $\mathcal{T}$ is the set of *multitables*, Rep is a mapping, Rep: $\mathcal{T} \to \mathcal{I}$ (recall that $\mathcal{I}$ is the set of all nonempty homogeneous sets of multirelations), Ω is a set of relational operators, and a certain natural condition, to be defined at the end of this section, is satisfied. Roughly speaking, this condition asserts that there is a way, consistent with respect to operators in Ω, to define $\mathbf{f}(\mathbf{T})$ for any Ω-expression $\mathbf{f}$ and any multitable $\mathbf{T} \in \mathcal{T}$.

First, however, let us give some intuitive explanations concerning the components of a representation system.

A multitable is usually a "generalized multirelation" with tuples allowed to contain not only values in appropriate attribute domains, but also some special symbols ("null values" of various kinds). Most of the notions and notation concerning relations and multirelations, such as a tuple, $\alpha(\mathbf{r})$, or $t[Y]$, carry over to multitables. The set Rep(T) of multirelations defines the information contained in multitable T; that is, it specifies the set of possibilities represented by T.

Suppose $\mathcal{X} \in \mathcal{I}$ represents our information about a certain unknown $\mathbf{r}^* \in \mathcal{X}$ and let $\mathbf{f}$ be an Ω-expression with $\alpha(\mathbf{f}) = \alpha(\mathcal{X})$. Clearly, our information about $\mathbf{f}(\mathbf{r}^*)$ is then represented by

$$\mathbf{f}(\mathcal{X}) = \{\mathbf{f}(\mathbf{r}) : \mathbf{r} \in \mathcal{X}\}.$$

In this way, any Ω-expression $\mathbf{f}$ can be treated in a natural way as a mapping $\mathbf{f}$: $\mathcal{I} \to \mathcal{I}$ (more exactly, a partial mapping defined only for those $\mathcal{X} \in \mathcal{I}$ with $\alpha(\mathcal{X}) = \alpha(\mathbf{f})$).

Suppose now that we want to give a natural definition of multitable $\mathbf{f}(\mathbf{T})$ where $\mathbf{T} \in \mathcal{T}$ and $\mathbf{f}$ is an Ω-expression ($\alpha(\mathbf{T}) = \alpha(\mathbf{f})$, where $\alpha(\mathbf{T})$ can be defined to be $\alpha(\text{Rep}(\mathbf{T}))$). If we think of T as representing in an incomplete way some unknown $\mathbf{r}^* \in \text{Rep}(\mathbf{T})$, then ideally we could expect that there exist the same relation between $\mathbf{f}(\mathbf{T})$ and $\mathbf{f}(\mathbf{r}^*)$, so that $\mathbf{f}(\text{Rep}(\mathbf{T})) = \text{Rep}(\mathbf{f}(\mathbf{T}))$; that is, the following diagram commutes:

$$\begin{array}{ccc} \mathcal{T} & \xrightarrow{\text{Rep}} & \mathcal{I} \\ \mathbf{f} \downarrow & & \downarrow \mathbf{f} \\ \mathcal{T} & \xrightarrow[\text{Rep}]{} & \mathcal{I} \end{array} \tag{3.1}$$

(for multitables of appropriate type). Unfortunately, this approach is usually not feasible, since in most practical situations the structure of the set $\mathbf{f}(\text{Rep}(\mathbf{T}))$ is not "regular" enough to be representable by any $\mathbf{U} \in \mathcal{T}$ (see, however, an exception at the end of Section 9). In other words, there is no $\mathbf{U} \in \mathcal{T}$ such that $\text{Rep}(\mathbf{U}) = \mathbf{f}(\text{Rep}(\mathbf{T}))$.

Clearly, if we are to define $\mathbf{f}(\mathbf{T})$ in a semantically meaningful way, then we should require that $\text{Rep}(\mathbf{f}(\mathbf{T}))$ approximate the information given by $\mathbf{f}(\text{Rep}(\mathbf{T}))$ in some natural sense (and we should precisely state in which sense). Before we describe what we consider to be a natural notion of "equivalence" between $\text{Rep}(\mathbf{f}(\mathbf{T}))$ and $\mathbf{f}(\text{Rep}(\mathbf{T}))$, we give some examples illustrating different kinds of equivalences between sets of multirelations.

Example 3.1. Let $\mathcal{X}$ consists of all those relations that contain at least one of the following two relations:

$$\begin{array}{|cc|} \hline a & b \\ a' & b' \\ \hline \end{array}\,, \qquad \begin{array}{|cc|} \hline a & b \\ a' & b'' \\ \hline \end{array}\,.$$

(Note: Here, and in all other examples in this paper, different symbols denoting values in attribute domains always stand for different values.)

Let $\mathcal{Y}$ be the set of all relations containing tuple ab (clearly $\mathcal{X} \subsetneq \mathcal{Y}$). In a way, $\mathcal{X}$ and $\mathcal{Y}$ are equivalent: if we assume $\mathbf{r}^* \in \mathcal{X}$, then the only tuple that can be concluded to be in $\mathbf{r}^*$ is ab, and the same is true for $\mathcal{Y}$.

However, $\mathcal{X}$ provides the information that $a' \in \pi_A(\mathbf{r}^*)$, whereas $\mathcal{Y}$ does not. Hence $\mathcal{X}$ and $\mathcal{Y}$ are not "equivalent with respect to projection." □

Example 3.2. Let $\mathcal{X}$ consist of all those relations that contain at least one of the following two relations:

$$\begin{array}{|ccc|} \hline a & b & c \\ \hline \end{array}\,, \qquad \begin{array}{|ccc|} \hline a & b' & c' \\ a' & b & c' \\ \hline \end{array}\,,$$

and let $\mathcal{Y}$ be defined in the same way by relations

$$\begin{array}{|ccc|} \hline a & b & c \\ \hline \end{array}\,, \qquad \begin{array}{|ccc|} \hline a & b' & c' \\ a' & b & c'' \\ \hline \end{array}\,.$$

It is easy to see that $\mathcal{X}$ and $\mathcal{Y}$ are equivalent with respect to projection, in the sense of the previous example. However, $\mathbf{r}^* \in \mathcal{X}$ implies

$$ab \in \pi_{AB}(\pi_{AC}(\mathbf{r}^*) \bowtie \pi_{BC}(\mathbf{r}^*)),$$

whereas this conclusion cannot be made under the assumption that $\mathbf{r}^* \in \mathcal{Y}$. Hence, $\mathcal{X}$ and $\mathcal{Y}$ are not equivalent "with respect to PJ-expressions." □

Example 3.3. Let $X = ABC$ and let

$$\mathcal{Z} = \{r \in \mathcal{R}(X) : abc \in r \lor ab'c \in r\}.$$

Define

$$\mathcal{X} = \{\langle r, r\rangle : r \in \mathcal{Z}\},$$
$$\mathcal{Y} = \{\langle r, s\rangle : r, s \in \mathcal{Z}\}.$$

It is not difficult to prove that $\mathcal{X}$ and $\mathcal{Y}$ are equivalent with respect to all PS-expressions (because PS-expressions involve only unary operators). However, they are not equivalent with respect to PJ-expressions. Indeed, $\langle r^*, s^*\rangle \in \mathcal{X}$ implies

$$ac \in \pi_{AC}(r^* \bowtie s^*)$$

(notice that $r^* \bowtie s^* = r^* \cap r^* = r^*$), whereas this conclusion cannot be made under the assumption that $\langle r^*, s^*\rangle \in \mathcal{Y}$. □

The above examples suggest the following definition. For a relational multi-expression $\mathbf{f}$ and $\mathcal{X} \in \mathcal{I}$ ($\alpha(\mathbf{f}) = \alpha(\mathcal{X})$) define the **f**-*information* in $\mathcal{X}$, denoted by $\mathcal{X}^{\mathbf{f}}$, to be

$$\mathcal{X}^{\mathbf{f}} = \bigcap \mathbf{f}(\mathcal{X})$$

(if $\mathbf{f} = \langle f_1, \ldots, f_k\rangle$, then $\bigcap \mathbf{f}(\mathcal{X})$ is understood as $\langle \bigcap f_1(\mathcal{X}), \ldots, \bigcap f_k(\mathcal{X})\rangle$). In other words, $\mathcal{X}^{\mathbf{f}}$ is the largest multirelation $\mathbf{s}$ such that $\mathbf{s} \subseteq \mathbf{f}(\mathbf{r}^*)$ for all $\mathbf{r}^* \in \mathcal{X}$. Putting it still another way, if $\mathcal{X}^{\mathbf{f}} = \langle s_1, \ldots, s_k\rangle$, then $t \in s_i$ means that from $\mathbf{r}^* \in \mathcal{X}$ we may conclude that $t \in f_i(\mathbf{r}^*)$.

Let $\mathcal{X}, \mathcal{Y} \in \mathcal{I}, \alpha(\mathcal{X}) = \alpha(\mathcal{Y})$. We say that $\mathcal{X}$ and $\mathcal{Y}$ are Ω-*equivalent* (in symbols $\mathcal{X} \equiv_\Omega \mathcal{Y}$) if $\mathcal{X}^{\mathbf{f}} = \mathcal{Y}^{\mathbf{f}}$ for any Ω-expression $\mathbf{f}$ with $\alpha(\mathbf{f}) = \alpha(\mathcal{X})$. Note that in Example 3.1, $\mathcal{X} \equiv_\varnothing \mathcal{Y}$ (we consider expressions of the form $f(R_1, \ldots, R_n)$

$= R_i$ to be the only relational $\varnothing$-expressions), but $\mathscr{X} \not\equiv_P \mathscr{Y}$; in Example 3.2, $\mathscr{X} \equiv_P \mathscr{Y}$, but $\mathscr{X} \not\equiv_{PJ} \mathscr{Y}$; in Example 3.3, $\mathscr{X} \equiv_{PS} \mathscr{Y}$, but $\mathscr{X} \not\equiv_{PJ} \mathscr{Y}$.

A multitable **T** is said to *Ω-represent* $\mathscr{X}$ if Rep(**T**) $\equiv_\Omega \mathscr{X}$.

We are now ready to complete the definition of a representation system. A triple $\langle \mathscr{T}, \text{Rep}, \Omega \rangle$, where $\mathscr{T}$, Rep, Ω are as described before, is a representation system if, for any Ω-expression **f** and for any multitable $\mathbf{T} \in \mathscr{T}$ $(\alpha(\mathbf{f}) = \alpha(\mathbf{T}))$, there is a multitable $\mathbf{U} \in \mathscr{T}$ that Ω-represents **f**(Rep(**T**))—in other words, if **f**(**T**) can be defined for every Ω-expression **f** and multitable $\mathbf{T} \in \mathscr{T}$ $(\alpha(\mathbf{f}) = \alpha(\mathbf{T}))$ in such a way that

$$\text{Rep}(\mathbf{f}(\mathbf{T})) \equiv_\Omega \mathbf{f}(\text{Rep}(\mathbf{T})). \tag{3.2}$$

Two multitables **T**, **U** are called *Ω-equivalent* if Rep(**T**) $\equiv_\Omega$ Rep(**U**) and *Rep-equivalent* if Rep(**T**) = Rep(**U**). Notice that for a given **T** and **f** there may exist many Ω-equivalent multitables $\mathbf{U} \in \mathscr{T}$ that Ω-represent **f**(Rep(**T**)).

There are two more conditions satisfied by most representation systems considered in this paper (these conditions are not part of the formal definition of a representation system). The first one is that any multirelation is—or at least can be identified with—a multitable, so that we may assume $\mathscr{R} \subseteq \mathscr{T}$. This reflects the fact that we are interested only in systems that extend the usual relational algebra. The second assumption (not valid in Section 9) is that for any multitable **T** and for any $\mathbf{r}, \mathbf{s} \in \mathscr{R}$

$$\mathbf{r} \in \text{Rep}(\mathbf{T}) \wedge \mathbf{s} \supseteq \mathbf{r} \Rightarrow \mathbf{s} \in \text{Rep}(\mathbf{T}). \tag{3.3}$$

This condition—which is essentially the *open world assumption* of Reiter [26]—is equivalent to saying that we are not able to represent negative information; that is, the knowledge that a relationship expressed by a certain tuple t is definitely *not* true in the real world $\mathbf{r}^*$ (or in $\mathbf{f}(\mathbf{r}^*)$, where **f** is some relational expression). An intuitive consequence of this assumption is that for any $\mathbf{r} \in \mathscr{R}$

$$\text{Rep}(\mathbf{r}) = \{\mathbf{s} \in \mathscr{R} : \mathbf{s} \supseteq \mathbf{r}\}.$$

We conclude this section by the following simple lemma.

LEMMA 3.1. *If Ω contains only unary operators, then $\langle \mathscr{T}, Rep, \Omega \rangle$ is a representation system iff $f(\mathbf{T})$ can be defined for every relational (rather than multirelational) Ω-expression f and every $\mathbf{T} \in \mathscr{T}$ with $\alpha(\mathbf{T}) = \alpha(f)$, in such a way that $Rep(f(\mathbf{T})) \equiv_\Omega f(Rep(\mathbf{T}))$.*

The easy proof is omitted.

4. *Codd Tables*

In this section we prove that the usual tables with null values @ (see [7]) provide a basis for a representation system with Ω = PS. We also show that these tables can support neither Ω = PSU nor Ω = PJ.

By a *@-tuple* on X we mean any function t that associates a value $t(A) \in D(A) \cup \{@\}$ with every $A \in X$. A *Codd table* on X is any finite set of @-tuples on X, and a *Codd multitable* of type $\langle X_1, \ldots, X_n \rangle$ is any sequence $\mathbf{T} = \langle T_1, \ldots, T_n \rangle$ where T_i is a Codd table on X_i, $1 \le i \le n$. The set of all Codd multitables is denoted by $\mathscr{T}_@$.

Let us define a partial order $\le$ on $D \cup \{@\}$ in such a way that $@ < a$, $a \in D$ are the only nontrivial relationships. For two @-tuples t, t' on X, we write $t \le t'$ if $t(A) \le t'(A)$ for every $A \in X$, that is, if t and t' agree on every $A \in X$ such that $t(A) \ne @$. For any Codd table T on X we define

$$\text{Rep}(T) = \{r \in \mathscr{R}(X) : \text{for every } t \in T \text{ there is } t' \in r \text{ such that } t \le t'\},$$

and for every Codd multitable $\mathbf{T} = \langle T_1, \ldots, T_n \rangle$,

$$\text{Rep}(\mathbf{T}) = \text{Rep}(T_1) \times \cdots \times \text{Rep}(T_n).$$

Intuitively, $\mathbf{r} \in \text{Rep}(\mathbf{T})$ iff **r** contains a multirelation obtained from **T** by replacing all occurrences of @ by some values in appropriate attribute domains (different occurrences may be replaced by different values, but equal values are allowed as well).

Let us now have a closer look at the notion of Ω-equivalence of homogeneous sets of multirelations for some simple cases of Ω.

We first note the following trivial fact:

$$\mathscr{X} \equiv_\varnothing \mathscr{Y} \Leftrightarrow \bigcap \mathscr{X} = \bigcap \mathscr{Y}. \tag{4.1}$$

Let us now consider the case of Ω = P.

THEOREM 4.1. *Any $\mathscr{X} \in \mathscr{I}$ can be P-represented by a Codd multitable.*

PROOF. Let us begin with the simple case where $\alpha(\mathscr{X}) = X$. For any $Y \subseteq X$, let $Q(Y)$ be obtained from $\mathscr{X}^{*Y}$ by extending with @'s every tuple $t \in \mathscr{X}^{*Y}$ to a @-tuple $\bar{t}$ on X (notice that $Q(\varnothing) = \varnothing$ if $\varnothing \in \mathscr{X}$ and $Q(\varnothing)$ consists of a tuple of @, otherwise). Define $T = \bigcup_{Y \subseteq X} Q(Y)$. We shall prove that $\text{Rep}(T) \equiv_P \mathscr{X}$. Indeed, consider an arbitrary $Y \subseteq X$. If $t \in \mathscr{X}^{*Y}$, then clearly T contains a @-tuple t' that agrees with t on Y, and consequently every $r \in \text{Rep}(T)$ contains a tuple u that agrees with t on Y; that is, $t \in \text{Rep}(T)^{*Y}$. Conversely, assume that $t \notin \mathscr{X}^{*Y}$, $\alpha(t) = Y$. Then no @-tuple in T agrees with t on Y, and consequently there exists a relation $r \in \text{Rep}(T)$ not containing any tuple agreeing with t on Y (r may be obtained by replacing every null value in T by a value in the corresponding attribute domain, in such a way that if $A \in Y$ then the value replacing an occurrence of @ in column A of T is different from $t(A)$). Hence $t \notin \text{Rep}(T)^{*Y}$, which concludes the proof that $\text{Rep}(T) \equiv_P \mathscr{X}$.

In the general case, in which $\alpha(\mathscr{X}) = \langle X_1, \ldots, X_n \rangle$, we construct tables T_i such that $\text{Rep}(T_i) \equiv_P \text{pr}_i(\mathscr{X})$, $1 \le i \le n$. It is then easily seen that $\mathbf{T} = \langle T_1, \ldots, T_n \rangle$ P-represents $\mathscr{X}$. □

Let us note the following simple fact concerning the P-equivalence of Codd multitables.

THEOREM 4.2. *Any two P-equivalent Codd multitables are Rep-equivalent.*

In other words, if P ∈ Ω, then $\mathbf{T} \equiv_\Omega \mathbf{U}$ iff $\mathbf{T} \equiv \mathbf{U}$. The easy proof is omitted.

Clearly, two Codd multitables $\langle T_1, \ldots, T_n \rangle$, $\langle U_1, \ldots, U_n \rangle$ of the same type are Rep-equivalent iff $T_i \equiv U_i$, $1 \le i \le n$. The following structural characterization of Rep-equivalence of Codd tables was proved by Biskup [3]:

THEOREM 4.3. *For any Codd tables T, U of the same type $T \equiv U$ iff for every $t \in T$ there is $u \in U$ such that $t \le u$ and for every $u \in U$ there is $t \in T$ such that $u \le t$.*

The S-equivalence is even simpler than the P-equivalence, since it turns out to coincide with the $\varnothing$-equivalence (see (4.1)). Before we prove this, notice that $\sigma_E(r)$ may be expressed as $r \cap \sigma_E(\mathbb{1}_Y)$, where $Y = \alpha(r)$ and $\mathbb{1}_Y = \times_{A \in Y} D(A)$, and this is true for arbitrary conditions E: $\mathbb{1}_Y \rightarrow$ {**true**, **false**}, not only for those generated by atomic conditions of the form $(A = a)$, $(A = B)$.

THEOREM 4.4. *For any* $\mathscr{X}, \mathscr{Y} \in \mathscr{I}$ *of the same type,*

$$\mathscr{X} \equiv_S \mathscr{Y} \Leftrightarrow \mathscr{X} \equiv_\varnothing \mathscr{Y}.$$

PROOF. Let $\mathscr{X}, \mathscr{Y} \in \mathscr{I}$, and let $f(R_1, \ldots, R_n) = \sigma_E(R_i)$ be an arbitrary relational S-expression $(\alpha(\mathscr{X}) = \alpha(\mathscr{Y}) = \alpha(f))$. If $\mathscr{X} \equiv_\varnothing \mathscr{Y}$ then, by (4.1), $\bigcap \mathscr{X} = \bigcap \mathscr{Y}$, which implies $\bigcap \mathrm{pr}_i(\mathscr{X}) = \bigcap \mathrm{pr}_i(\mathscr{Y})$. Hence

$$\mathscr{X}^f = \bigcap_{r \in \mathrm{pr}_i(\mathscr{X})} \sigma_E(r) = \bigcap_{r \in \mathrm{pr}_i(\mathscr{X})} (r \cap \sigma_E(\mathbb{1}_{\alpha(r)})) = \sigma_E(\mathbb{1}_{\alpha(r)}) \cap \bigcap \mathrm{pr}_i(\mathscr{X})$$
$$= \sigma_E(\mathbb{1}_{\alpha(r)}) \cap \bigcap \mathrm{pr}_i(\mathscr{Y}) = \mathscr{Y}^f,$$

which easily implies $\mathscr{X} \equiv_S \mathscr{Y}$. □

Notice that the S-equivalence coincides with the $\varnothing$-equivalence even if we allow arbitrary functions E: $\mathbb{1}_Y \rightarrow$ {**true**, **false**} as selection conditions. Clearly, by Theorem 4.4, $\mathscr{X} \equiv_P \mathscr{Y}$ implies $\mathscr{X} \equiv_S \mathscr{Y}$. However, the PS-equivalence does not coincide with the P-equivalence on $\mathscr{I}$, as shown by the following example.

Example 4.1. Let

$$\mathscr{X} = \{\lceil abc \rceil, \lceil ab'c| \}, \qquad \mathscr{Y} = \{\lceil abc|, \lceil ab'c'| \}.$$

We have $\mathscr{X} \equiv_P \mathscr{Y}$ since both $\mathscr{X}$ and $\mathscr{Y}$ can be P-represented by $T = \boxed{a@@}$. Consequently, also $\mathscr{X} \equiv_S \mathscr{Y}$. But $\mathscr{X} \not\equiv_{PS} \mathscr{Y}$, since for the PS-expression

$$f(R) = \pi_A(\sigma_{(B=b)\vee(C=c)}(R))$$

we have

$$\mathscr{X}^f = \{a\} \neq \varnothing = \mathscr{Y}^f.$$

In other words, $\mathscr{X}$ and $\mathscr{Y}$ are not distinguishable by either P-expressions or S-expressions, but *are* distinguishable by PS-expressions. □

Before we prove that $\langle \mathscr{T}_@, \mathrm{Rep}, \mathrm{PS} \rangle$ is indeed a representation system, let us note the following two simple facts:

LEMMA 4.1. *Every PSUJR-expression* **f** *is monotone; that is,* $\mathbf{r} \subseteq \mathbf{s} \Rightarrow \mathbf{f}(\mathbf{r}) \subseteq \mathbf{f}(\mathbf{s})$.

The easy proof, by induction on the number of operators in **f**, is omitted.

Let $\mathscr{X}, \mathscr{Y} \in \mathscr{I}, \alpha(\mathscr{X}) = \alpha(\mathscr{Y})$. We say that $\mathscr{X}$ and $\mathscr{Y}$ are *coinitial* (in symbols, $\mathscr{X} \approx \mathscr{Y}$) if for any $\mathbf{r} \in \mathscr{X}$ there is $\mathbf{s} \in \mathscr{Y}$ such that $\mathbf{s} \subseteq \mathbf{r}$, and for any $\mathbf{s} \in \mathscr{Y}$ there is $\mathbf{r} \in \mathscr{X}$ such that $\mathbf{r} \subseteq \mathbf{s}$. Obviously, for any monotone **f**

$$\mathscr{X} \approx \mathscr{Y} \Rightarrow \mathbf{f}(\mathscr{X}) \approx \mathbf{f}(\mathscr{Y}). \tag{4.2}$$

LEMMA 4.2. *If* $\mathscr{X}$ *and* $\mathscr{Y}$ *are coinitial, then* $\mathscr{X} \equiv_{PSUJR} \mathscr{Y}$.

PROOF. Let $\mathscr{X} \approx \mathscr{Y}$. Then for every $\mathbf{r} \in \mathscr{X}$ there is a $\varphi(\mathbf{r}) \in \mathscr{Y}$ such that $\varphi(\mathbf{r}) \subseteq \mathbf{r}$. By using the previous lemma, for any PSUJR-expression **f** we have

$$\mathscr{X}^{\mathbf{f}} = \bigcap_{\mathbf{r} \in \mathscr{X}} \mathbf{f}(\mathbf{r}) \supseteq \bigcap_{\mathbf{r} \in \mathscr{X}} \mathbf{f}(\varphi(\mathbf{r})) \supseteq \bigcap_{\mathbf{s} \in \mathscr{Y}} \mathbf{f}(\mathbf{s}) = \mathscr{Y}^{\mathbf{f}},$$

and similarly $\mathscr{Y}^{\mathbf{f}} \supseteq \mathscr{X}^{\mathbf{f}}$. □

We are now ready to prove the main result of this section.

THEOREM 4.5. *It is possible to correctly evaluate PS-expressions over Codd tables; more formally,* $\langle \mathscr{T}_@, Rep, PS \rangle$ *is a representation system.*

PROOF. By Lemma 3.1, it is sufficient to show that for any $\mathbf{T} \in \mathscr{T}_@$ and any relational PS-expression f with $\alpha(f) = \alpha(T)$ it is possible to define $f(\mathbf{T})$ in such a way that $\mathrm{Rep}(f(\mathbf{T})) \equiv_{PS} f(\mathrm{Rep}(\mathbf{T}))$.

We define $f(\mathbf{T})$ inductively, by using the following rules:

$$\text{If } \mathbf{T} = \langle T_1, \ldots, T_n \rangle, \text{ then } \mathrm{pr}_i(\mathbf{T}) = T_i,$$
$$\pi_Y(T) = \{t[Y] : t \in T\},$$
$$\sigma_E(T) = \{t \in T : E_*(t) = \mathbf{true}\},$$

where

$$E_*(t) = \begin{cases} \mathbf{true} & \text{if } E(u) \text{ for every } u \in \mathrm{Compl}(t), \\ \mathbf{false} & \text{otherwise,} \end{cases}$$

and Compl(t) denotes the set of all tuples u (not containing null values) such that $t \leq u$.

By Lemma 4.2, it is now sufficient to prove that

$$\mathrm{Rep}(f(\mathbf{T})) \approx f(\mathrm{Rep}(\mathbf{T})) \tag{4.3}$$

for all f and $\mathbf{T}$. Let us first notice that

$$\text{if } \mathbf{T} = \langle T_1, \ldots, T_n \rangle, \text{ then } \mathrm{Rep}(\mathrm{pr}_i(\mathbf{T})) = \mathrm{pr}_i(\mathrm{Rep}(\mathbf{T})), \tag{4.4}$$

and that for any Codd table T

$$\mathrm{Rep}(\pi_Y(T)) = \pi_Y(\mathrm{Rep}(T)), \tag{4.5}$$
$$\mathrm{Rep}(\sigma_E(T)) \approx \sigma_E(\mathrm{Rep}(T)). \tag{4.6}$$

We show (4.6) ((4.4) and (4.5) are obvious).

Let $r \in \mathrm{Rep}(\sigma_E(T))$. Then r contains a relation $s \in \sigma_E(\mathrm{Rep}(T))$ obtained by replacing nulls in the @-tuples $t \in T$ that belong to $\sigma_E(T)$ in such a way that the resulting tuples are in r, and by replacing nulls in every $t \in T \backslash \sigma_E(T)$ so as to obtain a tuple t^* with $E(t^*) = \mathbf{false}$ (this is possible since for every $t \in T \backslash \sigma_E(T)$, $E_*(t) = \mathbf{false}$).

Conversely, let $s \in \sigma_E(\mathrm{Rep}(T))$. Then s contains a relation $r \in \mathrm{Rep}(\sigma_E(T))$ obtained from T by replacing those @-tuples in T that belong to $\sigma_E(T)$ so as to obtain tuples in s, and by omitting the remaining @-tuples.

The desired formula (4.3) now easily follows by induction on the number of operators in f. We show, as an example, the inductive step in the case in which $f = \sigma_E g$, under the inductive assumption $\mathrm{Rep}(g(\mathbf{T})) \approx g(\mathrm{Rep}(\mathbf{T}))$:

$$\mathrm{Rep}(f(\mathbf{T})) = \mathrm{Rep}(\sigma_E(g(\mathbf{T}))) \approx \sigma_E(\mathrm{Rep}(g(\mathbf{T})))$$
$$\approx \sigma_E(g(\mathrm{Rep}(\mathbf{T}))) = f(\mathrm{Rep}(\mathbf{T}))$$

(we made use of (4.6) and then of (4.2)). □

Note that in Theorem 4.5 selection can be arbitrary, on the basis of an arbitrary function from tuples to {**true**, **false**}. This includes as a special case selection based on arbitrary Boolean combinations generated by atomic conditions of the form $(A \leq a)$, $(A \leq B)$ $(A, B \in \mathscr{U}, a \in D(A)$; we assume that the attribute domains are linearly ordered). These cases are treated in more detail in the next section.

The next two theorems say that, roughly speaking, our representation system based on Codd tables cannot, in addition, handle either union or join.

THEOREM 4.6. *It is not possible to correctly evaluate PSU-expressions over Codd tables; more formally* $\langle \mathcal{T}_{@}, Rep, PSU\rangle$ *is not a representation system.*

PROOF. We now give an example of a PSU-expression **f** and a Codd table T such that $\mathbf{f}(\mathrm{Rep}(T))$ is not PSU-representable by any Codd multitable. Let

$$\mathbf{f}(R) = \langle \sigma_{A=a}(R), \sigma_{A\neq a}(R)\rangle \qquad (\alpha(\mathbf{f}) = AB,\ a \in D(A)),$$

and let $T = \boxed{@b}$. Suppose that $\mathbf{U} = \langle U_1, U_2\rangle$ PSU-represents $\mathbf{f}(\mathrm{Rep}(T))$. Then obviously $\mathbf{U}$ P-represents $\mathbf{f}(\mathrm{Rep}(T))$. But the multitable $\langle \varnothing, \varnothing\rangle$ is easily seen to P-represent $\mathbf{f}(\mathrm{Rep}(T))$ (see the construction in the proof of Theorem 4.1), so that by Theorems 4.2 and 4.3, $\mathbf{U} = \langle \varnothing, \varnothing\rangle$.

Consider the relational expression $g(S_1, S_2) = \pi_B(S_1 \cup S_2)$. We have

$$\mathbf{f}(\mathrm{Rep}(T))^g = \cap\ g\mathbf{f}(\mathrm{Rep}(T)) = \cap\ \pi_B(\mathrm{Rep}(T)) = \{b\} \neq \varnothing = \mathrm{Rep}(\mathbf{U})^g,$$

that is, $\mathbf{U}$ does not PSU-represent $\mathbf{f}(\mathrm{Rep}(T))$, contrary to our assumption. □

It may be noted that if we restrict ourselves to the case in which all relational PSU-expressions considered involve only one relation symbol, then $f(\mathrm{Rep}(T))$ can always be PSU-represented by a Codd table U (see [13]). This is a simple consequence of the fact that any PSU-expression f involving only one relation symbol can be transformed into an equivalent PS-expression of the form $\pi_Y(\sigma_E(R))$. The easy proof of this fact, by induction on the number of operators in f, is omitted.

THEOREM 4.7. *It is not possible to correctly evaluate PJ-expressions over Codd tables; more formally,* $\langle \mathcal{T}_{@}, Rep, PJ\rangle$ *is not a representation system.*

PROOF. We give an example of a Codd table T and a PJ-expression f such that $f(\mathrm{Rep}(T))$ is not PJ-representable by any Codd table. Let

$$T = \{a@c,\ a'@c'\} \qquad (a \neq a',\ c \neq c')$$
$$f(R) = \pi_{AC}(R) \bowtie \pi_B(R).$$

It is easy to see that $f(\mathrm{Rep}(T)) \equiv_{\mathrm{P}} \mathrm{Rep}(T)$. By Theorem 4.2, if there is a Codd table U PJ-representing $f(\mathrm{Rep}(T))$, then $T \equiv U$, and consequently $f(\mathrm{Rep}(T)) \equiv_{\mathrm{PJ}} \mathrm{Rep}(T)$.

This last equivalence is, however, not true. Indeed, let

$$g(R) = \pi_{AC}(\pi_{AB}(R) \bowtie \pi_{BC}(R)).$$

We have

$$\mathrm{Rep}(T)^g = \begin{array}{|cc|} a & c \\ a' & c' \end{array}\,,$$

while

$$f(\mathrm{Rep}(T))^g = \begin{array}{|cc|} a & c \\ a' & c' \\ a & c' \\ a' & c \end{array}\,. \qquad \square$$

A representation system with $\Omega \supseteq \mathrm{PJ}$ is considered in Section 6.

Now we compare our approach to that of Biskup [3]. Roughly speaking, Biskup defines the union of two Codd tables to be the usual set-theoretical union, so that

$$\mathrm{Rep}(T \cup U) = \{r \cup s : r \in \mathrm{Rep}(T) \wedge s \in \mathrm{Rep}(U)\},$$

and he defines the join of two Codd tables in such a way that

$$\mathrm{Rep}(T \bowtie U) \equiv_{\mathrm{P}} \{r \bowtie s : r \in \mathrm{Rep}(T) \wedge s \in \mathrm{Rep}(U)\}. \tag{4.7}$$

His definition of join is based on the following informal matching rule:

$$@ \neq @, \qquad @ \neq a.$$

(In fact, it may be shown that the sets on both sides of (4.7) are coinitial so that they are PSUJ-equivalent.)

These definitions of union and join are semantically correct only if we assume that both arguments are independent; that is, every substitution of values in appropriate attribute domains for the null values in T and U is meaningful. This is clearly not the case when we want to correctly evaluate relational expressions such as

$$f(R) = \sigma_{A=a}(R) \cup \sigma_{A\neq a}(R),$$
$$g(R) = \pi_{AB}(R) \bowtie \pi_{AC}(R),$$

over a Codd table. Consequently, Biskup's approach does not generalize to arbitrary relational expressions, though in a sense, it does give correct results for single relational operators. On the other hand, Biskup's approach is more general in that it allows "universal" null values in addition to the usual "existential" null values @.

5. *Evaluating a Selection over a Codd Table*

Recall that the selection of a Codd table is defined by

$$\sigma_E(T) = \{t \in T : E_*(t) = \mathbf{true}\},$$

where $E_*(t) = \mathbf{true}$ iff $E(t') = \mathbf{true}$ for every $t' \in \mathrm{Compl}(t)$. Of course, we should have a more efficient method of computing $E_*(t)$ than that involving the computation of $E(t')$ for every $t' \in \mathrm{Compl}(t)$. ($\mathrm{Compl}(t)$ may be infinite if attribute domains are infinite.)

In this section we always assume that the selection condition E is of the form of an arbitrary Boolean combination (using $\neg$, $\vee$, $\wedge$) of certain atomic conditions. The case in which these conditions are of the form (A IN F), $F \subseteq D(A)$ and in which subset entries of the form G, $G \subseteq D(A)$, meaning "an unknown value in G," are allowed in the table, instead of just @, "an unknown value in $D(A)$," was extensively studied in [19], [20], and [21].

Here we sketch a method of computing $E_*(t)$ in the case in which the atomic conditions are of the form $(A = a)$, $(A = B)$, $(A \leq a)$, $(A \leq B)$ $(A, B \in \mathcal{U}, a \in D(A)$; in the third and fourth cases we assume a linear order on the corresponding attribute domains). The conditions $(A = a)$, $(A \leq a)$ are called *unary*, whereas $(A = B)$, $(A \leq B)$ are called *binary*. For simplicity, throughout this section we assume that every attribute domain is the same set D.

Note that we may "precompute" $E_*(t)$ by substituting in E the value $t(A)$ for every occurrence of A, for every A such that $t(A) \neq @$. This has the effect that some of the binary conditions become unary, and some conditions are reduced to $(a = b)$ or $(a \leq b)$, which can be replaced by **true** or **false** and then eliminated by using the absorption-type Boolean axioms. Let E' be the resulting condition. Clearly, the whole process can be carried out in time linear in the length of E. In this way our problem is reduced to evaluating $E'_*(t')$ where t' is a tuple of null values. This is obviously equivalent to testing whether E' is a tautology.

Let us begin with the case involving only conditions of the form $(A = a)$, $(A = B)$. We transform E' into a conjunctive normal form $\bigwedge_i \bigvee_j E_{ij}^{\epsilon_{ij}}$, where E_{ij} is an atomic condition, and $E_{ij}^{\epsilon_{ij}}$ denotes E_{ij} or $\neg E_{ij}$, depending on whether ϵ_{ij} is 1 or 0, respectively; we may also assume that no disjunct of this normal form contains both an equality and the negation to this equality. E' is a tautology iff for every i, $\bigvee_j E_{ij}^{\epsilon_{ij}}$ is a tautology. A disjunction of the form $\bigvee_j E_j^{\epsilon_j}$ is a tautology iff $\bigwedge_j E_j^{1-\epsilon_j}$ is not satisfiable. The satisfiability of this last conjunction can be tested in the following way. We construct a (nondirected) graph with vertices corresponding to attributes and constants occurring in $\bigwedge_j E_j^{1-\epsilon_j}$ (different occurrences of the same constant or attribute correspond to the same vertex), two vertices x, y joined by an edge iff the (nonnegated) condition $(x = y)$ appears in our conjunction.

It is clear that the conjunction is satisfiable iff every connected component of our graph contains at most one vertex corresponding to a constant. Obviously, finding the connected components can be done in time linear with respect to the number of vertices and edges of our graph, that is, $O(n)$, where n is the length of our conjunction (see, e.g., [11]). (Identifying *different* occurrences of attributes and constants may require $\Omega(n \log n)$ time.) The most complex part of this algorithm is, however, the transformation into a conjunctive normal form, since in the worst case it may involve an exponential growth of the length of our expression. We should not expect a substantially more efficient algorithm to evaluate $E_*(t)$, since it obviously contains as a special case the problem of deciding whether a Boolean expression is a tautology, a problem that is known to be NP-hard (see, e.g., [9]).

We now consider the case in which all four types of atomic conditions are allowed. Since

$$(x = y) \Leftrightarrow (x \le y) \wedge (y \le x), \tag{5.1}$$

our problem is reduced, in a similar way as before, to testing for the satisfiability of a conjunction $\bigwedge_j E_j$, where each E_j is either of the form $(x \le y)$ or $(x < y)$. (It may be noted, however, that using (5.1) to eliminate equality may be not the most efficient approach.) Let us construct a directed graph with vertices corresponding to different attributes occurring in $\bigwedge_j E_j$, with an $<$-edge or $\le$-edge $\langle x, y\rangle$ from x to y iff $(x < y)$ or $(x \le y)$, respectively, occurs in our conjunction. We associate with every vertex x an interval $I(x)$ with the beginning

$$b(x) = \max\{y \in D : (y < x) \text{ or } (y \le x) \text{ appears in } \textstyle\bigwedge_j E_j\}$$

and end

$$e(x) = \min\{y \in D : (x < y) \text{ or } (x \le y) \text{ appears in } \textstyle\bigwedge_j E_j\}$$

($b(x)$ is included into $I(x)$ iff $(b(x) < x)$ appears in the conjunction; similarly for $e(x)$).

We find strongly connected components of the graph consisting of $\le$-edges (see, e.g., [25]; x and y are in the same strongly connected component iff there is a path from x to y and a path from y to x).

For every strongly connected component, we identify all vertices of the component and replace them with a single vertex x_C with $I(x_C) = \bigcap_{y \in C} I(y)$, where C is the set of vertices of the component. (In the resulting graph, there is an edge from $x_{C'}$ to $x_{C''}$, $C' \neq C''$, iff there was an edge from some $x' \in C'$ to some $x'' \in C''$ in the original graph.) The graph obtained is always acyclic and we test for the satisfiability of our conjunction in the following way. We try to assign a value $v(x) \in I(x)$ to every vertex x in such a way that $v(x) < v(y)(v(x) \le v(y))$ if there is a $<$-edge ($\le$-edge, respectively) $\langle x, y\rangle$. Let us assume, for simplicity, that our graph contains only $\le$-edges, and that every $I(x)$ contains both $b(x)$ and $e(x)$ (the general case can be treated in a similar way). We set initially $v(x) = b(x)$ for any x, and we perform a breadth-first search (see, e.g., [11]) starting from the set of sources (i.e., vertices with no incoming edges). For any edge $\langle x, y\rangle$ processed by the search we set $v(y) := \max(v(y), v(x))$. If at any stage of the process this results in $v(y) > e(y)$, then clearly our conjunction is not satisfiable. Otherwise, the process determines an assignment of values to attributes that makes our conjunction true. We leave the details to the reader.

Example 5.1. Let our conjunction be

$$(A_1 \le 50) \wedge (A_4 \ge 100) \wedge (A_3 \le 200) \wedge (A_1 \le A_5)$$
$$\wedge (A_5 \le A_2) \wedge (A_5 \le A_4) \wedge (A_4 \le A_3) \wedge (A_3 \le A_5)$$

(the domain of each attribute is the set of integers).

Our graph has the form

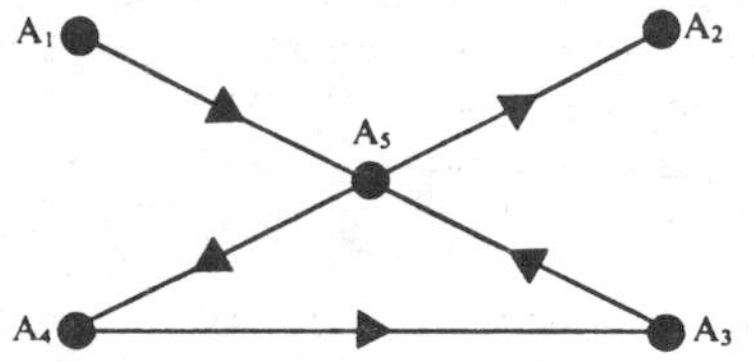

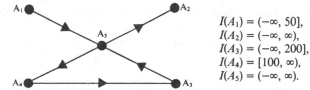

$$I(A_1) = (-\infty, 50],$$
$$I(A_2) = (-\infty, \infty),$$
$$I(A_3) = (-\infty, 200],$$
$$I(A_4) = [100, \infty),$$
$$I(A_5) = (-\infty, \infty).$$

The strongly connected components have vertex sets $\{A_1\}$, $\{A_2\}$, $\{A_3, A_4, A_5\}$, and our graph is transformed into

$$I(A_{345}) = [100, 200].$$

The breadth-first search produces $v(A_1) = -\infty$, $v(A_{345}) = 100$, $v(A_2) = 100$, which means that our conjunction is satisfiable. □

6. *V-Tables*

One of the reasons for the inability of Codd tables to correctly support the join operation appears to be the fact that we are not able to represent the information that two different occurrences of @ represent the same value. In this section we consider tables where, for any $A \in \mathcal{U}$, we have an infinite set of possible "null values." The interpretation of such a table is that the values represented by two occurrences of the same null value, though unknown, are the same. Such tables will turn out to be suitable for a representation system with $\Omega = \mathrm{PS^+UJ}$.

Formally, for every $A \in \mathcal{U}$, let $V(A)$ be a countably infinite set of symbols called *variables*. We assume that $V(A) \cap D = \varnothing$, $V(A) \cap V(B) = \varnothing$ if $D(A) \neq D(B)$, and $V(A) = V(B)$ if $D(A) = D(B)$. By a *V-tuple* on X, we mean any mapping t that associates an element $t(A) \in D(A) \cup V(A)$ with every $A \in X$. A *V-table* on X is any finite set of V-tuples on X, and a *V-multitable* of type $\langle X_1, \ldots, X_n\rangle$ is any sequence $\mathbf{T} = \langle T_1, \ldots, T_n\rangle$ where T_i is a V-table on X_i, $1 \le i \le n$ (notice that the same variable may occur in several T_i's). The set of all V-multitables is denoted by $\mathcal{T}_V$.

Let $V = \bigcup_{A \in \mathcal{U}} V(A)$. By a *valuation*, we mean any mapping v: $V \to D$ such that $x \in V(A)$ implies $v(x) \in D(A)$. Any valuation can be extended to the set of constants by putting $v(c) = c$ for every $c \in D$; to V-tuples, by defining, for any V-tuple t on

$v(t)$ to be the tuple on X satisfying

$$(v(t))(A) = v(t(A)) \qquad \text{for every} \quad A \in X; \tag{6.1}$$

to V-tables,

$$v(T) = \{v(t) : t \in T\}; \tag{6.2}$$

and finally to V-multitables $\mathbf{T} = \langle T_1, \ldots, T_n \rangle$,

$$v(\mathbf{T}) = \langle v(T_1), \ldots, v(T_n) \rangle. \tag{6.3}$$

The intuition given at the beginning of this section can now be formalized by defining, for any V-multitable, $\mathbf{T} = \langle T_1, \ldots, T_n \rangle$ of type $\langle X_1, \ldots, X_n \rangle$:

$$\text{Rep}(\mathbf{T}) = \{\mathbf{r} \in \mathscr{R}(X_1, \ldots, X_n) : \text{there exists a valuation } \mathbf{v} \text{ such that } v(\mathbf{T}) \subseteq \mathbf{r}\}. \tag{6.4}$$

Note that in view of this definition, any Codd multitable can informally be identified with a V-multitable obtained by replacing any occurrence of @ by a different variable.

Let us associate with a V-multitable $\mathbf{T} = \langle T_1, \ldots, T_n \rangle$ a first-order formula $\phi(\mathbf{T})$ (of a many-sorted predicate calculus) defined as

$$\exists x_1 \cdots \exists x_m \bigwedge_t \phi(t)$$

where t ranges over all V-tuples appearing in $\mathbf{T}$ and, for $t \in T_i$, $\phi(t)$ is $R_i(t)$, where R_i is a predicate symbol of a suitable type and $x_1, \ldots, x_m$ are all variables occurring in $\mathbf{T}$. It is easy to see that Rep($\mathbf{T}$) is simply the set of all finite models of $\phi(\mathbf{T})$ (over a fixed universe given by $D(A)$, $A \in \mathscr{U}$).

In this section we always assume that all attribute domains are infinite.

The following is the main result of this paper.

THEOREM 6.1. *It is possible to correctly evaluate PS⁺UJ-expressions over V-tables; more formally* $\langle \mathscr{T}_V, Rep, PS^+UJ \rangle$ *is a representation system.*

This theorem is proved in the next section, in which we develop a suitable formal notion: that of a *conditional table* (see also another proof in [23]). Here we only give the relevant definitions of the relational operators over V-tables.

For any V-multitable $\mathbf{T} = \langle T_1, \ldots, T_n \rangle$ we put

$$\text{pr}_i(\mathbf{T}) = T_i, \qquad 1 \le i \le n. \tag{6.5}$$

The definition of projection is the "natural one,"

$$\pi_Y(T) = \{t[Y] : t \in T\}, \tag{6.6}$$

and so is the definition of join of two V-tables T, W on X, Z, respectively:

$$T \bowtie W = \{t : \alpha(t) = X \cup Z \wedge t[X] \in T \wedge t[Z] \in W\}. \tag{6.7}$$

The union operator acts on V-tables as the usual set-theoretical union.

Finally,

$$\sigma_E(T) = \{t \in T : E_*(t) = \mathbf{true}\} \tag{6.8}$$

where

$$E_*(t) = \begin{cases} \mathbf{true} & \text{if } E(v(t)) = \mathbf{true} \text{ for every valuation } v, \\ \mathbf{false} & \text{otherwise.} \end{cases}$$

Note that, if E is positive, then $E_*(t)$ can be computed in a very simple way by using the following rule: We evaluate every atomic condition $(A = B)$ in E to **true** if $t(A) = t(B)$ and to **false** otherwise; we evaluate every atomic condition $(A = a)$ to **true** if $t(A) = a$ and to **false** otherwise; and then we use $\vee$, $\wedge$ in the natural way. In other words,

$$(A = B)_*(t) = \begin{cases} \mathbf{true} & \text{if } t(A) = t(B), \\ \mathbf{false} & \text{otherwise,} \end{cases}$$
$$(A = a)_*(t) = \begin{cases} \mathbf{true} & \text{if } t(A) = a, \\ \mathbf{false} & \text{otherwise,} \end{cases}$$
$$(E \vee E')(t) = E_*(t) \vee E'_*(t),$$
$$(E \wedge E')(t) = E_*(t) \wedge E'_*(t).$$

The correctness of this rule follows easily from the fact that, if there is a valuation v such that $E(v(t)) = \mathbf{false}$, then $E(v'(t)) = \mathbf{false}$ for any valuation v' such that $v'(x) \neq v'(y)$ for $x \neq y$ and $v'(x)$ does not appear in E for any $x \in V$. Note that this rule does *not* evaluate $E_*(t)$ correctly if E contains negation, or if attribute domains are finite.

The above rules, together with the obvious rule

$$\mathbf{f}(\mathbf{T}) = \langle f_1(\mathbf{T}), \ldots, f_k(\mathbf{T}) \rangle \tag{6.9}$$

for any $\mathbf{f} = \langle f_1, \ldots, f_k \rangle$, define inductively $\mathbf{f}(\mathbf{T})$ for any multirelational PS⁺UJ-expression $\mathbf{f}$ and any V-multitable $\mathbf{T}$ ($\alpha(\mathbf{T}) = \alpha(\mathbf{f})$).

To sum up, we evaluate PS⁺UJ-expressions over V-tables in *exactly the same way* as if the variables were values in the attribute domains. Let us emphasize that the fact that this simple method of evaluating PS⁺UJ-expressions gives correct results is not quite trivial (see the proof in the next section).

Example 6.1. Let us evaluate

$$f(T) = \pi_{AC}(\pi_{AB}(T) \bowtie \sigma_{(B=C)\vee(C=c)}(\pi_{BC}(T))),$$

where T is the following V-table:

A	B	C
x	y	c
a	b	c
a'	b'	c'
a	y	z
x	d	d

We get

$$\pi_{AB}(T) = \{xy, ab, a'b', xy, xd\},$$
$$\pi_{BC}(T) = \{yc, bc, b'c', yz, dd\},$$
$$\sigma_{(B=C)\vee(C=c)}(\pi_{BC}(T)) = \{yc, bc, dd\},$$
$$\pi_{AB}(T) \bowtie \sigma_{(B=C)\vee(C=c)}(\pi_{BC}(T)) = \{xyc, abc, xdd\},$$
$$f(T) = \{xc, ac, xd\}. \qquad \square$$

Rather suprisingly, it turns out that V-multitables, which are "more powerful" than Codd multitables, cannot support a representation system with Ω = PS.

THEOREM 6.2. *It is not possible to correctly evaluate PS-expressions over V-tables; more formally,* $\langle \mathscr{T}_V, Rep, PS \rangle$ *is not a representation system.*

PROOF. Let T be the following V-table:

A	B	C
a	y	c
a'	y	c

and let f be the following PS-expression—in fact, an S-expression:

$$f(R) = \sigma_{(A=a)\wedge(B=b)\vee(A=a')\wedge(B\neq b)}(R) \qquad (a \neq a').$$

We claim that there is no V-table U PS-representing $f(\mathrm{Rep}(T))$. Indeed, let

$$g(R) = \pi_C(\sigma_{(A=a)\vee(A=a')}(R)).$$

Notice that $f(\mathrm{Rep}(T))$ is coinitial with

$$\mathscr{X} = \{\boxed{abc}\} \cup \{\boxed{a'dc} : d \in D(B)\setminus\{b\}\},$$

so that $f(\mathrm{Rep}(T))^g = \mathscr{X}^g = \{c\}$.

If there is a V-tuple $pqv \in U$, where $p \in D(A)$, then $p \in \mathrm{Rep}(U)^{\pi_A} \neq \mathscr{X}^{\pi_A} = \varnothing$. If for every $pqr \in U$, p is a variable (in particular, if $U = \varnothing$), then clearly $\mathrm{Rep}(U)^g = \varnothing$, although we have already noted that $f(\mathrm{Rep}(T))^g = \{c\}$. Hence, in both cases, U does not PS-represent $f(\mathrm{Rep}(T))$. □

The apparent contradiction in the inability of V-multitables to support PS-expressions can be intuitively explained in the following way: $\langle \mathscr{T}, \mathrm{Rep}, \Omega\rangle$ is a representation system if the class $\mathscr{T}$ of multitables is a "fixpoint" with respect to Ω-expressions, in the sense that if we take any Ω-expression $\mathbf{f}$ and any $\mathbf{T} \in \mathscr{T}$, then to Ω-represent $\mathbf{f}(\mathrm{Rep}(\mathbf{T}))$ we do not need any more "representation power" than that available in $\mathscr{T}$. If we consider an arbitrary $\mathscr{T}' \supseteq \mathscr{T}$, there is no reason for $\mathscr{T}'$ to be also such a fixpoint.

7. *Conditional Tables*

By a conditional table we mean a V-table extended by one additional special column, called *con*, which contains for any tuple a *condition* from a set $\mathscr{L}$.

More precisely, $\mathscr{L}$ is the set of all expressions built up from atomic conditions of the form $(x = a)$, $(x = y)$, **false** and **true**, where for some $A \in \mathscr{U}$, $a \in D(A)$, $x, y \in V(A)$, by means of $\neg$, $\vee$, and $\wedge$. A condition is *positive*, if it does not contain $\neg$.

By a C-tuple on X we mean any mapping t defined on $X \cup \{\mathrm{con}\}$ such that $t[X]$ is a V-tuple and $t(\mathrm{con}) \in \mathscr{L}$. A *conditional table* (or *C-table*) on X is any finite set T of C-tuples on X. (Note: We assume that con is not part of $\alpha(t)$ or $\alpha(T)$.) A *conditional multitable* (or *C-multitable*) of type $\langle X_1, \ldots, X_n\rangle$ is any sequence $\mathbf{T} = \langle T_1, \ldots, T_n\rangle$ where T_i is a C-table on X_i, $1 \le i \le n$. The set of all C-multitables is denoted by $\mathscr{T}_C$.

Any valuation can be extended in the natural way to conditions.

For any valuation v, any C-table T on X, and any C-multitable $\mathbf{T} = \langle T_1, \ldots, T_n\rangle$ of type $\langle X_1, \ldots, X_n\rangle$, we define

$$v(T) = \{v(t[X]) : v(t(\mathrm{con})) = \mathbf{true}\}, \tag{7.1}$$
$$v(\mathbf{T}) = \langle v(T_1), \ldots, v(T_n)\rangle, \tag{7.2}$$

and finally

$$\mathrm{Rep}(\mathbf{T}) = \{\mathbf{r} \in \mathscr{R}(X_1, \ldots, X_n) : \text{there exists a valuation } v \text{ such that } v(\mathbf{T}) \subseteq \mathbf{r}\}. \tag{7.3}$$

We say that conditions $\gamma, \delta \in \mathscr{L}$ are *equivalent*, and we write $\gamma \approx \delta$, if $v(\gamma) = v(\delta)$ for any valuation v. It can easily be shown that $\gamma \approx \delta$ iff γ can be transformed into δ by using the axioms of Boolean algebra and the axioms of equality. It should be clear that if we (a) replace each of the conditions in a C-table T by an equivalent one, (b) delete all $t \in T$ with $t(\mathrm{con}) \approx$ **false**, and (c) replace some $t_1, \ldots, t_k \in T$ such that $t_1[X] = \cdots = t_k[X]$ $(X = \alpha(T))$ by a single C-tuple t such that $t[X] = t_1[X]$ and $t(\mathrm{con}) = \mathbf{W}_{i=1}^{k} t_i(\mathrm{con})$, then the resulting C-table U will be Rep-equivalent to T (i.e., $\mathrm{Rep}(T) = \mathrm{Rep}(U)$, see Section 3). We freely make use of the equivalent transformations of this kind; in particular, we use rule (c) to *normalize* a C-table T on X, that is, to replace T by a Rep-equivalent C-table T^0 on X not containing different C-tuples agreeing on X. In what follows we assume all C-tables to be normalized.

THEOREM 7.1. *It is possible to correctly evaluate PSUJ-expressions over C-tables; more formally, $\langle \mathscr{T}_C$, Rep, PSUJ$\rangle$ is a representation system.*

PROOF. We give definitions of the relational operators over C-tables that inductively define $\mathbf{f}(\mathbf{T})$ for any C-multitable $\mathbf{T}$ and PSUJ-expression $\mathbf{f}(\alpha(\mathbf{T}) = \alpha(\mathbf{f}))$, in such a way that

$$\mathbf{f}(\mathrm{Rep}(\mathbf{T})) \equiv_{\mathrm{PSUJ}} \mathrm{Rep}(\mathbf{f}(\mathbf{T})). \tag{7.4}$$

For any C-multitable $\mathbf{T} = \langle T_1, \ldots, T_n\rangle$ we put

$$\mathrm{pr}_i(\mathbf{T}) = T_i, \qquad 1 \le i \le n, \tag{7.5}$$

and for any C-tables T, W on X, Z, respectively, we define

$$\pi_Y(T) = \{t[Y \cup \{\mathrm{con}\}] : t \in T\}^0, \tag{7.6}$$
$$\sigma_E(T) = \{\sigma_E(t) : t \in T\}, \tag{7.7}$$

where $\sigma_E(t)$ is the C-tuple on X with

$$\sigma_E(t)[X] = t[X],$$
$$\sigma_E(t)(\mathrm{con}) = t(\mathrm{con}) \wedge E(t).$$

($E(t)$ is the result of substituting $t(A)$ for A in E, for every $A \in X$), and

$$T \bowtie W = \{t \bowtie w : t \in T \wedge w \in W\}^0, \tag{7.8}$$

where $t \bowtie w$ is the C-tuple on $X \cup Z$ with

$$(t \bowtie w)(A) = \begin{cases} t(A) & \text{if } A \in X, \\ w(A) & \text{if } A \in Z\setminus X, \end{cases}$$
$$(t \bowtie w)(\mathrm{con}) = t(\mathrm{con}) \wedge w(\mathrm{con}) \wedge \bigwedge_{A\in X\cap Z} (t(A) = w(A)).$$

If $X = Z$, then

$$T \cup W = (T \cup W)^0, \tag{7.9}$$

where $\cup$ on the left-hand side denotes the relational union operator that we define on C-tables, and $\cup$ on the right-hand side is the usual set-theoretical union.

Finally, if $\mathbf{f} = \langle f_1, \ldots, f_k\rangle$, then

$$\mathbf{f}(\mathbf{T}) = \langle f_1(\mathbf{T}), \ldots, f_k(\mathbf{T})\rangle. \tag{7.10}$$

We now prove that under the definition of $\mathbf{f}(\mathbf{T})$ given by (7.5)–(7.10),

$$v(\mathbf{f}(\mathbf{T})) = \mathbf{f}(v(\mathbf{T})) \tag{7.11}$$

for any valuation v. (On the right-hand side, $\mathbf{f}(v(\mathbf{T}))$ is understood as the result of performing $\mathbf{f}$ over the multirelation $v(\mathbf{T})$ in the usual way.) Clearly, (7.11) implies $\mathrm{Rep}(\mathbf{f}(\mathbf{T})) \approx \mathbf{f}(\mathrm{Rep}(\mathbf{T}))$, which by Lemma 4.2, proves (7.4).

We show (7.11) by verifying that

$$\begin{aligned} v(\mathrm{pr}_i(\mathbf{T})) &= \mathrm{pr}_i(v(\mathbf{T})), \\ v(\pi_Y(T)) &= \pi_Y(v(T)), \\ v(T \bowtie W) &= v(T) \bowtie v(W), \\ v(T \cup W) &= v(T) \cup v(W) \qquad (\alpha(T) = \alpha(W)), \end{aligned}$$

for any C-multitable $\mathbf{T}$ and any C-tables T, W.

Let $\alpha(T) = X$, $\alpha(W) = Z$. In the case of projection, $t \in v(\pi_Y(T))$ iff there is a C-tuple $t' \in \pi_Y(T)$ such that $v(t'[Y]) = t$, $v(t'(\mathrm{con})) = \mathbf{true}$; that is, iff there exists a C-tuple $t'' \in T$ such that $\pi_Y(v(t''[X])) = t$, $v(t''(\mathrm{con})) = \mathbf{true}$, which is exactly the condition for t to be in $\pi_Y(v(T))$.

In the case of selection, $t \in v(\sigma_E(T))$ iff there is a $t' \in T$ such that $v(t'(\mathrm{con})) = \mathbf{true}$, $v(E(t')) = \mathbf{true}$, and $t = v(t'[X])$, that is, iff $t \in \sigma_E(v(T))$.

In the case of join, a tuple t of type $X \cup Z$ is in $v(T \bowtie W)$ iff there are tuples $t' \in T$, $w' \in W$ such that $v((t' \bowtie w')(\mathrm{con})) = \mathbf{true}$, $v((t' \bowtie w'([X \cup Z]) = t$, and this is clearly equivalent to $t \in v(T) \bowtie v(W)$.

The case of union is obvious. □

Example 7.1. Let us evaluate

$$f(R) = \sigma_{C=c}(\pi_{AC}(\pi_{AB}(R) \bowtie \pi_{BC}(R)))$$

over the following C-table·

$T =$

A	B	C	con
a	b	z	$z \neq c$
a	y	c	$y \neq b$
x	b	c	$x \neq a$

We have

$U = \pi_{AB}(T) \bowtie \pi_{BC}(T) =$

A	B	C	con
a	b	z	$(z \neq c) \wedge (z \neq c) \wedge (b = b)$
a	b	c	$(z \neq c) \wedge (y \neq b) \wedge (b = y)$
a	b	c	$(z \neq c) \wedge (x \neq a) \wedge (b = b)$
a	y	z	$(y \neq b) \wedge (z \neq c) \wedge (y = b)$
a	y	c	$(y \neq b) \wedge (y \neq b) \wedge (y = y)$
a	y	c	$(y \neq b) \wedge (x \neq a) \wedge (y = b)$
x	b	z	$(x \neq a) \wedge (z \neq c) \wedge (b = b)$
x	b	c	$(x \neq a) \wedge (y \neq b) \wedge (b = y)$
x	b	c	$(x \neq a) \wedge (x \neq a) \wedge (b = b)$

$\equiv$

A	B	C	con
a	b	z	$(z \neq c)$
a	b	c	$(z \neq c) \wedge (y \neq b)$
a	y	c	$(y \neq b)$
x	b	z	$(x \neq a) \wedge (z \neq c)$
x	b	c	$(x \neq a)$

$W = \pi_{AC}(U) =$

A	C	con
a	z	$(z \neq c)$
a	c	$(y \neq b)$
x	z	$(x \neq a) \wedge (z \neq c)$
x	c	$(x \neq a)$

and finally

$\sigma_{C=c}(W) =$

A	C	con
a	z	$(z \neq c) \wedge (z = c)$
a	c	$(y \neq b) \wedge (c = c)$
x	z	$(x \neq a) \wedge (z \neq c) \wedge (z = c)$
x	c	$(x \neq a) \wedge (c = c)$

$\equiv$

A	C	con
a	c	$(y \neq b)$
x	c	$(x \neq a)$

□

Let T be a C-table on X. As usual we assume that no two different tuples in T agree on X. We define the *unconditional part* of T to be

$$T_* = \{t \in T : t(\mathrm{con}) \approx \mathbf{true}\}.$$

The unconditional part of a C-multitable $\mathbf{T} = \langle T_1, \ldots, T_n \rangle$ is defined as $\mathbf{T}_* = \langle T_{1*}, \ldots, T_{n*} \rangle$.

A C-multitable $\mathbf{T} = \langle T_1, \ldots, T_n \rangle$ is called *positive* if for every T_i and every $t \in T_i$, $t(\mathrm{con})$ is positive.

Lemma 7.1. *Let all attribute domains be infinite, and let* $\mathbf{T}$ *be a positive* C-*multitable. Then*

$$\bigcap \mathit{Rep}(\mathbf{T}) = \bigcap \mathit{Rep}(\mathbf{T}_*).$$

Proof. Obviously, we may restrict ourselves to the case where $\mathbf{T}$ is a single C-table, T.

Clearly $\mathrm{Rep}(T) \subseteq \mathrm{Rep}(T_*)$, and consequently $\bigcap \mathrm{Rep}(T_*) \subseteq \bigcap \mathrm{Rep}(T)$, so that it is sufficient to prove the converse inclusion.

Suppose $t \notin \bigcap \mathrm{Rep}(T_*)$. It means that there is a valuation v such that $t \notin v(T_*)$. Let v' be a valuation such that $v'(x) = v'(y)$ for $x \neq y$ and for every variable x appearing in T, $v'(x)$ does not appear in T or t (the existence of such a valuation v' is an obvious consequence of the assumption that the attribute domains are infinite). Clearly, v' makes all atomic conditions (which are positive, by our assumption) false, and consequently it makes false all conditions $t(\mathrm{con})$, $t \in T \setminus T_*$. Since $t \notin v(T_*)$, it follows that T_* does not contain any tuple agreeing with t on $\alpha(t)$. The valuation v' associates constants different from those appearing in t to variables in T, so that it cannot produce t; that is, $t \notin v'(T)$. Consequently, $t \notin \bigcap \mathrm{Rep}(T)$. □

We are now going to prove, as we promised in the previous section, that $\langle \mathcal{T}_V, \mathrm{Rep}, \mathrm{PS^+UJ} \rangle$ is a representation system.

A C-multitable $\mathbf{T}$ is called *unconditional* if $\mathbf{T}_* = \mathbf{T}$. Let $\mathbf{T} = \langle T_1, \ldots, T_n \rangle$ be an unconditional C-multitable and let $\mathbf{U}$ be the V-multitable obtained from $\mathbf{T}$ by deleting the con column from every T_i, $1 \le i \le n$. Then

$$\mathbf{Rep}(\mathbf{T}) = \mathbf{Rep}(\mathbf{U}),$$

where Rep(T) is computed according to (7.1)–(7.3) and Rep(U) according to (6.1)–(6.4). In what follows we always identify an unconditional C-multitable with the corresponding V-multitable. To avoid confusion, we write $\mathbf{f}^C(\mathbf{T})$ and $\mathbf{f}^V(\mathbf{T})$ for an expression f evaluated for an unconditional C-multitable T (identified with a V-multitable) according to the rules given for C-tables (see (7.5)–(7.10)) and V-tables (see (6.5)–(6.9)), respectively.

LEMMA 7.2. *Let all attribute domains be infinite, let* T *be a positive C-multitable and let* f *be a PS⁺UJ-expression with* $\alpha(\mathbf{f}) = \alpha(\mathbf{T})$. *Then*

$$\mathbf{f}^V(\mathbf{T}_*) = \mathbf{f}^C(\mathbf{T})_*.$$

PROOF. It is sufficient to prove that for any positive C-multitable $\mathbf{T} = \langle T_1, \ldots, T_n \rangle$

$$\mathrm{pr}_i^V(\mathbf{T}_*) = \mathrm{pr}_i^C(\mathbf{T})_*, \qquad 1 \le i \le n \tag{7.12}$$

and that for any positive C-tables T, W

$$\pi_Y^V(T_*) = \pi_Y^C(T)_*, \tag{7.13}$$
$$\sigma_E^V(T_*) = \sigma_E^C(T)_* \qquad \text{for } E \text{ positive}, \tag{7.14}$$
$$T_* \bowtie^V W_* = (T \bowtie^C W)_*, \tag{7.15}$$
$$T_* \cup^V W_* = (T \cup^C W)_*, \tag{7.16}$$

($X = \alpha(T)$, $Z = \alpha(W)$).

Before we verify these equalities, let us note the following simple fact concerning positive conditions:

For any positive conditions γ, δ

$$\gamma \vee \delta \approx \mathbf{true} \Rightarrow \gamma \approx \mathbf{true} \quad \text{or} \quad \delta \approx \mathbf{true}. \tag{7.17}$$

Indeed, it is easy to see that, if $\gamma \not\approx \mathbf{true}$ and $\delta \not\approx \mathbf{true}$, then $v(\gamma \vee \delta) = \mathbf{false}$, where v is any valuation such that $v(x) \ne v(y)$ for $x \ne y$ and $v(x)$ does not appear in $\gamma \vee \delta$ for any $x \in V$.

Since (7.12) is obvious, we now consider the case of projection. A V-tuple t is in $\pi_Y^V(T_*)$ iff there is a $t' \in T_*$ such that $t'[Y] = t[Y]$, that is, if there is a $t'' \in T$ such that $t''[Y] = t[Y]$ and $t''(\mathrm{con}) \approx \mathbf{true}$. On the other hand, $t \in \pi_Y^C(T)_*$ iff there are tuples $t_1, \ldots, t_k \in T$, $k \ge 1$ such that $t_i[Y] = t[Y]$, $1 \le i \le k$ and $\mathbf{W}_{i=1}^k t_i(\mathrm{con}) \approx \mathbf{true}$. But by (7.17) the last condition implies that $t_i(\mathrm{con}) \approx \mathbf{true}$ for some i, and we obtain exactly the same condition as before.

In the case of selection, $\sigma_E^V(T_*)$ consists of all tuples $t \in T$ such that for every valuation v, $v(t(\mathrm{con})) = \mathbf{true}$ and $v(E(t)) = \mathbf{true}$, which is exactly the condition for t to be in $\sigma_E^C(T)_*$. Notice that (7.14) holds true for any, not necessarily positive, condition E. The requirement that E be positive is needed only to guarantee that $\sigma_E^C(T)_*$ is positive, so that we could inductively prove the lemma using (7.12)–(7.16).

We now consider the case of join. It is obvious that $T_* \bowtie^V W_* \subseteq (T \bowtie^C W)_*$, so it is sufficient to prove the converse inclusion. Suppose $t \in (T \bowtie^C W)_*$. Then there are C-tuples $t_1, \ldots, t_k \in T$, $w_1, \ldots, w_k \in W$, $k \ge 1$, such that $t_i[X] = t[X]$, $w_i[Z \setminus X] = t[Z \setminus X]$, $1 \le i \le k$, and $\mathbf{W}_{i=1}^k (t_i \bowtie w_i)(\mathrm{con}) \approx \mathbf{true}$. By (7.17), for some i

$$t_i(\mathrm{con}) \wedge w_i(\mathrm{con}) \wedge \bigwedge_{A \in X \cap Z} (t_i(A) = w_i(A)) \approx \mathbf{true}.$$

This obviously means that $t_i \in T_*$, $w_i \in W_*$, and $t_i[X \cap Z] = w_i[X \cap Z]$; that is, $t \in T_* \bowtie^V W_*$.

Finally, in the case of union, $T_* \cup^V W_* \subseteq (T \cup^C W)_*$, and $t \in (T \cup^C W)_*$ implies that either $t \in T_*$ or $t \in W_*$ or there are $t' \in T$, $w' \in W$ with $t'[X] = w'[X] = t[X]$, $t'(\mathrm{con}) \vee w'(\mathrm{con}) \approx \mathbf{true}$. The last case is reduced, however, by (7.17), to either the first or the second one. □

We are now ready to give the promised proof of the fact that $\langle \mathcal{T}_V, \mathrm{Rep}, \mathrm{PS^+UJ} \rangle$ is a representation system.

PROOF OF THEOREM 6.1. We have to show that for any V-multitable T and any PS⁺UJ-expression f with $\alpha(\mathbf{f}) = \alpha(\mathbf{T})$,

$$\mathbf{Rep}(\mathbf{f}^V(\mathbf{T})) \equiv_{\mathrm{PS^+UJ}} \mathbf{f}(\mathbf{Rep}(\mathbf{T}));$$

that is, for any PS⁺UJ-expression g with appropriate $\alpha(\mathbf{g})$,

$$\mathbf{Rep}(\mathbf{f}^V(\mathbf{T}))^{\mathbf{g}} = \mathbf{f}(\mathbf{Rep}(\mathbf{T}))^{\mathbf{g}}. \tag{7.18}$$

The left-hand side of (7.18) can be transformed as follows:

$$\mathbf{Rep}(\mathbf{f}^V(\mathbf{T}))^{\mathbf{g}} = \bigcap_{\mathbf{r} \in \mathbf{Rep}(\mathbf{f}^V(\mathbf{T}))} \mathbf{g}(\mathbf{r}) = \bigcap \mathbf{g}(\mathbf{Rep}(\mathbf{f}^V(\mathbf{T}))).$$

By Theorem 7.1,

$$\mathbf{g}(\mathbf{Rep}(\mathbf{f}^V(\mathbf{T}))) \equiv_{\mathrm{PSUJ}} \mathbf{Rep}(\mathbf{g}^C(\mathbf{f}^V(\mathbf{T}))),$$

which implies the equality of the intersections

$$\bigcap \mathbf{g}(\mathbf{Rep}(\mathbf{f}^V(\mathbf{T}))) = \bigcap \mathbf{Rep}(\mathbf{g}^C(\mathbf{f}^V(\mathbf{T}))).$$

By applying Lemma 7.1 and then Lemma 7.2 to the right-hand side we get

$$\bigcap \mathbf{g}(\mathbf{Rep}(\mathbf{f}^V(\mathbf{T}))) = \bigcap \mathbf{Rep}(\mathbf{g}^C(\mathbf{f}^V(\mathbf{T}))_*) = \bigcap \mathbf{Rep}(\mathbf{g}\mathbf{f}^V(\mathbf{T})).$$

Again using Lemmas 7.2 and 7.1 and Theorem 7.1 we obtain

$$\bigcap \mathbf{Rep}(\mathbf{g}\mathbf{f}^V(\mathbf{T})) = \bigcap \mathbf{Rep}(\mathbf{g}\mathbf{f}^C(\mathbf{T})_*) = \bigcap \mathbf{Rep}(\mathbf{g}\mathbf{f}^C(\mathbf{T})) = \bigcap \mathbf{g}\mathbf{f}(\mathbf{Rep}(\mathbf{T}))$$

which is the same as the right-hand side of (7.18):

$$\mathbf{f}(\mathbf{Rep}(\mathbf{T}))^{\mathbf{g}} = \bigcap_{\mathbf{r} \in \mathbf{f}(\mathbf{Rep}(\mathbf{T}))} \mathbf{g}(\mathbf{r}) = \bigcap \mathbf{g}\mathbf{f}(\mathbf{Rep}(\mathbf{T})). \qquad \square$$

To conclude this section, we note that

$$\mathbf{f}(v(\mathbf{T})) \supseteq v(f(\mathbf{T})) \tag{7.19}$$

for any PS⁺UJ-expression f, any V-multitable T ($\alpha(\mathbf{T}) = \alpha(\mathbf{f})$), and any valuation v. This is proved easily by induction on the complexity of f. An immediate corollary is

$$\mathbf{Rep}(\mathbf{f}(\mathbf{T})) \supseteq \mathbf{f}(\mathbf{Rep}(\mathbf{T})). \tag{7.20}$$

An important fact about (7.20) is that it does not require any assumptions on the cardinality of attribute domains. Notice that, in the terminology of the Introduction, (7.20) says that the representation system based on V-multitables is always safe: Rep($\mathbf{f}$($\mathbf{T}$)) includes all "possible" $\mathbf{f}(\mathbf{r}^*)$, $\mathbf{r}^* \in$ Rep($\mathbf{T}$). The assumption that the attribute domains are infinite is only needed to prove its completeness.

8. *Renaming of Attributes, Conjunctive Queries*

It may be noted that the relational algebra based on Ω = PSUJD and a fixed finite set $\mathscr{U}$ of attributes is not relationally complete in the sense of Codd [6]. This is because our version of relational algebra is equivalent in expressive power to a many-sorted predicate calculus with only one variable available for each sort, and certain formulas of the usual (many-sorted) predicate calculus inherently need many "auxiliary variables" (cf. [14]). One way of making our algebra relationally complete is to add the operation of renaming attributes, and to consider an infinite set of attributes $\mathscr{U}$, which contains an infinite number of attributes for each sort (i.e., for every $A \in \mathscr{U}$, there exists different $A_1, A_2, \ldots$ with $D(A_i) = D(A)$). It is obvious that

$$s_B^A(\mathrm{Rep}(T)) = \mathrm{Rep}(s_B^A(T)), \tag{8.1}$$

where $s_B^A(T)$ (with T either a Codd table, V-table, or C-table) is defined in exactly the same way as $s_B^A(r)$. By (8.1), most of our results can easily be extended by adding renaming (R) to the set Ω of relational operators. In particular, by Theorem 6.1, we have the following corollary.

COROLLARY 8.1. *$\langle \mathscr{T}_V$, Rep, PS$^+$UJR$\rangle$ is a representation system.*

We now discuss another version of the relational algebra (see, e.g., [29]) where the type of a relation is defined as a *sequence*, rather than set, of attributes (repetitions are allowed). The relational operators are modified in the following way. In the projection operator, instead of a target attribute set we have a target sequence of positions (i.e., numbers of columns of the argument relation); in the selection condition, we refer to positions rather than to attributes; and instead of the natural join we consider the Cartesian product. The Cartesian product of two relations, r, s, of types $\langle A_1, \ldots, A_n\rangle$ and $\langle B_1, \ldots, B_m\rangle$, respectively, is a relation of type $\langle A_1, \ldots, A_n, B_1, \ldots, B_m\rangle$ defined as

$$r \times s = \{\langle a_1, \ldots, a_n, b_1, \ldots, b_m\rangle : \langle a_1, \ldots, a_n\rangle \in r \wedge \langle b_1, \ldots, b_m\rangle \in s\}. \tag{8.2}$$

Note that any relation, in the modified sense, of type $\langle A_1, \ldots, A_n\rangle$ can be uniquely represented by the usual relation of type $\{\langle A_1, 1\rangle, \ldots, \langle A_n, n\rangle\}$, and that (8.2) can be expressed by first renaming the attributes of s so that it is of type $\{\langle B_1, n+1\rangle, \ldots, \langle B_m, n+m\rangle\}$ and then performing the natural join. By Corollary 8.1, this easily implies the following theorem (where X stands for the Cartesian product):

THEOREM 8.1. *$\langle \mathscr{T}_V$, Rep, PS$^+$UX$\rangle$ is a representation system.*

Conversely, the join can easily be expressed by the Cartesian product, restriction, and projection, so that, by Theorem 4.7, the Codd tables cannot support Ω = PXE (E stands for restriction).

THEOREM 8.2. *$\langle \mathscr{T}_{@}$, Rep, PXE$\rangle$ is not a representation system.*

(Clearly, in Theorems 8.1 and 8.2 the notions of a V-table and Codd table are modified into a "column-ordered" form, in the same way as it was done for relations.)

Another important fact implied by Corollary 8.1 is that the system based on V-tables can handle arbitrary conjunctive queries [4]. Roughly speaking, a conjunctive query is defined by a conjunction of atomic relational formulas of the form $R_i(x_1, \ldots, x_p)$ (the R_i's are predicates corresponding to database relations), where each of the x_i is either a constant or variable, preceded by existential quantifiers binding some of the variables appearing in the conjunction. The mapping defined by a conjunctive query q can be defined, for any database state $\mathbf{r}$, by

$$q(\mathbf{r}) = \{\nu(s) : \nu \text{ is a valuation such that } \nu(\mathbf{Q}) \subseteq \mathbf{r}\} \tag{8.3}$$

where

$\mathbf{Q}$ is a suitable V-multitable (V-tuples appearing in $\mathbf{Q}$ correspond in the natural way to the atomic relational formulas in q; $\alpha(\mathbf{Q}) = \alpha(\mathbf{r}) = \alpha(q)$),
s is a V-tuple such that all variables occurring in s occur in $\mathbf{Q}$ ($\alpha(s) = \beta(q)$).

LEMMA 8.1. *For any conjunctive query q there is a PS$^+$JR-expression f such that $q(\mathbf{r}) = f(\mathbf{r})$ for every $\mathbf{r}$ ($\alpha(\mathbf{r}) = \alpha(f) = \alpha(q)$).*

SKETCH OF PROOF. Call a variable *repeated* if it occurs in at least two V-tuples in $\mathbf{Q}$, s, and a *target* variable if it occurs in s (see (8.3)). For every repeated variable x, let A_x be an attribute not appearing in $\mathbf{Q}$. Let $\mathbf{Q} = \langle Q_1, \ldots, Q_n\rangle$. For any V-tuple u in Q_i, let f_u be an expression consisting of a relation symbol R_i preceded by (from right to left)

(i) selections $\sigma_{A=a}$, for every $A \in \alpha(u)$ with $u(A) = a$, $a \in D$,
(ii) restrictions $\sigma_{A=B}$, for all $A, B \in \alpha(u)$ with $u(A) = u(B) = x$, a variable,
(iii) projection π_Y, where Y contains exactly one attribute A for any repeated variable x appearing in u ($u(A) = x$),
(iv) renaming $s_{A_x}^A$, for every $A \in Y$, where $x = u(A)$.

Let $h = \pi_X(\bowtie_u f_u)$, where u ranges over all V-tuples in $\mathbf{Q}$ and $X = \{A_x : x \text{ is a target variable}\}$. The required expression f is obtained from h by suitably renaming the attributes in X. Some easy modifications are required if s contains constants or multiple occurrences of the same variable. (A similarity of this construction to "shallow expressions" of [32] may be noted.) □

By Lemma 8.1, we obtain the following corollary.

COROLLARY 8.2. *The representation system $\langle \mathscr{T}_V$, Rep, PS$^+$UJR$\rangle$ can support arbitrary conjunctive queries; that is, for any conjunctive query q and any V-multitable $\mathbf{T}$ with $\alpha(\mathbf{T}) = \alpha(q)$ there is a V-table U such that Rep(U) $\equiv_{PS^+UJR}$ q(Rep($\mathbf{T}$)).*

Here we denote $q(\mathrm{Rep}(\mathbf{T})) = \{q(\mathbf{r}) : \mathbf{r} \in \mathrm{Rep}(\mathbf{T})\}$. The V-table U is obtained by finding the PS$^+$JR-expression f equivalent to q (see Lemma 8.1) and putting $U = f(\mathbf{T})$. The V-table U will also be denoted by $q(\mathbf{T})$.

By using the fact that in computing $f(\mathbf{T})$ we treat variables and constants in exactly the same way, and that the equivalence between q and f does not depend on the nature of the attribute domains, one can easily prove the following fact generalizing (8.3):

THEOREM 8.3. *For any conjunctive query q, given by a V-multitable* **Q** *and V-tuple s, and for any V-multitable* **T** *with* $\alpha(\mathbf{T}) = \alpha(\mathbf{Q})$

$$q(\mathbf{T}) = \{\rho(s) : \rho \text{ is a generalized valuation such that } \rho(\mathbf{Q}) \subseteq \mathbf{T}\},$$

where by a generalized valuation we mean any mapping $\rho: V \to V \cup D$ *such that* $x \in V(A)$ *implies* $\rho(x) \in V(A) \cup D(A)$.

9. *Closed World Interpretation of Tables*

The interpretation of multitables considered so far has been based on the open-world assumption [26, 27], which was embodied in the property

$$\mathbf{r} \in \mathrm{Rep}(\mathbf{T}) \wedge \mathbf{s} \supseteq \mathbf{r} \Rightarrow \mathbf{s} \in \mathrm{Rep}(\mathbf{T})$$

(see (3.3)). We now consider a different interpretation, which we call the *closed world interpretation.*

Let **T** be a *V*-multitable. The closed world interpretation of **T** is defined as follows:

$$\mathrm{rep}(\mathbf{T}) = \{\mathbf{r} : \text{there exists a valuation } v \text{ such that } v(\mathbf{T}) = \mathbf{r}\}, \tag{9.1}$$

where $v(\mathbf{T})$ is defined as before (see (6.1)–(6.3)). Similarly, for any *C*-multitable **T** we define rep(**T**) by formula (9.1), with $v(\mathbf{T})$ defined by (7.1) and (7.2). In the case of a Codd multitable **T**, we define

$$\mathrm{rep}(\mathbf{T}) = \mathrm{rep}(\mathbf{U}),$$

where **U** is any *V*-multitable obtained by replacing every occurrence of @ in **T** by a different variable. It seems that what Codd meant in [6] was in fact the closed world interpretation of Codd tables.

Notice that if a tuple *t* cannot be obtained by replacing nulls by constants in any @-tuple of a Codd table **T**, then **T** represents the "negative information" that the relationship expressed by *t* definitely does not hold, a fact not representable under the open world interpretation. The situation is similar in the case of *V*-tables and *C*-tables.

Clearly, for all three kinds of multitables,

$$\mathrm{rep}(\mathbf{T}) \subseteq \mathrm{Rep}(\mathbf{T});$$

moreover, rep(**T**) and Rep(**T**) are coinitial.

Let $\Omega \subseteq \mathrm{PSS^+UJR}$, **f** be an Ω-expression, **T** be a multitable of type $\alpha(\mathbf{f})$, and **U** be a multitable of type $\beta(\mathbf{f})$. Since $\mathrm{rep}(\mathbf{U}) \approx \mathrm{Rep}(\mathbf{U})$, $\mathrm{rep}(\mathbf{T}) \approx \mathrm{Rep}(\mathbf{T})$, by Lemma 4.2 we obtain

$$\mathrm{rep}(\mathbf{U}) \equiv_\Omega \mathrm{Rep}(\mathbf{U})$$

and

$$\mathbf{f}(\mathrm{rep}(\mathbf{T})) \equiv_\Omega \mathbf{f}(\mathrm{Rep}(\mathbf{T})).$$

Hence,

$$\mathrm{rep}(\mathbf{U}) \equiv_\Omega \mathbf{f}(\mathrm{rep}(\mathbf{T})) \quad \text{iff} \quad \mathrm{Rep}(\mathbf{U}) \equiv_\Omega \mathbf{f}(\mathrm{Rep}(\mathbf{T})).$$

This equivalence immediately implies that all results concerning representation systems developed under the open-world assumption carry over to the closed-world interpretation:

THEOREM 9.1. *Let* $\Omega \subseteq PSS^+UJR$ *and let* $\mathcal{T}$ *be either* $\mathcal{T}_@$ *or* $\mathcal{T}_V$ *or* $\mathcal{T}_C$. *Then*

$\langle \mathcal{T}, Rep, \Omega\rangle$ *is a representation system*
iff $\langle \mathcal{T}, rep, \Omega\rangle$ *is a representation system.*

Moreover, the correct operations on tables are the same under both interpretations.

It turns out that in the case of conditional tables we can handle all relational operations, including the difference, thus supporting the full strength of the relational algebra. Indeed, let *T*, *U* be two *C*-tables, $\alpha(T) = \alpha(U) = X$. For any $t \in T$, let us define t_U to be a *C*-tuple, $\alpha(t_U) = X$, such that

$$t_U[X] = t[X],$$
$$t_U(\mathrm{con}) = t(\mathrm{con}) \wedge \bigwedge_{u \in U} \bigvee_{A \in X} (t(A) \neq u(A)).$$

If we define

$$T - U = \{t_U : t \in T\},$$

then it is easily seen that

$$v(T - U) = v(T) - v(U)$$

for any valuation *v*, which, combined with (7.11), implies that

$$v(\mathbf{f}(\mathbf{T})) = \mathbf{f}(v(\mathbf{T}))$$

for any PSUJRD-expression **f**, any *C*-multitable **T** ($\alpha(\mathbf{T}) = \alpha(\mathbf{f})$), and any valuation *v*. Consequently,

$$\mathrm{rep}(\mathbf{f}(\mathbf{T})) = \mathbf{f}(\mathrm{rep}(\mathbf{T})), \tag{9.2}$$

that is, diagram (3.1) commutes. Let us state this as a theorem.

THEOREM 9.2. $\langle \mathcal{T}_C$, *rep, PSUJRD*$\rangle$ *is a representation system. Moreover, all relational operators can be defined on C-tables in such a way that* (9.2) *holds.*

10. *Conclusions*

We have proposed a general condition that should be satisfied if we want to evaluate relational expressions over "tables with nulls" in a semantically correct way.

Suppose that an instance of an incomplete information relational database is given by a multitable **T**, and let **f** be a relational query. While computing the response to **f**, we think of an unknown $\mathbf{r}^* \in \mathrm{Rep}(\mathbf{T})$—corresponding to the true state of the real world—being transformed by **f**, and we require that **f**(**T**) contain enough information to determine all tuples that surely (i.e., no matter which element of Rep(**T**) the multirelation $\mathbf{r}^*$ is) appear in $\mathbf{f}(\mathbf{r}^*)$.

In this way our approach is similar in spirit to the *external interpretation* and *lower value* $\|\cdot\|_*$ in [20] (see also [22]).

Note that the tuples that surely appear in $\mathbf{f}(\mathbf{r}^*)$ are given by $\mathrm{Rep}(\mathbf{T})^\mathbf{f}$, and it is easy to see that $\mathrm{Rep}(\mathbf{T})^\mathbf{f}$ can be obtained by deleting from **f**(**T**) all tuples containing nulls, both in the case of Codd tables and *V*-tables.

Another possibility is to treat **f**(**T**), rather than $\mathrm{Rep}(\mathbf{T})^\mathbf{f}$, as the response to query **f**. This has the advantage of providing more information; for instance, a tuple *a@c* (or *ayc*) appearing in the response can easily be shown to indicate that a tuple of the form *abc*, $b \in D(B)$ surely appears in $\mathbf{f}(\mathbf{r}^*)$. Moreover, this approach makes it possible to treat a response to query **f** as an intermediate step in computing the correct response to a more complex query **gf** (note that in general it is *not* possible to determine $\mathrm{Rep}(\mathbf{T})^{\mathbf{gf}}$ on the basis of $\mathrm{Rep}(\mathbf{T})^\mathbf{f}$ and **g**).

It should be noted that $\mathrm{Rep}(\mathbf{T})^\mathbf{f} = \mathrm{rep}(\mathbf{T})^\mathbf{f}$, so that by Theorem 9.1 the process of computing the response to a query is exactly the same under both open and closed world assumptions.

The results of the paper show that the devices suitable for representing incomplete information heavily depend on what processing of the information we are going to correctly perform, or, in more concrete terms, what relational operators are allowed. Our approach stresses the requirement for a correct evaluation of relational expressions, rather than just single relational operators, as was usually the case in previous attempts in the literature to correctly handle null values.

From the practical point of view an especially appealing system seems to be one based on *V*-tables, supporting projection, positive selection, union, join, and renaming, which allows for processing arbitrary conjunctive queries. The reason is that all these relational operators and queries can be evaluated over *V*-tables in *exactly the same way* as in the case of the usual relations.

There are several important problems that have not been treated here. One is how to handle dependencies in our framework. It turns out that functional, multivalued, and join dependencies—more exactly, arbitrary implicational dependencies [2] ("generalized dependencies" in [29])—can be *represented* in any *V*-table, in the sense that for any *V*-table T and any set Σ of such dependencies, there is a *V*-table U such that $\mathrm{Rep}(U) \equiv_{PS^+UJ} \mathrm{Rep}(T) \cap \mathrm{Sat}(\Sigma)$, where $\mathrm{Sat}(\Sigma)$ is the set of all relations satisfying the dependencies in Σ (see [12, 13, 16]). This is another argument for the usefulness of the representation system based on *V*-tables.

Another interesting topic is the relation between *V*-tables and the tableaux of Aho, Sagiv, and Ullman [1]. Roughly speaking, a tableau for a relational PSJ-expression f (with only selection of the form $\sigma_{A=a}$ allowed) can be treated as a *V*-table representing the inverse image of the summary of the tableau with respect to f (see [15]). It also turns out that for any PSJ-expression f (with only selection of the form $\sigma_{A=a}$) and every *V*-multitable $\mathbf{T}$ ($\alpha(\mathbf{T}) = \alpha(\mathbf{f})$), there is a *V*-multitable $\mathbf{U}$ such that $\mathrm{Rep}(\mathbf{U}) = \mathbf{f}^{-1}(\mathrm{Rep}(\mathbf{T}))$. This fact has several interesting applications (see [17]).

ACKNOWLEDGMENTS. Several comments and suggestions by J. Łoś, W. M Turski, and the referees are gratefully acknowledged.

REFERENCES

1. Aho, A. V., Sagiv, Y., and Ullman, J. D. Equivalences among relational expressions. *SIAM J. Comput. 8*, 2 (May 1979), 218–246.
2. Beeri, C., and Vardi, M. Y. Formal systems for tuple and equality generating dependencies. *SIAM J. Comput. 13*, 1 (Feb. 1984), 76–98.
3. Biskup, J. A formal approach to null values in database relations. In *Advances in Database Theory*, H. Gallaire, J. Minker, and J. M. Nicolas, Eds. Plenum Press, New York, 1981, pp. 299–341.
4. Chandra, A. K., and Merlin, P. M. Optimal implementation of conjunctive queries in relational data bases. In *Proceedings of the 9th Annual ACM Symposium on Theory of Computing* (Boulder, Col., May 2–4). ACM, New York, 1977, pp. 77–90.
5. Codd, E. F. A relational model for large shared data banks. *Commun. ACM 13*, 6 (June 1970), 377–387.
6. Codd, E. F. Relational completeness of data base sublanguages. In *Data Base Systems*, R. Rustin, Ed. Prentice-Hall, Englewood Cliffs, N.J., 1972, pp. 65–98.
7. Codd, E. F. Understanding relations (Installment #7). *FDT Bull. of ACM-SIGMOD 7*, 3–4 (Dec. 1975), 23–28.
8. Codd E. F. Extending the database relational model to capture more meaning. *ACM Trans. Database Syst. 4*, 4 (Dec. 1979), 397–434.
9. Garey, M. R., and Johnson, D. S. *Computers and Intractability: A Guide to the Theory of NP-completeness*. Freeman, San Francisco, Calif., 1979.
10. Grant, J. Null values in a relational data base. *Inf. Process. Lett. 6*, 5 (Oct. 1977), 156–157.
11. Horowitz, E., and Sahni, S. *Fundamentals of Computer Algorithms*. Computer Science Press, Potomac, Md., 1979.
12. Imieliński, T. Problems of representing information in relational databases (in Polish). Ph.D. Thesis, Institute of Computer Science, Polish Academy of Sciences, 1981.
13. Imieliński, T., and Lipski, W. On representing incomplete information in a relational data base. In *Proceedings of the 7th International Conference on Very Large Data Bases* (Cannes, France, Sept. 9–11) ACM, New York, 1981, pp. 388–397.
14. Imieliński, T., and Lipski, W. The relational model of data and cylindric algebras. *J. Comput. System Sci. 28*, 1 (Feb. 1984), 80–102.
15. Imieliński, T., and Lipski, W. A technique for translating states between database schemata. In *Proceedings of the ACM SIGMOD International Conference on Management of Data* (Orlando, Fla., June 2–4). ACM, New York, 1982, pp. 61–68.
16. Imieliński, T., and Lipski, W. Incomplete information and dependencies in relational databases. In *Proceedings of the ACM SIGMOD International Conference on Management of Data* (San Jose, Calif., May 23–26). ACM, New York, 1983, pp. 178–184.
17. Imieliński, T., and Lipski, W. Inverting relational expressions—a uniform and natural technique for various database problems. In *Proceedings of the ACM SIGACT-SIGMOD Symposium on Principles of Database Systems* (Atlanta, Ga., March 21–23). ACM, New York, 1983, pp. 305–311.
18. Lacroix, M., and Pirotte, A. Generalized joins. *ACM-SIGMOD Record 8*, 3 (Sept. 1976), 14–15.
19. Lipski, W. Informational systems with incomplete information. In *Proceedings of the 3rd International Colloquium on Automata, Languages and Programming* (Edinburgh, Scotland, July 20–23). Edinburgh University Press, Edinburgh, Scotland, 1976, pp. 120–130.
20. Lipski, W. On semantic issues connected with incomplete information databases. *ACM Trans. Database Syst. 4*, 3 (Sept. 1979), 262–296.
21. Lipski, W. On databases with incomplete information. *J. ACM 28*, 1 (Jan. 1981), 41–70.
22. Lipski, W. Logical problems related to incomplete information in databases. Tech. Rep. 138, Laboratoire de Recherche en Informatique, Université de Paris-Sud, Centre d'Orsay, Sept. 1983.
23. Lipski, W. On relational algebra with marked nulls. In *Proceedings of the 3rd ACM SIGACT-SIGMOD Symposium on Principles of Database Systems* (Waterloo, Ont., Canada, April 2–4). ACM, New York, 1984, pp. 201–203.
24. Maier, D., Ullman, J. D., and Vardi, M. Y. On the foundations of the universal relation model. *ACM Trans. Database Syst. 9*, 2 (June 1984), 283–308.
25. Reingold, E. M., Nievergelt, J., and Deo, N. *Combinational Algorithms: Theory and Practice*. Prentice Hall, Englewood Cliffs, N.J., 1977.
26. Reiter, R. On closed world databases. In *Logic and Data Bases*, H. Gallaire and J. Minker, Eds. Plenum Press, New York, 1978, pp. 55–76.
27. Reiter, R. Towards a logical reconstruction of relational database theory. In *Conceptual Modelling, Perspectives from Artificial Intelligence, Databases and Programming Languages*, M. L. Brodie, J. Mylopoulos, and J. Schmidt, Eds. Springer-Verlag, New York, 1984, pp. 191–233.
28. Siklóssy, L. Efficient query evaluation in relational databases with missing values. *Inf. Process. Lett. 13*, 4/5 (End 1981), 160–163.
29. Ullman, J. D. *Principles of Database Systems*. 2nd ed. Computer Science Press, Potomac, Md., 1982.
30. Vassiliou, Y. Null values in data base management: A denotational semantics approach. In *Proceedings of the ACM-SIGMOD International Symposium on Management of Data* (Boston, Mass., May 30–June 1). ACM, New York, 1979, pp. 162–169.
31. Vassiliou, Y. Functional dependencies and incomplete information. In *Proceedings of the 6th International Conference on Very Large Data Bases* (Montreal, Ont., Canada, Oct. 1–3). ACM, New York, 1980, pp. 260–269.
32. Yannakakis, M., and Papadimitriou, C. H. Algebraic dependencies. *J. Comput. Syst. Sci. 25*, 1 (Aug. 1982), 2–41.
33. Zaniolo, C. Relational views in a data base system support for queries. In *Proceedings of the IEEE Computer Software and Applications Conference* (Chicago, Ill., Nov. 8–11). IEEE, New York, 1977, pp. 267–275.
34. Zaniolo, C. Database relations with null values. In *Proceedings of the ACM SIGACT-SIGMOD Symposium on Principles of Database Systems* (Los Angeles, Calif., March 29–31). ACM, New York, 1982, pp. 27–33.

Epilogue

The main contribution of this paper, as I see it now, is the *correctness* criterion and methodology for extending relational algebra operations onto tables with different types of null values. This criterion was further clarified by Lipski in [Lipski 84] and can be applied to a much wider range of databases than we initially expected: Null values form just a special case of *complex objects* occuring in relations and the notion of representation systems introduced in the paper applies equally to extensions of relational algebra on *any* tables with *complex objects* not just tables with null values. Unfortunately, the part of the paper which introduces this general criterion is the least understood one and in the last 4 years I have seen many papers in which incorrect attempts of extending relational algebra on various types of tables have been made; the usual error is to define algebraic operations in an arbitrary way, ignoring the semantics of tables under consideration as well as the semantics of operations. Therefore, in this short note, I decided to explain the above mentioned criterion in terms more suitable for current "complex objects" orientation. I would like also to provide a simple example which illustrates common errors.

Let us assume that information in the database is represented in the form of tables which are extensions of relations possibly containing some other "objects" such as null values, sets (with "or" or "and" interpretations), variables, conditions etc. With each such table T we associate the value of a representation function rep(T) which is the set of *possible worlds* represented by this table. Possible worlds are standard "flat" relations (we can generalize our approach easily to the case when possible worlds also contain complex objects) . Now, having represented our data in such a tabular form, we want to process queries expressed in relational algebra (or relational calculus). To this end we have to *extend* relational algebra operations on these tables. Obviously we cannot do this extension in the arbitrary way - we have to "be faithful" to the underlying semantics. Let f be an arbitrary relational expression, and T an arbitrary table. The best way to define the extension f(T) of f over T would be to satisfy

$$\text{rep}(f(T)) = f(\text{rep}(T)) = \{f(S): S \in \text{rep}(T)\}$$

Indeed, in such a case f(T) would preserve all information about possible values of f(S)[1]. Unfortunately, as explained in the paper, this will be too restrictive. Fortunately it is also unnecessary; we can require less as explained in [Imielinski 84] and later reformulated more elegantly in [Lipski 84] . By a *True set* of the set of worlds X we mean $\cap X$, i.e the set of all tuples which belong to all relations in X. Here are our modified requirements for a *faithful* extension of relational algebra operations from Ω on tables T:

(1) Preservation of True Sets:

For any relational algebra expression f built from operations from Ω: $\cap\text{rep}(f(T)) = \cap f(\text{rep}(T))$: i.e. the table f(T) should preserve information about all tuples which for sure belong to $f(S^*)$ according to the table rep(T).

(2) Recursivness:

$$f(g(T)) = (fg)(T)$$

[1]according to the original table the real state of the world - S^* is one of possible worlds in rep(T), therefore the "real" state of the answer $f(S^*)$ is one of the possible worlds in f(rep(T))

This states that we should preserve the important feature of relational algebra - the intermediate results of subexpressions of a given expressions can be stored as "views" which can be later used to the computation of the full expressions without necessarilly starting from scratch.

The requirements (1) and (2) are equivalent to the representation systems requirement from [Imielinski 84]. I feel that (1) and (2) are really minimal acceptable requirements for any reasonable "extension" of relational algebra. As the paper indicates they are still pretty restrictive - i.e. extensions of some operations over some types of tables will be simply impossible. Intuitvely: *The expressive power of a given type of a table must be sufficient to represent the results of all relational algebra expressions from the set of expressions under consideration.* In many cases, in order to correctly extend a given set of operations on a given set of tables it is necessary to "enrich" the table itself, add to its expressive power. In the paper this was the case for V-tables which had to be extended to conditional tables in order to support all positive relational algebra expressions. Similarly Codd tabels had to be extended to V-tables in order to correctly support Project-Join expressions.

Many authors extend relational operations in an arbitrary way totally ignoring the above semantical considerations. The following example illustrates both the common mistake and the application of the criterion:

Example

Let us consider the set of tables admitting, additionally to domain constants, finite sets as entries. The occurence of a set $X=\{a_1,...a_n\}$ is interpreted disjunctively - at least one of the values in X is the "real" value[2]. Such sets are called OR-sets and naturally correspond to restricted nulls; for instance a tuple <John, {Manager, Supervisor, Director}> in a table R[Employee, Position] means that John is a manager or a supervisor or a director. Given a table T with OR-sets the representation function rep(T) is defined in a straightforward way following described above semantics of OR-sets. In order to process queries we have to extend relational algebra operations on these tables. Let us concentrate on just two operations - projection and join.

First we are going to show that the straightforward way of extending join operation fails: Let us define join by extending "equality" over OR-sets:

An OR-set is not "equal" to any other OR-set nor to any domain constant

The rationale for such a defintion is that given an OR-set $X=\{a_1,...a_n\}$ and an individual constant, say b (which might be an element of X), it is always possible that "the real" unknown value for which A stands will be different from "b". Similar rationale justifies the case of inequality two OR-sets. The following example illustrates that such an extension will not preserve "True sets" (the first part of our criterion) and therefore will loose information.

Let

R =

A	B
a	$\{b_1, b_2, b_3\}$

[2]This is contrary to the sets interpreted conjunctively, as in nested relations

and let

S =

B	C
b_1	c
b_2	c
b_3	c

Let f = $\pi_{AC}(R \bowtie S)$, where $\bowtie$ stands for natural join. If we extend join according to the above rule than f(R,S) will result in an empty table. However <a,c> $\in \cap$f(rep(R), rep(S)). Therefore, this extension of join will not be complete with respect to the underlying semantics and the requirement (1) fails. We can also show that the proposed extension does not satisfy the recursivness requirement. Indeed, let

R =

A	B	C
a	$\{b_1, b_2\}$	c

and let f= $\pi_{AC}(\pi_{AB}(R) \bowtie \pi_{BC}(R))$. If projection is extended naturally over tables with OR-sets (essentially the same as projection on relations) and join is extended the way we described before then the f(R) = $\emptyset$, while we have to have f(R) = {<a,c>} (this is a true set of f(rep(R)). Indeed, after computing two projections join will not unify two OR-sets[3]. Notice that the proposed operation of join would be correct if our set of operations contained *only* join and no other operations. It is the interaction of join with projection which causes problems. The common mistake in extending relational algebra is to consider correctness of each operation separately ignoring their interaction with other operations. These interactions are captured by the recursivness requirement.

Clearly join can no longer be defined "locally" just on the level of individual tuples - in this example four tuples contributed to <a,c> in the result, this number could be arbitrary large. What is therefore a correct and complete extension of projection and join which would preserve true sets and be recursive, i.e. satisfy both our requirements? Suprisingly, the answer is negative - there is *no* such extension; the expressive power of tables with OR-sets is not sufficient to support both projection and join. In order to demonstrate this informally we will construct two tables R and S with OR-sets and a relational algebra expressionn f such that f(T) would have to represent "arbitrary" disjunction:

R =

A	B
a	$\{b_1, b_2\}$

S =

B	C
b_1	c_1
b_2	c_2

B C D

[3]In order to fix this we would have to introduce marked nulls. This was done in [Imielinski 84] in the concept of V-tables

U =

B	C	D
b_1	c_1	d
b_2	c_2	d

In order to represent rep(R) ⋈ rep(S) by some table T we would have to represent a disjunction of the form "<a,b_1,c_1> or <a,b_2,c_2>" in T. Indeed, otherwise we could not correctly perform a project-join expression of hypothetical table T with U (i.e π_{AD}(T ⋈ U)) = {<a,d>}. Unfortunately the disjunction <a, b_1,c_1> or <a, b_2, c_2> cannot be represented by any table with OR-sets. In order to represent such disjunction we would have to extend the notion of a table with OR-sets into a table with "OR-tuples" of the form

<a, {<b_1,c_1>, <b_2, c_2>}>

The formal proof is presented in [Imielinski 87] and follows the general methodology of [Imielinski 84]. In [Imielinski 87] we also discuss tables which have both "OR-sets" and "AND-sets", i.e. sets with conjunctive interpretation.

■

The above example illustrates the usefullness of our criterion in checking whether it is possible at all to extend certain operations on certain types of tables. One has to be very careful in dealing with complex objects in tables since even such simple extension as the one shown here leads to problems with such simple operations as projection and join. Additionally, our criterion gives an indication how a given type of a table has to be extended in order to support a given set of operations. It is an interesting research direction to examine various types of tables with complex objects (both with complete and incomplete data) with respect to extendability of relational algebra expressions. We see the faithfulness criterion and techniques from [Imielinski 84] as playing major role in such investigations.

References

[Imielinski 84] Imielinski, T. , Lipski, W.
Incomplete Information in Relational Databases.
JACM 31(4):761-791, October, 1984.

[Imielinski 87] Imielinski,T.
Databases with OR-objects.
May, 1987.

[Lipski 84] Lipski,W.
Algebra on Tables with Null Values.
In *ACM PODS Symposium.* 1984.

Chapter 3

Performance Issues

This chapter considers algorithms, structures, and techniques for the core functions of database and knowledge-base systems. These implementation issues focus largely on systems' efficiency and robustness. The chapter contains 17 papers organized into four topic sections: Retrieval, Deduction, and Query Processing; Data/Knowledge Base Integrity; Implementation Techniques; and Data/Knowledge Management Systems.

3.1 Retrieval, Deduction, and Query Processing

A data/knowledge base is useful only to the extent that it is provided with retrieval operations. Retrieval has been studied in terms of query evaluation with respect to a database, and deductive question answering with respect to a knowledge base. Indeed, the primary use of a data/knowledge base is for query and search. Query capabilities are generally combined with features to define and update databases. A few database languages have come to dominate conventional DBMSs (e.g., SQL from System R [ABCE76], QUEL from INGRES [SWKH76], and Query by Example [ZLOO77]). More advanced database languages are discussed in Chapter 2. Considerable research has been invested in database-query languages (e.g., see [AU79], [BANC78], [BFN82], [CF81], [CACC78], [DEMO80], [DEMO81], and [ULLM85]). [KRB85] is an excellent book containing recent papers from major contributors to query-processing technology. There is also much work on retrieval in AI (e.g., see [COOP64], [RAPH64], [LM67], [VANE78], [KING80], [AF83], [BB83], [PBL84], and [MCT87]). [WILL84] presents retrieval by reformulation that uses frame-based techniques from AI in conjunction with database concepts. This section focuses on database querying and on knowledge-base retrieval.

This section begins with two survey papers intended to aid readers in finding their way around the labyrinth of literature on database-query processing. The first survey paper (3.1.1), "A Framework for Choosing a Database Query Language" by Matthias Jarke and Yannis Vassiliou, presents a thorough account of the issues that arise in selecting a query language for an application. It also describes the features of such languages from a user's perspective. The second paper (3.1.2), "An Amateur's Introduction to Recursive Query Processing" by Francois Bancilhon and Ragu Ramakrishnan, is an excellent survey of recursive query-processing techniques. In the early 1980s, recursive query processing was viewed as a fundamental feature required for databases to support new application domains, such as knowledge-based systems (e.g., rule processing in databases) and engineering data structures (e.g., parts hierarchies). Considerable research was done to support general and linear recursion, which is similar to computing recursive joins in relational databases (see [SM80], [NH80], [MN82], [HN84], [HR85], [IOAN85], [BANC86], and [AGRA87]). [RHDM86] is a less theoretical treatment, but is proposed as applying to a wider class of practical recursion situations than that addressed by most of the approaches discussed in the works referenced here. In 1988, it became widely accepted that the much more costly general recursion was not necessary for database support of typical rule executions or parts-hierarchy traversals. This research may still be applicable to complex recursive data structures and to optimization of logical database queries.

The third paper in this section (3.1.3), Ray Reiter's "Deductive Question-Answering on Relational Data Bases," raises the question of how queries can be processed with respect to a database that contains extensional and intensional facts. The paper treats this question in a many-sorted logical setting. The paper is noteworthy because it points out, for the first time, the problem of processing recursive queries. It also offers the idea of "compiling" general axioms in the database so that queries translate to retrieval operations on ground facts. Much of the work that followed on query processing with respect to a deductive database essentially provides answers to variations of the basic question raised by Reiter.

The fourth and final paper of this section (3.1.4), "Knowledge Retrieval as Limited Inference" by A. Frisch and James Allen, suggests an interesting middle ground between the data retrieval and the deductive question-answering views of query processing. The authors adopt a logic that is syntactically identical with first-order logic but has a different semantics. As a consequence, the decision problem for this logic is decidable and amounts to some form of a retrieval operation. Retrieval then can be viewed as deduction, provided one appropriately changes the meaning of the formulas in the information base. A similar conclusion is drawn in [PATE85] and [PATE87], although the starting point is substantially different.

A Framework for Choosing a Database Query Language

MATTHIAS JARKE and YANNIS VASSILIOU

Computer Applications and Information Systems Area, Graduate School of Business Administration, New York University, New York, N.Y. 10006

This paper presents a systematic approach to matching categories of query language interfaces with the requirements of certain user types. The method is based on a trend model of query language development on the dimensions of functional capabilities and usability. From the trend model the following are derived: a classification scheme for query languages, a criterion hierarchy for query language evaluation, a comprehensive classification scheme of query language users and their requirements, and preliminary recommendations for allocating language classes to user types.

The method integrates the results of existing human factors studies and provides a structured framework for future research in this area. Current and expected developments are exemplified by the description of "new generation" database query languages. In a practical query language selection problem, the results of this paper can be used for preselecting suitable query language types; the final selection decision will also depend on organization-specific factors, such as the available database management system, hardware and software strategies, and financial system costs.

Categories and Subject Descriptors: D.3.2 [**Programming Languages**]: Language Classifications—*very high-level languages*; H.1.2 [**Models and Principles**]: User/Machine Systems—*human factors*; H.2.3 [**Database Management**]: Languages; H.3.3 [**Information Storage and Retrieval**]: Information Search and Retrieval—*query formulation*

General Terms: Human Factors, Languages

Additional Key Words and Phrases: Databases, language evaluation, query language, user classification

CONTENTS

INTRODUCTION
1. QUERY LANGUAGE SELECTION PROCEDURE
2. TRENDS IN QUERY LANGUAGE DEVELOPMENT
   2.1 A Model of Query Language Development
   2.2 Query Language Taxonomy
3. USER CLASSIFICATION
4. HUMAN FACTORS RESEARCH IN QUERY LANGUAGES
5. EVALUATION CRITERIA FOR QUERY LANGUAGES
   5.1 Usability Criteria
   5.2 Functional Capabilities Criteria
6. EVALUATION OF LANGUAGE CLASSES AND USER REQUIREMENTS
   6.1 Query Language Evaluation
   6.2 Determining User Requirement Profiles
7. RECOMMENDATIONS OF QUERY LANGUAGES FOR USER TYPES
8. SUMMARY AND CONCLUSIONS
ACKNOWLEDGMENTS
REFERENCES

INTRODUCTION

A *query language* (QL) is defined as a high-level computer language for the retrieval and modification of data held in databases or files [Samet 1981]. It is usually interactive, on line, and able to support queries that are ad hoc (not predefined). It is often assumed that the main users of QLs have limited technical expertise, so user interaction tends to be of limited complexity and the displayed answer is usually relatively short.

Many different query language interfaces can be built on top of the standard languages offered by a database management system (DBMS) manufacturer. In fact, the number and variety of query language interfaces available or under development have grown so rapidly that a framework for evaluating query languages in terms of their functionality and usability by different types of users is needed. The goal of this paper is to propose a methodology for selecting a type of query language interface on the basis of its functionality and "user friendliness" characteristics, a goal that has not been attempted in previous surveys and categorizations of QLs [Brodie and Schmidt 1982; Lacroix and Pirotte 1977, 1980; Lehmann and Blaser 1979; Leavenworth and Sammet 1974; Lochovsky and Tsichritzis 1984; McDonald and McNally 1982; Samet 1981; Stonebraker and Rowe 1977]. In order to avoid becoming outdated before its publication, the paper concentrates on general query interface types rather than on specific language systems currently on the market.

In order to reach this goal, well-structured taxonomies of query languages and language users are developed. The proposed methodology for selecting a type of query language provides a framework for contrasting both taxonomies and combining them with existing technical and human factors research to recommend the types of language best suited for a known user class. However, as the existing human factors research—traditionally focused on specific systems—does not suffice for generalized conclusions, the main contribution of this paper is the proposed framework that can be seen as a structured set of hypotheses for future studies. The usefulness of our methodology has been demonstrated by its application in the development of evaluation schemes for a set of major empirical studies comparing natural versus formal query languages [Jarke et al. 1986a; Turner et al. 1984].

The next section is an overview of the proposed methodology; subsequently, each of its steps will be considered in more detail.

1. QUERY LANGUAGE SELECTION PROCEDURE

Our approach to query language evaluation can be understood as a specialized *cost-benefit analysis* method. It is a cost–benefit analysis in the sense that multiple evaluation criteria are based on a simple economic model of query language usage and the trade-off between costs and benefits depends on the user type. The method is specialized toward the specific task of evaluating query languages from the viewpoint of a single user.

This approach has the advantage of permitting specific recommendations with available data from technical and human factors research. On the other hand, most of the cost and benefit criteria are non-quantifiable, or at least very difficult to measure precisely. Consequently, one can only expect a preselection of "usable" language types from such a method. When confronted with the actual language selection problem, the user community must still consider costs, available hardware, compatibility with existing software systems, the type of "host" programming languages, and common use by different user types. In other words, the user may not always have a choice of what query language to use, or his or her choice may be limited to a few prespecified alternatives. It may often be possible, however, to construct more suitable specialized query language interfaces on top of existing ones via application programs in order to accommodate different user classes simultane-

ously. The proposed methodology is geared toward selecting those end-user query interfaces rather than the underlying programming languages.

However, the fact that the query language is only a part, although a central one, of the *total interface* between the user and the computer system should not be overlooked. For instance, one problem arises for programming users whose QL may be embedded in a host programming language. Such users require compatibility and smooth data transfer between the two languages. Lacroix and Pirotte [1980] differentiate among four types of embedding, which are listed here in ascending order of integration between host and query language: (1) subroutine calls, for example, DL/I [IBM 1975] and TOTAL-IQ [CINCOM Systems 1978]; (2) simple extension, for example, COBOL/DML [CODASYL 1971]; (3) procedural operators, for example, C/QUEL [Stonebraker et al. 1976] and APL/EDBS [Lochovsky and Tsichritzis 1977]; and (4) full integration, for example, PASCAL/R [Schmidt 1977] and ADAPLEX [Smith et al. 1981].

Having stated these limitations of the approach, we now present an overview of the method of selecting query languages. An outline of the proposed method is given in Figure 1.

The general problem of query language selection is characterized by a large and rapidly growing number of alternatives (query languages) and an even larger number of decision makers (potential users). The first step in the evaluation scheme is to develop an abstraction mechanism that generates a limited number of classes. To achieve this, well-structured taxonomies of both query languages and users are developed in Sections 2 and 3. A summary of recent human factors research in the area of query languages using these taxonomies is given in Section 4.

The next step in the evaluation scheme is the development of a hierarchy of evaluation criteria. The goals for developing good evaluation criteria are

- measuring all important costs and benefits of QL usage,
- discriminating clearly among both user and language types, and
- yielding simple criteria at the lowest level of the criteria hierarchy.

These goals are achieved by relating the evaluation criteria hierarchy to the dimensions of functional capabilities (benefit) and usability (cost) of the QL taxonomy (Section 5). The costs and benefits of a particular QL are not usually quantifiable. Roughly speaking, the "costs" are determined by the initial training effort (the user's investment) and the effort of continuing work with the language (the production costs). The "benefits" derive from language functions, such as result selection and composition, output presentation, and flexibility of interaction.

After establishing evaluation criteria, the method proceeds in Section 6 to apply them to both users (determine requirement profiles for each user type) and languages (characterize usability and functional capabilities of each language class). By matching user profiles with language profiles, the final step derives recommendations for the selection of query languages (Section 7). Note that it may be appropriate from a practical viewpoint to select several query language interfaces for several classes of users, because, on the one hand, many users with different needs will access the same DBMS and, on the other, many current DBMSs offer multiple query and/or programming languages that allow easy construction of a variety of interfaces. Therefore, the above analysis can be conducted for each major user group. The results of the final "optimization step" as presented in Section 7 are supported by results of human factors studies and by knowledge of technical restrictions, but can be only preliminary because of insufficient empirical research in the area.

In summary, the proposed preselection methodology includes three major processes, corresponding to the levels shown in Figure 1: (a) classification of users and languages, and establishment of evaluation criteria (the *technical* process, shown in the upper two levels of Figure 1); (b) evaluation of language types and determination of user requirements (the *evaluation* process in the third level); (c) matching user requirements with query language evaluations (the final *choice* process).

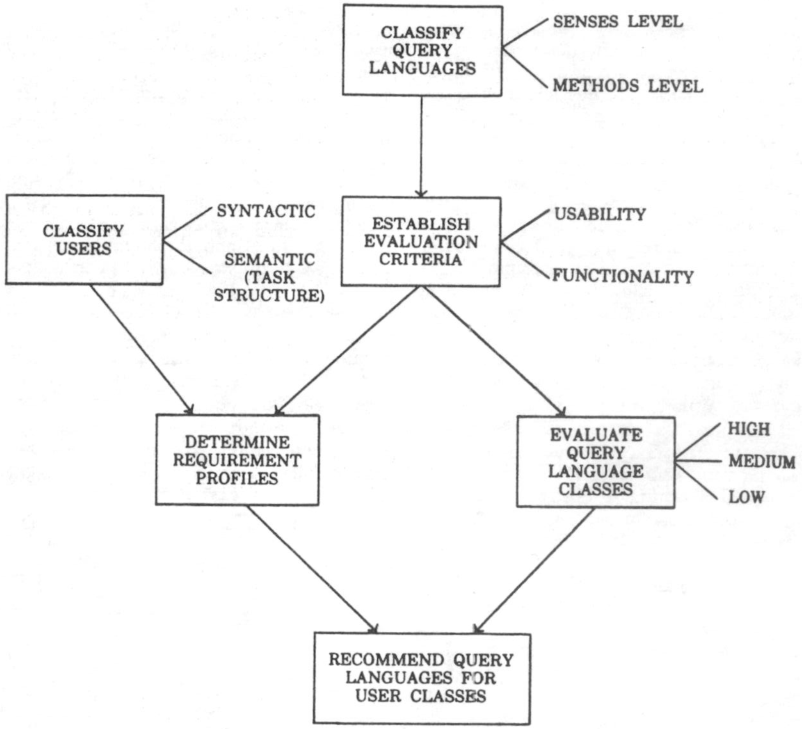

Figure 1. Evaluation methodology for query languages.

In a practical decision situation, additional studies must follow this preselection of language types. In particular, the hardware and software strategies of the organization (e.g., choice of manufacturer, hardware, programming languages, and software packages) must be taken into account. Furthermore, sunk costs of existing investments, or high financial costs of the "optimal" language may reduce the choices. These further steps are not specific to query languages and are therefore omitted here (see, e.g., King and Schrems [1978] for an overview of the uses of cost–benefit analysis in information systems).

The evaluation of language types centers around several tables. For generating and filling these tables a simple Delphi-like method was used, which also served as a validity check. The evaluation parameters in the tables (the column headings) were agreed upon after surveying the literature, extracting and generalizing important contributions, and reconciling differences for precise definitions. The tables were filled independently with the direct or indirect application of available human factors research results. In cases in which empirical data were not available, experience and common sense were relied upon. The common sense approach may be misleading [Moran 1981]; it is often cited as "armchair psychology." Therefore, in these cases the evaluations should be considered *testable hypotheses*.

2. TRENDS IN QUERY LANGUAGE DEVELOPMENT

The purpose of this section is to develop an understanding of some trends underlying QL development, and to apply this knowledge to the construction of an evaluation-oriented classification scheme for query languages.

2.1 A Model of Query Language Development

A review of existing QLs [Vassiliou and Jarke 1984] revealed that their development stems from two different sources: from the need for simple end user interfaces, and from theoretical conceptions of programming language or database research. The relationship between these areas is not yet fully understood but is the subject of increasing current research.

The development of QLs can be illustrated by a two-dimensional representation with the axes denoting the functional capabilities of a system and its usability. Roughly speaking, functional capabilities refer to what one can do with the system, whereas usability refers to the effort of actually doing it. Clearly, usability can only be valued with a specific user group in mind.

Figure 2 summarizes our QL development trend analysis. One group of QL developers, originating from the disciplines of programming languages and database theory, concentrates on the syntactic form and semantic meaning of database interactions. Languages developed by these disciplines are characterized by the full specification of an operation by a command or a sequence of commands. Starting from formal, mathematically oriented language concepts, this group of developers has moved to "English-like" keyword languages and finally restricted natural languages. The overall trend has been toward more "user friendliness" while preserving general functional capabilities.

The second group of language developers started from the ergonomic analysis of the interaction of computer-naive end users with computer systems. Whereas simple systems use function keys or line-by-line prompting, more complex systems involve the use of menu selection or graphical interaction with the database. These developments represent a trend toward more functional capabilities while remaining novice oriented.

These two query language development approaches have evolved fairly independently, with one serving the more and the other the less sophisticated user. The languages that have been developed are referred to as *previous generation QLs*. Recent developments, however, are leading to an overlap of the usage area for both language groups. The challenge is to integrate both approaches into functionally powerful query languages for relatively unsophisticated users, the *new generation QLs*.

The emergence of new generation query languages is not coincidental. Rather, it has followed (and, in terms of decreasing development costs, has been greatly assisted by) advances in many related areas:

(a) *Hardware Technology Developments*. Microprocessor technology and new devices, such as video disks, content addressable memories, holographic memories, and optical storage devices, allow for increased capabilities in storing and accessing data in several forms. Additionally, voice recognizers and synthesizers and eye-tracking and pointing devices lead to increased use of multimedia interactions.

(b) *Developments in Graphics and Artificial Intelligence*. The ability to display information in the most natural and dense form, that of an image, coupled with high-resolution display devices and the use of color, greatly contributes to the immediate comprehension of query output and the direct representation and manipulation of objects of interest [Foley and Van Dam 1982; Moorhead 1976; Newman and Sproull 1979]. Research in artificial intelligence—particularly in natural language processing, expert systems, and robotics—assists

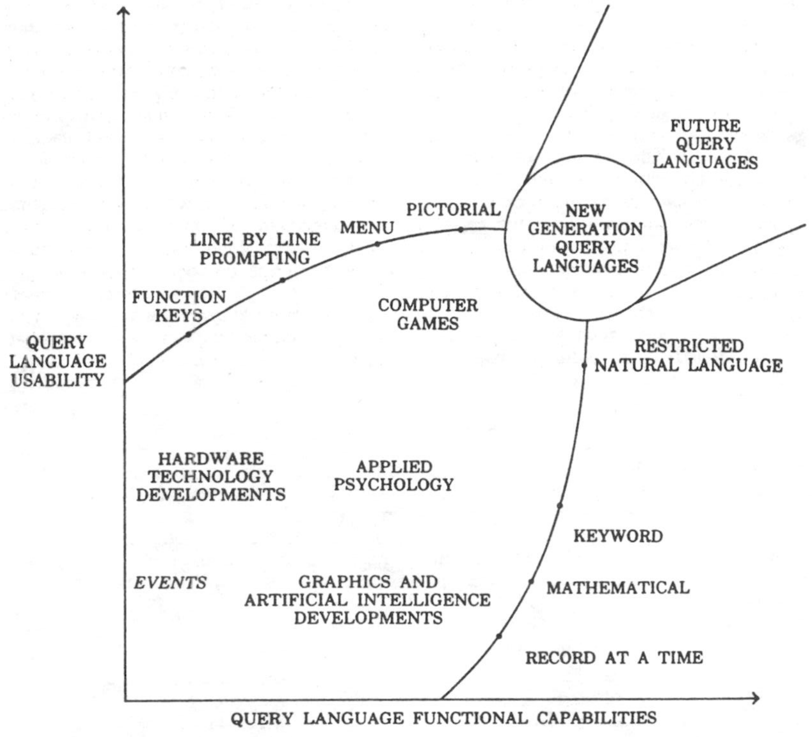

Figure 2. Query language development trends.

in query formulation and user feedback [Gable and Page 1980].

(c) *Developments in Applied Psychology and Related Sciences*. There is a new interest in "bridging the gap" between researchers concerned with the human factors aspects of query languages and their colleagues who are primarily concerned with the technology of query language design. Because of the tremendous possibilities for interaction with new generation query languages, the need for scientific methods to deal with the complex considerations of "convenience," "friendliness," and "effectiveness" of QLs becomes apparent. Several psychological studies of QLs have recently been reported [Brosey and Shneiderman 1978; Jarke et al. 1985; Reisner 1975, 1981; Shneiderman 1978; Small and Weldon 1983; Vassiliou et al. 1983; Welty and Stemple 1981], and considerable interest is evidenced by new professional meetings and special issues of publications focusing on human factors in computer systems [Moran 1981; Vassiliou 1984].

(d) *Success of Computer Games*. The pleasant and simple interaction of computer games has revolutionized the way in which people perceive interfaces to computer systems and helped remove many psychological barriers that people have when faced with a computer system. *Nat-*

urally, the success of computer games influ-*ences* designers of QLs [Malone 1982].

Future query language systems are expected to make increasingly sophisticated use of these developments.

2.2 Query Language Taxonomy

The analysis of QL development trends leads to a two-level taxonomy [Vassiliou and Jarke 1984] of query languages (Figure 3). The two levels are orthogonal, with the horizontal level focusing on the *methods* used in existing QLs and the vertical exploring the differences between previous and new generation languages. The latter is called the *senses* level because the use of more senses for the interaction is one of the main distinguishing factors between the two classes.[1]

2.2.1 *Previous Generation Query Languages: The Methods Level*

The previous generation query languages are classified in two groups (ergonomically oriented and programming-language-oriented languages) of four classes each: (1) function key, line-by-line prompting, menu selection, and graphic or pictorial and (2) record-at-a-time, mathematical, linear keyword, and restricted natural languages.

The first three language classes are typically exemplified by custom-made languages for specific applications.

The use of *function keys* is a limited but effective method of interaction for inexperienced users. By pressing a special key on the keyboard, a previously prepared transaction or report is processed.

Line-by-line prompting, also called parameterized interaction [Lehmann and Blaser 1979], is a simple system-driven dialogue. In the typical case, the user will be prompted to enter (line at a time) the name of the object of interest, a field name, a comparison value, etc. The query is built up from the user's responses.

A more sophisticated system-driven dialogue is *menu selection*. Here, users are required to point to their choice from a menu of options offered by the system. Menus are structured hierarchically; the choice of an option may cause the presentation of a new menu [Ellis and Nutt 1980].

In *graphic* or *pictorial* query languages the user can manipulate visual symbols to formulate queries. The entities and relationships in the database are represented by specific geometric shapes [McDonald 1975; Senko 1978; Tsichritzis 1976]. This group could be considered an early version of new generation languages that did not fully succeed because the necessary hardware and understanding of user needs were not yet available.

This concludes the discussion of ergonomically oriented languages. Next we discuss four language types evolving from the realm of programming language and database theory.

Conventional file management systems and many early database systems use a *record-at-a-time* logic for data retrieval. This approach is mentioned for completeness and because most QLs still use it for modification operations.

The introduction of the relational model [Codd 1970] led to set-oriented data retrieval. Some query languages use the precise notation of *mathematical* formalism for short and succinct expression of powerful operations. Examples include ALPHA [Codd 1971], PASCAL/R [Schmidt 1977], and ISBL [Todd 1976]. These languages are especially suited as target languages for very high-level user interfaces. Languages that use the position of the command operators and operands to convey meaning [Boyce et al. 1975] are also included in this group.

The majority of query languages available today fall into the category of *linear keyword*. These languages use statements that are similar to a programming language like COBOL but more English-like. The commands have a definite syntax, and only words from a specific reserved list can be used. Some typical examples of linear keyword languages are SQL [Astrahan et al. 1976] and QUEL [Stonebraker et al. 1976].

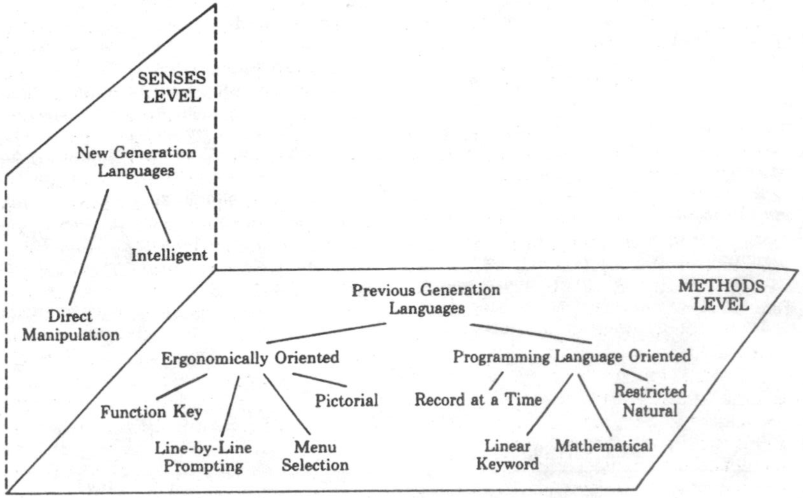

Figure 3. Query language taxonomy levels.

The *restricted natural language* mode has attracted interest in recent years. The intention is that the user can employ native natural language (e.g., English, German, French) for the interaction with the database. At least one such QL system is commercially available [Artificial Intelligence Corporation 1982; Harris 1977], and several others are under development in research laboratories [Bates and Bobrow 1983; Codd 1974; Hendrix et al. 1978; Hoeppner et al. 1983; Lehmann et al. 1978; Plath 1976; Thompson et al. 1983; Waltz 1978; Woods et al. 1972].

Some natural language systems will engage in a dialogue with the user to resolve any ambiguity in requests [Codd 1978]. Nevertheless, the natural language communication in all such state-of-the art QL systems is still far from close to person-to-person communication; this is the reason for using the prefix "restricted." Restrictions of current natural language query systems are at least twofold [Woods 1984]. On the one hand, most systems do not understand a sufficient range of complex grammatical constructs. On the other hand, all successful natural language systems thus far have been restricted to very narrow semantic domains of discourse and frequently do not degrade gracefully if the user exceeds their capabilities.

In summary, previous generation QLs provide only a restricted interactive environment. The user has a limited hardware interface (terminal, keyboard), and a relatively artificial conceptual model of formatted data and their organization. The user also has a formal query language syntax (the rules of the game), and uses experience and mastery of the system to accomplish a task (how to play and win the game).

The user's visual ability while interacting with the database is limited; the objects of interest are rarely displayed directly. Rather, they are represented by formatted text, thereby not giving the user any iconic clues (what the data look like) or spatial clues (where the data are) to help the querying process. Furthermore, the user does not fully employ his or her senses and cognition; for instance, query formulation does

[1] It is noted that the choice of communication media used for the interaction (keyboard, audio, etc.) is somewhat independent of the choice of methods (menu, function key, etc.). The taxonomy is designed to reflect this independence by placing the two levels orthogonally.

not use voice, touch, hearing, or gesture. Finally, the interaction is "static." A previous generation query system shows little or no "intelligence" in deducing answers from incomplete, yet obvious representations of user intentions. The user may still perform a task but with limited productivity and at the possible expense of more stress, less interest, and less pleasure.

2.2.2 *New Generation Query Languages: Advances at the Senses Level*

New generation QL systems attempt to incrementally utilize a person's instincts and senses. One subclass of these QL systems is referred to as "direct manipulation systems" [Shneiderman 1984]. Another subclass is that of "intelligent" QL systems, which use artificial intelligence techniques (e.g., knowledge bases) to bring man-machine interaction closer to communication between people.

Shneiderman [1984] identifies the basic features of *direct manipulation* QL systems: (a) object of interest visibility, (b) rapid reversible actions, and (c) replacement of command language syntax by direct manipulation of objects. The following examples indicate the directions taken in direct manipulation language development.

A prototype system based on the principle of spatial database management, called SDMS, has been developed and implemented at Computer Corporation of America [Herot 1981, 1984]. The advantages of this query system include the ability to locate objects of interest by browsing and zooming, and the use of icons, color, highlighting, and a natural arrangement of objects in the database.

The environment of Cedar [Brown et al. 1981] offers another example of a new generation QL. The language was developed at Xerox Palo Alto Research Center as a derivative of the Smalltalk [Goldberg and Robson 1981] family. It is object oriented and views data primarily through an entity-based browser with the help of dynamic windows. Window managers, in particular, are becoming standard in powerful small computer systems (often called workstations), and it is projected that windows will be a principal component in future query languages.

The Architecture Machine group at Massachusetts Institute of Technology [Schmandt and Hulteen 1982] is experimenting with a voice and gesture interactive system called "Put-That-There." The scenario calls for the database user to issue commands by intermixing voice, gesture (e.g., pointing), and eye positioning at the desirable object.

Query-by-Example (QBE) [Zloof 1977] is a commercially available direct manipulation QL that is based on the relational model of data. In contrast to keyword languages such as SQL, QBE makes relations directly visible as objects (table schemas) to be manipulated on the screen, and the user moves the cursor freely along the rows and columns of the tables. Query formulation is done through the use of examples, often considered a natural education process [Thomas and Gould 1975]. Several extensions of QBE have been proposed, for example, query by pictorial example (QBPE [Chang and Fu 1979]), and QBE-like systems have been developed in related areas such as office systems.

The other major class of new generation QLs is that of *intelligent* QL systems. Most of these QL systems address important aspects of the human–computer interactions such as (a) the (semi-) automatic refinement of queries based on feedback [Codd 1978], (b) the ability of the user to ask questions about the logical structure of the database and about the use of the language, (c) the ability of the system to explain query failures and understand (to some degree) the context of the interaction [Woods 1984], and (d) the automatic modification of queries to obtain meaningful results [Motro 1984]. The examples that follow illustrate these aspects.

Advisory Systems [Schank and Slade 1984] support a natural language user interface by the application of stored knowledge that is acquired by experience. For example, the story-understanding system IPP [Lebowitz 1980] acquires its experience by reading stories in its domain of knowledge. Additionally, such systems also try to infer the user's intentions [Carbonell 1979]. In these respects, advisory systems go beyond conventional natural language front ends and can therefore be called new generation. Learning by experience rather than relying on a given set of stored rules also distinguishes these systems from simpler deductive front ends to databases [Jarke and Vassiliou 1984] in which the knowledge has to be programmed.

RABBIT [Tou et al. 1982] is a QL system developed at Xerox Palo Alto Research Center that assists the user in formulating a query. The basic principle underlying RABBIT's design philosophy is "retrieval by reformulation," a paradigm derived from a psychological theory of long-term memory. Roughly speaking, RABBIT initially provides the partial description of an example instance from the database. The user manipulates this instance and its associated descriptors to incrementally construct the next iteration of the query. The mechanism used in RABBIT is termed "perspective" for the query and is a way of viewing objects while highlighting only certain attributes. In formulating the next query iteration, the user works on a perspective for the query and a database instance. The user may modify the query descriptors by specifying "required" attributes, "prohibited" attributes, specializations of the given descriptors, etc. At any time during the interaction, the user may ask for descriptions of descriptors (metadata).

Although slightly outside the boundaries of query language interfaces, languages for the conceptual design of data-intensive information systems should also be briefly mentioned as examples of intelligent database languages using knowledge representation mechanisms. Users of such languages are programmers rather than novice end users. An early language of this type is TAXIS [Mylopoulos et al. 1980], which, in order to support a paradigm of database software development by specialization of data and procedures (as opposed to stepwise decomposition used in structured programming), relies heavily on the inheritance mechanisms provided by generalization hierarchies of data and transaction structures.

A more recent design language, Galileo [Albano et al. 1985], also offers type inheritance but, in addition, provides an interactive prototyping environment for database applications, which is integrated with a generator for application-dependent form-based query language interfaces. In contrast, the language CML [Borgida et al. 1986] consciously avoids being close to a system implementation but instead extends the TAXIS ideas by modeling real-world concepts such as objects, time, or precision of knowledge representation. This approach recognizes the need for multiple interfaces for requirements modeling, database design, and database usage, and tries to control the interaction among these languages via a knowledge-based system [Jarke et al. 1986b].

In Table 1 some features of the new generation languages described in the above examples are compared with those of the previous generation languages discussed in the preceding section. The table demonstrates that the sparse set of input and output media available in previous generation QLs is substantially expanded in the new interface types and that these expanded media also result in a few new method types (e.g., browsing) that are not meaningful without the additional media. The other major difference between the two generations of QLs, the intelligence acquired from an underlying deduction system, is less visible from the external interface features presented in the table, but no less important. A more detailed comparison and evaluation of both language types is given by Vassiliou and Jarke [1984].

A word of caution is needed. New generation QLs provide a new burden of responsibility for the application developer. For instance, the appropriate icons to represent objects, the use of color and highlighting, and the "natural" arrangements of the objects in the database greatly influence the success of the system. Application designers may need additional skills, which are not found in the traditional systems analysis education.

3. USER CLASSIFICATION

Many criteria for classifying users have been proposed [Codd 1974; Cuff 1980; Lehmann and Blaser 1979; Shneiderman

Table 1. Characteristics of Previous and New Generation Languages

Query formulation		Output presentation	
Medium	Method	Medium	Method
Previous generation query languages			
Keyboard	Function key use	Screen	Lists
Function keys	Line-by-line prompting	Printer	Tables
			Forms
			Text
	Menu selection		
	Graphic		
	Keyword command		
	Restricted natural language		
New generation query languages			
Keyboard	Keyword command	Screen	Lists
Function keys	Menus	Voice synthesizer	Tables
Picking devices	Windows	Color graphics	Forms
Touch screens	Gesture	Video display	Templates
Voice recognizers	Eye positioning	Printer	Icons
Gesture tracking devices	Zooming	Plotter	Color
Eye-positioning tracking	Voice		Highlighting
	Browsing		Images
	By example		Sounds (voice)
	Touch		Arrangement
	Deduction		Text

1980; Yormark 1977; Zloof 1978]. Even though the classifications have several common points, their relationships have hardly been studied. Shneiderman [1980] uses a two-dimensional scheme classified by syntactic and semantic knowledge. The analysis in this section is related to this idea but includes other criteria that have been proposed elsewhere. The criteria fall into four classifications: familiarity with programming concepts, frequency of query language usage, knowledge about the application, and range of operations required.

Familiarity with programming concepts is a more general concept than the often-cited distinction between programmers and nonprogrammers, which may lead to different and at times inconsistent interpretations [Cuff 1980; Greenblatt and Waxman 1978; Moran 1981]. "High" familiarity with programming concepts characterizes a user who is not afraid of computers and has acquired logical or algorithmic problem-solving abilities.

The dimension *frequency of system usage* [Lehmann and Blaser 1979] is one of the most important dimensions in that many of the other dimensions appearing in the literature are derived from it. Frequency of use directly determines the acceptable amount of training; the more one wants to use the system, the greater an initial investment is justified. The amount of training in turn determines the typical skill level after the training period.

In the authors' opinion the transient skill levels during the QL training phase are of interest only if the frequency of use is so low that each use of the system requires relearning or if the turnover of users is extremely high. Thus the distinction between "novice" user (task: learning) and "expert" (task: routine skill) made in Moran [1981] and Schneider [1984] can be reduced to the frequency of usage dimension. We therefore use the term "novice" not only for new users but also for other infrequent users with little programming knowledge.

In combination, these two dimensions determine the user's ability to technically interact with the system, or "syntactic knowledge" [Shneiderman 1980]. The relationship between the two basic dimensions and the level of *interaction skill* is shown in Table 2a. Three user types are derived. Note that the "skilled" user is one who has a "high" score for either of the two dimensions and a "low" score for the other.

Table 2a. User Types: Interaction Capability (Syntactic Knowledge) as a Function of Familiarity with Programming Concepts and Frequency of System Usage

Frequency of system usage	Familiarity with programming concepts: Low	High
Low	Low (novice user)	Medium (skilled user)
High	Medium (skilled user)	High (professional user)

Table 2b. User Types: Task Structure (Semantic Knowledge) as a Function of Application Knowledge and Range of Operations

Range of operations	Application knowledge: General	Detailed
Narrow	Casual user	Clerical user
Broad	Managerial user	Application specialist user

The semantic dimensions are concerned with application knowledge and range of operations of the user. In the database context, *application knowledge* refers to the precision of the user's conceptual model about the structure and contents of the database. The other dimension, *range of operations*, describes how many different types of queries the user requires. Together, these two dimensions give a picture of the *task structure* (semantic knowledge) of the user (Table 2b). By combining high or low scores on the two underlying dimenions, four user types are derived from this classification: (1) casual users who approach the system without real interest to achieve a narrowly defined set of functions, (2) clerical users who perform a narrowly defined set of tasks but have detailed knowledge of their application, (3) managerial users who have little interest in details but require broad functionality, and (4) application specialists who have excellent application knowledge and need to fulfill a fairly broad range of tasks. In Section 7, the requirements of these user types are outlined in more detail.

4. HUMAN FACTORS RESEARCH IN QUERY LANGUAGES

One of the most important sources of information for determining the users' QL requirements are human factors experiments. Below, recent human factors research relevant in this context is briefly reviewed. The major results are displayed in Table 3. It is not the intention of this paper to critique these experiments (see, e.g., Reisner [1981] and Shneiderman [1980]). The reader should note, however, that many studies have not been "controlled" experiments that deliver statistically sound and generalizable results.

Since the now classic experiments of Reisner et al. [1975] and Thomas and Gould [1975], a number of laboratory studies and field experiments of human factors in use of query languages have been reported. For the purposes of this paper, these studies are classified either as comparisons between languages that use different methods (as defined in Section 2.2) or as studies of usability of certain features within a language type.

The first group of experiments consists of comparisons of keyword versus new generation languages [Greenblatt and Waxman 1978; Thomas and Gould 1975], keyword versus positional languages [Reisner et al. 1975], and keyword versus restricted natural languages [Jarke et al. 1985; Shneiderman 1978; Small and Weldon 1983; Vassiliou et al. 1983]. The reader is cautioned, however, that the majority of these experiments were not directed toward a general comparison of methods but rather toward specific comparisons of languages.

The second group of experiments concentrates on the usability of certain languages or language features within a given method. One focal point of laboratory experiments has been the keyword language SQL [Reisner 1977; Thomas 1976; Welty 1979; Welty and Stemple 1981], and another has been the influence of conceptual data models [Brosey and Shneiderman 1978; Lochovsky 1976; Lochovsky and Tsichritzis 1977]. In addition, there have been a number of field studies concerned with the usability of restricted natural languages

Table 3. Human Factors Experiments with Query Languages and Features

Reference	Type of experiment	User classes	Research question	Tasks and tests	Major results
Greenblatt and Waxman [1978]	Laboratory	Novices	Learnability of QBE vs. SQL	Composition	Formulation in QBE is faster
Jarke et al. [1985]	Field	Novice application specialists (advisors)	Productivity of natural language vs. SQL	Problem-solving Query acceptance	SQL has higher success rate; natural language less effort to use
Reisner et al. [1975]	Laboratory	Programmers Nonprogrammers	Learnability of SQL vs. SQUARE	Composition	Programmers are superior; SQL is better than SQUARE for beginners
Shneiderman [1978]	Laboratory	Novices	Productivity of natural vs. SQL subset	Query generation	Natural language user generated more invalid queries
Small and Weldon [1983]	Laboratory with simulated processor	Novices	Productivity of natural vs. SQL subset	Interactive problem solving	Formulation in SQL is faster
Turner et al. [1984]	Laboratory	Novice application specialists (advisors)	Learnability of natural language vs. SQL	Composition	Natural language and SQL about equal in error rates
Vassilliou et al. [1983]	Laboratory	Novices	Learnability of natural language vs. SQL	Composition	Natural language less verbose; manageable language subset used
Brosey and Shneiderman [1978]	Laboratory	Programmers Nonprogrammers	Relational vs. hierarchical model	Comprehension Memorization Problem solving	Programmers are better on relations than nonprogrammers; hierarchies are good for natural tree applications
Gould and Ascher [1975]	Laboratory	Novices	Query formulation process (IQF)	Composition	Influence of task complexity and ambiguity
Lochovsky and Tsichritzis [1977]	Laboratory	Programmers Nonprogrammers	Comparison of three data models embedded in APL	Composition Debugging	Programmers are superior; relational model best for nonprogrammers
Reisner [1977]	Laboratory	Programmers Nonprogrammers	Feature analysis of SQL	Composition	Recommended layered structure for novice and skilled user
Thomas [1976]	Laboratory	Novices	Use of quantifiers	Various noncomputerized tasks	Universal quantification is difficult for novices
Thomas and Gould [1975]	Laboratory	Novices	Learnability of QBE	Composition	67 percent successful after short training
Welty and Stemple [1981]	Laboratory	Programmers Nonprogrammers	Learnability of TABLET vs. SQL (procedurality)	Composition Retention	Programmers are superior; TABLET is better for hard queries
Damerau [1979]	Field	Novice application specialists	Productivity of TQA/REQUEST	Problem solving	65 percent accepted queries
Harris [1977]	Field	Application specialists	Productivity of ROBOT	Problem solving	80–90 percent accepted queries
Krause [1982]	Field	Skilled application specialists	Productivity of USL	Problem solving	More than 90 percent successful after adaptation
Lehmann et al. [1978]	Field	Skilled application specialists	Functions of USL	Problem solving	Statistics on use of various functions
Woods et al. [1972]	Field	Novice application specialists	Usability of LSNLIS (LUNAR)	Problem solving	Good success rate for application-specific system

in various settings [Damerau 1979; Harris 1977; Jarke et al. 1985; Krause 1982; Lehmann et al. 1978; Woods et al. 1972].

As concerns user types, most studies in the syntactic knowledge (interaction capability) dimension focus on the novice user. Virtually all laboratory experiments are learning and retention tests and therefore apply mainly to infrequent users. In addition, most experimenters explicitly chose subjects with little knowledge of programming concepts, often contrasting them with another group having more programming background. All experiments of this design show better performance for users with programming background [Reisner et al. 1975; Lochovsky and Tsichritzis 1977; Turner et al. 1984; Welty and Stemple 1981]. Some of the results of these experiments indicate that novices

- have difficulties with explicit quantification [Thomas 1976],
- perform better with a relational model of data than with a network or hierarchy when using a keyword language embedded in APL [Lochovsky and Tsichritzis 1977],
- learn a new generation language (QBE) faster than a keyword language (SQL) of similar power [Greenblatt and Waxman 1978; Thomas and Gould 1975],
- perform better on hard queries with a more procedural approach (TABLET versus SQL) for problem solving than a keyword language [Welty and Stemple 1981],
- can be offered a (closed) subset in a layered language [Reisner 1977].

The semantic classification of experimental subjects is less clear. Although the subjects of most laboratory experiments are students, whose semantic knowledge is difficult to establish, the thrust of the field experiments is more often toward the application specialist than the managerial user [Damerau 1979; Harris 1979; Jarke et al. 1985; Krause 1980].

The goal of this paper is to suggest classes of languages for known user types. The above survey demonstrates that the existing human factors research in query languages is insufficient for the solution of the pressing problem of language selection. Experiments have been criticized for sloppiness, very few repetitions, and limited coverage of issues. Most important for the purposes of this paper, little emphasis has been given to the consideration of language methods (classes) in connection with user types.

5. EVALUATION CRITERIA FOR QUERY LANGUAGES

The proposed methodology for QL selection (depicted in Figure 1; see Section 1) proceeds with the development of evaluation criteria for QLs. Like the QL taxonomy, the evaluation scheme is related to the trend analysis of QL development in that it relies on the same two dimensions: usability and functional capabilities. These basic dimenions must be refined further, however, in order to yield practical evaluation criteria.

The *functional capabilities* determine to a large degree the value of the information ("benefit") that one can get from the system. In a QL context, this can be described by the language power and the alternatives that the user has for output presentation. On the other hand, the *usability* of a system (the effort or "cost" to work with it) is mainly related to the process of query formulation.

Figure 4 is an overview of a criterion hierarchy derived from these considerations. All criteria are described below.

5.1 Usability Criteria

Query formulation effort describes the overall effort of the user to work with the system. The total effort is the sum of the initial training effort to learn the QL system and the repeated efforts to perform productive tasks on it. The relative importance of these two parts is determined by the frequency of system usage, in the sense that both repeated training may be necessary for infrequent users and training time accounts for a large percentage of overall effort for that group.

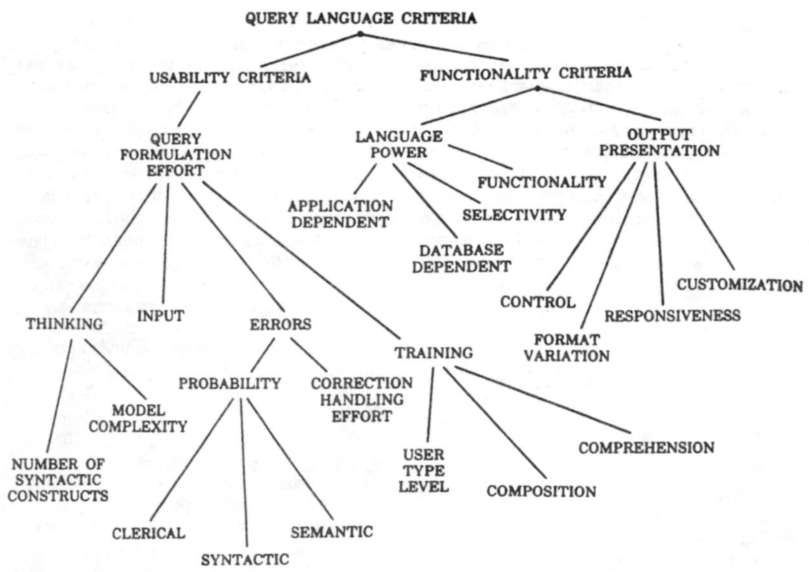

Figure 4. Query language evaluation parameters.

The analysis of a language's suitability for performing tasks is based on the simple query language interaction model presented in Figure 5 [Stohr et al. 1982]. It can be seen that productivity is determined by think time, input effort, and error handling time. Although this model captures the effort of query formulation fairly well, it does not completely reflect the overall productivity in performing a task; productivity also improves through increased functional capabilities that reduce the number of queries necessary for solving a problem.

Thinking effort includes the requirement that users remember *syntactic constructs.* Issues that influence this factor are command names and abbreviations, the number of different constructs, and the syntax for the composition of complex commands [Schneider 1984]. In addition to these static properties of a query language interface, the dynamics of how it allows a user to formulate a query also influences thinking effort. Reisner [1981] introduces the notion of a "model of the process of query writing" that users develop. This refers to the strategy that the user adopts to express the request. The *complexity* of this model is also part of the thinking effort.

Input refers to the amount of clerical effort required to express the request. When the interaction is via a keyboard, this may be measured by the number of keystrokes. When pointing devices are used, a good measure of input is the number of pointed objects [Lochovsky and Tsichritzis 1984].

Major system usage costs are induced by the efforts to detect and handle *errors.* The overall effort can be described as a combination of the error *probability* and the *correction handling effort* required for detecting and correcting an error that has occurred. As can be seen from Figure 5, three main types of error may occur during query formulation: *clerical* (e.g., typos), *syntactic* (not following the correct syntax of the language), and *semantic* (formulation of a syntactically correct query that does not solve the task at hand).

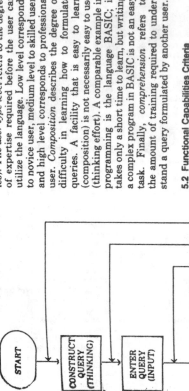

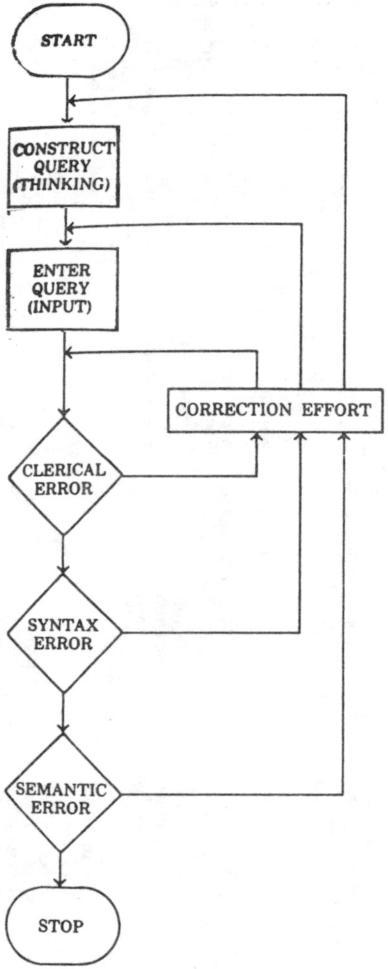

Figure 5. Query language interaction model.

The amount of *training* necessary for the user to perform useful tasks is a very important consideration in language selection. Training depends upon who learns (*user type level*) and what has to be learned (*composition* and *comprehension* of queries). The *user type level* refers to the degree of expertise required before the user can utilize the language. Low level corresponds to novice user, medium level to skilled user, and high level corresponds to professional user. *Composition* describes the degree of difficulty in learning how to formulate queries. A facility that is easy to learn (composition) is not necessarily easy to use (thinking effort). A comparable example in programming is the language BASIC; it takes only a short time to learn, but writing a complex program in BASIC is not an easy task. Finally, *comprehension* refers to the amount of training required to understand a query formulated by another user.

5.2 Functional Capabilities Criteria

Besides usability, there are two other criteria groups for query language evaluation: language power (how much a user can do with the language) and the alternatives that the user has for output presentation. These criteria are concerned with input to and output from the system. The first functional capability parameter for query language evaluation is *language power,* which can be described in terms of four parameters: application dependency, database dependency, selectivity, and functionality.

Application dependency is the sensitivity of a QL to the application domain: the degree to which the language has to change when it is used in a different application. Application dependency is common in many of the ergonomically oriented QLs, which optimize the user interface for specific narrow tasks. For instance, the keywords or labels on function keys of a query language interface may depend on the application, as may the sequencing and structural composition of menus.

Similarly, *database dependency* refers to the degree of language dependence on the underlying database model (e.g., network, relational). In early discussions [Codd 1970], network models were associated with navigational query languages, whereas the relational model offered nonprocedural access descriptions. Today, database dependency is a question of specific DBMS products, rather than one of principal limitations of the underlying database model.

In principle, the user interface design decision can be largely decoupled from the choice of a database model. For example, Codd [1972] and Pirotte [1978] have shown that the various forms of relational query languages (mapping, tuple and domain relational calculus, relational algebra) are essentially equivalent in expressive power. There are also optimizing translation algorithms that allow the installation of efficient navigational interfaces on relational systems [Katz and Wong 1982], and of relational query languages on network databases [Rosenthal and Reiner 1985]; see Larson [1983] for an overview. However, a specific DBMS product may not offer these facilities and thus introduce database dependency for the user.

For the other two criteria (functionality and selectivity), database theory has developed more formal methods of evaluation based on complexity theory. *Functionality* broadly refers to the range of different tasks for which the language can be used (e.g., queries, browsing, zooming, report generation, inserts, deletes, updates).

Selectivity is the availability of operators that allow the user to specify as precisely as possible what data he or she wishes to retrieve. Codd [1972] introduced the notion of relational completeness that has long served as a yardstick of selectivity. A QL is called relationally complete if it allows the expression of any query that is expressible in a single predicate of the so-called relational calculus, a query language based on first-order logic.

Zloof [1977] and Aho and Ullman [1979] were among the first to point out simple queries that were not expressible in relationally complete languages, and to propose language extensions. For example, the "transitive closure" of a relation cannot be expressed in relational calculus; among other things, this prevents answering queries such as "Is there a train connection between two cities?" from a database that contains the direct train connections. Chandra and Harel [1982] developed a complete hierarchy of QL expressiveness (Table 4). The levels below (appearing "before" in the table) relational completeness have been used to identify special cases in

Table 4. Query Language Expressiveness Hierarchy

Propositional calculus
Tableau queries
Conjunctive queries
Existential queries
FIRST-ORDER QUERIES (RELATIONALLY COMPLETE)
Fixpoint queries (Horn clause queries)
Full first-order logic and disjunction/negation
Second-order queries
Computable queries (full programming capabilities)

query optimization [Jarke and Koch 1984] or to offer simple query interfaces, for example, in microcomputer DBMSs.

Queries at the level of *propositional calculus* only allow access to a single file. Connections among different files have to be implemented in a programming language environment, or established manually by the user. *Tableau queries* are those that can be represented in a special tabular representation called tableaus [Aho et al. 1979]; owing to their mathematical properties (see below), they have caused much interest in the database theory community and have laid the foundation for "universal relation databases," which are characterized by the property that users need not know the partitioning of a database into its different relations. Instead, the user interface of a universal relation database is a single large table from which query results are constructed by projection on certain columns.

Conjunctive queries inherit their name from the fact that no "or's" are allowed in their specification. For example, the query "Give me the managers of age less than 35 and salary above $80,000" is conjunctive, whereas "List the students older than 30 and the Ph.D. students" is disjunctive; it is equivalent to the query "List all students whose age is greater than 30 or whose status is Ph.D. student." *Existential queries* allow disjunctive query conditions but require that the query be at least decomposable into a set of conjunctive queries. First-order (or, equivalently, relationally complete) queries that are not existential include those that contain universal quantification in their query condition, for example, "List the students who have taken *all* the courses in the database area."

The levels beyond relational completeness in Table 4 only recently have received the attention of language designers. For example, the *fixpoint* query level is exactly the level of queries available in Horn clause-based deductive query languages, such as Prolog [Clocksin and Mellish 1982]. Beyond this level, *full first-order logic* allows the representation of incomplete knowledge [Levesque 1984]; this permits the statement and querying of disjunctive information, such as "John is in New York or in Toronto" (but it is unknown in which of the two). *Second-order logic* allows queries about the relations, such as "Which tables contain information about John?" Although no QL offers this capability in general, many systems allow access to stored metadata that help to answer certain queries of this type.

Finally, the set of *computable queries* would provide full programming language capabilities *in the QL* and thus constitute the upper bound on selectivity. For complexity reasons, existing database systems can offer these capabilities at best in their host programming environment. Only a small set of efficiently computable functions has traditionally been built into QLs (e.g., count, sum, average). Broader capabilities (in which much of the responsibility for efficiency rests with the user) are provided by the so-called fourth generation languages, in which high-level programming language operators are offered the opportunity to execute more general functions on database data.

The other major functionality criterion for QL comparison is the quality of *output presentation*. This is subdivided into *control* (ability of the user to control the pace at which the output is presented), *format variation* (flexibility in selecting an output presentation format and/or redirecting output to alternative devices), *responsiveness* (how rapid and consistent the system's response is), and *customization* (the ability to have the best suited output for the application).

Again, these parameters tend to depend on the system rather than the language type. For example, a query compilation approach will usually lead to faster response times and better customization than a purely interpretive approach, especially in the case of repetitive query patterns, where query processing can be supported by access paths. However, the philosophy behind certain language types leads to a more natural adaptation of an appropriate output feature than others.

Moreover, it turns out that the expressiveness hierarchy in Table 4 is closely related to a hierarchy of query complexity [Chandra and Harel 1982]. Query complexity imposes a worst-case lower bound on responsiveness. It can be measured as data complexity (a function of operand size) or as expression complexity (a function of query length). Vardi [1982] found that expression complexity in query languages tends to be one exponential higher than data complexity.

Immerman [1982] has provided a theoretical underpinning to the use of Horn clause query languages (such as Prolog) by proving that the fixpoint queries can be computed with polynomial data complexity. Similarly, a subclass of tableau queries called simple queries can be optimally simplified in polynomial time [Aho et al. 1979], and a subclass of conjunctive queries called tree queries [Goodman and Shmueli 1982] can be processed with polynomial expression complexity.

Beyond these boundaries, execution times—in the worst case—may grow exponentially with the size of the expression or even of the database. Moreover, the higher levels of queries and data/knowledge representation (e.g., full first-order logic), which use theorem proving rather than finite search for question answering, run into decidability problems that may prevent the construction of a complete answer altogether [Brachman and Levesque 1984].

6. EVALUATION OF LANGUAGE CLASSES AND USER REQUIREMENTS

The results of applying the 18 evaluation criteria at the leaves of the hierarchy to the 9 language classes defined in Section 1 are shown in Table 5. In addition, the 12 user classes that result by combining interaction

Table 5. Evaluation of Query Languages at the Methods Level

QL parameters — Query formulation

QL types	Thinking: No. of syntactic constructs	Thinking: Model complexity	Input	Errors: Probability of error: Clerical	Errors: Probability of error: Syntactic	Errors: Probability of error: Semantic	Errors: Correction handling effort	Training: User type level	Training: Composition	Training: Comprehension
Function-key use	Low	Low	Low	Low	Low	Low	Low	Low	Low	Medium
Menu selection	Low	Low	Low	Low	Low	Low-medium	Low-medium	Low-medium	Low	Low-medium
Line-by-line prompting	Medium	Low	Medium	Medium	Low	Low-medium	High	Medium	Medium	Medium
Graphic or pictorial	Medium	Medium	Low-medium	Low-medium	Medium	Low-medium	Medium	Medium	Medium-high	Medium
Restricted natural	Low-high	Low	High	High	Low-medium	High	High	Low-medium	Low-medium	Low
Linear keyword	High	Medium-high	High	High	Medium-high	Medium-high	High	Medium	Medium-high	Low-medium
Positional keyword	High	High	Medium-high	High	High	High	High	Medium-high	High	Medium-high
Mathematical	High	High	Medium	High	High	Medium-high	High	High	Medium-high	Medium-high
New generation	Medium	Low	Medium	Low-medium	Low-medium	Medium-high	Medium-high	Low-medium	Low	N/A
Optimal	Low	Low	Low	Low	Low	Low	Low	N/A	Low	Low

QL Parameters — Language power and Output presentation

QL types	Language power: Application dependence	Language power: Database dependence	Language power: Selectivity	Language power: Functionality	Output presentation: Control	Output presentation: Format variation	Output presentation: Responsiveness	Output presentation: Customization	Examples
Function-key use	High	Low	Low	Low	Low	Low	Low-medium	High	Application dependent
Menu selection	High	Low	Low-medium	Low-medium	Low-medium	Low	High	High	Application dependent
Line-by-line prompting	High	Low	Low-medium	Low-high	Low	Low	Medium-high	Medium-high	Application dependent
Graphic or pictorial	Low	Medium-high	Medium-high	Low-medium	Low-high	Low-medium	High	Medium	LSL, CUPID
Restricted natural	Medium-high	Low	Medium	Medium	Low	Low	Low	Medium	INTELLECT, USL, RENDEZVOUS
Linear keyword	Low	High	High	High	Medium	Medium	Low	Low-medium	SQL, DL/I, NOMAD
Positional keyword	Low	High	High	High	Medium	Medium	Low	Low	SQUARE
Mathematical	Low	High	High	High	Medium	Medium	Low	Low	ISBL, PASCAL/R
New generation	Medium	Low	Medium-high	Low-medium	High	High	High	High	SDMS, VGQF, QBE
Optimal	Low	Low	High	High	High	High	High	High	

capability and task structure are related to the evaluation criteria in Table 6 (see Section 6.2). In filling the table entries for usability criteria, empirical data (if available) from the human factors area were used. Functionality criteria evaluations were based on technical restrictions of language classes.

As can be seen, the tables use a simple three-point scale (low, medium, high) for all criteria. A few finer distinctions are made by using intermediate values (low-medium, medium-high). There are several reasons to restrict oneself to such a simple structure. On the one hand, a finer scale would be problematic for several usability criteria in which empirical data for supporting the entries are missing or can only be applied indirectly.

On the other hand, any scoring method like this requires a uniform representation of criterion values. Therefore, it seemed wise to choose a simple, uniform range of values for all criteria, even though more detailed information from empirical data or formal analysis was available for some of them.

6.1 Query Language Evaluation

Technical language specifications determine the values in Table 5 that relate to functional capabilities. In that table, the row labeled "optimal" indicates which values of a criterion are considered "good" and which are considered "bad" from the user's viewpoint. For the usability criteria, an effort was made to apply results from human factors research. The application of such results was mostly indirect. For instance, Thomas and Gould [1975] indicate short training requirements for the composition of correct QBE queries. A generalization of this result places a "low" score for composition in new generation QLs (the class in which QBE belongs).

There are inherent dangers of misinterpretation, overgeneralization, and reliance on experiments of dubious validity. Reiterating, these values should be taken as testable hypotheses in a homogeneous framework where the evaluation variables have been set out carefully.

The entries in Table 5 give a more structured and precise description of the language classes introduced in Section 2. For example, it can be seen that the main advantages of new generation query languages are in the areas of output presentation, training, and query formulation. On the other hand, mathematical languages are strong in language power but awkward in query formulation and often awkward in output presentation. Thus these two language groups can be envisioned as complementary tools for different tasks.

6.2 Determining User Requirement Profiles

An abstraction of the evaluation criteria to the basic categories of usability and functionality is made in Table 6. At this level of abstraction, the user requirements are mostly inherent in the definition of a user class as given in this paper. For example, the range of operations determines the necessary selectivity and functionality. Similarly, the criterion "user type level" determines the prerequisites for working with a language directly in terms of interaction capability.

In other cases, the relationship is more indirect but still fairly obvious. For instance, users with only a general application knowledge will require a high quality of output presentation to understand the answers they get from the database.

A third possibility is that the user classification only determines the relative importance of evaluation criteria. The previously cited trade-off between training effort and day-to-day productivity is such a case.

7. RECOMMENDATIONS OF QUERY LANGUAGES FOR USER TYPES

In this section, languages are related to user types, and preliminary recommendations for allocating language classes to user types are offered. In order to improve readability, highlights of the users' minimal requirement profiles are discussed together with recommendations. A summary of these recommendations is given in Table 7, which is a combination of Tables 5 and 6. As an illustration of its development, consider the entries of Table 7 corresponding to the novice–casual user. From Table 6, the minimal requirements of this user class are determined. A consultation of Table 5 shows that these requirements are met in varying degrees, by menu selection, line-by-line prompting, new generation QLs, and function keys; these constitute the entries in Table 7.

The results are discussed for each user type and then summarized by language class.

The *casual user* is characterized as having only a general idea about structure and content of the database; the range of needed operations is also limited so that he or she may not require the full power of a query language [Reisner 1977]. Typical examples are the users of external databases like videotex [Lochovsky and Tsichritzis 1984] or electronic funds transfer systems. Most casual users are not familiar with programming concepts (which is why the lower left field of Table 7 is nearly empty), but their frequency of system usage may vary. The system must guide the infrequent casual user (novice) by offering simple menu choices or line-by-line prompts, whereas

Table 6. Minimal Requirements by User Type

User type		Evaluation criteria		
Interaction capability	Task structure	Query formulation effort	Language power	Output presentation
Novice (low)	Casual	Low-medium	Low	Low-medium
	Managerial	Low	Medium	Medium-high
	Clerical	Low-medium	Low-medium	Low-medium
	Application specialist	Medium	Medium	Medium-high
Skilled (medium)	Casual	Low-medium	Low-medium	Low-medium
	Managerial	Low	Medium-high	High
	Clerical	Low-medium	Low-medium	Medium
	Application specialist	Low-medium	High	Medium-high
Professional (high)	Casual	Medium	Low-medium	Low-medium
	Managerial	Low-medium	Medium-high	High
	Clerical	Medium-high	High	Medium
	Application specialist	Medium-high	High	High

Table 7. Relating Language Methods to User Types

Interaction capability (syntactic knowledge)	Task structure (semantic knowledge)			
	Casual user	Managerial user	Clerical user	Application specialist user
Novice user	Menu selection Line-by-line prompting New generation Function keys	New generation Menu selection Restricted natural	Function keys Menu selection Line-by-line prompting	New generation Restricted natural Menu selection Keyword
Skilled user	Menu selection New generation Function keys Line-by-line prompting	New generation Restricted natural Menu selection	Menu selection Keyword Function keys Graphic/pictorial	Keyword Restricted natural Graphic/pictorial
Professional user	(New generation)	Keyword Graphic/pictorial New generation Restricted natural	Mathematical Keyword Function keys	Mathematical New generation Keyword Positional

the more frequent user (skilled) may wish to adopt a more active role (new generation languages) or at least a faster sequence of actions (use of function keys).

The *managerial user* is probably the most demanding user type. Unwilling to "waste" time to acquire detailed knowledge of the database, he or she still wants to perform quite complicated and varied tasks, for example, generating summary information. Today, menu systems can be used for simple tasks, and intermediaries must handle complex ones unless the manager has programming background and uses the database routinely (professional managerial user).

A more direct path to the database is the great promise of advanced language concepts such as new generation QLs or restricted natural language. Studies of the use of natural language show, however, that novice users may have problems with the syntactic restrictions of the language [Jarke et al. 1985] or the semantic restrictions of the database [Brosey and Shneiderman 1978]. For this reason, restricted natural language is positioned in third place for novice managerial users. Some field studies indicate that more frequent users of this type can adapt to the limitations [Krause 1980].

Similar to the casual user, the *clerical user* (or parametric user) has to perform only a limited number of operations on the database, but may have detailed knowledge about the available data. The use of function keys or menus with little system guidance improves productivity for day-to-day tasks.

For the more computer-oriented or more frequent clerical user, keyword languages or even the more concise mathematical languages allow for powerful operations. Many studies exist for this user type in general (e.g., Embley and Nagy [1981]), but little has been published on tailoring query languages to clerical users.

As the range of operations becomes broader, the clerical user turns into an *application specialist user* (the synonymous "professional user" is assigned to another category). This type of user may have detailed knowledge of the database and requires multiple operations (data analysis, decision support) but often lacks programming background.

Whereas conventional programming and query languages mainly support the professional application specialist (frequent user with programming background), much of the recent research focuses on novice and skilled application specialists, who are expected to become a dominant group of computer users [Shneiderman 1984].

Studies of the use of natural language interfaces thus far have been inconclusive. The authors hypothesize that natural language is competitive if restricted to a narrow domain [Woods et al. 1972], relatively simple or tailored database structures [Damerau 1979; Harris 1977], or frequent users who adapt to the limitations [Krause 1982; Lehmann et al. 1978]. It appears that more novice users have trouble if their knowledge of the data is limited and if the quality of the overall interface (e.g., operating system command language) does not match that of the query language itself [Jarke et al. 1985]. As systems are improved, the somewhat optimistic preference for restricted natural language over keyword languages in the upper right field will become more realistic. For skilled users, natural language offers concise formulation of some queries, but in general a keyword language or a mathematical language with its more powerful operators is preferable. The inclusion of new generation languages at the lower right results from their rapid reversible actions, which support exploratory use of the database [Shneiderman 1984]. A promising research direction for natural language systems is their combined use with other media, such as menus [Thompson et al. 1983] or direct manipulation, for those tasks where natural language is too ambiguous. Essentially, this enhancement moves natural language interfaces to new generation QLs.

This section concludes with a summary of recommendations by language class. Interestingly, the pattern of query language development outlined in Section 2 repeats in the usage distribution of methods.

Formal query languages (keyword and mathematical) center around the lower right of Table 7, that is, around skilled or professional users with detailed database knowledge. Keyword languages have a more general scope than mathematical languages, which in turn may be more efficient for specialized task structures such as application programming. Natural language can be thought of as an extension of this kind of previous generation language intended for less sophisticated users.

Another line of development starts with choosing from a limited set of functions prompted by the system and then gradually enriching this set to accommodate more skilled or ambitious users.

From Table 7, it can be seen that the higher levels of both developments, new generation languages, restricted natural language, and, to a lesser degree, keyword languages and sophisticated menu selection, overlap in their usage. Currently, there is competition rather than cooperation, but the long-term trend should be toward integration.

8. SUMMARY AND CONCLUSIONS

A methodology for choosing a database query language category for particular user classes has been developed and its application indicated. The proposed framework is based on a new interpretation model of the development of database query languages as evolving along two lines, one influenced by the areas of programming language and database theory, the other by human factors engineering.

This observation immediately leads to a two-level classification of query languages: by the senses employed by the user and by the language methods. It was demonstrated that this classification can serve as a tool for evaluating query languages in a structured manner. The model can also be related to a comprehensive classification scheme of query language users from which most existing user categorizations can be derived. Finally, the query language development model forms the base for a hierarchy of criteria to be used for evaluating language types and determining user requirements.

The language and user evaluations taken together lead to recommendations for assigning suitable language methods to user types and applications. However, the recommendations cannot be fully general at this time, since—as the paper demonstrates—there are substantial gaps in empirical query language evaluation research. Scientifically sound human factors experiments are sparse. Furthermore, conclusive research to support the user profiles and language selection recommendations is not presently available. Until more empirical data are collected, however, it is the authors' opinion that this work is a useful tool for query language developers and users.

For the practitioner interested in fast solutions, the preliminary recommendations may serve as a preselection of possible query language types for which the software selection process can proceed. The actual selection of a query language must also include (and may be dominated by) financial and organizational considerations. A practitioner planning a major investment based on QL technology may want to follow the methodology outlined in this paper to do an analysis, possibly with specialized usability and functionality criteria and more refined user classes.

Finally, researchers may use the framework proposed here for defining empirical or theoretical studies to clarify issues that had to be left open in this paper owing to a lack of data or precise metrics. There is much need for such work. Perhaps the most important contribution of this paper, therefore, is the identification of a well-structured framework for testing the recommendations presented in Section 7 as research hypotheses.

A few examples of important hypotheses that need further study follow. As noted, few experiments in the field have been directed toward comparison at the general methods level, and experiments with natural language systems have not been conclusive. Thus the conclusions in Section 7, based on existing experiments with specific languages, may be overgeneralized. Similarly, development of "deep psychological models" of query formulation is only in the initial stage. There seems to be little research on database usage for clerical users and the long-term performance of skilled users. Finally, new generation languages are in too early a stage of development for the differentiation of methods within this group to be clearly understandable. It is hoped that the framework developed in this paper contributes to a refinement of research questions in this field.

Each single language type will have problems accommodating the variety of user types discussed in this paper. The authors envision that future query languages will employ multiple interaction modes in order to have a broader coverage and usability. For data consistency and system efficiency, such user interfaces must be integrated with well-understood formal query or database programming languages, and provide facilities allowing users to customize the interaction to their own needs and preferences.

ACKNOWLEDGMENTS

The authors are indebted to Margi Olson, Ron Weber, Associate Editor Sal March, and the anonymous referees for a large number of useful comments on earlier versions of this paper.

REFERENCES

AHO, A. V., AND ULLMAN, J. D. 1979. Universality of data retrieval languages. In *Proceedings of the 6th ACM Symposium on Principles of Programming Languages* (Jan. 29–31, San Antonio, Tex.). ACM, New York, pp. 110–120.

AHO, A. V., SAGIV, Y., AND ULLMAN, J. D. 1979. Efficient optimization of a class of relational expressions. *ACM Trans. Database Syst. 4*, 4 (Dec.), 435–454.

ALBANO, A., CARDELLI, L., AND ORSINI, R. 1985. Galileo: A strongly-typed, interactive conceptual language. *ACM Trans. Database Syst. 10*, 2 (June), 230–260.

ARTIFICIAL INTELLIGENCE CORPORATION, 1982. Intellect Query System, Reference Manual.

ASTRAHAN, M. M., BLASGEN, M. W., CHAMBERLIN, D. D., ESWARAN, K. P., GRAY, J. N., GRIFFITHS, P. P., KING, W. F., LORIE, R. A., MCJONES, P. R., MEHL, J. W., PUTZOLU, G. R., TRAIGER, I. L., WADE, B. W., AND WATSON, V. 1976. System-R: Relational approach to database management. *ACM Trans. Database Syst. 1*, 2 (June), 97–137.

BATES, M., AND BOBROW, R. J. 1983. A transportable natural language interface for information retrieval. In *Proceedings of the 6th Annual International ACM-SIGIR Conference on Research and Development in Information Retrieval* (Bethesda, Md., June 6–8). ACM, New York, pp. 81–86.

BORGIDA, A., GREENSPAN, S., MYLOPOULOS, J., AND VASSILIOU, Y. 1986. Towards a knowledge description language. In *On Knowledge Base Management Systems*, J. Mylopoulos and M. L. Brodie, Eds. Springer-Verlag, New York (in press).

BRACHMAN, R., AND LEVESQUE, H. J. 1984. What makes a knowledge base knowledgeable? A view of databases from the knowledge level. In *Proceedings of the 1st International Workshop on Expert Database Systems* (Kiawah Island, S.C., Oct. 24–27), L. Kershberg, Ed., pp. 30–39.

BOYCE, R. E., CHAMBERLIN, D. D., KING, W. F., AND HAMMER, M. M. 1975. Specifying queries as relational expressions: The SQUARE data sublanguage. *Commun. ACM 18*, 11 (Nov.), 621–628.

BRODIE, M., AND SCHMIDT, J. W., Eds. 1982. Final report of the ANSI/X3/SPARC DBS-SG relational database task group. *ACM SIGMOD Record 12*, 4.

BROSEY, M., AND SHNEIDERMAN, B. 1978. Two experimental comparisons of relational and hierarchical database models. *Int. J. Man-Mach. Stud. 10*.

BROWN, R. M., CATTELL, R. G. G., AND SUZUKI, N. 1981. The Cedar DBMS: A preliminary report. In *Proceedings of the International Conference on Management of Data* (Ann Arbor, Mich., Apr. 29–May 1). ACM, New York, pp. 205–211.

CARBONELL, J. 1979. Subjective understanding: Computer models of belief systems. Unpublished Ph.D. dissertation, Computer Science Dept., Yale Univ., New Haven, Conn.

CHANDRA, A., AND HAREL, D. 1982. Structure and complexity of relational queries. *J. Comput. Syst. Sci. 25*, 2, 99–128.

CHANG, N. S., AND FU, K. S. 1979. Query-by-pictorial example. In *IEEE Proceedings of the 3rd International Computer Software and Application Conference*. IEEE, New York.

CINCOM SYSTEMS, INC. 1978. Total Information System, The Next Generation of Software.

CLOCKSIN, W. F., AND MELLISH, C. S. 1982. *Programming in PROLOG*. Springer-Verlag, New York.

CODASYL DATA BASE TASK GROUP, 1971. Final report. In *Conference on Data System Languages* (Apr.). ACM, New York.

CODD, E. F. 1970. A relational model of data for large shared data banks. *Commun. ACM 13*, 6 (June), 377–387.

CODD, E. F. 1971. A data base sublanguage founded on the relational calculus. In *Proceedings of the ACM SIGFIDET Workshop on Data Description, Access and Control* (San Diego, Calif.). ACM, New York, pp. 35–68.

CODD, E. F. 1972. Relational completeness of data base sublanguages. In *Data Base Systems*, R. Rustin, Ed. Prentice-Hall, Englewood Cliffs, N.J., pp. 65–98.

CODD, E. F. 1974. Seven steps to Rendezvous with the casual user. In *Data Base Management*, J. W. Klimbie and K. L. Koffeman, Eds. North-Holland, New York, pp. 179–199.

CODD, E. F. 1978. How about recently? In *Databases: Improving Usability and Responsiveness*, B. Shneiderman, Ed. Academic Press, Orlando, Fla., pp. 3–29.

CUFF, R. N. 1980. On casual users. *Int. J. Man-Mach. Commun. 12*, 2, 163–187.

DAMERAU, F. J. 1979. The transformational question answering (TQA) system operating statistics. IBM Res. Rep., RC 7739, IBM Thomas J. Watson Research Laboratory, Yorktown Heights, N.Y.

ELLIS, C. A., AND NUTT, G. J. 1980. Office information systems and computer science. *ACM Comput. Surv. 12*, 1 (Mar.), 27–60.

EMBLEY, D. W., AND NAGY, G. 1981. Behavioral aspects of text editors. *ACM Comput. Surv. 13*, 1 (Mar.), 33–70.

FIELDS, C., AND NEGROPONTE, N. 1976. Using new clues to find data. In *Proceedings of the 2nd International Conference on Very Large Data Bases*.

FOLEY, J. D., AND VAN DAM, A. 1982. *Fundamentals of Interactive Computer Graphics*. Addison-Wesley, Reading, Mass.

GABLE, A., AND PAGE, C. V. 1980. The use of artificial intelligence techniques in computer-assisted instruction. *Int. J. Man-Mach. Stud. 12*, 3, 259–282.

GOLDBERG, A., AND ROBSON, 1981. Special issue on Smalltalk. *BYTE* (Aug.).

GOODMAN, N., AND SHMUELI, O. 1982. Tree queries: A simple class of relational queries. *ACM Trans. Database Syst. 7*, 4 (Dec.), 653–677.

GOULD, J. D., AND ASCHER, R. 1975. Use of an IQF-like query language by nonprogrammers. Tech. Rep. RC5279, IBM Thomas J. Watson Research Center, Yorktown Heights, N.Y.

GREENBLATT, D., AND WAXMAN, J. 1978. A study of three database query languages. In *Databases: Improving Usability and Responsiveness*, B. Shneiderman, Ed. Academic Press, Orlando, Fla., pp. 77–97.

HARRIS, L. R. 1977. User oriented database query with the ROBOT natural language query system. *Int. J. Man-Mach. Stud. 9*, 6, 697–713.

HENDRIX, G. G., SACERDOTI, E. D., SAGALOWICZ, D., AND SLOCUM, J. 1978. Developing a natural language interface to complex data. *ACM Trans. Database Syst. 3*, 2 (June), 105–147.

HEROT, C. F. 1980. Spatial management of data. *ACM Trans. Database Syst. 5*, 4 (Dec.), 493–513.

HEROT, C. F. 1984. Graphical user interfaces. In *Human Factors and Interactive Computer Systems*, Y. Vassiliou, Ed. Ablex, Norwood, N.J., pp. 83–103.

HOEPPNER, W., CHRISTALLER T., MARBURGER, H., MORIK, K., NEBEL, B., O'LEARY, M., AND WAHLSTER, W. 1983. Beyond domain-independence: Experience with the development of a German language access system to highly diverse background systems. In *Proceedings of the 8th International Joint Conference on Artificial Intelligence* (Karlsruhe, West Germany), pp. 588–594.

IBM, 1975. IBM Information Management System/Virtual Storage (IMS/VS). General Information Manual, G 20-1260-3, IBM Corp.

IMMERMAN, N. 1982. Relational queries computable in polynomial time. In *Proceedings of the 14th ACM Symposium on Theory of Computing* (San Francisco, Calif., May 5–7). ACM, New York, pp. 147–152.

JARKE, M., AND KOCH, J. 1984. Query optimization in database systems. *ACM Comput. Surv. 16*, 2 (June), 111–152.

JARKE, M., AND VASSILIOU, Y. 1984. Coupling expert systems with database management systems. In *Artificial Intelligence Applications for Business*, W. Reitman, Ed. Ablex, Norwood, N.J., p. 65–85.

JARKE, M., TURNER, J. A., STOHR, E. A., VASSILIOU, Y., WHITE, N. H., AND MICHIELSEN, K. 1985. A field evaluation of natural language for data retrieval. *IEEE Trans. Softw. Eng. SE-11*, 1, 97–114.

JARKE, M., KRAUSE, J., AND VASSILIOU, Y. 1986a. Studies in the evaluation of a domain-independent natural language system. In *Cooperative Interfaces to Information Systems*, L. Bolc and M. Jarke, Eds. Springer-Verlag, New York, (in press).

JARKE, M., MYLOPOULOS, J., SCHMIDT, J. W., AND VASSILIOU, Y. 1986b. KBMS for software development. In *Logic and Knowledge Base Management Systems*, C. Thanos and J. W. Schmidt, Eds. Springer-Verlag, New York (in press).

KATZ, R. H., AND WONG, E. 1982. Decompiling CODASYL DML into relational queries. *ACM Trans. Database Syst. 7*, 1 (Mar.), 1–23.

KING, J. L., AND SCHREMS, E. L. 1978. Cost–benefit

analysis of information systems development and operation. *ACM Comput. Surv. 10*, 1 (Mar.), 19–34.

KRAUSE, J. 1980. Natural language access to information systems: An evaluation study of its acceptance by end users. *Inf. Syst. 4*, 297–318.

KRAUSE, J. 1982. *Mensch-Maschine-Kommunikation in natuerlicher Sprache*. Niemeyer, Tübingen, West Germany.

LACROIX, M., AND PIROTTE, A. 1977. Domain-oriented relational languages. In *Proceedings of the 3rd International Conference on Very Large Data Bases* (Tokyo, Oct. 6–8). IEEE, New York, pp. 370–378.

LACROIX, M., AND PIROTTE, A. 1980. User interfaces for database application programming. Tech. Rep., Phillips MBLE Research Laboratory, Brussels, Belgium.

LARSON, J. A. 1983. Bridging the gap between relational and network databases. *IEEE Comput. 16*, 9, 82–92.

LEAVENWORTH, B. M., AND SAMMET, J. 1974. An overview of nonprocedural languages. In *Proceedings of a Symposium on Very High Level Languages. SIGPLAN Not. 9*, 4 (Apr.), 1–12.

LEBOWITZ, M. 1980. Generalization and memory in an integrated understanding system. Unpublished Ph.D. dissertation, Computer Science Dept., Yale Univ., New Haven, Conn.

LEHMANN, H., AND BLASER, A. 1979. Query languages in data base systems. TR 79.07.004, IBM Heidelberg Scientific Center, Heidelberg, West Germany.

LEHMANN, H., OTT, N., AND ZOEPPRITZ, M. 1978. User experiments with natural language for data base access. In *Proceedings of the 7th International Conference on Computational Linguistics* (Bergen, Norway).

LEVESQUE, H. J. 1984. The logic of incomplete knowledge bases. In *On Conceptual Modeling*, M. L. Brodie, J. Mylopoulos, and J. W. Schmidt, Eds. Springer-Verlag, New York, pp. 165–186.

LOCHOVSKY, F. H. 1976. Data base management system user performance variables. Ph.D. dissertation, Computer Science Dept., Univ. of Toronto, Toronto, Ontario, Canada.

LOCHOVSKY, F. H., AND TSICHRITZIS, D. C. 1977. User performance considerations in DBMS selection. In *Proceedings of the International Conference on Management of Data* (Toronto, Ontario, Aug. 3–5). ACM, New York, pp. 128–134.

LOCHOVSKY, F. H., AND TSICHRITZIS, D. C. 1984. Querying external databases. In *Human Factors and Interactive Computer Systems*, Y. Vassiliou, Ed. Ablex, Norwood, N.J., pp. 117–140.

MALONE, T. 1982. Heuristics for designing enjoyable user interfaces: Lessons from computer games. In *Proceedings of the Conference on Human Factors in Computer Systems* (Gaithersburg, Md.), pp. 63–68.

MCDONALD, N. H. 1975. CUPID: A graphic oriented facility for support of nonprogrammer interactions with a database. Ph.D. dissertation, Computer Science Dept., Univ. of California, Berkeley.

MCDONALD, N. H., AND MCNALLY, L. P. 1982. Query language feature analysis by usability. Unpublished paper, Computer Science Dept., University of South Florida.

MOORHEAD, W. G. 1976. GXRAM—A relational data base interface for graphics. Tech. Rep. RJ1735, IBM Research Laboratory, San Jose, Calif.

MORAN, T. P. 1981. Guest editor's introduction: An applied psychology of the user. *ACM Comput. Surv. 13*, 1 (Mar.), 1–11.

MOTRO, A. 1984. Query generalization: A technique for handling query failure. In *Proceedings of the 1st International Workshop on Expert Database Systems* (Kiawah Island, S.C., Oct. 24–27), L. Kershberg, Ed., pp. 314–326.

MYLOPOULOS, J., BERNSTEIN, P. A., AND WONG, H. K. T. 1980. A language facility for designing interactive database-intensive applications. *ACM Trans. Database Syst. 5*, 2 (June), 185–207.

NEWMAN, W. S., AND SPROULL, R. F. 1979. *Principles of Interactive Computer Graphics*. McGraw-Hill, New York.

PIROTTE, A. 1978. High-level database query languages. In *Logic and Databases*, H. Gallaire and J. Minker, Eds. Plenum, New York, pp. 409–436.

PLATH, W. J. 1976. REQUEST: A natural language question answering system. *IBM J. Res. Dev. 20*.

REISNER, P. 1977. Use of psychological experimentation as an aid to development of query languages. *IEEE Trans. Softw. Eng. SE-3*, 3, 218–229.

REISNER, P. 1981. Human factors studies of database query languages: A survey and assessment. *ACM Comput. Surv. 13*, 1 (Mar.), pp. 13–31.

REISNER, P., BOYCE, R. F., AND CHAMBERLIN, D. D. 1975. Human factors evaluation of two data base query languages—Square and Sequel. In *Proceedings of the National Computer Conference* (Anaheim, Calif., May 19–22), vol. 44. AFIPS Press, Reston, Va., pp. 447–452.

ROSENTHAL, A., AND REINER, D. 1985. Querying relational views of networks. In *Query Processing in Database Systems*, W. Kim, D. Reiner, and D. Batory, Eds. Springer-Verlag, New York, pp. 109–126.

SAMET, J., Ed. 1981. Query languages—A unified approach. Report of the British Computer Society Query Languages Group. Heyden University Press, Cambridge, England.

SCHANK, R. C., AND SLADE, S. 1984. Advisory systems. In *Artificial Intelligence Applications for Business*, W. Reitman, Ed. Ablex, Norwood, N.J., pp. 249–265.

SCHMANDT, C., AND HULTEEN, E. A. 1982. The intelligent voice-interactive interface. In *Proceedings of the Conference on Human Factors in Computer Systems* (Gaithersburg, Md.).

SCHMIDT, J. W. 1977. Some high-level language constructs for data of type relation. *ACM Trans. Database Syst. 2*, 3 (Sept.), 247–261.

SCHNEIDER, M. 1984. Ergonomic considerations in the design of control languages. In *Human Factors and Interactive Computer Systems*, Y. Vassiliou, Ed. Ablex, Norwood, N.J., pp. 141–161.

SENKO, M. E. 1977. DIAM II with FORAL LP: Making pointed queries with a light pen. In *Proceedings of the International Federation of Information Processing* (Toronto, Ontario). North-Holland, Amsterdam, pp. 635–640.

SHIPMAN, D. W. 1981. The functional data model and the data language DAPLEX. *ACM Trans. Database Syst. 6*, 1 (Mar.), 140–173.

SHNEIDERMAN, B. 1978. Improving the human factors aspect of database interactions. *ACM Trans. Database Syst. 3*, 4 (Dec.), 417–439.

SHNEIDERMAN, B. 1980. *Software Psychology*. Winthrop, Cambridge, Mass.

SHNEIDERMAN, B. 1984. The future of interactive systems and the emergence of direct manipulation. In *Human Factors and Interactive Computer Systems*, Y. Vassiliou, Ed. Ablex, Norwood, N.J., pp. 1–27.

SMALL, D. W., AND WELDON, L. J. 1983. An experimental comparison of natural and structured query languages. *Human Factors 25*, 3, 253–263.

SMITH, J. M., FOX, S., AND LANDERS, T. 1981. Reference manual for ADAPLEX. Tech. Rep. CCA-81-02, Computer Corporation of America, Cambridge, Mass.

STOHR, E. A., TURNER, J. A., VASSILIOU, Y., AND WHITE, N. H. 1982. Research in natural language retrieval systems. In *Proceedings of the 15th International Conference on System Sciences* (Honolulu, Hawaii).

STONEBRAKER, M. R., AND ROWE, L. A. 1977. Observations on data manipulation languages and their embedding in general purpose programming languages. In *Proceedings of the 3rd International Conference on Very Large Data Bases* (Tokyo, Oct. 6–8). IEEE, New York, pp. 128–143.

STONEBRAKER, M., WONG, E., KREPS, P., AND HELD, G. 1976. The design and implementation of INGRES. *ACM Trans. Database Syst. 1*, 3 (Sept.), 189–222.

THOMAS, J. C. 1976. Quantifiers and question-asking. IBM Res. Rep. RC 5866, T. J. Watson Research Laboratory, Yorktown Heights, N. Y.

THOMAS, J. C., AND GOULD, J. D. 1975. A psychological study of Query by Example. In *Proceedings of the National Computer Conference* (Anaheim, Calif., May 19–22), vol. 44. AFIPS Press, Reston, Va., pp. 439–445.

THOMPSON, C. W., ROSS, K. M., TENNANT, H. R., AND SAENZ, R. M. 1983. Building usable menu-based natural language interfaces to databases. In *Proceedings of the 9th International Conference on Very Large Data Bases* (Florence, Italy, Oct.). VLDB Endowment, Saratoga, Calif., pp. 43–55.

TODD, S. J. P. 1976. The Peterlee Relational Test Vehicle—A system overview. *IBM Syst. J. 15*, 4, 285–308.

TOU, F. N., WILLIAMS, M. D., FIKES, R. E., HENDERSON, D. A., AND MALONE, T. W. 1982. Rabbit: An intelligent database assistant. In *Proceedings of the National Conference on Artificial Intelligence* (Menlo Park, Calif.). AAAI, Menlo Park, Calif., pp. 314–318.

TSICHRITZIS, D. C. 1976. LSL: A link and selector language. In *Proceedings of the International Conference on Management of Data* (Washington, D.C., June 2–4). ACM, New York, pp. 123–134.

TURNER, J. A., JARKE, M., STOHR, E. A., VASSILIOU, Y., AND WHITE, N. H. 1984. Using restricted natural language for data retrieval—A plan for field evaluation. In *Human Factors and Interactive Computer Systems*, Y. Vassiliou, Ed. Ablex, Norwood, N.J., pp. 163–190.

VARDI, M. 1982. The complexity of relational query languages. In *Proceedings of the 14th Annual ACM Symposium on Theory of Computing* (San Francisco, Calif., May 5–7). ACM, New York, pp. 137–146.

VASSILIOU, Y., Ed. 1984. *Human Factors and Interactive Computer Systems*. Ablex, Norwood, N.J.

VASSILIOU, Y., AND JARKE, M. 1984. Query languages—A taxonomy. In *Human Factors and Interactive Computer Systems*, Y. Vassiliou, Ed. Ablex, Norwood, N.J., pp. 47–81.

VASSILIOU, Y., JARKE, M., STOHR, E. A., TURNER, J. A., AND WHITE, N. H. 1983. Natural language for database queries: A laboratory study. *Manage. Inf. Syst. Q. 7*, 4 (Dec.), 47–61.

WALTZ, D. L. 1978. An English language question answering system for a large relational database. *Commun. ACM 21*, 7 (July), 526–539.

WELTY, C. 1979. A comparison of a procedural and a non-procedural query language: Syntactic metrics and human factors. Ph.D. dissertation, Computer Science Dept., Univ. of Massachusetts, Amherst, Mass.

WELTY, C., AND STEMPLE, D. W. 1981. Human factors comparison of a procedural and a nonprocedural query language. *ACM Trans. Database Syst. 6*, 4 (Dec.), 626–649.

WOODS, W. A. 1984. Natural language communication with machines: an ongoing goal. In *Artificial Intelligence Applications for Business*, W. Reitman, Ed. Ablex, Norwood, N.J., pp. 195–209.

WOODS, W. A., KAPLAN, R. M., AND NASH-WEBBER, B. 1972. The lunar sciences natural language information system. Tech. Rep., Bolt Beranek and Newman, Cambridge, Mass.

YORMARK, B. 1977. The ANSI/X3/SPARC/SGDBMS architecture. In *The ANISI/SPARC DBMS Model*, Jardine, Ed. North-Holland Publ., Amsterdam, p. 521.

ZLOOF, M. 1977. Query By Example: A data base language. *IBM Syst. J. 16*, 4, 324–343.

ZLOOF, M. 1978. Design aspects of the Query-by-Example data base management language. In *Databases: Improving Usability and Responsiveness*, B. Shneiderman, Ed. Academic Press, Orlando, Fla.

An Amateur's Introduction to Recursive Query Processing Strategies †

Francois Bancilhon (1)
Raghu Ramakrishnan (2)

(1): Altair
BP 105, 78153 Le Chesnay Cedex, France

(2): Computer Sciences Department
University of Wisconsin-Madison, Madison, 53706, USA

ABSTRACT

This paper surveys and compares various strategies for processing logic queries in relational databases. The survey and comparison is limited to the case of Horn Clauses with evaluable predicates but without function symbols. The paper is organized in three parts. In the first part, we introduce the main concepts and definitions. In the second, we describe the various strategies. For each strategy, we give its main characteristics, its application range and a detailed description. We also give an example of a query evaluation. The third part of the paper compares the strategies on performance grounds. We first present a set of sample rules and queries which are used for the performance comparisons, and then we characterize the data. Finally, we give an analytical solution for each query/rule system. Cost curves are plotted for specific configurations of the data.

1. Introduction

The database community has recently manifested a strong interest in the problem of evaluating "logic queries" against relational databases. This interest is motivated by two converging trends: (i) the desire to integrate database technology and artificial intelligence technology i.e., to extend database systems, to provide them with the functionality of expert systems thus creating "knowledge base systems" and (ii) the desire to integrate logic programming technology and database technology, i.e., to extend the power of the interface to the database system to that of a general purpose language. The second goal is of a somewhat different nature and has found in its ranks proponents of object oriented, functional and imperative as well as logic based programming languages. The logic programming camp is relying on the fact that logic programming and relational calculus have the same underlying mathematical model, namely first order logic.

Of course, database researchers already know how to evaluate logic queries: the view mechanism, as offered by most relational systems, is a form of support of a restricted set of logic queries. But those logic queries are restricted to be non-recursive and the problem of efficiently supporting recursive queries is still open.

In the past five years, following the pioneering work by Chang, Shapiro and McKay, and Henschen and Naqvi, numerous strategies have been proposed to deal with recursion in logic queries. The positive side of this work is that there are a lot of algorithms offered to solve *the* problem. The negative side is that we do not know how to make a choice of an algorithm. It seems reasonable to say that all these strategies can

† This is a revised version of a paper that appeared under the same title in the proceedings of SIGMOD 86.
This work was performed while the first author was at MCC, Austin, and the second author was at the University of Texas at Austin and visiting MCC.

only be compared on three grounds: functionality (i.e., application domain), performance and ease of implementation. However, each of these algorithms is described at a different level of detail, and it is sometimes difficult to understand their differences. In fact, we shall claim later in this paper that some of them are indeed identical. Each comes with little or no performance analysis, and the application domain is not always easy to identify. We try in this paper to evaluate these algorithms with respect to these three criteria. We describe all the algorithms at the same level of detail and demonstrate their behavior on common examples. This is not always easy to do since some of them are fairly well formalized while others are merely sketched as an idea.

For each one of them, we state in simple terms the application domain. Finally, we give a first simple comparison of the performance of these algorithms. Choosing a simple set of typical queries, a simple characterization of the data and a simple cost function, we give an analytical evaluation of the cost of each strategy. The results give a first insight into the respective value of all the proposed strategies.

The rest of the paper is organized as follows: In section 2 we present our definitions and notations, and introduce the main ideas. In section 3 we present the main features of the strategies, and describe each one individually, and finally, in section 4, we present the performance evaluation methodology and results.

2. Logic Databases

2.1. An Example

Let us start by discussing informally an example. Here is what we call a ''logic database'':

parent(cain,adam).
parent(abel,adam).
parent(cain,eve).
parent(abel,eve).
parent(sem,abel).
ancestor(X,Y) :- ancestor(X,Z),ancestor(Z,Y).
ancestor(X,Y) :- parent(X,Y).
generation(adam,1).
generation(X,I) :- generation(Y,J), parent(X,Y),J=I-1.
generation(X,I) :- generation(Y,J), parent(Y,X),J=I+1.

Note that this is a purely syntactic object. In this database, we have a set of predicate or relation names (parent, ancestor and generation), a set of arithmetic predicates (I=J+1, I=J-1) and a set of constants (adam, eve, cain, sem and abel). Finally, we have a set of variables (X,Y and Z). The database consists of a set of sentences ending with a period. ''parent(cain,adam)'' is a fact, and ''ancestor(X,Y) :- parent(X,Y)'' is a rule.

Let us now associate a meaning with the database. We first associate with each constant an object from the real world: thus, with ''adam'' we associate the individual whose name is ''adam''. Then, we associate with each arithmetic predicate name the corresponding arithmetic operator. Then we can interpret intuitively each fact and each rule. For instance we interpret ''parent(cain,adam)'' by saying that the predicate parent is true for the couple (cain,adam), and we interpret the rule

ancestor(X,Y) :- ancestor(X,Z), ancestor(Z,Y).

by saying that if there are three objects X, Y and Z such that ancestor(X,Z) is true and ancestor(Z,Y) is true then ancestor(X,Y) is true.

This leads to an interpretation which associates with each predicate a set of tuples. For instance with the predicate ancestor we associate the interpretation {(cain,adam), (abel,adam), (cain,eve), (abel,eve), (sem,abel), (sem,adam), (sem,eve)}, and with the predicate generation we associate the interpretation {(adam,1), (eve,1), (cain,2), (abel,2), (sem,3)}

The problem is to answer queries, given the logic database. For instance given a query of the form generation(sem,?) or ancestor(?,adam), how do we find the answer: generation(sem,3) and {ancestor(cain,adam), ancestor(abel,adam), ancestor(sem,adam)}?

Let us now formalize all the notions encountered in this example and define a logic database. We first define it syntactically, then we attach an interpretation to this syntax.

2.2. Syntax of a Logic Database

We first define four sets of names: *variable* names, *constant* names, *predicate* or *relation* names and *evaluable predicate* names.

We adopt the Prolog convention of denoting variables by strings of characters starting with an upper case letter and constants by strings of characters starting with a lower case letter or integers. For instance X1, Father and Y are variables, while john, salary and 345 are constants.

We use identifiers starting with lower case letters for predicates names and relation names (evaluable and non-evaluable).

We use the term relation (from database terminology) and predicate (from logic terminology) indifferently to represent the same object. We shall however interpret them differently: a relation will be interpreted by a set of tuples and a predicate by a true/false function. There is a fixed arity associated with each relation/predicate.

The set of evaluable predicate names is a subset of the set of predicate names. We will not be concerned with their syntactic recognition; in the examples it will be clear from the name we use. The main examples of evaluable predicate names are arithmetic predicates. For instance, sum, difference and greater-than are examples of evaluable predicates of arity 3, 3 and 2 respectively, while parent and ancestor are non-evaluable predicates of arity 2.

A *literal* is of the form p(t1,t2,...,tn) where p is a predicate name of arity n and each ti is a constant or a variable. For instance father(john,X), ancestor(Y,Z), id(john,25,austin) and sum(X,Y,Z) are literals. An *instantiated* literal is one which does not contain any variables. For instance id(john,doe,25,austin) is an instantiated literal, while father(john,Father) is not.

We allow ourselves to write evaluable literals using functions and equality for the purpose of clarity. For instance, Z = X+Y denotes sum(X,Y,Z), I = J+1 denotes sum(J,1,I), and X > 0 denotes greater-than(X,0).

If p(t1,t2,...,tn) is a literal, we call (t1,t2,...,tn) a *tuple*.

A *rule* is a statement of the form

p :- q1,q2,...,qn.

where p and the qi's are literals such that the predicate name in p is a non-evaluable predicate. p is called the *head* of the rule, and each of the qi's is called a *goal*. The conjunction of the qi's is the *body* of the rule. We have adopted the Prolog notation of representing implication by ':-' and conjunction by ','. For instance

uncle(john,X) :- brother(X,Y), parent(john,Y).

is a rule with head "uncle(john,X)" and body "brother(X,Y), parent(john,Y)".

A *ground clause* is a rule in which the body is empty. A *fact* is a ground clause which contains no variables. For instance

loves(X,john).
loves(mary,susan).

are ground clauses, but only the second of these is a fact.

A *database* is a set of rules; note that this set is not ordered. Given a database, we can partition it into a set of facts and the set of all other rules. The set of facts is called the *extensional* database, and the set of all other rules is called the *intensional* database.

2.3. Interpretation of a Logic Database

Up to now our definitions have been purely syntactical. Let us now give an interpretation of a database. This will be done by associating with each relation name in the database a set of instantiated tuples. We first assume that with each evaluable predicate p is associated a set natural(p) of instantiated tuples which we call its *natural interpretation*. For instance, with the predicate *sum* is associated an infinite set of all the 3-tuples (x,y,z) of integers such that the sum of x and y is z. In general the natural interpretation of an evaluable predicate is infinite.

Given a database, an *interpretation* of this database is a mapping which associates with each relation name a set of instantiated tuples.

A *model* of a database is an interpretation I such that:

1. for each evaluable predicate p, I(p) = natural(p), and,
2. for any rule, p(t) :- q1(t1),q2(t2),...,qn(tn), for any instantiation σ of the variables of the rule such that σ(ti) is in the interpretation of qi for all i then σ(t) is is in the interpretation of p.

This is simply a way of saying that, in a model, if the right hand side is true then the left hand side is also true. This implies that for every fact p(x) of the database the tuple x belongs to the interpretation of p.

Of course, for a given database there are many models. The nice property of Horn Clauses is that among all these models there is a *least* one (least in the sense of set inclusion), which is the one we choose as *the* model of the database (Van Emden and Kowalski [1976]). Therefore from now on, when we talk about the model or the interpretation of a database, we mean its least model.

Notice that because of the presence of evaluable arithmetic predicates the minimal model is, in general, not finite.

Let p be an n-ary predicate. An *adornment* of p is a sequence *a* of length n of b's and f's (Ullman [1985]). For instance bbf is an adornment of a ternary predicate, and fbff is an adornment of predicate of arity 4. An adornment is to be interpreted intuitively as follows: the i-th variable of p is bound (respectively free) if the i-th element of *a* is b (respectively f). Let p(x1,x2,...,xn) be a literal, an adornment a1a2...an of that literal is an adornment of p such that :

(i) if xi is a constant then ai is b,
(ii) if xi = xj then ai = aj

We denote adornments by superscripts. A *query form* is an adorned predicate. Examples of query forms are $father^{bf}$, id^{bffb}.

A *query* is a query form and an instantiation of the bound variables. We denote it by an adorned literal where all the bound positions are filled with the corresponding constants and the free positions are filled by distinct free variables. Therefore $father^{bf}$(john,X) and id^{bffb}(john,X,Y,25) are queries. The distinction between queries and query forms are that query forms are actually compiled, and at run-time their parameters will be instantiated. Notice that father(X,X) is not a query form in this formalism.

The *answer* to a query q(t) is the set: {q(σ(t)) | σ is an instantiation of t, and σ(t) is in the interpretation of q}.

2.4. Structuring and Representing the Database

A predicate which only appears in the intensional database is a *derived* predicate. A predicate which appears only in the extensional database or in the body of a rule is a *base* predicate.

For performance reasons, it is good to decompose the database into a set of pure base predicates (which can then be stored using a standard DBMS) and a set of pure derived predicates. Fortunately, such a decomposition is always possible, because every database can be rewritten as an "equivalent" database containing only base and derived predicates. By equivalent, we mean that all the predicate names of the original database appear in the modified database and have the same interpretation.

We obtain this equivalent database in the following way: consider any predicate p that is neither base nor derived. By definition, we have a set of facts for p, and p appears on the left of some rules. So we simply introduce a new predicate p_ext and do the following:

1. replace p by p_ext in each fact of p,
2. add a new rule of the form p(X1,X2,...,Xn) :- p_ext(X1,X2,...,Xn) where n is the arity of p.

Example:

```
father(a,b).
parent(b,c).
grandfather(b,d).
grandfather(X,Y) :- father(X,Z),parent(Z,Y).
```

becomes:

```
father(a,b).
parent(b,c).
grandfather_ext(b,d).
grandfather(X,Y) :- father(X,Z),parent(Z,Y).
grandfather(X,Y) :- grandfather_ext(X,Y).
```

Most authors have chosen to describe a set of rules through some kind of graph formalism. Predicate Connection Graphs, as presented in McKay and Shapiro [1981], represent the relationship between rules and predicates. Rule/goal graphs, as presented in Ullman [1985], carry more information because predicates and rules are adorned by their variable bindings. We have chosen here to keep the rule/goal graph terminology while using unadorned predicates.

The *rule/goal* graph has two sets of nodes: square nodes which are associated with predicates, and oval nodes which are associated with rules. If there is a rule of the form

r: p:- p1,p2,...,pn

in the intensional database, then there is an arc going from node r to node p, and for each predicate pi there is an arc from node pi to node r.

Here is an example of an intensional database. For the sake of simplicity, we have omitted the variables in the rules:

r1	p1 :- p3,p4	r5	p3 :- p6
r2	p2 :- p4,p5	r6	p5 :- p5,p7
r3	p3 :- p6,p4,p3	r7	p5 :- p6
r4	p4 :- p5,p3	r8	p7 :- p8,p9

The rule/goal graph is:

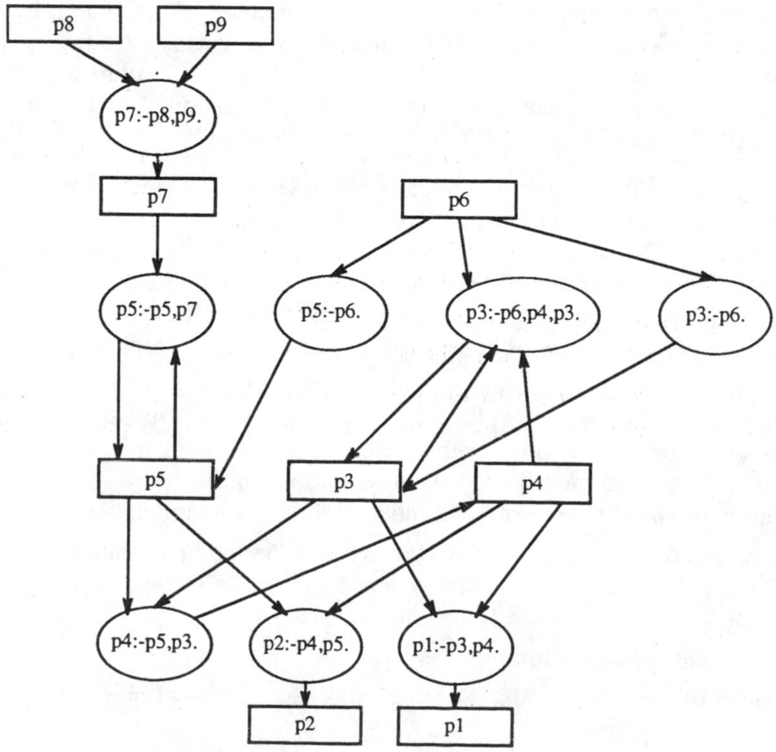

2.5. Recursion

Recursion is often discussed in the single rule context. For the purpose of clarity and simplicity, let us first give some temporary definitions in this context. We say that a rule is recursive if it is of the form

p(t) :- ...,p(t'),... .

For instance the rule

ancestor(X,Y) :- ancestor(X,Z),parent(Z,Y).

is recursive.

An interesting subcase is that of linear rules. Linear rules play an important role because (i) there is a belief that most "real life" recursive rules are indeed linear, and (ii) algorithms have been developed to handle them efficiently.

We say that a rule is linear if it is recursive, and the recursive predicate appears once and only once on the right. This property is sometime referred to as regularity (Chang [1981]). We believe the term linear to be more appropriate, and we think that regularity should be kept for another concept (which is not defined here).

For instance the rule:

sg(X,Y) :- p(X,XP),p(Y,YP),sg(XP,YP).

is linear, while the rule

ancestor(X,Y) :- ancestor(X,Z),ancestor(Z,Y).

is not.

These definitions are fairly simple in the single rule context. They are a little more involved in the context of a set of rules where properties have to be attached to predicates instead of rules. Consider the following database:

p(X,Y) :- b1(X,Z),q(Z,Y).
q(X,Y) :- p(X,Z),b2(Z,Y).

Neither of the rules are recursive according to the above definition, while clearly both predicates p and q are recursive.

We now come to the general definitions of recursion in the multirule context. Let p and q be two predicates. We say that p *derives* q (denoted p $\rightarrow$ q) if it occurs in the body of a rule whose head predicate is q. We define $\rightarrow$+ to be the transitive closure (*not* the reflexive transitive closure) of $\rightarrow$. A predicate p is said to be *recursive* if p $\rightarrow$+ p. Two predicates p and q are *mutually recursive* if p $\rightarrow$+ q and q $\rightarrow$+ p. It can be easily shown that mutual recursion is an equivalence relation on the set of recursive predicates. Therefore the set of recursive predicates can be decomposed into disjoint blocs of mutually recursive predicates.

Given a set of rules, we say that the rule
p :- p1,p2,...,pn is *recursive* iff there exists pi in the body of the rule which is mutually recursive to p.

A recursive rule p :- p1,p2,...,pn is *linear* if there is one and only one pi in the body of the rule which is mutually recursive to p. A set of rules is *linear* if every recursive rule in it is linear. For instance, the following system is linear:

r1 p(X,Y) :- p1(X,Z),q(Z,Y).
r2 q(X,Y) :- p(X,Z),p2(Z,Y).
r3 p(X,Y) :- b3(X,Y).
r4 p1(X,Y) :- b1(X,Z),p1(Z,Y).
r5 p1(X,Y) :- b4(X,Y).
r6 p2(X,Y) :- b2(X,Z),p2(Z,Y).
r7 p2(X,Y) :- b5(X,Y).

The set of recursive predicates is {p,q,p1,p2}, the set of base predicates is {b1,b2,b3,b4,b5}. The blocks of mutually recursive predicates are {[p,q],[p1],[p2]}. The recursive rules are r1, r2, r4 and r6, and the system is linear even though rules r1 and r2 both have two recursive predicates on their right.

We say that two recursive rules are mutually recursive iff the predicates in their heads are mutually recursive. This defines an equivalence relation among the recursive rules.

Thus mutual recursion defines an equivalence class among recursive predicates and among the recursive rules, (Bancilhon [1985]). Therefore, it groups together all predicates which are mutually recursive to one another, i.e which must be evaluated as a whole. It also groups together all the rules which participate in evaluating those blocks of predicates. Let us now see how this can be represented in the rule/goal graph. We define the *reduced rule/goal graph* as follows:

Square nodes are associated with non-recursive predicates or with blocks of mutually recursive predicates and, oval nodes are associated with non-recursive rules or with blocks of mutually recursive rules. The graph essentially describes the non-recursive part of the database by grouping together all the predicates which are mutually recursive to one another and isolating the recursive parts. For every non-recursive rule of the form r: p:- p1,p2,...,pn, there is an arc going from node r to node p (if p is non-recursive), or to node [p], which is the node representing the set of predicates mutually recursive to p (if p is recursive). For each non-recursive predicate pi, there is an arc from the node pi to the node r, and for each recursive predicate pj there is an arc going from [pj] the node representing the set of predicates mutually recursive to pj.

Finally, each bloc of recursive rules [r] is uniquely associated to a set of mutually recursive predicates [p], and we draw an arc from [p] to [r] and an arc from [r] to [p]. We also draw an arc from q (if q is non-recursive) or from [q] (if q is recursive) to [r] if there is a rule in [r] which has q in its body. This grouping of recursive predicates in blocks of strongly connected components is presented in Morris et al. [1986].

Here is the representation of the previous database:

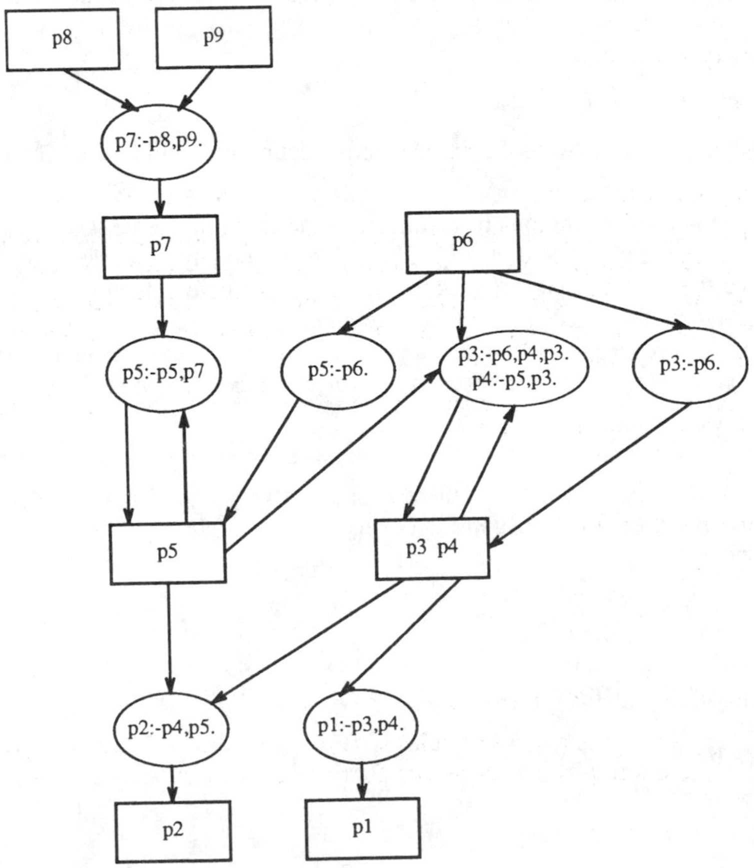

2.6. Safety of Queries

Given a query q in a database D, we say that q is *safe* in D if the answer to q is finite. Obviously unsafe queries are highly undesirable.

Sources of unsafeness are of two kinds

(i) the evaluable arithmetic predicates are interpreted by infinite tables. Therefore they are unsafe by definition. For instance the query greater-than(27,X) is unsafe.

(ii) rules with free variables in the head which do not appear in the body are a source of unsafeness in the presence of evaluable arithmetic predicates (the arithmetic predicates provide an infinite underlying domain, and the variable from the head of the rule which does not appear on the right ranges over that domain). Thus for instance, in the system

```
good-salary(X) :- X > 100000.
like(X,Y) :- nice(X).
nice(john).
```

the query like(john,X)? is unsafe because, in the minimal model of the database like(john,x) is true for every integer x. Note that if the first rule was not there, like(john,X)? would be safe and have answer like(john,john).

The problem of safety has received a lot of attention recently (Afrati et al. [1986], Kifer and Lozinskii [1987], Krishnamurthy et al. [1988], Ramakrishnan et al. [1987], Ullman [1985], Ullman and Van Gelder [1985], Van Gelder and Topor [1987], Zaniolo [1986]). We shall not survey those results here but merely present some simple sufficient syntactic conditions to guarantee safety. A rule is *range restricted* if every variable of the head appears somewhere in the body. Thus in this system:

```
r1   loves(X,Y) :- nice(X).
r2   loves(X,Y) :- nice(X),human(Y).
```

r1, which corresponds to "nice people love everything", is not range restricted while r2, which corresponds to "nice people love all humans", is. Obviously, every ground rule which is not a fact is not range restricted. For instance

```
loves(john,X).
```

is not range restricted.

A set of rules is range restricted if every rule in this set is range restricted.

It is known (Reiter [1978]) that if each evaluable predicate has a finite natural interpretation, and if the set of rules is range restricted, then every query defined over this set of rules is safe. This applies obviously to the case where there are no evaluable predicates. However, if there are evaluable predicates with infinite natural interpretations, safety is no longer assured. We now present a simple sufficient condition for safety in the presence of such predicates.

A rule is *strongly safe* iff: (1) it is range restricted, and (2) every variable in an evaluable predicate term also appears in at least one base predicate.

For example, the rule

```
well-paid(X) :- has-salary(X,Y), Y > 100K.
```

is strongly safe, whereas

```
great-salary(X) :- X > 100K.
```

is not strongly safe.

A set of rules is strongly safe if every rule in this set is strongly safe.

Any query defined over a set of strongly safe rules is safe. However, while this is a sufficient condition, it is not necessary. We can develop better conditions for testing safety, or leave it to the user to ensure that his queries are safe.

2.7. Effective Computability.

Safety, in general, does not guarantee that the query can be effectively computed. Consider for instance:

```
p1(1,X,Y) :- X≥Y.
p2(X,Y,2) :- X≤Y.
p(X,Y) :- p1(X,Z,Z),p2(Z,Z,Y).
```

The query p(X,Y) is safe (the answer is {p(1,2)}), but there is no general evaluation strategy which will compute the answer and terminate.

However, strongly safe rules are guaranteed to be safe *and* effectively computable.

In fact, while we might often be willing to let the user ensure that his queries are safe, it is desirable to ensure that the query can be computed without materializing "infinite" intermediate results. We now present a sufficient condition for ensuring this.

We first need some information about the way arithmetic predicates can propagate bindings. So we characterize each arithmetic predicate by a set of *finiteness constraints* (Zaniolo [1986], Ramakrishnan et al. [1987]). A finiteness constraint is a couple ($X \rightarrow Y$) where X is a set of attributes and Y is a set of attributes. It is to be interpreted intuitively as "if the values of the X attributes are fixed then there is a finite number of values of the Y attributes associated with them". Therefore, while their semantics is different from that of functional dependencies, they behave in the same fashion (and have the same axiomatization). Of course, we assume that the natural interpretation of the evaluable predicate satisfies the set of finiteness constraints.

For instance, the ternary arithmetic predicate "sum" has the finiteness constraints:

$\{1,2\} \rightarrow \{3\}$
$\{1,3\} \rightarrow \{2\}$
$\{2,3\} \rightarrow \{1\}$

while the arithmetic predicate "greater than" has only trivial finiteness constraints.

Now consider a rule, and define each variable in the body to be *secure* if it appears in a non-evaluable predicate in the body or if it appears in position i in an evaluable predicate p and there is a subset I of the variables of p which are secure and $I \rightarrow \{i\}$. Note that the definition is recursive.

A rule is *bottom-up evaluable* if

1. it is range restricted, and
2. every variable in the body is secure.

For instance:

```
p(X,Y) :- Y=X+1, X=Y1+Y2, p(Y1,Y2).
```

is bottom-up evaluable because (i) Y1 and Y2 are secure (they appear in p which is non-evaluable), (ii) in X=Y1+Y2, the finiteness constraint $\{Y1,Y2\} \rightarrow \{X\}$ holds, therefore X is secure, and (iii) in Y=X+1, the finiteness constraint $\{X\} \rightarrow \{Y\}$ holds, therefore Y is secure.

On the contrary

```
p(X,Y) :- X>Y1, q(Y1,Y).
```

is not bottom-up evaluable because X is not secure.

A set of rules is bottom-up evaluable if every rule in this set is bottom-up evaluable.

Any computation using only a set of bottom-up evaluable rules can be carried out without materializing infinite intermediate results. The computation proceeds in a strictly bottom-up manner, using values for the body variables to produce values for the head variables. The bottom-up evaluability criterion ensures that the set of values for body variables is finite at each step. However, there may be an infinite number of steps. For example, if we repeatedly apply the bottom-up evaluable rule given above, at each step we have a finite number of values (in this case, a unique value) for Y1 and Y2, and hence for X and Y. However, we can apply the rule an infinite number of times, producing new values for X and Y at each step.

3. Classification of the Strategies

In the past five years, a large number of strategies to deal with Horn rules have been presented in the literature. A strategy is defined by (i) an application domain (i.e., a class of rules for which it applies) and (ii) an algorithm for replying to queries given such a set of rules.

In studying the strategies, we found that the methods were described at different levels of detail and using different formalisms, that they were sometimes very difficult to understand (and sometimes were understood differently by subsequent authors), that the application domain was not always very clearly defined, and that no performance evaluation was given for any of the strategies, which left the choice of a given strategy completely open when the application domain was the same. Finally, we found that some of the strategies were in fact the same.

We think that the strategies should be compared according to the following criteria (i) size of the application domain, (the larger the better), (ii) performance of the strategy, (the faster the better) and (iii) ease of implementation (the simpler the better). While the last criterion is somehow subjective, the first two should be quantifiable. In this section, we give a complete description of our understanding of the strategies and of their application domains, and we demonstrate each one of them through an example. As much as possible, we have tried to use the same example, except for some ''specialized'' strategies where we have picked a specific example which exhibits its typical behavior.

3.1. Characteristics of the Strategies

3.1.1. Query Evaluation vs. Query Optimization

Let us first distinguish between two approaches: one first class of strategies consists of an actual query evaluation algorithm, i.e. a program which, given a query and a database, will produce the answer to the query. We will call these *methods.* Representatives of this class are: *Henschen-Naqvi, Query/Subquery (QSQ)* or *Extension Table, APEX, Prolog, Naive Evaluation* and *Semi-Naive Evaluation.*

The strategies in the second class assume an underlying simple strategy (which is in fact naive or semi-naive evaluation) and optimize the rules to make their evaluation more efficient. They can all be described as *term rewriting systems.* These include: *Aho-Ullman, Counting and Reverse Counting, Magic Sets, Generalized Magic Sets* and *Kifer-Lozinskii.*

Note that this distinction is somehow arbitrary: each of the optimization strategies could be described as a method (when adding to it naive or semi-naive evaluation). However, this decomposition has two advantages: (i) it *might* make sense from an implementation point of view to realize the optimization strategies as term rewriting systems on top of an underlying simpler method such as naive evaluation, and (ii) from a pedagogical standpoint, they are much easier to understand this way, because presenting them as term rewriting systems indeed captures their essence.

The subsequent characteristics only relate to pure methods.

3.1.2. Interpretation vs. Compilation

A method can be *interpreted* or *compiled.* The notion is somehow fuzzy, and difficult to characterize formally. We say that the strategy is compiled if it consists of two phases: (i) a compilation phase, which accesses only the intensional database, and which generates an ''object program'' of some form, and (ii) an execution phase, which executes the object program against the facts only. A second characteristic of compiled methods is that all the database query forms (i.e., the query forms on base relations which are directly sent to the DBMS) are generated during the compilation phase. This condition is very important, because it allows the DBMS to precompile the the query forms. Otherwise the database query forms are repetitively compiled by the DBMS during the execution of the query, which is a time consuming operation. If these two conditions do not hold, we say that the strategy is interpreted. In this case, no object code is produced and there is a fixed program, the ''interpreter'', which runs against the query, the set of rules and the set of facts.

3.1.3. Recursion vs. Iteration

A rule processing strategy can be *recursive* or *iterative*. It is iterative if the "target program" (in case of a compiled approach) or the "interpreter" (in case of the interpreted approach) is iterative. It is recursive if this program is recursive, i.e., uses a stack as a control mechanism. Note that in the iterative methods, the data we deal with is statically determined. For instance, if we use temporary relations to store intermediate results, there are a finite number of such temporary relations. On the contrary, in recursive methods the number of temporary relations maintained by the system is unbounded.

3.1.4. Potentially Relevant Facts

Let D be a database and q be a query. A fact p(a) is *relevant* to the query iff there exists a derivation p(a) $\rightarrow^*$ q(b) for some b in the answer set. The notion of relevant fact was introduced in Lozinskii [1985], we use it here with a somewhat different meaning. If we know all the relevant facts in advance, instead of using the database to reply to the query, we can use the relevant part of the database only, thus cutting down on the set of facts to be processed. A *sufficient set of relevant facts* is a set of facts such that replacing the database by this set of facts gives the same answer to the query. Unfortunately, in general there does not exist a unique minimal set of facts as the following example shows:

```
suspect(X) :- long-hair(X).
suspect(X) :- alien(X).
long-hair(antoine).
alien(antoine).
```

Minimal sets of facts with respect to the query suspect(X)? are {long-hair(antoine)} and {alien(antoine)}. The second unfortunate thing about relevant facts is that it is in general impossible to find all the relevant facts in advance without spending as much effort as in replying to the query. Thus, all methods have a way of finding a super-set of relevant facts. We call this set the *set of potentially relevant facts.* A set of potentially relevant facts is *valid* if it contains a sufficient set of relevant facts. An obvious but not very interesting valid set is the set of all facts of the database.

3.1.5. Top Down vs. Bottom Up

Consider the following set of rules and the query:

```
ancestor(X,Y) :- parent(X,Z), ancestor(Z,Y).
ancestor(X,Y) :- parent(X,Y).
query(X) :- ancestor(john,X).
```

We can view each of these rules as productions in a grammar. In this context, the database predicates (parent in this example) appear as terminal symbols, and the derived predicates (ancestor in this example) appear as the non-terminal symbols. Finally, to pursue the analogy, we shall take the distinguished symbol to be query(X). Of course, we know that the analogy does not hold totally, for two reasons: (i) the presence of variables and constants in the literals and (ii) the lack of order between the literals of a rule (for instance "parent(X,Z), ancestor(Z,Y)" and "ancestor(Z,Y), parent(X,Z)" have the same meaning). But we shall ignore these differences, and use the analogy informally.

Let us now consider the language generated by this "grammar". It consists of

```
{parent(john,X);
parent(john,X),parent(X,X1);
parent(john,X),parent(X,X1),parent(X1,X2);
...}
```

This language has two interesting properties: (i) it consists of first order sentences involving only base predicates, i.e., each word of this language can be directly evaluated against the database, and (ii) if we evaluate each word of this language against the database and take the union of all these results, we get the answer to the query.

There is a minor problem here: the language is not finite, and we would have to evaluate an infinite number of first order sentences. To get out of this difficulty, we use termination conditions which tell us when to stop. An example of such a termination condition is: if one word of the language evaluates to the empty set, then all the subsequent words will also evaluate to the empty set, so we can stop generating new words. Another example of a termination condition is: if a word evaluates to a set of tuples, and all these tuples are already in the evaluation of the words preceding it, then no new tuple will ever be produced by the evaluation of any subsequent word, thus we can stop at this point.

All query evaluation methods in fact do the following:

(i) generate the language, (ii) while the language is generated, evaluate all its sentences and (iii) at each step, check for the termination condition.

Therefore, there are essentially two classes of methods: those which generate the language bottom up, and those which generate the language top-down. The bottom-up strategies start from the terminals (i.e., the base relations) and keep assembling them to produce non-terminals (i.e derived relations) until they generate the distinguished symbol (i.e., the query). The top-down strategies start from the distinguished symbol (the query) and keep expanding it by applying the rules to the non-terminals (derived relations). As we shall see, top-down strategies are often more efficient because they "know" which query is being solved, but they are more complex. Bottom up strategies are simpler, but they compute a lot of useless results because they do not know what query they are evaluating.

4. The Methods

We shall use the same example for most of the methods. The intensional database and query are:

```
R1  ancestor(X,Y) :- parent(X,Z),ancestor(Z,Y).
R2  ancestor(X,Y) :- parent(X,Y).
R3  query(X) :- ancestor(aa,X).
```

The extensional database is:

```
parent(a,aa).
parent(a,ab).
parent(aa,aaa).
parent(aa,aab).
parent(aaa,aaaa).
parent(c,ca).
```

4.1. Naive Evaluation

Naive Evaluation is a bottom-up, compiled, iterative strategy.

Its application domain is the set of bottom-up evaluable rules.

In a first phase, the rules which derive the query are compiled into an iterative program. The compilation process uses the reduced rule/goal graph. It first selects all the rules which derive the query. A temporary relation is assigned to each derived predicate in this set of rules. A statement which computes the value of the output predicate from the value of the input predicates is associated with each rule node in the graph. With each set of mutually recursive rules, there is associated a loop which applies the rules in that set until no new tuple is generated. Each temporary relation is initialized to the empty set. Then computation proceeds from the base predicates capturing the nodes of the graph.

In this example, the rules which derive the query are {R1, R2, R3}, and there are two temporary relations: ancestor and query. The method consists in applying R2 to parent, producing a new value for ancestor, then applying R1 to ancestor until no new tuple is generated, then applying R3.

The object program is:

begin
initialize ancestor to the empty set;
evaluate (ancestor(X,Y) :- parent(X,Y));
insert the result in ancestor;
while "new tuples are generated" **do**
  begin
  evaluate (ancestor(X,Y) :- parent(X,Z), ancestor(Z,Y)) using the current value of ancestor;
  insert the result in ancestor
  end;
evaluate (query(X) :- ancestor(aa,X));
insert the result in query
end.

The execution of the program against the data goes as follows:

Step 1: Apply R2.
The resulting state is:
ancestor = {(a,aa), (a,ab), (aa,aaa), (aa,aab), (aaa,aaaa), (c,ca)}
query = {}

Step 2: Apply R1.
The following new tuples are generated:
ancestor: {(a,aaa), (a,aab), (aa,aaaa)}
And the resulting state is:
ancestor = {(a,aa), (a,ab), (aa,aaa), (aa,aab), (aaa,aaaa), (c,ca), (a,aaa), (a,aab), (aa,aaaa)}
query = {}

New tuples have been generated so we continue:

Step 3: Apply R1.
The following tuples are generated:
ancestor: {(a,aaa), (a,aab), (aa,aaaa), (a,aaaa)}
The new state is:

ancestor = {(a,aa), (a,ab), (aa,aaa), (aa,aab), (aaa,aaaa), (c,ca), (a,aaa), (a,aab), (aa,aaaa), (a,aaaa)}
query = {}

Because (a,aaaa) is new, we continue:

Step 4: Apply R1.
The following tuples are generated:
ancestor: {(a,aaa), (a,aab), (aa,aaaa), (a,aaaa)}

Because there are no new tuples, the state does not change and we move to R3.

Step 5: Apply R3.
The following tuples are produced:
query: {(aa,aaa), (aa,aaaa)}
The new state is:
ancestor = {(a,aa), (a,ab), (aa,aaa), (aa,aab), (aaa,aaaa), (c,ca), (a,aaa), (a,aab), (aa,aaaa), (a,aaaa)}
query = {(aa,aaa), (aa,aaaa), (aa,aab)}.

The algorithm terminates.

In this example, we note the following problems: (i) the entire relation is evaluated, i.e., the set of potentially relevant facts is the set of facts of the base predicates which derive the query, and (ii) step 3 completely duplicates step 2.

Naive evaluation is the most widely described method in the literature. It has been presented in a number of papers under different forms. The inference engine of SNIP, presented in McKay and Shapiro [1981], is in fact an interpreted version of naive evaluation. The method described in Chang [1981], while based on a very interesting language paradigm and restricted to linear systems, is a compiled version of naive evaluation based on relational algebra. The method in Marque-Pucheu [1983] is a compiled version of naive evaluation using a different algebra of relations. The method in Bayer [1985] is another description of naive evaluation. The framework presented in Delobel [1986] also uses naive evaluation as its inference strategy. SNIP is, to our knowledge, the only existing implementation in the general case.

4.2. Semi-Naive Evaluation

Semi-naive evaluation is a bottom-up, compiled and iterative strategy.

Its application range is the set of bottom-up evaluable rules.

This method uses the same approach as naive evaluation, but tries to cut down on the number of duplications. It behaves exactly as naive evaluation, except for the loop mechanism where it tries to be smarter.

Let us first try to give an idea of the method as an extension of naive evaluation. Let p be a recursive predicate; consider a recursive rule having p as a head predicate and let us write this rule:

$$p :- \phi(p1,p2,...,pn,q1,q2,...,qm).$$

where ϕ is a first order formula, p1,p2,...,pn are mutually recursive to p, and q1,q2,..,qm are base or derived predicates, which are not mutually recursive to p.

In the naive evaluation strategy, all the qi's are fully evaluated when we start computing p and the pi's. On the other hand p and the pi's are all evaluated inside the same loop (together with the rest of predicates mutually recursive to p).

Let pj(i) be the value of the predicate pj at the i-th iteration of the loop. At this iteration, we compute

$$\phi(p1(i),p2(i),...,pn(i),q1,q2,...,qm).$$

During that same iteration each pj receives a set of new tuples. Let us call this new set dpj(i). Thus the value of pj at the beginning of step (i+1) is pj(i) + dpj(i) (where + denotes union).

At step (i+1) we evaluate

$$\phi((p1(i)+dp1(i)),...,(pn(i)+dpn(i)),q1,...,qm),$$

which, of course, recomputes the previous expression (because ϕ is monotonic).

The ideal however, is to compute only the *new* tuples i.e the expression:

$$d\phi(p1(i),dp1(i),...,pn(i),dpn(i),q1,...,qm) = \\ \phi((p1(i)+dp1(i)),...,(pn(i)+dpn(i)),q1,...,qm) - \phi(p1(i),...,pn(i),q1,...,qm)$$

The basic principle of the semi-naive method is the evaluation of the differential of ϕ instead of the entire ϕ at each step. The problem is to come up with a first order expression for $d\phi$, which does not contain any difference operator. Let us assume there is such an expression, and describe the algorithm. With each recursive predicate p are associated four temporary relations p.before, p.after, dp.before and dp.after. The object program for a loop is as follows:

```
while "the state changes" do
  begin
  for all mutually recursive predicates p do
    begin
    initialize dp.after to the empty set;
    initialize p.after to p.before;
    end
  for each mutually recursive rule do
    begin
    evaluate dφ(p1,dp1,...,pn,dpn,q1,...,qn) using the current values of
    pi.before for pi and of dpi.before for dpi;
    add the resulting tuples to dp.after;
    add the resulting tuples to p.after
    end
  end.
```

All we have to do now is provide a way to generate dφ from φ. The problem is not solved in its entirety and only a number of transformations are known. In Bancilhon [1985], some of them are given in terms of relational algebra.

It should be noted however, that for the method to work, the only property we have to guarantee is that:

$$\phi(p1+dp1,...) - \phi(p1,...) \subseteq d\phi(p1,dp1,...) \subseteq \phi(p1+dp1,...)$$

Clearly, the closer dφ(p1,dp1,...) is to (φ(p1+dp1,...) - φ(p1,...)), the better the optimization is. In the worse case, where we use φ for dφ, semi-naive evaluation behaves as naive evaluation. Here are some simple examples of rewrite rules:

if φ(p,q) = p(X,Y),q(Y,Z), **then** dφ(p,dp,q) = dp(X,Y),q(Y,Z)

More generally when φ is linear in p, the expression for dφ is obtained by replacing p by dp.

if φ(p1,p2) = p1(X,Y),p2(Y,Z),
then dφ(p,dp) = p1(X,Y),dp2(Y,Z)+dp1(X,Y),p2(Y,Z)+dp1(X,Y),dp2(Y,Z)

Note that this is not an exact differential but a reasonable approximation.

The idea of semi-naive evaluation underlies many papers. A complete description of the method based on relational algebra is given in Bancilhon [1985]. The idea is also present in Bayer [1985].

It should also be pointed out that, in the particular case of linear rules, because the differential of φ(p) is simply φ(dp), it is sufficient to have an inference engine which only uses the new tuples. Therefore many methods which are restricted to linear rules do indeed use semi-naive evaluation. Note also that when the rules are not linear, applying naive evaluation only to the "new tuples" is an incorrect method (in the sense that it does not produce the whole answer to the query). This can be easily checked on the recursive rule:

ancestor(X,Y) :- ancestor(X,Z),ancestor(Z,Y).

In this case, if we only feed the new tuples at the next stage, the relation which we compute consists of the ancestors whose distance to one another is a power of two.

To our knowledge, outside of the special case of linear rules, the method as a whole has not been implemented.

4.3. Iterative Query/Subquery

Iterative Query/Subquery (QSQI) is an interpreted, top-down strategy.

Its application domain is the set of range restricted rules without evaluable predicates.

The method associates a temporary relation with every relation which derives the query, but the computation of the predicates deriving the query is done at run time. QSQI also stores a set of queries which are currently being evaluated. When several queries correspond to the same query form, QSQI stores and executes them as a single object. For instance, if we have the queries p(a,X) and query p(b,X), we can view this as query p({a,b},X). We call such an object a *generalized query.* The state memorized by the algorithm is a couple <Q,R>, where Q is a set of generalized queries, and R is a set of derived relations, together with their current values.

The iterative interpreter is as follows:

```
Initial state is <{query(X)},{}>
while the state changes do
 for all generalized queries in Q do
   for all rules whose head matches the generalized query do
      begin
      unify rule with the generalized query;
      (i.e propagate the constants. this generates new generalized queries for
      each derived predicate in the body by looking up the base relations.)
      generate new tuples;
      (by replacing each base predicate on the right by its value and every
      derived predicate by its current temporary value.)
      add these new tuples to R;
      add these new generalized queries to Q
      end
```

Let us now run this interpreter against our example logic database:

The initial state is: <{query(X)},{}>

Step 1

We try to solve query(X). Only rule R3 applies. The unification produces the generalized query ancestor({aa},X). This generates temporary relations for query and ancestor with empty set values. Attempts at generating tuples for this generalized query fail.

The new state vector is:

<{query(X),ancestor(aa,X)}, {ancestor={},query={}}>

Step 2

A new generalized query has been generated, so we go on. We try to evaluate each of the generalized queries: query(X) does not give anything new, so we try ancestor({aa},X).
Using rule R2, and unifying, we get parent(aa,X). This is a base relation, so we can produce a set of tuples. Thus we generate a value for ancestor which contains all the tuples of parent(aa,X) and the new state vector is:

<{query(X),ancestor(aa,X)}, {ancestor={(aa,aaa),(aa,aab)},query={}}>

We now solve ancestor(aa,X) using R1. Unification produces the expression :

parent(aa,Z),ancestor(Z,Y).

We try to generate new tuples from this expansion and the current ancestor value but get no tuples. We also generate new generalized queries by looking up parent and instantiating Z. This produces the new expression:

parent(aa,{aaa,aab}),ancestor({aaa,aab},Z).

This creates two new queries which are added to the generalized query and the new state is:

<{query(X),ancestor({aa,aaa,aab},X)}, {ancestor={(aa,aaa),(aa,aab)},query={}}>

Step 3

New generalized queries and new tuples have been generated so we continue. We first solve query(X) using R3 and get the value {(aa,aaa), (aa,aab)} for query. The resulting new state is:

<{query(X),ancestor({aa,aaa,aab},X)}, {ancestor={(aa,aaa),(aa,aab)}, query={(aa,aaa),(aa,aab)}}>

We now try to solve ancestor({aa,aaa,aab},X). Using R2, we get parent({aa,aaa,aab),X) which is a base relation and generates the following tuples in ancestor: {(aa,aaa),(aa,aab),(aaa,aaaa)}. This produces the new state:

<{query(X),ancestor({aa,aaa,aab},X)}, {ancestor={(aa,aaa),(aa,aab),(aaa,aaaa)},
query={(aa,aaa),(aa,aab)}}>

We now solve ancestor({aa,aaa,aab},X)} using R1 and we get: parent({aa,aaa,aab},Z),ancestor(Z,Y). We bind Z by going to the parent relation, and we get: parent({aa,aaa,aab},{aaa,aab,aaaa}), ancestor({aaa,aab,aaaa},Y). This generates the new generalized query ancestor({aaa,aab,aaaa},Y) and the new state:

<{query(X),ancestor({aa,aaa,aab,aaaa},X)}, {ancestor={(aa,aaa),(aa,aab),(aa,aaaa),(aaa,aaaa)},
query={(aa,aaa),(aa,aaaa),(aa,aab)}}>

Step 4

A new generalized query has been generated, so we continue. Solving the ancestor queries using R2 will not produce any new tuples, and solving it with R3 will not produce any new generalized query nor any tuples. The algorithm terminates.

Concerning the performance of the method, one can note that (i) the set of potentially relevant facts is better than for naive (in this example it is optimal), and (ii) QSQI has the same duplication problem as naive evaluation: each step entirely duplicates the previous strategy.

Iterative Query/Subquery is presented in Vieille [1986]. To our knowledge it has not been implemented.

4.4. Recursive Query/Subquery or Extension Tables

Recursive Query/Subquery (QSQR) is a top-down interpreted recursive strategy.

The application domain is the set of range restricted rules without evaluable predicates.

It is of course a recursive version of the previous strategy. As before, we maintain temporary values of derived relations and a set of generalized queries. The state memorized by the algorithm is still a couple <Q,R>, where Q is a set of generalized queries and R is a set of derived relations together with their current values. The algorithm uses a selection function which, given a rule, can choose the first and the next derived predicate in the body to be "solved".

The recursive interpreter is as follows:

```
procedure evaluate(q)  (* q is a generalized query *)
begin
while "new tuples are generated" do
  for all rules whose head matches the generalized query do
   begin
   unify the rule with the generalized query; (i.e., propagate the constants)
   until there are no more derived predicates on the right do
     begin
```

choose the first/next derived predicate according to the selection function;
generate the corresponding generalized query;
(This is done by replacing in the rule each base predicate by its value
and each previously solved derived predicate by its current value).
eliminate from that generalized query the queries that are already in Q;
this produces a new generalized query q';
add q' to Q;
evaluate(q')
end;
replace each evaluated predicate by its value and evaluate the generalized query q;
(This can be done in some order without waiting for all predicates to be evaluated.)
add the results in R;
return the results
end
end.
Initial state is <{query(X)},{}>
evaluate(query(X)).

It is important to note that this version of QSQ is very similar to Prolog. It solves goals in a top-down fashion using recursion, and it considers the literals ordered in the rule (the order is defined by the selection function). The important differences with Prolog are: (i) the method is set-at-a-time instead of tuple-at-a-time, through the generalized query concept, and (ii) as pointed out in Dietrich and Warren [1985], the method uses a dynamic programming approach of storing the intermediate results and re-using them when needed. This dynamic programming feature also solves the problem of cycles in the facts: while Prolog will run in an infinite loop in the presence of such cycles, QSQR will detect them and stop the computation when no new tuple is generated. Thus, QSQR is complete over its application domain whereas Prolog is not.

Here is the ancestor example:

evaluate(query(X))
use rule R3
query(X) :- ancestor(aa,X)
this generates the query ancestor({aa},X)
new state is: <{ancestor({aa},X), query(X)},{}>
evaluate(ancestor({aa},X)
Step 1 of the iteration
use rule R1
ancestor({aa},Y) :- parent({aa},Z), ancestor(Z,Y).
by looking up parent we get the bindings {aaa,aab} for Z.
this generates the query ancestor({aaa,aab},X)
new state is: <{ancestor({aa,aaa,aab},X), query(X)},{}>
evaluate (ancestor({aaa,aab},X))
(this is a recursive call)
Step 1.1
use R1
ancestor({aaa,aab},Y) :- parent({aaa,aab},Z),ancestor(Z,Y).
by looking up parent we get the binding {aaaa} for Z
new state is: <{ancestor({aa,aaa,aab,aaaa},X), query(X)},{}>
evaluate(ancestor({aaaa},X))
(this is a recursive call)
Step 1.1.1
use R1
ancestor({aaaa},Y) :- parent({aaaa},Z),ancestor(Z,Y).
by looking up parent we get no binding for Z
use R2

ancestor({aaaa},Y) :- parent({aaaa},Y)
this fails to return any tuple
end of **evaluate**(ancestor({aaaa},X))
Step 1.1.2
nothing new is produced
end of **evaluate**(ancestor({aaaa},Y))
use R2
ancestor({aaa,aab},Y) :- parent({aaa,aab},Y)
this returns the tuple ancestor(aaa,aaaa)
new state is: <{ancestor({aa,aaa,aab,aaaa},X),
query(X)}, {ancestor={(aaa,aaaa)}}>
Step 1.2
same as Step 1, nothing new produced
end of **evaluate** (ancestor({aaa,aab},X))
(popping from the recursion in rule R1, we have:)
a new tuple generated - ancestor(aa,aaaa)
new state is: <{ancestor({aa,aaa,aab,aaaa},X), query(X)},
{ancestor={(aaa,aaaa), (aa,aaaa)}}>
use rule R2
ancestor({aa},X) :- parent({aa},Y)
returns the tuples ancestor(aa,aaa) and ancestor(aa,aab)
new state is: <{ancestor({aa,aaa,aab,aaaa},X), query(X)},{ancestor={(aaa,aaaa),(aa,aaaa),(aa,aaa),(aa,aab)}}>
Step 2
nothing new produced
end of **evaluate**({aa},X)
generate tuples from R3
new state is: <{ancestor({aa,aaa,aab,aaaa},X), query(X)},{ancestor={(aaa,aaaa),
(aa,aaaa),(aa,aaa),(aa,aab)},query=(aa,aaaa), (aa,aaa),(aa,aab)}}>
end of **evaluate**(query(X))

Recursive Query/Subquery is described in Vieille [1986]. A compiled version has been implemented on top of the INGRES relational system. In Dietrich and Warren [1985], along with a good survey of some of these strategies, a method called "extension tables" is presented. It is, up to a few details, the same method.

4.5. Henschen-Naqvi

Henschen-Naqvi is a top-down, compiled and iterative method.

The application domain is that of linear range restricted rules.

The method has a compilation phase which generates an iterative program. That iterative program is then run against the data base. The general strategy is fairly complex to understand, and we shall restrict ourselves to describing it in the "typical case" which is:

p(X,Y) :- up(X,XU),p(XU,YU),down(YU,Y).
p(X,Y) :- flat(X,Y).
query(X) :- p(a,X).

Note that the relation names *up* and *down* are not to be confused with the notions "top-down" or "bottom-up", which are characteristics of evaluation strategies. Let us introduce some simple notation, which will make reading the algorithm much simpler. Since we are only dealing with binary relations, we can view these as set-to-set mappings. Thus, the relation r associates with each set A a set B, consisting of all the elements related to A by r. We denote A.r the image of A by r, and we have:

$$A.r = \{ y \mid r(x,y) \text{ and } x \in A \}$$

If we view relations as mappings, we can compose them, and we shall denote r.s the composition of r and s. Therefore:

A.(r.s) = (A.r).s

This approach is similar to the formalism described in Gardarin and Maindreville [1986]. We shall denote the composition of relation r n times with itself r^n. Finally we shall denote set union by '+'. Once this notation is introduced, it is easy to see that the answer to the query is

$\{a\}$.flat + $\{a\}$.up.flat.down + $\{a\}$.up.up.flat.down.down + ... + $\{a\}$.up^n.flat.down^n + ...

The state memorized by the algorithm is a couple <V,E>, where V is a the value of a unary relation and E is an expression. At each step, using V and E, we compute some new tuples and compute the new values of V and E.

The iterative program is as follows:

```
V :={a};
E := λ;        /* the empty string */
while "new tuples are generated in V" do
  begin
  /* produce some answer tuples */
  answer := answer + V.flat.E;
  /* compute the new value */
  V := V.up ;
  /* compute the new expression */
  E := E | .down;
  end.
```

Note that E is an *expression*, and is augmented each time around the loop by concatenating ".down" to it through the "cons" operator. As can be seen from this program, at step i, the value V represents $\{a\}$.up^i and the expression E represents down^i. Therefore the produced tuples are:

$\{a\}$.up^i.flat.down^i.

This is not meant to be a complete description of the method, but a description of its behavior in the typical case.

The Henschen-Naqvi method is described in Henschen and Naqvi [1984]. The method has been implemented in the case described here. This implementation can be found in Laskowski [1984]. An equivalent strategy is described using a different formalism in Gardarin and Maindreville [1986]. The performance of the strategy is compared to Semi-Naive evaluation and another method (not described here) in Han and Lu [1986].

4.6. Prolog

Prolog (Roussel [1975]) is a top-down, interpreted and recursive method.

The application domain of Prolog is difficult to state precisely: (i) it is data dependent in the sense that the facts have to be acyclic for the interpreter to terminate, and (ii) there is no simple syntactic characterization of a terminating Prolog program. The job of characterizing the "good" rules is left to the programmer.

We consider its execution model to be well known and will not describe it. In fact Prolog is a programming language and not a general strategy to evaluate Horn clauses. We essentially mention Prolog for the sake of completeness and because it is interesting to compare its performance to the other strategies.

4.7. APEX

APEX is a strategy which is difficult to categorize. It is partly compiled in the sense that a graph similar to the predicate connection graph is produced from the rules, which takes care of some of the preprocessing needed for interpretation. It is not fully compiled in the sense that the program which runs against the database is still unique (but driven by the graph). It is, however, clearly recursive, because the interpreter program is recursive. Finally, it is partly top-down and partly bottom-up as will be seen in the interpreter.

The application domain of APEX is the set of range restricted rules which contain no constants and no evaluable predicates.

The interpreter takes the form of a recursive procedure, which, given a query, produces a set of tuples for this query. It is as follows:

```
procedure solve(query,answer)
begin
answer := {};
if query q is on a base relation
then evaluate q against the date base
else
  begin
  select the relevant facts for q in the base predicates;
  put them in relevant;
  while new tuples are generated do
    begin
    for each rule do (this can be done in parallel)
      begin
      instantiate the right predicates with the relevant facts and produce tuples for the left predicate;
      add these tuples to the set of relevant facts;
      initialize the set of useful facts to the set of relevant facts;
      for each literal on the right do (this can be done in parallel)
        begin
        for each matching relevant fact do
          begin
          plug the fact in the rule and propagate the constants;
          this generates a new rule and a new set of queries;
          for all these new queries q' do
            begin
            solve(q',answer(q')) (this is the recursion step)
            add answer(q') to the useful facts
            end
          end
        instantiate the right predicates with the useful facts;
        produce tuples for the left predicate;
        add these to the relevant facts;
        extract the answer to q from the relevant facts.
        end
      end
    end
  end.
end;
solve(query(X),answer).
```

Let us now run this program against our ancestor example. We cannot have a constant in the rules and we must modify our rule set and solve directly the query ancestor(aa,X):

solve (ancestor(aa,X), answer)
we first select the relevant base facts.
relevant = {parent(aa,aaa),parent(aa,aab)};
we now start the main iteration:
Step 1
rule R1
ancestor(X,Y) :- parent(X,Z), ancestor(Z,Y)

```
we cannot produce any new tuple from this rule because ancestor
does not yet have any relevant fact
useful = {parent(aa,aaa),parent(aa,aab)};
process parent(X,Z)
  use parent(aa,aaa)
    the new rule is
    parent(aa,aaa),ancestor(aaa,Y)
    solve(ancestor(aaa,Y),answer1)
    ... (this call is not described)
    this returns
    {ancestor(aaa,aaaa)}, which we add to useful
    useful = {parent(aa,aaa),parent(aa,aab),ancestor(aaa,aaaa)};
  use parent(aa,aab)
    the new rule is
    parent(aa,aab),ancestor(aab,Y)
    solve(ancestor(aab,Y),answer2)
    ... (this call is not described)
    this returns nothing
process ancestor(Z,Y)
we instantiate parent and ancestor with the useful facts.
this produces ancestor(aa,aaaa)
we add it to the relevant facts:
relevant = {parent(aa,aaa),parent(aa,aab), ancestor(aa,aaaa)};

rule R2
  ancestor(X,Y) :- parent(X,Y)
  using the relevant facts we produce {ancestor(aa,aaa),ancestor(aa,aab)}
  we add these to relevant:
  relevant = {parent(aa,aaa),parent(aa,aab), ancestor(aa,aaa), ancestor(aa,aab), ancestor(aa,aaaa)};
  this rule does not produce any subquery

Step 2
  will not produce anything new,
  and so the algorithm stops.
```

The APEX method is described in Lozinskii [1985]. The method has been implemented.

5. The Optimization Strategies

We now turn to the description of the second class of strategies: the optimization strategies.

The main drawbacks of the naive evaluation method are:

1. The potential set of relevant facts is too large (i.e., it does not make good use of the query bindings), and
2. It generates a lot of duplicate computation.

A number of optimization strategies have recently been proposed to overcome these two difficulties.

5.1. Aho-Ullman

Aho and Ullman (Aho and Ullman [1979]) present an algorithm for optimizing recursive queries by commuting selections with the least fixpoint operator (LFP). The input is an expression

$$\sigma_F(\mathrm{LFP}(r=f(r))$$

where f(r) is a monotonic relational algebra expression (under the ordering of set inclusion) and contains at most one occurrence of r. The output is an equivalent expression where the selection has been pushed through as far as possible.

We introduce their notation and ideas through an example. Consider:

a(X,Y) :- a(X,Z), p(Z,Y).

a(X,Y) :- p(X,Y).

q(X) :- a(john,X).

Aho-Ullman write this as:

$\sigma_{a_1=john}(LFP(a = a.p \cup p))$

In this definition, *a* is a relation which is defined by a *fixpoint* equation in relational algebra, and *p* is a base relation. If we start with *a* empty and repeatedly compute *a* using the rule a = a.p ∪ p, at some iteration, there is no change (since the relation *p* is finite). Because the function used in the fixpoint equation is monotonic, this is the *least fixpoint* of the fixpoint equation (Tarski [1955]). It is the smallest relation *a* which satisfies the equation, i.e. contains every tuple which can be generated by using the fixpoint rule, and no tuple which cannot. The query is simply the selection a_1=john applied to this relation. Thus, the query is a selection applied to the transitive closure of p.

We now describe how the Aho-Ullman algorithm optimizes this query. We use '.' to denote composition, which is a join followed by projecting out the join attributes. We begin with the expression

$\sigma_{a_1=john}(a)$

and by replacing a by f(a) we generate

$\sigma_{a_1=john}(a.p \cup p))$

By distributing the selection across the join, we get

$\sigma_{a_1=john}(a.p) \cup \sigma_{a_1=john}(p)$.

Since the selection in the first subexpression only involves the first attribute of a, we can rewrite it as

$\sigma_{a_1=john}(a) . p$

We observe that this contains the subexpression

$\sigma_{a_1=john}(a)$

which was the first expression in the series. If we denote this by E, the desired optimized expression is then

$LFP(E = E.p \cup \sigma_{a_1=john}(p))$

This is equivalent to the Horn Clause query:

a(john,Y) :- a(john,Z), p(Z,Y).
a(john,Y) :- p(john,Y).
q(X) :- a(john,X).

The essence of the strategy is to construct a series of equivalent expressions starting with the expression $\sigma_F(r)$ and repeatedly replacing the single occurrence of r by the expression f(r). Note that each of these expressions contains just one occurrence of R. In each of these expressions, we push the selection as far inside as possible. Selection distributes across union, commutes with another selection and can be pushed ahead of a projection. However, it distributes across a Cartesian product Y × Z only if the selection applies to components from just one of the two arguments Y and Z. The algorithm fails to commute the selection with the LFP operator if the (single) occurrence of r is in one of the arguments of a Cartesian product across which we cannot distribute the selection. We stop when this happens or when we find an expression of the form $h(g(\sigma_F(r)))$ and one of the previous expressions in the series is of the form $h(\sigma_F(r))$. In the latter case, the equivalent expression that we are looking for is h(LFP(s=g(s))), and we have succeeded in pushing the selection ahead of the LFP operator.

We note in conclusion that the expression f(r) must contain no more than one occurrence of r. For instance, the algorithm does not apply in this case:

$$\sigma_{a_1=john}(LFP(a = a.a \cup p))$$

Aho and Ullman also present a similar strategy for commuting projections with the LFP operator, but we do not discuss it here.

5.2. Static Filtering

The Static Filtering algorithm is an extension of the Aho-Ullman algorithm described above. However, rules are represented as rule/goal graphs rather than as relational algebra expressions, and the strategy is described in terms of *filters* which are applied to the arcs of the graph. It is convenient to think of the data as flowing through the graph along the arcs. A *filter* on an arc is a selection which can be applied to the tuples flowing through that arc, and is used to reduce the number of tuples that are generated. Transforming a given rule/goal graph into an equivalent graph with (additional) filters on some arcs is equivalent to rewriting the corresponding set of rules.

The execution of a query starts with the nodes corresponding to the base relations sending all their tuples through all arcs that leave them. Each axiom node that receives tuples generates tuples for its head predicate and passes them on through all its outgoing arcs. A relation node saves all new tuples that it receives and passes them on through its outgoing arcs. Computation stops (with the answer being the set of tuples in the query node) when there is no more change in the tuples stored at the various nodes at some iteration. We note that this is simply Semi-Naive evaluation.

Given filters on all the arcs leaving a node, we can 'push' them through the node as follows. If the node is a relation node, we simply place the disjunction of the filters on each incoming arc. If the node is an axiom node, we place on each incoming arc the strongest consequence of the disjunction that can be expressed purely in terms of the variables of the literal corresponding to this arc.

The objective of the optimization algorithm is to place the "strongest" possible filters on each arc. Starting with the filter which represents the constant in the query, it repeatedly pushes filters through the nodes at which the corresponding arcs are incident. Since the number of possible filters is finite, this algorithm terminates. It stops when further pushing of filters does not change the graph, and the graph at this point is equivalent to the original graph (although the graph at intermediate steps may not). Note that since the disjunction of 'true' with any predicate is 'true', if any arc in a loop is assigned the filter 'true', all arcs in the loop are subsequently assigned the filter 'true'.

Consider the transitive closure example that we optimized using the Aho-Ullman algorithm. We would represent it by the following axioms:

R1 a(X,Y) :- a(X,Z), p(Z,Y).
R2 a(X,Y) :- p(X,Y).
R3 q(X) :- a(john,X).

Given below is the corresponding system graph, before and after optimization (We have omitted the variables in the axioms for clarity):

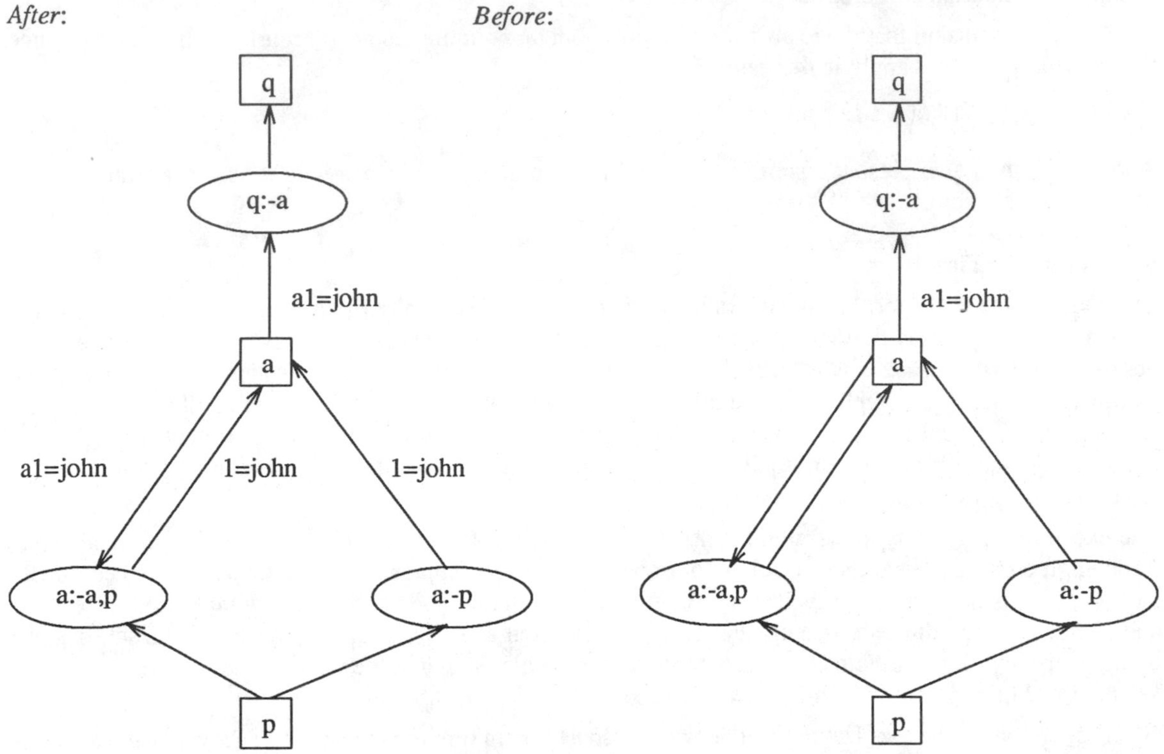

We begin the optimization by pushing the selection through the relation node a. Thus the arcs from R1 to *a* and from R2 to *a* both get the filter '1=john' (We have simplified the conventions for keeping track of variables - '1' refers to the first attribute of the corresponding head predicate). We then push these filters through the corresponding axiom nodes, R1 and R2. Pushing '1=john' through node R2 puts the filter 'p_1=john' on the arc from *p* to R2. Pushing '1=john' through node R1 puts the filter 'a_1=john' on the arc from *a* to R1. Note that it does not put anything on the arc from *p* to R1 (empty filters are equivalent to 'true'). There are no arcs entering *p*, and the filter on the arc from *a* to R1 does not change the disjunction of the filters on arcs leaving *a* (which is still 'a_1=john'). So the algorithm terminates here.

The analogy with the Aho-Ullman algorithm is easily seen when we recognize that a filter is a selection, pushing through a relation node is distribution across a $\cup$ and pushing through an axiom node is distribution across a Cartesian product. In general, the optimizations achieved by the two algorithms are identical. However, the Static Filtering algorithm is more general in that it successfully optimizes some expressions containing more than one occurrence of the defined predicate. An example is the expression

$$\sigma_{a_1=john}(\mathrm{LFP}(a = (a.p \cup a.q \cup p)))$$

The Aho-Ullman algorithm does not apply in this case because there are two occurrences of R in f(R). The Static Filtering algorithm optimizes this to

$$\mathrm{LFP}((\sigma_{a_1=john}(a)\ .\ p) \cup (\sigma_{a_1=john}(a)\ .\ q) \cup (\sigma_{a_1=john}(p)))$$

Essentially, it improves upon the Aho-Ullman algorithm in that it is able to distribute selection across some unions where both arguments contain r.

Further, the algorithm can work directly upon certain mutually recursive rules, for example

R1 r(X,Y) :- b(X), s(X,Y).
R2 s(X,Y) :- c(X), r(X,Y).
R3 q(X) :- r(X,john).

Before applying the Aho-Ullman algorithm, these rules must be rewritten as follows

R1 r(X,Y) :- b(X), c(X), r(X,Y).
R2 q(X) :- r(X,john).

Note that the Static Filtering algorithm fails to optimize both

$\sigma_{a_1=john}(LFP(a = a.a \cup p))$, and

$\sigma_{a_1=john}(LFP(a = a.p \cup p.a \cup p))$

In this description, we have treated only the "static" filtering approach of Kifer and Lozinskii. Elsewhere, they have also proposed "dynamic" filters (Kifer and Lozinskii [1986b]), which are not determined at compile time but are computed at run time, and this approach is similar to Generalized Magic Sets, discussed later in this section.

5.3. Magic Sets

The idea of the Magic Sets optimization is to simulate the sideways passing of bindings a la Prolog by the introduction of new rules. This cuts down on the number of potentially relevant facts.

The application domain is the set of bottom-up evaluable rules.

We shall describe the strategy in detail, using as an example a modified version of the same-generation rule set:

sg(X,Y) :- p(X,XP),p(Y,YP),sg(YP,XP).
sg(X,X).
query(X) :- sg(a,X).

Note that in this version the two variables XP and YP have been permuted. Note also that the second rule is not range restricted. The first step of the magic set transformation is the introduction of adornments and the generation of adorned rules.

Given a system of rules, the *adorned rule system* (Ullman [1985]) is obtained as follows:
For each rule r and for each adornment *a* of the predicate on the left, generate an adorned rule: Define recursively an argument of a predicate in the rule r to be *distinguished* (Henschen and Naqvi [1984]) if either it is bound in the adornment *a*, or it is a constant, or it appears in a base predicate occurrence that has a distinguished variable. Thus, the sources of bindings are (i) the constants and (ii) the bindings in the head of the rule. These bindings are propagated through the base predicates. If we consider each distinguished argument to be bound, this defines an adornment for each derived literal on the right. The adorned rule is obtained by replacing each derived literal by its adorned version.

If we consider the rule

sg(X,Y) :- p(X,XP),p(Y,YP),sg(YP,XP).

with adornment bf on the head predicate, then X is distinguished because it is bound in sg(X,Y), XP is distinguished because X is distinguished and p(X,XP) is a base predicate; these are the only distinguished variables. Thus the new adorned rule is

sg^{bf} (X,Y) :- p(X,XP),p(Y,YP),sg^{fb} (YP,XP).

If we consider a set of rules, this process generates a set of adorned rules. The set of adorned rules has size K.R where R is the size of the original set of rules and K is a factor exponential in the number of attributes per derived predicate. So, for instance, if every predicate has three attributes, then the adorned system is eight times larger than the original system. However, we do not need the entire adorned system and we only keep the adorned rules that derive the query. In our example the reachable adorned system is:

$sg^{bf}(X,Y)$:- p(X,XP),p(Y,YP),$sg^{fb}(YP,XP)$.
$sg^{fb}(X,Y)$:- p(X,XP),p(Y,YP),$sg^{bf}(YP,XP)$.
$sg^{bf}(X,X)$.
$sg^{fb}(X,X)$.
$query^{f}(X)$:- $sg^{bf}(a,X)$.

Clearly, this new set of rules is equivalent to the original set in the sense that it will generate the same answer to the query.

The magic set optimization consists in generating from the given set of rules a new set of rules, which are equivalent to the original set with respect to the query, and such that their bottom-up evaluation is more efficient. This transformation is done as follows: (i) for each occurrence of a derived predicate on the right of an adorned rule, we generate a magic rule. (ii) For each adorned rule we generate a modified rule.

Here is how we generate the magic rule: (i) choose an adorned literal predicate p on the right of the adorned rule r, (ii) erase all the other derived literals on the right, (iii) in the derived predicate occurrence replace the name of the predicate by magic.p^{a} where a is the literal adornment, and erase the non distinguished variables, (iv) erase all the non distinguished base predicates, (v) in the left hand side, erase all the non distinguished variables and replace the name of the predicate by *magic.p* $1^{a'}$, where p1 is the predicate on the left, and a' is the adornment of the predicate p1, and finally (vi) exchange the two magic predicates.

For instance the adorned rule:

$sg^{bf}(X,Y)$:- p(X,XP),p(Y,YP),$sg^{fb}(YP,XP)$.

generates the magic rule:

$magic^{fb}(XP)$:- p(X,XP), $magic^{bf}(X)$.

Note that the magic rules simulate the passing of bound arguments through backward chaining. (We have dropped the suffix ''sg'' in naming the magic predicates since it is clear from the context.)

Here is how we generate the modified rule: For each rule whose head is p.a, add on the right hand side the predicate magic.p.a(X) where X is the list of distinguished variables in that occurrence of p. For instance the adorned rule:

$sg^{bf}(X,Y)$:- p(X,XP),p(Y,YP),$sg^{fb}(YP,XP)$.

generates the modified rule:

$sg^{bf}(X,Y)$:- p(X,XP),p(Y,YP),$magic^{bf}(X)$, $sg^{fb}(YP,XP)$.

Finally the complete modified set of rules for our example is:

$magic^{fb}(XP)$:- p(X,XP), $magic^{bf}(X)$.
$magic^{bf}(YP)$:- p(Y,YP),$magic^{fb}(Y)$.
$magic^{bf}(a)$.
$sg^{bf}(X,Y)$:- p(X,XP),p(Y,YP),$magic^{bf}(X)$,$sg^{fb}(YP,XP)$.
$sg^{fb}(X,Y)$:- p(X,XP),p(Y,YP),$magic^{fb}(Y)$,$sg^{bf}(YP,XP)$.
$sg^{bf}(X,X)$:- $magic^{bf}(X)$.
$sg^{fb}(X,X)$:- $magic^{bf}(X)$.
query.f(X) :- $sg^{bf}(a,X)$.

The idea of the magic set strategy was presented in Bancilhon et al [1986] and the precise algorithm is described in Bancilhon et al [1986a]. A generalized version (Generalized Magic Sets, see below) has been implemented at MCC.

5.4. Counting and Reverse Counting.

Counting and Reverse Counting are derived from the magic set optimization strategy.

They apply under two conditions: (i) the data is acyclic and (ii) there is at most one recursive rule for each predicate, and it is linear.

We first describe counting using the ''typical'' single linear rule system:

```
p(X,Y) :- flat(X,Y).
p(X,Y) :- up(X,XU),p(XU,YU),down(YU,Y).
query(Y) :- p(a,Y).
```

The idea consists in introducing magic sets (called *counting* sets) in which elements are numbered by their distance to the element a. Remember that the magic set essentially marks all the *up* ancestors of a and then applies the rules in a bottom-up fashion to only the marked ancestors. In the counting strategy, at the same time we mark the ancestors of john, we number them by their distance from a. Then we can ''augment'' the p predicate by numbering its tuples and generate them by levels as follows:

```
counting(a,0).
counting(X,I) :-counting(Y,J),up(Y,X),I=J+1.
p'(X,Y,I) :- counting(X,I),flat(X,Y).
p'(X,Y,I) :- counting(X,I),up(X,XU), p'(XU,YU,J),down(YU,Y),I=J-1.
query(X) :- p'(a,X,0).
```

Thus at each step, instead of using the entire magic set, we only use the tuples of the correct level, thus minimizing the set of relevant tuples. But in fact, it is useless to compute the first attribute of the p predicate. Thus the system can be further optimized into:

```
counting(a,0).
counting(X,I) :-counting(Y,J),up(Y,X),I=J+1.
p''(Y,I) :- counting(X,I),flat(X,Y).
p''(Y,I) :- p''(YU,J),down(YU,Y),I=J-1,J>0.
query(X) :- p''(Y,0).
```

It is interesting to notice that this new set of rules is in fact simulating a stack.

Reverse counting is another variation around the same idea. It works as follow: (i) first compute the magic set, then (ii) for each element b in the magic set number all its *down* descendants and its *up* descendants and add to the answer all the *down* descendants having the same number as a (because a is in the *up* descendants). This gives the following equivalent system:

```
magic(a).
magic(Y) :- magic(X),up(X,Y).
des.up(X,X,0) :- magic(X).
des.down(X',Y,0) :- magic(X'),flat(X',Y).
des.up(X',X,I) :- des.up(X',Y,J),up(X,Y),I=J+1.
des.down(X',X,I) :- des.down(X',Y,J),down(Y,X),I=J+1.
query(Y) :- des.up(X',a,Y),des.down(X',Y,I).
```

This can be slightly optimized by limiting ourselves to the b's that will join with *flat* and restricting the *down* des's to be in the magic set. This generates the following system:

```
magic(a).
magic(Y) :- magic(X),up(X,Y).
des.up(X,X,0) :- magic(X),flat(X,Y).
des.down(X',Y,0) :- magic(X'),flat(X',Y).
des.up(X',X,I) :- magic(X),des.up(X',Y,J),up(X,Y),I=J+1.
des.down(X',X,I) :- des.down(X',Y,J),down(Y,X),I=J+1.
sg(a,Y) :- des.up(X',a,Y),des.down(X',Y,I).
```

Note that we still have the problem of a "late termination" on *down* because we number *all* the descendants in *down*, even those of a lower generation than a.

The idea of counting was presented in Bancilhon et al [1986] and a formal description of counting and of an extension called "magic counting" was presented in the single rule case in Sacca and Zaniolo [1986a]. Counting was extended to progams containing function symbols in Sacca and Zaniolo [1986b]. Reverse counting is described in Bancilhon et al. [1986a]. A generalized version of Counting (Generalized Counting, Beeri and Ramakrishnan [1987]) has been implemented at MCC.

5.5. Generalized Magic Sets

This is a generalization of the Magic Sets method and is described in Beeri and Ramakrishnan [1987]. The intuition is that thc Magic Sets method works essentially by passing bindings obtained by solving body predicates "sideways" in the rule to restrict the computation of other body predicates. The notion of *sideways information passing* is formalized in terms of labeled graphs. A sideways information passing graph is associated with each rule, and these graphs are used to define the Magic Sets transformation. (In general, many such graphs exist for each rule, each reflecting one way of solving the predicates in the body of the rule; and we may choose any one of these and associate it with the rule.)

There are examples, such as transitive closure defined using double recursion, in which the original Magic Sets transformation achieves no improvement over Semi-Naive evaluation. Intuitively, this is because the only form of sideways information passing that it implements consists of using base predicates to bind variables. Thus, in the same generation example discussed earlier, the predicate p is used to bind the variable XP. The method, however, fails to pass information through derived predicates, and so it fails with transitive closure expressed using double recursion (since the recursive rule contains no base predicates in the body). Consider the rule:

a(X,Y) :- a(X,Z), a(Z,Y).

Given a query a(john,Y), the Magic Sets method recognizes that X is bound (since it is bound in the adornment *bf* corresponding to the head of the rule). However, Z is considered free. So it generates the following adorned rule:

a^{bf} (X,Y) :- a^{bf} (X,Z), a^{ff} (Z,Y).

Clearly, the method computes the entire ancestor relation. To succeed in binding Z, the first occurrence of a in the body must be used.

The generalized version of the method succeeds in passing information through derived predicates as well.

As with the original Magic Sets strategy, a set of *adorned rules* is first obtained from the given rules, and these adorned rules are then used to produce the optimized set of rules. Both these steps are now directed, however, by the notion of *sideways information passing graphs* (sips). A sip corresponding to the above rule that binds Z is:

$h \rightarrow_X a.1,\ h, a.1 \rightarrow_Z a.2$

The predicate h denotes the bound part of the head. This graph indicates that the head binds X and this is used in solving the first occurrence of a, and further, this solution is used to bind Z in solving the second occurrence of a. This generates the adorned rule:

a^{bf} (X,Y) :- a^{bf} (X,Z), a^{bf} (Z,Y).

The magic rules corresponding to the two occurrences of a are:

magic(X) :- magic(X).
magic(Z) :- magic(X), a^{bf} (X,Z).

The first rule is trivial and may be discarded. In addition, we obtain the rule magic(john) from the query. The modified rules are obtained exactly as in the Magic Sets method, by adding magic predicates to the bodies of the original rules.

We do not present the details here. The reader is referred to Beeri and Ramakrishnan [1987], where Counting and variants of both Magic Sets and Counting are generalized as well. Generalized Magic Sets and Generalized Counting have been implemented at MCC.

The work in Beeri and Ramakrishnan [1987] still imposes one restriction on rules: every variable that appears in the head of a rule must also appear in the body. This ensures that every tuple produced in a bottom-up execution is ground. † On the other hand, this restriction disallows the use of certain effective logic programming techniques, such as difference lists, and makes it difficult to utilize partially bound arguments. This restriction is lifted in Ramakrishnan [1988], and thus, it is shown that the rewriting techniques (i.e., Magic Sets, Counting, etc.) can be generalized to deal with arbitrary logic programs.

The "Alexander" strategy described in Rohmer et al. [1986] is essentially a variant of the Generalized Magic Sets strategy.

The dynamic filtering approach of Kifer and Lozinskii is similar to the Generalized Magic Sets strategy, although it cannot implement some sideways information passing graphs. The dynamic filters essentially perform as magic sets, but this is a run-time strategy, and the overhead of computing and applying the filters falls outside our framework. We do not discuss dynamic filtering further in this paper.

6. Summary of Strategy Characteristics.

A summary of the characteristics of each strategy is presented in Table 1. We emphasize that this table contains some approximations and refer the reader to the actual descriptions for clarifications. For example, although Magic Sets and Generalized Magic Sets have the same application range, the latter succeeds in optimizing some queries in this range that the former cannot. (Magic Sets essentially reduces to Semi-Naive evaluation in these cases.) Several of these strategies have been further developed since this paper was written. We refer the reader to Beeri and Ramakrishnan [1987], Ramakrishnan [1988], Kifer and Lozinskii [1986b, 1988], Sacca and Zaniolo [1987] and Vieille [1988] for some of these further developments. (We also note that there has been significant related research that cannot be viewed as development of work discussed in this paper. It is outside the scope of this paper to review this work, and the interested reader is urged to consult the recent database literature. The collection of papers in Minker [1988] is a good starting point.)

Table 1: Summary of Strategy Characteristics

Method	*Application Range*	*Top down vs. Bottom Up*	*Compiled vs. Interpreted*	*Iterative vs. Recursive*
Naive Evaluation	Bottom-up Evaluable	Bottom Up	Compiled	Iterative
Semi-Naive Evaluation	Bottom-up Evaluable	Bottom Up	Compiled	Iterative
Query/Subquery	Range Restricted No Arithmetic	Top Down	Interpreted	Iterative
Query/Subquery	Range Restricted No Arithmetic	Top Down	Interpreted	Recursive
APEX	Range Restricted No Arithmetic Constant Free	Mixed	Mixed	Recursive
Prolog	User responsible	Top Down	Interpreted	Recursive

† The reader who is familiar with logic programs should note that this restriction makes an important optimization possible - the expensive operation of *unification* can always be replaced by the less expensive operation of *matching*, since one of the two arguments to the unification procedure is always ground, given that all generated tuples are ground.

Henschen-Naqvi	Linear	Top Down	Compiled	Iterative
Aho-Ullman	Strongly Linear	Bottom Up	Compiled	Iterative
Kifer-Lozinskii	Range Restricted No Arithmetic	Bottom Up	Compiled	Iterative
Counting	Strongly Linear	Bottom Up	Compiled	Iterative
Magic Sets	Bottom-up evaluable	Bottom Up	Compiled	Iterative
Generalized M. Sets	Bottom-up evaluable	Bottom-up	Compiled	Iterative

7. Framework for Performance Evaluation

We now turn to the problem of comparing the above strategies. To perform a comparison of the strategies we must:

1. Choose a set of rules and queries which will represent our benchmark.
2. Choose some test data which will represent our extensional database.
3. Choose a cost function to measure the performance of each strategy.
4. Evaluate the performance of each query against the extensional databases.

We first describe the four queries used as ''typical'' intensional databases. Then, we present our characterization of the data. Each relation is characterized by four parameters and it is argued that a number of familiar data structures, e.g. trees, can be described in this framework. We describe our cost metric, which is the size of the intermediate results before duplicate elimination. We present analytical cost functions for each query evaluation strategy on each query. The cost functions are plotted for three sets of data - tree, inverted tree and cylinder. We discuss these results informally.

7.1. Workload: Sample Intensional Databases and Queries

Instead of generating a general mix, we have chosen four queries that have the properties of exercising various important features of the strategies. We are fully aware of the fact that this set is insufficient to provide a complete benchmark, but we view this work as a first step towards a better understanding of the performance behavior of the various strategies.

The queries are three different versions of the ancestor query and a version of the same-generation query. The first one is just a classical ancestor rule and query with the first attribute bound.

Query 1
```
a(X,Y) :- p(X,Y).
a(X,Y) :- p(X,Z),a(Z,Y).
query(X) :- a(john,X).
```

Because most strategies are representation dependent, we have studied the same example with the second attribute bound instead of the first. This will allow us to determine which strategies can solve both cases.

Query 2
```
a(X,Y) :- p(X,Y).
a(X,Y) :- p(X,Z),a(Z,Y).
query(X) :- a(X,john).
```

The third version of the ancestor example specifies ancestor using double recursion. This enables us to see how the strategies react to the non linear case. This example being fully symmetric, it is sufficient to test it with its first attribute bound.

Query 3
```
a(X,Y) :- p(X,Y).
a(X,Y) :- a(X,Z),a(Z,Y).
```

query(X) :- a(john,X).

Finally, to study something more complex than transitive closure, we have chosen a generalized version of the same generation example, bound on its first attribute.

Query 4 p(X,Y) :- flat(X,Y).
p(X,Y) :- up(X,XU),p(XU,YU), down(YU,Y).
query(X) :- p(john,X).

7.2. Characterizing Data: Sample Extensional Databases

Because we decided on an analytical approach, we had to obtain tractable formulae for the cost of each strategy against each query. Therefore, each relation must be characterized by a *small* set of parameters. Fortunately, because of the choice of our workload, we can restrict our attention to binary relations.

We represent every binary relation by a directed graph and view tuples as edges and domain elements as nodes. Nodes are arranged in layers and each edge goes from a node in one layer to a node in the next. Note that in these graphs each node has at least one in-edge or one out-edge. Nodes in the first layer have no incoming edges and nodes in the last layer have no outgoing edges. We assume that edges are randomly distributed with a uniform distribution.

This formalism does not represent cycles. Nor does it represent short cuts, where a short cut is the existence of two paths of different length going from one point to another. Clearly, they would violate our assumption that nodes were arranged in layers with edges going from nodes in one layer to the next.

Let R be a binary relation and A be a set. Recall that we denote by A.R the set:

$$A.R = \{y \mid x \in A \text{ and } R(x,y)\}$$

We characterize a binary relation R by:

(1) F_R the *fan-out* factor,
(2) D_R the *duplication* factor,
(3) h_R the *height*, and
(4) b_R the *base*.

F_R and D_R are defined as follows: given a "random" set A of n nodes from R, the size of A.R is n F_R before duplicate elimination. D_R is the duplication factor in A.R, i.e. the ratio of the size of A.R before and after duplicate elimination. Thus the size of A.R after duplicate elimination is n F_R/D_R.

We call $E_R = F_R/D_R$ the *expansion* factor of R.

The base b_R is the number of nodes that do not have any antecedents. The height h_R is the length of the longest chain in R.

When no confusion is possible, we shall simply use F, D, h and b instead of F_R, D_R, h_R and b_R.

The typical structure consists of a number of layers. There are (h_R+1) layers of nodes in the structure, numbered from top to bottom (as 0 to h). There are b_R nodes in level 0.

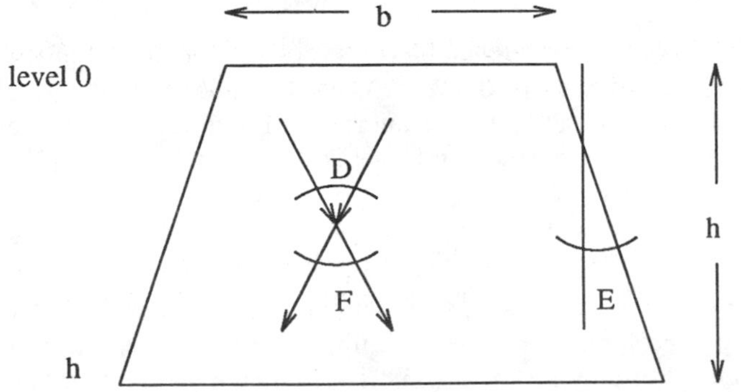

This "parametrized structure" is fairly general and can represent a number of typical configurations:

A binary balanced tree of height k is defined by:

F=2; D=1; h=k; b=1

The same binary tree upside down is defined by:

F=1; D=2; h=k, $b=2^k$

A list of length k is defined by:

F=1; D=1; h=k; b=1

A set of n lists of length k is defined by:

F=1; D=1; h=k; b=n

A parent relation, where each person has two children and each child has two parents is defined by:

F=2; D=2; h=number of generations; b=number of people of unknown parentage

We emphasize that we assume the data to be *random*, with a uniform distribution. Thus, the values F and D are average values. Our characterization of a binary tree, for instance, describes a random (but layered) data structure in which the average values of F and D are 2 and 1 respectively. An actual binary tree has a regular pattern (*each* internal node has exactly one incoming and two outgoing edges incident on it) and this is not captured by our characterization.

Our assumption that the duplication factor is independent of the size is a very crude approximation. For instance it implies that if you start from one node you still generate some duplicates. Obviously the duplication factor increases with the size of the start set. Therefore, our approximation overestimates the number of duplicates. However, it becomes reasonable as the size of the start set becomes large. It is also dependent upon our assumption that the data is random and not regular.

Let us now turn to the problem of characterizing inter-relation relationships. Let A and B be two sets. The *transfer ratio* of A with respect to B, denoted $T_{A.B}$ is the number such that given a random set of n nodes in A, the size of $A \cap B$ after duplicate elimination is n $T_{A.B}$. In other words, given a set of nodes in A, the transfer ratio is the fraction of these nodes that also appear in set B. Note that $0 \leq T \leq 1$.

This definition can be extended to binary relations by considering only the columns of the relations. We shall denote the i-th column of R by Ri. Thus, given two binary relations R and S, the number of tuples in the (ternary) result of the join of R and S is n $T_{R2.S1}$, where n is the number of tuples in R.

7.3. The Cost Metrics

We have chosen for our cost measure the number of *successful inferences* performed by the system.

Consider a rule:

p :- $q1, q2, \ldots, qn$

A *successful inference* (or *firing*) associated with this rule is of the form (*id, t, t1, t2, ... , tn*), where *t1* through *tn* are (ground) tuples in *q1* through *qn* and *t* is a tuple in *p*. It denotes that the truth of *t1* through *tn* is used to establish that *t* is true, by applying the given rule. There is (conceptually) an identifier *id* associated with this inference because it is possible that this inference is repeatedly made, and we wish to measure this.

The simplest way to obtain this cost function is to measure the size of the intermediate results *before* duplicate elimination.

We note that this cost measure does not count *unsuccessful* inferences, i.e. uses of the rule in which the tuples *t1* through *tn* fail to establish *t* (for example, because they do not agree on the values they assign to common variables). Also, since the cost measure is independent of the number of *q*'s, in this model the measure of complexity of the join, the cartesian product, intersection and selection is the size of the result; the measure of complexity of union is the sum of the sizes of the arguments (each tuple present in both argument is going to fire twice); and the measure of complexity of projection is the size of the argument. Readers familiar with performance evaluation of relational queries might be surprised by these measures.

Our concern, however, is primarily with recursive queries. In particular, all but one of our queries (ancestor using double recursion) are *linear*, i.e., the body of each recursive rule contains exactly one occurrence of the recursive predicate. We justify our measurement of only successful inferences by the observation that the number of successful inferences (for the recursive predicate) at one step constitutes the operand at the next step. We justify the approximation in estimating the cost of a join in terms of the size of just one of the operands as follows. The join represented by the predicates in the body of a rule may be thought of as a fixed "operator" that is repeatedly applied to the relation corresponding to the recursive predicate. It is reasonable to assume that the cost of each such application is proportional to the size of this relation (the operand). By measuring the size of this intermediate relation over all steps, we obtain a cost that is proportional to the actual cost.

In essence, our cost is a measure of one important factor in the performance of a query evaluation system, the number of successful inferences, rather than a measure of the actual run-time performance. This cost model is studied further in Bancilhon [1985].

8. Notation and Preliminary Derivations

In this section, we explain the notation and terminology used in analytically deriving the cost functions. We also derive some expressions that are used in the analysis of some of the strategies. The derivations of these expressions are of some interest in their own right, since they are good examples of the techniques we use in subsequent analyses.

We denote multiplication by simply juxtaposing the operands. Where there is ambiguity, parentheses are used to clarify the expression, or we use * to denote multiplication.

We denote the number of nodes at level i in relation R by $n_R(i)$, the total number of nodes in R by N_R, and the total number of edges in R (which is the number of tuples in R) by A_R. Where no confusion is possible, we drop the subscripts.

We denote the sum of the (h+1)st elements of the geometric series of ratio E by gsum(E,h), thus:

$$\text{gsum}(E,h) = (1 + E + E^2 + E^3 + \ldots + E^h)$$

From the definition of the expansion factor E, we have n(i+1)=n(i)E. So the total number of nodes is:

$$\begin{aligned} N &= b(1 + E + E^2 + E^3 + \ldots + E^h) \\ &= (b)\text{gsum}(E,h) \end{aligned}$$

Clearly, the number of edges entering level i is n(i-1)F, and the number of edges leaving level i is n(i)F. Thus the total number of edges is:

$$\begin{aligned} A &= bF + bEF + bE^2F + \ldots + bE^{(h-1)}F \\ &= bF(1 + E + E^2 + \ldots + E^{(h-1)}) \\ &= (bF)\text{gsum}(E,h-1) \end{aligned}$$

We denote by h' the *average* level:

$$h' = h - \left\lfloor \frac{\sum_{i=1}^{h}(i*n(i))}{N} \right\rfloor$$

It denotes the mean level at which we pick a node, assuming nodes are uniformly distributed. We have actually defined h' as the distance of the mean level from the highest level h for notational convenience, since this is a quantity we use extensively.

We define the length of an arc (a,b) in the transitive closure of R (which we denote by R*) to be the length of the path of R that generates it. (Note that this is well-defined because there are no short-cuts.)

Since an arc is represented by its end points, the number of arcs of length k with a given first node can be computed as the number of distinct nodes reachable from the given node by a path of length k. So, starting from a given node, on the average we can reach E distinct nodes by a path of length 1, E^2 distinct nodes by a path of length 2, and so on. The number of arcs of length k going from level i to level (i+k) is thus:

$$n(i)E^k = n(i+k)$$

Of course, if D is not one, this is an approximation that depends on our assumption of random data. In particular, it breaks down for regular data, such as an actual inverted tree. The intuition is as follows. The parameters F and D are used to estimate the number of *arcs* of length k, as opposed to the number of *paths* of length k. Several paths may generate the same arc (i.e., they have the same end points). Thus, we use the parameters F and D to estimate this "duplication" of arcs. This approximation depends upon the randomness of data - in an inverted tree, for instance, the number of paths is exactly the number of arcs because there is a unique path between any two points. The inverted tree is one instance of a family of data structures with given values of F (=1) and D (=2), and in this particular instance, due to the regular pattern in the data, the above approximation breaks down. In general, however, for such a structure the number of paths is *not* equal to the number of arcs; and if the data is randomly (and uniformly) distributed, our approximation is accurate.

We denote by $a_{R*}(k)$ the number of arcs of length exactly k in R*. Where the context is clear, we write a(k).

a(k) is obtained by summing all the arcs of length k that enter level i for i = k to h. Thus:

$$\begin{aligned} a(k) &= n(k) + n(k+1) + \ldots + n(h) \\ &= n(k)\ \mathrm{gsum}(E,h-k) \end{aligned}$$

Finally, given a relation R(A,B), its transpose $R^T(B,A)$ is defined to be such that $R^T(B,A)$ holds iff R(A,B) holds, for all pairs (A,B). We have the following relationships:

$$\begin{aligned} &F_{R^T} = D_R, \\ &D_{R^T} = F_R, \\ &E_{R^T} = 1/E_R, \\ &h_{R^T} = h_R, \\ &h'_{R^T} = h_R - h'_R, \text{ and} \\ &b_{R^T} = b_R E_R^{h_R}. \end{aligned}$$

9. Cost Evaluation

For each strategy and for each query, we have analytically evaluated the cost of computing the given query using the given strategy. The cost is expressed as a function of the data parameters F, D, h and b. The formulae are listed in Appendix 1, and their derivations are contained in Bancilhon and Ramakrishnan [1988]. To compare these fairly complex formulae, we have plotted a number of curves, some of which are included in the appendix.

10. Graphical Comparison of the Costs

The curves shown in the appendix show the relative performance of the various strategies on each of the sample queries for three sets of data. They are relations in which the tuples are arranged in a tree structure, an inverted tree structure, and a "cylinder". A cylinder is a structure in which each layer has b nodes and each node has on the average two incoming and two outgoing arcs. We present below a sample relation of each type:

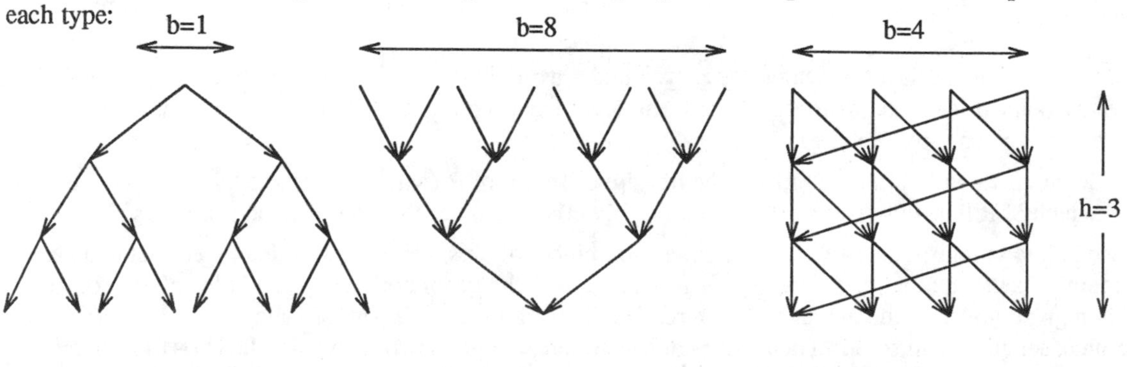

Tree, F=2, D=1   Inverted tree, F=1, D=2   Cylinder, F=2, D=2

The choice of these structures was made in order to study the effects of uneven distribution of the data and the effects of duplication. We have fixed the sizes of all relations at 100,000 tuples. For the tree structure, we vary the shape by changing the fan-out F while keeping the number of arcs (which is the number of tuples) constant. Clearly, decreasing the fan-out increases the depth of the structure and vice-versa. Similarly, the shape of the inverted tree is varied by varying the duplication factor. The shape of the cylinder is varied by varying the ratio of breadth b to height h, again keeping the number of arcs constant.

For each query and data structure, we plot the cost of each strategy against the shape of the data (measured in terms of the parameter used to vary it). Thus, for each query, we plot cost vs. F for the tree, cost vs. D for the inverted tree, and cost vs. b/h for the cylinder. We do this for each strategy. The cost is computed using the cost functions listed in the appendix. We have sometimes displayed a subset of the curves (for the same query and data structure) over a different range, to allow a better comparison.

For the ancestor queries, we plot the cost of each strategy for the cases when the parent relation has 100,000 tuples and the data in it has the shape of a tree, an inverted tree and a cylinder.

For the same generation example, we have assumed that the relations *up* and *down* are identical and that the fan-out and duplication for the relation flat are both equal to 1. We have also assumed that the transfer ratio from up to flat is equal to the transfer ratio from flat to down. We have assumed that all three relations (*up*, *flat* and *down*) have 100,000 tuples. We plot the cost of each strategy as the shape of *up* and *down* varies for a total of six cases: the cases when the structure is a tree, an inverted tree and a cylinder, with the transfer ratio equal to 1 and 0.01 (100% and 1% respectively).

10.1. Summary of the Curves

There are several important points to be seen in the curves. For a given query, there is a clear ordering of the various strategies that usually holds over the entire range of data. The difference in performance between strategies is by orders of magnitude, which emphasizes the importance of choosing the right strategy. The cost of the optimal strategy is less than 10,000 in each of the queries we have considered, over the entire range of data. The size of the data is 100,000 tuples. This indicates that recursive queries can be implemented efficiently.

We present a summary of the ordering of the strategies, as seen in the corresponding curves. We use ≪ to denote an order of magnitude or greater difference in performance, and for a given query, we list in parentheses those strategies that perform identically for all data. We refer to the various strategies using the following acronyms for brevity: HN (Henschen-Naqvi), C (Counting), MS (Magic Sets), GMS (Generalized Magic Sets), QSQR, QSQI, APEX, P (Prolog), SN (Semi-Naive), N (naive) and SF (Static Filtering).

Query 1 (Ancestor.bf)

Tree: (HN,C) ≪ (QSQR,APEX) = P ≈ (MS,GMS) ≪ QSQI ≪ (SN,SF) ≪ N

Inverted tree: (HN,C) ≪ (QSQR,APEX) ≈ (MS,GMS) ≪ P ≪ QSQI ≪ (SN,SF) ≪ N

Cylinder: (HN,C) ≪ (QSQR,APEX) ≈ (MS,GMS) ≪ QSQI ≪ (SN,SF) ≪ N ≪ P

Query 2 (Ancestor.fb)

All Data: (HN,MS,GMS,QSQR,SF) ≪ APEX ≈ QSQI ≪ SN ≪ N ≈ P

Query 3 (Ancestor.bf, non-linear)

All data: QSQR ≈ GMS ≪ QSQI ≪ APEX ≪ (SN,MS,SF) ≪ N

(HN, Counting and Prolog do not apply)

Query 4 (Same Generation.bf)

Tree: C ≪ HN ≈ (MS,GMS) ≪ QSQR = P ≪ APEX ≪ QSQI ≪ (SN,SF) ≪ N

Inverted tree: C ≪ HN ≈ (MS,GMS) ≪ QSQR ≈ APEX ≪ P ≈ QSQI ≪ (SN,SF) ≪ N

Cylinder: C ≪ HN ≈ (MS,GMS) ≪ QSQR ≪ APEX ≪ QSQI ≪ (SN,SF) ≪ N ≪ P

To summarize the ancestor results, the following order is seen to hold for the ancestor queries:

(HN, C) ≪ QSQR ≈ (MS,GMS) ≪ APEX ≈ QSQI ≪ SN ≪ N

There are some exceptions and additions to the above ordering. In the non-linear case, Henschen-Naqvi and Counting do not apply, and Magic Sets reduces to Semi-Naive. Static Filtering performs like Semi-Naive, except in the case where the second argument is bound, and in this case it performs like QSQR. APEX performs like QSQR in the case where the first argument is bound. Prolog performs poorly when it cannot propagate the constant in the query (the case where the second argument is bound), as expected. When it can propagate the constant, its performance degrades sharply with duplication, especially as the depth of the data structure increases. This is readily seen from the curves for the cylinder.

To summarize the same generation results, we have:

$C \ll HN \approx (MS,GMS) \ll QSQR \ll APEX \ll QSQI \ll (SN, SF) \ll (P, N)$

Prolog behaves like QSQR when there is no duplication (tree). With duplication, its performance degrades so sharply with an increase in the depth of the data structure that we have classified it with Naive, although it performs better than Semi-Naive over a wide range.

10.2. Interpreting the Results

These results indicate that the following three factors greatly influence the performance:

1. The amount of *duplication* of work,
2. The size of the set of *relevant facts*, and
3. The size (number and arity) of intermediate relations.

By duplication of work, we refer to the repeated firing of a rule on the same data. This can occur due to duplication in the data (e.g. Prolog), or due to an iterative control strategy that does not remember previous firings (e.g. QSQI and Naive). Consider the second factor. A fact p(a) is *relevant* to a given query q iff there exists a derivation p(a) →* q(b) for some b in the answer set. If we know all the relevant facts in advance, instead of using the database to reply to the query, we can use the relevant part of the database only, thus cutting down on the set of facts to be processed. It is in general impossible to find all the relevant facts in advance without spending as much effort as in replying to the query. Thus, all methods have a way of finding a super-set of relevant facts. We call this set the *set of potentially relevant facts*. As this set becomes smaller, i.e., contains fewer and fewer facts that are *not* relevant, the work done in evaluating the query clearly decreases. The third factor is hard to define precisely. Strategies that only look at sets of nodes rather than sets of arcs perform better than those that look at sets of arcs, by an order of magnitude or more. They are less generally applicable since this often involves a loss of information. This usually leads to non-termination unless the database has certain properties, such as linearity of rules and acyclicity of the extensional database. And of course, strategies that create more intermediate relations pay for it in increased costs, since the addition of a tuple to a relation (intermediate or otherwise) represents a firing.

The following discussion is intended to clarify these concepts, as well as to explain the performance of the various strategies in terms of these three factors.

10.2.1. The Ancestor Queries

We begin by looking at the ancestor queries. The effect of duplication is seen by considering Prolog and QSQI, both of which do duplicate work, for different reasons. When the first argument is bound, Prolog performs like QSQR on a tree data structure, where exactly one arc enters each node (equivalently, there is exactly one way of deriving a given answer). With duplication (i.e. on the average more than one arc enters a given node) performance degrades dramatically. Prolog's performance for the same query on a cylinder is comparable to Naive evaluation, a difference of several orders of magnitude! We note that the set of relevant facts is comparable in the two cases, being the set of nodes reachable from the node denoting the constant in the query (which will henceforth be referred to as the query node). However, in the case of the cylinder, these nodes can be reached along several paths and Prolog infers them afresh along each path. QSQI performs duplicate computation for a different reason, which is that its iterative control strategy does not remember previous firings. Essentially, there are as many steps (executions of the control loop) as the longest path from the query node, and all nodes reached by a path of length less than or equal to i are recomputed at all steps after the ith. This can be seen by comparing QSQR and QSQI and noting that QSQI is orders of magnitude worse in all cases. QSQR uses the same set of relevant facts (the reachable nodes) and differs only in that it has a recursive control strategy that avoids precisely this duplication. Naive evaluation also does a lot of duplicate work, for the same reason as QSQI, i.e., it does not remember previous firings. Semi-Naive differs from Naive only in that it remembers all previous firings and does not repeat them. Thus, the effect of duplication can also be seen in the difference between Naive and Semi-Naive.

The effect of a smaller set of relevant facts can be seen in the vast difference between Magic Sets and Semi-Naive. Magic Sets is simply Semi-Naive applied to the set of relevant facts, which is determined to be the set of reachable nodes except in the doubly recursive case. In this case, the first phase of the Magic Sets strategy, which computes the set of relevant facts, fails and the Magic Sets strategy degenerates to Semi-Naive. This effect can also be seen in the behavior of Prolog on a tree data structure (which means we eliminate the effect of duplication) when the first argument is free. Prolog's depth first strategy is unable to propagate the constant in the second argument of the query. In other words, it must consider all facts in the database, and its performance degrades by several orders of magnitude. Similarly, the Static Filtering strategy degenerates to Semi-Naive when the optimization algorithm fails to push down the constant in the query. We note that pushing the constant (i.e., the selection that it represents) is equivalent to cutting down on the number of relevant facts.

QSQR succeeds in restricting the set of relevant facts to the set of nodes reachable from the query node even in the non-linear version of ancestor. It does this at the cost of implementing the recursive control, which is a cost that we do not understand at this stage. QSQI also succeeds in restricting the set of relevant facts, but performs a great deal of duplicate computation. The Magic Sets algorithm uses the entire parent relation for the set of relevant facts and so degenerates to Semi-Naive. APEX, for reasons explained below, also uses a much larger set of relevant facts. So, although it improves upon Semi-Naive computation in this case, it is much worse than QSQR. The Generalized Magic Sets strategy, however, succeeds in restricting the set of relevant facts to those reachable from the query node, thus illustrating its wider applicability. Henschen-Naqvi and Counting do not apply and Prolog does not terminate.

The behavior of APEX illustrates the interesting distinction between the set of relevant facts and the set of *useful* facts. The first step in the APEX strategy is to find what APEX calls the set of relevant facts (which is actually a subset of the set of relevant facts as we have defined it, since it does not include all facts than could derive an answer). In the ancestor examples, these are facts from the relation parent, and the firing of the first rule adds them to the ancestor relation. Subsequently, these facts are substituted (in turn) into both the parent and ancestor predicates in the body of the second rule. Except in the first case, this leads to subqueries whose answers are not relevant. For example, in the case where the second argument is bound to john, the set of relevant (a la APEX) facts is the set of facts p(X,john). By substituting these into the parent predicate in the second rule, we generate the query a(john,?). This computes the ancestors of john, whereas the given query a(?,john) asks for the descendants of john. This is because APEX does not make the distinction that facts of the form p(X,john) are relevant to the query a(?,john) only when substituted into the ancestor predicate in the second rule. This is a distinction that the Magic Sets strategy makes, and it thereby reduces the number of useless firings.

We now consider the third factor, the arity of the intermediate relations. The two strategies that use unary intermediate relations are the Henschen-Naqvi and Counting strategies. In essence, at step i they compute the set of relevant facts that is at a distance i from the query node. Let us denote this set by Si. At the next step, they compute the set of those nodes in parent to which there is an arc from a node in Si. Thus, they compute all nodes reachable from john, and further they compute each node at most D times where D is the duplication factor. However, the unary relations strategy fails to terminate if the query node is in a cycle. Also, neither the Henschen-Naqvi nor the Counting strategy applies when there are non-linear rules.

Magic Sets computes exactly the same set of relevant facts and does no duplicate work. However, in the second phase at step i it computes all arcs in the transitive closure of parent (restricted to the set of relevant facts) of length i. In particular, this includes all arcs of length i rooted at john. This is the answer, and this is essentially all that the more specialized methods, Henschen-Naqvi and Counting, compute. Everything else that the Magic Sets strategy does is useless computation. Thus, the cost of the Magic Sets strategy is the number of arcs in the transitive closure of the subtree rooted at john (i.e. the subtree of nodes reachable from john).

The recursive control of QSQR generates subqueries using precisely the nodes in set Si at step i, and the answer to each of these subqueries is the set of all nodes in the subtree rooted at that node. By induction, it is easy to see that the total cost involved in computing a query is the number of arcs in the transitive closure of the subgraph rooted at that query node. (The cost is thus similar to that of Magic Sets.) The intermediate relations here are the (binary) sets of answers to each subquery. This seems to indicate the power of a recursive control strategy since it succeeds in reducing both the set of relevant facts and the amount of duplicate work.

10.2.2. The Same Generation Query

We conclude this discussion by explaining the performance of the various strategies in the same generation query in terms of these three factors. Counting has the best performance since it uses the smallest set of relevant facts (the nodes of *up* that are reachable from the query node), does not do duplicate computation, and further, uses unary intermediate relations. It executes the query in two phases. In the first phase, at step i, it computes the set of all nodes in *up* that are reachable from the query node via a path of length i. In the second phase, it first computes the nodes of *down* that are reachable from this set via an arc of flat, still retaining the distance of each set from the query node. In subsequent iterations, it steps through *down* once each time, such that each node in a set that is i steps away from the query node in *up* is the root of paths of length i in *down*.

Henschen-Naqvi uses the same set of relevant facts, and is a unary strategy, but it does a lot of duplicate work. It is a single phase algorithm that does the same amount of work as the first phase of Counting in computing sets of *up* nodes along with their distances from the query node. However, it steps through *down* i times for each set at a distance i from the query node in *up*. Since it does not keep track of the work it does in step i at step i+1, it repeats a lot of the work in stepping through *down*. (Unless, of course, the data is such that there is no duplication of work. This corresponds to the data configuration in the worst case for Counting - the additional book-keeping done by Counting is unnecessary since the data ensures that there is no duplication of work in stepping through *down*.)

The set of relevant facts for Magic Set and QSQR is again the set of *up* nodes reachable from the query node. They do not perform duplicate computation. However, they work with binary relations, in effect computing all paths with equal lengths in *up* and *down* linked by a single arc in flat. Thus, their performance is inferior to that of Counting. Further, QSQR's left to right strategy forces us to create intermediate relations for up^* and $up^*.sg$, where up^* denotes the transitive closure of *up*. Since the Magic Set strategy does not impose any order of evaluation, we can do with the single intermediate relation *sg*. The cost of the additional inferences required to create the intermediate relations causes a large difference in the costs of the two strategies.

Our graphs show the performance of Magic Set to be identical to that of Henschen-Naqvi. It is to be expected that they perform similarly since the duplicate work done by Henschen-Naqvi is offset by the fact that they work with binary relations. However, their performance is not really identical. It appears to be so in our curves for two reasons. The first is our approximation of the number of arcs of length l to n(l)gsum(E,h-l). The second is the fact that we plot the curves for cases where *up* and *down* are identical. Under these conditions, the expressions for the performance of these methods become identical.

QSQI is similar to QSQR except that at each step, it duplicates the work of the previous steps, and so it is inferior to Magic Set and QSQR. Semi-Naive uses binary relations, and although it does not do duplicate work, this is outweighed by the fact that the set of relevant facts is all the nodes in *up*. So it performs worse than QSQI. Static Filtering degenerates to Semi-Naive since the optimization strategy fails to make any improvements to the system graph. Prolog is similar to QSQR when there is no duplication in the data, but its cost increases exponentially with the depth of the data structure when there is duplication. Naive evaluation uses the entire set of nodes in *up* as relevant facts, does duplicate work since it does not remember firings, and uses binary intermediate relations. With the exception of Prolog over a certain range, it is clearly the worst strategy.

Finally, we note that when the transfer ratio T is 0.01 (1%), the cost of computing the answer by Naive or Semi-Naive evaluation is essentially that of computing all arcs in the relation *flat*, and so the two methods perform almost identically.

11. Related Work

The performance issue was addressed informally through the discussion of a set of examples in Bancilhon et al. [1986b]. Han and Lu [1986] contains a study of the performance of a set of four evaluation strategies (including Naive and Henschen-Naqvi and two others not considered here) on the same generation example, using randomly generated data. Their model is based on the selectivity of the join and select operations and the sizes of the data relations. They consider both CPU and IO cost. We have chosen to concentrate on one aspect of the problem, which is the number of successful firings (measured using the sizes of the intermediate relations), and have studied a wider range of strategies, queries and data.

12. Conclusions and Caveats

We have presented a performance comparison of ten methods. Even though the "benchmark" we have used is incomplete, the cost measure too elementary and the approximations crude, we found the results to be valuable. The robustness of the results (at least on our workload), both in terms of the order of magnitude differences between the costs of the strategies and in terms of invariance of the results to the parameters that we varied, was a surprise. We have also been able to explain most of our results through three factors: duplication, relevant facts and unary vs. binary. While the first two factors were well known, the third one came as a surprise, even though it was probably already understood in Sacca and Zaniolo [1986].

Our conclusions may be summarized as follows:

1. For a given query, there is a clear ordering of the strategies.
2. The more specialized strategies perform significantly better.
3. Recursion is a powerful control structure which reduces the number of relevant facts and eliminates duplicate work.
4. The choice of the right strategy is critical since the differences in performance are by orders of magnitude.
5. Three factors which greatly influence performance are: (i) duplication of work, (ii) the set of relevant facts, and (iii) the number and arity of the intermediate relations.

The results seem robust in that the performance of the various strategies usually differ by orders of magnitude, which allows a wide latitude for the approximations in the model and cost evaluation. Also, the curves rarely intersect, which means that the relative ordering of the strategies is maintained in most cases over the entire range of data.

However, it must be emphasized that our cost function makes some crude approximations. The cost of join is linear in the size of the result, a consequence of our using the size of intermediate relations as the cost measure. We also ignore the cost of disk accesses, and the cost of implementing a recursive control strategy. Our model suffers from the approximation that duplication is independent of the size of the start set.

Finally, our sample data and queries are limited, and the results must be extrapolated to other data and queries with caution, especially since the results show some variance in the relative performance of the strategies for different sets of data and queries. In particular, our benchmark is limited to the type of data and query where there is a *large* amount of data and the size of the answer to the query is *small*. This clearly favors the "smart" strategies and obscures, for instance, the fact that Semi-Naive performs as well as any other strategy when computing the entire transitive closure of a relation (Bancilhon [1986]).

Further, our data contains no cycles or shortcuts. This is an important limitation since it favors some of the specialized strategies. We emphasize the importance of this limitation since it is possible to (mis-)interpret our results as evidence for the uniform superiority of the Henschen-Naqvi and Counting methods. For example, cycles in the data make Counting inapplicable. The presence of shortcuts may well make these methods considerably more expensive. For instance, there are cases where Counting performs worse than Magic Sets (Bancilhon et al. [1986a]).

13. Acknowledgements

We wish to thank Bill Alexander, Patrick Valduriez and Ken Smith for careful proofreading of parts of the manuscript. We are extremely grateful to Paris Kanellakis, Eliezer Lozinskii, Jeff Ullman, Laurent Vieille and Carlo Zaniolo who provided enlightening comments and suggested many corrections and improvements to the paper. We thank the anonymous referees of Bancilhon and Ramakrishnan [1988] for numerous comments which improved the technical content and presentation of this paper.

14. References

1. F. Afrati, C. Papadimitriou, G. Papageorgiou, A. Roussou, Y. Sagiv and J.D. Ullman [1986], "Convergence of Sideways Query Evaluation," *Proc. 5th ACM SIGMOD-SIGACT Symposium on Principles of Database Systems, 1986.*

2. A. Aho and J. D. Ullman [1979], "Universality of Data Retrieval Languages," *Proc. 6th ACM Symposium on Principles of Programming Languages, 1979, pp 110-120.*

3. F. Bancilhon [1986], "Naive Evaluation of Recursively Defined Relations," in *On Knowledge Base Management Systems - Integrating Database and AI Systems, Brodie and Mylopoulos, Eds., Springer-Verlag, 1986, pp 165-178.*

4. F. Bancilhon [1985], "A Note on the Performance of Rule Based Systems," *MCC Technical Report DB-022-85, 1985.*

5. F. Bancilhon, D. Maier, Y. Sagiv and J.D. Ullman [1986a], "Magic Sets and Other Strange Ways to Implement Logic Programs," *Proc. 5th ACM SIGMOD-SIGACT Symposium on Principles of Database Systems, 1986, pp 1-15.*

6. F. Bancilhon, D. Maier, Y. Sagiv and J.D. Ullman [1986b], "Magic Sets: Algorithms and Examples," *Unpublished Manuscript, 1986.*

7. F. Bancilhon and R. Ramakrishnan [1988], "Performance Evaluation of Data Intensive Logic Programs", In *Foundations of Deductive Databases and Logic Programming, Ed. J. Minker, Morgan Kaufman, 1988.*

8. R. Bayer [1985], "Query Evaluation and Recursion in Deductive Database Systems," *Unpublished Manuscript, 1985.*

9. C. Beeri and R. Ramakrishnan [1987], "On the Power of Magic," *Proc. 6th ACM SIGMOD-SIGACT-SIGART Symposium on Principles of Database Systems, 1987, pp 269-283.*

10. C. Chang [1981], "On the Evaluation of Queries Containing Derived Relations in Relational Databases," In *Advances in Data Base Theory, Vol.1, H.Gallaire, J. Minker and J.M. Nicolas, Plenum Press, New York, 1981, pp 235-260.*

11. C. Delobel [1986], "Bases de Donnees et Bases de Connaissances: Une Approche Systemique a l'Aide d'une Algebre Matricielle des Relations," *Journees Francophones, Grenoble, January 1986, pp 101-134.*

12. S.W. Dietrich and D.S. Warren [1985], "Dynamic Programming Strategies for the Evaluation of Recursive Queries," *Unpublished Report, 1985.*

13. H. Gallaire, J. Minker and J.-M. Nicolas [1984], "Logic and Data Bases: A Deductive Approach," *Computing Surveys, Vol. 16, No 2, June 1984, pp 153-185.*

14. G. Gardarin and Ch. de Maindreville [1986], "Evaluation of Database Recursive Logic Programs as Recurrent Function Series," *Proc. SIGMOD 86, Washington, D.C., May 1986, pp 177-186.*

15. J. Han and H. Lu [1986], "Some Performance Results on Recursive Query Processing in Relational Database Systems," *Proc. Data Engineering Conference, Los Angeles, February 1986, pp 533-539.*

16. L. Henschen and S. Naqvi [1984], "On Compiling Queries in Recursive First-Order Data Bases," *JACM, Vol 31, January 1984, pp 47-85.*

17. M. Kifer and E. Lozinskii [1986a], "Filtering Data Flow in Deductive Databases," *Proc. International Conference on Database Theory, Lecture Notes in Computer Science, No. 243, Springer-Verlag, 1986, pp 186-202.*

18. M. Kifer and E. Lozinskii [1986b], "A Framework for an Efficient Implementation of Deductive Databases," *Proc. 6th Advanced Database Symposium, 1986, pp 109-116.*

19. M. Kifer and E. Lozinskii [1988], "SYGRAF: Implementing Logic Programs in a Database Style," *To appear, IEEE Trans. on Software Engineering, 1988.*

20. R. Krishnamurthy, R. Ramakrishnan and O. Shmueli [1988], "A Framework for Testing Safety and Effective Computability of Extended Datalog," *To appear, Proc. ACM-SIGMOD Conference, 1988.*

21. K. Laskowski [1984], "Compiling Recursive Axioms in First Order Databases," *Masters Thesis, Northwestern University, 1984*

22. E. Lozinskii [1985], "Evaluating Queries in Deductive Databases by Generating," *Proc. 11th International Joint Conference on Artificial Intelligence, 1985, pp 173-177.*

23. G. Marque-Pucheu [1983], "Algebraic Structure of Answers in a Recursive Logic Database," *To appear in Acta Informatica.*

24. G. Marque-Pucheu, J. Martin-Gallausiaux and G. Jomier [1984], "Interfacing Prolog and Relational Database Management Systems," *in New Applications of Databases, Gardarin and Gelenbe Eds, Academic Press, London, 1984.*

25. D. McKay and S. Shapiro [1981], "Using Active Connection Graphs for Reasoning with Recursive Rules," *Proc. 7th International Joint Conference on Artificial Intelligence, 1981, pp 368-374.*

26. J. Minker [1988], "Foundations of Deductive Databases and Logic Programming," *Ed. J. Minker, Morgan Kaufmann, 1988.*

27. K. Morris, J. Ullman and A. Van Gelder [1986], "Design Overview of the NAIL! System," *Proceedings of the 3rd International Conference on Logic Programming, London, July 1986.*

28. R. Ramakrishnan [1988], "Magic Templates: A Spell-Binding Approach to Logic Programs," *Technical Report, Computer Sciences Department, Univ. of Wisconsin-Madison, 1988.*

29. R. Ramakrishnan, F. Bancilhon and A. Silberschatz [1987], "Safety of Horn Clauses with Infinite Relations," *Proc. 6th ACM SIGMOD-SIGACT Symposium on Principles of Database Systems, 1987.*

30. J. Rohmer, R. Lescoeur and J.M. Kerisit [1986], "The Alexander Method: A Technique for the Processing of Recursive Axioms in Deductive Databases," *New Generation Computing 4, 3, 1986, pp 273-285.*

31. A. Rosenthal, S. Heiler, U. Dayal and F. Manola [1986], "Traversal Recursion: A Practical Approach to Supporting Recursive Applications," *Proc. ACM-SIGMOD Conference, 1986.*

32. P. Roussel [1975], "PROLOG, Manuel de Reference et de Utilisation," *Groupe Intelligence Artificielle, Universite Aix-Marseille II, 1975.*

33. D. Sacca and C. Zaniolo [1986a], "On the Implementation of a Simple Class of Logic Queries for Databases," *Proc. 5th ACM SIGMOD-SIGACT Symposium on Principles of Database Systems, 1986, pp 16-23.*

34. D. Sacca and C. Zaniolo [1986b], "The Generalized Counting Method for Recursive Logic Queries," *Proc. First International Conference on Database Theory, 1986.*

35. D. Sacca and C. Zaniolo [1987], "Magic Counting Methods," *Proc. ACM-SIGMOD Conference, 1987, pp 49-59.*

36. S. Shapiro and D. McKay [1980], "Inference with Recursive Rules," *Proc. 1st Annual National Conference on Artificial Intelligence, August, 1980.*

37. S. Shapiro, J. Martins and D. McKay [1982], "Bi-Directional Inference," *Proc. 4th Annual Conference of the Cognitive Science Society, Ann Arbor, Michigan, 1982.*

38. A. Tarski [1955], "A Lattice Theoretical Fixpoint Theorem and its Applications" *Pacific Journal of Mathematics 5, 1955, pp 285-309*

39. J.D. Ullman [1985], "Implementation of Logical Query Languages for Databases," *Transactions on Database Systems, Vol. 10, No. 3, 1985, pp 289-321.*

40. J. Ullman and A. Van Gelder [1985], "Testing Applicability of Top-Down Capture Rules," *Technical Report, Stanford University, STAN-CS-85-1046, 1985.*

41. P. Valduriez and H. Boral [1986], "Evaluation of Recursive Queries Using Join Indices," *Proc. First Intl. Conference on Expert Database Systems, Charleston, 1986.*

42. M. Van Emden and R. Kowalski [1976], "The Semantics of Predicate Logic as a Programming Language," *JACM, Vol 23, No 4, October 1976, pp 733-742.*

43. A. Van Gelder and R. Topor [1987], "Safety and Correct Translation of Relational Calculus Formulas," *Proc. 6th ACM SIGMOD-SIGACT Symposium on Principles of Database Systems, 1987.*

44. L. Vieille [1986], "Recursive axioms in Deductive Databases: The Query/Subquery Approach," *Proc. First Intl. Conference on Expert Database Systems, Charleston, 1986, pp 179-194.*

45. L. Vieille [1988], "From QSQ towards QoSaQ: Global Optimization of Recursive Queries," *To appear in "Proc. 2nd Intl. Conf. on Expert Database Systems", Ed. L. Kerschberg, 1988.*

46. C. Zaniolo [1985], "The Representation and Deductive Retrieval of Complex Objects," *Proc. 11th Int. Conference on Very Large Data Bases, Stockholm, September 1985.*

47. C. Zaniolo [1986], "Safety and Compilation of Non-Recursive Horn Clauses," *Proc. First Intl. Conference on Expert Database Systems, Charleston, 1986.*

15. Appendix 1: The Cost Functions

Query 1 (Ancestor.bf)

1.1 Naive evaluation $D\sum_{i=1}^{h}(h-i+1).a(i) + E.gsum(E,h'-1).$

1.2 Semi-Naive Evaluation $D\sum_{i=1}^{h}a(i) + E.gsum(E,h'-1).$

1.3 QSQ, Iterative $E.gsum(E,h'-1) + F.\sum_{i=1}^{h'}(h'-i+1).i.E^{i-1}$

1.4 QSQ, Recursive $(F+E).gsum(E,h'-1) + D\sum_{i=1}^{h'}E^{i}.gsum(E,h'-i)$

1.5 Henschen-Naqvi $(F+E).gsum(E,h'-1)$

1.6 Prolog $gsum(F,h') + E.gsum(E,h'-1) + \sum_{i=1}^{h'}(F^{i}).gsum(F,h'-i)$

1.7 APEX $(F+E).gsum(E,h'-1) + D\sum_{i=1}^{h'}E^{i}.gsum(E,h'-i)$

1.8 Kifer-Lozinskii $D\sum_{i=1}^{h}a(i)+E.gsum(E,h'-1)$

1.9 Magic Sets $(F+E).gsum(E,h'-1) + D\sum_{i=1}^{h'}E^{i}.gsum(E,h'-i)$

1.10 Counting $(F+E).gsum(E,h'-1)$

Query 2 (Ancestor.fb)

2.1 Naive evaluation	$D\sum_{i=1}^{h}(h-i+1).a(i) + (1/E).gsum(1/E,h\text{-}h'\text{-}1)$
2.2 Semi-Naive Evaluation	$D\sum_{i=1}^{h}a(i) + (1/E).gsum(1/E,h\text{-}h'\text{-}1)$
2.3 QSQ, Iterative	$(1/E).gsum(1/E,h\text{-}h'\text{-}1) + D.\sum_{i=1}^{h-h'}(h-h'-i+1).i.(1/E)^{i-1}$
2.4 QSQ, Recursive	$1 + (1/E).gsum(1/E,h\text{-}h'\text{-}1) + F.\sum_{i=1}^{h-h'}(1/E)^{i}.gsum(1/E,h-h'-i)$
2.5 Henschen-Naqvi	$(D+1/E).gsum(1/E,h\text{-}h'\text{-}1)$
2.6 Prolog	$(1/E).gsum(1/E,h\text{-}h'\text{-}1) + \sum_{i=1}^{h}n(i).gsum(F,h-i)$
2.7 APEX	$(1/E)^{(h-h')}.(E.gsum(E,h-1)+D\sum_{i=1}^{h}E^{i}.gsum(E,h-i))$
2.8 Kifer-Lozinskii	$(D+1/E).gsum(1/E, h\text{-}h'\text{-}1)$
2.9 Magic Sets	$1 + (1/E).gsum(1/E,h\text{-}h'\text{-}1) + F.\sum_{i=1}^{h-h'}(1/E)^{i}.gsum(1/E,h-h'-i)$
2.10 Counting	$(D+1/E).gsum(1/E,h\text{-}h'\text{-}1)$

Query 3 (Ancestor.bf, Non-Linear Version)

3.1 Naive evaluation	$E.gsum(E,h'\text{-}1) + D\sum_{i=1}^{h}(\log(h/i)+1).(i-1).a(i)$
3.2 Semi-Naive Evaluation	$E.gsum(E,h'\text{-}1) + D\sum_{i=1}^{h}(i-1).a(i)$
3.3 QSQ, Iterative	$E.gsum(E,h'\text{-}1) + F.\sum_{i=1}^{h'}(h'-i+1).i.E^{i-1}$
3.4 QSQ, Recursive	$F+E.gsum(E,h'-1)+D\sum_{i=2}^{h'}(i-1).E^{i}$
3.5 Henschen-Naqvi	Does not apply.
3.6 Prolog	Does not terminate.
3.7 APEX	$E.gsum(E,h'\text{-}1) + (1/E)^{h-h'}.(D\sum_{i=1}^{h}(i-1).E^{i}.gsum(E,h-i))$
	$+ E^{h'}.(F\sum_{i=1}^{h}(i-1).(1/E)^{i}.gsum(1/E,h-i))$

3.8 Kifer-Lozinskii $E.gsum(E,h'-1) + D\sum_{i=1}^{h}(i-1).a(i)$

3.9 Magic Sets $E.gsum(E,h'-1) + D\sum_{i=1}^{h}(i-1).a(i)$

3.10 Counting Does not apply.

Query 4 (Same Generation.bf)

In the following expressions, $h'_{up.down} = \min(h'_{up}, h'_{down})$, and $h_{up.down} = \min(h_{up}, h_{down})$.

4.1 Naive evaluation

$$A_{flat} + T_{up2.flat1}.E_{flat}.T_{flat2.down1}.D_{down}.\sum_{i=1}^{h_{up.down}}(h_{up.down}-i+1).a_{up}(i).E^{i}_{down} +$$

$$T_{up2.flat1}.E_{flat}.T_{flat2.down1}.F_{down}.\sum_{i=1}^{h'_{up.down}}(E_{up}.E_{down})^{i}$$

4.2 Semi-Naive Evaluation

$$A_{flat} + T_{up2.flat1}.E_{flat}.T_{flat2.down1}.D_{down}.\sum_{i=1}^{h_{up.down}}a_{up}(i).E^{i}_{down} +$$

$$T_{up2.flat1}.E_{flat}.T_{flat2.down1}.F_{down}.\sum_{i=1}^{h'_{up.down}}(E_{up}.E_{down})^{i}$$

4.3 QSQ, Iterative

$$(h'_{up.down}+1).F_{flat} +$$

$$T_{up2.flat1}.F_{flat}\sum_{i=1}^{h'_{up.down}}(h'_{up.down}-i+1).E_{up}{}^{i} +$$

$$E_{flat}.T_{up2.flat1}.T_{flat2.down1}.F_{down}.\sum_{i=1}^{h'_{up.down}}(h'_{up.down}-i+1).E^{i}_{up}.gsum(E_{down},i-1) +$$

$$T_{up2.flat1}.E_{flat}.T_{flat2.down1}.F_{down}.\sum_{i=1}^{h'_{up.down}}(E_{up}.E_{down})^{i}$$

4.4 QSQ, Recursive

$$F_{up}.gsum(E_{up},h'_{up}-1) + E_{up}.gsum(E_{up},h'_{up}-1).T_{up2.flat1}.F_{flat} +$$

$$T_{up2.flat1}.E_{flat}.T_{flat2.down1}.D_{down}.\sum_{i=1}^{h'_{up.down}}E^{i}_{up}.gsum(E_{up},h'_{up}-i).E^{i}_{down} +$$

$$T_{up2.flat1}.E_{flat}.T_{flat2.down1}.F_{down}.\sum_{i=1}^{h'_{up.down}}(E_{up}.E_{down})^{i}$$

4.5 Henschen-Naqvi

$$F_{up}.gsum(E_{up},h'_{up}-1) +$$

$$\sum_{i=1}^{h'_{up.down}}(E^{i}_{up}.T_{up2.flat1}.F_{flat} + T_{up2.flat1}.E_{flat}.T_{flat2.down1}.F_{down}.E^{i}_{up}.gsum(E_{down},i-1)) +$$

$$T_{up2.flat1}.E_{flat}.T_{flat2.down1}.F_{down}.\sum_{i=1}^{h'_{up.down}}(E_{up}.E_{down})^{i}$$

4.6 Prolog

$$gsum(F_{up},h'_{up}-1) + F_{up}.gsum(F_{up},h'_{up}-1).T_{up2.flat1}.F_{flat} +$$
$$T_{up2.flat1}.F_{flat}.T_{flat2.down1}.\sum_{i=1}^{h'_{up.down}} F^i_{up}.gsum(F_{up},h'_{up}-i).F^i_{down} +$$
$$T_{up2.flat1}.E_{flat}.T_{flat2.down1}.F_{down}.\sum_{i=1}^{h'_{up.down}} (E_{up}.E_{down})^i$$

4.7 APEX

$$F_{up}.gsum(E_{up},h'_{up}-1) + E_{up}.gsum(E_{up},h'_{up}-1).T_{up2.flat1}.F_{flat} +$$
$$T_{up2.flat1}.E_{flat}.T_{flat2.down1}.D_{down}.\sum_{i=1}^{h'_{up.down}} E^i_{up}.gsum(E_{up},h'_{up}-i).E^i_{down} +$$
$$T_{up2.flat1}.E_{flat}.T_{flat2.down1}.F_{down}.\sum_{i=1}^{h'_{up.down}} (E_{up}.E_{down})^i$$

4.8 Kifer-Lozinskii

$$A_{flat} + T_{up2.flat1}.E_{flat}.T_{flat2.down1}.D_{down}.(\sum_{i=1}^{h_{up.down}} (a_{up}(i).E^i_{down}) +$$
$$T_{up2.flat1}.E_{flat}.T_{flat2.down1}.F_{down}.\sum_{i=1}^{h'_{up.down}} (E_{up}.E_{down})^i$$

4.9 Magic Sets

$$F_{up}.gsum(E_{up},h'_{up}-1) + E_{up}.gsum(E_{up},h'_{up}-1).T_{up2.flat1}.F_{flat} +$$
$$T_{up2.flat1}.E_{flat}.T_{flat2.down1}.D_{down}.\sum_{i=1}^{h'_{up.down}} E^i_{up}.gsum(E_{up},h'_{up}-i).E^i_{down} +$$
$$T_{up2.flat1}.E_{flat}.T_{flat2.down1}.F_{down}.\sum_{i=1}^{h'_{up.down}} (E_{up}.E_{down})^i$$

4.10 Counting

$$F_{up}.gsum(E_{up},h'_{up}-1) +$$
$$T_{up2.flat1}.F_{flat}(1+E_{up}gsum(Eu,h'_{up}-1)) +$$
$$\sum_{i=1}^{h'_{up.down}} T_{up2.flat1}.E_{flat}.T_{flat2.down1}.D_{down}.(E_{up}.E_{down})^i +$$
$$T_{up2.flat1}.E_{flat}.T_{flat2.down1}.F_{down}.\sum_{i=1}^{h'_{up.down}} (E_{up}.E_{down})^i$$

Appendix 2: The Curves

Query 1, Tree data

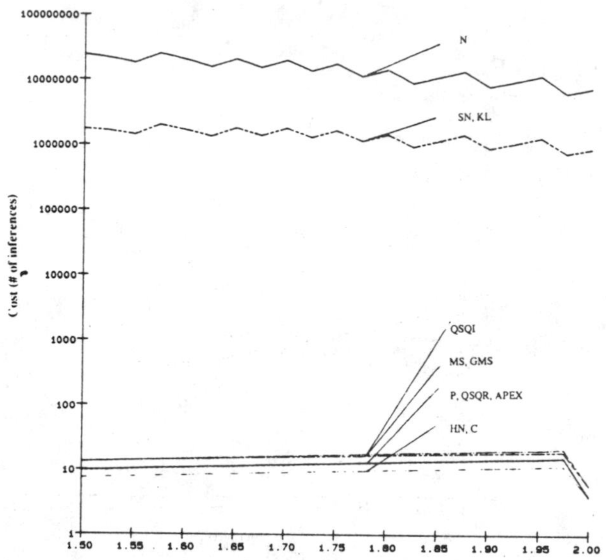

Fanout F

Query 1, Cylinder data

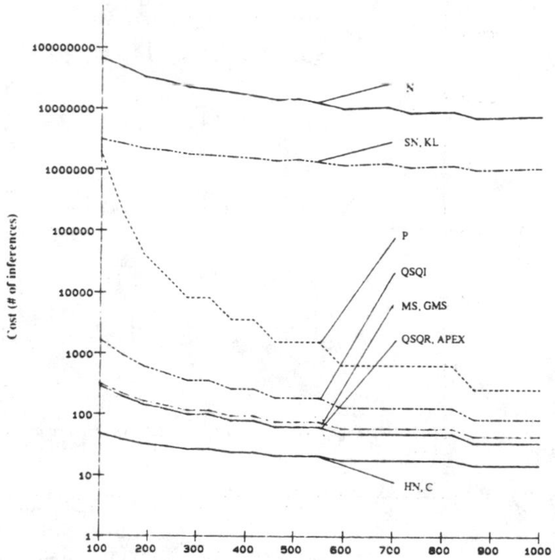

Breadth (b)/Height (h)

ABF_INV

Query 1, Inverted tree data

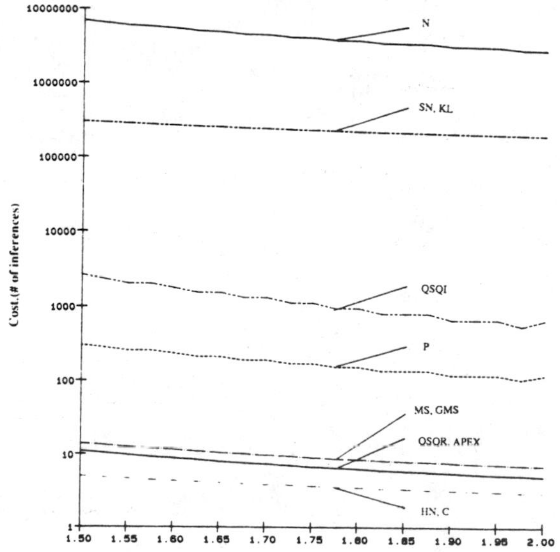

Duplication D

Query 2, Cylinder data

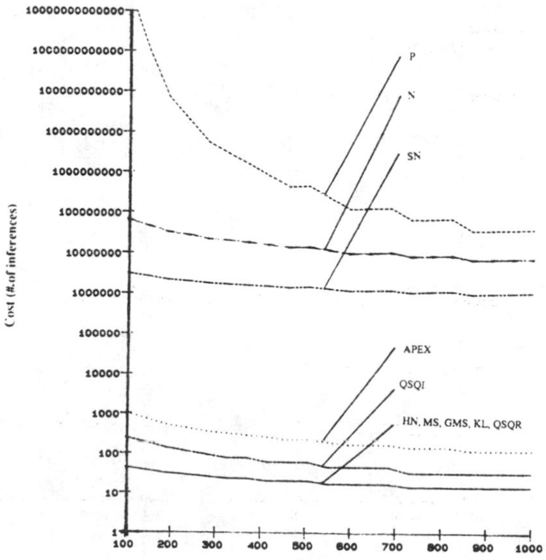

Breadth (b)/Height (h)

Query 2, Tree data

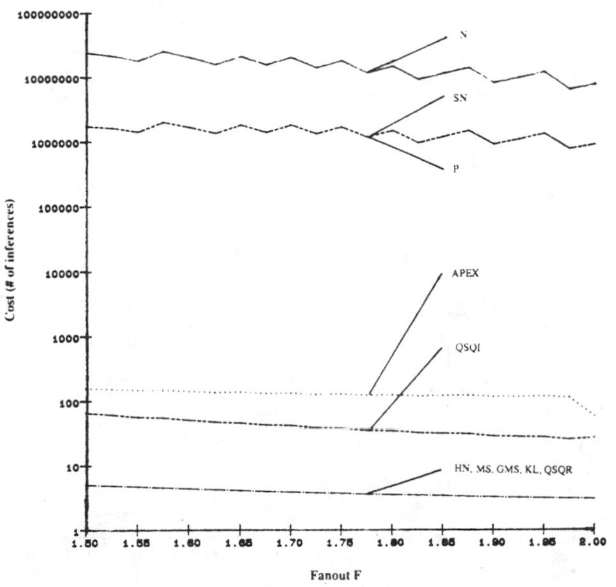

Query 3, Cylinder data

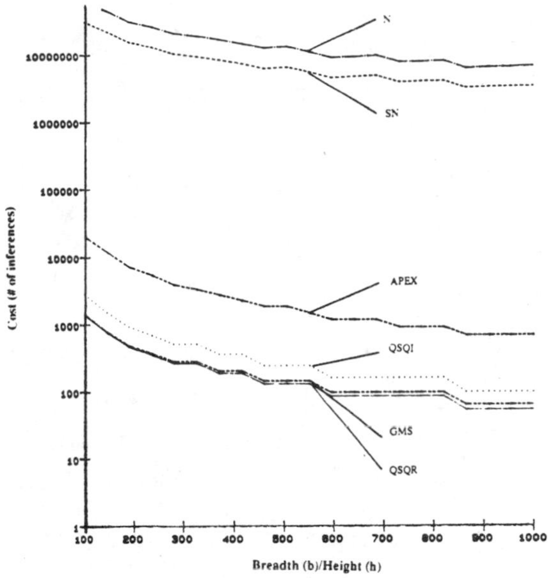

Query 3, Tree data

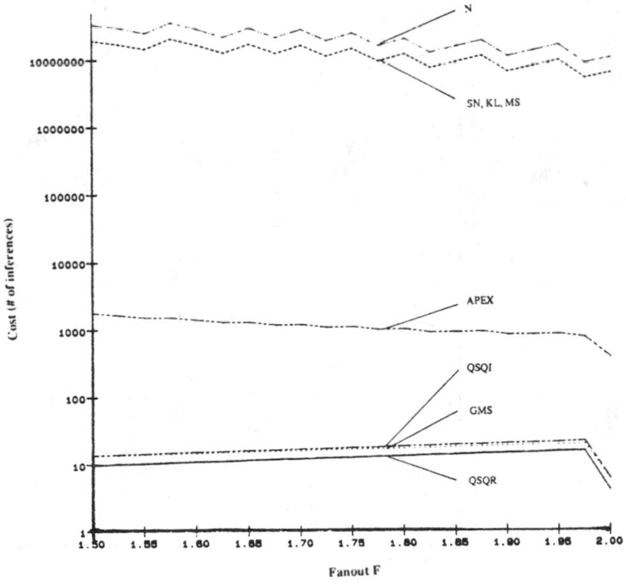

Query 4, Cylinder data with Join Selectivity = 100%

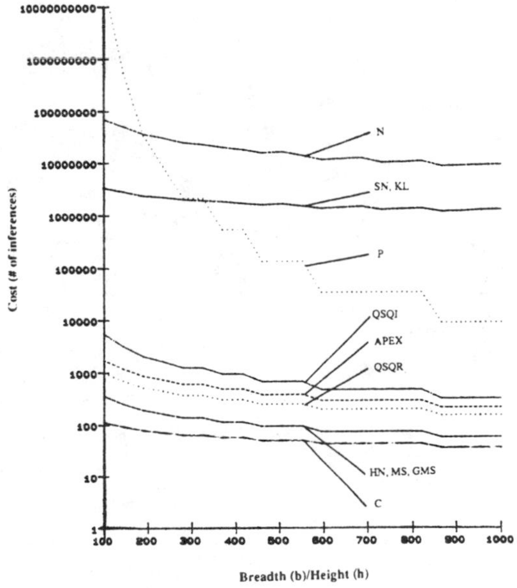

Query 4, Tree data with Join Selectivity = 100%

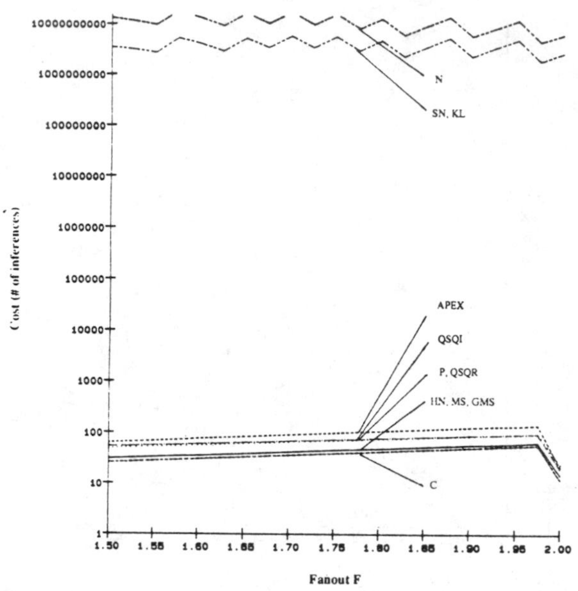

Query 4, Inverted tree data with Join Selectivity = 1%

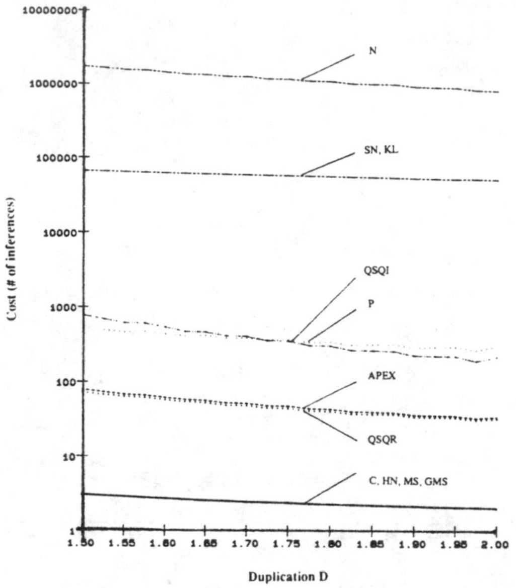

SG_INV

Query 4, Tree data with Join Selectivity = 100%

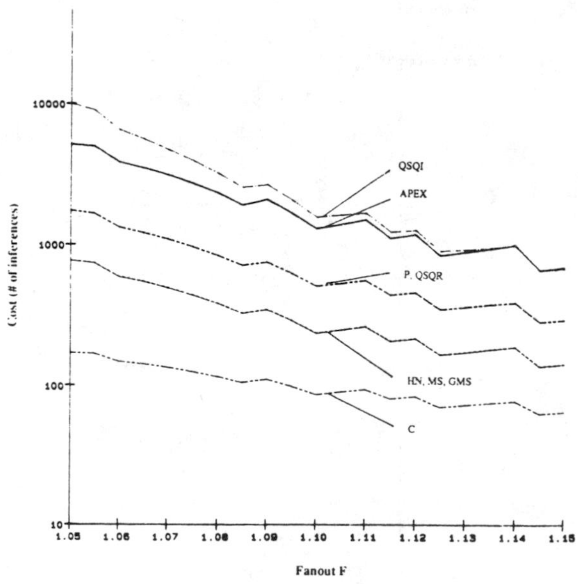

Query 4, Inverted tree data with Join Selectivity = 100%

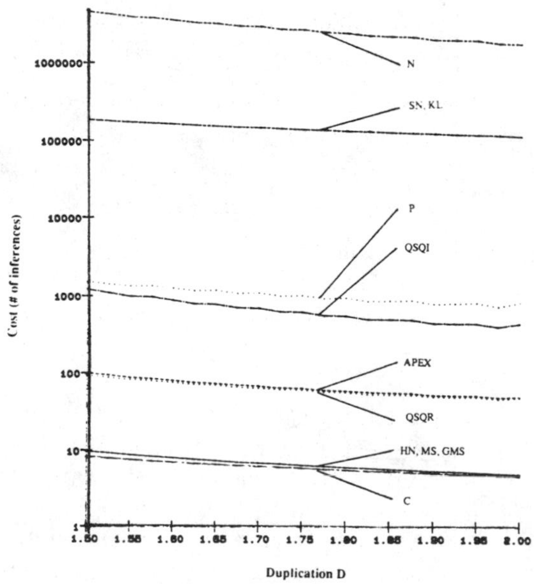

Epilogue

Recursive queries have received a great deal of attention recently, and the preceding survey does not touch upon several interesting developments. In this epilogue, we provide some pointers to further work in this area. In order to be as comprehensive as possible, we have chosen to present an annotated bibliography, but even this is far from complete. However, this should provide a starting point for the interested reader. †

Projects

Two of the major research projects in this area have been carried out at MCC in Austin and at Stanford University. An overview of these projects is provided in the following references.

K. Morris, J.F. Naughton. Y. Saraiya, J.D. Ullman and A. Van Gelder [1987], "YAWN! (Yet Another Window on NAIL!)," *Bull. Data Engineering, Vol. 10, No. 4, Dec. 1987.*

D. Chimenti, T. O'Hare, R. Krishnamurthy, S. Naqvi, S. Tsur, C. West and C. Zaniolo [1987], "An Overview of the LDL System," *Bull. Data Engineering, Vol. 10, No. 4, Dec. 1987.*

Some of the other influential efforts include projects at ECRC in Munich, the ESPRIT projects, Honeywell-Bull, INRIA, SUNY-StonyBrook, the University of Maryland and the University of Melbourne. The work at ECRC, ESPRIT, and the Univ. of Melbourne is surveyed in the following references.

H. Gallaire and J.-M. Nicolas [1987], "Logic Approach to Knowledge and Data Bases at ECRC," *Bull. Data Engineering, Vol. 10, No. 4, Dec. 1987.*

D. Sacca, M. Dispinzeri, A. Mecchia, C. Pizzuti, C. Del Gracco and P. Naggar [1987], "The Advanced Database Environment of the KIWI System," *Bull. Data Engineering, Vol. 10, No. 4, Dec. 1987.*

K. Ramamohanarao, J. Shepherd, I. Balbin, G. Port, L. Naish, J. Thom, J. Zobel and P. Dart [1987], "The NU-Prolog Deductive Database System," *Bull. Data Engineering, Vol. 10, No. 4, Dec. 1987.*

While we are not aware of any overviews of the other projects, pointers may be found in the following references: Rohmer et al. [1986] (Honeywell-Bull), Gardarin and de Maindreville [1986] (INRIA) and Kifer and Lozinskii [1988] (StonyBrook). Pointers to the work at Maryland may be found in the following reference, which also provides a historical survey of the field.

J. Minker [1987], "Perspectives in Deductive Databases," *Proc. PODS 87, San Diego.*

Projects at CCA and Bell Labs have focussed on transitive closure and related path problems. The following references provide further pointers.

U. Dayal, A. Buchmann, D. Goldhirsch, S. Heiler, F. Manola, J. Orenstein and A. Rosenthal [1986], "PROBE- a Research Project in Knowledge-Oriented Database Systems: Preliminary Analysis," *Technical Report, CCA-85-03, July 1985.*

R. Agrawal and H.V. Jagadish [1987], "Direct Algorithms for Computing the Transitive Closure of Database Relations," *Proc. Conf. on Very Large Data Bases 87.*

Query Evaluation

We present brief descriptions of some recent work. Ullman [1985] presented the "capture rules" framework for planning the evaluation of a recursive query. An alternative framework, with a comparison, is proposed in Krishnamurthy et al. [1988]. In essence, it is proposed that all strategies be implemented by rewriting (e.g., using Generalized Magic Sets) followed by bottom-up evaluation. Testing capturability is now similar to testing for safety, and a general testing algorithm is presented. Aly and Ozsoyoglu [1987] presents a Petri-net based model for describing logic queries and the flow of control in algorithms for evaluating them.

Kifer and Lozinskii [1986b, 1988] extend the original "static" filtering algorithm to deal with general recursion and rules containing function symbols. They also consider the issue of safety. The method in the

† The references for some of the papers discussed in this epilogue appear in the list of references for the survey paper.

most general form is comparable to Generalized Magic Sets. Nejdl [1987] presents a recursive algorithm related to QSQ. Vieille [1988] extends the QSQ method and discusses its relationship to the generalized versions of Magic Sets and Counting. Grahne et al. [1987] consider efficient evaluation of a simple class of programs ("binary chain programs") and also consider the use of their algorithm to deal with more general programs. Sippu and Soisalon-Soininen [1988a] proposes an algorithm similar to the Generalized Magic Sets algorithm, but such that the rules defining the "magic sets" are simplified and separated from the other rules. The trade-off is that the magic sets so computed may be less restrictive. Gardarin [1987] presents a functional-style algorithm extending the results in Gardarin and de Maindreville [1986]. Sacca and Zaniolo [1987] addresses the issue of how to adapt the Counting method to the Magic Sets method when it is discovered that the former is not applicable. Ramakrishnan [1988] extends the Generalized Magic Sets to deal with arbitrary programs by treating rules in which some head variables do not appear in the body (even in the rewritten program). Such rules give rise to partial data structures, and allow the utilization of partially bound arguments and of data structures such as difference lists. Haddad and Naughton [1988] proposes an efficient way to adapt Counting in the presence of cyclic data. Marchetti-Spaccamela et al. [1987] presents a worst-case analysis of three algorithms (Counting, Magic Sets, and a method similar to Henschen-Naqvi), and suggests a modification to deal with Counting in the presence of cyclic data. Much of this work may be viewed as attempting to "push" selections through recursive rules. In Beeri et al. [1987], this was formalized as transforming a binary chain program with a selection query into an equivalent monadic program (i.e., all derived predicates have exactly one argument). This problem was shown to be undecidable (since it is equivalent to testing whether a context free grammar defines a regular language).

Sagiv [1987] introduced the notion of "uniform equivalence" of programs and showed that it was decidable to test whether two programs were uniformly equivalent. He also considered the deletion of rules and literals under uniform equivalence. The problem of pushing projections through recursive rules was studied in Ramakrishnan et al. [1988]. The problem was shown to be undecidable, using the result in Beeri et al. [1987]. Several optimization algorithms for dealing with projections were presented, including a sufficient condition for deleting rules under "uniform query equivalence". Naughton [1987] introduces a class of programs which permit efficient evaluation strategies. This class of programs generalizes transitive closure in a natural way. Han and Henschen [1987] discusses related strategies (as part of a more general study of how to reduce redundant computation).

Zhang and Yu [1987] presents an algorithm to obtain a linear recursive rule which is equivalent to a doubly recursive rule, when the latter satisfies certain conditions. Ceri et al. [1986], Ceri and Tanca [1987], and Ioannidis and Wong [1988] consider algebraic formalisms for representing and manipulating recursive queries. Ioannidis and Wong [1987] considers the use of simulated annealing to deal with large access plan spaces in recursive query evaluation. Whang and Navathe [1987] proposes an Extended Disjunctive Normal Form for recursive queries and considers evaluation strategies based on translation into this form, which allows recognition of common subexpressions in the evaluation of multiple rules. Raschid and Su [1986] presents an evaluation strategy based on evaluating a series of non-recursive expressions (generated by repeatedly expanding recursive rules) in parallel. Jagadish et al. [1987] show that linearly recursive rules can be translated into relational algebra augmented with transitive closure, but, in general, this involves taking cross-products of relations.

H. Aly and Z.M. Ozsoyoglu [1987], "Non-deterministic Modelling of Logical Queries in Deductive Databases," *Proc. ACM-SIGMOD Conference, 1987.*

C. Beeri, P. Kanellakis, F. Bancilhon and R. Ramakrishnan [1987], "Bounds on the Propagation of Selection into Logic Programs," *Proc. 6th ACM SIGACT-SIGMOD-SIGART Symposium on Principles of Database Systems, 1987.*

S. Ceri, G. Gottlob and L. Lavazza [1986], "Translation and Optimization of Logic Queries: The Algebraic Approach," *Proc. 12th Inter. Conf. on Very Large Data Bases, 1986.*

S. Ceri and L. Tanca [1987], "Optimization of Systems of Algebraic Equations for Evaluating Datalog Queries," *Proc. 13th Inter. Conf. on Very Large Data Bases, 1987.*

L. Raschid and S.Y.W. Su [1986], "A Parallel Processing Strategy for Evaluating Recursive Queries," *Proc. 12th Inter. Conf. on Very Large Data Bases, 1986.*

G. Gardarin [1987], "Magic Functions: A Technique to Optimize Extended Datalog Recursive Programs," *Proc. 13th Inter. Conf. on Very Large Data Bases, 1987.*

G. Grahne, S. Sippu and E. Soisalon-Soininen [1987], "Efficient Evaluation for a Subset of Recursive Queries," *Proc. 6th ACM SIGACT-SIGMOD-SIGART Symposium on Principles of Database Systems, 1987.*

R.W. Haddad and J.F. Naughton [1988], "Counting Methods for Cyclic Relations," *Proc. 7th ACM SIGACT-SIGMOD-SIGART Symposium on Principles of Database Systems, 1988.*

J. Han and L. Henschen [1987], "Handling Redundancy in the Processing of Recursive Queries," *Proc. ACM-SIGMOD Conference, 1987.*

Y.E. Ioannidis and E. Wong [1987], "Query Optimization by Simulated Annealing," *Proc. ACM-SIGMOD Conference, 1987.*

H.V. Jagadish, R. Agrawal and L. Ness [1987], "A Study of Transitive Closure as a Recursion Mechanism," *Proc. ACM-SIGMOD Conference, 1987.*

A. Marchetti-Spaccamela, A. Pelaggi and D. Sacca [1987], "Worst-case Complexity Analysis of Methods for Logic Query Implementation," *Proc. 6th ACM SIGACT-SIGMOD-SIGART Symposium on Principles of Database Systems, 1987.*

J.F. Naughton [1986], "Redundancy in Function-Free Recursive Rules," *Proc. 3rd IEEE Symposium on Logic Programming, 1986.*

J.F. Naughton [1987], "One-Sided Recursions," *Proc. 6th ACM SIGACT-SIGMOD-SIGART Symposium on Principles of Database Systems, 1987.*

W. Nejdl [1987], "Recursive Strategies for Answering Recursive Queries - The RQA/FQI Strategy," *Proc. 13th Inter. Conf. on Very Large Data Bases, 1987.*

R. Ramakrishnan, C. Beeri and R. Krishnamurthy [1988], "Optimizing Existential Datalog Programs," *Proc. 7th ACM SIGACT-SIGMOD-SIGART Symposium on Principles of Database Systems, 1988.*

Y. Sagiv [1988], "Optimizing Datalog Programs," *Proc. 6th ACM SIGACT-SIGMOD-SIGART Symposium on Principles of Database Systems, 1987.*

S. Sippu and E. Soisalon-Soininen [1988a], "An Optimization Strategy for Recursive Queries in Logic Databases," *Proc. 4th Data Engineering Conf., 1988.*

K.-Y. Whang and S. Navathe [1987], "An Extended Disjunctive Normal Form Approach for Optimizing Recursive Logic Queries in Loosely Coupled Environments," *Proc. 13th Inter. Conf. on Very Large Data Bases, 1987.*

W. Zhang and C.T. Yu [1987], "A Necessary Condition for a Doubly Recursive Rule to be Equivalent to a Linear Recursive Rule," *Proc. ACM-SIGMOD Conference, 1987.*

Transitive Closure

There has been considerable effort on optimizing the evaluation of transitive closure queries. Most of the work has concentrated on evaluating the entire transitive closure of a relation. Much of the effort has been to reduce the I/O cost when the relations are sufficiently large that they must reside mostly on disk. Agrawal and Jagadish [1987] discusses the implementation of well-known algorithms (Warshall, Warren) based on matrix-multiplication with careful blocking to reduce I/O. (Lu et al. [1987] also consider these algorithms, but their implementation did not utilize blocking.) Agrawal et al. [1987] extends this work to deal with path computations, such as the shortest paths between pairs of nodes. Their work (in particular, the formalism), as well as that of Ioannidis and Ramakrishnan [1988] is influenced by the work of Carre [1979]. Ioannidis and Ramakrishnan [1988] presents an algorithm based on depth-first traversal. The algorithm can be viewed as a refinement of the Seminaive and Schmitz algorithms, and can deal with path computations and selections. The Schmitz algorithm, also based on depth-first traversal, is unable to deal with path computations. Ioannidis [1986] and Valduriez and Boral [1986] present an algorithm called the "Logarithmic" or "Smart" algorithm that is an iterative algorithm like Seminaive, but converges in fewer iterations. Ioannidis derived this algorithm based on an algebraic formulation of queries, which is further developed in Ioannidis and Wong [1986, 1988]. Lu [1987] presents a refinement of Seminaive based on using hash-joins, dynamically reducing the size of intermediate relations, and aggressively processing in-memory tuples. Sippu and Soisalon-Soininen [1988b] considers a generalization of transitive closure, based on a generalization of the composition (join) operation from binary to n-ary relations. The references below also contain pointers to related work such as transforming general queries into transitive closure computations, and pushing selections in the special case of transitive closure.

R. Agrawal, S. Dar and H.V. Jagadish [1987], "Transitive Closure Algorithms Revisited: The Case for Path Computations," *Manuscript, 1987.*

B. Carre [1979], "Graphs and Networks," *Clarendon Press, Oxford, England, 1979.*

Y.E. Ioannidis [1986], "On the Computation of the Transitive Closure of Relational Operators," *Proc. 12th Inter. Conf. on Very Large Data Bases, 1986.*

Y.E. Ioannidis and R. Ramakrishnan [1988], "Efficient Transitive Closure Algorithms," *Manuscript, 1988.*

Y.E. Ioannidis and E. Wong [1986], "An Algebraic Approach to Recursive Inference," *Proc. of the 1st Inter. Conf. on Expert Database Systems, 1986.*

Y.E. Ioannidis and E. Wong [1988], "Transforming Nonlinear Recursion into Linear Recursion," *To appear in Proc. 2nd Inter. Conf. on Expert Database Systems, 1988.*

H. Lu [1987], "New Strategies for Computing the Transitive Closure of a Database Relation," *Proc. 13th Inter. Conf. on Very Large Data Bases, 1987.*

H. Lu, K. Mikkilineni, and J.P. Richardson [1987], "Design and Evaluation of Algorithms to Compute the Transitive Closure of a Database Relation," *Proc. of the 3rd Inter. Data Engineering Conf., 1987.*

L. Schmitz [1983], "An Improved Transitive Closure Algorithm," *Computing, Vol. 30, 1983.*

S. Sippu and E. Soisalon-Soininen [1988b], "A Generalized Transitive Closure for Relational Queries," *Proc. 7th ACM SIGACT-SIGMOD-SIGART Symposium on Principles of Database Systems, 1988.*

Negation and Sets

The database approach to negation has differed significantly from the logic programming approach. The notion of "stratification" was proposed in Apt, Blair and Walker [1988], Naqvi [1986] and Van Gelder [1988]. The idea, intuitively, is that if predicate p is defined in terms of $\neg q$, then q must not depend on p. (Thus, we can think of the predicates in a program as being partioned into *strata* - p and q would be in different strata.) Przymusinski [1988] extends this notion by considering ground instances of rules ("local stratification"). Lifshitz [1988] considers the relationship between stratification and circumscription. Apt and Pugin [1987] considers the maintenance of materialized views based on stratified programs. Beeri et al. [1987], Balbin et al. [1987a] and Balbin et al. [1987b] consider the evaluation of stratified programs using Generalized Magic Sets. Beeri et al. [1987] also presents a description of sets and negation in the LDL language. Shmueli et al. [1988] considers the use of rewriting to implement set terms. Kuper [1987] presents another proposal for incorporating sets in a logic-based language, and Kuper [1988] considers the expressive power of these (and other) proposals. A more general overview of the expressive power of query languages is provided in Chandra [1988]. Kolaitis and Papadimitriou [1988] and Abiteboul and Vianu [1988] propose another semantics for negation, based on "inflationary fixpoints" (essentially, a fact once deduced is never discarded). Yet another proposal for dealing with negation, which properly includes local stratification, is presented in Van Gelder et al. [1988]. Imielinski and Naqvi [1988] suggest that there may be no one natural semantics for negation, and instead propose a rule algebra as a way to specify a limited amount of control, whereby a number of distinct semantics for negation may be realized by the user.

S. Abiteboul and V. Vianu [1988], "Procedural and Declarative Database Update Languages, *Proc. 7th ACM SIGACT-SIGMOD-SIGART Symposium on Principles of Database Systems, 1988.*

K.R. Apt, H. Blair and A. Walker [1988], "Towards a Theory of Declarative Knowledge," *In "Foundations of Deductive Databases and Logic Programming," Ed. J. Minker, Morgan Kaufmann, 1988.*

K.R. Apt and J.-M. Pugin [1987]. "Maintenance of Stratified Databases Viewed as a Belief Revision System," *Proc. 6th ACM SIGACT-SIGMOD-SIGART Symposium on Principles of Database Systems, 1987.*

I. Balbin, G.S. Port and K. Ramamohanarao [1987a], "Magic Set Computation of Stratified Databases," *Technical Report 87/3, University of Melbourne, 1987.*

I. Balbin, K. Meenakshi and K. Ramamohanarao [1987b], "An Efficient Labelling Algorithm for Magic Set Computation on Stratified Databases," *Technical Report 88/1, University of Melbourne, 1988.*

C. Beeri, S. Naqvi, R. Ramakrishnan, O. Shmueli and S. Tsur [1987], "Sets and Negation in a Logic Database Language (LDL1)," *Proc. 6th ACM SIGACT-SIGMOD-SIGART Symposium on Principles of Database Systems, 1987.*

A. Chandra [1988], "Theory of Database Queries," *Proc. 7th ACM SIGACT-SIGMOD-SIGART Symposium on Principles of Database Systems, 1988, invited paper.*

T. Imielinski and S. Naqvi [1988], "Explicit Control of Logic Programs Through Rule Algebra," *Proc. 7th ACM SIGACT-SIGMOD-SIGART Symposium on Principles of Database Systems, 1988.*

P.G. Kolaitis and C.H. Papadimitriou [1988], "Why not Negation by Fixpoint?," *Proc. 7th ACM SIGACT-SIGMOD-SIGART Symposium on Principles of Database Systems, 1988.*

G. Kuper [1987], "Logic Programming with Sets," *Proc. 6th ACM SIGACT-SIGMOD-SIGART Symposium on Principles of Database Systems, 1987.*

G. Kuper [1988], "On the Expressive Power of Logic Programming Languages with Sets," *Proc. 7th ACM SIGACT-SIGMOD-SIGART Symposium on Principles of Database Systems, 1988.*

V. Lifschitz [1988], "On the Declarative Semantics of Logic Programs with Negation," *In "Foundations of Deductive Databases and Logic Programming," Ed. J. Minker, Morgan Kaufmann, 1988.*

S. Naqvi [1986], "A Logic for Negation in Database Systems," *In preprints of the Workshop on the Foundations of Deductive Databases and Logic Programming, Washington, 1986.*

T.C. Przymusinski [1988], "On the Declarative Semantics of Deductive Databases and Logic Programs," *In "Foundations of Deductive Databases and Logic Programming," Ed. J. Minker, Morgan Kaufmann, 1988.*

A. Van Gelder [1988], "Negation as Failure Using Tight Derivations for Logic Programs," *In "Foundations of Deductive Databases and Logic Programming," Ed. J. Minker, Morgan Kaufmann, 1988.*

A. Van Gelder, K. Ross and J.S. Schlipf [1988], "Unfounded Sets and Well-founded Semantics for General Logic Programs," *Proc. 7th ACM SIGACT-SIGMOD-SIGART Symposium on Principles of Database Systems, 1988.*

Bounded Recursion

A set of Horn clauses is called *bounded* if it is equivalent to a finite number of nonrecursive ones. A recursive Horn clause is *uniformly bounded* if it is uniformly equivalent to a finite number of nonrecursive ones. One can easily show that a recursive Horn clause is uniformly bounded if and only if its combination with any nonrecursive Horn clause is bounded. Thus, uniform boundedness implies boundedness, but the converse is not true.

Minker and Nicolas originally gave a sufficient condition for characterizing uniformly bounded recursion in a class of recursive Horn clauses (Minker and Nicolas [1983]). Representing a Horn clause by a tableau, and under various restrictions on the form of the tableau, Sagiv gives necessary and sufficient conditions for a set of Horn clauses to be uniformly bounded (Sagiv [1985]). Similar results have also been presented in Cosmadakis and Kanellakis [1986]. Necessary and sufficient conditions for a single linear recursive Horn clause to be uniformly bounded within an assortment of restricted classes of Horn clauses have been presented in Ioannidis [1986] and Naughton [1986]. Naughton has also dealt with the problem of (nonuniform) boundedness within the same classes [Naughton 86]. Recently this assortment of classes has been unified into a more abstract (super)class of recursive Horn clauses, where the characterization of Ioannidis and Naughton holds (Naughton and Sagiv [1987]). For general programs, both boundedness and uniform boundedness have been proven undecidable (Gaifman et al. [1987], Vardi [1987]). Finally, it has been shown that boundedness is decidable but NP-complete for programs which contain a single linear recursive Horn clause (Kanellakis [1986] and Vardi [1988]). The boundedness problem is decidable but EXPTIME-hard for monadic problems, and PSPACE-complete for linear monadic programs (Cosmadakis et al. [1988]).

J. Minker and J.-M. Nicolas [1983], "On Recursive Axioms in Deductive Databases," *Information Systems, Vol. 8, No. 1, 1983.*

Y.E. Ioannidis [1986], "A Time Bound on the Materialization of Some Recursively Defined Views," *Algorithmica, Vol. 1, No. 4, October 86.*

S.S. Cosmadakis and P.C. Kanellakis [1986], "Parallel Evaluation of Recursive Rule Queries," *Proc. of the 5th ACM SIGMOD-SIGACT Symposium on Principles of Database Systems, 1986.*

P.C. Kanellakis [1988], "Logic Programming and Parallel Complexity," *In "Foundations of Deductive Databases and Logic Programming," Ed. J. Minker, Morgan Kaufmann, 1988.*

J.F. Naughton [1986], "Data Independent Recursion in Deductive Databases," *Proc. of the 5th ACM SIGMOD-SIGACT Symposium on Principles of Database Systems, 1986.*

Y. Sagiv [1985], "On Computing Restricted Projections of Representative Instances," *Proc. of the 4th ACM SIGMOD-SIGACT Symposium on Principles of Database Systems, 1985.*

J.F. Naughton and Y. Sagiv [1987], "A Decidable Class of Bounded Recursions," *Proc. of the 6th ACM SIGMOD-SIGACT Symposium on Principles of Database Systems, 1987.*

M.Y. Vardi [1988] "Decidability and Undecidability Results for Boundedness of Linear Recursive Queries," *Proc. of the 7th ACM SIGMOD-SIGACT Symposium on Principles of Database Systems, 1988.*

H. Gaifman, H. Mairson, Y. Sagiv, and M.Y. Vardi [1987], "Undecidable Optimization Problems for Database Logic Programs," *Proc. 2nd Inter. Symposium on Logic in Computer Science, 1987.*

S.S. Cosmadakis, H. Gaifman, P.C. Kanellakis and M.Y. Vardi [1988], "Decidable Optimization Problems for Database Logic Programs," *Manuscript.*

Conclusions

We have attempted to provide a roadmap for the adventurous reader. The objective of the epilogue has been to complement the survey, and work which has been mentioned in the survey has been omitted (even work which has not been adequately discussed, e.g., the recent work on safety). Exigencies of space and time have also precluded mention of work in other important areas, e.g., updates, intelligent query answering, the expressive power of logic-based query languages and connections to logic programming. A good starting point in these areas is the collection of papers in Minker [1988] and the proceedings of PODS 88.

The area of recursive query processing has progressed very rapidly in the last few years, and we now have a good insight into both the theoretical and practical aspects of the field. The area is extremely vigorous, as evidenced by the large numbers of papers in this area appearing in recent database and logic programming conferences. We observe however, that a critical note has recently been raised: Do we really need more general forms of recursion than transitive closure in a database query language? (This question is raised, for example, in Laguna Beach [1988], and partly underlies the decision of the CCA, Bell Labs and other projects to focus on transitive closure.) This is an important question, and will not be completely settled until the community has had the opportunity to use and experiment with some of the more expressive recursive query languages such as LDL. While research in this area will continue to be productive, and is interesting from a theoretical point of view and for its relevance to the field of logic programming, the importance of general recursive query processing for database applications remains to be established. In fact, settling this question is, in our opinion, an important research objective.

Laguna Beach Participants [1988], "Future Directions in DBMS Research," *Manuscript.*

Acknowledgements

Yannis Ioannidis helped to compile the section on bounded recursion. Ioannidis and Jeff Naughton also provided comments on a draft version of the epilogue.

DEDUCTIVE QUESTION-ANSWERING ON RELATIONAL DATA BASES

Raymond Reiter

The University of British Columbia

Vancouver, British Columbia

ABSTRACT

The principal concern of this paper is the design of a retrieval system which combines current techniques for query evaluation on relational data bases with a deductive component in such a way that the interface between the two is both clean and natural. The result is an approach to deductive retrieval which appears to be feasible for data bases with very large extensions (i.e. specific facts) and comparatively small intensions (i.e. general facts). More specifically, a suitably designed theorem prover "sweeps through" the intensional data base, extracting all information relevant to a given query. This theorem prover never looks at the extensional data base. The end result of this sweep is a set of queries, each of which is extensionally evaluated. The union of answers returned from each of these queries is the set of answers to the original query.

One consequence of this decomposition into an intensional and extensional processor is that the latter may be realized by a conventional data base management system. Another is that the intensional data base can be compiled using a theorem prover as a once-only compiler.

This paper is essentially an impressionistic survey of some results which are rigorously treated elsewhere. As such, no proofs are given for the theorems stated, and the basic system design is illustrated by means of an extended example.

INTRODUCTION

The principal concern of this paper is the design of a retrieval system which combines current techniques for query evaluation on relational data bases, e.g. Codd [1972] with a deductive component in such a way that the interface between the two is both clean and natural. The result is an approach to deductive retrieval which appears to be feasible for data bases with very large extensions (i.e. specific facts) and comparatively small intensions (i.e. general facts). More specifically, a suitably designed theorem prover "sweeps through" the intensional data base, extracting all information relevant to a given query. In particular, this theorem prover never looks at the extensional data base. The end result of this sweep is a set of queries, each of which is extensionally evaluated. The union of answers returned from each of these queries is a set of answers to the original query.

There are two important consequences of this decomposition of the question-answering task into a theorem prover computing on the intensional data base, and an extensional processor computing on the extensional data base:

1. The extensional processor can be realized by a conventional data base management system.

2. Because the theorem prover never accesses the extensional data base, the intensional data base can be compiled using the theorem prover as a once-only compiler. This means that at query evaluation time there is no need for a theorem prover, nor are there the usual problems involving search which can plague a theorem proving system.

This paper is essentially a survey of some of the results in Reiter [1977]. As such, it is necessarily impressionistic, so that no proofs are given for the theorems stated, and the basic approach to query evaluation which decouples the theorem prover from the extensional processor is described by means of an extended example. A rigorous presentation is contained in Reiter [1977] to which the interested reader is referred for the painful details.

DATA BASES

The results of this paper apply only to first order data bases with the following properties:

(i) The data base consists of finitely many twffs (typed well-formed formulae). For example, in an inventory domain, such a twff might be

$$(x/\text{Manufacturer})(y/\text{Part})(z/\text{Part})\text{manufactures } x,y \wedge \text{Subpart } z,y \supset \text{Supplies } x,z$$

i.e., every manufacturer of a part supplies all its subparts. The restricted universal quantifier (y/Part) may be read "for every y which is a Part". The restrictions Manufacturer and Part are called types and are distinguished monadic predicates. If τ is such a type, then $(x/\tau)W$ is an abbreviation for $(x)\tau x \supset W$. We shall later require the notion of a restricted existential quantifier (Ex/τ) which may be read "there is an x in τ". $(Ex/\tau)W$ is an abbreviation for $(Ex)\tau x \wedge W$. We denote by $|\tau|$ the set of all constants which satisfy the type τ. Thus, |Part| might be {gadget-1, widget-3, bolt-49, ...,}. In general, a twff has the form $(x_1/\tau_1)\ldots(x_n/\tau_n)W$ for $n \geq 0$ where W is any quantifier free ordinary first order formula containing no function signs, and $\tau_1,\ldots,\tau_n$ are types. Notice that no existential quantifiers are permitted - all twffs are universally quantified. In the case that the twff has no quantifiers, it is an ordinary ground first order formula.

(ii) There are only finitely many constant signs. Constant signs denote individuals of the data base e.g. bolt-49, Acme-manufacturers, etc.

(iii) Equality is a distinguished predicate. We assume that the data base contains the following equality axioms:

E1. $(x)x=x$
E2. $(x)(y)\ x=y \supset y=x$
E3. $(x)(y)(z)\ x=y \wedge y=z \supset x=z$
E4. For each n-ary predicate sign P
$(x_1)\ldots(x_n)(x_1')\ldots(x_n')\ x_1=x_1' \wedge\ldots\wedge x_n=x_n' \wedge$

$Px_1,\ldots,x_n \supset Px_1',\ldots,x_n'$

In addition, if $c_1,\ldots,c_p$ are all of the constant signs of the data base, then the following domain closure axiom applies:

DC. $(x)[x=c_1 \vee x=c_2 \vee \ldots \vee x=c_p]$

The domain closure axiom restricts the universe of discourse to just those individuals denoted by the constant signs of the theory. In the intended interpretation, answers to queries will be formulated exclusively in terms of these finitely many individuals.

Finally, we assume that for each constant sign c, the ground equality literal c=c is in the data base, and for each pair of distinct constant signs c,c' the inequality literal $c \neq c'$ is in the data base. Intuitively, as far as the data base is concerned, two constant signs are treated as equal iff they are identical syntactic objects.

Let DB be a data base as defined above, and let EDB be the set of ground literals of DB. EDB will be called the extensional data base. The intensional data base is defined to be IDB = DB - EDB. Intuitively, the EDB is a set of specific facts like "John Doe teaches Calculus 103", while the IDB is a set of general facts like "All widgets are manufactured by Foobar Inc." or "John Doe teaches Calculus 102 or Bill Jones teaches Calculus 103 (but I don't know which)" together with the equality and domain closure axioms.

QUERIES AND ANSWERS

A query is any expression of the form

$$< x_1/\tau_1,\ldots,x_n/\tau_n | (q_1y_1/\theta_1)\ldots(q_my_m/\theta_m)W(x_1,\ldots,x_n,y_1,\ldots,y_m)> \quad (1)$$

where (q_iy_i/θ_i) is (y_i/θ_i) or (Ey_i/θ_i), the τ's and θ's are types, and $W(x_1,\ldots,x_n,y_1,\ldots,y_m)$ is a quantifier-free formula containing no function signs and whose variables are $x_1,\ldots,x_n,y_1,\ldots,y_m$. For brevity, we shall usually denote the typical query (1) by $<\vec{x}/\vec{\tau} | (q\vec{y}/\vec{\theta})W(\vec{x},\vec{y})>$.

Intuitively, (1) denotes the set of all n-tuples $\vec{x}$ such that $\vec{x} \in |\vec{\tau}|^*$ and such that $(q\vec{y}/\vec{\theta})W(\vec{x},\vec{y})$ is true.

As an example, consider an inventory domain and the request "Give those manufacturers who supply all widgets". This might be represented in our query language by

$<x/\text{Manufacturer} | (y/\text{Widget})\text{Supplies } x,y>$

Formally, let DB be a data base as defined in the previous section, and $Q = <\vec{x}/\vec{\tau} | (q\vec{y}/\vec{\theta})W(\vec{x},\vec{y})>$ a query. A set of n-tuples $\{\vec{c}^{(1)},\ldots,\vec{c}^{(r)}\}$ is an answer to Q (with respect to DB) iff

1. $\vec{c}^{(i)} \in |\vec{\tau}| \quad i=1,\ldots,r$ and
2. $DB \vdash \bigvee_{i\leq r} (q\vec{y}/\vec{\theta})W(\vec{c}^{(i)},\vec{y})$

Notice that if $\{\vec{c}^{(1)},\ldots,\vec{c}^{(r)}\}$ is an answer to Q and $\vec{c}$ is any n-tuple of constants such that $\vec{c} \in |\vec{\tau}|$ then so also is $\{\vec{c}^{(1)},\ldots,\vec{c}^{(r)},\vec{c}\}$ an answer to Q. This suggests the need for the following definitions:

A is a minimal answer to Q iff no proper subset of A is an answer to Q. If A is minimal, then if $|A| = 1$, A is a definite answer to Q. Otherwise A is an indefinite answer to Q. Instead of denoting an indefinite answer by $\{\vec{c}^{(1)},\ldots,\vec{c}^{(r)}\}$, we prefer the more suggestive notation $\vec{c}^{(1)}+\ldots+\vec{c}^{(r)}$. Indefinite answers have interpretation:
$\vec{x} = \vec{c}^{(1)}$ or $\vec{x} = \vec{c}^{(2)}$ or...or $\vec{x} = \vec{c}^{(r)}$ but there is not enough information, given DB, to determine which. We shall sometimes refer to expressions of the form $\vec{c}^{(1)}+\ldots+\vec{c}^{(r)}$ as disjunctive tuples. Finally, we denote by $\|Q\|$ the set of minimal answers to Q.

The use of types in deductive question-answering has been independently proposed in McSkimin [1976], McSkimin and Minker [1977], who refer to types as primitive categories. Typically, types are used to block certain unifications, and to maintain data base integrity.

---

* If $\vec{\tau} = \tau_1,\ldots,\tau_n$ is a sequence of types, then $|\vec{\tau}| = |\tau_1| \times\ldots\times |\tau_n|$

In order to better understand why the possibility of indefinite answers must be entertained, consider the following fragment of a kinship data base:

Example 1

IDB (x/Male)(y/Human)Brother x,y ⊃ Sibling x,y

(xz/Male)(y/Human)(w/Female)Uncle x,y ∧ Father z,y ∧ Mother w,y ⊃ Brother x,z ∨ Brother x,w

EDB Uncle a,b Father c,b Mother d,b Brother a,e

Consider the query "Who are all of a's siblings?"

$Q = < x/Human|Sibling\ a,x >$

Then $\|Q\| = \{e, c+d\}$

i.e. e is a sibling of a. Moreover either c is a sibling of a or d is, but there is not enough information available to determine which is the case.

EXISTENTIAL QUERIES AND EQUALITY

Recall that a data base was defined, in part, to contain the equality axioms E1 - E4, and the domain closure axiom DC. The presence of these axioms will clearly prove disastrous for any theorem proving approach to query evaluation. The use of proof procedures with "built in" equality e.g. paramodulation (Robinson and Wos [1969]) will be of little value since the domain closure axiom will still be present and for data bases with a large number of constants, this axiom will inevitably lead to unfeasible computations. Fortunately, for existential queries i.e. queries of the form $<\vec{x}/\vec{\tau}|(E\vec{y}/\vec{\theta})W(\vec{x},\vec{y})>$, these axioms turn out to be irrelevant.

Theorem 1

Let E(DB) be the equality and domain closure axioms of a data base DB, and let Q be an existential query. Then A is an answer to Q with respect to DB iff it is an answer to Q with respect to DB - E(DB) i.e. the equality and domain closure axioms are irrelevant to existential query evaluation.

REDUCTION OF ARBITRARY QUERIES TO EXISTENTIAL QUERIES

As we saw in the previous section, equality poses no difficulties for existential queries. Unfortunately, Theorem 1 fails for arbitrary queries. To see why, consider the following data base:

Equality axioms E1 - E4

DC (x)x=a

Pa,a

$|\tau| = \{a\}$

i.e., a data base with a single constant a and a single type τ. Then $\|< x/\tau|(y/\tau)Px,y>\| = \{a\}$. But $(y/\tau)Pa,y$, i.e., $(y)\tau y \supset Pa,y$ is not provable without the domain closure axiom DC.

The approach which we adopt is to reduce arbitrary queries to existential ones by invoking the "projection" and "division" operators which we now define. Let $Q = < \vec{x}/\vec{\tau}, z/\psi|(q\vec{y}/\vec{\theta})W(\vec{x},\vec{y},z) >$. The quotient of $\|Q\|$ by z, $\Delta_z\|Q\|$, is a set of disjunctive tuples and is defined as follows:

$\vec{c}^{(1)} +\ldots+ \vec{c}^{(m)} \in \Delta_z\|Q\|$ iff

1. For all $\vec{a} \in |\psi|^m$, $(\vec{c}^{(1)},a_1)+\ldots+(\vec{c}^{(m)},a_m)$ is an answer (not necessaryily minimal) to Q (and hence some sub-disjunctive tuple of $(\vec{c}^{(1)},a_1)+\ldots+(\vec{c}^{(m)},a_m)$ is an element of $\|Q\|$), and
2. for no i, $1 \le i \le m$, does $\vec{c}^{(1)} +\ldots+ \vec{c}^{(i-1)} + \vec{c}^{(i+1)} +\ldots+ \vec{c}^{(m)}$ have property 1. (There is a slight abuse of notation here. If $\vec{c} = (c_1,\ldots,c_n)$, then $(\vec{c},a)$ is intended to denote $(c_1,\ldots,c_n,a)$.) The operator Δ_z is called the division operator with respect to z and is an appropriate generalization of the division operator of Codd [1972].

The projection of Q with respect to z, $\pi_z\|Q\|$, is a set of disjunctive tuples and is defined as follows:

$\vec{c}^{(1)} +\ldots+ \vec{c}^{(m)} \in \pi_z\|Q\|$ iff

1. There exist constant signs $a_j^{(i)} \in |\psi|, j=1,\ldots,r_i$ $i=1,\ldots,m$ such that $\sum_{j \le r_i,\ i \le m} (\vec{c}^{(i)}, a_j^{(i)}) \in \|Q\|$ and
2. For no i, $1 \le i \le m$, does $\vec{c}^{(1)} +\ldots+ \vec{c}^{(i-1)} + \vec{c}^{(i+1)} +\ldots+ \vec{c}^{(m)}$ have property 1.

The operator π_z is called the projection operator with respect to z and is an appropriate generalization of the projection operator of Codd [1972].

The following theorem indicates the importance of these operators:

<u>Theorem 2</u>

If $W(\vec{x},y)$ is a (not necessarily quantifier-free) formula with free variables $\vec{x}$ and y, then

1. $\| < \vec{x}/\vec{\tau} \,|\, (y/\theta) W(\vec{x},y) > \| = \Delta_y \| < \vec{x}/\vec{\tau}, y/\theta \,|\, W(\vec{x},y) > \|$

2. $\| < \vec{x}/\vec{\tau} \,|\, (Ey/\theta) W(\vec{x},y) > \| = \pi_y \| < \vec{x}/\vec{\tau}, y/\theta \,|\, W(\vec{x},y) > \|$

Using Theorem 2 we can now represent an arbitrary query as the appropriate application of projection and division operators to an existential query. For example,

$$\| < x/\tau_1 \,|\, (Ey/\tau_2)(z/\tau_3)(Ew/\tau_4) W(x,y,z,w) > \| =$$

$$\pi_y \Delta_z \| < x/\tau_1, y/\tau_2, z/\tau_3 \,|\, (Ew/\tau_4) W(x,y,z,w) > \|$$

In view of Theorem 2 it is sufficient to devise techniques for evaluating existential queries only, in which case, by Theorem 1, we can eliminate the equality and domain closure axioms from the data base.

ANSWERING EXISTENTIAL QUERIES

The approach of this paper is designed for very large data bases in which the vast majority of facts are extensional i.e. $|EDB| \gg |IDB|$ with $|EDB|$ very large. Under these circumstances, conventional theorem proving approaches (e.g., Minker et al. [1972]) are likely to be quite inefficient since the theorem prover is intermingling access to both the IDB and EDB. As an alternative, Figure 1 illustrates our proposed system design. There are several points worth noting:

1. As its name implies, the extensional query evaluator evaluates queries in our query language, but only with respect to the EDB. As such, it need not be a conventional theorem prover.

2. The most significant observation is that the EDB and IDB processors are completely decoupled. The IDB, but <u>not</u> the EDB, is invoked during the theorem proving process. Since, in applications to large data bases, we can expect $|EDB| \gg |IDB|$, the last thing we want is to require of the theorem prover that it have to look at the EDB. Moreover, there are far more efficient non theorem proving techniques for extensional query evaluation, e.g. relational query evaluation (Palermo [1974], Reiter [1976]). In effect, this decoupling of the EDB and IDB processors relegates the search task over the IDB to the theorem prover, and the "search-free computational" task over the EDB to the extensional query evaluator.

3. The result of the theorem proving process is a proof search tree from which a set of queries $Q_1, \ldots, Q_m$ can be extracted. These are extensionally evaluated and the results unioned to obtain the answers to the original query Q.

We cannot in the limited space of this paper, formally describe and justify the approach to deductive question-answering of Figure 1. Instead, we shall try to convey its basic flavour by means of an example. The interested reader is referred to Reiter [1977] for particulars.

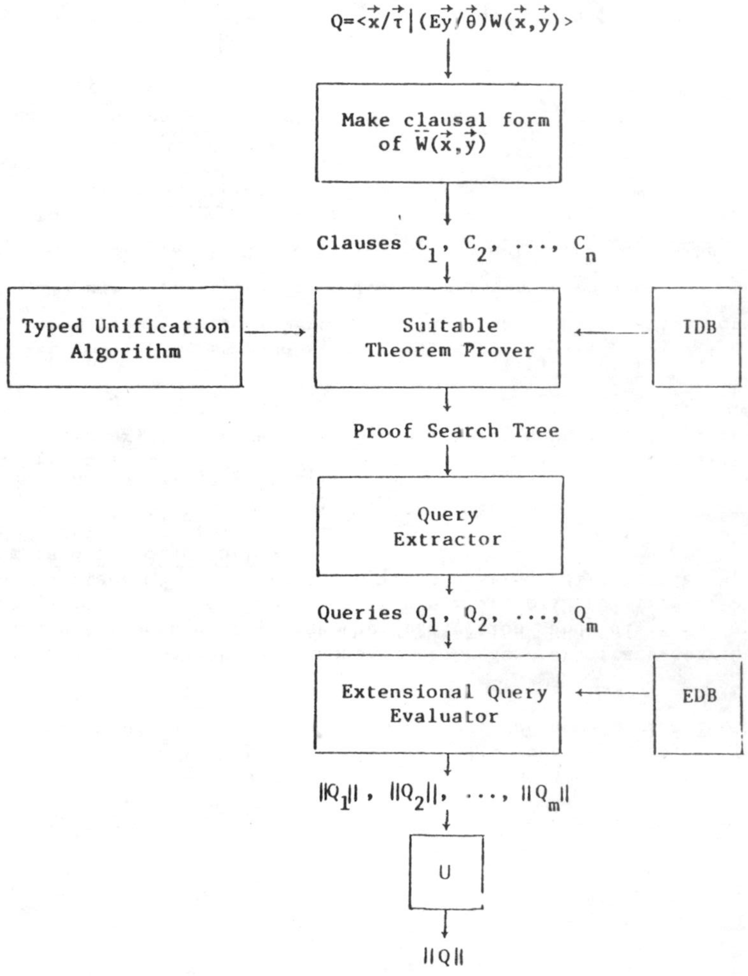

Figure 1. System Overview

Example 2

We consider a simple fragment of an education domain.

IDB (1) A teaches all calculus courses.

(z/Calculus)Teach A,z

(2) B teaches all computer science courses

(y/CS)Teach B,y

(3) If teacher u teaches course v and student w is enrolled in v, then u is a teacher of w.

(u/Teacher)(v/Course)(w/Student)Enrolled w,v $\wedge$ Teach u,v $\supset$ Teacher-of w,u

EDB

Teach	x	y
	A	P100
	B	P200
	C	P300
	D	H100
	D	H200

Enrolled	x	y
	a	C100
	a	P300
	a	CS100
	b	C200
	b	CS200
	b	CS300
	c	H100
	c	C100
	d	H200
	d	P200
	d	P300

|Teacher| = {A,B,C,D}

|Student| = {a,b,c,d}

|Course| = {C100,C200,CS100,CS200,CS300,H100,H200,P100,P200,P300}

|Calculus| = {C100,C200}

|CS| = {CS100,CS200,CS300}

Consider the query "Who are a's teachers?"

Q = < x/Teacher|Teacher-of a,x >

We start by treating (Ex/Teacher)Teacher-of a,x as a theorem to be proved with DB as hypothesis. Using the usual refutation approach, we create the clausal form of its negation i.e. $\overline{\text{Teacher-of}}$ a,x and associate, with the variable x of this clause, the type Teacher. Now consider attempting a linear refutation using $\overline{\text{Teacher-of}}$ a,x as top clause. There are two possibilities:

(i) This top clause could be resolved against a unit of the EDB, or

(ii) It could be resolved against a clause (in this case the clausal form* of (3)) of the IDB.

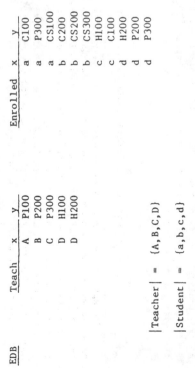

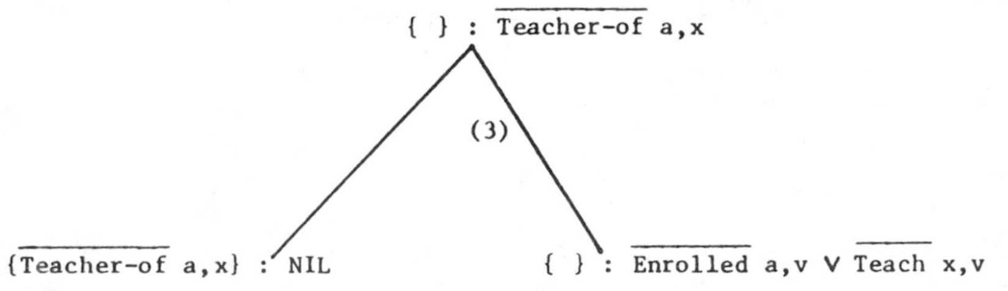

Figure 3. Deduction Step Continued

Our approach is to admit both possibilities, as in Figure 2, but to perform just the second. Literals enclosed in curly brackets represent literals which possibly might have been, but were not, resolved away against the EDB. The label on the right branch of Figure 2 indicates that clause of the IDB against which $\overline{\text{Teacher-of}}$ a,x was resolved. The left branch is unlabeled, indicating that we could have tried to resolve Teacher-of a,x against the EDB, but we have postponed this attempt by instead placing the literal within curly brackets. This left node is now closed, since there are no remaining literals to resolve against the IDB. The right node, with clause $\overline{\text{Enrolled}}$ a,v V $\overline{\text{Teach}}$ x,v remains open. Again there are two possibilities:

(i) Resolve $\overline{\text{Teach}}$ x,v against the EDB, or

(ii) Resolve it against clauses (1) or (2) of the IDB.

Figure 3 represents these possibilities, again postponing the resolution operation against the EDB, as indicated by the unlabeled left branch. The branches labeled (1) and (2) correspond to possibility (ii).

It is clear that we can continue expanding nodes in this way. If

$$N = \{E_1,\ldots,E_k\} : L_1 \vee\ldots\vee L_p$$

is a typical such node, then N will have successors $N_o, N_1, \ldots, N_r$ where

$$N_o = \{E_1,\ldots,E_k,L_p\} : L_1 \vee\ldots\vee L_{p-1}$$

* In converting IDB formulae to clausal form, one eliminates the quantifiers. Since all quantifiers are restricted by types, these types must be associated with their corresponding variables in the clausal form.

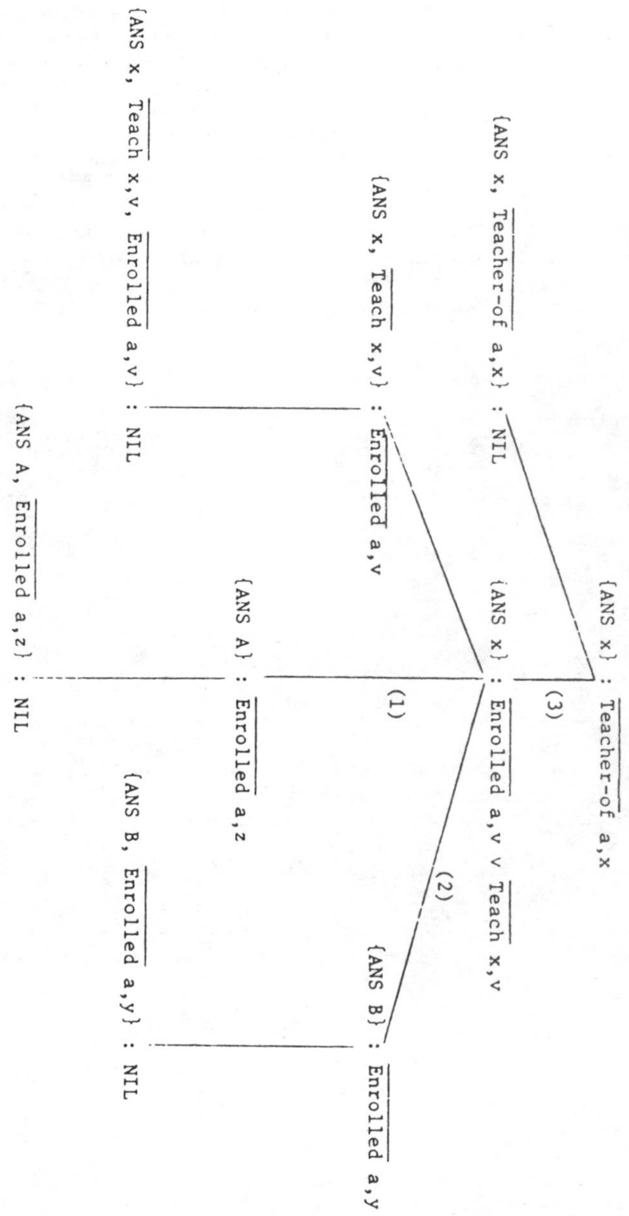

Figure 4. Deduction Steps and Answer Extraction.

indicating that we are postponing any attempted resolution of L_p against a unit of the EDB. For i=1,...,r

$$N_i = \{E_1\sigma_i, \ldots, E_k\sigma_i\} : R_i$$

where R_i is the resolvent obtained by resolving the clause $L_1 \vee \ldots \vee L_p$ upon its rightmost literal L_p against a clause of the IDB and σ_i is the corresponding unifying substitution. Notice that we are here using a clause ordering linear resolution strategy in which only rightmost literals in a deduction are resolved upon. When suitably formalized, such a strategy can be shown to be complete (Reiter [1971]).

For the example at hand, we can continue expanding nodes until eventually no further expansion is possible. Figure 4 shows the resulting fully expanded tree. The only new feature in this figure is the introduction of an answer literal ANS x (Green [1969]) whose function is to record the substitutions being made for the variable x. Clearly there is a need for this bookkeeping device since any substitution made for x is a possible answer to Q.

Now consider a typical terminal node in Figure 4, say {ANS x, Enrolled a,v, Teach x,v} : NIL. This means that the non answer literals have yet to be resolved away against the EDB. In other words, the query

Q_1 = < x/Teacher|(Ev/Course)Enrolled a,v ∧ Teacn x,v >

when extensionally evaluated yields a set of answers to the original query Q. Similarly, the remaining terminal nodes yield the following queries for extensional evaluation:

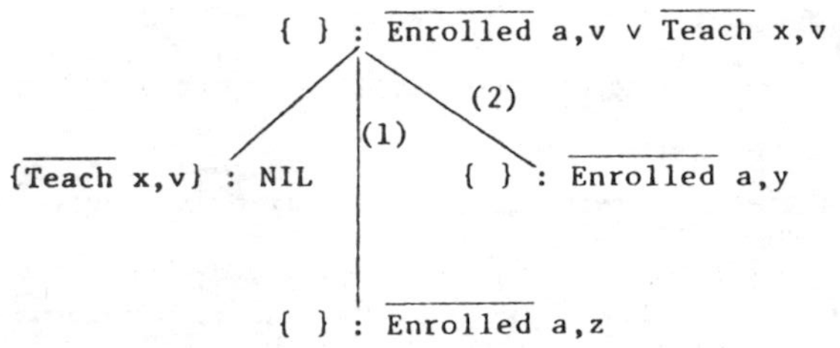

Figure 2. Deduction Step

Q_2 = < x/Teacher|Teacher-of a,x >

Q_3 = < x/Teacher|(Ez/Calculus)Enrolled a,z ∧ x=A >

Q_4 = < x/Teacher|(Ey/CS)Enrolled a,y ∧ x=B >

These queries have respective extensional values $\{C\}$, ϕ, $\{A\}$, $\{B\}$, the union of which yields

$$\|Q\| = \{A,B,C\}$$

Notice how the intensional and extensional processors are totally decoupled under this approach. Figure 4 represents the first phase of query evaluation. This is the only task allocated to the theorem prover and nowhere in this process does the theorem prover probe the EDB. The second phase requires the extensional evaluation of the queries Q_1, Q_2, Q_3 and Q_4 . This can be done by a relational data base management system and is certain to be far more efficient for large EDBs than any theorem proving technique. For an approach to extensional query evaluation designed for the query language of this paper and which optimizes for equality see Reiter [1976].

COMPLETENESS OF THE QUERY EVALUATION PROCESS

As this paper is necessarily impressionistic, we have been deliberately vague in the previous section (Answering Existential Queries) about the nature of the theorem prover that is required. Moreover, there are a number of features which the simple example of that section fails to illustrate:

1. The derivation of indefinite answers.

2. How the types associated with the variables of a clause affect the unification algorithm.

3. The treatment of multiple clauses arising from a query.

In Reiter [1977] all of these issues are made precise. Once this has been done, it is possible to prove the following completeness result:

> Provided the extensional query evaluator returns all and only the answers to a given query and provided an appropriate theorem prover is used for the intensional processing, then the approach of this paper is complete i.e. all and only the answers to a given query will be returned, including indefinite answers should they arise.

In a very real sense, this completeness result must be taken with a grain of salt, for in order to properly make use of it the proof search tree generated by the theorem prover must be finite, as indeed that of Figure 4 is. Clearly we cannot expect finite search trees in the presence of recursive axioms. For example, an axiom defining the transitivity of a relation R

$$(x,y,z/\tau)Rx,y \wedge Ry,z \supset Rx,z$$

will lead to an infinite search tree for the query $< x/\tau, y/\tau\ Rx,y >$. Under such circumstances an heuristic approach could be adopted. For example, the search tree could be truncated at some predefined level bound in which case a set of answers is returned with a warning to the user that some answers might be missing. We favour a different approach, one which guarantees that all search trees will be finite. There are two arguments in favour of this approach:

(i) The user will be assured that all answers to a query will be returned.

(ii) When all search trees are finite, the IDB can be compiled. (See the section on Compiling the IDB below.)

One way of guaranteeing finite search trees is to appropriately <u>structure</u> the data base. In Reiter [1978a] an approach to data base structuring is described. Briefly, this first involves characterizing those circumstances under which infinite deductive paths can arise. This can be done in terms of certain sequences, called <u>cycles</u>, of IDB formulae. Intuitively, a cycle can be viewed as a possible recursive application of its formulae in the process of searching for a proof. It turns out that cycles can be "cut", and hence infinite deductive paths eliminated, by representing, in the EDB, certain sub-extensions of appropriately designated predicates. In effect, what we are proposing is a criterion by means of which the following question can be answered: In designing a data base, what information should be represented extensionally, and what intensionally? The structuring proposal is to represent enough information extensionally so as to "cut" all of the cycles of the data base, thereby quaranteeing finite search trees.

Although this process of filling in sub-extensions of suitably chosen predicates can always be invoked to cut cycles, this can occasionally be too drastic a remedy. In certain special cases, the particular structure of a cycle can be exploited to prove that it cannot lead to an infinite deduction path, in which case there is no need to enlarge the extensional data base. For example, consider the following recursive intensional fact: "All parts suppliers also provide subparts for those parts."

$$(x,y,z/Part)Subpart\ y,z \wedge Supplies\ x,y \supset Supplies\ x,z$$

Because the Subpart relation is transitive, it is possible to prove that this intension cannot lead to an infinite deductive path. Many other such examples exist.

These last remarks suggest an alternate view of data base structuring. For what they amount to is proving the "correctness" of a data base, where "correct" is taken to mean "all deductive paths will be finite". Under this view, a necessary condition that a data base be well structured is that it has been proved correct. For an elaboration of these ideas, see Reiter [1978a].

COMPILING THE IDB

We have shown that query evaluation may be decomposed into an intensional processor involving a theorem prover which computes only on the IDB, and an extensional processor computing only on the EDB. One very nice feature of this decomposition is that it is now possible to <u>compile</u> the IDB using the theorem prover as a once-only compiler.

The basic idea is quite simple. For each predicate of the data base, say the predicate Teach of the example, determine all "proofs" with top clause Teach x,y as well as with top clause $\overline{\text{Teach}}$ x,y. Notice that these "proofs" involve only clauses of the IDB. Next store all such trees, for all predicates, on an external file, and discard both the IDB and the theorem prover. Then at query evaluation time, read in all of the "proofs" for those signed predicates occurring in the query. These trees can then be appropriately combined to yield all of the "proofs" required by the query.

It turns out that this compilation process together with the resulting query evaluation are considerably simplified under the so-called closed world assumption (CWA). In order to illustrate what is involved we shall assume that the reader is familiar with the material and notation in Reiter [1978b]. In particular, we shall exploit the fact that the set of CWA answers to an arbitrary query can be computed by applying the set operations of union, intersection and difference and the relational algebra operation of projection to the open world assumption (OWA) answers to atomic queries. Thus, CWA query evaluation reduces to OWA evaluation for atomic queries. Now an atomic query has the form

$$Q = < \vec{x}/\vec{\tau} \,|\, (E\vec{y}/\vec{\theta})Pt_1,\ldots,t_n >$$

where each t is an x, a y, or a constant, and P is a predicate sign. Suppose that we had available all "proofs" of the literal $Pu_1,\ldots,u_n$ using only the clauses of the IDB, where each variable u_i has type U, the universal type i.e. $|U|$ = the set of all constants. Then to compute $\|Q\|_{OWA}$ simply substitute t_i for u_i in these proofs ensuring that the type of t_i is consistent with the type of u_i. Then, as in the section on Answering Existential Queries, form appropriate queries using the terminal nodes in the resulting proof tree, and extensionally evaluate these queries. The method is best explained by an example.

<u>Example 3</u>

We shall treat the data base of Example 2 in closed world mode. To begin, we compile the predicate Teach i.e. we determine all "proofs" of Teach u_1,u_2 i.e. all "refutations" with top clause $\overline{\text{Teach}}$ u_1,u_2. Here u_1 and u_2 both have type U. The "refutations" use only the clauses of IDB just as we did in the section on Answering Existential Queries. Figure 5 shows the resulting fully

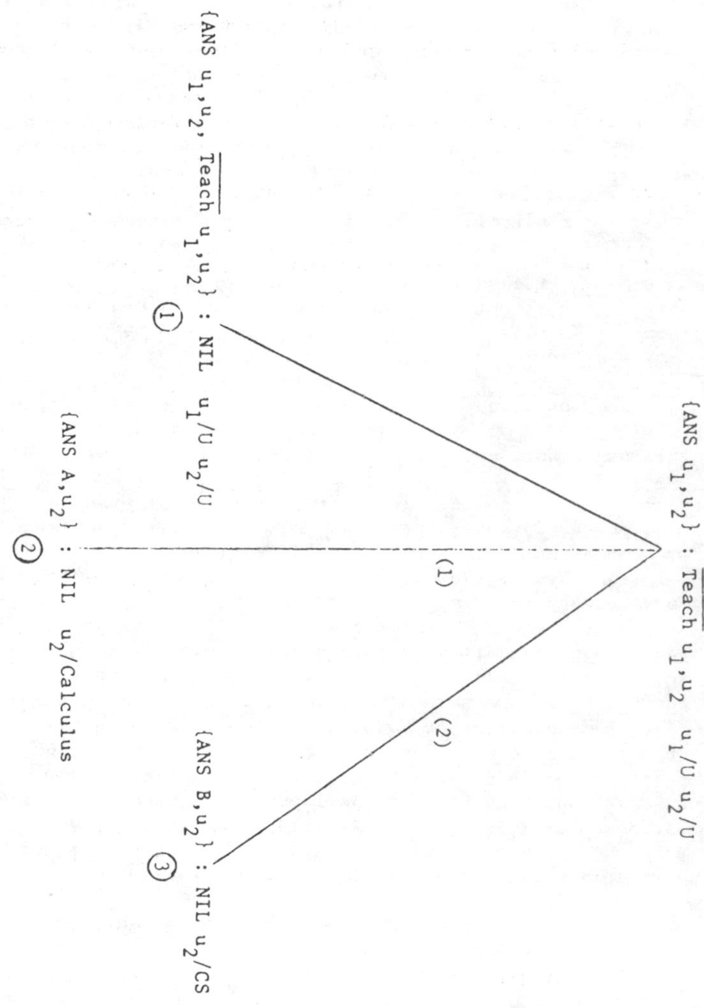

Figure 5. The refutation search tree for Teach.

expanded search tree. The types associated with each free variable at a given node are indicated. Now suppose we wish to determine $\|Q\|_{OWA}$ where

$$Q = < x/\text{Teacher} \mid \text{Teach } x,\text{CS100} >$$

To do so, substitute x of type Teacher for u_1 and substitute CS100 for u_2 in Figure 5. The substitution of x for u_1 satisfies the type restrictions on u_1 throughout the tree. The substitution of CS100 for u_2 violates the type restriction on u_2 at node 2 since CS100 $\notin$ |Calculus|, so node 2 cannot contribute to the evaluation of Q. Nodes 1 and 3 do contribute, so we form the two queries:

$$Q_1 = < x/\text{Teacher} \mid \text{Teach } x,\text{CS100} >$$

$$Q_3 = < x/\text{Teacher} \mid x = B >$$

Q_1 and Q_3 extensionally evaluate to ϕ and B respectively, whence $\|Q\|_{OWA} = \{B\}$.

It should be clear that we had no use for the entire tree of Figure 5 - only the terminal nodes were necessary. Moreover, the relevant information contained in these nodes is more succinctly representable by the following three formulae with free variables u_1 and u_2

(i) Teach u_1,u_2 u_1/U u_2/U

(ii) $u_1 = A \wedge u_2 = u_2$ u_1/U $u_2/\text{Calculus}$

(iii) $u_1 = B \wedge u_2 = u_2$ u_1/U u_2/CS

We shall refer to these three formulae as the <u>compiled form</u> of the predicate Teach As a further example consider

$$Q = <x/\text{Teacher} \mid (Ey/\text{CS})\text{Teach } x,y >$$

Substitute x of type Teacher for u_1 and y of type CS for u_2 in (i), (ii) and (iii) above. This yields a type inconsistency in (ii), so we obtain two queries:

$$Q_1 = < x/\text{Teacher} \mid (Ey/\text{CS})\text{Teach } x,y >$$

$$Q_3 = < x/\text{Teacher} \mid (Ey/\text{CS})x = B \wedge y = y >$$

These extensionally evaluate to ϕ and {B} respectively, whence $\|Q\|_{OWA} = \{B\}$

Next we compile the predicate Teacher-of. Figure 6 contains the refutation search tree. From its terminal nodes we obtain the following compiled form for Teacher-of:

Teacher-of u_1,u_2 u_1/U u_2/U

$(Ev/\text{Course})\text{Teach } u_2,v \wedge \text{Enrolled } u_1,v$ $u_1/\text{Student}$ $u_2/\text{Teacher}$

$(Ev/\text{Calculus})\text{Enrolled } u_1,v \wedge u_2 = A$ $u_1/\text{Student}$

$(Ev/\text{CS})\text{Enrolled } u_1,v \wedge u_2 = B$ $u_1/\text{Student}$

Consider evaluating

$$Q = < x/\text{Student} \mid \text{Teacher-of } x,B >$$

Substituting x for u_1 and B for u_2 in the compiled form of Teacher-of yields the following queries for extensional evaluation:

$$Q_1 = < x/\text{Student} \mid \text{Teacher-of } x,B >$$

$$Q_2 = < x/\text{Student} \mid (Ev/\text{Course})\text{Teach } B,v \wedge \text{Enrolled } x,v >$$

$$Q_3 = < x/\text{Student} \mid (Ev/\text{Calculus})\text{Enrolled } x,v \wedge B = A >$$

$$Q_4 = < x/\text{Student} \mid (Ev/\text{CS})\text{Enrolled } x,v \wedge B = B >$$

These extensionally evaluate to ϕ , {d}, ϕ and {a,b} whence $\|Q\|_{OWA} = \{a,b,d\}$.

Finally, consider evaluating the following non atomic query under the CWA:

$$Q = < x/\text{Teacher} \mid \text{Teacher-of } a,x \wedge \overline{\text{Teach}}\ x,\text{CS100} >$$

Then

$$\|Q\|_{CWA} = \|Q_1\|_{OWA} \cap (|\text{Teacher}| - \|Q_2\|_{OWA})$$

where

$$Q_1 = < x/\text{Teacher} \mid \text{Teacher-of } a,x >$$

$$Q_2 = < x/\text{Teacher} \mid \text{Teach } x,\text{CS100} >$$

Evaluating Q_1 using the compiled form of Teacher-of yields {A,B,C}. We have already evaluated Q_2 at the beginning of this example, yielding {B}. Hence $\|Q\|_{CWA} = \{A,C\}$.

There are a number of advantages to this approach of compiling the IDB:

(i) The time required for query evaluation is reduced since there is no need to search for all possible proofs.

(ii) Compilation completely eliminates the need for a theorem prover at query evaluation time.

(iii) The compilation process can be effected by a suitably designed interactive theorem prover. This can provide for a far greater measure of control over the deductive mechanism than is currently possible under autonomous theorem proving systems. In particular, the data base designer will be in a position to interactively exploit his or her knowledge of the semantics of the domain to prune fruitless or infinite deduction paths, to apply optimizing transformations, and to recognize redundant or duplicate deductions. Moreover, the design of such an interactive system is far simpler than that of an autonomous theorem prover and requires significantly less code. Finally, since efficiency considerations for such an interactive theorem prover are irrelevant given that it is functioning as a once-only compiler, it's implementation is even further simplified. And of course, once the compilation is completed, the compiler may be expunged from the system.

(iv) The query language of this paper is set oriented i.e. we seek all answers to a given query. Moreover the techniques for query evaluation which we have proposed are specifically directed at computing sets of answers. One might conclude from this that the evaluation of "single answer" queries will require a substantially different approach. By a "single answer" query we mean one whose appropriate answer is "yes", "no" or "I don't know". (This latter cannot arise under the CWA.) For example, "Is A a teacher of b?" i.e. Teacher-of b,A or "Does A teach calculus?" i.e. (Ex/Calculus)Teach A,x. It should be clear, however, that if the IDB is compiled, it is trivial to evaluate "single answer" queries. Merely instantiate in turn each formula of the appropriate compiled forms of the predicates, and send that formula off to the extensional evaluator to extensionally test its truth value. For example, to evaluate Teacher-of b,A we retrieve the compiled form of Teacher-of and extensionally test each of the following formulae in turn, returning "yes" if and when one of them tests true:

Teacher-of b,A

(Ev/Course)Teach A,v ∧ Enrolled b,v

(Ev/Calculus)Enrolled b,v ∧ A = A

(Ev/CS)Enrolled b,v ∧ B = A

The evaluation of "single answer" queries in the case of "compound" queries is slightly more complicated. By a compound query we mean one with more than one literal. For example, "Is anyone a teacher of both a and b?" i.e.

(Ex/Teacher)Teacher-of a,x ∧ Teacher-of b,x.

In this case one must form all possible conjunctions of pairs of formulae in the compiled form of Teacher-of, and extentionally test each of these in turn. Thus we must test

(Ex/Teacher)Teacher-of a,x ∧ Teacher-of b,x

(Ex/Teacher)Teacher-of a,x ∧ (Ev/Course)Teach x,v ∧ Enrolled b,v

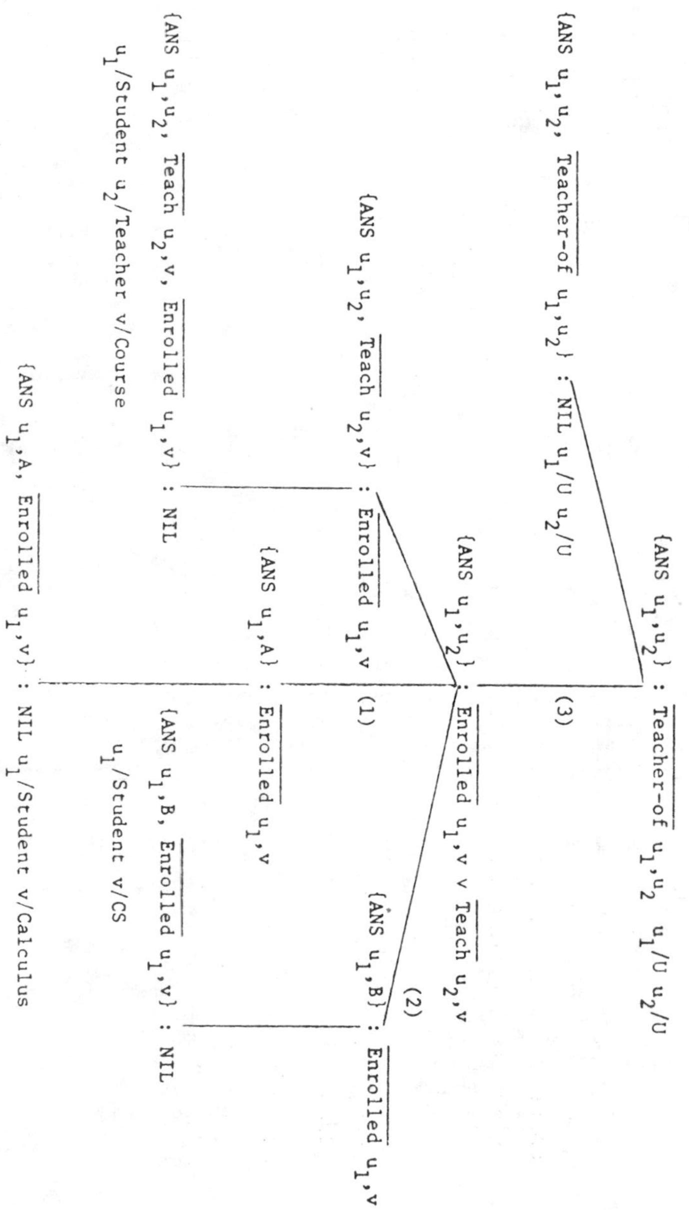

Figure 6. The refutation search tree for Teacher-of.

$(Ex/Teacher)Teacher\text{-}of\ a,x \wedge (Ev/Course)Enrolled\ b,v \wedge x=A$

etc.

Of course, the ability to compile the IDB relies upon the absence of recursive axioms. In the section on Completeness of the Query Evaluation Process we argued that the effects of recursive axioms must be neutralized by appropriately structuring the data base in order to guarantee that the theorem prover will return with all answers to a query. Since such a data base can also be compiled, we have a second argument in favour of recursion elimination.

One last point. Notice that the concept of a compiler for the IDB is feasible only under an approach to deductive question-answering which completely decouples the IDB and EDB theorem proving processors, as described earlier (Answering Existential Queries). Any attempt at deductive question-answering by means of a theorem prover which intermingles access to both the IDB and EDB can only run "interpretively" since the set of all possible proofs corresponding to a predicate P will in general be impossibly large in the presence of any sizeable EDB.

DISCUSSION

This paper has addressed a variety of problems that arise in deductive question-answering. It is appropriate at this point to summarize the issues that have been raised, to draw comparisons with other approaches in the literature, and to point out certain difficulties which remain to be resolved.

Indefinite Answers

The possibility of indefinite answers (section on Queries and Answers) has long been recognized in other theorem proving applications (Green [1969]) but seems to have been overlooked or ignored in the deductive question-answering literature. Nevertheless, they are real (see Example 1) and must be taken into account in any proposed theory of deductive retrieval. It is just such answers which make the definitions of the projection and division operators (see Reduction of Arbitrary Queries to Existential Queries) more complicated than their counterparts in relational algebra. Although not described in this paper, there is a satisfactory computational approach to indefinite answers (Reiter [1977]).

As far as I can determine, all current deductive retrieval systems assume only definite answers, and indeed, such answers do make life much simpler. But it seems to me that we need a theory which <u>quarantees</u> that this assumption is warranted. A few such results are known. If the data base is Horn, and the query positive, then no indefinite answers can arise (Reiter [1977]). Moreover, for query evaluation under the closed world assumption, all answers will be definite (Reiter [1978b]).

Interfacing with a Data Base Management System

Both Chang [1977] and Kellogg et al. [1978] have independently proposed interfacing a theorem prover with a data base management system for processing the EDB. Both of these systems use a theorem prover to transform a given query containing virtual relations into one containing only base relations. (A <u>virtual</u> relation has no representation in the EDB, i.e. all of the information about that relation is contained in the IDB. A <u>base</u> relation is one whose total extension is explicitly represented in the EDB. In Example 2, Enrolled is a base relation, Teacher-of is virtual, and Teach is neither.) A data base management system then returns the answers to the transformed query. Since Kellogg, Klahr and Travis are not concerned with returning all answers to a given query, their overall system design differs somewhat from ours. Chang is concerned with retrieving sets of answers and accordingly proposes a similar system architecture. The most significant distinction between our proposal and those of Kellogg et al. and Chang is that we do not require, as they do, that a given relation be either virtual or base, i.e. we permit information about a relation to be contained in both the EDB and IDB. Thus, in Example 2, Teach is neither a virtual nor base relation. In general, this provides for a greater measure of flexibility in representing information about a given domain.

Equality

The whole question of equality in automatic deduction is a thorny one. Although a firm theoretical foundation exists for the treatment of equality (Robinson and Wos [1969]) no feasible computational approach is known for a general first order theory. Nevertheless, there is a definite need for the equality relation in deductive question-answering. For example, the intension "Distinct offspring of the same parent are siblings" cannot be expressed without it:

$$(x,y,z/Human)Parent\ y,x \wedge Parent\ z,x \wedge y \neq z \supset Siblings\ y,z$$

To my knowledge, no work in deductive question-answering has addressed the equality issue. In this paper I have taken what amounts to a first cut at an efficient computational treatment of equality, but at the expense of generality. Specifically, generality is sacrificed in the following ways:

(i) All constants are assumed pairwise distinct i.e. $c_i \neq c_j$ for $i \neq j$.

(ii) More significantly, <u>no function signs are permitted</u> either in the data base or in queries. Since existential quantifiers implicitly lead to function signs (Skolem functions), no intension is permitted to have an existential quantifier in its prenex normal form.

Under these conditions, equality poses no difficulties whatever for existential queries (Theorem 1). If we relax either of conditions (i) or (ii), Theorem 1 fails in which case all of the computational problems associated with equality which plague general purpose theorem provers will arise in the context of deductive question-answering.

What is a Data Base?

An issue which arises as a natural extension of the equality problem has to do with just what is meant by a data base. The definition of a data base in this paper does not admit function signs, in part because of the difficulties they create with respect to equality. There is another compelling reason for adopting a function-free definition of a data base - without some such restriction, any first order theory is a data base. No distinction can be drawn between an inventory domain, and point set topology, despite the fact that reasoning with real world non mathematical domains should not require the full inferential capabilities of a mathematician. The choice of a function-free theory, while not entirely satisfactory, more closely approximates my own intuitive concept of a data base than does an arbitrary first order theory. Perhaps this latter point deserves elaboration. In a function-free theory, answers to queries involve only constants (but not Skolem constants). Another way of expressing this is that all answers are extensional i.e. they involve only known individuals (the constants). This, of course, is in agreement with conventional data base management systems which also treat only extensional entities, so that the concept of a data base defined in this paper can be viewed as an appropriate generalization of these conventional systems. On the other hand, an arbitrary first order theory admits intensional entities i.e. descriptions of new entities in terms of old. Typically, the way such descriptions are formed is by means of functions (usually Skolem functions) whose extensions are not completely known. For example, although we may not know who John's father is, we can nevertheless form the description father(John) - a perfectly respectable, though unknown, individual. It is precisely such intensional entities that lead to all of the problems associated with equality, since different descriptions might denote the same entity. This, in turn, prevents any reasonable notion of the completeness of answer extraction techniques in those cases where all answers to a given query are to be returned, an issue which is further discussed in the following section (Returning All Answers to a Query).

One way that functions might be admitted into the formalism of this paper without opening the door to arbitrary first order theories is to require that the functions so admitted be extensional i.e. we know or can compute their values for all of their arguments. Another is to admit only functions with a free interpretation (Clark [1978]). In the first case, equality of two descriptions reduces to equality of their values. In the second case, two descriptions are equal iff they are syntactically identical. Although such an approach will circumvent the problems associated with equality, it can affect a system's ability to return all answers to a given query in those situations where infinitely many answers arise, an issue which is discussed in the following section

To my knowledge, all other current research on deductive question-answering (e.g. Minker [1978], Kellogg et al. [1978], Chang [1977]) relies on the concept of a data base as an arbitrary first order theory. What is being argued here is that this concept should be suitably restricted in order to guarantee completeness of the query evaluator, and to provide a computationally feasible treatment of the equality relation.

Returning All Answers to a Query

The approach of this paper, like that of Chang [1977], is designed to return all answers to a given query. In addition, we have a completeness result to the effect that all answers will be returned (section on Completeness of the Query Evaluation Process). It seems to me important that users of a deductive question-answering system be assured, on formal grounds, that all answers to their queries will be returned. Moreover, there are many applications which demand all answers, not simply one or a few. Under these circumstances, systems designed to return single answers (e.g. Kellogg et al. [1978]) or a few answers (e.g. Minker [1978]) can be easily modified to continue searching for more answers once the first has been found. In the case of Kellogg, the underlying proof procedure is incomplete so that we cannot be quaranteed, on a priori grounds, that all answers will be returned. Minker's system does rely on a complete proof procedure and therefore could conceivably be used to return all answers. However, since for both Minker and Chang a data base can be any first order theory, it is difficult to see just what a completeness result for answers might be. For one thing, infinitely many answers are possible. As an example, consider the following data base:

$P0$

$(x)Px \supset Pf(x)$

and the query "Find all x such that Px". The answer set is the infinite set $\{0,f(0),f(f(0)),\ldots,\}$ and this cannot be computed by continuing the search for more answers each time a new answer is found. Clearly, under these circumstances, a deductive Q/A system must be capable of returning set intensions i.e. descriptions of sets, rather than their extensions.

A second, seemingly insurmountable obstacle to the possibility of guaranteeing completeness of answer sets in arbitrary first order theories stems from the equality problem. If by an answer set we mean the set of all distinct answers, then no completeness guarantee is possible, since the question of determining the equality of terms in a general first order theory is recursively undecidable.

The issue of completeness reflects on our earlier discussion of a previous section - What is a Data Base? - i.e. just what should be admitted as a reasonable notion of a data base. It is clear from the above example that if we admit even one function sign, then infinitely many answers are possible, in which case to guarantee completeness we will require a theory of answer extraction which returns set intensions. If we preclude function signs, but admit infinitely many constants, other pathologies can arise.

For example, infinitely long indefinite answers may occur (Reiter [1977, Appendix 1]). Moreover, it is not difficult to construct examples with infinite answer sets, so that set intensions must be returned. In general then, it would appear that any natural extension of the concept of a data base beyond that of this paper will require, at the very least, a theory of set intensions whenever sets of answers are to be returned.

Universal Quantification and the Domain Closure Axiom

Recall that in defining the notion of a data base we postulated a domain closure axiom DC which, in essence, states that the only existing individuals are the constants. In the section on Existential Queries and Equality we showed that this axiom is irrelevant for existential query evaluation. For queries with universal quantifiers, however, the presence or absence of DC is crucial. To see why, consider the data base of Example 2 augmented by the type extension $|History| = \{H100, H200\}$, and consider the query "Does D teach all of the history courses?" Since D indeed teaches both H100 and H200, we would intuitively expect the answer to be "yes", corresponding to a successful proof of (x/History)Teach D,x i.e. to a successful proof of (x)History x ⊃ Teach D,x . But in the absence of a domain closure axiom, no such proof exists! The reason is clear enough - without domain closure there are models of the data base containing additional individuals which are History courses but which are not taught by D. The difficulty can be traced to the semantics of "for all". If the intended interpretation of "(x)" is "for all x that you know about" then the domain closure axiom is required. On the other hand, if we mean "for all x, even those whose possible existence you may not be aware of" then no such axiom is in force.

With the exception of Chang [1977] all of the work that I know of in deductive question-answering does not make the domain closure assumption, in which case their treatment of universally quantified queries may be suspect. Chang, on the other hand, implicitly invokes the domain closure axiom by not skolemizing universally quantified variables in queries or existentially quantified variables in axioms, and by assuming that the underlying data base management system treats the constants as the only existing individuals.

ACKNOWLEDGMENT

This paper was written with the financial support of the **National Research Council of Canada under grant A7642.**

REFERENCES

1. Chang, C.L. [1978] DEDUCE 2: Further Investigations on Deduction in Relational Data Bases, In *Logic and Data Bases* (H. Gallaire and J. Minker, Eds.), Plenum Press, N.Y., 1978, 201-236.

2. Clark, K. [1978] Negation as Failure, In *Logic and Data Bases* (H. Gallaire and J. Minker, Eds.), Plenum Press, New York, New York, 1978, 293-322.

3. Codd, E. F. [1972] Relational Completeness of Data Base Sublanguages, In *Data Base Systems* (R. Rustin, Ed.), Prentice-Hall, Englewood Cliffs, N.J., 1972, 65-98.

4. Green, C. C. [1969] Theorem Proving by Resolution as a Basis for Question Answering Systems, In *Machine Intelligence, Vol. 4* (B. Meltzer and D. Michie, Eds.), American Elsevier Publishing Co., New York, N.Y., 1969, 183-208.

5. Kellogg, C. Klahr, P. and Travis, L. [1978] Deductive Planning and Pathfinding for Relational Data Bases, In *Logic and Data Bases* (H. Gallaire and J. Minker, Eds.), Plenum Press, New York, N.Y., 1978, 179-200.

6. McSkimin, J. R. [1976] "The Use of Semantic Information in Deductive Question-Answering Systems," Ph.D. Thesis, Department of Computer Science, University of Maryland, College Park, Maryland, 1976.

7. McSkimin, J. R. and Minker, J. [1977] The Use of a Semantic Network in a Deductive Question-Answering System, *Proceedings IJCAI-77*, Cambridge, Massachusetts, 1977, 50-58.

8. Minker, J. [1978] An Experimental Relational Data Base System Based on Logic, In *Logic and Data Bases* (H. Gallaire and J. Minker, Eds.), Plenum Press, New York, New York, 1978, 107-147.

9. Minker, J., Fishman, D. H., and McSkimin, J. R. [1973] The Q* Algorithm - A Search Strategy for a Deductive Question-Answering System, *Artificial Intelligence 4*, (1973), 225-243.

10. Palermo, F. P. [1974] A Data Base Search Problem, In *Information Systems* (J. T. Tou, Ed.), Plenum Press, New York, N.Y., 1974. 67-101.

11. Reiter, R. [1971] Two Results on Ordering for Resolution with Merging and Linear Format, *JACM 18*, 4(October 1971), 630-646.

12. Reiter, R. [1976] Query Optimization for Question-Answering Systems, *Proceedings COLING*, Ottawa, Canada, June 28 - July 2, 1976.

13. Reiter, R. [1977] An Approach to Deductive Question-Answering, *BBN Tech. Report 3649* , Bolt Beranek and Newman, Inc., Cambridge, Mass., Sept. 1977, 161 pp.

14. Reiter, R. [1978a] On Structuring a First Order Data Base, *Proceedings of the Canadian Society for Computational Studies of Intelligence, Second National Conference* (R. Perrault, Ed.), Toronto, July 19-21, 1978.

15. Reiter, R. [1978b] On Closed World Data Bases, In *Logic and Data Bases* (H. Gallaire and J. Minker, Eds.), Plenum Press, New York, N.Y., 1978, 55-76.

16. Robinson, G. A., and Wos, L. [1969] Paramodulation and Theorem Proving in First Order Theories with Equality, In *Machine Intelligence , Vol. 4* (B. Meltzer and D. Michie, Eds.), American Elsevier, New York, N.Y., 1969, 135-150.

Knowledge Retrieval as Limited Inference

Alan M. Frisch
James F. Allen

Computer Science Department
The University of Rochester
Rochester, NY 14627

Abstract

Artificial intelligence reasoning systems commonly employ a knowledge base module that stores a set of facts expressed in a representation language and provides facilities to retrieve these facts. A retriever could range from a simple pattern matcher to a complete logical inference system. In practice, most fall in between these extremes, providing some forms of inference but not others. Unfortunately, most of these retrievers are not precisely defined.

We view knowledge retrieval as a limited form of inference operating on the stored facts. This paper is concerned with our method of using first-order predicate calculus to formally specify a limited inference mechanism and to a lesser extent with the techniques for producing an efficient program that meets the specification. Our ideas are illustrated by developing a simplified version of a retriever used in the knowledge base of the Rochester Dialog System. The interesting property of this retriever is that it performs typical semantic network inferences such as inheritance but not arbitrary logical inferences such as modus ponens.

1. INTRODUCTION

Artificial intelligence reasoning systems commonly employ a knowledge base module (KB) that stores a set of facts expressed in a representation language and provides facilities to retrieve these facts. Such a module is then used by the reasoner in performing its task-specific inference. In designing a knowledge base, it is important to maintain a fine balance between efficiency and usefulness. The module should perform only those inferences for which it has adequate control knowledge to perform efficiently. For instance, we present a KB that performs inheritance as found in semantic networks but not general logical inference such as modus ponens.

Thus, the fundamental issue in designing a KB retriever is how to limit inference. One possibility is to limit the expressive power of the representation language so that an efficient search space is produced. This is a bad idea as the reasoner may depend on being able to represent and retrieve arbitrary facts. The other alternative is to leave the representation language completely general and to limit the inferences that could occur during retrieval. This paper describes our methodology for specifying such a limited inference process.

The methodology uses first-order predicate calculus (FOPC) as the specification formalism. The use of FOPC notation in a representation language is not uncommon (Nilsson, 1980). And, as the study of logic programming (Kowalski, 1979) tells us, a retrieval algorithm can be specified in logic. Though the representation logic and the retrieval logic are different, they are not independent! In particular, the representation logic must have a well-defined semantics in order to be useful to the reasoner. The retrieval logic must respect this semantics by specifying only valid inferences. An example of a relationship between the two logics that meets this criteria is expressed by the statement, "The sentence '$\alpha \wedge \beta$' can be retrieved if and only if the sentence 'α' and the sentence 'β' each can be retrieved."

We continue this paper by refining our notion of retrieval and then present our method of using FOPC to give a functional specification of a retriever. We illustrate these methodological points by a two-part presentation of a simplified version of the knowledge base module of the Rochester Dialog System (Allen, 1980). The first part of the presentation considers a retriever based on logical inference and the second part extends the system to handle semantic-network inference. We conclude with a brief discussion of techniques for implementing an efficient program that meets the specification.

This paper uses conventional notation for FOPC. The symbol used for logical implication or entailment is $\Rightarrow$ and the statement it forms is called a *sequent*. The symbol used for logical equivalence or bi-directional entailment is $\equiv$ and the statement it forms is called an *equivalence*. As is traditional, the order of precedence of the logical symbols from highest to lowest is; $\sim, \wedge, \vee, \rightarrow, \leftrightarrow, \forall, \exists$. In logical formulae, variables appear in lower case while constant symbols (predicates and functions) appear in upper case. Greek letters are used in schemata as variables that range over formulae or constant symbols.

2. WHAT IS RETRIEVAL?

At any point the KB will have a set of facts called its base facts, on the basis of which it responds to queries made by the reasoner. The issues addressed by this section are what form a query should take and what the retriever should do to respond to the query. We will characterize two extreme positions that can be taken and then present our position as lying somewhere between them.

At one extreme the set of base facts can be treated as an abstract data structure and queries as calls to utilities for examining it. This approach neither prevents a reasoner from performing any kind of operations it wants nor commits a reasoner to any kind of operation it doesn't want. Yet such a retriever doesn't provide much assistance. Presumably, there are operations that can be factored out of the reasoner to be done automatically and efficiently by the retriever on each query.

At the other extreme the set of base facts can be treated as a representation and a query as a request to determine if a given sentence logically follows. This approach has several difficulties that are caricatured by the fact that there is no assurance that the retrieval process will ever terminate. Allocating the retriever such power is putting the muscle of the system in the wrong place. It is the reasoner that is specialized for appropriately controlling inference in its task domain.

Our viewpoint is that retrieval must respect the semantics of the representation language and is therefore inference. A query is a request for the retriever to attempt to infer a specified sentence of the representation language. (For purposes of this paper we will assume that the sentence is closed. It is a trivial extension (Green, 1969; Luckham and Nilsson, 1971) to consider a query as a request to prove an instance, or even all instances, of an open sentence and to return the instance.) If this attempt to infer the queried sentence must be guaranteed to terminate then either the representation language must be severely restricted or the inference engine must be severely restricted and thus incomplete. Restricting the representation language would be a serious mistake. The role of a representation is to define the set of valid inferences that *could* be made, not those that *are* made. Even if the retriever only makes a small portion of all valid inferences the remaining possibilities must be available for the reasoner to consider. Our refusal to restrict the representation language leaves us with the problem of designing a limited inference engine.

One common approach to limiting inference is to restrict the amount of resources used in the computation (Norman and Bobrow, 1975; Bobrow and Winograd, 1977; Robinson and Sibert, 1980). This can be done by restricting computation time, the total number of inference steps taken, or the depth of the inference. These approaches are unsuitable for knowledge retrieval because they limit all forms of inference uniformly. For example, if inference is limited to a depth of 5, then properties cannot be inherited down 6 levels of a type hierarchy. In general, there may be some kinds of inference that we want to be to be computed completely and others that we want to be ignored completely. A methodology for limiting inference should provide the knowledge base designer with enough control to pick and choose the inferences that he wants done.

Another class of limited inference systems are the incomplete theorem provers that are fairly common in the literature - for example, (Brown, 1978). Typically, these systems are not guaranteed to terminate. They often have the undesirable property that the prover has a base fact yet cannot respond to the query that consists of that very fact. It is not surprising that these inference systems are ill-suited for knowledge retrieval - they were not designed for that purpose.

For a while we attempted to design a specialized resolution theorem prover suited for knowledge retrieval. We tried to conjure up a scheme for limiting the resolutions in the search space. The attempt failed, again because it was so difficult to limit inference and yet have all base facts retrievable.

It is instructive to consider why it is so difficult to restrict a traditional proof system without infringing on the retrievability of the base facts. Posit the base fact $P \rightarrow Q$ and also the query $P \rightarrow Q$. A common way of proving the query is to assume P and derive Q by modus ponens. If modus ponens is not restricted then the retriever may not terminate but if it is restricted then $P \rightarrow Q$ may not be retrievable. Situations similar to this are pervasive since theorem provers typically prove a complex sentence by using inference to recursively constuct the sentence from its constituent parts. We seek a proof technique that can respond to a query simply by noticing that it is a base fact.

3. SPECIFYING LIMITED INFERENCE

Our method of specifying limited inference requires a shift in viewpoint from an algorithmic description of the inference engine to a higher level functional description. This is done by focussing on the retriever's query set, Q(B), which is the set of queries that succeed given a particular set of base axioms, B. A specification of Q(B) is more appropriate than a specification of its decision procedure for certain puposes, such as proving that the retrieval system has properties like the ones we are about to discuss.

The previous section argued informally that a retriever must have certain properties. We now examine these more closely from the new viewpoint. The first requirement is derived from the stipulation that all retrievals must terminate. A set is recursive if and only if there is an algorithm that in finite time determines whether any given object is a member of the set. This places the following requirement on the query set:

(Req_1) Q(B) is recursive.

It is this requirement which necessitates limitations on a retriever's inference. If the retriever is a complete theorem prover, then Q(B) is not necessarily recursive.

The second of the requirements is that if a query is in the query set then it logically follows from the base axioms.

(Req_2) $Q(B) \subseteq \{q \mid B \Rightarrow q\}$

This essentially states that the KB retrieval mechanism is sound. The third and final requirement is that all base facts can be retrieved. That is, Q(B) contains B.

(Req_3) $Q(B) \supseteq B$

Our method for specifying representation language retrievability (i.e., Q(B)) is somewhat analogous to the way in which object language provability is traditionally expressed in a meta-language. Because we do not introduce a meta-language term to name each base fact, we use the expressions "representation language" and "retrieval language" rather than "object language" and "meta-language."

The specification of a retriever has two components: a mapping, M, of representation language sentences to retrieval language sentences, and a set of retrieval axioms, R. (On occasion, M will be applied to a set, in which case it designates the set derived by applying the mapping to each member.) A query, q, succeeds if and only if its retrieval language representation, M(q), logically follows from the retrieval language representation of the base axioms, M(B), and the retrieval axioms, R. The retriever does not try to decide the truth of B ⇒ q but rather the much simpler decision of the truth of M(B) ∪ R ⇒ M(q). Retrieval is *limited* inference since the latter sequent implies the first, but not vice-versa.

It will be seen that a quite elaborate retriever can be specified clearly and succinctly with this method. This is possible because the mapping allows representation language constructs to be embedded in the retrieval language, rather than interpreted by it. For example, it would suffice to require that representation language sentences are mapped to retrieval language sentences by quotation. However, doing so would require that a universally quantified variable be given its meaning in the retrieval language by defining operations such as substitution. This is what we have referred to as *interpretation*. On the other hand, the meaning of a universally quantified variable could be *embedded* in the retrieval language simply by mapping representation language variables to retrieval language variables. Interpretation is a more general technique but, when possible, embedding will be used for its simplicity.

It is crucial to observe that in our system everything is mapped to the retrieval language and it is there that retrievability is decided. For all intents and purposes, the representation language has been discarded. This is in contrast to FOL (Weyhrauch, 1980) which uses reflection rules to map back and forth to its META representation when desired and the Bowen and Kowalski (1981) proposal which allows meta-language and object language to be mixed freely.

4. A LOGICAL RETRIEVAL SYSTEM

In this section we develop a logical retrieval system by specifying M and R. We call it a *logical* system because the mappings and retrieval axioms deal specifically with each logical symbol but treat all non-logical symbols uniformly. We have *deliberately* made this system quite weak because it has no control knowledge of how to handle any specific predicate or function symbols. We strengthen the system in section 5 by dealing explicitly with a small set of predicates used to structure semantic networks.

The mapping, M, which takes representation language sentences to retrieval language sentences, will be explained by demonstrating how it handles several sample formulae. A literal in the representation language maps to a term in the retrieval language by mapping predicate symbols and function symbols to corresponding function symbols and the logical operator ~ to the function symbol NOT. Thus the representation language literal ~DRINKS(JB,BEER) maps to the retrieval language term NOT(DRINKS(JB,BEER)). Since representation language and retrieval language are never mixed, we adopt the convention of mapping function symbols and predicate symbols to retrieval language function symbols of the same name. It should always be clear from context which language a given formula is in.

A representation language disjunction of literals is mapped to the retrieval language as a set of terms. For example, ~DRINKS(JB,MILK) ∨ DRINKS(JB,BEER) maps to the term {NOT(DRINKS(JB,MILK)),DRINKS(JB,BEER)}. By virtue of sets being *unordered* collections, the retrieval language accounts for the fact that representation language ∨ is commutative and associative.

Now consider how the base fact

(1) DRINKS(JB,MILK) → DRINKS(JB,BEER)

is mapped to the retrieval language. First the base fact is put into prenex conjunctive normal form, which in this case yields the single conjunct:

(2) ~DRINKS(JB,MILK) ∨ DRINKS(JB,BEER)

This disjunction of literals is then mapped to a retrieval language term that is then asserted to be retrievable with the predicate RET. Thus (2) is mapped to the atomic sentence

(3) RET({NOT(DRINKS(JB,MILK)),DRINKS(JB,BEER)})

If the sentence to be mapped has more than one conjunct, such as

(4) DRINKS(ALAN,MILK) ∧ DRINKS(ALAN,BEER)

then each conjunct is mapped as before. The resulting atomic sentences are then made into a conjunction. Thus, mapping (4) would result in the retrieval language sentence

(5) RET({DRINKS(ALAN,MILK)}) ∧ RET({DRINKS(ALAN,BEER)})

It can be seen that object language conjunction is mapped to retrieval language conjunction. This method of defining the meaning of a representation language construct by mapping it directly to its corresponding retrieval language construct is what we have referred to as embedding.

Object language quantification is also embedded in the retrieval language. Consider the sentence

(6) ∀x (∃y DRINKS(x,y)) ∧ (∃y ~DRINKS(x,y))

which in prenex conjunctive normal form becomes

(7) ∀x ∃y ∃z DRINKS(x,y) ∧ ~DRINKS(x,z)

The matrix is mapped as before with the additional consideration that variables are mapped to corresponding variables. The prefix remains essentially unchanged by the mapping except for the mapping of variables to corresponding variables. Thus, mapping (7) to the retrieval language results in

(8) ∀x ∃y ∃z RET({DRINKS(x,y)}) ∧ RET({NOT(DRINKS(x,z))})

Observe that since the representation language connectives $\vee$ and ~ have been mapped to retrieval language function symbols, their meaning will be interpreted by the retrieval language. There will be axioms which enable deductions to be made with the terms constructed from NOT and { }. These will mimic sound representation language inferences. However, the representation language proof system must not be totally mimicked by the retrieval language axioms if (Req_1) is to be met. OR and NOT will be given much weaker interpretations than $\vee$ and ~. On the other hand, representation language $\wedge$ and quantification has been mapped to retrieval language $\wedge$ and quantification. This embedding gives these representation language constructs their full-blown logical meaning.

Before considering retrieval axioms, let us examine this retriever with no retrieval axioms. It can immediately be seen that this retriever meets (Req_3). It also meets the first two requirements, but showing so involves more subtlety than can be dealt with in this paper.

But the query set contains much more than just the base axioms! For example, the query

(9) $\sim\exists x\,(\forall y\,\text{DRINKS}(x,y)) \vee (\forall y\,\sim\text{DRINKS}(x,y))$

would succeed in a KB that had (6) as a base fact. Though not immediately obvious, (6) and (9) both map to (8) in the retrieval language and are therefore logically equivalent. The normalization process that accounts for this by equating many logical paraphrases is a powerful technique. Mapping disjunctions to sets is also a form of normalization because it makes the retrieval language insensitive to the ordering of representation language disjunction. Thus, if A $\vee$ B were added to the KB, the query B $\vee$ A would succeed.

In addition, the embedding of representation language variables and conjunction means that these will be handled with their full logical meaning. For example, the query

(10) $\exists x\,\exists y\,\text{DRINKS}(x,y)$

can be answered positively by this KB if either (4) or (7) had been added. The retrieval language representation of this query,

(11) $\exists x\,\exists y\,\text{RET}(\{\text{DRINKS}(x,y)\})$

logically follows from (5), the retrieval language representation of (4), or from (8), the retrieval language representation of (7).

Because there are no retrieval axioms that chain base facts together (i.e., use more than one base fact in an inference) this system has the property that

($Prop_1$) A query succeeds *only if* each conjunct of the query follows from one conjunct of one base fact.

We will now look at ways of strengthening this system by adding retrieval axioms. These retrieval axioms strengthen the system but not so much as to destroy ($Prop_1$). The first retrieval axiom is based on the fact that disjunction is monotonic. That is, if a disjunct is true, then adding additional disjuncts to it cannot change its truth value. This inspires the logical retrieval axiom:

(R_1) $\forall y\,(\exists x\,\text{RET}(x) \wedge x \subseteq y) \rightarrow \text{RET}(y)$

The above retrieval axiom allows a set to be manipulated in a manner consistent with the meaning of the disjunction it encodes. The next retrieval axiom does the same for NOT and the negation it encodes. It says that an atomic sentence and its negation cannot both be retrievable.

(R_2) $\forall x\,\sim\text{RET}(\{x\}) \vee \sim\text{RET}(\{\text{NOT}(x)\})$

(R_2) does not change the query set of the current retriever but it is needed in the semantic network retrieval system.

Because ($Prop_1$) is a desirable design objective, (R_1) and (R_2) are the only logical retrieval axioms used. There will be other retrieval axioms, such as those derived from the study of semantic networks undertaken in the next section. Although we consider the three requirements which we presented to be constraints on all KB designs, the design objective was chosen based on our particular task. We shall now discuss the rationale for this design objective.

As discussed before, and as can be seen clearly now, the KB has no special knowledge of any representation language predicates. It therefore treats them uniformly and this is what we mean when we say that the KB is domain independent. Without such knowledge, a strong inferencial component cannot perform effectively and thus we have taken a conservative approach to inference. In this sense the system presented here can be viewed as a KB kernel on top of which a more powerful, and possibly domain-dependent KB could be built. A reasoner can compensate for a KB that is efficient but deductively weak by making deductions of its own. However, it is hard for a reasoner to compensate for a KB whose excessive deductive power leads to inefficiency.

5. A SEMANTIC NETWORK RETRIEVAL SYSTEM

In this section, we investigate a very simple semantic network system by formalizing it in FOPC. This investigation yields a primitive set of predicates that can be used to structure knowledge and a set of axioms relating these predicates. This formalization takes place without consideration of the role that the axioms should play in a KB. We then take up the problem of how to integrate these axioms into the KB so that the retriever can use them to make the kind of inferences typically performed by semantic network interpreters.

The fact that our KB uses the notation of FOPC for the representation language is methodologically important yet it says little about how a domain should be represented. Modern semantic networks - those since (Woods, 1975) - have made steps in suggesting knowledge-structuring primitives, though a great deal of freedom still remains in choosing how to represent a domain. Others have referred to these knowledge-structuring primitives as epistemological primitives (Brachman, 1979), structural relations (Shapiro, 1979) and system relations (Shapiro, 1971).

Elsewhere (Frisch, 1981; Allen and Frisch, 1982), we have shown how semantic networks can motivate a logic with a fixed set of predicates and how the relationship between these predicates can be axiomatized. Here we use a much simpler scheme that has 4 predicates, TYPE, SUBTYPE, ROLE, and =, and 3 axioms, labelled (Asn-1), (Asn-2), and (Asn-3). We then integrate these axioms into the KB so that they can drive the retriever.

The use of type hierarchies is characteristic of semantic networks. The domain of individuals is divided into sets called types. TYPE(I,T) asserts that an individual I belongs to a type T and SUBTYPE(T,T') asserts that the type T is a subset of the type T'. There are two axioms involving these predicates:

(Asn_1) ∀x,t,t' TYPE(x,t') ∧ SUBTYPE(t',t) → TYPE(x,t)

(Asn_2) ∀x,t',t SUBTYPE(t',x) ∧ SUBTYPE(x,t) → SUBTYPE(t',t)

If events such as 'Jellybean drank milk' are represented as DRANK(JB,MILK) then, as pointed out by Davidson (1967), there is no way to quantify over events and their components. This prevents the representation of assertions such as 'The actor of an action causes that action.' For this reason and for the purpose of making all relations binary, semantic networks traditionally represent 'Jellybean drank milk' as

(12) TYPE(DRANK01,DRANKEVENT) ∧ ACTOR(DRANK01,JB) ∧ OBJECT(DRANK01,MILK)

Thus, 'The actor of an event causes that event' can be expressed as

(13) ∀x,y TYPE(x,ACTION) ∧ ACTOR(x,y) → CAUSE(y,x)

However, in this representation, there is no way to state 'Role fillers are unique' or to query 'Is there an event involving Jellybean and milk.' Because we do not restrict ourselves to binary relations, we can generalize the above representation by making roles into objects in their own right. Thus, (12) becomes

(14) TYPE(DRANK01,DRANKEVENT) ∧ ROLE(ACTOR,DRANK01,JB) ∧
ROLE(OBJECT,DRANK01,MILK)

and the query 'Is there an event involving Jellybean and milk' is represented as:

(15) ∃e,r,r' TYPE(e,EVENT) ∧ ROLE(r,e,JB) ∧ ROLE(r',e,MILK)

Notice that (15) logically follows from (14).

The third and final semantic network axiom states that role fillers are unique and can now be expressed as:

(Asn_3) ∀r,e,f,f' ROLE(r,e,f) ∧ ROLE(r,e,f') → f = f'

How can (Asn_1), (Asn_2) and (Asn_3) be integrated into the KB so that they can be used by the retriever in its deductions? We would like to obtain the property that the query set is closed with respect to the derivation of true sentences from these axioms.

First of all, these axioms should be added to the set of base facts in the KB. Mapping them to the retrieval language yields:

(16) ∀x,t,t' RET({NOT(TYPE(x,t')),NOT(SUBTYPE(t',t)),TYPE(x,t)})

(17) ∀x,t',t RET({NOT(SUBTYPE(t',x)),NOT(SUBTYPE(x,t)),SUBTYPE(t',t)})

(18) ∀r,e,f,f' RET({NOT(ROLE(r,e,f)),NOT(ROLE(r,e,f')),f = f'})

But this is not enough. Let us consider the situation in which TYPE(JB,DOG) and SUBTYPE (DOG,MAMMAL) are also base facts and the query that we wish to succeed is TYPE(JB,MAMMAL). Thus, in the retrieval language there are two base facts,

(19) RET({TYPE(JB,DOG)})

(20) RET({SUBTYPE(DOG,MAMMAL)})

and the query

(21) RET({TYPE(JB,MAMMAL)})

But notice that (21) does not follow from the base facts. The query fails because disjunction in (Asn_1) is weakened when mapped to (16) in the retrieval logic. We can get the query to succeed by using the following retrieval axiom based on (Asn_1):

(R_3) ∀x,t,t' RET({NOT(TYPE(x,t'))}) ∨ RET({NOT(SUBTYPE(t',t))}) ∨ RET({TYPE(x,t)})

(21) now logically follows from (19), (20), (R_2) and (R_3). The increased power of the retriever is due to the fact that the disjunction in (Asn_1) has been mapped to a disjunction in (R_3) rather than a set as was done in (16).

Likewise, the two other semantic network axioms are made into retrieval axioms:

(R_4) ∀x,t',t RET({NOT(SUBTYPE(t',x))}) ∨ RET({NOT(SUBTYPE(x,t))}) ∨
RET({SUBTYPE(t',t)})

(R_5) ∀r,e,f,f' RET({NOT(ROLE(r,e,f))}) ∨ RET({NOT(ROLE(r,e,f'))}) ∨ RET({f = f'})

However, a deficiency still remains. Consider the situation in which 'All mammals drink a liquid' is added to the above KB and the query 'Jellybean drinks a liquid' is made. Adding

(22) ∀m TYPE(m,MAMMAL) → ∃l TYPE(l,LIQUID) ∧ DRINKS(m,l)

yields the retrieval language base fact

(23) ∀m ∃l RET({NOT(TYPE(m,MAMMAL)),TYPE(l,LIQUID)}) ∧
RET{NOT(TYPE(m,MAMMAL)),DRINKS(m,l)})

Though (21) logically follows, (23) is not strong enough to logically imply the queried sentence

(24) $\exists l\ \mathrm{RET}(\{\mathrm{TYPE}(l,\mathrm{LIQUID})\}) \land \mathrm{RET}(\{\mathrm{DRINKS}(\mathrm{JB},l)\})$

More generally, the KB as it now stands cannot infer a property of an individual based on a property asserted of all members of one of its types. The problem is that M combines TYPE atoms with other atoms thus subjecting types to the system's inference limitations. The problem could be solved by altering M to factor out appropriate representation language TYPE atoms into their own retrieval language RET atoms. For example, the query, (24), would succeed if (22) were mapped to the retrieval language as

(25) $\forall m\ \exists l\ \mathrm{RET}(\{\mathrm{TYPE}(m,\mathrm{MAMMAL})\}) \rightarrow \mathrm{RET}(\{\mathrm{TYPE}(l,\mathrm{LIQUID})\}) \land \mathrm{RET}(\{\mathrm{DRINKS}(m,l)\})$

Rather than complicating the mappings to recognize and factor out the appropriate type information, the representation language is extended so that certain type information can be written in a factored-out manner initially. The extended language, called typed first-order predicate calculus or TFOPC, includes formulae of the form $\forall x{:}\tau\ \varphi$ and $\exists x{:}\tau\ \varphi$, where φ is a formula and τ is the name of a type. The meaning of this notation is defined by two equivalence schemata:

(26) $\forall x{:}\tau\ \varphi \equiv \forall x\ \mathrm{TYPE}(x,\tau) \rightarrow \varphi$

(27) $\exists x{:}\tau\ \varphi \equiv \exists x\ \mathrm{TYPE}(x,\tau) \land \varphi$

Thus, (22) could be written in TFOPC as

(28) $\forall m{:}\mathrm{MAMMAL}\ \exists l{:}\mathrm{LIQUID}\ \mathrm{DRINKS}(m,l)$

M is appropriately modified to handle the extended representation language. As before, the representation language base fact or query is put in prenex conjunctive normal form. The same process that converts a FOPC sentence to prenex conjunctive normal form (Robinson, 1979) also converts a TFOPC sentence. Here's why: The conversion process is based on many equivalence schemata, six of which deal with quantification. There are six corresponding TFOPC schemata that can easily be proved and therefore, quantifiers can be moved about as if the types weren't even there.

Once the query or base fact is in prenex conjunctive normal form, it is mapped as before but with the additional consideration that formulae of the form $\forall x{:}\tau\ \varphi$ map to

(29) $\forall x\ \mathrm{RET}(\{\mathrm{TYPE}(x,\tau)\}) \rightarrow M(\varphi)$

and those of the form $\exists x{:}\tau\ \varphi$ map to

(30) $\exists x\ \mathrm{RET}(\{\mathrm{TYPE}(x,\tau)\}) \land M(\varphi)$

Therefore, applying the complete M mapping to the base fact (28) yields

(31) $\forall m\ \mathrm{RET}(\{\mathrm{TYPE}(m,\mathrm{MAMMAL})\}) \rightarrow \exists l\ \mathrm{RET}(\{\mathrm{TYPE}(l,\mathrm{LIQUID})\}) \land \mathrm{RET}(\{\mathrm{DRINKS}(m,l)\})$

The query 'Jellybean drinks a liquid,' which can be stated in TFOPC as

(32) $\exists l{:}\mathrm{LIQUID}\ \mathrm{DRINKS}(\mathrm{JB},l)$

gets mapped to the retrieval language as

(33) $\exists l\ \mathrm{RET}(\{\mathrm{TYPE}(l,\mathrm{LIQUID})\}) \land \mathrm{RET}(\{\mathrm{DRINKS}(\mathrm{JB},l)\})$

And finally, the deficiency stated at the outset has been overcome. The example situation now behaves as desired since (33) logically follows from (19), (20), (31), and the retrieval axioms.

As a final observation, notice that typing existential variables has not extended the power of the system as has typing universal variables. This is due to the fact that a type on an existential variable is an abbreviation for a conjunction and the limited inference handles conjunction fully. Typed existential variables have been added to the language for the sake of uniformity.

The semantic-network retriever presented in this section meets (Req_1), (Req_2) and (Req_3). Though the retriever can now chain base facts together in deriving TYPE and SUBTYPE relations, Q(B) is still recursive because the type hierarchy is finite.

6. IMPLEMENTING RETRIEVAL

The KB module of the Rochester Dialog System has a retriever that is an extended version of the semantic-network retriever presented here. The representation language has been extended with a set of abbreviations tailored to our domain and the semantic network retrieval axioms have been extended to handle a larger set of knowledge-structuring primitives (Allen and Frisch, 1982; Frisch, 1981). All communication with the KB is in the representation language - the retrieval language is totally invisible. We will only briefly discuss the techniques used in the implementation since we have not yet proved their correctness.

Our method of producing a program that meets the specification developed in this paper is to map queries and base facts to the retrieval language and treat the specification as the logic component of an algorithm (Kowalski, 1979). This logic component can then be transformed to an equivalent specification - one for which we can produce an efficient control component. The transform we employ makes all retrieval language sentences into Horn clauses. Notice that all of the semantic-network retrieval axioms are disjunctions of positive RET literals of singleton sets. For concreteness consider

(R_3) ∀x,t,t' RET({NOT(TYPE(x,t'))}) ∨ RET({NOT(SUBTYPE(t',t))}) ∨ RET({TYPE(x,t)})

There are three sentences that have a single positive literal which logically follow from (ASN_1) and

(R_2) ∀x ~RET({x}) ∨ ~RET({NOT(x)})

They are:

(34) ∀x,t,t' RET({NOT(TYPE(x,t'))}) ∨ ~RET({(SUBTYPE(t',t))}) ∨ ~RET({NOT(TYPE(x,t))})

(35) ∀x,t,t' ~RET({TYPE(x,t')}) ∨ RET({NOT(SUBTYPE(t',t))}) ∨ ~RET({NOT(TYPE(x,t))})

(36) ∀x,t,t' ~RET({(TYPE(x,t'))}) ∨ ~RET({SUBTYPE(t',t)}) ∨ RET({TYPE(x,t)})

Thus all sentences of *n* literals are rewritten into *n* sentences, each of which has one positive literal and *n-1* negative literals. Once the rewritting is completed (R_2) is no longer needed. This rewriting is clearly sound and, in general, incomplete. The important question remains open: Is this rewriting technique complete for our class of theories? The new set of sentences need not be equivalent to the original set of sentences - it need only preserve the truth of the sequent M(B) ∪ R ⇒ M(q). We point out that this rewriting is related to Meltzer's proposal (1966) and appears to yield a system equivalent to linear input resolution (Loveland, 1978).

It can be seen that these rewritten sentences can then trivially be made into Horn clauses. We then use a PROLOG-like theorem prover called HORNE (Allen and Frisch, 1981) to interpret the clauses. Failure to prove a query is construed as meaning that the query is not in Q(B) (Clark, 1978). We now discuss the selection and search strategies (Van Emden, 1977) that we use to control the theorem-prover.

Since all clauses that result from retrieval axioms are fixed, we manually order the literals within the clauses to take advantage of HORNE's left-to-right selection strategy. As discussed by Clark and McCabe (1979), several orderings are specified for each clause depending on which variables are bound. Cuts are also manually added to these clauses based on the bindings. Ordering of literals within base facts is not crucial since they are atomic with the exception of the TYPE literals. Ordering of literals within a query is crucial and must be done dynamically. Nothing has been done in this regard but some thought has been given to using a method similar to Chat-80's query optimization (Warren and Pereira, 1981).

Search strategy plays a relatively minor role in the retriever's performance. When the retriever is looking for all answers to a query or when there are no answers to a query, the entire search space must be examined. These situations are not unusual and clearly search strategy is irrelevant in them. Therefore, HORNE's depth-first search is a good choice because it lends itself to efficient implementation through the use of stack allocation. The order that branches are chosen is arbitrary.

However, if our search space were dynamically pruned, search strategy would be a factor. Not only could dynamic pruning eliminate deductive paths guaranteed to fail (Perreira and Porto, 1980) but it could eliminate deductive paths guaranteed to yield redundant solutions.

We have realized great improvements in efficiency by using TFOPC as the retrieval language and accordingly extending HORNE to handle TFOPC Horn clauses. Type checking is done on unification by recursively calling the retriever to test the appropriate TYPE and SUBTYPE relations. This organization reorders the goals in a proof and appears to result in a much smaller search space. The rationale for this is that, when possible, the retriever reasons about classes of individuals rather than about the individuals themselves. This is a minimum commitment strategy similar to that obtained in MOLGEN (Stefik, 1981) by the use of constraints.

ACKNOWLEDGEMENTS

We thank Pat Hayes for his insightful comments on this paper and the Artificial Intelligence Study Group for patiently hearing our arguments and providing valuable counterarguments. This research has been supported in part by NSF grant IST-801248 and ONR grant N00014-80-C-0197.

REFERENCES

Allen, J. F., The Rochester natural language understanding project. *1980-81 Computer Science and Computer Engineering Research Review.* Computer Science Department, University of Rochester, 1980.

Allen, J. F. and Frisch, A. M., What's in a semantic network? Submitted to 20th Annual Meeting of the Association for Computational Linguistics, 1982.

Allen, J. F. and Frisch, A. M., HORNE user's manual. Internal report, Computer Science Department, University of Rochester, 1981.

Bobrow, D. G. and Collins, A. M. (Eds.), *Representation and understanding.* New York: Academic Press, 1975.

Bobrow, D. G. and Winograd, T., An overview of KRL, a knowledge representation language. *Cognitive Science,* 1977, *1,* 3-46.

Bowen, K. A. and Kowalski, R. A., *Amalgamating language and metalanguage in logic programming*. Technical Report, School of Information and Computer Science, Syracuse University, 1981.

Brachman, R. J., On the epistemological status of semantic networks. In Findler, 1979.

Brown, F. M., Towards the automation of set theory and its logic. *Artificial Intelligence*, 1978, 10, 281-316.

Clark, K. L., Negation as failure. In Gallaire and Minker, 1978.

Clark, K. L., and McCabe, F. G., The control facilities of IC-PROLOG. In Michie, 1979.

Davidson, D., The logical form of action sentences. In Rescher, 1967.

Elcock, E. W. and Michie, D. (Eds.), *Machine intelligence 8*. Chichester, England: Ellis Horwood, 1977.

Findler, N. V. (Ed.), *Associative networks: Representation and use of knowledge by computers*. New York: Academic Press, 1979.

Frisch, A. M., A formal study of knowledge representation and retrieval. Ph.D. thesis proposal, Computer Science Department, University of Rochester, 1981.

Gallaire, H. and Minker, J. (Eds.), *Logic and data bases*. New York: Plenum Press, 1978.

Green, C., Theorem-proving by resolution as a basis for question-answering systems. In Meltzer and Michie, 1969.

Kowalski, R. A., *Logic for problem solving*. New York: North Holland, 1979.

Loveland, D. W., *Automated theorem proving: A logical basis*. Amsterdam: North-Holland, 1978.

Luckham, D. C., and Nilsson, N. J., Extracting information from resolution proof trees. *Artificial Intelligence*, 1971, 2, 27-54.

Meltzer, B., Theorem-proving for computers: Some results on resolution and renaming. *Computer Journal*, 1966, *8*, 341-343.

Meltzer, B., and Michie, D. (Eds.), *Machine intelligence 4*. Ediburgh: Edinburgh University Press, 1969.

Michie, D. (Ed.), *Expert systems in the micro electronic age*. Ediburgh: Edinburgh University Press, 1979.

Nilsson, N. J., *Principles of artificial intelligence*, Palo Alto, CA.: Tioga, 1980.

Norman, D. A., and Bobrow, D. G., On data-limited and resource-limited processes. *Cognitive Psychology*, 1975, 7, 44-64.

Pereira, L. M., and Porto, A., Selective backtracking for logic programs. *5th Conference on Automated Deduction Proceedings*, Springer-Verlag, 1980.

Rescher, N. (Ed.), *The logic of decision and action*. Pittsburgh: U. of Pittsburgh Press, 1967.

Robinson, J. A., *Logic: Form and function*. New York: North Holland, 1979.

Robinson, J. A., and Sibert, E. E., LOGLISP - An alternative to PROLOG. Technical Report, School of Computer and Information Science, Syracuse University, December, 1980.

Shapiro, S. C., The SNePS semantic network processing system. In Findler, 1979.

Shapiro, S. C., A net structure for semantic information storage, deduction and retrieval. *Proceedings of the 2nd International Joint Conference on Artificial Intelligence*, 1971.

Stefik, M. J., Planning with constraints. *Artificial Intelligence*, 1981, *16*, 111-140.

Van Emden, M. H., *Programming with resolution logic*. In Elcock and Michie, 1977.

Warren, D. H. D., and Pereira, F. C. N., An efficient easily adaptable system for interpreting natural language queries. DAI Research Paper No. 155, Department of Artificial Intelligence, University of Ediburgh, 1981.

Weyhrauch, R. W., Prolegomena to a theory of mechanized formal reasoning. *Artificial Intelligence*, 1980, *13*, 133-170.

Woods, W. A., What's in a link: Foundations for semantic networks. In Bobrow and Collins, 1975.

Knowledge Retrieval Then and Now

An Epilogue to "Knowledge Retrieval as Limited Inference"

Alan M. Frisch [1]

In "Knowledge Retrieval as Limited Inference"—henceforth KRLI—James Allen and I address a well-known dilemma that confronts anyone building a system that responds to queries on the basis of a corpus of information stored in a knowledge base (KB). It is impossible to allow the query and KB to be stated in a highly-expressive language and simultaneously to have an effective procedure that uses complete deduction to respond to the query. In general, increased expressivity in the representation results in decreased efficiency in query processing. Something must be sacrificed.

Traditional data bases opt for a complete, efficient system for responding to queries while sacrificing expressiveness. However, many artificial intelligence applications demand extremely expressive representations; in such cases it seems reasonable to opt for expressiveness and sacrifice the power of the retrieval system. KRLI investigates this route, discussing the properties required of a limited inference system that is to be used for retrieval and proposing a system that meets the requirements.

To the best of my knowledge, KRLI is the first serious study of the use of limited inference for knowledge retrieval. This is not to say that no one in AI had used limited inference systems to access a KB; indeed it appears to have been a common practice in the semantic-network systems of the late 1970's. At that time, however, inference, like many bodily functions, was not discussed in public. Witness the near-total absence of such discussion in *Associative Networks* [Findler, 1979], a collection of papers on state-of-the-art semantic-network systems.

Though I am proud of KRLI's claim to being the first study of its kind, I am pleased that the paper has long relinquished any claim to being the best. KRLI marks the beginning of the Ph.D. research on this topic that I conducted under the supervision of James Allen. Simultaneously other researchers in AI pursued closely-related research on knowledge retrieval and related topics.

The Ph.D. thesis that resulted from that research [Frisch, 1986a] contains a notably improved investigation into knowledge retrieval, though, in certain aspects, it bears a striking resemblance to KRLI. Our original intuitions of what form of inference constitutes retrieval have stood over time.

[1] Author's address: Department of Computer Science, University of Illinois, 1304 West Springfield Avenue, Urbana, IL 61801. Phone: (217) 244-6024 Email: frisch@a.cs.uiuc.edu

Consequently, the two retrievers specified in KRLI and in the thesis are similar.[2] Furthermore, the later study follows the example of the earlier one by concentrating on what is retrievable before considering how the retriever is to operate.

KRLI and the thesis differ significantly in the specification method employed. Whereas the KRLI specification is syntactic—what is called interpretation and embedding there—the later specification is entirely model-theoretic. A three-valued model theoretic semantics is given for the sentences of first order logic, and the entailment relation of that model theory is used as the specification of the retriever. In the terminology of KRLI, Q(B) is the set of all sentences that are entailed by B in the three-valued model theory.

Unlike the bald presentation of the specification found in KRLI, the specification in the thesis is derived from certain fundamental intuitions and then proved to capture those intuitions. The use of a model theoretic specification means that the intuitions can be permeated uniformly throughout the specification and also facilitates proving certain properties of the retriever. The guiding intuition is that a retriever is, at least in simple cases, a pattern matcher, though in more complex cases it may perform selected inferences such as inheritance.

Like the KRLI specification, the thesis specification is developed in two stages, the first specifying an extremely weak logical retriever and the second adding taxonomic inference to the retriever. The first stage captures the pattern-matching intuition by making sure that the system meets the no-chaining restriction, a formally-stated restriction that is much like ($Prop_1$) of KRLI. The retriever that is developed is proved to be the strongest inference system that does no chaining. The second stage of the specification augments the retriever with the ability to perform taxonomic inferences, almost identical to the inferences incorporated in the second stage of the KRLI retriever. The thesis proves that the specified retriever is able to infer all consequences of its taxonomic knowledge without otherwise chaining.

[2] Though syntactic differences make direct comparisons difficult, it appears that the latter retriever differs little, if any, from the KRLI retriever if one were to remove

$$(R_2) \quad \forall x\, \neg RET(\{x\}) \vee \neg RET(\{NOT(x)\})$$

and add

$$\forall x\, RET(\{x, NOT(x)\}).$$

The thesis also presents algorithms that provably meet each of the specifications. The ultimate algorithm is of interest in that it performs all taxonomic inference during unification. The theoretical underpinnings of the method used to build taxonomic inference into unification are under further study and the method is being integrated into other inference systems [Frisch, 1988, Frisch, 1986b].

Interest in limited inference has mushroomed in the study of knowledge retrieval, as well as in other areas of AI. For example, at the 1985 International Joint Conference on AI, the Computers and Thought Award Lecture [Levesque, 1986] discussed—among other things—limited inference, and the best paper award went to a paper on limited inference [Fagin and Halpern, 1985].

Space precludes discussion of this expanding body of work. However, some of this work is so closely related to and has so strongly influenced the work discussed here that neglecting it would constitute malpractice. The work to which I am referring is based on Belnap's [1975, 1977] four-valued semantics for relevance logic, where the four values are a superset of those employed in the thesis specification. Patel-Schneider [1987] has specified a retriever extremely close to the thesis retriever, though the use of a four-valued semantics weakens the system so that it does not perform all inferences that require no chaining. The issue of limited inference also arises in reasoning about the beliefs of another agent. We can no more expect an agent to conclude all the consequences of his beliefs than we can expect a retriever to compute all consequences of the KB. Using Belnap's four-valued semantics, Levesque [1984] has built a propositional logic of belief, and Lakemeyer [1986, 1987] has extended it to handle quantifiers and iterated beliefs—beliefs about belief.

If the past six years are any indication of what lies ahead, we can expect limited inference to grow in importance in the study of knowledge retrieval, as well as in other areas of AI.

References

[Belnap, 1975] Nuel D. Belnap, Jr. How a computer should think. In *Contemporary Aspects of Philosophy: Proceedings of the Oxford International Symposium*, pages 30–56, 1975.

[Belnap, 1977] Nuel D. Belnap, Jr. A useful four-valued logic. In G. Epstein and J. M. Dunn, editors, *Modern Uses of Multiple-Valued Logic*, pages 8–37, Reidel, 1977.

[Fagin and Halpern, 1985] Ronald Fagin and Joseph Y. Halpern. Belief, awareness, and limited reasoning: preliminary report. In *Proceedings IJCAI-85*, pages 491–501, Los Angeles, California, August 1985.

[Findler, 1979] Nicholas V. Findler, editor. *Associative Networks: Representation and Use of Knowledge by Computers.* Academic Press, New York, 1979.

[Frisch, 1986a] Alan M. Frisch. *Knowledge Retrieval as Specialized Inference.* PhD thesis, Computer Science Department, University of Rochester, August 1986.

[Frisch, 1986b] Alan M. Frisch. Parsing with restricted quantification: an initial demonstration. *Computational Intelligence*, 2(3):142–150, 1986.

[Frisch, 1988] Alan M. Frisch. A general approach to deduction in sorted logic: fundamental results. To appear, 1988.

[Lakemeyer, 1986] Gerhard Lakemeyer. Steps towards a first-order logic of explicit and implicit belief. In Joseph Y. Halpern, editor, *Theoretical Aspects of Reasoning About Knowledge: Proceedings of the 1986 Conference*, pages 325–340, Monterey, California, Morgan Kaufmann, Los Altos, California, March 1986.

[Lakemeyer, 1987] Gerhard Lakemeyer. Tractable meta-reasoning in propositional logics of belief. In *Proceedings IJCAI-87*, pages 402–408, Milan, Italy, August 1987.

[Levesque, 1984] Hector J. Levesque. A logic of implicit and explicit belief. In *Proceedings of the National Conference on Artificial Intelligence*, pages 198–202, William Kaufmann, Los Altos, CA, August 1984.

[Levesque, 1986] Hector J. Levesque. Making believers out of computers. *Artificial Intelligence*, 30(1):81–108, October 1986.

[Patel-Schneider, 1987] Peter F. Patel-Schneider. *Decidable, Logic-Based Knowledge Representation.* PhD thesis, Department of Computer Science, University of Toronto, February 1987.

3.2 Data/Knowledge Base Integrity

Integrity checking has been a nonissue for databases and knowledge bases alike, although for quite different reasons. Integrity checking for a database (i.e., checking that a database conforms to a set of integrity constraints) was deemed for a long time computationally too expensive to be of practical use. Attempts were made to improve the precision of the data model ([HM75], [BROD80a], and [LS87]), and to find corresponding efficient implementation techniques [HS78], as we shall describe. Several researchers have used logic to improve database integrity checking (see [NY78], [REIT81], and the fourth paper in this section [NICO82]).

For knowledge bases, integrity checking usually amounts to checking that a set of logical formulas is inconsistent, which is computationally undecidable. Recently, the subject has received some attention, although it remains more of a theoretical rather than a practical interest. Integrity-checking mechanisms need to address two basic problems. First, they need to detect inconsistencies in the data/knowledge base. Second, they must provide means for dealing with the inconsistency. This work is related to the complex and important problem of truth maintenance in a knowledge base [DOYL79].

The first paper in this section (3.2.1), "Fast Maintenance of Integrity Assertions Using Redundant Aggregate Data" by Phil Bernstein, Barbara Blaustein, and E. Clarke, is an excellent example of the approaches to database integrity checking. Although the technique is relatively fast, it is inherently limited in its optimization capabilities as it does not consider the semantics of the transactions and constraints. A more powerful but less tractable approach, based on theorem proving, was proposed in [GM79] and is being pursued [SS86]. [CRMN88] presents a recent attempt to apply the framework proposed by Bernstein and colleagues for integrity checking with respect to a semantic data model. [LS87] examines the problem of expressing and checking *dynamic* integrity constraints (i.e., constraints on admissible sequences of database states).

The second paper (3.2.2), "A Sophisticate's Introduction to Database Normalization Theory" by Catriel Beeri, Phil Bernstein, and Nat Goodman, offers a second approach to database integrity checking. Ted Codd offered database normalization, together with use of the relational data model, as syntactic analytical tests of a database schema to identify potential errors in the operation of the corresponding database. The general rule is to represent all facts (represented using *functional dependencies*) nonredundantly and independently of other facts (two excellent ideas). Violating these rules in designing a database schema may lead to anomolous behaviour on database update. Due to the lack of other database-design techniques at the time, normalization received considerable attention and was proposed, by some researchers, to be a complete database-design methodology. Indeed, relational-database schemas can be synthesized from definitions of facts, and potential errors can be identified syntactically in existing relational schemas given the definition of the intended facts. Researchers now generally recognize that normalization offers excellent techniques to identify potential errors in record-based (not just relational) schemas, but that these techniques address only a small part of the semantics of database schemas. Fully normalized databases (i.e., those without the identifiable potential problems) are generally not optimal with respect to the transaction loads to be executed over the database. Hence, normalization is not always appropriate. However, identification of the potential errors permits the development of alternative means of avoiding them. The seminal paper on normalization algorithms is [BERN76]. Other work includes [FAGI77] and [BB79].

The third paper in this section (3.2.3), "The Programming Language Aspects of ThingLab, a Constraint-Oriented Simulation Laboratory" by Alan Borning, addresses the problem of restoring a knowledge base to a consistent state, after an inconsistency has been introduced. This is one of the best examples of a paper addressing constraint propagation, a topic that has been studied extensively in AI (see also [MACK77] for a different perspective on the subject).

The fourth and final paper in this section (3.2.4), "Logic for Improving Integrity Checking in Relational Databases" by Jean-Marie Nicolas, shows how we can handle integrity checking efficiently for relational databases, by using deductive techniques. An extension of Nicolas' integrity-checking algorithm for deductive databases is described in [LT85], whereas [DECK86] presents new important results on the issue of integrity checking for deductive databases. Related work can be found in [NY78], [REIT81], and [HMN84].

FAST MAINTENANCE OF SEMANTIC INTEGRITY ASSERTIONS USING REDUNDANT AGGREGATE DATA*

Philip A. Bernstein
Barbara T. Blaustein
Edmund M. Clarke

Aiken Computation Laboratory
Harvard University
Cambridge, MA 02138

Abstract

Semantic integrity assertions are predicates that define consistent database states. To enforce such assertions, a database system must prevent any update from mapping a consistent state to an inconsistent one. In this paper, we describe an enforcement method that is efficient for a large class of relational calculus assertions. The method automatically selects minima and maxima of certain sets to maintain as redundant data in the database. This redundant data is sufficient for enforcing all of the assertions in the class, yet it can be easily maintained. Correctness proofs are expressed in Hoare's program logic.

1. Introduction

Accuracy is an important property of any database. One way to prevent inaccurate data from being stored in a database is to use *semantic integrity assertions*. These assertions are predicates on database states; a database state is *consistent* with these assertions if all assertions hold in that state. By defining a collection of semantic integrity assertions, a user specifies consistent states. The database system is responsible for ensuring database consistency by rejecting updates that produce inconsistent states.

The main components of an implementation of semantic integrity assertions are a *specification language* for defining assertions and *enforcement algorithms* for guaranteeing database consistency relative to those assertions. Expressive power is an asset for such a language, since it allows many types of constraints to be stated; but it is also a liability, since complicated assertions are often expensive to enforce. One language that is richly expressive is relational calculus [Codd 72]. However, since many applications do not need the full power of relational calculus to express semantic integrity assertions, and since arbitrary relational calculus assertions can be quite expensive to enforce, we focus on a restricted class of assertions. Our restricted class is sufficiently general to express many common assertions, yet simple enough to be enforced efficiently.

Efficient enforcement depends not only on the complexity of the assertions, but also on the structure of the database. One method for improving the efficiency of enforcement algorithms is to augment the database, D, with stored redundant information, D', that summarizes the contents of D. If D' is cleverly designed, it will contain sufficient information for testing the consistency of most assertions during updates. However, D' itself must be kept consistent relative to the database, D, it is intended to describe. So, there is a trade-off between the work saved during consistency testing by exploiting D' and the extra effort required to keep D' consistent with respect to D. For D' to be effective, its benefit for consistency testing must exceed the cost of maintaining it.

We have adopted the use of redundant data to reduce the cost of testing consistency. The redundant data that we typically add to the database is aggregate information that characterizes a set of values in the database, such as the greatest lower bound of a set. We test consistency using the stored aggregate data rather than all the individual values in the set. The aggregate information is designed to be quickly accessed and easily maintained.

The enforcement method that is the subject of this paper includes: A formal definition of the class of assertions it can enforce; a procedure that selects the appropriate aggregate information to store for each assertion in the class; a procedure that determines the proper run-time test for each type of update and assertion; and a procedure that generates an efficient program for maintaining the correctness of the redundant aggregate information during database updates. Each of these procedures requires little more than a table look-up. The method requires no mechanical theorem proving, and can exploit the full capabilities of the database system's query processor (as in [Stonebraker 75]).

This method represents a qualitatively different approach to integrity enforcement than other published methods. We do not simply incorporate heuristics in a general purpsoe integrity enforcement mechanism and apply the heuristics whenever they seem cost effective. Rather, we define a class of assertions for which the heuristic--maintaining aggregate data--is virtually guaranteed to be cost effective. We can then conclude that any assertion in our class will be enforced efficiently by out method.

Section 2 defines the database model and the restricted class of assertions we consider in this paper. Section 3 presents algorithms to generate fast consistency tests. We use Hoare's program logic [Hoare 69; Hoare and Wirth 73] to prove that these tests are sufficient to guarantee consistency. Implementation issues of accessing and maintaining aggregate data are discussed in Section 4. Finally, in Section 5, we compare our approach with previous work and argue that our approach has low cost.

*This work was supported by the National Science Foundation under grants MCS-77-05314, MCS-79-07762, and MCS-79-08365,

2. Modelling Databases, Assertions and Updates

2.1 Relational Data Model

We use relations as our underlying data model. A database is described by a *database schema*, which consists of a set of relation schemas. Each *relation schema* consists of a relation name, say R, and a set of attributes, say $\{A_1,\ldots,A_n\}$, and is denoted by $R(A_1,\ldots,A_n)$. An example database schema that we use throughout this paper appears in Fig. 1.

A *state* of a relation schema $R(A_1\ldots,A_n)$ is a relation, R, which is a subset of $dom(A_1)\times\ldots\times dom(A_1)$ where $dom(A_i)$ is the *domain* of values for A_i. A *database state* D of database schema $D=\{R_1,\ldots R_n\}$ is a set of relations $\{R_1,\ldots,R_n\}$ where R_i is a state of R_i, i = 1,...n.

2.2 The Assertion Language

We express assertions in a language much like relational calculus [Codd 72]. The symbols of our language include

variables
- -relation symbols (e.g., R,S);
- -tuple variable symbols (e.g., r, which denotes a tuple of a relation);
- -indexed tuple variable symbols (e.g., r.B, which denotes the B attribute of tuple r);

parameters
- -constant symbols (including "true", "false", and the rational numbers);
- - function symbols, including arithmetic functions (e.g., +,×,-);
- -predicate symbols, including arithmetic relations (e.g., =,≤ , etc.);
- -the quantifiers ∀ and ∃ ;
- -boolean operators (e.g.,¬ , ∧,∨ , ⇒).

Assertions are well-formed formulas (abbr. wffs) as in relational calculus, where terms are indexed tuple variables and constants and clauses are formed in the usual way. (Unlike relational calculus, the range of a quantifier can only be a single relation.) A[x/y] denotes a wff A with x substituted for all occurrences of y,

A *structure* for our language interprets the parameters and assigns a universe to the variables. It assigns a value to each constant symbol, a function to each function symbol (with the standard interpretation of arithmetic function symbols), a relation to each predicate symbol (with the standard interpretation of arithmetic relations), and a set of relations to each relation symbol (the set of possible states of each relation schema). An *interpretation* of our language includes a structure and a database state. In what follows, we assume a fixed structure; only the database state can change as a result of program execution.

Example 1 - Assertions

(a) English assertion: No item may be sold at a loss.
Assertion:* ∀buys∈BUYS ∀sells∈SELLS
(buys.ITEM=sells.ITEM ⇒ buys.COST<sells.PRICE)

(b) English assertion: Items can only be bought by cases.
Assertion: ∀buys∈BUYS ∃packs∈PACKS
(buys.ITEM=packs.ITEM∧buys.QUANTITY÷packs.#PER-CASE)
where x ÷ y ≡ x is an integer multiple of y. □

(We will use ≡ to abbreviate "is defined as")

Figure 1
An Example Database Schema

DATABASE SCHEMA: D = {BUYS,SELLS,PACKS}
RELATION SCHEMAS:

BUYS(INVOICE#,DEPT,ITEM,QUANTITY,COST)
An invoice entry records a department buying a quantity of an item at a certain cost per item.

SELLS(INVOICE#,DEPT,ITEM,QUANTITY,PRICE)
An invoice entry records a department selling a quantity of an item at a certain price per item.

PACKS(ITEM,CASE-TYPE,#-PER-CASE)
A certain number of items are packed in each type of case (e.g., 'economy', 'jumbo', etc.)

ATTRIBUTES:

Attribute name	Domain
DEPT,ITEM,CASE-TYPE	Alphanumeric strings
INVOICE#,QUANTITY,#-PER-CASE	Nonnegative integers
COST,PRICE	Positive real numbers with two decimal places

2.3 A New Class of Assertions

Our assertion language is very powerful, making it potentially quite expensive to preserve the consistency of an arbitrary assertion. The purpose of this paper is to demonstrate methods for preserving the consistency of a restricted class of assertions, called two-free assertions.

An assertion is *two-free* if it is of the form: 1)∀r∈R∀s∈S(P(r,s) ⇒ r.A≤s.B), or 2) ∀r∈R∃s(P(r,s) ∧r.A≤s.B), or 3) ∃r∈R∀s∈S(P(r,s) ∧ r.A≤s.B), where r.A and s.B have the same underlying domain, P is a wff, r and s are the only free tuple variables in P, and no bound tuple variable in P has the same range as r or s.* □

We will only consider updates to relations whose tuple variables are free in P. In our examples, P is a function of r and s only. If R and S are the same relation, we perform tests for an update to R and for an update to S.

The assertions in Ex. 1 are two-free. In Ex. 1b,

∀buys ∈BUYS ∃packs ∈PACKS(buys.ITEM=packs.ITEM
∧ buys.QUANTITY ÷ packs.#-PER-CASE),

integer division defines a partial order. While we could denote the partial order by the symbol ≤, we use ÷ to avoid confusion with the standard arithmetic ordering.

* We use ∀buys ∈ BUYS(...) to abbreviate the more complex but formally correct (∀buys)(BUYS(buys) ⇒(...)).

In this paper, "assertion" refers only to two-free assertions. Assertions of forms 1, 2, and 3 are called ∀∀-assertions, ∀∃-assertions, and ∃∀-assertions, respectively. We fix the order of the quantifiers and require that the r quantifier precede the s quantifier.

2.4 Simple Updates

In this paper we consider only *simple* updates: single-tuple insertions and single-tuple deletions. An in-place modification of an existing tuple is modelled currently by a deletion followed by an insertion; techniques for handling these updates directly will appear in a future paper. We model updates with assignment statements. Given a tuple r_0 and a relation R, "$R:=R \cup r_0$" denotes an insertion of r_0 into R, and "$R:=R- r_0$" denotes a deletion of r_0 from R. (We have dropped the usual set brackets, "{}", from enclsing r_0 to avoid confusion with the notation of Hoare's logic that follows.) Assignments to R have no effect on other relations in the database.

2.5 Hoare's Logic

We use Hoare's program logic [Hoare 69· Hoare and Wirth 73] to analyze the effects of updates on assertions. Formulas in the logic include formulas of the assertion language and formulas of the form P{u}Q, where P and Q are formulas and u is a program. In our case, u will always be a database update. A *formula* P{u}Q *is true in an interpreation* $I=(\mathcal{S},D)$, where $\mathcal{S}$ is a structure and D is a database state, denoted $\models_I P\{u\}Q$, if whenever *precondition* P is true in I before the update then *postcondition* Q is true in $(\mathcal{S},u(D))$, where u(D) is the database state after u executes. The logic is a set of axioms and inference rules that permits us to determine, whenever provable, if a formula is true in all database states (see Fig.2). We use $\vdash P\{u\}Q$ to denote that the formula P{u}Q is provable in the logic.

Figure 2
Axioms of Hoare's Program Logic

General form: $\dfrac{E_1 E_2 \ldots E_n}{E}$ **if** $E_1 \wedge E_2 \wedge \ldots \wedge E_n$ **then** E

Assignment Axiom: $\vdash P[y/x]\{x:=y\}P$

Composition Axiom: $\dfrac{\vdash P\{Q_1\}R_1 \quad \vdash R_1\{Q_2\}R}{\vdash P\{Q_1;Q_2\}R}$

Conditional Axiom: $\dfrac{\vdash P \wedge B\{S\}Q \quad \vdash P \wedge \neg B \Rightarrow Q}{\vdash P\{\textbf{if}\ B\ \textbf{then}\ S\}Q}$

Alternative Axiom: $\dfrac{\vdash P \wedge B\{S_1\}Q \quad \vdash P \wedge \neg B\{S_2\}Q}{\vdash P\{\textbf{if}\ B\ \textbf{then}\ S_1\ \textbf{else}\ S_2\}Q}$

Consequence Rule: $\dfrac{\vdash P\{Q\}R \quad \vdash S \Rightarrow P \quad \vdash R \Rightarrow T}{\vdash S\{Q\}T}$

----

* Assertions of the above form prefixed by ∃r∈R∃s∈S can also be handled by our method. However, extra technical machinery is required to do so. Since examples of such assertions are few and, for the most part, contrived, we choose not to discuss them in this paper.

It follows from the soundness of the logic that if $\vdash P\{u\}Q$, then for all database states D, $\models_{(\mathcal{S},D)} P\{u\}Q$ [Clarke 79].

A database state D is *consistent* with an assertion A iff $\models_{(\mathcal{S},D)} A$. An update u *preserves the consistency* of D with respect to (abbr. w.r.t.) A iff $\models_{(\mathcal{S},D)} A\{u\}A$. We say u *preserves* A if, for all database states D, u preserves the consistency of D w.r.t. A. Note that if $\vdash A\{u\}A$, then u preserves A.

We assume that the database state is consistent prior to the update. ∃∀-assertions are the only ones for which the empty database state is inconsistent. In this case only, we assume that consistency tests for each update are suppressed until an initial consistent state is reached

3. Determining Whether Updates Preserve Consistency

3.1 General Strategy

One way to test that an update, u, preserves the consistency of an assertion A, in a particular state is to perform u and then evaluate A in the new state. If the new state is consistent, then the update is backed-out, thereby undoing its effects.

In view of this potential back-out, it may be preferable to test that u preserves A before u is acutally executed. To accomplish this, we construct a *consistency test*, t, that, for each database state, D, determines whether u preserves D w.r.t. A. We can check that we correctly constructed t by proving the theorem: $\vdash A\{\textbf{if}\ t\ \textbf{then}\ u\}A$. This theorem verifies that t is a correct test for all database states. (If t(D) = false, then u is not executed and the database state is unchanged.) We adopt this strategy of testing consistency before permitting the update. We note that this strategy is essentially the one used in the query modification method proposed by Stonebraker [75].

To *enforce* an assertion A, a database system must provide a consistency test for each update. Assuming the enforcement method is a compile-time algorithm that cannot access the database state, then enforcement amounts to an algorithms that maps each assertion. A and update u into a test t, such that $\vdash A\{\textbf{if}\ t\ \textbf{then}\ u\}A$ and $\vdash A\{\textbf{if}\ \neg t\ \textbf{then}\ u\}\neg A$. For the tests in this paper, the proof of $\vdash A\{\textbf{if}\ t\ \textbf{then}\ u\}\neg A$ should be clear from the proof of $\vdash A\{\textbf{if}\ t\ \textbf{then}\ u\}A$.

To determine a test t for A and u, we could begin by finding the weakest precondition sufficient to ensure the truth of A after u executes, denoted wp(A,u) [Dijkstra 76]; so, $\vdash$wp(A,u){u}A. However, wp(A,u) assumes we know nothing about the database state before u executes. In fact, we *do* know that A holds in that state. So, we can substitute any test t for wp(A,u) such that $\vdash(A \wedge t) \Rightarrow wp(A,u)$. One method for determining t is to substitute the Boolean constant true in each clause of wp(A,u) that A implies; the resulting formula is a correct test (although not necessarily a "minimal" one).

3.2 Trivial Tests

For some combination of two-free assertions and updates, the assertion implies the weakest precondition. That is, $\vdash A \Rightarrow wp(A,u)$. In this case, the consistency test is trivial-- it is simply true, because $\vdash$A{<u>if</u> true <u>then</u> u}A. A trivial consistency test for a particular assertion and update means that the update preserves the assertion. For such updates, the database system does not need to do any work to enforce the assertion.

<u>Example 2</u> - <u>A Trivial Test</u>

<u>Assertion</u>: (as in Ex. 1a)
<u>Update</u>: SELLS:=SELLS-sells$_0$, where sells$_0$ is an arbitrary tuple in SELLS
<u>Claim</u>: The update preserves A, so no consistency test is required. Formally stated,
$\vdash$A{SELLS:=SELLS-sells$_0$}A

<u>Proof</u>.

1. $\forall$buys$\in$BUYS$\forall$sells$\in$SELLS P(buys,sells)
   $\Rightarrow$ $\forall$buys$\in$BUYS$\forall$sells$\in$(SELLS-sells$_0$)P(buys,sells)
   ; by def. of two-free, there are no variables other than buys and sells bound to BUYS and SELLS in P.
2. $\vdash$A $\Rightarrow$ A[SELLS-sells$_0$/SELLS]
   ; 1 and def. of substitution
3. $\vdash$A[SELLS-sells$_0$/SELLS]{SELLS:=SELLS-sells$_0$}A
   ; Assignment axiom.
4. $\vdash$A{SELLS:=SELLS-sells$_0$}A
   ; 1,2, and Consequence Rule. □

3.3 Using Stored Aggregates to Simplify Consistency Tests

We can simplify all nontrivial consistency tests further, provided certain aggregate values--minima and maxima of certain domains--are maintained.

Let V be a set whose domain is partially ordered by $\leq$. We define $MIN(V,\leq) \equiv \{v\in V | \neg(\exists v'\in V)(v'<v)\}$, where (v'<v) abbreviates $((v'\leq v) \wedge (v'\neq v))$. Similarly, $MAX(V,\leq) \equiv \{v\in V | \neg(\exists v'\in V)(v<v')\}$. Note that MIN and MAX are sets, not necessarily singletons. We assume MIN and MAX are non-empty. When $|MIN(V,\leq)|=1$, we use MIN(V,$\leq$) to abbreviate the unique element in the set (similarly for MAX). When the relevant partial order is clear in context, we drop $\leq$ as a parameter to MIN and MAX.

<u>Example 3</u> - <u>Using a Stored Aggregate to Simplify a Consistency Test</u>

<u>Assertion</u>: same as Ex.1a.
<u>Update</u>: BUYS:=BUYS$\cup$buys$_0$,
where buys$_0$=(494,'toy','whistle',100,.20)
<u>Claim</u>: If A is true before the update then
TEST$\equiv$($\forall$m$\in$MIN({sells.PRICE|sells$\in$SELLS $\wedge$sells.ITEM=buys.ITEM})(buys.COST$\leq$m))
is sufficient to ensure consistency. Formally stated
$\vdash$A{<u>if</u> TEST <u>then</u> BUYS:=BUYS$\cup$buys$_0$}A.

<u>Proof</u>.

1. A$\wedge$A[buys$_0$/BUYS] $\Rightarrow$ A[BUYS$\cup$buys$_0$/BUYS]
   ; defs. of A and U
2. TEST $\Rightarrow$ A[buys$_0$/BUYS]
   ; defs. of A, TEST, and MIN
3. $\vdash$A$\wedge$TEST$\Rightarrow$A[BUYS$\cup$buys$_0$/BUYS]
   ; 1. and 2
4. $\vdash$A[BUYS$\cup$buys$_0$/BUYS]{BUYS:=BUYS$\cup$buys$_0$}A
   ; Assignment axiom
5. $\vdash$A$\wedge$TEST{BUYS:=BUYS$\cup$buys$_0$}A
   ; 3, 4, and Consequence rule
6. $\vdash$A{<u>if</u> TEST <u>then</u> BUYS:=BUYS$\cup$buys$_0$}A
   ; 5 and Conditional axiom

Since we design our tests to promote efficiency, let us briefly discuss here the cost of this method (a fuller discussion is in Section 5.2). If the minimum PRICE of all 'whistle' tuples in SELLS is available, we only need one comparison to evaluate TEXT. By constrast, note that query modification [Stonebraker 75] sets out to prove $\vdash$A{BUYS:=BUYS$\cup$buys$_0$}A and uses the Assignment Axiom to produce the precondition $\forall$sells$\in$SELLS ('whistle'=sells.ITEM$\Rightarrow$.20$\leq$sells.PRICE). Assuming no inverted files, this formula entails searching the entire SELLS relation, checking the ITEM values, and comparing .20 to the PRICE value for every tuple with ITEM='whistle'. If SELLS is inverted on ITEM, then the test must still be made on all 'whistle' tuples in SELLS.

In general, for any two-free assertion A and any simple update u, there is an efficient test t such that $\vdash$A{<u>if</u> t <u>then</u> u}A. Figure 3 shows the test t for each type of assertion and update. In all cases where t is nontrivial, t relies on a MIN or MAX value that must be maintained as redundant information in the database. Efficient methods for locating and maintaining these MIN and MAX values are discussed in Section 4.

The proof of $\vdash$A{<u>if</u> t <u>then</u> u}A for each case included in Fig. 3 is similar to those in Examples 2 and 3; proofs appear in [Bernstein and Blaustein 80].

Figure 3
Consistency test t for assertion A and update u such that $\vdash A\{\underline{if}\ t\ \underline{then}\ u\}A$

Assertion: $\forall r \in R \forall s \in S (P(r,s) \rightarrow r.A \leq s.B)$
Update:

$R:=R \cup r_0$	$\forall m \in MIN(\{s.B \mid s \in S \wedge P(r_0,s)\})\ r_0.A \leq m$
$S:=S \cup s_0$	$\forall m \in MAX(\{r.A \mid r \in R \wedge P(r,s_0)\})\ m \leq s_0.B$
$R:=R-r_0$	TRUE
$S:=S-s_0$	TRUE

Assertion: $\forall r \in R \exists s \in S (P(r,s) \wedge r.A \leq s.B)$
Update:

$R:=R \cup r_0$	$\exists m \in MAX(\{s.B \mid s \in S \wedge P(r_0,s)\})\ r_0.A \leq m$
$S:=S \cup s_0$	TRUE
$R:=R-r_0$	TRUE
$S:=S-s_0$	$\forall r \in \{r \in R \mid P(r,s_0)\}(\exists m \in MAX(\{s.B \mid s \in S-s_0 \wedge P(r,s)\})\ r.A \leq m)$

Assertion: $\exists r \in R \forall s \in S (P(r,s) \wedge r.A \leq s.B)$
Update:

$R:=R \cup r_0$	TRUE
$S:=S \cup s_0$	$\exists m \in MIN(\{r.A \mid r \in R \wedge P(r,s_0) \wedge \forall s \in S (P(r,s) \wedge r.A \leq s.B)\})\ m \leq s_0.B$
$R:=R-r_0$	$\exists m \in MIN(\{r.A \mid r \in R-r_0 \wedge \forall s (P(r,s) \wedge r.A \leq s.B\})\ \forall n \in MIN(\{s.B \mid s \in S\})\ m \leq n$
$S:=S-s_0$	TRUE

3.4 Special Cases

The tests in Fig. 3 are sufficiently general to handle MIN and MAX as sets. The cost of performing a test, then, depends principally on the size of the MIN or MAX set. However, in most common cases MIN and MAX each consist of a single value. Consistency tests for these cases require at most on comparison per update.

Lemma 1. *If $\leq$ defines a lattice and X is a finite set, then there is a single value v which is the greatest lower bound of* MIN(X,$\leq$). *Similarly, there is a single value v' which is the least upper bound of* MAX(X,$\leq$). □

Note that Lemma 1 is only useful for ∀∀-assertions.

Lemma 2. *If $\leq$ defines a total ordering, then* $|MIN(X,\leq)| = |MAX(X,\leq)| = 1$. □

Examples 1-3 use a partial ordering that is also a total ordering. The following example applies our strategy to a different partial order, integer division, and illustrates a case where the MAX values are sets.

Example 4 - A Different Type of Partial Order

Assertion: same as Ex.1b.
Update: PACKS:=PACKS-packs$_0$,
where packs$_0$ = ('whistle','economy',100)

Application of Figure 3:
For a ∀∃-assertion and a deletion from S, Fig. 3 gives TEST ≡ $\forall r \in \{r \in R \mid P(r,s_0)\}(\exists m \in MAX(\{s.B \mid s \in S-s_0 \wedge P(r,s)\})\ r.A \leq m)$ where $\vdash A\{\underline{if}$ TEST $\underline{then}$ $S:=S-s_0\}A$.

Substituting BUYS,PACKS and packs$_0$ for R, S, and s_0 respectively, we obtain:

TEST=∀buys∈{buys∈BUYS|buys.ITEM='whistle'
(∃m∈MAX({packs.#-PER-CASE|packs∈PACKS-packs$_0$
∧packs.ITEM='whistle'})buys.QUANTITY≤m)

This simplifies to

MAX({buys.QUANTITY|buys∈BUYS∧buys.ITEM='whistle'})
≤ MAX({packs.#-PER-CASE
|packs∈PACKS-packs$_0$∧packs.ITEM='whistle'})

Integer division defines our partial order (m ÷ n means that n divides m), so MAX contains the least common divisors in the set. We take the MAX (or least common divisors) of QUANTITY values of tuples in BUYS with ITEM='whistle' and try to find an integer divisor for each such QUANTITY value from the set of least common divisors of #-PER-CASE values of PACKS tuples with ITEM='whistle'.

4. Implementation

Having discussed our general strategy, we now focus on implementing a system based on this strategy. For any assertion and any update, Fig.3 gives a consistency test. For trivial tests, the update preserves the assertion, so there is nothing to implement. For nontrivial tests, MIN and MAX values are needed. So, to support nontrivial tests, the system must create MIN and MAX values in the database when an assertion is defined, and must maintain these values during updating.

When an assertion is defined and added to the system, the following steps must be taken.

A1. Augment the data description to include appropriate MIN or MAX sets needed for all nontrivial tests.

A2. Compute these MIN and MAX values.

A3. Test that the new assertion is true in the current database state. When an update is processed, the following steps must be taken for each assertion:

U1. Find the appriate test in Fig. 3.

U2. Locate the correct MIN or MAX value.

U3. Perform the test. If it fails, reject the update. Otherwise perform U4 and U5.

U4. Do any necessary bound maintenance.

U5. Execute the update.

We now explain how to perform each of the above steps.

4.1 Identifying Bounds

Step A1 uses Fig.3 to determine which bounds must be included in the data description for non-trivial tests. Suppose Fig. 3 specifies that a MAX of the set {s∈S|P(r,s)} is needed to test consistency when some r∈R is deleted. So, the MAX of this set must be incorporated in the database. It appears that each r∈R has its own set{s∈S|P(r,s)} and its own MAX. Fortunately, fewer sets and MAX's are usually sufficient. The smaller number of sets is obtained by grouping together R tuples that satisfy P for precisely the same S values, since each of these R tuples has the same associated set. For formalize this idea, we define the *equivalence set* of r_0∈R w.r.t. P in state D to be P_{r_0}(D) ≡ {r∈R|in state D, ∀s∈S(P(r_0,s) ⇔ P(r,s))}. We will drop D as a parameter when it is clear in context.

Example 5 - Equivalence Sets of Tuples

Assertion: same as Ex.1b.
Update: (as in Example 4) PACKS:=PACKS-$packs_0$, where $packs_0$= ('whistle','economy',100)

n Ex. 4 we need the MAX of the set {packs.#-PER-CASE |packs∈PACKS-$packs_0$∧packs.ITEM='whistle'}.

This set is simply the projection of P_{packs_0}(D) on #-PER-CASE, where P=(buys.ITEM=packs.ITEM) and D is the state after the deletion. In words, P_{packs_0} is the set of remaining PACKS tuples with ITEM='whistle'. □

Equivalence sets can be indexed by the attributes referenced in P, called *P-attributes*. Let $A_1,\ldots,A_m$ be all the P-attributes for R. Since P is a formula on indexed tuple variables and constants, each $A_1,\ldots,A_m$ value uniquely identifies an equivalence set of R tuples. Therefore, each equivalence set and its relevant bounds can be indexed by P-attribute values.

Example 6 - Identifying Aggegate Values

Assertion: same as Ex.1a.

All BUYS tuples with the same ITEM value are equivalent with respect to this assertion, as are SELLS tuples. We store bounds of COST values indexed by ITEM values for BUYS tuples and bounds of PRICE values indexed by ITEM values for SELLS tuples. □

Executing A1, then, involves identifying the P-attributes of the relations in the assertion and using these P-attribute values to identify stored bound values. A2 computes the MIN or MAX of all tuples in the relation having the same P-attributes. A3 then compares bound values to test the current state. We proceed in Section 4.2 to show how to decide which values must be compared with each other.

4.2 Locating the Correct MIN and MAX Values

The tests in Fig. 3 show which aggregates to store for assertions of each type. Steps A3 and U2 depend on accessing particular bound values. Once the appropriate values are accessed, A3 and U3 simply compare them. Using equivalence sets of tuples reduces the number of bounds stored, and these bounds are easy to locate because they are indexed by attribute values. The only remaining difficulty is to find pairs of equivalence sets from R and S that *simultaneously* satisfy P. That is, given an assertion and P-attribute values for one relation (the one being updated), we need to find the (set of) P-attribute values in the other relation that satisfy P. In this paper, we assume that each tuple has a unique associated equivalence set in the other relation*. Essentially, P is being interpreted as a query.

Example 7 - P as a Query

Assertion: same as Ex.1a.
Update: BUYS:=BUYS $buys_0$, where
$buys_0$=(324,'toy','whistle',100,.10)

Before we can compare .10 with the minimum PRICE value, we must evaluate P(BUYS.ITEM=sells.ITEM), with $buys_0$ substituted for buys, to find the ITEM-value in SELLS which indexes the correct equivalence set. Thus, P acts as a query which finds an ITEM-value in SELLS given a tuple in BUYS.

Even had we not used equivalence sets, it would have been necessary to compare .10 with PRICE values for all tuples satisfying ∀sells∈SELLS('whistle'=sells.ITEM⇒.10≤sells.PRICE). P would have had to be evaluated in exactly the same way. Consistency checking methods must all evaluate the query P and can all use the same mechanism to do so. □

Interpreting P is basic to all consistency testing methods. It is essentially a query optimization problem and can be abstracted from other aspects of consistency verification. We choose to treat it in this way and do not discuss it further in this paper.

4.3 Maintaining Bounds

If an update preserves consistency (the test in U3 succeeds), then we may need to change the bound value of the updated tuple's equivalence set (in step U4). It is not enough for the assertion A to be true after the update; the stored bound value must also be accurate relative to the new database state produced by the update. In effect, we are adding a new precondition and postcondition that describe the accuracy of our bounds. Formally, we must define a formula B that is true in a database state iff the stored bound is accurate in that

*Although our examples deal only with assertions where P is a single equality formula, methods handling general expressions have been developed and will appear in a later paper.

state. We then augment the given update, u, by another update, u_b, that maintains the consistency of the bounds. That is,

$\vdash A \wedge B\{\underline{\text{if}}\ t\ \underline{\text{then}}\ (u_b;u)\}\ A \wedge B.$

For our method to be cost effective, the cost of bound maintenance must not exceed the savings gained in using those bounds to test the consistency of assertions. So, bound maintenance must be efficient. This efficiency is obtained by combining bound maintenance with the consistency test. This combined activity helps when a tuple update does not affect the bound of its equivalence set. Since consistency only depends on bound values, if the bound is unchanged, then the database must be consistent and no consistency test is needed. In such cases, bound maintenance subsumes the consistency test.

Example 9 - Combining Bound Maintenance and Consistency Tests

Assertion: same as Ex.1a.
Update: BUYS:=BUYS∪$buys_0$, where

$buys_0$ = (434,'toy','whistle',500,.05).

Claim: Let MX be the BUYS aggregate used to test consistency of insertions into BUYS. Let B ≡ (MX=MAX({buys.COST |buys∈BUYS∧buys.ITEM='whistle'})). B is an assertion that describes states in which MX has the intended value . We claim that if A ∧ B hold before the update and the update does not force a recalculation of MX, then no consistency test is required. Formally stated

```
⊢A∧B{if .05≤MX then BUYS:=BUYS∪buys₀
       else if .05≤MIN({sells.PRICE
                |sells∈SELLS∧sells.ITEM='whistle'})
            then begin MX:=.05; BUYS:=BUYS∪buys₀ end}A∧B
```

In the above program, if .05≤MX, then the assertion is satisfied, the existing bound (MX) is still correct, and no SELLS tuples need be accessed. If not, a consistency test is performed and, if it yields true, then the stored bound is changed and the update is executed.

Sketch of Proof. Let T1 ≡ (.05≤MAX({buys.COST |buys∈BUYS∧buys.ITEM='whistle'})) and T2 ≡ (.05≤MIN({sells.PRICE |sells∈SELLS∧sells.ITEM='whistle'})).
The proof follows immediately from
⊢A∧B∧T1{BUYS:=BUYS∪$buys_0$}A∧B and
⊢A∧B∧¬T1∧T2{MX:=.05}A[BUYS∪$buys_0$/BUYS] ∧B[BUYS∪$buys_0$/BUYS], using the axioms in Fig. 2.□

Using techniques such as that of Ex. 8, we have produced algorithms that combine consistency testing and bound maintenance for each type of assertion and update. The algorithms are defined by two procedures: CHECK to test consistency and maintain bounds, and MAINT to maintain bounds only (used for trivial tests). These procedures use two consistency tests, called TEST1 and TEST2, and a recalculation of bounds, called BOUND, which are defined in Fig. 4.

```
CHECK(A,U,TEST1,TEST2,BOUND) ≡
begin
/*first compare tuple with its own equivalence set*/
if TEST1 then U;
/*test against other relations and maintain bound*/
else if TEST2 then (call BOUND;U;)
end

MAINT(A,U,TEST1,BOUND) ≡
begin
/*do maintenance if necessary*/
if TEST1 then call BOUND;
U;
end
```

$MX_{P_{r_0}}$ is defined MAX({r.A|r∈P_{r_0}}); similarly for $MN_{P_{r_0}}$, $MX_{P_{s_0}}$ and $MN_{P_{s_0}}$, and $MN_{P_{s_0}}$. $MN'_{P_{r_0}}$ is defined MIN({r.A|r∈P_{r_0} ∧∀s∈S(P(r,s)∧r.A≤s.B)}).

Each combined consistency check and bound maintenance algorithm given by Fig. 4 and the above procedure definitions ensures that A is true and the stored bound is correct after the algorithm is executed.

Figure 4
Comined Integrity Checking and Bound Maintenance

Assertion type: ∀r∀s

UPDATE: R:=R∪r_0; PROCEDURE: CHECK

$TEST1 \equiv (\exists m \in MX_{P_{r_0}})(r_0.A \leq m)$

$TEST2 \equiv (\forall m \in MIN(\{s.B \mid s \in S \wedge P(r_0,s)\}))(r_0.A \leq m)$

$BOUND \equiv MX_{P_{r_0}} := (MX_{P_{r_0}} - \{m \in MX_{P_{r_0}} \mid m < r_0.A\}) \cup \{r_0.A\}$

UPDATE: S:=S∪s_0; PROCEDURE: CHECK

$TEST1 \equiv (\exists m \in MN_{P_{s_0}})(m \leq s_0.B)$

$TEST2 \equiv (\forall m \in MAX(\{r.A \mid r \in R \wedge P(r,s_0)\}))(m \leq s_0.B)$

$BOUND \equiv MN_{P_{s_0}} := (MN_{P_{s_0}} - \{m \in MN_{P_{s_0}} \mid s_0.B < m\}) \cup \{s_0.B\}$

UPDATE: R:=R-r_0; PROCEDURE: MAINT

$TEST1 \equiv r_0.A \in MX_{P_{r_0}}$

$BOUND \equiv MX_{P_{r_0}} := MAX(\{r.A \mid r \in P_{r_0} - r_0\})$

S:=S-s_0; PROCEDURE: MAINT

$TEST1 \equiv s_0.B \in MN_{P_{s_0}}$

$BOUND \equiv MN_{P_{s_0}} := MIN(\{s.B \mid s \in P_{s_0} - s_0\})$

Assertion type: $\forall r \exists s$

$R := R \cup r_0$; PROCEDURE; CHECK

TEST1 $\equiv (\exists m \in MX_{P_{r_0}})(r_0.A \leq m)$

TEST2 $\equiv (\exists m \in MAX(\{s.B \mid s \in S \wedge P(r_0, s)\}))(r_0.A \leq m)$

BOUND $\equiv MX_{P_{r_0}} := (MX_{P_{r_0}} - \{m \in MX_{P_{r_0}} \mid m < r_0.A\}) \cup \{r_0.A\}$

UPDATE: $S \cup s_0$; PROCEDURE; MAINT

TEST1 $\equiv \neg(\exists m \in MX_{P_{s_0}})(s_0.B \leq m)$

BOUND $\equiv MX_{P_{s_0}} := (MX_{P_{s_0}} - \{m \in MX_{P_{s_0}} \mid m < s_0.B\}) \cup \{s_0.B\}$

UPDATE: $R := R - r_0$; PROCEDURE; MAINT

TEST1 $\equiv r_0.A \in MX_{P_{r_0}}$

BOUND $\equiv MX_{P_{r_0}} := MAX(\{r.A \mid r \in P_{r_0} - r_0\})$

UPDATE: $S := S - s_0$; PROCEDURE; CHECK

TEST1 $\equiv \neg(s_0.B \in MX_{P_{s_0}})$

TEST2 $\equiv (\forall m \in MAX(\{r.A \mid r \in R \wedge P(r, s_0)\})$
$\quad \exists n \in MAX(\{s.B \mid s \in P_{s_0} - s_0\}))\ (m \leq n)$

BOUND $\equiv MX_{P_{s_0}} := MAX(\{s.B \mid s \in P_{s_0} - s_0\})$

Assertion type: $\exists r \forall s$

UPDATE: $R := R \cup r_0$; PROCEDURE; MAINT

TEST1 $\equiv \neg(\exists m \in MN'_{P_{r_0}})(m \leq r_0.A)$

BOUND $\equiv MN'_{P_{r_0}} := (MN'_{P_{r_0}} - \{m \in MN'_{P_{r_0}} \mid r_0.A < M\}) \cup \{r_0.A\}$

UPDATE: $S := S \cup s_0$; PROCEDURE: CHECK

TEST1 $\equiv (\exists m \in MN_{P_{s_0}})(m \leq s_0.B)$

TEST2 $\equiv (\exists m \in MIN(\{r.A \mid r \in R \wedge \forall s \in S \quad P(r, s\ )\})$
$\quad \forall n \in MN_{P_{s_0}})\ (m \leq n)$

BOUND $\equiv MN_{P_{s_0}} := (MN_{P_{s_0}} - \{m \in MN_{P_{s_0}} \mid s_0.B < m\}) \cup \{s_0.B\}$

UPDATE: $R := R - r_0$; PROCEDURE; CHECK

TEST1 $\equiv \neg(r_0.A \in MN'_{P_{r_0}})$

TEST2 $\equiv (\exists m \in MIN(\{r.A \mid r \in P_{r_0} - r_0$
$\quad \wedge \forall s \in S(P(r,s) \wedge r.A \leq s.B)\})$
$\quad \forall n \in MIN(\{s.B \mid s \in S \wedge \overline{P}(r_0, s)\}))\quad (m \leq n)$

BOUND $MN'_{P_{r_0}} := MIN(\{r.A \mid r \in P_{r_0} - r_0$
$\quad \wedge \forall s \in S(P(r,s) \Rightarrow r.A \leq s.B)\})$

UPDATE: $S := S - s_0$; PROCEDURE: MAINT

TEST1 $\equiv s_0.B \in MN_{P_{s_0}}$

BOUND $\equiv MN_{P_{s_0}} := MIN(\{s.B \mid s \in P_{s_0} - s_0\})$

---

5. Comparison with Previous Work

5.1 Comparing Approaches

Few systematic approaches to the implementation of semantic integrity assertions have been published; two well-known examples are the query modification method of Stonebraker [75] and the heuristic program analysis of Hammer and Sarin [78]. Let us compare our method to each of these two.

Comparing our method to [Stonebraker 75], we see three main differences: the types of assertions studied, the role of aggregates in assertopms and the cost of consistency testing.

Our class of assertions is a subset of those studied by Stonebraker [75]. We studied only two-variable assertions with certain forms (two-free assertions). Stonebraker studied assertions with any number of variables and with any logical structure. He divided assertions into categories based on the number of variables in the assertion and on the role in the assertion of the relation being updated. Our class of two-free assertions is not directly comparable to his categories, in that two-free assertions include two-variable assertions from each of these categories. We note that the categorization of assertions by Hammer and McLeod [75] is similar to that of [Stonebraker 75], and the above comments apply to their categorization as well.

The impact of aggregates on consistency tests is markedly different in each method. In query modification, assertions involving aggregates are among the most difficult to test, because testing the assertion requires calculating the aggregate. In contrast, our method maintains stored aggregates; often, it is even cost beneficial to transform assertions without aggregates into assertions involving aggregates.

The cost of testing consistency also differs from method to method. In query modification, the modified update often requires significantly more work for evaluation than does the original update. For example, for multivariate assertions with more than one tuple ranging over the relating being updated, the number of clauses to be evaluated is exponential in the number of variables ranging over the relation being updated. This usually leads to a high cost of evaluating the assertion. Even when the number of clauses is small, the modified update may access many tuples of relations referenced in the assertion.

Example 9 - Update Modification

Assertion: same as Ex.1a.
Update: SELLS:=SELLS∪(432,'toy','whistle',30,.75).
Modified Update: Insert (432,'toy','whistle',30,.75) into SELLS where
∀buys∈BUYS(buys.ITEM='whistle')⇒buys.COST≤.75).

All tuples in BUYS must be checked for ITEM≠'whistle' or COST≤.75 before the insertion is done. If BUYS is inverted on ITEM, then |BUYS[ITEM='whistle']| tuples must accessed, compared to only one tuple in our method. □

Section 5.2 discusses cost comparisons more fully.

Hammer and Sarin [Sarin 77; Hammer and Sarin 78] discuss faster methods of evaluating assertions by using knowledge about the update transaction and the assertion to identify specific conditions which may cause a semantic integrity violation. Testing these conditions is often less costly than evaluating the complete assertion on the current database state. This method depends on an analysis of the particular assertion and update transaction. And, the analytic technique is essentially mechanical theorem proving, which is typically slow. By contrast, our algorithms apply to all simple updates and a given class of assertions. And, they do not require any prior analysis of the actual update transaction; all of the analysis is done *a priori* and can be summarized in a table. At run-time, the analysis is no more complex than a table look-up to obtain the appropriate procedures.

5.2 Cost Estimates

It is difficult to quantify the cost of different integrity enforcement methods, yet this task is essential for precisely comparing them. As with any cost model, it is difficult to capture all the factors which affect the final cost and to assign relative costs to each factor. Integrity enforcement costs cannot be accurately determined independent of an actual machine and database because they depend on such factors as the structure of the assertion to be verified, the type and frequency of updates, the storage structure of the database, and even on the actual values in the database and in the update.

Although we cannot define a general and mathematically precise cost model, we can focus on several of the major factors affecting cost. The role of each of these factors in different verification methods helps to determine the condition under which each method works best. The cost of our method is chiefly dependent on:

1. the type of assertion (∀∀, ∀∃, etc.)
2. the ratio of deletions to insertions
3. the probability that the bound of an equivalent set will not change with each update
4. the average size of equivalence sets, and
5. the cost of evaluating P.

With the caveat that our cost equations are only rough estimates, we proceed to characterize the impact of the above factors. We use the resulting formulas only to help compare relative costs and do not try to derive absolute costs from them.

Cost Constants:

Q_S = cost of evaluating P for an updated tuple r_0, i.e., of finding $\{s \in S | P(r_0,s)\}$

Q_R = cost of evaluating P for an updated tuple s_0, i.e., of finding $\{r \in R | P(r,s_0)\}$

M_R = average size of P_{r_0}

M_S = average size of P_{s_0}

c = cost of comparing (≤) two values
d = cost of one database access
P_R = probability that an update changes an R bound
P_S = probability that an update changes an S bound.

Using the algorithms in Section 4.2 and Fig.4, we can derive cost formulas. We describe the derivation for insertions and deletions of R tuples for ∀∀-assertions, and list the formulas for other types of assertions and updates later. We assume that Lemma 1 or 2 holds, so that we have only bound value for each equivalence set (this usually seems to hold in practice since the underlying domain is the set of integers, reals, etc.) Thus, each MIN and MAX set contains only one element. So, accessing a bound costs d and testing a tuple against a bound costs c. Also, assume that P produces one equivalence set per relation (this is only relevant for ∀∃-assertions.)

The algorithm for inserting r_0 for a ∀∀-assertion is CHECK(A,R:=R r_0TEST1 ,TEST2,BOUND). Filling in the appropriate tests and bound assignments we get:

1. <u>if</u> ∃m∈MX≡MAX({r.A|r∈P_{r_0} })r_0.A≤m <u>then</u> R:=R∪r_0;
2. <u>else</u> <u>if</u> ∀m∈MIN({s.B|s∈S∧P(r_0,s)})r_0.A≤m
3. <u>then</u> <u>begin</u> MX:=(MX={m∈MX|m r_0.A})∪{r_0.A};
4. R:=R∪r_0;
<u>end</u>

Evaluating Line 1 involves accessing the stored bound and comparing it to r_0.A, for a cost of d+c.

Line 2 is only executed if the bound must be changed (r_0.A>MAX({r.a|r∈P_{r_0}})), so it only adds to the total cost with probability p_R. Evaluating Line 2 involves evaluating P to find the correct S equivalence set, accessing the stored bound, and comparing it with r_0.A, Thus, line 2 costs $p_R(Q_S+d+c)$.

The rest of the algorithm adds no significant cost. If the test succeeds and Line 3 is executed, we simply store the new bound value. We have already accessed the proper equivalence set, and changing the bound involves no new computation. Line 4 is just the cost of inserting the tuple.

Query modification for insertion to R for a ∀∀-assertion requires evaluating P, accessing each S tuple which satisfies P, and comparing it to the inserted tuple. In our system, the S tuples satisfying P would constitute an equivalence set, so we can denote the number of these S tuples as M_S. Therefore, the cost formula is $Q_S+M_S \cdot d \cdot c$.

Cost formulas for other types of assertions are: 1) Insert to relation with universally quantified tuple variable, d+c+p(Q+d+c), 2) Insert to relation with existentially quantified tuple variable d+c, 3) Delete from relation with univerally quantified tuple variable, d+c+p(Mdc), and 4) Delete from relation with existentially quantified tuple variable, d+c+p(Q+Mdc+c). By Fig. 3, the test for deletion for ∀∀-assertions is trivial, so the cost of query modification in this case is 0.

Note that for ∀∀-assertions, insertion and deletion of S tuples are exactly analogous to those of R tuples.

In performing a comparison of the two methods, we make the following simplifying assumptions: 1) each operation (insert to R, insert to S, delete from R, delete from S) occurs with the same frequency; 2) the average equivalence set size is the same for R as for S ($M_R=M_S$; we will use $M=M_R=M_S$); 3) the query processor is equally efficient given and R tuple or an S tuple ($Q_R=Q_S$; we will use Q to mean either Q_R or Q_S); 4) c is a unit cost, and evaluating P costs more than a database access, which in turn is more than c ($c<d<Q$); and 5) the probability that the bound of an equivalence set will change with a given update is 1/M. Assumption 1 allows us to simply add together the costs for each operation. We drop the c in each formula by Assumption 4 and make the simplifications in Assumption 2, 3, and 5.

Query modification: 2(q+Md)

Our method: 2(d+1/m(Q+d)+d+(1/M)Md
= 2(Q/M+(3+1/M)d)

Comparing these formulas, we see that our method is more efficient (given all the assumptions), when the average equivalence set size is 3 or more. Depending on the cost of evaluating P relative to the cost of a database access, our method may also be efficient for M=2.

Under other assumptions, our method may be even more efficient. For example, if Assumption 1 were changed to model a situation where insertions outnumber deletions, our method would compare even more favorably to query modification. On insertions a bound change only requires comparison with the previous bound; it is not necessary to access all the tuples in the equivalence set. Deletions that cause bound changes are more costly, in that each tuple in the equivalence set must be accessed; but even this process only involves accessing the same number of tuples that query modification accessses on each insertion (i.e., the set of tuples which satisfy P). Furthermore, in most cases ($p_R<1$) bound maintenance will not have to be done for each deletion.

Although the above formulas yield no absolute cost values, they help identify the conditions under which our method is most useful. Whenever stored aggregates of values in an equivalence set can be used frequently to avoid accessing tuples individually, the efficiency of checking integrity offsets the cost of maintaining bounds.

6. Conclusion

The approach to semantic integrity we have described consists of designing a class of assertions that can be efficiently enforced using suitable tactics, and then fully analyzing the compile-time and run-time enforcement algorithms. In this paper, we worked through the analysis for two-free assertions using redundant aggregate data as a tactic. We have carried out this analysis on other classes of assertions with equal success. We believe this approach offers the best hope of developing a semantic integrity subsystem for a database system with acceptable performance.

Acknowledgements

We gratefully acknowledge Marco Casanova, Nathan Goodman, John Smith and Umeshwar Dayal, whose careful reviews of early drafts led to many terminological and organizational improvements. We also wish to thank the referees for their helpful comments and suggestions.

References

[Berstein and Blaustein 80]
Bernstein, P. A.; and Blaustein, B. T., "Efficient Maintenance of Semantic Integrity Assertions Containing Two Tuple Variables", Technical Report Aiken Computation Laboratory, Harvard University, to appear.

[Clarke 79]
Clarke, E. M., "Programming Language Constructs for Which It Is Impossible to Obtain Good Hoare Axiom Systems", JACM 26, 1 (Jan. 1979), 129-147.

[Codd 72]
Codd, E. F., "Relational Completeness of Data Base Sublanguages", in *Data Base Systems*, Courant Computer Science Symposia Seris, Vol.6, Prentice-Hall, Englewood Cliffs, NJ 1972, pp.65-90.

[Dijkstra 76]
Dijkstra, E. W., *A Discipline of Programming*, Prentice-Hall, Englewood Cliffs, NJ, 1976.

[Hammer and McLeod 75]
Hammer, M. M.; and McLeod, D. J., "Semantic Integrity in a Relational Data Base System", in *Proceedings First International Conference on Very Large Data Bases*, 1975, pp.25-47.

[Hammer and Sarin 78]
Hammer, M. M. and Sarin, S., "Efficient Monitoring of Database Assertions", *Proceedings of 1978 SIGMOD Conference on Management of Data*, ACM, NY , 1978.

[Hoare 69]
Hoare, C. A. R., "An Axiomatic Basis for Computer Programming", in *CACM*, Vol.12, No.10, October, 1969.

[Hoare and Wirth 73]
Hoare, C. A. R., and Wirth, N., "An Axiomatic Definition of the Programming Language PASCAL", in *Acta Informatica*, Vol.2, 1973, pp.335-355.

[Sarin 77]
Sarin, S. K., "Automatic Synthesis of Efficient Procedures for Database Integrity Checking", Master's Thesis, Massachusetts Institute of Technology, Sept., 1977.

[Stonebraker 75]
Stonebraker, M., "Implementation of Integrity Constraints and Views by Query Modification", *Proceedings 1975 ACM-SIGMOD Conference*, pp.65-78.

Epilogue

When this paper was first published in 1981, one of its main contributions was its demonstration that a rigorous proof technique, Hoare's program logic, could be used to validate tests of database consistency constraints. Now, at a time when rule-based systems and logic programming are much more widespread, this idea seems to require less emphasis. Perhaps now the proposed strategies for devising efficient tests should receive more attention than the details needed to prove the sufficiency of the tests.

Efficient tests are essential whenever predefined predicates must be evaluated over a partially changing set of data, whether to enforce consistency constraints, process views, monitor exceptions, or enforce security or management policies. We believe that the use of summary or aggregate data, materialized views, and simplified sufficient tests are powerful techniques. More work is needed to devise automated or semi-automated means of identifying, using, and maintaining aggregate data to simplify the evaluations of particular classes of predicates. As more sophisticated and intelligent systems are designed, simplified sufficient tests become even more attractive. If a system can tolerate and even repair certain occasional inconsistencies, then it can benefit from a greater optimistic use of efficient partial tests. The possibility exists for tuning the system, for trading constant consistency and higher overhead for occasional inconsistency and much lower processing time.

A SOPHISTICATE'S INTRODUCTION TO DATABASE NORMALIZATION THEORY[†]

Catriel Beeri

Computer Science Department
The Hebrew University
Jerusalem, ISRAEL

Philip A. Bernstein

Aiken Computation Lab.
Harvard University
Cambridge, MA 02138

Nathan Goodman

Computer Corp. of America
575 Technology Square
Cambridge, MA 02139

Abstract

Formal database semantics has concentrated on dependency constraints, such as functional and multivalued dependencies, and on normal forms for relations. Unfortunately, much of this work has been inaccessible to researchers outside this field, due to the unfamiliar formalism in which the work is couched. In addition, the lack of a single set of definitions has confused the relationships among certain results. This paper is intended to serve the two-fold purpose of introducing the main issues and theorems of formal database semantics to the uninitiated, and to clarify the terminology of the field.

1. INTRODUCTION

1.1 Database Semantics

A database is a collection of information about some enterprise in the world. The role of *database semantics* is to ensure that stored information accurately represents the enterprise. Database semantics studies the creation, maintenance, and interpretation of databases as models of external activities. A wide variety of database semantic tools exist, ranging from *data type* constraints, to *integrity constraints*, to semantic modelling structures used in Artificial Intelligence [26,36,39].

This paper is concerned with a specific type of database semantic tool, namely *data dependencies*--both functional and multi-valued dependencies. This paper surveys the major results in this area. Our aim is to provide a unified framework for understanding these results.

1.2 Database Models

Most work on data dependencies uses the *relational* data model, with which we assume reader familiarity at the level of [16]. Briefly, a relational database consists of a set of *relations* defined on certain *attributes*. R(X) is our notation for a relation named R defined on a set of attributes X.[1] The relation R(X) is a set of m-*tuples*, where $m=|X|$. A relation can be visualized as a *table* whose columns are labelled with attributes and whose rows depict tuples. Fig. 1 illustrates a relation in this way. The data manipulation operators used in this paper are *projection* and *natural join*. The projection of relation R(X) on attributes T is denoted R[T]. If V=X-T, $R[T] = \{\langle t\rangle \mid \langle t,v\rangle \in R(X)\}$, and is defined iff $T \subseteq X$. (If we visualize R as a table, R[T] is those columns of R labelled with elements of T.) The natural join of relations R and S is denoted R*S. Given R(X,Y) and S(Y,Z), where X,Y,Z are disjoint sets, $R*S = \{\langle x,y,z\rangle \mid \langle x,y\rangle \in R \text{ and } \langle y,z\rangle \in S\}$.

Functional and multivalued dependencies are predicates on relations. Intuitively, a *functional dependency* (abbr. FD) $f:X\rightarrow Y$ holds in R(X,Y,Z) iff each value of X in R is associated with exactly one value of Y (see Fig. 1). The truth-value of f can of course vary over time, since the contents of R can vary over time. A multivalued dependency (abbr. MVD) $g:X\twoheadrightarrow Y$ holds in R iff each X-value in R is associated with a set of Y-values in a way that does not depend on Z-values (see Fig. 1). FDs and MVDs are defined formally in the next section.

FIGURE 1. A relation with functional and multi-valued dependencies

Relation: RENTAL-UNITS
Attributes: LANDLORD,ADDRESS,APT#,RENT,OCCUPANT,PETS
Functional dependencies:
ADDRESS,APT# → RENT--Each unit has one rental
OCCUPANT → ADDRESS,APT#--Every occupant lives in one unit
Multivalued dependencies:
LANDLORD ↠ ADDRESS--Each landlord can own many buildings
OCCUPANT ↠ PETS --Each occupant may have several pets
Tuples:

LANDLORD,	ADDRESS,	APT#,	RENT,	OCCUPANT,	PETS
Wizard,	Oz,	#3,	$ 50,	Tinman,	Oilcan
Wizard,	Oz,	#1,	$ 50,	Witch,	Bat
Wizard,	Oz,	#1,	$ 50,	Witch,	Snake
Wizard,	Oz,	#2,	$ 75,	Lion,	Mouse
Codd,	3 NF St,	#1,	$500,	Beeri,	Fish
Codd,	3 NF St,	#1,	$500,	Bernstein,	Dog
Codd,	3 NF St,	#1,	$500,	Bernstein,	Rhino
Codd,	3 NF St,	#2,	$600,	Goodman,	Cat

[†]This work was supported in part by the National Science Foundation under Grant MCS-77-05314.

[1]More generally, the notation R(X,Y,Z,...) denotes relation R defined on $X \cup Y \cup Z \cup \ldots$.

1.3 Description vs. Content

The interplay between database *description* and database *content* is a major theme in database semantics. A database description is called a *schema*, and contains descriptions for each relation in the database. The description of a single relation is called a *relation scheme* and consists of the relation name, its attributes and a set of data dependencies. $\underline{R}$=<T,Γ> denotes a relation scheme $\underline{R}$ with attributes T and dependencies Γ (see Fig. 2). We sometimes use the notation $\underline{R}$(T) when Γ is either unknown or irrelevant.

FIGURE 2. Formal notation for a relation scheme based on Figure 1.

```
RENTAL-UNITS =
  <{LANDLORD,ADDRESS,APT#,RENT,OCCUPANT,PETS},
   {ADDRESS,APT# → RENT;
    OCCUPANT → ADDRESS,APT#;
    LANDLORD →→ ADDRESS;
    OCCUPANT →→ PETS}>
```

The contents of a relation is called the *state* or *extension* of the corresponding scheme, and is a set of tuples as stated above. R(T) denotes an extension of $\underline{R}$ = <T,Γ>. If R(T) satisfies all dependencies in Γ, it is called an *instance* of $\underline{R}$ (notationally, R denotes an instance of $\underline{R}$). A *relational database* for a schema is a collection of instances, one for each relation scheme in the schema.

In summary, *schema* and *scheme* are syntactic objects; *database* and *relation* refer to database content. The distinction between schema-related and content-related concepts is often subtle yet important, and we keep it sharp in this paper.

1.4 The Universal Relation Assumption

Most work on data dependencies assumes that all relations in a database are projections of a single relation. Formally, suppose $R_1(T_1)$, $R_2(T_2),\ldots,R_n(T_n)$ is a database of interest, and let $T = \bigcup_{1\leq i\leq n} T_i$. It is assumed that a *universal relation* U(T) exists, such that $R_i = U[T_i]$ for $1\leq i\leq n$.

This "universal relation assumption" is a controversial issue in the field. On the one hand, it has formal advantages: it permits us to specify relations solely in terms of their attributes; also it supports the FD and MVD *uniqueness* rule which states that syntactically identical dependencies are semantically equivalent. On the other hand, many practical applications do not naturally conform to the assumption; to force these applications into the universal relation mold places an added burden on the database administrator, and can obscure desired relationships in the database. The reader should note that all results in this paper make the universal relation assumption, and in some cases they do not extend to alternative frameworks.

1.5 Topics

Formal work in database semantics falls roughly into the areas of *schema design* and *data manipulation*. We limit our attention to the first area, though some of the work we cover has application in the second area also. The problem of schema design is: Given an initial schema, find an *equivalent* one that is *better* in some respect. As we will see, different definitions of "equivalent" and "better" lead to startlingly different results.

The paper is organized as follows. Section 2 formally defines data dependencies and reviews their basic properties. Section 3 states the schema design problem more precisely. Then Sections 4, 5 and 6 examine several definitions of schema "equivalence" and several criteria for one schema to be "better" than another. Section 7 ties these ideas together by looking at specific schema design methods. We conclude with an historical look at our field and predications for its future.

2. DATA DEPENDENCIES

2.1 Definition and Basic Properties

An FD is a statement of the form F:X→Y, where X and Y are sets of attributes. f is *defined* for a relation R(T) or a relation scheme $\underline{R}$(T) if X and Y are subsets of T. If f is defined for R, then f is a predicate on R's state; f is *valid* in R iff every two tuples of R that have the same X-value also have the same Y-value. From the definition we see that f's validity depends only on the values assigned to X and Y. We say that FDs enjoy the *projectivity* and *inverse projectivity* properties: For sets $X,Y \subseteq T' \subseteq T$, X→Y is valid in R(T) iff it is valid in R[T'].

An MVD is a statement of the form g:X→→Y. g is *defined* for R(T) or $\underline{R}$(T) if X and Y are subsets of T. Let $Z = T-(X \cup Y)$. For a Z-value, z, we define $Y_{xz} = \{y \mid <x,y,z> \in R\}$. g is *valid* in R iff $Y_{xz} = Y_{xz'}$ for each x,z,z' such that Y_{xz} and $Y_{xz'}$ are nonempty. This definition implies that g's validity depends on values assigned to Z, not just X and Y. If g is valid in R(T), then it is valid in all projections of R(T); the converse, however, does not hold. MVDs thus enjoy the *projectivity* property but *not inverse projectivity*.

The FD X→Y states that a unique Y-value is associated with each X-value; the MVD X→→Y states that a unique *set* of Y-values is associated with each X-value. So essentially, an FD is just an MVD plus a functionality condition.

2.2 Inference Rules for Dependencies

Given a set of dependencies in a relation, it is often possible to deduce other dependencies that also hold in that relation. Consider once again the relation in Fig. 1. By examining its contents we see that OCCUPANT→RENT and LANDLORD→ADDRESS hold, although neither is expressly stated. This is not coincidental; these two FDs are logical consequences of the given set of FDs and MVDs.

Given a schema $\underline{R}$ = <T,Γ>, and a dependency g, Γ *implies* g *in* $\underline{R}$ if g holds in every instance of R. Note that a dependency g' may hold in *some* instances of $\underline{R}$ without being implied by Γ. For example, ADDRESS→LANDLORD holds in Fig. 1 although it is *not* implied by the given dependencies.

It is possible to tell whether g is implied by Γ using systems of *inference rules* [3,6]. Inference rules permit us to derive new dependencies implied by a given set. A system of inference rules is *complete* if (a) every g derivable from Γ is in fact implied by Γ, and (b) every g implied by Γ is derivable using the rules. Fig. 3 shows three complete systems of inference rules for FDs and MVDs. The FD-rules are complete when FDs only are considered. The MVD-rules are complete for MVDs. When FDs and MVDs are considered, all three systems are needed for completeness. Fig. 3 also presents other rules that are useful, though not needed.

FIGURE 3. Inference rules for FDs and MVDs [3,6]

FD-rules:

FD_1 (reflexivity): If $Y \subseteq X$ then $X \to Y$.

FD_2 (augmentation): If $Z \subseteq W$ and $X \to Y$ then $XW \to YZ$.

FD_3 (transitivity): If $X \to Y$ and $Y \to Z$ then $X \to Z$.

Other useful rules:

FD_4 (pseudo-transitivity): If $X \to Y$ and $YW \to Z$ then $XW \to Z$.

FD_5 (union): If $X \to Y$ and $X \to Z$ then $X \to YZ$.

FD_6 (decomposition): If $X \to YZ$ then $X \to Y$ and $X \to Z$.

MVD-rules:

MVD_0 (complementation): Let $X+Y+Z=U$ and $Y \cap Z \subseteq X$; then $X \twoheadrightarrow Y$ iff $X \twoheadrightarrow Z$.

MVD_1 (reflexivity): If $Y \subseteq X$ then $X \twoheadrightarrow Y$.

MVD_2 (augmentation): If $Z \subseteq W$ and $X \twoheadrightarrow Y$ then $XW \twoheadrightarrow YZ$.

MVD_3 (transitivity): If $X \twoheadrightarrow Y$ and $Y \twoheadrightarrow Z$ then $X \twoheadrightarrow Z-Y$.

Other useful rules:

MVD_4 (pseudo-transitivity): If $X \twoheadrightarrow Y$ and $YW \twoheadrightarrow Z$ then $XW \twoheadrightarrow Z-YW$.

MVD_5 (union): If $X \twoheadrightarrow Y$ and $X \twoheadrightarrow Z$ then $X \twoheadrightarrow YZ$.

MVD_6 (decomposition): If $X \twoheadrightarrow Y$ and $X \twoheadrightarrow Z$ then $X \twoheadrightarrow Y \cap Z$, $X \twoheadrightarrow Y-Z$, $X \twoheadrightarrow Z-Y$.

FD-MVD rules:

$FD\text{-}MVD_1$: If $X \to Y$ then $X \twoheadrightarrow Y$.

$FD\text{-}MVD_2$: If $X \twoheadrightarrow Z$ and $Y \to Z'$, $Z' \subseteq Z$, and if Y and Z are disjoint, then $X \to Z'$.

Another useful rule:

$FD\text{-}MVD_3$: If $X \twoheadrightarrow Y$ and $XY \to Z$ then $X \to Z-Y$.

The set of all dependencies derivable from Γ using a complete system of rules is called the *closure of* Γ, denoted Γ^+. From the foregoing it should be clear that Γ^+ is the exact set of dependencies implied by Γ.

2.3 The Membership Problem

Given a set of dependencies Γ and a dependency g, the *membership problem* is to tell whether $g \in \Gamma^+$. For $g: X \to Y$ and Γ containing just FDs this problem is solved by determining the *maximum* set Z such that $X \to Z$ is in Γ^+. Then (by rules FD_5 and FD_6, Fig.3), $g \in \Gamma^+$ iff $Y \subseteq Z$. Z can be computed as follows:

1. Initialize $Z := X$. (Since $X \to X$ by FD_1.)
2. If $U \to V$ is in Γ and $U \subseteq Z$, then set $Z := Z+V$.
3. Repeat step 2 until more attributes can be added to Z.

A straightforward implementation yields an $O(n^2)$ time algorithm [7]; linear time implementation of this algorithm is described in [5].

For MVDs the best known membership algorithm requires $O(n^4)$ time [4].

2.4 Coverings

A *covering* of Γ is any set $\hat{\Gamma}$ such that $\hat{\Gamma}^+ = \Gamma^+$. $\hat{\Gamma}$ is *nonredundant* if no proper subset of it is a covering. One can obtain a nonredundant covering of Γ as follows. A dependency $g \in \Gamma$ is redundant iff $g \in (\Gamma - \{g\})^+$. For each $g \in \Gamma$ the above test is performed using the membership algorithm, and g is removed from Γ if it is found to be redundant.

2.5 Inherently Difficult Dependency Problems

We list here two inherently difficult dependency problems. Other such problems are presented in [5,28].

Key Finding: Given a set of FDs F over attributes U, a relation scheme $\underline{R}(X)$ where $X \subseteq U$, and a subset of R's keys, determine whether $\underline{R}$ has any other keys. This problem is NP-complete [5] (i.e., probably requires exponential time [2]).

Key Listing: Given F and $\underline{R}$ as above, list all keys of $\underline{R}$. This problem has exponential worst-case time since there are relation schemes with an exponential number of keys [40].

3. THE SCHEMA DESIGN PROBLEM

We now return to the problem of schema design. Our treatment considers one particular schema design scenario. We assume that a schema S_ϕ containing a single relation scheme is given. The problem is to design a schema S_D that is *equivalent* to S_ϕ, but is *better* in some specified way. Let $S_\phi = \{\underline{U} = \langle T, \Gamma \rangle\}$ and $S_D = \{\underline{R_i} = \langle T_i, \Gamma_i \rangle \mid i=1,\ldots,n\}$. In our scenario S_D contains "projections" of $\underline{U}$; i.e., each $T_i \subseteq T$ and Γ_i is "inherited" from Γ. For FDs, "inheritance" means Γ_i is a covering of the FDs in Γ^+ that are defined for $\underline{R_i}$. For MVDs, the situation is more complicated and will not be elaborated here. An instance U of $\underline{U}$ is represented in S_D's database by $\{U[T_i] \mid i=1,\ldots,n\}$.

Our study of schema design can now be considered to be a study of the mapping between S_ϕ and S_D and between the set of instances of S_ϕ and the sets of instances of S_D.

4. THE PRINCIPLE OF REPRESENTATION

A clear requirement for schema S_D to replace S_ϕ is that S_D and S_ϕ be equivalent; that is, S_D must *represent the same information* as S_ϕ. Different researchers formulate this concept in different ways--ways that lead to startingly different conclusions. In the following, let $S_\phi = \{\underline{U} = \langle T, \Gamma \rangle\}$ and $S_D = \{\underline{R_i} = \langle T_i, \Gamma_i \rangle \mid i=1,\ldots,n\}$.

Definition Rep1. S_D represents the same information as S_ϕ if they contain the same attributes; that is, if $\cup_{i=1}^{n} T_i = T$.

This definition is inadequate because it ignores relationships among attributes. By this definition, the schemas in Figs. 4 and 5 are equivalent to the one in Fig. 2, even though they contain no data dependencies.

FIGURE 4. A schema equivalent to one in Fig. 2 under Def. Rep1.

$$S_D = \{\underline{R}_1, \underline{R}_2, \underline{R}_3\}$$

$\underline{R}_1$ = <{LANDLORD,RENT,PETS},{}>

$\underline{R}_2$ = <{ADDRESS,APT#},{}>

$\underline{R}_3$ = <{OCCUPANT},{}>

FIGURE 5. Another schema equivalent to one in Fig. 2 under Rep1.

$$S_D = \{\underline{R}_1, \underline{R}_2, \underline{R}_3, \underline{R}_4, \underline{R}_5, \underline{R}_6\}$$

$\underline{R}_1$ = <LANDLORD,{}>

$\underline{R}_2$ = <RENT,{}>

$\underline{R}_3$ = <ADDRESS,{}>

$\underline{R}_4$ = <APT#,{}>

$\underline{R}_5$ = <OCCUPANT,{}>

$\underline{R}_6$ = <PETS,{}>

Definition Rep2. S_D represents the same information as S_ϕ if they have the same attributes and the same data dependencies.

When only FDs are involved, this definition can be made precise. The FDs of S_ϕ are Γ^+. The FDs of S_D are $(\cup_{i=1}^{n}\Gamma_i)^+$. S_D represents S_ϕ if $\Gamma^+ = (\cup_{i=1}^{n}\Gamma_i)^+$, i.e., if $(\cup_{i=1}^{n}\Gamma_i)$ is a covering of Γ.

However, there is a problem with the definition as stated. The inference rules in Sec. 2 are only defined with respect to dependencies in a *single* relation. Since S_D involves *multiple* relations, it is not obvious that those inference rules can validly be applied to it. Suppose, $S_\phi = \{\underline{U} = \langle T = \{X,Y,Z\}, \Gamma = \{X \to Y; Y \to Z\}\rangle$, and $S_D = \{\underline{R}_1 = \langle T_1 = \{X,Y\}, \Gamma_1 = \{X \to Y\}\rangle; \underline{R}_2 = \langle T_2 = \{Y,Z\}, \Gamma_2 = \{Y \to Z\}\rangle\}$. Notice that $X \to Z$ is in Γ^+ and that S_D represents S_ϕ by the above definition. Yet S_D does not even contain a relation scheme in which $X \to Z$ is defined!

This problem is rectified by the "universal relation assumption" (Sec. 1) and the "inverse projectivity property of FDs" (Sec. 2). Let R_1 and R_2 be instances of $\underline{R}_1$ and $\underline{R}_2$; define $\underline{R}_{12} = \langle T_{12} = T_1 \cup T_2, \Gamma_{12} = \Gamma_1 \cup \Gamma_2\rangle$; and define $R_{12} = R_1 * R_2$. From the inverse projectivity property it can be shown that R_{12} is an instance of $\underline{R}_{12}$ if R_1 and R_2 are instances of $\underline{R}_1$ and $\underline{R}_2$. Thus the FD $X \to Z$ (which is in Γ_{12}^+) is valid in R_{12}. Moreover, by the universal relation assumption R_1 and R_2 are projections of U, as is $R_{12}[XZ]$. Consequently the user can obtain the "extension" of $X \to Z$ from S_D, even though $X \to Z$ is not explicitly represented. In fact, all FD inference rules can be "simulated" by relational operators applied to relations containing the FDs. It follows that all FDs in Γ^+ can be retrieved from S_D if S_D's schemes contain a covering of Γ.

MVDs, on the other hand, do not possess the inverse projectivity property, and definition Rep2 is not easily generalized to them. More research is needed to formulate a suitable generalization of Rep2 for MVDs.

Definition Rep3. S_D represents the same information as S_ϕ if they have the same attributes and the databases of S_D contain the same data as the databases of S_ϕ.

In contrast to Rep2, this definition stresses the data component of equivalence. Two schemas are equivalent under Rep3 if at all times their databases contain the same information, albeit in different formats.

The definition is formalized by the concept of *lossless join* [1]. Suppose U(T) is an instance of $\underline{U}$ and the corresponding set of instances of S_D is $\{R_i(T_i) = U[T_i] \mid i=1,\ldots,n\}$. To answer a query involving, say, all attributes of T, we must reconstruct U from $\{R_i\}$ via the join operator. If $U = R_1 * \ldots * R_n$, then U can be precisely reconstructed from its projections. If, however, $U \subset R_1 * \ldots * R_n$, the join contains tuples that are not in U, and $\{R_i\}$ is not a faithful representation. This phenomenon is called a *lossy join* and is illustrated in Fig. 6.

FIGURE 6. An Example of a lossy join.

Let S_ϕ = {RENTAL-UNITS} defined in Fig. 2, with instance of Fig. 1.

Let S_D = {LAND-APT#,APT#-RENT,PERSON-PETS}

LAND-APT# = <{LANDLORD,APT#},{}>
APT#-RENT = <{APT#,RENT},{}>
PERSON-PETS = <{OCCUPANT,PETS,ADDRESS}, {OCCUPANT→ADDRESS;OCCUPANT→→PETS}>

Instances corresponding to Fig. 1 are

LAND-APT#(LANDLORD,APT#)

LANDLORD	APT#
Wizard,	#1
Wizard,	#1
Wizard,	#2
Codd,	#1
Codd,	#2

APT#-RENT(APT#,RENT)

APT#	RENT
#3,	$ 50
#1,	$ 50
#2,	$ 75
#1,	$500
#2,	$600

LAND-APT#*APT#-RENT =

Attributes: LANDLORD, APT#, RENT

Tuples:

LANDLORD	APT#	RENT
Wizard,	#3,	$ 50
Wizard,	#1,	$ 50
Wizard,	#1,	$500
Wizard,	#2,	$ 75
Wizard,	#2,	$600

FIGURE 6 continued

Attributes:	LANDLORD,	APT#,	RENT
Tuples:	Codd,	#1,	\$ 50
	Codd,	#1,	\$500
	Codd,	#2,	\$ 75
	Codd,	#2,	\$600

Note that each LANDLORD is associated with RENTs charged by the other.

Formally we say that S_D has the *lossless join property* if for each instance U of U,

$$U = \mathop{*}_{i=1}^{n} U[T_i].$$

When only pairs of relations are considered, we have the following results.

FACT 1: If $\underline{U} = \langle T,F \rangle$ (that is, only FDs are given) then for sets T_1, T_2 such that $T_1 \cup T_2 = T$, $\{\underline{R}_1(T_1), \underline{R}_2(T_2)\}$ has the lossless join property iff either $T_1 \cap T_2 \rightarrow T_1$ or $T_1 \cap T_2 \rightarrow T_2$ is in Γ^+ [33].

FACT 2: For $\underline{U} = \langle T,\Gamma \rangle$ and for T_1, T_2 as above, $\{\underline{R}_1(T_1), \underline{R}_2(T_2)\}$ has the lossless join property iff $T_1 \cap T_2 \twoheadrightarrow T_1$ (and, by rule MVD_0, $T_1 \cap T_2 \twoheadrightarrow T_2$) is in Γ^+ [23].

These facts are stated as properties of universally quantified sets of instances; i.e., the conditions of Facts 1 & 2 hold iff *all* instances of the given schemas have lossless joins. It is possible, though, for the conditions not to hold, yet for *specific* instances to have lossless joins, nonetheless. Facts 1 & 2 can be adapted for specific instances as follows.

FACT 1': Given $\underline{U} = \langle T,\Gamma \rangle$, and T_1, T_2 as above. An instance $U = U[T_1]*U[T_2]$ if (but *not* only if) $T_1 \cap T_2 \rightarrow T_1$ or $T_1 \cap T_2 \rightarrow T_2$ holds in U.

FACT 2': Given $\underline{U} = \langle T,\Gamma \rangle$, and T_1, T_2 as above. An instance $U = U[T_1]*U[T_2]$ iff $T_1 \cap T_2 \twoheadrightarrow T_1$ (and by MVDs $T_1 \cap T_2 \twoheadrightarrow T_2$) holds in U.

When more than pairs of relations are considered, the situation is more complex. An algorithm for deciding the lossless join property in general is presented in [1]. The algorithm requires polynomial time for FDs but may require exponential time for MVDs. Another interesting result is that for all $n > 2$ there are sets of n relation schemes that have the lossless join property, for which no proper subset has this property.

Definition Rep4. S_D represents the same information as S_ϕ iff there exists a one-to-one mapping between the databases of S_ϕ and databases of S_D.

Rep4 combines definitions Rep2 and Rep3. Rep3 says that every database of S_ϕ is represented by a unique database of S_D. Rep2 says that every database of S_D satisfies the same dependencies as S_ϕ, and hence represents a legal database of S_ϕ. Together, Rep2 and Rep3 imply Rep4.

If only FDs are given, Rep4 is identical to the notion of *independent components* [31], and the following is proved:

Let $\underline{U} = \langle T,F \rangle$, $\underline{R}_1 = \langle T_1,F_1 \rangle$ and $\underline{R}_2 = \langle T_2,F_2 \rangle$. $\{R_1,R_2\}$ are independent components of $\underline{U}$ iff (a) $(F_1 \cup F_2)^+ = F^+$, and (b) F^+ contains $T_1 \cap T_2 \rightarrow T_1$ or $T_1 \cap T_2 \rightarrow T_2$ [31].

Comparison of Definitions. Fig. 5 illustrated a schema equivalent to the schema of Fig. 2 by Rep1 but not by Rep2, Rep3, or Rep4. Fig. 7 differentiates between Rep2 and Rep3. Fig. 7(a) is similar to an example in [16, p. 165]. S_D is equivalent to S_ϕ under Rep3 but not Rep2; it would be considered a good design by [16,23], but not by [7]. In Fig. 7(b), S_D is equivalent to S_ϕ by Rep2 but not by Rep3; it would be approved by [7], but not [23,37]. These differences of opinion are examined further in later sections.

FIGURE 7. Situations where Rep2 differs from Rep3.

S_ϕ = {DWELLER = <{ADDRESS,APT#,OCCUPANT},
{ADDRESS,APT# → OCCUPANT;
OCCUPANT → ADDRESS; OCCUPANT → APT#}>}

S_D = {ADD-OCC = <{ADDRESS,OCCUPANT},
{OCCUPANT → ADDRESS}>;
APT-OCC <{APT#,OCCUPANT},{OCCUPANT → APT#}>}

S_D does not Rep2-represent S_ϕ. S_D Rep3-represents S_ϕ.

S_ϕ = {RENTAL = <{LANDLORD,ADDRESS,APT#,OCCUPANT},
{LANDLORD → ADDRESS;
ADDRESS,APT# → OCCUPANT;
OCCUPANT → ADDRESS; OCCUPANT → APT#}>}

S_D = {OWNER = <{LANDLORD,ADDRESS},
{LANDLORD → ADDRESS}>;
DWELLER = <{ADDRESS,APT#,OCCUPANT},
{ADDRESS,APT# → OCCUPANT;
OCCUPANT → ADDRESS; OCCUPANT → APT#}>}

S_D Rep2-represents S_ϕ. S_D does not Rep3-represents S_ϕ.

5. THE PRINCIPLE OF SEPARATION

The next question is to understand how S_D can be "better than" S_ϕ. One way is for "independent relationships" to be represented by S_D in independent relation schemes. To illustrate this point, let S_ϕ be the RENTAL-UNITS scheme of Figs. 1 & 2, and suppose we want to add a new LANDLORD to the database. This can only be done if values for other attributes are given, too. The new LANDLORD must be associated with an ADDRESS; the ADDRESS must be associated with an APT#; the ADDRESS, APT# pair requires a RENT and an OCCUPANT; and the OCCUPANT needs PETS. So to add a new LANDLORD, S_ϕ forces us to add information that is at most distantly related to him. By the same token, when the last PET of the last OCCUPANT of the last APT# of a given ADDRESS runs away, the association between LANDLORD and ADDRESS is also destroyed.

Another problem with S_ϕ is data redundancy. Each LANDLORD is represented in four tuples although each only owns one building. To change the building owned by Codd, say, requires that all four tuples with ADDRESS = "3 NF St" be updated. If some of these tuples were forgotten, the database would be *inconsistent*, meaning that some dependencies would no longer hold. In this case, LANDLORD $\twoheadrightarrow$ ADDRESS would no longer hold.

These difficulties are caused by a lack of separation in S_ϕ. To overcome these difficulties, a series of *database normal forms* have been proposed, four of which are of interest. Before defining them, we present several preliminary concepts.

Let $S = \{\underline{R}_i = <T_i, \Gamma_i> | i = 1,\ldots,n\}$ be a schema and let $\Gamma = (\bigcup_{i=1}^{n} \Gamma_i)$. (1) *Superkey*--Let $X \subseteq T_i$; X is a superkey of $\underline{R}_i$ if $X \rightarrow T_i$ is in Γ^+. (2) *Key*--Let $X \subseteq T_i$; X is a key of $\underline{R}_i$ if X is a superkey and no $X' \subset X$ is. (3) *Prime attribute*--Let $A \in T_i$; A is prime in $\underline{R}_i$ if A is in any key of $\underline{R}_i$. (4) *Transitive dependence*--Let $A \in T_i$ and $X \subseteq T_i$; A is transitively dependent on X in $\underline{R}_i$ if there exists $Y \subseteq T_i$ such that $X \rightarrow Y \in \Gamma^+$, $Y \rightarrow A \in \Gamma^+$, $Y \rightarrow X \notin \Gamma^+$, and $A \notin Y$. (5) *Trivial FD*--$X \rightarrow Y$ is trivial, meaning it holds in *all* relations, if $Y \subseteq X$. (6) *Trivial MVD*--$X \twoheadrightarrow \phi$ and $X \twoheadrightarrow T_i - X$ are trivial in $\underline{R}_i(T_i)$.

We now define four normal forms of interest.

1. Third Normal Form (abbr. 3NF)*: [14] $\underline{R}_i \in S$ is in 3NF if none of its nonprime attributes is transitively dependent on any of its keys
2. Boyce-Codd Normal Form (BCNF): [15] Let $f: X \rightarrow Y$ be any nontrivial FD in Γ^+, defined on $\underline{R}_i \in S$. $\underline{R}_i$ is in BCNF if for all such f, X is a superkey of $\underline{R}_i$.
3. Weak Fourth Normal Form (W4NF): Let $g: X \twoheadrightarrow Y \in \Gamma^+$ be any nontrivial MVD in $\underline{R}_i \in S$. $\underline{R}_i$ is in W4NF if it is in 3NF and all such g are FDs.
4. Fourth Normal Form (4NF): [23] Let $g: X \twoheadrightarrow Y \in \Gamma^+$ be any nontrivial MVD in $\underline{R}_i \in S$. $\underline{R}_i$ is in 4NF if for all such g, X is a superkey of $\underline{R}_i$.

Notice that 3NF is a weak version of BCNF, and W4NF is a weak version of 4NF. Also W4NF implies 3NF and 4NF implies BCNF. BCNF and 4NF always succeed in separating independent relationships into separate schemes. This is illustrated in Fig. 8. Notice that S_D in Fig. 8 Rep2-represents RENTAL-UNITS. There are cases, though, where the stronger normal forms cannot be achieved and we must settle for the weaker forms. Fig. 9 shows an example of this sort. The following formalize this observation. Let $S_\phi = \{\underline{U} = <T,F>\}$.

FACT 3: There always exists a 3NF schema that Rep2-represents S_ϕ [7].

FACT 4: There need not exist a BCNF schema that Rep2-represents S_ϕ. Moreover the question, "Is schema S in BCNF?" is NP-hard [5].

FACT 5: There need not exist a 4NF schema that Rep2-represents S_ϕ. (Follows from Fact 4 when $G = \phi$.) It is not known whether a W4NF scheme Rep2-representing S_ϕ need always exist.

*1NF simply requires that relations be "flat", non-hierarchical. 2NF is a weak form of 3NF and is subsumed by it [14,16].

FACT 6: There always exists a 4NF schema that Rep3-represents S [23]. It follows that a BCNF schema Rep3-representing S_ϕ is always achievable, too.

FIGURE 8. 4NF schema and instance corresponding to RENTAL-UNITS (Figs. 1 & 2)

S_D = {OWNS, CHARGES, LIVES, LOVES}

OWNS = <{LANDLORD, ADDRESS}, {LANDLORD $\twoheadrightarrow$ ADDRESS}>
CHARGES = <{ADDRESS, APT#, RENT}, {ADDRESS, APT# $\rightarrow$ RENT}>
LIVES = <{OCCUPANT, ADDRESS, APT#}, {OCCUPANT $\rightarrow$ ADDRESS, APT#}>
LOVES = <{OCCUPANT, PETS}, {OCCUPANT $\twoheadrightarrow$ PETS{>

OWNS (LANDLORD, ADDRESS)

Wizard	Oz
Codd	3 NF St

CHARGES (ADDRESS, APT#, RENT)

Oz,	#3	$ 50
Oz,	#1	$ 50
Oz,	#2	$ 75
3 NF St,	#1	$500
3 NF St,	#2	$600

LIVES (OCCUPANT, ADDRESS, APT#)

Tinman,	Oz,	#3
Witch,	Oz,	#1
Lion,	Oz,	#2
Beeri,	3 NF St,	#1
Bernstein,	3 NF St,	#1
Goodman,	3 NF St,	#2

LOVES (OCCUPANTS, PETS)

Tinman,	Oilcan
Witch,	Bat
Witch,	Snake
Lion,	Mouse
Beeri,	Fish
Bernstein,	Dog
Bernstein,	Rhino
Goodman,	Cat

FIGURE 9. W4NF schema and instance.

S_ϕ = {RENTAL-UNITS' =
<{LANDLORD, ADDRESS, APT#, RENT, OCCUPANT, PETS},
{ADDRESS, APT# $\rightarrow$ RENT; OCCUPANT $\rightarrow$ ADDRESS, APT#,
LANDLORD $\twoheadrightarrow$ ADDRESS; OCCUPANT $\twoheadrightarrow$ PETS;
ADDRESS, APT# $\rightarrow$ LANDLORD}>

S_D = {OWNS', CHARGES, LIVES, LOVES}, CHARGES, LIVES, LOVES same as in Fig. 8.

OWNS' = <{LANDLORD, ADDRESS, APT#}, {LANDLORD $\twoheadrightarrow$ ADDRESS; ADDRESS, APT# $\rightarrow$ LANDLORD}>

CHARGES, LIVES, LOVES in 4NF (from Fig. 8)

OWNS' in W4NF since LANDLORD $\rightarrow$ ADDRESS implied by S_ϕ's dependencies:

(1) OCCUPANT $\rightarrow$ ADDRESS, APT# $\Rightarrow$ OCCUPANT $\rightarrow$ ADDRESS (FD_6)
(2) LANDLORD $\twoheadrightarrow$ ADDRESS and OCCUPANT $\rightarrow$ ADDRESS $\Rightarrow$ LANDLORD $\rightarrow$ ADDRESS ($FD\text{-}MVD_2$)

Extension of OWNS', given data in Figs. 1 and 8.

OWNS' (LANDLORD, ADDRESS, APT#)

Wizard,	Oz,	#3
Wizard,	Oz,	#1
Wizard,	Oz,	#2
Codd,	3 NF St,	#1
Codd,	3 NF St,	#2

Another observation to make from Fig. 9 is that W4NF doesn't achieve total separation in the way 4NF does. OWNS' has redundant information and suffers the same kind of update anomalies as RENTAL-UNITS does. The same is true of 3NF vs. BCNF. And since 4NF and BCNF cannot always be achieved under Rep2 (Facts 4 & 5), we must conclude that Rep2 and total separation are incompatible concepts. This result is both surprising and fundamental; it holds for non-computerized databases as well as computerized ones, and has applicability in all data models.

This result has been interpreted differently by some workers [16,24] who argue that BCNF and 4NF schemas should be obtained even if Rep2 is not achieved. We saw such a case in Fig. 7(a), which we replicate in Fig. 10. In that example, S_D violates Rep2 because it does not include ADDRESS,APT# → OCCUPANT. Without this FD legal instances of S_D can correspond to illegal instances of S_ϕ, and may represent illegal conditions in the real world (see Fig. 10(b)). It is suggested in [16] that these illegal instances be prevented by adding ADDRESS,APT# → OCCUPANT to S_D as an "interrelational constraint." However, because Rep2 is incompatible with BCNF in this case, this suggestion is futile. If we add the suggested interrelational constraint, the two *relations* can no longer be updated independently, which simply defeats the original goal of separation.

In other words, while total separation is a goal of schema design, there simply are cases where it cannot be achieved.

FIGURE 10. An instance of S_D that is not an instance of S_ϕ.

S_ϕ = {DWELLER = <{ADDRESS,APT#,OCCUPANT} {ADDRESS,APT# → OCCUPANT; OCCUPANT→ADDRESS; OCCUPANT→APT#}>}

S_D = {<u>ADD-OCC</u> = <{ADDRESS,OCCUPANT}; {OCCUPANT → ADDRESS}>;

<u>APT-OCC</u> = <{APT#,OCCUPANT}; {OCCUPANT → APT#}>}.

S_D does not Rep2-represent S_ϕ. S_D Rep3-represents S_ϕ.

(a)

Relation: ADD-OCC

Attributes: <u>ADDRESS,OCCUPANT</u>

Tuples:

Oz,	Tinman
Oz,	Witch
Oz,	Lion
Oz,	Scarecrow

Relation: APT-OCC

Attributes: <u>APT#, OCCUPANT</u>

Tuples:

#3,	Tinman
#1,	Witch
#2,	Lion
#2,	Scarecrow

Each relation has legal contents--all dependencies hold. But, ADDRESS,APT# → OCCUPANT does not hold in ADD-OCC*APT-OCC.

ADD-OCC*APT-OCC =

Attributes: <u>ADDRESS, APT#, OCCUPANT</u>

Tuples:

Oz,	#3,	Tinman
Oz,	#1,	Witch
Oz,	#2,	Lion
Oz,	#2,	Scrarecrow

(b)

6. THE PRINCIPLE OF MINIMAL REDUNDANCY

Another goal in designing S_D is *minimal redundancy*; S_D must contain the information needed to represent S_ϕ but it should not contain the information redundantly. The meaning of minimal redundancy depends on the definition of representation. Only by knowing what it means to represent information can we judge whether a certain representation is redundant.

Virtually all work on schema design adopts some notion of minimal redundacy, although often this point is addressed intuitively. Consequently our treatment of redundancy must be sketchier than the previous sections. We present here different definitions of redundancy analogous to the definitions of representation in Sec. 4. In the following, let $S_D = \{\underline{R_i} = \langle T_i, \Gamma_i \rangle \mid i = 1, \ldots, n\}$.

<u>Definition Red1</u>. $\underline{R_i} \in S_D$ is redundant if $T_i \subseteq \bigcup_{j=1, j\neq i}^{n} T_j$. This approach, like Definition Rep1, is unsatisfactory since it does not account for relationships among attributes. Also, minimal redundancy under Red1 is always attained in S_ϕ since each attribute appears only once.

<u>Definition Red2</u>. $\underline{R_i} \in S_D$ is redundant if $\underline{R_i}$'s data dependencies are represented by the other schemes. For the case of FDs, the definition can be made formal. $\underline{R_i} \in S_D$ is redundant if $(\bigcup_{j=1}^{n} \Gamma_j)^+ = (\bigcup_{j=1, j\neq i}^{n} \Gamma_j)^+$. Note that the FDs of Γ_i need not be explicitly represented. Rather, they need only be derivable from the FDs in the other schemes. As for Rep2, this definition does not easily generalize to MVDs since rules for manipulating MVDs in different relations are not known.

<u>Definition Red3</u>. $R_i \in S_D$ is redundant if for each database of S_D, the data in R_i is contained in $\{R_j \mid j = 1, \ldots, n, j \neq i\}$. For this definition to be meaningful, a database of S_D must be viewed as a set of related relations, since if relations can assume independent values, no relation scheme is ever redundant. The universal relation assumption (Sec.1) provides the necessary connection and leads to the following. $\underline{R_i}$ is redundant in S_D if $\overset{n}{\underset{j=1}{*}} R_j = \overset{n}{\underset{j=1, j\neq i}{*}} R_j$, for all databases of S_D.

<u>Definition Red4</u>. $\underline{R_i} \in S_D$ is redundant if there is a one-to-one correspondence between the set of instances of S_D and the set of instances of $S_D - \{\underline{R_i}\}$. This definition, like Rep1, combines data and dependency aspects of schema design.

We note, in conclusion, that other approaches to redundancy are possible, e.g., using as a measure the number of data items in relations, etc.

7. SCHEMA DESIGN METHODS

Traditionally, schema design has been called "database normalization" in the literature in this area and two approaches are prominent: *synthesis* [5,7], and *decomposition* [14,20,21,25,41]. This section describes both approaches, explaining how they interpret and achieve the schema design principles discussed earlier.

The key difference between synthesis and decomposition lies in the definition of *representation* that each adopts. In synthesis S_D *Rep2-represents* input S_ϕ, whereas with decomposition S_D *Rep3-represents* S_ϕ.* This difference leads to a series of other discrepancies between the methods: (1) Since Rep2 is not compatible with total separation (Sec.5), synthesis can only achieve 3NF and not higher normal forms; decomposition, on the other hand, is not limited in this way. (2) Rep2 leads to the Red2 definition of redundancy, while Rep3 leads to Red3; therefore synthesis strives for minimality of dependencies while decomposition strives for minimality of data content. (3) Because definitions Rep2 and Red2 do not easily extend to MVDs, it is not known how (or if) synthesis can handle MVDs; decomposition, on the other hand, is straightforwardly extendable to MVDs. (4) Finally, as explained in Sec. 5, Rep3 does not guarantee that all instances of S_D correspond to legal instances of S_ϕ; thus schemas produced by decomposition admit instances that would not be permitted by synthesized schemas. These differences are summarized in Figure 11.

FIGURE 11. Differences between principal Normalization Methods

Method	Synthesis	Decomposition	Decomposition
Described by	Bernstein [7]	Fagin [25]	Rissanen [31]
Definition of Representation	Rep2, "S_D has same dependencies as S_ϕ"	Rep3, "S_D has same data content as S_ϕ"	Rep4, "S_D and S_ϕ databases are 1-to-1"
Dependencies	FDs	FDs + MVDs	FDs
Normal Form	3NF	4NF, BCNF	3NF
Definition of Redundancy	Red2, "redundancy of dependencies" (attained)	Red3, "redundancy of data content" (not attained by current algorithms)	Red4, "both Red2 + Red3" (not attained by current algorithms)
Instances admitted by S_D	Same as S_ϕ	More than S_ϕ	Same as S_ϕ

7.1 The Synthesis Approach

We discuss the synthesis approach in terms of the specific method of [7]. A central concept of this method is *embodied* FDs, which are FDs implied by keys. Formally, given $\underline{R_i} = \langle T_i, \Gamma_i \rangle$, $X \rightarrow A$ is embodied in $\underline{R_i}$ if $X \rightarrow A \in \Gamma_i$, and X is a superkey of R_i. Fig. 12 presents a simplified synthesis algorithm (called SYN1) that uses embodied FDs to construct an S_D Rep2-representing S_ϕ. SYN1 is a first step towards a correct synthesis algorithm. SYN1 is not yet correct because S_D is not necessarily in 3NF, so transitive dependencies can be exhibited within *individual* FDs, due to *extraneous attributes* in their left hand sides. An attribute is extraneous in an FD if it could be eliminated from the FD without affecting the closure (F^+).

FIGURE 12. Simplified Synthesis Algorithm

Algorithm SYN1

Input: $S_\phi = \{\underline{U} = \langle T, F \rangle\}$

Output: $S_D = \{\underline{R_i} = \langle T_i, F_i \rangle\}_{i=1,\ldots,n}$

1. (Find Covering). Find a nonredundant covering $\hat{F}$ of F.
2. (Partition). Partition $\hat{F}$ into "groups", F_i, $i = 1,\ldots,n$, such that all FDs in each F_i have the same left hand side, and no two groups have the same left hand side.
3. (Construct Relations). For each F_i construct a relation scheme $\underline{R_i} = \langle T_i, F_i \rangle$ where T_i = all attributes appearing in F_i.

Important Fact: The left hand side of every FD in F_i is a *superkey* of $\underline{R_i}$; each FD in F_i is *embodied* in $\underline{R_i}$.

Let us precede SYN1 with a step that eliminates extraneous attributes from the left sides of FDs in F, and call the resulting algorithm SYN1'. SYN1' produces schemas that Rep2-represent the input and are guaranteed to be in 3NF. Algorithm SYN1' thus meets the representation and separation goals of schema synthesis.

The next step is to achieve minimality. Let $\hat{F}$ be the nonredundant covering of F obtained by SYN1' after excising extraneous attributes, and suppose $\hat{F}$ includes $V \rightarrow W$ and $X \rightarrow Y$, $X \neq V$. Clearly these FDs will be embodied in different relation schemes. But suppose V and X are *equivalent*; i.e., $V \rightarrow X$ and $X \rightarrow V$ are in F^+. Then $V \rightarrow X$ and $X \rightarrow V$ can be embedded in one relation scheme with *both* V and X as keys. Doing so reduces the number of synthesized schemes and makes explicit the equivalence of X and V.

So, we add a stage to SYN1' to find and merge all relation schemes with equivalent keys. Unfortunately, this modification takes a step backward: it no longer produces 3NF schemes! When we merge relation schemes we also add FDs to $\hat{F}$ from

*A decomposition approach is suggested by [Rissanen,77] in which S_D Rep4-represents S_ϕ. This approach is algorithmically similar to the other decomposition approaches so will not be discussed separately.

$(F^+-\hat{F})$ which may thereby cause F to become redundant. A final stage is needed to eliminate this redundancy. This modification brings us to algorithm SYN2 (Fig. 13), which is our final schema synthesis algorithm. The following facts, are proved in [7], establishing that SYN2 achieves the three schema design principles. Given $S_\phi = \{\underline{U} = \langle T,F\rangle\}$ and S_D = the result of applying SYN2 to S_ϕ.

FACT 7: S_D Rep2-represents S_ϕ.

FACT 8: S_D is in 3NF.

FACT 9: S_D is minimally redundant under definition Red2. In fact S_D is minimal in an even stronger sense. Let $S_D = \{S_D' \mid S_D'$ Rep2-represents S_ϕ and all FDs in S_D' are *embodied* FDs$\}$. S_D contains no more relation schemes than any other scheme in S_D. In other words, S_D is the smallest schema that can Rep2-represent S_ϕ using just keys.

FIGURE 13. A Correct Synthesis Algorithm [5].

Algorithm SYN2

Input: $S_\phi = \{\underline{U} = \langle T,F\rangle\}$

Output: $S_D = \{\underline{R}_i = \langle T_i,F_i\rangle \mid i = 1,\ldots,n\}$

1. (Eliminate Extraneous Attributes) Eliminates extraneous attributes from the left side of each FD in F, producing the set F'.
2. (Find Covering) Find a nonredundant covering $\hat{F}$ of F'.
3. (Partition) Partition $\hat{F}$ into groups F_i, $i = 1,\ldots,n$, as in step 2 of SYN1.
4. (Merge Equivalent Keys) Set $J:=\emptyset$. For each pair of groups F_i, F_j with left hand sides X_i, X_j do the following: If $X_i \rightarrow X_j \in F^+$ and $X_j \rightarrow X_i \in F^+$, merge F_i and F_j, add $X_i \rightarrow X_j$ and $X_j \rightarrow X_i$ to J, and remove them from $\hat{F}$.
5. (Eliminate Transitive Dependencies) Find a minimal $\hat{F}' \subseteq \hat{F}$ such that $(\hat{F}+J)^+ = (\hat{F}'+J)$. Delete each element of $\hat{F}-\hat{F}'$ from the group in which it appears. For each $X_i \rightarrow X_j$ in J, add it to the corresponding group.
6. (Construct Relations) For each F_i construct a relation scheme $\underline{R}_i = \langle T_i,F_i\rangle$ where T_i = all attributes appearing in F_i.

7.2 The Decomposition Approach

Fig. 14 shows a typical decomposition algorithm (which we call algorithm DEC) adapted from [25]. DEC achieves the representation and separation goals of decomposition but does not achieve minimal redundancy. These conclusions are stated formally as follows. Given $S_\phi = \{\underline{U} = \langle T,\Gamma\rangle\}$ and S_D = the result of applying DEC to S_ϕ.

FACT 10: S_D Rep3-represents S_ϕ.

Reason: Whenever a scheme $\underline{R}$ is decomposed into $\underline{R}_1$ and $\underline{R}_2$ (in step 3 of DEC) $\underline{R}_1,\underline{R}_2$ has the lossless join property (by Fact 2).

FIGURE 14. Basic Decomposition Algorithm

Algorithm DEC

Input: $S_\phi = \{\underline{U} = \langle T,\Gamma\rangle\}$

Output: $S_D = \{\underline{R}_i = \langle T_i,\Gamma_i\rangle \mid i=1,\ldots,n\}$

1. (Initialize) Set $k:=\emptyset$.
2. (Test for Separation) If all schemes in S_k are in 4NF, then output $S_D:=S_k$.
3. (Decompose) Set $S_{k+1}:=\emptyset$. Let $\underline{R}_i = \langle T_i,\Gamma_i\rangle$ be any non-4NF scheme in S_k, and set $S_k:=S_k-\underline{R}_i$. Decompose $\underline{R}_i$ into $\underline{R}_{i,1}$ and $\underline{R}_{i,2}$ as follows: (1) Let $X \rightarrow\rightarrow Y$ be any non-trivial MVD in Γ defined on $\underline{R}_1$. (2) Let $\underline{R}_{i,1}:=\langle X \cup Y,\{g \in \Gamma_i \mid g$ is defined on $\underline{R}_{i,1}\}$. (3) Define $\underline{R}_{i,2} = \langle T_i - Y$ $\{g \in \Gamma_i \mid g$ is defined on $\underline{R}_{i,2}\}$. (4) Set $S_{k+1}:=S_{k+1} \cup \{\underline{R}_{i,1},\underline{R}_{i,2}\}$. (5) Repeat for all $\underline{R}_i \in S_k$.
4. (Eliminate Some Redundancy) For each $\underline{R}_i,\underline{R}_j \in S_{k+1}$. If $T_i \subseteq T_j$ set $S_{k+1}:=S_{k+1} - \{\underline{R}_i\}$.
5. (Iterate) Set $k:=k+1$. Go to step 2.

FACT 11: S_D is in 4NF.

Reason: DEC will not stop until S_D is in 4NF.

FACT 12: S_D is *not* necessarily minimally redundant under Rep3 (or most other reasonable definitions).

Reason: Fig. 15 shows two ways DEC could decompose the same schema, one of which is minimal and one of which is not. Few minimality facts have been established regarding decomposition, and it is not even known whether minimal schemas can be produced by *non-deterministic* decomposition. Also, it is not known whether decomposition can consider *coverings* of dependencies rather than entire *closures*; in the specific case of Fig. 15(a) minimality would be guaranteed if S_ϕ were decomposed using a nonredundant, nonextraneous covering of Γ.

Algorithmic aspects of decomposition have not been considered fully either, and current algorithms have high computational complexity. For example, DEC is probably very slow, because the question "Is schema S in 4NF?" is NP-hard and DEC asks this question repeatedly. A related problem is caused by using closures rather than coverings. Closures can be exponentially large and their use can lead to exponential worst case running time.

Another problem is that decompositions are not unique. At each stage the algorithm may have several decomposition choices with different choices leading to very different outputs (e.g., Fig. 15). Some choices produce "natural looking" schemas while other choices may lead to bizarre results (see Fig. 16). Also, the dependencies in the output schema can depend idiosyncratically on the input and the algorithm (see Fig. 17).

Notice in Fig. 17 that S_D^1 Rep3-represents S_ϕ^1, S_D^2 Rep3-represents S_ϕ^2, and S_ϕ^1 and S_ϕ^2 both Rep3-represent a third schema $S_\phi = \{\underline{U} = \langle T, (F^1+F^2)^+$. Nonetheless, S_D^1 and S_D^2 have substantially different sets of legal instances. Heuristics for choosing "good" decompositions are suggested in [41] but no rules are known to work in all cases.

FIGURE 15. Algorithm D does not achieve minimal redundancy (italicized attributes become relations schemes).

$S_\phi = \{\underline{U} = \langle T = \{A,B,C,D\},\ \Gamma = \{B \twoheadrightarrow C; D \twoheadrightarrow B; BC \twoheadrightarrow A\}\rangle\}$

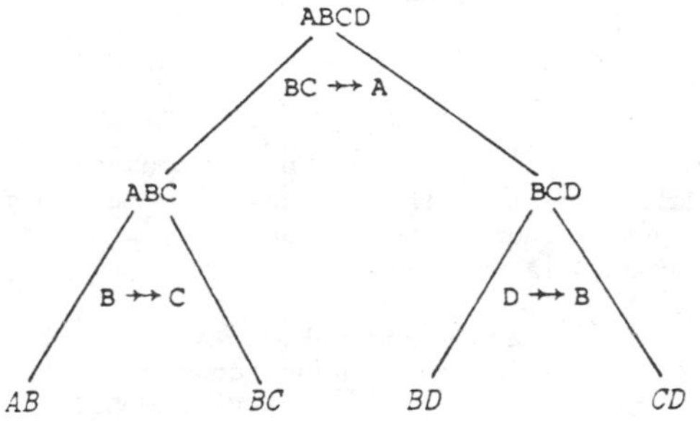

(a)

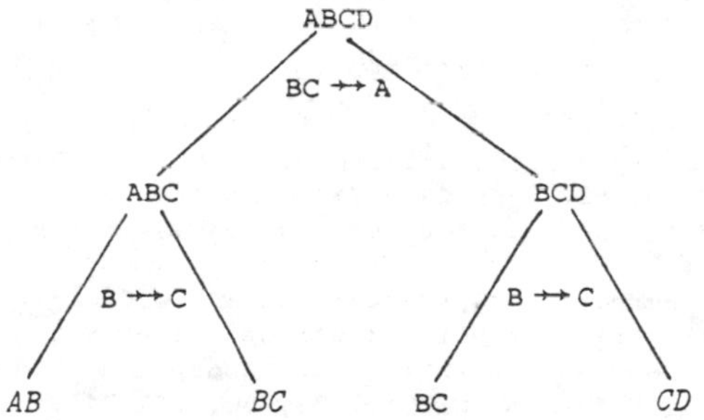

(b)

FIGURE 16. Natural and unnatural 4NF schemas produced by decomposition.

$S = \langle T = \{\text{LANDLORD,ADDRESS,APT\#,RENT,OCCUPANT,PETS}\} = \{\text{LANDLORD} \twoheadrightarrow \text{ADDRESS}; \text{ADDRESS,APT\#} \rightarrow \text{RENT}; \text{OCCUPANT} \rightarrow \text{ADDRESS,APT\#}; \text{OCCUPANT} \twoheadrightarrow \text{PETS}\}\rangle$

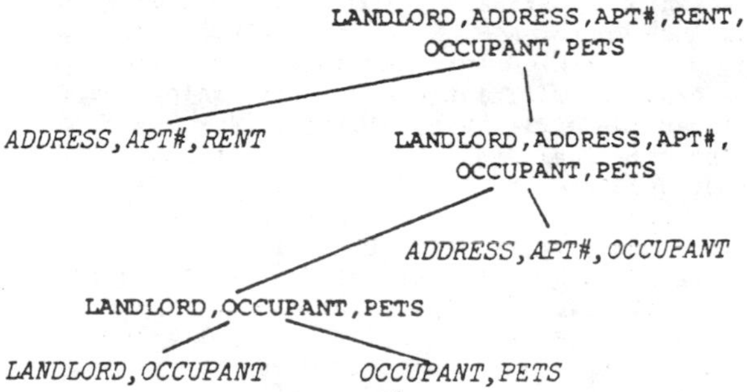

(a) S_D^1

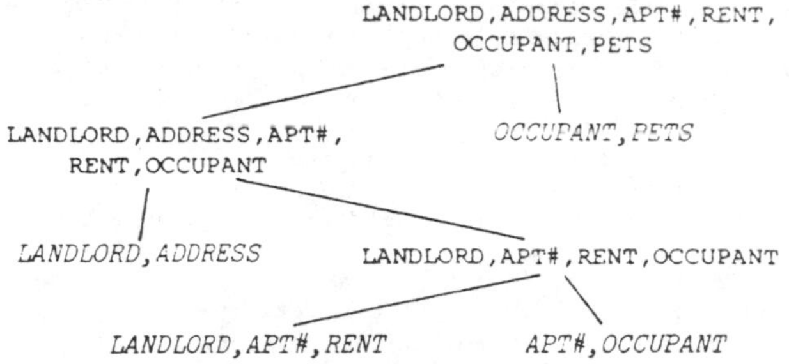

(b) S_D^2

FIGURE 17. Idiosyncratic behavior of decomposition

$S_\phi^1 = \{\underline{U}^1 = \langle T = \{ABCD\}, F^1 = \{A\rightarrow B; A\rightarrow C; A\rightarrow D, B\rightarrow C, B\rightarrow D, D\rightarrow C\},$

$S_\phi^2 = \{\underline{U}^2 = \langle T = \{ABCD\}, F^2 = \{A\rightarrow BCD; B\rightarrow CD; C\rightarrow D\}.$

(Note: $(F^1)^+ = (F^2)^+$).

$$\begin{aligned} S_D^1 = \{&\underline{R}_1^1 = \langle T_1 = \{AB\},\ F_1^1 = \{A\rightarrow B\}\rangle \\ &\underline{R}_2^1 = \langle T_2 = \{BC\},\ F_2^1 = \{B\rightarrow C\}\rangle \\ &\underline{R}_3^1 = \langle T_3 = \{CD\},\ F_3^1 = \{C\rightarrow D\}\rangle\} \end{aligned}$$

$$\begin{aligned} S_D^2 = \{&\underline{R}_1^1 = \langle T_1 = \{AB\},\ F_1^2 = \{\}\rangle \\ &\underline{R}_2^2 = \langle T_2 = \{BC\},\ F_2^2 = \emptyset\rangle\{\}\rangle \\ &\underline{R}_3^2 = \langle T_3 = \{CD\},\ F_3^2 = \{C\rightarrow D\}\rangle\}\ . \end{aligned}$$

8. HISTORY, CONCLUSIONS, AND FUTURE WORK

The history of database normalization theory begins with Codd's early work [14]. Codd introduced the notion of FD, but did not formalize it. The first mathematizations of FDs were by Delobel [17], Rissanen and Delobel [33], and Delobel and Casey [20]; these authors concentrated on formal properties of dependencies and their relationship to the decomposition approach. They were followed by Armstrong [3] who introduced the notion of completeness of inference rules and proved the completeness of a set of rules for FDs. This work laid the groundwork for the formal theory that has developed since. The earliest synthesis algorithm was an informal one described by Wang and Wedekind [38]. Bernstein [17] followed with a synthesis algorithm that used Armstrong's theory to prove properties of synthesized schemas. Bernstein's algorithm was the first to use a formal definition of representation. This algorithm was subsequently enhanced by Bernstein and Beeri [5,8] who improved its running time.

The first generalization of FDs was the concept of first order hierarchical decomposition by Delobel [18] and Delobel and Leonard [21]. The related concept of MVD was introduced by Fagin [23] and Zaniolo [41], and 4NF was introduced by Fagin

[23]. Completeness of inference rules for MVDs is treated by Beeri, Fagin and Howard [6] and Mendelzohn [29], and algorithmic questions about MVDs by Beeri [4]. Recently, attention has been directed to the representation principle by the work of Aho, Beeri, and Ullman [1] and Rissanen [31].

These references are a mere sketch of the history of normalization theory; a more complete bibliography follows.

A variety of important results appear in these papers, but the lack of uniform definitions has obscured the relationships among many works. We hope the paper will clear up some of the confusion by comparing the major definitions and outlining a general framework in which all can be embedded.

Our main theme is that schema design is directed by the three principles of representation, separation, and minimal redundancy. A goal of research in schema design is to develop a design methodology that satisfies these three principles. Specific formulations of the principles depend upon the types of constraints involved, so a thorough understanding of the formal properties of FDs and MVDs is a prerequisite for achieving this goal.

Many questions still remain unanswered. We list four important areas where more work is needed:

1. *Other dependency structures*--An MVD can hold in a projection of a relation, although it does not hold in the entire relation [19,25]. These *embedded* MVDs (abbr. EMVD) may appear when decomposing a relation scheme into smaller schemes. While some inference rules for EMVDs have appeared, a complete set is not currently known [19].

MVDs characterize lossless joins between two relations. Dependency structures that characterize lossless joins among N relations have recently been suggested, and should be integrated into the theory [30,32]. In addition, the concept of representation (particularly Rep2, Rep4) has only been developed for FDs. Representation questions about MVDs and other dependency structures are open.

2. *Semantic operations on dependencies*--Dependency structures can be used to guide correct retrievals given only minimal logical access path information [11,34]. However, the influence of dependency structures on data operations and the constraints that hold in a relation constructed by operations are only known for special cases.

3. *Universal relation assumption*--This assumption simplifies many theoretical problems but apparently does not hold in practice. It should either be abandoned or adapted for practical situations in some way.

4. *Design tools*--Mechanical procedures must be developed to assist the database designer. A schema synthesis algorithm that takes FDs *and* MVDs as input could be one such design aid. Mechanical mappings from high level data descriptions (e.g., [36]) into dependency structures are also needed. The true test of the theory is demonstrating its effectiveness in solving day to day database design problems. On this metric the theory will live or die.

REFERENCES

1. A.V. Aho, C. Beeri, and J.D. Ullmann, "The Theory of Joins in Relational Databases," Proc. 18th IEEE Symp. on Foundations of Computer Science, Oct. 1977.

2. A.V. Aho, J.E. Hopcroft, and J.D. Ullman, *The Design and Analysis of Computer Algorithms*, Addison-Wesley, Reading, Mass., 1974.

3. W.W. Armstrong, "Dependency Structures of Database Relationships," Proc. IFIP 74, North Holland, 1974, pp. 580-583.

4. C. Beeri, "On the Membership Problem for Multivalued Dependencies in Relational Databases," TR-229, Dept. of Elec. Eng. and Comp. Science, Princeton Univ., Princeton, N.J., Sept. 1977.

5. Beeri, C. and P.A. Bernstein, "Computational Problems Regarding the Design of Normal Form Relational Schemas," *ACM Trans. on Database Sys.*, to appear.

6. C. Beeri, R. Fagin, and J.H. Howard, "A Complete Axiomatization for Functional and Multivalued Dependencies," Proc. ACM-SIGMOD Conf., Toronto, Aug. 1977, pp. 47-61.

7. P.A. Bernstein, "Synthesizing Third Normal Form Relations from Functional Dependencies," *ACM Trans. on Database Sys.*, Vol. 1, No. 4 (Dec. 1976), pp. 277-298.

8. P.A. Bernstein and C. Beeri, "An Algorithmic Approach to Normalization of Relational Database Schemas," TR CSRG-73, Computer Systems Research Group, Univ. of Toronto, Sept. 1976.

9. P.A. Bernstein, J.R. Swenson, and D.C. Tsichritzis, "A Unified Approach to Functional Dependencies and Relations," Proc. ACM-SIGMOD Conf., San Jose, Cal., 1975, pp. 237-245.

10. J-M. Cadiou, "On Semantic Issues in the Relational Model of Data," Proc. Intern. Symp. on Math. Foundations of Comp. Science, Gdansk, Poland, Sept. 1975, Springer-Verlag Lecture Notes in Computer Science.

11. Carlson, C.R. and R.S. Kaplan, "A Generalized Access Path Model and its Application to a Relational Database Systems," Proc. 1976 ACM-SIGMOD Conf., ACM, N.Y., pp. 143-156.

12. P.P-S. Chen, "The Entity-Relationship Model: Toward a Unified View of Data," *ACM Trans. on Database Sys.*, Vol. 1, No. 1 (Sept. 1976), pp. 9-36.

13. E.F. Codd, "A Relational Model for Large Shared Data Bases," *CACM*, Vol. 13, No. 6 (June, 1970), pp. 377-387.

14. E.F. Codd, "Further Normalization of the Data Base Relational Model," in *Data Base Systems* (R. Rustin, ed.), Prentice-Hall, Englewood Cliffs, N.J., 1972, pp. 33-64.

15. E.F. Codd, "Recent Investigations in Relational Data Base Systems," Proc. IFIP 74, North-Holland, 1974, pp. 1017-1021.

16. C.J. Date, *An Introduction to Database Systems* (2nd ed.), Addison-Wesley, Reading, MA, 1977.

17. C. Delobel, "A Theory About Data in an Information Systems," IBM Res. Rep. RJ964, Jan. 1972.

18. C. Delobel, "Contributions Théoretiques à la Conception d'un Système d'Informations," Ph.D. Thesis, Univ. of Grenoble, Oct. 1973.

19. C. Delobel, "Semantics of Relations and Decomposition Process in the Relational Data Model," Computer Laboratory, Univ. of Grenoble, 1977.

20. C. Delobel and R.C. Casey, "Decomposition of a Data Base and the Theory of Boolean Switching Functions," *IBM J. of Res. and Dev.*, 17:5 (Sept. 1972), pp. 370-386.

21. C. Delobel and M. Leonard, "The Decomposition Process in a Relational Model," Int. Workshop on Data Structures, IRIA, Namur (Belgium), May 1974.

22. R. Fadous and J. Forsythe, "Finding Candidate Keys for Relational Data Bases," Proc. 1st ACM-SIGMOD Conf., pp. 203-210, San Jose, Cal., 1975.

23. R. Fagin, "Multivalued Dependencies and a New Normal Form for Relational Databases," *ACM Trans. on Database Sys.*, Vol. 2, No. 3 (Sept. 1977), pp. 262-278.

24. R. Fagin, "The Decomposition Versus the Synthetic Approach to Relational Database Design," Proc. 3rd VLDB Conf., Tokyo, Oct. 1977, pp. 441-446.

25. R. Fagin, "Functional Dependencies in a Relational Database and Propositonal Logic," *IBM J. of Res. and Dev.*, Vol. 21, No. 6, (Nov. 1977), pp. 534-544.

26. M.M. Hammer and D.J. McLeod, "Semantic Integrity in a Relational Database System," Int. Conf. on Very Large Data Bases, ACM, N.Y., pp. 25-47, 1975.

27. W. Kent, "A Primer of Normal Forms," IBM Sys. Dev. Div., TR02.600, San Jose, Cal., 1973.

28. C.L. Lucchesi and S.L. Osborn, "Candidate Keys for Relations," Tech. Rep. Univ. of Waterloo, Waterloo, Ontario, Canada, 1976.

29. A. O. Mendelzon, "On Axiomatizing Multivalued Dependencies in Relational Databases," Dept. of Electr. Eng. and Computer Science, Princeton Univ., Princeton, N.J., July 1977.

30. J.M. Nicolas, "Mutual Dependencies and Some Results on Undecomposable Relations," ONERA-CERT, Toulouse, France, Feb. 1978.

31. J. Rissanen, "Independent Components of Relations," *ACM Trans. on Database Sys.*, Vol. 2, No. 4 (Dec. 1977), pp. 317-325.

32. J. Rissanen, "Theory of Relations for Databases--A Tutorial Survey," IBM Research Lab., San Jose, Cal., Apr. 1978.

33. J. Rissanen and C. Delobel, "Decomposition of Files--A Basis for Data Storage and Retrieval," IBM Res. Rep. RJ1220, San Jose, Cal., May 1973.

34. K.L. Schenk and J.R. Pinkert, "An Algorithm for Servicing Multi-Relational Queries," Proc. 1977 ACM-SIGMOD Conf., ACM, N.Y., pp. 10-19.

35. H.A. Schmid and J.R. Swenson, "On the Semantics of the Relational Data Model," Proc. 1975 ACM-SIGMOD Conf., San Jose, Cal., pp. 211-223.

36. J.M. Smith and D.C.P. Smith, "Database Abstractions: Aggregation and Generalization," *ACM Trans. on Database Sys.*, Vol. 2, No. 2 (June 1977), pp. 105-133.

37. Y. Tanaka and T. Tsuda, "Decomposition and Composition of a Relational Database," Proc. 3rd VLDB Conf., Tokyo, Oct. 1977, pp. 454-461.

38. C.P. Wang and H.H. Wedekind, "Segment Synthesis in Logical Data Base Design," *IBM J. of Res. and Dev.*, Vol. 19, No. 1 (Jan. 1975), pp. 71-77.

39. H.K.T. Wong and J. Mylopoulos, "Two Views of Data Semantics: A Survey of Data Models in Artificial Intelligence and Data Management," Tech. Rep., Computer Science Dept., Univ. of Toronto, 1977.

40. C.T. Yu and D.T. Johnson, "On the Complexity of Finding the Set of Candidate Keys for a Given Set of Functional Dependencies," *Information Processing Letters*, Vol. 5, No. 4 (oct. 1976), pp. 100-101.

41. C. Zaniolo, "Analysis and Design of Relational Scemata for Database Systems," Tech. Rep. UCLA-ENG-7769, Dept. of Computer Science, UCLA, July 1976.

Acknowledgments

We gratefully acknowledge the assistance of Renate D'Arcangelo for her expert preparation of this manuscript.

The Programming Language Aspects of ThingLab, a Constraint-Oriented Simulation Laboratory

ALAN BORNING
Xerox Palo Alto Research Center

The programming language aspects of a graphic simulation laboratory named ThingLab are presented. The design and implementation of ThingLab are extensions to Smalltalk. In ThingLab, *constraints* are used to specify the relations that must hold among the parts of the simulation. The system is object-oriented and employs *inheritance* and *part-whole* hierarchies to describe the structure of a simulation. An interactive, graphic user interface is provided that allows the user to view and edit a simulation.

Key Words and Phrases: constraints, constraint satisfaction, object-oriented languages, inheritance, part-whole hierarchies, Smalltalk, ThingLab
CR Categories: 3.69, 4.22, 8.1, 8.2

1. INTRODUCTION

This paper describes the programming language aspects of a simulation laboratory named ThingLab. The principal research issue addressed is the representation and satisfaction of *constraints*. A constraint specifies a relation that must be maintained. For example, suppose that a user desires that the value of some integer always be displayed as a piece of text at a certain location on the screen. In a conventional language, one must remember to update the text whenever the value of the integer is changed, and to update the integer if the text is edited. In a constraint-oriented system such as ThingLab, the user can specify the relation between the text and the integer and leave it to the system to maintain that relation. If additional constraints are placed on the integer or the text, the system takes care of keeping these satisfied as well.

The notion of an *object* provides a basic organizational tool; in particular, the modularity gained by the use of object-oriented programming techniques is important for constraint satisfaction, where it is essential to know what is affected by a given change. Nonprimitive objects are constructed hierarchically from *parts*, which are themselves other objects. As is shown below, constraints provide a natural way to express the relations among parts and subparts. Methods are also described for integrating the use of constraints with *inheritance hierarchies*, allowing new kinds of objects to be described in terms of existing ones. Finally, an interactive, graphic user interface is described that is integrated with the constraint, part-whole, and inheritance mechanisms, allowing a user to view and edit objects conveniently.

The concept of constraints, combined with inheritance and part-whole hierarchies, is one that could add significant power to programming languages. While ThingLab is not a general-purpose language, many of the concepts and techniques described here would be useful in such a context. A promising direction for future research is to explore the design of a full constraint-oriented programming language.

ThingLab is an extension to the Smalltalk-76 programming language [6, 7] and runs on a personal computer. This paper is based on the author's Stanford Ph.D. dissertation [2].

This work was supported in part by the Xerox Corporation.

Author's present address: Department of Computer Science, FR-35, University of Washington, Seattle, WA 98195.

1.1 The ThingLab System

The original question addressed by the research described in this paper is as follows: "How can we design a computer-based environment for constructing interactive, graphic simulations of experiments in physics and geometry?" Examples of the sorts of things that a user should be able to simulate are simple electrical circuits and mechanical linkages. However, the underlying system should be general. Rather than a program with knowledge built into it about electrical circuit components and linkages, we envisioned a sort of kit-building kit, in which environments tailored for domains such as electrical circuit simulations or geometric figures could be constructed. There would thus be two kinds of users of the system. The first kind would employ ThingLab to construct a set of building blocks for a given domain; for example, for use in simulating electrical circuits, such a user would construct definitions of basic parts such as resistors, batteries, wires, and meters. The second kind of user could then employ these building blocks to construct and explore particular simulations.

Another requirement on the system was that it have an appropriate user interface, particularly for the second kind of user working in a particular domain. For example, to create a geometric object such as a triangle, the user should be able simply to draw it on the screen, rather than having to type in its coordinates or (worse) write some code. Similarly, making changes to an object should also be natural. To move a vertex of the triangle, the user should be able to point to it on the screen and drag it along with a pointing device, seeing it in continuous motion, rather than pointing to the destination and having the triangle jump suddenly, or (again, worse) typing in the coordinates of the destination.

As specified in the above problem description, ThingLab provides an environment for constructing dynamic models of experiments in geometry and physics, such as simulations of constrained geometric objects, simple electrical circuits, mechanical linkages, and bridges under load. However, the techniques developed in ThingLab have wider application and have also been used to model other sorts of objects, such as a graphic calculator, and documents with constraints on their layout and contents. Examples of the system in operation are presented in Section 2.

1.2 Constraints

The range of relations that can be specified in ThingLab using constraints is broad. Some examples of constraints that have been defined by various users are

(1) that a line be horizontal;

(2) that the height of a bar in a bar chart correspond to an entry in a table;
(3) that one triangle be twice as big as another;
(4) that a resistor obey Ohm's law;
(5) that a beam in a bridge obey Hooke's law;
(6) that the gray-scale level of an area on the computer's display correspond to a number between zero and one;
(7) that a rectangle on the display be precisely big enough to hold a given paragraph.

The representation of constraints reflects their dual nature as both descriptions and commands. Constraints in ThingLab are represented as a *rule* and a set of *methods* that can be invoked to satisfy the constraint. The rule is used by the system to construct a procedural test for whether or not the constraint is satisfied and to construct an error expression that indicates how well the constraint is satisfied. The methods describe alternate ways of satisfying the constraint; if any one of the methods is invoked, the constraint will be satisfied.

It is up to the user to specify the constraints on an object, but it is up to the system to satisfy them. Satisfying constraints is not always trivial. A basic problem is that constraints are typically multidirectional. For example, the text-integer constraint mentioned above is allowed to change either the text or the integer. Thus, one of the tasks of the system is to choose among several possible ways of locally satisfying each constraint. One constraint may interfere with another; in general, the collection of all the constraints on an object may be incomplete, circular, or contradictory. Again, it is up to the system to sort this out.

Further, the user interface as specified in the problem description demands that constraint satisfaction be rapid. Consider the case of the user continuously moving some part of a complex geometric figure. Every time the part moves, the object's constraints may need to be satisfied again. To meet this speed requirement, constraint satisfaction techniques have been implemented that incrementally analyze constraint interactions and compile the results of this analysis into executable code. When possible, the system compiles code that satisfies the constraints in one pass. Constraint satisfaction thus takes place in two stages: there is an initial planning stage, in which a constraint satisfaction plan is formulated and compiled; then at run time this compiled code is invoked to update the object being altered.

Constraint representation is described in Section 4; constraint satisfaction is discussed in Section 5.

1.3 Object-Oriented Language Techniques

Smalltalk, in which ThingLab is written, is a language based on the idea of objects that communicate by sending and receiving messages. This object-centered factorization of knowledge provides one of the basic organizational tools. For example, in representing a geometric construction, the objects used in the representation are things such as points, lines, and triangles. This provides a natural way of bundling together the information and procedures relevant to each object. Each object holds its own state and is also able to send and receive messages to obtain results.

Object descriptions and computational methods are organized into *classes*. Every object is an *instance* of some class. In broad terms, a class represents a generic concept, while an instance represents an individual. A class holds the similarities among a group of objects; instances hold the differences. More specifically, a class has a description of the internal storage required for each of its instances and a dictionary of messages that its instances understand, along with *methods* (i.e., procedures) for computing the appropriate responses. An instance holds the particular values that distinguish it from other instances of its class.

A new class is normally defined as a subclass of an existing class. The subclass inherits the instance storage requirements and message protocol of its superclass. It may add new information of its own and may override inherited responses to messages.

One of the important features of Smalltalk is the sharp distinction it makes between the inside and the outside of an object. The internal aspects of an object are (1) its class and (2) its instance fields and their contents; the external aspects are the messages that it understands and its responses. Since other parts of the system and the user interact with the object by sending and receiving messages, they need not know about its internal representation. This makes it easier to construct modular systems. For example, the class Rectangle defines the message *center*. It makes no difference to the user of this message whether a rectangle actually has a center stored as one of its instance fields or whether the center is computed on demand (in fact, it is computed on demand).

ThingLab extends Smalltalk in a number of respects. The principal extension is the inclusion of constraints and constraint satisfaction mechanisms. The other significant extensions are provision for multiple superclasses rather than just a single superclass; a part–whole hierarchy with an explicit, symbolic representation of shared substructure; the use of *paths* for symbolic references to subparts and *prototypes* for the representation of default instances; and a facility for class definition by example. The latter extensions are discussed in Section 3.

Object-oriented languages generally emphasize a very localized approach to interaction within a program: an object interacts with other parts of the system only by sending and receiving messages to other objects that it knows about. On the other hand, it is very difficult to do constraint satisfaction in a purely local way: there are problems of circularity and the like that are better spotted by a more global analysis. There is consequently a tension between the object and constraint metaphors; the integration of these approaches in ThingLab is one of its points of interest.

1.4 The User Interface

Considerable effort has been spent on designing a good user interface to the system. Some quite general graphic editing tools are provided, and purely graphic objects, such as a triangle, can be constructed using graphic techniques only. The user interface allows objects to be viewed in other ways as well, for example, as a structural description or as a table of values.

The user interface allows smooth access to the constraint mechanism and to the inheritance and part–whole hierachies. Thus, when the user edits an object, say by selecting a point and moving it with the cursor, the constraint satisfaction mechanism is invoked automatically to keep all the constraints satisfied. New classes may be defined by example, that is, by constructing a typical instance. The structural descriptions provided by the interface present the part–whole hierarchy, the constraints, and so forth.

1.5 Relation to Other Work

One of the principal influences on the design of ThingLab has been Sketchpad [16], a general-purpose system for drawing and editing pictures on a computer. In Sketchpad the user interacts directly with the display, using a light pen for adding, moving, and deleting parts of the drawing. ThingLab has adopted much of Sketchpad's flavor of user interaction, and the Sketchpad notions of constraints and of recursive merging have been central to its design. ThingLab has extended Sketchpad's constraint mechanism in a number of respects, most notably by integrating it with an inheritance hierarchy, by allowing local procedures for satisfying a constraint to be included as part of its definition, and by incrementally compiling the results of constraint satisfaction planning into Smalltalk code.

The other principal ancestor of ThingLab is Smalltalk. Not only is ThingLab written in Smalltalk, but the important ideas in Smalltalk—objects, classes and instances, and messages—are all used directly in ThingLab. As prevously described, ThingLab adds a number of new features to the language. Smalltalk has proved to be an excellent language to support research of this sort, in terms of both linguistic constructs and programming environment.

ThingLab is also related to some very interesting work on constraint languages done at M.I.T. by Guy Steele and Gerald Sussman [13]. The ThingLab representation of an object in terms of parts and subparts, with explicit representation of shared parts, is nearly isomorphic to the representation independently developed by Steele and Sussman. Their system has a built-in set of primitive constraints, such as adders and multipliers, from which compound constraints can be constructed. This is similar to the method used in the ThingLab calculator example described in Section 2.2. To handle constraints that cannot be satisfied using a one-pass ordering, they employ multiple redundant views that can cooperate in solving the problem; in their previous work, symbolic algebraic manipulation techniques were employed. Their use of multiple views has been adopted in ThingLab. Among the differences between the two systems is that Steele and Sussman's language retains dependency information, that is, a record of the justifications for each conclusion, for producing explanations and for implementing efficient backtracing when search is needed (dependency-directed backtracking). On the other hand, their system has no graphics capabilities. Also, ThingLab has two significant advantages in regard to efficiency. First, it compiles plans into the base language, whereas in Steele and Sussman's system constraint satisfaction is done interpretively. Compilation is essential if constraint languages are to become practical tools. Second, ThingLab has a class-instance mechanism, including multiple inheritance, that allows information common to several objects to be factored out, while their system uses a macro facility for abstraction, which has the disadvantage that a complete copy of the constraint network is required for each instance.

Steele's recent Ph.D. dissertation [12], completed after the work described above and the author's own dissertation, gives a clear statement of design goals for a complete, general-purpose language organized around constraints and describes further progress toward implementing such a language. The system deals explicitly with the problem of behaving properly in the presence of contradictions, which is important for the interactive construction of large systems, and further develops the notions of assumptions and defaults. While its usual mode of operation is interpretive, it also includes a constraint compiler like that used in ThingLab.

Other related work on languages includes SIMULA [3], which is one of the principal ancestors of Smalltalk. The distinction that Smalltalk makes between the inside and the outside of an object is also closely related to the data-abstraction mechanisms in languages such as MESA [10], CLU [9], and ALPHARD [17]. These languages separate the interface specification of a type from its internal implementation, just as Smalltalk distinguishes the external message protocol of an object from its internal aspects. Thus, in programs in these data-abstraction languages, changes to the implementation of a type (but not its interface) do not affect the users of that type; so more modular systems result.

ABSET [4] is a set-oriented language developed at the University of Aberdeen with a number of constraint-like features; for example, given the statement $A + B = 3$ AND $A = 1$, it can deduce B's value. Also, it emphasizes the avoidance of unnecessary ordering restrictions in the statement of a program. The ACTOR languages [5] use and extend the notion of objects that communicate by passing messages. Representation languages for artificial intelligence work, such as KRL [1], develop the notion of multiple inheritance. ThingLab's facility for class definition by example is related to work on programming by example [8, 11].

There is a large body of work in artificial intelligence on reasoning and problem-solving systems of various kinds. Most of these systems are concerned with more complex problem-solving tasks than those tackled in ThingLab. By contrast, in ThingLab much of the emphasis has been on finding ways of generalizing plans and compiling them as procedures so that they may be used efficiently in a graphic environment. However, the problem-solving techniques developed in these other systems may well prove useful if ThingLab's constraint satisfaction abilities are to be strengthened.

This artificial intelligence work includes a number of systems that use constraints and constraint satisfaction as such. Steels [14] has constructed a reasoning system, modeled on a society of communicating experts, that uses propagation of constraints in its reasoning process. Unlike either ThingLab or Steele and Sussman's system, Steels' system is description-oriented and does not require that constraint satisfaction yield a unique value. Stefik [15] uses the technique of constraint posting in MOLGEN, a system for planning experiments in molecular genetics. His system uses hierarchical planning and dynamically formulates and propagates constraints during its planning process.

2. SOME EXAMPLES

Before plunging into a technical discussion of the system, it is useful to present some examples of its operation. A brief description of the operation of the ThingLab user interface is needed first. The user interacts with ThingLab via a *window*, a rectangular area on the computer's display. The window notion is central to Smalltalk's user interface philosophy. The ThingLab window described here is typically one of several windows on the screen, with other windows being available for debugging, editing system code, freehand sketching, and so on.

The ThingLab window is divided into five panes: the *class pane*, the *format pane*, the *messages pane*, the *arguments pane*, and the *picture pane*. The class pane is a *menu* of names of classes that may be viewed and edited. Once a class has been selected, a menu of formats in which it can display itself appears in the *format pane* immediately to the right. The class shows itself in the chosen format in the large *picture pane* at the bottom of the window.

The two remaining panes, messages and arguments, contain menus used for graphic editing of the class' prototype. All editing operations are performed by sending a message to the object being edited; the ThingLab window allows us to compose and send certain kinds of editing messages graphically. The messages pane contains a list of message names, such as *insert* and *delete*, while the arguments pane contains a list of possible classes for the message argument. The argument itself will be an instance of that class, either newly created or selected from among the parts in the picture.

The user communicates with the system primarily by means of a *mouse* and secondarily by use of a keyboard. The mouse is a small box-shaped object that can be moved about on the user's desk top; as it moves, its relative position is tracked by a cursor on the screen (the arrow in the illustrations). If some graphic object on the screen is "attached" to the cursor, that object moves as well. The mouse also has three buttons on it, which serve as control keys.

In the menu panes, a black stripe indicates a selected item. Thus, in Figure 1, *Triangle* and *prototype's picture* have been selected. Since a menu may be too long to fit in its pane, all the menus can be *scrolled* up or down so that the user can view and select any of the items. To make a selection, the user positions the cursor over the item to be selected and pushes a button on the mouse.

2.1 A Geometric Example

As an introductory example, we use ThingLab to construct a quadrilateral and to view it in several ways. We then use the system to demonstrate a theorem about quadrilaterals.

2.1.1 *Defining the Class of Quadrilaterals.* First, we define the class of quadrilaterals. New classes are always defined as a subclass of some more general class; if nothing better is available, they can be made subclasses of class Object, the most general class in the system. In this case, we create the new class Quadrilateral as a subclass of GeometricObject.

One of the important features of the ThingLab environment is that the user can define classes by example. To be more precise, the structural aspects of a class (its part descriptions and constraints) may be specified incrementally by editing its prototypical instance. We define the class Quadrilateral in this way.

First, we ask to view the picture of the prototype Quadrilateral. So far, the prototype has no parts, and so its picture is blank. We now edit the prototype by adding and connecting four sides. Using the mouse, we select the word *insert* in the messages pane and the word *Line* in the arguments pane. When we move the cursor into the bottom pane, a blinking picture of a line appears, attached to the cursor by one of its endpoints. As the cursor is moved, the entire line follows. When the endpoint attached to the cursor is in the desired location, we press a button. This first endpoint stops moving, and the cursor jumps to the second endpoint. The second endpoint follows the cursor, but this time the first endpoint remains stationary. We press the button again to position the second endpoint (Figure 2).

We insert another line in the same way. To connect the new line to the first, we position the endpoint attached to the cursor near one of the endpoints of the first line. When the two points are close together, the moving point locks onto the stationary point, and the line stops blinking. This indicates that the two points will merge if the button is pressed. We press the button and the points merge.

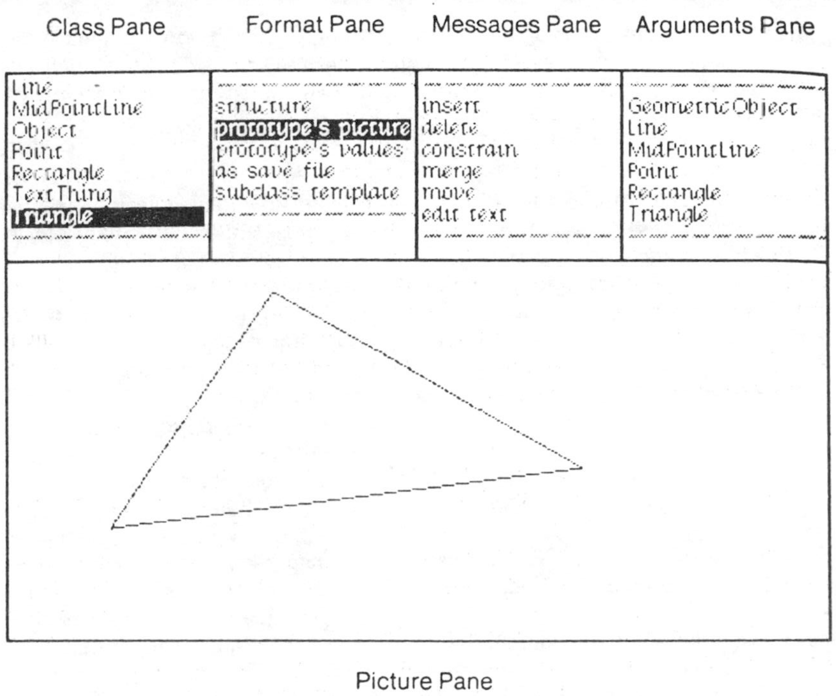

Fig. 1. Panes of the ThingLab window.

The two lines now share a common endpoint. Also, a record of the merge is kept by the class Quadrilateral. Similarly, we position the other endpoint and insert the remaining two lines (Figure 3).

During this editing session, the system has been updating the structure common to all quadrilaterals that is stored in the class Quadrilateral, as well as saving the particular locations of the prototype's sides. To see the structure of the class Quadrilateral, we select *structure* in the menu of formats. The class responds by listing its name, superclasses, part descriptions, and constraints (Figure 4). We may also view the values stored in the prototype by selecting *prototype's values* (Figure 5).

2.1.2 *Demonstrating a Geometry Theorem.* We may now use the new class in demonstrating a geometry theorem. The theorem states that, given an arbitrary quadrilateral, if one bisects each of the sides and draws lines between the adjacent midpoints, the new lines form a parallelogram.

To perform the construction, we make a new class named *QTheorem.* As before, we create it as a subclass of GeometricObject and define it by example. We first add an instance of class Quadrilateral as a part. We select *insert* and *Quadrilateral.* As we move the cursor into the bottom pane, a blinking picture of a quadrilateral, whose shape has been copied from the prototype, appears. We position the quadrilateral and press a button.

The next step is to add midpoints to the sides of the quadrilateral. To do this, we use four instances of the class MidPointLine. This class specifies that each of

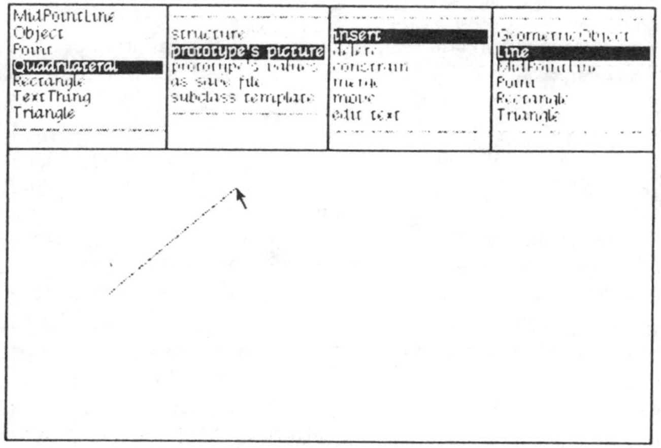

Fig. 2. Positioning the second endpoint of a line.

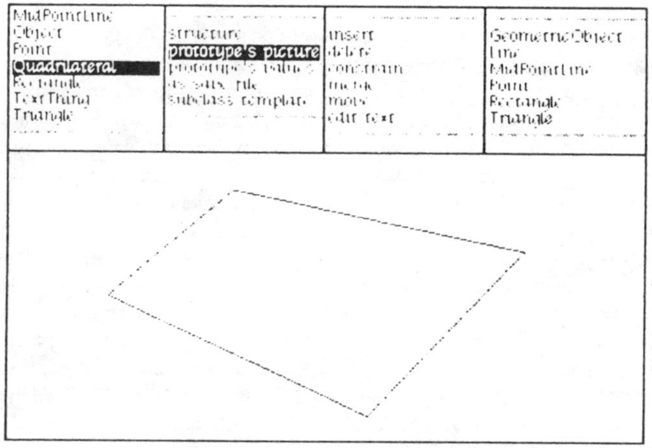

Fig. 3. The completed quadrilateral.

its instances has two parts: a line and a point. In addition, it has a constraint that, for each instance, the point be halfway between the endpoints of the line. As we insert each instance of MidPointLine, we move it near the center of one of the sides of the quadrilateral and merge the line part of the MidPointLine with the side of the quadrilateral (Figure 6). The last step is to add four lines connecting the midpoints to form the parallelogram.

Once the construction is complete, we may move any of the parts of the prototype QTheorem and observe the results. In general, it is not enough for the system simply to move the selected part; because of the constraints we have placed on the object, other parts, such as the midpoints, may need to be moved as well to keep all the constraints satisfied. Suppose we want to move a vertex. We select the message *move* and the argument *Point.* A blinking point appears in the picture that is attached to the cursor. We position it over the vertex to be moved and hold down a button. The vertex follows the cursor until the button is released (Figure 7). (The first time we try to move the vertex, there will be a long pause as the system plans how to satisfy the constraints.) We notice that indeed the lines connecting the midpoints form a parallelogram no matter how the quadrilateral is deformed. The theorem remains true even when the quadrilateral is turned inside out!

2.1.3 *Constraint Satisfaction.* The user described how QTheorem should behave in terms of the midpoint constraint and the various merges, but not by writing separate methods for moving each part of QTheorem. The midpoint constraint (as defined by an experienced user) describes methods that can be invoked to satisfy itself. Three such methods were specified: the first asks the midpoint to move to halfway between the line's endpoints; the second asks one of the line's endpoints to move; and the third asks the other endpoint to move. It was up to QTheorem to decide which of these methods to invoke, and when and in what order to use them.

In general, the constraints on an object might specify its behavior incompletely or redundantly, or they might be unsatisfiable. QTheorem, for example, is underconstrained. The behavior we observed was only one way of moving the vertex while satisfying the constraints. Two other possibilities would have been for the entire object to move, or for the midpoints to remain fixed while the other vertices moved. Neither of these responses would have been as pleasing to us as human observers. (If we had wanted the entire object to move, we would have specified *move QTheorem* instead.) Therefore, besides the more mathematical techniques for finding *some* way of satisfying its constraints, or for deciding that they are unsatisfiable, an object can also take the user's preferences into account in deciding its behavior. In this case, the midpoint constraint specified that the midpoint was to be moved in preference to one of the endpoints of the line.

We might override the preference specified in the midpoint constraint by anchoring the midpoints, as in Figure 8. (Anchor is a subclass of Point, with an added constraint that its instances may not be moved during constraint satisfaction.)

2.2 Constructing a Program for a Graphic Calculator

In this second example, we construct some graphic programs for a simulated calculator. In the process, we use a number of classes from a "calculator kit." One simple but important class is NumberNode. An instance of NumberNode has two

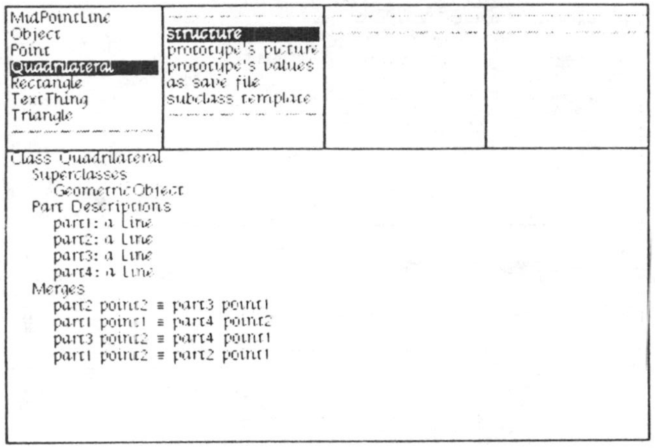

Fig. 4. Structure described by the class Quadrilateral.

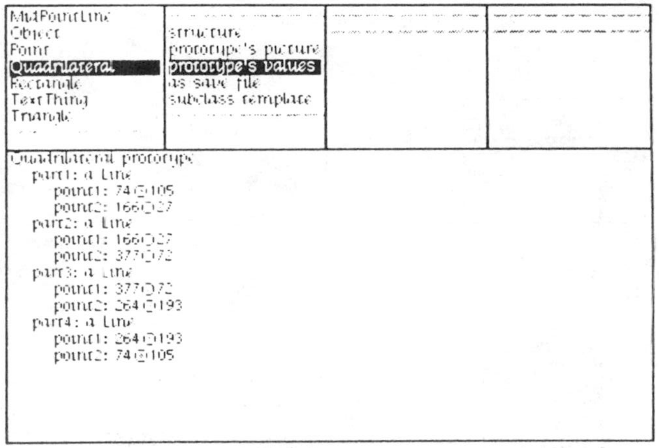

Fig. 5. Values of the prototype Quadrilateral.

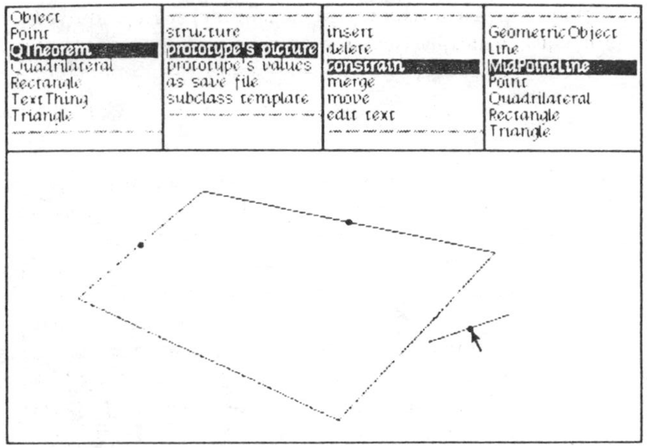

Fig. 6. Adding a midpoint.

parts: a real number and a point. Its purpose is to provide a graphic representation of a register in the calculator. Another class is NumberLead, consisting of a number node and an attached line. As with leads on electrical components, it is used to connect parts of the calculator. Also, classes that represent the various arithmetic operations have been defined. There is a general class Number-Operator, whose parts are a frame containing the operator's symbol and three number leads that terminate on the edges of the frame. Four subclasses of NumberOperator are defined, namely, Plus, Minus, Times, and Divide. Plus, for example, has three number leads with number nodes at the ends, which are inherited from NumberOperator (Figure 9). It has an added constraint that the number at the node on the right always be the sum of the numbers at the leads on the left. The classes for Minus, Times, and Divide prototypes have been defined analogously.

To view and edit a number at a node, the class NumberPrinter has been constructed. Its parts are a number lead and an editable piece of text. Also, it has a constraint that the number at its node correspond to that displayed in the text. If the node's number changes, the text is updated; if the text is edited, the node's number is changed correspondingly. A special kind of NumberPrinter is a Constant. For constants, the constraint is unidirectional. The text may be edited, thus changing the number; but the number may not be changed to alter the text.

2.2.1 *Constructing a Celsius-to-Fahrenheit Converter*. Using these parts, let us construct a Celsius-to-Fahrenheit converter. After creating a new class, TemperatureConverter, we select *insert* and *Times*. As we move the cursor into the picture pane, a blinking picture of an instance of the class Times appears. We position the frame that holds the multiplication symbol, and then the three nodes. Next, we insert a Plus operator in the same manner, connecting its addend node to the product node of the times operator. (The connection is made by merging the nodes, in the same way that the endpoints of the sides of the quadrilateral were connected.) Finally, we insert two instances of Constant, connecting them

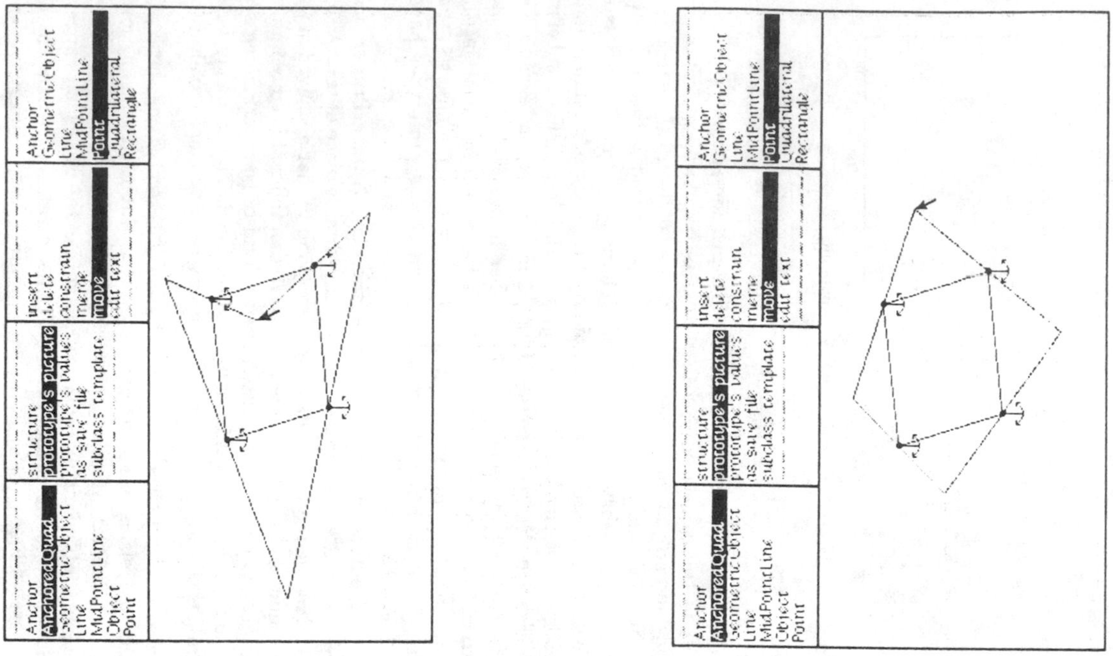

Fig. 8. A quadrilateral with anchored midpoints.

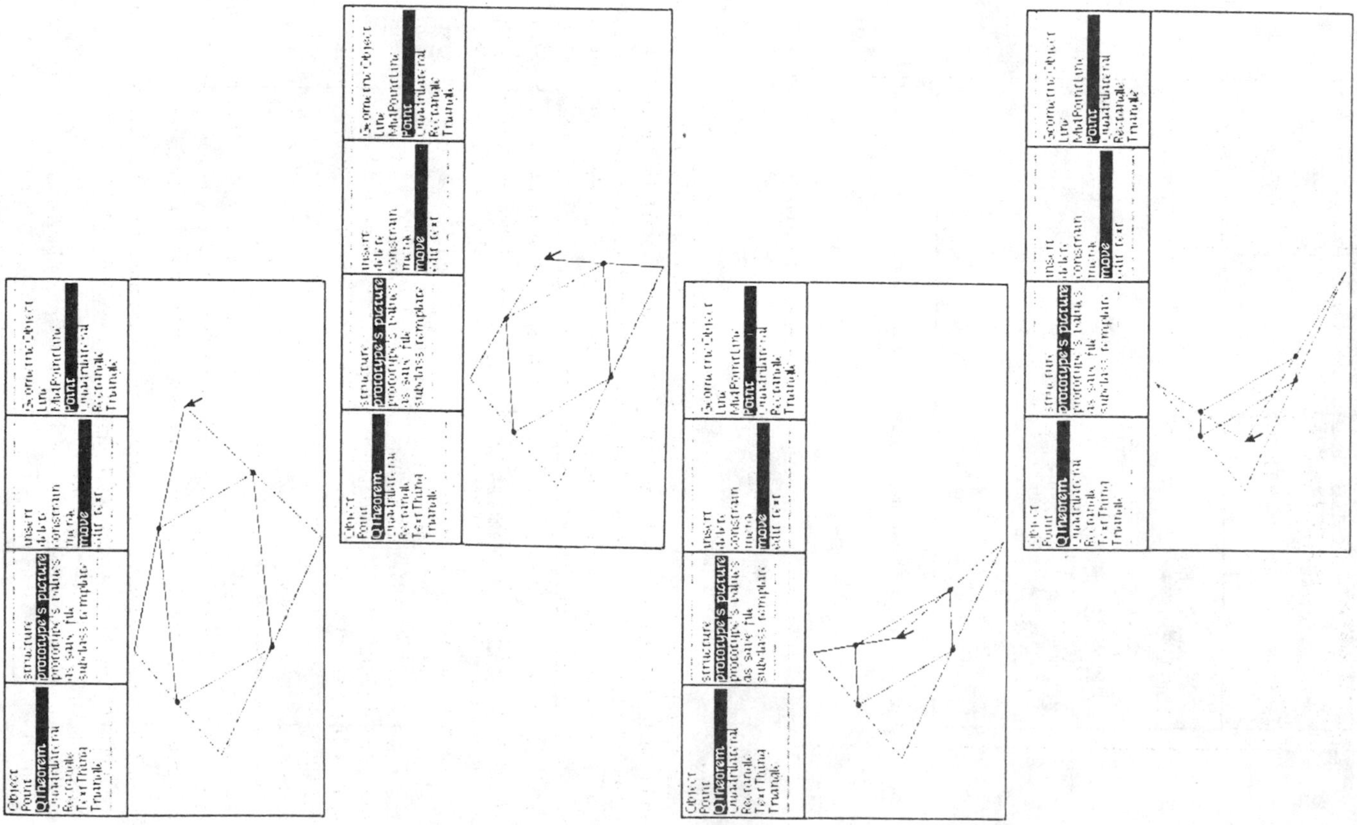

Fig. 7. Moving a vertex of the quadrilateral.

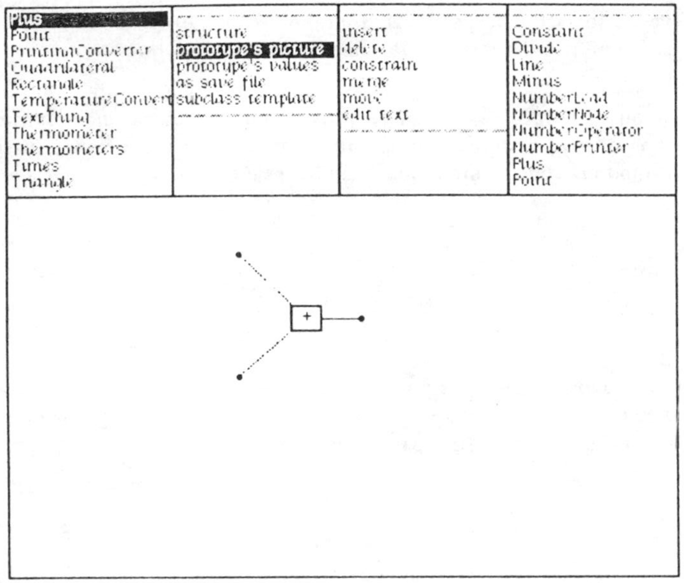

Fig. 9. Picture of the prototype for Plus.

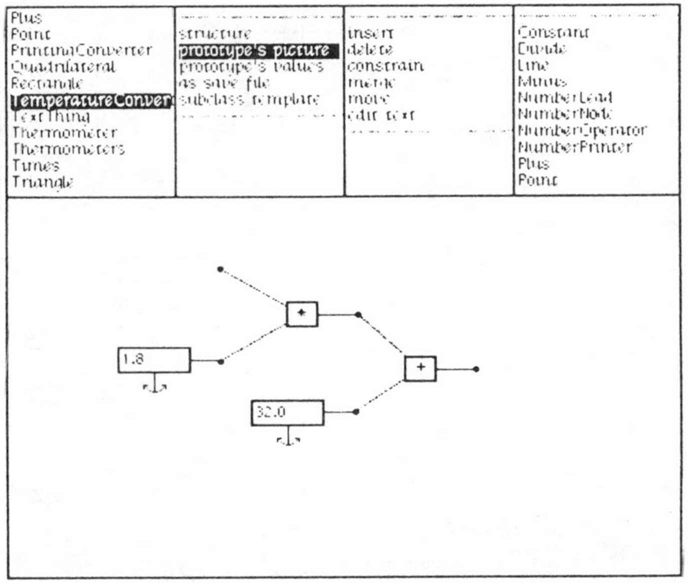

Fig. 10. Picture of the completed Celsius-to-Fahrenheit Converter.

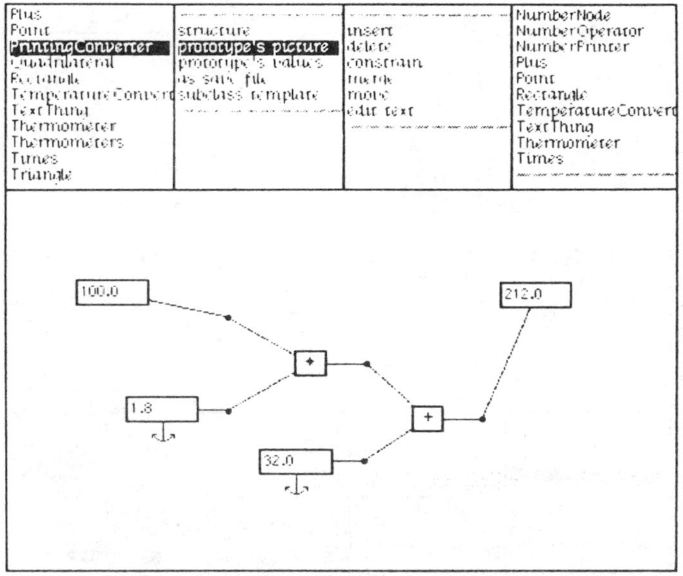

Fig. 11. A PrintingConverter.

to the appropriate nodes of the operators. We then invoke the *edit text* message and change the constants to 1.8 and 32.0. The result is shown in Figure 10.

Once the converter has been defined, we may use it as a part of other objects (i.e., as a subroutine). As an example, we define a new class PrintingConverter. We add an instance of TemperatureConverter as a part, and also two instances of NumberPrinter to display the Celsius and Fahrenheit temperatures (Figure 11). If we edit the Celsius temperature, the PrintingConverter satisfies its constraints by updating the numbers at its nodes and the Fahrenheit temperature displayed in the frame on the right.

However, because of the multiway nature of the constraints, the device works backward as well as forward! Thus, we can edit the Fahrenheit temperature, and the Celsius temperature is updated correspondingly (Figure 12). This demonstrates the need for the special class Constant: without it, the system could equally well have satisfied the constraints by changing one of these coefficients rather than the temperatures.

We may also connect the converter to other types of input/output devices, for example, a simulated thermometer. We can select *move* and *Point* and grab either of the columns of mercury with the cursor. When we move one of the columns up or down, the other column moves correspondingly (Figure 13).

2.2.2 *Solving a Quadratic Equation.* After experimenting with the converter, we might try building a more complex device, such as the network for solving quadratic equations shown in Figure 14.

When we edit any of the constants, the value in the frame on the left changes to satisfy the equation. In the picture, the coefficients of the equation $x^2 - 6x + 9 = 0$ have been entered, and a solution, $x = 3$, has been found. This case is unlike the temperature converter examples: the system was unable to find a one-pass ordering for solving the constraints and has resorted to the relaxation method. Relaxation will converge to one of the two roots of the equation, depending on the initial value of x.

Now let us try changing the constant term c from 9 to 10. This time, the system puts up an error message, protesting that the constraints cannot be satisfied. Some simple algebra reveals that the roots of this new equation are complex; but the number nodes hold real numbers, and so the system was unable to satisfy the constraints.

A better way of finding the roots of a quadratic equation is to use the standard solution to the quadratic equation $ax^2 + bx + c = 0$, namely, $x = (-b \pm (b^2 - 4ac)^{\frac{1}{2}}) / 2a$. The system can be told about this canned formula by defining a class QuadraticSolver whose parts include four NumberNodes a, b, c, and x and a constraint that $x = (-b + (b^2 - 4ac)^{\frac{1}{2}}) / 2a$. (Since the class NumberNode does not allow multiple values, in the QuadraticSolver's constraint one of the roots has been chosen arbitrarily as the value for x. A more general solution would be to define a class MultipleRoots and set up the constraint so that it determined both the number of roots and their values.)

We can insert an instance of QuadraticSolver into the network, merging its number nodes with the appropriate existing nodes in the network (Figure 15). Now, the system can find a simple one-pass ordering for satisfying the constraints and does not need to use relaxation.

In inserting an instance of QuadraticSolver into the network, we have added another view of the constraints on x. In the sense that the permissible values of x are the same with or without it (ignoring the multiple-root problem), the new constraint adds no new information. However, QuadraticSolver's constraint is computationally better suited to finding the value of x. This technique of introducing multiple redundant constraints on an object is an important way of dealing with circularity.

3. OBJECTS

3.1 The Part–Whole Relationship

In ThingLab, an object is composed of named parts, each of which is in turn another object. The parts are thus composed of subparts, and so on. The recursion stops with primitive objects such as integers and strings. Consider a line:

Line
  *point*1: *a Point*
    x: 50
    y: 100
  *point*2: *a Point*
    x: 200
    y: 200.

The line is composed of two parts that are its endpoints. Each endpoint is in turn composed of an x and a y value; these are primitive objects (integers). An object is sometimes referred to as the *owner* of its parts. For example, the above line owns its endpoints.

3.1.1 *Part Descriptions.* A *PartDescription* is an object that describes the common properties of the corresponding parts of all instances of a class. Every

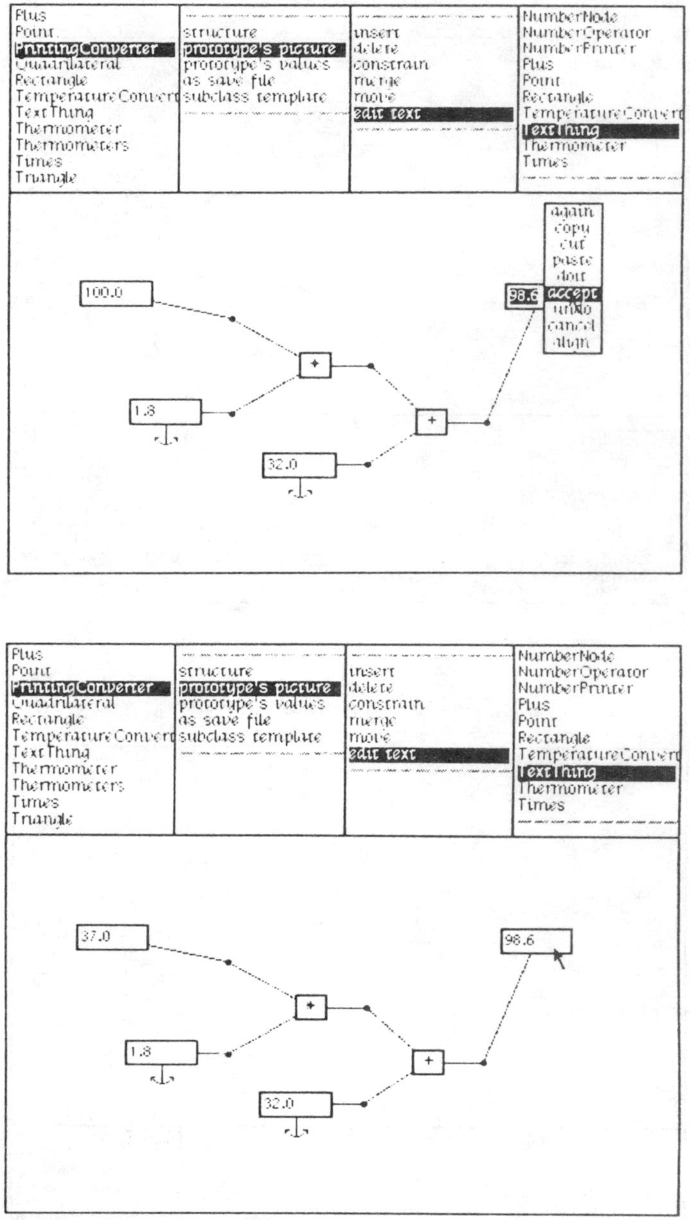

Fig. 12. Editing the Fahrenheit temperature.

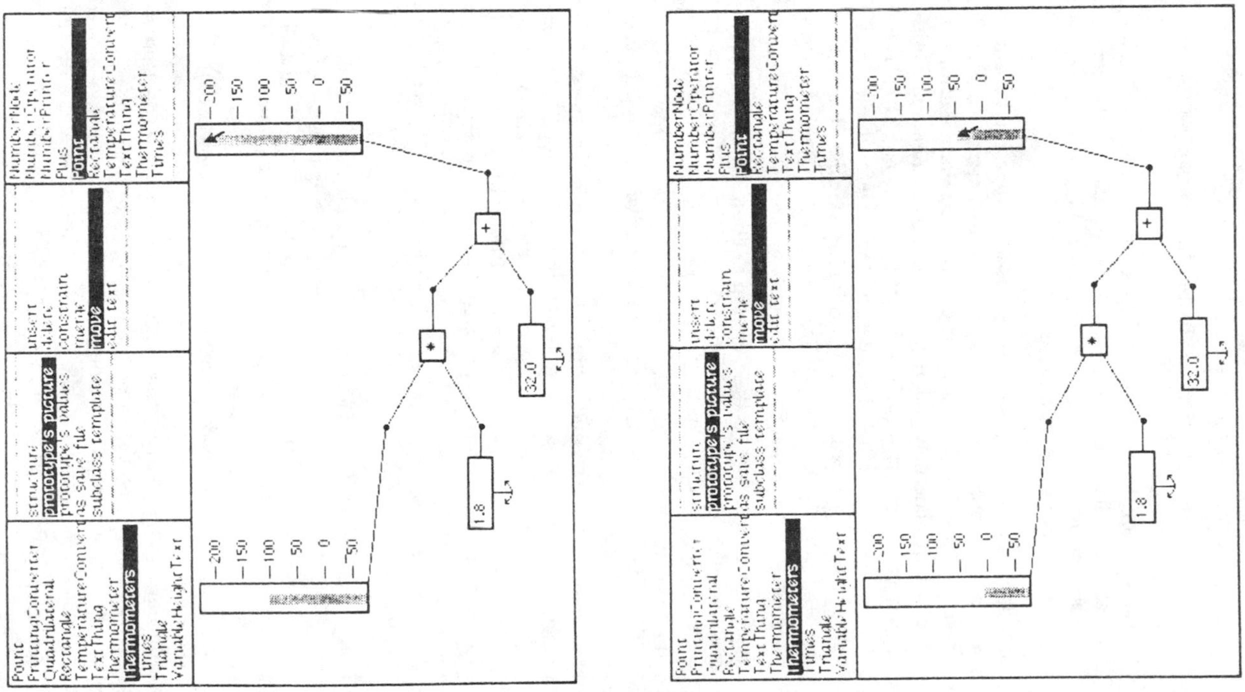

Fig. 13. The temperature converter with thermometers for input and output.

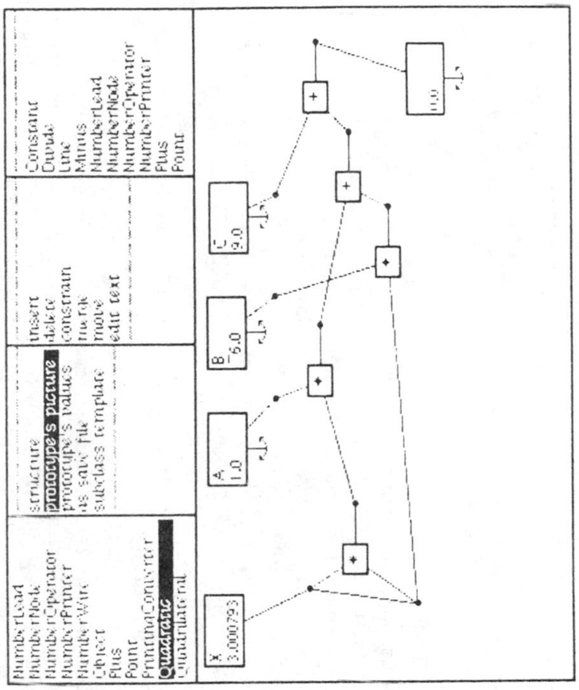

Fig. 14. A quadratic equation network.

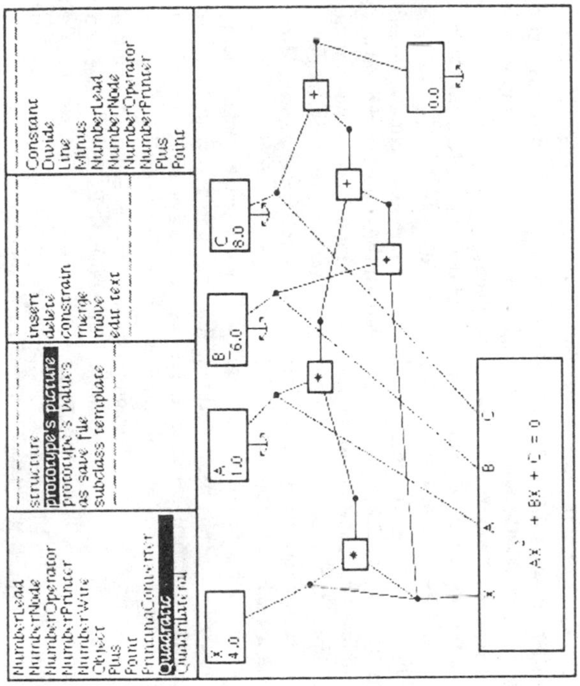

Fig. 15. The network after adding an instance of QuadraticSolver.

class has a list of part descriptions, one for each part owned by its instances. The following things are associated with each part description:

name an identifier;
constraints the set of constraints that apply to the corresponding part of each instance;
merges the set of merges that apply to the corresponding part of each instance;
class the class of the corresponding part of each instance. This is more restrictive than in Smalltalk, where the class of the contents of an instance field is not declared. Imposing this restriction makes the job of constraint satisfaction easier.

When a part description is added to a class, messages are compiled automatically in the class' message dictionary to read and write the part.

For example, the class Line has two part descriptions that describe the parts of each instance of Line. The first part description has the name *point*1. It has no constraints or merges, and it specifies that the *point*1 part of each line be an instance of class Point. The other part description is defined analogously. For a class that specifies some constraints, for example, the class HorizontalLine, the *point*1 part description would also indicate that there was a constraint that applied to the *point*1 part of each of its instances.

3.1.2 *Insides and Outsides.* As described in Section 1.3, one of the important features of Smalltalk is the sharp distinction it makes between the inside and the outside of an object. In ThingLab, the notion of having a part has implications for both the internal and external aspects of the object that owns the part. Internally, the object must have an instance field in which the part is stored, as well as a corresponding part description in its class; externally, the object should understand messages to read and write the part. However, these internal and external aspects are separate. A *virtual part*, as proposed in [2], is an example of the use of this separation. Such a part would have all the external manifestations of a part, that is, messages to read and write it. Internally, however, there would be no corresponding field; rather, the part would be computed as needed. (Smalltalk already has virtual parts; the proposed mechanism would add the necessary declarative superstructure so that the constraint satisfaction mechanism could know about them.)

3.1.3 *Paths.* A *path* is a ThingLab object that represents a symbolic reference to a subpart. Each path is a hierarchical name, consisting of a list of part names that indicates a way to get from some object to one of its subparts. The path itself does not own a pointer to the object to which it is applied; this must be supplied by the user of the path. Thus the same path can be used to refer to the corresponding subpart of many different objects. For example, *point*1 *x* is a path to get to the *x* value of the first endpoint of any line. Typically, the path as such is used only during compilation; this path would compile code that sent the message *point*1 to a line and then sent the message *x* to the result.

While the definition of a path is simple, the idea behind it has proved quite powerful and has been essential in allowing the constraint- and object-oriented metaphors to be integrated. As mentioned above, Smalltalk draws a distinction between the inside and the outside of an object. The notion of a path helps strengthen this distinction by providing a protected way for an object to provide external references to its parts and subparts. For example, if a triangle wishes to allow another object to refer to one of its vertices, it does so by handing back a path such as *side2 point*1, rather than by providing a direct pointer to the vertex. If this other object wants to change the location of the vertex, it must do so by routing the request through the triangle, rather than by simply making the change itself. This allows the triangle to decide whether or not to accept the change; if it does accept it, it knows what has been altered, so that it can update its other parts as necessary to satisfy all its constraints.

In addition to these semantic considerations, a major pragmatic benefit of this discipline is that no backpointers are needed. (If the triangle did hand out a direct pointer to its vertex, the vertex would need a pointer back to the triangle so that it could inform the triangle when it changed.) Access to parts is somewhat slower using this technique, since each access involves following a path. However, an access via a path can often be moved out of the inner loops by the constraint compiler. Another pragmatic consideration is that constraints and merges can be represented symbolically using paths, so that they apply to all instances of a class, rather than to a particular instance. This allows the system to compile constraint satisfaction plans in the form of standard Smalltalk methods.

ThingLab's constraint satisfaction techniques all depend on noticing when one constraint applies to the same subpart as another. Paths are used to specify which parts or subparts of an object are affected by the constraint. Two paths *overlap* if one can be produced from the other by adding zero or more names to the end of the other's list. The following paths overlap the path *side*1 *point*1:

*side*1 *point*1 *x*
*side*1 *point*1
*side*1
(*the empty path*)

The following paths do not overlap *side*1 *point*1:

*side*1 *point*2
*side*2

To test if two constraints apply to the same subpart, the system checks to see if any of their paths overlap.

3.2 Inheritance

A new class may be defined as a subclass of one or more existing classes. The subclass inherits the part descriptions, constraints, merges, and message protocol of its superclasses. It may add new information of its own, and it may override inherited responses to messages. Every class (except class Object) must be a subclass of at least one other class.

The superclasses of an object are represented by including an instance of each superclass as a part of the object. The field descriptions for such parts are instances of SuperclassDescription, a subclass of PartDescription. These parts may have constraints and merges applied to them in the usual way; among other things, this allows the user to indicate that parts inherited from several superclasses are in fact to be represented by only a single part in the subclass. The only difference between these instances of superclasses and ordinary parts is that messages are forwarded to them automatically. (The actual implementation is somewhat more arcane, to take advantage of the efficient single-superclass mechanism built into Smalltalk. However, the effect is as described, and the reader should think of it in this way.)

3.2.1 *Class Object.* The most general class in both Smalltalk and ThingLab is class Object. As part of the ThingLab kernel, a large number of methods have been added to this class. These methods provide defaults for adding or deleting parts, merging parts, satisfying constraints, showing in a ThingLab window, and so on. In general, these methods treat an object as the sum of its parts. For example, to show itself, an object asks each of its parts to show; to move itself by some increment, the object asks each of its parts to move by that increment. This strict hierarchy is, however, modified by the object's constraints and merges. Thus, when an object decides exactly how to move, it must watch for overlap between its parts due to merges, and it must also keep all its constraints satisfied.

3.2.2 *Message Behavior.* When an object receives a message, the object's class first checks its own message dictionary. If a corresponding method is found, that method is used. If not, the class asks each of its superclasses if any of them has an appropriate method. In turn, each superclass, if it does not itself define the method, will ask *its* superclasses, and so forth, thus implementing inheritance through multiple levels of the hierarchy. If there is a single inherited method for that message, then that method is used. If there is no method, or if there are several conflicting inherited methods, an error occurs. Note that the overriding of inherited methods is still allowed; it is an error only if a class with no method of its own inherits different methods via two or more of its immediate superclasses. If the user wants to choose among conflicting messages, or to combine them somehow, an appropriate method for doing this should be defined in the subclass. To avoid this search the next time the message is received, the class automatically compiles a *message forwarder* that will intercept that message in the future and relay it directly to the appropriate superclass part.

As an example of the use of multiple superclasses, suppose that a user has available a class of horizontal lines and another class of lines of constant length. The class of horizontal lines of constant length may then be defined as a subclass of both of these.

Multiple superclasses also provide a way of implementing multiple representations of objects. For example, suppose the user desires to represent a point in both Cartesian and polar forms. This may be done as follows:

Class CartesianPoint
  Superclasses
    GeometricObject
  Part Descriptions
    x: a Real
    y: a Real
Class PolarPoint
  Superclasses
    GeometricObject
  Part Descriptions
    r: a Real
    theta: a Real
Class MultiplyRepresentedPoint
  Superclasses
    C: CartesianPoint
    P: PolarPoint
  Constraints
    C = P asCartesian
      C ← P asCartesian
      P ← C asPolar

The constraint on MultiplyRepresentedPoint keeps the parts representing the two superclasses in coordination. It makes use of an auxiliary message to PolarPoint that returns its Cartesian equivalent, and of an analogous message to CartesianPoint.

3.2.3 *Prototypes.* For a given class, a prototype is a distinguished instance that owns default or typical parts. All classes understand the message *prototype* and respond by returning their prototypical instance. If the user does not specify otherwise, the prototype has nil in each of its instance fields. However, if the user has defined the class by example, the prototype holds the particular values from the example. These values may also be set by writing an initialization message.

Prototypes provide a convenient mechanism for specifying default instance values. Thus, in the introductory example, when a new line was being inserted into the quadrilateral, its initial length and orientation were copied from the prototype Line. Such defaults are essential in graphic editing, since every object needs *some* appearance.

More important, a prototype serves as a representative of its class. ThingLab distinguishes between messages that have no side effects for the receiver (read-only messages), messages that alter the values stored in the receiver, and messages that alter the receiver's structure. Any instance accepts read-only or value-altering messages, but only prototypes accept structure-altering messages. The reason is that this latter type of message affects the class. The prototype is in charge of its class and is willing to alter it, but, for instances other than the prototypical one, the class is read-only. Requests to move a side of a polygon, or even turn it inside out, are examples of value-altering messages. On the other hand, requests to add or delete a side, edit a constraint, or merge two points are structure-altering messages.

3.2.4 *Defining Classes by Example.* When the user defines a class by example, the editing messages are always sent to the prototype, rather than sometimes to the class and sometimes to one of its instances. The prototype takes care of separating the generic information that applies to all instances of its class from the specific information that applies only to the default values that it holds in its fields. With its class it associates the number and class of the parts, the constraints, and the merges. With its own instance fields it associates the default values for its parts.

It is not possible to define all classes by example; some, such as classes for new constraint types and abstract classes like GeometricObject, must be entered by writing an appropriate Smalltalk class definition. In general, there are many possible classes that could be abstracted from a given example; which one *should* be abstracted depends on the user's purposes. The ThingLab facility for definition by example provides a reasonable default, but it is not a general solution to this problem. If the user wants some other sort of class, he or she should write an appropriate definition.

4. CONSTRAINT REPRESENTATION

This section describes the representation of ThingLab constraints. To support constraints, some new kinds of objects were implemented. In Smalltalk, objects communicate by sending and receiving messages; an object's response to a message is implemented by a method (i.e., a procedure). ThingLab objects are described that stand for Smalltalk messages and methods. The purpose of this additional mechanism is to provide tools for reasoning about messages and methods, and in particular about the interactions among messages and constraints.

4.1 Message Plans

A message plan is an abstraction of the Smalltalk notion of sending a message. A message plan does not stand for a particular act of sending a message; rather, it is a template for any number of messages that might be sent. A message plan is itself an object: an instance of class *MessagePlan*. The parts of a message plan include a *receiver*, a *path*, an *action*, and zero or more *arguments*. The receiver is normally a particular object, although for some uses it may be nil or may be a prototype representing any instance of a class of objects that might receive the message. The path tells how to get to one of the receiver's subparts, which will be called the *target* of the message plan. The action is a *selector* for a Smalltalk method understood by the target. The arguments may be either actual or symbolic. Actual arguments are pointers to other objects; symbolic arguments are simply names (strings). The arguments correspond to the arguments passed at run time to the Smalltalk method invoked by the action. For example, here is a message plan asking a triangle to move one of its vertices right by ten screen dots:

*triangle side*1 *point*2 *moveby:* 10@0.

The receiver is *triangle*, the path is *side*1 *point*2, the action is *moveby:*, and the argument is the point 10@0.

An important use of message plans is to describe the methods for satisfying a constraint. If a message plan is used in this way, the plan will have several Boolean flags and a pointer to the constraint that generated it, in addition to the parts listed above. The flags are the following:

- *uniqueState* — true if there is only one state of the target that will satisfy the constraint (given that all other parts of the receiver are fixed). See Section 4.3.2 below;
- *referenceOnly* — true if the action described by the message plan only references its target, rather than altering it;
- *compileTimeOnly* — true if the message plan is used only during constraint satisfaction planning and not in producing executable code.

4.2 Methods

In ThingLab, an explicit class *Method* has been defined. The parts of a method are a list of *keywords*, a matching list of symbolic *arguments*, a list of *temporaries*, and a procedural *body*. The selector for the method is constructed by concatenating the keywords. These parts are the same as those of a Smalltalk method, the only difference being that in Smalltalk the method is stored as text, and the parts must be found by parsing the text. One reason for defining an explicit class in ThingLab is to simplify access to the parts of a method. This is useful because methods are often generated by the system rather than being entered by the user, with different parts of the method coming from different parts of the system. Also, some methods have their own special properties. For example, all the methods that an object has for showing itself are indexed in a table used by the ThingLab user interface.

After a ThingLab method has been constructed, it is usually asked to add itself to some class' method dictionary. In the implementation, the method does this by constructing a piece of text and handing it to the regular Smalltalk compiler. The Smalltalk compiler in turn produces a byte-coded string for use at run time and indexes it in the class' method dictionary.

4.3 The Structure of a Constraint

As described in Section 1, a constraint represents a relation among the parts of an object that must always hold. Constraints are themselves objects. New kinds of constraints are defined by specifying both a *rule* and a set of *methods* for satisfying the constraint. Adding or modifying a constraint is a structural change; Constraints are indexed in several tables in the prototype's class for easy retrieval during constraint satisfaction.

The constraint's methods describe alternate ways of satisfying the constraint; if any one of the methods is invoked, the constraint will be satisfied. These methods are represented as a list of instances of class Method. The constraint also has a matching list of instances of MessagePlan. Each message plan specifies how to invoke the corresponding method and describes its effects. When the constraint satisfier decides that one of the methods will need to be invoked at run time, the message plan that represents that method is asked to generate code that will send the appropriate Smalltalk message to activate the method. Exactly which methods are used depends on the other constraints and on the user's preferences as to what should be done if the object is underconstrained.

The rule is used to construct a procedural test for checking whether or not the constraint is satisfied and to construct an error expression that indicates how well the constraint is satisfied. Both the test and the error expression are instances of class Method. These methods are constructed in a fairly simple-minded way. If the constraint's rule equates numbers or points, the test checks that the two sides of the equation are equal to within some tolerance; the error will be the difference of the two sides of the equation. If the constraint is nonnumerical, the rule is used directly to generate the test; the error will be zero if the constraint is satisfied and one if it is not. If the user wants to override these default methods, he or she can replace them with hand-coded Smalltalk methods.

4.3.1 *Example of a Constraint.* Consider the structure described by the class MidPointLine used in the quadrilateral example.

Class MidPointLine
Superclasses
Geometric Object
Part Descriptions
line: *a Line*
midpoint: a Point
Constraints
midpoint = (*line point*1 + *line point*2)/2
midpoint ← (*line point*1 + *line point*2)/2
*line point*1 ← *midpoint* * 2 − *line point*2
*line point*2 ← *midpoint* * 2 − *line point*1

The class MidPointLine has a constraint that the midpoint lie halfway between the endpoints of the line. The constraint has three alternate ways of satisfying itself, as described by the methods listed under the rule. The first method alters the midpoint, the second one alters one endpoint of the line, and the third alters the other endpoint.

The user may want one method to be used in preference to another if there is a choice. This is indicated by the order of the methods: if the system has a choice about which method to use to satisfy the constraint, the first one on the list is used. In the case of the midpoint, the user preferred that the constraint be satisfied by moving the midpoint rather than by moving an end of the line.

4.3.2 *Relations Among the Parts of a Constraint.* The relations among the parts of a constraint are fairly rigidly defined. Each of the methods, if invoked, must cause the constraint to be satisfied. For every part that is referenced by the rule, there must be either a method that alters that part or a dummy method referencing it. Currently, it is up to the user to see that these requirements are met; none of this is checked by the system.

As has been previously discussed, Smalltalk makes a strong distinction between the inside and the outside of an object. A method for satisfying a constraint is internal to the constraint and its owner, while the message plan that describes the method is the external handle of that method. It is the message plan that is used by the constraint satisfier in planning how to satisfy an object's constraints.

In particular, the path of a message plan describes the side effects of its method. The constraint satisfier uses this information to detect overlap in the parts affected by the various methods. Therefore, the more precisely one can specify which subparts are affected by the method, the more information the constraint satisfier has to work with. Also, the constraint satisfier can do more with a method if it is known that there is only one state of the subpart affected by the method that satisfies the constraint, given the states of all other parts. This is described by the Boolean variable *uniqueState* listed previously; in the example above, *uniqueState* is true.

This way of describing constraints allows the representation of relations that are not very tractable analytically. Any sort of relation can be expressed as a constraint, if a procedural test exists and some algorithm can be specified for satisfying the relation. In the most extreme case of analytical intractability, the constraint has a single method that affects the entire object that owns the constraint, and this message is not *uniqueState*. However, in such a case, the constraint satisfier has little to work with, and only one such constraint can be handled.

4.4 Merges

An important special case of a constraint is a *merge*. When several parts are merged, they are constrained to be all equal. For efficiency, they are usually replaced by a single object, rather than being kept as several separate objects. The owner of the parts maintains a symbolic representation of the merge for use by constraint satisfiers, as well as for reconstruction of the original parts if the merge is deleted. There are two principal uses of merging, both of which were illustrated by the introductory example in Section 2.1. The first use is to represent connectivity, for example, to connect the sides of the quadrilateral. The other is for applying predefined constraints, as was done with the midpoint constraint. As with constraints, adding or modifying a merge is a structural change; so only prototypes allow their merges to be edited. The process of merging is the same for both these uses. The object that owns the parts to be merged (e.g., QTheorem) is sent the message *merge: paths*, where *paths* is a list of paths to the parts to be merged.

When it can be done, the replacement of several merged objects by a single object yields a more compact storage format and speeds up constraint satisfaction considerably, since information need not be copied back and forth between the parts that have been declared equal. It does not result in any loss of information, since the owner of the parts keeps a symbolic representation of the merge that contains enough information to reconstruct the original parts. On the other hand, it is slower to merge or unmerge parts, since more computation is required; so, for applications in which the structure of the object changes frequently, equality constraints would be more efficient. Another efficiency consideration is that a single merge can apply to an indefinite number of objects, while constraints have built into them the number of objects to which they apply. Thus, it is simple to make five separate points be equal using merges. To do this with equality constraints would require either that four separate constraints be used or that a special equality constraint be defined for use with five objects.

The most difficult parts of the ThingLab system to program and debug were those that deal with adding and deleting merges, due especially to interactions among merges at different levels of the part–whole hierarchy. For example, in the quadrilateral construction presented in Section 2.1, when merging the line part of the MidPointLine with the side of the quadrilateral, the system not only had to substitute a new line for the two line parts, but because of the merges connecting the sides of the quadrilateral it also had to substitute a new endpoint for the two connecting sides. In fact, at one point the author gave up in disgust and always represented merges by using equality constraints; but he eventually backtracked on this choice because it made things too slow for typical uses of ThingLab. Future implementers of systems using merges are hereby warned!

5. CONSTRAINT SATISFACTION

5.1 Overview

Constraint satisfaction is divided into two stages: planning and run time. Planning commences when an object is presented with a message plan. This message plan is not an actual request to do something; rather, it is a declaration of intent: a description of a message that might be sent to the object. Given this description, the object generates a plan to be used at run time for receiving such messages, while satisfying any constraints that might be affected. The results of this planning are compiled as a Smalltalk method. Directions for calling the compiled method are returned as a new message plan.

Consider the quadrilateral example described in Section 2.1. When the user selects *move Point* and first positions the cursor over a vertex of the quadrilateral, the ThingLab window composes a message plan and presents it to the quadrilateral. The quadrilateral decides how to move its vertex while still keeping all the midpoint constraints satisfied and embeds this plan in a compiled Smalltalk method. It then returns another message plan that gives directions for invoking that method. As the user pulls on the vertex with the cursor, the window repeatedly sends the quadrilateral a message asking it to update its position. This message invokes the Smalltalk method that was just compiled.

During planning, the object that is presented with the message plan creates an instance of ConstraintSatisfier to handle all the work. The constraint satisfier gathers up all the constraints that might be affected by the change and plans a method for satisfying them. The constraint satisfier first attempts to find a one-pass ordering for satisfying the constraints. There are two techniques available for doing this: propagation of degrees of freedom and propagation of known states. If there are constraints that cannot be handled by either of these techniques, the constraint satisfier asks the object for a method for dealing with circularity. Currently, relaxation is the only such method available. If relaxation is used, the user is warned, so that perhaps some other redundant constraints can be supplied that eliminate the need for relaxation. Relaxation is described in Section 5.2.3.

5.2 Constraint Satisfaction Methods

The constraint satisfaction methods used in ThingLab are now described in more detail. To illustrate the operation of the methods, an electrical circuit example is used (Figure 16). Briefly, the classes involved are as follows. Instances of class Node are connection points. The parts of a node are a voltage and a set of currents flowing into that node; there is also a constraint that the sum of the currents be zero. (This is Kirchhoff's current law.) A subclass of Node is Ground, which has an additional constraint that its voltage be zero. Instances of Lead, like their physical counterparts, are used to connect devices. The parts of a lead are a node and a current; there is a constraint that the current belong to the node's set of currents flowing into it. Leads are connected by merging their nodes. There is a general class TwoLeadedObject, whose parts are two instances of Lead, and which has a constraint that the currents in the lead be equal and opposite. A number of subclasses of TwoLeadedObject are defined, including Resistor, Battery, Wire, and Meter; Meter in turn has subclasses Ammeter and Voltmeter. All these objects have appropriate constraints on their behavior: a resistor must obey the Ohm's law constraint relating its resistance, the current flowing through it, and the voltage across it; an ammeter must display the current flowing through it; and so forth. A complete listing of the ThingLab classes for building electrical circuit simulations is given in [2].

5.2.1 *Propagation of Degrees of Freedom.* In propagating degrees of freedom, the constraint satisfier looks for a part with enough degrees of freedom so that it can be altered to satisfy all its constraints. If such a part is found, that part and all the constraints that apply to it can be removed from further consideration. Once this is done, another part may acquire enough degrees of freedom to satisfy all its constraints. The process continues in this manner until either all constraints have been taken care of or no more degrees of freedom can be propagated.

Because of the difficulty of giving a precise definition of degrees of freedom for nonnumeric objects, the constraint satisfier uses a simpleminded criterion for deciding if a part has enough degrees of freedom to satisfy its constraints: it has enough degrees of freedom if there is only one constraint that affects it. It does not matter whether or not the constraint determines the part's state uniquely (removes all its degrees of freedom).

In deciding when a constraint affects a part, the part–whole hierarchy must be taken into account. The set of constraints that affect a given part is found by checking whether the path to the part overlaps the paths of any of the message plans generated by the constraints. Thus, a constraint on the first endpoint of a line affects the line as a whole, the first endpoint, and the x coordinate of the first endpoint; but it does not affect the line's second endpoint.

ACM Transactions on Programming Languages and Systems, Vol. 3, No. 4, October 1981.

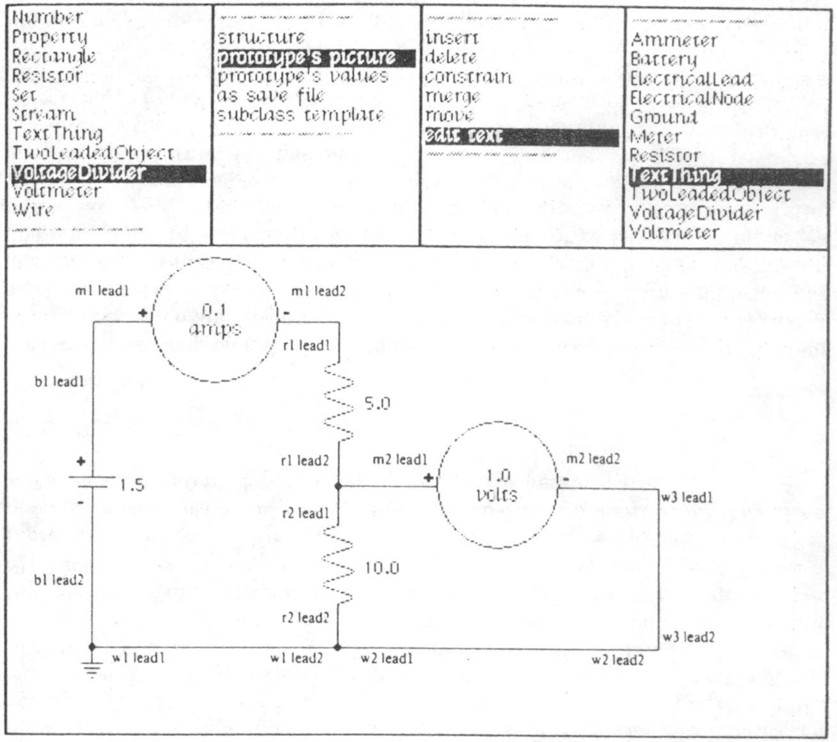

Fig. 16. A voltage divider.

In the voltage divider example, the text that displays the voltmeter's reading has only a single constraint on it: that it correspond to the voltage drop between *m*2 *lead*1 *node* and *m*2 *lead*2 *node*. Similarly, the text in the ammeter is constrained only by its relation to *m*1 *lead*1 *current*. Therefore, these pieces of text can be updated after the voltage drop and current are determined, and their constraints can be removed from further consideration. In this case, there are no propagations that follow.

5.2.2 *Propagation of Known States.* This method is very similar to the previous one. In propagating known states, the constraint satisfier looks for parts whose state will be completely known at run time, that is, parts that have no degrees of freedom. If such a part is found, the constraint satisfier looks for one-step deductions that will allow the states of other parts to be known at run time, and so on recursively. For the state of part A to be known (in one step) from the state of part B, there must be a constraint that connects A and B and that determines A's state uniquely. This is indicated by the *uniqueState* flag on the message plan whose target is A. When propagating known states, the constraint satisfier can use information from different levels in the part–whole hierarchy: if the state of an object is known, the states of all its parts are known; if the states of all the parts of an object are known, the state of the object is known.

If the state of a part is uniquely determined by several different constraints, one of the constraints is used to find its state, and run-time checks are compiled to see if the other constraints are satisfied.

In the example, this method would be used as follows. By the constraint on the ground, at run time *b*1 *lead*2 *node voltage* is known. (Actually, it was already known during planning, but the constraint satisfier does not use this information.) Also, by the battery's constraint, *b*1 *lead*1 *node voltage* is known, and it is the same as *m*1 *lead*1 *node voltage*. The ammeter has a constraint that there be no voltage drop across it, and so *m*1 *lead*2 *node voltage* is known. Similarly, the voltmeter has a constraint that it draw no current, and so the current in its leads and connecting wires is known. Finally, by the constraint on the wires, *w*1 *lead*2 *node voltage*, *w*2 *lead*2 *node voltage*, and *w*3 *lead*1 *node voltage* are all known.

The voltage at the node between the resistors, and all the other currents, are still unknown.

5.2.3 *Relaxation*. If there are constraints that cannot be handled by either of these techniques, the constraint satisfier asks the object for a method for dealing with circularity. Currently, relaxation is the only such method available (unless the user supplies more information; see below). Relaxation can be used only with objects that have all numeric values; also, the constraints must be such that they can be adequately approximated by a linear equation.

When relaxation is to be used, a call on an instance of Relaxer is compiled. At run time, the relaxer changes each of the object's numerical values in turn so as to minimize the error expressions of its constraints. These changes are determined by approximating the constraints on a given value as a set of linear equations and finding a least-mean-squares fit to this set of equations. The coefficients of each linear equation are calculated by noting the initial error and by numerically finding the derivative of the error expressions with respect to the value. Relaxation continues until all the constraints are satisfied (all the errors are less than some cutoff), or until the system decides that it cannot satisfy the constraints (the errors fail to decrease after an iteration).

Often, many more parts would be relaxed than need to be. To help ease this situation, a trick is used during planning. The trick is to try assuming that the state of one of the parts to be relaxed, say P, is known. This part P is chosen by looking for the part with the largest number of constraints connecting it to other still unknown parts. P is placed in a set S. Then the method of propagation of known states is invoked to see if the states of any other parts would become known as a result. All the parts which would become known, along with P itself, are eliminated from the set of parts to be relaxed. The process is repeated until the set of parts to be relaxed is empty. At run time, only the parts in S are relaxed. As each part P in S is relaxed, the system also computes the new states of the parts which had become known as a result of assuming that P was known. In computing the error in satisfying the constraints on P, the system considers the errors in satisfying the constraints on both P itself and also these other parts.

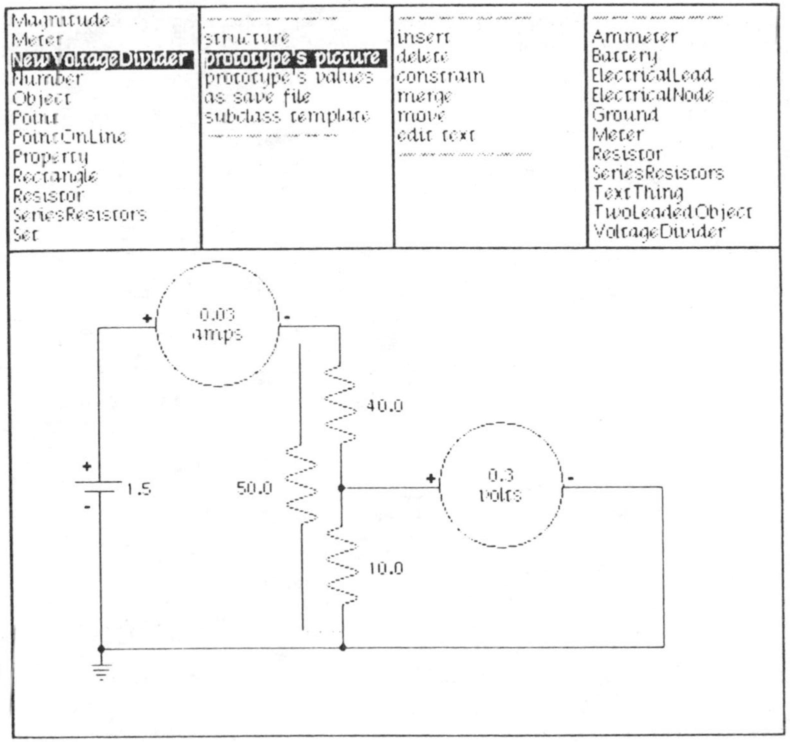

Fig. 17. The voltage divider with an added instance of SeriesResistors.

In the voltage divider, *r*2 *lead*1 *current* has three constraints connecting it to other unknowns: the Ohm's law constraint on *r*2, *r*2's constraint inherited from TwoLeadedObject, and the Kirchhoff's law constraint on *r*2 *lead*1 *node*. No other unknown has more constraints, and so the system tries assuming that it is known. Given its value, *r*2 *lead*1 *node voltage* and all the other currents would be known. Therefore, at run time, only *r*2 *lead*1 *current* is relaxed.

5.2.4 *Using Multiple Views to Avoid Relaxation*. Using the method employed by Steele and Sussman [13], another view of the voltage divider may be added that obviates the need for relaxation. First, a new class SeriesResistors is defined that embodies the fact that two resistors in series are equivalent to a single resistor. An instance of SeriesResistors has three parts: resistors *rA* and *rB*, which are connected in series, and an equivalent single resistor *rSeries*. There is a constraint that the resistance of *rSeries* be equal to the sum of *rA*'s resistance and *rB*'s resistance.

To add this new description to the voltage divider, an instance of SeriesResistors is inserted in the circuit (call it *series*), and the resistors *rA* and *rB* of *series* are merged with the existing resistors *r*1 and *r*2 in the circuit (Figure 17).

Using this additional description, all the constraints can be satisfied in one pass. As previously described, *m1 lead2 node voltage* and *w1 lead2 node voltage* are both known. These are the same as *series rSeries lead1 node voltage* and *series rSeries lead2 node voltage*, respectively. Thus, by the Ohm's law constraint on *series rSeries*, *series rSeries lead1 current* is known. But this is the same current as *series rA lead1 current* and also the same as *r1 lead1 current*. Again by Ohm's law, the voltage at the midpoint, *r1 lead2 node voltage*, is known. All the other currents are also known.

It is appropriate to apply this redundant view to a pair of resistors in series only if there is no significant current flowing from the center node of the resistors. If this is not the case, then some of the constraints are not satisfiable, and the user is notified. However, in the present implementation there is no explicit representation of the fact that a redundant description has been provided; the system could do a better job of describing the reason that the constraints could not be satisfied if it knew about the use of such descriptions.

6. CONCLUSION

This paper has described ThingLab, a simulation laboratory. The system uses a number of concepts and techniques (in particular, constraints) that could add significant power to programming languages. A promising direction for future research is to explore the design of a full constraint-oriented programming language; work on this topic is underway, both by the author and by other researchers. Constraints will be taking an increasingly prominent position in our paradigms for programming in the years to come.

ACKNOWLEDGMENTS

Among the many people who have helped with this research, I would particularly like to thank all the members of the Learning Research Group at Xerox Palo Alto Research Center and my dissertation advisor, Terry Winograd. Thanks also to the referees for their useful comments.

REFERENCES

1. Bobrow, D., and Winograd, T. An overview of KRL, a Knowledge Representation Language. *Cognitive Sci. 1*, 1 (Jan. 1977), 3–46.
2. Borning, A. ThingLab—A Constraint-Oriented Simulation Laboratory. Ph.D. dissertation, Dep. Computer Science, Stanford Univ., Stanford, Calif., March 1979 (revised version available as Rep. SSL-79-3, Xerox PARC, Palo Alto, Calif., July 1979).
3. Dahl, O.-J., and Nygaard, K. SIMULA—An ALGOL-based simulation language. *Commun. ACM 9*, 9 (Sept. 1966), 671–678.
4. Elcock, E.W., Foster, J.M., Gray, P.M.D., McGregor, J.J., and Murray, A.M. ABSET, a programming language based on sets: Motivation and examples. In *Machine Intelligence*, vol. 6, B. Meltzer and D. Michie (Eds.). Edinburgh University Press, Edinburgh, Scotland, 1971, pp. 467–492.
5. Hewitt, C. Viewing control structures as patterns of passing messages. *Artif. Intell. 8*, 3 (June 1977), 323–364.
6. Ingalls, D.H.H. The Smalltalk-76 programming system: Design and implementation. In Conf. Rec., 5th Ann. ACM Symp. Principles of Programming Languages, Tucson, Ariz., Jan. 23–25, 1978, pp. 9–16.
7. Kay, A., and Goldberg, A. Personal dynamic media. *Computer 10*, 3 (March 1977), 31–42.
8. Lieberman, H., and Hewitt, C. A session with TINKER: Interleaving program testing with program design. In Proc. 1980 LISP Conf., Stanford Univ., Stanford, Calif., Aug. 1980, pp. 90–99.
9. Liskov, B., Snyder, A., Atkinson, R., and Shaffert, C. Abstraction mechanisms in CLU. *Commun. ACM 20*, 8 (Aug. 1977), 564–576.
10. Mitchell, J., Maybury, W., and Sweet, R. Mesa language manual. Rep. CSL-79-3, Xerox PARC, Palo Alto, Calif., April 1979.
11. Smith, D. PYGMALION: A creative programming environment. Rep. AIM-260, Dep. Computer Science, Stanford Univ., June 1975.
12. Steele, G. The Definition and Implementation of a Computer Programming Language Based on Constraints. Ph.D. dissertation, Dep. Electrical Engineering and Computer Science, M.I.T., Cambridge, Mass., Aug. 1980 (available as MIT-AI TR 595, Aug. 1980).
13. Steele, G.L., Jr., and Sussman, G.J. Constraints. MIT AI Lab. Memo 502, M.I.T., Cambridge, Mass., Nov. 1978. Also in APL '79: Conf. Proc., *APL Quote Quad* (ACM SIGPLAN/STAPL) *9*, 4 (June 1979), part 1, pp. 208–225.
14. Steels, L. Reasoning modelled as a society of communicating experts. MIT-AI TR 542, M.I.T., Cambridge, Mass., 1979.
15. Stefik, M. Planning with constraints (MOLGEN: part 1). *Artif. Intell. 16*, 2 (May 1981), 111–139.
16. Sutherland, I. Sketchpad: A Man-Machine Graphical Communication System. Ph.D. dissertation, Dep. Electrical Engineering, M.I.T., Cambridge, Mass., 1963.
17. Wulf, W.A., London, R., and Shaw, M. An introduction to the construction and verification of Alphard programs. *IEEE Trans. Softw. Eng. SE-2*, 4 (Dec. 1976), 253–264.

Logic for Improving Integrity Checking in Relational Data Bases*

Jean-Marie Nicolas

ONERA-CERT, Département d'Informatique 2, avenue Edouard Belin, F-31055 Toulouse, France

Summary. When an "updating" operation occurs on the current state of a data base, one has to ensure the new state obeys the integrity constraints. So, some of them have to be evaluated on this new state. The evaluation of an integrity constraint can be time consuming, but one can improve such an evaluation by taking advantage from the fact that the integrity constraint is satisfied in the current state. Indeed, it is then possible to derive a simplified form of this integrity constraint which is sufficient to evaluate in the new state in order to determine whether the initial constraint is still satisfied in this new state. The purpose of this paper is to present a simplification method yielding such simplified forms for integrity constraints. These simplified forms depend on the nature of the updating operation which is the cause of the state change. The operations of inserting, deleting, updating a tuple in a relation as well as transactions of such operations are considered. The proposed method is based on syntactical criteria and is validated through first order logic. Examples are treated and some aspects of the method application are discussed.

0. Introduction

Integrity constraints on relational data bases define the intension of relations [3, 24]; otherwise stated they express time independent properties of relations [6]. On another hand a data base state provides an extension (set of tuples) for each of the considered relations. Obviously, intension and extension of relations have to be compatible; i.e. only valid data base states, those that obey the integrity constraints, are relevant.

Given a (valid) data base state, the current state, a new state is obtained either by inserting, deleting or updating a tuple in a relation extension or by applying a sequence, called transaction [13, 17], of such operations which is

* The work reported in this paper was supported by the D.R.E.T.

In an interpretation with domain $\mathscr{E}$, a closed wff is either true or false, while a (open) wff with n ($n \geqq 1$) free variables determines a set of n-tuples (i.e. a relation) on $\mathscr{E}^n$. Each of these n-tuples is such that when its components are substituted for the corresponding free variables in the open wff then the closed wff which is obtained is true in this interpretation. If the set of n-tuples is empty then the open wff is said to be false, and if the set of n-tuples coincides with $\mathscr{E}^n$ then the open wff is said to be true.

Finally, an interpretation of a set of wffs $\mathscr{W}$ is called a *model* of $\mathscr{W}$ if and only if every wff of $\mathscr{W}$ is true in this interpretation.

1.2.2. Another view of an interpretation

For convenience in the proof of some theorems stated in the following sections, we will present another way to look at an interpretation of logical formulas and to evaluate wffs under Skolem standard form. Readers not interested in the validation of the simplification method (presented in paragraph 4.1.4) can skip this section.

Let W be a function free wff in prenex conjunctive normal form. We shall emphasize that arguments of atomic formulas in W, are either constants or variables (universally or existentially quantified).

Now, let us consider SW, the Skolem standard form of W obtained by substituting adequate Skolem terms for existentially quantified variables in W and erasing existential quantifiers. SW is a conjunction of clauses, and arguments of literals in SW are either variables (universally quantified), constants or Skolem terms. In order to avoid any confusion between Skolem constant and non Skolem ones, which may occur in SW, the former will be referred to as (0-ary) Skolem functions or Skolem terms, while the latter will be referred to as constants or elements.

Assume I is an interpretation of W. Because of the Skolem functions, I is a non complete interpretation of SW. However, W is true in I iff there is a valuation on I of the Skolem functions occurring in SW (an F-valuation), such that SW is true in I (under the F-valuation). Let us make more precise this equivalence. For that purpose, another way to look at the interpretation I is given below [7].

For any n-ary predicate symbol R in W, let us also refer to its assigned relation in I as R. The interpretation I can be looked at as its set of elements $\mathscr{E}(I)$ together with a set of (ground) literals $\mathscr{L}(I)$ defined as follows. For any n-ary predicate symbol R in W and for any tuple $\langle e_1, \ldots, e_n \rangle \in \mathscr{E}(I)^n$: if $\langle e_1, \ldots, e_n \rangle \in R$, then $R(e_1, \ldots, e_n) \in \mathscr{L}(I)$ else $\neg R(e_1, \ldots, e_n) \in \mathscr{L}(I)$; no other literal belongs to $\mathscr{L}(I)$.

If we make explicit the variables occurring in SW by writing it as $SW(x_1, \ldots, x_p)$ then, according to that view of an interpretation, W is true in I iff there is an F-valuation on I, such that for any tuple

$$\langle e_1, \ldots, e_p \rangle \in \mathscr{E}(I)^p$$

at least one literal of each of the (ground) clauses in $FSW(e_1, \ldots, e_p)$ belongs to $\mathscr{L}(I)$. $FSW(e_1, \ldots, e_p)$ is obtained from $SW(e_1, \ldots, e_p)$ by replacing each Skolem term by its value according to the F-valuation.

As an example, suppose W is the following formula:

$$W\colon \forall x \exists y((\neg P(x) \vee Q(x,y)) \wedge R(y)),$$

its Skolem standard form is:

$$SW(x)\colon \forall x((\neg P(x) \vee Q(x, f(x))) \wedge R(f(x))).$$

Let I be the interpretation of W defined as follows:

$\mathscr{E}(I) = \{a, b\}$

$P(x)$
a

$Q(x,y)$
a b
b a

$R(x)$
b

The reader can verify that W is true in I.

Now, $\mathscr{L}(I) = \{P(a), \neg P(b), Q(a,b), Q(b,a), \neg Q(a,a), \neg Q(b,b), R(b), \neg R(a)\}$ and four F-valuations can be defined on I:

$$f(a)=a,\quad f(b)=a;\qquad f(a)=a,\quad f(b)=b;$$
$$f(a)=b,\quad f(b)=a;\qquad f(a)=b,\quad f(b)=b.$$

Finally, one gets:

$$SW(a)\colon (\neg P(a) \vee Q(a, f(a))) \wedge R(f(a))$$
$$SW(b)\colon (\neg P(b) \vee Q(b, f(b))) \wedge R(f(b))$$

and, according to the latest of the above F-valuations:

$$FSW(a)\colon (\neg P(a) \vee Q(a,b)) \wedge R(b)$$
$$FSW(b)\colon (\neg P(b) \vee Q(b,b)) \wedge R(b).$$

At least one literal of each clause in both of them belongs to $\mathscr{L}(I)$.

2. Integrity Constraints as Logical Formulas

In a relational data base, integrity constraints are assertions data base states are compelled to obey. One usually distinguishes state constraints from transition constraints. The former deal with data which belong to a same data base state, whereas the latter concern data occurring in two consecutive data base states. In the following, we will mainly be concerned with state constraints.

2.1. On a Logical View of Integrity Constraints

It is now well established that integrity constraints can be expressed by logical formulas. Moreover it has been shown [22, 24] that any state of a database can be viewed as an interpretation of a set of logical formulas expressing the integrity constraints, the valid database states corresponding then to the models of the set of logical formulas. Consequently, updating relation extensions (changing data base states) corresponds to a change of interpretation for the considered set of logical formulas: and integrity checking consists in verifying whether the new interpretation is still a model of the set of logical formulas (i.e.: an interpretation in which all these formulas are satisfied).

The simplification method which is developed in this paper is based upon the above logical view. But there is another (and complementary) way to exploit this logical view for improving integrity checking. It is sketched below.

A lot of work has been done, in the context of database design, on the problem of characterizing "good" relation schemes for representing information of the world to be modeled. This led to the so-called normal forms. However little has been done on another aspect of database design which consists in choosing a "good" set of integrity constraints. In this latter case "good" is intended to mean easy to maintain and easy to check.

The above logical view of integrity constraints provides an adequate framework for studying such a problem. Indeed, let $\mathscr{W}$ be the set of logical formulas corresponding to the integrity constraints of a given database and let us denote as $\mathscr{W}^*$ the closure of $\mathscr{W}$, namely the set of all formulas logically implied by $\mathscr{W}$. Any set of formulas $\overline{\mathscr{W}}$ such that $\overline{\mathscr{W}}^* = \mathscr{W}^*$ ($\overline{\mathscr{W}}$ is said to be a cover of $\mathscr{W}$) admits the same models as $\mathscr{W}$. Otherwise stated the integrity constraints corresponding to the formulas in $\overline{\mathscr{W}}$ characterize exactly the same valid database states as $\mathscr{W}$. Consequently, anyone of the covers of $\mathscr{W}$ can be retained as the set of integrity constraints to be enforced on the database. Then choosing, for example, a cover with a reduced number of constraints may reduce the cost of integrity checking.

Now, as mentioned in [24], once an adequate set of constraints has been chosen, say $\mathscr{W}$, it may happen that a new constraint w is to be asserted. At that time, one may want to determine whether w has to be effectively added to $\mathscr{W}$. To do that, one can check whether w or $\neg w$ is logically implied by $\mathscr{W}$. In the first case, it will be useless to add w to $\mathscr{W}$, since $\mathscr{W} \cup \{w\}$ characterizes exactly the same valid database states as $\mathscr{W}$[3]. In the second case, the adjunction of w would lead to an inconsistent set of constraints. But if none of w or $\neg w$ is logically implied by $\mathscr{W}$, then w is independent from $\mathscr{W}$ and hence has to be added to $\mathscr{W}$.

As a conclusion, let us note that the simplification method developed in the paper works for any set of integrity constraints whether or not it has been "optimized" in the above mentioned sense.

2.2. On the Form of Formulas Corresponding to Integrity Constraints

Logical formulas corresponding to integrity constraints are closed wffs, so, in the following "wffs" will mean "closed wffs". Moreover, we can suppose, without loss of generality [22], that these wffs are free from n-ary $(n>0)$

[3] As a particular case, a tautology (i.e. a theorem of the predicate calculus) is true in any interpretation, it then appears as a useless integrity constraint since it is satisfied in any database state

function symbols, apart from Skolem function symbols when Skolem standard forms are considered.

Since relations, in relational data bases, are defined on different domains, many-sorted (sorts $\simeq$ types) formulas [12] are, a priori, more appropriate for expressing integrity constraints. In fact (one-sorted) wffs, as those used in this paper, can also be retained and it appears that in such a case only a subclass of wffs, characterized in [26] and termed range restricted wffs, is needed. A *range restricted wff* is a wff satisfying the range restricted property as defined below.

A wff under prenex conjunctive normal form satisfies the *range restricted property* iff:

- each of its universally quantified variables appears in at least one negated atomic formula in any disjunction where the variable occurs;

and

- for each of its existentially quantified variables which occurs in a negated atomic formula, there is a disjunction containing only non negated atomic formulas, all of them having the variable as argument.

Intuitively, a range restricted wff is structured in such a way that, in an interpretation, the range of its variables is restricted to the elements which occur in the extensions of the relations that the formula involves. We note that this notion is similar to the notions of range separable formulas [10] and of safe formulas [32].

A complete discussion of the wff formulation of integrity constraints would be out of the scope of this paper (see [26]). We will merely mention two points; the second point emphasizing why range restricted wffs are of interest with regard to the validation of the simplification method.

i) First, the formulation of integrity constraints as wffs rather as many-sorted formulas is retained here mainly for convenience in the proof of theorems which validate the simplification method. We note that this formulation does not introduce many ad hoc range predicates, since such wffs are, as one might say, naturally range restricted.

For example, in Table 1, some integrity constraints are listed. Most of them are borrowed from [8]. Each of these integrity constraints has an English formulation and two logical formulations, the latter one (b) corresponding to wffs under prenex conjunctive normal form. The reader can check that they all satisfy the range restricted property and that no ad hoc range predicate occurs.

ii) Second, range restricted wffs satisfy with regard to truth value preservation, the property stated in the following theorem.

Theorem [26]. *Let W be a wff under prenex conjunctive normal form which satisfies the range restricted property. Given any interpretation I of W and any interpretation I* obtained from I only by adding a new element to its set of elements then:*

W is true in I iff W is true in I.*

This theorem means that if $R_1 \ldots R_n$ are all the relations involved in a range restricted formula F then the truth value of F in an interpretation only depends on the R_i's extensions. Otherwise stated F takes the same truth value in all interpretations which coincide on the R_i's extensions. Thus range restricted wffs can be viewed as domain independant formulas [14].

Let us now briefly explain to what extent the above result is important with regard to the validation of the simplification method proposed herein.

Consider a data base in a given state (the current state) and suppose that a tuple, say $\langle \mathbf{e}_1, \ldots, \mathbf{e}_n \rangle$, is inserted into a relation extension. It may happen that, for example, the element $\mathbf{e}_j$ does not occur in any relation extension in the current state. So, this operation of inserting a tuple has the side effect of adding the new element $\mathbf{e}_j$ to the data base. In a similar way the operation of deleting a tuple from a relation extension may have the side effect of suppressing an element, and these two possibilities are combined for an updating operation. The above theorem precisely states that such side effects have no impact on integrity constraints. This result will be used in the proof of theorems which provide the validation of the simplification method.

Let us conclude this section by pointing out that from now on, we will use "integrity constraints" and "(range restricted) wffs" interchangeably as "data base state" and "interpretion".

3. Introduction to the Simplification Method

When a peculiar integrity constraint is considered, it is quite easy to characterize, on semantic grounds, a simplified form of this constraint which is sufficient to evaluate for a given data base state change. In this section, we will first illustrate the preceding point and then provide an intuitive introduction to the simplification method.

Suppose that all integrity contraints listed in Table 1 are satisfied in a given (the current) data base state. Let us consider some of them successively and *independently*.

i) *Integrity constraint* (1)

Suppose that a new tuple, say $\langle D, I \rangle$ is inserted into the (extension of the) relation SALE. On semantic grounds, it is clear that this integrity constraint will be satisfied in the new state iff the following simplified constraint is satisfied: "*There is a company which supplies department D with item I*" (i.e.: $\exists z \, \mathrm{SUPPLY}(z, D, I)$). Therefore it is sufficient to evaluate this latter one.

ii) *Integrity constraint* (5)

Suppose that a new tuple, say $\langle C, D, I \rangle$, is inserted into the relation SUPPLY. Now again, it is sufficient to evaluate on the new state the simplified integrity constraint: "*Company C does not supply another department than D with item I*" (i.e.: $\neg \exists z (\mathrm{SUPPLY}(C, z, I) \wedge (D \neq z))$), in order to determine whether the initial integrity constraint is satisfied.

iii) *Integrity constraint* (6)

Suppose that the new tuple $\langle E_1, E_2 \rangle$ is inserted into the extension of relation SUBORD. In order to check whether this integrity constraint is

Table 1

Relations	Intended meaning:	
SUPPLY (COMP, DEPT, ITEM)	$\langle C, D, I\rangle \in$ SUPPLY	$\Leftrightarrow$ Company C supplies departement D with item I.
CLASS (ITEM, TYPE)	$\langle I, T\rangle \in$ CLASS	$\Leftrightarrow$ I is a type T item.
SALE (DEPT, ITEM)	$\langle D, I\rangle \in$ SALE	$\Leftrightarrow$ Department D sells item I.
SUBORD (EMP, MNG)	$\langle E_1, E_2\rangle \in$ SUBORD	$\Leftrightarrow$ Employee E_1 is a subordinate of E_2.

Integrity Constraints

(1) *When a department sells an item then there is a company which supplies it with this item.*

a) $\forall x \forall y(\mathrm{SALE}(x, y) \rightarrow \exists z\, \mathrm{SUPPLY}(z, x, y))$

b) $\forall x \forall y \exists z(\neg \mathrm{SALE}(x, y) \vee \mathrm{SUPPLY}(z, x, y))$

(2) *No other companies than company C supplies type T_4 items.*

a) $\forall x(\exists z(\exists y\, \mathrm{SUPPLY}(x, y, z) \wedge \mathrm{CLASS}(z, T_4)) \rightarrow (x = C))$

b) $\forall x \forall y \forall z(\neg \mathrm{SUPPLY}(x, y, z) \vee \neg \mathrm{CLASS}(z, T_4) \vee (x = C))$

(3) *Any company that supplies guns also supplies bullets.*

a) $\forall x(\exists y\, \mathrm{SUPPLY}(x, y, \mathrm{guns}) \rightarrow \exists z\, \mathrm{SUPPLY}(x, z, \mathrm{bullets}))$

b) $\forall x \forall y \exists z(\neg \mathrm{SUPPLY}(x, y, \mathrm{guns}) \vee \mathrm{SUPPLY}(x, z, \mathrm{bullets}))$

(4) *Any company that supplies type T_1 items also supplies type T_2 items.*

a) $\forall x(\exists y(\exists z\, \mathrm{SUPPLY}(x, z, y) \wedge \mathrm{CLASS}(y, T_1)) \rightarrow \exists y'(\exists z'\, \mathrm{SUPPLY}(x, z', y') \wedge \mathrm{CLASS}(y', T_2)))$

b) $\forall x \forall y \forall z \exists y' \exists z'((\neg \mathrm{SUPPLY}(x, y, z) \vee \neg \mathrm{CLASS}(y, T_1) \vee \mathrm{SUPPLY}(x, z', y'))$
$\wedge(\neg \mathrm{SUPPLY}(x, y, z) \vee \neg \mathrm{CLASS}(y, T_1) \vee \mathrm{CLASS}(y', T_2)))$

(5) *No company must supply two different departments with item I.*

a) $\neg \exists x \exists y \exists z(\mathrm{SUPPLY}(x, y, I) \wedge \mathrm{SUPPLY}(x, z, I) \wedge (y \neq z))$

b) $\forall x \forall y \forall z(\neg \mathrm{SUPPLY}(x, y, I) \vee \neg \mathrm{SUPPLY}(x, z, I) \vee (y = z))$

(6) *Whenever an employee is a subordinate of another employee which is itself a subordinate of a third one then the first one is a subordinate of the latter one.*

a) $\forall x \forall y(\exists z(\mathrm{SUBORD}(x, z) \wedge \mathrm{SUBORD}(z, y)) \rightarrow \mathrm{SUBORD}(x, y))$

b) $\forall x \forall y \forall z(\neg \mathrm{SUBORD}(x, z) \vee \neg \mathrm{SUBORD}(z, y) \vee \mathrm{SUBORD}(x, y))$

(7) *There is at least one type T_3 item which is supplied by every company.*

a) $\exists x'(\mathrm{CLASS}(x', T_3) \wedge \forall x(\exists y \exists z\, \mathrm{SUPPLY}(x, y, z) \rightarrow \exists y'\, \mathrm{SUPPLY}(x, y', x')))$

b) $\exists x' \forall x \exists y' \forall y \forall z(\mathrm{CLASS}(x', T_3) \wedge (\neg \mathrm{SUPPLY}(x, y, z) \vee \mathrm{SUPPLY}(x, y', x')))$

satisfied in the new state, one has only to determine whether *all the subordinates of E_1 are subordinates of E_2 and all managers of E_2 are managers of E_1*, i.e.

$$\forall x \forall y((\mathrm{SUBORD}(x, E_1) \rightarrow \mathrm{SUBORD}(x, E_2)) \wedge (\mathrm{SUBORD}(E_2, y) \rightarrow \mathrm{SUBORD}(E_1, y))).$$

Finally, we will consider two border-line cases. On the one hand, the case where the simplified form is in fact always satisfied and, on the other hand, the case where it coincides with the initial constraint.

iv) *Integrity constraint* (2)

Suppose that a new tuple, say $\langle I, T_2\rangle$, is inserted into the relation CLASS. This time, intuitively the considered integrity constraint is unaffected by the inserting operation. In such a case, the simplified inferred integrity constraint can be viewed as a special one which is always satisfied.

v) *Integrity constraint* (7)

Suppose the new tuple $\langle C, D, I\rangle$ is inserted into the relation SUPPLY. If C is not a new company then the integrity constraint will also be satisfied on the new state. Otherwise, if I is not a type T_3 item then it will be falsified. But in the case where C is a new company and I is a type T_3 item, one has to determine whether I is (one of) the type T_3 item which is supplied by all the other companies. Due to this latter case (as far as the type T_3 items which are supplied by all the companies, in the current state, are not memorized)[4], the whole integrity constraint has to be evaluated to determine whether it is satisfied in the new state. Thus, this time, the "simplified form" coincides in fact with the initial constraint.

The preceding examples point out how integrity constraints can be simplified before evaluating them. But these simplifications are based upon semantical considerations and thus are applicable only for particular integrity constraints. As opposed, the simplification method we will propose is based upon syntactic criteria. So, this is a general method which can be applied on any integrity constraint. Therefore, when implemented in a data base management system, it enables us to automatically generate the simplified forms of integrity constraints, whatever the application is. In Sect. 5, the method will be applied on the preceding examples and we will see that it generates the same simplified forms as those obtained here from semantical considerations.

We will give now an intuitive introduction to the simplification method. The basic idea is quite simple and can be illustrated as follows.

Let us consider integrity constraint (1) and its associated wffs. The fact that this wff is true in the current state means that for every couple $\langle x_i, y_i\rangle$ belonging to the (extension of the) relation SALE there exists a triple $\langle z_i, x_i, y_i\rangle$ in the relation SUPPLY. In so far as the new state is obtained merely by inserting the tuple $\langle D, I\rangle$ into SALE, the possible falsification of the integrity constraint only depends on this new tuple. So, it is sufficient for determining whether it is actually falsified, to evaluate the instance obtained from it by substituting D for x and I for y, i.e. to evaluate:

$$\mathrm{SALE}(D, I) \rightarrow \exists z\, \mathrm{SUPPLY}(z, D, I)$$

Moreover, according to the insert operation, it is known that $\mathrm{SALE}(D, I)$ is true in the new state. Thus, due to the evaluation rules of the implication connective, it is sufficient to evaluate the right hand side of the above formula, i.e. $\exists x\, \mathrm{SUPPLY}(z, D, I)$ which is in fact the simplified form obtained in i).

It then appears that the basic principle of the method relies upon the instantiation of formulas obtained by substituting for some of their variables the (or some of the) constants occurring in the inserted (or deleted, or updated) tuple. The problem is then to find the right substitutions.

[4] Memorizing extra data for an efficient evaluation of a restricted class of integrity constraints has been considered in [4]

4. Definition and Validation of the Simplification Method

When a database state change happens, not all constraints are subject to falsification. For example, whenever the operation is dealing with the extension of a relation R, integrity constraints in which R does not occur are unaffected (see the theorem of Sect. 2). Furthermore, it has been shown in [23] that integrity constraints (considered in prenex conjunctive normal form) which do not contain R in a negated atomic formula (respectively, a nonnegated atomic formula) are unaffected when a tuple is inserted (respectively, deleted) into (from) the extension of R[5]. For example, the insertion of a tuple into the relation SUPPLY cannot falsify the integrity constraint (1) whereas the insertion of a tuple into SALE can falsify it. In the following, only constraints subject to falsification will be considered.

The simplified forms which can be generated for a given integrity constraint depend on the nature of the operation which leads to the new state. We will consider successively the operations of inserting a tuple, deleting a tuple and transactions of such operations; updating operations beeing treated as special transactions. In each of these cases we will define three simplified forms for a given integrity constraint. Their respective advantages will be discussed in Sect. 5.

Before defining the simplified forms, two notions need to be introduced.

Substitution

A (ground) substitution σ is a set of pairs $\{v_1/c_1, \ldots, v_p/c_p\}$, where v_i's are distinct variables and c_i's are constants. Applying σ to a wff W leads to the wff $W(\sigma)$ (called an instance of W) where each variable which appears both in W and in σ, has been replaced in W by the associated constant in σ. Whenever σ is the empty set, $W(\sigma)$ is W itself and we will refer to this peculiar substitution as the *identity substitution* (noted as $\mathcal{I}$).

Subsumption

Given two substitutions σ and σ', σ *subsumes* σ' iff $\sigma \subseteq \sigma'$; namely iff for each pair v_j/c_j in σ there is a pair v_i'/c_i' in σ' such that $v_i' = v_j$ and $c_i' = c_j$. Note that $\mathcal{I}$ subsumes any substitution.

4.1. *Inserting a Tuple*

Let W be a range restricted wff in prenex conjunctive normal form (i.e. an integrity constraint) which contains at least one negated atomic formula with R as (n-ary) predicate symbol. Let I be an interpretation in which W is true (the current data base state) and I_+ the interpretation (the new state) obtained from I by inserting into the extension of R the tuple $\langle \mathbf{e}_1, \ldots, \mathbf{e}_n \rangle$ where $\mathbf{e}_i$ is not necessarily distinct from $\mathbf{e}_j$ for $i \neq j$.

The simplified forms of W are built by applying to W substitutions which are defined according to the inserted tuple and the negated occurrences of R in W. We will first characterize this set of substitutions. Then we will successively introduce the main simplified form of W, noted $S^+(W)$, and two auxiliary simplified forms referred to as $W(\gamma^+)$ and $T^+(W)$. Finally, we will prove that each of them is valid, namely that it is true in I_+ iff W is also true in I_+.

4.1.1. *Definition of the substitutions*

Since the possible falsification of W only depends on the negated occurrences of R, it is those occurrences which govern the construction of the substitutions.

Suppose there are p negated occurrences of R in W. We denote them $\neg R(t_1^i, \ldots, t_n^i)$, $1 \leqq i \leqq p$, where t_j^i stands either for a variable or for a constant (interpreted in I, and in the same way in I_+). For each $\neg R(t_1^i, \ldots, t_n^i)$ and according to the inserted tuple $\langle \mathbf{e}_1, \ldots, \mathbf{e}_n \rangle$ a substitution γ_i is (possibly) defined as follows.

Definition of γ_i

1) γ_i is defined iff:
- whenever t_j^i ($j \in [1, n]$) is a constant then $t_j^i = \mathbf{e}_j$;

and
- whenever there exist j and j' (j and $j' \in [1, n]$) such that $t_j^i = t_{j'}^i$, then $\mathbf{e}_j = \mathbf{e}_{j'}$.

2) When γ_i is defined then:

$\gamma_i = \{t_j^i/\mathbf{e}_j\}$ for $j = 1, \ldots, n$ such that t_j^i is a universally quantified variable not governed[6] by an existentially quantified one in W.

We will call Γ the set of the above *defined* substitutions γ_i.

Some comments can now be made with regard to the above definition. First, it appears that a given γ_i is not defined:
- either when one of the argument of the negated occurrence of R which is considered, is a constant which differs from the corresponding component in the inserted tuple;
- or when the negated occurrence of R which is considered, contains two identical arguments while the corresponding components in the inserted tuple are different.

When this is the case, it means that no instance of W can be such that the negated occurrence of R which is considered coincides with $\neg R(\mathbf{e}_1, \ldots, \mathbf{e}_n)$. Thus, the possible falsification of W cannot depend on this occurrence of $\neg R$. If no γ_i is defined then W is unaffected by the database modification.

For example, consider the integrity constraint (2) and suppose that the new tuple $\langle I, T_2 \rangle$ is inserted into the relation CLASS. As there is only one occurrence of $\neg$CLASS in this constraint, only one substitution could be defined. But, since $T_4 \neq T_2$, it is in fact not defined. Thus constraint (2) will remain satisfied after the insertion.

Now, when γ_i is defined, it deals only with some of the universally quantified variables of W. The two following simple examples give the reason why.

[5] These results can in fact, as we will see, be corroborated by the proof of theorems which validate the simplification method

[6] Otherwise stated, there is no variable x in W such that $\exists x$ occurs before $\forall t_j^i$ in W

First consider the formula $\exists x(S(x) \wedge \neg P(x))$ and assume it is true in a given interpretation. That means that there exists at least one x_i such that $S(x_i) \wedge \neg P(x_i)$ is true. Suppose now that a constant a is inserted into the extension of P. The instance of the considered formula obtained by substituting a for x (i.e. $S(a) \wedge \neg P(a)$) will be false in the new interpretation whereas, in general, the formula itself will remain true (except if there was only one x_i which furthermore was coinciding with a). Thus substituting components of the inserted tuple for existentially quantified variables does not lead to valid instances.

As a second example, consider the formula $\exists y \forall x(\neg P(x) \vee Q(x, y))$ and assume it is true in a given interpretation. That means that there exists at least one y_j such that for every x_k which satisfies P, the tuple $\langle x_k, y_j \rangle$ satisfies Q. Suppose now that a constant a is inserted into the extension of P. Once again the truth values, in the new interpretation, of the formula and of its instance $\exists y(\neg P(a) \vee Q(a, y))$ are not garanteed to be the same. For example, if there are y_i's which satisfy $Q(a, y_i)$ but such that none of them coincides with one of the above characterized y_j's, the instance will be true while the formula itself will be false. Thus only substitutions of components of the inserted tuple for universally quantified variables not governed by an existentially quantified one are to be considered.

Considering the set Γ, several remarks are now in order. First, if no γ_i is defined, then $\Gamma = \emptyset$. Second, as Γ is a set, whenever γ_i is identical to γ_j (for $i \neq j$) then only one of them belongs to Γ. Third, the identity substitution $\mathscr{I}$ may belong to Γ. And finally, one can notice that wffs which do not include R as a negated atomic formula could have been considered here by associating to them, as set Γ, the empty set. In this case, Theorem 1, which is proven in the paragraph 4.1.4, corroborates the fact that such wffs are unaffected by a tuple insertion into R (see the beginning of the present section).

4.1.2. *Definition of the simplified form $S^+(W)$*

According to the way the substitutions are defined, W shall be true in I_+ iff for each γ_i in Γ, $W(\gamma_i)$ is true in I_+. But it may happen that two substitutions in Γ, say γ_i and γ_j, be such that whenever $W(\gamma_i)$ is true in I_+ then so is $W(\gamma_j)$. In such a case $W(\gamma_j)$ is in fact redundant with regard to $W(\gamma_i)$ and then γ_j can be eliminated. So is the case when γ_i subsumes γ_j.

Example. Consider the formula F: $\forall x \forall y(\neg P(x, b) \vee \neg P(x, y) \vee Q(x, y))$ and suppose that the tuple $\langle a, b \rangle$ is inserted into the extension of P. One gets then two substitutions $\sigma_1 = \{x/a\}$ and $\sigma_2 = \{x/a, y/b\}$; the former subsuming the latter. Now, if $F(\sigma_1)$ (i.e.: $\forall y(\neg P(a, b) \vee \neg P(a, y) \vee Q(a, y))$ is true in an interpretation, it is true in particular for $y = b$ and therefore $F(\sigma_2)$ (i.e.: $(\neg P(a, b) \vee \neg P(a, b) \vee Q(a, b))$ is also true in that interpretation.

The above motivates the following definition:

Definition of $\Gamma_R^+(W)$. Γ_R^+ is the reduced set of substitutions obtained from Γ by erasing in Γ each substitution which is subsumed by another substitution in Γ.

$$\Gamma_R^+ = \{\gamma_i / \gamma_i \in \Gamma \text{ and } \nexists \gamma_j \in \Gamma (j \neq i) \text{ such that } \gamma_j \text{ subsumes } \gamma_i\}.$$

$$\Gamma_R^+(W) \text{ stands for } \begin{cases} \mathbb{T}, \textbf{ if } \Gamma_R^+ = \emptyset; \ (\mathbb{T} \text{ is a particular wff which is true in any interpretation}); \\ W(\gamma_1) \wedge \ldots \wedge W(\gamma_\ell), \textbf{ otherwise}. \ (\gamma_1 \ldots \gamma_\ell \text{ are all the substitutions in } \Gamma_R^+). \end{cases}$$

Note that $\Gamma_R^+ = \{\mathscr{I}\}$ iff $\mathscr{I} \in \Gamma$, and that $\Gamma_R^+ = \emptyset$ iff $\Gamma = \emptyset$.

In the case where $\Gamma_R^+(W)$ differs from $\mathbb{T}$, this formula can be further simplified by taking advantage of the fact that the truth-value on I_+ of some ground literals it contains can be known without evaluating them on I_+ (i.e. without any access to the database state). So is the case for the literal $R(\mathbf{e}_1, \ldots, \mathbf{e}_n)$ which is known to be true in I_+ because of the updating operation, and for ground literals whose predicate symbol corresponds to comparison operators like $=$, $\neq$, $<$, ... (e.g.: $5 \leqq 20$). Such literals, that we call *pre-valued literals*, can be replaced in $\Gamma_R^+(W)$ by their truth-value ($\mathbb{T}$ or $\mathbb{F}$) while preserving the truth-value of the formula on I_+. Moreover, this formula can then be reduced by applying the following absorption rules where $\mathbb{T}$ stands for True, $\mathbb{F}$ stands for False and A stands for any formula.

Absorption rules:

$$\neg\mathbb{T} \Rightarrow \mathbb{F}; \quad \neg\mathbb{F} \Rightarrow \mathbb{T}$$
$$\mathbb{T} \vee A \Rightarrow \mathbb{T}; \ \mathbb{F} \vee A \Rightarrow A$$
$$\mathbb{T} \wedge A \Rightarrow A; \ \mathbb{F} \wedge A \Rightarrow \mathbb{F}.$$

The formula obtained by applying, as much as possible, the above rules (which obviously are truth-value preserving), either reduces to $\mathbb{T}$ or $\mathbb{F}$ or consists in a formula free of these symbols.

Examples. i) Consider the formula $\forall x \forall y(\neg P(x, y) \vee \neg Q(y) \vee P(a, y))$ and suppose that the tuple $\langle a, b \rangle$ is inserted into the extension of P. One then gets the substitution $\{x/a, y/b\}$ which applied to the formula leads to the instance $(\neg P(a, b) \vee \neg Q(b) \vee P(a, b))$. Replacing the pre-valued literals by their truth-value yields $(\neg\mathbb{T} \vee \neg Q(b) \vee \mathbb{T})$. Finally, applying the absorption rules produces the formula $\mathbb{T}$ which means that the constraint will remain satisfied on the new database state.

ii) Consider now the formula $\forall x \forall y(\neg P(x, y) \vee (x = y) \vee Q(x, y))$ and suppose again that the tuple $\langle a, b \rangle$ is inserted into the extension of P. Applying the same process as above leads successively to:

$$(\neg P(a, b) \vee (a = b) \vee Q(a, b))$$
$$(\ \neg\mathbb{T} \quad \vee \quad \mathbb{F} \quad \vee Q(a, b))$$
$$(Q(a, b)).$$

Finally, a last simplification step can be applied when the formula obtained at this stage still consists in several (possibly reduced by the former simplification) instances of W. Indeed, it may turn out that two such instances $W(\gamma_i)$ and $W(\gamma_j)$ are identical up to a permutation of the disjunctions, a permutation of literals and a renaming of variable. In such a case, $W(\gamma_i)$ and $W(\gamma_j)$ are obviously equivalent and one of them can be erased without affecting the truth value of the formula in I_+.

Example. Let W be: $\forall x \forall y \forall z(\neg R(x,y) \vee \neg R(x,z) \vee (y=z))$ and suppose the tuple $\langle a,b \rangle$ is inserted into the extension of R; then $\Gamma_R^+(W)$ is:

$$(\forall z(\neg R(a,b) \vee \neg R(a,z) \vee (b=z)) \wedge \forall y(\neg R(a,y) \vee \neg R(a,b) \vee (y=b)).$$

Processing the pre-valued literals yields:

$$\forall z(\neg R(a,z) \vee (b=z)) \wedge \forall y(\neg R(a,y) \vee (y=b)).$$

The two sub-formulas being identical up to the renaming of z as y, one finally obtains: $\forall y(\neg R(a,y) \vee (y=b))$.

We have just described and motivated the different stages which, given the inserted tuple, lead from W to $S^+(W)$; they are summarized in the following algorithm.

Step 1. Construct the set Γ of substitutions γ_i according to the occurrences of $\neg R$ in W and the inserted tuple $\langle \mathbf{e}_1, \ldots, \mathbf{e}_n \rangle$.

If $\Gamma = \emptyset$, **then** $S^+(W) = \mathbb{T}$ (i.e. W is satisfied in the new interpretation), **Stop**.

Step 2. Erase in Γ any substitution which is subsumed by another one. Let Γ_R^+ be the resulting set. Define $\Gamma_R^+(W)$ as the conjunction $W(\gamma_1) \wedge \ldots \wedge W(\gamma_\ell)$, where $\gamma_1, \ldots, \gamma_\ell$ are all substitutions in Γ_R^+.

If $\Gamma_R^+ = \{\mathscr{I}\}$, **then** $S^+(W) = W$, **Stop**.

Step 3[7]. Replace in $\Gamma_R^+(W)$ each pre-valued literal by its truth value in I_+ and apply, as much as possible, the absorption rules.

If the formula reduces to $\mathbb{T}$ (respectively, $\mathbb{F}$), **then** $S^+(W) = \mathbb{T}$ (respectively, $S^+(W) = \mathbb{F}$); i.e. W is satisfied (respectively, falsified) in the new interpretation **stop**.

Step 4. Erase in the formula so obtained any $W(\gamma_i)$ such that there is a $W(\gamma_j)$ $(j \neq i)$ identical to $W(\gamma_i)$ up to a permutation of the disjunctions, a permutation of the atomic formulas and a renaming of variable. $S^+(W)$ is the obtained formula, **stop**.

As a conclusion, the evaluation of $S^+(W)$ on the new database state can be substituted for the evaluation of W. But we shall emphasize that in some cases (when $S^+(W) = \mathbb{T}$ or $\mathbb{F}$) no evaluation at all is needed and that in some other cases (when no occurrences of R remain in $S^+(W)$) the evaluation of $S^+(W)$ can be run on the current state, before the update is done, thus avoiding to have to undo the update if it turns out to be non-valid.

4.1.3. Definitions of the simplified forms $W(\gamma^+)$ and $T^+(W)$

Roughly, $S^+(W)$ has been obtained by replacing as many variables as possible in W by constants, while guaranteeing that $S^+(W)$ and W will take the same truth value in I_+. But, despite the various simplification steps, $S^+(W)$ may sometimes consist of the conjunction of several instances of W. In some cases, it may be interesting (see Sect. 5) to deal with simplified forms which contain a smaller number of instances of W than $S^+(W)$, although these instances are less instantiated[8] than the one is $S^+(W)$. We define below two such auxiliary simplified forms. The first one, noted $W(\gamma^+)$, always consists of a single instance of W. The second one, noted $T^-(W)$, is intermediate between $W(\gamma^+)$ and $S^+(W)$. Finally, we note that both are defined (and needed) only when the set of substitution Γ_R^+ is not empty.

As seen in the previous paragraph, subsumed substitutions lead to redundant instances. Thus, a substitution which subsumes all the substitutions in Γ_R^+ will yield a simplified form containing only one instance of W; hence the following definition.

Definition of $W(\gamma^+)$. Let γ^+ be the substitution obtained as the intersection of all the substitutions in Γ_R^+. Then $W(\gamma^+)$ is the wff resulting from applying this substitution to W, possibly reduced by the third simplification step of the algorithm given in 4.1.2.

Between $W(\gamma^+)$ and $S^+(W)$, other simplified forms can be defined containing less instances of W than $S^+(W)$ but more instantiated than the one in $W(\gamma^+)$. This can be done by replacing some subsets of Γ_R^+ by a substitution which subsumes all the substitutions in the subset. $T^+(W)$ is such a simplified form which in fact coincides with $W(\gamma^+)$ when $\gamma^+ \neq \mathscr{I}$ and with $S^-(W)$ when all the substitutions in Γ_R^+ are pairwise disjoint.

Definition of $T^+(W)$. Let us first define procedurally the set of substitutions T^+ as follows:

- Initialize T as Γ_R^+.
- Consider those subsets of T (including T) such that, for each of them, the intersection of all the substitutions it contains is non-empty.

If there is no such subsets (but singletons) **then** $T^+ = T$, **stop**.
Else choose anyone of the largest ones,
let σ be the intersection of all its substitutions,
erase in T any substitution which is subsumed by σ, insert σ in T and iterate.

Now $T^+(W)$ stands for the conjunction of $W(\gamma_k)$'s for all substitutions γ_k in T^+, possibly reduced by the two last simplification steps which lead from $\Gamma_R^+(W)$ to $S^+(W)$.

Example. Consider the integrity constraint:

$$\forall x \forall y \forall z(\neg P(x,y,c,z,e) \vee \neg P(x,y,c,d,z) \vee \neg P(a,x,y,d,e) \vee Q(x,y,z))$$

and suppose that the tuple $\langle a,b,c,d,e \rangle$ is inserted into the extension of P. Then the following three substitutions are defined:

$$\gamma_1 = \{x/a, y/b, z/d\},$$
$$\gamma_2 = \{x/a, y/b, z/e\},$$
$$\gamma_3 = \{x/b, y/c\}.$$

[7] The presentation of Step-3 given here is inspired from the presentation of the method which is given in [19]

[8] To instantiate means to substitute constants for variables

As none of them subsumes another one, $\Gamma_R^+ = \{\gamma_1, \gamma_2, \gamma_3\}$ and $\gamma^+ = \gamma_1 \cap \gamma_2 \cap \gamma_3 = \mathscr{I}$.

In this example, T^+ is obtained in one step. There is only one subset of Γ_R^+ whose substitutions have a non-empty intersection: $\{\gamma_1, \gamma_2\}$. Thus $\sigma = \gamma_1 \cap \gamma_2 = \{x/a, y/b\}$ and $T^+ = \{\{x/a, y/b\}, \{x/b, z/c\}\}$.

4.1.4. Validation of the simplified forms of W

The central point for validating the simplified forms of W for the inserting operation consists in the validation of $\Gamma_R^+(W)$. It is provided for by theorem-1 below. But proving theorem-1 requires the following lemma which validates the elimination of subsumed substitutions.

Lemma. *Given a wff F in prenex normal form and any interpretation I of F. Given two substitutions σ_i and σ_j which deal, on the one hand with variables in F which are universally quantified variables but not governed by an existentially quantified one, and on the other hand with elements in I. If σ_i subsumes σ_j then:*

if $F(\sigma_i)$ is true in I then so is $F(\sigma_j)$.

Proof. Let us write $F(\sigma_i)$ as $F(\sigma_i)(x_1, \ldots, x_q)$ where $x_1, \ldots, x_q$ are the variables in $F(\sigma_i)$ which occur in σ_j (but not in σ_i). These variables are universally quantified variables in $F(\sigma_i)$ but not governed by an existentially quantified one. Therefore, $F(\sigma_i)$ is true in I iff for any tuple $\langle e_1, \ldots, e_q \rangle$ in $\mathscr{E}(I)^q$ so is $F(\sigma_i)(e_1, \ldots, e_q)$. Since the elements associated with $x_1, \ldots, x_q$ in σ_j constitute a tuple in $\mathscr{E}(I)^q$, then $F(\sigma_j)$ is formally identical to one of the above $F(\sigma_i)(e_1, \ldots, e_q)$. Consequently, if $F(\sigma_i)$ is true in I then so is $F(\sigma_j)$. □

Theorem 1. *if W is true in I then:*

W is true in I_+ iff $\Gamma_R^+(W)$ is true in I_+.

Proof. Because W satisfies the range restricted property, one can assume, without loss of generality (see Sect. 2), that each element in $\langle \mathbf{e}_1, \ldots, \mathbf{e}_n \rangle$ belongs to $\mathscr{E}(I)$.

Therefore, one can write:

$$\mathscr{E}(I_+) = \mathscr{E}(I)$$

$$\mathscr{L}(I_+) = \mathscr{L}(I) - \{\neg R(\mathbf{e}_1, \ldots, \mathbf{e}_n\} \cup \{R(\mathbf{e}_1, \ldots, \mathbf{e}_n)\}$$

In the following, $\Gamma(W)$ stands for a wff which is defined from Γ in the same way as $\Gamma_R^+(W)$ was defined from Γ_R^+. Now we will distinguish two cases depending on whether Γ_R^+ is the empty set or not.

1) $\Gamma_R^+ = \emptyset$

First let us note that $\Gamma_R^+ = \emptyset$ iff $\Gamma = \emptyset$. In such a case we have to prove that if W is true in I then so is W in I_+. For this purpose, let us consider the Skolem standard from $SW(x_1, \ldots, x_p)$ of W; $x_1, \ldots, x_p$ are all the variables occurring in SW.

Suppose W is true in I, then there is an F-valuation in I such that for any tuple $\langle e_1, \ldots, e_p \rangle \in \mathscr{E}(I)^p$, at least one literal in each clause of $FSW(e_1, \ldots, e_p)$ belongs to $\mathscr{L}(I)$.

According to the construction of Γ, if $\Gamma = \emptyset$, then whatever $\langle e_1, \ldots, e_p \rangle$ is in $\mathscr{E}(I)^p$, none of the clauses in $FSW(e_1, \ldots, e_p)$ contains the literal $\neg R(\mathbf{e}_1, \ldots, \mathbf{e}_n)$. Therefore, as $\mathscr{L}(I_+)$ includes all literals in $\mathscr{L}(I)$ but $\neg R(\mathbf{e}_1, \ldots, \mathbf{e}_n)$, for the same F-valuation, at least one literal of each of these clauses belongs to $\mathscr{L}(I_+)$. Consequently W is true in I_+.

2) $\Gamma_R^+ \neq 0$

Hypothesis: W is true in I.

- *Only if part:* assume W is true in I_+, then $W(\mathscr{I})$ which is identical to W, is also true in I_+. Since, $\mathscr{I}$ subsumes any substitution in Γ_R^+ then, according to the lemma, $\Gamma_R^+(W)$ is true in I_+.

- *if part:* assume $\Gamma_R^+(W)$ is true in I_+. Since all substitutions in Γ are subsumed by substitutions in Γ_R^+, then $\Gamma(W)$ is true in I_+. So, for any $\gamma_i \in \Gamma$, $W(\gamma_i)$ is true in I_+.

We have to prove that W is true in I_+; that is for any substitution σ_k in Σ, $W(\sigma_k)$ is true in I_+, where Σ is the set of substitutions defined as follows:

Let $x_1, \ldots, x_q$ be the universally quantified variables in W not governed by an existentially quantified one. For each tuple $\langle e_1^k, \ldots, e_q^k \rangle$ in $\mathscr{E}(I_+)^q (\equiv \mathscr{E}(I)^q)$:

$$\sigma_k = \{x_1/e_1^k, \ldots, x_q/e_q^k\}.$$

Note that, by construction, for any γ_i its set of variables is a subset of $\{x_1, \ldots, x_q\}$. Now let us consider any one of the substitutions σ_k. Two cases can occur:

Case 1. There is a substitution $\gamma_i \in \Gamma$ which subsumes σ_k. Then, by applying the lemma, as $W(\gamma_i)$ is true in I_+, so is $W(\sigma_k)$.

Case 2. There is no $\gamma_i \in \Gamma$ which subsumes σ_k. That means that, for any negated atomic formula $\neg R(t_1^i, \ldots, t_n^i)$ in $W(\sigma_k)$, at least one of the two following conditions holds:

a) one of the t_j^i is a constant but different from $\mathbf{e}_j$;

or

b) there are some j and j' such that $t_j^i = t_{j'}^i$ and $\mathbf{e}_j \neq \mathbf{e}_{j'}$ (let us recall that $W(\sigma_k)$ is not necessarily a ground instance).

Indeed, suppose there is an atomic formula $\neg R(t_1^i, \ldots, t_n^i)$ in $W(\sigma_k)$ such that neither a) nor b) hold. Then, a fortiori, neither a) nor b) hold in the corresponding atomic formula in W. Therefore, according to the way the substitutions in Γ are defined, γ_i is defined. Moreover the variables which occur in γ_i are those which both belong to the atomic formula and to $\{x_1, \ldots, x_q\}$. If there is no such variable then $\gamma_i = \mathscr{I}$. Otherwise, as each t_j^i (in $\neg R(t_1^i, \ldots, t_n^i)$ in $W(\sigma)$) which is a constant is $\mathbf{e}_j$, then those variables are associated with the same element both in γ_i and in σ_k. Therefore in any cases γ_i subsumes σ_k, what contradicts the hypothesis.

Hence, for any atomic formula $\neg R(t_1^i, \ldots, t_n^i)$ in $W(\sigma_k)$, at least one of the conditions a) or b) holds. Therefore, none of the instantiations of variables in $W(\sigma_k)$ with elements of $\mathscr{E}(I)$ (or $\mathscr{E}(I_+)$) may lead to a formula which contains the literal $\neg R(\mathbf{e}_1, \ldots, \mathbf{e}_n)$. Therefore the fact that $W(\sigma_k)$ is true in I does not depend on the fact that $\neg R(\mathbf{e}_1, \ldots, \mathbf{e}_n)$ is true in I. So, as I_+ differs from I only because $\neg R(\mathbf{e}_1, \ldots, \mathbf{e}_n)$ is false in it, $W(\sigma_k)$ is true in I_+.

At last, since for any substitution $\sigma_k \in \Sigma$, $W(\sigma_k)$ is true in I_+ then so is W. □

Theorem-1 constitutes the foundation of the validation of the simplification method. The two last simplification steps which lead from $\Gamma_R^+(W)$ to $S^+(W)$ were shown to be valid while presenting them. As for the validity of $W(\gamma^+)$ and $T^+(W)$ it directly follows from the above and from the lemma. These results are summarized in the inserting theorem.

Inserting theorem: *If W is true in I then:*

i) *W is true in I_+ iff $\Gamma_R^+(W)$ is true in I_+;*
ii) *W is true in I_+ iff $W(\gamma^+)$ is true in I_+;*
iii) *W is true in I_+ iff $T^+(W)$ is true in I_+;*
iv) *W is true in I_+ iff $S^+(W)$ is true in I_+.*

4.2. Deleting a Tuple

Let W be a wff in prenex conjunctive normal form satisfying the range restricted property and which contains at least one non negated atomic formula with R as (n-ary) predicate symbol. Let I be an interpretation in which W is true and I_- the interpretation obtained from I merely by deleting from the extension of R the tuple $\langle \mathbf{e}_1, \ldots, \mathbf{e}_n \rangle$, where for $i \neq j$, $\mathbf{e}_i$ is not necessarily distinct from $\mathbf{e}_j$.

Because W satisfies the range restricted property, one can assume, without loss of generality, that each element in $\langle \mathbf{e}_1, \ldots, \mathbf{e}_n \rangle$ remains in $\mathscr{E}(I_-)$. Therefore one can write:

$$\mathscr{E}(I_-) = \mathscr{E}(I),$$
$$\mathscr{L}(I_-) = \mathscr{L}(I) - \{R(\mathbf{e}_1, \ldots, \mathbf{e}_n)\} \cup \{\neg R(\mathbf{e}_1, \ldots, \mathbf{e}_n)\}.$$

Now, the set Γ_R^- can be defined by applying the same reasoning as in paragraph 4.1 while replacing: negated atomic formula by non negated atomic formula (and vice-versa), $\neg R(\mathbf{e}_1, \ldots, \mathbf{e}_n)$ by $R(\mathbf{e}_1, \ldots, \mathbf{e}_n)$ (and vice-versa), $\neg R(t_1^i, \ldots, t_n^i)$ by $R(t_1^i, \ldots, t_n^i)$, I_+ by I_-, and Γ_R^+ by Γ_R^-.

Theorem 2. *If W is true in I then*

W is true in I_- iff $\Gamma_R^-(W)$ is true in I_-.

Proof. The same as theorem 1 provided the substitutions mentioned above are done. □

The simplified forms $W(\gamma^-)$ and $T^-(W)$ are defined in the same way from Γ_R^- as the simplified forms $W(\gamma^+)$ and $T^+(W)$ were defined from Γ_R^+. The last two simplification steps leading from $\Gamma_R^+(W)$ to $S^+(W)$ (and possibly applied to $T^+(W)$) can be reproduced here, while considering that time that the value of $R(\mathbf{e}_1, \ldots, \mathbf{e}_n)$ in I_- is $\mathbb{F}$. So is obtained $S^-(W)$. Consequently the deleting theorem can be stated as follows.

Deleting theorem: *If W is true in I then:*

i) *W is true in I_- iff $\Gamma_R^-(W)$ is true in I_-;*
ii) *W is true in I_- iff $W(\gamma^-)$ is true in I_-;*
iii) *W is true in I_- iff $T^-(W)$ is true in I_-;*
iv) *W is true in I_- iff $S^-(W)$ is true in I_-.*

4.3. Updating a Tuple and Transactions

From a logical point of view one can consider the operation of updating a tuple in a relation extension as a peculiar transaction which consists of the two operations of deleting the tuple and entering a new one with adequate components. Thus we will now focus our attention on transactions.

4.3.1. Some comments on transactions

First, let us recall that a transaction is a sequence of (now, inserting and/or deleting) operations which is indivisible with regard to integrity checking. That is, considering a valid data base state S and a transaction which leads to the final state S_f, one is concerned only with the validity of the final state, whether the transient states are valid or not.

In the preceding paragraphs, we assumed implicity that the considered operations of inserting and of deleting led to effective insertions and deletions of tuples into and from the data base. When this is not the case, the new state is in fact identical to the current state and then integrity constraints are necessarily satisfied. In the same way, we will consider here that all operations in a transaction lead to effective insertions and deletions of tuples. Thus, if two opposed operations dealing with the same tuple appear in a transaction, they can be both erased without changing the final state. In the following we will assume that transactions are free from such opposed operations. So, the order of the operations in a transaction is immaterial.

4.3.2 The transaction theorem

Let W be a wff under prenex conjunctive normal form satisfying the range restricted property and I an interpretation of W. Now consider a transaction to be applied on I which leads to an interpretation I_f. With regard to W, the set of operations in the transaction can be partitioned into two subsets θ_u and θ. θ_u is the subset of operations which do not affect W. An operation belongs to θ_u iff it is an inserting (respectively deleting) operation dealing with a relation R and R does not occur as a negated (respectively non-negated) atomic formula in W. The subset θ is the complement of θ_u in the transaction. As the order of operations is immaterial, one can suppose that the operations in θ_u are applied first on I leading to the transient interpretation I_t and next the operations in θ are applied on I_t leading to I_f. It is clear that if W is true in I then it is true in I_t. Furthermore, it turns out that if $\theta_u = \emptyset$ then $I_t = I$ and if θ

$=\emptyset$ then $I_t = I_f$. In this latter case, W is unaffected by the transaction; therefore up to now we will assume that θ is non-empty.

For each operation in θ, let Γ_R^i (either Γ_R^{+i} or Γ_R^{-i}) be its associated set of substitutions with regard to W, defined as in paragraphs 4.1 and 4.2. Let Γ^* be the union of all Γ_R^i's.

According to the results proven in the preceding paragraphs, those Γ_R^i which are empty (if any) correspond to operations in θ which do not affect the truth-value of W; let $\theta_{u'}$ be the set of these operations. Now, starting from I_t and applying successively the operations in $\theta_{u'}$ leads to an interpretation $I_{t'}$ in which W is true (if W is true in I). Note that whenever all Γ_R^i are the empty set ($\Gamma^* = \emptyset$) then $I_{t'} = I_f$.

Let us now consider the set θ_r of operations in θ which do not belong to $\theta_{u'}$ ($\theta_r = \theta - \theta_{u'}$). To each operation in θ_r let us associate a literal defined as follows. If the operation consists in inserting (respectively, deleting) a tuple, say $\langle \mathbf{e}_1, \ldots, \mathbf{e}_n \rangle$, into (from) a relation, say R, the literal associated to this operation is then $R(\mathbf{e}_1, \ldots, \mathbf{e}_n)$ (respectively, $\neg R(\mathbf{e}_1, \ldots, \mathbf{e}_n)$). Let us call $\mathscr{L}_a$ this set of literals and $\mathscr{L}_s$ the set of literals obtained by taking the negation of each literal $\mathscr{L}_a$; hence one can write:

$$\mathscr{E}(I_f) = \mathscr{E}(I_{t'}),$$
$$\mathscr{L}(I_f) = \mathscr{L}(I_{t'}) - \mathscr{L}_s \cup \mathscr{L}_a.$$

Let Γ_R^* be the set of substitutions obtained from Γ^*, in the same way as Γ_R^+ was obtained from Γ and let us define $\Gamma_R^*(W)$ from Γ_R^* as was $\Gamma_R^+(W)$ from Γ_R^+.

Theorem 3. *If W is true in I then:*

W is true in I_f iff $\Gamma_R^*(W)$ is true in I_f.

Proof. As whenever W is true in I then it is true in $I_{t'}$, it remains to prove that if W is true in $I_{t'}$ then the equivalence holds.

Based on proofs of Theorem 1 and Theorem 2, the proof can be obtained in a similar way, but reasoning now with Γ^*, Γ_R^* and literals in $\mathscr{L}_s$ (see [25]). □

The simplified forms of W for a transaction: $W(\gamma^*)$, $T^*(W)$ and $S^*(W)$ are defined from Γ_R^* in the same way as $W(\gamma^+)$, $T^+(W)$ and $S^+(W)$ were defined from Γ_R^+. But this time, these are the literals in $\mathscr{L}_s$, obviously false in I_f, which have to be considered for the third simplification step (Step-3) in the algorithm).

Finally, the transaction theorem can be stated as follows:

Transaction theorem. *If W is true in I then:*
i) *W is true in I_f iff $\Gamma_R^*(W)$ is true in I_f;*
ii) *W is true in I_f iff $W(\gamma^*)$ is true in I_f;*
iii) *W is true in I_f iff $T^*(W)$ is true in I_f;*
iv) *W is true in I_f iff $S^*(W)$ is true in I_f.*

4.4. Comments on the Structure of wffs

We will conclude this section by making two comments on the choice of a "good" structure of wffs with regard to the simplification method.

The first remark deals with the way wffs are put into prenex normal form. Doing so consists in shifting the quantifiers to the front of the wffs by applying adequate transformation rules. In general, a wff admits several prenex normal forms which may differ by the order in which quantifiers occurs. The simplification method proposed here allows one to instantiate in the wff, only universally quantified variables which are not governed by existentially quantified ones. Consequently, in order to get, through the method, the more instantiated wff as possible, it will be better to retain as prenex normal form the one where, as many as possible, existential quantifiers appear on the right. For instance, the prenex normal form (b) given for the formula (3) in Table 1 is a "better" prenex form for the wff (3) than the following one:

$$\forall x \exists z \forall y(\neg \text{SUPPLY}(x, y, \text{guns}) \vee \text{SUPPLY}(x, z, \text{bullets}))$$

The second remark is concerned with the decomposition of a wff into independent sub-formulas. Consider a wff in prenex conjunctive normal form. Such a wff can be decomposed into independent sub-formulas iff its matrix can be partitioned into two sub-conjunctions (possibly reduced to a single disjunction) such that none of the existentially quantified variables which occur in one of them also occur in the other one. If so is the case, the two subformulas whose matrix is one of the two sub-conjunctions and quantifiers are each of the relevant quantifiers in the initial wff, can be evaluated independently in an interpretation; the initial wff being true iff they are both true. The decomposition of a wff into its smallest[9] independent sub-formulas is straightforward. As an example, let us consider the integrity constraint: *Each item supplied by company C_6 or sold by department D_6 is a type T_6 item.* The corresponding wff is:

$$\forall x((\exists y \text{SUPPLY}(C_6, y, x) \vee \text{SALE}(D_6, x)) \rightarrow \text{CLASS}(x, T_6))$$

and its prenex conjunctive normal form is:

$$\forall x \forall y((\neg \text{SUPPLY}(C_6, y, x) \vee \text{CLASS}(x, T_6)) \wedge (\neg \text{SALE}(D_6, x) \vee \text{CLASS}(x, T_6)))$$

the above wff can be decomposed into the two sub-formulas:

$$\forall x \forall y(\neg \text{SUPPLY}(C_6, y, x) \vee \text{CLASS}(x, T_6))$$
$$\forall x \quad (\neg \text{SALE}(D_6, x) \vee \text{CLASS}(x, T_6)).$$

Clearly each of them corresponds to one of the two integrity constraints:

Each item supplied by company C_6 is a type T_6 item

and

Each item sold by department D_6 is a type T_6 item.

The simplification method can be applied to wffs whether they are decomposable or not. But it may be more interesting to deal with wffs which have been decomposed. So is the case in the preceding example with regard to inserting a tuple into the relation SUPPLY. The reader can verify that all wffs in Table 1 are undecomposable.

[9] i.e. sub-formulas which cannot themselves be decomposed

5. Applying the Simplification Method

The purpose of this section is twofold. On the one hand the application of the method is discussed in general. On the other hand it is exemplified on some particular examples.

5.1. Discussion

The main problem which remains to be discussed is whether the simplification method enables us to effectively reduce the cost (in time) of integrity checking.

We will a priori consider that the time needed for generating the simplified form can be neglected compared with the cost of secondary storage accesses needed for evaluating the integrity constraints (the initial constraints as well as their simplified forms). So it remains to determine whether the evaluation of a simplified form is less time consuming than the evaluation of the initial constraint it comes from.

To do so, let us consider an integrity constraint (wffs) W and denote $W(\gamma)$, $T(W)$ and $S(W)$ its three simplified forms, independently from the nature of the operation which causes the state change. If one neglects (which disadvantages simplified forms) the elimination of some atomic formulas (step 3 of the algorithm), each of these simplified forms appears as a conjunction of instances of W. Remember that these instances are obtained by substituting constants for universally quantified variables. It is clear that the evaluation cost of such an instance of W is necessarily less than or equal to the evaluation cost of W and this, whatever the way data are stored and how the evaluation module works. According to its definition, $W(\gamma)$ always consists of a single instance of W and then its evaluation cost is less than or equal to the one of W. Thus, the problem is now shifted one step and deals with the choice of one simplified form among $W(\gamma)$, $T(W)$ and $S(W)$.

In the case where either $S(W) \equiv \mathbb{F}$ or $S(W) \equiv \mathbb{T}$, the answer is very simple as no evaluation is needed for $S(W)$. From a general point of view, it appears that the more a simplified form is instantiated (i.e. the more constants have been substituted for variables) and the less it contains instances of W, better it is. $S(W)$ contains the most instantiated (as possible) instances of W, but possibly several ones. As for $W(\gamma)$ it always contains a single instance of W but less instantiated than those in $S(W)$. Therefore, when $S(W)$ consists of a single instance of W, the choice is then clear, and we shall notice that, accounting to the simplicity of integrity constraints in most real applications [10], this case will be rather frequent.

In the less frequent case where $S(W)$ contains several (n) instances of W, the choice depends both on the value of n, and on the way data are stored and how the evaluation module works. Let us first make some comments on the possible values of n. For this purpose, the three basic operations of inserting, deleting and updating have to be distinguished from transactions. Concerning the former ones the value of n is in general small. Indeed, it is limited by the number of occurrences, in the integrity constraint, of the relation the operation is dealing with and integrity constraints where a given relation occurs more than three times (with a given sign) are quite rare. Now with respect to transactions, all values are possible depending on whether many or few operations in the transaction deal with relations occurring in W. Let us consider now the second parameter the choice between $W(\gamma)$ and $S(W)$ is depending on. This latter parameter can only be taken into account through criteria which reflect the physical organization of data, criteria which will be proper to the data base management system in which the simplification method is implemented. However, one can avoid to appeal to such criteria by systematically choosing a simplified form of W which realizes a trade-off between the number of instances of W it contains and their "degree" of instantiation. The simplified form $T(W)$ symbolizes such a trade-off. At this point we shall emphasize that $W(\gamma)$, $T(W)$ and $S(W)$ constitute, in a way, basic simplified forms for W. $W(\gamma)$ and $S(W)$ appear as the two extremes of the simplified forms of W, the former with regard to the number of instances, the latter with regard to their instantiation degree. But, based upon the set of substitutions Γ_R and according to the lemma proven in Sect. 4.1.4, a lot of intermediate simplified forms can be defined for W. Among them, we retained $T(W)$ because this is the one which, for us, better symbolizes the above mentioned trade-off.

We will conclude this section by making four last remarks. First, the simplification method requires that formulas be in prenex conjunctive normal form. But the process of putting wffs into this form is quite simple and need to be applied only once; for example, when a new integrity constraint is entered. Second, the simplified forms generated by the method are also in prenex conjunctive normal form. But, once they have been obtained, nothing requires them to be evaluated under this form, and query evaluation optimizing techniques (e.g. see [1, 9, 28]) can then be applied. Third, the method indicates that an integrity constraint may be falsified in the new state only if the range of its variables has been modified by the operation which occurred. Hence, before evaluating the simplified integrity constraints, one can envisage to determine, by a partial evaluation on the new state, whether the range of its variables is actually modified. But this is another problem... . Finally, if the validation of the simplification method may appear as rather complex, the method in itself is quite simple, and its implementation does not raise any difficulties. The reader interested in such an implementation is referred to [19].

5.2. Application to Examples

In this sub-section, we will, in particular, take again the examples treated in the third section and show that applying the simplification method leads to the same results as those obtained from semantical considerations in that section. The reader is also referred to [27] where the simplification method is applied to the special family of integrity constraints constituted by dependency statements.

i) *Integrity constraint* (1)

Inserting the tuple $\langle D, I \rangle$ into the relation SALE leads, for this integrity constraint, to the sets of substitutions:

$$\Gamma = \Gamma_R^+ = \{\{x/D, y/I\}\}; \quad \{\gamma^+\} = T^+ = \Gamma_R^+.$$

Consequently:

$$\Gamma_R^+((1)) \equiv \exists z(\neg \mathrm{SALE}(D,I) \vee \mathrm{SUPPLY}(z,D,I))$$

and finally:

$$(1)(\gamma^+) \equiv T^+((1)) \equiv S^+((1)) \equiv \exists z\, \mathrm{SUPPLY}(z,D,I)$$

ii) *Integrity constraint* (5)

Assume the tuple $\langle C,D,I \rangle$ is inserted into the relation SUPPLY then:

$$\Gamma = \Gamma_R^+ = \{\{x/C, y/D\}, \{x/C, z/D\}\}; \{\gamma^+\} = T^+ = \{\{x/C\}\}$$

$$\Gamma_R^+((5)) \equiv \forall z(\neg \mathrm{SUPPLY}(C,D,I) \vee \neg \mathrm{SUPPLY}(C,z,I) \vee (D=z))$$
$$\wedge \forall y(\neg \mathrm{SUPPLY}(C,y,I) \vee \neg \mathrm{SUPPLY}(C,D,I) \vee (y=D))$$

Then applying the two last simplification steps leads to:

$$S^+((5)) = \forall z(\neg \mathrm{SUPPLY}(C,z,I) \vee (D=z)).$$

The reader will note that the above wff differs from the wff obtained in Sect. 3 merely by the negation distribution.

The other simplified forms are:

$$(5)(\gamma^+) \equiv T^+((5)) \equiv \forall y \forall z(\neg \mathrm{SUPPLY}(C,y,I) \vee \neg \mathrm{SUPPLY}(C,z,I) \vee (y=z))$$

iii) *Integrity constraint* (6)

The tuple $\langle E_1, E_2 \rangle$ is inserted into the relation SUBORD.

$$\Gamma = \Gamma_R^+ = \{\{x/E_1, z/E_2\}, \{z/E_1, y/E_2\}\}; \quad \gamma^+ = \mathscr{I}; \quad T^+ = \Gamma_R^+$$

$$\Gamma_R^+((6)) \equiv \forall y(\neg \mathrm{SUBORD}(E_1,E_2) \vee \neg \mathrm{SUBORD}(E_2,y) \vee \mathrm{SUBORD}(E_1,y))$$
$$\wedge \forall x(\neg \mathrm{SUBORD}(x,E_1) \vee \neg \mathrm{SUBORD}(E_1,E_2) \vee \mathrm{SUBORD}(x,E_2))$$

$$S^+((6)) \equiv \forall y(\neg \mathrm{SUBORD}(E_2,y) \vee \mathrm{SUBORD}(E_1,y))$$
$$\wedge \forall x(\neg \mathrm{SUBORD}(x,E_1) \vee \mathrm{SUBORD}(x,E_2))$$

iv) *Integrity constraint* (2)

The tuple $\langle I, T_2 \rangle$ is inserted into the relation CLASS. In this case, no substitution is defined, hence $\Gamma_R^+ = \emptyset$ and then $S^+((2)) \equiv \mathbb{T}$, namely the formula which is true in any interpretation.

v) *Integrity constraint* (7)

The tuple $\langle C,D,I \rangle$ is inserted into the relation SUPPLY. In this case, a substitution is defined, but it is the empty one. Then $\Gamma_R^+ = \{\mathscr{I}\}$ and therefore $\Gamma_R^+((7)) \equiv S^+((7)) \equiv (7)$.

At last, let us consider globally all integrity constraints in Table 1 and suppose the tuple $\langle I, T_2 \rangle$ in relation CLASS is updated into $\langle I, T_3 \rangle$. Only integrity constraints where CLASS occurs either as a negated or a non negated atomic formula may be falsified by this updating operation. For each of them the simplified form which is obtained is the following one.

For the integrity constraints (2) and (7), Γ_R^* is the empty set; so, they remain necessarily satisfied in the new data base state.

$$(S^*((2)) \equiv S^*((7)) \equiv \mathbb{T}).$$

For the integrity constraint (4) because of the deletion of the tuple $\langle I, T_2 \rangle$ then $\Gamma_R^* = \{\mathscr{I}\}$. Therefore the whole integrity constraint has to be evaluated on the new state.

6. Conclusion

A simplification method for integrity constraints on data base relations has been proposed and validated. For any integrity constraint, this method yields simplified forms that it is sufficient to check when a data base state change occurs. These simplified forms depend on the operation which is the cause of the data base state change. One of them $(W(\gamma))$, may be the less interesting one, has an evaluation cost which is less than or equal to that of the initial constraint whatever it is and whatever the way data are stored and how the evaluation module works. But, due to the simplicity of most integrity constraints, the a priori most interesting of them $(S(W))$ can be retained without implementation hypotheses in most cases. However some cases remain where choosing the best among them to evaluate can be done only according to criteria which reflect the physical organization of data, unless a third simplified form $(T(W))$ which realizes a trade-off between the two former ones be, in such cases, systematically chosen.

The integrity constraints we have considered were state integrity constraints, as opposed to transition ones [13, 17, 23]. Transition integrity constraints link together relations extensions in two different data base states. So, they cannot, a priori, be expressed by wffs which admit a data base state as an interpretation. However, it has been shown in [23] that, by extending the data base with ad hoc relations, called action relations, that can in fact be done. Transition integrity constraints are then expressed as wffs in which an action relation appears. Whenever an operation occurs on a data base state, transition constraints which might be falsified by this operation, are determined according to their action relation. Since the extension of such action relations contains at most one tuple, the simplification of such integrity constraints by instantiation does not seem to be worthwhile.

At last, the simplification method as defined can be implemented directly (e.g. see [19]) in a database management system, the data manipulation language of which is predicate calculus oriented with individual variables [2, 11, 29]. We think that it can also be adapted, to other systems, in as much as their data manipulation language is assertional. A similar method has been recently defined in [5] for integrity constraints expressed in the tuple relational calculus.

Acknowledgments. The author is thankful to H. Gallaire for his helpful comments on this paper and to A. Fahmy, K. Yazdanian and B. Jacobs for fruitful discussions he had with them. Thanks are also due to D.S. Parker and P.V. Homeier for the implementation of the method which has been realized at U.C.L.A. Furthermore valuable comments of the referees were greatly appreciated.

References

1. Aho, A.V., Sagiv, Y., Ullman, J.D.: Efficient optimization of a class of relational expressions. Presented at the ACM-SIGMOD Conf., Austin, (June, 1978). ACM-TODS (4.4). 1979
2. Artaud, A., Nicolas, J.-M.: An experimental query system: SYNTEX. Proc. of the International Computing Symposium, Davos, 1973, North-Holland, 1974
3. Beeri, C., Bernstein, P.A., Goodman, N.: A sophisticate's introduction to data base normalization theory. Proc. of the 4th VLDB Conf. Berlin, 1978
4. Bernstein, P.A., Blaustein, B.T., Clarke, E.M.: Fast maintenance of semantic integrity assertions using redondant aggregate data. Proc. of the 6th VLDB Conf., Montreal, 1980
5. Blaustein, B.T.: Enforcing database assertions: Techniques and Applications. Ph. D. Thesis, Cambridge: Harvard University, 1981
6. Cadiou, J.-M.: On semantic issues in the relational model of data. In: Math. Found. Comput. Sci. Mazurkiewiez, A. (ed.). Vol. 45, Berlin Heidelberg New York: Springer 1976
7. Chang, C.L., Lee, R.C.T.: Symbolic logic and mechanical theorem proving. Comput. Sci. Appl. Math. Academic Press, 1973
8. Chang, C.L., DEDUCE 2: Further investigations of deduction in relational data bases. In: [16]
9. Chandra, A.K., Merlin, P.M.: Optimal implementation of conjunctives queries in relational Data Banks. Proc. 9th Annual ACM-Symp. Theory Comput. 1976
10. Date, C.J.: An introduction to data base systems. (Second edition), Addison-Wesley Publ. Comp., 1977
11. Demolombe, R., Lemaître, M., Nicolas, J.-M.: The language of SYNTEX-2, an implemented relational-like DBMS. In: Informat. Technol. Moneta, J. (ed.). JCIT3, Amsterdam: North-Holland Pub. Comp., 1978
12. Enderton, H.B.: A mathematical introduction to logic. Academic Press, 1972
13. Eswaran, K.P., Chamberlin, D.D.: Functional specifications of a sub-system for Data Base Integrity. Proc. 1st VLDB Conf., Framingham, 1975
14. Fagin, R.: Horn clauses and database dependencies. Proc. 12th Annual ACM Symp. Theor Comput., 1980
15. Gallaire, H.: Impacts of Logic on Databases. Proc. 7th VLDB Conf., Cannes, 1981
16. Gallaire, H., Minker, J. (eds.): Logic and databases. New York: Plenum Press, 1978
17. Hammer, M.M., McLeod, D.J.: Semantic integrity in a relational data base system. Proc. 1st VLDB Conf., Framingham, 1975
18. Hammer, M., Sarin, S.K.: Efficient monitoring of data base assertions. Presented at the ACM-SIGMOD 78 Conf., Austin, 1978
19. Homeier, P.V.: Simplifying Integrity constraints in a relational database: an implementation. Master thesis, Comput. Sci. Dept., Los Angeles: University of California, 1981
20. Kowalski, R.: Logic for Problem solving. Elsevier North-Holland, New York, 1979
21. Mendelson, E.: Introduction to mathematical logic. D. van Nostrand, 1964
22. Nicolas, J.-M., Gallaire, H.: Data base: theory vs. interpretation. In: [16]
23. Nicolas, J.-M., Yazdanian, K.: Integrity checking in deductive data bases. In: [16]
24. Nicolas, J.-M.: First order logic formalization for functional, multivalued and mutual dependencies. Proc. ACM-SIGMOD Conf., Austin, 1978
25. Nicolas, J.-M.: Logical formulas and integrity constraints: the range restricted property and a simplification method. T-R CERT-LBD/79-1, Toulouse, 1979
26. Nicolas, J.-M.: A property of logical formulas corresponding to integrity constraints on data base relations. Preprints of the Workshop on "Formal bases for data bases", Toulouse, 1979
27. Nicolas, J.-M.: Applying a simplification method for integrity constraints to Dependency statements. T.R. CERT, 1979
28. Palermo, F.P.: A data base search problem: In: Informat. Syst. COINS IV. Tou, J.T. (ed.). New York- Plenum Press, 1974
29. Pirotte, A.: High level data base query languages. In: [16]
30. Stonebraker, M.: High level integrity assurance in relational data base management systems. Mem. ERL-M473, University of California, Berkeley, 1974
31. Stonebraker, M.: Implementation of integrity constraints and views by query modification. Proc. ACM-SIGMOD Conf., San Jose, 1975
32. Ullman, J.D.: Principles of Database systems. Computer Science Press, Potomac, MD, 1980

3.3 Implementation Techniques

Data/knowledge base systems issues for which implementation techniques have been developed include concurrency control, query optimization, security, view processing, data structures and algorithms, performance evaluation, database-systems reliability, distributed databases, and systems architectures. These topics are discussed in [Brodie and Manola, 1.1]. This section deals with four key data/knowledge base implementation techniques: query optimization, database concurrency control, database view processing and security, and knowledge-base pattern matching. There is extensive literature on the implementation techniques not covered in this section (e.g., security [GW76]; data structures and algorithms [SAME84]; indexing [BM72], [BF79], [BENT75], [GUTT84]; buffering [CD85], [SCHK86]; robustness [ES83]; and recovery [VERH78]). AI implementation techniques are not nearly as well developed as are database techniques. Although there are correspondences between database and knowledge-base implementation problems (c.f., database query processing and control strategies in AI, such as described in [KDSJ77]), little has been done to apply results in one area to problems in the other [MB86].

The first paper (3.3.1), "Access Path Selection in a Relational DBMS" by Pat Selinger-Griffiths, Morton Astrahan, Don Chamberlin, Raymond Lorie, and T.G. Price, is the classic paper on query optimization (QO). Query processing is still based on the techniques proposes in this paper. QO is a fundamental technique in DBMSs on which much work has been done. [KRB85] is an excellent book on the topic. QO has been considered in many contexts (e.g., distributed databases [DAYA85]; spatial databases [OREN86]; recursion [Bancilhon, 3.1.2]; and knowledge-base systems [CFM86], [Bocca, 3.4.5]). AI techniques are now being applied to QO to take greater advantage of knowledge of the query processing and the system state [FREY87].

The second paper (3.3.2), "The Notions of Consistency and Predicate Locks in a Database System" by Kapali Eswaren, Jim Gray, Raymond Lorie, and Irv Traiger, is the concurrency-control classic. Concurrency is required to support one of the primary principles of databases—namely, data sharing. The idea is to lock out other users from reading data while you are updating those data, to ensure that others see the data correctly updated rather than in a potentially inconsistent intermediate form. The paper introduces the key notions of *predicate locking* and *two-phase commit*. A predicate lock is what gets set as a result of stating, in a predicate, which data you intend to update. Two-phase commit, the basis of conventional concurrency control, involves one phase of acquiring locks on all items to be updated and one phase of committing the updates to the database once all updates have been completed sucessfully, and then releasing the locks. A companion paper [GLPG75] presents the first *two-phase locking* algorithm to support two-phase commit. [BHG87] presents a thorough treatment of concurrency control issues. Related work includes [BADA79], [BSR80], [BG81], and [BHAR82]. Although concurrency control for conventional DBMSs is well understood (please, no more papers), advanced DBMSs, such as discussed in the next section, reopen the book on concurrency control (and, no doubt, will spawn many more papers!).

The third paper (3.3.3), Mike Stonebraker's "Implementation of Integrity Constraints and Views by Query Modification," describes a classic database implementation technique for security checking and view processing. It has been used in several commercial DBMSs. It is fair to add, however, that it has now been improved by methods that are more secure (e.g., data are not brought into buffers). Related work can be found on security [CHEH81], [LAND81] and on view processing [IOAN85], [RS79].

The fourth and final paper in this section (3.3.4) is "RETE: A Fast Algorithm for the Many Pattern/Many Object Pattern Match Problem" by C.L. Forgy. It presents the now-famous RETE match algorithm, which is a relatively (by AI standards) efficient means for matching the patterns of a set of production rules against the objects in the workspace of a production system. [MIRA89] presents a successor to the RETE algorithm and studies the latter's performance on a parallel computer. RETE is related to view processing (i.e., view materialization) in databases [HANS87]. It is likely that knowledge-base search techniques can benefit considerably from the database search techniques developed over the past 10 years.

Access Path Selection in a Relational Database Management System

P. Griffiths Selinger
M. M. Astrahan
D. D. Chamberlin
R. A. Lorie
T. G. Price

IBM Research Division, San Jose, California 95193

ABSTRACT: In a high level query and data manipulation language such as SQL, requests are stated non-procedurally, without reference to access paths. This paper describes how System R chooses access paths for both simple (single relation) and complex queries (such as joins), given a user specification of desired data as a boolean expression of predicates. System R is an experimental database management system developed to carry out research on the relational model of data. System R was designed and built by members of the IBM San Jose Research Laboratory.

1. Introduction

System R is an experimental database management system based on the relational model of data which has been under development at the IBM San Jose Research Laboratory since 1975 <1>. The software was developed as a research vehicle in relational database, and is not generally available outside the IBM Research Division.

This paper assumes familiarity with relational data model terminology as described in Codd <7> and Date <8>. The user interface in System R is the unified query, data definition, and manipulation language SQL <5>. Statements in SQL can be issued both from an on-line casual-user-oriented terminal interface and from programming languages such as PL/I and COBOL.

In System R a user need not know how the tuples are physically stored and what access paths are available (e.g. which columns have indexes). SQL statements do not require the user to specify anything about the access path to be used for tuple retrieval. Nor does a user specify in what order joins are to be performed. The System R optimizer chooses both join order and an access path for each table in the SQL statement. Of the many possible choices, the optimizer chooses the one which minimizes "total access cost" for performing the entire statement.

This paper will address the issues of access path selection for queries. Retrieval for data manipulation (UPDATE, DELETE) is treated similarly. Section 2 will describe the place of the optimizer in the processing of a SQL statement, and section 3 will describe the storage component access paths that are available on a single physically stored table. In section 4 the optimizer cost formulas are introduced for single table queries, and section 5 discusses the joining of two or more tables, and their corresponding costs. Nested queries (queries in predicates) are covered in section 6.

2. Processing of an SQL statement

A SQL statement is subjected to four phases of processing. Depending on the origin and contents of the statement, these phases may be separated by arbitrary intervals of time. In System R, these arbitrary time intervals are transparent to the system components which process a SQL statement. These mechanisms and a description of the processing of SQL statements from both programs and terminals are further discussed in <2>. Only an overview of those processing steps that are relevant to access path selection will be discussed here.

The four phases of statement processing are parsing, optimization, code generation, and execution. Each SQL statement is sent to the parser, where it is checked for correct syntax. A query block is represented by a SELECT list, a FROM list, and a WHERE tree, containing, respectively the list of items to be retrieved, the table(s) referenced, and the boolean combination of simple predicates specified by the user. A single SQL statement may have many query blocks because a predicate may have one operand which is itself a query.

If the parser returns without any errors detected, the OPTIMIZER component is called. The OPTIMIZER accumulates the names of tables and columns referenced in the query and looks them up in the System R catalogs to verify their existence and to retrieve information about them.

The catalog lookup portion of the OPTIMIZER also obtains statistics about the referenced relations, and the access paths available on each of them. These will be used later in access path selection. After catalog lookup has obtained the datatype and length of each column, the OPTIMIZER rescans the SELECT-list and WHERE-tree to check for semantic errors and type compatibility in both expressions and predicate comparisons.

Finally the OPTIMIZER performs access path selection. It first determines the evaluation order among the query blocks in the statement. Then for each query block, the relations in the FROM list are processed. If there is more than one relation in a block, permutations of the join order and of the method of joining are evaluated. The access paths that minimize total cost for the block are chosen from a tree of alternate path choices. This minimum cost solution is represented by a structural modification of the parse tree. The result is an execution plan in the Access Specification Language (ASL) <10>.

After a plan is chosen for each query block and represented in the parse tree, the CODE GENERATOR is called. The CODE GENERATOR is a table-driven program which translates ASL trees into machine language code to execute the plan chosen by the OPTIMIZER. In doing this it uses a relatively small number of code templates, one for each type of join method (including no join). Query blocks for nested queries are treated as "subroutines" which return values to the predicates in which they occur. The CODE GENERATOR is further described in <9>.

During code generation, the parse tree is replaced by executable machine code and its associated data structures. Either control is immediately transfered to this code or the code is stored away in the database for later execution, depending on the origin of the statement (program or terminal). In either case, when the code is ultimately executed, it calls upon the System R internal storage system (RSS) via the storage system interface (RSI) to scan each of the physically stored relations in the query. These scans are along the access paths chosen by the OPTIMIZER. The RSI commands that may be used by generated code are described in the next section.

3. <u>The Research Storage System</u>

The Research Storage System (RSS) is the storage subsystem of System R. It is responsible for maintaining physical storage of relations, access paths on these relations, locking (in a multi-user environment), and logging and recovery facilities. The RSS presents a tuple-oriented interface (RSI) to its users. Although the RSS may be used independently of System R, we are concerned here with its use for executing the code generated by the processing of SQL statements in System R, as described in the previous section. For a complete description of the RSS, see <1>.

Relations are stored in the RSS as a collection of tuples whose columns are physically contiguous. These tuples are stored on 4K byte pages; no tuple spans a page. Pages are organized into logical units called segments. Segments may contain one or more relations, but no relation may span a segment. Tuples from two or more relations may occur on the same page. Each tuple is tagged with the identification of the relation to which it belongs.

The primary way of accessing tuples in a relation is via an RSS scan. A scan returns a tuple at a time along a given access path. OPEN, NEXT, and CLOSE are the principal commands on a scan.

Two types of scans are currently available for SQL statements. The first type is a segment scan to find all the tuples of a given relation. A series of NEXTs on a segment scan simply examines all pages of the segment which contain tuples from <u>any</u> relation, and returns those tuples belonging to the given relation.

The second type of scan is an index scan. An index may be created by a System R user on one or more columns of a relation, and a relation may have any number (including zero) of indexes on it. These indexes are stored on separate pages from those containing the relation tuples. Indexes are implemented as B-trees <3>, whose leaves are pages containing sets of (key, identifiers of tuples which contain that key). Therefore a series of NEXTs on an index scan does a sequential read along the leaf pages of the index, obtaining the tuple identifiers matching a key, and using them to find and return the data tuples to the user in key value order. Index leaf pages are chained together so that NEXTs need not reference any upper level pages of the index.

In a segment scan, all the non-empty pages of a segment will be touched, regardless of whether there are any tuples from the desired relation on them. However, each page is touched only once. When an entire relation is examined via an index scan, each page of the index is touched only once, but a data page may be examined more than once if it has two tuples on it which are not "close" in the index ordering. If the tuples are inserted into segment pages in the index ordering, and if this physical proximity corresponding to index key value is maintained, we say that the index is <u>clustered</u>. A clustered index has the property that not only each index page, but also each data page containing a tuple from that relation will be touched only once in a scan on that index.

An index scan need not scan the entire relation. Starting and stopping key values may be specified in order to scan only those tuples which have a key in a range of index values. Both index and segment scans may optionally take a set of predicates, called search arguments (or SARGS), which are applied to a tuple before it is returned to the RSI caller. If the tuple satisfies the predicates, it is returned; otherwise the scan continues until it either finds a tuple which satisfies the SARGS or exhausts the segment or the specified index value range. This reduces cost by eliminating the overhead of making RSI calls for tuples which can be efficiently rejected within the RSS. Not all predicates are of the form that can become SARGS. A <u>sargable predicate</u> is one of the form (or which can be put into the form) "column comparison-operator value". SARGS are expressed as a boolean expression of such predicates in disjunctive normal form.

4. <u>Costs for single relation access paths</u>

In the next several sections we will describe the process of choosing a plan for evaluating a query. We will first describe the simplest case, accessing a single relation, and show how it extends and generalizes to 2-way joins of relations, n-way joins, and finally multiple query blocks (nested queries).

The OPTIMIZER examines both the predicates in the query and the access paths available on the relations referenced by the query, and formulates a cost prediction for each access plan, using the following cost formula:

COST = PAGE FETCHES + W * (RSI CALLS).

This cost is a weighted measure of I/O (pages fetched) and CPU utilization (instructions executed). W is an adjustable weighting factor between I/O and CPU. RSI CALLS is the predicted number of tuples returned from the RSS. Since most of System R's CPU time is spent in the RSS, the number of RSI calls is a good approximation for CPU utilization. Thus the choice of a minimum cost path to process a query attempts to minimize total resources required.

During execution of the type-compatibility and semantic checking portion of the OPTIMIZER, each query block's WHERE tree of predicates is examined. The WHERE tree is considered to be in conjunctive normal form, and every conjunct is called a <u>boolean factor</u>. Boolean factors are notable because every tuple returned to the user must satisfy every boolean factor. An index is said to match a boolean factor if the boolean factor is a sargable predicate whose referenced column is the index key; e.g., an index on SALARY matches the predicate 'SALARY = 20000'. More precisely, we say that a predicate or set of predicates <u>matches</u> an index access path when the predicates are sargable and the columns mentioned in the predicate(s) are an initial substring of the set of columns of the index key. For example, a NAME, LOCATION index matches NAME = 'SMITH' AND LOCATION = 'SAN JOSE'. If an index matches a boolean factor, an access using that index is an efficient way to satisfy the boolean factor. Sargable boolean factors can also be efficiently satisfied if they are expressed as search arguments. Note that a boolean factor may be an entire tree of predicates headed by an OR.

During catalog lookup, the OPTIMIZER retrieves statistics on the relations in the query and on the access paths available on each relation. The statistics kept are the following:

For each relation T,
- NCARD(T), the cardinality of relation T.
- TCARD(T), the number of pages in the segment that hold tuples of relation T.
- P(T), the fraction of data pages in the segment that hold tuples of relation T. P(T) = TCARD(T) / (no. of non-empty pages in the segment).

For each index I on relation T,
- ICARD(I), number of distinct keys in index I.
- NINDX(I), the number of pages in index I.

These statistics are maintained in the System R catalogs, and come from several sources. Initial relation loading and index creation initialize these statistics. They are then updated periodically by an UPDATE STATISTICS command, which can be run by any user. System R does not update these statistics at every INSERT, DELETE, or UPDATE because of the extra database operations and the locking bottleneck this would create at the system catalogs. Dynamic updating of statistics would tend to serialize accesses that modify the relation contents.

Using these statistics, the OPTIMIZER assigns a <u>selectivity factor</u> 'F' for each boolean factor in the predicate list. This selectivity factor very roughly corresponds to the expected fraction of tuples which will satisfy the predicate. TABLE 1 gives the selectivity factors for different kinds of predicates. We assume that a lack of statistics implies that the relation is small, so an arbitrary factor is chosen.

TABLE 1 SELECTIVITY FACTORS

```
column = value
        F = 1 / ICARD(column index) if there is an index on column
        This assumes an even distribution of tuples among the index key
        values.
        F = 1/10    otherwise

column1 = column2
        F = 1/MAX(ICARD(column1 index), ICARD(column2 index))
            if there are indexes on both column1 and column2
        This assumes that each key value in the index with the smaller
        cardinality has a matching value in the other index.
        F = 1/ICARD(column-i index) if there is only an index on column-i
        F = 1/10    otherwise

column > value (or any other open-ended comparison)
        F = (high key value - value) / (high key value - low key value)
        Linear interpolation of the value within the range of key values
        yields F if the column is an arithmetic type and value is known at
        access path selection time.
        F = 1/3 otherwise (i.e. column not arithmetic)
        There is no significance to this number, other than the fact that
        it is less selective than the guesses for equal predicates for
        which there are no indexes, and that it is less than 1/2. We
        hypothesize that few queries use predicates that are satisfied by
        more than half the tuples.

column BETWEEN value1 AND value2
        F = (value2 - value1) / (high key value - low key value)

        A ratio of the BETWEEN value range to the entire key value range is
        used as the selectivity factor if column is arithmetic and both
        value1 and value2 are known at access path selection.
        F = 1/4 otherwise
        Again there is no significance to this choice except that it is
        between the default selectivity factors for an equal predicate and
        a range predicate.

column IN (list of values)
        F = (number of items in list) * (selectivity factor for column =
        value)
        This is allowed to be no more than 1/2.

columnA IN subquery
        F = (expected cardinality of the subquery result) /
            (product of the cardinalities of all the relations in the
        subquery's FROM-list).
        The computation of query cardinality will be discussed below.
        This formula is derived by the following argument:
        Consider the simplest case, where subquery is of the form "SELECT
        columnB FROM relationC ...". Assume that the set of all columnB
        values in relationC contains the set of all columnA values. If all
        the tuples of relationC are selected by the subquery, then the
        predicate is always TRUE and F = 1. If the tuples of the subquery
        are restricted by a selectivity factor F', then assume that the set
        of unique values in the subquery result that match columnA values
        is proportionately restricted, i.e. the selectivity factor for the
        predicate should be F'. F' is the product of all the subquery's
        selectivity factors, namely (subquery cardinality) / (cardinality
        of all possible subquery answers). With a little optimism, we can
        extend this reasoning to include subqueries which are joins and
        subqueries in which columnB is replaced by an arithmetic expression
        involving column names. This leads to the formula given above.

(pred expression1) OR (pred expression2)
        F = F(pred1) + F(pred2) - F(pred1) * F(pred2)
```

```
(pred1) AND (pred2)
        F = F(pred1) * F(pred2)
        Note that this assumes that column values are independent.

NOT pred
        F = 1 - F(pred)
```

Query cardinality (QCARD) is the product of the cardinalities of every relation in the query block's FROM list times the product of all the selectivity factors of that query block's boolean factors. The number of expected RSI calls (RSICARD) is the product of the relation cardinalities times the selectivity factors of the <u>sargable</u> boolean factors, since the sargable boolean factors will be put into search arguments which will filter out tuples without returning across the RSS interface.

Choosing an optimal access path for a single relation consists of using these selectivity factors in formulas together with the statistics on available access paths. Before this process is described, a definition is needed. Using an index access path or sorting tuples produces tuples in the index value or sort key order. We say that a tuple order is an <u>interesting order</u> if that order is one specified by the query block's GROUP BY or ORDER BY clauses.

For single relations, the cheapest access path is obtained by evaluating the cost for each available access path (each index on the relation, plus a segment scan). The costs will be described below. For each such access path, a predicted cost is computed along with the ordering of the tuples it will produce. Scanning along the SALARY index in ascending order, for example, will produce some cost C and a tuple order of SALARY (ascending). To find the cheapest access plan for a single relation query, we need only to examine the cheapest access path which produces tuples in each "interesting" order and the cheapest "unordered" access path. Note that an "unordered" access path may in fact produce tuples in some order, but the order is not "interesting". If there are no GROUP BY or ORDER BY clauses on the query, then there will be no interesting orderings, and the cheapest access path is the one chosen. If there are GROUP BY or ORDER BY clauses, then the cost for producing that interesting ordering must be compared to the cost of the cheapest unordered path <u>plus</u> the cost of sorting QCARD tuples into the proper order. The cheapest of these alternatives is chosen as the plan for the query block.

The cost formulas for single relation access paths are given in TABLE 2. These formulas give index pages fetched plus data pages fetched plus the weighting factor times RSI tuple retrieval calls. W is the weighting factor between page fetches and RSI calls. Some situations give several alternative formulas depending on whether the set of tuples retrieved will fit entirely in the RSS buffer pool (or effective buffer pool per user). We assume for clustered indexes that a page remains in the buffer long enough for every tuple to be retrieved from it. For non-clustered indexes, it is assumed that for those relations not fitting in the buffer, the relation is sufficiently large with respect to the buffer size that a page fetch is required for every tuple retrieval.

TABLE 2 COST FORMULAS

<u>SITUATION</u>	<u>COST</u> (<u>in pages</u>)
Unique index matching an equal predicate	1 + 1 + W
Clustered index I matching one or more boolean factors	F(preds) * (NINDX(I) + TCARD) + W * RSICARD
Non-clustered index I matching one or more boolean factors	F(preds) * (NINDX(I) + NCARD) + W * RSICARD or F(preds) * (NINDX(I) + TCARD) + W * RSICARD if this number fits in the System R buffer
Clustered index I not matching any boolean factors	(NINDX(I) + TCARD) + W * RSICARD
Non-clustered index I not matching any boolean factors	(NINDX(I) + NCARD) + W * RSICARD or (NINDX(I) + TCARD) + W * RSICARD if this number fits in the System R buffer
Segment scan	TCARD/P + W * RSICARD

5. Access path selection for joins

In 1976, Blasgen and Eswaran <4> examined a number of methods for performing 2-way joins. The performance of each of these methods was analyzed under a variety of relation cardinalities. Their evidence indicates that for other than very small relations, one of two join methods were always optimal or near optimal. The System R optimizer chooses between these two methods. We first describe these methods, and then discuss how they are extended for n-way joins. Finally we specify how the join order (the order in which the relations are joined) is chosen. For joins involving two relations, the two relations are called the _outer_ relation, from which a tuple will be retrieved first, and the _inner_ relation, from which tuples will be retrieved, possibly depending on the values obtained in the outer relation tuple. A predicate which relates columns of two tables to be joined is called a _join predicate_. The columns referenced in a join predicate are called _join columns_.

The first join method, called the _nested loops_ method, uses scans, in any order, on the outer and inner relations. The scan on the outer relation is opened and the first tuple is retrieved. For each outer relation tuple obtained, a scan is opened on the inner relation to retrieve, one at a time, all the tuples of the inner relation which satisfy the join predicate. The composite tuples formed by the outer-relation-tuple / inner-relation-tuple pairs comprise the result of this join.

The second join method, called _merging scans_, requires the outer and inner relations to be scanned in join column order. This implies that, along with the columns mentioned in ORDER BY and GROUP BY, columns of equi-join predicates (those of the form Table1.column1 = Table2.column2) also define "interesting" orders. If there is more than one join predicate, one of them is used as the join predicate and the others are treated as ordinary predicates. The merging scans method is only applied to equi-joins, although in principle it could be applied to other types of joins. If one or both of the relations to be joined has no indexes on the join column, it must be sorted into a temporary list which is ordered by the join column.

The more complex logic of the merging scan join method takes advantage of the ordering on join columns to avoid rescanning the entire inner relation (looking for a match) for each tuple of the outer relation. It does this by synchronizing the inner and outer scans by reference to matching join column values and by "remembering" where matching join groups are located. Further savings occur if the inner relation is clustered on the join column (as would be true if it is the output of a sort on the join column). "Clustering" on a column means that tuples which have the same value in that column are physically stored close to each other so that one page access will retrieve several tuples.

N-way joins can be visualized as a sequence of 2-way joins. In this visualization, two relations are joined together, the resulting composite relation is joined with the third relation, etc. At each step of the n-way join it is possible to identify the outer relation (which in general is composite) and the inner relation (the relation being added to the join). Thus the methods described above for two way joins are easily generalized to n-way joins. However, it should be emphasized that the first 2-way join does not have to be completed before the second 2-way join is started. As soon as we get a composite tuple for the first 2-way join, it can be joined with tuples of the third relation to form result tuples for the 3-way join, etc. Nested loop joins and merge scan joins may be mixed in the same query, e.g. the first two relations of a three-way join may be joined using merge scans and the composite result may be joined with the third relation using a nested loop join. The intermediate composite relations are physically stored only if a sort is required for the next join step. When a sort of the composite relation is not specified, the composite relation will be materialized one tuple at a time to participate in the next join.

We now consider the order in which the relations are chosen to be joined. It should be noted that although the cardinality of the join of n relations is the same regardless of join order, the cost of joining in different orders can be substantially different. If a query block has n relations in its FROM list, then there are n factorial permutations of relation join orders. The search space can be reduced by observing that that once the first k relations are joined, the method to join the composite to the k+1-st relation is independent of the order of joining the first k; i.e. the applicable predicates are the same, the set of interesting orderings is the same, the possible join methods are the same, etc. Using this property, an efficient way to organize the search is to find the best join order for successively larger subsets of tables.

A heuristic is used to reduce the join order permutations which are considered. When possible, the search is reduced by consideration only of join orders which have join predicates relating the inner relation to the other relations already participating in the join. This means that in joining relations t1,t2,...,tn only those orderings ti1,ti2,...,tin are examined in which for all j (j=2,...,n) either
(1) tij has at least one join predicate

with some relation tik, where k < j, or (2) for all k > j, tik has no join predicate with ti1,ti2,...,or ti(j-1). This means that all joins requiring Cartesian products are performed as late in the join sequence as possible. For example, if T1,T2,T3 are the three relations in a query block's FROM list, and there are join predicates between T1 and T2 and between T2 and T3 on different columns than the T1-T2 join, then the following permutations are not considered:

T1-T3-T2
T3-T1-T2

To find the optimal plan for joining n relations, a tree of possible solutions is constructed. As discussed above, the search is performed by finding the best way to join subsets of the relations. For each set of relations joined, the cardinality of the composite relation is estimated and saved. In addition, for the unordered join, and for each interesting order obtained by the join thus far, the cheapest solution for achieving that order and the cost of that solution are saved. A solution consists of an ordered list of the relations to be joined, the join method used for each join, and a plan indicating how each relation is to be accessed. If either the outer composite relation or the inner relation needs to be sorted before the join, then that is also included in the plan. As in the single relation case, "interesting" orders are those listed in the query block's GROUP BY or ORDER BY clause, if any. Also every join column defines an "interesting" order. To minimize the number of different interesting orders and hence the number of solutions in the tree, equivalence classes for interesting orders are computed and only the best solution for each equivalence class is saved. For example, if there is a join predicate E.DNO = D.DNO and another join predicate D.DNO = F.DNO, then all three of these columns belong to the same order equivalence class.

The search tree is constructed by iteration on the number of relations joined so far. First, the best way is found to access each single relation for each interesting tuple ordering and for the unordered case. Next, the best way of joining any relation to these is found, subject to the heuristics for join order. This produces solutions for joining pairs of relations. Then the best way to join sets of three relations is found by consideration of all sets of two relations and joining in each third relation permitted by the join order heuristic. For each plan to join a set of relations, the order of the composite result is kept in the tree. This allows consideration of a merge scan join which would not require sorting the composite. After the complete solutions (all of the relations joined together) have been found, the optimizer chooses the cheapest solution which gives the required order, if any was specified. Note that if a solution exists with the correct order, no sort is performed for ORDER BY or GROUP BY, unless the ordered solution is more expensive than the cheapest unordered solution plus the cost of sorting into the required order.

The number of solutions which must be stored is at most 2**n (the number of subsets of n tables) times the number of interesting result orders. The computation time to generate the tree is approximately proportional to the same number. This number is frequently reduced substantially by the join order heuristic. Our experience is that typical cases require only a few thousand bytes of storage and a few tenths of a second of 370/158 CPU time. Joins of 8 tables have been optimized in a few seconds.

<u>Computation of costs</u>

The costs for joins are computed from the costs of the scans on each of the relations and the cardinalities. The costs of the scans on each of the relations are computed using the cost formulas for single relation access paths presented in section 4.

Let C-outer(path1) be the cost of scanning the outer relation via path1, and N be the cardinality of the outer relation tuples which satisfy the applicable predicates. N is computed by:

N = (product of the cardinalities of all relations T of the join so far) * (product of the selectivity factors of all applicable predicates).

Let C-inner(path2) be the cost of scanning the inner relation, applying all applicable predicates. Note that in the merge scan join this means scanning the contiguous group of the inner relation which corresponds to one join column value in the outer relation. Then the cost of a nested loop join is

C-nested-loop-join(path1,path2)=
C-outer(path1) + N * C-inner(path2)

The cost of a merge scan join can be broken up into the cost of actually doing the merge plus the cost of sorting the outer or inner relations, if required. The cost of doing the merge is

C-merge(path1,path2)=
C-outer(path1) + N * C-inner(path2)

For the case where the inner relation is sorted into a temporary relation none of the single relation access path formulas in section 4 apply. In this case the inner scan is like a segment scan except that the merging scans method makes use of the fact that the inner relation is sorted so that it is not necessary to scan the entire inner relation looking for a match. For this case we use the following formula for the cost of the inner scan.

C-inner(sorted list) =
TEMPPAGES/N + W*RSICARD

where TEMPPAGES is the number of pages

required to hold the inner relation. This formula assumes that during the merge each page of the inner relation is fetched once.

It is interesting to observe that the cost formula for nested loop joins and the cost formula for merging scans are essentially the same. The reason that merging scans is sometimes better than nested loops is that the cost of the inner scan may be much less. After sorting, the inner relation is clustered on the join column which tends to minimize the number of pages fetched, and it is not necessary to scan the entire inner relation (looking for a match) for each tuple of the outer relation.

The cost of sorting a relation, C-sort(path), includes the cost of retrieving the data using the specified access path, sorting the data, which may involve several passes, and putting the results into a temporary list. Note that prior to sorting the inner table, only the local predicates can be applied. Also, if it is necessary to sort a composite result, the entire composite relation must be stored in a temporary relation before it can be sorted. The cost of inserting the composite tuples into a temporary relation before sorting is included in C-sort(path).

Example of tree

We now show how the search is done for the example join shown in Fig. 1. First we find all of the reasonable access paths for single relations with only their local predicates applied. The results for this example are shown in Fig. 2. There are three access paths for the EMP table: an index on DNO, an index on JOB, and a segment scan. The interesting orders are DNO and JOB. The index on DNO provides the tuples in DNO order and the index on JOB provides the tuples in JOB order. The segment scan access path is, for our purposes, unordered. For this example we assume that the index on JOB is the cheapest path, so the segment scan path is pruned. For the DEPT relation there are two access paths, an index on DNO and a segment scan. We assume that the index on DNO is cheaper so the segment scan path is pruned. For the JOB relation there are two access paths, an index on JOB and a segment scan. We assume that the segment scan path is cheaper, so both paths are saved. The results just described are saved in the search tree as shown in Fig. 3. In the figures, the notation C(EMP.DNO) or C(E.DNO) means the cost of scanning EMP via the DNO index, applying all predicates which are applicable given that tuples from the specified set of relations have already been fetched. The notation Ni is used to represent the cardinalities of the different partial results.

Next, solutions for pairs of relations are found by joining a second relation to

EMP

NAME	DNO	JOB	SAL
SMITH	50	12	8500
JONES	50	5	15000
DOE	51	5	9500

DEPT

DNO	DNAME	LOC
50	MFG	DENVER
51	BILLING	BOULDER
52	SHIPPING	DENVER

JOB

JOB	TITLE
5	CLERK
6	TYPIST
9	SALES
12	MECHANIC

```
SELECT  NAME, TITLE, SAL, DNAME
FROM    EMP, DEPT, JOB
WHERE   TITLE='CLERK'
AND     LOC='DENVER'
AND     EMP.DNO=DEPT.DNO
AND     EMP.JOB=JOB.JOB
```

"Retrieve the name, salary, job title, and department name of employees who are clerks and work for departments in Denver."

Figure 1. JOIN example

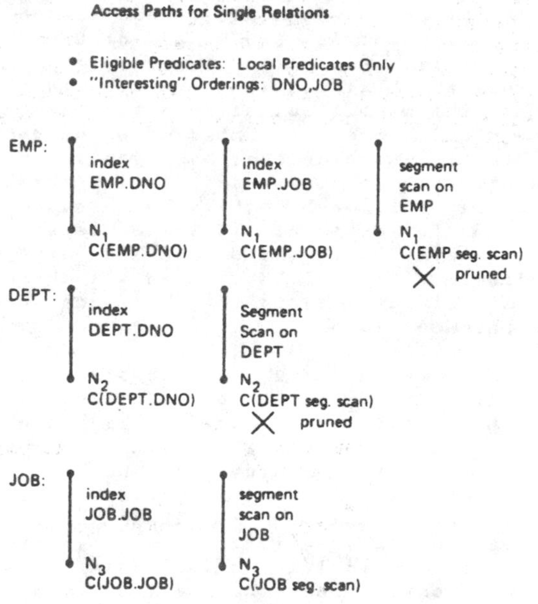

Figure 2.

the results for single relations shown in Fig. 3. For each single relation, we find access paths for joining in each second relation for which there exists a predicate connecting it to the first relation. First we consider access path selection for nested loop joins. In this example we assume that the EMP-JOB join is cheapest by accessing JOB on the JOB index. This is likely since it can fetch directly the tuples with matching JOB (without having to scan the entire relation). In practice the cost of joining is estimated using the formulas given earlier and the cheapest path is chosen. For joining the EMP relation to the DEPT relation we assume that the DNO index is cheapest. The best access path for each second-level relation is combined with each of the plans in Fig. 3 to form the nested loop solutions shown in Fig. 4.

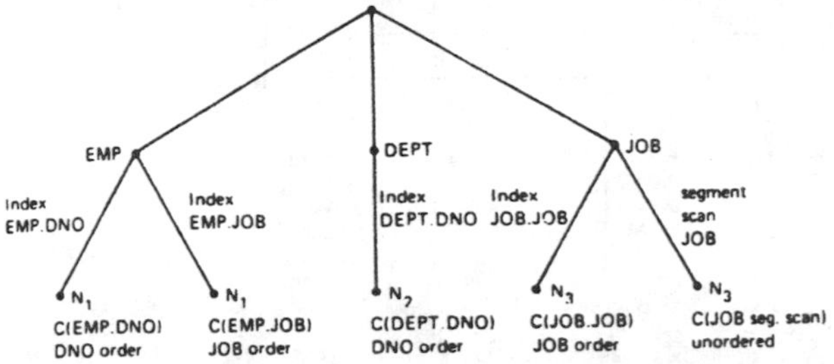

Figure 3. Search tree for single relations

Next we generate solutions using the merging scans method. As we see on the left side of Fig. 3, there is a scan on the EMP relation in DNO order, so it is possible to use this scan and the DNO scan on the DEPT relation to do a merging scans join, without any sorting. Although it is possible to do the merging join without sorting as just described, it might be cheaper to use the JOB index on EMP, sort on DNO, and then merge. Note that we never consider sorting the DEPT table because the cheapest scan on that table is already in DNO order.

For merging JOB with EMP, we only consider the JOB index on EMP since it is the cheapest access path for EMP regardless of order. Using the JOB index on JOB, we can merge without any sorting. However, it might be cheapter to sort JOB using a relation scan as input to the sort and then do the merge.

Referring to Fig. 3, we see that the access path chosen for the the DEPT relation is the DNO index. After accessing DEPT via this index, we can merge with EMP using the DNO index on EMP, again without any sorting. However, it might be cheaper to sort EMP first using the JOB index as input to the sort and then do the merge. Both of these cases are shown in Fig. 5.

As each of the costs shown in Figs. 4 and 5 are computed they are compared with the cheapest equivalent solution (same tables and same result order) found so far, and the cheapest solution is saved. After this pruning, solutions for all three relations are found. For each pair of relations, we find access paths for joining in the remaining third relation. As before we will extend the tree using nested loop joins and merging scans to join the third relation. The search tree for three relations is shown in Fig. 6. Note that in one case both the composite relation and the table being added (JOB) are sorted. Note also that for some of the cases no sorts are performed at all. In these cases, the composite result is materialized one tuple at a time and the intermediate composite relation is never stored. As before, as each of the costs are computed they are compared with the cheapest solution found so far and the cheapest solution is saved. After all of the solutions have been evaluated we are left with the best solution.

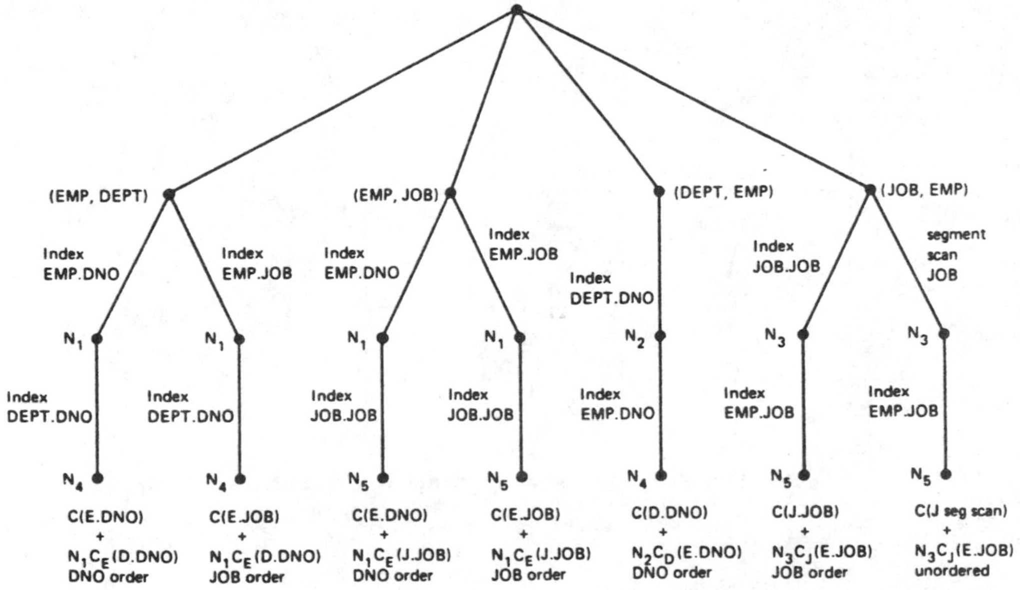

Figure 4. Extended search tree for second relation (nested loop join)

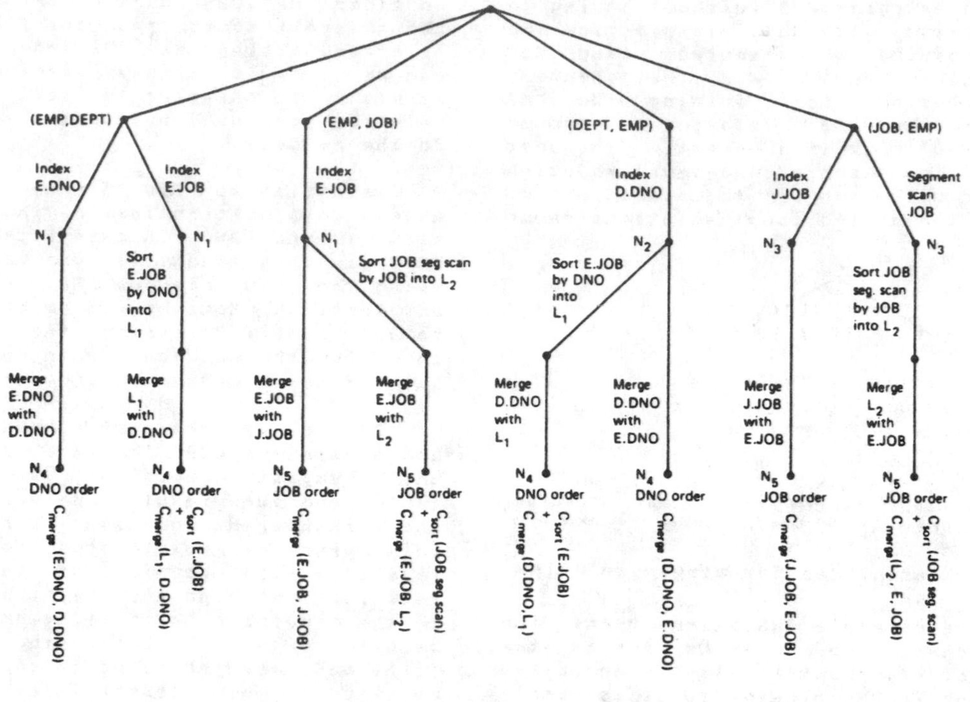

Figure 5. Extended search tree for second relation (merge join)

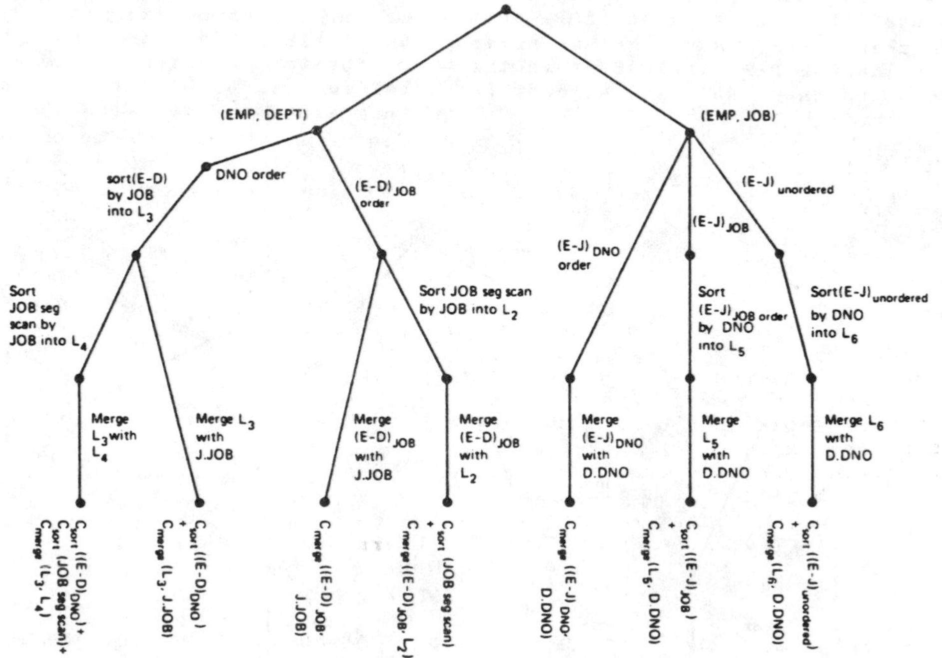

Figure 6. Extended search tree for third relation

6. Nested Queries

A query may appear as an operand of a predicate of the form "expression operator query". Such a query is called a Nested Query or a Subquery. If the operator is one of the six scalar comparisons (=, ¬=, >, >=, <, <=), then the subquery must return a single value. The following example using the "=" operator was given in section 2:

```
SELECT NAME
FROM EMPLOYEE
WHERE SALARY =
    (SELECT AVG(SALARY)
     FROM EMPLOYEE)
```

If the operator is IN or NOT IN then the subquery may return a set of values. For example:

```
SELECT NAME
FROM EMPLOYEE
WHERE DEPARTMENT_NUMBER IN
    (SELECT DEPARTMENT_NUMBER
     FROM DEPARTMENT
     WHERE LOCATION='DENVER')
```

In both examples, the subquery needs to be evaluated only once. The OPTIMIZER will arrange for the subquery to be evaluated before the top level query is evaluated. If a single value is returned, it is incorporated into the top level query as though it had been part of the original query statement; for example, if AVG(SAL) above evaluates to 15000 at execution time, then the predicate becomes "SALARY = 15000". If the subquery can return a set of values, they are returned in a temporary list, an internal form which is more efficient than a relation but which can only be accessed sequentially. In the example above, if the subquery returns the list (17,24) then the predicate is evaluated in a manner similar to the way in which it would have been evaluated if the original predicate had been DEPARTMENT_NUMBER IN (17,24).

A subquery may also contain a predicate with a subquery, down to a (theoretically) arbitrary level of nesting. When such subqueries do not reference columns from tables in higher level query blocks, they are all evaluated before the top level query is evaluated. In this case, the most deeply nested subqueries are evaluated first, since any subquery must be evaluated before its parent query can be evaluated.

A subquery may contain a reference to a value obtained from a candidate tuple of a higher level query block (see example below). Such a query is called a correlation subquery. A correlation subquery must in principle be re-evaluated for each candidate tuple from the referenced query block. This re-evaluation must be done before the correlation subquery's parent predicate in the higher level block can be tested for acceptance or rejection of the candidate tuple. As an example, consider the query:

```
SELECT NAME
FROM EMPLOYEE X
WHERE SALARY > (SELECT SALARY
                FROM EMPLOYEE
                WHERE EMPLOYEE_NUMBER=
                      X.MANAGER)
```

This selects names of EMPLOYEE's that earn more than their MANAGER. Here X identifies the query block and relation which furnishes the candidate tuple for the correlation. For each candidate tuple of the top level query block, the MANAGER value is used for evaluation of the subquery. The subquery result is then returned to the "SALARY >" predicate for testing acceptance of the candidate tuple.

If a correlation subquery is not directly below the query block it references but is separated from that block by one or more intermediate blocks, then the correlation subquery evaluation will be done before evaluation of the highest of the intermediate blocks. For example:

```
level 1   SELECT NAME
          FROM EMPLOYEE X
          WHERE SALARY >
level 2       (SELECT SALARY
               FROM EMPLOYEE
               WHERE EMPLOYEE_NUMBER =
level 3           (SELECT MANAGER
                   FROM EMPLOYEE
                   WHERE EMPLOYEE_NUMBER =
                         X.MANAGER))
```

This selects names of EMPLOYEE's that earn more than their MANAGER's MANAGER. As before, for each candidate tuple of the level-1 query block, the EMPLOYEE.MANAGER value is used for evaluation of the level-3 query block. In this case, because the level 3 subquery references a level 1 value but does not reference level 2 values, it is evaluated once for every new level 1 candidate tuple, but not for every level 2 candidate tuple.

If the value referenced by a correlation subquery (X.MANAGER above) is not unique in the set of candidate tuples (e.g., many employees have the same manager), the procedure given above will still cause the subquery to be re-evaluated for each occurrence of a replicated value. However, if the referenced relation is ordered on the referenced column, the re-evaluation can be made conditional, depending on a test of whether or not the current referenced value is the same as the one in the previous candidate tuple. If they are the same, the previous evaluation result can be used again. In some cases, it might even pay to sort the referenced relation on the referenced column in order to avoid re-evaluating subqueries unnecessarily. In order to determine whether or not the referenced column values are unique, the OPTIMIZER can use clues like NCARD > ICARD, where NCARD is the relation cardinality and ICARD is the index cardinality of an index on the referenced column.

7. Conclusion

The System R access path selection has been described for single table queries, joins, and nested queries. Evaluation work on comparing the choices made to the "right" choice is in progress, and will be described in a forthcoming paper. Preliminary results indicate that, although the costs predicted by the optimizer are often not accurate in absolute value, the true optimal path is selected in a large majority of cases. In many cases, the ordering among the estimated costs for all paths considered is precisely the same as that among the actual measured costs.

Furthermore, the cost of path selection is not overwhelming. For a two-way join, the cost of optimization is approximately equivalent to between 5 and 20 database retrievals. This number becomes even more insignificant when such a path selector is placed in an environment such as System R, where application programs are compiled once and run many times. The cost of optimization is amortized over many runs.

The key contributions of this path selector over other work in this area are the expanded use of statistics (index cardinality, for example), the inclusion of CPU utilization into the cost formulas, and the method of determining join order. Many queries are CPU-bound, particularly merge joins for which temporary relations are created and sorts performed. The concept of "selectivity factor" permits the optimizer to take advantage of as many of the query's restriction predicates as possible in the RSS search arguments and access paths. By remembering "interesting ordering" equivalence classes for joins and ORDER or GROUP specifications, the optimizer does more bookkeeping than most path selectors, but this additional work in many cases results in avoiding the storage and sorting of intermediate query results. Tree pruning and tree searching techniques allow this additional bookkeeping to be performed efficiently.

More work on validation of the optimizer cost formulas needs to be done, but we can conclude from this preliminary work that database management systems can support non-procedural query languages with performance comparable to those supporting the current more procedural languages.

Cited and General References

<1> Astrahan, M. M. et al. System R: Relational Approach to Database Management. ACM Transactions on Database Systems, Vol. 1, No. 2, June 1976, pp. 97-137.

<2> Astrahan, M. M. et al. System R: A Relational Database Management System. To appear in Computer.

<3> Bayer, R. and McCreight, E. Organization and Maintenance of Large Ordered Indices. Acta Informatica, Vol. 1, 1972.

<4> Blasgen, M.W. and Eswaran, K.P. On the Evaluation of Queries in a Relational Data Base System. IBM Research Report RJ1745, April, 1976.

<5> Chamberlin, D.D., et al. SEQUEL2: A Unified Approach to Data Definition, Manipulation, and Control. IBM Journal of Research and Development, Vol. 20, No. 6, Nov. 1976, pp. 560-575.

<6> Chamberlin, D.D., Gray, J.N., and Traiger, I.L. Views, Authorization and Locking in a Relational Data Base System. ACM National Computer Conference Proceedings, 1975, pp. 425-430.

<7> Codd, E.F. A Relational Model of Data for Large Shared Data Banks. ACM Communications, Vol. 13, No. 6, June, 1970, pp. 377-387.

<8> Date, C.J. An Introduction to Data Base Systems, Addison-Wesley, 1975.

<9> Lorie, R.A. and Wade, B.W. The Compilation of a Very High Level Data Language. IBM Research Report RJ2008, May, 1977.

<10> Lorie, R.A. and Nilsson, J.F. An Access Specification Language for a Relational Data Base System. IBM Research Report RJ2218, April, 1978.

<11> Stonebraker, M.R., Wong, E., Kreps, P., and Held, G.D. The Design and Implementation of INGRES. ACM Trans. on Database Systems, Vol. 1, No. 3, September, 1976, pp. 189-222.

<12> Todd, S. PRTV: An Efficient Implementation for Large Relational Data Bases. Proc. International Conf. on Very Large Data Bases, Framingham, Mass., September, 1975.

<13> Wong, E., and Youssefi, K. Decomposition - A Strategy for Query Processing. ACM Transactions on Database Systems, Vol. 1, No. 3 (Sept. 1976) pp. 223-241.

<14> Zloof, M.M. Query by Example. Proc. AFIPS 1975 NCC, Vol. 44, AFIPS Press, Montvale, N.J., pp. 431-437.

Management Applications
H. Morgan Editor

The Notions of Consistency and Predicate Locks in a Database System

K.P. Eswaran, J.N. Gray, R.A. Lorie, and I.L. Traiger
IBM Research Laboratory
San Jose, California

In database systems, users access shared data under the assumption that the data satisfies certain consistency constraints. This paper defines the concepts of transaction, consistency and schedule and shows that consistency requires that a transaction cannot request new locks after releasing a lock. Then it is argued that a transaction needs to lock a logical rather than a physical subset of the database. These subsets may be specified by predicates. An implementation of predicate locks which satisfies the consistency condition is suggested.

Key Words and Phrases: consistency, lock, database, concurrency, transaction

CR Categories: 4.32, 4.33

1. Introduction

In database systems, users access shared data under the assumption that the data satisfies certain consistency assertions. For simplicity consider a system with a fixed set of named resources called *entities*. Each entity has a name and a value. Examples of such assertions are

"*A*" is equal to "*B*",
"*C*" is the count of the free cells in "*D*",
"*E*" is an index for "*F*".

Most such assertions are never explicitly stated in designing or using a system, and yet all programs and users depend on the correctness of these assertions whenever they deal with the system state.

The assertions above are quite simple; however, in practice, assertions become extremely complex. A complete set of assertions about a system would no doubt be as large as the system itself. In practice, there is little reason for explicitly enumerating all such assertions, but for the purposes of this discussion we presume that a set of assertions, hereafter called *consistency constraints*, is explicitly defined and we say that the *state is consistent* if the contents of the entities of the state satisfy all the consistency constraints.

The system state is not static. It is continually undergoing changes due to *actions* performed by processes on the entities. Read and write are examples of such actions. We assume that actions are atomic; that is, if two processes concurrently perform actions, the effect will be as though one of the actions were performed before the other.

One might think that consistency constraints could be enforced at each action but this is not true. One may need to temporarily violate the consistency of the system state while modifying it. For example, in moving money from one bank account to another there will be an instant during which one account has been debited and the other not yet credited. This violates a constraint that the number of dollars in the system is constant. For this reason, the actions of a process are grouped into sequences called *transactions* which are units of consistency. In general, consistency assertions cannot be enforced before the end of a transaction. In this paper it is assumed that each transaction, when executed alone, transforms a consistent state into a new consistent state; that is, transactions preserve consistency.

Having grouped actions into transactions, we are interested in the problem of running transactions with maximal concurrency by interleaving actions from several transactions while continuing to give each transaction a consistent view of the system state. In such an environment, each transaction must employ a locking protocol to insure that it and others do not access data which is temporarily inconsistent. This lock protocol results in an additional set of actions called lock and unlock. A particular sequencing of the actions of a set of transactions is called a *schedule*. A schedule which gives each transaction a consistent view of the state is called a *consistent schedule*.

Not all consistent schedules for a set of transactions give exactly the same state (i.e. consistency is a weaker property than determinacy). For example, in an airlines reservation system if a set of transactions each requests a seat on a particular flight, then each consistent schedule will have the property that no seat is sold twice and no request is denied if there is a free seat, but two distinct consistent schedules may differ in the details of the seat assignment.

In the next section, we consider the problems of

Authors' address: IBM Corp., Monterey and Cottle Roads, San Jose, CA 95193.

locking and consistency in more detail. The discussion is applicable to database systems and to more conventional environments such as operating systems. The principal result is that consistency requires that a transaction must be constructed to have a growing and a shrinking phase. During the growing phase it can request new locks. However, once a lock has been released, the transaction cannot request a new one.

After this general discussion, a second section considers the peculiarities of locking in a database system. A phenomenon called *phantoms* seems to imply that one must lock logical subsets of the database rather than locking individual records present in the database. An implementation of logical locks satisfying the requirements of consistency is then proposed. For definiteness, this section is couched in terms of a relational model of data.

2. General Properties of Locking

To see the problems associated with running transactions concurrently consider the two transactions $\mathbf{T}_1$ and $\mathbf{T}_2$ of Figure 1 (below):

T_1:	T_2:
$A + 100 \rightarrow A$	$A * 2 \rightarrow A$
$B + 100 \rightarrow B$	$B * 2 \rightarrow B$

Suppose that the only assertion about the system state is that $A = B$. Although when considered alone both $\mathbf{T}_1$ and $\mathbf{T}_2$ conserve consistency, they have the following properties:

temporary inconsistency—after the first step of $\mathbf{T}_1$ or $\mathbf{T}_2$, $A \neq B$ and so the state is inconsistent. (1a)

conflict—if transaction $\mathbf{T}_2$ is scheduled to run between the first and second steps of $\mathbf{T}_1$, then the end result is $A \neq B$, which is an inconsistent state. (1b)

The problem of temporary inconsistency is inherent. Conflict on the other hand is not inherent and is undesirable.

If transactions are run one after another with no concurrency then conflict never arises. Each transaction starts in a consistent state and, since transactions preserve consistency, each transaction ends in a consistent state. Any inconsistencies seen by an in-progress transaction are due to changes it has made to the state. If transactions were instantaneous, there would be no penalty for a serial schedule for transactions. However, transactions are not instantaneous and substantial performance gains may be obtained by running several transactions in parallel.

In most cases, a particular transaction depends only on a small part of the system state. Therefore one technique for avoiding conflict is to partition entities into disjoint classes. One can then schedule transactions concurrently only if they use distinct classes of entities. Transactions using common parts of the state must still be scheduled serially. If such a policy is adopted, then each transaction will see a consistent version of the state. Unfortunately, it is usually impossible to examine a transaction and decide exactly which subset of the state it will use. For this reason the "partition" scheme described above is abandoned in favor of a more flexible scheme where individual entities are locked dynamically. In this system, transactions lock entities for several reasons. In terms of the above discussion, they want to prevent conflict with other transactions (i.e. lock out changes made by other transactions) and they may want to temporarily suspend consistency assertions on the locked entities. Still another motive for locking is reproducibility of reads. Unless a transaction locks an entity, successive reads of the entity may yield distinct values reflecting updates by concurrent transactions. This has little to do with consistency constraints; rather it rests on the notion that entities hold their values until updated.

Recovery and transaction backup provide an additional motive for locking. Database systems usually maintain a log of all changes made by each transaction. This log forms an audit trail. It may also be used for backup. Backup arises not only from deadlock-preemption but also from protection violations, hardware errors, and human errors. One backup procedure for a transaction $\mathbf{T}$ is to undo all of its updates as recorded in the log. Then all entities locked by $\mathbf{T}$ may be unlocked and $\mathbf{T}$ may be reset to its initial state. As Davies and Bjork [1, 2] point out, this procedure may not work correctly after $\mathbf{T}$ has unlocked (committed) any entities which it has modified. This implies that (update) locks should be held to the end of a transaction.

For simplicity, this section ignores the distinction between shared and exclusive access to an entity. It assumes that each action (other than lock and unlock) modifies the entity. The generalization of this section to the case of shared access is straightforward and is mentioned parenthetically as the section develops.

If transaction $\mathbf{T}_1$ attempts to lock entity e_1 which is already locked by transaction $\mathbf{T}_2$ then either $\mathbf{T}_1$ must wait for $\mathbf{T}_2$ to unlock e_1 or $\mathbf{T}_1$ must preempt e_1 from $\mathbf{T}_2$. If $\mathbf{T}_1$ waits and then $\mathbf{T}_2$ attempts to lock an entity e_2 locked by $\mathbf{T}_1$ then $\mathbf{T}_2$ must wait or preempt. If both $\mathbf{T}_1$ and $\mathbf{T}_2$ wait, then deadlock arises. The question of when to wait and when to preempt is not the subject of this paper. The paper by Chamberlin, Boyce, and Traiger [3] presents a scheme for deciding which transaction to preempt. When a resource is preempted, the preempted transaction must be backed up.

To insure that each transaction sees a consistent state, a transaction must not request a new lock after releasing some lock. To state and prove this result we must proceed more formally. However, for the sake of simplicity, we assume in the sequel that *all* transactions have the property that they do not relock an entity at step i which is already locked at step i, that they do not unlock an entity at step i which is not locked through step i, and that they end with no locks set.

A *transaction* is a sequence[1]: $\mathbf{T} = ((T, a_i, e_i))_{i=1}^{n}$ of n steps where T is the transaction name, a_i is the *action* at step i and e_i is the entity acted upon at step i.

A transaction has *locked entity e through step i* if

for some $j \leq i$, a_j = lock and $e_j = e$, and (2a)
there is no $k, j < k < i$, such that
a_k = unlockand $e_k = e$. (2b)

A transaction **T** is *well-formed* if

for each step $i = 1, \ldots, n$, (3a)
if a_i = lock then e_i is not locked by **T** through step $i - 1$,
if $a_i \neq$ lock then e_i is locked by **T** through step i,

and

at step n, only e_n is still locked by **T** and a_n = unlock. (3b)

Figure 2 shows two well-formed versions of transaction $\mathbf{T}_1$ from Figure 1.

Any sequence obtained by collating the actions of transactions $\mathbf{T}_1, \ldots, \mathbf{T}_n$ is called a *schedule* for $\mathbf{T}_1, \ldots, \mathbf{T}_n$. If the schedule takes actions from one transaction at a time it is called a *serial* schedule. More formally, a *schedule* for a set of transactions $\mathbf{T}_1, \ldots, \mathbf{T}_n$ is any sequence $\mathbf{S} = ((T_i, a_i, e_i))_{i=1}^{m}$ such that

for each $j = 1, \ldots, n$, (4a)
$\mathbf{T}_j = ((T_i, a_i, e_i) \in \mathbf{S} \mid T_i = T_j)_{i=1}^{m}$

and

The length of **S**, m, is the sum of the lengths of the transactions $T_1, \ldots, T_n$ (i.e. **S** contains only elements of $T_1, \ldots, T_n$). (4b)

Note that m is the number of steps in *all* transactions.

A schedule **S** is *serial* if for some permutation π, $\mathbf{S} = \mathbf{T}_{\pi(1)}\mathbf{T}_{\pi(2)} \ldots \mathbf{T}_{\pi(n)}$ (i.e. **S** is the concatenation of the transactions). Figure 3 gives three examples of schedules for a set of three transactions.

Nonserial schedules run the risk of giving a transaction an inconsistent view of the state. So we are particularly interested in those schedules which are "equivalent" to serial schedules. The equivalence between schedules hinges on the dependency relation of a schedule.

The *dependency* relation induced by schedule **S**, $DEP(\mathbf{S})$, is a ternary relation on $T \times E \times T$ (where T is the set of all transaction names in **S** and E is the set of all entities) defined by $(T_1, e, T_2) \in DEP(\mathbf{S})$ iff for some $i < j$

$\mathbf{S} = (\ldots, (T_1, a_i, e), \ldots, (T_2, a_j, e), \ldots)$, and (5a)
there is no k such that $i < k < j$ and $e_k = e$. (5b)

[1] The sequence $\mathbf{S} = s_1, \ldots, s_n$ is denoted $(s_i)_{i=1}^{n}$. The subsequence of elements satisfying condition C is denoted $(s_i \in \mathbf{S} \mid C(s_i))_{i=1}^{n}$ by analogy with the notation for sets. The ith element of **S** is denoted by $\mathbf{S}(i)$.

Informally, if (T_1, e, T_2) is in $DEP(\mathbf{S})$ then entity e is an output of $\mathbf{T}_1$ and an input of $\mathbf{T}_2$ and $\mathbf{T}_1$ gives e to $\mathbf{T}_2$. Again, we are assuming that each action on an entity modifies the entity. If one distinguishes "read-share" actions, then the dependency relation must be modified so that entities which are only read by a transaction are not recorded as outputs of the transaction (i.e. adjoin the clause "and a_i or a_j is an update action" to (5a) and adjoin the clause "and a_k is an update action" to (5b)).

Two schedules, $\mathbf{S}_1$ and $\mathbf{S}_2$ are *equivalent* if $DEP(\mathbf{S}_1) = DEP(\mathbf{S}_2)$ and a schedule $\mathbf{S}_1$ is *consistent* if it has an equivalent serial schedule. Figure 4 illustrates these definitions. It shows three schedules, where $\mathbf{S}_1$ is consistent, $\mathbf{S}_2$ is not consistent and $\mathbf{S}_3$ is serial (therefore consistent). Since a serial schedule starts with a consistent state and since each transaction (when run alone) transforms a consistent state into a new consistent state, a serial schedule gives each transaction a consistent set of inputs. If a set of transactions is consistently scheduled, then each transaction sees the same state it would see in the corresponding serial schedule (i.e. a consistent state). These observations justify the dual use of the term consistency to describe states and schedules.

It is very easy to explain the effect of a serial schedule. The user thinks of a complete transaction as being an "atomic" transformation of the state just as the scheduler thinks each action is an atomic transformation of the state. He sees all the changes made by transactions "before" his transaction starts and none of the changes of transactions "after" his transaction completes (i.e. he sees a consistent state). This observation yields the following important properties of serial schedules:

If $\mathbf{T}_1$ and $\mathbf{T}_2$ are any two transactions and e_1 and e_2 are any entities, then $(T_1, e_1, T_2) \in DEP(\mathbf{S})$ implies $(T_2, e_2, T_1) \notin DEP(\mathbf{S})$. (6a)

More generally,

The binary relation $<$ on the set of transactions is defined by: $T_1 < T_2$ if and only if $(T_1, e, T_2) \in DEP(\mathbf{S})$ for some entity e. Then $<$ is an acyclic relation which may be extended to a total order of the transactions. (6b)

Any consistent schedule also has these properties because it has the same dependency set as some serial schedule. Conversely, it will later be shown that any schedule with property (6b) is consistent.

We would like to further characterize those nonserial schedules which are consistent. To do this it is necessary to consider the lock and unlock actions of each step. Entity e is said to be *locked by transaction* **T** *through step k of schedule* **S** if

there is a $j \leq k$ such that $\mathbf{S}(j) = (T, \text{lock}, e)$ and (7a)
there is no j', $j < j' < k$ such that $\mathbf{S}(j') = (T, \text{unlock}, e)$. (7b)

Fig. 2. Two well-formed versions of transaction T_1 of Fig. 1.

T_{11}:

T_{11}	LOCK		A
T_{11}	A + 100	→	A
T_{11}	UNLOCK		A
T_{11}	LOCK		B
T_{11}	B + 100	→	B
T_{11}	UNLOCK		B

T_{12}:

T_{12}	LOCK		A
T_{12}	A + 100	→	A
T_{12}	LOCK		B
T_{12}	UNLOCK		A
T_{12}	B + 100	→	B
T_{12}	UNLOCK		B

Fig. 3. Schedules for three transactions T_1, T_2, T_3. S_2 is a serial schedule. Each small rectangle represents a transaction step.

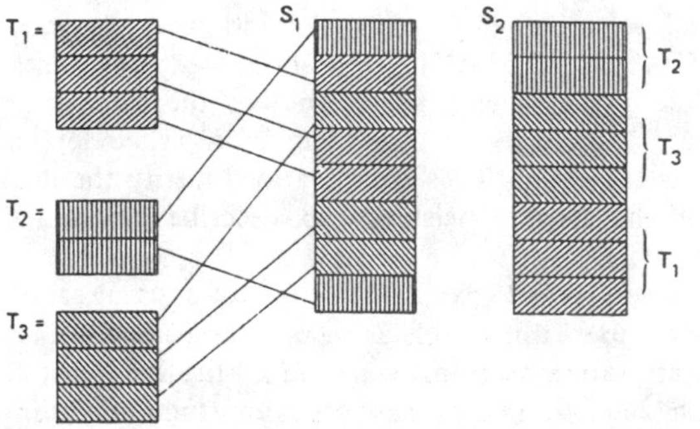

Fig. 4. Three schedules for T_1, T_2 of Fig. 1. S_1 is equivalent to serial schedule S_3 and hence is consistent. S_2 is inconsistent.

S_1:

T_1	A + 100	→	A	$DEP(S_1) = \{(T_1, A, T_2), (T_1, B, T_2)\}$
T_2	A * 2	→	A	
T_1	B + 100	→	B	
T_2	B * 2	→	B	

S_2:

T_1	A + 100	→	A	$DEP(S_2) = \{(T_1, A, T_2), (T_2, B, T_1)\}$
T_2	A * 2	→	A	
T_2	B * 2	→	B	
T_1	B + 100	→	B	$DEP(S_3) = DEP(S_1)$

S_3:

T_1	A + 100	→	A
T_1	B + 100	→	B
T_2	A * 2	→	A
T_2	B * 2	→	B

Schedule S is *legal* if for all k, if $S(k) = (T, a, e)$ and e is locked by T, through step k, then e is not locked by any other transaction through step k. Legal schedules observe the lock protocol that a transaction attempting to lock an already locked entity must wait. A schedule gives a history of how transactions were processed. As the processing is being done, we imagine a scheduler at each instant choosing a particular transaction step from the set of all next steps of all incomplete transactions. This scheduler allows lock actions on free entities but never chooses a lock action on an already locked entity. Such a scheduler only produces legal schedules, since it never chooses to run a lock step on an already locked entity.

The example schedule of Figure 5 shows that not every legal schedule is consistent. It is very important to know how transactions must be constructed so that any legal schedule is consistent.

Clearly, if legality is to insure consistency in all contexts, then it is necessary that each transaction lock each entity before otherwise acting on it and that the transaction ultimately unlock each such locked entity. More formally, using the definition of well-formed transactions (3a), (3b):

Consistency requires that transactions be well-formed. Unless all transactions are well-formed, it is possible to construct a legal but inconsistent schedule. (8a)

To prove this, consider any transaction $\mathbf{T}_1 = (T_1, a_i, e_i)_{i=1}^{n}$ which is not well-formed. Then for some step k, $\mathbf{T}_1$ does not have e_k locked through step k. Consider the (two-phase well-formed) transaction $\mathbf{T}_2 = ((T_2, \text{lock}, e_k), (T_2, \text{read}, e_k), (T_2, \text{write}, e_k), (T_2, \text{unlock}, e_k))$. The schedule $\mathbf{S} = (\mathbf{T}_1(i))_{i=1}^{k-1}\, \mathbf{T}_2(1), \mathbf{T}_2(2), \mathbf{T}_1(k), \mathbf{T}_2(3), \mathbf{T}_2(4), (\mathbf{T}_1(k))_{i=k+1}^{n}$ is legal. Since (T_1, e_k, T_2) and (T_2, e_k, T_1) are both in $DEP(\mathbf{S})$, S is not equivalent to any serial schedule (by property (6a)). So S is not a consistent schedule and (8a) is established. Intuitively, T_1 could change e_k after T_2 read it but before T_2 wrote it. This would not be possible in a serial (i.e. consistent schedule).

A less obvious fact is that consistency requires that a transaction be divided into a growing and a shrinking phase. During the growing phase the transaction is allowed to request locks. The beginning of the shrinking phase is signaled by the first unlock action. After the first unlock, a transaction cannot issue a lock action on any entity. More formally, transaction $\mathbf{T} = ((T, a_i, e_i))_{i=1}^{n}$ is *two-phase* if for some $j < n$,

$i < j$ implies $a_i \neq$ unlock,
$i = j$ implies $a_i =$ unlock,
$i > j$ implies $a_i \neq$ lock.

Steps $1, \ldots, j-1$ are called the *growing phase* and steps $j, \ldots, n$ are the *shrinking phase* of T.

Transaction $\mathbf{T}_{11}$ of Figure 2 is not two-phase since it locks B after releasing A. Transaction $\mathbf{T}_{12}$ of Figure 2 is well-formed and two-phase. To see that $\mathbf{T}_{11}$ may see an inconsistent state, consider the legal schedule S shown in Figure 5. In the schedule S, $\mathbf{T}_{12}$ sees A from $\mathbf{T}_{11}$ and $\mathbf{T}_{11}$ sees B from $\mathbf{T}_{12}$. So S is not equivalent to any serial schedule and hence S is inconsistent. This construction can be generalized to prove:

Consistency requires that transactions be two-phase. That is, unless all transactions are two-phase, it is possible to construct a legal but inconsistent schedule. (8b)

Conversely,

If each transaction in the set of transactions $T = \{\mathbf{T}_1, \ldots, \mathbf{T}_n\}$ is well-formed and two-phase then any legal schedule for T is consistent. (8c)

A sketch of the proof for this is fairly simple. Let S be any schedule for T. Define the binary relation '$<$' on T by $\mathbf{T}_i < \mathbf{T}_j$ iff $(T_i, e, T_j) \in DEP(\mathrm{S})$ for some entity e. One can prove a lemma that $<$ may be extended to a total order $\ll$ on T as follows.

First define the integer $SHRINK(\mathbf{T}_i)$ for each transaction $\mathbf{T}_i$ to be the least integer j such that $\mathbf{T}_i$ unlocks some entity at step j of S:

$$SHRINK(\mathbf{T}_i) = \min \{j \mid \mathrm{S}(j) = (T_i, \text{unlock}, e) \text{ for some entity } e\}.$$

If each transaction $\mathbf{T}_i$ is non-null then $SHRINK(\mathbf{T}_i)$ is well-defined because each $\mathbf{T}_i$ is well-formed.

We now argue that for any transactions $\mathbf{T}_1$ and $\mathbf{T}_2$ and entity e, if $(T_1, e, T_2) \in DEP(\mathrm{S})$ then $SHRINK(\mathbf{T}_1)$ is less than $SHRINK(\mathbf{T}_2)$. For if $(T_1, e, T_2) \in DEP(\mathrm{S})$ then by definition of $DEP(S)$ there are integers i and j such that $\mathrm{S} = (\ldots, (T_1, a_i, e), \ldots, (T_2, a_j, e), \ldots)$ and so that for any integer k between i and j, $e_k \neq e$ by Definition (5). Since S is legal, e must be locked only by $\mathbf{T}_1$ through step i of S and since $\mathbf{T}_2$ is well formed e must be locked only by $\mathbf{T}_2$ through step j of S. So a_i = unlock and a_j = lock. This immediately implies that $SHRINK(\mathbf{T}_1)$ is less than or equal to i. Since $\mathbf{T}_2$ is two-phase, no unlock by $\mathbf{T}_2$ precedes step j of S so $SHRINK(\mathbf{T}_2)$ is greater than j.

Thus we have shown that if $\mathbf{T}_1 < \mathbf{T}_2$ then $SHRINK(\mathbf{T}_1)$ is less than $SHRINK(\mathbf{T}_2)$. This implies property (6b) and hence $<$ can be extended to a total order $\ll$ on T.

Assume without loss of generality that $\mathbf{T}_1 \ll \mathbf{T}_2 \ll \ldots \ll \mathbf{T}_n$. Induce on n to show that S is equivalent to the serial schedule $\mathbf{T}_1, \ldots, \mathbf{T}_n$. If $n = 1$ the result is trivial. The induction step follows in two steps.

First show that S is equivalent to the schedule

$$\mathrm{S}' = \mathbf{T}_1((T_i, a_i, e_i) \in \mathrm{S} \mid T_i \neq T_1)_{i=1}^{m}.$$

Then note that by hypothesis

$$((T_i, a_i, e_i) \in \mathrm{S} \mid T_i \neq T_1)_{i=1}^{m} \text{ is equivalent to } \mathbf{T}_2, \ldots, \mathbf{T}_n.$$

So S′ is equivalent to $\mathbf{T}_1, \mathbf{T}_2, \ldots, \mathbf{T}_n$. But $\mathbf{T}_1, \ldots, \mathbf{T}_n$ is a serial schedule so S is equivalent to a serial schedule and is consistent. Figure 6 gives a graphic illustration of the construction of a serial schedule from S. To summarize then,

If the transactions $\mathbf{T}_1, \ldots, \mathbf{T}_n$ are each well-formed and two-phase then any legal schedule is consistent. (8d)

Unless transaction T is well-formed and two-phase there is a transaction T′, which is well-formed and two-phase, such that T and T′ have a legal but inconsistent schedule. (8e)

Fig. 5. A schedule for transactions $\mathbf{T}_{11}$ and $\mathbf{T}_{12}$ which is legal but not consistent because $\mathbf{T}_{11}$ is not two-phase.

T_{11}	LOCK	A	
T_{11}	UPDATE	A	
T_{11}	UNLOCK	A	
T_{12}	LOCK	A	T_{11} gives A to T_{12}
T_{12}	LOCK	B	
T_{12}	UPDATE	A	
T_{12}	UPDATE	B	
T_{12}	UNLOCK	B	
T_{12}	UNLOCK	A	T_{12} gives B to T_{11}
T_{11}	LOCK	B	
T_{11}	UPDATE	B	
T_{11}	UNLOCK	B	

$DEP(S) = \{(T_{11}, A, T_{12}), (T_{12}, B, T_{11})\}$

Clearly a transaction run alone is consistent. Further, any set of transactions which do not interact (i.e. $DEP(\mathrm{S}) = \emptyset$) can be consistently scheduled in any order without locking. Even if the transactions interact, the two-phase restriction may be too strong. If, for example, transaction $\mathbf{T}_{12}$ of Figure 2 had updated entity C rather than entity B, then any legal schedule for $\mathbf{T}_{11}$ and $\mathbf{T}_{12}$ would be consistent even though neither transaction is two-phase. However, if one added a transaction $\mathbf{T}_{13}$ which accesses entities A, B, and C, then the new transaction set would have legal but inconsistent schedules. It therefore seems difficult to give nontrivial necessary conditions for all legal schedules for a set of transactions to be consistent ((8d) is sufficient). We can make the following assertion: if one intends to run a transaction concurrently with an *unknown* set of other transactions then, to guarantee that all legal schedules be consistent, all transactions must be well-formed and two-phase.

3. Predicate Locks

Section 2 introduced the notions of consistency and locking; it explored the locking protocols required by consistency. The discussion was quite general and applies to any system which supports the concepts of transaction and shared entity. Next we consider locking in a database environment. Aside from the problem of scale (millions of entities rather than hundreds or thousands), there are substantial differences in the unit of locking. These differences stem from associative addressing of entities by transactions in a database environment. It is not uncommon for a transaction to want to lock the set of all entities with a certain value (i.e. "key" addressing). Updating a seemingly unrelated entity may add it to such a set, creating the problem of "phantom" records. This section explains this problem and proposes a solution.

For definiteness we adopt the relational model of data (Codd [4]). The database consists of a collection of relations, $R_1, R_2, \ldots, R_n$. Each relation can be thought of as a table or flat file. Each column of the relation is called a *domain* and each element of the relation (row) is called a *tuple* (record). Each tuple consists of a fixed number of *fields*. Each domain has a name. Figure 7 shows an example of such a database.

One approach would be to lock whole relations or domains whenever any member of the relation or domain is referenced. However, since there are many more tuples than relations or domains, this will not produce much concurrency. For example, two transactions making deposits in different accounts could not run concurrently if required to lock whole relations.

This suggests that locks should apply to as small a unit as possible so that transactions do not lock information they do not need. Therefore the natural unit of locking is the field or tuple of a relation. However, a tuple is not an entity in the sense of Section 2, since it has no name which is separate from its value. This may seem odd at first, but it stems from the fact that tuples are referenced by value rather than by the address of the storage they occupy.

To illustrate this point, consider the example of a transaction T_1, on the database of Figure 7. The transaction checks the assertion that the sum of Napa account balances is equal to the sum of Napa assets by:

Fig. 6. A graphic illustration of the construction of a serial schedule from a consistent schedule. The arrows show the dependencies of S. $T_1 \ll T_2 \ll T_3$ and so S' has the same dependencies as S. The induction hypothesis applies to S' to give T_1, T_2, T_3.

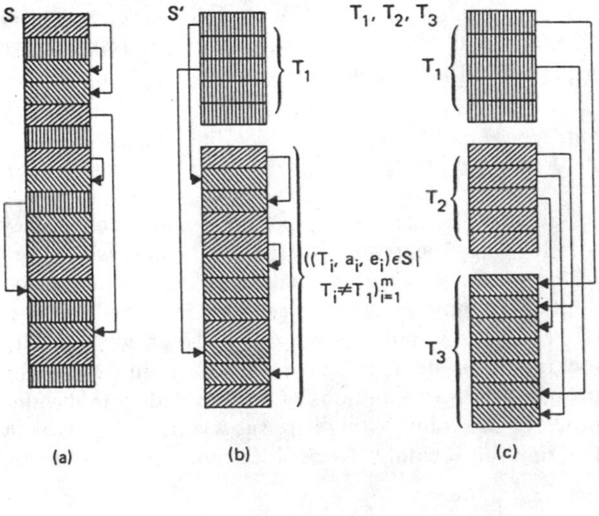

Associately addressing the *ACCOUNTS* relation, locking any accounts located in Napa. (9a)

Summing the balances in the locked accounts. (9b)

Locking the Napa tuple in *ASSETS* and comparing its value with the computed sum. (9c)

Releasing all locks. (9d)

If a second transaction T_2 inserts a new tuple in *ACCOUNTS* with Location = Napa and adds the deposit to the Napa assets and if T_2 is scheduled between steps (9b) and (9c) of T_1, then T_1 will see an inconsistent state: T_1 will see the balance of the new account reflected in the *ASSETS* but will not have seen the account in the *ACCOUNTS* relation. A similar problem arises if T_2 merely transferred an account from St. Helena to Napa.

A still more elementary example is the test for the existence of a tuple in a relation. If the tuple exists, it is to be locked to insure that no other transaction will delete it before the first transaction terminates. If the tuple does not exist, "it" should be locked to insure that no other transaction will create such a tuple before the first transaction terminates. In this case the "nonexistence" of the tuple is being locked. Such nonexistent tuples are called *phantoms*. Inspection of the earlier example shows that T_1 should lock not only all existing Napa accounts but also all phantom ones.

As argued in the previous section, consistency requires that a transaction lock all tuples examined, both real and phantom (i.e. it be well formed). The set of all possible Napa accounts is the Cartesian product: $\{\text{Napa}\} \times INTEGERS \times INTEGERS$. This set is infinite so there is little hope of locking each individual tuple of the set. Rather it seems natural to lock the set of tuples and phantoms satisfying the predicate: Location = Napa. More generally, if P is a predicate on tuples t of relation R then P defines the set S where $t \in S$ iff $P(t)$. Transactions will be allowed to lock any subset of a relation by specifying such a predicate. We only require that the truth or falsity of P depend only on t.

If such predicates are used as the unit of locking, then a list of locks becomes a (much smaller) list of sets identified by their predicates. Locking the entire relation is achieved by using the predicate *'TRUE'* while locking the tuple (NAPA, 32123, 1050) is achieved by the predicate $P(t) \triangleq t = (\text{NAPA}, 32123, 1050)$. However, one cannot directly apply the formulation of locking and consistency in the previous section, because entities were assumed to be uniquely named objects. In this section we extend the results on scheduling and consistency to apply to locks on possibly overlapping sets of tuples.

First of all, if predicates are arbitrarily complex there is little hope of deciding whether two distinct predicates define overlapping sets of tuples (and hence whether they conflict as locks). In fact the problem is

Fig. 7. The sample database.

ACCOUNTS

Location	Number	Balance
NAPA	32123	1050
ST HELENA	36592	506
NAPA	5320	287

ASSETS

Location	Total
NAPA	1337
ST HELENA	506

Assertions: 1) Account numbers are unique.

2) The sum of balances of accounts at a location is equal to the total assets at that location.

recursively unsolvable (Kleene [5]), so it is not clear how to make predicate locks "work." A method for scheduling predicate locks is introduced first by example and then more abstractly.

In the sample database of Figure 7 suppose that transaction T_1 is interested in all tuples in *ACCOUNTS* for which Location = Napa. A transaction T_2 starts during the processing of T_1. T_2 is interested in all tuples in *ACCOUNTS* with Location = Sonoma. When T_1 declares its intent to access Napa accounts by executing the action

T_1 *LOCK ACCOUNTS*: Location = Napa,

this predicate lock is associated with T_1 and with the *ACCOUNTS* relation. Later when T_2 declares its intent to access Sonoma accounts by executing the action

T_2 *LOCK ACCOUNTS*: Location = Sonoma,

this predicate lock is also associated with the *ACCOUNTS* relation. Before T_2 can be granted access to the Sonoma accounts, the lock controller must check that T_2's lock does not conflict with locks held by other transactions. In the case above, the controller must decide that the predicates Location = Napa and Location = Sonoma are mutually exclusive. In general, the controller must compare the requested predicate lock against the outstanding predicate locks of other transactions on this relation. If two such predicates are mutually satisfiable (i.e. have an existing or phantom tuple in common), then there is conflict and the request must wait or preempt; otherwise, the request can be granted immediately.

That is more or less how predicate locks work. It does not explain how sharing works and finesses the fact that predicate satisfiability is recursively unsolvable. In order to give a more complete explanation of how predicate locks "work," it is necessary to define how an action is allowed or prohibited by a lock and how two locks may conflict. First we need to decide on the lockable entities. In [8] a field was chosen as the basic unit of locking. This choice gives maximal concurrency but presents many notational complexities. For the sake of simplicity, the formal development of predicate locks here is done for tuple-level locking rather than field-level locking. After a formal development of tuple-level predicate locks the generalization to field-level predicate locks is informally discussed.

A particular *action* on a single tuple may be denoted by (R, t, a), meaning that tuple t of relation R is accessed in mode a. Two modes are distinguished here:

a = read allows sharing with other readers,

while

a = write requires an exclusive lock on tuple t (update, insert, delete are all examples of write access).

The action *reads* tuple t if a = read and it *writes* tuple t if a = write.

Reading the balance of account number 32123 would be an action

(*ACCOUNTS*, (Napa, 32123, 1050), read)

An update of the balance by $50 would involve two actions and *two* tuples, first

(*ACCOUNTS*, (Napa, 32123, 1050), write)

and also

(*ACCOUNTS*, (Napa, 32123, 1100), write)

because *both* tuples are written by the *atomic* update operation (one is "deleted" and the other "inserted"). Further, consistency requires that the Napa ASSETS tuple be updated by $50.

In the model of actions described above, the action specifies a tuple by providing the values of all fields of the tuple. Although this is formally correct, the examples above show that it is inappropriate for the context at hand. The first example wants to read the balance of account number 3123 and cares nothing about the location of the account. Yet the model requires that the action specify both the balance and location of the account as well as the account number. Similarly the second transaction wants to read the balance and location of account number 32123 and then add $50 to the balance of the account and to the assets of the account's location.

If one considers the problem of reading the Napa tuple of *ASSETS* without a priori knowing its current balance, the problem and its solution become quite clear. The concept of action must be generalized to the concept of *access*, which acts on all tuples satisfying a given predicate. This notion is consistent with the idea of associative addressing which returns the set of all tuples with designated values in given fields. To access account number 32123, one specifies the access:

(*ACCOUNTS*, Number = 32123, read)

which refers to either a single tuple or no tuples, since account numbers are unique. An access which updates the balance of account number 32123 would be denoted by

(*ACCOUNTS*, Number = 32123, write).

Consistency assertions require that such an access be followed by an access

(*ASSETS*, Location = 'Napa', write),

since we require that the assets be the sum of the balances at each location.

An access to find the numbers of all Napa accounts would return a set of tuples and would be denoted by

(*ACCOUNTS*, Location = 'Napa', read).

To proceed more formally we need the following definitions. If the relation R is drawn from the Cartesian product of sets $S_1, S_2, \ldots S_n$ ($R \subseteq \times_{i=1}^{n} S_i$), then any predicate P defined on all tuples $(s_1, \ldots, s_n) \in \times_{i=1}^{n} S_i$ is an *admissible predicate* for R. We ask that P be an effective test: given a tuple t, $P(t) = TRUE$ or $P(t) = FALSE$.

A particular *access* on relation R is denoted by (R, P, a) where P is an admissible predicate. Such an access is equivalent to the (possibly infinite) set of actions (R, t, a) where $P(t) = TRUE$, and where t ranges over the Cartesian product underlying R. In particular, it *reads* all such tuples if a = read and *writes* all such tuples if a = write. A *predicate lock* on relation R is denoted by (R, P, a) where P is an admissible predicate for R and a is an access mode.

An action (R, t, a) is said to *satisfy* predicate lock (R', P', a') if

$$R = R' \text{ and} \qquad (10a)$$
$$P'(t) = TRUE \text{ and} \qquad (10b)$$
$$a = a' \text{ or } a' = \text{write.} \qquad (10c)$$

In the second clause of (10c) we are assuming that write access implies read and write access.

The action *conflicts* with the predicate lock if

$$R = R' \text{ and} \qquad (11a)$$
$$P'(t) = TRUE \text{ and} \qquad (11b)$$
$$a = \text{write or } a' = \text{write.} \qquad (11c)$$

To give an example, the predicate lock

L = (*ACCOUNTS*, Location = Napa, read)

is satisfied by the action

(*ACCOUNTS*, (Napa, 3213, 1050), read)

and conflicts with the action

(*ACCOUNTS*, (Napa, 3213, 1050), write).

Satisfiability and conflict are defined analogously for accesses. Access $A = (R, P, a)$ *satisfies* predicate lock L if and only if for each tuple t in the Cartesian product underlying R, if $P(t)$ is true then action (R, t, a) satisfies L. Access A *conflicts* with L if for some tuple t in the Cartesian product underlying R, $P(t)$ is true and action (R, t, a) conflicts with L.

As an example, the access which moves account 23175 from Napa to Sonoma would be denoted

(*ACCOUNTS*, (Location = 'Napa' ∨ Location = 'Sonoma') ∧ Number = 23175, write).

This access would require that the transaction have a lock on the *ACCOUNTS* relation of the form (*ACCOUNTS*, P, write), where the predicate P must be satisfied by the tuples (Napa, 23175, *) and (Sonoma, 23175, *). That is, the lock predicate P must cover both the old and new values.

Note that we require an access to be covered by a single predicate lock. If one holds *two* locks, one for Napa and another for Sonoma, then the access would not satisfy either one and so would not be allowed. It is possible to relax this restriction so that an access is allowed if it satisfies the union of the locks held by a transaction.

Two predicate locks are said to *conflict* if there is some action which satisfies one of them and conflicts with the other; that is, if one lock allows an access which is prohibited by the other lock.

Given these definitions, the notions of the previous section generalize as follows. A transaction is a sequence of (transaction name, access) pairs. A transaction is well-formed if each access it makes satisfies some predicate lock it holds through that step. A transaction is two-phase if it does not request predicate locks after releasing a predicate lock.

A schedule for a set of transactions is any collating (merging) of the transaction sequences. The dependency relation is defined by choosing (tuple, relation) pairs as the entities (for all tuples in the Cartesian products underlying the relations). Let E be the set of all such entities. The notion of an access reading or writing such entities has already been introduced. If **S** is a schedule for the set of transactions T, then the dependency set of **S** is defined to be the set of triples

$$(T_1, e, T_2) \in T \times E \times T$$

such that for some integers $i < j$:

$\mathbf{S}(i) = (T_1, A_1)$ and A_1 reads or writes entity e, (12a)

$\mathbf{S}(j) = (T_2, A_2)$ and A_2 reads or writes entity e (12b) and not both A_1 and A_2 simply reads e,

for any k between i and j, if $\mathbf{S}(k) = (T_3, A_3)$ (12c) then A_3 does *not* write entity e.

The generalization of tuple-level predicate locks to field-level predicate locks can be done as follows (see [8] for a formal development of this notion): A particular field-level access to a relation reads, writes, or ignores each of the fields of the relation specified by the access predicate. A field-level predicate lock locks particular fields of the tuples covered by the predicate. Fields are either ignored by the lock or are locked in read or write mode. Two predicate locks conflict if their predicates are mutually satisfiable and one demands write access to a field locked in read or write mode by the other. A field-level access satisfies a predicate lock if it only accesses tuples covered by the predicate lock and it only reads fields locked in read mode

Fig. 8. An example of the *LOCK* table.

LOCK	
Transaction	Predicate Lock
T_1	(ACCOUNTS, Location=Napa, write)
T_2	(ACCOUNTS, Balance <500, read)

by the lock and only writes fields locked in write mode by the predicate lock. Similarly, an access conflicts with a predicate lock if the two predicates are mutually satisfiable and the access reads a field of a tuple locked by the lock in write mode or it writes a field locked by the predicate lock in read or write mode. Given these definitions of access, satisfiability, and conflict, the development of this section generalizes to field-level predicate locks.

To give concrete examples, the reading of an account balance is denoted by the access

(*ACCOUNT*, Number = 32123, {(Number, read), (Balance, write)})

which ignores the Location field, reads the Number field, and updates the Balance field. This access satisfies the predicate lock

(*ACCOUNT*, Number = 32123, {(Number, write), (Balance, write)})

and this predicate lock conflicts with the predicate lock

(*ACCOUNT*, Number = 32123, {(Number, read)}).

The access does not satisfy the latter predicate above.

We now return to the simpler model where locks apply to whole tuples. To implement arbitrary predicate locks, associate with the database a table called *LOCK* which is a binary relation between transactions and predicate locks (see Figure 8).

The legal lock scheduler functions as follows. Transactions are presumed to be two-phase and well-formed; the scheduler enforces this rule. Any growing transaction may request any predicate lock. When this happens, the scheduler tries to enter the transaction name and predicate lock into the *LOCK* table. If the predicate lock does not conflict with any other predicate lock in the table, it may be entered and granted immediately. If the predicate lock does conflict with one or more locks held by other transactions, then the requestor must wait for the other locks to be released or he must preempt the locks (or be preempted). As commented earlier, this is a scheduling decision and not the proper topic of this paper. Any transaction may release any predicate lock belonging to it. This deletes the lock from *LOCK* and marks the transaction as shrinking. If other transactions are waiting for tuples released by this lock then they may be started. Each time a transaction T^* makes an action or access A the LOCK table is examined to find the set

$$YES = \{(T, L) \in LOCK \mid A \text{ satisfies } L \text{ and } T = T^*\}$$

YES is a list of all the reasons T^* should be allowed to make the access. If *YES* is empty then T^* is not well-formed and it should be given an error.

It is clear that the scheduler described above checks the following properties:

All transactions are well-formed and two-phase. (13a)

If transaction T locks predicate P on relation R, then for any tuple t in the Cartesian product underlying R such that $P(t) = TRUE$, no other transaction may insert, delete or modify t until T releases the predicate lock. *That is, predicate locks solve the problem of phantoms.* (13b)

So the scheduler described produces legal schedules and by the results of the previous section, gives each transaction a consistent view of the state of the system.

Thus far we have ignored the details of how the scheduler decides whether or not two predicate locks conflict. In general this is a recursively unsolvable problem (even if predicates are restricted to using the arithmetic operators $+, *, -, \div$ as shown by Gödel (see Kleene [5])). The problem then is to find an interesting class of predicates for which it is easily decidable whether two predicates "overlap." We propose the following simple class of predicates.

A *simple* predicate is any Boolean combination of atomic predicates. *Atomic* predicates have the form

$$\langle\text{field name}\rangle \begin{Bmatrix} `<' \\ `=' \\ `\neq' \\ `>' \end{Bmatrix} \langle\text{constant}\rangle$$

where *constant* is a string or number and *field name* is the name of some field of the relation. For example,

((Location = 'Napa' ∨ Location = 'Santa Rosa') ∧ ((Balance < 200) ∧ (Balance > 10))

is a simple predicate with four atomic predicates.

Again, Presburger (see Kleene [5]) showed a procedure to decide if two predicates overlap for a class of predicates slightly more general than simple predicates (he allowed $+, -, <, =, \neq, >$, mod and allowed *any* Boolean combination of these operators and operands on integers). However, his decision procedure is much more complicated than the procedure for this simple set of predicates.

To decide whether two simple predicate locks L and L' conflict is a fairly straightforward matter. Suppose $L = (R, P, a)$ and $L' = (R', P', a')$ are two predicate locks. Then

If $R \neq R'$ there is no conflict as the locks apply to different relations. (14a)

If neither a = write nor a' = write then there is no conflict. (14b)

Otherwise, there will be no conflict only if there is no tuple t such that $P \wedge P'(t)$ is *TRUE*. (14c)

Similarly, deciding whether access $A = (R', P', a')$ conflicts with lock L above consists of testing (14a), (14b) and (14c) above for access A. A will satisfy L if it passes the tests

$R = R'$, and (15a)
$a' = a$ or a = write (15b)
For any tuple t, if $P'(t)$ is *TRUE* then $P(t)$ is (15c)
TRUE (i.e. $P' \Rightarrow P$ or equivalently $P' \wedge \sim P$
is not satisfiable).

Thus the conflict-satisfiability questions for both accesses and locks have been reduced to the question of deciding whether a particular simple predicate is satisfiable. But simple predicates are defined to have an easy decision procedure.

The procedure is to organize $P \wedge P'$ of case (c) into disjunctive normal form (Kleene [5]) and then for each disjunct see whether it is satisfiable or not. Each such disjunct will be a conjunct of atomic predicates and so this is trivial. Consider the example

P = (Location = 'Napa' $\vee$ Location = 'Santa Rosa')
$\wedge$ (Balance $<$ 500 $\wedge$ Balance $>$ 10)
P' = Location = 'Napa' $\wedge$ Balance = 700.

Then the disjunctive normal form of $P \wedge P'$ is

Location = ('Napa' $\wedge$ Balance $<$ 500 $\wedge$ Balance $>$ 10
$\wedge$ Balance = 700)
$\vee$ (Location = 'Santa Rosa' $\wedge$ Location = 'Napa'
$\wedge$ Balance $<$ 500 $\wedge$ Balance $>$ 10 $\wedge$ Balance = 700).

The first disjunct is not satisfied because Balance = 700 contradicts Balance $<$ 500, while the second has the added contradiction that Location = 'Napa' and Location = 'Santa Rosa'. So $P \wedge P'$ is not satisfiable and there is no conflict. To give an example of conflict, suppose

P = (Location = 'Napa') and P' = (Balance $>$ 500).

Then $P \wedge P'$ is satisfiable by the tuple (Napa, 0, 501) and so the predicates "overlap" and allow conflict.

In summary then, if only simple predicates are allowed in accesses and predicate locks, then predicate locks can be scheduled in the same way ordinary locks are scheduled.

As mentioned before, predicate locks solve the problem of phantom records. When coupled with the results on consistency, predicate locks can be used to construct consistent legal schedulers. The degenerate form of predicates, locking entire relations with the predicate which is always *TRUE* or locking a particular tuple by the predicate which is only *TRUE* for that tuple gives the more conventional forms of locking. If the desired set is not describable by a simple predicate then any "larger" simple predicate (i.e. a simple predicate which is implied by the desired predicate) will be a suitable predicate for the lock. If only simple predicates are used then predicate locks can be legally scheduled.

There are simple analogs to predicate locks in existing data-base systems. For example in hierarchial systems such as IMS (IBM [6]) it is common to lock a subtree of the hierarchy. This subtree is a logical set of records (i.e. those with a given parent). Similarly, in a network model it is desirable to lock all members of a "set" in the DBTG [7] sense although DBTG lacks such a facility.

Last, we observe that locking is a very dynamic form of authorization. All the techniques we have described (predicate locks, simple predicates, the *YES* set, . . .) apply to the problem of doing value dependent authorization of access to database records at the granularity of a field.

4. Summary

Section 2 introduced a very simple data model and discussed the notions of transaction, consistency and locking. It was argued that consistency requires that transactions be two-phase and well-formed, and conversely that if all transactions are well-formed and two-phase then any legal schedule is consistent.

Section 3 was couched in terms of the relational model of data. The problems that associative addressing introduces were described: namely phantom records entering and leaving the set of records locked by a transaction. Predicate locks are proposed as a solution to this problem. To schedule and enforce these locks, predicates are restricted to the class of simple predicates. It is possible to schedule simple predicate locks in the same way "ordinary" locks are scheduled.

Acknowledgments. The concept of consistency presented here grew out of discussions with Ray Boyce, Don Chamberlin, and Frank King. An earlier draft of the paper was polished by helpful comments from Rudolph Bayer, Paul McJones, Gianfranco Putzolu, and by the referees.

Received December 1974; revised August 1975

References

1. Bjork, L.A. Recovery scenario for a DB/DC system. Proc. ACM 73 Nat. Conf., Atlanta, Ga., pp. 142–146.
2. Davies, C.T. Recovery semantics for a DB/DC system. Proc. ACM 73 Nat. Conf., Atlanta, Ga., pp. 136–141.
3. Chamberlin, D.D., Boyce, R.F., Traiger, I.L. A deadlock-free scheme for resource locking in a data-base environment, Information Processing 74, North-Holland Pub. Co., Amsterdam, 1974, pp.340–343.
4. Codd, E.F. A relational model for large shared data banks. *Comm. ACM 14*, 6 (June 1970), pp. 377–387.
5. Kleene, S.C. *Introduction to Metamathematics*. Van Nostrand, Princeton, N.J., 1952, p. 204.
6. IBM Information Management System for Virtual Storage (IMS/VS), Conversion and Planning Guide. Form No. SH20-9034, IBM, Armonk, N.Y., 1973, pp. 38–44.
7. CODASYL, Data Base Task Group Report. ACM, N.Y., 1971.
8. Eswaran, K.P., Gray, J.N., Lorie, R.A., and Traiger, I.L. On the notions of consistency and predicate locks in a data base system. Res. Rep., RJ 1487, IBM Res. Lab., San Jose, Calif., 1974.

IMPLEMENTATION OF INTEGRITY CONSTRAINTS AND VIEWS BY QUERY MODIFICATION

Michael Stonebraker

Department of Electrical Engineering and Computer Sciences
and the Electronics Research Laboratory
University of California, Berkeley, California 94720

Because the user interface in a relatonal data base management system may be decoupled from the storage representation of data, novel, powerful and efficient integrity control schemes are possible. This paper indicates the mechanism being implemented in one relational system to prevent integrity violations which can result from improper updates by a process. Basically each interaction with the data is immediately modified at the query language level to one guaranteed to have no integrity violations. Also, a similar modification technique is indicated to support the use of "views," i.e. relations which are not physically present in the data base but are defined in terms of ones that are.

I INTRODUCTION

Integrity of stored data can be corrupted in at least two ways: 1) By concurrent update by two or more processes; 2) by inadvertant, improper or malicious update by a process.

The first mechanism is a well known operating system problem [1] which is addressed in [2,3] in the context of a relational data base system. In this paper we shall focus only on the second mechanism.

These corruptions can result from access violations, i.e. an unauthorized user updates the data base in an unapproved way. In a recent paper [4] we indicated that user interactions with a data base could be efficiently modified into ones guaranteed to have no access violations. However, integrity can also be destroyed by inadvertant update by an authorized user. For example, a data base containing salaries of employees might be inadvertantly updated to give some employee a negative salary. Such an update would violate a constraint which might be put on a data base that all salaries be non negative. Other possible constraints are that employees with a job classification of Assistant Professor must make between $12,000 and $16,000 and that department chairman must be full professors. In this paper we will show that a wide variety of integrity constraints can be effectively guaranteed using the same interaction modification technique indicated in [4].

We also show that support for "views" (i.e. virtual relations which are not actually present in the data base) can be handled effectively in the identical manner.

The solution of these problems at the user language level should be contrasted with lower level solutions (such as providing data base procedure calls in the access paths to data [5,6,7] where they will be called repeatedly).

The observation is made in [8] and [9] that integrity constraints should be predicates in a high level language. However, neither suggests an implementation scheme. The specification of our integrity constraints are very similar to those in [8] and [9]; however, we indicate reasonably efficient implementation algorithms. The suggestion is made in [9] that views can also be stated in a high level language. Again, our contribution is the indication of an implementation algorithm.

These mechanisms are being implemented in a relational data base system [10,11] under development (and now mostly operational) at Berkeley. This system, INGRES, must be briefly described to indicate the setting for the algorithms to be presented. Of particular relevance is the query language, QUEL, which will be discussed in the next section.

II QUEL

QUEL (QUEry Language) has points in common with Data Language/ALPHA [12], SQUARE [13] and SEQUEL [14] in that it is a complete [15] query language which frees the programmer from concern for how data structures are implemented and what algorithms are operating on stored data. As such it facilitates a considerable degree of data independence [16]. We assume that the reader is familiar with standard relational terminology [17] and now indicate the relations which will be used in the examples of this paper.

	NAME	DEPT	SALARY	MANAGER	AGE
EMPLOYEE	Smith	toy	10000	Jones	25
	Jones	toy	10000	Johnson	32
	Adams	candy	12000	Baker	36
	Johnson	toy	14000	Harding	29
	Baker	admin	20000	Harding	47
	Harding	admin	40000	none	58

Indicated above is an EMPLOYEE relation with domains NAME, DEPT, SALARY, MANAGER and AGE. Each employee has a manager (except for Harding who is presumably the company president), a salary, an age and is in a department.

The second relation utilized will be a DEPARTMENT relation as follows. Here, each department is on a floor, has a certain number of employees and has a sales volume in thousands of dollars.

	DEPT	FLOOR#	#EMP	SALES
DEPARTMENT	toy	8	10	1,000
	candy	1	5	2,000
	tire	1	16	1,500
	admin	4	10	0

A QUEL interaction includes at least one RANGE statement of the form;

```
RANGE OF variable-list IS relation-name
```

The symbols declared in the range statement are variables which will be used as arguments for tuples. These are called TUPLE VARIABLES. The purpose of this statement is to specify the relation over which each variable ranges.

Moreover, an interaction includes one or more statements of the form:

```
COMMAND Result-name (Target-list)
        WHERE Qualification
```

Here, COMMAND is either RETRIEVE, APPEND, REPLACE, or DELETE. For RETRIEVE and APPEND, Result-name is the name of the relation which qualifying tuples will be retrieved into or appended to. For REPLACE and DELETE, Result-name is the name of a tuple variable which, through the qualification, identifies tuples to be modified or deleted. The Target-list is a list of the form

```
Result-domain = Function, ...
```

Here, the Result-domain's are domain names in the result relation which are to be assigned the value of the corresponding function.

The following suggest valid QUEL interactions. A complete description of the language is presented in [10] and [18].

Example 2.1. Find the birth date of employee Jones.

```
RANGE OF E IS EMPLOYEE
RETRIEVE INTO W(BDATE = 1975 - E.AGE)
WHERE E.NAME = 'Jones'
```

Here, E is a tuple variable which ranges over the EMPLOYEE relation and all tuples in that relation are found which satisfy the qualification E.NAME = 'Jones'. The result of the query is a new relation, W, which has a single domain, BDATE, that has been calculated for each qualifying tuple. If the result relation is omitted, qualifying tuples are printed on the user's terminal. Also in the target list, the 'Result-domain =' may be omitted if the function is a simple domain (i.e. NAME = E.NAME may be written as E.NAME - see example 2.6).

Example 2.2. Insert the tuple (Jackson,candy,13000,Baker,30) into EMPLOYEE.

```
APPEND TO EMPLOYEE(NAME = 'Jackson', DEPT = 'candy', SALARY = 13000, MGR = 'Baker', AGE = 30)
```

Here, the result relation EMPLOYEE is formed by adding the indicated tuple to the EMPLOYEE relation.

Example 2.3. Delete the information about employee Jackson.

```
RANGE OF E IS EMPLOYEE
DELETE E WHERE E.NAME = 'Jackson'
```

Here, the tuples corresponding to all employees named Jackson are deleted from EMPLOYEE.

Example 2.4. Give a 10 percent raise to Jones.

```
RANGE OF E IS EMPLOYEE
REPLACE E(SALARY BY 1.1 * E.SALARY)
WHERE E.NAME = 'Jones'
```

Here, E.SALARY is to be replaced by 1.1*E.SALARY for those tuples in EMPLOYEE where E.NAME = 'Jones'. (Note that the keywords IS and BY may be used interchangeably with '=' in any QUEL statement.)

Also, QUEL contains aggregation operators including COUNT, COUNT', SUM, SUM', AVG, AVG', MAX, MIN, and the set operators, SET and SET'. Two examples of the use of aggregation follow.

Example 2.5. Replace the salary of all toy department empolyees by the average toy department salary.

```
RANGE OF E IS EMPLOYEE
REPLACE E(SALARY BY AVG'(E.SALARY WHERE E.DEPT = 'toy')) WHERE E.DEPT = 'toy'
```

here, AVG' is to be taken of the salary domain for those tuples satisfying the qualification E.DEPT = 'toy.' Note that AVG'(E.SALARY WHERE E.DEPT = 'toy') is scalar valued and consequently will be called an AGGREGATE. For the example chosen this aggregate has the value (1/3)*(10000+10000+14000) which equals 11,333. It is sometimes useful to allow aggregates to be taken in such a way that duplicates tuples are not included. Non primed aggregates (SET, AVG, COUNT, and SUM) perform this function. For example, AVG(E.SALARY WHERE E.DEPT = 'toy') has a value 12,000.

More general aggregations are possible as suggested by the following example.

Example 2.6. Find those departments whose average salary exceeds the company wide average salary, both averages to be taken only for those employees whose salary exceeds $10000.

```
RANGE OF E IS EMPLOYEE
RETRIEVE INTO HIGHPAY(E.DEPT)
WHERE AVG'(E.SALARY BY E.DEPT WHERE E.SALARY > 10000) >
      AVG'(E.SALARY WHERE E.SALARY>10000)
```

Here, AVG'(E.SALARY BY E.DEPT WHERE E.SALARY>10000) is an AGGREGATE FUNCTION and takes a value for each of E.DEPT. This value is the aggregate AVG'(E.SALARY WHERE E.SALARY>10000 AND E.DEPT = value) as indicated below.

E.DEPT	AVG'(E.SALARY BY E.DEPT WHERE E.SALARY>10000)
toy	14000
candy	12000
admin	30000

The qualification expression for the statement is then true for departments for which this aggregate function exceeds the aggregate AVG'(E.SALARY WHERE E.SALARY>10000). The later is simply the scalar 21,500. Hence, admin is the only qualifying department.

As with aggregates, aggregate functions can have duplicates deleted with an unprimed operator.

In the sequel there will be several integrity control algorithms applied to APPEND, DELETE and REPLACE statements. Consequently, we indicate their general form and interpretation at this time.

An APPEND statement is of the following general form:

```
RANGE OF X1 IS R1
RANGE OF X2 IS R2
        .
        .
        .
RANGE OF XN IS RN
APPEND R(D1=f1,...,Dr=fr)        WHERE Q
```

Here, X1,...,XN are tuple variables over relations R1,...,RN

R is the name of the result relation and may or may not be Ri for some i.

D1,...,Dr are the names of ALL domains in R. They may be defaulted as indicated earlier.

f1,...,fr are valid QUEL alpha-functions. For a discussion of alpha-functions, see [10].

Q is a qualification statement in variables X1,...,XN, i.e. Q = Q(X1,...,XN), or a subset thereof.

Conceptually, the interpretation of an APPEND statement is the following:

1) Issue the statement

```
RANGE OF X1 is R1
RANGE OF X2 IS R2
        .
        .
        .
RANGE OF XN IS RN
RETRIEVE INTO TEMP (D1=f1,...,Dr=fr) WHERE Q
```

An error results if TEMP and R do not have identical domains. Also, if Q is absent and f1,...,fr are simply the domains from a given relation, then step 1) would be a copy operation. Hence, it need not be done in this case.

2) Perform a set union of TEMP and R into R

The general form of a DELETE statement is the following:

```
RANGE OF X1 IS R1
RANGE OF X2 IS R2
        .
        .
        .
RANGE OF XN IS RN
DELETE X1 WHERE Q
```

The interpretation is the following:

1) Issue the statement

```
RANGE OF X1 IS R1
RANGE OF X2 IS R2
        .
        .
        .
RANGE OF XN IS RN
RETRIEVE INTO TEMP(X1.ALL) WHERE Q
```

Here, ALL is a keyword indicating all domains.

2) Perform the relative complement of R1 and TEMP into R1

The general form of a REPLACE statement is the following:

```
RANGE OF X1 IS R1
RANGE OF X2 IS R2
        .
        .
        .
RANGE OF XN IS RN
REPLACE X1(D1=f1,...,Ds=fs)  WHERE Q
```

Here, D1,...,Ds are a subset of the domains in R1.

The interpretation is the following:

1) Issue the statement

```
RANGE OF X1 IS R1
RANGE OF X2 IS R2
        .
        .
        .
RANGE OF XN IS RN
RETRIEVE INTO TEMP(X1.TID,f1,...,fs) WHERE Q
```

Here, TID is a tuple identifier which is guaranteed to be unique to a tuple.

2) For each tuple in TEMP, obtain the tuple in R1 identified by TID, substitute f1,...,fs for D1,...,Ds and replace the tuple. Should there be more than one tuple in the TEMP with a given TID, the update is

NON-FUNCTIONAL and is aborted. This problem is discussed further in [3].

A RETRIEVE statement is processed by breaking it into a sequence of RETRIEVE statements each of which involves only a single tuple variable. This decomposition is discussed in [10] and a similar one in [19]. These single variable queries involve only one relation and can be directly executed (in the worst case by a sequential scan of the relation tuple by tuple). Often the relation will be stored in such a way that a complete scan is not needed. Also, secondary indices which can profitably be used to speed access are utilized.

The actual processing of update commands follows the general flavor indicated above. However, where possible, the creation of TEMP is avoided and steps 1 and 2 performed at once.

III INTEGRITY CONSTRAINTS

For each data base we allow ASSERTIONS to be stored. Each assertion is (logically) a RANGE statement and a valid QUEL qualification in variables specified in the RANGE statement. This qualification is true or false for each tuple in the Cartesian product of the relations specified by variables in the RANGE statement. In the next four sections we indicate algorithms which guarantee that the qualification is TRUE for all tuples in the product space after each update. The general mechanism is to modify each user interaction so that updates which violate an assertion are disallowed. In the remainder of this section we indicate examples of possible assertions.

Example 3.1. Employee salaries must be positive

```
RANGE OF E IS EMPLOYEE
INTEGRITY E.SALARY>0
```

Example 3.2. Everyone in the toy department must make more than $8000

```
RANGE OF E IS EMPLOYEE
INTEGRITY E.SALARY>8000 OR E.DEPT ≠ 'toy'
```

Example 3.3. Employees must earn less than ten times the sales volume of their department if their department has a positive sales

```
RANGE OF E IS EMPLOYEE
RANGE OF D IS DEPARTMENT
INTEGRITY E.SALARY < 10*D.SALES
          OR E.DEPT ≠ D.DEPT
          OR D.SALES = 0
```

Example 3.4. No employee can make more than his manager

```
RANGE OF E,M IS EMPLOYEE
INTEGRITY E.SALARY ≤ M.SALARY
          OR E.MANAGER ≠ M.NAME
```

Example 3.5. Harding must make more than twice the average employee salary

```
RANGE OF E IS EMPLOYEE
INTEGRITY E.NAME ≠ 'Harding'
          OR E.SALARY > 2*AVG'(E.SALARY)
```

Example 3.6. Name must be a primary key

```
RANGE OF E IS EMPLOYEE
INTEGRITY COUNT(E.TID) = COUNT(E.NAME)
```

Example 3.7. Floor# is functionally dependent [20] on DEPT

```
RANGE OF D IS DEPT
INTEGRITY COUNT(D.FLOOR# BY D.DEPT) = 1
```

There will be four algorithms of increasing complexity (and cost) for dealing with:

1) one variable aggregate-free assertions as in Examples 3.1-3.2.

2) multivariate aggregate-free assertions with only one tuple variable on the relation being updated as in Example 3.3.

3) multivariate aggregate-free assertions with two or more tuple variables on the relation being updated as in Example 3.4.

4) assertions involving aggregates as in Examples 3.5-3.7.

We deal with each case individually in the next four sections. For all sections we deal with APPEND, DELETE and REPLACE in their general form indicated in Section 2. Hence, notation introduced in Section 2 will be used throughout.

IV ENFORCEMENT OF ONE VARIABLE AGGREGATE-FREE ASSERTIONS

Intuitively, a one variable aggregate free assertion specifies a condition which is true or false for each tuple in a relation. Hence, integrity assurance reduces to checking each tuple that is inserted or modified to ensure the truth of the assertion. Tuples may, of course, be deleted with no checking whatsoever. As a result, a DELETE statement can be processed with no regard for such integrity constraints.

The following algorithm must be applied to APPEND statements.

ALGORITHM 1

a) Find all one variable aggregate-free assertions with RANGE OF Y IS R for some tuple variable Y. Call the corresponding qualifications Q1(Y),...,Qh(Y).

b) Replace Q, the given qualification, by Q AND Q* where

```
Q* = Q1(f1,...,fr)
     AND Q2(f1,...,fr)
     AND
       .
       .
       .
     AND Qh(f1,...,fr)
```

Here, Qj(f1,...,fr) results from Qj(Y) by replacing Y.Dk by fk whenever Y.Dk appears in Qj.

The APPEND statement can be processed normally assured that R will satisfy all one variable aggregate free assertions after execution. The result of the RETRIEVE portion of the algorithm to execute APPEND statements will contain only tuples which satisfy the constraints; R, of course, satisfies the constraints; hence, the set union of R and this result will also.

The tuples which are not APPENDED to R because of an integrity violation can be easily found as follows:

```
RANGE OF X1 IS R1
RANGE OF X2 IS R2
           .
           .
           .
RANGE OF XN IS RN
RETRIEVE INTO MISTAKE(D1 = f1,...,Dr = fr) WHERE Q AND NOT Q*
```

The algorithm for REPLACE statements differs only slightly from the algorithm above.

Algorithm 2

a) same as step a) for Algorithm 1

b) Replace Q by Q AND Q* for which Qj(f1,...,fs) is formed by replacing Y by X1 then by replacing X1.Dk by fk wherever X1.Dk appears in Qj.

The tuples which cannot be altered are found by:

```
RANGE OF X1 IS R1
RANGE OF X2 IS R2
           .
           .
           .
RANGE OF XN IS RN
RETRIEVE INTO MISTAKE(X1.ALL) WHERE Q AND NOT Q*
```

Two examples illustrate these algorithms at work. Here, we enforce the constraint on positive salaries given in Example 3.1.

Example 4.1. Insert the tuple (Jackson, candy, 13000, Baker, 30) into EMPLOYEE

```
APPEND TO EMPLOYEE(NAME = 'Jackson', DEPT = 'candy',
              SALARY = 13000, MGR = 'Baker', AGE = 30)
```

This is exactly Example 2.2 and becomes after application of the algorithm:

```
APPEND TO EMPLOYEE(NAME = 'Jackson', DEPT = 'candy',
               SALARY = 13000, MGR = 'Baker', AGE = 30)
                    WHERE 13000>0
```

Hence, Jackson's tuple will be added only if he has a positive salary. Tuples disallowed by the integrity constraint would be found by:

```
RETRIEVE INTO MISTAKE(NAME = 'Jackson', DEPT = 'candy',
   SALARY = 13000, MGR = 'Baker', AGE = 30)
      WHERE NOT 13000>0
```

In fact, the following format issues both statements at once:

```
APPEND TO EMPLOYEE(NAME = 'Jackson', DEPT = 'candy',
              SALARY = 13000, MGR = 'Baker', AGE = 30)
ERRORS TO MISTAKE
```

Example 4.2. Give a 500 dollar paycut to Jones

```
RANGE OF E IS EMPLOYEE
REPLACE E(SALARY = E.SALARY-500) WHERE E.NAME = 'Jones'
ERRORS TO MISTAKE
```

Upon modification, this becomes:

```
RANGE OF E IS EMPLOYEE
REPLACE E(SALARY = E.SALARY - 500) WHERE E.NAME = 'Jones'
     AND E.SALARY-500 > 0

RETRIEVE INTO MISTAKE(E.ALL) WHERE E.NAME = 'Jones'
     AND NOT E.SALARY-500 > 0
```

V ENFORCEMENT OF MULTIVARIATE AGGREGATE-FREE ASSERTIONS, I

Here, we consider the case that all assertions have two or more tuple variables but only one ranging over the relation being updated. In this case each tuple which is inserted or modified will add or change many tuples in the product space for which the assertion must be guaranteed. As a result the algorithms in this section are more complex than previously. Note, however, that tuples may still be deleted from a relation with no checking.

The following algorithm must be applied to APPEND statements:

Algorithm 3

a) Find all multivariable assertions which contain RANGE OF Y IS R for some Y. Let these qualifications be Q1,...,Qh.

If f1,...,fr are simple domains with only a single tuple variable, say Xm, then do b), otherwise do b1) and b2).

b) Append Q* to the users qualification where Q*=Q1* AND ... AND Qh* and where Qi* is found as follows. Let Qi be qualification in variables Y, U1,...,Uq, i.e. Qi = Qi(Y,U1,...,Uq). Then Qi* is:

```
COUNT(U1.TID,...,Uq.TID BY Xm.TID
         WHERE Qi(Xm,U1,...,Uq))
         =
COUNT(U1.TID,...,Uq.TID)
```

b1) Do step 1 of the algorithm to process APPEND statements therefy creating TEMP (as noted in Section 2).
b2) Issue the interaction

```
RANGE OF Z IS TEMP
APPEND INTO R(Z.ALL) WHERE Q*
```

Here, Q* is the qualification Q1* AND ... AND Qh* where Qi* is:

```
COUNT(U1.TID,...,Uq.TID BY Z.TID
    WHERE Qi(Z, U1,...,Uq))
         =
COUNT(U1.TID,...,Uq.TID)
```

The algorithm for REPLACE statements is the following.

Algorithm 4

a) Find all multivariate assertions which contain RANGE OF Y IS R for some Y. Let these qualification be Q1,...,Qh.

b) For the i-th qualification, let Qi have tuple variables Y, U1,...,Uq, i.e. Qi = Qi(Y, U1,...,Uq).

c) Replace Q, the given qualification, by Q and Q1* AND ... AND Qh* where Qi* is:

```
COUNT(U1.TID,...,Uq.TID BY X1.TID
     WHERE Qi(f1,...,fs, U1,...,Uq))
          =
COUNT(U1.TID,...,Uq.TID)
```

Here, note that Qi(f1,...,fs, U1,...,Uq) is Qi with Y replaced by X1 then X1.Dk replaced by fk wherever it appears.

The following examples illustrates these algorithms.

Suppose one wants to enforce the constraint of Example 3.3 that an employee must earn less than 10 times the sales volume of his department if sales volume is positive.

Suppose the employee tuple for Jackson is in a relation W and is to be added to EMPLOYEE as follows.

Example 5.1.

```
RANGE OF Y IS W
APPEND TO EMPLOYEE(Y.ALL) WHERE Y.NAME = 'Jackson'
```

Upon modification this becomes:

```
RANGE OF Y IS W
RANGE OF D IS DEPARTMENT
APPEND TO EMPLOYEE(Y.ALL) WHERE Y.NAME = 'Jackson'

       AND    COUNT(D.TID BY Y.TID
              WHERE Y.SALARY < 10*D.SALES
                  OR Y.DEPT ≠ D.DEPT
                OR D.SALES = 0)
                   =
              COUNT(D.TID BY Y.TID)
```

The algorithm applied to Example 4.2 now follows.

Example 5.2. Give a 500 dollar paycut to Jones

```
RANGE OF E IS EMPLOYEE
REPLACE E(SALARY = E.SALARY-500) WHERE E.NAME = 'Jones'
```

Upon modification this becomes:

```
RANGE OF E IS EMPLOYEE
RANGE OF D IS DEPARTMENT
REPLACE E(SALARY = E.SALARY-500) WHERE E.NAME = 'Jones'

       AND   COUNT(D.TID BY E.TID
             WHERE E.SALARY-500 < 10*D.SALES
               OR E.DEPT ≠ D.DEPT
               OR D.SALES = 0
                   =
             COUNT(D.TID BY E.TID)
```

VI ENFORCEMENT OF MULTIVARIATE AGGREGATE-FREE ASSERTIONS, II

We now consider the case of assertions such as Example 3.4 which contain two or more tuple variables ranging over the relation to be updated. This situation differs from the cases considered previously in the following respect. In effect, integrity control was exercised by examining each tuple to be updated, allowing updates for those tuples satisfying the assertions and denying them otherwise. Unfortunately, updates subject to the assertions considered in this section must be allowed or disallowed as a whole, and decisions cannot be made incrementally. The following example illustrates the problem which arises.

Consider the combination of two relations on employees (which might happen if two companies merge) i.e.

```
RANGE OF N IS NEWEMP
APPEND TO EMPLOYEE(N.ALL)
```

Moreover, suppose one wants to enforce the constraint of Example 3.4, i.e. that each employee must make less than his manager. Lastly, suppose most of all of the employees in the relation NEWEMP violate this condition.

Now, suppose one inserts tuples from NEWEMP into EMPLOYEE in an order such that each employee is inserted before his manager. Each employee who is not a manager can be inserted without a violation while each manager will not be allowed. On the other hand, if managers are inserted first, at least one will satisfy the constraints while all non managers will fail. Hence, the order in which the tuples are inserted will affect which ones are in violation of the constraints. Since ordering of tuples in a relation should not affect the outcome of any operation, one must treat an update subject to this form of integrity constraint as an entity and allow or disallow the whole procedure. Consequently, the algorithms are somewhat different than those in the previous sections.

It can again be noted that DELETES can be processed with no checking; the integrity assurance algorithm for APPENDS now follows.

Algorithm 5

a) Find all multivariate assertions which have two or more tuple variables ranging over R. Let these qualifications be Q1,...,Qh.

b) Do step one of the algorithm to process APPEND statements, thereby creating TEMP

c) Issue the interaction:

```
RANGE OF Z IS TEMP
APPEND TO R(Z.ALL) WHERE Q*
```

Here, Q* = Q1* AND ... AND Qh* and where Qi* is found as follows. Let Qi have tuple variables Y1,...,Ym, U1,...,Uq where Yj ranges over R and Uj does not for all j.

Then Qi* is the following:

```
  AND   . . .  AND    COUNT(V1.TID,...,Vm.TID, U1.TID,...,Uq.TID
 V1 in        Vm in
{R,TEMP}     {R,TEMP}          WHERE Qi(V1,...,Vm, U1,...,Uq))

                                       =

                       COUNT(V1.TID,...,Vm.TID, U1.TID,...,Uq.TID)
```

The reader should note several points concerning this algorithm:

1) the COUNT term when Vi=R for all i can be eliminated since R satisfies the constraint before the update.

2) when Vi=TEMP for all i, only one of the m permutations need be included since the rest would be redundant.

3) new tuple variables are required in the second APPEND statement because of the introduction of Q*.

4) aggregates appear in this algorithm instead of the aggregate functions in algorithms 3 and 4. In this way Q* has either the value TRUE or FALSE and the update as a whole is either allowed or disallowed as a result.

The reader can also note the changes which must be made to create a working algorithm for REPLACE statements. We now indicate an example of the algorithm at work ensuring Example 3.4.

Example 6.1. Add Jackson to EMPLOYEE

```
RANGE OF Y IS W
APPEND TO EMPLOYEE(Y.ALL) WHERE Y.NAME = 'Jackson'
```

Upon modification this becomes:

```
        RANGE OF Y IS W
        RETRIEVE INTO TEMP(Y.ALL) WHERE Y.NAME = 'Jackson'

        RANGE OF T, T2 IS TEMP
        RANGE OF E IS EMPLOYEE
        APPEND TO EMPLOYEE(T.ALL) WHERE

        COUNT(T.TID,T2.TID WHERE
            T.SALARY < T2.SALARY
              OR T.MANAGER ≠ T2.NAME)
          =
        COUNT(T.TID, T2.TID)
AND     COUNT(T.TID, E.TID WHERE
            T.SALARY < E.SALARY
              OR T.MANAGER ≠ E.NAME)
          =
        COUNT(T.TID, E.TID)
AND     COUNT(E.TID, T.TID WHERE
            E.SALARY < T.SALARY
              OR E.MANAGER ≠ T.NAME)
          =
        COUNT(E.TID,T.TID)
```

VII CONSTRAINTS INVOLVING AGGREGATES

The reader can note that constraints involving aggregates have the same problem that occurred with the previous class of constraints, namely updates must be allowed or disallowed as a whole. Again the reason is that the tuples which violate the constraints depend on the order in which they are changed or added. There is, however, a more serious problem.

For example, the assertion AVG'(X.SALARY) < 14000 might be applied to the following update.

```
        RANGE OF Y IS W
        APPEND INTO EMPLOYEE(Y.ALL)
```

as follows

```
        RANGE OF Y IS W
        RANGE OF E IS EMPLOYEE
        APPEND INTO EMPLOYEE(Y.ALL) WHERE
                      SUM'(E.SALARY) +SUM'(Y.SALARY)
                      ----------------------------  < 14000
                      COUNT(E.TID) + COUNT(Y.TID)
```

In this fashion the revised average salary would be computed and checked for the integrity constraint during the update. Unfortunately, there may be tuples in W which are also in EMPLOYEE.

If so, the APPEND statement will, of course, delete the duplicate tuples when it performs a set union of EMPLOYEE and W. However, the added qualification is, in effect, the integrity statement with the duplicates present. There is no way in QUEL to express the fact that the constraint should be taken with duplicates deleted.

Therefore, the algorithm for constraints involving aggregates must be to try the update, test the resulting relation for the integrity constraint and then undo the update if one is not satisfied.

VIII EFFICIENCY CONSIDERATIONS

The addition of single variable aggregate-free integrity constraints will usually result in the same decomposition to a sequence of one-variable queries that would have resulted otherwise. Each such one variable query is further qualified by one or more integrity qualifications. Such one variable queries are usually at least as efficient to process as those without constraints. In fact, the added qualification may be employable to speed access. Hence, the cost of integrity for one variable aggregate-free assertions should be negligible.

Unfortunately, this is not the case for the other forms of constraints. All involve testing for equality, pairs of aggregates or aggregate functions. These operations are usually very costly. Consequently, the user may enforce more complex controls but only at considerable cost.

Note that our algorithms generally have the effect of testing constraints for only small subrelations on each update. Of course, this is to be preferred to examining the whole relation each time.

Also, if controls are desired at each update, we believe the proper approach is to append them at as high a level as possible. In this way checks in the access paths are avoided, and any information available can be utilized to perform the update as efficiently as possible. Note also that schemes which append integrity controls at lower levels have considerable difficulty enforcing complex controls (such as those involving more than a single tuple variable).

Lastly, note that the power of RETRIEVE statements can also be used to ascertain the truth of integrity constraints. Thus, users who do not wish to pay the price of checking each update may less frequently make their own checks and take appropriate action.

IX SUPPORT FOR VIEWS

"Views" or virtual relations are relations which do not physically exist in the data base but may be definable in terms of ones which do exist.

One such view might be the relation EMPTOY with domains NAME, SALARY, AGE, and DEPT defined as follows:

```
RANGE OF E IS EMPLOYEE
DEFINE EMPTOY(NAME=E.NAME,SALARY=E.SALARY,AGE=E,AGE,DEPT=E.DEPT)
       WHERE E.DEPT = 'toy'
```

Note again that defaults could have been used for the names of the domains in EMPTOY.

In INGRES any user is allowed to define views for his own use. Moreover, the data base administrator can define views which apply to others. The syntax of a DEFINE statement is identical to a RETRIEVE statement and is parametrically:

```
RANGE OF X1 IS R1
RANGE OF X2 IS R2
            .
            .
            .
RANGE OF XN IS RN
DEFINE VIEWNAME(D1=f1,...,Dj=fj)  WHERE Q
```

Note that the RANGE statement of a view can involve a relation which is itself a view. Views are supported for two reasons.

1) user convenience as a 'MACRO' facility

2) the stored relations may change over time and views allow previous relations to be defined in terms of current ones. Hence, programs written for previous versions of the data base can continue to be supported (with certain restrictions to be discussed presently).

Our view algorithm now follows.

Algorithm 6

For each tuple variable V specified in a user interaction which ranges over a view defined by a target list Tv and qualification Qv:

1) Delete V from the RANGE statement of the user interaction and add all tuple variables in the view definition (modifying them to have unique names if necessary).

2) If VIEWNAME is the relation in a DELETE statement from which tuples will be deleted, then replace V by Xm in the Result-name portion of the interaction if f1,...,fj have only a single tuple variable, say Xm. Otherwise, abort the command.

Similarly, if VIEWNAME is the relation to which tuples are to be added by an APPEND statement and if f1,...,fj involve only a single tuple variable, say Xm, then replace VIEWNAME by Rm, the relation over which Xm ranges, as the result relation. If f1,...,fj involve more than one tuple variable, abort the interaction in this situation.

Lastly, in REPLACE statements for which V indicates that VIEWNAME is to be modified, then append V to each domain name to the left of an equals sign in the target list; do step 6 of the algorithm; then factor out the tuple variable again. If more than one tuple variable results to the left of an equals sign then abort the command.

3) Abort all REPLACE statements which update a domain appearing in Qv. In this case several problems are

present. One is the possibility of updating a tuple in such a way that it is deleted from the view (for example by updating DEPT in the previous example). This anomoly should not be allowed.

4) Append

```
AND Qv
```

to the user's qualification.

5) Append Qv to the qualificaiton portion of any aggregate or aggregate function which contains V unless V appears as part of the BY argument in the qualification portion of the user's interaction. In this case the variable is not local to the aggregate in question. Hence, step 4 appropriately conditions such functions.

6) Replace each domain V.Dj in the user interaction with fj from the target list of the view definition.

The following points should be carefully noted concerning this algorithm:

1) The algorithm translates interactions on views into interactions on real relations.

2) The resulting interaction may be syntactically illegal. For example, APPEND and DELETE statements may be so modified that TEMP created in step 1 of the execution algorithm (see Section 2) does not have the correct domains. Such an interaction will be aborted automatically.

3) In step 2 of the view algorithm an abort occurs because a SINGLE interaction on a view must be translated into MORE THAN ONE interaction on real relations. Such a translation is, in general, impossible as noted in [21].

The following examples illustrate the algorithm at work.

<u>Example 9.1</u> Give Jones a 10 percent raise

```
RANGE OF Y IS EMPTOY
REPLACE Y(SALARY = 1.1*Y.SALARY)  WHERE Y.NAME = 'Jones'
```

Upon application of algorithm 6 this becomes:

```
RANGE OF E IS EMPLOYEE
REPLACE E(SALARY = 1.1*E.SALARY)
      WHERE      E.NAME = 'Jones' AND E.DEPT = 'toy'
```

<u>Example 9.2</u>

The following statements define a second view of EMPLOYEE.

```
RANGE OF E IS EMPLOYEE
DEFINE EMPOTHER(NAME=E.NAME, PROGRESS=E.SALARY/E.AGE)
```

The update

```
RANGE OF O IS EMPOTHER
REPLACE O(PROGRESS=1.1*O.PROGRESS)
```

becomes

```
RANGE OF E IS EMPLOYEE
REPLACE E(SALARY/AGE =1.1*E.SALARY/E.AGE)
```

which is syntactically illegal and is aborted.

<u>Example 9.3</u>

The following statements define a view involving both EMPLOYEE and DEPARTMENT.

```
RANGE OF E IS EMPLOYEE
RANGE OF D IS DEPARTMENT
DEFINE COMBEMP(NAME=E,NAME, SALARY=E.SALARY, FLOOR#=D.FLOOR#)
    WHERE E.DEPT=D.DEPT
```

The update

```
        RANGE OF C IS COMBEMP
        REPLACE C(FLOOR#=3) WHERE C.NAME = 'Jones'
becomes
        RANGE OF E IS EMPLOYEE
        RANGE OF D IS DEPARTMENT
        REPLACE D(FLOOR#=3)
                WHERE E.NAME = 'Jones' AND E.DEPT=D.DEPT
```

which is processed correctly.

The following table summarizes the actions of the view algorithm.

	(A) The view is a restriction[15] of an existing relation	(B) f1,...,fj involve a single tuple variable but (A) is not satisfied	(C) f1,...,fj involve more than a single relation
	(Example 8.1)	(Example 8.2)	(Example 8.3)
REPLACE (tuples in the view)	correct (unless disallowed by 3)	correct (unless disallowed by 3 or syntactically illegal)	correct (unless disallowed by 2 or 3 or syntactically illegal)
APPEND (to the view)	correct	syntactically illegal (point 2)	disallowed by 2
DELETE (from the view)	correct	syntactically illegal (point 2)	disallowed by 2
RETRIEVE (and all other updates)	correct	correct	correct

The notion of "correct" is the following . If the view were materalized (by replacing the DEFINE with a RETRIEVE and issueing the query) and the interaction were processed; the result would be the same as would be obtained by applying the view algorithm to the interaction, then processing the interaction which results and materalizing the view.

Note that this algorithm processes all RETRIEVES and many REPLACES correctly; APPENDS and DELETES are usually disallowed. Moreover, it is easy to implement and involves the same sort of processing needed for protection and integrity constraints. Note lastly that more elaborate algorithms are possible which will handle more cases than algorithm 6. In fact, supporting APPENDS and DELETES for certain views in the second column above does not appear difficult. However, the difficulty of handling most other disallowed cases appears very great, and in some cases there may be no possible procedure.

X SUMMARY

The advantages of these integrity control and view support algorithms are briefly recapitulated here.

1) In both cases control is placed at the source language level. As such, access control, integrity checks and support for views can all be accomplished at once. Also, at this level the algorithms are conceptually simple and easy to implement. This should be contrasted with lower level schemes (such as [2,5]).

2) Little storage space is required to store integrity assertions and view definitions.

3) These algorithms involve small overhead at least in the simpler (and presumably more common) cases.

ACKNOWLEDGEMENT

Research sponsored by the National Science Foundation Grant GK-43024X and the Naval Electronic Systems Command Contract N00039-75-C-0034.

REFERENCES

[1] Brinch Hansen, P., Operating Systems Principles, Prentice Hall, Englewood Cliffs, N.J., 1973.

[2] Chamberlin, D., et al. "A Deadlock-Free Scheme for Resource Locking in a Data Base Environment," IBM Research Laboratory, San Jose, Ca., March 1974.

[3] Stonebraker, M., "High Level Integrity Assurance in Relational Data Base Systems," University of California, Electronics Research Laboratory, Memorandum M473, August 1974.

[4] Stonebraker, M. and Wong, E., "Access Control in a Relational Data Base Management System by Query Modification," Proc. 1974 ACM National Conference, San Diego, Ca., Nov. 1974.

[5] Committee on Data Systems Languages, "Data Description Language," U.S. Dept. of Commerce, National Bureau of Standards, Handbook #112, January, 1974.

[6] Hoffman, L., "The Formulary Model for Flexible Privacy and Access Control," Proc. 1971 Fall Joint Computer Conference, Las Vegas, Nev., November 1971.

[7] Fossum, B., "Data Base Integrity as Provided for by a Particular Data Base Management System," Proc. 1974 IFIP Conference on Data Base Management Systems, Cargese, Corsica, April 1974.

[8] Florentin, J., "Consistency Auditing of Data Bases," The Computer Journal, vol. 17, no. 1, February 1974.

[9] Chamberlin, D. and Boyce, R., "Using a Structured English Query Language as a Data Definition Facility," IBM Research Report RJ 1318, San Jose, Ca. December 1973.

[10] Held, G., et al., "INGRES - A Relational Data Base System," Proc. 1975 National Computer Conference, Anaheim, Ca., May 1975. (to appear).

[11] Held, G. and Stonebraker, M., "Storage Structures and Access Methods in the Relational Data Base Management System, INGRES," Proc. ACM-PACIFIC-75 San Francisco, Ca., April 1975.

[12] Codd, E., "A Data Base Sublanguage Founded on the Relational Calculus," Proc. 1971 ACM-SIGFIDET Workshop on Data Description, Access and Control, San Diego, Ca., November 1971.

[13] Boyce, R. et al., "Specifying Queries as Relational Expressions: SQUARE," Proc. ACM SIGPLAN-SIGIR Interface Meeting, Gaithersberg, Md., November 1973.

[14] Chamberlin, D. and Boyce, R., "SEQUEL: A Structured English Query Language," Proc. 1974 ACM-SIGFIDET Workshop on Data Description, Access and Control, Ann Arbor, Mich., May 1974.

[15] Codd, E., "Relational Completeness of Data Base Sublanguages," Courant Computer Science Symposium, May 1971.

[16] Stonebraker, M., "A Functional View of Data Independence," Proc. 1974 ACM-SIGFIDET Workshop on Data Description, Access and Control, Ann Arbor, Mich, May 1974.

[17] Codd, E., "A Relatonal Model of Data for Large Shared Data Banks," CACM, 13 6 (June 1970).

[18] McDonald, N. and Stonebraker, M., "CUPID - A Friendly Query Language," Proc. ACM-PACIFIC-75, San Francisco, Ca., April 1975.

[19] Rothnie, J., "An Approach to Implementing a Relational Data Base Management System," Proc. 1974 ACM-SIGFIDET Workshop on Data Description, Access and Control, Ann Arbor, Mich., May 1974.

[20] Codd, E., "Normalized Data Base Structure: A Brief Tutorial," Proc. 1971 ACM-SIGFIDET Workshop on Data Description, Access and Control, San Diego, Ca. November 1971.

[21] Codd, E., "Recent Investigations in Relational Data Base Systems," Information processing '74, North Holland, 1974.

Rete: A Fast Algorithm for the Many Pattern/Many Object Pattern Match Problem*

Charles L. Forgy

Department of Computer Science, Carnegie-Mellon University, Pittsburgh, PA 15213, U.S.A.

Recommended by Harry Barrow

ABSTRACT

The Rete Match Algorithm is an efficient method for comparing a large collection of patterns to a large collection of objects. It finds all the objects that match each pattern. The algorithm was developed for use in production system interpreters, and it has been used for systems containing from a few hundred to more than a thousand patterns and objects. This article presents the algorithm in detail. It explains the basic concepts of the algorithm, it describes pattern and object representations that are appropriate for the algorithm, and it describes the operations performed by the pattern matcher.

1. Introduction

In many pattern/many object pattern matching, a collection of patterns is compared to a collection of objects, and all the matches are determined. That is, the pattern matcher finds every object that matches each pattern. This kind of pattern matching is used extensively in Artificial Intelligence programs today. For instance, it is a basic component of production system interpreters. The interpreters use it to determine which productions have satisfied condition parts. Unfortunately, it can be slow when large numbers of patterns or objects are involved. Some systems have been observed to spend more than nine-tenths of their total run time performing this kind of pattern matching [5]. This article describes an algorithm that was designed to make many pattern/many object pattern matching less expensive. The algorithm was developed for use in production system interpreters, but since it should be useful for other languages and systems as well, it is presented in detail.

This article attends to two complementary aspects of efficiency: (1) designing an algorithm for the task and (2) implementing the algorithm on the computer. The rest of Section 1 provides some background information. Section 2 presents the basic concepts of the algorithm. Section 3 explains how the objects and patterns should be represented to allow the most efficient implementations. Section 4 describes in detail a very fast implementation of the algorithm. Finally, Section 5 presents some of the results of the analyses of the algorithm.

1.1. OPS5

The methods described in this article were developed for production system interpreters, and they will be illustrated with examples drawn from production systems. This section provides a brief introduction to the language used in the examples, OPS5. For a more complete description of OPS5, see [6].

A production system program consists of an unordered collection of If-Then statements called *productions*. The data operated on by the productions is held in a global data base called *working memory*. By convention, the If part of a production is called its *LHS* (left-hand side), and its Then part is called its *RHS* (right-hand side). The interpreter executes a production system by performing the following operations.

(1) *Match*. Evaluate the LHSs of the productions to determine which are satisfied given the current contents of working memory.

(2) *Conflict resolution*. Select one production with a satisfied LHS; if no productions have satisfied LHSs, halt the interpreter.

(3) *Act*. Perform the actions in the RHS of the selected production.

(4) Goto 1.

OPS5 working memories typically contain several hundred objects, and each object typically has between ten and one hundred associated attribute-value pairs. An object together with its attribute-value pairs is called a *working memory element*. The following is a typical, though very small, OPS5 working memory element; it indicates that the object of class Expression which is named Expr17 has 2 as its first argument, '*' as its operator, and X as its second argument.

(Expression ↑Name Expr17 ↑Arg1 2 ↑Op * ↑Arg2 X)

The ↑ is the OPS5 operator that distinguishes attributes from values.

The LHS of a production consists of a sequence of patterns; that is, a sequence of partial descriptions of working memory elements. When a pattern P describes an element E, P is said to *match* E. In some productions, some of

*This research was sponsored by the Defense Advanced Research Projects Agency (DOD), ARPA Order No. 3597, monitored by the Air Force Avionics Laboratory under Contract F33615-78-C-1551.

The views and conclusions contained in this document are those of the author and should not be interpreted as representing the official policies, either expressed or implied, of the Defense Advanced Research Projects Agency or the US Government.

Artificial Intelligence 19 (1982) 17–37

the patterns are preceded by the negation symbol, –. An LHS is satisfied when

(1) Every pattern that is not preceded by – matches a working memory element, and

(2) No pattern that is preceded by – matches a working memory element.

The simplest patterns contain only constant symbols and numbers. A pattern containing only constants matches a working memory element if every constant in the pattern occurs in the corresponding position in the working memory element. (Since patterns are partial descriptions, it is not necessary for every constant in the working memory element to occur in the pattern.) Thus the pattern

(Expression ↑Op * ↑Arg2 0)

would match the element

(Expression ↑Name Expr86 ↑Arg1 X ↑Op * ↑Arg2 0)

Many non-constant symbols are available in OPS5 for defining patterns, but the two most important are variables and predicates. A variable is a symbol that begins with the character '⟨' and ends with the character '⟩'—for example ⟨X⟩. A variable in a pattern will match any value in a working memory element, but if a variable occurs more than once in a production's LHS, all occurrences must match the same value. Thus the pattern

(Expression ↑Arg1 ⟨VAL⟩ ↑Arg2 ⟨VAL⟩)

would match either of the following

(Expression ↑Name Expr9 ↑Arg1 Expr23 ↑Op * ↑Arg2 Expr23)
(Expression ↑Name Expr5 ↑Arg1 0 ↑Op – ↑Arg2 0)

but it would not match

(Expression ↑Name Expr8 ↑Arg1 0 ↑Op * ↑Arg2 Expr23)

The predicates in OPS5 include = (equal), <> (not equal), < (less than), > (greater than), <= (less than or equal), and >= (greater than or equal). A predicate is placed between an attribute and a value to indicate that the value matched must be related in that way to the value in the pattern. For instance,

(Expression ↑Op <>*)

will match any expression whose operand is not *. Predicates can be used with variables as well as with constant values. For example, the following pattern

(Expression ↑Arg1 ⟨LEFT⟩ ↑Arg2 <> ⟨LEFT⟩)

will match any expression in which the first argument differs from the second argument.

The RHS of a production consists of an unconditional sequence of actions. The only actions that need to be described here are the ones that change working memory. MAKE builds a new element and adds it to working memory. The argument to MAKE is a pattern like the patterns in LHSs. For example,

(MAKE Expression ↑Name Expr1 ↑Arg1 1)

will build an expression whose name is Expr1, whose first argument is 1, and whose other attributes all have the value NIL (the default value in OPS5). MODIFY changes one or more values of an existing element. This action takes as arguments a pattern designator and a list of attribute-value pairs. The following action, for example

(MODIFY 2 ↑Op NIL ↑Arg2 NIL)

would take the expression matching the second pattern and change its operator and second argument to NIL. The action REMOVE deletes elements from working memory. It takes pattern designators as arguments. For example

(REMOVE 1 2 3)

would delete the elements matching the first three patterns in a production.

An OPS5 production consists of (1) the symbol P, (2) the name of the production, (3) the LHS, (4) the symbol -->, and (5) the RHS, with everything enclosed in parentheses. The following is a typical production.

```
(P Time 0x
    (Goal ↑Type Simplify ↑Object ⟨X⟩)
    (Expression ↑Name ⟨X⟩ ↑Arg1 0 ↑Op *)
-->
    (MODIFY 2 ↑Op NIL ↑Arg2 NIL))
```

1.2. Work on production system efficiency

Since execution speed has always been a major issue for production systems, several researchers have worked on the problem of efficiency. The most common approach has been to combine a process called *indexing* with direct interpretation of the LHSs. In the simplest form of indexing, the interpreter begins the match process by extracting one or more features from each working memory element, and uses those features to hash into the collection of productions. This produces a set of productions that might have satisfied LHSs. The interpreter examines each LHS in this set individually to determine whether it is in fact satisfied. A more efficient form of indexing adds memory to the process. A typical scheme involves storing a count with each pattern. The counts are all zero when execution of the system begins. When an element enters working memory, the indexing function is executed with the new element as its only input, and all the patterns that are reached have their counts increased by one. When an element leaves working memory, the index is again executed, and the patterns that are reached have their counts decreased by one. The interpreter performs the direct interpretation step only on those LHSs that have non-zero counts for all their patterns. Interpreters using this scheme—in some cases combined with other efficiency measures—have been described by McCracken [8], McDermott, Newell, and Moore [9], and Rychener [10].

The algorithm that will be presented here, the Rete Match Algorithm, can be described as an indexing scheme that does not require the interpretive step. The indexing function is represented as a network of simple feature recognizers. This representation is related to the graph representations for so-called structured patterns. (See for example [2] and [7]). The Rete algorithm was first described in 1974 [3]. A 1977 paper [4] described some rather complex interpreters for the networks of feature recognizers, including parallel interpreters and interpreters which delayed evaluation of patterns as long as possible. (Delaying evaluation is useful because it makes it less likely that patterns will be evaluated unnecessarily.) A 1979 paper [5] discussed simple but very fast interpreters for the networks. This article is based in large part on the 1979 paper.

2. The Rete Match Algorithm—Basic Concepts

In a production system interpreter, the output of the match process and the input to conflict resolution is a set called the *conflict set.* The conflict set is a collection of ordered pairs of the form

⟨Production, List of elements matched by its LHS⟩

The ordered pairs are called *instantiations.* The Rete Match Algorithm is an algorithm for computing the conflict set. That is, it is an algorithm to compare a set of LHSs to a set of elements in order to discover all the instantiations. The algorithm can efficiently process large sets because it does not iterate over the sets.

2.1. How to avoid iterating over working memory

A pattern matcher can avoid iterating over the elements in working memory by storing information between cycles. The step that can require iteration is determining whether a given pattern matches any of the working memory elements. The simplest interpreters determine this by comparing the pattern to the elements one by one. The iteration can be avoided by storing, with each pattern, a list of the elements that it matches. The lists are updated when working memory changes. When an element enters working memory, the interpreter finds all the patterns that match it and adds it to their lists. When an element leaves working memory, the interpreter again finds all the patterns that match it and deletes it from their lists.

Since pattern matchers using the Rete algorithm save this kind of information, they never have to examine working memory. The pattern matcher can be viewed as a black box with one input and one output.

(Changes to Working Memory)

↓

Black Box

↓

(Changes to the Conflict Set)

The box receives information about the changes that are made to working memory, and it determines the changes that must be made in the conflict set to keep it consistent. For example, the black box might be told that the element

(Goal ↑Type Simplify ↑Object Expr19)

has been added to working memory, and it might respond that production TimexN has just become instantiated.

2.1.1. *Tokens*

The descriptions of working memory changes that are passed into the black box are called *tokens.* A token is an ordered pair of a *tag* and a list of data elements. In the simplest implementations of the Rete Match Algorithm, only two tags are needed, + and −. The tag + indicates that something has been added to working memory. The tag − indicates that something has been deleted from working memory. When an element is modified, two tokens are sent to the black box; one token indicates that the old form of the element has been deleted from working memory, and the other that the new form of the element has been added. For example, if

(Expression ↑Name Expr41 ↑Arg1 Y ↑Op + ↑Arg2 Y)

was changed to

(Expression ↑Name Expr41 ↑Arg1 2 ↑Op * ↑Arg2 Y)

the following two tokens would be processed.

⟨−(Expression ↑Name Expr41 ↑Arg1 Y ↑Op + ↑Arg2 Y)⟩
⟨+(Expression ↑Name Expr41 ↑Arg1 2 ↑Op * ↑Arg2 Y)⟩

2.2. How to avoid iterating over production memory

The Rete algorithm avoids iterating over the set of productions by using a tree-structured sorting network or index for the productions. The network, which is compiled from the patterns, is the principal component of the black box. The following sections explain how patterns are compiled into networks and how the networks perform the functions of the black box.

2.2.1. *Compiling the patterns*

When a pattern matcher processes a working memory element, it tests many features of the element. The features can be divided into two classes. The first class, which could be called the intra-element features, are the ones that involve only one working memory element. For an example of these features, consider the following pattern.

(Expression ↑Name ⟨N⟩ ↑Arg1 0 ↑Op + ↑Arg2 ⟨X⟩)

When the pattern matcher processes this pattern, it tries to find working memory elements having the following intra-element features.

- The class of the element must be Expression.
- The value of the Arg1 attribute must be the number 0.
- The value of the Op attribute must be the atom +.

The other class of features, the inter-element features, results from having a variable occur in more than one pattern. Consider Plus0x's LHS.

```
(P Plus0x
    (Goal   ↑Type Simplify   ↑Object ⟨N⟩)
    (Expression   ↑Name ⟨N⟩   ↑Arg1 0   ↑Op +   ↑Arg2 ⟨X⟩)
-->· · ·)
```

The intra-element features for the second pattern are listed above. A similar list can be constructed for the first pattern. But in addition to those two lists, the following inter-element feature is necessary because the variable ⟨N⟩ occurs twice.

- The value of the Object attribute of the goal must be equal to the value of the Name attribute of the expression.

The pattern compiler builds a network by linking together nodes which test elements for these features. When the compiler processes an LHS, it begins with the intra-element features. It determines the intra-element features that each pattern requires and builds a linear sequence of nodes for the pattern. Each node tests for the presence of one feature. After the compiler finishes with the intra-element features, it builds nodes to test for the inter-element features. Each of the nodes has two inputs so that it can join two paths in the network into one. The first of the two-input nodes joins the linear sequences for the first two patterns, the second two-input nodes joins the output of the first with the sequence for the third pattern, and so on. The two-input nodes test every inter-element feature that applies to the elements they process. Finally, after the two-input nodes, the compiler builds a special terminal node to represent the production. This node is attached to the last of the two-input nodes. Fig. 1 shows the network for Plus0x and the similar production Time0x. Note that when two LHSs require identical nodes, the compiler shares parts of the network rather than building duplicate nodes.

2.2.2. *Processing in the network*

The root node of the network (at the top in Fig. 1) is the input to the black box. This node receives the tokens that are sent to the black box and passes copies of the tokens to all its successors. The successors of the top node, the nodes to perform the intra-element tests, have one input and one or more outputs. Each node tests one feature and sends the tokens that pass the test to its successors. The two-input nodes compare tokens from different paths and join them into bigger tokens if they satisfy the inter-element constraints of the LHS. Because of the tests performed by the other nodes, a terminal node will receive only tokens that instantiate the LHS. The terminal node sends out of the black box the information that the conflict set must be changed.

For an example of the operation of the nodes, consider what happens in the network in Fig. 1 when the following two elements are put into an empty working memory.

```
(Goal   ↑Type Simplify   ↑Object Expr17)
(Expression   ↑Name Expr17   ↑Arg1 0   ↑Op *   ↑Arg2 X)
```

First the token

⟨+(Goal ↑Type Simplify ↑Object Expr17)⟩

is created and sent to the root of the network. This node sends the token to its successors. One of the successors (on the right in Fig. 1) tests it and rejects it because its class is not Expression. This node does not pass the token to its successor. The other successor of the top node accepts the token (because its class is Goal) and so sends it to its successor. That node also accepts the token (since its type is Simplify), and it sends the token to its successors, the two-input nodes. Since no other tokens have arrived at the two-input nodes, they can perform no tests; they must just store the token and wait.

When the token

⟨+(Expression ↑Name Expr17 ↑Arg1 0 ↑Op * ↑Arg2 X)⟩

is processed, it is tested by the one-input nodes and passed down to the right input of Time0x's two-input node. This node compares the new token to the earlier one, and finding that they allow the variable to be bound consistently, it creates and sends out the token

```
⟨+(Goal   ↑Type Simplify   ↑Object Expr17)
  (Expression   ↑Name Expr17   ↑Arg1 0   ↑Op *   ↑Arg2 X)⟩
```

```
(P PlusOx
        (Goal   ↑Type Simplify   ↑Object (N))
        (Expression   ↑Name (N)   ↑Arg1 0   ↑Op +   ↑Arg2 (X))
-->     · · ·)

(P TimeOx
        (Goal   ↑Type Simplify   ↑Object (N))
        (Expression   ↑Name (N)   ↑Arg1 0   ↑Op *   ↑Arg2 (X))
-->     · · ·)
```

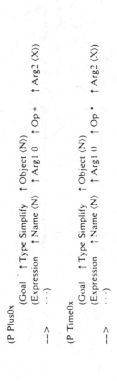

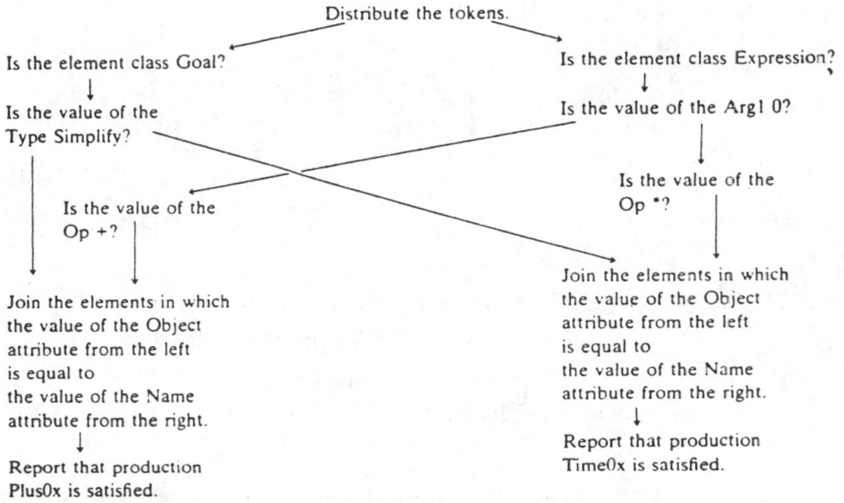

Distribute the tokens.
Is the element class Goal?
Is the value of the Type Simplify?
Is the value of the Op +?
Join the elements in which the value of the Object attribute from the left is equal to the value of the Name attribute from the right.
Report that production PlusOx is satisfied.
Is the element class Expression?
Is the value of the Arg1 0?
Is the value of the Op *?
Join the elements in which the value of the Object attribute from the left is equal to the value of the Name attribute from the right.
Report that production TimeOx is satisfied.

FIG. 1. The network for PlusOx and TimeOx.

When its successor, the terminal node for TimeOx, receives this token, it adds the instantiation of TimeOx to the conflict set.

2.2.3. *Saving information in the network*

As explained above, the black box must maintain state information because it must know what is in working memory. In simple Rete networks all such state is stored by the two-input nodes. Each two-input node contains two lists called its left and right memories. The left memory holds copies of the tokens that arrived at its left input, and the right memory holds copies of the tokens that arrived at its right input. The tokens are stored as long as they are useful. The next section explains how the nodes determine when the tokens are no longer useful.

2.2.4. *Using the tags*

The tag in a token indicates how the state information is to be changed when the token is processed. The + and − tokens are processed identically except:

- The terminal nodes use the tags to determine whether to add an instantiation to the conflict set or to remove an existing instantiation. When a + token is processed, an instantiation is added; when a − token is processed, an instantiation is removed.
- The two-input nodes use the tags to determine how to modify their internal memories. When a + token is processed, it is stored in the internal memory; when a − token is processed, a token with an identical data part is deleted.
- The two-input nodes use the tags to determine the appropriate tags for the tokens they build. When a new output is created, it is given the tag of the token that just arrived at the two-input node.

2.3. Completing the set of node types

The network in Fig. 1 contained four kinds of nodes: the root node, the terminal nodes, the one-input nodes, and the two-input nodes. Certainly one could define many more kinds of nodes, but only a few more are necessary to have a complete and useful set. In fact, only two more kinds of nodes are necessary to interpret OPS5.

A second kind of two-input node is needed for negated patterns (that is, patterns preceded by −). The new two-input node stores a count with each token in its left memory. The count indicates the number of tokens in the right memory that allow consistent variable bindings. The tokens in its right memory contain the elements that match the negated pattern—or, more precisely, the tokens contain the elements that have the intra-element features that the negated pattern requires. The node allows the tokens with a count of zero to pass.

The last node type that needs to be defined is a variant of the one-input nodes described earlier. Those nodes tested working memory elements for constant features (testing, for example, whether a value was equal to a given atomic symbol). The new one-input nodes compare two values from a working memory element. These nodes are used to process patterns that contain two or more occurrences of a variable. The following, for example, would require one of these nodes because ⟨X⟩ occurs twice.

(Expression   ↑Arg1 ⟨X⟩   ↑Op +   ↑Arg2 ⟨X⟩)

3. Representing the Network and the Tokens

This section describes representations for tokens and nodes that allow very fast interpreters to be written.

3.1. Working memory elements

The representation chosen for the working memory elements should have two properties.

- The representation should make it easy to extract values from elements because every test involves extracting one or more values.
- The representation should make it easy to perform the tests once the values are available.

To make extracting the values easy, each element should be stored in a contiguous block in memory, and each attribute should have a designated index in the block. For example, if elements of class Ck had seventeen attributes, A1 through A17, they should be stored as blocks of eighteen values. The first value would be the class name (Ck). The second value would be the value of attribute A1. The third would be the value of attribute A2, and so on. The particular assignment of indices to attributes is unimportant; it is important only that each attribute have a fixed index, and that the indices be assigned at compile time. This allows the compiler to build the indices into the nodes. Thus instead of a node like the following:

Is the value of the Status attribute Pending?

the compiler could build the node

Is the value at location 8 Pending?

With this representation, each value can be accessed in one memory reference, regardless of the number of attributes possessed by an element.

To make the tests inexpensive, the representation should have explicit type bits. One obvious way to represent a value is to use one word for the type and one or more words for the value proper. But more space-efficient representations are also possible. For example, consider a production system language that supports three data types, integers, floating point numbers, and atoms. A representation like the following might be used: One word would be allocated to each value. For integers and atoms, the low order sixteen (say) bits would hold the datum and the seventeenth bit would be a type bit. For floating point numbers, the entire word would be used to store a normalized floating point number. A floating point number would be recognized by having at least one non-zero in the high order bits.

3.2. The network

This section explains how to represent nodes in a form similar to von Neumann machine instructions. This representation was chosen because it allows the network interpreter to be organized like the interpreters for conventional von Neumann architectures.

3.2.1. *An assembly language notation*

To make it easier to discuss the representation for the nodes, an assembly language notation is used below. A one-input node like

Is the value of locating 8 Pending?

becomes

TEQA 8, Pending

The T, which stands for test, indicates that this is a one-input node. The EQ indicates that it is a test for equality. (It is also necessary to have NE for not equals, LT for less than, etc.). The A indicates the node tests data of type atom. (There is also a type N for integer values, a type F for floating point, and a type S for comparing two values in the same working memory element). Two-input nodes are indicated by lines like the following.

L001 AND (2) = (1)

L001 is a label. AND indicates that this is a two-input node for non-negated patterns. The sequence (2) = (1) indicates that the node compares the second value of elements from the left and the first value of elements from the right; the = indicates that it performs a test for equality. The terminal nodes contain the type TERM and the name of the production. For example

TERM Plus0x

As will be explained below, the ROOT node is not needed in this representation.

3.2.2. *Linearizing the network*

To make the nodes like the instructions for a von Neumann machine, it is necessary to eliminate the explicit links between nodes. Many of the explicit links can be eliminated simply by linearizing the network, placing a node and its successor in contiguous memory locations. However, since some nodes have more than one successor, and others (the two-input nodes) have more than one predecessor, linearizing is not sufficient in itself: two new node types must be defined to replace some of the links. The first of the new nodes, the FORK, is used to indicate that a node has more than one successor. The FORK node contains the address of one of the successors. The other successor is placed immediately after the FORK. For example, the FORK in the following indicates that the node L003 has two successors.

```
L003  TEQA 0, Expression
      FORK L004
      TEQA 3, +
      . . .
L004  TEQA 3, *
```

The other new node type, the MERGE, is used where the network has to grow back together—that is, before two-input nodes. The two-input node is placed after one of its predecessors (say its left predecessor) and the MERGE is placed after the other. The MERGE, which contains the address of the two-input node, functions much like an unconditional jump. Fig. 2 shows the effect of the linearization process; it contains the productions from Fig. 1 and the linearized network for their LHSs.

3.2.3. *Representing the nodes in memory*

This section shows how the nodes could be represented on a computer which has a thirty-two bit word length. The thirty-two bit word length was chosen because it is typical of today's computers; the precise word length is not critical, however. Since the network can be rooted at a FORK (see the example in Fig. 2) it is not necessary to have an explicit root node for the network. Hence only seven classes of nodes are needed; FORKs, MERGEs, the two kinds of one-input nodes, the two kinds of two-input nodes, and the terminal nodes.

FORKs and MERGEs could be represented as single words. Six bits could be used for a type field (that is, a field to indicate what the word represents) and the remaining twenty-six bits could be used for the address of the node pointed to. FORKs and MERGEs would thus be represented:

TYPE	ADDRESS
(6 bits)	(26 bits)

Both kinds of one-input nodes could be represented as single words that are divided into three fields. The first field would hold the type of the node. The second field would hold the index of the value to test. The third field would hold either a constant or a second index. The bits in a word could be allocated as follows.

TYPE	INDEX	CONSTANT or INDEX
(6 bits)	(10 bits)	(16 bits)

A sixteen-bit field is required to represent an integer or an atom using the format of Section 3.1. Since a floating point number cannot be represented in sixteen bits, in nodes that test floating point numbers, this field would hold not the number, but the address of the number.

```
(P Plus0x
        (Goal   ↑Type Simplify   ↑Object (N))
        (Expression   ↑Name (N)   ↑Arg1 0   ↑Op +   ↑Arg2 (X))
-->     ...)

(P Time0x
        (Goal   ↑Type Simplify   ↑Object (N))
        (Expression   ↑Name (N)   ↑Arg1 0   ↑Op *   ↑Arg2 (X))
-->     ...)


ROOT    FORK L003               ; Root node of the network
        TEQA 0, Goal            ; Is the element class Goal?
        TEQA 1, Simplify        ; Is the Type Simplify?
        FORK L002
L001    AND (2) = (1)           ; Two-input node for Plus0x
        TERM Plus0x             ; Report Plus0x is satisfied
L002    AND (2) = (1)           ; Two-input node for Time0x
        TERM Time0x             ; Report Time0x is satisfied
L003    TEQA 0, Expression      ; Is the element class Expression?
        TEQN 2, 0               ; Is the Arg1 0?
        Fork L004
        TEQA 3, +               ; Is the Op +?
        MERGE L001
L004    TEQA 3, *               ; Is the Op *?
        MERGE L002
```

FIG. 2. A compiled network.

The terminal nodes could also be stored in single words. These nodes contain two fields, the usual type field plus a longer field for the index or address of the production that the node represents.

TYPE	PRODUCTION
(6 bits)	(26 bits)

The length of a two-input node would depend on the number of value pairs tested by the node. Each node could have one word of basic information plus one word for each value pair. The first word would contain a type field, a pointer to the memory for the left input, a pointer to the memory for the right input, and a field indicating how many tests are performed by the node. The bits in the word could be allocated as follows.

TYPE	COUNT	MEMORY POINTER	MEMORY POINTER
(6 bits)	(4 bits)	(11 bits)	(11 bits)

The word for each test would contain three fields. Two fields would hold the indices of the two elements to test. The remaining field would indicate the test to perform; that is, it would indicate whether the node is to test for equality of the two elements, for inequality, or for something else. The bits in the word might be allocated as follows.

```
 _____________________________________________________________________
|           |                         |                               |
|   TEST    |          INDEX          |             INDEX             |
|           |                         |                               |
|_|_|_|_|_|_|_|_|_|_|_|_|_|_|_|_|_|_|_|_|_|_|_|_|_|_|_|_|_|_|_|_|_|_|_|
  (6 bits)          (13 bits)                   (13 bits)
```

Note that the index fields here are longer than the index fields in the one-input nodes. This is necessary because the indices in the two-input nodes must designate elements in the tokens as well as values in the elements.

3.3. The tokens

This section describes a space-efficient representation for tokens. This representation is not suitable for all interpreters; it requires the interpreter to process only one working memory change at a time, and it requires that certain parts of the network be traversed depth first. Fortunately, these are not serious restrictions. The simplest way to perform the match is process one token at a time, traversing the entire network depth first. Section 4 describes an interpreter that operates in this manner.

If the interpreter operates this way, then it can use a stack to represent its tokens. When a token has to be built, first the tag for the token is pushed onto the stack, and then the working memory elements are pushed onto the stack in order. When tokens have to be extended (a very common operation—see the code in Section 4) the additional working memory elements are just pushed onto the stack.

The one-input nodes will be more efficient if they do not use this stack. Since all the one-input nodes will process the same working memory element—the element that was just added to or deleted from working memory—the element should be made easily available. The element could be copied into a dedicated location in memory, or the address of the element could be loaded into a dedicated base register. Either of these would make it possible for the one-input nodes to access the element without going through the stack.

3.4. The interpreter's state

In addition to the stack for tokens, the interpreter must maintain another stack for its state information. One reason for the stack is to allow the interpreter to find its way about in the network. When the interpreter passes a FORK, it pushes the pointer it does not follow onto the stack. Then when it reaches the end of a path it pops a pointer from the stack and follows it. Another reason for the stack is to provide a place for the two-input nodes to keep their local information. As will be seen in the next section, the two-input nodes sometimes have to suspend themselves while their successors are processed. The stack holds the information that is needed to resume processing the two-input nodes.

4. The Network Interpreter

This section provides a concrete description of the operations performed by the network interpreter. One node from each class has been selected, and the code to interpret the nodes has been written. It might be noted that since the code sequences are short and simple, they could easily be written in microcode.

The code is written in a PASCAL-like language which has literal labels and field extraction. Field extraction is indicated by putting two numbers within angle brackets; the first number is the index of the high order bit in the field, and the second number is the index of the low order bit. The assumption will be made that the bits are numbered from right to left, with the low order bit being bit zero. Thus the expression SELF⟨31:26⟩ indicates that the high order six bits of the value of the variable SELF are to be extracted and right justified.

The main loop of the interpreter is very simple: the interpreter fetches the next node from memory and dispatches on its type field. Let the segment of memory that holds the nodes be called NODE_MEMORY and let the pointer to the current node be called NC. The main loop is then:

```
MAIN:   SELF := NODE_MEMORY[NC];
        CASE SELF⟨31:26⟩ OF    !Type field is high order 6 bits
          0: GOTO FORK;
          1: GOTO MERGE;
          2: GOTO TERM;
          3: GOTO TEQA;
          . . .
          END;
```

The node is copied into the variable SELF so that the node programs can examine it. The assignment of numbers to the various node types is arbitrary. Goto's are used instead of procedure calls because these examples make all the state of the interpreter explicit, and not hidden in PASCAL's stack.

TEQA is typical of the one-input nodes for testing constants. If the segment of memory that holds the working memory element being processed is called CURRENT, then TEQA is as follows.

```
TEQA:   TEMP := CURRENT[SELF⟨25:16⟩];        !Get the word pointed to
                                             !by the index field
```

```
IF (TEMP⟨31:16⟩ = 0) AND          !Test type bits
   (TEMP⟨15:0⟩ = SELF⟨15:0⟩)      !Test value
THEN GOTO SUCC
ELSE GOTO FAIL:
```

Either SUCC or FAIL is executed after each one-input node. SUCC is executed when the test succeeds, and FAIL is executed when the test fails. SUCC increments the node counter to point to the next node.

```
SUCC:  NC := NC + 1;
       GOTO MAIN;
```

FAIL tries to get a node from the stack of unprocessed nodes; if it cannot, it halts the match. Assuming the stack is named NS and the pointer to the top of the stack is called NSTOP, the code is:

```
FAIL:  IF NSTOP < 0 THEN GOTO EXIT_MATCH;
       NC := NS[NSTOP];
       NSTOP := NSTOP - 1;
       GOTO MAIN;
```

The one-input nodes for comparing pairs of values are similar to the other one-input nodes. TEQS is typical of these nodes.

```
TEQS:  IF CURRENT[SELF⟨25:16⟩] = CURRENT[SELF⟨9:0⟩]
       THEN GOTO SUCC
       ELSE GOTO FAIL;
```

FORK pushes an address onto NS and then passes control to the following node.

```
FORK:  NSTOP := NSTOP + 1;
       NS[NSTOP] := SELF⟨25:0⟩;
       GOTO SUCC;
```

A two-input node must be able to determine whether it was reached over its left input or its right input. This can be indicated to the node by a global variable which usually has the value LEFT, but which is temporarily set to RIGHT when a MERGE passes control to a two-input node. If this global variable is called DIRECTION, the code for the MERGE is

```
MERGE:  DIRECTION := RIGHT;
        NC := SELF⟨25:0⟩;
        GOTO MAIN;
```

The two kinds of two-input nodes are very similar, so only AND is shown here. In order not to obscure the more important information, some details of the program are omitted. The code does not show how the variables are tested, nor does it show how tokens are added to and removed from the node's memories. Assuming the token stack is called TS and the pointer to the top element is called TSTOP, the program is as follows.

```
!  Control can reach this point many times during the processing
!  of a token. The node needs to update its state and put
!  information on NS only once, however.
!
AND:IF NS[NSTOP] <> NC                          !If the state is not in NS
      THEN                                      !Then put it there
        BEGIN
        NSTOP := NSTOP + 4;
        NS[NSTOP] := NC;
        NS[NSTOP - 1] := DIRECTION;
        NS[NSTOP - 2] := MEMORY_CONTENTS
                           (OPPOSITE(DIRECTION));
        NS[NSTOP - 3] := TSTOP;
        MODIFY_MEMORY(DIRECTION);               !Store the token
        DIRECTION := LEFT;                      !Reset to the default
        END;
!
!  Go process the tokens
!
      IF NS[NSTOP] - 1] = RIGHT THEN GOTO RLOOP
        ELSE GOTO LLOOP;
!  Compare the token to the elements in the right memory
!
LLOOP:  REPEAT
            TEMP := NEXT_POSITION(NS[NSTOP - 2]);
            IF TEMP = NIL                       !If right memory is empty
            THEN                                !Then clean up and exit
              BEGIN
              TSTOP := NS[NSTOP - 3];
              NSTOP := NSTOP - 4;
              GOTO FAIL;
              END
          UNTIL PERFORM_AND_TEST(TEMP,LEFT);
!
!  Fall out of the loop when the test succeeds so that
!  the successors of this node can be activated
!
```

```
        !Extend the token
        TSTOP := NS[NSTOP - 3] + 1; TS[NSTOP] := TEMP;
        !Prepare NS so that control will return to this node
        NSTOP := NSTOP + 1; NS[NSTOP] := NC;
        !Pass control to the successors of this node
        NC := NC + SELF(25:22) + 1; GOTO MAIN;
!
! Compare the token the elements in the left memory
!
RLOOP:
```

This is similar to LLOOP.

The only remaining node type is the TERM node. Since updating the conflict set is a language-dependent operation, that detail of the TERM node cannot be shown. The rest of the processing of the node is as follows.

```
TERM:  UPDATE_CONFLICT_SET(SELF(25 : 0));
       GOTO FAIL;
```

5. Performance of the Algorithm

Extensive studies have been made of the efficiency of the Rete Match Algorithm. Both analytical studies (which determined the time and space complexity of the algorithm) and empirical studies have been made. This section presents some of the results of the analytical studies. Because of space constraints, it was not possible to present the empirical results or the proofs of the analytical results. The proofs and detailed results of some empirical studies can be found in [5].

Table 1 summarizes the results of the analytical studies of the algorithm. The usual notation for asymptotic complexity is used in this table [1]. Writing that a cost is $O(f(x))$ indicates that the cost varies as $f(x)$ plus perhaps some smaller terms in x. The smaller terms are ignored because the $f(x)$ term will dominate when x is large. Writing that a cost is O(1) indicates that the cost is unaffected by the factor being considered. It should be noted that all the complexity results in Table 1 sharp; production systems achieving the bounds are described in [5].

TABLE 1. Space and time complexity

Complexity measure	Best case	Worst case
Effect of working memory size on number of tokens	O(1)	$O(W^C)$
Effect of production memory size on number of nodes	$O(P)$	$O(P)$
Effect of production memory size on number of tokens	O(1)	$O(P)$
Effect of working memory size on time for one firing	O(1)	$O(W^{2C-1})$
Effect of production memory size on time for one firing	$O(\log_2 P)$	$O(P)$

C is the number of patterns in a production.
P is the number of productions in production memory.
W is the number of elements in working memory.

6. Conclusions

The Rete Match Algorithm is a method for comparing a set of patterns to a set of objects in order to determine all the possible matches. It was described in detail in this article because enough evidence has been accumulated since its development in 1974 to make it clear that it is an efficient algorithm which has many possible applications.

The algorithm is efficient even when it processes large sets of patterns and objects, because it does not iterate over the sets. In this algorithm, the patterns are compiled into a program to perform the match process. The program does not have to iterate over the patterns because it contains a tree-structured sorting network or index for the patterns. It does not have to iterate over the data because it maintains state information: the program computes the matches and partial matches for each object when it enters the data memory, and it stores the information as long as the object remains in the memory.

Although the Rete algorithm was developed for use in production system interpreters, it can be used for other purposes as well. If there is anything unusual about the pattern matching of production systems, it is only that the pattern matching takes place on an unusually large scale. Production systems contain rather ordinary patterns and data objects, but they contain large numbers of them, and invocations of the pattern matcher occur very frequently during execution. If programs of other kinds begin to use pattern matching more heavily, they could have the same efficiency problems as production systems, and it could be necessary to use methods like the Rete Match Algorithm in their interpreters as well. Certainly the algorithm should not be used for all match problems; its use is indicated only if the following three conditions are satisfied.

- The patterns must be compilable. It must be possible to examine them and determine a list of features like the lists in Section 2.2.1.
- The objects must be constant. They cannot contain variables or other non-constants as patterns can.
- The set of objects must change relatively slowly. Since the algorithm maintains state between cycles, it is inefficient in situations where most of the data changes on each cycle.

ACKNOWLEDGMENT

The author would like to thank Allen Newell and Robert Sproull for many useful discussions concerning this work, and Allen Newell, John McDermott, and Michael Rychener for their valuable comments on earlier versions of this article.

REFERENCES

1. Aho, A.V., Hopcroft, J.E., and Ullman, J.D., *The Design and Analysis of Computer Algorithms* (Addison-Wesley, Reading, MA, 1974).
2. Cohen, B.L., A powerful and efficient structural pattern recognition system, *Artificial Intelligence* **9** (1977) 223–255.
3. Forgy, C.L., A network match routine for production systems, Working Paper, 1974.
4. Forgy, C.L., A production system monitor for parallel computers, Department of Computer Science, Carnegie-Mellon University, 1977.
5. Forgy, C.L., On the efficient implementation of production systems. Ph.D. Thesis, Carnegie-Mellon University, 1979.
6. Forgy, C.L., OPS5 user's manual, Department of Computer Science, Carnegie-Mellon University, 1981.
7. Hayes-Roth, F. and Mostow, D.J., An automatically compilable recognition network for structured patterns, *Proc. Fourth Internat. Joint Conference on Artificial Intelligence* (1975) 246–251.
8. McCracken, D., A production system version of the Hearsay-II speech understanding system, Ph.D. Thesis, Carnegie-Mellon University, 1978.
9. McDermott, J., Newell, A., and Moore, J., The efficiency of certain production system implementations, in: Waterman, D.A. and Hayes-Roth, F. (Eds.), *Pattern-Directed Inference Systems* (Academic Press, New York, 1978) 155–176.
10. Rychener, M.D., Production systems as a programming language for Artificial Intelligence applications, Ph.D. Thesis, Carnegie-Mellon University, 1976.

Received May 1980; revised version received April 1981

3.4 Data/Knowledge Management Systems

This section presents papers that describe prototype implementations of DBMSs, extended DBMSs, and knowledge-base–management systems. Many DBMSs have been developed. Conventional DBMSs include IBM's System R [ABCE76], [CABG81] and the University of California at Berkeley's (UCB's) INGRES [SWKH76], [STON80]. Distributed DBMSs included Computer Corporation of America's (CCA's) SDD-1 [RBF80], DDM [CDFG83], and MULTIBASE [LR82]; as well as IBM's R* [DSHL82], [WDHL82], and [LHMW82]. DBMSs based on extended data models include CCA's ADAPLEX (descibed in [Chan et al., 3.4.2]) and IBM's DEDUCE [CHAN78], which is based on logic. Object-oriented and extensible prototype DBMSs include CCA's PROBE [MD86]; UCB's Postgres (described in [Stonebraker, 3.4.4], [SR86], and [STON86a]); IBM's Starburst [LMP87]; and the University of Wisconsin's EXODUS [CDFG86], [GD87].

Due to the lack of emphasis on system building in AI (compared with in the database area), AI systems tend to be less generic (i.e., applicable to a smaller problem domain) and less robust than are their database counterparts. Prototype AI systems include MYCIN [SHOR76], OPS [FM77], INTERNIST [MPM84], ASK [TT83], KL-ONE [BS85], TAXIS [MGBM86], STROBE-IMPULSE [SC86], ISIS [FS84], KODIAK [WILE84], and ARGON [PBL84]. There are now over 400 commercial DBMSs (e.g., IBM's DB2, Relational Technology's INGRES, and Oracle's Oracle) and hundreds of commercial knowledge-base–system and expert system shells (e.g., Intellicorp's KEE, Carnegie Group's Knowledge Kraft, Tecknowledge's S.1, Inference Corporation's ART).

The first paper in this section (3.4.1) is "System R: Relational Approach to Database Management" by Morton Astrahan and the System R team at IBM San Jose. It describes System R, one of the most ambitious and successful DBMS implementation projects, started in 1974 and completed in 1979–1980. In 1980–1981, 10 years after Codd's original paper [CODD70], System R evolved into an IBM product, SQL/Data System, which ran in the DOS/VSE operating-system environment. Only in 1985 did IBM release DB2, the relational DBMS that runs in most IBM environments and is coming to dominate the DBMS market. [CABG81] describes the history and evaluation of the System R project. System R became the base from which subsequent IBM DBMS projects sprang (i.e., R*, a distributed DBMS; Starburst [LMP87], an extensible DBMS).

The second paper (3.4.2) is "Storage and Access Structures to Support a Semantic Data Model" by Arvola Chan and the ADAPLEX project team at CCA. It describes the implementation of ADAPLEX, an extension of ADA that provides database facilities. This paper is a sequel to [Shipman, 2.2.2] since the DAPLEX model and query language were adopted for the design of ADAPLEX [SFL83], [FLRR84]. ADAPLEX was one of the few DBMSs to be built based on a semantic data model prior to the wave, starting in 1986, of extensible and object-oriented DBMSs. CCA attempted but failed to turn ADAPLEX into a commercial product. During the developement of the ADAPLEX product, the semantic data-model interface was replaced with SQL, the standard language for relational DBMSs. The information-systems world was not ready, in 1987, for powerful semantic data models and languages. Similarly, a Burroughs commercial DBMS, based in part on a semantic data model [HM81], has not been widely accepted. ADAPLEX, or more strictly DAPLEX, became the base for subsequent CCA DBMS projects (e.g., distributed DBMSs, SDD-1, DDM, and MULTIBASE; and the object-oriented, extensible DBMS PROBE).

The third paper (3.4.3) is "A Modular Toolkit for Knowledge Management" by Gilles Lafue and Reid Smith of the STROBE-IMPULSE team at Schlumberger. It describes the user environment developed around the knowledge-representation language STROBE, initially designed and implemented by the second author at the Schlumberger–Dole research lab. The environment, intended for the developer of knowledge-based systems, includes database-management facilities such as an integrity checker and a file manager [LAFU85]. The STROBE system and its environment are being used routinely by Schlumberger in the development of knowledge-based systems for oil-drilling applications. [SC86] offers a comprehensive account of the STROBE programming environment. In 1987–1988, Schlumberger worked with Sun Microsystems to transfer the STROBE-IMPULSE system into a Sun knowledge-base–system shell product called the Symbolic Programming Environment (SPE).

The section ends with two relatively recent papers describing advanced DBMSs knowledge-base–management systems. Research in this general area is described in [Brodie and Manola, 1.1]. The fourth paper in this section (3.4.4) is Mike Stonebraker's "Inclusion of New Types in

Relational Database Systems." It describes a key aspect of extending a DBMS to handle a wider class of data structures. It provides rather atypical facilities for adding new data types to the data model and for supporting POSTGRES DBMS. The POSTGRES project, based at the UCB, is an extension of the INGRES project, which resulted in one of the most successful implementations of a relational DBMS. The theme of the POSTGRES project is to develop a more powerful DBMS, offering a variety of features (e.g., rule processing, abstract data types, extensibility) required to support new application domains such as AI and engineering. [SR86] presents an overview of some of the features under consideration and of their proposed implementation.

The fifth and final paper of the section (3.4.5) is Jorge Bocca's "On the Evaluation Strategy of EDUCE." It describes an advanced DBMS and knowledge-base–management system consisting of a deductive database front end coupled to a conventional relational DBMS, INGRES. EDUCE is running at the European Computer-Industry Research Centre (ECRC). It is providing a base for further investigations of coupling of deductive and conventional DBMSs, and for supporting advanced, logic-based knowledge-base systems. [BDNV86] presents an overview of this and related ECRC projects.

System R: Relational Approach to Database Management

M. M. ASTRAHAN, M. W. BLASGEN, D. D. CHAMBERLIN,
K. P. ESWARAN, J. N. GRAY, P. P. GRIFFITHS,
W. F. KING, R. A. LORIE, P. R. McJONES, J. W. MEHL,
G. R. PUTZOLU, I. L. TRAIGER, B. W. WADE, AND V. WATSON

IBM Research Laboratory

System R is a database management system which provides a high level relational data interface. The system provides a high level of data independence by isolating the end user as much as possible from underlying storage structures. The system permits definition of a variety of relational views on common underlying data. Data control features are provided, including authorization, integrity assertions, triggered transactions, a logging and recovery subsystem, and facilities for maintaining data consistency in a shared-update environment.

This paper contains a description of the overall architecture and design of the system. At the present time the system is being implemented and the design evaluated. We emphasize that System R is a vehicle for research in database architecture, and is not planned as a product.

Key Words and Phrases: database, relational model, nonprocedural language, authorization, locking, recovery, data structures, index structures
CR categories: 3.74, 4.22, 4.33, 4.35

CONTENTS

1. INTRODUCTION
   Architecture and System Structure
2. THE RELATIONAL DATA SYSTEM
   Host Language Interface
   Query Facilities
   Data Manipulation Facilities
   Data Definition Facilities
   Data Control Facilities
   The Optimizer
   Modifying Cursors
   Simulation of Nonrelational Data Models
3. THE RELATIONAL STORAGE SYSTEM
   Segments
   Relations
   Images
   Links
   Transaction Management
   Concurrency Control
   System Checkpoint and Restart
4. SUMMARY AND CONCLUSION
APPENDIX I. RDI Operators
APPENDIX II. SEQUEL Syntax
APPENDIX III. RSI Operators
ACKNOWLEDGMENTS
REFERENCES

1. INTRODUCTION

The relational model of data was introduced by Codd [7] in 1970 as an approach toward providing solutions to various problems in database management. In particular, Codd addressed the problems of providing a data model or view which is divorced from various implementation considerations (the data independence problem) and also the problem of providing the database user with a very high level, nonprocedural data sublanguage for accessing data.

To a large extent, the acceptance and value of the relational approach hinges on the demonstration that a system can be built which can be used in a real environment to solve real problems and has performance at least comparable to today's existing systems. The purpose of this paper is to describe the overall architecture and design aspects of an experimental prototype database management system called System R, which is currently being implemented and evaluated at the IBM San Jose Research Laboratory. At the time of this writing, the design has been completed and major portions of the system are implemented and running. However, the overall system is not completed. We plan a complete performance evaluation of the system which will be available in later papers.

The System R project is not the first implementation of the relational approach [12, 30]. On the other hand, we know of no other relational system which provides a complete database management capability—including application programming as well as query capability, concurrent access support, system recovery, etc. Other relational systems have focused on, and demonstrated, feasibility of techniques for solving various specific problems. For example, the IS/1 system [22] demonstrated the feasibility of supporting the relational algebra [8] and also developed optimization techniques for evaluating algebraic expressions [29]. Techniques for optimization of the relational algebra have also been developed by Smith and Chang at the University of Utah [27]. The extended relational memory (XRM) system [19] developed at the IBM Cambridge Scientific Center has been used as a single user access method by other relational systems [2]. The SEQUEL prototype [1] was originally developed as a single-user system to demonstrate the feasibility of supporting the SEQUEL [5] language. However, this system has been extended by the IBM Cambridge Scientific Center and the MIT Sloan School Energy Laboratory to allow a simple type of concurrency and is being used as a component of the Generalized Management Information System (GMIS) [9] being developed at MIT for energy related applications. The INGRES project [16] being developed at the University of California, Berkeley, has demonstrated techniques for the decomposition of relational expressions in the QUEL language into "one-variable

Authors' address: IBM Research Laboratory, San Jose, CA 95193.

queries." Also, this system has investigated the use of query modification [28] for enforcing integrity constraints and authorization constraints on users. The problem of translating a high level user language into lower level access primitives has also been studied at the University of Toronto [21, 26].

Architecture and System Structure

We will describe the overall architecture of System R from two viewpoints. First, we will describe the system as seen by a single transaction, i.e. a monolithic description. Second, we will investigate its multiuser dimensions. Figure 1 gives a functional view of the system including its major interfaces and components.

The Relational Storage Interface (RSI) is an internal interface which handles access to single tuples of base relations. This interface and its supporting system, the Relational Storage System (RSS), is actually a complete storage subsystem in that it manages devices, space allocation, storage buffers, transaction consistency and locking, deadlock detection, backout, transaction recovery, and system recovery. Furthermore, it maintains indexes on selected fields of base relations, and pointer chains across relations.

The Relational Data Interface (RDI) is the external interface which can be called directly from a programming language, or used to support various emulators and other interfaces. The Relational Data System (RDS), which supports the RDI, provides authorization, integrity enforcement, and support for alternative views of data. The high level SEQUEL language is embedded within the RDI, and is used as the basis for all data definition and manipulation. In addition, the RDS maintains the catalogs of external names, since the RSS uses only system generated internal names. The RDS contains an optimizer which chooses an appropriate access path for any given request from among the paths supported by the RSS.

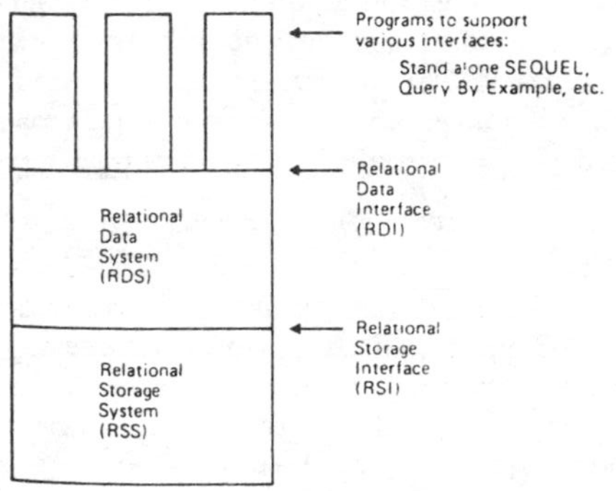

FIG. 1. Architecture of System R

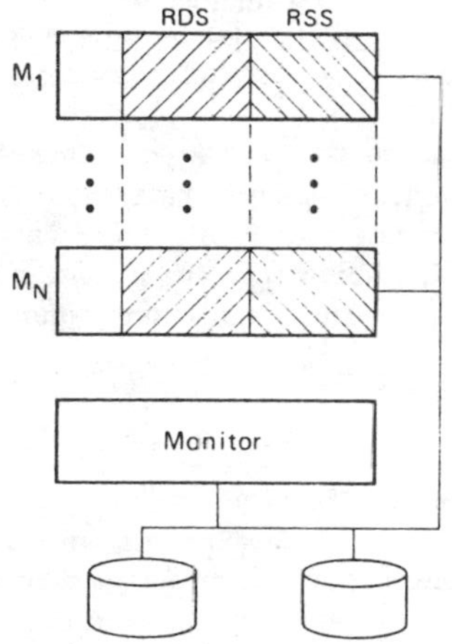

FIG. 2. Use of virtual machines in System R

The current operating system environment for this experimental system is VM/370 [18]. Several extensions to this virtual machine facility have been made [14] in order to support the multiuser environment of System R. In particular, we have implemented a technique for the selective sharing of read/write virtual memory across any number of virtual machines and for efficient communication among virtual machines through processor interrupts. Figure 2 illustrates the use of many virtual machines to support concurrent transactions on shared data. For each logged-on user there is a dedicated *database machine*. Each of these database machines contains all code and tables needed to execute all data management functions; that is, services are not reserved to a centralized machine.

The provision for many database machines, each executing shared, reentrant code and sharing control information, means that the database system need not provide its own multitasking to handle concurrent transactions. Rather, one can use the host operating system to multithread at the level of virtual machines. Furthermore, the operating system can take advantage of multiprocessors allocated to several virtual machines, since each machine is capable of providing all data management services. A single-server approach would eliminate this advantage, since most processing activity would then be focused on only one machine.

In addition to the database machines, Figure 2 also illustrates the Monitor Machine, which contains many system administrator facilities. For example, the Monitor Machine controls logon authorization and initializes the database machine for each user. The Monitor also schedules periodic checkpoints and maintains usage and performance statistics for reorganization and accounting purposes.

In Sections 2 and 3 we describe the main components of System R: the Relational Data System and the Relational Storage System.

2. THE RELATIONAL DATA SYSTEM

The Relational Data Interface (RDI) is the principal external interface of System R. It provides high level, data independent facilities for data retrieval, manipulation, definition, and control. The data definition facilities of the RDI allow a variety of alternative relational views to be defined on common underlying data. The Relational Data System (RDS) is the subsystem which implements the RDI. The RDS contains an optimizer which plans the execution of each RDI command, choosing a low cost access path to data from among those provided by the Relational Storage System (RSS).

The RDI consists of a set of operators which may be called from PL/I or other host programming languages. (See Appendix I for a list of these operators.) All the facilities of the SEQUEL data sublanguage [5] are available at the RDI by means of the RDI operator called SEQUEL. (A Backus-Naur Form (BNF) syntax for SEQUEL is given in Appendix II.) The SEQUEL language can be supported as a stand-alone interface by a simple program, written on top of the RDI, which handles terminal communications. (Such a stand-alone SEQUEL interface, called the User-Friendly Interface, or UFI, is provided as a part of System R.) In addition, programs may be written on top of the RDI to support other relational interfaces, such as Query by Example [31], or to simulate nonrelational interfaces.

Host Language Interface

The facilities of the RDI are basically those of the SEQUEL data sublanguage, which is described in [5] and in Appendix II. Several changes have been made to SEQUEL since the earlier publication of the language; they are described below.

The illustrative examples used in this section are based on the following database of employees and their departments:

```
EMP(EMPNO, NAME, DNO, JOB, SAL, MGR)
DEPT(DNO, DNAME, LOC, NEMPS)
```

The RDI interfaces SEQUEL to a host programming language by means of a concept called a *cursor*. A cursor is a name which is used at the RDI to identify a set of tuples called its *active set* (e.g. the result of a query) and furthermore to maintain a position on one tuple of the set. The cursor is associated with a set of tuples by means of the RDI operator SEQUEL; the tuples may then be retrieved, one at a time, by the RDI operator FETCH.

Some host programs may know in advance exactly the degree and data types of the tuples they wish to retrieve. Such a program may specify, in its SEQUEL call, the program variables into which the resulting tuples are to be delivered. The program must first give the system the addresses of the program variables to be used by means of the RDI operator BIND. In the following example, the host program identifies variables *X* and *Y* to the system and then issues a query whose results are to be placed in these variables:

```
CALL BIND('X', ADDR(X));
CALL BIND('Y', ADDR(Y));
CALL SEQUEL(C1,   'SELECT NAME:X,  SAL:Y
                   FROM EMP
                   WHERE JOB = ''PROGRAMMER''');
```

The SEQUEL call has the effect of associating the cursor C1 with the set of tuples which satisfy the query and positioning it just before the first such tuple. The optimizer is invoked to choose an access path whereby the tuples may be materialized. However, no tuples are actually materialized in response to the SEQUEL call. The materialization of tuples is done as they are called for, one at a time, by the FETCH operator. Each call to FETCH delivers the next tuple of the active set into program variables *X* and *Y*, i.e. NAME to *X* and SAL to *Y*:

```
CALL FETCH(C1);
```

A program may wish to write a SEQUEL predicate based on the contents of a program variable—for example, to find the programmers whose department number matches the contents of program variable *Z*. This facility is also provided by the RDI BIND operator, as follows:

```
CALL BIND('X', ADDR(X));
CALL BIND('Y', ADDR(Y));
CALL BIND('Z', ADDR(Z));
CALL SEQUEL(C1,   'SELECT NAME:X, SAL:Y
                   FROM EMP
                   WHERE JOB = ''PROGRAMMER''
                   AND DNO = Z');
CALL FETCH(C1);
```

Some programs may not know in advance the degree and data types of the tuples to be returned by a query. An example of such a program is one which supports an interactive user by allowing him to type in queries and display the results. This type of program need not specify in its SEQUEL call the variables into which the result is to be delivered. The program may issue a SEQUEL query, followed by the DESCRIBE operator which returns the degree and data types. The program then specifies the destination of the tuples in its FETCH commands. The following example illustrates these techniques:

```
CALL SEQUEL(C1,   'SELECT *
                   FROM EMP
                   WHERE DNO = 50');
```

This statement invokes the optimizer to choose an access path for the given query and associates cursor *C*1 with its active set.

```
CALL DESCRIBE(C1, DEGREE, P);
```

P is a pointer to an array in which the description of the active set of *C*1 is to be returned. The RDI returns the degree of the active set in DEGREE, and the data types and lengths of the tuple components in the elements of the array. If the array (which contains an entry describing its own length) is too short to hold the description of a tuple, the calling program must allocate a larger array and make another call to DESCRIBE.

Having obtained a description of the tuples to be returned, the calling program may proceed to allocate a structure to hold the tuples and may specify the location of this structure in its FETCH command:

```
CALL FETCH(C1, Q);
```

Q is a pointer to an array of pointers which specify where the individual components of the tuple are to be delivered. If this "destination" parameter is present in a FETCH command, it overrides any destination which may have been specified in the SEQUEL command which defined the active set of *C*1.

A special RDI operator OPEN is provided as a shorthand method to associate a cursor with an entire relation. For example, the command

```
CALL OPEN(C1, 'EMP');
```

is exactly equivalent to

```
CALL SEQUEL(C1, 'SELECT * FROM EMP');
```

The use of OPEN is slightly preferable to the use of SEQUEL to open a cursor on a relation, since OPEN avoids the use of the SEQUEL parser.

A program may have many cursors active at the same time. Each cursor remains active until an RDI operator CLOSE or KEEP is issued on it. CLOSE simply deactivates a cursor. KEEP causes the tuples identified by a cursor to be copied to form a new permanent relation in the database, having some specified relation name and field names.

The RDI operator FETCH_HOLD is included for the support of interfaces which provide for explicit locking. FETCH_HOLD operates in exactly the same way as FETCH except that it also acquires a "hold" on the tuple returned, which prevents other users from updating or deleting it until it is explicitly released or until the holding transaction has ended. A tuple may be released by the RELEASE operator, which takes as a parameter a cursor positioned on the tuple to be released. If no cursor is furnished, the RELEASE operator releases all tuples currently held by the user.

Query Facilities

In this section we describe only the most significant changes made to the SEQUEL query facilities since their original publication [5]. The changes correct certain deficiencies in the original syntax and facilitate the interfacing of SEQUEL with a host programming language. One important change deals with the handling of block labels. The following example, illustrating the original version of SEQUEL, is taken from [5]. (For simplicity, "CALL SEQUEL(. . .)" has been deleted from the next several examples.)

Example 1(a). List names of employees who earn more than their managers.

```
B1: SELECT NAME
    FROM   EMP
    WHERE SAL )
              SELECT SAL
              FROM   EMP
              WHERE EMPNO = B1.MGR
```

Experience has shown that this block label notation has three disadvantages:

(1) It is not possible to select quantities from the inner block, such as: "For all employees who earn more than their manager, list the employee's name and his manager's name."

(2) Since the query is asymmetrically expressed, the optimizer is biased toward making an outer loop for the first block and an inner loop for the second block. Since this may not be the optimum method for interpreting the query, the optimization process is made difficult.

(3) Human factors studies have shown that the block label notation is hard for nonprogrammers to learn [24, 25].

Because of these disadvantages, the block label notation has been replaced by the following more symmetrical notation, which allows several tables to be listed in the FROM clause and optionally referred to by variable names.

Example 1(b). For all employees who earn more than their managers, list the employee's name and his manager's name.

```
SELECT X.NAME, Y.NAME
FROM   EMP X, EMP Y
WHERE  X.MGR = Y.EMPNO
AND    X.SAL > Y.SAL
```

Example 1(b) illustrates the SEQUEL notation for the JOIN operator of the relational algebra. The tables to be joined are listed in the FROM clause. A variable name may optionally be associated with each table listed in the FROM clause (e.g. *X* and *Y* above). The criterion for joining rows is given in the WHERE clause (in this case, *X*.MGR = *Y*.EMPNO). Field names appearing in the query may stand alone (if unambiguous) or may be qualified by a table name (e.g. EMP.SAL) or by a variable (e.g. *X*.SAL).

In the earlier report [5], the WHERE clause is used for two purposes: it serves both to qualify individual tuples (e.g. "List the employees who are clerks") and to qualify groups of tuples (e.g. "List the departments having more than ten employees"). This ambiguity is now eliminated by moving group qualifying predicates to a separate HAVING clause. Queries are processed in the following order:

(1) Tuples are selected by the WHERE clause;

(2) Groups are formed by the GROUP BY clause;

(3) Groups are selected which satisfy the HAVING clause, as shown in the example below.

Example 2. List the DNOs of departments having more than ten clerks.

```
SELECT DNO
FROM   EMP
WHERE JOB = 'CLERK'
GROUP BY DNO
HAVING COUNT(*) > 10
```

Two more query features have been added to the ones described in [5]. The first allows the user to specify a value ordering for his query result.

Example 3 (Ordering). List all the employees in Dept. 50, ordered by their salaries.

```
SELECT *
FROM   EMP
WHERE DNO = 50
ORDER BY SAL
```

The other new feature, which is useful primarily to host language users of the RDI, allows a query to qualify tuples by comparing them with the current tuple of some active cursor:

Example 4 (Cursor reference). Find all the employees in the department indicated by cursor *C*5.

```
SELECT *
FROM   EMP
WHERE DNO = DNO OF CURSOR C5 ON DEPT
```

The evaluation of this reference to the content of cursor *C*5 occurs when the query is executed (by a SEQUEL call). Thereafter, moving the cursor *C*5 does not affect the set of tuples defined by the query. The optional phrase "ON DEPT" indicates to the optimizer that it can expect the cursor *C*5 to be positioned on a tuple of the DEPT table. This information may be useful in selecting an access path for the query.

Since elimination of duplicates from a query result is an expensive process and is not always necessary, the RDS does not eliminate duplicates unless explicitly requested to do so. For example, "SELECT DNO, JOB FROM EMP" may return duplicate DNO, JOB pairs, but "SELECT UNIQUE DNO, JOB FROM EMP" will return only unique pairs. Similarly, "SELECT AVG(SAL) FROM EMP" allows duplicate salary values to participate in the average, while "SELECT COUNT (UNIQUE JOB) FROM EMP" returns the count only of different job types in the EMP relation.

Data Manipulation Facilities

The RDI facilities for insertion, deletion, and update of tuples are also provided via the SEQUEL data sublanguage. SEQUEL can be used to manipulate either one tuple at a time or a set of tuples with a single command. The current tuple of a particular cursor may be selected for some operation by means of the special predicate CURRENT TUPLE OF CURSOR. The values of a tuple may be set equal to constants, or to new values computed from their old values, or to the contents of a program variable suitably identified by a BIND command. These facilities will be illustrated by a series of examples. Since no result is returned to the calling program in these examples, no cursor name is included in the calls to SEQUEL.

Example 5 (Set oriented update). Give a 10 percent raise to all employees in Dept. 50.

```
CALL SEQUEL('UPDATE EMP
              SET SAL = SAL × 1.1
              WHERE DNO = 50');
```

Example 6 (Individual update).

```
CALL BIND('PVSAL', ADDR(PVSAL));
CALL SEQUEL('UPDATE EMP
              SET SAL = PVSAL
              WHERE CURRENT TUPLE OF CURSOR C3');
```

Example 7 (Individual insertion). This example inserts a new employee tuple into EMP. The new tuple is constructed partly from constants and partly from the contents of program variables.

```
CALL BIND('PVEMPNO', ADDR(PVEMPNO));
CALL BIND('PVNAME', ADDR(PVNAME));
CALL BIND('PVMGR' ADDR(PVMGR));
CALL SEQUEL('INSERT INTO EMP:
              ⟨PVEMPNO, PVNAME, 50, ''TRAINEE'', 8500, PVMGR⟩');
```

An insertion statement in SEQUEL may provide only some of the values for the new tuple, specifying the names of the fields which are provided. Fields which are not provided are set to the null value. The physical position of the new tuple in storage is influenced by the "clustering" specification made on associated RSS access paths (see below).

Example 8 (Set oriented deletion). Delete all employees who work for departments in Evanston.

```
CALL SEQUEL('DELETE EMP
              WHERE DNO =
                     SELECT DNO
                     FROM   DEPT
                     WHERE LOC = ''EVANSTON''');
```

The SEQUEL assignment statement allows the result of a query to be copied into a new permanent or temporary relation in the database. This has the same effect as a query followed by the RDI operator KEEP.

Example 9 (Assignment). Create a new table UNDERPAID consisting of names and salaries of programmers who earn less than $10,000.

```
CALL SEQUEL('UNDERPAID(NAME, SAL) ←
       SELECT  NAME, SAL
       FROM    EMP
       WHERE   JOB = ''PROGRAMMER''
       AND     SAL < 10,000');
```

The new table UNDERPAID represents a snapshot taken from EMP at the moment the assignment was executed. UNDERPAID then becomes an independent relation and does not reflect any later changes to EMP.

Data Definition Facilities

System R takes a unified approach to data manipulation, definition, and control. Like queries and set oriented updates, the data definition facilities are invoked by means of the RDI operator SEQUEL. Many of these facilities have been described in [4] and [15].

The SEQUEL statement CREATE TABLE is used to create a new base (i.e. physically stored) relation. For each field of the new relation, the field name and data type are specified.[1] If desired, it may be specified at creation time that null values are not permitted in one or more fields of the new relation. A query executed on the relation will deliver its results in system determined order (which depends upon the access path which the optimizer has chosen), unless the query has an ORDER BY clause. When a base relation is no longer useful, it may be deleted by issuing a DROP TABLE statement.

System R currently relies on the user to specify not only the base tables to be stored but also the RSS access paths to be maintained on them. (Database design facilities to automate and adapt some of these decisions are also being investigated.) Access paths include images and binary links,[2] described in Section 3. They may be specified by means of the SEQUEL verbs CREATE and DROP. Briefly, images are value orderings maintained on base relations by the RSS, using multilevel index structures. The index structures associate a value with one or more Tuple Identifiers (*TIDs*). A *TID* is an internal address which allows rapid access to a tuple, as discussed in Section 3. Images provide associative and sequential access on one or more fields which are called the *sort fields* of the image. An image may be declared to be UNIQUE, which forces each combination of sort field values to be unique in the relation. At most one image per relation may have the *clustering* property, which causes tuples whose sort field values are close to be physically stored near each other.

Binary links are access paths in the RSS which link tuples of one relation to

[1] The data types of INTEGER, SMALL INTEGER, DECIMAL, FLOAT, and CHARACTER (both fixed and varying length) are supported.

[2] Unary links, described in Section 3, are used for internal system purposes only, and are not exposed at the RDI.

related tuples of another relation through pointer chains. In System R, binary links are always employed in a value dependent manner: the user specifies that each tuple of Relation 1 is to be linked to the tuples in Relation 2 which have matching values in some field(s), and that the tuples on the link are to be ordered in some value dependent way. For example, a user may specify a link from DEPT to EMP by matching DNO, and that EMP tuples on the link are to be ordered by JOB and SAL. This link is maintained automatically by the system. By declaring a link from DEPT to EMP on matching DNO, the user implicitly declares this to be a one-to-many relationship (i.e. DNO is a key of DEPT). Any attempts to define links or to insert or update tuples in violation of this rule will be refused. Like an image, a link may be declared to have the *clustering* property, which causes each tuple to be physically stored near its neighbor in the link.

It should be clearly noted that none of the access paths (images and binary links) contain any logical information other than that derivable from the data values themselves. This is in accord with the relational data model, which represents all information as data values. The RDI user has no explicit control over the placement of tuples in images and links (unlike the "manual sets" of the DBTG proposal [6]). Furthermore, the RDI user may not explicitly use an image or link for access to data; all choices of access path are made automatically by the optimizer.

The query power of SEQUEL may be used to define a view as a relation derived from one or more other relations. This view may then be used in the same ways as a base table: queries may be written against it, other views may be defined on it, and in certain circumstances described below, it may be updated. Any SEQUEL query may be used as a view definition by means of a DEFINE VIEW statement. Views are dynamic windows on the database, in that updates made to base tables immediately become visible via the views defined on these base tables. Where updates to views are supported, they are implemented in terms of updates to the underlying base tables. The SEQUEL statement which defines a view is recorded in a system maintained catalog where it may be examined by authorized users. When an authorized user issues a DROP VIEW statement, the indicated view and all other views defined in terms of it disappear from the system for this user and all other users.

If a modification is issued against a view, it can be supported only if the tuples of the view are associated one-to-one with tuples of an underlying base relation. In general, this means that the view must involve a single base relation and contain a key of that relation; otherwise, the modification statement is rejected. If the view satisfies the one-to-one rule, the WHERE clause of the SEQUEL modification statement is merged into the view definition; the result is optimized and the indicated update is made on the relevant tuples of the base relation.

Two final SEQUEL commands complete the discussion of the data definition facility. The first is KEEP TABLE, which causes a temporary table (created, for example, by assignment) to become permanent. (Temporary tables are destroyed when the user who created them logs off.) The second command is EXPAND TABLE, which adds a new field to an existing table. All views, images, and links defined on the original table are retained. All existing tuples are interpreted as having null values in the expanded fields until they are explicitly updated.

Data Control Facilities

Data control facilities at the RDI have four aspects: transactions, authorization, integrity assertions, and triggers.

A transaction is a series of RDI calls which the user wishes to be processed as an atomic act. The meaning of "atomic" depends on the level of consistency specified by the user, and is explained in Section 3. The highest level of consistency, Level 3, requires that a user's transactions appear to be serialized with the transactions of other concurrent users. The user controls transactions by the RDI operators BEGIN_TRANS and END_TRANS. The user may specify save points within a transaction by the RDI operator SAVE. As long as a transaction is active, the user may back up to the beginning of the transaction or to any internal save point by the operator RESTORE. This operator restores all changes made to the database by the current transaction, as well as the state of all cursors used by this transaction. No cursors may remain active (open) beyond the end of a transaction. The RDI transactions are implemented directly by RSI transactions, so the RDI commands BEGIN_TRANS, END_TRANS, SAVE, and RESTORE are passed through to the RSI, with some RDS bookkeeping to permit the restoration of its internal state.

The System R approach to authorization is described in [15]. System R does not require a particular individual to be the database administrator, but allows each user to create his own data objects by executing the SEQUEL statements CREATE TABLE and DEFINE VIEW. The creator of a new object receives full authorization to perform all operations on the object (subject, of course, to his authorization for the underlying tables, if it is a view). The user may then grant selected capabilities for his object to other users by the SEQUEL statement GRANT. The following capabilities may be independently granted for each table or view: READ, INSERT, DELETE, UPDATE (by fields), DROP, EXPAND, IMAGE specification, LINK specification, and CONTROL (the ability to specify assertions and triggers on the table or view). For each capability which a user possesses for a given table, he may optionally have GRANT authority (the authority to further grant or revoke the capability to/from other users).

System R relies primarily on its view mechanism for read authorization. If it is desired to allow a user to read only tuples of employees in Dept. 50, and not to see their salaries, then this portion of the EMP table can be defined as a view and granted to the user. No special statistical access is distinguished, since the same effect (e.g. ability to read only the average salary of each department) can be achieved by defining a view. To make the view mechanism more useful for authorization purposes, the reserved word USER is always interpreted as the user-id of the current user. Thus the following SEQUEL statement defines a view of all those employees in the same department as the current user:

```
DEFINE VIEW VEMP AS:
        SELECT *
        FROM   EMP
        WHERE  DNO =
               SELECT DNO
               FROM   EMP
               WHERE  NAME = USER
```

The third important aspect of data control is that of integrity assertions. The System R approach to data integrity is described in [10]. Any SEQUEL predicate may be stated as an assertion about the integrity of data in a base table or view. At the time the assertion is made (by an ASSERT statement in SEQUEL), its truth is checked; if true, the assertion is automatically enforced until it is explicitly dropped by a DROP ASSERTION statement. Any data modification, by any user, which violates an active integrity assertion is rejected. Assertions may apply to individual tuples (e.g. "No employee's salary exceeds $50,000") or to sets of tuples (e.g. "The average salary of each department is less than $20,000"). Assertions may describe permissible *states* of the database (as in the examples above) or permissible *transitions* in the database. For this latter purpose the keywords OLD and NEW are used in SEQUEL to denote data values before and after modification, as in the example below.

Example 10 (Transition assertion). Each employee's salary must be non-decreasing.

```
ASSERT ON UPDATE TO EMP: NEW SAL ≥ OLD SAL
```

Unless otherwise specified, integrity assertions are checked and enforced at the end of each transaction. Transition assertions compare the state before the transaction began with the state after the transaction concluded. If some assertion is not satisfied, the transaction is backed out to its beginning point. This permits complex updates to be done in several steps (several calls to SEQUEL, bracketed by BEGIN_TRANS and END_TRANS), which may cause the database to pass through intermediate states which temporarily violate one or more assertions. However, if an assertion is specified as IMMEDIATE, it cannot be suspended within a transaction, but is enforced after each data modification (each RDI call). In addition, "integrity points" within a transaction may be established by the SEQUEL command ENFORCE INTEGRITY. This command allows a user to guard against having a long transaction completely backed out. In the event of an integrity failure, the transaction is backed out to its most recent integrity point.

The fourth aspect of data control, triggers, is a generalization of the concept of assertions. A trigger causes a prespecified sequence of SEQUEL statements to be executed whenever some triggering event occurs. The triggering event may be retrieval, insertion, deletion, or update of a particular base table or view. For example, suppose that in our example database, the NEMPS field of the DEPT table denotes the number of employees in each department. This value might be kept up to date automatically by the following three triggers (as in assertions, the keywords OLD and NEW denote data values before and after the change which invoked the trigger):

```
DEFINE TRIGGER EMPINS
      ON INSERTION OF EMP:
            (UPDATE  DEPT
             SET     NEMPS = NEMPS + 1
             WHERE   DNO = NEW EMP.DNO)

DEFINE TRIGGER EMPDEL
      ON DELETION OF EMP:
            (UPDATE DEPT
             SET    NEMPS = NEMPS - 1
             WHERE  DNO = OLD EMP.DNO)
DEFINE TRIGGER EMPUPD
      ON UPDATE OF EMP:
            (UPDATE  DEPT
             SET     NEMPS = NEMPS - 1
             WHERE   DNO = OLD EMP.DNO;
             UPDATE  DEPT
             SET     NEMPS = NEMPS + 1
             WHERE   DNO = NEW EMP.DNO)
```

The RDS automatically maintains a set of catalog relations which describe the other relations, views, images, links, assertions, and triggers known to the system. Each user may access a set of views of the system catalogs which contain information pertinent to him. Access to catalog relations is made in exactly the same way as other relations are accessed (i.e. by SEQUEL queries). Of course, no user is authorized to modify the contents of a catalog directly, but any authorized user may modify a catalog indirectly by actions such as creating a table. In addition, a user may enter comments into his various catalog entries by means of the COMMENT statement (see syntax in Appendix II).

The Optimizer

The objective of the optimizer is to find a low cost means of executing a SEQUEL statement, given the data structures and access paths available. The optimizer attempts to minimize the expected number of pages to be fetched from secondary storage into the RSS buffers during execution of the statement. Only page fetches made under the explicit control of the RSS are considered. If necessary, the RSS buffers will be pinned in real memory to avoid additional paging activity caused by the VM/370 operating system. The cost of CPU instructions is also taken into account by means of an adjustable coefficient, H, which is multiplied by the number of tuple comparison operations to convert to equivalent page accesses. H can be adjusted according to whether the system is compute-bound or disk access-bound.

Since our cost measure for the optimizer is based on disk page accesses, the physical clustering of tuples in the database is of great importance. As mentioned earlier, each relation may have at most one clustering image, which has the property that tuples near each other in the image ordering are stored physically near each other in the database. To see the importance of the clustering property, imagine that we wish to scan over the tuples of a relation in the order of some image, and that the number of RSS buffer pages is much less than the number of pages used to store the relation. If the image is not the clustering image, the locations of the tuples will be independent of each other and in general a page will have to be fetched from disk for each tuple. On the other hand, if the image is the clustering image, each disk page will contain several (usually at least 20) adjacent tuples, and the number of page fetches will be reduced by a corresponding factor.

The optimizer begins by classifying the given SEQUEL statement into one of several statement types, according to the presence of various language features such as join and GROUP BY. Next the optimizer examines the system catalogs to find the set of images and links which are pertinent to the given statement. A rough decision procedure is then executed to find the set of "reasonable" methods of executing the statement. If there is more than one "reasonable" method, an expected cost formula is evaluated for each method and the minimum-cost method is chosen. The parameters of the cost formulas, such as relation cardinality and number of tuples per page, are obtained from the system catalogs.

We illustrate this optimization process by means of two example queries. The first example involves selection of tuples from a single relation, and the second involves joining two relations together according to a matching field. For simplicity we consider only methods based on images and relation scans. (A relation scan in the RSS accesses each of the pages in a data segment in turn (see Section 3), and selects those tuples belonging to the given relation.) Consideration of links involves a straightforward extension of the techniques we will describe.

Example 11 will be used to describe the decision process for a query involving a single relation:

Example 11. List the names and salaries of programmers who earn more than $10,000.

```
SELECT NAME, SAL
FROM   EMP
WHERE  JOB = 'PROGRAMMER'
AND    SAL > 10,000
```

In planning the execution of this example, the optimizer must choose whether to access the EMP relation via an image (on JOB, SAL or some other field) or via a relation scan. The following parameters, available in the system catalogs, are taken into account:

- R relation cardinality (number of tuples in the relation)
- D number of data pages occupied by the relation
- T average number of tuples per data page (equal to R/D)
- I image cardinality (number of distinct sort field values in a given image)
- H coefficient of CPU cost ($1/H$ is the number of tuple comparisons which are considered equivalent in cost to one disk page access).

An image is said to "match" a predicate if the sort field of the image is the field which is tested by the predicate. For example, an image on the EMP relation ordered by JOB (which we will refer to as an "image on EMP.JOB") would match the predicate JOB = 'PROGRAMMER' in Example 11. In order for an image to match a predicate, the predicate must be a simple comparison of a field with a value. More complicated predicates, such as EMP.DNO = DEPT.DNO, cannot be matched by an image.

In the case of a simple query on a single relation, such as Example 11, the optimizer compares the available images with the predicates of the query, in order to determine which of the following eight methods are available:

Method 1: Use a clustering image which matches a predicate whose comparison-operator is '='. The expected cost to retrieve all result tuples is $R/(T \times I)$ page accesses (R/I tuples divided by T tuples per page).

Method 2: Use a clustering image which matches a predicate whose comparison operator is not '='. Assuming half the tuples in the relation satisfy the predicate, the expected cost is $R/(2 \times T)$.

Method 3: Use a nonclustering image which matches a predicate whose comparison operator is '='. Since each tuple requires a page access, the expected cost is R/I.

Method 4: Use a nonclustering image which matches a predicate whose comparison-operator is not '='. Expected cost to retrieve all result tuples is $R/2$.

Method 5: Use a clustering image which does not match any predicate. Scan the image and test each tuple against all predicates. Expected cost is $(R/T) + H \times R \times N$, where N is the number of predicates in the query.

Method 6: Use a nonclustering image which does not match any predicate. Expected cost is $R + H \times R \times N$.

Method 7: Use a relation scan where this relation is the only one in its segment. Test each tuple against all predicates. Expected cost is $(R/T) + H \times R \times N$.

Method 8: Use a relation scan where there are other relations sharing the segment. Cost is unknown, but greater than $(R/T) + H \times R \times N$, because some pages may be fetched which contain no tuples from the pertinent relation.

The optimizer chooses a method from this set according to the following rules:

1. If Method 1 is available, it is chosen.
2. If exactly one among Methods 2, 3, 5, and 7 is available, it is chosen. If more than one method is available in this class, the expected cost formulas for these methods are evaluated and the method of minimum cost is chosen.
3. If none of the above methods are available, the optimizer chooses Method 4, if available; else Method 6, if available; else Method 8. (Note: Either Method 7 or Method 8 is always available for any relation.)

As a second example of optimization, we consider the following query, which involves a join of two relations:

Example 12. List the names, salaries, and department names of programmers located in Evanston.

```
SELECT NAME, SAL, DNAME
FROM   EMP, DEPT
WHERE  EMP.JOB = 'PROGRAMMER'
AND    DEPT.LOC = 'EVANSTON'
AND    EMP.DNO = DEPT.DNO
```

Example 12 is an instance of a join query type, the most general form of which involves restriction, projection, and join. The general query has the form:

> Apply a given restriction to a relation R, yielding R1, and apply a possibly different restriction to a relation S, yielding S1. Join R1 and S1 to form a relation T, and project some fields from T.

To illustrate the optimization of join-type queries, we will consider four possible methods for evaluating Example 12:

Method 1 (use images on join fields): Perform a simultaneous scan of the image on DEPT.DNO and the image on EMP.DNO. Advance the DEPT scan to obtain the next DEPT where LOC is 'EVANSTON'. Advance the EMP scan and fetch all the EMP tuples whose DNO matches the current DEPT and whose JOB is 'PROGRAMMER'. For each such matching pair of DEPT, EMP tuples, place the NAME, SAL, and DNAME fields into the output. Repeat until the image scans are completed.

Method 2 (sort both relations): Scan EMP and DEPT using their respective clustering images and create two files W1 and W2. W1 contains the NAME, SAL, and DNO fields of tuples from EMP which have JOB = 'PROGRAMMER'. W2 contains the DNO and DNAME fields of tuples from DEPT whose location is 'EVANSTON'. Sort W1 and W2 on DNO. (This process may involve repeated passes over W1 and W2 if they are too large to fit the available main memory buffers.) The resulting sorted files are scanned simultaneously and the join is performed.

Method 3 (multiple passes): DEPT is scanned via its clustering image, and the DNO and DNAME fields (a subtuple) of those DEPT tuples which have LOC = 'EVANSTON' are inserted into a main memory data structure called W. If space in main memory is available to insert a subtuple (say S), it is inserted. If there is no space and if S.DNO is less than the current highest DNO value in W, the subtuple with the highest DNO in W is deleted and S inserted. If there is no room for S and the DNO in S is greater than the highest DNO in W, S is discarded. After completing the scan of DEPT, EMP is scanned via its clustering image and a tuple E of EMP is obtained. If E.JOB = 'PROGRAMMER', then W is checked for the presence of the E.DNO. If present, E is joined to the appropriate subtuple in W. This process is continued until all tuples of EMP have been examined. If any DEPT subtuples were discarded, another scan of DEPT is made to form a new W consisting of subtuples with DNO value greater than the current highest. EMP is scanned again and the process repeated.

Method 4 (*TID* algorithm): Using the image on EMP.JOB, obtain the *TID*s of tuples from EMP which satisfy the restriction JOB = 'PROGRAMMER'. Sort them and store the *TID*s in a file W1. Do the same with DEPT, using the image on DEPT.LOC and testing for LOC = 'EVANSTON', yielding a *TID* file W2. Perform a simultaneous scan over the images on DEPT.DNO and EMP.DNO, finding the *TID* pairs of tuples whose DNO values match. Check each pair (*TID*1, *TID*2) to see if *TID*1 is present in W1 and *TID*2 is in W2. If they are, the tuples are fetched and joined and the NAME, SAL, and DNAME fields placed into the output.

These methods should be considered as illustrative of the techniques considered by the optimizer. The optimizer will draw from a larger set of methods, including methods which use links to carry out the join.

A method cannot be applied unless the appropriate access paths are available. For example, Method 4 is applicable only if there are images on EMP.DNO and EMP.JOB, as well as on DEPT.DNO and DEPT.LOC. In addition, the performance of a method depends strongly on the clustering of the relations with respect to the access paths. We will consider how the optimizer would choose among these four methods in four hypothetical situations. These choices are made on the basis of cost formulas which will be detailed in a later paper.

Situation 1: There are clustering images on both EMP.DNO and DEPT.DNO, but no images on EMP.JOB or DEPT.LOC. In this situation, Method 1 is always chosen.

Situation 2: There are unclustered images on EMP.DNO and DEPT.DNO, but no images on EMP.JOB or DEPT.LOC. In this case, Method 3 is chosen if the entire working file W fits into the main memory buffer at once; otherwise Method 2 is chosen. It is interesting to note that the unclustered images on DNO are never used in this situation.

Situation 3 :There are clustering images on EMP.DNO and DEPT.DNO, and unclustered images on EMP.JOB and DEPT.LOC. In this situation, Method 4 is always chosen.

Situation 4: There are unclustered images on EMP.DNO, EMP.JOB, DEPT.DNO, and DEPT.LOC. In this situation, Method 3 is chosen if the entire working file W fits into the main memory buffer. Otherwise, Method 2 is chosen if more than one tuple per disk page is expected to satisfy the restriction predicates. In the remaining cases, where the restriction predicates are very selective, Method 4 should be used.

After analyzing any SEQUEL statement, the optimizer produces an Optimized Package (OP) containing the parse tree and a plan for executing the statement. If the statement is a query, the OP is used to materialize tuples as they are called for by the FETCH command (query results are materialized incrementally whenever possible). If the statement is a view definition, the OP is stored in the form of a Pre-Optimized Package (POP) which can be fetched and utilized whenever an access is made via the specified view. If any change is made to the structure of a base table or to the access paths (images and links) maintained on it, the POPs of all views defined on that base table are invalidated, and each view must be reoptimized from its defining SEQUEL code to form a new POP.

When a view is accessed via the RDI operators OPEN and FETCH, the POP for the view can be used directly to materialize the tuples of the view. Often, however, a query or another view definition will be written in terms of an existing view. If the query or view definition is simple (e.g. a projection or restriction), it can sometimes be *composed* with the existing view (i.e. their parse trees can be merged and optimized together to form a new OP for the new query or view). In more complex cases the new statement cannot be composed with the existing view definition. In these cases the POP for the existing view is treated as a formula for materializing tuples. A new OP is formed for the new statement which treats the existing view as a table from which tuples can be fetched in only one way: by interpreting the existing POP. Of course, if views are cascaded on other views in several levels, there may be several levels of POPs in existence, each level making reference to the next.

Modifying Cursors

A number of issues are raised by the use of the insertion, deletion, and update facilities of System R. When a modification is made to one of the tuples in the active set of a cursor, the modification may change the ordinal position of the tuple or even disqualify it entirely from the active set. It should be noted here that a user operating at Level 3 consistency is automatically protected against having his cursors affected by the modifications of other users. However, even in Level 3 consistency, a user may make a modification which affects one of his own active cursors.

If the cursor in question is open on a base relation, the case is simple: the modification is done and immediately becomes visible via the cursor. Let us consider a case in which the cursor is not on a base relation, but rather on the result of a SEQUEL query. Suppose the following query has been executed:

```
SELECT *
FROM   EMP
WHERE DNO = 50
ORDER BY SAL
```

If the system has no image ordered on SAL, it may execute this query by finding the employees where DNO = 50 and sorting them by SAL to create an ordered list of answer tuples. Along with this list, the system will keep a list of the base relations from which the list was derived (in this case, only EMP). The effect resembles that of performing a DBTG KEEP verb [6] on the underlying base relations: if any tuple in an underlying relation is modified, the answer list is marked "potentially invalid." Now any fetch from this list will return a warning code since the tuple returned may not be up to date. If the calling program wishes to guarantee accuracy of its results, it must close its cursor and reevaluate the query when this warning code is received.

Simulation of Nonrelational Data Models

The RDI is designed in such a way that programs can be written on top of it to simulate "navigation oriented" database interfaces. These interfaces are often characterized by collections of records connected in a hierarchic [17] or network [6] structure, and by the concept of establishing one or more "current positions" within the structure (e.g. the currency indicators of DBTG). In general our strategy will be to represent each record type as a relation and to represent information about ordering and connections between records in the form of explicit fields in the corresponding relations. In this way all information inserted into the database via the "navigational" interface (including information about orderings and connections) is available to other users who may be using the underlying relations directly. One or more "current positions" within the database may then be simulated by means of one or more RDI cursors.

We will illustrate this simulation process by means of an example. Suppose we wish to simulate the database structure shown in Figure 3, and wish to maintain a "current position" in the structure. The hierarchical connections from DEPT to EMP and from DEPT to EQUIP may be unnamed in a hierarchic system such as IMS [17], or they may represent named set types in a network oriented system such as DBTG [6].

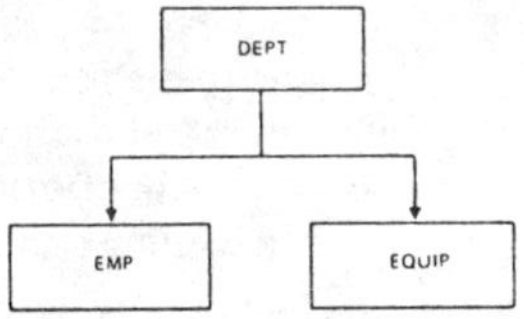

FIG. 3. Example of a hierarchic data structure

At database definition time, a relation is created to simulate each record type. The DEPT relation must have a sequence-number field to represent the ordering of the DEPT records. The EMP and EQUIP relations must have, in addition to a sequence-number field, one or more fields which uniquely identify their "parent" or "owner" records (let us assume the key of DEPT is DNO). If a record had several "owners" in different set types, several "owner's key" fields would have to appear in the corresponding relation.

Also at database definition time, a view definition is entered into the system which will represent the "currently visible" tuples of each relation at any point in time. The view definitions for our example are given below:

```
DEFINE VIEW VDEPT AS
    SELECT *
    FROM   DEPT
    ORDER BY ⟨sequence field⟩
DEFINE VIEW VEMP AS
    SELECT *
    FROM   EMP
    WHERE DNO = DNO OF CURSOR C1 ON DEPT
    ORDER BY ⟨sequence field⟩
DEFINE VIEW VEQUIP AS
    SELECT *
    FROM   EQUIP
    WHERE DNO = DNO OF CURSOR C1 ON DEPT
    ORDER BY ⟨sequence field⟩
```

The definitions of VEMP and VEQUIP call for tuples of EMP and EQUIP which have the same DNO as cursor *C*1; furthermore they promise that, when these views are used, cursor *C*1 will be active on the DEPT relation. These view definitions are parsed and optimized, and stored in the form of POPs. During this optimization process, any direct physical support for the hierarchy (such as a link from DEPT to EMP by matching DNO) will be discovered.

At run time, when a position is to be established on a DEPT record, the cursor *C*1 is opened on the view VDEPT. If the "current position" then moves downward to an EMP record, the view VEMP is opened. The exact subset of EMP tuples made available by this view opening depends on the location of the cursor *C*1 in the "parent" relation. If the "current position" moves upward again to DEPT, the view VEMP is closed, to be reopened later as needed. Any insertion, deletion, or update operations issued against the hierarchy are simulated by SEQUEL INSERT, DELETE, and UPDATE operations on the corresponding relations, with appropriate sequence-number and parent-key values generated, if necessary, by the simulator program. At the end of the transaction, all cursors are closed.

Following this general plan, it is expected that hierarchic oriented or network oriented interfaces can be simulated on top of the RDI. It should be particularly noted that no parsing or optimization is done in response to a command to move the "current position"; the system merely employs the POP for the view which was optimized at database definition time. For any connections which are given direct physical support in the form of a binary link, the optimizer will take advantage of the link to provide good performance. The system is also capable of simulating connections which have no direct physical support, since the optimizer will automatically find an appropriate access path.

3. THE RELATIONAL STORAGE SYSTEM

This section is concerned with the Relational Storage System or RSS, the database management subsystem which provides underlying support for System R. The RSS supports the RSI which provides simple, tuple-at-a-time operators on base relations. Operators are also supported for data recovery, transaction management, and data definition. (A list of all RSI operators can be found in Appendix III.) Calls to the RSI require explicit use of data areas called segments and access paths called images and links, along with the use of RSS-generated, numeric identifiers for data segments, relations, access paths, and tuples. The RDS handles the selection of efficient access paths to optimize its operations, and maps symbolic relation names to their internal RSS identifiers.

In order to facilitate gradual database integration and retuning of access paths, the RSI has been designed so that new stored relations or new indexes can be created at any time, or existing ones destroyed, without quiescing the system and without dumping and reloading the data. One can also add new fields to existing relations, or add or delete pointer chain paths across existing relations. This facility, coupled with the ability to retrieve any subset of fields in a tuple, provides a degree of data independence at a low level of the system, since existing programs which execute RSI operations on tuples will be unaffected by the addition of new fields.

As a point of comparison, the RSS has many functions which can be found in other systems, both relational and nonrelational, such as the use of index and pointer chain structures. The areas which have been emphasized and extended in the RSS include dynamic definition of new data types and access paths, as described above, dynamic binding and unbinding of disk space to data segments, multipoint recovery for in-process transactions, a novel and efficient technique for system checkpoint and restart, multiple levels of isolation from the actions of other concurrent users, and automatic locking at the level of segments, relations, and single tuples. The next several subsections describe all of these RSS functions and include a sketch of the implementation.

Segments

In the RSS, all data is stored in a collection of logical address spaces called *segments*, which are employed to control physical clustering. Segments are used for storing user data, access path structures, internal catalog information, and intermediate results generated by the RDS. All the tuples of any relation must reside within a single segment chosen by the RDS. However, a given segment may contain several relations. A special segment is dedicated to the storage of transaction logs for backing out the changes made by individual transactions.

Several types of segments are supported, each with its own combination of functions and overhead. For example, one type is intended for storage of shared data, and has provisions for concurrent access, transaction backout, and recovery of the segment's contents to a previous state. Another segment type is intended for low overhead storage of temporary relations, and has no provision for either concurrent access or segment recovery. A maximum length is associated with each segment; it is chosen by a user during initialization of the system.

The RSS has the responsibility for mapping logical segment spaces to physical extents on disk storage, and for supporting segment recovery. Within the RSS, each segment consists of a sequence of equal-sized *pages*, which are referenced and formatted by various components of the RSS. Physical page slots in the disk extents are allocated to segments dynamically upon first reference, by checking and modifying bit maps associated with the disk extents. Physical page slots are freed when access path structures are destroyed or when the contents of a segment are destroyed. This dynamic allocation scheme allows for the definition of many large sized segments, to accommodate large intermediate results and growing databases. Facilities are provided to cluster pages on physical media so that sequential or localized access to segments can be handled efficiently.

The RSS maintains a page map for each segment, which is used to map each segment page to its location on disk. Such a map is maintained as a collection of equal-sized *blocks*, which are allocated statically. A page request is handled by allocating space within a main memory buffer shared among all concurrent users. In fact two separate buffers are managed, one for the page map blocks and one for the segment pages themselves. Both pages and blocks are fixed in their buffer slots until they are explicitly freed by RSS components. Freeing a page makes it available for replacement, and when space is needed the buffer manager replaces whichever freed page was least recently requested.

The RSS provides a novel technique to handle segment recovery, by associating with each recoverable segment *two* page maps, called current and backup. When the OPEN_SEGMENT operator is issued, to make the segment available for processing, these page maps have identical entries. When a component of the RSS later requests access to a page, with intent to update (after suitable locks have been acquired), the RSS checks whether this is the first update to the page since the OPEN or since the last SAVE_SEGMENT operation. If so, a new page slot is allocated nearby on disk, the page is accessed from its original disk location, and the current page map is then modified to point to the new page slot. When the page is later replaced from the buffer, it will be directed to the new location, while the backup page and backup page map are left intact.

When the SAVE_SEGMENT operator is issued, the disk pages bound to segments are brought up to date by storing through all buffer pages which have been updated. Both page maps are then scanned, and any page which has been modified since the last save point has its old page slot released. Finally the backup page map entries are set equal to the current page map entries, and the cycle is complete.

With this technique, the RESTORE_SEGMENT operation is relatively simple, since the backup page map points to a complete, consistent copy of the segment. The current page map is simply set equal to the backup one, and newly allocated page slots are released. The SAVE_SEGMENT and RESTORE_SEGMENT functions are useful for recovering a previous version of private data, and also for support of system checkpoint and restart, as explained below. However, the effect of restoring a segment of public data segment may be to undo changes made by several transactions, since each of them may have modified data since the segment was last saved. An entirely different mechanism is therefore used to back out only those changes made by a single transaction, and is explained below.

Note that our recovery scheme depends on the highly stylized management of two page maps per segment, and on our ability to control when pages are stored through from main memory to disk. These particular requirements led to the decision to handle our own storage management and I/O for RSS segments, rather than relying on the automatic paging of virtual memory in the operating system.

Relations

The main data object of the RSS is the *n*-ary *relation*, which consists of a time-varying number of tuples, each containing *n* fields. A new relation can be defined at any time within any segment chosen by the RDS. An existing relation and its associated access path structures can be dropped at any time, with all storage space made reusable. Even after a relation is defined and loaded, new fields may be added on the right, without a database reload and without immediate modification to existing tuples.

Two field types are supported: fixed length and variable length. For both field types, a special protocol is used at the RSI to generate an undefined value. This feature has a number of uses, but a particularly important one is that when the user adds new fields to an existing relation, values for those fields in each existing tuple are treated as undefined until they are explicitly updated.

Operators are available to INSERT and DELETE single tuples, and to FETCH and UPDATE any combination of fields in a tuple. One can also fetch a sequence of tuples along an access path through the use of an RSS cursor or *scan*. Each scan is created by the RSS for fetching tuples on a particular access path through execution of the OPEN_SCAN operator. The tuples along the path may then be accessed by a sequence of NEXT operations on that scan. The access paths which are supported include a value determined ordering of tuples through use of an image, an RDS determined ordering of tuples through use of a link (see below for discussions of images and links), and an RSS determined ordering of tuples in a relation. For all of these access paths the RDS may attach a search argument to each NEXT operation. The search argument may be any disjunctive normal form expression where each atomic expression has the form ⟨field number, operator, value⟩. The value is an explicit byte string provided by the RDS, and the operator is '=', '≠', '<', '>', '≤', or '≥'.

Associated with every tuple of a relation is a *tuple identifier* or *TID*. Each tuple identifier is generated by the RSS, and is available to the RDS as a concise and efficient means of addressing tuples. *TID*s are also used within the RSS to refer to tuples from index structures, and to maintain pointer chains. However, they are not intended for end users above the RDS, since they may be reused by the RSS after tuple deletions and are reassigned during database reorganization.

The RSS stores and accesses tuples within relations, and maintains pointer chains to implement the links described below. Each tuple is stored as a contiguous sequence of field values within a single page. Field lengths are also included for variable length fields. A prefix is stored with the tuple for use within the RSS. The prefix contains such information as the relation identifier, the pointer fields (*TID*s) for link structures, the number of stored data fields, and the number of pointer fields. These numbers are employed to support dynamic creation of new fields and links to existing relations, without requiring immediate access or modification to the existing tuples. Tuples are found only on pages which have been reserved as data pages. Other pages within the segment are reserved for the storage of index or internal catalog entries. A given data page may contain tuples from more than one relation, so that extra page accesses can be avoided when tuples from different relations are accessed together. When a scan is executed on a relation (rather than an image or link), an internal scan is generated on all nonempty data pages within the segment containing that relation. Each such data page is touched once, and the prefix of each tuple within the page is checked to see if it belongs to the relation.

The implementation of tuple identifier access is a hybrid scheme, similar to one used in such systems as IDS [11] and RM [20], which combines the speed of a byte address pointer with the flexibility of indirection. Each tuple identifier is a concatenation of a page number within the segment, along with a byte offset from the bottom of the page. The offset denotes a special entry or "slot" which contains the byte location of the tuple in that page. This technique allows efficient utilization of space within data pages, since space can be compacted and tuples moved with only local changes to the pointers in the slots. The slots themselves are never moved from their positions at the bottom of each data page, so that existing *TID*s can still be employed to access the tuples. In the rare case when a tuple is updated to a longer total value and insufficient space is available on its page, an overflow scheme is provided to move the tuple to another page. In this case the *TID* points to a tagged overflow record which is used to reference the other page. If the tuple overflows again, the original overflow record is modified to point to the newest location. Thus, a tuple access via a *TID* almost always involves a single page access, and never involves more than two page accesses (plus possible accesses to the page map blocks).

In order to tune the database to particular environments, the RSS accepts hints for physical allocation during INSERT operations, in the form of a tentative *TID*. The new tuple will be inserted in the page associated with that *TID*, if sufficient space is available. Otherwise, a nearby page is chosen by the RSS. Use of this facility enables the RDS to cluster tuples of a given relation with respect to some criterion such as a value ordering on one or more fields. Another use would be to cluster tuples of one relation near particular tuples of another relation, because of matching values in some of the fields. This clustering rule would result in high performance for relational join operations, as well as for the support of hierarchical and network applications.

Images

An *image* in the RSS is a logical reordering of an *n*-ary relation with respect to values in one or more sort fields. Images combined with scans provide the ability to scan relations along a value ordering, for low level support of simple views. More importantly, an image provides associative access capability. The RDS can rapidly fetch a tuple from an image by keying on the sort field values. The RDS can also open a scan at a particular point in the image, and retrieve a sequence of tuples or subtuples with a given range of sort values. Since the image contains all the tuples and all the fields in a relation, the RDS can employ a disjunctive normal form search argument during scanning to further restrict the set of tuples which is returned. This facility is especially useful for situations where SEQUEL search predicates involve several fields of a relation, and at least one of them has image support.

A new image can be defined at any time on any combination of fields in a relation. Furthermore, each of the fields may be specified as ascending or descending. Once defined, an image is maintained automatically by the RSS during all INSERT, DELETE, and UPDATE operations. An image can also be dropped at any time.

The RSS maintains each image through the use of a multipage index structure. An internal interface is used for associative or sequential access along an image, and also to delete or insert index entries when tuples are deleted, inserted, or updated. The parameters passed across this interface include the sort field values along with the *TID* of the given tuple. In order to handle variable length, multifield indexes efficiently, a special encoding scheme is employed on the field values so that the resulting concatenation can be compared against others for ordering and search. This encoding eliminates the need for costly padding of each field and slow field-by-field comparison.

Each index is composed of one or more pages within the segment containing the relation. A new page can be added to an index when needed as long as one of the pages within the segment is marked as available. The pages for a given index are organized into a balanced hierarchic structure, in the style of B-trees [3] and of Key Sequenced Data Sets in IBM's VSAM access method [23]. Each page is a node within the hierarchy and contains an ordered sequence of index entries. For nonleaf nodes, an entry consists of a ⟨sort value, pointer⟩ pair. The pointer addresses another page in the same structure, which may be either a leaf page or another nonleaf page. In either case the target page contains entries for sort values less than or equal to the given one. For the leaf nodes, an entry is a combination of sort values along with an ascending list of *TID*s for tuples having exactly those sort values. The leaf pages are chained in a doubly linked list, so that sequential access can be supported from leaf to leaf.

Links

A *link* in the RSS is an access path which is used to connect tuples in one or two relations. The RDS determines which tuples will be on a link and determines their relative position, through explicit CONNECT and DISCONNECT operations. The RSS maintains internal pointers so that newly connected tuples are linked to previous and next twins, and so that previous and next twins are linked to each other when a tuple is disconnected. A link can be scanned using a sequence of OPEN SCAN and NEXT operations, with the optional search arguments described above.

A unary link involves a single relation and provides a partially defined ordering of tuples. Unary links can be used to maintain tuple ordering specifications which are not supported by the RSS (i.e. not value ordered). Another use is to provide an efficient access path through all tuples of a relation without the time overhead of an internal page scan.

The more important access path is a binary link, which provides a path from single tuples (parents) in one relation to sequences of tuples (children) in another relation. The RDS determines which tuples will be children under a given parent, and the relative order of children under a given parent, through the CONNECT and DISCONNECT operators. Operators are then available to scan the children of a parent or go directly from a child to its parent along a given link. In general, a tuple in the parent relation may have no children, and a tuple in the child relation may have no parent. Also, tuples in a relation may be parents and/or children in an arbitrary number of different links. The only restriction is that a given tuple can appear only once within a given link. Binary links are similar to the notion of an owner coupled set with manual membership found in the DBTG specifications for a network model of data [6].

The main use of binary links in System R is to connect child tuples to a parent based on value matches in one or more fields. With such a structure the RDS can access tuples in one relation, say the Employee relation, based on matching the Department Number field in a tuple of the Department relation. This function is especially important for supporting relational join operations, and also for supporting navigational processing through hierarchical and network models of data. The link provides direct access to the correct Employee tuples from the Department tuple (and vice versa), while use of an image may involve access to several pages in the index. A striking advantage is gained over images when the child tuples have been clustered on the same page as the parent, so that no extra pages are touched using the link, while three or more pages may be touched in a large index.

Another important feature of links is to provide reasonably fast associative access to a relation without the use of an extra index. In the above example, if the Department relation has an image on Department Number, then the RDS can gain associative access to Employee tuples for a given value of Department Number by using the Department relation image and the binary link—even if the Department tuple is not being referenced by the end user.

Links are maintained in the RSS by storing *TID*s in the prefix of tuples. New links can be defined at any time. When a new link is defined for a relation, a portion of the prefix is assigned to hold the required entries. This operation does not require access to any of the existing tuples, since new prefix space for an existing tuple is formatted only when the tuple is connected to the link. When necessary, the prefix length is enlarged through the normal mechanisms used for updates and new data fields. An existing link can be dropped at any time. When this occurs, each tuple in the corresponding relation(s) is accessed by the RSS, in order to invalidate the existing prefix entries and make the space available for subsequent link definitions.

Transaction Management

A *transaction* at the RSS is a sequence of RSI calls issued in behalf of one user. It also serves as a unit of consistency and recovery, as will be discussed below. In general, an RSS transaction consists of those calls generated by the RDS to execute all RDI operators in a single System R transaction, including the calls required to perform such RDS internal functions as authorization, catalog access, and integrity checking. An RSS transaction is marked by the START_TRANS and

END_TRANS operators. Various resources are assigned to transactions by the RSS, using the locking techniques described below. Also, a transaction recovery scheme is provided which allows a transaction to be incrementally backed out to any intermediate save point. This multipoint recovery function is important in applications involving relatively long transactions when backup is required because of errors detected by the user or RDS, because of deadlock detected by the RSS, or because of long periods of inactivity or system congestion detected by the Monitor.

A transaction save point is marked using the SAVE_TRANS operator, which returns a save point number for subsequent reference. In general, a save point may be generated by any one of the layers above the RSS. An RDI user may mark a save point at a convenient place in his transaction in order to handle backout and retry. The RDS may mark a save point for each new set oriented SEQUEL expression, so that the sequence of RSI calls needed to support the expression can be backed out for automatic retry if any of the RSI calls fails to complete.

Transaction recovery occurs when the RDS or Monitor issues the RESTORE_TRANS operator, which has a save point number as its input parameter, or when the RSS initiates the procedure to handle deadlock. The effect is to undo all the changes made by that transaction to recoverable data since the given save point. Those changes include all the tuple and image modifications caused by INSERT, DELETE, and UPDATE operations, all the link modifications caused by CONNECT and DISCONNECT operations, and even all the declarations for defining new relations, images, and links. In order to aid the RDS in continuing the transaction, all scan positions on recoverable data are automatically reset to the tuples they were pointing to at the time of the save. Finally, all locks on recoverable data which have been obtained since the given save point are released.

The transaction recovery function is supported through the maintenance of time ordered lists of log entries, which record information about each change to recoverable data. The entries for each transaction are chained together, and include the old and new values of all modified recoverable objects along with the operation code and object identification. Modifications to index structures are not logged, since their values can be determined from data values and index catalog information.

At each transaction save point, special entries are stored containing the state of all scans in use by the transaction, and the identity of the most recently acquired lock. During transaction recovery, the log entries for the transaction are read in last-in-first-out order. Special routines are employed to undo all the listed modifications back to the recorded save point, and also to restore the scans and release locks acquired after the save point.

The log entries themselves are stored in a dedicated segment which is used as a ring buffer. This segment is treated as a simple linear byte space with entries spanning page boundaries. Entries are also archived to tape to support audits and database reconstruction after system failure.

Concurrency Control

Since System R is a concurrent user system, locking techniques must be employed to solve various synchronization problems, both at the logical level of objects like relations and tuples and at the physical level of pages.

At the *logical* level, such classic situations as the "lost update" problem must be handled to insure that two concurrent transactions do not read the same value and then try to write back an incremented value. If these transactions are not synchronized, the second update will overwrite the first, and the effect of one increment will be lost. Similarly, if a user wishes to read only "clean" or committed data, not "dirty" data which has been updated by a transaction still in progress and which may be backed out, then some mechanism must be invoked to check whether the data is dirty. For another example, if transaction recovery is to affect only the modifications of a single user, then mechanisms are needed to insure that data updated by some ongoing transaction, say T1, is not updated by another, say T2. Otherwise, the backout of transaction T1 will undo T2's update and thus violate our principle of isolated backout.

At the *physical* level of pages, locking techniques are required to insure that internal components of the RSS give correct results. For example, a data page may contain several tuples with each tuple accessed through its tuple identifier, which requires following a pointer within the data page. Even if no logical conflict occurs between two transactions, because each is accessing a different relation or a different tuple in the same relation, a problem could occur at the physical level if one transaction follows a pointer to a tuple on some page while the other transaction updates a second tuple on the same page and causes a data compaction routine to reassign tuple locations.

One basic decision in establishing System R was to handle both logical and physical locking requirements within the RSS, rather than splitting the functions across the RDS and RSS subsystems. Physical locking is handled by setting and holding locks on one or more pages during the execution of a single RSI operation. Logical locking is handled by setting locks on such objects as segments, relations, *TIDs*, and key value intervals and holding them until they are explicitly released or to the end of the transaction. The main motivation for this decision is to facilitate the exploration of alternative locking techniques. (One particular alternative has already been included in the RSS as a tuning option, whereby the finest level of locking in a segment can be expanded to an entire page of data, rather than single tuples. This option allows pages to be locked for both logical and physical purposes, by varying the duration of the lock.) Other motivations are to simplify the work of the RDS and to develop a complete, concurrent user RSS which can be tailored to future research applications.

Another basic decision in formulating System R was to automate all of the locking functions, both logical and physical, so that users can access shared data and delegate some or all lock protocols to the system. For situations detected by the end user or RDS where locking large aggregates is desirable, the RSS also supports operators for placing explicit share or exclusive locks on entire segments or relations.

In order to provide reasonable performance for a wide spectrum of user requirements, the RSS supports multiple levels of consistency which control the isolation of a user from the actions of other concurrent users (see also [13]). When a transaction is started at the RSI, one of three consistency levels must be specified. (These same consistency levels are also reflected at the RDI.) Different consistency levels may be chosen by different concurrent transactions. For all of these levels, the RSS guarantees that any data modified by the transaction is not modified by any other until the given transaction ends. This rule is essential to our transaction recovery scheme, where the backout of modifications by one transaction does not affect modifications made by other transactions.

The differences in consistency levels occur during read operations. Level 1 consistency offers the least isolation from other users, but causes the lowest overhead and lock contention. With this level, dirty data may be accessed, and one may read different values for the same data item during the same transaction. It is clear that execution with Level 1 consistency incurs the risk of reading data values that violate integrity constraints, and that in some sense never appeared if the transaction which set the data values is later backed out. On the other hand, this level may be entirely satisfactory for gathering statistical information from a large database when exact results are not required. The HOLD option can be used during read operations to insure against lost updates or dirty data values.

In a transaction with Level 2 consistency, the user is assured that every item read is clean. However, no guarantee is made that subsequent access to the same item will yield the same values or that associative access will yield the same item. At this consistency level it is possible for another transaction to modify a data item any time after the given Level 2 transaction has read it. A second read by the given transaction will then yield the new value, since the item will become clean again when the other transaction terminates. Transactions running at Level 2 consistency still require use of the HOLD option during read operations preceding updates, to insure against lost updates.

For the highest consistency level, called Level 3, the user sees the logical equivalent of a single user system. Every item read is clean, and subsequent reads yield the same values, subject of course to updates by the given user. This repeatability feature applies not only to a specific item accessed directly by tuple identifier, but even to sequences of items and to items accessed associatively. For example, if the RDS employs an image on the Employee relation, ordered by Employee Name, to find all employees whose names start with 'B', then the same answer will occur every time within the same transaction. Thus, the RDS can effectively lock a set of items defined by a SEQUEL predicate and obtained by any search strategy, against insertions into or deletions from the set. Similarly, if the RDS employs an image to access the unique tuple where Name = 'Smith', and no such tuple exists, then the same nonexistence result is assured for subsequent accesses.

Level 3 consistency eliminates the problem of lost updates, and also guarantees that one can read a logically consistent version of any collection of tuples, since other transactions are logically serialized with the given one. As an example of this last point, consider a situation where two or more related data items are periodically updated, such as the mean and variance of a sequence of temperature measurements. With Level 3 consistency, a reader is assured of reading a consistent pair—rather than, say, a new variance and an old mean. Although one could use the HOLD option to handle this particular problem, many such associations may not be understood in a more complex database environment, even by relatively experienced programmers.

The RSS components set locks automatically in order to guarantee the logical functions of these various consistency levels. For example, in certain cases the RSS must set locks on tuples, such as when they have been inserted or updated. Similarly, in certain cases the RSS must set locks on index values or ranges of index values, even when the values are not currently present in the index—such as in handling the case of 'Smith' described above. In both of these cases the RSS must also acquire physical locks on one or more pages, which are held at least during the execution of each RSI operation, in order to insure that data and index pages are accessed and maintained correctly.

The RSS employs a single lock mechanism to synchronize access to all objects. This synchronization is handled by a set of procedures in every activation of the RSS, which maintains a collection of queue structures called *gates* in shared, read/write memory. Some of these gates are numbered and are associated by convention with such resources as the table of buffer contents, or the availability of the database for processing. However, in order to handle locks on a potentially huge set of objects like the tuples themselves, the RSS also includes a named gate facility. Internal components can request a lock by giving an eight-character name for the object, using such names as a tuple identifier, index value, or page number. If the named resource is already locked it will have a gate. If not, then a named gate will be allocated from a special pool of numbered gates. The named gate will be deallocated when its queue becomes empty.

An internal request to lock an object has several parameters: the name of the object, the mode of the lock (such as shared, exclusive, or various other modes mentioned below), and an indication of lock duration, so that the RSS can quickly release all locks held for a single RSI call, or all locks held for the entire transaction. The duration of a lock is also used for scheduling purposes, such as to select a transaction for backout when deadlock is detected.

The choice of lock duration is influenced by several factors, such as the type of action requested by the user and the consistency level of the transaction. If a tuple is inserted or updated by a transaction at any consistency level, then an exclusive lock must be held on the tuple (or some superset) until the transaction has ended. If a tuple is deleted, then an exclusive lock must be held on the *TID* of that tuple for the duration of the transaction, in order to guarantee that the deletion can be undone correctly during transaction backout. For any of these cases, as well as for the ones described below, an additional lock is typically set on the page itself to prevent conflict of transactions at the physical level. However, these page locks are released at the end of the RSI call.

In the case of a transaction with Level 3 consistency, share locks must be maintained on all tuples and index values which are read, for the duration of the transaction, to insure repeatability. For transactions with Level 2 consistency, read accesses require a share lock with immediate duration. Such a lock request is enqueued behind earlier exclusive lock requests so that the user is assured of reading clean data. The lock is then released as soon as the request has been granted, since reads do not have to be repeatable. Finally, for transactions with Level 1 consistency, no locks are required for read purposes, other than short locks on pages to insure that the read operation is correct.

Data items can be locked at various granularities, to insure that various applications run efficiently. For example, locks on single tuples are effective for transactions which access small amounts of data, while locks on entire relations or even entire segments are more reasonable for transactions which cause the RDS to access large amounts of data. In order to accommodate these differences, a dynamic lock hierarchy protocol has been developed so that a small number of locks can be used to lock both few and many objects [13]. The basic idea of the scheme is that separate locks are associated with each granularity of object, such as segment, relation, and tuple. If the RDS requests a lock on an entire segment in share or exclusive mode, then every tuple of every relation in the segment is implicitly locked in the same mode. If the RDS requests a lock on a single relation, say in exclusive mode, but does not wish exclusive access to the entire segment, then the RSS first generates an automatic request for a lock in *intent-exclusive* mode on the segment, before requesting an exclusive lock on the relation. This intent-exclusive lock is compatible with other intent locks but incompatible with share and exclusive locks. The same protocol is extended to include locks on individual tuples, through automatic acquisition of intent locks on the segment and relation, before a lock is acquired on the tuple in share or exclusive mode.

Since locks are requested dynamically, it is possible for two or more concurrent activations of the RSS to deadlock. The RSS has been designed to check for deadlock situations when requests are blocked, and to select one or more victims for backout if deadlock is detected. The detection is done by the Monitor, on a periodic basis, by looking for cycles in a user-user matrix. The selection of a victim is based on the relative ages of transactions in each deadlock cycle, as well as on the durations of the locks. In general the RSS selects the youngest transaction whose lock is of short duration, i.e. being held for the duration of a single RSI call, since the partially completed call can easily be undone. If none of the locks in the cycle are of short duration, then the youngest transaction is chosen. This transaction is then backed out to the save point preceding the offending lock request, using the transaction recovery scheme described above. (To simplify the code, special provisions are made for transactions which need locks and are already backing up.)

System Checkpoint and Restart

The RSS provides functions to recover the database to a consistent state in the event of a system crash. By a consistent state we mean a set of data values which would result if a set of transactions had been completed, and no other transactions were in progress. At such a state all image and link pointers are correct at the RSS level, and more importantly all user defined integrity assertions on data values are valid at the RDS level, since the RDS guarantees all integrity constraints at transaction boundaries.

In the RSS, special attention has been given to reduce the need for complete database dumps from disk to tape to accomplish a system checkpoint. The database dump technique has several difficulties. Since the time to copy the database to tape may be long for large databases, checkpoints may be taken infrequently, such as overnight or weekly. System restart is then a time consuming process, since many database changes must be reconstructed from the system log to restore a recent database state. In addition, before the checkpoint is performed, all ongoing transactions must first be completed. If any of these are long, then no new transactions are allowed to initiate until the long one is completed and the database dump is taken.

In the RSS, two system recovery mechanisms have been developed to alleviate these difficulties. The first mechanism uses disk storage to recover in the event of a "soft" failure which causes the contents of main memory to be lost; it is oriented toward frequent checkpoints and rapid recovery. The second mechanism uses tape storage to recover in the relatively infrequent case that disk storage is destroyed; it is oriented toward less frequent checkpoints. In both mechanisms, checkpoints can be made while transactions are still in progress.

The disk oriented recovery mechanism is heavily dependent on the segment recovery functions described above, and also on the availability of transaction logs. The Monitor Machine has the responsibility for scheduling checkpoints, based on parameters set during system startup. When a checkpoint is required, the Monitor quiesces all activity within the RSS at a point of physical consistency: transactions may still be in progress, but may not be executing an RSI operation. The technique for halting RSS activity is to acquire a special RSS lock in exclusive mode, which every activation of the RSS code acquires in share mode before executing an RSI operation, and releases at the end of the operation. The Monitor then issues the SAVE_SEGMENT operator to bring disk copies of all relevant segments up to date. Finally, the RSS lock is released and transactions are allowed to resume.

When a soft failure occurs, the RESTORE_SEGMENT operator is used to restore the contents of all saved segments. Recall that the restore function is a relatively simple one involving the setting of current page map values equal to the backup page map values and the releasing of pages allocated since the save point. The log segment, which is saved more frequently than normal data segments, is effectively saved at the end of each transaction, and contains "after" values as well as "before" values of modified data. Therefore transactions completing after the last database save, but before the last log save, can be redone automatically. In addition, the transaction logs are used to back out transactions which were incomplete at the checkpoint and cannot be redone, in order that a consistent database state is reached.

Our tape oriented recovery scheme is an extension of the above one. In order to recover in the event of lost disk data, some technique is required to get a sufficient copy of data and log information to tape. The technique we have chosen is to have the Monitor schedule certain checkpoints as "long" rather than standard short ones. A long checkpoint performs the usual segment save operations described above, but also initiates a process which copies the saved pages from disk to tape. Thus the checkpoint to tape is incremental.

4. SUMMARY AND CONCLUSION

We have described the overall architecture of System R and also the two main components: the Relational Data System (RDS) and the Relational Storage System (RSS). The RSS is a concurrent user, data management subsystem which provides underlying support for System R. The Relational Storage Interface (RSI) has operations at the single tuple level, with automatic maintenance of an arbitrary number of value orderings, called *images*, based on values in one or more fields. Images are implemented through the use of multilevel index structures. The

RSS also supports efficient navigation from tuples in one relation to tuples in another, through the maintenance of pointer chain structures called *links*. Images and links, along with physical scans through RSS pages, constitute the access path primitives which the RDS employs for efficient support of operators on the relational, hierarchical, and network models of data. Furthermore, to facilitate gradual integration of data and changing performance requirements, the RSS supports dynamic addition and deletion of relations, indexes, and links, with full space reclamation, and the addition of new fields to existing relations—all without special utilities or database reorganization.

Another important aspect of the RSS is full support of concurrent access in a multiprocessor environment, through the use of gate structures in shared, read/write memory. Several levels of consistency are provided to control the interaction of each user with others. Also locks are set automatically within the RSS, so that even unsophisticated users can write transactions without explicit lock protocols or file open protocols. These locks are set on various granularities of data objects, so that various types of application environments can be accommodated.

In the area of recovery, transaction backout is provided to any one of an arbitrary number of user specified save points, to aid in the recovery of long application programs. Backout may also be initiated by the RSS during automatic detection of deadlock. A new recovery scheme is provided at the system level, so that both checkpoint and restart operations can be performed efficiently.

The RDS supports the Relational Data Interface (RDI), the external interface of System R, and provides the user with a consistent set of facilities for data retrieval, manipulation, definition, and control. The RDI is designed as a set of operators which may be called directly from a host program. It is expected that programs will be written on top of the RDI to implement various stand-alone relational interfaces and other, possibly nonrelational, interfaces.

The most important component of the RDS is the optimizer, which makes plans for efficient execution of high level operations using the RSS access path primitives. Of great importance in optimizing queries is the method by which tuples are arranged in physical storage. The RDS provides the RSS with clustering hints during insert operations, so that the tuples of a relation are physically clustered according to some value ordering, or placed near associated tuples along a binary link. Given the cluster properties of stored relations, the optimizer uses an access path strategy with the main emphasis on reducing the number of I/O operations between main memory and on-line, direct access storage.

In addition to the optimizer, the RDS contains components for various other functions. The authorization component allows the creator of a relation or view to grant or revoke various capabilities. The integrity system automatically enforces assertions about database values, which are entered through SEQUEL commands. A similar mechanism is employed to trigger one or more database actions when a given action is detected. The SEQUEL language may also be used to define any query as a named view. The access plan to materialize this view is selected by the optimizer, and can be stored away as a Pre-Optimized Package (POP) for subsequent execution. POPs are especially important for the support of transactions which are run repetitively, since they avoid much of the overhead usually associated with a high level of data independence.

APPENDIX I. RDI OPERATORS

Square brackets [ ] are used below to indicate optional parameters.

```
Operators for data definition and manipulation:

    SEQUEL ( [ <cursor name>,] <any SEQUEL statement> )

    FETCH ( <cursor name> [, <pointers to I/O locations>] )

    FETCH_HOLD ( <cursor name> [, <pointers to I/O locations> ] )

    OPEN ( <cursor name>, <name of relation or view> )

    CLOSE ( <cursor name> )

    KEEP ( <cursor name>, <new relation name>,

           <list of new field names> )

    DESCRIBE ( <cursor name>, <degree>, <pointers to I/O

           locations> )

    BIND ( <program variable name>, <program variable address> )


Operators on transactions and locks:

    BEGIN_TRANS ( <transaction id>, <consistency level> )

    END_TRANS

    SAVE ( <save point name> )

    RESTORE ( <save point name> )

    RELEASE ( <cursor name> )
```

APPENDIX II. SEQUEL SYNTAX

The following is a shortened version of the BNF syntax for SEQUEL. It contains several minor ambiguities and generates a number of constructs with no semantic support, all of which are (hopefully) missing from our complete, production syntax. Square brackets [ ] are used to indicate optional constructs.

```
statement  ::=  query
              | dml-statement
              | ddl-statement
              | control-statement

dml-statement  ::=  assignment
                  | insertion
                  | deletion
                  | update

query  ::=  query-expr [ ORDER BY  ord-spec-list ]

assignment  ::=  receiver <- query-expr

receiver  ::=  table-name [ ( field-name-list ) ]

insertion  ::=  INSERT  INTO  receiver  :  insert-spec

insert-spec  ::=  query-expr
                | literal
                | constant

field-name-list  ::=  field-name
                    | field-name-list  ,  field-name
```

```
deletion  ::=  DELETE table-name [ var-name ]  [ where-clause ]

update  ::=  UPDATE  table-name [ var-name ] set-clause-list
                [ where-clause ]

where-clause  ::=  WHERE  boolean
                |  WHERE  CURRENT  [ TUPLE ]  OF
                        [ CURSOR ] cursor-name

set-clause-list  ::=  set-clause
                   |  set-clause-list  ,  set-clause

set-clause  ::=  SET  field-name  =  expr
              |  SET  field-name  =  ( query-expr )

query-expr  ::=  query-block
              |  query-expr  set-op  query-block
              |  ( query-expr )

set-op  ::=  INTERSECT  |  UNION  |  MINUS

query-block  ::=  select-clause  FROM  from-list
                        [ WHERE boolean ]
                        [ GROUP BY  field-spec-list
                            [ HAVING boolean ] ]

select-clause  ::=  SELECT [ UNIQUE ] sel-expr-list
                 |  SELECT [ UNIQUE ] *

sel-expr-list  ::=  sel-expr
                 |  sel-expr-list  ,  sel-expr

sel-expr  ::=  expr [ : host-location ]
            |  var-name  .  *  |  table-name  *

from-list  ::=  table-name [ var-name ]
             |  from-list  ,  table-name [ var-name ]

field-spec-list  ::=  field-spec
                   |  field-spec-list  ,  field-spec

ord-spec-list  ::=  field-spec [ direction ]
                 |  ord-spec-list  ,  field-spec [ direction ]

direction  ::=  ASC  |  DESC

boolean  ::=  boolean-term
           |  boolean  OR  boolean-term

boolean-term  ::=  boolean-factor
                |  boolean-term  AND  boolean-factor

boolean-factor  ::=  [ NOT ] boolean-primary

boolean-primary  ::=  predicate
                   |  ( boolean )

predicate  ::=  expr  comparison  expr
             |  expr  BETWEEN  expr  AND  expr
             |  expr  comparison  table-spec
             |  < field-spec-list >  =  full-table-spec
             |  < field-spec-list >  [ IS ]  IN  full-table-spec
             |  IF  predicate  THEN  predicate
             |  SET ( field-spec-list )  comparison
                    full-table-spec
             |  SET ( field-spec-list )  comparison
                    SET ( field-spec-list )
             |  table-spec  comparison  full-table-spec

full-table-spec  ::=  table-spec
                   |  ( entry )
                   |  constant

table-spec  ::=  query-block
              |  ( query-expr )
              |  literal

expr  ::=  arith-term
        |  expr  add-op  arith-term

arith-term  ::=  arith-factor
              |  arith-term  mult-op  arith-factor

arith-factor  ::=  [ add-op ] primary

primary  ::=  [ OLD | NEW ]  field-spec
           |  set-fn  ( [ UNIQUE ] expr )
           |  COUNT  (  *  )
           |  constant
           |  (  expr  )

field-spec  ::=  field-name
              |  table-name  .  field-name
              |  var-name  .  field-name

comparison  ::=  comp-op
              |  CONTAINS
              |  DOES NOT CONTAIN
              |  [  IS  ]  IN
              |  [  IS  ]  NOT IN

comp-op  ::=  =  | ¬=  |  >  |  >=  |  <  |  <=

add-op  ::=  +  |  -

mult-op  ::=  *  |  /

set-fn  ::=  AVG  |  MAX  |  MIN  |  SUM  |  COUNT  |  identifier

literal  ::=  (  lit-tuple-list  )
           |  (  entry-list  )
           |  lit-tuple

lit-tuple-list  ::=  lit-tuple
                  |  lit-tuple-list  ,  lit-tuple

lit-tuple  ::=  <  entry  >
             |  <  entry-list  >

entry-list  ::=  entry  ,  entry
              |  entry-list  ,  entry

entry  ::=  [ constant ]

constant  ::=  quoted-string
            |  number
            |  host-location
            |  NULL
            |  USER
            |  DATE
            |  field-name  OF CURSOR  cursor-name
                    [ ON  table-name ]

table-name  ::=  name

image-name  ::=  name

link-name  ::=  name

asrt-name  ::=  name

trig-name  ::=  name

name  ::=  [ creator  . ] identifier

creator  ::=  identifier

user-name  ::=  identifier

field-name  ::=  identifier

var-name  ::=  identifier

cursor-name  ::=  identifier

host-location  ::=  identifier

integer  ::=  number
```

```
ddl-statement  ::=  create-table
                 |  expand-table
                 |  keep-table
                 |  create-image
                 |  create-link
                 |  define-view
                 |  drop
                 |  comment

create-table  ::=  CREATE  [ perm-spec ]  [ share-spec ]  TABLE
                     table-name  :  field-defn-list

perm-spec  ::=  PERMANENT  |  TEMPORARY

share-spec  ::=  SHARED  |  PRIVATE

field-defn-list  ::=  field-defn
                   |  field-defn-list  ,  field-defn

field-defn  ::=  field-name  ( type [ , NONULL ] )

type  ::=  CHAR  ( integer )
        |  CHAR ( * )
        |  INTEGER
        |  SMALLINT
        |  DECIMAL ( integer , integer )
        |  FLOAT

expand-table  ::=  EXPAND  TABLE  table-name  ADD
                         FIELD  field-defn

keep-table  ::=  KEEP  TABLE  table-name

create-image  ::=  CREATE  [ image-mod-list ]  IMAGE  image-name
                      ON  table-name  ( ord-spec-list )

image-mod-list  ::=  image-mod
                  |  image-mod-list  image-mod

image-mod  ::=  UNIQUE
             |  CLUSTERING

create-link  ::=  CREATE  [ CLUSTERING ]  LINK  link-name
                    FROM  table-name ( field-name-list )
                    TO  table-name ( field-name-list )
                    [ ORDER BY ord-spec-list ]

define-view  ::=  DEFINE  [ perm-spec ]  VIEW  table-name
                [ ( field-name-list ) ]  AS  query

drop  ::=  DROP  system-entity  name

comment  ::=  COMMENT ON  system-entity  name  :  quoted-string
          |  COMMENT ON FIELD  table-name . field-name
                :  quoted-string

system-entity  ::=  TABLE  |  VIEW  |  ASSERTION
                 |  TRIGGER  |  IMAGE  |  LINK

control-statement  ::=  asrt-statement
                     |  enforcement
                     |  define-trigger
                     |  grant
                     |  revoke

asrt-statement  ::=  ASSERT  asrt-name [ IMMEDIATE ]
                       [ ON asrt-condition ]  :  boolean

asrt-condition  ::=  action-list
                  |  table-name  [ var-name ]

action-list  ::=  action
               |  action-list  ,  action

action  ::=  INSERTION OF  table-name [ var-name ]
          |  DELETION OF  table-name [ var-name ]
          |  UPDATE OF  table-name [ var-name ]
                [ ( field-name-list ) ]

enforcement  ::=  ENFORCE  INTEGRITY
               |  ENFORCE ASSERTION  asrt-name

define-trigger  ::=  DEFINE TRIGGER  trig-name
                        ON trig-condition  :  ( statement-list )

trig-condition  ::=  action
                  |  READ OF  table-name [ var-name ]

statement-list  ::=  statement
                  |  statement-list  ;  statement

grant  ::=  GRANT [ auth ] table-name  TO  user-list
                  [ WITH GRANT OPTION ]

auth  ::=  ALL RIGHTS ON
        |  operation-list  ON
        |  ALL BUT  operation-list  ON

user-list  ::=  user-name
             |  user-list  ,  user-name
             |  PUBLIC

operation-list  ::=  operation
                  |  operation-list  ,  operation

operation  ::=  READ
             |  INSERT
             |  DELETE
             |  UPDATE [ ( field-name-list ) ]
             |  DROP
             |  EXPAND
             |  IMAGE
             |  LINK
             |  CONTROL

revoke  ::=  REVOKE [ operation-list ON ] table-name
                 FROM  user-list
```

APPENDIX III. RSI OPERATORS

The RSI operators are oriented toward the use of formatted control blocks. Rather than explain the detailed conventions of these control blocks, we list below an approximate but hopefully readable form for the operators. Square brackets [ ] are used to indicate optional parameters.

```
Operators on segments:

    OPEN_SEGMENT ( <segid> )

    CLOSE_SEGMENT ( <segid> )

    SAVE_SEGMENT ( <segid> )

    RESTORE_SEGMENT ( <segid> )


Operators on transactions and locks:

    START_TRANS ( <consistency level> )

    END_TRANS

    SAVE_TRANS, RETURNS ( <saveid> )

    RESTORE_TRANS ( <saveid> )

    LOCK_SEGMENT ( <segid>, <mode: SHARE or EXCLUSIVE or SIX> )

    LOCK_RELATION ( <segid>, <relid>, <mode, as above> )

    RELEASE_TUPLE ( <segid>, <tid> )
```

```
Operators on tuples and scans:

    FETCH ( <segid>, <relid>, <identifier: tid or scanid or imageid,
            key values>, <field list>, <pointers to I/O locations>
            [, HOLD] )
    INSERT ( <segid>, <relid>, <pointers to I/O locations>
            [, <nearby tid> ] ),   RETURNS ( <tid> )
    DELETE ( <segid>, <relid>, <identifier, as above> )
    UPDATE ( <segid>, <relid>, <identifier, as above>,
            <field list>, <pointers to I/O locations> )
    OPEN_SCAN ( <segid>, <path: relid or imageid or linkid>,
            <start-point: key values for image, or tid for link,
            or scanid for link> ),
              RETURNS ( <scanid> )
    NEXT ( <segid>, <scanid>, <field list>, <pointers to I/O locations>
          [, <search argument>] [, HOLD] )
    CLOSE ( <segid>, <scanid> )
    PARENT ( <child segid>, <linkid>, <identifier for new tuple, as
            above>, <field list>, <pointers to I/O locations>
            [, HOLD] )
    CONNECT ( <child segid>, <linkid>, <identifier for new tuple, as
            above>, <neighbor relid>, <neighbor tid>,
            <location: BEFORE or AFTER> )
    DISCONNECT ( <child segid>, <linkid>, <identifier for child, as
            above> )

Operators for data definition:

    CREATE ( <segid>, <object type: REL or IMAGE or LINK >, <specs> ),
            RETURNS ( <object identifier: relid or imageid or linkid> )
    DESTROY ( <segid>, <object identifier, as above> )
    CHANGE ( <segid>, <object identifier, as above>,
            <new specs> )
    READSPEC ( <segid>, <object identifier, as above>,
            <pointer to I/O location> )
```

ACKNOWLEDGMENTS

The authors wish to acknowledge many helpful discussions with E.F. Codd, originator of the relational model of data, and with L.Y. Liu, manager of the Computer Science Department of the IBM San Jose Research Laboratory. We also wish to acknowledge the extensive contributions to System R of Phyllis Reisner, whose human factors experiments (reported in [24, 25]) have resulted in significant improvements in the SEQUEL language.

REFERENCES

1. ASTRAHAN, M.M., AND CHAMBERLIN, D.D. Implementation of a structured English query language. *Comm. ACM 18*, 10 (Oct. 1975), 580–588.
2. ASTRAHAN, M.M., AND LORIE, R.A. SEQUEL-XRM: A relational system. Proc. ACM Pacific Conf., San Francisco, Calif., April 1975, pp. 34–38.
3. BAYER, R., AND MCCREIGHT, E.M. Organization and maintenance of large ordered indexes. *Acta Informatica 1* (1972), 173–189.
4. BOYCE, R.F., AND CHAMBERLIN, D.D. Using a structured English query language as a data definition facility. Res. Rep. RJ 1318, IBM Res. Lab., San Jose, Calif., Dec. 1973.
5. CHAMBERLIN, D.D., AND BOYCE, R.F. SEQUEL: A structured English query language. Proc. ACM SIGFIDET Workshop, Ann Arbor, Mich., May 1974, pp. 249–264.
6. CODASYL DATA BASE TASK GROUP. April 1971 Rep. (Available from ACM, New York.)
7. CODD, E.F. A relational model of data for large shared data banks. *Comm. ACM 13*, 6 (June 1970), 377–387.
8. CODD, E.F. Relational completeness of data base sublanguages. In *Courant Computer Science Symposia, Vol. 6: Data Base Systems*, G. Forsythe, Ed., Prentice-Hall, Engelwood Cliffs, N.J., 1971, pp. 65–98.
9. DONOVAN, J.J., FESSEL, R., GREENBERG, S.S., AND GUTENTAG, L.M. An experimental VM/370 based information system. Proc. Internat. Conf. on Very Large Data Bases, Framingham, Mass., Sept. 1975, pp. 549–553. (Available from ACM, New York.)
10. ESWARAN, K.P., AND CHAMBERLIN, D.D. Functional specifications of a subsystem for data base integrity. Proc. Internat. Conf. on Very Large Data Bases, Framingham, Mass., Sept. 1975, pp. 48–68. (Available from ACM, New York.)
11. Feature analysis of generalized data base management systems. CODASYL Systems Committee Tech. Rep., May 1971. (Available from ACM, New York.)
12. GOLDSTEIN, R.C., AND STRNAD, A.L. The MACAIMS data management system. Proc. ACM SIGFIDET Workshop on Data Description and Access, Houston, Tex., Nov. 1970, pp. 201–229.
13. GRAY, J.N., LORIE, R.A., PUTZOLU, G.R., AND TRAIGER, I.L. Granularity of locks and degrees of consistency in a shared data base. Proc. IFIP Working Conf. on Modelling of Data Base Management Systems, Freudenstadt, Germany, Jan. 1976, pp. 695–723.
14. GRAY, J.N., AND WATSON, V. A shared segment and inter-process communication facility for VM/370. Res. Rep. RJ 1579, IBM Res. Lab., San Jose, Calif., Feb. 1975.
15. GRIFFITHS, P.P., AND WADE, B.W. An authorization mechanism for a relational data base system. Proc. ACM SIGMOD Conf., Washington, D.C., June 1976 (to appear).
16. HELD, G.D., STONEBRAKER, M.R., AND WONG, E. INGRES: A relational data base system. Proc. AFIPS 1975 NCC, Vol. 44, AFIPS Press, Montvale, N.J., pp. 409–416.
17. Information Management System, General Information Manual. IBM Pub. No. GH20-1260, IBM Corp., White Plains, N.Y., 1975.
18. Introduction to VM/370. Pub. No. GC20-1800, IBM Corp., White Plains, N.Y., Jan. 1975.
19. LORIE, R.A. XRM—An extended (*n*-ary) relational memory. IBM Scientific Center Rep. G320-2096, Cambridge, Mass., Jan. 1974.
20. LORIE, R.A., AND SYMONDS, A.J. A relational access method for interactive applications. In *Courant Computer Science Symposia, Vol. 6: Data Base Systems*, G. Forsythe, Ed., Prentice-Hall, Engelwood Cliffs, N.J., 1971, pp. 99–124.
21. MYLOPOULOS, J., SCHUSTER, S.A., AND TSICHRITZIS, D. A multi-level relational system. Proc. AFIPS 1975 NCC, Vol. 44, AFIPS Press, Montvale, N.J., pp. 403–408.
22. NOTLEY, M.G. The Peterlee IS/1 System. IBM UK Scientific Center Rep. UKSC-0018, March 1972.
23. Planning for Enhanced VSAM under OS/VS. Pub. No. GC26-3842, IBM Corp., White Plains, N.Y., 1975.
24. REISNER, P. Use of psychological experimentation as an aid to development of a query language. Res. Rep. RJ 1707, IBM Res. Lab., San Jose, Calif., Jan. 1976.
25. REISNER, P., BOYCE, R.F., AND CHAMBERLIN, D.D. Human factors evaluation of two data base query languages: SQUARE and SEQUEL. Proc. AFIPS 1975 NCC, Vol. 44, AFIPS Press, Montvale, N.J., pp. 447–452.

26. SCHMID, H.A., AND BERNSTEIN, P.A. A multi-level architecture for relational data base systems. Proc. Internat. Conf. on Very Large Data Bases, Framingham, Mass., Sept. 1975, pp. 202–226. (Available from ACM, New York.)
27. SMITH, J.M., AND CHANG, P.Y. Optimizing the performance of a relational algebra database interface. *Comm. ACM 18*, 10 (Oct. 1975), 568–579.
28. STONEBRAKER, M. Implementation of integrity constraints and views by query modification. Proc. ACM SIGMOD Conf., San Jose, Calif., May 1975, pp. 65–78.
29. TODD, S. PRTV: An efficient implementation for large relational data bases. Proc. Internat. Conf. on Very Large Data Bases, Framingham, Mass., Sept. 1975, pp. 554–556. (Available from ACM, New York.)
30. WHITNEY, V.K.M. RDMS: A relational data management system. Proc. Fourth Internat. Symp. on Computer and Information Sciences, Miami Beach, Fla., Dec. 1972, pp. 55–66.
31. ZLOOF, M.M. Query by Example. Proc. AFIPS 1975 NCC, Vol. 44, AFIPS Press, Montvale, N.J., pp. 431–437.

Received November 1975; revised February 1976

Epilogue

System R: A Relational Approach to Database Management

Donald D. Chamberlin
IBM Almaden Research Center
San Jose, California

The System R project continued in existence at IBM's San Jose Research Laboratory (now Almaden Research Center) for several years after the publication of this paper. The interfaces and relational database technology developed by System R were ultimately incorporated into several products announced by IBM and have had an influence on products announced by other manufacturers as well.

A series of evolutionary changes to the syntax of the SEQUEL language described in this paper were published in the *IBM Journal of Research and Development* in November 1976 [CHAM 76]. The name of the language was later changed to SQL, and a summary of user experience with the early implementations of the language was published in 1980 [CHAM 80].

The most important architectural change in System R after the publication of this paper was a change from an interpreter to a compiler strategy. The Relational Data Interface is described here as a static collection of calls from a programming language to an interpreter that accepts SQL statements. This approach was ultimately replaced by a "compiler" approach in which System R was divided into two separate and distinct parts:

1. A precompiler that operates on a user's source program, finding SQL statements and replacing each one with a call to a compiled "access module" containing a pre-optimized access path.
2. A run-time system that is called by the user's object program to load and execute the pre-optimized access modules.

The benefits of the compilation approach are obvious for transactions that are executed repetitively, since access path selection need not be done at run-time and the user's program is provided with a very efficient machine-language module for processing the transaction. It was less obvious that the compilation approach also made sense for queries that are specified interactively and executed only once or a few times; however, experiments revealed that the efficiency of compiled code would often pay back the cost of compilation during the process of executing even an ad-hoc query. The techniques and tradeoffs developed for processing ad-hoc queries and pre-compiled transactions in System R were described in a 1981 paper in *ACM Transactions on Database Systems* [CHAM 81a]. Details of the optimization and access path selection process were described in [SELI 79].

Near the end of the System R project, several overview papers were published describing the architectural evolution of the system, the results of its first experimental installations, and its development into a supported product. These papers include [BLAS 81] and [CHAM 81b].

The first IBM product to incorporate System R technology was SQL/Data System [IBM 81], announced in 1981 in the DOS/VSE environment and later in the VM/370 environment. This product was followed in 1984 by DB2, a high-performance implementation of SQL in the MVS environment [IBM 84], and Query Management Facility (QMF) [IBM 86], which provides an interactive query and report generation facility on top of both SQL/DS and DB2. More recently, an implementation of SQL was announced as part of the OS/2 Extended Edition operating system for IBM's Personal System/2 [IBM 87a].

In addition to the IBM products mentioned above, implementations of the SQL database language have been announced by several other manufacturers, and the language has been the subject of both national and international standardization. An SQL standard was adopted by the American National Standards Institute (ANSI) in 1986 [ANSI 86] and by the International Organization for Standardization (ISO) in 1987 [ISO 87]. SQL has also been incorporated by IBM as one of the interfaces in its Systems Application Architecture [IBM 87b].

The Almaden Research Center continues to be actively involved in research in relational database management technology. After the completion of System R, a prototype distributed relational database system called R* was designed and implemented [WILL 82]. More recently, a project called Starburst [LIND 87] has been investigating issues of extensibility in workstation-based relational database management systems. The database department at Almaden is also conducting research in database machines, highly available database systems, high-volume transaction systems, relational database theory, and other related areas.

References

[ANSI 86] ANSI Standard X3.135-1986: Database Language SQL. American National Standards Institute, 1986.

[BLAS 81] M. Blasgen, M. Astrahan, D. Chamberlin, J. Gray, W. King, B. Lindsay, R. Lorie, J. Mehl, T. Price, G. Putzolu, M. Schkolnick, P. Selinger, D. Slutz, H. Strong, I. Traiger, B. Wade, and R. Yost. "System R: An Architectural Overview" *IBM Systems Journal*, Vol. 20, No. 1, February 1981, p. 41.

[CHAM 76] D. Chamberlin, M. Astrahan, K. Eswaran, P. Griffiths, R. Lorie, J. Mehl, P. Reisner, and B. Wade. "SEQUEL 2: A Unified Approach to Data Definition, Manipulation, and Control" *IBM Journal of Research and Development*, November 1976, p. 560. (Also see errata in January 1977 issue.)

[CHAM 80] D. Chamberlin. "A Summary of User Experience with the SQL Data Sublanguage" *Proc of International Conference on Data Bases*, Aberdeen, Scotland, July 1980.

[CHAM 81a] D. Chamberlin, M. Astrahan, W. King, R. Lorie, J. Mehl, T. Price, M. Schkolnick, P. Selinger, D. Slutz, B. Wade, and R. Yost. "Support for Repetitive Transactions and Ad-Hoc Queries in System R" *ACM Transactions on Database Systems*, Vol. 6, No. 1, March 1981, p. 70.

[CHAM 81b] D. Chamberlin, M. Astrahan, M. Blasgen, J. Gray, W. King, B. Lindsay, R. Lorie, J. Mehl, T. Price, G. Putzolu, M. Schkolnick, P. Selinger, D. Slutz, I. Traiger, B. Wade, and R. Yost. "A History and Evaluation of System R" *Communications of the ACM*, Vol. 24, No. 10 (October 1981) pp. 632-646.

[IBM 81] SQL/Data System General Information Manual. IBM Publication GH24-5012 (1981).

[IBM 84] DB2 General Information Manual. IBM Publication GC26-4073 (1984).

[IBM 86] Query Management Facility: User's Guide and Reference. IBM Publication SC26-4232 (1986).

[IBM 87a] OS/2 Extended Edition Database Manager. IBM Publication Z360-2787 (1987).

[IBM 87b] Systems Application Architecture: Common Programming Interface Database Reference. IBM Publication SC26-4348 (1987).

[ISO 87] ISO Standard 9075-1987(E): Database Language SQL. International Organization for Standardization, 1987.

[LIND 87] B. Lindsay, J. McPherson, and H. Pirahesh. "Data Management Extension Architecture" *Proc. ACM SIGMOD Conference*, 1987.

[SELI 79] P. Selinger, M. Astrahan, D. Chamberlin, R. Lorie, and T. Price. "Access Path Selection in a Relational Database Management System," *Proc. ACM SIGMOD Conference*, 1979.

[WILL 82] R. Williams, D. Daniels, L. Haas, G. Lapis, B. Lindsay, P. Ng, R. Obermarck, P. Selinger, A. Walker, P. Wilms, and R. Yost. "R*: An Overview of the Architecture" in *Improving Database Usability and Responsiveness*, edited by P. Scheuerman, Academic Press (1982) pp. 1-27.

Storage and Access Structures to Support a Semantic Data Model

Arvola Chan
Sy Danberg
Stephen Fox
Wen-Te K. Lin
Anil Nori
Daniel Ries

Computer Corporation of America
575 Technology Square
Cambridge, Massachusetts 02139

Abstract

This paper describes the design of storage and access structures for a high performance Ada* compatible database management system. This system supports the database application programming language ADAPLEX [Smith81, Smith82], which is the result of embedding the database sublanguage DAPLEX [Shipman81] in the general purpose language Ada [DoD80]. A prominent feature of the underlying data model is its support for generalization hierarchies [Smith77] which are intended to simplify the mapping from conceptual entities to database objects. An in-depth discussion of the rationale behind our choice of storage and access structures to support semantics intrinsic to the data model and to permit physical database organization tuning is provided in this paper.

1. INTRODUCTION

We are presently engaged in the development of a distributed database management system that is compatible with the programming language Ada [DoD80]. This system supports the general purpose database application programming language ADAPLEX [Smith82], which is the result of embedding the database sublanguage DAPLEX [Shipman81] in Ada. This DBMS is intended to go beyond systems like INGRES and System R, which are based on the older relational technology, in terms of modelling capabilities and ease of use. Two versions of the DBMS are being developed. A centralized DBMS, called the Local Database Manager (LDM), is designed for high performance and for use as a stand-alone system. A distributed DBMS, called the Distributed Database Manager (DDM), interconnects multiple LDMs in a computer network in order to provide rapid access to data for users who are geographically separated. This paper describes the set of storage and access structures supported in the LDM implementation.

The version of DAPLEX used in the formation of ADAPLEX is a simplification of the language described in [Shipman81]. However, all the key concepts have been retained. The semantics of database structure is defined in terms of entity types and relationships between entity types. Aside from the use of functional notations for expressions that significantly enhance the naturalness and readability of programs, the most prominent language feature that distinguishes ADAPLEX from other database languages is its support for the notion of generalization hierarchies [Smith77]. In this paper, we present our design for a set of storage and access structures that supports semantics intrinsic to the data model and permits the tuning of physical database organization. Section 2 provides a summary of the data model underlying the ADAPLEX language. Section 3 identifies our design objectives and presents an in-depth discussion of the rationale behind our design decisions.

2. DATA MODEL SUMMARY

The basic modelling constructs in ADAPLEX are entities and functions. These are intended to correspond to conceptual objects and their properties. Entities with similar generic properties are grouped together to form entity sets. Functions may be single-valued or set-valued. They may also be total or partial. Each (total) function, when applied to a given entity, returns a specific property of that entity. Each property is represented in terms of either a single value or a set of values. Such values can be drawn from noncomposite, Ada-supported data types and character strings, or they can refer to (composite) entities stored in the database as values.

This research was jointly supported by the Defense Advanced Research Projects Agency of the Department of Defense and the Naval Electronic Systems Command under Contract Number N00039-80-C-0402. The views and conclusions contained in this paper are those of the authors and should not be interpreted as necessarily representing the official policies, either expressed or implied, of the Defense Advanced Research Projects Agency, the Naval Electronic Systems Command, or the U.S. Government.

*Ada is a trademark of the Department of Defense (Ada joint program office).

Consider a university database modelling students, instructors, departments, and courses. Figure 2.1 is a graphical representation of the logical definition for such a database in ADAPLEX. The big rectangles depict (composite) entity types and the smaller rectangles indicate (noncomposite) Ada data types. The single and double arrows represent respectively single-valued and set-valued functions that map entities from their domain types into their corresponding range types.

One notable difference between the data model underlying ADAPLEX and the relational data model is that referential constraints [Date81], which are extremely general and fundamental in database applications but not easily specifiable in relational contexts, are directly supported in ADAPLEX. In other words, the definition of the range of a function in our model is much more precise than the definition of the domain of a column in the relational model. At the same time, for functions that range over noncomposite values, we are able to exploit Ada's type definition facilities and avoid the need to introduce a separate domain definition facility [McLeod76], as has been proposed for a relational environment.

In relational systems, a real-world entity that plays several roles in an application environment is typically represented by tuples in a number of relations. In the example university database, we might have an instructor named John Doe and a student also named John Doe, who are in fact the same person in real life. In this case, we might want to impose the constraint that the age of John Doe as an instructor should agree with the age of John Doe as a student. This constraint can be more simply expressed in ADAPLEX by declaring a new entity type called person, indicating that student and instructor are subtypes of person, and that age is a function applicable to person. The function inheritance semantics of ADAPLEX automatically guarantees the consistency of age information on student and age information on instructor since age is a function inherited from the supertype person. At the same time, inherited functions can be applied directly to an entity in ADAPLEX data manipulation constructs, without the need for tedious explicit joining operations. Figure 2.2 is a graphical representation of the revised database definition. The double-edged arrows represent is-a relationships (e.g., each student is-a person). A person entity has properties common to both student and instructor entities, specifically name and age. Each student entity not only possesses properties specific to student (i.e., enrollments and advisor), but also inherits the properties of name and age by virtue of being a person. Similarly, each instructor entity has properties specific to instructor (i.e., dept and rank), in addition to the properties name and age inherited from being a person. The actual ADAPLEX syntax used in the definition of this database is shown in Figure 2.3. Notice that the degree of overlap between the extents of two entity types is explicitly constrained. Such overlaps can be total or partial. The overlapping of the person, student, and instructor entity sets in the above example is illustrated graphically in Figure 2.4. The outer circle represents the set of person entities. The two inner circles represent the subset of person entities that are also student entities and instructor entities, respectively. The intersection of these two inner circles represents the

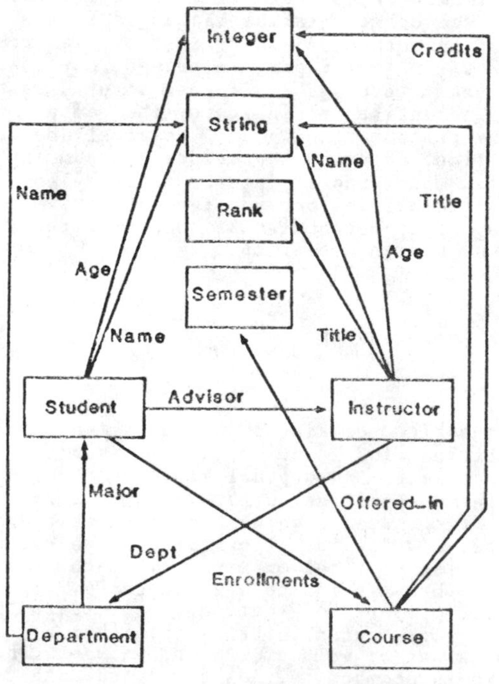

Figure 2.1 An ADPAPELX Database

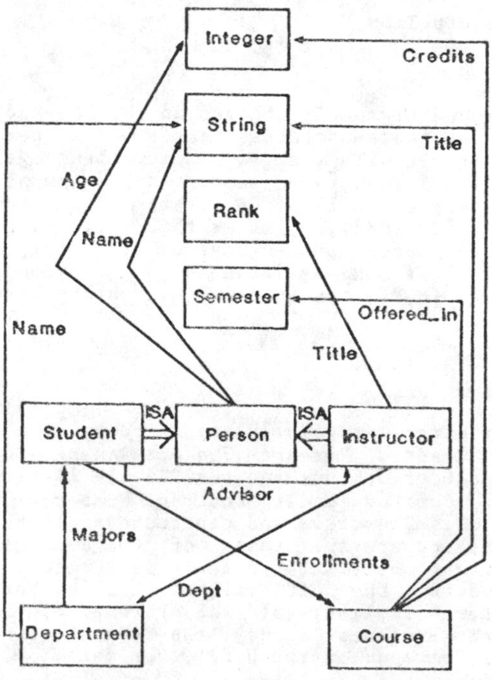

Figure 2.2 An ADPAPELX Database with Type Overlap

```
database UNIVERSITY is

type RANK is
  (ASST_PROF, ASSOC_PROF, FULL_PROF);

type SEMESTER is
  (F, W, S);

type DEPARTMENT;

type COURSE;

type PERSON is entity
  NAME: STRING(1..30);
  AGE: INTEGER;
end entity;

type INSTRUCTOR is entity
  TITLE: RANK;
  DEPT: DEPARTMENT;
end entity;

type STUDENT is entity
  ADVISOR: INSTRUCTOR partial;
  ENROLLMENTS: set of COURSE;
end entity;

type COURSE is entity
  TITLE: STRING(1..30);
  OFFERED_IN: SEMESTER;
  CREDITS: INTEGER range 1..4;
end entity;

type DEPARTMENT is entity
  NAME: STRING(1..30);
  MAJORS: set of STUDENT;
end entity;

unique NAME within PERSON;
unique NAME within DEPARTMENT;
unique TITLE within COURSE;
contain INSTRUCTOR in PERSON;
contain STUDENT in PERSON;
share INSTRUCTOR with STUDENT;

end UNIVERSITY;
```

Figure 2.3 Definition of an Example Database

subset of person entities that are both student entities and instructor entities.

Aside from general integrity constraints that may be explicitly declared as part of the database definition and that are enforced at the end of each database transaction, there are a number of invariant properties implied by the data model. These latter are in some sense treated as being more fundamental. Their validity is enforced at the end of each user-specified database interaction, rather than at the grosser transaction level. These fundamental constraints include:

- Referential/range constraint. The range of an entity-valued function may be another entity type in the database. When an entity of the latter type is deleted, it is necessary to ensure that there are no dangling references. For scalar and string functions, Ada provides the facilities for constraining the range of

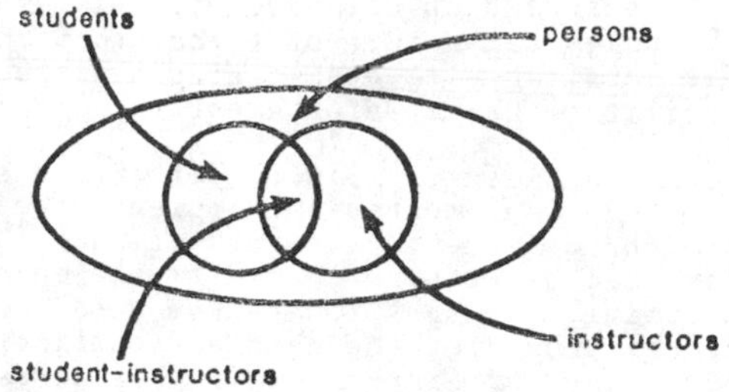

Figure 2.4 Example of Entity Set Overlap

possible values in the underlying value set. For example, the range of integers, the precision of real numbers, and the enumeration of values in a discrete type can all be defined.

- Extent overlap constraint. An entity can be included into the extent of an entity type only if overlaps among the extents of all of the types to which it currently belongs, and the extent of the type to which it is to be included, are permissible. At the same time, excluding an entity from the extent of a specified type will also exclude it from the extent of all subtypes whose extents are completely contained in the extent of the type in question.

- Totality constraint. A total function must be defined for all elements in its domain at all times; when a new entity is created, all of its values for various total functions must be known.

- Uniqueness constraint. One or more groups of single-valued functions within an entity type may optionally be declared to be unique. That is, each group of functions will yield distinct combinations of values when applied to distinct entities of the underlying type. This type of constraint is enforced automatically on insertions and updates.

This concludes our overview of the ADAPLEX data model. The interested readers are referred to [Smith81, Smith82] for more details on the syntax and semantics of the ADAPLEX language.

3. STORAGE AND ACCESS STRUCTURE DESIGN

Our choice for the set of data structures and implementation options to incorporate in the LDM has been motivated primarily by three considerations:

- Support for high-level ADAPLEX modelling constructs. Our data model provides several functional capabilities not supported by models used in contemporary systems. In particular, we need to devise new structures to efficiently represent information concerning entities that belong to multiple overlapping entity types.

- Maintenance of fundamental semantic integrity constraints. The underlying data model implies several fundamental constraints that must be enforced on database updates. Because of the universal nature of these constraints, it is desirable to design special structures to facilitate their enforcement.

- Performance tuning. Since different structures and implementation options are best suited for different patterns of use, efficiency can be attained only through organization tuning. We seek to achieve good performance by providing the database designer with a good range of implementation alternatives that he can choose to match against the requirements of his applications.(1)

We are assuming an environment where the bulk of the database is stored on conventional block-oriented storage devices. In this context, two fundamental design issues are: the appropriate clustering of information often used together to maximize the locality of reference, and the efficient support for frequently traversed associative access paths to minimize the amount of sequential searching required. More specifically, we are concerned with:

- Grouping of information concerning entities into logical records. Logical records of the same type are assumed to store the same set of fields.

- Placement of logical records into physical files. Each file is a linear address space that is mapped into physical blocks of storage devices. Logical records of the same type may optionally be divided into groups, each of which may then be stored in different files, possibly using different placement strategies. We will refer to each of these groups of logical records as a storage record type. Different storage record types that originate from the same generalization hierarchy may also be stored in the same file to achieve the desired clustering of information.

- Support for efficient associative access to stored records. The primary organization or placement strategy for the stored records in a file will determine the primary access path to these records. In addition, auxiliary access structures can be maintained in order to provide direct access based on secondary key fields that are not used to determine record placement.

3.1 Representing Entities and Entity Functions

The basic modelling concepts in ADAPLEX are those of entities and entity functions. To represent entity functions (in particular, entity-valued functions), it is important that entities be uniquely identifiable. However, the data model does not require that each entity be uniquely identifiable externally. That is, for entities of a given type, there does not necessarily exist a function (or a combination of functions) that yields a distinct value (or a distinct combination of values) when applied to each of the entities. Therefore, for internal unique identification purposes, an entity identifier is assigned to each entity upon creation. This entity identifier then serves to stand for the entity in the representation of functions.(2)

The set of functions that are applicable to an entity depends on the entity type(s) to which it belongs. Three different categories of information about an entity need to be stored:

- Values for applicable functions. This corresponds to values for attributes relevant to the entities in question and is typical of information accessed by applications in current database systems.

- Typing information. Given an entity, it is often necessary to determine the set of entity types (among a set of overlapping types) to which it belongs. Such a capability is essential for determining whether a function can legally be applied to the entity on hand. For example, in looping through entities of the type person, it is legal to apply the enrollments function to an entity only if that entity is also included in the type student.

- Additional control information. The deletion semantics of ADAPLEX requires that upon excluding an entity from an entity type, that entity must no longer be referenced by other entities (i.e., it is no longer in the active range of entity-valued functions). An efficient way to check for the satisfaction of such constraints is through the maintenance of reference counts that indicate the number of times each entity is referred to by entity functions, one for each entity type to which it belongs.(3)

Below, we describe our representation schemes for the above categories of function. We will first describe the mapping of entity functions into logical records and then introduce the notion of an entity directory as a receptacle for the remaining typing and reference count information.

3.1.1 Mapping Function Values Into Logical Records

As mentioned earlier, an important performance consideration is the clustering of information often needed together. In terms of the representation of functions, there are a number of obvious clustering alternatives:

---

(1) Our desire for tunability must, however, be balanced against the complexity and size of required software. Besides, in the absence of powerful design aids, we must ensure that the design freedom we provide to designers can be exploited effectively.

(2) Of course, given an entity identifier, it should be possible to obtain efficiently all information known about the corresponding entity.

(3) An exclusion operation is legal only if the corresponding reference count is zero.

- The no grouping approach. Each entity function is stored as a binary relation (i.e., a two-attribute file).

- The complete grouping approach. The values for all functions that are applicable to an entity (independent of entity types within a generalization hierarchy) are stored in the same record.

- The semantic grouping approach. The values for all (noninherited) functions applicable to an entity from the viewpoint of a particular entity type are stored in the same record.

- The arbitrary grouping approach. The values for functions applicable to an entity are stored in an arbitrary number of records to suit the usage pattern.

Our decision here is to use a combination of the semantic grouping approach and the no grouping approach. As a default, we will use the semantic grouping approach and store values for all noninherited applicable functions from the same entity-type viewpoint in the same record. In cases where we have arbitrarily long (repeating/varying length) fields that might complicate storage allocation, we provide for the option of storing such fields as individual secondary records. Our rationale for such a choice is that while the no grouping approach results in an overly fragmented database,(4) the complete grouping approach has the opposite effect.(5) As we shall see later, when coupled with the horizontal partitioning and clustering options, our approach is flexible enough to permit the grouping together of all information known about all entities of a given type, while being completely isolated from other irrelevant information.(6) By clustering all of the record types that store information on a set of entities from different viewpoints, an organization that approximates the complete grouping approach can also be obtained as a special case. Finally, we disallow arbitrary grouping of functions because we fear that this may result in too enormous a physical design space, one which a human database designer may not be able to utilize effectively. Besides, a significant increase in software complexity may also result.

In summary, to store the values of functions applicable to entities, there will be one primary logical record type corresponding to each entity type. Typically, each primary logical record includes one field for the identifier of the entity being represented, and a number of repeating or nonrepeating fields for each set-valued or single-valued function (as applied to the entity in question and not specified for separate representation). In addition, there may be zero or more secondary logical records for separately represented functions. Only the primary logical records may be considered for further horizontal partitioning and clustering. Each type of secondary logical record will be stored as a separate two-attribute file(7) that will permit efficient associative access based on entity identifiers. In case an entity belongs to multiple entity types, there will be one primary logical record for each entity type to which it belongs.

(4) It is frequently true that values for multiple functions applied to the same entity are often needed together.

(5) The end result is that unnecessary data transfers often have to be made.

(6) An entity type that is lower in a generalization hierarchy conceptually inherits all the functions applicable to its ancestors in the hierarchy. Rather than duplicating such information, we allow the use of clustering to appropriately juxtapose the related information.

3.1.2 Entity Directory

To keep the remaining information concerning entities, an entity directory is maintained for each generalization hierarchy. The information stored in the entity directory is essentially redundant and can be obtained through sequential searching of logical records that represent entities. The purpose of the entity directory, however, is to centralize all information known about entities in order to permit efficient access. In the entity directory, there will be one entry for each entity that belongs to at least one of the types in the underlying generalization hierarchy. In addition to the typing information and the reference count information, the directory entry for each entity will also contain physical pointers to the primary storage records that store values for applicable functions, one for each entity type to which it belongs. Thus, given an entity identifier, all stored information concerning the entity can be located either directly in the entity directory itself or indirectly through it.

Occasionally, an entity may belong to an arbitrary number of types in a generalization hierarchy. Thus, an entry in an entity directory may have to store a varying number of pointers. We use a varying length record representation for the entries to reduce storage overhead. The organization of the entries also must support efficient associative access based on entity identifiers. Furthermore, to permit the inclusion of new entities and to reuse the space occupied by entries for defunct entities, it is important that a dynamic file organization be used. For this reason, we choose to organize the entity directory using linear hashing [Larson80, Litwin80]. Each associative retrieval of an entry based on entity identifier can typically be made in one page access, regardless of growth or shrinkage of the directory.

3.2 Horizontal Partitioning of Primary Logical Records

In order to achieve better inter and intra entity type information clustering, we support

(7) That is, the entity identifier will be included as one of the attributes.

have an optimization scheme for approximating the performance characteristics of static file organizations through the storage of hybrid pointers (combination of logical and physical pointers).

From an alternate viewpoint, we can distinguish between organizations based on address calculation (randomization) and those that use tree-structured directories. Typically, a tree-structured organization provides the capability of accessing records in key order, which is not feasible in randomized organizations. On the other hand, a randomized organization is usually more efficient for accessing individual records. To accommodate a range of applications, we have decided to support both randomized and tree-structured organizations. Thus, the dynamic organizations we support initially will include B*-tree [Bayer72, Comer79] and linear hashing [Larson80, Litwin80].

It should be noted that the choice of primary organization is allowed for only in the case of primary storage records. Secondary storage records will always be organized using linear hashing since the predominant access mode will be keyed on individual entity identifiers.

3.4 Clustering of Storage Record Types

In addition to positioning criteria based purely on record contents, we also support the placement of records dependent on the position of related records. For example, we may want to store a student storage record next to a person storage record when they represent the same underlying entity. In particular, we may combine clustering with horizontal partitioning to achieve better juxtapositioning of information within the same generalization hierarchy. For example, we may map person logical records into storage records for person who is also an instructor, and storage records for person who is not an instructor, and then cluster the instructor storage records with the first group of person storage records. In this way, all the information concerning instructor entities will be readily accessible together.

In the above example, the clustering is based on a one-to-one relationship, namely, records representing the <u>same</u> entity are to be stored close to each other. In this case, we require the related records to be stored adjacently on the <u>same</u> page, so that a single page access will suffice for their simultaneous access.(11) We will call such clustering <u>contiguous</u>. As a special case, if we cluster both student records and instructor records with the corresponding person records, we effectively have a scheme very similar to one that is obtained by storing values for all applicable functions in the same record.(12) In general, we allow multiple storage records representing the same underlying entity to be clustered together. We also allow multiple storage record types that originate from the the same logical record type to provide the functions for determining record placement.

Besides contiguous clustering based on one-to-one relationships, it is possible to perform clustering based on one-to-many relationships. For example, if there is a one-to-many relationship between department and employee (department is a single-valued function applicable to employee entities), we may require each employee record to be stored close to the corresponding department record. In this case, it may not always be possible to store all of the employee records related to a particular department record on the same page. Rather, it may be more reasonable to require that they be stored only in the same general vicinity (a small fraction of the file space). We will call this type of clustering <u>noncontiguous</u>. One practical way to implement noncontiguous clustering is in conjunction with a static file organization. Instead of requiring that all related records be found on the same page, related records are localized only on pages assigned to the same bucket. In this case, all related records can be located by a sequential scan of the entire bucket. As in contiguous clustering, multiple types of records may be clustered. For example, we may want to store Employee records close to the related Department records, and to store Dependent records close to corresponding Employee records. However, in view of our decision not to support static organization initially, we must also postpone support for noncontiguous clustering.

3.5 Auxiliary Access Structures

In addition to primary access paths provided by record placement strategies, often it is desirable to support associative access based on additional criteria. As in conventional systems, we permit the maintenance of simple and combined indices on logical records of a given type. Conceptually, an index provides a mapping from an indexed key value (or combination of values) to a set of pointers to the storage records that contain the indexed value (or combination of values). (As will be seen in the next section,

---

(11) In fact, we will construct a hybrid record to combine the information from the original records representing the same underlying entity. In general, a (hybrid or nonhybrid) record may consist of a fixed length portion followed by a varying length portion. We require only that the fixed length portion of the combined record not span page boundaries.

(12) A single record header is used to describe a group of records that represent the same underlying entity that is being clustered together. This header will also replicate the typing information in order to eliminate access to the entity directory when it is necessary to obtain information about an entity from the viewpoints of several overlapping entity types, and this information is already clustered in the same hybrid record. Pointers from the entity directory point to the combined record instead of to the individual records.

the options of mapping one primary logical record type into several disjoint storage record types, and also the option of clustering multiple storage record types originating from the same generalization hierarchy in the same file.

Consider the following generalization hierarchy involving the entity types persons, students, and instructors.(8) Assume that students and instructors do not overlap (i.e., a person cannot be both a student and an instructor). An alternative to storing all the person records in the same file is to divide the person records into disjoint groups, and to store the groups of records in different files. If we view all of the logical records of a given type as a table, then the grouping may be viewed as partitioning this table horizontally. Instead of horizontal partitioning based on arbitrary criteria, we require that the partitioning be based on properties of overlapping type membership only. In the above generalization hierarchy, we can divide person records into records for:

- person who is a student
- person who is an instructor
- person who is neither a student nor an instructor

Alternatively, to suit a different usage pattern, we can divide the person records into records for:

- person who is an instructor
- person who is not an instructor

Now consider a generalization hierarchy where student and instructor do overlap. Here we may want to divide person records into:

- person who is a student but is not an instructor
- person who is an instructor but is not a student
- person who is both a student and an instructor.
- person who is neither a student nor an instructor.

In essence, the blocks of a horizontal partitioning scheme are defined by a number of nonoverlapping block definition predicates. Each block definition predicate may consist of a conjunction of type inclusion/noninclusion conditions involving types that overlap with the type in question.(9) In addition to the blocks defined by each of these predicates, a complementary block is also induced by the complement of their disjunction when this complement is satisfiable. That is, records that do not satisfy any of the block definition predicates will be stored in the complementary block.

(8) That is, each student is also a person and each instructor is also a person.

(9) The use of disjunction of subtype membership properties to define blocks is in effect supported since we allow the placement of two or more blocks from the same horizontal partitioning scheme in the same file.

3.3 Placement of Storage Records

The primary organization of a file determines how records are to be positioned within the file. In general, the placement criteria may be based on:

- The entity identifier of the record
- One or more other fields stored in the record
- The positioning of related records

Typical file organizations may be dichotomized as static versus dynamic. In a static organization, records do not move once they have been inserted in the file. When the original (primary) space assigned to the file runs out, overflow space (typically additional pages chained onto the original pages) is used to accommodate the subsequently inserted records.(10) Contrarily, in a dynamic organization, the amount of primary space assigned to a file grows or shrinks dynamically in response to insertions and deletions. Records are moved as a result of page splitting and merging operations (used to maintain a certain loading factor) and to guarantee a certain level of associative access efficiency and uniformity.

For an infrequently updated file, a static organization typically is faster than a dynamic organization. However, the amount of overflow in a statically organized file is liable to become excessive and unbalanced, requiring costly periodic reorganization of the whole file. This will result in the file's inaccessibility while reorganization is in progress. In a dynamically organized file, reorganization is performed incrementally and continuously, so that performance and accessibility tends to be more uniform. The drawback with having to move records around in response to insertions and deletions is that pointers to these records cannot readily be maintained. On the other hand, the storage of such pointers is often necessary in auxiliary access structures in order to provide additional access paths to the records. As we shall see in subsequent discussions, it is possible to replace physical pointers to records with logical pointers consisting of entity identifiers in order to minimize the impact of record relocation. However, this will require indirection through the entity directory for each access.

It is our belief that there will be situations where a static organization is more desirable than a dynamic one, and vice versa. However, in an attempt to limit the size and complexity of the system, we have decided to support dynamic organizations only in the initial implementation. Our rationale is that stability is often more critical than performance, and that the need to initiate reorganization is too much of a burden on users in many applications [Stonebraker80]. As will be discussed in Section 3.6,

(10) The distinction between primary and overflow is that access to a record in the overflow space can be made only by first accessing other records in the primary space. Thus, it is more expensive to access a record in the overflow space.

we will use only logical and hybrid pointers to point to dynamically organized records.) As for the organization for the index file(13) the options of using either a B*-tree organization or a linear hashing organization may both be useful. (There is no advantage for using a static organization for the index file since records in this file are not pointed to by records in other files.) A linear hashing organization provides more efficient access based on an equality search. Typically, a single access is all that is needed to locate a particular index entry. A B*-tree organization, on the other hand, requires one access for each level of the tree, while providing a fuller range of functional capabilities: the ability to access index entries in key order makes it useful in the resolution of range queries. In addition, it is also possible to use such an index to retrieve all records in key order. Both types of organizations are allowed for in the LDM implementation.

Another relevant organizational issue is how a pointer list should be represented. While most contemporary systems use a sorted array representation, there are also some which automatically convert an array representation to a bit-map representation when a list gets long. The advantage of the latter scheme is that it results in a much more compact representation on which bitwise operations can be performed in order to implement set operations on pointer lists. However, it may be more difficult to intersect pointer lists that use different representation. For the sake of software simplicity, we restrict our initial implementation to the array representation only.

3.6 Hybrid Pointers

Pointers in data structures are essential for supporting associative access. These pointers may be of a logical nature, or they may be physically oriented. A logical pointer has the advantage of providing a higher level of data independence. However, once a logical pointer is obtained, an extra level of searching must be performed to acquire an actual physical pointer to the desired information. In our context, the entity identifier serves as a logical pointer, with the entity directory providing the indirection. When a storage record that stores information concerning an entity has to be relocated, only the corresponding entry in the entity directory needs to be updated; all other records that store the entity identifier of the affected entity need not be modified. For indices that point to dynamically organized records, it would be appropriate to store logical pointers to simplify pointer maintenance.

As a physical pointer, we use the page number together with the direct or indirect(14) offset of the record within the page. Physical pointers have the advantage of directness. However, the price we pay is pointer maintenance when records are relocated. Since we support only dynamic organizations, we do not permit the use of physical pointers in isolation in secondary indices or in the representation of functions.

As an optimization, however, we support the option of combining a physical pointer with a logical pointer to form a hybrid pointer. For example, when representing a function from course to student, it may be useful to store both the student entity identifier, and the physical pointer to the student record. The rationale is that often when the student function is applied to the course entity, one is interested only in the student aspects of the target entity. Similarly, in the index on age for the student record type, we can store both the entity identifiers and the physical pointers to the student records. In general, we can follow the physical portion of a hybrid pointer to find the pointed-to record, and then compare the entity identifier stored there against the logical pointer portion of the hybrid pointer on hand. If the two entity identifiers do not match, we know that the pointed-to record has been relocated. In this case, the corresponding entry in the entity directory should be examined to determine the new address of the relocated record, and the hybrid pointer should be updated. The advantage of this scheme is that records can be relocated without regard to the pointers that point to them. Only the entity directory needs to be updated. The hybrid pointers are revalidated when they are next used. Thus in a high update situation, a record may be relocated many times before pointers pointing to it need be updated.

4. SUMMARY

We have presented a set of storage and access structures for supporting a semantic data model. The prominent features of this data model, which are intended to capture more application semantics than constructs found in conventional data models, include the notions of generalization hierarchies and referential constraints. Our design allows for the flexible tuning of database organizations to match application requirements. The design space encompasses such options as horizontal and vertical partitioning of information within an entity type, as well as the clustering of information across entity types within the same generalization hierarchy. Dynamic file organizations are used for the storing of data records, and the concept of hybrid pointers is introduced for the

---

(13) Each record in this file consists of an indexed key value and an associated pointer list.

(14) In the case of varying length records, it is often desirable to be able to relocate a record within a page without having to update all pointers that point to the relocated record. The indirection of the physical pointer can solve the problem by means of indexing information stored at the bottom of the same page.

purpose of pointing to dynamically relocatable records in the representation of inverted lists in secondary indices, and in the representation of interentity relationships. The underlying DBMS that supports the discussed set of storage and access structures is being developed by the Computer Corporation of America. It is scheduled to be completed in 1983.

5. ACKNOWLEDGEMENTS

We are indebted to Professor Philip Bernstein, Professor Nathan Goodman, Dr. Randy Katz, Terry Landers, Frank Manola, Dr. James Rothnie, Dr. Diane Smith, and Dr. John Smith for providing us with invaluable input and feedback during the design of the Local Database Manager to support the ADAPLEX language.

6. REFERENCES

[Bayer72]
Bayer, R., C. McCreight, "Organization and Maintenance of Large Ordered Indexes," Acta Informatica, Vol. 1, No. 3, 1972.

[Comer79]
Comer, D., "The Ubiquitous B-Tree," ACM Computing Surveys, Vol. 11, No. 2, June, 1979.

[Date81]
Date, C. J., "Referential Integrity," VLDB Conference Proceedings, 1981.

[DoD80]
United States Department of Defense, "Reference Manual for the Ada Programming Language," Proposed Standard Document, July 1980.

[Larson80]
Larson, P., "Linear Hashing With Partial Expansions," VLDB Conference Proceedings, 1980.

[Litwin80]
Litwin, W., "Linear Hashing: A New Tool for File and Table Addressing," VLDB Conference Proceedings, 1980.

[McLeod76]
McLeod, D. J., "High Level Domain Definition in a Relational Database," Proceedings for ACM SIGPLAN/SIGMOD Conference on Data: Abstraction, Definition, and Structure, 1976.

[Shipman81]
Shipman, D., "The Functional Data Model and the Data Language DAPLEX," ACM Transactions on Database Systems, Vol. 6, No. 1, March 1981.

[Smith77]
Smith, J. M., D. C. P. Smith, "Database Abstractions: Aggregation and Generalization," ACM Transactions on Database Systems, Vol. 2, No. 2, June, 1977.

[Smith81]
Smith, J. M., S. Fox, T. Landers, "Reference Manual for ADAPLEX," Technical Report CCA-81-02, Computer Corporation of America, January 1981.

[Smith82]
Smith, J. M., S. Fox, T. Landers, "ADAPLEX: The Integration of the DAPLEX Database Language with the Ada Programming Language," Technical Report, Computer Corporation of America, in preparation.

[Stonebraker80]
Stonebraker, M., "Retrospection on a Database System," ACM Transactions on Database Systems, Vol. 5, No. 2, June 1980.

A Modular Tool Kit For Knowledge Management

Gilles M. E. Lafue *Reid G. Smith*

Schlumberger-Doll Research
Old Quarry Road
Ridgefield, CT 06877-4108
USA

ABSTRACT

We describe an integrated programming environment for developing knowledge-based systems. The environment contains a variety of general-purpose tools: a rule interpretation system, a semantic integrity manager, a task representation system and a file manager. Although the tools have different origins (*e.g.*, rule-based systems, database management, process control), an object-oriented foundation lends modularity and consistency to the tool kit.

I. INTRODUCTION

By now the value of powerful tool kits for developing knowledge-based systems is well-understood. Such tools act as *substrates* – computational bases that allow system builders to concentrate on the problems of acquiring and formalizing domain knowledge. In this paper we discuss a number of specific tools that we have found to be useful. We also argue for the utility of an object-oriented foundation that ties the individual tools together in a coherent fashion.

The foundation for our tool kit is an object-oriented knowledge representation system called *Strobe* [5, 6]. It has been used in a variety of applications, most recently in *Crystal* [9], a system that supports interactive manual and automatic interpretation of well-logs, (*i.e.*, measurements made in boreholes). This system was developed for two main classes of users: end-users (*i.e.*, log interpreters) doing interactive well-log interpretation, and interpretation program developers. It combines graphic display and manipulation of logs with graphic editors and menus. It controls distributed execution of interpretation programs either on the Xerox workstations or on Ethernet-connected Vaxes. These programs have been written from a variety of computational perspectives (*e.g.*, statistical, pattern recognition, symbolic) and in a variety of programming languages. Strobe and Crystal provide the *glue* that binds these heterogeneous components together.

The Crystal knowledge bases incorporate a number of subsystems that are neither specific to the Crystal application nor to well-log interpretation. These subsystems are the tools of a modular, general-purpose knowledge-management tool kit that can be used to extend Strobe. Each tool is incorporated into a basic Strobe knowledge base by adding slots to one of the initial domain-independent objects, or by adding one or a few objects. Each tool is modular in that it doesn't require modifying slots or functions defined by other tools.

This paper describes a rule interpretation system, a semantic integrity manager, a task representation system, and a file manager for storing and retrieving objects. These tools implement the interpretation of the declarative representations for the entities they manage: rules, integrity constraints, tasks, files. The salient features of Strobe needed for the presentation of the tools are introduced in the next section. Each tool is then described, first through examples of the declarations it supports – drawn primarily from Crystal – and then by showing the objects that implement it.

II. STROBE

A Strobe *knowledge base* is a collection of *objects* of two types: *classes*, which can be specialized, and *individuals* which cannot. Objects are organized into taxonomic hierarchies (which may be tangled) along which properties are inherited (alternative inheritance paths are also supported).

A Strobe object has properties called *slots*, and a slot has properties called *facets*. Both slots and facets may be inherited. Some facets, namely, *Value* and *Datatype*, are system-defined and exist for all slots; others are user-defined. Message-passing and event-oriented computation are supported.

Strobe supports multiple knowledge bases in the same address space. Also, messages can be sent to objects in any knowledge base, even if that knowledge base is on another machine connected by Ethernet. (Indeed, any Strobe operation can be performed across the network.) To further support distribution and computational heterogeneity, Strobe had been implemented in a variety of languages: Interlisp-D on Xerox workstations, Mainsail, CommonLisp and C on Vaxes. This paper concentrates on the Interlisp-D version.

Interlisp-D Strobe has a display-oriented editor called *Impulse* [4]. This editor is itself built as a collection of Strobe objects. As a result, it can be specialized to suit the needs of Strobe applications, based on the types of declarations supported by the tools discussed here. An example of such a specialization is presented in [9].

A. User-defined Datatypes

A datatype in Strobe is itself implemented as an object. Datatyping provides another form of inheritance in that a slot may inherit some of its facets, typically operations, from its datatype. More precisely, receivers for messages sent to facets may be inherited from slots in the datatype object. Such slots are characterized by the fact that their name starts with the atom "DATUM ". For instance, a message sent to the *Put* facet of a slot is forwarded to the *DATUM-Put* slot of the object implementing the datatype of the slot if no receiver can be found through standard taxonomic inheritance.

B. User-defined Facets

User-defined facets are useful for meta-data encoding. They have been used extensively in Crystal to support communication between knowledge bases. By agreeing on the meaning of a relatively small number of facets, knowledge bases can interpret each other's objects and slots without detailed knowledge of each other's domain of application (*e.g.*, object and slot names). For example, a part of an entity may be identified based on a *Role* facet set to *Part* rather than on the name of the part. Each of our tools defines some facets and incorporates an interpreter for them.

C. Initial Objects

A Strobe knowledge base starts with a few general objects which are organized in the generalization hierarchy shown in Figure II 1. DATATYPE is the ancestor of all datatype objects. Initially, it comes with a few slots that contain functions for implementing basic operations such as putting a value into a slot, getting, printing or editing a slot value. The message handlers for some of these slots (*e.g.*, DATUM-Edit or DATUM-Print) are defined in the descendants of DATATYPE: BITMAP, TEXT, LISP (for Interlisp-D functions and lambda expressions), EXPR (for arbitrary s-expressions) and OBJECT (for slots whose value points to Strobe objects).

```
Object: DATATYPE
Type: Class
Generalizations: ROOT
  DATUM-Edit:
  DATUM-Print:
  DATUM-Get: sys/mgetvalue
  DATUM-Put: sys/mputvalue
```

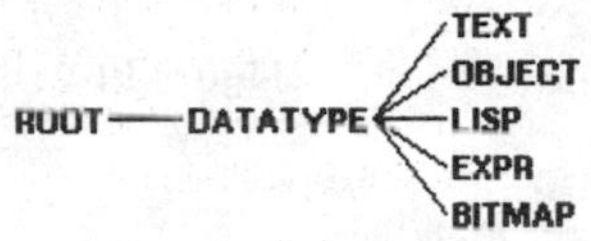

Figure II-1: Initial Strobe Knowledge Base Objects[1]

III. RULE INTERPRETATION

The rule interpreter [7] included in our tool kit applies rules in a forward-chained manner. The rule syntax supports a number of types of match variable instantiation in the left-hand side. In addition, the system provides support for user extensions to the syntax. A form of rule compilation can be used to generate code and speed up rule application. Rules can be grouped into *Rulesets* and control structures defined for attempting and firing rules associated with rulesets. Uncertainty is currently handled according to the EMYCIN model [10]. There is also a simple mechanism for generating natural language rule translations. Finally, and most important, rules written for this system can access domain knowledge encoded as Strobe objects.[2]

A. Declarations For Rule Interpretation

Each rule in the system is itself a Strobe object - an instance of the class *Rule*. Figure III-1 shows a sample rule (taken in concept from the *Dipmeter Advisor*[*] system [8]).

```
Object: NormalFault9
Type: Individual
Generalizations: Rule
  IF: (Condition1 Condition2)
  THEN: (Action1 Action2)
  Condition1: (THERE-EXISTS :Y NormalFaultZone)
  Condition2: (THERE-EXISTS :Z RedPattern
               ($< ($LENGTH :Z) RedLength))
               ($ABOVE :Z :Y Overlap Gap)
               ($PERPENDICULAR (THE Azimuth :Z)
                               (THE Strike :Y)
                               Tolerance))
  Action1: ($SPECIALIZE :Y to be a LateFaultZone)
  Action2: ($ASSIGN DirectionToDownthrownBlock of :Y to be
               (THE Azimuth :Z))
  TRANSLATION:
  IF:
  (1) there exists an instance of the class
        NormalFaultZone (:Y), and
  (2) there exists an instance of the class RedPattern (:Z)
       such that the Length of :Z < RedLength, and
       such that :Z is above :Y within [Overlap,Gap], and
       such that the Azimuth of :Z is perpendicular to
         the Strike of :Y within Tolerance degrees
  THEN:
  (1) specialize :Y to be a LateFaultZone
  (2) the DirectionToDownthrownBlock of :Y _the Azimuth of :Z
```

Figure III-1: Late Fault Rule

Clauses may refer to Strobe objects (*e.g.*, via the THE function, in Figure III-1, which accesses a slot of an object) as well as other Lisp data structures. They may also bind variables that can be accessed during the matching and execution of the rule. We have defined an initial rule language of approximately 50 left-hand-side predicates and 10 right-hand-side actions. The rule language may be augmented as desired by end-users by defining Interlisp functions (and translation templates, if desired).

To match NormalFault9 against the database, the rule interpreter attempts to find a normal fault zone and a zone characterized by a signal pattern known as a red pattern, such that the two zones together satisfy the predicates associated with Condition2. The rule interpreter attempts to match the rule by sequentially instantiating the match variables. As each match variable is instantiated, the truth value of the clause is tested. If true, then the instantiation process continues, but if false, then the process backtracks to the last variable instantiated that has untried values in its domain and reinstantiates it to its next value.[3]

---

[1] Figures showing objects are to be read as follows. General information about the object (such as its synonyms, whether it is a class or an individual, its immediate generalizations) is shown first. Slots are then shown indented with respect to the object information, and when shown, the facets of a slot are indented with respect to the slot name. The value (if any) is printed following the slot name. Names in curly brackets are synonyms for the slot with which they are associated.

[2] The ability to integrate rules and structured objects as well as the ability to extend the rule syntax in a flexible way are not easily managed in existing rule interpreters, like OPS5 [1]. We have opted for the *flexibility* end of the flexibility/speed spectrum.

[*] Mark of Schlumberger

[3] Note that there may be several zone pairs for which the conditions are satisfied. To find them all, some form of iteration is required. This is performed automatically, as desired, by the rule interpreter.

There are several forms of *quantified-condition* clauses. In the standard case, the domain of a match variable is the set of instances of a specified class (as in Figure III-1). Alternatively, it can be the set of instances of a class and of all its subclasses. Other possibilities can be defined by the user. Another type of quantified-condition clause that we have found useful is illustrated by the rule in Figure III-2. This rule expresses the fact that a tidal flat is characterized by a number of signal patterns known as blue patterns, that have alternating azimuth. We do not know *a priori* how many such patterns there will be – their number depends on the thickness of the flat. Set quantification in a single rule appears to provide a useful match to the way that variable thickness units are conceptualized and detected by our domain specialists.

Rules are grouped into *Rulesets*. A ruleset defines the control structure to attempt and fire the rules it contains. It can eliminate the need for clauses often found in flat rule systems that are aimed at setting the context for rule application. Figure III-3 shows a ruleset used for stratigraphic interpretation of dipmeter data.

The simplest ruleset contains a single list of rules called NORMAL-RULES. These rules are attempted one at a time according to their order in the list. Each time a rule fires, the content of the CONTROL-STRATEGY slot determines whether scanning is to continue with the next rule (ContinueAfterFiring) or is to begin again with the first rule (ReStartAfterFiring)[4]. This iteration continues until no rules can be successfully fired. (This default termination condition can be overridden in particular rulesets.)

A ruleset can also contain the following lists of rules. FIRE-ONCE-RULES can only be fired once for each invocation of the ruleset. They can be used to initialize the execution of a ruleset. FIRE-ALWAYS-RULES are attempted on each iteration regardless of the control strategy. They can be used to *respond* to the firing of other rules (*e.g.*, to update dependent relationships). Unlike NORMAL-RULES and FIRE-ONCE-RULES, FIRE-ALWAYS-RULES can be fired more than once with the same match variable bindings within a single ruleset invocation.

To assist in explanation and debugging, the execution history of each ruleset invocation is recorded as an instance of the ruleset class. It retains information such as the rules that were attempted and fired (together with their match variable bindings and the objects created or modified as a result of their firing).

B. Rule Interpretation Subsystem

The rule interpreter is implemented via the Rule object and the Ruleset object (Figure III-4). (Not all of their slots are shown.)

An additional feature has proved quite useful for hypothesis testing. In applying a ruleset (or a rule), the caller is allowed to pass in a set of bindings. These bindings are analogous to lambda bindings and allow ruleset invocation to be considered as a form of function invocation. Match variable bindings may be included in this list, in which case, the rule interpreter tries to fill in the remaining instantiations.

[4]The ReStartAfterFiring option is useful when the actions of an individual rule could interact with the conditions of other rules. It is often used in combination with a rule ordering that places the most specific rules before the most general rules. The ContinueAfterFiring option is useful when individual rule actions are independent or additive. (It is the default strategy.)

```
Object: Tidal1
Type: Individual
Generalizations: Rule
  IF: (Condition1 Condition2)
  THEN: (Action1 Action2 Action3 Action4)
  Condition1: (THERE-EXISTS :X Transition/InnerShelfZone
                 ($= (THE Influence :X) 'Wave/TideDominated))
  Condition2: (THERE-EXISTS-SET :Z BluePattern
                 ($WITHIN ($NEW :Z) :X)
                 ($ABOVE ($LAST :Z) ($NEW :Z) Overlap Gap)
                 ($OPPOSITE-DIRECTION (THE Azimuth ($NEW :Z))
                                      (THE Azimuth ($LAST :Z))
                                      Tol)
            FINALLY ($> (LENGTH :Z) 1))
  Action1: ($CREATE :ZZ as a TidalFlatZone
  Action2: ($ASSIGN Top of :ZZ to be (THE Depth ($FIRST :Z)))
  Action3: ($ASSIGN Bottom of :ZZ to be (THE Depth ($LAST :Z)))
  Action4: ($ASSIGN Axis of :ZZ to be (THE Azimuth ($LAST :Z)))
  TRANSLATION:
IF:
(1) there exists an instance of the class
      Transition/InnerShelfZone (:X)
    such that the Influence of :X = Wave/TideDominated, and
(2) there exists a set of instances of the class BluePattern
      (:Z)
    such that the current candidate for :Z is within :X, and
    such that the last item of :Z is above the current
      candidate for :Z within [Overlap,Gap], and
    such that the Azimuth of the current candidate for :Z is
      opposite to the Azimuth of the last item of :Z within
        Tol degrees, and
    such that the size of the set :Z > 1
THEN:
(1) create a TidalFlatZone (:ZZ)
(2) the Top of :ZZ _the Depth of the first item of :Z
(3) the Bottom of :ZZ _the Depth of the last item of :Z
(4) the Axis of :ZZ _the Azimuth of the last item of :Z
```

Figure III-2: Tidal Flat Rule

```
Object: DEEP-MARINE-RULESET
Type: INDIVIDUAL
Generalizations: Ruleset
  NORMAL-RULES: MARINE-20 MARINE-21 MARINE-22 MARINE-23
                MARINE-24 MARINE-27
  CONTROL-STRATEGY: ReStartAfterFiring
```

Figure III-3: Deep Marine Ruleset

```
Object: Rule                        Object: Ruleset
Type: CLASS                         Type: CLASS
Generalizations: ROOT               Generalizations: ROOT
  IF:                                 NORMAL-RULES:
  THEN:                               FIRE-ONCE-RULES:
  RULESET:                            FIRE-ALWAYS-RULES:
  TRANSLATE: TranslateRule            CONTROL-STRATEGY:
  TRANSLATION:                        TERMINATION-CONDITION:
  Apply: ApplyRule                    KNOWLEDGE-BASE:
  Match: MatchRule                    Apply: ApplyRuleset
  MatchAll: MatchRuleAll
  Execute: ExecuteRule
```

Figure III-4: Rule Interpretation Objects

IV. SEMANTIC INTEGRITY MANAGEMENT

The integrity management system allows the user to define constraints on slots of objects, and to define actions to be taken in case of constraint violation or satisfaction (with appropriate defaults). The system analyzes the constraints and derives the information it needs to check them at run time (*i.e.*, the constraint variables and the operations that require checking). Currently, our constraint language is a combination of Interlisp-D and Strobe.

A. Declarations For Integrity Management

We distinguish several types of integrity constraints. A *single-slot constraint* involves a single-slot. A *datatype constraint* applies to all slots having a particular datatype. A *multi-slot constraint* involves several slots, in one or several objects. Since slots can be set-valued, constraints are divided into *element constraints* (that apply to the elements of a slot value) and *set constraints* (that apply to a slot value as a set).

Two alternatives for encoding a constraint are supported: *(i)* as slots of an object and *(ii)* as facets of a slot. In this section, we discuss constraints encoded as objects. For a presentation of slot encoding, and criteria for choosing between the two alternatives, see [2] and [3].

Figure IV-1 shows the object that defines a well location in terms of a town, county, state, country and continent. The `Continent` slot is subject to a (single-slot) constraint that its value must belong to the set of names enumerated in the `Candidates` facet. The constraint is implemented in the `ContinentConstraint` object (Figure IV-2) whose *Condition* slot encodes the constraint definition and *Correction* slot the correction of violations (here, simply an error message).

```
Object: WellLocation
Type: Class
Generalizations:  OBJECT
  Well:
  TOWN: {Township}
  COUN: {County Parish}
  STAT: {State Province}
  NATI: {Nation Country}
  CONT: {Continent}
    Datatype: EXPR
    Candidates: (Europe North-America South-America Asia Africa
                 Australia)
    PutElementConditions: ContinentConstraint
    AddElementConditions: ContinentConstraint
```

Figure IV-1: The WellLocation Object

```
Object: ContinentConstraint
Type: Class
Generalizations: SingleSlotConstraint
  Condition: (MEMBER Value Candidates)
  Correction: (Error Value "is not one of:" Candidates)
  SetOrElementConstraint: Element
  ConstrainedObject: WellLocation
  ConstrainedSlot: Continent
  Facets: Candidates
```

Figure IV-2: Single-Slot Constraint On Continent

Figure IV-3 shows the `Measurement` datatype object and one of its constraints: the `InternalUnitsConstraint`, implemented in the object shown in Figure IV-4. The constraint states that if slots whose datatype is a measurement specify the units for their values – their `internal units` – the values they are assigned must be in those units. The *Correction* slot contains the code to make the conversion if necessary.

```
Object: Measurement
Synonyms: DimensionedQuantity
Type: Class
Generalizations: DATATYPE
  UnitsConversion:
  InternalUnitsConstraint: InternalUnitsConstraint
    Datatype: DatatypeConstraint
  PutElementConditions: InternalUnitsConstraint
  AddElementConditions: InternalUnitsConstraint
```

Figure IV-3: The Measurement Object

```
Object: InternalUnitsConstraint
Type: Class
Generalizations: DatatypeConstraint
  Condition: (EQ (fetch UNITS of Value) InternalUnits)
  Correction: (MESSAGE Datatype 'UnitsConversion
                 (LIST (fetch UNITS of Value) InternalUnits))
  SetOrElementConstraint: Element
  DatatypeObject: Measurement
  ConstraintSlot: InternalUnitsConstraint
  Facets: InternalUnits
```

Figure IV-4: Datatype Constraint For Internal Units

Figure IV-5 shows the *Condition* slot of an object that implements a multi-slot constraint involving several objects. The constraint is between different regions, or components, of a geological fault, referred to as the upper and lower distortion regions (or blocks) and the breccia region (the zone between the blocks characterized by crushed rocks). It states that the upper distortion region of a fault is above its breccia region which, in turn, is above its lower distortion region. It assumes that there exist *(i)* `Fault` objects with `UpperDistortionRegion`, `LowerDistortionRegion` and `BrecciaRegion` slots, and *(ii)* `DistortionRegion` and `BrecciaRegion` objects with `Fault`, `Top` and `Bottom` slots.

```
Object: DistortionBrecciaConstraint
Type: Class
Generalizations:  MultiSlotConstraint
  Condition:
    (OR (≠ (THE Fault DistortionRegion)
           (THE Fault BrecciaRegion))
        (if (= DistortionRegion (THE UpperDistortionRegion
                                  (THE Fault BrecciaRegion)))
         then ($ABOVE (THE Bottom DistortionRegion)
                      (THE Top BrecciaRegion)))
        (if (= DistortionRegion (THE LowerDistortionRegion
                                  (THE Fault BrecciaRegion)))
         then ($ABOVE (THE Bottom BrecciaRegion)
                      (THE Top DistortionRegion))))
```

Figure IV-5: Multi-Slot Constraint Between Fault Regions

The user fills the *Condition* slot and optionally, the *Correction* and *Action* slots (the latter states a side effect of constraint satisfaction). These slots can contain function names, lambda expressions or s-expressions. They can reference slots and facets as free variables rather than by using Strobe access functions. In single-slot and datatype constraints, *Value* refers to the current slot value. In multi-slot constraints involving several objects, the *THE* function references slots in relation to their objects.

The checking declarations generated and used by the system basically consist of identifiers of the constraint variables to allow *(i)* insertion of triggers from the variables to the constraints at analysis time and *(ii)* efficient binding of the variables at run time.

A single-slot constraint object has a *ConstrainedObject* slot and a *ConstrainedSlot* slot. A datatype constraint object has a *DatatypeObject* slot and a *ConstraintSlot* slot. Since these constraints can involve facets other than *Value* (*e.g.*, `InternalUnits` in `InternalUnitsConstraint`) such facets are declared in a *Facets* slot. A *Slots* slot in a datatype constraint declares the slots of the datatype object involved in the constraint, and in a multi-slot constraint, it declares the constrained slots together with their respective objects.

A trigger associated with a slot is implemented by a facet that points to single or multi-slot constraints. The facet name indicates the operations on the slot that require checking (*Put, Add, Remove*)[5]. It also indicates whether the constraints are set or element constraints. This allows the user to reset the order in which constraints are checked (*e.g.*, element constraints before set constraints) and the system to efficiently order the constraints to check at run time. For example, the *PutElementConditions* facet of the `Continent` slot (Figure IV-1) indicates that `ContinentConstraint` must be checked when a value is put in the slot.

A trigger associated with a datatype object is a slot that points to the constraints for the datatype. Its name encodes the same information as trigger facets. The *AddElementConditions* slot of `Measurement` shows that `InternalUnitsConstraint` must be checked when a value is added to a slot whose datatype is some measurement.

B. Integrity Management Subsystem

The integrity management system consists of slots added to the *DATATYPE* object (Figure IV-6) and of constraint objects. The constraint objects are organized in a taxonomic hierarchy. The *Constraint* object is shown in Figure IV-7.

The *DATUM-Put*, *DATUM-Add*, and *DATUM-Remove* slots of *DATATYPE* contain the operations for which integrity may be checked. These operations are also declared in the *OperationsWithIntegrity* slot of *Constraint*. *DefaultOperations* declares the default operations for which integrity is checked.

```
Object: DATATYPE
Type: Class
Generalizations: ROOT
   DATUM-Edit:
   DATUM-Print:
   DATUM-Get: sys/mgetvalue
   DATUM-Put: DatatypePut
   DATUM-Add: DatatypeAdd
   DATUM-Remove: DatatypeRemove
   DATUM-AnalyzeConstraints: DatatypeAnalyzeConstraints
   ConstraintCheckingOrder: (DatatypeElementConstraints
                             ElementConstraints
                             DatatypeSetConstraints
                             SetConstraints)
```

Figure IV-6: DATATYPE Object For Integrity Management

```
Object: Constraint
Type: Class
Generalizations: DATATYPE
Specializations: (SingleSlotConstraint DatatypeConstraint
                  MultiSlotConstraint)
   OperationsWithIntegrity: (Put Add Remove)
   DefaultOperations: (Put Add)
   Analyze:
   Verify:
```

Figure IV-7: The Constraint Object

The *DATUM-AnalyzeConstraints* slot of *DATATYPE* and the *Analyze* slot of *Constraint* provide alternative ways of analyzing constraints. The former is a message handler for analyzing constraints encoded in slots. The latter is a message handler for analyzing constraint objects. For example, an *AnalyzeConstraints* message sent to the `PutElementConditions` slot of `Measurement` results in filling the *DatatypeObject*, *ConstraintSlot* and *Facets* slots of `InternalUnitsConstraint`. An *Analyze* message to the `InternalUnitsConstraint` object results in filling the same slots as well as the *PutElementConditions* and *AddElementConditions* slots of `Measurement`.

[5] Currently, the identification of the operations that may cause a constraint violation is based on heuristic, rather than formal, analysis, and can be overridden by the user.

The *Verify* slot in *Constraint* verifies whether a hypothetical value for a slot violates the constraints that apply to the slot. Instead of executing the corrections associated with the violated constraints, it returns an association list of the names of those constraints and the bindings of their variables. The *ConstraintCheckingOrder* slot declares the default order in which constraints are checked and can be reset in any datatype.

V. TASK REPRESENTATION

Declarative task representation has been successfully used to capture component function and structure in a number of domains: hardware design, fault detection, well-log interpretation. Our motivation for task declaration is to provide a structure within which *(i)* a knowledge-based system can reason about tasks, *(ii)* a unified mechanism can control task execution, and *(iii)* code written from a variety of computational perspectives and in a variety of programming languages can be integrated. An example is described in [9]. It shows how the Crystal knowledge base responsible for the user interface interprets information about tasks to guide the user through their execution and how it prompts him for the necessary input. To date, we have concentrated on task/subtask relationships, data description and control flow.

A. Declarations For Task Representation

In our formalism, task declarations are made in subclasses of the *Module* object. The execution history of a task is recorded as an instance of its class (analogous to ruleset invocation). Figure V-1 shows some of the slots of a task called `Eigen` which represents a principal component analysis on the logs identified in the `ActiveLogs` slot for the well identified in `Well` from `TopDepth` to `BottomDepth`. Among the outputs are principal component logs, represented by the `PCLogs` slot.

A task can be a substask of another task, which is called its *abstraction*. It points to that abstraction via a slot whose *Role* facet is set to *Abstraction*. For example, the `Faciolog` slot of an `Eigen` instance points to an instance of a module, called `Faciolog`* – a program that finds zones of similar log responses in a well, and whose first subtask is the principal component analysis carried out by `Eigen`. Conversely, a task points to its subtasks via slots whose *Role* facet is set to *Expansion*. Slots representing expansions also have an *Order* facet that indicates the relative (partial) order in which each expansion is normally to be executed. (`Eigen` has no expansions.)

The slots representing input and output parameters of a task are denoted by a *Role* facet set to *Port* and a *Direction* facet set to *In*, *Out* or *(In Out)*. These slots also have an *Order* facet that indicates to the system the relative (partial) order in which each input parameter should get its value. The *Origin* facet identifies where the value for the slot can be obtained. It may *(i)* identify the user (which in Crystal causes the user interface knowledge base to take charge); *(ii)* specify a slot of another object; or *(iii)* indicate

*Mark of Schlumberger

that the task will compute the value itself. The *Default* facet contains an s-expression that evaluates to a default value, and the *Candidates* facet evaluates to a set of possible values. These two facets are used by the user interface knowledge base in its prompting of the user (*e.g.*, by presenting a menu if there are candidate values). Other facets are discussed in [9].

The other facets associated with an input port are for integrity management. The `ActiveLogs` slot, for example, is subject to an

```
Object: Eigen
Type: Class
Generalizations: Module
  Faciolog:
    Datatype: Faciolog Role: Abstraction
  Well:
    Datatype: Well      Role: Port        Direction: In
  ActiveLogs:
    Datatype: Log       Role: Port        Direction: In
    Order: 2            Origin: User
    Cardinality: (1 . 30)
    Candidates: (MESSAGE Well 'Logs)
    Condition: (MEMBER Value Candidates)
    Facets: Candidates
    Operations: (Put Add)
    Correction: (Retry Value "isn't in" Well)
    SetCondition:(≥ 1 (for Log in Value count Log when
                    (Generalization? Log 'GammaRay)))
    SetCorrection: (Retry "You cannot select more than one
                    Gamma Ray log.")
    SetOperations: (Put Add)
  TopDepth:
    Datatype: Depth     Role: Port        Direction: In
    Order: 4            Origin: User
    PutMultiSlotConditions: TopBottomConstraint
    Default: (MESSAGE ActiveLogs 'TopDepth)
  BottomDepth:
    Datatype: Depth     Role: Port        Direction: In
    Order: 4            Origin: User
    PutMultiSlotConditions: TopBottomConstraint
    Default: (MESSAGE ActiveLogs 'BottomDepth)
  TopBottomConstraint: (> BottomDepth TopDepth)
    Datatype: Lisp      Role: MultiSlotCondition
    Slots: (TopDepth BottomDepth)
    Correction: (Retry "Bottom depth must be greater than top
                  depth.")
  PCLogs:
    Datatype: Log       Role: Port        Direction: Out
```

Figure V-1: Eigen Module

element constraint that each value be drawn from the logs associated with the Well, and to a set constraint such that no more than one log can be of type GammaRay. Furthermore, its `Cardinality` is limited to 30.

B. Task Declaration Subsystem

The mechanism to control task execution is implemented in the `Module` object (Figure V-2). (Only some slots are shown.)

```
Object: Module
Type: Class
Generalizations: OBJECT
  Code:
    Datatype: Lisp  File:
    Address: {crystal$node}crystal$disk:<crystal.users>
  RemoteExecutionObject:
    Host: crystal$node            KB: VLDB
  ReturnControl:
  Control: ModuleControl
    Datatype: Lisp  Iterate: NIL  Interactive: T  PauseOnEntry: NIL
```

Figure V-2: Module Object

The computation carried out by a task may execute either on the Xerox workstation or on a remote machine, in a language other than Interlisp-D. In the former case, the computation is specified in the `Code` slot, which typically contains a function name. In the latter case, it is specified in the `RemoteExecutionObject` slot. The value of that slot points to a Strobe object on the remote machine (identified in the *Host* facet) which is responsible for calling the foreign language program. That object (written in Mainsail, CommonLisp, or C Strobe if it resides on a Vax) exchanges input and output parameters with the current module object written in Interlisp-D Strobe.

The `ReturnControl` slot identifies where control is to be passed next (in terms of a host, knowledge base, object, slot and facet).

A task executes when its `Control` slot receives a message. This slot contains the function that implements the task execution control mechanism. Basically, that function *(i)* acquires the input parameters; *(ii)* instantiates and executes expansions as required, if there are expansions, or else, executes the task computation; and *(iii)* passes control to the next module. Dynamic alteration of control flow is supported by resetting `ReturnControl` slots on the fly. Note also that the `Control` slot has facets to modify control flow (*e.g.*, to iterate through a task or to pause for interaction before starting a task). Of course, the default values for these facets defined in the `Module` object can be overridden in its specializations.

VI. FILE MANAGEMENT

Strobe manages objects in virtual memory. At the end of a session, all objects in a knowledge base are generally stored on the same file. Subsets of objects from a knowledge base may also be loaded and stored. The file management tool extends this basic capability in that *(i)* it allows more generality in specifying the subsets of objects (by description as well as by name), and *(ii)* it keeps track of the files on which such collections are stored. Our goal is to provide DBMS-like facilities to cope with increasing numbers of objects as knowledge bases scale up.

A. Declarations For File Management

The filing mechanism is implemented via *file indexes*. A file index is defined as a conjunction of slot names. It maps values of that conjunction into file names. For example, a file index may be defined by the conjunction `(Well CreationDate)` and an index value may be `(WellA 23-Oct-84)`. The object implementing that file index associates `(WellA 23-Oct-84)` with the name of one or several files that contain objects whose `Well` slot value is `WellA` and whose `CreationDate` slot value is `23-Oct-84`.

Figure VI-1 shows a file index whose conjunction, defined in the `Index` slot, is `(Well CreationDate)`. The slots `IndexValue1`, `IndexValue2` and `IndexValue3` represent index entries, *i.e.*, tuples of the mapping between index values and file names. The *Value* facet of such a slot is an index value, *e.g.*, `(WellA 23-Oct-84)`, and its *Files* facet points to the files that contain objects corresponding to its value[6]. Slots implementing index entries are created and managed automatically by the system and are of no more concern to the user than the implementation of

---

[6] An index value may point to several files because it is our policy to avoid duplication of objects on several files. As a result, an object corresponding to two index values (for two different indexes) is stored in only one of the two corresponding files, and that file must be pointed to by the other index value.

B-trees in a DBMS. The user need only be concerned with loading and storing objects, not with the system's implementation of those operations.

```
Object: WellIndex
Type: Individual
Generalizations: FileIndex
  Index: (Well CreationDate)
  IndexValue1: (WellA 23-Oct-84)
    Datatype: EXPR      Files: WellA.obs;1
  IndexValue2: (WellA 2-Dec-84)
    Datatype: EXPR      Files: (WellA.obs;1 truc.obs;1)
  IndexValue3: (WellB 2-Dec-84)
    Datatype: EXPR      Files: WellB.obs;1
```

Figure VI-1: WellIndex object

B. File Management Subsystem

The file management subsystem is implemented in the FileIndex object (Figure VI-2). Its specializations are individual user-defined objects representing file indexes such as WellIndex. Address specifies the host, device, and directory where the files are actually found. LoadObjects contains a function that takes an index value as argument and loads the objects corresponding to that index value. Similarly, StoreObjects stores the objects corresponding to an index value.

```
Object: FileIndex
Type: Class
Generalizations: ROOT
  Index:
  Address: {crystal$node}:crystal$disk:<crystal.wells>
  LoadObjects: FileIndexLoadObjects
  StoreObjects: FileIndexStoreObjects
```

Figure VI-2: FileIndex Object

VII. CONCLUSION

We have described the implementation of knowledge management tools for Strobe knowledge bases and presented examples of the capabilities they offer. Each tool is confined to a few general domain-independent objects which can be added to an initial knowledge base. The addition of a new tool is modular in that it consists only of defining new objects or new slots of an existing object. Figure VII-1 shows the initial taxonomic hierarchy of a knowledge base incorporating all tools described in this paper.

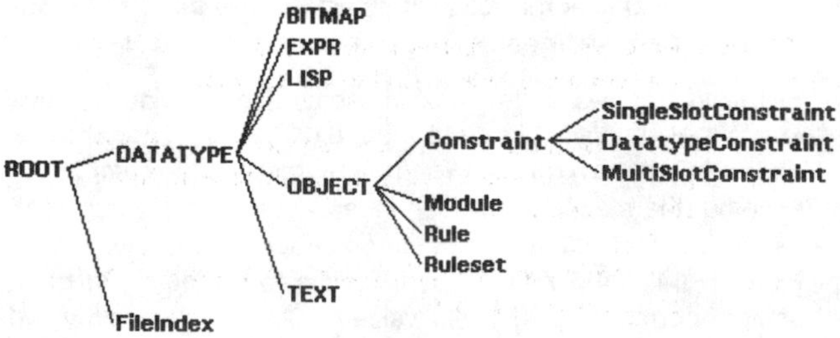

Figure VII-1: Initial Objects For Knowledge Management Tools

Implementation of the tools has been unified through an object-oriented foundation. This foundation also helps to unify access to the tools – through invocation via message. This is a simple, yet powerful concept that helps to integrate objects, rules, tasks, and procedures.

Tool kits such as ours offer a number of alternative styles of programming: Rulesets, modules, constraints, and procedures. While they do help integrate these various styles, criteria for selecting among the alternatives for any given task are not always clear. For instance, a computation to be carried out as the result of an operation on a slot could be encoded as a constraint (possibly with maintenance actions), or as a ruleset, or as a module whose invocation is triggered by a demon associated with that slot. Our intention, then, is to use the tool kit both as a development vehicle for knowledge-based systems and as an exploration vehicle for seeking selection principles.

ACKNOWLEDGMENTS: We gratefully acknowledge the Crystal team for providing the context for this work. Eric Schoen built Impulse, parts of the task representation system and lower-level tools such as the networking and Strobe Vax execution environment. Robert Young made a number of valuable suggestions.

REFERENCES

1. C. L. Forgy. *The OPS5 User's Manual.* Tech. Rept. CMU-CS-81-135, Carnegie-Mellon University, July, 1981.

2. Lafue G. M. E. *Integrity Constraints for Strobe Knowledge Bases.* Research Note SYS-85, Schlumberger-Doll Research, 1985.

3. G. M. E. Lafue and R. G. Smith. Implementation of An Integrity Manager With A Knowledge Representation System. *Expert Database Systems*, 1985.

4. E. Schoen and R. G. Smith. Impulse, A Display-Oriented Editor for Strobe. *Proceedings of the National Conference on Artificial Intelligence*, August, 1983, pp. 356-358.

5. R. G. Smith. Strobe: Support For Structured Object Knowledge Representation. *Proceedings of the Eighth International Joint Conference on Artificial Intelligence*, August, 1983, pp. 855-858.

6. R. G. Smith. *Structured Object Programming In Strobe.* Research Note SYS-84-08, Schlumberger-Doll Research, March, 1984.

7. R. G. Smith. *Programming With Rules In Strobe.* Research Note SYS-84-12, Schlumberger-Doll Research, December, 1984.

8. R. G. Smith and R. L. Young. The Design Of The Dipmeter Advisor System. *Proceedings of the ACM Annual Conference*, ACM, New York, October, 1984, pp. 15-23.

9. R. G. Smith, G. M. E. Lafue, E. Schoen, and S. C. Vestal. "Declarative Task Description As A User Interface Structuring Mechanism." *Computer 17*, 9 (September 1984), 29-38.

10. W. VanMelle, A. C. Scott, J. S. Bennett, and M. Peairs. *The Emycin Manual.* Tech. Rept. STAN-CS-81-885 (HPP-81-16), Dept. Of Computer Science, Stanford University, October, 1981.

INCLUSION OF NEW TYPES IN RELATIONAL DATA BASE SYSTEMS

Michael Stonebraker
EECS Dept.
University of California, Berkeley

Abstract

This paper explores a mechanism to support user-defined data types for columns in a relational data base system. Previous work suggested how to support new operators and new data types. The contribution of this work is to suggest ways to allow query optimization on commands which include new data types and operators and ways to allow access methods to be used for new data types.

1. INTRODUCTION

The collection of built-in data types in a data base system (e.g. integer, floating point number, character string) and built-in operators (e.g. +, -, *, /) were motivated by the needs of business data processing applications. However, in many engineering applications this collection of types is not appropriate. For example, in a geographic application a user typically wants points, lines, line groups and polygons as basic data types and operators which include intersection, distance and containment. In scientific application, one requires complex numbers and time series with appropriate operators. In such applications one is currently required to simulate these data types and operators using the basic data types and operators provided by the DBMS at substantial inefficiency and complexity. Even in business applications, one sometimes needs user-defined data types. For example, one system [RTI84] has implemented a sophisticated date and time data type to add to its basic collection. This implementation allows subtraction of dates, and returns "correct" answers, e.g.

"April 15" - "March 15" = 31 days

This definition of subtraction is appropriate for most users; however, some applications require all months to have 30 days (e.g. programs which compute interest on bonds). Hence, they require a definition of subtraction which yields 30 days as the answer to the above computation. Only a user-defined data type facility allows such customization to occur.

Current data base systems implement hashing and B-trees as fast access paths for built-in data types. Some user-defined data types (e.g. date and time) can use existing access methods (if certain extensions are made); however other data types (e.g. polygons) require new access methods. For example R-trees [GUTM84], KDB trees [ROBI81] and Grid files are appropriate for spatial objects. In addition, the introduction of new access methods for conventional business applications (e.g. extendible hashing [FAGI79, LITW80]) would be expeditied by a facility to add new access methods.

This research was sponsored by the U.S. Air Force Office of Scientific Research Grant 83-0254 and the Naval Electronics Systems Command Contract N39-82-C-0235

A complete extended type system should allow:

1) the definition of user-defined data types
2) the definition of new operators for these data types
3) the implementation of new access methods for data types
4) optimized query processing for commands containing new data types and operators

The solution to requirements 1 and 2 was described in [STON83]; in this paper we present a complete proposal. In Section 2 we begin by presenting a motivating example of the need for new data types, and then briefly review our earlier proposal and comment on its implementation. Section 3 turns to the definition of new access methods and suggests mechanisms to allow the designer of a new data type to use access methods written for another data type and to implement his own access methods with as little work as possible. Then Section 4 concludes by showing how query optimization can be automatically performed in this extended environment.

2. ABSTRACT DATA TYPES

2.1. A Motivating Example

Consider a relation consisting of data on two dimensional boxes. If each box has an identifier, then it can be represented by the coordinates of two corner points as follows:

```
create box (id = i4, x1 = f8, x2 = f8, y1 = f8, y2 = f8)
```

Now consider a simple query to find all the boxes that overlap the unit square, ie. the box with coordinates (0, 1, 0, 1). The following is a compact representation of this request in QUEL:

```
retrieve (box.all) where not
  (box.x2 <= 0 or box.x1 >= 1
  or box.y2 <= 0 or box.y1 >= 1)
```

The problems with this representation are:

The command is too hard to understand.

The command is too slow because the query planner will not be able to optimize something this complex.

The command is too slow because there are too many clauses to check.

The solution to these difficulties is to support a box data type whereby the box relation can be defined as:

```
create box (id = i4, desc = box)
```

and the resulting user query is:

```
retrieve (box.all) where box.desc !! "0, 1, 0, 1"
```

Here "!!" is an overlaps operator with two operands of data type box which returns a boolean. One would want a substantial collection of operators for user defined types. For example, Table 1 lists a collection of useful operators for the box data type.

Fast access paths must be supported for queries with qualifications utilizing new data types and operators. ·uently, current access methods must be extended to : in this environment. For example, a reasonable ıg sequence for boxes would be on ascending area, and a storage structure could be built for boxes using this ce. Hence, queries such as

rieve (box.all) where box.desc AE "0,5,0,5"

operator	symbol	left operand	right operand	result
s	!!	box	box	boolean
ed in	<<	box	box	boolean
e left of	<L	box	box	boolean
e right of	>R	box	box	boolean
:tion	??	box	box	box
e	"	box	box	float
ıs than	AL	box	box	boolean
uals	AE	box	box	boolean
eater	AG	box	box	boolean

operator	symbol	operand	result
	AA	box	float
	LL	box	float
	HH	box	float
al	DD	box	line

Operators for Boxes

Table 1

use this index. Moreover, if a user wishes to optimize for the !! operator, then an R-tree [GUTM84] may be a ıble access path. Hence, it should be possible to add a :fined access method. Lastly, a user may submit a query all pairs of boxes which overlap, e.g:

ıge of b1 is box
ıge of b2 is box
:rieve (b1.all, b2.all) where b1.desc !! b2.desc

y optimizer must be able to construct an access plan for queries which contains user defined operators.

/e turn now to a review of the prototype presented in 83] which supports some of the above function.

DEFINITION OF NEW TYPES

o define a new type, a user must follow a registration which indicates the existence of the new type, gives the of its internal representation and provides input and conversion routines, e.g:

```
fine type-name length = value,
               input = file-name
               output = file-name
```

:w data type must occupy a fixed amount of space, since ced length data is allowed by the built-in access methods in INGRES. Moreover, whenever new values are input from a program or output to a user, a conversion routine must be called. This routine must convert from character string to the new type and back. A data base system calls such routines for built-in data types (e.g. ascii-to-int, int-to-ascii) and they must be provided for user-defined data types. The input conversion routine must accept a pointer to a value of type character string and return a pointer to a value of the new data type. The output routine must perform the converse transformation.

Then, zero or more operators can be implemented for the new type. Each can be defined with the following syntax:

```
define operator token = value,
                left-operand = type-name,
                right-operand = type-name,
                result = type-name,
                precedence-level like operator-2,
                file = file-name
```

For example:

```
define operator token = !!,
                left-operand = box,
                right-operand = box,
                result = boolean,
                precedence like *,
                file = /usr/foobar
```

All fields are self explanatory except the precedence level which is required when several user defined operators are present and precedence must be established among them. The file /usr/foobar indicates the location of a procedure which can accept two operands of type box and return true if they overlap. This procedure is written in a general purpose programming language and is linked into the run-time system and called as appropriate during query processing.

2.3. Comments on the Prototype

The above constructs have been implemented in the University of California version of INGRES [STON76]. Modest changes were required to the parser and a dynamic loader was built to load the required user-defined routines on demand into the INGRES address space. The system was described in [ONG84].

Our initial experience with the system is that dynamic linking is not preferable to static linking. One problem is that initial loading of routines is slow. Also, the ADT routines must be loaded into data space to preserve sharability of the DBMS code segment. This capability requires the construction of a non-trivial loader. An "industrial strength" implementation might choose to specify the user types which an installation wants at the time the DBMS is installed. In this case, all routines could be linked into the run time system at system installation time by the linker provided by the operating system. Of course, a data base system implemented as a single server process with internal multitasking would not be subject to any code sharing difficulties, and a dynamic loading solution might be reconsidered.

An added difficulty with ADT routines is that they provide a serious safety loophole. For example, if an ADT routine has an error, it can easily crash the DBMS by overwriting DBMS data structures accidentally. More seriously, a malicious ADT routine can overwrite the entire data base with zeros. In addition, it is unclear whether such errors are due to bugs in the user routines or in the DBMS, and finger-pointing between the DBMS implementor and the ADT implementor is likely to result.

ADT routines can be run in a separate address space to solve both problems, but the performance penalty is severe. Every procedure call to an ADT operator must be turned into a round trip message to a separate address space. Alternately, the DBMS can interpret the ADT procedure and guarantee safety, but only by building a language processor into the run-time system and paying the performance penalty of interpretation. Lastly, hardware support for protected procedure calls (e.g. as in Multics) would also solve the problem.

However, on current hardware the prefered solution may be to provide two environments for ADT procedures. A protected environment would be provided for debugging purposes. When a user was confident that his routines worked correctly, he could install them in the unprotected DBMS. In this way, the DBMS implementor could refuse to be concerned unless a bug could be produced in the safe version.

We now turn to extending this environment to support new access methods.

3. NEW ACCESS METHODS

A DBMS should provide a wide variety of access methods, and it should be easy to add new ones. Hence, our goal in this section is to describe how users can add new access methods that will efficiently support user-defined data types. In the first subsection we indicate a registration process that allows implementors of new data types to use access methods written by others. Then, we turn to designing lower level DBMS interfaces so the access method designer has minimal work to perform. In this section we restrict our attention to access methods for a single key field. Support for composite keys is a straight forward extension. However, multidimensional access methods that allow efficient retrieval utilizing subsets of the collection of keys are beyond the scope of this paper.

3.1. Registration of a New Access Method

The basic idea which we exploit is that a properly implemented access method contains only a small number of procedures that define the characteristics of the access method. Such procedures can be replaced by others which operate on a different data type and allow the access method to "work" for the new type. For example, consider a B-tree and the following generic query:

retrieve (target-list) where relation.key OPR value

A B-tree supports fast access if OPR is one of the set:

{=, <, <=, >=, >}

and includes appropriate procedure calls to support these operators for a data type (s). For example, to search for the record matching a specific key value, one need only descend the B-tree at each level searching for the minimum key whose value exceeds or equals the indicated key. Only calls on the operator "<=" are required with a final call or calls to the

TEMPLATE-1	AM-name	condition
	B-tree	P1
	B-tree	P2
	B-tree	P3
	B-tree	P4
	B-tree	P5
	B-tree	P6
	B-tree	P7

TEMPLATE-2	AM-name	opr-name	opt	left	right	result
	B-tree	=	opt	fixed	type1	boolean
	B-tree	<	opt	fixed	type1	boolean
	B-tree	<=	req	fixed	type1	boolean
	B-tree	>	opt	fixed	type1	boolean
	B-tree	>=	opt	fixed	type1	boolean

Templates for Access Methods

Table 2

AM	class	AM-name	opr	generic name	opr-id opr	Ntups	Npages
	int-ops	B-tree	=	=	id1	N / Ituples	2
	int-ops	B-tree	<	<	id2	F1 * N	F1 * NUMpages
	int-ops	B-tree	<=	<=	id3	F1 * N	F1 * NUMpages
	int-ops	B-tree	>	>	id4	F2 * N	F2 * NUMpages
	int-ops	B-tree	>=	>=	id5	F2 * N	F2 * NUMpages
	area-op	B-tree	AE	=	id6	N / Ituples	3
	area-op	B-tree	AL	<	id7	F1 * N	F1 * NUMpages
	area-op	B-tree	AG	>	id8	F1 * N	F1 * NUMpages

The AM Relation

Table 3

routine supporting "=".

Moreover, this collection of operators has the following properties:

P1) key-1 < key-2 and key-2 < key-3 then key-1 < key-3
P2) key-1 < key-2 implies not key-2 < key-1
P3) key-1 < key-2 or key-2 < key-1 or key-1 = key-2
P4) key-1 <= key-2 if key-1 < key-2 or key-1 = key-2
P5) key-1 = key-2 implies key-2 = key-1
P6) key-1 > key-2 if key-2 < key-1
P7) key-1 >= key-2 if key-2 <= key-1

In theory, the procedures which implement these operators can be replaced by any collection of procedures for new operators that have these properties and the B-tree will "work" correctly. Lastly, the designer of a B-tree access method may disallow variable length keys. For example, if a binary search of index pages is performed, then only fixed length keys are possible. Information of this restriction must be available to a type designer who wishes to use the access method.

The above information must be recorded in a data structure called an access method template. We propose to store templates in two relations called TEMPLATE-1 and TEMPLATE-2 which would have the composition indicated in Table 2 for a B-tree access method. TEMPLATE-1 simply documents the conditions which must be true for the operators provided by the access method. It is included only to provide guidance to a human wishing to utilize the access method for a new data type and is not used internally in the system. TEMPLATE-2, on the other hand, provides necessary information on the data types of operators. The column "opt" indicates whether the operator is required or optional. A B-tree must have the operator "<=" to build the tree; however, the other operators are optional. Type1, type2 and result are possible types for the left operand, the right operand, and the result of a given operator. Values for these fields should come from the following collection;

a specific type, e.g. int, float, boolean, char
fixed, i.e. any type with fixed length
variable, i.e. any type with a
prescribed varying length format
fix-var, i.e. fixed or variable
type1, i.e. the same type as type1
type2, i.e. the same as type2

After indicating the template for an access method, the designer can propose one or more collections of operators which satisfy the template in another relation, AM. In Table 3 we have shown an AM containing the original set of integer operators provided by the access method designer along with a collection added later by the designer of the box data type. Since operator names do not need to be unique, the field opr-id must be included to specify a unique identifier for a given operator. This field is present in a relation which contains the operator specific information discussed in Section 2. The fields, Ntups and Npages are query processing parameters which estimate the number of tuples which satisfy the qualification and the number of pages touched when running a query using the operator to compare a key field in a relation to a constant. Both are formulas which utilize the variables found in Table 4, and values reflect approximations to the computations found in [SELI79] for the case that each record set occupies an individual file. Moreover, F1 and F2 are surogates for the following quantities:

F1 = (value - low-key) / (high-key - low-key)
F2 = (high-key - value) / (high-key - low-key)

With these data structures in place, a user can simply modify relations to B-tree using any class of operators defined in the AM relation. The only addition to the modify command

Variable	Meaning
N	number of tuples in a relation
NUMpages	number of pages of storage used by the relation
Ituples	number of index keys in an index
Ipages	number of pages in the index
value	the constant appearing in: rel-name.field-name OPR value
high-key	the maximum value in the key range if known
low-key	the minimum value in the key range if known

Variables for Computing Ntups and Npages

Table 4

is a clause "using class" which specifies what operator class to use in building and accessing the relation. For example the command

modify box to B-tree on desc using area-op

will allow the DBMS to provide optimized access on data of type box using the operators {AE,AL,AG}. The same extension must be provided to the index command which constructs a secondary index on a field, e.g:

index on box is box-index (desc) using area-op

To illustrate the generality of these constructs, the AM and TEMPLATE relations are shown in Tables 5 and 6 for both a hash and an R-tree access method. The R-tree is assumed to support three operators, contained-in (<<), equals (==) and contained-in-or-equals (<<=). Moreover, a fourth operator (UU) is required during page splits and finds the box which is the union of two other boxes. UU is needed solely for maintaining the R-tree data structure, and is not useful for search purposes. Similarly, a hash access method requires a hash function, H, which accepts a key as a left operand and an integer number of buckets as a right operand to produce a hash bucket as a result. Again, H cannot be used for searching purposes. For compactness, formulas for Ntups and Npages have been omitted from Table 6.

3.2. Implementing New Access Methods

In general an access method is simply a collection of procedure calls that retrieve and update records. A generic abstraction for an access method could be the following:

open (relation-name)

This procedure returns a pointer to a structure containing all relevant information about a relation. Such a "relation control block" will be called a descriptor. The effect is to make the relation accessible.

close (descriptor)

This procedure terminates access to the relation indicated by the descriptor.

get-first (descriptor, OPR, value)

This procedure returns the first record which satisfies the qualification

..where key OPR value

get-next (descriptor, OPR, value, tuple-id)

TEMPLATE-1	AM-name	condition
	hash	Key-1 = Key-2 implies H(key1) = H(key-2)
	R-tree	Key-1 << Key-2 and Key-2 << Key-2 implies Key-1 << key-3
	R-tree	Key-1 << Key-2 implies not Key-2 << Key-1
	R-tree	Key-1 <<= Key-2 implies Key-1 << Key-2 or Key-1 == Key-2
	R-tree	Key-1 == Key-2 implies Key-2 == Key-1
	R-tree	Key-1 << Key-1 UU Key-2
	R-tree	Key-2 << Key-1 UU Key-2

TEMPLATE-2	AM-name	opr-name	opt	left	right	result
	hash	=	opt	fixed	type1	boolean
	hash	H	req	fixed	int	int
	R-tree	<<	req	fixed	type1	boolean
	R-tree	==	opt	fixed	type1	boolean
	R-tree	<<=	opt	fixed	type1	boolean
	R-tree	UU	req	fixed	type1	boolean

Templates for Access Methods

Table 5

AM	class	AM-name	opr name	generic opr	opr-id	Ntups	Npages
	box-ops	R-tree	==	==	id10		
	box-ops	R-tree	<<	<<	id11		
	box-ops	R-tree	<<=	<<=	id12		
	box-ops	R-tree	UU	UU	id13		
	hash-op	hash	=	=	id14		
	hash-op	hash	H	H	id15		

The AM Relation

Table 6

This procedure gets the next tuple following the one indicated by tuple-id which satisfies the qualification.

get-unique (descriptor, tuple-id)

This procedure gets the tuple which corresponds to the indicated tuple identifier.

insert (descriptor, tuple)

This procedure inserts a tuple into the indicated relation

delete (descriptor, tuple-id)

This procedure deletes a tuple from the indicated relation.

replace (descriptor, tuple-id, new-tuple)

This procedure replaces the indicated tuple by a new one.

build (descriptor, keyname, OPR)

Of course it is possible to build a new access method for a relation by successively inserting tuples using the insert procedure. However, higher performance can usually be obtained by a bulk loading utility. Build is this utility and accepts a descriptor for a relation along with a key and operator to use in the build process.

There are many different (more or less similar) access method interfaces; see [ASTR76, ALLC80] for other proposals. Each DBMS implementation will choose their own collection of procedures and calling conventions.

If this interface is publicly available, then it is feasible to implement these procedures using a different organizing principle. A clean design of open and close should make these routines universally usable, so an implementor need only construct the remainder. Moreover, if the designer of a new access method chooses to utilize the same physical page layout as some existing access method, then replace and delete do not require modification, and additional effort is spared.

The hard problem is to have a new access method interface correctly to the transaction management code. (One commercial system found this function to present the most difficulties when a new access method was coded.) If a DBMS (or the underlying operating system) supports transactions by physically logging pages and executing one of the popular concurrency control algorithms for page size granules, (e.g. [BROW81, POPE81, SPEC83, STON85] then the designer of a new access method need not concern himself with transaction management. Higher level software will begin and end transactions, and the access method can freely read and write pages with a guarantee of atomicity and serializability. In this case the access method designer has no problems concerning transactions, and this is a significant advantage for transparent transactions. Unfortunately, much higher performance will typically result if a different approach is taken to both crash recovery and concurrency control. We now sketch roughly what this alternate interface might be.

With regard to crash recovery, most current systems have a variety of special case code to perform logical logging of events rather than physical logging of the changes of bits. There are at least two reasons for this method of logging. First, changes to the schema (e.g. create a relation) often require additional work besides changes to the system catalogs (e.g. creating an operating system file in which to put tuples of the relation). Undoing a create command because a transaction is aborted will require deletion of the newly created file. Physical backout cannot accomplish such extra function. Second, some data base updates are extremely inefficient when physically logged. For example, if a relation is modified from B-tree to hash, then the entire relation will be written to the log (perhaps more than once depending on the implementation of the modify utility). This costly extra I/O can be avoided by simply logging the command that is being performed. In the unlikely event that this event in the log must be undone or redone, then the modify utility can be rerun to make the changes anew. Of course, this sacrifices performance at recovery time for a compression of the log by several orders of magnitude.

If such logical logging is performed, then a new access method must become involved in logging process and a clean event-oriented interface to logging services should be provided. Hence, the log should be a collection of **events**, each having an event-id, an associated **event type** and an arbitrary collection of data. Lastly, for each event type, T, two procedures, REDO(T) and UNDO(T) are required which will be called when the log manager is rolling forward redoing log events and rolling backward undoing logged events respectively. The system must also provide a procedure,

LOG (event-type, event-data)

which will actually insert events into the log. Moreover, the system will provide a collection of **built-in event types**. For each such event, UNDO and REDO are available in system libraries. Built-in events would include:

replace a tuple
insert a tuple at a specific tuple identifier address
delete a tuple
change the storage structure of a relation
create a relation
destroy a relation

A designer of a new access method could use the built-in events if they were appropriate to his needs. Alternately, he could specify new event types by writing UNDO and REDO procedures for the events and making entries in a system relation holding event information. Such an interface is similar to the one provided by CICS [IBM80].

We turn now to discussing the concurrency control subsystem. If this service is provided transparently and automatically by an underlying module, then special case concurrency control for the system catalogs and index records will be impossible. This approach will severely impact performance as noted in [STON85]. Alternately, one can follow the standard scheduler model [BERN81] in which a module is callable by code in the access methods when a concurrency control decision must be made. The necessary calls are:

read (object-identifier)
write (object-identifier)
begin
abort
commit
savepoint

and the scheduler responds with yes, no or abort. The calls to begin, abort, commit and savepoint are made by higher level software, and the access methods need not be concerned with them. The access method need only make the appropriate calls on the scheduler when it reads or writes an object. The only burden which falls on the implementor is to choose the appropriate size for objects.

The above interface is appropriate for data records which are handled by a conventional algorithm guaranteeing serializability. To provide special case parallelism on index or system catalog records, an access method requires more control over concurrency decisions. For example, most B-tree implementations do not hold write locks on index pages which are split until the end of the transaction which performed the insert. It appears easiest to provide specific lock and unlock calls for such special situations, i.e:

lock (object, mode)
unlock (object)

These can be used by the access method designer to implement special case parallelism in his data structures.

The last interface of concern to the designer of an access method is the one to the buffer manager. One requires five procedures:

get (system-page-identifier)
fix (system-page-identifier)
unfix (system-page-identifier)
put (system-page-identifier)
order (system-page-identifier,
event-id or system-page-identifier)

The first procedure accepts a page identifier and returns a pointer to the page in the buffer pool. The second and third procedures pin and unpin pages in the buffer pool. The last call specifies that the page holding the given event should be written to disk prior to the indicated data page. This information is necessary in write-ahead log protocols. More generally, it allows two data pages to be forced out of memory in a specific order.

An access method implementor must code the necessary access method procedures utilizing the above interfaces to the log manager, the concurrency control manager and the buffer manager. Then, he simply registers his access method in the two TEMPLATE relations.

3.3. Discussion

A transparent interface to the transaction system is clearly much preferred to the complex collection of routines discussed above. Moreover, the access method designer who utilizes these routines must design his own events, specify any special purpose concurrency control in his data structures, and indicate any necessary order in forcing pages out of the buffer pool. An open research question is the design of a simpler interface to these services that will provide the required functions.

In addition, the performance of the crash recovery facility will be inferior to the recovery facilities in a conventional system. In current transaction managers, changes to indexes are typically not logged. Rather, index changes are recreated from the corresponding update to the data record. Hence, if there are n indexes for a given object, a single log entry for the data update will result in n+1 events (the data update and n index updates) being undone or redone in a conventional system. Using our proposed interface all n+1 events will appear in the log, and efficiency will be sacrificed.

The access method designer has the least work to perform if he uses the same page layout as one of the built-in access methods. Such an access method requires get-first, get-next, and insert to be coded specially. Moreover, no extra event types are required, since the built-in ones provide all the required functions. R-trees are an example of such an access method. On the other hand, access methods which do not use the same page layout will require the designer to write considerably more code.

4. QUERY PROCESSING AND ACCESS PATH SELECTION

To allow optimization of a query plan that contains new operators and types, only four additional pieces of information are required when defining an operator. First, a selectivity factor, Stups, is required which estimates the expected number of records satisfying the clause:

...where rel-name.field-name OPR value

A second selectivity factor, S, is the expected number of records which satisfy the clause

...where relname-1.field-1 OPR relname-2.field-2

Stups and S are arithmetic formulas containing the predefined variables indicated earlier in Table 4. Moreover, each variable can have a suffix of 1 or 2 to specify the left or right operand respectively.

Notice that the same selectivity appears both in the definition of an operator (Stups) and in the entry (Ntups) in AM if the operator is used in an index. In this case, Ntups from AM should be used first, and supports an if-then-else specification used for example in the [SELI79] for the operator "=" as follows:

selectivity = (1 / Ituples) ELSE 1/10

In this example selectivity is the reciprocal of the number of index tuples if an index exists else it is 1/10. The entry for Ntups in AM would be (N / Ituples) while Stups in the operator definition would be N / 10.

The third piece of necessary information is whether merge-sort is feasible for the operator being defined. More exactly, the existence of a second operator, OPR-2 is required such that OPR and OPR-2 have properties P1-P3 from Section 3 with OPR replacing "=" and OPR-2 replacing "<". If so, the relations to be joined using OPR can be sorted using OPR-2 and then merged to produce the required answer.

The last piece of needed information is whether hash-join is a feasible joining strategy for this operator. More exactly, the hash condition from Table 6 must be true with OPR replacing "=".

An example of these pieces of information for the operator, AE, would be:

```
define operator token = AE,
                left-operand = box,
                right-operand = box,
                result = boolean,
                precedence like *,
                file = /usr/foobar,
                Stups = 1,
                S = min (N1, N2),
                merge-sort with AL,
                hash-join
```

We now turn to generating the query processing plan. We assume that relations are stored keyed on one field in a single file and that secondary indexes can exist for other fields. Moreover, queries involving a single relation can be processed with a scan of the relation, a scan of a portion of the primary index, or a scan of a portion of one secondary index. Joins can be processed by iterative substitution, merge-sort or a hash-join algorithm. Modification to the following rules for different environments appears straigth-forward.

Legal query processing plans are described by the following statements.

1) Merge sort is feasible for a clause of the form:

relname-1.field-1 OPR relname-2.field-2

if field-1 and field-2 are of the same data type and OPR has the merge-sort property. Moreover, the expected size of the result is S. The cost to sort one or both relations is a built-in computation.

2) Iterative substitution is always feasible to perform the join specified by a clause of the form:

relname-1.field-1 OPR relname-2.field-2

The expected size of the result is calculated as above. The cost of this operation is the cardinality of the outer relation multiplied by the expected cost of the one-variable query on the inner relation.

3) A hash join algorithm can be used to perform a join specified by:

relname-1.field-1 OPR relname-2.field-2

if OPR has the hash-join property. The expected size of the result is as above, and the cost to hash one or both relations is another built-in computation.

4) An access method, A for relname can be used to restrict a clause of the form

relname.field-name OPR value

only if relname uses field-name as a key and OPR appears in the class used in the modify command to organize relname. The expected number of page and tuple accesses are given by the appropriate row in AM.

5) A secondary index, I for relname can be used to restrict a clause of the form:

relname.field-name OPR value

only if the index uses field-name as a key and OPR appears in the class used to build the index. The expected number of index page and tuple accesses is given by the appropriate row in AM. To these must be added 1 data page and 1 data tuple per index tuple.

6) A sequential search can always be used to restrict a relation on a clause of the form:

relname.field-name OPR value

One must read NUMpages to access the relation and the expected size of the result is given by Stups from the definition of OPR.

A query planner, such as the one discussed in [SELI79] can now be easily modified to compute a best plan using the above rules to generate legal plans and the above selectivities rather than the current hard-wired collection of rules and selectivities. Moreover, a more sophisticated optimizer which uses statistics (e.g. [KOOI82, PIAT84] can be easily built that uses the above information.

5. CONCLUSIONS

This paper has described how an abstract data type facility can be extended to support automatic generation of optimized query processing plans, utilization of existing access methods for new data types, and coding of new access methods. Only the last capability will be difficult to use, and a cleaner high performance interface to the transaction manager would be highly desirable. Moreover, additional rules in the query optimizer would probably be a useful direction for evolution. These could include when to cease investigating alternate plans, and the ability to specify one's own optimizer parameters, e.g. the constant W relating the cost of I/O to the cost of CPU activity in [SELI79].

REFERENCES

[ALLC80] Allchin, J. et. al., "FLASH: A Language Independent Portable File Access Method," Proc. 1980 ACM-SIGMOD Conference on Management of Data, Santa Monica, Ca., May 1980.

[ASTR76] Astrahan, M. et. al., "System R: A Relational Approach to Data," ACM-TODS, June 1976.

[BERN81] Bernstein, P. and Goodman, N., "Concurrency Control in Distributed Database Systems," ACM Computing Surveys, June 1981.

[BROW81] Brown, M. et. al., "The Cedar DBMS: A Preliminary Report," Proc. 1981 ACM-SIGMOD Conference on Management of Data, Ann Arbor, Mich., May 1981.

[FAGI79] Fagin, R. et. al., "Extendible Hashing: A Fast Access Method for Dynamic Files," ACM-TODS, Sept. 1979.

[GUTM84] Gutman, A., "R-trees: A Dynamic Index Structure for Spatial Searching," Proc. 1984 ACM-SIGMOD Conference on Management of Data, Boston, Mass. June 1984.

[IBM80] IBM Corp, "CICS System Programmers Guide," IBM Corp., White Plains, N.Y., June 1980.

[KOOI82] Kooi, R. and Frankfurth, D., "Query Optimization in INGRES," IEEE Database Engineering, September 1982.

[LITW80] Litwin, W., "Linear Hashing: A New Tool for File and Table Addressing," Proc. 1980 VLDB Conference, Montreal, Canada, October 1980.

[ONG84] Ong, J. et. al., "Implementation of Data Abstraction in the Relational System, INGRES," ACM SIGMOD Record, March 1984.

[PIAT84] Piatetsky-Shapiro, G. and Connell, C., "Accurate Estimation of the Number of Tuples Satisfying a Condition," Proc. 1984 ACM-SIGMOD Conference on Management of Data, Boston, Mass. June 1984.

[POPE81] Popek, G., et. al., "LOCUS: A Network Transparent, High Reliability Distributed System," Proc. Eighth Symposium on Operating System Principles, Pacific Grove, Ca., Dec. 1981.

[RTI84] Relational Technology, Inc., "INGRES Reference Manual, Version 3.0," November 1984.

[ROBI81] Robinson, J., "The K-D-B Tree: A Search Structure for Large Multidimensional Indexes," Proc. 1981 ACM-SIGMOD Conference on Management of Data, Ann Arbor, Mich., May 1981.

[SELI79] Selinger, P. et. al., "Access Path Selection in a Relational Database Management System," Proc. 1979 ACM-SIGMOD Conference on Management of Data, Boston, Mass., June 1979.

[SPEC83] Spector, A. and Schwartz, P., "Transactions: A Construct for Reliable Distributed Computing," Operating Systems Review, Vol 17, No 2, April 1983.

[STON76] Stonebraker, M. et al., "The Design and Implementation of INGRES," TODS 2, 3, September 1976.

[STON83] Stonebraker, M. et. al., "Application of Abstract Data Types and Abstract Indices to CAD Data," Proc. Engineering Applications Stream of Database Week/83, San Jose, Ca., May 1983.

[STON85] Stonebraker, M. et. al., "Interfacing a Relational Data Base System to an Operating System Transaction Manager," SIGOPS Review, January 1985.

On the Evaluation Strategy of EDUCE

Jorge Bocca

European Computer-Industry Research Centre GmbH

Arabellastr. 17

D-8000 Muenchen 81

West Germany

Abstract

Educe is a logic programming system for handling large knowledge bases. It was constructed by fully integrating the logic programming language Prolog and the relational data base management system Ingres. Educe uses a hybrid strategy for the evaluation of queries. This strategy is based on two contrasting strategies. The strategy known as *sets retrieval*, transforms recursive and non-recursive queries into a form suitable for evaluation by a relational data base management system. The other strategy, known as *one-tuple-at-a-time*, evaluates queries by imitating the evaluation strategy of the programming language Prolog. In earlier versions of Educe, users selected the strategy by using two different query languages. In order to remove this responsibility from the user, algorithms to map expressions from either of the languages into the other were implemented and added to Educe. This paper briefly reviews the implementation of both evaluators and the mappings, compares the basic strategies of evaluation, and then proceeds to explain Educe's own strategy.

1. Introduction

This paper discusses the design and implementation of Educe, a logic programming system capable of handling large knowledge bases. Educe uses a hybrid strategy for the evaluation of queries. This strategy is based on two contrasting strategies. The strategy known as *sets retrieval* transforms recursive and non-recursive queries into a form suitable for evaluation by a relational data base management system (RDBMS). The other strategy, known as *one-tuple-at-a-time*, evaluates queries by imitating the evaluation strategy of the programming language Prolog [prolog].

A number of alternatives for coupling/integrating Prolog and a relational DBMS are presented and discussed in [kb9, Ston85, Vass84, Venk85, cpdb, Zaniolo, SciWarr]. Educe was constructed by the coupling/integration of a deductive component and an external data base (EDB) component [kb9]. The programming language Prolog is at the centre of the deductive component, and the relational DBMS Ingres [ingres] was used for the EDB component [Gall85].

At the top level, Educe offers users two different languages: one following the non-procedural style of data manipulation language (DML) for RDBMSs, and one with a style close to Prolog. We refer to these languages as *loose* DML and *close* DML, respectively. Expressions in these languages can be freely mixed in Educe programs. In terms of implementation, there is a close correlation between these languages and the evaluation strategies outlined in the previous paragraph. It seems natural to use the *sets retrieval* strategy for the loose DML and the *one-tuple-at-a-time* strategy for the close DML.

Initially, Educe used a coupling between a Prolog interpreter and a relational DBMS for the implementation of the loose DML. Because of the problems that the evaluation of recursive queries causes [Bocca 85] in a coupled system, the close DML was implemented by integrating the low level access mechanism of the DBMS into the Prolog interpreter. Although, these two approaches might be thought antagonistic to each other, in Educe they co-exist and co-operate.

More recently, algorithms to map expressions from either of the languages into the other have been implemented. This allows Educe to decide for itself which is the (likely) best strategy for evaluation of a given query.

The motivations for the two languages in Educe and their particular syntax are discussed in detail in [Bocca 85]. This paper first presents a short review of the architecture of Educe, then describes its implementation, and finally discusses issues of performance.

The paper is divided into five sections. Section 1 is this introduction. In section 2, an outline of the architecture of Educe is given. Section 3 discusses the implementation of the loose and the close languages, the handling of those rules stored in the EDB and the mapping algorithms. An examination of the efficiency of Educe's particular implementation is undertaken in section 4. Finally, in section 5 conclusions are presented and future work discussed.

2. Architecture

In this section, an outline of the chosen architecture for Educe and the motivations behind it are presented. A detailed discussion of possible alternative architectures for Educe can be found in [Bocca 85].

From the point of view of the implementor, loose coupling presents itself as an obvious method for implementation. Provided that recursion is not allowed, a simple way to construct a loosely coupled system is by setting up two processes: one for the deductive component and one for the EDB component. These two processes exchange messages, i.e. queries and replies, through a channel of communication. Educe follows this approach for loose coupling, setting up one process for Prolog, as the deductive component, and one process for Ingres as the EDB component. Communication between the Prolog and the Ingres processes is by mean of two pipes [unix 83], one for queries and one for replies [Fig. 1].

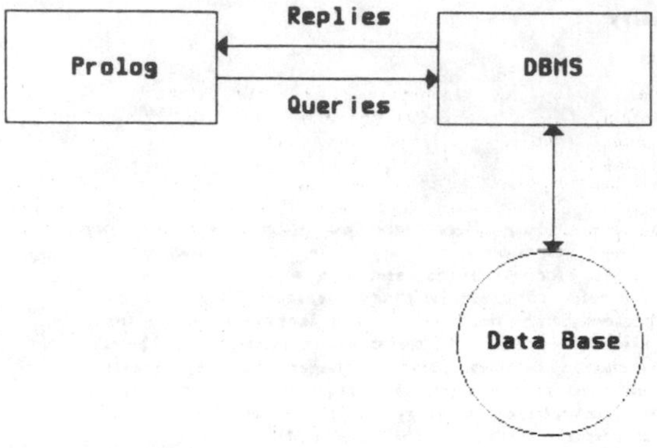

Figure 1

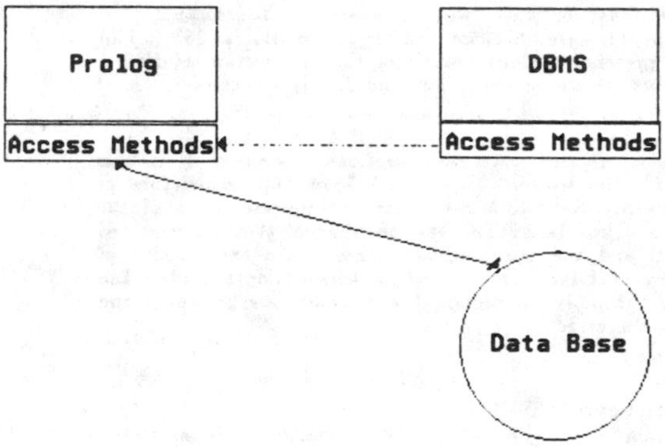

Figure 2

Unfortunately, the two processes in loose coupling would be very inefficient for an implementation of the close DML in Educe. This is apparent in systems that have adopted this as a solution [frog 85, Naish 83]. Because of this, we chose to integrate the deductive and the EDB components into one monolithic unit to handle the close DML. For this, the *access methods* module of the DBMS was detached from it and attached to Prolog [Fig. 2].

This allowed the multiple process configuration of loose coupling [Fig. 1] to be merged with the close integration configuration [Fig. 2] in a particularly coherent way. To explain this, let us start by considering two concurrent processes, each of which runs the DBMS on a common data base [Fig. 3].

When this configuration [Fig. 3] is merged with the two previous ones [Figs. 1 and 2] produces Educe's arhitecture [Fig. 4]. In the configuration depicted by Fig. 3, one of the occurences of the DBMS is replaced by the Prolog+AM configuration [Fig. 2]. This is possible, since the Access Methods module of the Prolog+AM and the DBMS are identical replicas. In other words, Educe appears as two concurrent DBMS's sharing access to a common data base.

It is important to note that this architecture does not impose any restrictions on recursion. On the contrary, it provides an efficient mechanism for the evaluation of multiple and recursive queries in either of the two languages, close and loose. Recursive definitions which include expressions in loose form are evaluated by a hybrid strategy. An evaluator has been implemented for this purpose. The evaluator uses loose coupling for the non-recursive part of the definition, and then, for the recursive part, it uses the route provided by close integration for retrievals from the intermediate results. Recently, a module which performs mappings from expressions in loose form into close form and vice versa, has been built. This module allows Educe to select a route, either coupling or integration, entirely on the basis of expected performance.

3. Implementation

The description of the implementation of Educe here presented follows the historical development of the system. In order to avoid dismantling the deductive and the EDB components, loose coupling was implemented in the first instance. The integration phase was postponed until we had gathered sufficient detail of the construction of these components. Rule storage and the transformation of expressions can be seen as important extensions of the basic capabilities of Educe.

3.1. Loose Coupling

Let us begin with the discussion of a relatively simple part of the implementation: the part that deals with loose coupling without recursion. This part of Educe was implemented as two related processes [Fig. 1]. One process acting as a master runs the Prolog interpreter, while the second process, the server, runs the DBMS. The Prolog interpreter used is a derived product of the Mu-Prolog interpreter [Naish 83]. The Ingres DBMS [Stonebraker 76] was chosen as the EDB component. Thus, in this set up, whenever the evaluation of a goal requires access to the EDB, all expressions requiring some form of syntactic analysis are parsed, and code is generated for them by the Prolog interpreter. The code generated is the equivalent QUEL expression. This QUEL expression, the query, is sent via a pipe to Ingres. Ingres in turn evaluates the query and produces a reply. This reply is piped back to Prolog which further processes it to bind variables to their respective values. In this part of the implementation, the control of processes and communication between them was written in C, while the parsing of queries and code generation was all done in Prolog.

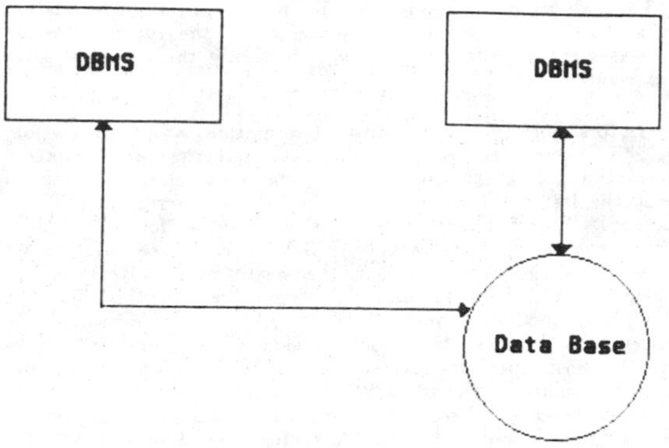

Figure 3

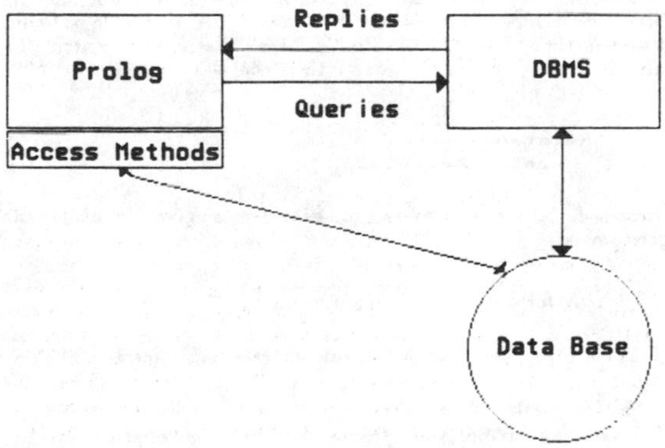

Figure 4

This scheme permits a more refined and efficient control of synchronization and communication between the processes.

The predicate *helpdb* is perhaps the simplest example of the theory of operation described above. This predicate is defined by the Prolog clause:

```
helpdb :-
        query(' help ').
```

The predicate *query(anIngresQuery)* takes the atom *anIngresQuery* and sends the string of characters forming the name of the atom down a pipe to Ingres. Then it waits for the evaluation of the query by Ingres and on completion returns *true*. Thus, by means of this mechanism, any arbitrary Ingres query can be sent to the server for evaluation. The predicate *query* was written in C and has been integrated into the Prolog interpreter.

A more complex situation develops when the mode of operation of Prolog differs from the mode of operation of the EDB. Take the case of *retrieve*:

```
retrieve( Atts, Boolean ) :-
        :
        :
    send_query( Rels, Atts, Boolean ),
        :
        :
    repeat,
    rel( P ),
    ( P = E,
       ( E = continue,
          !,
          fail
       )
       :
       :
       ;
       P =.. [ | OutAtts],
          value( Atts, OutAtts )
    )
```

Following the parsing of Atts, a query is sent to Ingres via *send_ query*. Typically, Ingres produces a whole relation as an answer to the query. Since Prolog requires only one tuple at a time, some adjustments have to be made. Basically, Ingres pipes the result relation to Prolog while Prolog takes one tuple each time from the pipe. In other words, the pipe acts as a queue. To take one tuple from the pipe, *rel(P)* is called. *P* is compared against the atom *continue* to check for the end of reply from Ingres. If it is not the end of reply (*continue*), then the tuple *P* is passed in suitable form to *value* which binds variables to attribute values.

It should also be mentioned that the syntax of *retrieve* allows uninstantiated variables in the conditions (*Boolean*) argument. Because of this, it is desirable to delay evaluation of the *retrieve* until the search criteria have been clearly established, so avoiding retrieval of unnecessary data.

3.2. Close Integration

It is not only for syntactic convenience that variables are necessary in the condition part of *retrieves*. Without them, it would be impossible to express recursion. Take for example the relation *parent(X, Y)*, defined by:

```
parent( X, Y) :-
    ( var(X), var(Y), !,
      retrieve([ father.is_ = X,
          father.of_ = Y],
      true)
    )
    ;
    ( atom(X), atom(Y), !,
          :
    ).

parent( X, Y) :-
        :
      retrieve([ mother.is_ = X,
          mother.of_ = Y],
      true)
        :
        .
```

Then we could define the derived relation *ancestor(X, Y)* recursively by:

```
ancestor( X, Y) :-
    parent( X, Y).
ancestor( X, Y) :-
    parent( X, Z),
    ancestor(Z, Y).
```

Unfortunately, the introduction of recursion and multiple queries brings new problems. It becomes necessary to relate replies to their originating queries. In order to evaluate a recursive definition such as *ancestor*, Educe first generates the relation *parent* (if virtual) and then proceeds to evaluate the recursive clause by using close access. But, before we discuss the details of how this is done in Educe, a description of the implementation of *close integration* is needed. The particular reasons for having close integration in Educe are discussed in [Bocca 85].

Because of its linkage to the low level *access methods*, the close DML is implemented mainly in C. At the top level, the Prolog predicate *retr* binds the C implemented parts, together. The implementation of this predicate is presented below:

```
retr( R ) :-
    R =.. [Rel | Atts],
    openr(D, O, Rel),
    setsearch( D, Atts),
    repeat,
    getvals(D, Atts, NewTuple),
    ( (  /* failed */
         NewTuple = O,
         closer(D),
         !, fail
      )
      ;
      true
    ).
```

An example of the use of *retr* is *?- retr(employee(john, Salary)).* In this example, the relation employee is searched for *john*'s *Salary*.

The program above starts by transforming the (only) argument of *retr* into a list. The head of the list is instantiated to the name of the relation (*Rel*) and the tail is instantiated to a list of attributes (*Atts*), some as variables and the others as constants, according to the particular retrieval condition. In our example, this list becomes *[employee, john, Salary]*. Once this is done, the relation *Rel* is opened by *openr* and the searching keys are set by *setsearch*. Only then the first tuple (if any exists) is retrieved by a call to *getvals*. The call to *repeat* is necessary to handle backtracking. The predicates *openr*, *setsearch*, *getvals* and *closer* are all implemented in C. The call to *openr* opens the file which contains the relation *Rel* and it also creates a descriptor, *D*. If the file for relation *Rel* was already open (for reading) then only the new descriptor D is created.

Descriptors not only keep static information about a relation, e.g. file name, degree, cardinality, etc, but they also maintain information of a dynamic type. In particular, information about the last tuple accessed is kept by the descriptors (TID of last tuple [Stonebraker 76]). This is essential for an efficient implementation of backtracking. Otherwise, Educe would need to re-access old tuples to get the next tuple. This use of descriptors is essential in recursive cases. Without the descriptors, recursive queries on a given relation would be restricted to as many levels of recursion as the numbers of files that the host operating system allows to keep opened at any particular time. As an additional bonus to the scheme of operation described here, the overhead of opening and closing files is greatly reduced. In fact, for recursive queries, this overhead is reduced to practically nothing.

3.3. Rules

Once the ability to handle large numbers of facts by the EDB component had been installed in Educe, the next logical step was to introduce facilities to store and maintain large numbers of deduction rules in the EDB. Thus a mechanism to serve this purpose was implemented. In Educe, deduction rules are stored like the schema of the data base, in a relation. This relation is named *rulerel*.

Obviously, the storage of rules in the EDB is not in itself enough to achieve the desired effect. Rules stored in the EDB must also be executed just like any other rule in main memory. For this, the top level Prolog interpreter was modified. Thus if, during the evaluation of a goal, an appropriate clause head is not found for it in main memory, then the *rulerel* relation is searched for it. If a rule with such a head is found in the EDB, then Educe executes it. If however the rule is not found in *rulerel* then Educe looks for a base relation to match the goal. If such a relation is found then the rule

```
Relation :-
    retr( Relation).
```

is asserted. More formally, to evaluate a given goal G the algorithm is:

1. Search for rule/fact in main memory.

2. If 1. fails then search for rule in relation *rulerel*.

3. If 2. fails then search for base relation with matching name and degree. If such a relation is found then assert the rule *G :- retr(G)*.

The algorithm above effectively makes the EDB component of Educe transparent to users of the close DML.

Unfortunately, this scheme of operation is not free of some (minor) side effects. The above algorithm implies an order of evaluation for rules and facts. In this implied order of evaluation, rules precede facts. However, since facts are a special case of rules (no body), they can be treated like a rule if so wanted by the user.

Still on the subject of evaluation precedence, a more important point is to note that Prolog inspects facts in a program in a top-down manner. In relational data base terms, this implies an ordering in the tuples of a given relation. This contradicts the definition of a relation. To avoid the problem, Educe adopts the semantic of *assert* when inserting tuples in a relation. Equivalences for *asserta* and *assertz* are purposedly excluded from Educe. However, this is not sufficient in the case of general rules. To keep close to Prolog semantic, users are asked to specify an order of evaluation for the rules kept by the EDB. For example, to add the definition of *anc* to the EDB component of Educe, one should proceed as follow:

```
?- nrule( 1,
     'anc(X,Y)  :- parent(X,Y).').
?- nrule( 2,
     'anc(X,Y)  :- parent(X,Z), anc(Z,Y).').
```

Once this is done, the EDB component of Educe becomes transparent to those users accessing the derived relation *anc*.

Finally, a point that has some bearing on efficiency and integrity: the evaluation algorithm described above retrieves rules from *rulerel* not only when the rule is activated for the first time, but also when backtracking takes place. From an efficiency point of view, this is a serious drawback. Also from the point of view of integrity, backtracking can cause some problems. In particular, the answers to a query would not be correct if another user were allowed to update part of the necessary definitions while they were still being used. Educe solves these two problems by pre-processing the top level query. Thus, given a goal to evaluate, Educe builds the whole evaluation tree for this query. Rules are then retrieved from the *rulerel* and the necessary *retr*'s rules are also asserted. Only when all this information has been obtained from the EDB. Educe proceeds to evaluate the query. Effectively, the EDB is only consulted once for the necessary rules, and all the definitions needed are frozen during the evaluation of the goal. Notice that with this scheme, other users are not prevented from updating the non-factual knowledge. For the factual knowledge (base relations), the EDB uses normal data base techniques for concurrent access to relations.

3.4. Mappings

Now we can go back to our example *ancestor* (sub-section 3.2 and see how recursive (and multiple) queries in loose form are handled in Educe. First, let us examine the program *$slowretr* below. This program is a preamble to a simple but not very efficient implementation of a query evaluator for the loose DML. However, this program is capable of handling multiple and recursive queries.

```
/* $slowretr -
   it uses same syntax as retrieve
   in Atts and Boolean
*/

$slowretr( Rels, Atts, Boolean) :-
      :
   /* Rels list is obtained
      from Atts and Boolean */
      :
   $q_and_s( IntRes, Rels,
             Atts, Boolean),
   !,         /* never backtrack */
   $quickretr( IntRes, Atts).
```

In this program, once the list of base relations *Rels* has been extracted from *Atts* and *Boolean*, the call to *$q_and_s* prepares a query in loose form and executes it, saving the result in the intermediate relation *IntRes*. We do not want to backtrack past this point, hence the cut (!). It is now up to *$quickretr* to produce the answer(s), one tuple at a time. This is done by *$quickretr* by querying the intermediate relation *IntRes* using the close DML. Finally, *$quickretr* matches the values in the returned tuple (close DML) to the non-positional projection specified by *Atts*.

The first and obvious problem in this strategy of evaluation is one of efficiency. In the case of recursive definitions, each time we backtrack on the non-recursive part of a definition, a new intermediate relation will be generated. This is easily solved though, by labeling the queries already answered with the name of the intermediate relation generated for it. Thus before proceeding to generate a new intermediate relation, we check whether the intermediate relation has been generated for the (intermediate) query. The program for this version of *retrieve* is given below. To stress the fact that this program also handles multiple relations and recursive definitions, we call it *mretrieve*.

```
/* mretrieve -
   handles multiple relations and
   recursive definitions in the
   loose DML.
   It uses same syntax as retrieve */

mretrieve( Atts, Boolean) :-
   $evaluated( Res, Atts, Boolean)
     -> $quickretr( Res, Atts)
     ;  $slowretr( Res, Atts, Boolean).
```

As can easily be imagined there are occasions when the above strategy to evaluate recursive queries can produce very slow responses. This problem is addressed in detail in the next section.

4. Efficiency

As was pointed out in [Bocca 85], users expect in the context of a Prolog interpreter to obtain a reply quickly. This reply normally corresponds to just one tuple in a relation (base or derived). During backtracking the same still holds true. By contrast, in a relational DBMS, users expect a whole relation, i.e. a set of tuples, to be generated as an answer. This dichotomy between the two types of system leads to two different types of evaluation strategy for queries.

Because DBMS evaluation techniques have been developed over a longer period of time, it is generally believed that they are more efficient than Prolog-type techniques. This belief is questionable, particularly in the case of recursive queries. A typical DBMS evaluation strategy is akin to batch processing, e.g. the emphasis on the generation of a set of tuples (a relation) as the result. In direct contradiction to this bias of DBMSs, a Prolog-type of system assumes an interactive environment. In this latter case, answers (or part of them) should be delivered as small units, so that users can logically grasp them. Hence, the smaller granularity of a "Prolog" answer, i.e. normally one tuple at a time.

In order to compare these two different modes of evaluating a query, a number of tests were performed. Equivalent queries in loose and close form were prepared and issued for evaluation by Educe. The queries were graded according to expected difficulty and were run on relations containing 50000 randomly generated tuples. The time taken by Educe to evaluate each query is given in Table 1.

As the figures in Table 1 show, it is not unusual for the *one-tuple-at-a-time* strategy (*method 3*) to outperform the *sets retrieval* strategy of DBMSs (*method 1*). This is particularly true in the case of recursive queries. The cases in which the *sets retrieval* strategy is the winner are normally explained by the way in which Prolog selects sub-goals for evaluation [Bocca 85]. This sometimes leads to the choice of the wrong index, which is then used until it gets exhausted, and only then the correct one might be chosen and used. To demonstrate this, query B in run 7 was re-formulated so as to favour an early selection of the correct index in the evaluation of the close query.

In loose coupling, queries are handed to the EDB component for evaluation. This is in effect an evaluation of queries by a DBMS (*method 1*). In all cases of queries involving several relations and/or recursion and in many cases of queries involving a single relation, e.g. aggregation, a number of intermediate relations are generated during the evaluation of these queries. It is the creation and manipulation of these intermediate relations that is the cause of major overheads in the evaluation of queries in loose form, particularly in the recursive case. Even if large buffers in main memory were used for these intermediate relations, it would still be necessary to use secondary memory (slow) to store considerable parts of these relations. Also there is an overhead attached to the creation and maintenance of the schemas for these relations.

The *one-tuple-at-a-time* strategy of Prolog does not need to create intermediate relations (*method 3*). All intermediate results are kept at all times in main memory. This is only possible because of the relatively small size of the intermediate results required by the *one-tuple-at-a-time* strategy. In other words, retrieval of data from secondary memory only occurs when base relations are consulted.

However, as was discussed in [Bocca 85], there are good reasons for using a loose DML to express queries. Also, as shown by a significative number of cases in Table 1, there are situations where the *sets retrieval* strategy of DBMSs outperforms the *one-tuple-at-a-time* strategy of Prolog. In Educe, all of these reasons are considered to be important and hence queries in loose form are supported. Moreover, a number of optimization techniques are applied to queries in loose form, in order to improve performance. In addition to the optimization techniques of the DBMS, Educe uses its own techniques. Particular attention is given to the recursive case, since this is an area outside the scope of conventional DBMSs. Four significant cases are here discussed.

The first case arises in queries involving one base relation and the boolean condition *true*. For example, consider the relation *employee* with attributes *name, address and dept*, and the goal

```
?- retrieve( [employee.name = Name,
        employee.dept = Dept],
    true).
```

This query is transformed into the equivalent "query" in the close DML:

```
employee( Name, Dept) :-
    retr( employee( Name, Dept, _)).

?- employee( Name, Dept).
```

This example is generalized to the case of any base relation being queried with the boolean condition set to *true*. The built-in predicate *$whole_base_r* makes the appropriate tests to decide on the applicability of this transformation rule. Although the case described seems trivial and unlikely to be presented to Educe by users, it often arises as an intermediate step in the evaluation of a recursive definition. For instance, in the loose DML version of our definition of *parent* [section 3.2], given the goal

```
/* see 3.2 */
?- ancestor( X, charles).
```

when the recursive clause is used, the goals to solve are *parent(X,Z)* and *ancestor(Z,charles)*. Since *X* and *Z* are not instantiated, to solve *parent(X,Z)* the goal *retrieve([parent.father.is_ =X,father.of_ =Y],true)* would have to be solved.

The second case for efficiency improvements occurs again very frequently in recursive queries. This is the case of intermediate queries that have already been evaluated, as discussed in 3.4, above. It should also be said here that, although this situation often arises during the evaluation of recursive queries, it is not exclusive to them.

The third case of importance occurs in conjunctive queries on a single relation. Again, this is a very common situation during the evaluation of recursive queries (top level). In this case the conjunctive query is first transformed into a normal form and then, from this normalized form, an equivalent query in close form is generated and evaluated.

The last but certainly not the least major optimization step takes place during the transformation of loose form into close form and during the instantiation of variables at the top level. For both of these processes it is necessary to access the schema of the relation involved. These accesses are speeded up by maintaining the data base schema in buffers in main memory. Obviously, some synchronization with the copies in secondary memory is necessary. This is a common solution in a conventional DBMS and Educe has adopted it. More seriously though, whenever a tuple is retrieved from a base relation, a number of variables have to be instantiated. To do this, the list of values in the retrieved tuple has to be matched with a list of variables (typically, the variables in the projection part of a *retrieve*). The list of variables is normally shorter than the list of values and their sequences do not match. For instance, a typical tuple in our relation *employee* might be *[john, munich, toys]* and the goal might be *retrieve([employee.dept=Dept, employee.name=Name],...)*. Obviously, the order and the length of the lists *[Dept, Name]* and *[john, munich, toys]* do not match. In general, to match the two lists every time a new tuple is retrieved is unnecessary. The problem is avoided by, firstly, creating a bogus list of variables, say *[X1, X2, X3]*, then matching this list only once to the projection list in the *retrieve*, and finally, each time a

Query \ Run->	1	2	3	4	5	6	7	8
1Aa	260	258	268	279	339	275	425	274
3Aa	3	5	4	4	4	14	–	3
1Ab	240	339	235	219	343	240	223	231
3Ab	16	12	15	14	12	25	–	11
1Ac	256	264	252	257	314	329	224	259
3Ac	13	436	11	11	10	22	–	12
1Bc	527	475	502	506	12316	12932	11835	11853
3Bc	581	34	857	633	327	322	327	320
1Cc	10	235	10	11	319	250	248	236
3Cc	5	8	4	4	5	5	8	1
1Dc	–	254	236	228	233	243	241	280
3Dc	–	4	2	2	2	2	1	2

+ Times are given in 100th's of a second

Table 5-1: Comparisons of Methods: DBMS and Prolog

Query \ Run->	1	2	3	4	5	6	7	8
1Aa	260	258	268	279	339	275	425	274
2Aa	6	6	6	7	6	17	4	5
3Aa	3	5	4	4	4	14	–	3
1Ab	240	339	235	219	343	240	223	231
2Ab	5	3	5	4	5	7	4	6
3Ab	16	12	15	14	12	25	–	11
1Ac	256	264	252	257	314	329	224	259
2Ac	3	3	4	3	4	3	4	3
3Ac	13	436	11	11	10	22	–	12
1Bc	527	475	502	506	12316	12932	11835	11853
2Bc	8	8	8	8	927	917	912	909
3Bc	581	34	857	633	327	322	327	320
1Cc	10	235	10	11	319	250	248	236
2Cc	6	4	4	4	4	3	4	4
3Cc	5	8	4	4	5	5	8	1
1Dc	–	254	236	228	233	243	241	280
2Dc	–	4	4	5	4	6	4	4
3Dc	–	4	2	2	2	2	1	2

+ Times are given in 100th's of a second

KEYS
****

METHOD:
1. Sets Retrieval (DBMS)
2. Educe's for loose DML
3. One-Tuple-At-A-Time (Prolog)

TASK:
A. Simple Selection
B. Selection + Projection + Join
C. Simple Recursion
D. Difficult Recursion

SIZE:
a. Small - 10 tuples
b. Fair - 1000 tuples
c. Large - 50000 tuples

The test programs were run eight times on a VAX 785. Constant values were changed from one run to the next. Also, in some runs the arguments were less (more) instantiated than in earlier runs. For further details of the tests, see Appendix.

Table 5-2: Comparisons of Methods: DBMS, Educe and Prol

tuple is retrieved from secondary memory, this bogus list is used to instantiate the real variables. A lot of unnecessary sorting is eliminated at a stroke!

The optimization steps described above have in fact led to a new strategy, the *Educe method.* This method integrates all the above optimization steps into a harmonized strategy of evaluation for queries expressed in loose form. The improvements obtained by the application of this method go well beyond the recursive case. In fact, the *Educe method* always give a performance close to the best of the other two methods (DBMSs and Prolog). This is clearly shown by the performance figures obtained in comparative tests of the three methods [see Table 2].

5. Conclusions

From a logical point of view two contrasting styles of query language are used in Educe. One is similar to query languages found in conventional DBMSs and the other follows the conventions of the programming language Prolog. According to their closeness to Prolog, they are referred to as *loose* and *close* DML, respectively. Both DMLs are necessary and complementary to each other.

The form of each language strongly suggests its mode of evaluation. The strategy known as *sets retrieval* used by conventional DBMS seems, at first, the most appropriate for the loose DML. Similarly, the *one-query-at-a-time* strategy of Prolog seems more suited for the close DML. However, our work on Educe points to a mixed strategy, specially in the case of queries expressed in loose form.

The *sets retrieval* strategy of conventional DBMSs produces a heavy overhead in the recursive case (and also in other non-recursive cases). The main problem is the creation and maintenance of relatively large numbers of temporary relations. By contrast, the *one-tuple-at-a-time* close integration strategy of evaluation does not require intermediate relations. This acquires special importance in the case of recursive queries. Precisely because of this, a capability to map expressions from one language into the other, according to performance requirements, was built into Educe. In particular, recursive queries using conjunctive conditions benefit from the transformation of loose into close form. Nevertheless, one should be aware of the limitations to possible optimizations that the Prolog order of evaluation (for sub-goals) imposes. This is indeed one more argument for a close DML based on pure Horn clauses, where a more flexible evaluation order could be adopted.

References

[Appelrath 85] Appelrath, H-J., Bense, H. and Rose, T. CPDB - A Data Base based Prolog System Incorporating Meta-Knowledge. *Unpublished* , September, 1985. ETH Zurich, Dept. of Computer Science, Switzerland.

[Bocca 85] Bocca, J.B. *EDUCE - A Marriage of Convenience: Prolog and a Relational DBMS.* Internal Report KB-9, European Computer-Industry Research Centre, Munich, September, 1985.

[frog 85] Ducasse, M., Faget, J. and Gumbach, A. FROG - Implementation of a Language merging Functional Relational Programming Styles, via an Object Type Driven Evaluation. 1985. Laboratories Marcoussis.

[Gallaire 85] Gallaire, H. Logic Programming: Further Developments. In *Proc. 1985 Symposium on Logic Programming.* pages 88-96. Boston, USA, July, 1985.

[Naish 83] Naish. L. *MU-PROLOG 3.0 reference manual* Melbourne University. Computer Sc., Melbourne, Australia, 1983.

[prolog 81] Clocksin, W.F. and Mellish, C.S. *Programming in Prolog.* Springer-Verlag. Berlin-Heidelberg-New York, 1981.

[SciWarr 84] Sciore. E. and Warren. D.S. Towards an Integrated Database-Prolog System. In *Proceedings First International Workshop on Expert Database Systems.* pages 801-815. Kiawah Island. South Carolina, USA. October. 1984.

[Stonebraker 76] Stonebraker. M., Wong, E., Kreps. P. and Held. G. The Design And Implementation Of Ingres. *ACM Transactions on Database Systems* 1(3):189-222. September. 1976.

[Stonebraker 85] Stonebraker. M. Inference in Data Base Systems Using Lazy Triggers. In *Proc. of the Islamorada Workshop on Large Scale Knowledge Base and Reasoning Systems*, pages 295-310. Islamorada, Florida, USA, February, 1985.

[unix 83] *Unix Programmer's Manual* 4.2 Berkeley Software Distribution (copyright 1979, Bell Telephone Laboratories, Inc.) edition, Dept. of Electrical Engineering and Computer Science, University of California, Berkeley, California, USA, 1983.

[Vassiliou 84] Vassiliou, Y., Clifford, J and Jarke, M.
Access to Specific Declarative Knowledge by Expert Systems: The Impact of Logic Programming.
Decision Support Systems 1(1), 1984.

[Venken 85] Venken, R.
The Interaction between Prolog and Relational Databases.
Unpublished , Early, 1985.
Report on ESPRIT Pilot Project 107.

[Zaniolo 84] Zaniolo, C.
Prolog: a Database Query Language for All Seasons.
In *Proceedings First International Workshop on Expert Database Systems*, pages 63-73.
Kiawah Island, South Carolina, USA, October, 1984.

```
/***********************************
   TEST PERFORMANCE OF EDUCE
***********************************

SCHEMA:
*******

parent( anc, child)
  + entered by hand +
   pkey   -- ISAM on anc
   Tuples              -- 10
   Recursion Levels-- 9

parenta( name, father, mother)
  + random generator +
   pkey   -- HASH on name
   indexes:
      x2parenta - ISAM
         on [father, name]
      x3parenta - ISAM
         on [mother, name]
   Tuples -- 1000
   Recursion Levels-- 3

parentb( name, father, mother)
  + random generator +
   pkey -- HASH on name
   indexes:
      x2parentb - ISAM
         on [father, name]
      x3parentb - ISAM
         on [mother, name]
   Tuples                    -- 50000
   Recursion Levels-- 10


Method
******
(Explicit use of mretr, fretr
and retr to force use of wanted
method of evaluation)

1. Uses straight DBMS techniques
   (Loose coupling).
2. Loose --> Close DML and optimizes
   new expression.
3. Close Integration.


Task
****

Query A : Simple Selection
Query B : Selection + Projection
          + Join
Query C : Simple Recursion
Query D : Difficult Recursion
          (slow in Prolog)


Size
****

Size a : 10 tuples
Size b : 1000 tuples
Size c : 50000 tuples
************************************/


/*
   Derived relations
```

```
Explicit use of indexes for better
control of test.
*/

par1b( X,Y) :-
   /* derived from
   parenta relation
   1000 + 1000 tuples */

par1c( X,Y) :-
   /* derived from
   parentb relation
   50000 + 50000 */

par2b( X,Y) :-
   /* derived from
   parenta relation
   Method 2
   1000 + 1000 tuples */

par2c( X,Y) :-
   /* derived from
   parentb relation
   Method 2
   50000 + 50000 tuples */

par3b(X,Y) :-
   /* derived from
   parenta relation
   Method 3
   1000 + 1000 tuples */

par3c(X,Y) :-
   /* derived from
   parentb relation
   Method 3
   50000 + 50000 tuples */

brother1Bc( X, Y) :-
   par1c(X, P),
   par1c(Y, P),
   X ~= Y.
brother2Bc( X, Y) :-
   par2c(X, P),
   par2c(Y, P),
   X ~= Y.
brother3Bc( X, Y) :-
   par3c(X, P),
   par3c(Y, P),
   X ~= Y.

anc1( X, Y) :-
   par1c(X, Y).
anc1(X, Y) :-
   par1c(X, Z),
   anc1(Z,Y).

anc2( X, Y) :-
   par2c(X, Y).
anc2(X, Y) :-
   par2c(X, Z),
   anc2(Z,Y).

anc3( X, Y) :-
   par3c(X, Y).
anc3(X, Y) :-
   par3c(X, Z),
   anc3(Z,Y).


/************************
        QUERIES
************************/
/***************
Case A - Select
***************/
/*
   Method 1.
   mretr -- is basic DBMS method
      + obvious optimisation steps
*/

query1Aa :-
   /* size a:  10 tuples */
   write('1Aa -- '),
   etime(_),
   mretr([parent.anc = Parent],
      parent.child = mary),
   etime(X), writeln(X), !.

query1Ab :-
   /* size b:  1000 tuples */
   write('1Ab -- '),
   etime(_),
   mretr([parenta.mother = Mother],
      parenta.name = 235),
   etime(X), writeln(X), !.

query1Ac :-
   /* size c: 50000 tuples */
   write('1Ac -- '),
   etime(_),
   mretr([parentb.mother = Mother],
      parentb.name = 235),
   etime(X), writeln(X), !.

/*
   Method 2.
   fretr -- loose is mapped into close
      + high level optimization
*/
query2Aa :-
   /* size a */
   write('2Aa -- '),
   etime(_),
   fretr([parent.anc = Parent],
   parent.child = mary),
   etime(X), writeln(X), !.

query2Ab :-
   /* size b */
   write('2Ab -- '),
   etime(_),
   fretr([parenta.mother = Mother],
   parenta.name = 235),
   etime(X), writeln(X), !.

query2Ac :-
   /* size c */
   write('2Ac -- '),
   etime(_),
   fretr([parentb.mother = Mother],
      parentb.name = 235),
   etime(X), writeln(X), !.

/*
   Method 3.
   Close Integration (Prolog)
*/
query3Aa :-
   /* size a */
   write('3Aa -- '),
   etime(_),
   retr( parent( Parent, mary)),
   etime(X), writeln(X), !.
```

```
query3Ab :-
    /* size b */
    write('3Ab -- '),
    etime(_),
    retr( parenta( 235, Father,
        Mother)),
    etime(X), writeln(X), !.

query3Ac :-
    /* size c */
    write('3Ac -- '),
    etime(_),
    retr( parentb( 235, Father,
        Mother)),
    etime(X), writeln(X), !.


/******************
Case B: S + P + J
******************/
/*
    A comparison of Methods 1, 2 and 3.
    Join + Select + Project operators
    Only 1 size tested: 50000 tuples.
*/

query1Bc :-
    /* 1.  basic DBMS method */
    write('1Bc -- '),
    etime(_),
    brother1Bc(248, 919),
    etime(X), writeln(X), !.
query1Bc :-
    /* on failure */
    etime(X), writeln(X), !.

query2Bc :-
    /* 2.  Loose --> Close */
    write('2Bc -- '),
    etime(_),
    brother2Bc(248, 919),
    etime(X), writeln(X), !.
query2Bc :-
    /* on failure */
    etime(X), writeln(X), !.


query3Bc :-
    /* 3.  Close DML */
    write('3Bc -- '),
    etime(_),
    brother3Bc(248, 919),
    etime(X), writeln(X), !.
query3Bc :-
    /* on failure */
    etime(X), writeln(X), !.
```

```
/************************
Case C:  Simple Recursion
************************/
/*
    Compare Methods 1, 2 and 3.
    Simple recursion
    Larguish size:  50000 tuples
*/

query1Cc :-
    /* 1.  DBMS method */
    write('1Cc -- '),
    etime(_),


    anc1(255, _),
    etime(X), writeln(X), !.

query2Cc :-
    /* 2.  Loose --> Close */
    write('2Cc -- '),
    etime(_),
    anc2(255, _),
    etime(X), writeln(X), !.

query3Cc :-
    /* 3. Close DML */
    write('3Cc -- '),
    etime(_),
    anc3(255, _),
    etime(X), writeln(X), !.


/***************************
Case D: Difficult Recursion
***************************/
/*
    Again compare methods 1, 2 and 3
    Hard recursion (for Prolog)
    Only largish size  50000
*/

query1Dc :-
    /* 1.  DBMS method */
    write('1Dc -- '),
    etime(_),
    anc1( 255, 4095),
    etime(X), writeln(X), !.

query2Dc :-
    /* 2.  Loose --> Close */
    write('2Dc -- '),
    etime(_),
    anc2( 255, 4095),
    etime(X), writeln(X), !.

query3Dc :-
    /* 3.  Close DML */
    write('3Dc -- '),
    etime(_),
    anc3( 255, 4095),
    etime(X), writeln(X), !.
```

Epilogue

Following the implementation of Educe , we assessed the relative importance of a number of factors which contribute to performance and usability of systems of the Educe type. Early applications of Educe provided us with the preliminary information about candidate factors to be studied in isolation. We performed tests on the relative importance of performance and usability factors, then we analysed the results and derived the elements of design for Educe*. This is a follow up system to Educe and it relies on compiled code to be maintained by the external storage subsystem, instead of the classical solution based on the interpretation of source code managed by the external DBMS.

Our studies of performance related issues in Educe showed that three factors can affect performance rather badly whenever rules stored in the External DB (EDB) are in use: the use of an interpreter instead of a compiler, poor selectivity on the retrieval of rules stored in the External DB and frequent assertion (and erase) in main memory of rules stored in the External DB. All of these three factors point towards the usage of some form of compiled code to be stored for rules in the external relational storage, as shown below:

1. The differences in performance between compilation and interpretation have been clearly established by the relatively recent appearance of Prolog compilers. It is not unusual to have performance increased by a factor of more than 20-30 times when moving from an interpreter to a compiler generating native code (for the host machine, as oppose to some virtual machine). However, in the context of an integrated Prolog - Relational DBMS system, this sort of compilation is not possible due to the need for garbage collection of externally stored compiled code. More realistically, one could consider the possibility of storing code for a specially adapted virtual machine based on a well known and proven design - such as the Warren Abstract Machine (WAM), which must be extended to handle associative addresses to avoid garbage collection of external storage. Typical improvements from interpreted Prolog code to compiled code for a virtual machine are of the order of 10 to 20 times. This type of compilation is also attractive because of the ease with which the interpretation mechanism of a Relational DBMS would fit with the emulator for the virtual machine (and its resolution of associative addresses).

2. In a system such as Educe, the obvious way of storing rules in the External DBMS was to store them in source form. In addition, Educe stored some extra information to make the retrieval of rules more selective. In a system using a compiler for Prolog, it is possible to use the compiler itself to collect all sorts of information to help in the latter process of retrieval, so improving its selectivity.

3. Assertion of Prolog clauses, whether rules or facts is a very expensive operation in terms of cpu time. However, in a system that stores rules in the EDB in source form it is an unavoidable operation. In order to use rules kept in the EDB, they have to be searched for in the EDB, asserted (if in source form), executed and finally erased to make room for the next rule(s) to come from the EDB. Notice that potentially a given rule can be asserted and erased thousands of times into (from) main memory. Compiled code stored externally makes these assertions almost completely unnecessary and also considerably simplifies the erasure. The very time consuming activity of parsing general logic terms is not required at all when loading from the external DBMS.

Given the above arguments about compilation and the WAM in particular, it might have seemed very attractive to adopt the WAM as the compilation model without further questioning. However, this was not so obvious when the characteristics of current relational DBMS's were brought into consideration. There is a fundamental difference in the principles of operation of the WAM and the query evaluation engine of relational DBMS's. The WAM is directed to handle code for one Prolog term at a time, while the retrieval engine of relational DBMS's is goal orientated. The design of Educe* is the result of a close examination of the interaction of these two components.

The design and implementation of Educe* is strongly linked to the development of EKS - a new Knowledge Base System currently being developed at ECRC. Educe* provides efficient primitives to support the facilities for inference, for handling large facts and rules bases in external storage, and for debugging during the development of EKS.

Epilogue

This chapter contains one paper by Michael L. Brodie on the motivations, requirements, status, importance, and challenges in AI-DB Integration. The paper is based on invited talks at the 1988 National Conference of the American Association of Artificial Intelligence (AAAI) held in St. Paul, Minnesota, and at the 1988 International Conference on Very Large Data Bases (VLDB) held in Long Beach, California. The invitations and talks, which were attended by more than 3,000 people, are indications of the importance of AI-DB Integration. Of particular interest in the paper are the results of an extensive survey on AI-DB Integration conducted in 1988 in which more than 400 AI and DB researchers and practitioners from around the world participated. The paper argues that AI-DB Integration is critical not only for the effective application of AI technology and the extension of DB technology but also for the next generation of computing.

Future Intelligent Information Systems: AI and Database Technologies Working Together

Michael L. Brodie
GTE Laboratories Incorporated

ABSTRACT

AI-DB Integration is critical not only for the effective application of much AI technology, and the development of DB technology, but also for the next generation of computing, which will support Intelligent Information Systems and which will be based on distributed cooperative work. Hence, AI-DB Integration will significantly contribute to the Infrastructure for Science and Technology and to business and humanitarian applications of computers. Due to these potential contributions, AI-DB Integration is considerably more important than might be assumed from its contribution to the enhancement of AI and DB technologies alone.

This paper presents a vision of future computing that provides a framework and goals for AI-DB Integration. Short-term and long-term benefits are illustrated, and the critical need for progress is emphasized. Progress over the past 30 years is discussed. The applicability of existing DB techniques to AI systems and of AI techniques to DB systems is described. Open problems are identified along with promising and challenging research directions. To reinforce these views, the paper presents the results of a survey of more than 400 AI and DB researchers and practitioners from over 12 countries. The results express expert opinions on the need, importance, and status of AI-DB Integration and on the next generation of computing.

1. INTRODUCTION

The effective application of Artificial Intelligence (AI) technology and the development of future computing systems require the integration of AI and Database (DB) technologies. The integration will benefit both technologies and will substantially advance the state of computing.

Information Systems (ISs) are among the greatest potential beneficiaries of AI technology. For example, what if advanced reasoning capabilities could be added to any IS? What if intelligent systems interfaces could replace unfriendly interfaces? What if AI techniques were used to extend DB management functionality? At the same time, AI technology will benefit dramatically from DB technology. For example, what if knowledge could be shared concurrently by existing and unanticipated applications (*knowledge sharing* and *reuse*)? What if AI systems could contain hundreds of thousands of rules and access millions of facts? What if new reasoning techniques could be directly applied to existing knowledge bases (KBs)? What if knowledge could be augmented or reorganized, independently of existing applications, to extend a KB and to optimize for current usage (*knowledge representation independence*)? What if AI systems development involved simply incremental augmentation of existing knowledge-based systems (KBSs)? What if AI systems could cooperate with other remote KBs (*distributed KBs*)? What if AI systems were as robust as on-line transaction processing systems?

Future computing systems will require AI and DB technology to work together with other technologies. These systems will consist of large numbers of heterogeneous, distributed agents that have varying abilities to work cooperatively. Each will have its own knowledge and reasoning schemes, languages, and capabilities. Data, procedures, knowledge, and objects in these systems may be shared, incomplete, and inconsistent with those of other agents, but they will certainly persist and will together form a massive distributed information base.[1] The current trend toward interconnectivity and interoperability — one system accessing another via standard interfaces — will evolve into **Intelligent Interoperability** — intelligent cooperation among systems to optimally achieve specified goals.

Future computing systems pose major challenges for both AI and DB technologies. Many of these challenges (e.g., managing, structuring, searching, sharing, and modifying objects; reasoning about tasks and in specific domains) are present in simpler forms in current AI and DB systems. Extending existing solutions to new contexts requires a deep understanding of both technologies, their requirements, their capabilities, and their limitations. Difficulties with current research and commercial AI systems, let alone future systems, are due, in part, to a lack of such a deep understanding.

AI-DB Integration has been of interest since the beginnings of the AI and DB fields 30 years ago. Since then, AI and DBs have evolved into two mature research fields with associated general results and generic technologies (e.g., DBMSs, symbolic programming, KBS shells, theorem provers). There have been no comparable significant results in AI-DB Integration.

---

[1]The term information base is used to refer to both DBs and KBs. DB/KB (i.e., database/knowledge base) will also be used to emphasize the currently disjoint components.

Effective AI-DB Integration requires a deep understanding by AI people of what DB technology could offer and by DB people of the requirements of AI systems. This understanding has yet to happen. Unfortunately, there has been little effective communication or technology transfer between AI scientists and practitioners and their DB colleagues. The following recent, real tales are typical of the situation.

Tale 1 *There was once (not so long ago) a major contributor to AI research who constructed several systems to provide DB support for AI systems. (A commercial DBMS is now based on one of the systems.) In discussion with DB researchers, the AI researcher was surprised to find that the system did not support DB concurrency control. As a result, multiple applications accessing a DB simultaneously could lose data or access inconsistent data. The AI researcher did not, but now will, place more importance on basic DB functions. (The DBMS marketplace will probably force a resolution of the problem with the commercial product. Initially, this may be difficult for AI customers to judge.)*

Tale 2 *Once upon a time, there were two workshops on AI-DB Integration in the same kingdom (i.e., AAAI '88). "Very Large Multi-Functional Knowledge Bases" was organized by AI researchers. "Databases in Large AI Systems" was organized by DB researchers. Organizers and some participants of both workshops knew of the other workshop but made no effort to ride over to the other camp, even when encouraged to do so. I was the only person at both workshops. The AI [DB] people knew little about DB [AI] technology and made little progress in that direction. It is clear that AI [DB] people are not able to judge the difficulty or value of DB [AI] problems or contributions. All claimed AI-DB results by DB [AI] people should be evaluated by AI [DB] people.*

Tale 3 *In a faire land not so far away, BigBucks, an ambitious, appealing AI-DB Integration project, was proposed for all to see. A one-day proposal evaluation with the 10 or so AI researchers who proposed the research made two things clear to me. First, they did not understand the related DB issues. Second, they did not understand that they did not understand the DB issues. It would be a waste of national resources for AI [DB] people to reinvent DB [AI] technology. Every AI-DB Integration project should have adequate representation from both the AI and DB communities.*

Tale 4 *Once (February 1988) upon a (Laguna) beach, 16 leading DB researchers met to identify future DB research directions. The meeting and resulting report [NS88] discussed AI only in terms of Prolog and "Rule Systems." This oversimplification and oversight was strongly criticized by many DB researchers at a public discussion of the report (at a panel discussion at VLDB 1988).*

Progress on AI-DB Integration requires changes from the AI and DB communities. The following proposals relate to each of the above tales and are illustrated throughout the paper.

Prop 1 *AI [DB] researchers will inevitably encounter DB [AI] problems as they improve their systems. There are 30 years of DB [AI] results and technology to address these problems. Do not ignore that work. Identify relevant results and adapt or extend them to address the problems faced in the new context. At the AAAI '88 workshop on AI-DB Integration organized by the AI community, almost all problems raised in the context of KBs were encountered 20 to 30 years earlier in the DB community in the context of data.*

Prop 2 *AI-DB Integration work should be conducted by people with adequate knowledge of AI and DB technologies rather than by researchers from one field conducting redundant or possibly second-rate work in the other field.*

Prop 3 *DB [AI] technology is immediately applicable to some AI-DB problems. Other AI-DB problems require major DB [AI] research. Related research has been going on in the DB [AI] community for some time. Some understanding and partial results exist.*

Prop 4 *AI-DB Integration requires theoretical and experimental work. Experimental AI-DB systems should be developed now to help identify difficult issues and to build a technology base for AI-DB Integration. Do not wait for the difficult theoretical problems to be solved before constructing AI-DB systems.*

Prop 5 *AI [DB] researchers should express their requirements of DB [AI] technology so as to influence DB [AI] development to meet their needs. Otherwise AI will end up with DB standards, such as the relational DB language SQL, that may not adequately serve AI.*

Section 2 presents a vision of future computing as a framework for AI-DB Integration. It also introduces an extensive survey conducted to report the state of and need for AI-DB Integration around the world. Section 3 describes the various types of AI-DB Integration and the potentially vast benefits for AI, DB, and IS technologies, and for the future of computing. Section 4 expresses basic DB objectives in AI terminology, AI requirements of DB technology [Prop 5], and related DB research problems. Section 5 presents uses of AI to enhance and extend DB technology and lists open AI-DB Integration research problems. Section 6 concludes with a discussion of the potential role of AI-DB Integration in future computing and one such role called *Intelligent Interoperability.*

2. THE NEXT GENERATION OF COMPUTING

The current popular vision of future computing is networking over heterogeneous computers and systems to provide access to remote resources such as computer cycles and systems [Figure 1]. The popular term **interoperability** suggests connecting the current "islands of automation."

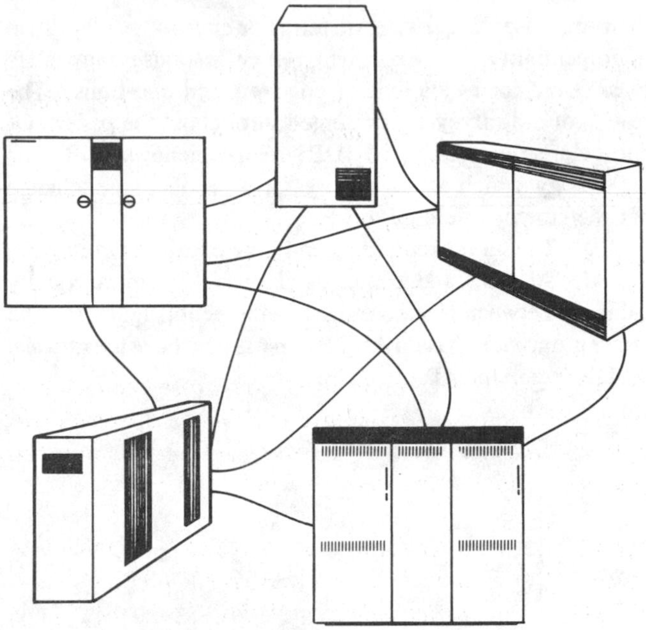

Figure 1. Networking and Interoperability

As is often the case with systems technology [BM88], much of the vision and progress in interoperability comes from industry rather than from universities. Vast numbers of computers and systems products that support networking and interoperability are announced daily, or so it seems. In reality, there is much more talk than progress. The computer industry has been very slow to connect heterogeneous computers and systems. Interoperability is long overdue and is still a long way off.

Interoperability is only 10% of the vision of future computing. It ensures that systems can communicate (e.g., via messages). It provides no guarantee that messages are mutually understood. Interoperability is a step toward **intelligent interoperability** in which systems which communicate via interoperability act as intelligent agents that cooperate to solve critical problems. We need networks of agents since each agent, like a human agent, has unique resources (i.e., knowledge, data, functional capabilities). Future intelligent ISs should be able to use all resources in a network of intelligent agents regardless of where the resources are or the details of how to use the resource. AI-DB Integration is critical to achieving this vision.

Consider how complex tasks are executed in human organizations, such as a hospital. Each human agent (e.g., doctor, technician, nurse, receptionist) provides capabilities to cooperatively execute tasks. For a doctor to complete an analysis of a patient, the doctor may need the opinion of another doctor, the results of a laboratory test, and personal information about the patient. This requires that the analysis be broken into subtasks, appropriate agents be found for each subtask, each subtask be sent to the appropriate agents, required information be transmitted with each subtask in the correct formats, etc. Cooperating agents must analyze and complete the subtasks and return the results. The doctor must then analyze the results and combine them to complete the task. Such cooperative work is the basic paradigm for most human organizations and will be the basis of future ISs [BBLM88].

Interoperability in the hospital example is the ability of the doctor to establish communication with other agents [Figure 2]. Cooperative work requires considerable intelligent interaction between human agents using knowledge of who does what, what information is required, the form in which it is required, how to locate the appropriate agents, how to request capabilities, etc. The intelligent interaction of agents in the hospital illustrates intelligent interoperability. The example illustrates how interoperability is only a small part of future computing.

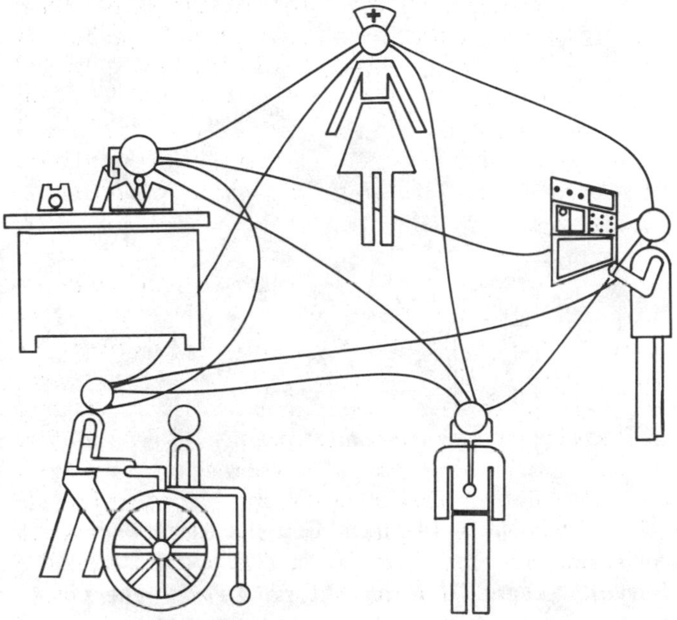

Figure 2. Intelligent Interoperability

The cost and quality of the products of most human organizations depend on the effectiveness of cooperation among agents. In hospitals, the quality and cost of health care, and indeed lives, depend on the effectiveness and speed of cooperation among agents. The cost and complexity of the human interactions argue for optimizing the interactions. The cost of a doctor's interactions are reduced by an infrastructure which makes the interactions transparent to the doctor (i.e., reduces the doctor's involvement) as much as possible. To avoid a doctor's having to contact potentially all agents directly and having the required information and capabilities, interactions are performed by less costly resource agents who are specialists in the necessary interactions [Figure 3]. We are concerned not only with the functionality of intelligent interoperability but also with its cost, which depends on how it is implemented.

Future computing will be based on intelligent cooperation similar to that shown in Figure 3. Future intelligent ISs will consist of many ISs, each an expert in a particular domain (e.g., keeping patient records). Each domain expert will be able to augment its capabilities transparently and efficiently through intelligent interoperability provided by a resource agent. Each resource agent will find and acquire resources (e.g., data, knowledge, methods) in a manner transparent to the domain agent [Figure 3]. Intelligent interoperability requires DB technology to efficiently manage resources, just as current DB technology manages data, and it requires AI technology to support reasoning in domains and cooperation among agents. Hence, the next generation of computing requires the integration of AI and DB technologies to achieve intelligent and transparent access to remote computing resources.

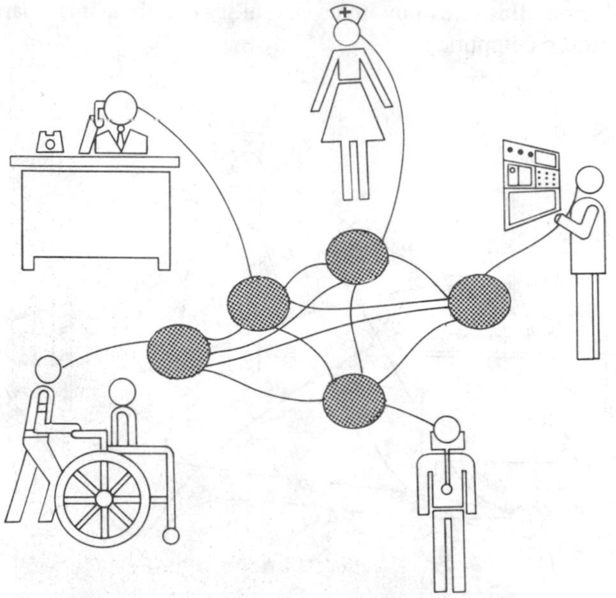

Figure 3. Intelligent Resource Agents

Survey of AI and DB Researchers and Practitioners

To evaluate the status, importance, and specific needs [Prop 5] of AI-DB Integration and of intelligent interoperability, I conducted a survey in the summer of 1988. The survey[2] was distributed to leading AI and DB researchers and developers in universities and industry, to leading KBS and DBMS practitioners in KBS and DBMS companies and their clients selected for their AI-DB experience, and to attendees of the AAAI '88 talk on which this paper is based. More than 400 AI and DB researchers and practitioners from the USA, Canada, UK, France, West Germany, Sweden, Switzerland, Italy, Israel, China, USSR, Scotland, Brazil, and Columbia responded. The large response indicates the importance of the topic. More than 50 individuals claimed to be unqualified to answer but replied to express their feelings on the importance of AI-DB Integration. Approximately 40% of the respondents attended a presentation of the ideas and the intended uses of the survey results prior to their response. Otherwise, no terms or questions, other than interoperability, were explained. Hence, responses may relate to different interpretations of concepts and questions. The results of the survey are presented throughout the paper. Of particular note are the AI [DB] requirements of DB [AI] technology which are necessary for a productive exchange between the two fields [Prop 5].

The survey represents a mixture of experts working in the AI, AI-DB, and DB areas [Figure 4][3] almost equally balanced between research and development [Figure 5]. The larger group were AI and AI-DB experts who have the greatest AI-DB requirements.

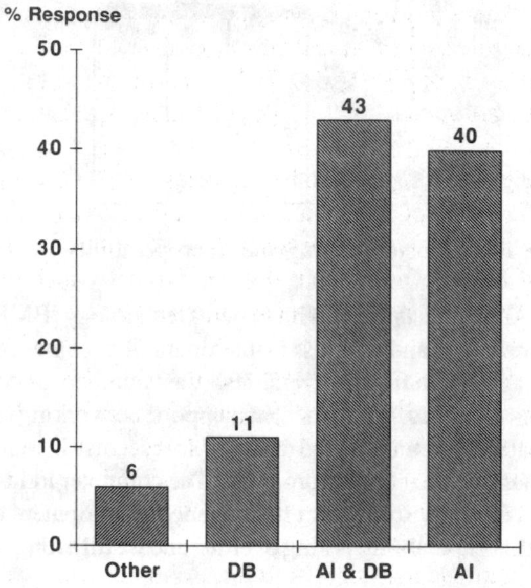

Figure 4. Work Areas

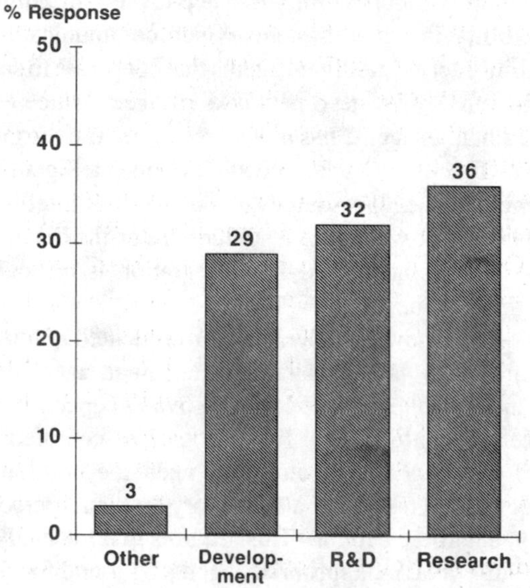

Figure 5. Work Types

[2]See Appendix A for the survey questionnaire.

[3]% Response, used as an axis in most charts, is with respect to the total number of respondents.

3. WHAT IS AI-DB INTEGRATION?

AI-DB Integration concerns reasoning over large or shared information bases. It involves any combination of AI and DB technologies. Some such systems are easy to imagine: a multiuser KBS that efficiently accesses multiple large shared DBs or file systems (e.g., a medical diagnosis expert accessing patient records and pathology DBs); a conventional IS augmented by KBS capabilities (e.g., an airline reservation system with intelligent routing selection which considers passenger preferences and notifies passengers of rerouting based on changing conditions such as flight availability and weather). The potential is much greater than these simple extrapolations.

There has been interest in AI-DB Integration since the pioneering days of AI and DBs more than 30 years ago. In 1951, Alan Turing's "Turing Test" involved a machine that might imitate human intelligence [TURI51]. A vast information base would be required here. Many early question-answering, learning, and other systems (e.g., McCarthy's Advice Taker [McCAR58] in 1958) assumed access to large, possibly shared, information bases. These systems implicitly assumed DB capabilities but did not explicitly address the issues. The pioneers' visions have not been realized in more than 30 years.

Since the late 1950's and early 1960's with the emergence of the first natural language interface to file systems, AI-DB Integration has been addressed explicitly. The early foci of interest concerned natural language interfaces and intelligent information retrieval [COOP64] [AS68] and deductive DBs (i.e., DBs and logic).

Current areas of AI-DB interaction involve not only the coupling of AI and DB systems but also the application of AI technology to DB technology and *vice versa*. Specific areas include knowledge representation and modelling [BMS84] [BL85], coupling of DBs and KBSs [JV83], knowledge base management [BM86] (KBMSs manage knowledge,[4] whereas DBMSs manage data[5]), and intelligent DBs (extending DBMSs by adding intelligence to traditional DB functions such as query optimization [CFM86] [FREY87]). Future interest in AI-DB Integration will focus on what one can do when the current AI-DB challenges are met. This includes intelligent interoperability and distributed computing [BBLM88].

Over the past 30 years, there has been a steady increase in interest in AI-DB Integration. The trend can be seen in the number of AI-DB papers published [Figure 6], and in the number of books published [BMS84] [BM86] [MB88] [KERS86] [KERS87] [KERS88] [[GM78] [GNM81] [GMN84] [GRAY84] [ULLM88], as well as in the number of conferences, workshops, and panels held (i.e., more than 30 during 1978-1988), the number of commercial products introduced (i.e., over 45 in 1987-1988), and the number of projects begun. A 1983 survey [KING83] identified 36 AI-DB projects begun. The current 1988 survey identified over 350 AI-DB projects. The average labour effort in person years per project per year rose from three in 1986 to five in 1988 and is projected to go to nine in 1990 [Figure 7]. More than 10 projects had 20 or more people per year. Based on the survey of only 400 individuals, at least 2,000 person years were spent on AI-DB projects in 1988. This is expected to rise to over 3,000 person years in 1990.

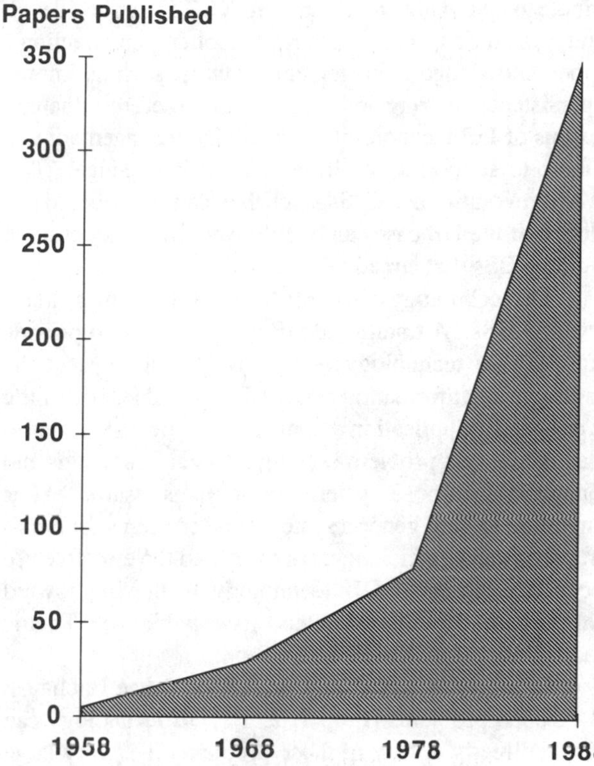

Figure 6. AI-DB Interaction History

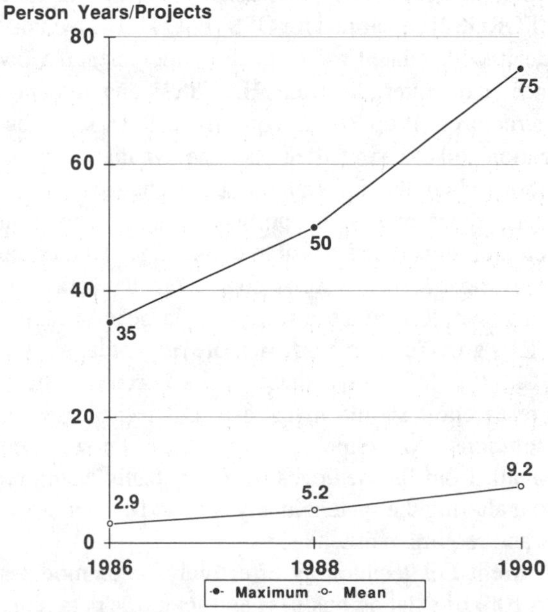

Figure 7. Average Effort Over 350 AI-DB Projects

[4]Whatever that means.

[5]Whatever that means.

AI-DB Integration Benefits [Prop 1, 3]

The large amount of activity in the AI-DB area indicates both the need for integrating the two technologies and a recognition of the potential benefits [Prop 5]. The primary benefit to AI of DB technology will be to scale up AI systems, particularly KBSs, to industrial strength. DB technology can contribute to knowledge management, KBS design and development, systems aspects, and to KBS cooperation. Section 3 describes knowledge management features, such as knowledge persistence, sharing, independence, and access, as natural extensions of DB technology. Knowledge management will contribute to supporting multiple uses of knowledge. This alone will revolutionize KBSs since they can be designed and developed, if the DB case can be followed, by augmenting or extending KBSs that already exist.

DB technology can contribute to improving systems aspects of KBSs. A traditional DB goal has been to provide general-purpose technology (e.g., DBMSs) to support the widest range of information processing possible, with little focus on specific application domains. In contrast, AI technology has focused on problem-solving in specific domains and not on general-purpose systems or systems issues. AI is moving more toward generic systems and concerns for architecture, robustness, efficiency, controls, and the effective use of secondary storage. DB technology is moving toward special-purpose domains to extend its capabilities. This is increasing interest in AI-DB Integration.

In his 1986 AAAI talk on KBSs, Bruce Buchanan listed 11 open problems [Prop 1, 2, 3]. DB technology can contribute directly to four of those problems (i.e., very large KBs, shared KBs, distributed KBs, and integration with existing operations such as DBs) and indirectly to four more (i.e., specialized representations and inference, dynamic reasoning such as monitoring, KB consistency and completeness, and KB compilation). Specifically, Buchanan mentioned the Rete structure [FORG82] developed for OPS [FM77]. DB technology has dealt with related topics such as incremental view maintenance and materialization [HANS87] and dynamic indexing structures [Prop 3]. In contrast to Rete, DB view materialization and indexing attempts to be dynamic to avoid recompilation when the information base changes and to support many types of search optimization (e.g., based on information maintained and possible clustering). Due to the small size of most KBSs, Rete is considered to work adequately. However, Rete will not scale up to large information bases. As KBs grow (e.g., to 1,000 or more rules or larger, see [BM84] [LPS85] [MPM84]), these issues become critical. Then, AI researchers should investigate DB technology for potential solutions. AI technology would benefit now, when KBs are small, from fast searches over constantly changing KBs without altering the system in any way and even more as KBs grow and require maintenance.

Current DB technology effectively accommodates only 5% to 10% of existing business and scientific data (e.g., it cannot adequately deal with engineering or AI data structures). Most DB research is directed at extending this to 50% or 80% by increasing the functionality of DB technology and the types of objects that can be managed. This is being done by examining the requirements of special-purpose domains (e.g., CAD/CAM, AI, software engineering) [Prop 5]. AI technology can contribute directly to these extensions in addition to providing application requirements for DBMSs to support [Prop 3].

ISs, which include DB applications, are the greatest potential beneficiaries of AI technology. The most obvious advantage is to add powerful representation and reasoning capabilities to new or existing ISs. However, AI technology can also provide deeper technology benefits in the areas of DB theory, functionality (e.g., information representation, KB management, user interfaces, and active DBs), performance (e.g., semantic query optimization, flexible concurrency control [BG84], and distributed DBs [GARC83]), and extensions of DB technology (e.g., intelligent DBs, expert DBs [KERS86, 87, 88], deductive DBs [GMN84a], KBMSs [BM86], and object-oriented DBMSs [DD86]). For example, DBMSs would benefit considerably from maintaining, reasoning about, and acting on currently available knowledge about their functionality and performance. For example, DBMSs would be more realistic if they were able to knowingly support inconsistency and incompleteness [BBLM88] [Prop 3].

Importance and Need for AI-DB Integration

There is considerable agreement on the need for and importance of AI-DB Integration. At National Science Foundation meetings in early 1988, senior U.S. scientists in computer science and other areas agreed unanimously on the positive potential impact of AI-DB Integration on the future of computing and on the infrastructure of science and technology in the United States. However, they disagreed on whether the area had matured enough to be able to achieve the desired goals in the near term. They also disagreed on approaches to achieving the goals. Some argued that general theories are required before results could be expected. However, as has been the case in many systems areas [BM88], AI-DB Integration systems building is critical in creating a technology base for AI-DB systems and in identifying issues for further research [Prop 4]. Theoretical and practical AI-DB research should be funded if researchers understand the relevant AI and DB technologies [Prop 2].

There has been considerable *talk* in the AI industry of the need for AI-DB Integration (largely KBS access to DBs). In 1986, most KBS shells and AI languages did not have connections to DB systems. By 1988, many such products provided simple, *ad hoc (versus* general-purpose) connections to DBMSs. Each connection provides access to a specific version of a DBMS product running under a specific operating system on a specific machine. Currently, these products, which are far from mainstream ISs, have very few users. The modest demand is due, in part, to the non-IS point of view of KBS developers not used to accessing large ISs and to the lack of adequate, easy-to-use technology. As shown in the survey results, KBSs do not differ from conventional ISs in their requirements to access DBs. Currently, most KBSs are small "islands of automation," as were ISs 20 to 30 years ago when DB technology was developed to provide data sharing and the resulting integration of IS applications.

In 1988, there are very few (by IS standards) practical KBS applications.[6] Very few of these systems access DBs or use products that support KBS-DB coupling. The importance and need for AI-DB Integration in IS will increase dramatically by 1990, when the value of KBSs becomes recognized. There will be a massive growth in the deployment of KBSs but not in their current form. KBSs must become integrated into traditional DB/IS technology to achieve access to large shared persistent information bases; to integrate KBSs into traditional IS architectures and environments; to make KBSs a robust technology; and to permit the by then large number of KBSs to communicate and possibly cooperate.

By 1992, the current DBMS vendors will be the primary deliverers of KBS facilities to the IS industry. DBMSs will be extended with simple inference techniques that will support 90% of all KBSs. KBS features will be made almost transparent by the addition of a few simple language constructs to traditional DB languages such as SQL. This will assist the rapid deployment of KBS technology since DB technology is part of traditional ISs.[7] DBMSs will very efficiently search small or very large KBs to identify applicable rules and execute the rules. It is an open question as to how much these DBMSs will support other KBS functionality (e.g., explanation, backtracking, truth maintenance). They will do well with linearly recursive rules but will not do well with general recursive rules, which account for less than 5% of most KBs. Most DBMS companies are currently extending their DBMSs to provide such support for tight coupling of AI and DB systems. AI companies will still have a role in providing more powerful KBS technology than DBMSs can effectively support. The resulting KBSs will be coupled with DBMSs and other systems via loose coupling techniques such as may be provided through intelligent interoperability technology.

Consider the opinions of the AI and DB researchers and practitioners surveyed on the importance and need of AI-DB Integration. While more than 80% of those surveyed expressed a need for AI-DB Integration both in the future (conceptually) and currently (practically) [Figure 8], all respondents expressed a moderately strong need[8] (6.4 and 6.7, respectively) for it. More than 60% were attempting (In Reality) to integrate AI and DB in their current systems. On average the efforts are very limited (5.2).

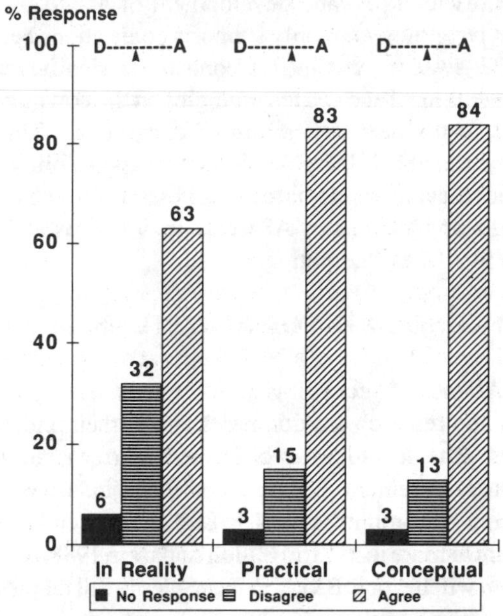

Figure 8. Need for AI-DB Integration

Whereas 58% of the respondents disagreed that AI-DB Integration is adequate for their needs, all respondents emphasized the inadequacy (2.8) [Figure 9]. Of the respondents, 45% felt that they knew the requirements; on average, however, all respondents felt that they did not know the requirements very well (5.1). Due to the lack of understanding across the AI-DB boundary, it is difficult for respondents to evaluate adequacy or requirements [Tales 1-4] [Prop 1-5]. The responses are probably optimistic.

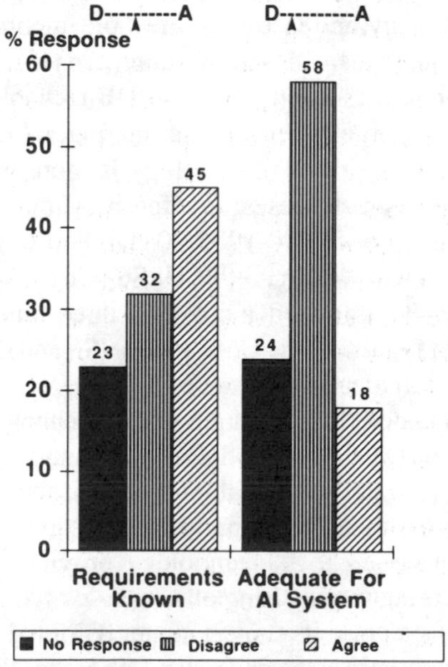

Figure 9. AI-DB Integration Status

---

[6]In his invited talk at AAAI '88, *The Results of a Study of the First Wave of Expert System Applications to Business,* Ed Fiegenbaum reported that there were less than 2,000 practical expert systems in production use, worldwide. The greatest difficulties involved the accessing of large DBs and the lack of acceptance by IS managers.

[7]There are more than 500,000 DBMSs in use in large-scale ISs and more than 3,000,000 DBMSs in use on personal computers in comparison with less than 10,000 KBSs in practical use.

[8]Respondents were asked to express their strength of agreement on most issues on a scale from 0 (disagree) to 9 (agree). In most subsequent figures, the mean strength of agreement across all respondents is illustrated by a bar on a line between D (disagree) and A (agree). D--------|-A illustrates a mean agreement of 8 in the scale of 0 to 9.

This section has described the growing need for integrating AI and DB systems and the increased perception of the importance of AI-DB Integration. There is now a dramatic growth in research into and development of AI-DB technology. This technology not only supports connections between AI and DB systems, but it also contributes significantly to improvements in AI and DB technologies on their own and will contribute to the next generation of computing. The next section describes basic DB objectives, their applicability to AI, and related research problems to be addressed. The subsequent section lists applications of AI technology to DBs and open problems in AI-DB Integration.

4. DB TECHNOLOGY FOR AI SYSTEMS

AI and DB technologies differ considerably in their industrial and research environments and in their underlying paradigms. The development of DB technology is driven, in part, by the requirements and nature of the IS industry. Of all money spent on computing, 70% to 80% is spent on ISs. This will amount to more than $150 billion dollars in 1988, of which $2.5 billion will be for DBMSs alone. Sales for all AI products will amount to $1.5 billion in 1988. Optimistic projections for 1990 are $6 billion for DBMSs and $4 billion for AI. There are approximately three million copies of DBMS products in use. The vast majority of these are on personal computers. There are more than 300,000 installations of DBMS on mainframes in large-scale applications. Although there are more than 400 DBMS products, the market is dominated by about 10-15 DBMSs.

In contrast to popular belief, most DBs are very small. DBs run in size from <1 MB on PCs to hundreds of gigabytes. Industrial-strength DB applications, on micros and mainframes, generally run in the 50-500 MB range [Table 1]. However, there is an enormous growth in the use of small DBs on PCs. The widest selling DBMSs are Ashton Tate's dBase products for PCs. In these cases, DB management, data sharing, efficiency, and ease of use are more important features of DB technology than DB size. Further, even if main memory becomes very cheap, large, and fast, DB technology will be required to support efficient access, sharing, robustness, etc.

Even though DB technology is more widely used, there has been a greater research effort in AI than in DB. For example, in the period 1970-1985, 204 DB Ph.D.'s were earned in comparison with 447 in AI [TAUL86]. In the same period, NSF and DARPA funded more than three times more AI research than DB research. Until 1987, NSF and DARPA had major AI research programs and no DB research programs.

An underlying paradigm of DB technology is that it provides a computational model of information focusing on generic (i.e., broadly applicable) systems and on systems issues such as robustness, performance, and concurrency [BM88]. In contrast, AI technology provides a semantic theory of information focusing on semantic accounts of a KB to relate its contents to its subject matter [BM86a]. The above differences may help in the understanding of the DB objectives described below.

Table 1. DB Technology for AI

DB sizes		
• Very large		100 GB
• Large		>500 MB
• Medium		50 to 500 MB
• Small		<50 MB
IS APPLICATION SIZES	**CURRENT (GB)**	**HISTORICAL (GB)**
Airline	40	120
Retailer	30	360
Aerospace	100	1000
Communications	100	1000

The Basic DB Paradigm As a New KB Paradigm

The basic DB paradigm, which underlies DB technology, involves an **information agent,** or **D/KBMS**[9] [Figure 10(b)], which handles all aspects of the information: entry, search, update, maintenance, etc. A client system (e.g., AI application) states what information it requires or what new information it wants to add to the information base and relies on the information agent to provide access to relevant portions of the information base. Client systems state their requests in suitably abstract terms and ignore all aspects of the information base, including maintaining the semantic integrity and information management. The D/KBMS permits client systems to focus on the problem-solving at hand. Another aspect of the DB paradigm is that client systems assume that the information base is **persistent** (i.e., permanently maintained independently of any application even when the information base is not being accessed). Persistence is illustrated in Figure 10 and subsequent figures by a drum, indicating a conventional DB, and by a head, indicating a persistent KB.

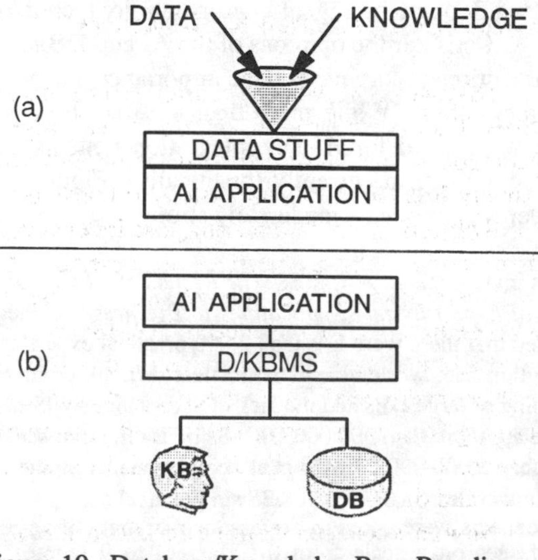

Figure 10. Database/Knowledge Base Paradigm

[9]D/KBMS refers to a system that provides DBMS and KBMS features.

To consider the applicability of DB objectives to AI, let's assume the notion of an information agent for KBs, hence a new KB paradigm. Correspondingly, let's consider DB objectives in KB terms (i.e., what KBs would be like if they were treated as DBs are now). In the absence of this new KB paradigm, as with current KBSs, an application must handle all aspects of dealing with data and knowledge [Figure 10(a)]. Data and knowledge is read in at run time and is lost or is saved in simple files when the system terminates execution. In the hospital example, this might compare with the information required by a doctor in examining a patient. To examine a patient, the doctor would acquire (from all known sources) all data concerning the patient and knowledge needed for the examination. The data and knowledge would all be forgotten at the end of the exam. Such practices are costly and prone to error, which in a hospital can be fatal. For example, the information may come from various, possibly redundant, sources, each of which may be updated at any time. The doctor must be responsible for ensuring that the information is up to date and is correct. Worse still, in a hospital this must be done for thousands of patients and hundreds of doctors. In reality, a doctor has information agents, or assistants, who handle the doctor's information requests. The doctor examines the patient while the assistants acquire and present information essential for the doctor's task.

The new KB paradigm leads to the need for a KB model with which to describe the information base, and for associated definition, access, and manipulation languages to permit client systems[10] to deal with the D/KBMS. It leads to other requirements such as techniques and tools for information base design. Providing DB/KB functionality in a D/KBMS rather than in each client system provides more opportunity for increased performance, robustness, control over data, off-loading of data-related functionality to the D/KBMS, and ease of information base access.

Basic DB Objectives As New KB Objectives

DB functionality can be considered in terms of six DB objectives. The objectives motivate successively higher levels of abstraction of the information agent or D/KBMS (i.e., successively less for the client system to consider). Three traditional objectives are data sharing, data independence, and data distribution. These objectives are described below in terms of their potential KB counterparts. Three new DB objectives being added to conventional DBMSs are support for objects of all types (e.g., AI structures), rather than only the simple structured record types; specific performance characteristics (e.g., real time, active DBs); and cooperation with client systems (e.g., intelligent interoperability discussed in Sections 1 and 6).

Now let's consider the three traditional DB objectives in KB terms, if the new KB paradigm were valid. The first KB objective would be **knowledge sharing**. Without sharing, each application must manage its own information base and cannot access those of other applications [Figure 11(a)]. Without sharing in the hospital example, doctors would have their own patient information, which they would not share with others. Multiple copies of the information could easily lead to inconsistencies and could, therefore, lead to critical errors in patient treatment. Compare a KBS to the doctor. Most current KBSs do not share information (i.e., data or knowledge); however, there is frequently information that could be shared between multiple KBSs.

In reality, different doctors who provide care for the same patients share some patient information and have some information that is unique to their needs. Under the new KB paradigm, all information that could be shared would be extracted from all applications to be managed by the information agent in a shared repository [Figure 11(b)]. At the same time, all code needed to access, search, and manage the information is extracted and becomes part of the KBMS. This off-loading of information agent functions from AI applications to the KBMS leads to a reduction of application coding, greater focus on AI applications problem-solving, and greater potential for correctness, robustness, and efficiency of information agent functions and for extending those functions independent of and for the benefit of all AI applications.

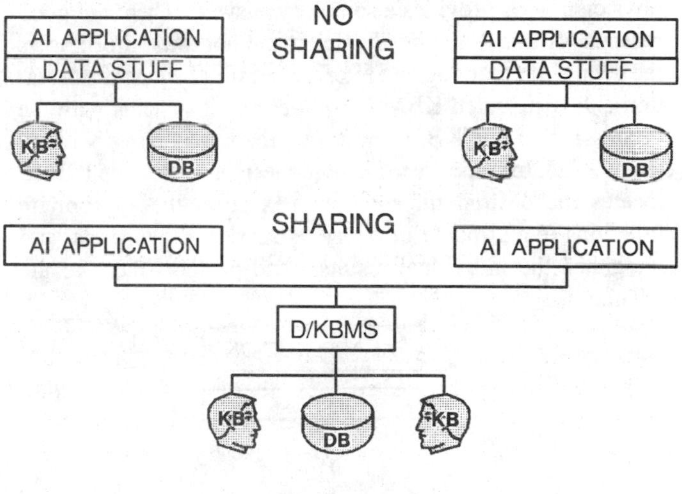

Figure 11. Knowledge Sharing

A shared KB leads to desirable KBS properties, including a common ontology, a common KB model and associated languages (or at least an ability to communicate between different models and languages), multiple uses of knowledge, and knowledge reuse. These properties would aid KBS development since a KBS would be developed using existing KBs. Knowledge sharing provides multiuser access to information which, for updates, requires concurrency control and a transaction concept to define logical, recoverable application units. Knowledge sharing could provide a basis for cooperative KBSs.

The second KB objective would be **knowledge representation independence.** The goal is to minimize the

[10]Use by multiple client systems is one distinction between the KB model and its associated languages, and between AI knowledge representation schemes.

negative effects of inevitable changes. KBs will evolve by logical changes (e.g., adding or modifying whole applications, knowledge, and data) or physical changes (e.g., adding or modifying physical storage or access details such as organization, storage devices, indexes, and access paths). These problems are faced to some degree by most KBSs but have become major challenges for large KBs (e.g., R1 [BM84], INTERNIST [MPM84] CYC [LPS85]). Ideally for such changes, each application that shares the KB would be insulated completely for KB features on which it does not depend and to varying degrees for KB features on which it does depend (e.g., completely for implementation changes, partly for semantic changes). This goal is the essence of this new KB paradigm, which would strive for complete transparency not only for applications but also for systems support provided by KB administrators. In the hospital example, doctors may ask information agents to add new types of information and whole new types of requests. As long as results were adequate, information agents could radically change the way they do their jobs without the doctor needing to know.

The third KB objective would be **knowledge distribution**. In the hospital example, consider how visitors obtain information about patients. Patients often have one responsible physician but many doctors (e.g., specialists). Rather than discussing the patient's condition with all doctors and coming to some conclusion, visitors speak to the responsible physician, who provides a summary answer. There are good reasons for this (e.g., the physician and not the visitor knows the details of obtaining and interpreting the pertinent information). A distributed KBMS provides client systems with the impression of one KB when in fact there may be very many [Figure 12]. In response to client requests, a distributed KBMS locates the desired information; executes the appropriate functions (e.g., update or query); translates, interprets, and integrates the individual results; and presents them to the client.

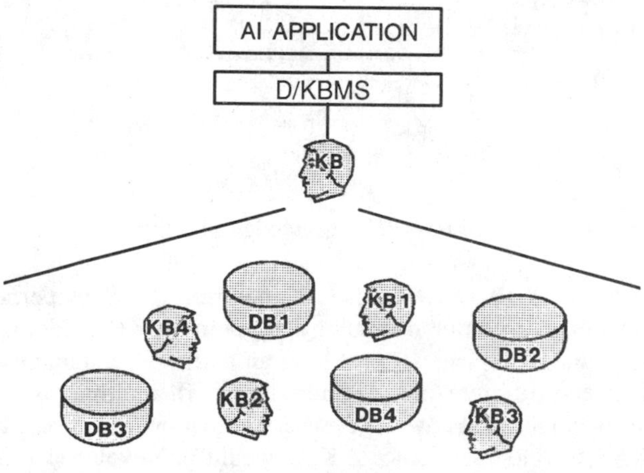

Figure 12. Distributed Knowledge Bases

The main benefit of knowledge distribution is that applications need not be aware of the locations, or even identities, of contributing information bases and the complexities of interacting with any one of them (e.g., locations, formats, communication protocols) or of integrating the results of interaction. Related benefits include integration of possibly remote and heterogeneous information bases (both KBs and DBs) through one logical view and improved systems features based on the fact that the KB consists of multiple systems which provide greater potential for robustness, reliability, extensibility, and availability. Knowledge distribution may provide another basis for cooperative KBSs.

DB and AI Levels

The above DB and KB objectives can be related in term of the levels used to discuss them in the DB and AI fields, respectively. The correspondence indicates similarities and differences between AI and DB and suggests potential contributions from one to the other. DB representation is expressed in terms of three levels [BM88]. The **DB level** concerns the instances of entities (e.g., records used to store patient data in a patient DB) that constitute the DB. The **schema level** concerns the data types used to define entities (e.g., patient, doctor), hence the allowable DBs. The **data model level** concerns the meta-types that define the types that can be used to define any schema under the given data model (e.g., the rules defining a relation in the relational data model). The DB representation levels are used in discussing data models and languages.

DB design is considered in (at least) three levels: conceptual, logical, and physical. Design by successive refinement begins at the **conceptual level** at which entities are designed using conceptual or semantic data models [BMS84] (e.g., entity-relationship [CHEN76]). The conceptual level concerns the design and analysis of the information content independent of representation and implementation issues. The resulting conceptual DB designs are translated down to the **logical level** into less abstract conventional data models (e.g., relational, network). Finally, logical DB designs are translated down to the **physical level** in terms of the specific data model provided on the target computer (e.g., the actual code used to implement a DB2 DB). DB design levels are used by DB administrators who are responsible for DB designs.

There are three levels in which AI is considered [NEWE82] [BPL85] [BL86] [BL86a]. The **architectural** or **organizational level** compares with DB administration at which systems organization issues, such as distribution, are considered. The **knowledge level** corresponds to the data model and conceptual levels in DBs which include DB topics such as DB and data model theory and conceptual DB design. The **symbol level** includes systems and representational issues such as algorithms and data structures (e.g., at the logical and physical DB design levels).

Survey Results on AI Requirements for DB Technology [Prop 5]

To design and build a KBMS, requirements must be defined by identifying the DB functions required to support KBSs. Proposals have been made for specific cases [WIED84]

[BM86] [ST88], but there is little agreement [BROD86]. AI and DB experts were asked to state their requirements. The responses provide a broad-based view of the requirements for and role of DB technology for AI systems.

While over 90% of those surveyed felt that DB is critical for the success of KBSs [Figure 13], the mean level of agreement was high (7.7). Surprisingly, almost 80% felt that DB was critical to non-KBS AI systems, with a somewhat strong mean agreement (6.4). Of the respondents, 80% felt that DB technology was applicable in their current system or work, with a strong mean agreement (7.4). A surprising 64% felt that they were currently applying DB technology in their AI system or work but, on average, only to a very small degree (6.0). The responses are probably optimistic [Tale 1].

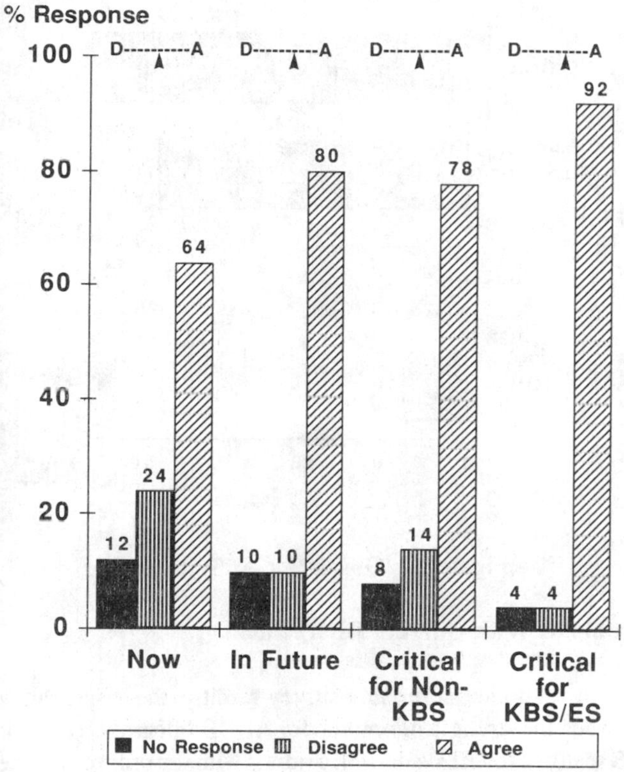

Figure 13. DB Technology for AI

There is a strong perceived need by those surveyed for both loose and tight coupling [Figure 14]. An important architectural consideration in DB support of KB requirements is the coupling between KB and DB systems. Tight coupling generally means that the DB component is an integral part of the KBS with potentially high efficiency, a transparent interface, and little flexibility for use by other systems (e.g., the data and KB in OPS). Loose coupling generally means that the DB system is external to the KBS (which uses an external DBMS interface), has low efficiency, but is accessible to other systems. Although most ISs access DBs through loose coupling achieved by external procedure calls, there are clearly good reasons for both types of coupling.

AI systems are similar to any IS in their potential data access requirements. Survey respondents need read-only and read-write access to all sizes of DBs [Figure 14]. They expressed a greater need to access small DBs [Figure 15], but a significant percent require access to medium and large DBs. Some require access to DBs of various sizes.

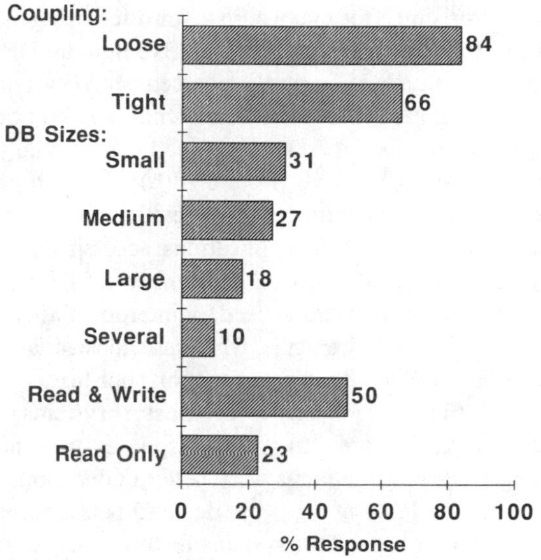

Figure 14. AI Access to DB Systems

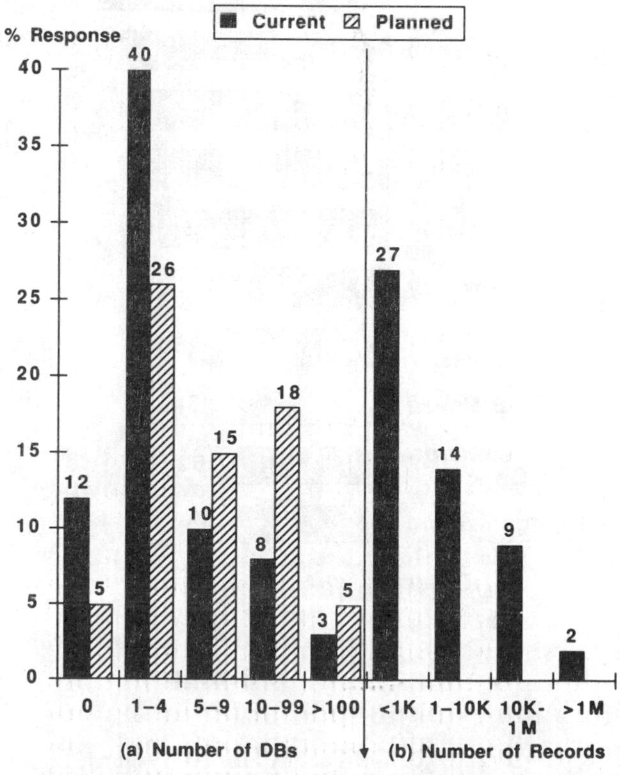

Figure 15. AI Access to DB Systems

In principle, AI applications need not differ from ISs in terms of the size of the DBs they could take advantage of accessing. However, the survey uncovered some surprising AI requirements for DB access. Concerning the number of DBs that an AI system needs to access, approximately 12% do not currently want access to any DBs [Figure 15(a)]. The greatest current preference (40%) was to access between one and four DBs. An amazing 21% need to access five or more, and 3% (i.e., 12 AI systems) need access to more than 100 DBs. Even more surprising is the major shift toward accessing many more DBs (e.g., 38% will want access to five or more DBs). Concerning the number of records accessed per AI system use, the greatest emphasis was placed on a small number; however a significant number of AI systems need to access large to very large numbers of records [Figure 15(b)]. Taken together, the above DB access requirements suggest[11] new requirements for DBs, namely, many AI applications accessing few records during each execution for large numbers of DBs of varying size. This suggests a strong need for interoperability. Without knowing these requirements, which are nonstandard for most current ISs, DBMSs may never support such features [Prop 5].

According to the survey, most AI systems need most DB features [Figure 16]. The responses may have been stronger if the DB features were better understood. The two most desired features were queries and persistence. Strong needs were expressed for systems features such as access to external DBs; security, integrity, and directory controls; access, search, and storage optimization; concurrency control for multiuser access; and robustness and recovery. Considering the potential software engineering value of multifunctional KBs, there is surprisingly little desire for DB/KB reuse and reorganization. These features, when they are realized, will revolutionize the design, development, use, and maintenance of KBSs[12] [Prop 1, 2].

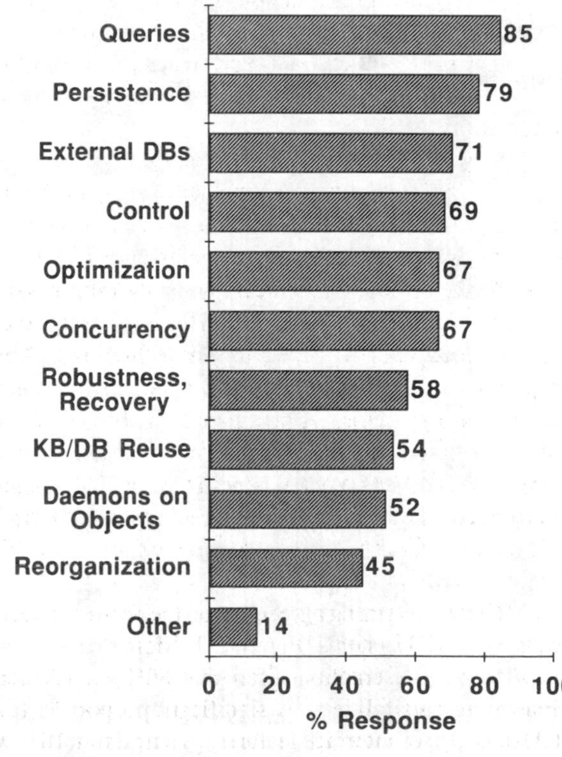

Figure 16. DB Features for AI Systems

[11]The related questions were asked independently.

Almost all AI systems need to access traditional DBs [Figure 17]. To take advantage of most computerized data (i.e., to integrate KBSs into traditional IS architectures and environments), KBSs will have to access file systems and DBs. More than 75% want KBs to store frames, rules, units, etc. Only 38% want the D/KBMS to manage systems code. Of the respondents, 16% want 30 other object types, including chemical structures, traces, logs, multimedia objects, and e-mail.

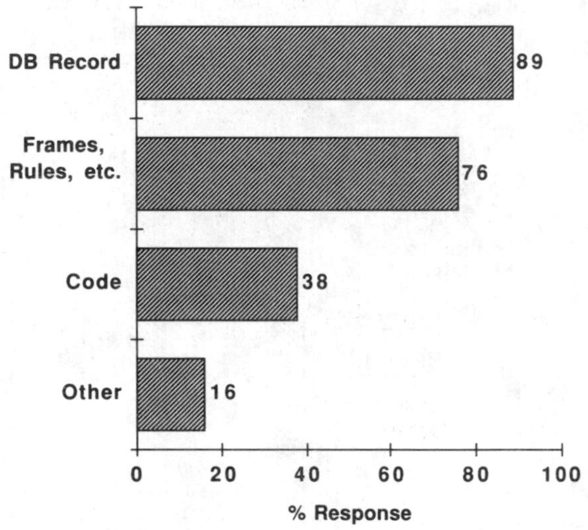

Figure 17. Objects for AI Systems

Problems With Current DB Technology

Another surprising survey result is the discrepancy between the strength of opinion for AI-DB Integration and for DB features for AI systems in contrast with the progress in the area. The survey questioned why AI systems are not currently coupled with DBMSs. The greatest perceived difficulty was accessing DBMSs [Figure 18]. DBMSs, unlike almost any other type of system, are designed to facilitate access by external systems and human users. DBMS interfaces and languages (e.g., SQL) have problems, but they are not difficult to use. The 70% response reflects other problems, such as the difficulty of accessing any system from within AI systems and languages. Most other problems with DBMSs concern their inability to store AI objects. To store AI objects in DB systems, the AI objects must be translated into and out of DB objects. DB objects are generally fixed-length record structures con-

[12]Many respondents claiming considerable practical KBS experience claim that KB and KBS maintenance will be the major potential benefit of AI-DB Integration.

sisting of fields based on a small set of data types (e.g., character string, integer, real, date, and time). A related problem is that current AI systems translate objects into and from their internal formats rather than referencing objects transparently. A simple alternative is to store AI objects in their native format directly in DBs as long character or bit strings, in which case most DBMS functionality (e.g., search for subobjects) is not available. A significant number of respondents (45% and 28%, respectively) felt that DB searches were not powerful enough and that DB integrity was too strict.

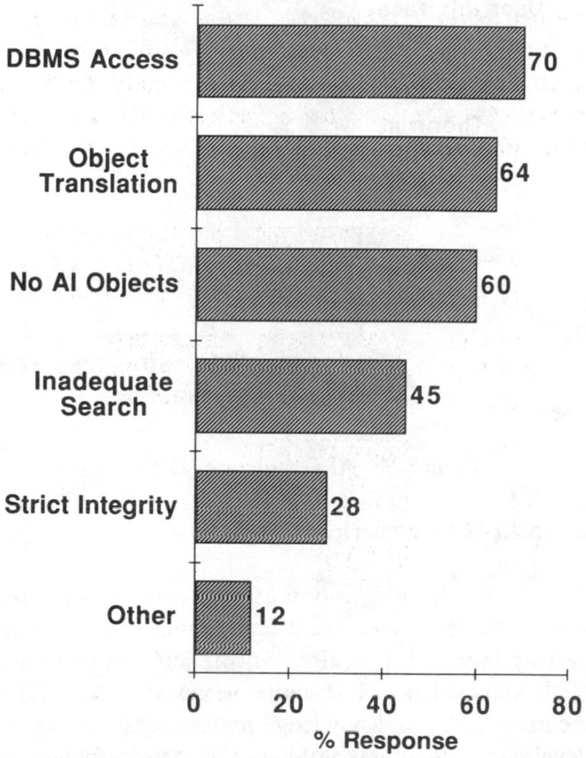

Figure 18. Problems with DB Systems

Expressing AI Requirements for DB Systems

The AI community would benefit significantly from expressing their requirements clearly to the DB community, both to take advantage of advances in DB technology and to direct it toward their needs [Prop 5]. To build a DBMS you must know the precise information, processing, and performance requirements of the intended applications. Information requirements concern the properties of the objects to be stored (e.g., the structures, their components, and their relationships). Processing requirements concern the DB operations to be executed over the objects and how they are grouped into programs (e.g., transactions). Performance requirements concern transaction loads (i.e., expected groupings of transactions — what the KBMS will really have to do), their frequency of execution, and the volumes of objects to be stored. Without experience with applications that make extensive use of KBs and DBs, it is difficult to estimate these requirements, let alone understand what an AI transaction might be over a DB or KB.

The majority of DB research, and a good deal of advanced DBMS development, is directed at extending DB technology to address the problems and issues described above [Prop 3]. The current foci for support of arbitrary objects and performance, mentioned earlier, and of means for tailoring DBMSs to meet new requirements will change DB technology dramatically. Requirements of nontraditional DB applications such as AI are providing major stimuli for DB research. The needed DB extensions will require fundamental changes in existing DB assumptions such as the closed-world assumption [REIT78], concurrent access based on serializability, single viewpoints, strictly enforcing a simple integrity and consistency (versus knowingly supporting inconsistency [BBLM88]), providing only simple exhaustive searches (versus heuristic search [KHIS86]) and simple data models. DB technology is considering AI technology to address some of the above research problems, as is described in the next section.

5. AI TECHNOLOGY FOR DB SYSTEMS AND OPEN AI-DB PROBLEMS

Let's now consider the application of AI technology to DB systems and DB requirements of AI (e.g., DB system access to AI systems) [Prop 5]. More than 70% of the respondents feel that AI is critical for enhancing DB technology [Figure 19],[13] with moderately strong (6.5) average strength of agreement. More than 60% believe that AI will be applicable in their future DB work, while all respondents believe, moderately strongly (6), that it will be applicable. Less than 45% of the respondents felt that AI was being applied in their current DB work. The average strength of agreement was low (4.5). The extent to which DB experts understand AI technology is an important factor in interpreting reasons for and accuracy of the results.

Respondents were asked about the types of AI systems access required for their DB applications. More than 60% feel that the ability of a DB application to access an AI system is desirable (with a strong average agreement of 7), but less than 50% feel such access is critical (with only a slight positive average agreement (5.5) [Figure 20]. This is in strong contrast with the perception of AI's need for DB technology. Almost all respondents (88%) want their DB applications to access KBSs or expert systems. A significant number (66%) want access to AI-based user interface systems. A deeper understanding of AI and its potential benefits (only 10% suggested alternative AI systems) would raise these responses [Prop 1, 2, 3]. AI system access by DB applications concerns both DBMS and programming language technology.

There was strong agreement on the desire for specific AI features for DB systems [Figure 21]. More than 85% want AI knowledge representation. More than 80% want AI search and reasoning capabilities. A significant proportion (62%) want AI-based user interface features. A surprising 18% want

[13]Many AI experts gave no response on the DB technology questions.

theorem proving capabilities.[14] Of the respondents, 12% listed 24 additional AI features, including learning, case-based reasoning, fuzzy sets, inference, induction, truth maintenance, temporal reasoning, and uncertainty management.

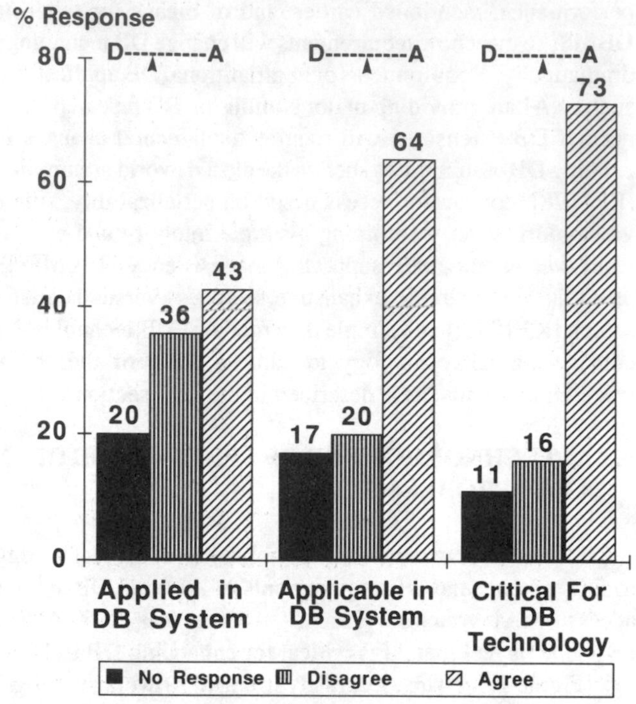

Figure 19. AI Technology for DB

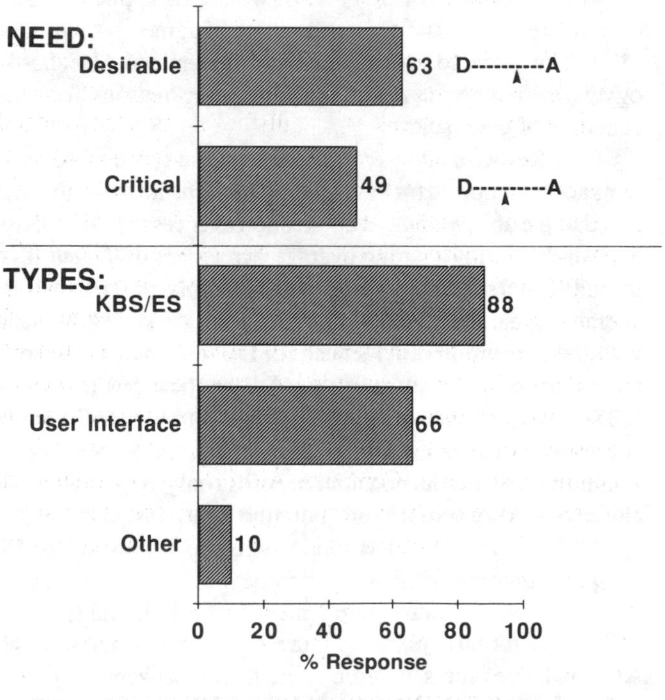

Figure 20. DB Access to AI Systems

[14]Hopefully for non-run-time analysis (e.g., [SS86]) rather than for run-time use, as this might seriously impact the performance goal of 1,000 transactions per second.

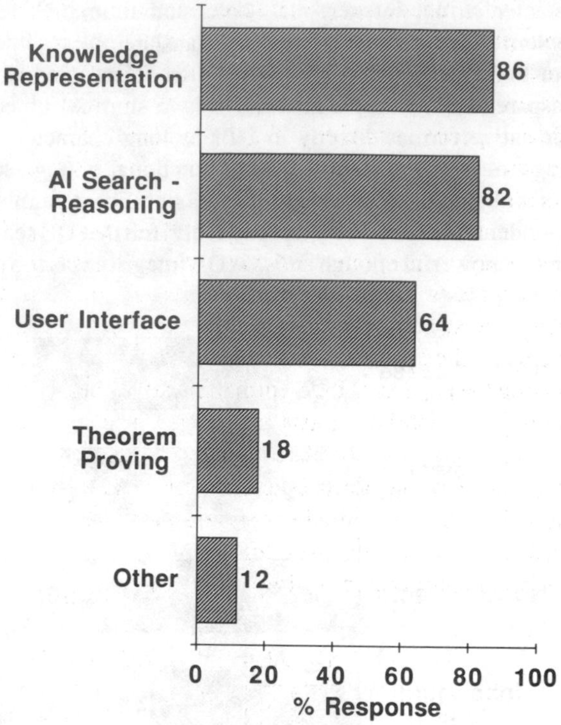

Figure 21. AI Features for DB Systems

Open AI-DB Research Problems

AI-DB Integration is a fertile, open research area with a wide range of theoretical and engineering challenges at varying levels of difficulty. Theoretical research topics include knowledge representation issues, deductive DBs, and recursion in DBs. Knowledge representation issues include developing a common ontology and semantics for heterogeneous representations, inconsistency and incompleteness, the closed-world assumption, new types of reasoning, and multiple viewpoints. Engineering issues include architecture, cooperation between systems, constraint management, implementation and performance issues associated with new requirements, and theoretical results. Architectural issues include accommodating heterogeneous systems, loose and tight coupling, extensibility of systems and architectures, and appropriate grain size of objects in an object-oriented architecture.

The difficulty of some of these issues can be seen in the cooperation and object boundary problems. Cooperation issues include the optimal allocation of functions between AI and DB systems; optimal planning, execution, monitoring, and possibly intervention of tasks between cooperating agents; and the optimal exchange of information among cooperating agents. Consider optimally splitting a search between a DB and an AI system. The objective is to have each system do the parts of the search it does best. DBs are excellent at exhaustive, first-order searches over large DBs. AI systems are good at heuristic and higher than first-order searches over small KBs. How is one search task decomposed to make optimal use of DB and AI searches? One alternative is to use the DB system to efficiently reduce the search space for the AI system. It is an open problem to decompose a search expression into these two parts. Related open problems are the following: What information must be exchanged between the systems to execute their respective searches? What additional information must be passed to maintain parallel tasks such as truth maintenance, backtracking, and explanation?

An open problem that underlies many AI-DB Integration issues is the Object Boundary Problem, which involves identifying what objects (e.g., records) or components of an object must be accessed to resolve an object reference and complete the operations associated with the reference. Minimizing the portion of the information base accessed to resolve an object reference assists in integrity maintenance and in minimizing access conflicts to increase performance. Identifying the minimal object boundary is comparable in complexity to the subgraph and subexpression matching problems. The problem is more complex for complex AI objects [Figure 22(b)] than for currently simple DB objects [Figure 22(a)].

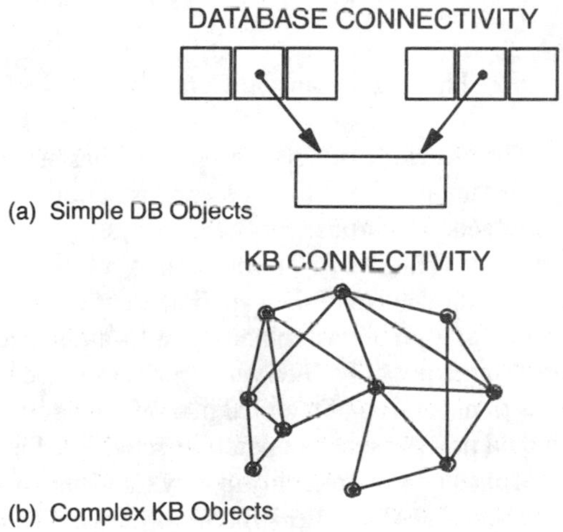

Figure 22. Object Boundary Problem

To illustrate the problem and some of its consequences, consider the concurrency control problem for complex objects. Conventional DB objects (e.g., entities) are simple in that they are logically related to very few other objects and are not composed of subobjects [Figure 22(a)] (i.e., have small object boundaries). Much DB technology is based on the assumption of simple objects. For example, logically related DB objects (i.e., objects and those in their boundaries) are grouped together for storage, caching, buffering, indexing, search, and data transfer between levels of memory on the assumption that they will be accessed together and cause few access conflicts. The simple object assumption is used in concurrency control as follows. Logically related objects are locked together to ensure that an update to one object occurs consistently across the related objects before other updates can access any object in the boundary. Small groups for simple objects mean that few concurrent updates will be blocked.

In contrast to simple DB objects, many AI objects, such as in semantic nets and frames, are complex or highly interrelated [Figure 22(b)]. Indeed, AI objects are often defined in terms of their relationships to many other objects. Sharing complex (AI) objects and making them persistent may lead, using traditional DB assumptions, to more difficult object boundary problems and to grouping and locking arbitrarily large portions of the KB. The groups may be so large, possibly major portions of the KB, that they defeat current DB transaction processing and related optimizations based on grouping. Complex object and related object boundary problems are open problems at the heart of many DB challenges [DEPP86] [LP83]. They arise in engineering and many areas in addition to AI [Prop 3]. Many DB assumptions must be loosened. DB theory and technology must be rethought to accommodate such changes. AI may be able to contribute solutions to these DB problems [Prop 3].

Approaches to AI-DB Integration

Two approaches to AI-DB Integration are the engineering approach and the deep synthesis approach. Deep synthesis attempts to develop sound frameworks on which to develop AI and DB technology. Frameworks include concepts for representation and systems, and related theories. Research problems related with deep synthesis are often difficult and have unpredictable progress. Such work is critical to ultimate success, as illustrated by successful frameworks such as the relational data model and first-order logic, and hoped-for frameworks for persistent programming languages and object-oriented systems.

The engineering approach attempts to couple AI and DB systems, provide DB capabilities in AI systems, and AI features in DB systems by actually building systems. Ideally, these systems can be generalized to develop effective AI-DB systems and to contribute to an AI-DB technology. The engineering approach helps to identify and prioritize difficult problems. Indeed, DB technology evolved following the engineering approach. Ten years of DBMS development and many early DBMSs were in existence before the term data model was defined and before DB research began in universities [BM88]. The engineering approach has been successful for heterogeneous, distributed DBs; distributed systems; and loosely coupled AI-DB systems. After five years in the engineering phase, Computer Aided Software Engineering (CASE) technology is becoming a topic for university research. Both engineering and deep synthesis approaches are required now [Prop 4].

6. AI-DB TECHNOLOGY FOR THE NEXT GENERATION OF COMPUTING

The next generation of computing will involve vast networks of highly intelligent, heterogeneous distributed agents which cooperate to optimally use the resources of all the agents in the network. The primary objective will be to transparently take advantage of any appropriate resource on any computer in the network. Just as new application requirements require fundamental changes to DBs, distributed cooperative work will have profound implications for changing much of computing.

Future computing will require the integration of many currently disjoint technologies, including AI, DB, programming languages, operating systems, heterogeneous distributed systems, and communications. In particular, AI technology will be required for special-purpose domains and for the complex problem of cooperation. DB technology will be required to manage and provide access to objects or resources wherever they are in the network, whether those objects are in DBs, KBs, or any other type of system. AI-DB technology will provide the basis for intelligent interoperability, which was introduced in Section 1 and is described in more detail below.

Currently, DBMSs manage distinct data repositories (i.e., DBs), which are provided as resources to client systems (e.g., DB applications). However, in support of future computing requirements, DB technology will be extended from management of data resources under DBMS control (i.e., a DB) to management of all types of shared resources, including data, knowledge, programs, or any software object of whatever size. Any object in any system in an attached network could, in principle, be shared. All objects that will be shared will form a large, distributed **Object Space** (OS).[15] The OS will be under the control of an **Object Space Management System** (OSMS).[16]

This future role of DB technology can be described as DBs without data. *DBs without data* refers to the notion that all objects in the OS do not reside in one repository under the control of the OSMS.[17] Objects can reside in the source system, which provides efficient, special-purpose techniques (e.g., control, data structures, methods). It may be too costly to translate and move objects to the OSMS.[18] Since an object's location will be transparent, the location (or locations for replicated objects as in [BENN87]) should be determined by requirements such as control and efficiency. A client system requiring OSMS services need not lose control of its objects. However, the extent to which it permits the OSMS access to its objects will determine the level of services to be provided. The level of control by the OSMS and many other properties (e.g., locations, authorization, formats, optimization hints) will be defined for each object when it is registered with the OSMS.

Intelligent interoperability will be a major objective of an OSMS. It is illustrated below in terms of the evolution of systems architectures and functions, which will depend heavily on AI-DB technology. Most computer systems are disjoint; they do not communicate [Figure 23(a)].[19] Those systems that are connected use *ad hoc* interfaces written for the particular connection [Figure 23(b)]. DBMSs are a major exception is this regard because they provide standard interfaces for communications with external systems.[20]

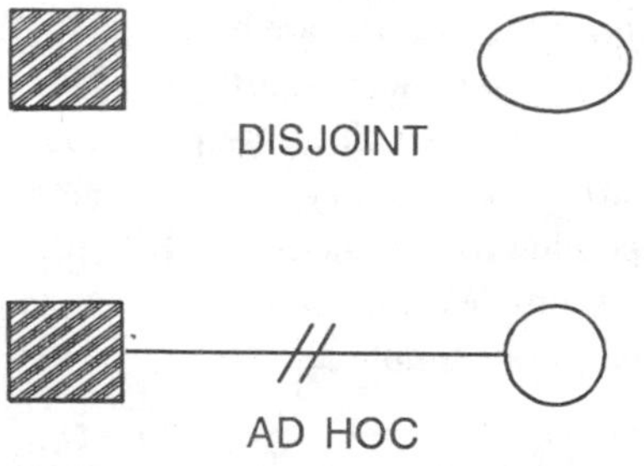

Figure 23. Current Connectivity

The onslaught of object orientation has brought with it an unsubstantiated hope that the encapsulation of systems will lead to general-purpose mechanisms (i.e., protocols) for interoperability [Figure 24]. The optimal use of such a connection requires knowledge of the capabilities of each system to provide the appropriate task planning, allocation, execution, monitoring, and, possibly, intervention between the systems. This leads to the notion of a global planner or resource agent which would provide such cooperation activities [Figure 25]. The global planner will work only in very small networks since its activity becomes a bottleneck for the (otherwise distributed) system. It may be required to be more intelligent and larger than any other component in the system.

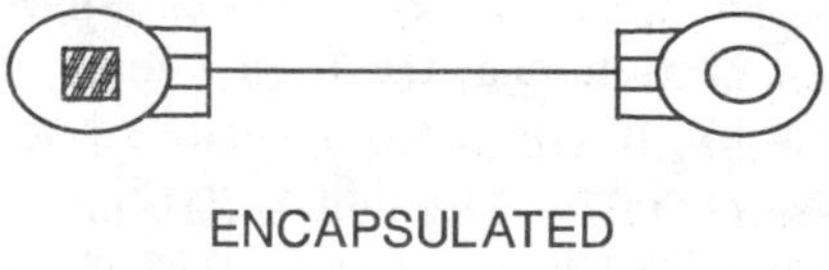

Figure 24. Object-Oriented Connectivity

---

[15]The term SPACE is intended to suggest objects anywhere in an n-dimensional space rather than residing in a single **base** as in a data**base**. The acronym OS suggests an affinity to operating system functions.

[16]Distributed Object Management (DOM) is also an appropriate term.

[17]Object-Oriented DBMS (OODBMSs) is a contradiction in terms and concepts. Objects are active (e.g., have methods) and take part in a particular context. OODBMSs attempt to extract objects from their native context, place them in a DB or object base, and treat them as passive.

[18]An objective here is to support long-term heterogeneity with facilities to integrate existing systems, as well as unanticipated future systems, into evolving OSs as transparently as possible. This is an extreme form of data and knowledge-representation independence.

[19]The differently shaped symbols in Figure 23 indicate that the two systems are heterogeneous (e.g., a DB system and a KBS).

[20]SQL, the standard DB interface language for relational DBMSs, is having a major impact on systems communication.

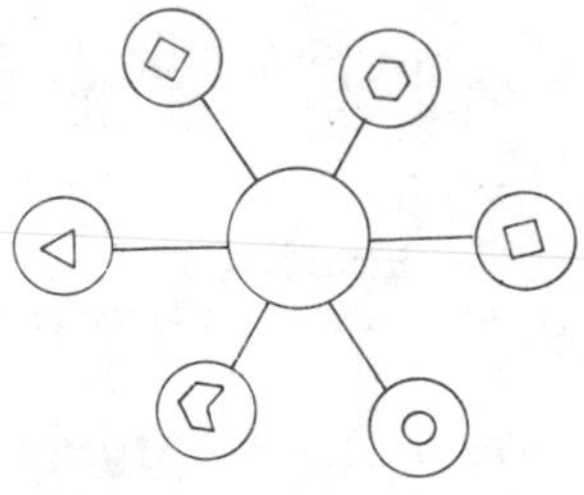

Figure 25. Global Planner

The final step toward intelligent interoperability is to distribute the functions of the global resource agent so that each system has its own resource agent[21] [Figure 26]. **Resource agents** will cooperate to acquire needed resources (i.e., to execute complex tasks). All resource agents, which themselves may be heterogeneous, will constitute the OSMS. Agents (i.e., computer systems in the network) would simply ask their resource agent for needed resources. This compares with the vision of intelligent interoperability illustrated in the hospital example in Section 1. The vision requires the extension of DB technology to general-purpose resource management and of AI technology to support distributed cooperative work. The vision is heavily dependent on AI-DB Integration.

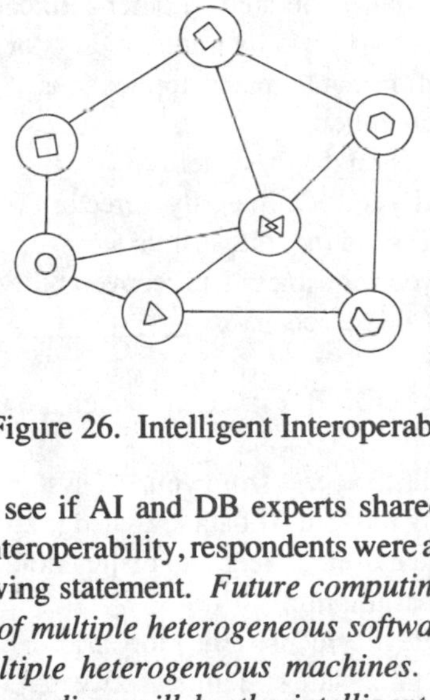

Figure 26. Intelligent Interoperability

To see if AI and DB experts shared this vision of intelligent interoperability, respondents were asked to respond to the following statement. *Future computing environments will consist of multiple heterogeneous software systems running on multiple heterogeneous machines. The dominant computing paradigm will be the intelligent cooperation of systems to execute tasks. This will be based on "intelligent interoperability," the ability to interconnect and share resources (e.g., functionality, objects) between arbitrary systems in ways unanticipated when the resources were created.*

Almost all respondents (90%) feel that intelligent interoperability is desirable, with a very strong mean agreement (8.2) [Figure 27]. Of the respondents, 80% agree that intelligent interoperability will be the computing paradigm of the future, with a moderately strong mean agreement (6.8). While only 71% desire intelligent interoperability in their current system, 80% desire it in systems they are planning. Of the respondents, 80% feel that AI-DB Integration is required for intelligent interoperability. On average, respondents felt that intelligent interoperability would be a practical reality in 7.6 years.

[21]Alternatively, Distributed Object Manager.

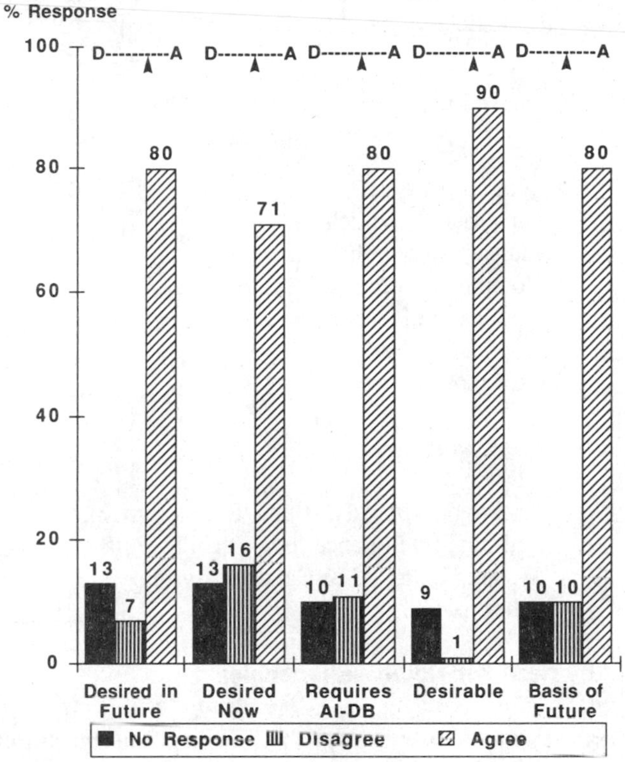

Figure 27. Intelligent Interoperability

The vision of the next generation of computing and the goal of intelligent interoperability are shared by almost all AI and DB experts. The vision expressed in this paper is simply a restatement, in current terminology, of the vision of AI and DB pioneers. The difference between 1958 and 1988 is that we are much closer to realizing the vision. It is easy to imagine potential benefits in simple extrapolations of existing systems. It is hard to imagine the benefits or nature of computing that will result from the paradigm shift to distributed cooperative work. As comparatively simple as they may be, intelligent DBMSs and ISs, and KBSs that can access information bases, are yet to be achieved. Solving these AI-DB Integration problems now will provide contributions toward The Next Generation of Computing.

7. REFERENCES

References cited in this paper are included in the bibliography of this book.

ACKNOWLEDGMENTS

I am grateful to Pam Talbourdet, Craig Yee, and Vivek Virmani for their assistance in conducting and analyzing the survey and to the more than 400 AI and DB researchers and practitioners who took the time to respond to the survey. I thank Frank Manola for his ideas and discussions concerning the content of the paper and Reid Smith for inviting me to discuss this topic at AAAI '88.

Appendix A: AI-DB Survey Questions

Check all your work type(s)

____ University Research
____ Industry Research
____ Commercial Product Development
____ Application Development
____ Application Use
____ Other (please specify): ____________

Check all your work area(s)

____ DBMSs
____ Knowledge-Based Systems/Expert Systems
____ Artificial Intelligence (other than KBSs/ESs)
____ Systems Using AI or Database Systems
____ Other (please specify): ____________

1. AI's Need For Database Technology

Note: (0-9) is a scale used to express gradation of (dis)agreement
0-2 = Disagree
3-6 = Slightly Disagree to Slightly Agree
7-9 = Agree

Database technology is (please enter number)

____(0-9) Critical for practical knowledge-based systems
____(0-9) Critical for practical AI systems (other than KBSs)
____(0-9) Applicable to your current AI work/project/system
____(0-9) Being applied in your current AI work/project/system

If each answer above is less than 3, go to Section 2 (next page).

1.1. Database/File System Access for Your AI System

Database/file system access is

____(0-9) Desirable
____(0-9) Critical

If each answer above is less than 3, go to Section 1.2

Check all desired couplings to databases

____ Loose (access to external databases)
____ Tight (database internal to your AI system)

Check estimated size of most important database/file

____ Small: < 50 MB
____ Medium: 50 to 500 MB
____ Large: >500 MB

Number of databases/files to be accessed (please enter number)

____ You have [*example*, 2]
____ You plan to have [*ex*, 3]

Name of DBMS or file system being/to be used (please enter name)

____________ You use [*ex*, ISAM]
____________ You plan to use [*ex*, DB2, Ingres, Oracle]

Database/file system access (estimated) requirement

____ Number of records accessed per AI system use [*ex*, 1000]
____ Access type: Read, Write, Read & Write [*ex*, R & W]

Check all object types to be stored in your data/knowledge-base

____ Database records
____ Frames, units, rules, etc.
____ Source or compiled code
____ Other (please specify): ____________

1.2. Database Functionality for Your AI System

Check all features desired for your knowledge base

____ Persistence of AI data/knowledge structures
____ Queries
____ Access data generated by other applications
____ Concurrent access by multiple users or applications
____ Reuse for unanticipated applications
____ Reorganization
____ Daemons on database items
____ Control: security, integrity, directory
____ Optimization (access, search, storage, etc.)
____ Improved robustness and recoverability
____ Other (please specify): ____________

Check all current DBMS restrictions which are unacceptable for your AI system

____ Difficult to access from your AI system
____ Inability to store AI data/knowledge structures
____ Inadequate search (e.g., no disjunction, closed world assumption)
____ Data integrity/consistency too strict
____ Need to translate structures between AI and DB systems
____ Other (please specify): ____________

2. Database's Need for AI Technology

AI technology is

____(0-9) Critical for enhancing database technology
____(0-9) Applicable to your current database work
____(0-9) Being applied in your current database work

If each answer above is less than 3, go to Section 3

2.1. AI Systems Access for Your Database Application

AI system access is
____(0-9) Desirable
____(0-9) Critical
If each answer above is less than 3, go to Section 2.2.

Check all AI system types desired to be accessed
____ Knowledge-based/expert system
____ User interface system (e.g., natural language)
____ Other (please specify): ____________________

2.2. AI Functionality/Techniques for Your Database System.

Check all AI features desired in your database system
____ Knowledge representation
____ AI search/reasoning techniques (e.g., heuristic, non-exhaustive)
____ Natural language/user interfaces
____ Theorem proving
____ Others (please specify): ____________________

3. AI-Database Integration Progress and Challenges

Most important progress to date has been (please specify)
[*ex*, Natural language interface to databases]
1. ____________________
2. ____________________
3. ____________________

Most important short-term challenge(s) (please specify)
[*ex*, Loose coupling between Expert System Shells and Databases]
1. ____________________
2. ____________________
3. ____________________

Most important long-term challenge(s) (please specify)
[*ex*, Knowledge base management]
1. ____________________
2. ____________________
3. ____________________

Problem domains in which AI-Database Integration is important (please specify)

Major AI Feature for Database System or Domain
Major Database Feature for AI System

[*ex*, AI Systems in Engineering] [*ex*, access to engineering data]
1. ____________________ ____________________
2. ____________________ ____________________
3. ____________________ ____________________

Current status
____(0-9) AI-Database requirements are known in your problem domain
____(0-9) Current AI-Database Integration practice is adequate for your needs

Please give information about your AI-DB project(s)/product(s)
1. Project/Product Name: ____________________
Application domain: ____________________
Effort in person years: 1986: __ 1988: __ 1990: __
Main Database Feature(s)(See 1.2): ____________________
Main AI Feature(s)(See 2.2): ____________________

2. Project/Product Name: ____________________
Application domain: ____________________
Effort in person years: 1986: __ 1988: __ 1990: __
Main Database Feature(s)(See 1.2): ____________________
Main AI Feature(s)(See 2.2): ____________________

4. Need for Interoperability

Please respond below to the following statement:

Future computing environments will consist of multiple heterogeneous software systems running on multiple heterogeneous machines. The dominant computing paradigm will be the intelligent cooperation of systems to execute tasks. This will be based on "intelligent interoperability," the ability to interconnect and share resources (e.g., functionality, objects) between arbitrary systems in ways unanticipated when resources are created.

____(0-9) Most future computing will be as described above.
____(0-9) Interoperability is desirable.
____(0-9) AI-Database Integration is critical for interoperability.
____(0-9) Your system requires integration with/access to other systems.
____(0-9) Interoperability is desired for your current systems.
____(0-9) Interoperability is desirable for systems you are planning.
____ How many years to the availability of practical interoperability? [*ex*, 10]

5. Other Comments: (e.g., Relevant thoughts not captured by this questionnaire)

Personal Statement: Computer Science and Concern for Our Planet

Michael L. Brodie

This message comes from my heart, from my spirit. Please consider with me some challenging questions for which I have no clear answers but which provide a source of creativity and inspiration in my professional and personal life:

- What kind of world are we creating with computers?
- What kind of world do you want to live in?
- How can you use computers, amongst other things, to create that world?
- Are you doing those things now? Or, at least, is your work consistent with your desired world view?
- Whatever you are doing with computers, you are changing our world. Is it for the better?*

Computers provide an enormous power on our planet. Moment by moment their power affects and influences you, me, nations, the world economy; and their power and influence will continue to grow enormously. Like all potent powers, computers can be used in many ways. As computer scientists, we play a key role in directing the future use of that power.

Computer scientists often accept jobs or funding to achieve tasks without considering whether these jobs or tasks are in keeping with their desired world view. At least, it is difficult for me to imagine that they want their children to live in the world that could result from their work. Such inattention to values and goals leads to monsters, waste of minds, waste of money, or just plain poor computer systems.

There are also computer scientists and detractors of computer science whose world views exclude many or even all applications of computers. Such myopia can prevent the *positive* deployment of the amazing power of computers. Computer scientists with this positive attitude may be unable to obtain funding for creative, positive applications of computers.

Where do *you* fall in this spectrum of concern for the effects of your work? What kind of world are *you* creating? Do you feel good about *your* work?

Over the past few years I have grown a great deal professionally and personally—in part, by considering these issues. My goal is to align my intellectual, spiritual, and physical beings. I want everything I do, without exception, to contribute to a world that I want to live in. Such a vision has provided me clear direction concerning what I want to do with computers and what I refuse to do

* A joyful, genuine expression of concern for these issues came from 2,500 computer scientists at the 1988 AAAI Conference who spontaneously applauded for one minute after these questions were posed.

with computers. A major consequence of the process is dramatic freedom of thought, inspiration, and creativity. I am more creative now than I have ever been before in my life. I'm having a blast!

I simply want to encourage you to align your mind, spirit, and body—to consider vigilantly how your work contributes to improving the world for all beings, to find the strength to refuse tasks that do not contribute to your world view, and to delight in the creativity that will come from this alignment. Each of us is capable of these things and much more! Our work in computer science is as important in its way as that of Mother Teresa. Let us strive to make our work worthy of such a comparison.

Michael L. Brodie, September 1988

Bibliography

[AB87] Altman, R.B. and B.G. Buchanan, "Partial Compilation of Strategic Knowledge," *Proc. Sixth National Conference on Artificial Intelligence,* Seattle, 1987, Morgan Kaufmann, 399–404.

[AB87a] Atkinson, M.P. and O. Peter Buneman, "Types and Persistence in Database Programming Languages," *ACM Computing Surveys 19,* No. 2, June 1987.

[ABCE76] Astrahan, M.M., M.W. Blasgen, D.D. Chamberlin, K.P. Eswaren, J.N. Gray, P.P. Griffiths, W.F. King, R.A. Lorie, P.R. McJones, J.W. Mehl, G.R. Putzolu, I.L. Traiger, B.W. Wade and V. Watson, "System R: Relational Approach to Database Management," *ACM Transactions on Database Systems 1,* 1976, 97–137.

[ABG84] Attar, R., P.A. Bernstein, and N. Goodman. "Site Initialization, Recovery, and Backup in a Distributed Database System," *IEEE Transactions on Software Engineering SE-10,* No. 6, November 1984, 645–650.

[ABM88] Atkinson M.P., O. Peter Buneman and R. Morrison (eds.), *Data Types and Persistence,* Springer-Verlag, New York, 1988.

[ABRI74] Abrial, J.R., "Data Semantics," in *Data Management Systems,* J.W. Klimbie and K.L. Koffeman (eds.), North Holland, 1974.

[AC86] Ariav, G. and J. Clifford (eds.), *New Directions for Database Systems,* Ablex, New York, 1986.

[ACO85] Albano, A., L. Cardelli and R. Orsini, "Galileo: A Strongly Typed, Interactive Conceptual Language," *ACM Transactions on Database Systems 10,* No. 2, March 1985.

[ADD85] Albano, A., V. Di Antonellis and A. Di Leva, *Computer-Aided Database Design: The DATAID Project,* North-Holland, 1985.

[AF83] Allen, J.F. and J.M. Frisch, "Knowledge Retrieval as Limited Inference," *Proc. Sixth Conference on Automated Deduction,* D.W. Loveland (ed.), *Lecture Notes in Computer Science,* Springer-Verlag, New York, 1982.

[AGHA86] Agha, G.A., *ACTORS: A Model of Concurrent Computation in Distributed Systems,* MIT Press, Cambridge MA, 1986.

[AGO88] Albano, A., G. Ghelli and R. Orsini, "The Implementation of Galileo's Persistent Values," in [ABM88], 253–264.

[AGRA87] Agrawal, R. "Alpha: An Extension of Relational Algebra to Express a Class of Recursive Queries," *Proc. IEEE Conference on Data Engineering,* Los Angeles, 1987.

[ALBA85] Albano, A., "Conceptual Languages: A Comparison of ADAPLEX, GALILEO, and Taxis," *Proc. International Workshop on Knowledge Base Management Principles,* Chania, 1985, 343–356; also in [ST88].

[ALLE83] Allen, J. "Maintaining Knowledge About Temporal Intervals," *Communications of the ACM 26,* No. 11, November 1983, 832–843.

[AN74] Artraud, A. and Nicolas, J.-M., "An Experimental Query System: SYNTEX," *Proc. International Computing Symposium,* Elsevier North-Holland, New York, 1974, 557–563.

[ANDE86] Anderson, T., E.F. Ecklund, Jr. and D. Maier, "PROTEUS: Objectifying the DBMS User Interface," in [DD86].

[ANSI75] ANSI/X3/SPARC, "Study Group on DBMS Interim Report," *SIGMOD FDT Bulletin. 7,* No. 2, 1975.

[ARMS74] Armstrong, W.W., "Dependency Structures of Database Relationships," *Proc. IFIP World Congress,* Elsevier North-Holland, New York, 1974, 580–583.

[AS68] Ash, W.L. and E.H. Sibley, "TRAMP: An Interpretive Associative Processor," *Proc. Twenty-Third ACM National Computer Conference,* Princeton, 1968.

[ASU79] Aho, A.V., Sagiv, Y. and Ullman, J.D., "Equivalences among Relational Expressions," *SIAM Journal of Computing 8,* No. 2, May 1979, 218–246.

[ASW87] Ayuso, D.B., V. Shaked, and R.M. Weischedel, "An Environment for Acquiring Semantic Information," *Proc. of the ACL Annual Conference,* Palo Alto, CA, 1987, 32–40.

[ATKI83] Atkinson, M.P., P.J. Bailey, W.P. Cockshott, K.J. Chisholm and R. Morisson, "An Approach to Persistent Programming," *Computer Journal 26,* No. 4, 1983, 360–365.

[AU79] Aho, A. and J. Ullman, "On the Universality of Data Retrieval Languages," *Proc. Sixth ACM Symposium on Principles of Programming Languages,* January 1979, 110–117.

[BACH73] Bachman, C.W., "The Programmer As Navigator," *Communications of the ACM 16,* No. 11, November 1973, 653–658.

[BACK78] Backus, J., "Can Programming be Liberated from the von Neumann Style? A Functional Style and Its Algebra of Programs," *Communications of the ACM 21,* No. 8, August 1978. (*Note:* This is the 1978 Turing award lecture.)

[BADA79] Badal, D. "Correctness of Concurrency Control and Implications in Distributed Databases," *Proc. COMPSAC-79 Conference,* Chicago, November 1979.

[BALZ80] Balzer, R., L. Erman, P. London and C. Williams, "HEARSAY-III: A Domain-Independent Framework for Expert Systems," *Proc. National Conference on Artificial Intelligence,* August 1980.

[BANC78] Bancilhon, F., "On the Completeness of Query Languages for Relational Database," *Proc. Seventh Symposium on Mathematical Foundations of Computer Science,* Springer-Verlag, Berlin and New York, 1978, 112–123.

[BANC86] Bancilhon, F. "Naive Evaluation of Recursively Defined Relations," in [BM86].

[BARR81] Barron, J., "Dialog and Process Design for Interactive Information Systems Using Taxis," *Proc. ACM SIGOA Conference on Office Information Systems,* Philadelphia, 1982, 12–20.

[BB79] Beeri, C. and P.A. Bernstein. "Computational Problems Related to the Design of Normal Form Schemas," *ACM TODS 4,* No. 1, March 1979.

[BB83] Bates, M. and R. Bobrow, "A Transportable Natural Language Interface for Information Retrieval," *Proc. Sixth International ACM SIGIR Conference,* 1983.

[BB84] Batory, D.S. and A.P. Buchmann. "Molecular Objects, Abstract Data Types and Data Models: A Framework," *Proc. Tenth International Conference on Very Large Databases,* 1984.

[BBC80] Bernstein, P., B. Blaustein, and E. Clarke, "Fast Maintenance of Integrity Assertions Using Redundant Aggregate Data," *Proc. Sixth International Conference on Very Large Databases,* October 1980.

[BBDM84] Brodie, M.L., B.T. Blaustein, U. Dayal, F.A. Manola and A.S. "CAD/CAM Database Management," *IEEE Database Engineering Newsletter,* R. Katz (ed.), *Special Issue on Engineering Data Management,* 1984.

[BBG78] Beeri, C., P.A. Bernstein, and N. Goodman, "A Sophisticate's Introduction to Database Normalization Theory," *Proc. 4th International Conference on Very Large Data Bases,* 1978.

[BBGS86] Batory, D.S., J.R. Barnett, J.F. Garza, K.P. Smith, K. Tsukuda, B.C. Twichell and T.E. Wise, "GENESIS: An Extensible Database Management System," *IEEE Transactions on Software Engineering,* (to appear); also technical report 86-07, Department of Computer Science, University of Texas at Austin, 1986.

[BBLM88] Brodie, M.L., D. Bobrow, V. Lesser, S. Madnick and D.C. Tsichritzis, "Future Artificial Intelligence Requirements For Database Systems," in [KERS88].

[BC75] Bobrow, D.B. and A. Collins (eds.), *Representation and Understanding,* Academic Press, New York, 1975.

[BC79] Buneman, O.P. and E.K. Clemons, "Efficiently Monitoring Relational Databases," *ACM Transactions on Database Systems 4,* No. 3, September 1979, 368–382.

[BDD84] Batini, C., V. De Antonellis and A. Di Leva. "Database Design Activities Within the DATAID Project," *IEEE Database Engineering 7,* No. 4, December 1984.

[BDM88] Bry, F., H. Decker and R. Mantley, "A Uniform Approach to Constraint Satisfaction in Deductive Databases," *Proc. International Conference on Extending Database Technologies,* Venice, March 1988.

[BEER88] Beeri, C. (ed.), *Proc. Third International Conference on Data and Knowledge Bases,* Israel, 1988.

[BENN87] Bennett, J.K., "The Design and Implementation of Distributed Smalltalk," in [MEYR87].

[BENT75] Bentley J.L. "Multidimensional Binary Search Trees Used for Associative Searching," *Communications of the ACM 18,* No. 9, 1975, 509–517.

[BENT80] Bentley, J.L. "Multidimensional Divide-and-Conquer," *Communications of the ACM 23,* No. 4, 1980, 214–229.

[BERN76] Bernstein, Philip A., "Synthesizing Third Normal Form Relations from Functional Dependencies," *ACM Transactions On Database Systems 1,* No. 4, December 1976.

[BF79] Bentley, J.L. and J.H. Friedman, "Data Structures for Range Searching," *ACM Computing Surveys 11,* No. 4, 1979, 397–410.

[BF81] Barr, A. and E. Feigenbaum (eds.), *Handbook of Artificial Intelligence,* William Kaufmann, Los Altos, 1981.

[BFL83] Brachman, R.J., R.E. Fikes and H.J. Levesque, "KRYPTON: A Functional Approach to Knowledge Representation," *IEEE Computer 16,* No. 10, 1983, 67–73.

[BFN82] Buneman, O.P., R.E. Frankel and R. Nikhil, "An Implementation Technique for Database Query Languages," *ACM Transactions on Database Systems 7,* No. 2, June 1982.

[BG81] Bernstein, P.A. and N. Goodman. "Concurrency Control in Distributed Database System," *ACM Computing Surveys 13,* No. 2, June 1981, 185–221.

[BG84] Boral, H. and I. Gold, "Towards a Self-Adapting Centralized Concurrency Control," *Proc. ACM SIGMOD International Conference on Management of Data,* 1984.

[BGM85] Borgida, A., S. Greenspan and J. Mylopoulos, "Knowledge Representation as the Basis for Requirements Specification," *IEEE Computer 18,* No. 4, 1985, 82–91.

[BGM85a] Bouzeghoub, M., G. Gardarin, E. Metais, "Database Design Tools: An Expert System Approach," *Proc. International Conference on Very Large Databases,* Stockholm, 1985.

[BGM86] Borgida, A., S. Greenspan and J. Mylopoulos, "A Requirements Modelling Language and Its Logic," in [BM86], 471–502.

[BGN84] Balzer, R., N. Goldman and R. Neches, "Specification-based Computing Environments for Information Management," *Proc. IEEE International Conference on Data Engineering,* Los Angeles, 1984, 454–458.

[BH80] Ball, E. and P. Hayes. "Representation of Task-Specific Knowledge in a Gracefully Interacting User Interface," *Proc. National Conference on Artificial Intelligence,* August 1980.

[BHAR82] Bhargava, B., "Resiliency Features of the Optimistic Concurrency Control Approach for Distributed Database Systems," *Proc. Second Symposium on Reliability in Distributed Software and Database Systems,* Pittsburgh, July 1982.

[BHG87] Bernstein, P.A., V. Hatzilakos and N. Goodman, *Concurrency Control and Recovery in Database Systems,* Addison-Wesley, Reading, MA, 1987.

[BJ86] Brodie, M.L. and M. Jarke, "On Integrating Logic Programming and Databases," in [KERS86].

[BJMS87] Borgida, A., M. Jarke, J. Mylopoulos, J.W. Schmidt and Y. Vassiliou, "The Software Development Process as a Knowledge Base Management Systems," *Proc. CIPS National Computer Conference,* Edmonton, November 1987.

[BK82] Bowen, K.A. and Kowalski, R.A., "Amalgamating Language and Metalanguage in Logic Programming," in *Logic Programming,* K.L. Clark and S.A. Tarnlund, (Eds.) Academic Press, New York, 1982, 153–172.

[BK85] Batory, D.S. and W. Kim. "Modeling Concepts for VLSI CAD Objects," *ACM Transactions on Database Systems 10,* No. 3, 1985.

[BKNT77] Bobrow, D.G., R.M. Kaplan, D.A. Norman, H. Thompson, and T. Winograd, "GUS, A Frame-Driven Dialog System," *Artificial Intelligence 8,* 1977, 155–173.

[BL85] Brachman, R. and H. Levesque, *Readings in Knowledge Representation,* Morgan Kaufmann, Los Altos, 1985.

[BL86] Brachman, R.J., H.J. Levesque, "What Makes a Knowledge Base Knowledgeable? A View of Databases from the Knowledge Level," in [KERS86], 69–78.

[BL86a] Brachman, R. and H. Levesque, "The Knowledge Level of KBMSs," in [BM86].

[BLAC64] Black, F.S., *A Deductive Question-Answering System,* Ph.D. dissertation, Harvard University, Division of Engineering and Applied Physics, Cambridge, MA, 1964.

[BLAS80] Blaser, A. (ed.), *Database Techniques for Pictorial Applications,* Springer-Verlag, New York, 1980.

[BLAU81] Blaustein, B.T., "Enforcing Database Assertions: Techniques and Applications," Ph.D. dissertation, Computer Science Department, Harvard University, Cambridge, MA, August 1981.

[BLNS82] Birrell, A.D., R. Levin, R.M. Needham, and M.D. Schroeder. "Grapevine: An Exercise in Distributed Computing," *Communications of the ACM 25,* No. 4, April 1982, 260–274.

[BM72] Bayer, R. and E. McCreight, "Organization and Maintenance of Large Ordered Indexes," *Acta Informatica 1, No. 3, (1972),* 173–189.

[BM80] Bentley, J.L. and H.A. Maurer, "Efficient Worst-Case Data Structures for Range Searching." *Acta Informatica 13,* 1980, 155–168.

[BM84] Bachant, J. and J. McDermott, "R1 Revisited: Four Years in the Trenches," *AI Magazine,* Vol. 5, No. 3, 1984.

[BM86] Brodie, M. and J. Mylopoulos, *On Knowledge Base Management Systems: Integrating Artificial Intelligence and Database Technologies,* Springer-Verlag, New York, 1986. (*Note:* This volume includes the proceedings of the Islamorada workshop held in February 1985 in Islamorada, FL.)

[BM86a] Brodie, M.L. and J. Mylopoulos, "Knowledge Bases and Databases: Semantic vs. Computational Theories of Information," in [AC86].

[BM88] Brodie, M.L. and F. Manola, "Database Management: A Survey," in [MB88] and [ST88].

[BMS84] Brodie, M.L., J. Mylopoulos and J.W. Schmidt (eds.). *On Conceptual Modelling: Perspectives from Artificial Intelligence, Databases, and Programming Languages,* Springer-Verlag, New York, 1984. (*Note:* This volumes includes the proceedings of the Intervale workshop held in June 1983 in Intervale, NH.)

[BMS86] Bates, M., M. Moser, and D. Stallard, "The IRUS Transportable Natural Language Database Interface," in [KERS86].

[BMW84] Borgida, A., J. Mylopoulos and H.K.T. Wong, "Generalization/Specialization as a Basis for Software Specification," in [BMS84].

[BN78] Biller, H. and E. Neuhold, "Semantics of Databases: The Semantics of Data Models," *Information Systems 3,* 1978, 11–30.

[BOBR86] Bobrow, D.B., K. Kahn, G. Kiszales, L. Masinter, M. Stefik and F. Zdybel, "COMMONLOOPS: Merging Lisp and Object-Oriented Programming," in [DD86].

[BOCC86] Bocca, J., "On the Evaluation Strategy of EDUCE," *Proc. 1986 SIGMOD Int'l Conference on Management of Data,* Washington, D.C., May 1986.

[BORG85] Borgida, A. "Flexible Mechanisms for Handling Exceptions in Information Systems," *ACM Transactions on Database Systems 10,* No. 4, 1985, 565–603.

[BORG85a] Borgida, A., "Features of Languages for the Development of Information Systems at the Conceptual Level," *IEEE Software 2,* No. 1, January 1985, 63–73.

[BORN81] Borning, A., "The Programming Language Aspects of Thinglab, a Constraint-Oriented Simulation Laboratory," *ACM Transactions on Programming Languages and Systems 3,* No. 4, 1981, 353–387.

[BPL85] Brachman, R., V. Pigman-Gilbert and H. Levesque, "An Essential Hybrid Reasoning System: Knowledge and Symbol Level Accounts of KRYPTON," *Proc. IJCAI-85,* Los Angeles, 1985, 532–539.

[BPP76] Bracchi, G., P. Paolini and G. Pelagatti, "Binary Logical Associations in Data Modelling," *Proc. IFIP TC-2 Working Conference,* Black Forest, 1976.

[BR84] Brodie, M.L. and D. Ridjanovic, "On the Design and Specification of Database Transactions," in [BMS84].

[BR86] Bancilhon, F. and R. Ramakrishnan, "An Amateur's Introduction to Recursive Query Processing," *Proc. ACM SIGMOD International Conference on Management of Data,* Washington, D.C., May 1986.

[BRAC79] Brachman, R.J., "On the Epistemological Status of Semantic Networks," in [FIND79].

[BROD80a] Brodie, M.L., "The Application of Data Types to Database Semantic Integrity," *Information Systems 5,* No. 4, 1980.

[BROD80b] Brodie, M.L. "Data Abstraction, Databases, and Conceptual Modeling," *Proc. Sixth International Conference on Very Large Databases,* Montreal, Canada, October 1980.

[BROD84] Brodie, M.L., "On the Development of Data Models," in [BMS84].

[BROD86] Brodie, M.L., "Knowledge Base Management Systems: Discussions from the Working Group," in [KERS86].

[BROD88] Brodie, M.L., "Future Intelligent Information Systems: AI and Database Technologies Working Together," in [MB88].

[BROW85] Brown, G.P., et al., "Program Visualization: Graphical Support for Software Development," *IEEE Computer 18,* No. 8, August 1985.

[BS84] Buchanan, B.G. and E.H. Shortliffe, *Rule-Based Expert Systems: The Mycin Experiments of the Stanford Heuristic Programming Project,* Addison-Wesley, Reading, MA, Series in Artificial Intelligence, 1984.

[BS85] Brachman, R. and J. Schmolze, "An Overview of the KL-ONE Knowledge Representation System," *Cognitive Science 9,* 1985.

[BS86] Ballard, B.W. and D.E. Stumberger, "Semantic Acquisition in TELI: A Transportable, User-Customized Natural Language Processor," *Proc. ACL Annual Conference,* 1986, 20–29.

[BSR80] Bernstein, P., D.W. Shipman, and J.B. Rothnie, Jr., "Concurrency Control in a System for Distributed Databases (SDD-1)," *ACM Transactions On Database Systems 5,* No. 1, March 1980.

[BUBE80] Bubenko, J., "Information Modelling in the Context of System Development," *Proc. IFIP World Congress,* 1980, 395–411.

[BURK83] Burkard, W.A., "Interpolation-Based Index Maintenance," *Proc. Second ACM SIGACT-SIGMOD Symposium on Principles of Database Systems,* 1983, 76–89.

[BUSH45] Bush, V., "As We May Think," *Atlantic Monthly 176,* No. 1, July 1945, 101–108.

[BUTL87] Butler, M.H. "Storage Reclamation in Object Oriented Database Systems," *Proc. ACM SIGMOD International Conference on Management of Data,* 1987.

[BW77] Bobrow, D.G. and T. Winograd, "An Overview of KRL, a Knowledge Representation Language," *Cognitive Science 1,* No. 1, 1977, 3–46.

[BW81] Borgida, A. and Wong, H.K.T., "Data Models and Data Manipulation Languages: Complementary Semantics and Proof Theory," *Proc. Seventh Conference on Very Large Databases,* Cannes, France, September 1981, 260–271.

[BZ81] Brodie, M.L. and S.N. Zilles, (eds.), *Proc. Workshop on Data Abstraction, Databases and Conceptual Modelling,* Joint Special Issue of *SIGPLAN Notices, SIGMOD Record,* and *SIGART Newsletter,* January 1981.

[CA84] Casanova, M. and J. Amarel de Sa, "Mapping Uninterpreted Schemes into Entity-Relationship Diagrams: Two Applications to Conceptual Schema Design," *IBM Journal of Research and Development 28,* No. 1, January 1984, 82–94.

[CABG81] Chamberlin, D.D., M.M. Astrahan, M.W. Blasgen, J.N. Gray, W.F. King, B.G. Lindsay, R. Lorie, J.W. Mehl, T.G. Price, F. Putzolu, P.G. Selinger, M. Schkolnick, D.R. Slutz, I.L. Traiger, B.W. Wade and R.A. Yost, "A History and Evaluation of System R," *Communications of the ACM 24,* No. 10, October 1981, 632–646.

[CACC78] Codd, E.F., R.S. Arnold, J.M. Cadiou, C.L. Chang and N. Roussopoulos,

"Rendezvous Version I: An Experimental English-Language Query Formulation System for Casual Users of Relational Databases," Research Report RJ2144, IBM Research Lab, San Jose, CA, January 1978.

[CALZ84] Calzolari, N., "Machine-Readable Dictionaries, Lexical Database and the Lexical System," *Proc. of Annual COLING Conference,* 1984.

[CB79] Casanova, M.A. and Bernstein, P.A., "The Logic of A Relational Data Manipulation Language," *Proc. Sixth ACM Symposium on Principles of Programming Languages,* San Antonio, TX, January 1979, 101–109.

[CB85] Chodorow M.S. and R. Byrd, "Extracting Semantic Hierarchies from a Large On-Line Dictionary," *Proc. ACL National Conference,* 1985, 299–304.

[CBMA83] Carbonell, J.G., W.M. Boggs, M.L. Mauldin and P.G. Anick, "The XCALIBUR Project, A Natural Language Interface to Expert Systems," *Proc. Eighth International Joint Conference on Artificial Intelligence,* Karlsruhe, 1983, 653–656.

[CCF82] deCastilho, J.M.V., M.A. Casanova and A.L. Furtado, "A Temporal Framework for Database Specifications," *Proc. Eighth International Conference on Very Large Databases,* 1982, 280–291.

[CD85] Chou, H.T. and D.J. DeWitt, "An Evaluation of Buffer Management Strategies for Relational Database," *Proc. International Conference on Very Large Databases,* Stockholm, August 1985, 127–141.

[CDFG83] Chan, A., U. Dayal, S. Fox, N. Goodman, D. Ries and D. Skeen, "Overview of an Ada Compatible Distributed Database Manager," *Proc. ACM SIGMOD International Conference on Management of Data,* San Jose, CA, May 1983.

[CDFG86] Carey, M.J., D.J. DeWitt, D. Frank, G. Graefe, M. Muralikrishna, J.E. Richardson and E.J. Shekita, "The Architecture of the EXODUS Extensible DBMS," in [DD86], 52–65.

[CDFL82] Chan, A., S. Danberg, S. Fox, W.K. Lin, A. Nori and D. Ries, "Storage and Access Structures to Support a Semantic Data Model," *Proc. International Conference on Very Large Databases,* Mexico City, Mexico, September 1982.

[CDH85] Chan, A., U. Dayal and M. Hsu, "Providing Database Management Capabilities for Mission Critical Applications," *Proc. International Workshop on High-Performance Transaction Systems,* Pacific Grove, CA, September 1985.

[CERI83] Ceri, S. (ed.), *Methodology and Tools for Database Design,* North-Holland, 1983.

[CEST86] Carbonell, J.G., D.A. Evans, D.S. Scott and R.H. Thomason, "On the Design of Biomedical Knowledge Bases," *Proc. Fifth Conference on Medical Informatics,* R. Salamon, B. Blum and M. Jorgensen (eds.), Elseview Science Pub., Washington D.C., 1986, 37–41.

[CF81] Chang, N.S. and K.S. Fu, "Picture Query Languages for Pictorial Database Systems," in [CHAN81], 23–33.

[CFM86] Chakravarthy, U.S., D.H. Fishman and J. Minker, "Semantic Query Optimization in Expert Systems and Database Systems," in [KERS86].

[CG85] Chan, T.A. and R. Gray, "Implementing Distributed Read-Only Transactions," *IEEE Transactions on Software Engineering SE-11,* No. 2, February 1985, 205–212.

[CH80] Chandra, A.K. and Harel, D., "Structure and Complexity of Relational Queries," *Proc. Twenty-First IEEE Symposium on Foundations of Computer Science,* Syracuse, October 1980, 333–347. Also in *Journal of Computing and Systems Science 25,* No. 1, August 1982, 99–128.

[CH82] Chandra, A. and D. Harel, "Horn Clause Queries and Generalization," *Proc. ACM SIGACT-SIGMOD Symposium on Principles of Database Systems Conference,* 1982.

[CHAM76] Chamberlin, D.D., "Relational Database Management Systems," in [SIBL76].

[CHAN70] Chang, C.L., "The Unit Proof and the Input Proof in Theorem Proving," *Journal of the ACM 17,* No. 4, October 1970, 698–707.

[CHAN77] Chang, S.K., et al., "A Relational Database System for Pictures," *Proc. IEEE Workshop on Picture Data Description Data and Management,* 1977.

[CHAN78] Chang, C.L., "DEDUCE 2: Further Investigations of Deduction in Relational Data Bases," in [GM78].

[CHAN81] Chang, C.L., "On Evaluation of Queries Containing Derived Relations in a Relational Database," in [GMN81], 235–260.

[CHAN81a] Chang, S.K. (ed.), *Pictorial Information Systems,* Special Issue, *IEEE Computer 14,* No. 11, 1981.

[CHEH81] Cheheyl, M.H., et.al., "Verifying Security," *ACM Computing Surveys 13,* No. 3, September 1981.

[CHEN76] Chen, P.P.-S., "The Entity-Relationship Model: Towards a Unified View of Data," *ACM Transactions on Database Systems 1,* No. 1, March 1976.

[CHEN79] Chen, P.P.-S. (ed.), *Proc. International Conference on Entity-Relationship Approach to Systems Analysis and Design,* Los Angeles, 1979.

[CHOC84] Chock, M., et al., "Database Structure and Manipulation Capabilities of a Picture Database Management System (PICDBMS)," *IEEE Transactions on Pattern Analysis and Machine Intelligence 6,* No. 4, 1984.

[CHRI84] Christodoulakis, S., "Implications of Certain Assumptions in Database Performance Evaluation," *ACM Transactions on Database Systems 9,* No. 2, 1984, 163–186.

[CHU83] Chu, K.C., et al., "VDD: A VLSI Design Database System," *Proc. ACM SIGMOD Conference on Engineering Design Applications,* 1983.

[CK84] Cosmadakis, S. and P. Kanellakis, "Functional and Inclusion Dependencies: A Graph-Theoretic Approach," in *Principles of Database Systems,* R. Fagin (ed.), Association of Computing Machinery, New York, 1984, 29–37.

[CL73] Chang, C.L. and Lee, R.C.T., *Symbolic Logic and Mechanical Theorem Proving,* Academic Press, New York, 1973.

[CLAR78] Clark, K.L., "Negation as Failure," in [GM87], 293–322.

[CLEM81] Clemons, E., "Design of an External Schema Facility to Define and Process Recursive Structures," *ACM Transactions on Database Systems 6,* No. 2, June 1981, 81–92.

[CM81] Clocksin, W.F. and C.S. Mellish, *Programming in PROLOG,* Springer-Verlag, New York, 1981.

[CM84] Copeland, G. and D. Maier, "Making Smalltalk A Database System," *Proc. ACM SIGMOD International Conference on Management of Data,* Boston, MA, June 1984, 316–324.

[CM85] Charniak, E. and D. McDermott, *Introduction to Artificial Intelligence,* Addison-Wesley, Reading, MA, 1985.

[CMS83] Cammarata, C., D. McArther and R. Steeb, "Strategies of Cooperation in Distributed Problem Solving," *Proc. IJCAI-83,* Karlsruhe, W. Germany, August 1983.

[CMT82] Chakravarthy, U.S., Minker, J. and Tran, D., "Interfacing Predicate Logic Languages and Relational Databases," *Proc. First Conference on Logic Programming,* Marseille, France, September 1982, 91–98.

[CODA69] *A Survey of Generalized Data Base Management Systems,* Technical Report of the CODASYL Systems Committee, ACM Press, May 1969.

[CODA71] *CODASYL Database Task Group Report,* Association of Computing Machinery, New York, 1971.

[CODD70] Codd, E.F., "A Relational Model for Large Shared Data Banks," *Communications of the ACM 13,* No. 6, June 1970, 377–387.

[CODD72] Codd, E.F., "Relational Completeness of Database Sublanguages," in *Database Systems,* R. Rustin, (ed.), Prentice-Hall, New York, 1972, 65–98.

[CODD79] Codd, E.F., "Extending the Database Relational Model to Capture More Meaning," *ACM Transactions on Database Systems 4,* No. 4, December 1979.

[COOP64] Cooper, W.S., "Fact Retrieval and Deductive Question-Answering Retrieval Systems," *Journal of the ACM,* April 1964.

[COX86] Cox, B.J., *Object Oriented Programming: An Evolutionary Approach,* Addison-Wesley, 1986.

[CP81] Colmerauer, A. and Pique, J.F., "About Natural Logic," in [GMN81], 343–365.

[CP84] Ceri, S. and G. Pelagatti, *Distributed Databases: Principles and Systems,* McGraw-Hill, 1984.

[CRMN88] Chung, L., D. Rios-Zertuche, J. Mylopoulos and B. Nixon, "Process Management and Assertion Enforcement for a Semantic Data Model," *Proc. International Conference on Extending Database Technology,* Venice, March 1988.

[CS84] Clancey, W.J. and E.H. Shortliffe, *Readings in Medical Artificial Intelligence: The First Decade.* Addison-Wesley, Reading, MA, 1984.

[CVF84] Casanova, M., P.A.S. Veloso and A.L. Furtado, "Formal Database Specification — An Eclectic Perspective," *Proc. Third Annual ACM Symposium on Principles of Database Systems,* 1984, 110–118.

[CW83] Clifford, J. and D.S. Warren, "Formal Semantics for Time in Databases," *ACM Transactions on Database Systems 8,* No. 2, June 1983, 214–254.

[DADA86] Dadam, P., et al., "A DBMS Prototype to Support Extended NF2 Relations: An Integrated View on Flat Tables and Hierarchies," *Proc. ACM SIGMOD International Conference on Management of Data,* Washington D.C., May 1986.

[DAHL82] Dahl, V., "On Database System Development Through Logic," *ACM Transaction on Database Systems 7,* No. 1, March 1982, 102–123.

[DAME85] Damerau, F., "Problems and Some Solutions in Customization of Natural Language Database Front Ends," *ACM Transactions on Office Information Systems 3,* No. 2, 1985.

[DARL65] Darlington, J.L., "Machine Methods for Proving Logical Arguments Expressed in English," *Mechanized Computational Linguistics 8,* 1965.

[DATE81] Date, C.J., *An Introduction to Database Systems,* 3rd edition, Addison-Wesley, Reading, MA, 1981.

[DATE83] Date, C.J., *An Introduction to Database Systems,* Volume II, Addison-Wesley, Reading, MA, 1983.

[DAYA85] Dayal, U., "Query Processing in a Multidatabase System," in *Query Processing in Database Systems,* W. Kim, D. Reiner, D. Batory (eds.), Springer-Verlag, New York, 1985.

[DB77] Davis, R. and Buchanan, B.G., "Meta-Level Knowledge: Overview and Applications," *Proc. IJCAI-77,* Cambridge, MA, in [BL85], 920–927.

[DBS77] Davis, R., Buchanan, B. and Shortliffe, E., "Production Rules as a Representation for a Knowledge-Based Consultation Program," *Artificial Intelligence 8,* No. 1, in [BL85], 15–45.

[DD86] Dittrich, K.R. and U. Dayal (eds.), *Proc. International Workshop on Object-Oriented Database Systems,* Pacific Grove, CA, September 1986.

[DEMA78] De Marco, T., *Structured Analysis and System Specification,* Yourdon Press, New York, 1978.

[DEMO80] Demolombe, R., "Estimation of the Number of Tuples Satisfying a Query Expressed in Predicate Calculus Language," *Proc. Sixth International Conference on Very Large Databases,* Montreal, October 1980, 55–63.

[DEMO81] Demolombe, R., "Assigning Meaning to Ill-Defined Queries Expressed in Predicate Calculus Language," in [GMN81a], 367–395.

[DEPP86] Deppisch, U., et al., "A Storage System for Complex Objects," in [DD86].

[DF86] Deering, M. and J. Faletti, "Database Support for Storage of AI Reasoning Knowledge," in [KERS86].

[DIXO87] Dixon G.N. and S.K. Shrivastava, "Exploiting Type-Inheritance Facilities to Implement Recoverability in Object-Based Systems," *Proc. Sixth IEEE Symposium on Distributed Software and Database Systems,* March 1987, 17–19.

[DK79] Deliyanni, A. and Kowalski, R.A., "Logic and Semantic Networks," *Communications of the ACM 22,* No. 3, March 1979, 184–192.

[DMF81] dosSantos, C.S., Maibaum, T.S.E. and Furtado, A.L., "Conceptual Modeling of Database Operations," *International Journal of Computing Information Science 10,* No. 5, 1981, 299–314.

[DN66] Dahl O.J. and K. Nygaard, "SIMULA—An Algol-based Simulation Language," *Communications of the ACM 9,* 1966, 671–678.

[DONE78] Donelson, W., *Spatial Management of Information, ACM Transactions on Computer Graphics 12,* No. 3, July 1978.

[DOYL79] Doyle, J., "A Truth Maintenance System," *Artificial Intelligence* 12, 1979, 231–272.

[DREY81] Dreyfus, H.L., "From Micro-Worlds to Knowledge Representation: AI at an Impasse," in Mind Design, J. Haugeland (ed.), Cambridge, MA, MIT Press, 1981, 161–204. Also in [BL85].

[DS83] Davis, R. and R.G. Smith, "Negotiation as a Metaphor for Distributed Problem Solving," *Artificial Intelligence 20,* 1983.

[DS84] D'Atri, A. and D. Sacca, "Equivalence and Mapping of Database Schemes," *Proc. Tenth International Conference on Very Large Databases,* Singapore, 1984, 187–195.

[DS86] Dayal, U. and J.M. Smith, "PROBE: A Knowledge-Oriented Database Management System," in [BM86].

[DSHL82] Daniels, D., P. Selinger, L. Haas, B. Lindsay, C. Mohan, A. Walker and P.L. Wilus, "An Introduction to Distributed Query Compilation in R*," in *Distributed Databases,* H.J. Schneider (ed.), North-Holland, 1982, 291–309.

[DZ81] De Antonellis V. and B. Zonta, "Modelling Events in Database Application Design," *Proc. International Conference on Very Large Databases,* 1981.

[EGLT76] Eswaran, K.P., J.N. Gray, R. Lorie and I.L. Traiger, "The Notions of Consistency and Predicate Locks in a Database System," *Communications of the ACM 19,* No. 11, November 1976.

[ER83] Etherington, D.W. and Reiter, R., "On Inheritance Hierarchies with Exceptions," *Proc. AAAI-83,* Washington, D.C., 1983, 104–108. Also in [BL85].

[ES83] Eager, D.L. and K.C. Sevcik, "Achieving Robustness in Distributed Database Systems," *ACM Transactions on Database Systems 8,* No. 3, September 1983, 354–381.

[ESWA76] Eswaran, K.P, "Aspects of a Trigger Subsystem in an Integrated Database System," *Proc. Second International Conference on Software Engineering,* October 1976, 243–250.

[ETHE88] Etherington, D., *Reasoning with Incomplete Knowledge,* Morgan Kaufmann, San Mateo, CA, 1988.

[FA82] Frisch, A.M. and J.F. Allen, "Knowledge Retrieval as Limited Inference," in D.W. Loveland (ed.) *Lecture Notes in Computer Science:*

Sixth Conference on Automated Deduction, Springer Verlag, New York, 1982.

[FAGI77] Fagin, R., "Multivalued Dependencies and a New Normal Form for Relational Databases," *ACM Transaction on Database Systems 2,* No. 3, September 1977, 262–278.

[FAGI82] Fagin, R., "Horn Clause and Database Dependencies," *Journal of the ACM 29,* No. 4, October 1982, 952–985.

[FAHL79] Fahlman, S., *NETL: A System for Representing and Using Real-World Knowledge,* MIT Press, Cambridge MA, 1979.

[FCKH80] Friedell, M., R. Carling, D. Kramlich and C.F. Herot, "The Management of Very Large Two-Dimensional Raster Graphics Environments," Workshop on *Picture Data Description and Management,* August 1980.

[FDS78] Futo, I., F. Darvas and Szeredi, "The Application of PROLOG to the Development of QA and DBM Systems," in [GM78].

[FEIG77] Feigenbaum, E. "The Art of Artificial Intelligence: Themes and Case Studies of Knowledge Engineering," *Proc. IJCAI-77,* Cambridge, MA, 1977, 1014–1029.

[FERR85] Ferrara, F.M., "Easy ER: An Integrated System for the Design and Documentation of Database Applications," *Proc. Fourth International Conference on Entity-Relationship Approach,* Chicago, IL, October 1985.

[FF63] Feigenbaum, E. and J. Feldman (eds.) *Computers and Thought,* McGraw Hill, New York, 1963.

[FIND79] Findler, N.V., *Associative Networks,* Academic Press, New York, 1979.

[FISH87] Fishman, D.H., et. al., "Iris: An Object-Oriented Database Management System," *ACM Transactions on Office Information Systems 5,* No. 1, January 1987.

[FK85] Fikes, R. and T. Kehler, "The Role of Frame-Based Representation in Reasoning," *Communications of the ACM 28,* No. 9, September 1985, 904–920.

[FLOR74] Florentin, J.J., "Consistency Auditing of Databases," *Computing Journal 17,* No. 1, 1974.

[FLRR84] Fox, S., T. Landers, D.R. Ries and R.L. Rosenberg, "ADAPLEX User's Manual," Technical Report CCA-84-01, Computer Corporation of America, Cambridge MA, 1984.

[FM77] Forgy, C.L. and J. McDermott, "OPS: A Domain-Independent Production System Language," *Proc. Fifth International Joint Conference on Artificial Intelligence,* Cambridge, MA, 1977.

[FM82] Fischer, M.J. and A. Michael, "Sacrificing Serializability to Attain High Availability of Data in an Unreliable Network," *Proc. Conference on Principles of Database Systems,* 1982, 70–75.

[FN86] Furtado, A.L. and E.J. Neuhold, *Formal Techniques for Database Design,* Springer-Verlag, Berlin, 1986.

[FORG79] Forgy, C.L., *On the Efficient Implementation of Production Systems,* Ph.D. Dissertation, Carnegie-Mellon University, Pittsburgh, PA, 1979.

[FORG82] Forgy, C.L., "Rete: A Fast Algorithm for the Many Pattern/Many Object Pattern Match Problem," *Artificial Intelligence 19,* No. 1, 1982.

[FREN85] Frenkel, K.A., "Toward Automating the Software-Development Cycle," *Communications of the ACM 28,* No. 6, June 1985.

[FREY87] Freytag, J.C., "A Rule-Based View of Query Optimization," *Proc. ACM SIGMOD International Conference on Management of Data,* 1987.

[FS76] Fry, J.P. and E.H. Sibley, "Evolution of Data-Base Management Systems," in [SIBL76].

[FS84] Fox, M. and S. Smith, "ISIS: A Knowledge-Based System for Factory Scheduling," *International Journal of Expert Systems 1,* No. 1, 1984.

[FUNT80] Funt, B.V., "Problem-Solving with Diagrammatic Representation," *Artificial Intelligence 13,* No. 3, 1980, 201–230. Also in [BL85].

[FURU77] Furukawa, K., "A Deductive Question-Answering System on Relational Databases," *Proc. Fifth International Joint Conference on Artificial Intelligence,* Cambridge, MA, August 1977, 59–66.

[FUV83] Fagin, R., Ullman, J.D. and Vardi, M.Y., "On the Semantics of Updates in Databases," *Proc. Second ACM Symposium on Principles of Database Systems,* Atlanta, GA, March 1983, 352–365.

[GALL81] Gallaire, H., "Impacts of Logic on Databases," *Proc. Seventh International Conference on Very Large Databases,* Cannes, France, September 1981, 248–259.

[GALL83] Gallaire, H., "Logic Databases vs. Deductive Databases," *Logic Programming Workshop,* Albufeira, Portugal, 1983, 608–622.

[GARC83] Garcia-Molina, H., "Using Semantic Knowledge for Transaction Processing in a Distributed Database," *ACM Transactions on Database Systems 8,* No. 2, June 1983.

[GASS87] Gasser, L., "The 1985 Workshop on Distributed Artificial Intelligence," *AI Magazine 8,* No. 2, Summer 1987.

[GD87] Graefe G. and D.J. DeWitt, "The EXODUS Optimizer Generator," *Proc. ACM SIGMOD International Conference on Management of Data,* May 1987.

[GELE63] Gelernter, H., "Realization of A Geometry-Theorem Proving Machine," in [FF63], 134–152.

[GHL63] Gelernter, H., Hansen, J.R. and Loveland, D.W., "Empirical Explorations of the Geometry-Theorem Proving Machine," in [FF63], 153–163.

[GIFF79] Gifford, D.K., "Weighted Voting for Replicated Data," *Proc. Seventh Symposium on Operating Systems Principles,* November 1979, 150–162.

[GJWC63] Green, B.F., Jr., A.K. Wolf, C. Chomsky and K. Laughery, "Baseball: An Automatic Question Answerer," in [FF63], 207–216.

[GLF81] Garvey, T.D., Lowrance, J.D. and Fischler, M.A., "An Inference Technique for Integrating Knowledge from Disparate Sources," *Proc. IJCAI-81,* Vancouver, B.C., August 1981, 319–325. Also in [BL85].

[GLP75] Gray, J.N., Lorie, R.A. and Putzolu, G.R., "Granularity of Locks in a Shared Database," *Proc. First International Conference on Very Large Databases,* Framingham, MA, 1975, 428–451.

[GM78] Gallaire, H. and J. Minker (eds.), *Logic and Databases,* Plenum Press, New York, 1978.

[GM79] Gardarin, G. and Melkanoff, M., "Proving Consistency of Database Transactions," *Proc. Fifth International Conference on Very Large Databases,* Rio de Janeiro, October 1979, 291–298.

[GM81] Grant, J. and Minker, J., "Optimization in Deductive and Conventional Relational Database Systems," in [GMN81], 195–234.

[GMN84] Gallaire, H., J. Minker and J. Nicolas, (eds.) *Advances in Database Theory,* Plenum Press, New York, 1984.

[GMN84a] Gallaire, H., J. Minker and J. Nicolas, (eds.) "Logic and Databases: A Deductive Approach," *ACM Computing Surveys 16,* No. 2, June 1987.

[GNM81] Gallaire, H., J. Nicolas and J. Minker, (eds.), *Advances in Database Theory,* Volume 1, Plenum Press, New York, 1981.

[GOGU84] Goguen, J.A. and J. Meseguer, "Equality, Types, Modules, and Generics for Logic Programming," *Proc. Second International Conference on Logic Programming,* Uppsala, 1984.

[GOLD84] Goldberg, A. *Smalltalk-80: The Interactive Programming Environment,* Addison-Wesley, Reading, MA, 1984.

[GOOD87] Goodman, D., *The Complete HyperCard Handbook,* Bantam Books, New York, 1987.

[GOTL86] Gotlieb, C.C., "Information Systems in the Small," *Proc. IFIP World Congress,* Dublin, 1986, 739–743.

[GR68] Green, C.C. and B. Raphael, "Research on Intelligent Question-Answering Systems," *Proc. Twenty-Third ACM National Computer Conference,* Princeton, 1968.

[GR83] Goldberg, A. and D. Robson, *Smalltalk-80: The Language and Its Implementation,* Addison-Wesley, Reading, MA, 1983.

[GRAY78] Gray, J.N., "Notes on Database Operating Systems," in *Lecture Notes on Computer Science 60,* Springer-Verlag, New York, 1978, 393–481.

[GRAY84] Gray, P. *Logic, Algebra, and Database*, John Wiley and Sons, New York, 1984.

[GREE69] Green, Cordell, "Theorem Proving by Resolution as a Basis for Question-Answering Systems," in *Machine Intelligence 4,* B. Meltzer and D. Michie (eds.), 1969, 183–205.

[GS82] Guttman, A. and M. Stonebraker, "Using a Relational Database Management System for Computer Aided Data," *IEEE Database Engineering Newsletter,* June 1982.

[GS84] Gifford, D.K. and A. Spector (eds.), "Case Study: The TWA Reservation System," *Communications of the ACM 27,* No. 7, July 1984, 650–665.

[GS87] Greif, I. and S.K. Sarin, "Data Sharing in Group Work," *ACM Transactions on Office Information Systems 5,* No. 2, April 1987.

[GSW86] Grosz, B., K. Sparck Jones and B.L. Webber *Readings in Natural Language Processing,* Morgan Kaufmann, Los Altos, CA, 1986.

[GUTT84] Guttman, A., "R-Trees: A Dynamic Index Structure for Spatial Searching," *Proc. ACM SIGMOD International Conference on Management of Data,* 1984.

[GW76] Griffiths, P.P and B.W. Wade, "An Authorization Mechanism for a Relational Data Base System," *ACM Transactions on Database Systems 1,* No. 3, September 1976.

[HAIL86] Hailpern, B., (ed.), "Special Issue on Multiparadigm Languages and Environments," *IEEE Software 3,* No. 1, January 1986,

[HANS87] Hanson, E., "A Performance Analysis of View Materialization Strategies," *Proc. ACM SIGMOD International Conference on Management of Data,* 1987.

[HARE79] Harel, D., "First Order Dynamic Logic," in *Lecture Notes in Computer Science 68,* Springer-Verlag, Berlin and New York, 1979.

[HARE80] Harel, D., "Review of Logic and Databases," H. Gallaire and J. Minker. *Computing Reviews 21,* No. 8, August 1980, 367–369.

[HARR77] Harris, L.R., "User-Oriented Database Query with the ROBOT Natural Language Query System," *Proc. Third International Conference on Very Large Databases,* October 1977.

[HARR79] Harris, L., "Experience with Natural Language Database Query Applications," *Proc. IJCAI-79,* 1979, 365–368.

[HAYE74] Hayes, P.J., "Some Problems and Non-Problems in Representation Theory," *Proc. AISB Summer Conference,* University of Sussex, 1974, 63–79. Also in [BL85].

[HAYE79] Hayes, P.J., "The Logic of Frames," in *Frame Conceptions and Text Understanding,* D. Metzing (ed.), Walter de Gruyter and Co., Berlin, 1979, 46–61. Also in [BL85].

[HAYE85] Hayes, P.J., "The Second Naive Physics Manifesto," in *Formal Theories of the Commonsense World,* J.R. Hobbs and R.C. Moore (eds.), Ablex, Norwood, NJ, 1985, 1–36. Also in [BL85].

[HCFK80] Herot, C.F., R. Carling, M. Friedell and D. Kramlich, "A Prototype Spatial Data Management System," *ACM Transactions on Computer Graphics 14,* No. 3, July 1980.

[HEWI71] Hewitt, C., "Planner: A Language for Proving Theorems in Robots," *Proc IJCAI-71,* London, 1971.

[HEWI72] Hewitt, C., "Description and Theoretical Analysis (Using Schemata) of PLANNER: A Language for Proving Theorems and Manipulating Models in A Robot," AI Memo No. 251, MIT Project MAC, Cambridge, MA, 1972.

[HEWI77] Hewitt, C., "Viewing Control Structures as Patterns of Passing Messages," *Artificial Intelligence 8,* No. 3, June 1977.

[HK87] Hull, R. and R. King, "Semantic Database Modelling: Survey, Applications and Research Issues," *ACM Computing Reviews 19,* No. 3, September 1987.

[HL82] Haskin, R.L. and R.A. Lorie, "On Extending the Functions of a Relational Database System," *Proc. ACM SIGMOD International Conference on Management of Data,* 1982, 207–212.

[HM75] Hammer, M.M. and D.J. McLeod, "Semantic Integrity in a Relational Data Base System," *Proc. International Conference on Very Large Databases,* September 1975.

[HM81] Hammer, M.M. and D.J. McLeod, "Database Description with SDM: A Semantic Database Model," *ACM Transactions on Database Systems 6,* No. 3, September 1981.

[HM85] Heimbigner, D. and D. McLeod, "A Federated Architecture for Information Management," *ACM Transaction on Office Information Systems 3,* No. 3, July 1985, 253–276.

[HMN84] Henschen, L.J., McCune, W.W. and Naqvi, S.A., "Compiling Constraint Checking Program from First Order Formulas," in [GMN84], 145–169.

[HN84] Henschen, L.J. and S.A. Naqvi, "On Compiling Queries in Recursive First Order Databases," *Journal of the ACM 31,* No. 1, October 1984, 47–85.

[HOAR72] Hoare, C.A.R., "Notes on Data Structuring," in *Structured Programming,* APIC Studies in Data Processing No. 8, Academic Press, New York, 1972.

[HOAR85] Hoare, C.A.R., *Communicating Sequential Processes,* Prentice-Hall, Englewood Cliffs, NJ, 1985.

[HR85] Heiler, S.I. and A. Rosenthal, "G-Whiz: A Visual Interface for the Functional Model with Recursion," *Proc. Eleventh International Conference on Very Large Databases,* 1985.

[HS78] Hammer, M.M. and S.K. Sarin, "Efficient Monitoring of Database Assertions," *ACM SIGMOD Conference Supplement,* June 1978.

[HUDS86] Hudson, S.E. and R. King, "CACTIS: A Database System for Specifying Functionally-Defined Data," in [DD86], 26–37.

[HULL84] Hull, R., "Relative Information Capacity of Simple Relational Database Schemata," *Principles of Database Systems,* R. Fagin (ed.), Association of Computing Machinery, 1984, 97–109.

[HWL83] Hayes-Roth, F., D.A. Waterman and D.B. Lenat, *Building Expert Systems,* Addison-Wesley, Reading, MA, 1983.

[HZ80] Hammer, M.T. and Zdonik, S.B., "Knowledge-Based Query Processing," *Proc. Sixth International Conference on Very Large Databases,* Montreal, October 1980, 137–147.

[IB84] Israel, D. and R.J. Brachman, "Some Remarks on the Semantics of Representation Languages," in [BMS84].

[IL81] Imielinski, T. and Lipski, W., "On Representing Incomplete Information in a Relational Database," *Proc. Seventh International Conference on Very Large Databases,* Cannes, France, September 1981, 389–397.

[IOAN85] Ioannides, Y., "A Time Bound on the Materialization of Some Recursively Defined Views," *Proc. Eleventh International Conference on Very Large Databases,* 1985.

[ISRA83] Israel, D., "Some Remarks on the Role of Logic in Knowledge Representation," Technical Report No. 5388, Bolt Beranek and Newman Inc., July 1983.

[ISRA86] Israel, D., "Inference: A Somewhat Skewed Survey," in [BM86].

[JANA79] Janas, J.M., "Towards More Informative User Interfaces," *Proc. Fifth International Conference on Very Large Databases,* Rio de Janeiro, October 1979, 17–23.

[JANA81] Janas, J.M., "On the Feasibility of Informative Answers," in [GMN81], 397–414.

[JCV84] Jarke, M., J. Clifford and Y. Vassiliou, "An Optimizing PROLOG Front-End to a Relational Query," *Proc. ACM SIGMOD International Conference on Management of Data,* 1984.

[JLL83] Jaffar, J., J.L. Lassez and J. Lloyd, "Completeness of the Negation by Failure Rule," *Proc. IJCAI-83,* Karlsruhe, W. Germany, August 1983, 500–506.

[JLS85] Jarke, M., V. Linnemann and J. Schmidt, "Data Constructors: On the Integration of Rules and Relations," *Proc. Eleventh International Conference on Very Large Databases,* 1985.

[JR86] Jones, M.B. and R.F. Rashid, "Mach and Matchmaker: Kernel and Language Support for Object-Oriented Distributed Systems," *Proc. Conference on Object-Oriented Programming Systems, Languages, and Applications,* Portland, OR, September 1986.

[JTSV85] Jarke, M., J. Turner, E. Stohr, Y. Vassiliou and N. White, "A Field Evaluation of Natural Language for Data Retrieval," *IEEE Transactions on Software Engineering SE-11,* No. 1, January 1985, 97–112.

[JV83] Jarke, M. and Y. Vassiliou, "Coupling Expert Systems with Database Management Systems," *NYU Symposium on Artificial Intelligence Application for Business,* May 1983.

[JV85] Jarke, M. and Y. Vassiliou, "A Framework for Choosing a Database Query Language," *ACM Computing Surveys 17,* No. 3, September 1985.

[KAEH86] Kaehler, T., "Virtual Memory on a Narrow Machine for an Object-Oriented Language," *Proc. Conference on Object-Oriented Programming Systems, Languages and Applications,* Portland, OR, September 1986, 87–106.

[KATZ85] Katz R.H., *Information Management for Engineering Design,* Springer-Verlag, New York, 1985.

[KBB83] Kaufman, C.W., J. Barnett and B.T. Blaustein, "The DACOS Forms-Based Query System," *Journal of Telecommunication Networks,* 1983, 463–482.

[KBDF71] Kellogg, C., J. Burger, T. Diller and K. Fogt, "The CONVERSE Natural Language Data Management System: Current Status and Plans," *Proc. Symposium on Information Storage and Retrieval,* University of Maryland, 1971.

[KBR86] Kaczmarek, T.S., R. Bates and G. Robins, "Recent Developments in NIKL," *Proc. Seventh National Conference on Artificial Intelligence,* Philadelphia, PA, 1986.

[KDSJ77] de Kleer, J., J. Doyle, G.L. Steele, Jr. and G.J. Sussman, "AMORD: Explicit Control of Reasoning," *Proc. Symposium on Artificial Intelligence and Programming Languages, SIGPLAN Notices 12,* and *SIGART Newsletter,* No. 8, in [BL85], No. 64, August 1977, 116–125.

[KE80] Kawaguchi, E. and T. Endo, "On a Method of Binary-Picture Representation and Its Application to Compression," *IEEE Transactions on Pattern Analysis and Machine Intelligence,* January 1980.

[KELL68] Kellogg, C., "A Natural Language Compiler for On-Line Data Management," *Proc. Fall Joint Computer Conference,* 1968, 473–492.

[KELL83] Kellogg, C., "Intelligent Assistants for Knowledge and Information Resources Management," *Proc. IJCAI-83,* Karlsruhe, August 1983, 170–172.

[KENT78] Kent, W., *Data and Reality,* North-Holland, Amsterdam, 1978.

[KENT79] Kent, W., "Limitations of Record-Based Information Models," *ACM Transactions on Database Systems 4,* No. 1, 1979, 107–131.

[KENT81] Kent, W., "Consequences of Assuming a Universal Relation," *ACM Transactions on Database Systems 6,* No. 4, December 1981.

[KERS85] Kerschberg, L., "Expert Database Systems (Workshop Review)," *Proc. ACM SIGMOD International Conference on the Management of Data,* Austin, TX, May 1985.

[KERS86] Kerschberg, L. (ed.), *Expert Database Systems: Proceedings from the First International Workshop,* Benjamin/Cummings, Menlo Park, CA, February 1986.

[KERS87] Kerschberg, L. (ed.), *Expert Database Systems: Proceedings from the First International Conference,* Benjamin/Cummings, Menlo Park, CA, 1987.

[KERS88] Kerschberg, L. (ed.), *Expert Database Systems: Proceedings from the Second International Conference,* Benjamin/Cummings, Menlo Park, CA, 1988.

[KHIS86] Kung, R., et al., "Heuristic Search in Data Base Systems," in [KERS86].

[KIM84] Kim, W., "Highly Available Systems for Database Applications," *ACM Computing Surveys 16,* No. 1, March 1984, 71–98.

[KING80] King, J.J., "Intelligent Retrieval Planning," *Proc. First National Conference on Artificial Intelligence,* August 1980, 243–245.

[KING81] King, J.J., "QUIST: A System for Semantic Optimization in Relational Databases," *Proc. Seventh Very Large Databases Conference,* Cannes, France, 1981, 510–517.

[KING83] King, J.J. (ed.), *Special Issue on AI and Database Research, ACM SIGART Newsletter,* October 1983.

[KK71] Kowalski, R.A. and D. Kuehner, "Linear Resolution with Selection Function," *Artificial Intelligence 2,* No. 3/4, 1971, 227–260.

[KKT78] Kellogg, C., Ph. Klahr and L. Travis, "Deductive Planning and Path Finding for Relational Databases," in [GM78].

[KKW84] Kunz, J.C., T.P. Kehler and M.D. Williams, "Applications Development Using a Hybrid AI Development System," *AI Magazine 5,* No. 3, Fall 1984, 41–54.

[KL88] Kim W. and F. Lochovsky (eds.), *Object-Oriented Languages, Applications, and Databases,* Addison-Wesley, Reading, MA, (to appear).

[KLUG79] Klug, A., "Entity-Relationship Views over Uninterpreted Enterprise Schemas," *Proc. International Conference on E-R Approach,* Los Angeles, CA, December 1979, 39–59.

[KM84] King, R. and D. McLeod, "A Unified Model and Methodology for Conceptual Database Design," in [BMS84].

[KM85] King, R. and D. McLeod, "Semantic Data Models," in *Principles of Database Design, Volume I: Logical Organizations,* S.B. Yao (ed.), Prentice-Hall, New York, 1985.

[KONO81] Konolige, K., "A Metalanguage Representation of Databases for Deductive Question-Answering Systems," *Proc. IJCAI-81,* Vancouver, B.C., August 1981, 469–503.

[KOWA74] Kowalski, R., "Predicate Logic as a Programming Language," *Proc. IFIP World Congress,* North-Holland, Amsterdam, 569–574.

[KOWA78] Kowalski, R.A., "Logic for Data Description," in [GM78], 77–103.

[KOWA78a] Kowalski, R., *Logic for Problem Solving,* North-Holland, Amsterdam, 1978.

[KP75] Kerschberg, L. and J.E.S. Pacheco, "A Functional Database Model," Monograph Series in Computer Science and Computer Applications, Department de Informatica, Pontificia Universita Catolica do Rio de Janeiro, Brazil, 1975.

[KRAM85] Kramer J. and J. Magee, "Dynamic Configuration for Distributed

Systems," *IEEE Transactions on Software Engineering SE-11,* No. 4, April 1985.

[KRB85] Kim, W., D. Reiner and D. Batory (eds.), *Query Processing in Database Systems,* Springer-Verlag, New York, February 1985.

[KS86] Kowalski, R. and M. Sergot, "A Logic-Based Calculus of Events," *New Generation Computing,* 1986.

[KT81] Kellogg, C. and Travis, "Reasoning with Data in a Deductively Augmented Data Management System," in [GNM81].

[KW87] Kim, W., K. Woelk, "Multimedia Information Management in an Object-Oriented Database System," *Proc. Thirteenth Very Large Databases Conference,* 1987, 319–329.

[LAFU85] Lafue, G. and R. Smith, "Implementation of an Integrity Manager with a Knowledge Representation System," in [KERS85].

[LAMP78] Lamport, L., "Time, Clocks, and the Ordering of Events in a Distributed System," *Communications of the ACM 21,* No. 7, July 1978, 558–565.

[LAND81] Landwehr, C.E., "Formal Models for Computer Security," *ACM Computing Surveys 13,* No. 3, September 1981.

[LB84] Levesque, H.J. and Brachman, R.J., "A Fundamental Tradeoff in Knowledge Representation and Reasoning (Revised Version)," Original version appeared as "A Fundamental Tradeoff in Knowledge Representation and Reasoning" (by Hector J.L.), *Proc. CSCSI-84,* London, Ontario, in [BL85] 1984, 141–152.

[LBEF82] Litwin, W., J. Baudenant, C. Esculier, A. Ferrier, A.M. Glorieux, J. La Chimia, K. Kabbai, C. Moulinoux, P. Rolin and C. Stranget, "SIRIUS Systems for Distributed Database Management," in *Distributed Databases,* H.J. Schneider (ed.), North-Holland, Amsterdam, 1982.

[LBS86] Lynch, N., B. Blaustein and M. Siegel, "Correctness Conditions for Highly Available Replicated Databases," *Proc. Fifth ACM Symp. on Principles of Distributed Computing,* August 1986.

[LENA83] Lenat, D.B., "The Role of Heuristics in Learning by Discovery: Three Case Studies," in *Machine Learning, An Artificial Intelligence Approach,* R.S. Michalski, J.G. Carbonell and T.M. Mitchell (eds.), Morgan Kaufmann, San Mateo, CA, 1983.

[LEVE81] Levesque, H.J., "The Interaction with Incomplete Knowledge Bases: A Formal Treatment," *Proc. IJCAI-81,* Vancouver, 1981, 240–245.

[LEVE84] Levesque, H., "The Logic of Incomplete Knowledge Bases," in [BMS84].

[LEVE87] Levesque, H. (ed.), "Taking Issue: A Critique of Pure Reason," *Computational Intelligence 3,* No. 3, August 1987.

[LHMW84] Lindsay, B.G., L.M. Haas, C. Mohan, P.F. Wilms and R.A. Yost, "Computation and Communication in R*: A Distributed Database Manager," *ACM Transactions on Computer Systems 2,* No. 1, 1984, 24–38.

[LIND63] Lindsay, R.K., "Inferential Memory as the Basis of Machines which Understand Natural Language," in [FF63], 217–233.

[LIND81] Lindsay, B.G., "Object Naming and Catalog Management for a Distributed Database Manager," *Proc. Second International Conference on Distributed Computing Systems,* April 1981, 31–40.

[LIPS79] Lipski, W., "On Semantic Issues connected with Incomplete Information System," *ACM Transaction on Database Systems 4,* No. 3, September 1979, 262–296.

[LISK81] Liskov, B., *CLU Reference Manual,* Lecture Notes in Computer Science 114, Springer-Verlag, New York, 1981.

[LISK88] Liskov, B., "Distributed Programming in Argus," *Communications of the ACM 31,* No. 3, March 1988.

[LITW80] Litwin, W., "Linear Hashing: A New Tool for File and Table Addressing," *Proc. Sixth International Conference on Very Large Databases,* 1980, 212–223.

[LM67] Levien, R.E. and M.E. Maron, "A Computer System for Inference Execution and Data Retrieval," *Communications of the ACM 10,* No. 11, November 1967.

[LM79] Levesque, H. and J. Mylopoulos, "A Procedural Semantics for Semantic Networks," in [FIND79].

[LM83] Lorie, R.A. and A. Meier, "Using a Relational DBMS for Geographical Databases," IBM Research Report RJ 3848 (43915), April, 1983, San Jose Research Center, CA.

[LMP87] Lindsay, B., J. McPherson and H. Pirahesh, "A Data Management Extension Architecture," *Proc. ACM SIGMOD International Conference on Management of Data,* May 1987, 220–226.

[LOCH85] Lochovsky F., (ed.), "Special Issue on Object-Oriented Database Systems," *Database Engineering 8,* No. 4, 1985.

[LOGI82] *Proc. First Conference on Logic Programming* 1982. Marseille, France, Universite d'Aix-Marseille-Luminy, Marseille. September 1982.

[LOGI83] *Proc. Logic Programming Workshop* 1983. Praia da Falesia, Algarve, Portugal. Department of Computer Science, University of Lisboa, Lisbon, Portugal, June 26-July 1, 1983.

[LORI77] Lorie, R.A., "Physical Integrity in a Large Segmented Database," *ACM Transactions on Database Systems 2,* No. 1, March 1977.

[LORI82] Lorie, R.A., "Issues in Database for Design Applications," J. Encarnacao and F.-L. Krause (eds.), *File Structures and Data Bases for CAD,* North-Holland, Amsterdam, 1982.

[LOVE69] Loveland, D., "Theorem Provers Combining Model Elimination and Resolution," in *Machine Intelligence,* Volume 4, B. Meltzer and D. Michie, (eds.) Elsevier North-Holland, New York, 1969, 73–86.

[LOVE70] Loveland, D., "A Linear Format for Resolution," *Proc. IRIA Symposium on Automatic Demonstration,* Springer-Verlag, Berlin and New York, 1970, 147–162.

[LOVE78] Loveland, D., "Automated Theorem Proving: A Logical Basis," Elsevier North-Holland, New York, 1978.

[LOZI85] Lozinski, E.L., "Evaluating Queries in Deductive Databases by Generating," *Proc. IJCAI-85,* Los Angeles, 1985 173–177.

[LP83] Lorie, R.A. and W. Plouffe, "Complex Objects and Their Use in Design Transactions," *ACM SIGMOD Database Week: Engineering Design Applications,* May 1983.

[LPS81] Lampson, B.W., M. Paul and H.J. Siegert (eds.), *Distributed Systems — Architecture and Implementation,* Springer-Verlag, New York, 1981.

[LPS85] Lenat, D.B., M. Prakash and M. Shepherd, "CYC: Using Common Sense Knowledge to Overcome Brittleness and Knowledge Acquisition Bottlenecks," *AI Magazine 6,* 1985, 65–85.

[LR82] Landers, T. and R. Rosenberg, "An Overview of MULTIBASE," *Proc. Second International Symposium on Distributed Databases*, Berlin, West Germany, September 1982.

[LS83] Liskov, B. and R. Scheifler, "Guardians and Actions: Linguistic Support for Robust, Distributed Programs," *ACM Transactions on Programming Languages and Systems 5,* No. 3, July 1983, 381–404.

[LS85] Lafue, G. and R. Smith, "A Modular Toolkit for Knowledge Management," *Proc. IJCAI-85,* Los Angeles, August 1985, 46-52.

[LS87] Lipeck, U.W. and G. Saake, "Monitoring Dynamic Integrity Constraints Based on Temporal Logic," *Information Systems 12,* No. 3, 1987, 255–269.

[LSBM83] Lohman, G.M., J.C. Stoltzfus, A.N. Benson, M.T. Martin and A.F. Cardenas, "Remotely Sensed Geophysical Databases: Experience and Implications for Generalized DBMS," *Proc. ACM SIGMOD International Conference on Management of Data,* 1983.

[LSP82] Lamport, L., R. Shostak and M. Pease, "The Byzantine Generals Problem," *ACM Transactions on Programming Languages and Systems 4,* No. 3, July 1982, 382–410.

[LT85] Lloyd, J. and R. Topor, "A Basis for Deductive Database Systems," *Journal of Logic Programming 2,* No. 2, July 1985, 93–110.

[LU77] Lien, Y.E. and D.F. Utter, Jr., "Design of an Image Database," *Proc. IEEE Workshop on Picture Data Description and Management,* 1977.

[LUM84] Lum, V., et al., "Designing DBMS Support for the Temporal Dimension," *Proc. ACM SIGMOD International Conference on Management of Data,* 1984, 115–130.

[LW85] Le Blanc, R.J. and C.J. Wilkes, "System Programming with Objects and Actions," *Proc. Fifth International Conference on Distributed Computing Systems,* May 1985.

[LY77] Liou, J.H. and S.B. Yao, "Multidimensional Clustering for Database Organization," *Information Systems 2,* No. 4, 1977, 187–198.

[LYNC83] Lynch, N. "Multilevel Atomicity: A New Correctness Criterion for Database Concurrency Control," *ACM Transactions on Database Systems 8,* No. 4, 1983, 484–502.

[LZ74] Liskov, B. and S. Zilles, "Programming with Abstract Data Types," *SIGPLAN Notices 9,* No. 4, April 1974, pp. 50-59.

[MACK77] Mackworth, A., "Consistency in Networks of Relations," *Artificial Intelligence 8,* No. 1, 1977, 99–118.

[MAIE83] Maier, D., *The Theory of Relational Databases,* Computer Science Press, Potomac, MD, 1983.

[MALL82] Mallgren, W.R., "Formal Specification of Graphic Data Types," *ACM Transactions on Programming Languages and Systems 4,* No. 4, October 1982.

[MB86] Manola, F.A. and M.L. Brodie, "On Knowledge-Based System Architectures," in [BM86].

[MB88] Mylopoulos, J. and M.L. Brodie, *Readings in Artificial Intelligence and Databases,* Morgan Kaufmann, San Mateo, CA, 1988.

[MBCR76] Mylopoulos, J., A. Borgida, P. Cohen, N. Roussopoulos, J. Tsotsos and H.K.T. Wong, "A Natural Language Understanding System for Data Management," *Proc. IJCAI-75,* Tbilisi USSR, September 1975.

[MBGM84] Mylopoulos, J., A. Borgida, S. Greenspan, C. Meghini and B. Nixon, "Information System Design at the Conceptual Level: The Taxis Project," *IEEE Database Engineering 7,* No. 4, December 1984.

[MBGM86] Mylopoulos, J., A. Borgida, S. Greenspan, C. Meghini and B. Nixon, "Knowledge Representation in the Software Development Process: A Case Study," in Winter, H. (ed.), *Artificial Intelligence and Man–Machine Systems,* Lecture Notes in Control and Information Sciences, No. 80, Springer-Verlag, Berlin, 1986, 23–44.

[MBW80] Mylopoulos, J., P. Bernstein and H.K.T. Wong, "A Language Facility for Designing Database-Intensive Applications," *Transactions on Database Systems 5,* No. 2, June 1980, 185–207.

[McCAR58] McCarthy, J., "Mechanization of Thought Processes," *Proc. Symposium of National Physical Laboratory,* London, November 1958, 77–84.

[McCAR68] McCarthy, J., "Programs with Common Sense," in *Semantic Information Processing,* M. Minsky (ed.), MIT Press, Cambridge, MA, 1968, in [BL85], 403–418.

[McCAR77] McCarthy, J., "Epistemological Problems in Artificial Intelligence," *Proc.*

IJCAI-77, Cambridge, MA, in [BL85], 1977, 1038–1044.

[McCAR79] McCarthy, J., "First Order Theories of Individual Concepts and Propositions," in *Machine Intelligence 9,* J.E. Hayes, D. Michie and L.I. Mikulich (eds.), Ellis Horwood, Ltd., in [BL85], Chichester, England, 1979, 129–147.

[McCAR80] McCarthy, J., "Circumscription—A Form of Non-Monotonic Reasoning," *Artificial Intelligence 13,* 1980, 27–39.

[McM77] McSkimin, J. and J. Minker, "The Use of A Semantic Network in A Deductive Question-Answering System," *Proc. IJCAI-77,* Cambridge, MA, August 1977, 50–58.

[McSKI76] McSkimin, J., "Techniques for Employing Semantic Information in Question-Answering Systems," Ph.D. dissertation, Department of Computer Science, University of Maryland, College Park, 1976.

[MCT87] Mauldin, M.L., J.G. Carbonell and R.H. Thomason, "Beyond the Keyword Barrier: Knowledge-Based Information Retrieval," *Proc. Annual Conference of the National Federation of Abstracting and Information Services,* North-Holland, Amsterdam, March 1987.

[MD86] Manola, F. and U. Dayal, "PDM: An Object-Oriented Data Model," in [DD86].

[MERR78] Merrett, T.H., "Multidimensional Paging for Efficient Database Querying," *Proc. International Conference on Management of Data,* Milan, 1978, 277–290.

[MERR84] Merrett, T.H., *Relational Information Systems,* Reston Publishing, Reston, VA, 1984.

[MEYR87] Meyrowitz, N. (ed.) *Proc. OOPSLA '87 Conference,* ACM, 1987. Published as *SIGPLAN Notices, 21,* No. 12, December 1987.

[MINK75] Minker, J., "Performing Inferences Over Relational Databases," *Proc. ACM SIGMOD International Conference on Management of Data,* San Jose, CA, May 1975, 79–91.

[MINK78] Minker, J., "Search Strategy and Selection Function for an Inferential Relational System," *ACM Transaction on Database System 3,* No. 1, March 1978, 1–31.

[MINK78a] Minker, J., "An Experimental Relational Database System Based on Logic," in [GM78], 107–147.

[MINK82] Minker, J., "On Indefinite Databases and the Closed World Assumption," *Proc. Sixth Conference on Automated Deduction,* Lecture Notes in Computer Science, Springer-Verlag, Berlin and New York, No. 138, 1982, 292–308.

[MINS63] Minsky, M., "Steps Toward Artificial Intelligence," in [FF63], 406–450.

[MINS68] Minsky, M. (ed.), *Semantic Information Processing,* MIT Press, Cambridge, MA, 1968.

[MINS75] Minsky, M., "A Framework for Representing Knowledge," in *The Psychology of Computer Vision,* P.H. Winston (ed.), McGraw-Hill, New York, 1975.

[MIRA89] Miranker, D., *TREAT: A New and Effective Match Algorithm for AI Production Systems,* Morgan Kaufmann, San Mateo, CA (to appear).

[ML84] Mylopoulos, J. and H. Levesque, "An Overview of Knowledge Representation," in [BMS84].

[MM77] Minker, J.R. and J. McSkimin, "The Use of Semantic Networks in a Deductive Question-Answering System," *Proc. IJCAI-77,* Cambridge, MA, August 1977, 50–58.

[MMC76] Michaels, A.S., B. Mittman and C.R. Carlson, "A Comparison of Relational and CODASYL Approaches to Data-Base Management," in [SIBL76].

[MMS79] Maier, D., A.O. Mendelzon and Y. Sagiv, "Testing Implications of Data Dependencies," *ACM Transaction on Database Systems 4,* No. 4, December 1979, 455–469.

[MN82] Minker, J. and J.M. Nicolas, "On Recursive Axioms in Deductive Databases," *Information System 8,* No. 1, January 1982, 1–13.

[MO86] Manola, F.A. and J.A. Orenstein. "Toward A General Spatial Data Model For An Object-Oriented DBMS," *Proc. Twelfth International Conference on Very Large Databases,* August 1986.

[MOOR81] Moore, R.C., "Problem in Logical Form," *Proc. Nineteenth Annual Meeting of the Association for Computational Linguistics,* Association for Computational Linguistics, June 1981, 117–124.

[MOOR82] Moore, R.C., "The Role of Logic in Knowledge Representation and Commonsense Reasoning," *Proc. AAAI National Conference on Artificial Intelligence,* Pittsburgh, PA, 1982, 428–433. Also in [BL85].

[MORE85] Morehouse, S., "ARC/INFO: A Geo-Relational Model for Spatial Information," *Proc. Seventh International Symposium on Computer-Assisted Cartography,* American Congress on Surveying and Mapping, 1985.

[MOSE83] Moser, M.G., "An Overview of NIKL, the New Implementation of KL-ONE," in C.L. Sidner (ed.), *Research in Knowledge Representation and Natural Language Understanding: Annual Report,* Bolt Beranek and Newman, Cambridge, MA, 1983.

[MP84] Minker, J. and Perlis, D., "Applications of Protected Circumscription," *Proc. Conference on Automated Deduction 7,* Napa, CA, Springer-Verlag, Berlin and New York, May 1984, 414–425.

[MPM84] Miller, R.A., H.E. Pople and J.D. Myers, "INTERNIST-1, An Experimental Computer-Based Diagnostic Consultant for General Internal Medicine," in *Readings in Medical Artificial Intelligence: The First Decade,* W.J. Clancey and E.H. Shortliffe, (eds.), Addison-Wesley, Menlo Park, CA, 1984, 190–209.

[MS82] Maida, A.S. and Shapira, S.C., "Intentional Concepts in Propositional Semantic Networks," *Cognitive Science 6,* No. 4, in [BL85], 1982, 291–330.

[MSOP86] Maier, D., J. Stein, A. Otis and A. Purdy, "Development of an Object-Oriented DBMS," *Proc. Conference on Object-Oriented Programming Systems, Languages and Applications,* Portland, OR, September, 1986, 472–482.

[MT83] Mantyla, M. and M. Tamminen, "Localized Set Operations for Solid Modeling," *ACM Computer Graphics 17,* No. 3, 1983, 279–288.

[MU83] Maier, D. and J.D. Ullman, "Maximal Objects and the Semantics of Universal Relation Databases," *ACM Transactions on Database Systems 8,* No. 1, March 1983, 1–14.

[MW80] Mylopoulos, J. and H. Wong, "Some Features of the TAXIS Data Model," *Proc. Sixth International Conference on Very Large Databases,* Montreal, October 1980.

[MYLO86] Mylopoulos, J., "On Knowledge Base Management Systems," in [BM86].

[MZ79] Melkanoff, M. and C. Zaniolo, "Decomposition of Relations and Synthesis of Entity-Relationship Diagrams," *Proc. International Conference on E-R Approach,* Los Angeles, CA, December 1979, 277–294.

[NCLB87] Nixon, B., L. Chung, D. Lauzon, A. Borgida, J. Mylopoulos and M. Stanley, "Implementation of a Compiler for a Semantic Data Model: Experiences with Taxis," *Proc. ACM SIGMOD International Conference on Management of Data,* 1987.

[NEWE61] Newell, A. (ed.), *Information Processing Language V Manual,* Prentice-Hall, Englewood Cliffs, NJ, 1961.

[NEWE82] Newell, A., "The Knowledge Level," *Artificial Intelligence 18,* No. 1, 1982, 87–127.

[NG78] Nicolas, J.-M. and Gallaire, H., "Database: Theory vs. Interpretation," in [GM78], 33–54.

[NH80] Naqvi, S.A. and Henschen, L.J., "Performing Inferences over Recursive Databases," *Proc. First Annual National Conference on Artificial Intelligence,* Stamford, CT, August 1980, 263–265.

[NHS84] Nievergelt, J., H. Hinterberger and K.C. Sevcik, "The Grid File: An Adaptable, Symmetric Multi-Key File Structure," *ACM Transactions on Database Systems 9,* No. 1, 1984, 38–71.

[NICO78] Nicolas, J.-M., "First Order Logic Formalization for Function, Multivalued and Mutual Dependencies," *Proc. ACM-SIGMOD International Conference on Management of Data,* Austin, TX, June 1978, 40–46.

[NICO82] Nicolas, J.-M., "Logic for Improving Integrity Checking in Relational Databases," *Acta Informatica 18,* 1982, 227–253.

[NII86] Nii, H.P., "Blackboard Systems: The Blackboard Model of Problem Solving and the Evolution of Blackboard Architectures," *AI Magazine 7,* No. 2, Summer 1986.

[NILS80] Nilsson, N.J., *Principles of Artificial Intelligence,* Morgan Kaufmann, San Mateo, CA, 1980.

[NS88] Neuhold E. and M. Stonebraker, "Future Directions in DBMS Research," To appear in SIGMOD Record, Fall 1988.

[NSS59] Newell, A., J.C. Shaw and H. Simon, "A General Problem-Solving Program for a Computer," *Computers and Automation 8,* No. 7, 1959, 10–16.

[NSS63] Newell, A., J.C. Shaw, and H.A. Simon, "Empirical Explorations with the Logic Theory Machine: A Case Study in Heuristics," in [FF63], 109–133.

[NW79] Nagy, G. and S. Wagle, "Geographic Data Processing," *ACM Computing Surveys 11,* No. 2, 1979, 139–181.

[NY78] Nicolas, J.-M. and Yazdanian, K., "Integrity Checking in Deductive Databases," in [GM78], 325–346.

[OBS86] O'Brien, P., B. Bullis and C. Schaffert, "Persistent and Shared Objects in Trellis/Owl," in [DD86].

[OLLE88] Olle, T.W., et al., *Information Systems Methodologies: A Framework for Understanding,* Addison-Wesley, Reading, MA, 1988.

[OM84] Orenstein, J.A. and T.H. Merrett, "A Class of Data Structures for Associative Searching," *Proc. Third ACM SIGACT-SIGMOD Symposium on Principles of Database Systems,* 1984, 181–190.

[OOPS86] *Proc. ACM Object-Oriented Systems and Programming Languages Conference,* Portland, OR, September 1986.

[OREN86] Orenstein, J.A., "Spatial Query Processing in an Object-Oriented Database System," *Proc. ACM SIGMOD International Conference on Management of Data,* Washington, D.C., May 1986.

[OST84] Olle, T.W., H.G. Sol and C.J. Tully (eds.), *Information Systems Design Methodologies: A Feature Analysis,* North-Holland, Amsterdam, 1984.

[PATE85] Patel-Schneider, P.F., "A Decidable First Order Logic for Knowledge Representation," *Proc. IJCAI-85,* Los Angeles, 1985, 455–458.

[PBL84] Patel-Schneider, P.F., R.J. Brachman and H.J. Levesque, "Argon: Knowledge Representation Meets Information Retrieval," *Proc. First Conference on Artificial Intelligence Applications,* Denver, 1984.

[PIRO78] Pirotte, A., "High Level Data Query Languages," in [GM78], 409–436.

[PM88] Peckham, J. and F. Maryanski, "Semantic Data Models," *ACM Comuting Surveys,* Vol. 20, No. 3, September 1988, 153–190.

[PPRS83] Parker, D.S., G.J. Popek, G. Rudisin, A. Stoughton, B.J. Walker, E. Walton, J.M. Chow, D. Edwards, S. Kiser and C. Kline, "Detection of Mutual Inconsistency in Distributed Systems," *IEEE Trans. Software Engineering* SE-9, No. 3, May 1983, 240–246.

[PRA76] Pratt, V.R., "Semantical Considerations on Floyd–Hoare Logic," *Proc. Seventeenth IEEE Symposium Foundations of Computer Science,* IEEE, New York, October 1976, 409–420.

[PSS82] Patil, R.S., P. Szolovits and W.B. Schwartz, "Information Acquisition in Diagnosis," *Proc. National Conference on Artificial Intelligence,* 1982, 345–348.

[QUIL67] Quillian, M.R., "Word Concepts: A Theory and Simulation of some Basic Semantic Capabilities," *Behavioral Science 12,* in [BL85], 1967, 410–430.

[RAPH64] Raphael, B., *SIR: A Computer Program for Semantic Information Retrieval,* Ph.D. dissertation, MIT, Department of Mathematics, Cambridge, MA, 1964.

[RBBF84] Reiner, D., M.L. Brodie, G. Brown, M. Friedell, D. Kramlich, J. Lehman and A.S. Rosenthal, "The Database Design and Evaluation Workbench (DDEW) Project at CCA," in [REIN84].

[RBFG80] Rothnie, J.B., P.A. Bernstein, S. Fox, N. Goodman, M. Hammer, T.A. Landers, C. Reeve, D.W. Shipman and E. Wong, "Introduction to a System for Distributed Databases (SDD-1)," *ACM Transactions on Database Systems 5,* No. 1, March 1980.

[REIT71] Reiter, R., "Two Results on Ordering for Resolution with Merging and Linear Format," *Journal of the ACM 18,* No. 4, October 1971, 630–646.

[REIN84] Reiner, D. (ed.), "Special Issue on Database Design Techniques, Tools, and Environments," *IEEE Database Engineering Newsletter,* December 1984.

[REIT78] Reiter, R., "On Closed World Databases," in [GM79].

[REIT78a] Reiter, R., "Deductive Question-Answering on Relational Databases," in [GM78], 1978, 149–178.

[REIT78b] Reiter, R., "On Structuring a First-Order Database," *Proc. Second Conference of the Canadian Society for Computational Studies of Intelligence,* Canada, July 1978.

[REIT78c] Reiter, R., "On Reasoning by Default," *Proc. TINLAP-2 Conference,* Urbana-Champaign, IL, July 1978.

[REIT80] Reiter, R., "Equality and Domain Closure in First-Order Databases," *Journal of the ACM 27,* No. 2, April 1980.

[REIT81] Reiter, R., "On the Integrity of First-Order Databases," in [GMN81], 137–158.

[REIT82] Reiter, R., "Circumscription Implies Predicate Completion (Sometimes)," *Proc. American Association for Artificial Intelligence National Conference,* Pittsburgh, PA, August 1982, 418–420.

[REIT83] Reiter, R., "A Sound and Sometimes Complete Query Evaluation Algorithm for Relational Databases with Null Values," Technical Report, Computer Science Department, University of British Columbia, Canada, June 1983.

[REIT84] Reiter, R, "Towards a Logical Reconstruction of Relational Database Theory," in [BMS84].

[REIT84a] Reitman, W. (ed.), *Artificial Intelligence for Business,* Ablex, Norwood, NJ, 1984.

[REIT87] Reiter, R., "Nonmonotonic Reasoning," *Annual Review of Computer Science,* 1987, 147–186.

[RGKM83] Reiter, R., H. Gallaire, J. King, J. Mylopoulos and B. Webber, "Panel on AI and Databases," *Proc. IJCAI-83,* Karlsruhe, 1983.

[RHDM86] Rosenthal, A.S., S.I. Heiler, U. Dayal and F.A. Manola, "Traversal Recursion: A Practical Approach to Supporting Recursive Applications," *Proc. ACM SIGMOD International Conference on Management of Data,* 1986.

[RHM84] Rosenthal, A.S., S.I. Heiler and F.A. Manola, "An Example of Knowledge-Based Query Processing in a CAD/CAM DBMS," *Proc. Tenth International Conference on Very Large Databases,* Singapore, August 1984, 363–370.

[RICH83] Rich, E., *Artificial Intelligence,* McGraw-Hill, New York, 1983.

[RICH87] Rich E., "LUKE: A Knowledge Base Management System," *Preprints of the NSF-ICOT Joint Symposium on AI,* Tokyo, Japan, December 1987.

[RIEG76] Rieger, C., "An Organization of Knowledge for Problem-Solving and Language Comprehension," *Artificial Intelligence 7,* No. 2, in [BL85], 1976, 89–127.

[RM75] Roussopoulos, N. and J. Mylopoulos, "Using Semantic Networks for Data Base Management," *Proc. First International Conference on Very Large Databases,* September 1975.

[ROBI65] Robinson, J.A., "A Machine-Oriented Logic Based on the Resolution Principle," *Journal of the ACM 12,* No. 1, January 1965, 23–41.

[ROBI81] Robinson, J.T., "The K-D-B Tree: A Search Structure for Large Multidimensional Dynamic Indexes," *Proc. ACM SIGMOD International Conference on Management of Data,* 1981, 10–18.

[ROUS75] Roussel, P., "PROLOG: Manuel de Reference et d'utilisation," Technical Report, Department d'Informatiques, Univresite d'Aix-Marseille-Luminy, Marseille, France, September 1975.

[ROUS76] Roussopoulos, N., *A Semantic Network Model of Databases,* Ph.D. dissertation, Department of Computer Science, University of Toronto, Toronto, 1976.

[ROUS79] Roussopoulos, N., "CSDL: A Conceptual Schema Definition Language for the Design of Database Applications," *IEEE Transactions on Software Engineering SE-5,* No. 5, September 1979, 481–496.

[ROWE86] Rowe, L.A., "A Shared Object Hierarchy," in [DD86], 160–171.

[RS79] Rowe, L.A. and K. Shoens, "Data Abstraction, Views and Updates in RIGEL," *Proc. ACM SIGMOD International Conference on Management of Data,* Boston, MA, 1979.

[SACL79] Selinger, P.G., M.M. Astrahan, D.D. Chamberlin, R.A. Lorie and T.G. Price, "Access Path Selection in a Relational Database Management System," *Proc. ACM-SIGMOD International Conference on Management of Data,* Boston, May 30–June 1, 1979, 23–34.

[SAME84] Samet, H., "The Quadtree and Related Hierarchical Data Structures," *ACM Computing Surveys 16,* No. 2, 1984.

[SARI87] Sarin S.K. (ed.), "Special Issue on Federated Database Systems," *Database Engineering 10,* No. 3, 1987.

[SB81] Schmolze, J.G. and R.J. Brachman (eds.), *Proc. 1981 KL-ONE Workshop,* Jackson NH, October 1981.

[SB83] Schmidt, J.W. and M.L. Brodie, *Relational Database Systems: Analysis and Comparison,* Springer-Verlag, New York, 1983.

[SB86] Stefik, M. and D.G. Bobrow, "Object-Oriented Programming: Themes and Variations," *AI Magazine 6,* No. 4, 1986, 40–62.

[SBDD85] Spector, A.Z., J. Butcher, D.S. Daniels, D.J. Duchamp, J.L. Eppinger, C.E. Fineman, A. Heddaya and P.M. Schwartz, "Support for Distributed Transactions in the TABS Prototype," *IEEE Transactions on Software Engineering SE-11,* No. 6, June 1985.

[SBK85] Sarin, S.K., B.T. Blaustein and C.W. Kaufman, "System Architecture for Partition-Tolerant Distributed Databases," *IEEE Trans. Computers C-34,* 12, December 1985, pp. 1158–1163.

[SBN84] Schroeder, M.D., A.D. Birrell and R.M. Needham, "Experience with Grapevine: The Growth of a Distributed System," *ACM Transactions on Computer Systems 2,* No. 1, 1984, 3–23.

[SC86] Smith, R.G. and P. Carando, "Structured Object Programming in STROBE," Technical Report SYS-86-23, Schlumberger-Doll Research, Ridgefield, CT, 1986.

[SCHA75] Schank, R.C., *Conceptual Information Processing,* North-Holland, Amsterdam, 1975.

[SCHK86] Schkolnick, M., "Buffer Management in Relational Database Systems," *ACM Transactions on Database Systems 11,* No. 4, December 1986.

[SCHM77] Schmidt, J.W., "Some High Level Language Constructs for Data of Type Relation," *ACM Transactions on Database Systems 2,* No. 3, 1977.

[SCHU76] Schubert, L. "Extending the Expressive Power of Semantic Networks," *Artificial Intelligence 7,* 1976, 163–198.

[SDPF81] Sagiv, Y., C. Delobel, D.S. Parker, Jr. and R. Fagin, "An Equivalence between Relational Database Dependencies and a Subclass of Propositional Logic," *Journal of the ACM 28,* No. 3, July 1981, 435–453.

[SENK75] Senko, M., "The DDL in the Context of a Multi-Level Structured Description: DIAM II with FORAL," in Douque and Nijssen (eds.), *Data Base Management,* North-Holland, Amsterdam, 1975.

[SFL83] Smith, J.M., S.A. Fox and T. Landers, "ADAPLEX Rationale and Reference Manual," Technical Report CCA-83-08, Computer Corporation of America, Cambridge, May 1983.

[SGC79] Schubert, L., R. Goebel and N. Cercone, "The Structure and Organization of a Semantic Net for Comprehension and Inference," in [FIND79], 122–172.

[SHIP81] Shipman, D., "The Functional Data Model and the Data Language DAPLEX," *ACM Transaction on Database Systems 6,* No. 1, March 1981, 140–173.

[SHNE80] Shneiderman, B., *Software Psychology,* Winthrop, Cambridge, MA, 1980.

[SHOR76] Shortliffe, E.H., *MYCIN: Computer-Based Medical Consultations,* American Elsevier, New York, 1976.

[SIBL76] Sibley, E.H. (ed.), "Special Issue: Data-Base Management Systems," *ACM Computing Surveys, 8,* No. 1, March 1976.

[SK88] Selman, B. and H. Kautz, "The Complexity of Model-Preference Default Theories," *Proc. Seventh Biennial Conference of the Canadian Society for Computational Studies of Intelligence,* Edmonton, Canada, June 1988, 102–109.

[SKS86] Sarin, S.K., C.W. Kaufman and J.E. Somers, "Using History Information to Process Delayed Database Updates," *Proc. Twelfth International Conference on Very Large Databases,* Kyoto, August 1986.

[SL76] Severance, D.G. and G.M. Lohman, "Differential Files: Their Application to the Maintenance of Large Databases," *ACM Transactions on Database Systems 1,* No. 3, September 1976, 256–267.

[SL82] Siklossy, L. and J.-L. Lauriere, "Removing Restrictions in the Relational Database Model: An Application of Problem Solving Techniques," *Proc. American Association for Artificial Intelligence 82 Conference,* Pittsburgh, PA, August 1982.

[SLOM75] Sloman, A., "Afterthoughts on Analogical Representation," *Proc. Theoretical Issues in Natural Language Processing,* Cambridge, MA, in [BL85], 1975, 164–168.

[SM80] Shapiro, S.E. and D.P. McKay, "Inference with Recursive Rule," *Proc. First Annual National Conference on Artificial Intelligence, AAAI,* Palo Alto, CA, 1980.

[SMIT78] Smith, J.M., "Comments on the papers: 'A Software Engineering View of Management' by A.I. Wasserman and 'A Software Engineering View of Systems' by H. Weber," *Proc. Fourth International Conference on Very Large Databases,* Berlin, September 1984.

[SMIT82] Smith, B.C., "Reflection and Semantics in a Procedural Language," Ph.D. thesis and Tech. Report MIT/LCS/TR-272, MIT, Cambridge, MA, 1982. Also in [BL85].

[SMIT85] Smith, J.M., "Large-Scale Knowledge Systems," *Proc. GI-Congress on Knowledge Based Systems,* Munich, Germany, October 1985.

[SMIT86] Smith, J.M., "Expert Database Systems: A Database Perspective," in [KERS86].

[SMIT87] Smith, R.G., "Report on the 1986 Workshop on Distributed AI," *AI Magazine 8,* No. 3, Fall 1987.

[SP82] Scheck, H.J. and P. Pistor, "Data Structures for an Integrated Data Base Management and Information Retrieval System," *Proc. Eighth International Conference on Very Large Databases,* 1982, 197–207.

[SR74] Schank, R.C. and C.J. Rieger, III, "Inference and the Computer Understanding of Natural Language," *Artificial Intelligence 5,* No. 4, in [BL85], 1974, 373–412.

[SR86] Stonebraker, M. and L.A. Rowe, "The Design of POSTGRES," *Proc. ACM SIGMOD International Conference on Management of Data,* Washington, D.C., May 1986, 340–355.

[SRG83] Stonebraker, M., B. Rubenstein and A. Guttman, "Application of Abstract Data Types and Abstract Indices to CAD Data," *Proc. ACM SIGMOD Conference on Engineering Design Applications,* 1983.

[SS75] Schmid, J. and J.R. Swenson, "On the Semantics of the Relational Model," *Proc. ACM SIGMOD International Conference on Management of Data,* San Jose, CA, May 1975.

[SS77] Smith, J.M. and D. Smith, "Data Abstraction: Aggregation," *Communications of the ACM 20,* No. 6, June 1977, 568–579.

[SS77a] Smith, J.M. and D. Smith, "Data Abstraction: Aggregation and Generalization," *ACM Transactions on Database Systems 2,* No. 2, June 1977, 105–133.

[SS78] Smith, J.M. and D.C.P. Smith, "Principles of Conceptual Database Design," *Proc. NYU Symposium on Database Design,* New York, May 1978, No. 6, June 1977, 568–579.

[SS79] Smith, J.M. and D.C.P. Smith, "Conceptual Database Design," *Proc. The Sixty-Second Infotech State of the Art Conference*, September 1979, Infotech Int'l., Maidenhead, England, 88–112.

[SS79a] Smith J.M. and D.C.P. Smith, "A Database Approach to Software Specification," in *Software Development Tools,* W.E. Riddle and R.E. Fairley (eds.), Springer-Verlag, New York, 1979.

[SS83] Spector, A.Z. and P.M. Schwarz, "Transactions: A Construct for Reliable Distributed Computing," *Operating Systems Review 17,* No. 2, April 1983, 18–35.

[SS86] Sheard, T. and D. Stemple, "Coping with Complexity in Automated Reasoning about Database Systems," *Proc. Eleventh International Conference on Very Large Databases,* Stockholm, August 1986, 426–435.

[ST85] Samet, H. and M. Tamminen, "Computing Geometric Properties of Images Represented by Linear Quadtrees," *IEEE Transactions on Pattern Analysis and Machine Intelligence 7,* No. 2, 1985.

[ST85a] Samet, H. and M. Tamminen, "Bintrees, CSG Trees and Time," *ACM SIGGRAPH 19,* No. 3, 1985.

[ST88] Schmidt, J.W. and C. Thanos (eds.), *Fundamentals of Knowledge Base Management Systems,,* Springer-Verlag, New York, 1988.

[STIC85] Stickel, M., "Automated Deduction by Theory Resolution," *Journal of Automated Reasoning 1,* 1985, 333–355.

[STON75] Stonebraker, M., "Implementation of Integrity Constraints and Views by Query Modification," *Proc. ACM SIGMOD International Conference on Management of Data,* San Jose, CA, May 1975.

[STON80] Stonebraker, M., "Retrospection on a Database System," *ACM Transactions* on *Database Systems 5,* No. 2, 225–240.

[STON86a] Stonebraker, M., "Object Management in POSTGRES Using Procedures," in [DD86].

[STON86b] Stonebraker, M., "The Case for Shared Nothing," *IEEE Database Engineering 9,* No. 1, March 1986, 4–10.

[STON86c] Stonebraker, M. and M.R. Stonebraker, "Inclusion of New Types in Relational Database Systems," *Proc. Second International Conference on Data Base Engineering,* Los Angeles, February 1986.

[SWKH76] Stonebraker, M., E. Wong, P. Kreps and G. Held, "The Design and Implementation of INGRES," *ACM Transactions on Database Systems 1,* No. 3, September 1976, 189–222.

[TAMA85] Tamassia, R., "New Layout Techniques for Entity-Relationship Diagrams," *Proc. Fourth International Conference on E-R Approach,* Chicago, October 1985.

[TAMM82] Tamminen, M. and R. Sulonen, "The EXCELL Method for Efficient Geometric Access to Data," *Proc. Nineteenth ACM Design Automation Conference,* 1982, 345–351.

[TAUL] Taulbee, O.E., "Annual U.S. Summaries of Ph.D. Production and Employment in Computer Science 1970–1985," *CIGSE Bulletin*, Vol. 18, No. 3, September 1986.

[TB83] Templeton, M. and J. Burger, "Problems in Natural Language Interface to DBMS with Examples from EUFID," *Proc. Conference on Applied Natural Language Processing,* 1983, 3–16.

[TEOR82] Teorey, T.J. and J.P. Fry, *Design of Database Structures,* Prentice-Hall, Englewood Cliffs, NJ, 1982.

[TF76] Taylor, R.W. and R.L. Frank, "CODASYL Data-Base Management Systems," in [SIBL76].

[TF80] Teorey, T.J. and J.P. Fry, "The Logical Record Access Approach to Database Design," *ACM Computing Surveys 12,* No. 2, 1980.

[TFGN87] Tsichritzis, D., E. Fiume, S. Gibbs and O. Nierstrasz, "KNOs: KNowledge Acquisition, Dissemination and Manipulation Objects," *Transactions on Office Information Systems 5,* No. 1, 1987, 96–112.

[THAT86] Thatte, S.M., "Persistent Memory: A Storage Architecture for Object-Oriented Database Systems," in [DD86], 148–159.

[THOM79] Thomas, R.H., "A Majority Consensus Approach to Concurrency Control for Multiple Copy Databases," *ACM Transactions on Database Systems 4,* No. 2, June 1979, 180–209.

[TL76] Tsichritzis, D.C. and F.H. Lochovsky, "Hierarchical Data-Base Management," in [SIBL76].

[TSIC88] Tsichritzis, D. (ed.), "Active Object Environments," Technical Report, Centre Universitaire D'Informatique, Universite de Geneve, 1988.

[TT83] Thompson, B.H. and F. Thompson, "Introducing ASK: A Simple Knowledgeable System," *Proc. Conference on Applied Natural Language Processing,* Santa Monica, CA, 1983

[TT85] Thompson, B. and F. Thompson, "ASK Is Transportable in Half a Dozen Ways," *ACM Transactions on Office Information Systems 3,* No. 2, 1985.

[TURI51] Turing, A.M., "Computing Machinery and Intelligence," in [FF63], 11–35.

[TURN84] Turner, R., *Logics for Artificial Intelligence,* Ellis Horwood, 1984.

[TYF86] Teorey, T.J., D. Yang and J.P. Fry, "A Logical Design Methodology for Relational Databases Using the Extended Entity-Relationship Model," *ACM Computing Surveys 18,* No. 2, 1986.

[ULLM82] Ullman, J.D., *Principles of Database Systems,* 2nd Edition, Computer Science Press, Potomac, MD, 1982,

[ULLM85] Ullman, J.D., "Implementation of Logical Query Languages for

Databases," *ACM Transactions on Database Systems,* 1985.

[ULLM88] Ullman, J.D., *Principles of Database and Knowledge-Base Systems,* Volume I, Computer Science Press, Potomac, MD, 1988.

[UM80] Uno, S. and H. Matsuka, "A Relational Database for Design Aids System," *Proc. Workshop on Picture Data Description and Management,* August 1980.

[VANE78] Van Emden, M.H., "Computation and Deductive Information Retrieval," in *Formal Description of Programming Concepts,* E. Neuhold (ed.), Elsevier North-Holland, New York, 1978, 421–440.

[VANM81] Van Melle, W., *System Aids in Constructing Consultation Programs,* UMI Research Press, Ann Arbor, MI, 1981.

[VASS79] Vassiliou, Y., "Null Values in Database Management: A Denotational Semantics Approach," *Proc. ACM SIGMOD International Conference on Management of Data,* 162–169.

[VASS80] Vassiliou, Y., "Functional Dependencies and Incomplete Information," *Proc. Sixth International Conference on Very Large Databases,* Montreal, October 1980, 260–269.

[VCJ83] Vassiliou, Y., J. Clifford and M. Jarke, "How Does an Expert System Get Its Data?" *Proc. Ninth International Conference on Very Large Databases,* 1983.

[VDF81] Veloso, P.A.S., J.M.V. De Castilho and A.L. Furtado, "Systematic Derivation of Complementary Specifications," *Proc. Seventh International Conference on Very Large Databases,* Cannes, France, September 1981, 409–421.

[VERH78] Verhofstad, J.S.M., "Recovery Techniques for Database Systems," *ACM Computing Surveys 10,* No. 2, June 1978.

[VILA85] Vilain, M., "The Restricted Language Architecture of a Hybrid Representation System," *Proc. Ninth International Joint Conference on Artificial Intelligence,* Los Angeles, 1985, 547–551.

[VK76] Van Emden, M.H. and R.A. Kowalski, "The Semantics of Predicate Logic as a Programming Language," *Journal of the ACM 23,* No. 4, October 1976, 733–742.

[VSZM83] Vesonder, G.T., S.J. Stolfo, J.E. Zielinski, F.D. Mille and D.H. Copp, "ACE: An Expert System for Telephone Cable Maintenance," *Proc. Eighth International Joint Conference on Artificial Intelligence,* 1983, 116–121.

[WARR81] Warren, D.H.D., "Efficient Processing of Interactive Relational Database Queries Expressed in Logic," *Proc. Seventh International Conference on Very Large Databasea,* Cannes, France, September 1981, 272–281.

[WDHL82] Williams, R., D. Daniels, L. Haas, G. Lapis, B. Lindsay, P. Ng, R. Obermarck, P. Selinger, A. Walker, P. Wilms and R. Yost, "R*: An Overview of the Architecture," *Proc. Second International Conference on Database Systems,* Jerusalem, 1982.

[WEYH80] Weyhrauch, R.W., "Prolegomena to a Theory of Mechanized Formal Reasoning," *Artificial Intelligence,* 13, No. 1, 2, in [BL85], 1980, 133–170.

[WIED83] Wiederhold, G., *Database Design,* 2nd Edition, McGraw-Hill, New York, 1983.

[WIED84] Wiederhold, G., "Knowledge and Database Management," *IEEE Software,* January 1984.

[WILE84] Wilensky, R., "KODIAK — A Knowledge Representation Language," *Proc. Sixth Annual Conference of the Cognitive Science Society,* 1984, 344–352.

[WILL84] Williams, M.D., "What Makes RABBIT Run?" *International Journal of Man–Machine Studies 21,* 1984, 333–352.

[WINO75] Winograd, T., "Frame Representations and the Declarative-Procedural Controversy," in [BC75].

[WINS75] Winston, P.H., "Learning Structural Descriptions from Examples," in *The Psychology of Computer Vision,* P.H. Winston (ed.), McGraw-Hill, New York, in [BL85], 1975, 157–209.

[WINS85] Winston, P. *Artificial Intelligence,* Addison-Wesley, Reading, MA, 1985.

[WM77] Wong, H.K.T. and J. Mylopoulos, "Two Views of Data Semantics: Data Models in Artificial Intelligence and Database Management," *INFOR 15,* No. 3, 1977.

[WOOD67] Woods, W.A., "Semantics for Question-Answering Systems," Ph.D. dissertation, Rep. NSF-19, Aiken Computation Laboratory, Harvard University, Cambridge, MA, 1967.

[WOOD68] Woods, W.A., "Procedural Semantics for a Question-Answering Machine," *Proc. Fall Joint Computer Conference,* 1968, 457–471.

[WOOD73] Woods, W.A., "Progress in Natural Language Understanding: An Application to Lunar Geology," *Proc. AFIPS Conference 42,* 1973, 441–450.

[WOOD75] Woods, W.A., "What's in a Link: Foundations for Semantic Networks," in *In Representation and Understanding: Studies in Cognitive Science,* D.G. Bobrow and A.M. Collins (eds.), Academic Press, New York, 1975, 35–82; Reprinted in *Readings in Knowledge Representation,* R.J. Brachman and H.J. Levesque (eds.), Morgan Kaufmann, Los Altos, CA, 1985, 217–241.

[WY76] Wong E. and K. Yosseffi, "Decomposition — A Strategy of Query Processing," *ACM Transactions on Database Systems 1,* No. 3, September 1976, 223–241.

[YOKO84] Yokota, H., et al., "An Enhanced Inference Mechanism for Generating Relational Algebra Queries," *Proc. ACM SIGACT-SIGMOD Symposium on Principles of Database Systems,* 1984.

[YP82] Yannakakis, M. and Papadimitriou, C., "Algebraic Dependencies," *Journal of the Computer and Systems Science 25,* No. 1, August 1982, 2–41.

[ZANI83] Zaniolo, C., "The Database Language GEM," *Proc. ACM SIGMOD Conference on Management of Data,* San Jose, CA, May 1983.

[ZDON85] Zdonik, S.B., "Object Management Systems for Design Environments," in [LOCH85].

[ZLOO75a] Zloof, M.M., "Query by Example: The Invocation and Definition of Tables and Forms," *Proc. First International Conference on Very Large Databases,* September 1975.

[ZLOO77] Zloof, M.M., "Query-by-Example: A Data Base Language," *IBM Systems Journal 16,* No. 4, 1977, 324–343.

[ZLOO82] Zloof, M.M., "Office-by-Example: A Business Language that Unifies Data and Word Processing and Electronic Mail," *IBM Systems Journal 21,* No. 3, 1982.

[ZM89] Zdonick, S.B. and D. Maier, *Readings in Object-Oriented Databases,* Morgan Kaufmann, San Mateo, CA (to appear).

[ZOBR77] Zobrist, A.L., "Elements of an Image-Based Information System," *Proc. IEEE Workshop on Picture Data Description and Management,* 1977, 55–60.

Credits

Astrahan, M.M., D. Chamberlin, M.W. Blasgen, et al., "System R: Relational Approach to Database Management," ACM Transactions on Database Systems, Vol. 1, 1976, pp. 97-137. © 1969, ACM. Reprinted with permission of the publisher and authors.

Bachman, C.W., "The Programmer as Navigator," Communications of the ACM, Vol. 16, No. 11, November, 1973, pp. 653-658. Turing Award Lecture. © 1973, ACM. Reprinted with permission of the publisher and author.

Bancilhon, F. and R. Ramakrishnan, "An Amateur's Introduction to Recursive Query Processing," Proceedings of the 1986 SIGMOD International Conference on Management of Data, Washington D.C., May 1986, pp. 16-52. © 1986, ACM. Reprinted with permission of the publisher and the authors.

Beeri, C., P.A. Bernstein, and N. Goodman, "A Sophisticate's Introduction to Database Normalization Theory," Proceedings of the 4th International Conference on Very Large Databases, 1978, pp. 113-124. © 1978, Alfonso Cardenas. Reprinted with permission of the publisher and authors.

Bernstein, P.A., B. Blaustein and N. Goodman, "Fast Maintenance of Integrity Assertions Using Redundant Aggregate Data," Proceedings of the 6th International Conference on Very Large Databases, October, 1980, pp. 126-136. © 1980, Alfonso Cardenas. Reprinted with permission of the publisher and authors.

Biller H. and E. Neuhold, "Semantics of Data Models: Database Semantics," Information Systems 3, 1978, pp. 11-30. © 1978, Pergamon Press. Reprinted with permission of the publisher and authors.

Bocca, J. "On the Evaluation Strategy of EDUCE," 1986 Proceedings of SIGMOD on Management of Data, Washington D.C., pp. 368-378. © 1986, ACM. Reprinted with permission of the publisher and author.

Borning, A. "The Programming Language Aspects of ThingLab, a Constraint-Oriented Simulation Laboratory," ACM Transactions on Programming Languages and Systems, Vol. 3, No. 4, 1981, pp. 353-387. © ACM, 1981. Reprinted with permission of the publisher and author.

Brachman, R. V. Pigman-Gilbert, and H. Levesque "An Essential Hybrid Reasoning System: Knowledge and Symbol Level Accounts of KRYPTON," IJCAI-85, Los Angeles, 1985, pp. 532-539. © IJCAI, 1985. Reprinted with permission of the publisher and authors.

Brachman, R.J. "An Overview of the KL-ONE Knowledge Representation System," Cognitive Science 9, 1985, pp. 171-216. c 1985, Ablex Publishing Corporation. Reprinted with permission of the publisher and author.

Brodie, M.L. & F. Manola "Database Management: A Survey," in Fundamental of Knowledge Base Management Systems, J.W. Schmidt and C. Thanos (eds.), Springer-Verlag, New York, to appear, 1988, pp. 1-24. © 1988, Springer-Verlag. Reprinted with permission of the publisher and authors.

Brodie, M.L. & D. Ridjanovic "On the Design and Specification of Database Transactions," in On Conceptual Modelling: Perspectives from Artificial Intelligence, Databases, and Programming Languages, M.L. Brodie, J. Mylopolous, and J.W. Schmidt (eds.), Springer-Verlag, New York, 1984, pp. 277-306. © 1984, Springer- Verlag. Reprinted with permission of the publisher and authors.

Chan, A.S., S. Danburg, S. Fox, W.K. Lin, A. Nori, and D. Ries "Storage and Access Structures to Support a Semantic Data Model," Proceedings of the 8th International Conference on very Large Databases, Mexico, 1982, pp. 122-130. © 1982, Alfonso Cardenas. Reprinted with permission of the publisher and authors.

Chen, P.P.S. "The Entity-Relationship Model: Towards a Unified View of Data," ACM Transactions on Database Systems Vol. 1, No. 9, 1976, pp. 9-36. © 1976, ACM. Reprinted with permission of the publisher and author.

Codd, E.F. "Relational Database: A Practical Foundation for Productivity," Communications of the ACM, Vol. 25, No. 2, February, 1982, pp.109-117. © 1982, ACM. Reprinted with permission of the publisher and author.

Eswaren, K.P., J.N. Gray, R. Lorie, and I.L. Traiger "The Notions of Consistency and Predicate Locks in a Database System," Communications of the ACM, Vol. 19, No. 9, 1976, pp. 624-633. © 1976, ACM. Reprinted with permission of the publisher and authors.

Forgy, C.L. "Rete: A Fast Algorithm for the Many Pattern/Many Object Pattern Match Problem," Artificial Intelligence, Vol. 19, No. 1, 1982, pp. 17-37. © 1982, AI Journal. This material originally appeared in Artificial Intelligence, an international journal published by North-Holland, and is reprinted here by permission of the publisher and author.

Frisch, A.M. and J.F. Allen "Knowledge Retrieval as Limited Inference," in Lecture Notes in Computer Science: Sixth Conference on Automated Deduction, D. Loveland (ed.), Springer-Verlag, New York, 1982, pp. 274-291. © 1982, Springer-Verlag. Reprinted with permission of the publisher and authors.

Gallaire, H. J. Minker, and J.-M. Nicolas "Logic and Databases: A Deductive Approach," ACM Computing Surveys, Vol. 16, No. 2, 1984, pp. 153-185. © 1984, ACM. Reprinted with permission of the publisher and authors.

Imielinski, T. and W. Lipski "On Representing Incomplete Information in a Relational Database," Proceedings of the Conference on Very Large Databases, Cannes, France, 1981, pp. 398-397. © 1981, Alfonso Cardenas. Reprinted with permission of the publisher and authors.

Jarke, M. and Y. Vassiliou "A Framework for Choosing a Database Query Language," ACM Computing Surveys, Vol. 17, No. 3, September, 1985. © 1985, ACM. Reprinted with permission of the publisher and authors.

Kent, W. "Limitations of Record-Based Information Models," ACM Transactions on Database Systems, Vol. 4, No. 1, 1979, pp. 108-131. © 1979, ACM. Reprinted with permission of the publisher and author.

Kowalski, R. "Logic for Data Description," in Logic and Data Bases, H. Gallaire and J. Minker (eds.), Plenum Press, New York, 1978, pp. 77-103. © 1978, Plenum Press. Reprinted with permission of the publisher and author.

Lafue, G. and R. Smith "A Modular Tool Kit for Knowledge Management," IJCAI-85, Los Angeles, 1985, pp. 46-52. © 1985, IJCAI. Reprinted with permission of the publisher and authors.

Levesque, H. J. "Making Believers Out of Computers," Artificial Intelligence, Vol. 30, 1986, pp. 81-108. © 1986, AI Journal. Reprinted with permission of the publisher and author.

Levesque, H.J. "The Logic of Incomplete Databases," In M.L. Brodie and J.W. Schmidt (eds.), On Conceptual Modelling: Perspectives from Artificial Intelligence, Databases, and Programming Languages, Springer-Verlag, 1984. © 1984, Springer-Verlag. Reprinted with permission of the publisher and author.

Levesque, H.J. "Knowledge Representation and Reasoning," Annual Review of Computer Science, Vol. 1, 1986, pp. 255-287. © 1986, Annual Reviews. Reprinted with permission of the publisher and author.

Mylopoulos, J., P.A. Bernstein, and H.K.T. Wong "A Language Facillity for Designing Interactive Data-Intensive Systems," ACM Transactions on Database Systems, Vol. 5, No. 2, 1980, pp. 185-207. © 1980, ACM. Reprinted with permission of the publisher and authors.

Nicolas, J.-M. "Logic for Improving Integrity Checking in Relational Databases," Acta Informatica, Vol. 18, No. 3, 1982, pp. 227-253. © 1982, Springer-Verlag. Reprinted with permission of the publisher and author.

Reiter, R. "Towards a Logical Reconstruction of Relational Database Theory," in On Conceptual

Modelling: Perspectives from Artifical Intelligence, Databases, and Programming Languages, M.L. Brodie, J. Mylopoulos, and J.W. Schmidt (eds.), Springer-Verlag, New York, 1984, pp. 191-238. © 1984, Springer-Verlag. Reprinted with permission of the publisher and author.

Reiter, R. "On Closed World Databases," in Logic and Data Bases, H. Gallaire, & J. Minker (eds.), Plenum Press, New York, 1978, pp. 55-76. © 1978, Plenum Press. Reprinted with permission of the publisher and author.

Reiter, R. "Reductive Question-Answering on Relational Data Bases," in Logic and Data Bases, H. Gallaire & J. Minker (eds.), Plenum Press, New York, 1978, pp. 149-176. © Plenum Press, 1978. reprinted with permission of the publisher and author.

Roussopoulos, N. & J. Mylopoulos, "Using Semantic Networks for Database Management," Proceedings of the International Conference on Very Large Databases, Framingham, MA, 1975, pp. 144-157. © 1975, Alfonso Cardenas. Reprinted with permission of the publisher and authors.

Selinger, P.G., M.M. Astrahan, D.D. Chamberlin, R.A. Lorie, and T.G. Price "Acces Path Selection in a Relational DBMS," Proceedings of the 1979 SIGMOD Conference, pp. 23-34. © 1979, ACM. Reprinted with permission of the publisher and author.

Shipman, D. "The Functional Data Model and the Data Language DAPLEX," ACM Transactions on Database Systems, Vol. 5, No. 1, 1981, pp. 140-173. © 1981, ACM. Reprinted with permission of the publisher and author.

Smith, J.M. and D.C.P. Smith, "Database Abstractions: Aggregation and Generalization," ACM Transactions on Database Systems, Vol. 2, No. 2, June, 1977, pp.105-133. © 1977, ACM. Reprinted with permission of the publisher and author.

Stonebraker, M. "Inclusion of New Types in Relational Database Systems," Proceedings of the 2nd International Conference on Data Engineering, Los Angeles, CA, 1986, pp. 262-269. © 1986, IEEE. Reprinted with permission of the publisher and author.

Stonebraker, M. "Implementation of Integrity Constraints and Views by Query Modification," ACM SIGMOD International Conference on Management of Data, 1975, pp. 65-78. © 1975, ACM. Reprinted with permission of the publisher and the author.

Index

A

ABox. *See* System, KRYPTON
Abstraction
    in ACM/PCM, 186
    conceptual, in DAPLEX, 174-75
    database, 12, 138-53, 198, 200
    generalization, 138-41
    in the SHM+, 187-88
Access
    to database records, 55-56
    design of, in ADAPLEX, 585-90
    methods of, and the inclusion of new data types, 600, 601-5
    shared, 56
Access path, selection of, in a relational DBMS, 511-22
ACM/PCM. *See* Modeling, active and passive component
Agent, in combined AI-DB systems, 623
Aggregation
    in conceptual modeling, 318-19
    in DAPLEX, 172-73
    DB, 138-53
    in the SHM+, 187
Aho-Ullman method, for query processing, 397-99
"Alexander" strategy, for query processing, 405
Algebra
    object, 204
    relational, "complex objects" orientation and, 357-60
Algorithm, Rete Match, 547-56
Answer
    deductive, of queries to relational DB, 431-43
    indefinite, and deductive question-answering, 441
    returning all, 442-43
APEX, for query processing, 395-97, 418, 419, 421
Application
    of DAPLEX, 177-79
    database-intensive, language for, 156-66
Architecture
    of computer-based information systems, 58
    DB, 11-12, 19
    DBMS, 25
    design level of, in AI, 631
Artificial intelligence (AI)
    and DB, 1-2, 623-641
        requirements for, 632-634
        technology for systems of, 630-634
    historical sketch of, 2-6
    integration of, with DB, 623-641
    levels of design, and DB, 632
    and QL development, 365
    technology
        and DB systems requirements, 635-36
        to benefit DB, 623
Assertion, integrity constraint and, 457-67, 538-42
Assumption
    closed world (CWA), 233
        DB and, 248-58
        if-and-only-if definitions and, 268
        knowledge base and, 339
        in relational DB, 319
    default, in KR, 39, 46-48
    domain closure, 233
    open world, and if-halves definitions, 268
    unique name, 233
    universal relation, data dependency and, 469
Attribute
    in record structures, 91
    renaming, 354-55
    storage, in DAPLEX, 177
Automation, of DB design, 59
Axiom
    domain closure, and universal quantification, 443
    KL schemata, 333
    retrieval, in a limited inference retriever, 445, 447, 448-49

B

Behavior
- in DB application, 185-86
- modeling, with SHM+, 189-95
- scheme, in transactions, 191-93
- specifications for, 193-95
- and structure, 202
- worst case, and KBS, 72-73

Belief
- KL-ONE and, 208-10
- and KR, 44-45, 293
- and worst case behavior, 73

Bounds, in semantic integrity assertions, 462-64

C

Calculation, graphic, in ThingLab, 484-88
Calculus, relational, 235
CALS. *See* Computer-Aided Logistics Support
Cancellation, in KL-ONE, 216
CASE. *See* Engineering, Computer Aided Software
Celsius, converting to Fahrenheit, in ThingLab, 485, 487, *488-89*
Circumscription, 48
Class, in TAXIS, 157-61, 162-65
Classification, in the SHM+, 187
Classifier, KL-ONE, 210, 215-16, 223-29
Combinatorial explosions, 72
Compiler, for System R, 581
Computability, effective, of queries in a DB, 384
Computer-Aided Logistics Support (CALS), 27
Computers, as believers, 69-82
Computing
- distributed, 627
- next generation, and AI-DB technology, 624-26, 637-39

Concept
- in KL-ONE, 209-12, 215-17
- level of, in DB design, 632

Concerning the Revolutions of the Celestial Spheres (Copernicus), 52
Concurrency control
- and access methods for new data types, 604
- and AI systems, 624, 628
- concurrency, in DBMS, 26
- structures for, in DAPLEX, 174
- in System R, 573-75

Consequence, logical, 36, 44
Consistency
- abstract data model and, 279-83
- of data, and the entity-relationship data model, *105-6*, 106
- in a DBS, 523-32
- locking and, 524-27
- tests of, 460-61
- updates and, 459-61

Constraint (*see also* Integrity constraint)
- aggregate and, 542
- in DAPLEX, 176
- defined, 480
- in ThingLab, 480-81
  - representation of, 491-93
  - satisfaction of, 484, *486*, 490, 493-96
  - structure of, 492-93

Contamination, in shared access multiprogramming, 56
Context, in a semantic network, 10-11
Cooperative work, distributed, 623, 625
Copernicus, 52, 53, 57
Corporation for Open Systems (COS), 58
COS. *See* Corporation for Open Systems
Cost-benefit analysis, for choosing a QL, 363-65
Cost (*see also* Efficiency)
- and degree of cooperation, 625
- of maintaining semantic integrity, 465-66
- query processing, 408-12, 418-24
- for single relation access paths, 513-15, 517-18, 522
- in System R, 566-68

Counting, for query processing, 403, 404, 418, 419, 421
- reverse, 403-4

Coupling
- loose
  - in EDUCE, 608-9
  - between KB and DB systems, 633
- tight, between KB and DB systems, 633

Crash recovery
- and access methods for new data types, 604
- System R and, 575

Credit card, DB language for verification of, 156
Cursor, modifying, in System R, 568-69
CWA. *See* Assumption, closed world

D

DAPLEX
- data definition in, 170-71
- data manipulation in, 171-74
- DB and, 176-77
- derived data in, 174-76
- in front-end applications, 177-78
- goals of, 168
- interface as, with network DB, 178, 179
- overview of, 168-69
- specification of, 179-84

Data
- application for handling, 631
- control, in System R, 565-66
- defining, in System R, 564-65
- derived, in DAPLEX, 174-76
- description
  - in DAPLEX, 176-77
  - and logic, 259-70
  - relational, 259-62
- distribution, 631
- entity-relationship model of, 83-84
- independence, 631
- manipulating
  - in DAPLEX, 171-74
  - in System R, 564
- multilevel views of, and the entity-relationship data model, 98, *99*
- order of, in DAPLEX, 171

redundant aggregate, for maintaining semantic integrity assertions, 457-67
sharing, 631
structures, 20
Database (DB)
abstraction of, 138-52
active, 631
AI technology and, 628
AI and, 1-2, 623-641
closed world, 248-58
completeness in, 442-43
concepts of, 10-11
consistency in, 523-32
content of, defined, 469
conventional, and logic, 234-39, 377-79
DAPLEX and, 176-77
deductive (logic), 627-28
defined, 239-40
definite (DDDB), 240-43
indefinite (IDDDB), 243
and logic, 239-44
departmental, described, 263-64
described, 442
description, schema as, 469
design, 14-15
and the entity-relationship data model, 103-4
and logic, 238-39
distinguished from a KB, 338-39
distributed, 628
dynamic, 323
early, 53
evolving, dynamics of, 266
expert, 628
extensional (EDB), and CWA, 250-52
function, and KB, 631-32
hardware, 21
incomplete information in, 307-8, 311-15
indefinite deductive (IDDDB), 243
intelligent, 627
intensional (IDB), compiling, for deductive question-answering, 438-41
KB paradigm, 631
KBS and, 627
KR and, 40-41
levels of design in, and AI, 632
and logic, 231-44
model theoretic perspective of, 302-9
deficienies in, 307-8
proof theoretic perspective of, 308-19
generalizing, 311-19
logical, 279-91
logic. *See* Database (DB), deductive
models of, 468
network, DAPLEX and, 178, 179
performance evaluation, 20
predicate locks in, 523-32
queries and, 248-49
query evaluation in, assumptions of, 233
real time, 631
relational
access path selection in, 511-22
criticisms of, 65-67
DAPLEX and, 177-78
deductive question-answering on, 431-43
defined, 305, 311
described, 468
extensions of, 308
future of, 67
including new types in, 599-606
and incomplete information, 342-60
integrity checking in, 497-508
locking and, 528-32
motivation for research in, 61
productivity and, 60-68
recursive query processing in, 376-430
representation systems in, 344-46
theories of, and logic, 301-24
relevant facts in, and query processing, 386
research into, 22
semantics of, 273-91
technology
for AI systems, 630-35
problems with current, and AI integration, 634-35
tools of, 11-13
transactions in
design of, 185-202
specifications for, 185, 193-98
Database management (DBM), 10-27, 53-54
incompletness in, 335-37
semantic networks for, 1-25
system (DBMS), 11
AI and, 631, 635-37
distributed (DDBMS), 21, 583
interfacing with, 441
object-oriented (OODBMS), 27, 628
programmers and, 52-59
relational, problems of, 1-2
spatial (SDMS), 367
Database Task Group (DBTG), 151
Data dependency, 469-70
defined, 469
inference rules for, 469-70
membership and, 470
properties of, 469
Data equivalence, 272
described, 273-75
Data model
components of, 62-63
conceptual, 632
DBM and, 15-19, 23
defining concepts of, 201
entity-relationship, 98-110
entity set, 98, 109-10
functional, and DAPLEX, 168-84
level, 632
naturalness of, 168n
network, 98, 108-9
relational, 17-18, 98, 106-8
definitions of, 343-44
distinguished from ADAPLEX, 584
and semantic integrity, 458
semantic, 18, 273-91, 632

storage and access structures for, 583-91
simulation of nonrelational, in System R, 569-70
Data services, in relational DB, 65-66
Data type
abstract, 599-601
definition of new, 600
including new in relational DBS, 599-606
prototype of new, 600-601
user-defined, in STROBE, 592-93
DBM. *See* Database management
DBMS. *See* Database management (DBM), system
DBTG. *See* Database Task Group
DDDB. *See* Database, definite deductive
Deduction
compilative, DB and, 242-43
interpretive, DB and, 242
KB capabilities of, 339
Default, values of, in KL-ONE, 216
Definition, if-and-only-if formulation of, 267-70
Deletion, simplification method and, 505
Dependency
functional (FV), 468, 469-70
multivalued, (MVD), 468, 469-70
and propositional logic, 238-39
in V-tables, 356
Derivability, in logic, 37
Description (*see also* Data, description)
in record structures, 87-88
structural, in KL-ONE, 217-20
Design
DB, logic and, 238-39
DB transactions, 185-202
incremental, 198-99
principles of, for TAXIS, 156-57
structure, procedure for, 201
Diagram
data-structure, 108-9
entity-relationship, system analysis and, 103
Differentiation, in KL-ONE, 214-15
Domain, notion of, 322

E

Editor, display oriented (Impulse), 592
Efficiency (*see also* Cost)
of EDUCE, 611-14
integrity constraints and, 542-43
and logical modeling, 324
production system, 548-49
of the Rete Match algorithm, 556
in semantic integrity maintenance, 467
Engineering, Computer Aided Software (CASE), 14, 24, 203-4
Entity
and the entity-relationship data model, 98-102
in record structures, 89-90
Equality, in automatic deduction, 441-42
Equation, quadratic, solving, in ThingLab, 487-88, *489*
Ethernet, 592
Evaluation
naive, for query processing, 387-89, 397, 418, 420
semi-naive, for query processing, 389-90, 418-20
Event
in DB applications, 201
representing, in relational DB, 316-17
Exceptions
handling, for DB transactions, 194-95
in TAXIS, 164-65
Expressions
in DAPLEX, 171, 173-74
in TAXIS, 164
Extensibility, in DBMS, 23

F

Facet, user-defined, in STROBE, 593
Facts, relevant, in record structures, 85-87, 88-88
Fahrenheit, converting to Celsius, in ThingLab, 485, 487, *488-89*
Field name, function of, in record structures, 88
File
management of, in STROBE, 597-98
sequential, 53
system, natural language interface to, 627
Filtering, static, for query processing, 399-401, 418-19, 421
FOL. *See* Logic, first-order
Frames
and KR, 43
in the SHM+, 187
Functionality, of query languages, 370-71
Function call, nested, in DAPLEX, 171-72
Function, in DAPLEX
defining by special operators, 176
evaluating, 173
inversion of, 170-71
naming, 171
FV. *See* Dependency, functional

G

Games, computer, and QL development, 365-66
Generalization
DB abstraction as, 138-53
and the proof theoretic perspective of relational DB, 311-19
in the SHM+, 187-88
Geometry, example of, in ThingLab, 483-84, *485-86*, 493
Graph-fitting (integration of information), in a semantic network, *9*, 10, 11
Graphics, and QL development, 365
Graphs, representing, 265

H

Hardware, and QL development, 365
Henschen-Naqvi method, for query processing, 394-95, 418-20
Hierarchy
generalization, 583
IS-A, 317
in TAXIS, 160-66
in relational DB, 323-24
Homogeneity, in record structures, 85-87, 89
Horn clause, 41-42, 267-68, 269

Hotel reservation program, 185, 190-92, 194-96
Human factors, research into, and QL, 368-69

I

IDB. *See* Database, intensional
IDDDB. *See* Database, indefinite deductive
Identifiers, in record structures, 91-94
I-D-S. *See* Integrated Data Store
IIS. *See* System, interactive information
Images, in RSS of System R, 571-72
Implementation
of EDUCE, 608-11
of a limited inference retrieval system, 449-50
of system to maintain semantic integrity, 461-64
techniques for, 510
Impulse, 592
Incompleteness, support for, in DBMS, 628
Inconsistency, support for, in DBMS, 628
Inference
limited
and knowledge retrieval, 444-54
to specify, 445-46
methods of, and DB access, 242-43
rules of
for data dependency, 469-70
for KL, 333
system for. *See* System, reasoning
Information
disjunctive, in DB, 307, 312-13
incomplete, and relational DB, 342-60
in record structures, 87-88
system (IS), intelligent, 626
future of, 623-39
Information resource management (IRM), 14
Inheritance, in ThingLab, 490-91
Insertion, simplification method and, 501-5, 507-8
Integrated Data Store (I-D-S), 54
Integration
AI-DB
approaches to, 637
benefits of, 628
described, 627-30
need for, 628-30
close, in EDUCE, 609-10
Integration proving, 623
Integrity
checking, in relational DB, 497-508
of data, and the entity-relationship data model, 104-5
DB
capacity for, in AI, 634
and CWA, 255
maintaining assertions of semantic, with redundant aggregate data, 457-67
maintenance of, in DB, 10-11, 20
semantic, in STROBE, 594-96
Integrity constraint
in ADAPLEX, 585
and DDDBs, 241-42
described, 537-38
implementation of, by query modification, 533-45
and logic, 262-63, 336-37
logical formulas as, 498-99
simplification method and, 499-508
in STROBE, 595-96
Interconnectivity, trend in, 623
Interface
access method, 603-4
KRYPTON, 294-97
natural language, 627
QL, 363, 364
Query-by-Example, 561
Relational Data (RDI), 563, 576
standardized, 58
user
AI technology and, 628
of ThingLab, 481, 482-83
User-Friendly (UFI), in System R, 561
Interference, in shared access multiprogramming, 56
International Organization for Standardization (ISO), 58
Interoperability
intelligent, 623, 625
trend in, 623, 625
Interpreter, network, pattern matching and, 554-56
IRM. *See* Information resource management
ISO. *See* International Organization for Standardization
Iteration, over memory, avoiding, 549-50
Iterative Query/Subquery (QSQI), for query processing, 391-92, 418-20

J

Join, access path selection for, 516-20

K

KBMS. *See* Knowledge base (KB), management system
KBS. *See* Knowledge base (KB), system
Knowledge
application for handling, 631
completeness of, 74, 76-78
design level of, in AI, 631
distribution, for cooperative KBS, 632
domain-dependent, 73-74
incompleteness of, 327
peripheral, on a semantic network, 8, 10
re-use of, 623, 631, 634
sharing, 623
tool kit for management of, 592-98
vividness of, 74-78
world, in relational DB, 308, 316-19
Knowledge base (KB)
compilation of, 628
completeness in, 628
consistency in, 628
and DB function, 631-32
DB paradigm, 630-31
definition language for, 334-35
described, 71
distinguished from a DB, 338-39
distributed, and DB technology, 228

first order, 329-30
incomplete, logic and, 328-39
knowledge sharing in, 631
in KRYPTON, 296-97
management system (KBMS), 22, 27, 627-28
new techniques for, 623
retrieval from, 444-54
and semantics, 1-2, 42-43
shared, and DB technology, 628
system (KBS), 36, 69-82
AI and, 623, 628
DB and, 627
design, 634
development, 634
maintenance, 634
modular tool kit for, 592-98
multiple, 631
multiuser, 627
shells, 624
very large, and DB technology, 628
Knowledge representation (KR)
AI-DB interaction and, 627
compromise in, 39-40
DB and, 2-12
defined, 35
hypothesis of, 36
incompletness in, 337-38
independence of, 623
KL-ONE system for, 207-21, 223-27
and logic, 36-40
models of limited reasoning for, 39, 44-46
and reasoning, 35-46
special-purpose language for, 39-44
system
KL-ONE, 207-21, 223-29
KRYPTON as, 293-99
system for, STROBE as, 592-98
theorem proving and, 38-39
KR. *See* Knowledge representation

L

Laboratory, simulation, ThingLab as, 480-96
Language
ABSET, 482
ACTOR, 482
ADAPLEX, 364, 583
ALPHA, 366
ALPHARD, 482
APL/EDBS, 364
assertional, in KL-ONE, 220
C, 592, 597
CAKE, 44
Cedar, 367
CLU, 482
CML, 367
COBOL, 366
COBOL/DML, 364
CommonLisp, 592, 597
constraint, ThingLab and, 482
C/QUEL, 364
DAPLEX, 168-84, 583
Data Definition, 151
data query, logic and, 262
for designing database-intensive applications, 156-66
DL/I, 364
first-order, 302-5, 306-7
Galileo, 367
Interlisp-D, 592, 594, 597
ISBL, 366
KL, proof theory for, 332-33
KL-ONE. *See* System, KL-ONE
KRL, 48, 482
KRYPTON KR, 43, 44
logical data (LDL), 289-91
logicial data definition (LDDL), 283-89
Mainsail, 592, 597
MESA, 482
natural
interface to file systems and, 627
sytems of, 366
object-oriented, 481
OPS5, 547-48
PASCAL/R, 364, 366
PLAIN, 165
PLANNER, 41, 42, 47
programming
for database, 23-24
logic for, 265
and ThingLab, 480-96
PROLOG, 41-42, 46n, 243, 263, 265, 371, 395, 418-19, 421
QBE, 372
QUEL (QUEry language), 366, 533-37
Query-By-Example (QBE), 367, 561
query. *See* Query language
for semantic integrity assertion, 458-59
SEQUEL, 562-64, 577-79. *See also* Language, SQL
SIMULA, 482
Smalltalk-76, 367, 480-81, 490
special-purpose, for KR, 39-44
SQL, 366, 368, 512, 582-83. *See also* Language, SEQUEL
TAXIS, 156-66, 367
TOTAL-IQ, 364 Law
deductive, and DDDBs, 241-42
general, for data description, 260-62
LDDL. *See* Language, logicial data definition
LDL. *See* Language, logical data
Leibniz, 36, 69
Level of design, in DB
and AI, 632
physical, 632
Link
in KRYPTON, 298-99
in System R's RSS, 572
Literature, publication policies and, 57
Localization, in ACM/PCM, 186, 188, 189
Lock, predicate, in a database system, 527-32
Locking, notion of, 524-27

Logic
applicability of, to relational DB theory, 320-21
and data description, 259-70
and DBM, 231-44
default, 47, 48
first-order (FOL), and dependencies, 238-39
formal
in KR, 36-38
Leibniz and, 36
formulas of, as integrity constraints, 498-99
for integrity checking in relational DB, 497-508
interpretations of, for integrity checking, 497-98
level of, in DB design, 632
mathematical, and DB, 232-33
monotonicity criticism of, 266-67
nonmonotonic, 47-48
nonstandard, for KR, 44
program
Hoare's, 459
KR and, 41-42
propositional, and DB design, 238
and relational DB theory, 301-24
relevance, 45-46, 47n, 81
and representation of knowledge, 36-40, 45-46, 47n
thinking and, 70-71

M

Magic Sets, for query processing, 401-2, 404-5, 418-19, 421
Mapping
in EDUCE, 611
in a limited inference retriever, 445-47
Merge, in ThingLab's constraint system, 493
Message plan, in ThingLab, 492
Metaclass, in TAXIS, 157, 158-59, 162-65
Metadata, updating, in DAPLEX, 177
Metadescription, in KL-ONE, 220-21
Method, in ThingLab, 492
Model
abstract data, and the standard interpretation, 276-77
extended semantic hierarchy (SHM+), 187-98 passim, 200
information, limitations of record-based, 85-96
relational data (RDM)
defined, 231-32
described, 62-63
extending, 323
Modeling
active and passive component (ACM/PCM), in database design, 186-87
behavior
concepts in, 201-2
SHM+ for, 189-95
conceptual
in ACM/PCM, 186
and relational DB, 316-19, 321
constructs of, in ADAPLEX, 583-84
with generic abstraction structures, 143-47
logical, and efficiency, 324
structure, for DB transactions, 187-89
transaction, in ACM/PCM, 186
types of, for DB transactions, 199
Monotonicity, criticism of, and logic DB, 266-67
Multiprogramming, shared access and, 55-57
Multitable, closed world interpretation of, 355
MVD. *See* Dependency, multivalued

N

Net, semantic, in a relational DB, 3-11
Network
procedural semantic (PSN), and TAXIS, 166
in the Rete Match algorithm, 550-51, 551-54
semantic
for DBM, 1-25
KR and, 8-9. *See also* Frames
structured inheritance, in KL-ONE, 210
Node, in semantic nets, 3-5
Node type, in the Rete Match algorithm, 551
Normal form, relations and, 150
Normalization
database. *See* Schema, design of
theory, 468-78
Notation, assembly language, for the Rete Match algorithm, 552
Null value
described, 323, 342, 357-60
disjunctive, 307-8, 313-15
logic and, 236

O

Object
initial, in STROBE, 593
inside and outside of, 481, 490
notion of, 480
in TAXIS, 157
in ThingLab, 487-88, 490-91
Object class, specifications for, in DB transactions, 195
Omniscience, logical, 44
Ontology, common, in KBS, 632
Operator
function-defining, in DAPLEX, 176
general-purpose, in DAPLEX, 174
modal, K, 339
semantic, in a relational DB, 17-23
Optimization
for query processing, 397-405, *406*
semantic query, AI technology and, 628
Optimizer, in System R, 566-68
Organization, design level of, in AI, 632
Outcomes, in KRYPTON, 296

P

Paradigm, DB/KB, 631-32
Part
special-purpose language for, 44
in ThingLab, 487-88, 490
Path, in ThingLab, 491. *See also* Access path
Pattern, compiling, 550

Pattern matching
algorithm for, 547-56
uses of, 547
PDM. *See* Probe Data Model
Performance, of relational databases, 66-67
Persistence, DB capabilities in, for AI, 634
Predicate, specifications, for DB transactions, 194-95
Primitive, epistemological, in KL-ONE, 209
Probe Data Model (PDM), 204
Procedure
attached, in KL-ONE, 221
co-operating decision, KR and, 44
Processing, relational, capability for, 63-64
Productivity, and relational DB, 60-68
Program
action (transaction), and behavior specification, 195-96
DB, and logic, 264-65
Programmer, functions of, in DBMS, 52-59
Project, TORUS, 2-3, 11
Property
inheritance of, in relational DB, 317, 323-24
in TAXIS, 158-60
uniform relational, language and, 64-65
Psychology, applied, and QL development, 365

Q

QBE. *See* Language, Query-By-Example
QL. *See* Query language
QuadraticSolver, ThingLab's, 488, 489
Quantification, of knowledge, in a DB, 11
Query language
for a KB, 330-31, 333-34
logic and, 235-36
Query language (QL)
choosing for a DB, 363-73
defined, 363
development of, 365-67
embedded, 364
evaluating, 364-65, 369-73
first-order, 306-7
hierarchy of expressiveness in, 371
and human factors research, 368-69
intelligent, 367
model of, 365-66
new generation, 365, 367, *368*
previous generation, 365, 366-67, *368*
research issues in choosing, 374
Query (*see also* Retrieval)
ancestor, in evaluating query processing strategies, 412-14, 418-20
conjunctive, 354-55
DB capabilities in, 248-49
for AI, 634
deductive answering of, in relational DB, 431-43
evaluation of
completness in, 437
and CWA, 252-55
in EDUCE, 607-18
vs. optimization, 385
existential, system for answering, 434-37
facilities for, in System R, 563-64
interpretation of, vs. compilation, 385
modification, 533-45
nested, and access path selection, 521
optimization of, 19-20, 25-26
and logic, 237-38
processing
and access methods for new data types, 605-6
evaluation of strategies for, 406-9
recursive, 376-430
top down vs. bottom up, 386-87
recursion, vs. iteration, 385
safety of, in a DB, 383-84
same generation, in evaluating query processing strategies, 414, 420-21
Questionnaire, on AI-DB integration, 640-41

R

RDI. *See* Interface, Relational Data
RDM. *See* Model, relational data
Reality, databases and, 275
Reasoning
and knowledge representation, 35-46
models of limited, for KR, 39, 44-46
nonmonotonic, and KR, 47-48
unsound, 78-79
Record
defined, 85
structure
assumptions behind, 85-87
semantics of, 94-96
traditional implementation of, 87-89
Recovery, DBMS, 20, 26
in AI, 634
Recursion, 381-82
Recursive Query/Subquery (QSQR), for query processing, 392-418, 419, 420
Reducibility, dilemma of, in record structure identifiers, 93-94
Redundancy, minimal, DB dependency and, 474-75
Registration, of students and courses, DB language for, 156
Relation
3NF, and the entity-relationship data model, 107-8
DB, operations on, 16-23
invariant, in DB abstraction, 147-50, 151
in RSS of System R, 571
virtual. *See* View
Relational Data System, in System R, 561-70
Relational Storage System (RSS), in System R, 570-75
Relationship
binary, in record structures, 90-91
entity, in DAPLEX, 171
and the entity-relationship data model, 98-102
Relaxation, in ThingLab, 494, 495-96
Re-organization, DB/KB, 634
Representation
of data, and logic, 260
DB dependency and, 470-72

knowledge. *See* Knowledge representation
in relational DB, 344-46
schema design and, 475-77
Research
open problems in AI-DB integration and, 636-37
on TAXIS, 166
Research Storage System (RSS), in System R, 512-13
Reservation, airline, DB language for, 156-66 passim
Residue, in KRYPTON, 297-98
Resolution, strategy, in KRYPTON, 298
Restriction, in KL-ONE, 212-15
Retrieval
of DB records, 54
and the entity-relationship data model, 105-6
implementation of, 449-50
as limited inference, 444-54
logical system for, 446-47
semantic network system for, 447-49
specification for limited inference, model-theoretic, 453-54
Retriever, specification of, 445-46
Robustness, DB capacity for, in AI, 634
Role, in KL-ONE, 212-15
RSS. *See* Relational Storage System; Research Storage System
Rules
deduction, in EDUCE, 610-11, 618
interpretation of, in STROBE, 593-94
Russell, Bertrand, 57

S

Scan, RSS, 512-13
Scenario, in semantic nets, 6-8, 9
Schema
conceptual, for computer-based information systems, 58, 59
DB
applications in, 201
description as, 469
design of, 470, 476-77
decomposition in, 475, 476-77
history of, 477-78
research issues in, 478
synthesis in, 475-76
LDDL, 288-89
relational, for a DB, 13-16
Scheme
behavior, in transactions, 191-93
object, in structure modeling, 188-89
Search tree, and access path selection, 517, 518-*520*
Security
DB capabilities in, 634
DBMS, 21
Segments, in RSS of System R, 570-71
Semantics
in DAPLEX, 179-84
data-equivalence problem in, 272
of data models, 105-6, 273-91
DB, 273-91, 468
defined, 275-79
of first-order languages, 303-5
in KRYPTON, 295-96
logic and, 232-33
Separation, DB dependency and, 472-75
SHARE (organization), 57
SHM+. *See* Model, extended semantic hierarchy
Simplification method, for integrity checking, 499-508
Specification, DB transaction
behavior, 193-95
design, 185, 193-98
functional, 196-97
State description
abstract, 277-78
real world, 275-76
Statement
DECLARE, in DAPLEX, 170
DEFINE, in DAPLEX, 174
SQL, processing, 511-12
Storage
design of, in ADAPLEX, 585-90
direct access, 53
Structure
and behavior, 202
in DB application, 185, 187-89
generic, for generalization, 141-47, 151
Subject, confusion of, in record structure identifiers, 94
Substitution, notion of, 501
Subsumption, notion of, 501
Surrogates, in record structures, 94
Survey, of AI and DB practitioners and researchers, 626, 640-41
Symbol, design level of, in AI, 632
Syntax
for action program design, 196
in DAPLEX, 171-72, 179, *180*
first-order theory, 233
in KRYPTON, 295
logical state description and, 278-79
of a logic DB, 378
SEQUEL, 576-78
System
Ada, 583
ADAPLEX, data model, discussed, 583-85
advisory, QL and, 367
AMORD, 47
CRYSTAL, 1, 2. *See also* System, STROBE
database management. *See* Database management (DBM), system
DB2, 581
EDUCE*, 617-18
EDUCE
architecture of, 607-8, *609*
query evaluation in, 607-18
test performance of, 615-17
EKS, 618
expert, and KB, 328
information. *See* Information, system
INGRES, 600
interactive information (IIS), 156-66 passim
IPP (story-understanding), 367

KL-ONE, 207-21
example of application of, 223-29
language structure of, 208-10
philosophy of, 208-10
as precursor to KRYPTON, 294
KLONE. *See* System, KL-ONE
knowledge-based. See Knowledge base (KB), system
knowledge representation. *See* Knowledge representation (KR), system
KRYPTON, 293-99
implementation of, 297-99
knowledge level of, 294-97
sample application of, 299-300
MOLGEN, 482
OS/2 Extended Edition, 581
"Put-That-There," 367
Query Management Facility, 581
R*, 582
RABBIT, 367
reasoning, hybrid, 293-99
Rochester Dialog, 444, 449-50
R. *See* System R
Sketchpad, 482
SQL/Data System, 581
Starburst, 582
STROBE, modular tool kit for, 592-98
ThingLab, described, 480 System R
access path selection in, 511-22
architecture and design of, 560-82
implementations of, 581
relational data system of, 561-70

T

Table
C-. *See* Table, conditional
Codd, 342-43, 346-49
conditional (C-table), 351-54
extension, for query processing, 392, 394
V-, 343, 349-51
Tag, in the Rete Match algorithm, 551
Task, declarative representation of, in STROBE, 596-97
Taxonomy
of KL-ONE, 210-12
of QL, 363, 366-67
TBox. *See* System, KRYPTON
Template, access method, for new data types, 602
Theorem
Codd table, 346-48
CWA, 251-54 passim
proofs of, 255-58
geometry, demonstrating in ThingLab, 483-84
relational DB, 310-11, 313, 315
transaction, 505-6
V-table, 350-51
Theorem prover, 439-40
in combined AI-DB systems, 624
incomplete, and limited inference, 445
resolution, for limiting inference, 445
Theorem-proving, connection graph, in KRYPTON, 297, 298
Theory, relational, of DB, and logic, 308-11
ThingLab
operation of, 482-88
other work related to, 482
programming language and, 480-96
Thought, computers and, 69-82
Time, special-purpose language for, 43-44
Token
in the Rete Match algorithm, 549, 550, 551, 554
in TAXIS, 157-58
Tool kit, modular, for knowledge management, 592-98
Transaction
behavior modeling and, 190-91
consistency in, and logic, 237
management of, in System R, 572-73
simplification method and, 505-6
in TAXIS, 159-60, 164
Truth maintenance, and KR, 47
Type, in record structures, 89-90

U

Updating
in DAPLEX, 173, 175-76, 177
and semantic integrity, 459
simplification method and, 505
Usability, of query languages, 369-70
Users, of query languages
classification of, 367-68
and evaluation of QL, 371-73
User view, in DAPLEX, 175

V

Variable, looping, in DAPLEX, 171, 172
Vax, 592, 597
View
implementation of, by query modification, 533, 543-45
maintenance of, DB technology and, 628
materialization, DB technology and, 628
in relational databases, 65-66

W

Weyerhaeuser Corporation, 57
Window, ThingLab, 482-*489*
World, possible, and KR, 44-46

X

Xerox workstation, 592, 597